THE HANDBOOK OF
Alternative
Education

THE HANDBOOK OF

Alternative Education

JERRY MINTZ
Editor-in-chief

RAYMOND SOLOMON
SIDNEY SOLOMON
Associate Editors

ALAN MUSCAT
Database Manager

A Solomon Press Book

MACMILLAN PUBLISHING COMPANY
NEW YORK

Maxwell Macmillan Canada
TORONTO

Maxwell Macmillan International
NEW YORK   OXFORD   SINGAPORE   SYDNEY

The editors, writers, and publishers of *The Handbook of Alternative Education* have provided this listing of schools, programs, and organizations solely as information. We do not endorse, or evaluate, any school, program, or organization listed or described in this book. Nor do we recommend to parents, teachers, students, or any other persons or organizations that they attend any listed school or program, or participate in activities sponsored by any such school. It is entirely up to the reader to evaluate or judge each school and program listed.

Macmillan Publishing Company   Maxwell Macmillan Canada, Inc.
866 Third Avenue   1200 Eglinton Avenue East
New York, NY 10022   Suite 200
                                      Don Mills, Ontario M3C 3N1

Macmillan Publishing Company is part of the Maxwell Communication Group of Companies

Library of Congress Catalog Card Number: 94-13903

Printed in the United States of America

Printing Number
1   2   3   4   5   6   7   8   9   10

Library of Congress Cataloging-in-Publication Data

The Handbook of alternative education / Jerry Mintz, editor-in-chief ;
Raymond Solomon, Sidney Solomon, associate editors ; Alan Muscat,
database manager.
p.   cm.
"A Solomon Press book."
Includes index.
ISBN 0-02-897303-8
1. Non-formal education—United States—Handbooks, manuals, etc.
2. Educational innovations—United States—Handbooks, manuals, etc.
I. Mintz, Jerry.   II. Solomon, Raymond.   III. Solomon, Sidney.
LC45.4.H36   1994
371'.04'0973—dc20   94-13903
                                                     CIP

The paper used in the publication meets the minimum requirements of American National Standard for Information Sciences—Permanence of Paper for Printed Library Materials. ANSI Z39.48-1984.∞ ™

BOOK DESIGN BY RAYMOND SOLOMON AND SIDNEY SOLOMON

Dedicated to OUIDA MINTZ,
whose patience, help,
and support have been
life-long
— *Jerry Mintz*

To CLARA FREEDMAN SOLOMON
Talented graduate
of an alternative
educational environment,
accomplished musician,
teacher, generous to all
My beloved, devoted wife
— *Sidney Solomon*

Dedicated to JUDY SOLOMON
"Let thy fountain be blessed
and have happiness with the
wife of thy youth."
(PROVERBS 5:18)
— *Raymond Solomon*

Contents

Part Three
Directory of Educational Alternatives

United States

Part Four
Vignettes of Alternative Schools

Part Five
Bibliography and Appendices

Part Six
Comprehensive Alphabetical Index   *401*

Preface

This is the first comprehensive directory of educational alternatives in the United States and Canada. It is our hope that by uniting educational alternatives under one cover we will communicate to the public the broad scope of this movement, as well as foster communication and networking within it.

The Handbook of Alternative Education was compiled and written as an atlas to action. Although it may be used by some for study and research, we expect that it will mainly serve to help those seeking to create a good educational environment for themselves, their children, or in which to teach. In some cases, the Handbook may be used as a guide to create a new school, a new program within an existing school, or a home-based learning program.

What educational alternatives generally have in common with each other is an approach that is more individualized, has more respect for the student, parent, and teacher, and is more experiential and interest-based. Once you decide that you are looking for alternatives to the traditional school system, you must find out which approach is most suitable for you. Several are discussed in the following pages, and the resource and bibliography sections point to more information available.

You may want to explore one of the fifty boarding or residential alternatives in the Handbook—a list of them can be found in the Appendix. Most of them are small, democratic, flexible. Many are not very expensive, and most offer scholarships.

But perhaps the best approach would be to visit several of the alternatives that are near where you live. Look for the ones nearest your zip code, and note the type of school when it is indicated. Virtually all welcome visitors. And seeing these schools first-hand fits well with the experiential realm of educational alternatives. Call ahead for an appointment. Remember, we do not judge the quality or make any specific evaluations of the schools. That is entirely up to you.

A wide variety of educational alternatives exists at the elementary, secondary, and college levels. These generally fall into four major categories: public choice, public at-risk, independent (or private), and home-based.

The public school options in this book number in the thousands. These include entirely separate schools in their own settings as well as classes, programs, and even semi-autonomous "schools within schools." Public choice options are open to all students in their communities (though some have waiting lists). Among these are the *magnet* schools, which attract students to particular themes, such as performing arts. Public at-risk schools are geared toward students who are having difficulty with school and have special needs (including potential dropouts, pregnant teens, returning students, etc.). Generally speaking, public school teachers must have state certification.

The existence of public alternatives often results in positive interactions between the traditional programs and the alternatives.

Independent schools have more flexibility in staff selection and educational approach. Montessori schools, in one form or another, are the most plentiful; we list more than 2500. Most of these are private, but an increasing number are public. In addition, we list over 100 Waldorf schools, based on the teachings of Rudolf Steiner, 60 Quaker or Friends schools, and over 500 other independent schools. The majority of independent schools offer at least partial scholarships.

Some families choose "none of the above" for educational, philosophical, or religious reasons, or if there appears to be no nearby educational alternative, and decide to have home-based education. If you are interested in this option, you can find help by connecting with one of the more than 700 home-based groups listed in the Handbook. Some call themselves *unschoolers,* for they follow an approach based on interest, rather than a set curriculum. Others enroll in "umbrella" schools which provide a curriculum to follow (see homeschool resource section). Those which are religious-based usually indicate so in their name, but most of those listed here are for homeschoolers of all backgrounds and philosophies.

There are also some interesting gray areas. For example, home-based educators have combined to create resource centers where they meet as often as three days a week, but whose members are all home-based. In some states, public school districts have set up programs for homeschoolers whereby they are considered enrolled, and have access to school resources and facilities. In Canada, some private schools receive public school funding. This is also being done in Milwaukee for low-income students.

Above and beyond all this, it is very possible, with help, to start an alternative school yourself! This is being done all over the world (see section on foreign schools) as groups of parents, teachers, and students come together to form new independent schools, or programs in existing schools. Another exciting area is opening up with the "charter" schools; combining private initiatives and state funding, these can be set up with specific purposes and supported without many of the usual state regulations. Minnesota, California, Massachusetts, and Colorado are some of the states where this is happening. Help for starting or changing schools can be found in the resource section. The Alternative Education Resource Organization, which aided in the production of this Handbook, is one such resource.

If you choose to create a new alternative, one of your first tasks will be to decide how decisions are to be made for the organization. This is crucial. As you browse through the listings, you will see that school governance can involve the local educational authority, a board, an administrator, teachers, parents, and the students themselves. Many combine these, for example, by having a policy-making board, with day-to-day decisions being made by a democratic school meeting.

It is being increasingly recognized that students learn better when they have real responsibility for their own education. In fact, some see this as a basic right. This philosophy is implemented in a wide variety of ways. Quaker schools work toward consensus at a school meeting, in which all participants come to a "sense of the meeting." At Montessori schools students continuously choose which materials they want to work with. In some independent community schools, the educational process and all basic decisions are made at a democratic school meeting, with each having a say. There are even schools in which the students participate in hiring their own teachers. An increasing number of schools base their curricula on the interests expressed by the learners, and some have noncompulsory class attendance.

Our advocacy of alternative styles in education does not negate the devotion and skills of the many thousands of excellent teachers and administrators in the mainstream of schooling. This cataloguing of educational alternatives does not imply that all that goes on in the mainstream educational system is bad. There are many good programs and untold numbers of effective individual teachers and administrators in the traditional schools, as well as millions of parents, teachers, and children happy with that choice. Also, everything does not always go perfectly in alternative schools, and results vary widely. Our point is to alert the general public to the fact *that these educational alternatives are a choice available for their consideration.* Furthermore, many mainstream schools have incorporated methods which might be considered alternative into their general approach, so the line between alternative and mainstream is becoming blurred. Perhaps that is good, for as Ted Sizer of the Coalition of Essential Schools once said, "I want to put an end to alternative education. What you offer should be available to all students."

We have created the Handbook because we feel it is of primary importance to help students learn how to learn, to stay open to that process, and to retain confidence in themselves as learners throughout their lives. Perhaps at one time it was possible to teach students just what was needed to be known for their future lives, but with today's explosion of information, the best thing we can do is help them maintain openness, curiosity, and flexibility as they face the challenge of the twenty-first century.

— *Jerry Mintz*

Acknowledgments

Our aims in producing the *Handbook* are to promote communication among people in the educational alternatives, to work toward a more cohesive movement, and ultimately make alternative education available to all learners. The Alternative Education Resource Organization was created to work toward these goals. It supported the development of the *Handbook*. AERO is the education arm of the 60-year-old School of Living, a non-profit corporation. It publishes *AERO-GRAMME,* a quarterly networking newsletter.

This project has had consistent support from the Alternative Education Conference and the new States Educational Alternatives League. All of the states which have alternative education organizations and attended the Conference committed themselves to help. Through additional state education contacts and *AERO-GRAMME* readers, we established representatives in 42 states. They have worked hard to funnel information to us. We also received help from every state education department in the United States, and most provincial education departments in Canada. Our heartfelt thanks for this cooperation.

The following other alternative education groups provided us with invaluable support and resources:

National Coalition of Alternative Community Schools
Association of Waldorf Schools of North America
Network of Progressive Educators
National Coalition of Education Activists
Montessori Foundation
Changing Schools (a magazine)
Holt Associates
Coalition of Essential Schools
School of Living
Public School Montessorian (a magazine)
Home Education Press
Global Alliance for Transforming Education
Magnet Schools of America
Resource Center for Redesigning Education
Natural Life Magazine
International Association for the Study of Cooperation in Education
Folk Education Association of North America
Canadian Alliance of Homeschoolers
North American Montessori Teachers Association.

Much of the sorting and mailing of questionnaires and newsletters was done by energetic interns at the AERO office, including Mike Lepore, Tom Morley Mischa Denisenko, David Hammerman, Jenifer Goldman, Lisa Harris, Asiba, Sunny, and Wakan Tupahache. Their enthusiasm and help with a tedious job was indeed welcome.

Lauren Most helped coordinate the issue of *AERO-GRAMME* which first announced the project, and also began entering the data from the returned questionnaires.

Alan Muskat, a recent Princeton graduate interested in alternative education, communities, and computers became a key asset as database manager. Through him we met efie womon, who also entered and edited data.

Traci Lachenmeyer first contacted us from California, and began editing, entering data, and swapping disks, eventually moving back to the New York area.

Carol Morley, a homeschool parent, edited virtually all of the Montessori questionnaires, and went on to do any other work we needed.

Another homeschool parent, Betty Lepore, also did editing.

David Sower of Floyd, VA, heard about the project through the intentional communities network, and also became an editor.

Debby Finn, in New York City, became our most recent editor.

Ouida Mintz coordinated most phone messages (which came in at all times of the day and night), and her advice and support were essential.

We are fortunate to include helpful articles written by some of the best-known leaders in alternative education. These include Ron Miller, founder of *Holistic Education Review* and Director of the Resource Center for Redesigning Education; Tim Seldin, Director of the Montessori Foundation and Headmaster Emeritus of the Barrie School; Dave Lehman, Principal of the Alternative Community School (Ithaca, NY) and President of the New York State Alternative Education Association; Professor Mary Ann Raywid of Hofstra University and the Center for the Study of Educational Alternatives; Pat Farenga, President of Holt Associates, Publisher of *Growing Without Schooling;* Dan Greenberg, a founder of Sudbury Valley School; Joan Barickman, Director of the Academic Community School; Michael Oliver, teacher at The New School of Northern Virginia; Joy Jensen of Jefferson County Open School; Katie McNeil of Snakefoot Educational Association; and Shelley Preston of the Audubon Expedition Institute. Their detailed accounts of what actually happens in alternative schools give us a better picture of daily life in a variety of settings.

Kip Shaw, of Pageworks in Delhi, NY, handled the typesetting tasks with high professional skill and unfailing patience. Krishnendu Mandal cheerfully gave advice and assistance in solving computer-related problems.

We are grateful to Phil Friedman, Publisher of Macmillan Reference, for his publishing wisdom, advice, and cooperation during the many months of development of the *Handbook*. A hearty thank you, Phil.

We are deeply appreciative of the overall guidance as well as close attention to detail offered by Andrew V. Ambraziejus, managing editor of Macmillan Reference.

Finally, our thanks to the thousands who provided information to us through questionnaires, telephone calls, faxes, letters, lists, and enthusiastic support.

Part One

INTRODUCTION

How to Use the Directory

Although we have nearly 7500 entries, that does not mean that we have found every single alternative school, program, or homeschool group; we hope to hear from those we missed, and those who create new alternatives, so we may list them in future editions. If you find an error in the listings or wish to include a new school or program in the next printing, write to Jerry Mintz, 417 Roslyn Rd., Roslyn Hts., NY 11577.

The schools, groups, and programs in this *Handbook,* although sometimes very different from each other, fall into categories which are generally considered to be educational alternatives. Our key purpose in listing them is to let the reader know they exist. Beyond that, we have given additional information, some of which came from the thousands of questionnaires which were returned to us. Some of it came from lists and other data sent to us by state education departments, Montessori, Waldorf, Quaker, community schools, and other alternative education organizations. Within tight space limitations, we provided what we could. Some may no longer be active; we didn't always hear back from everyone we tried to reach but decided that some unconfirmed leads might prove to be useful contacts. We do not evaluate any of the schools or programs. These listings should not be considered definitive, just indicative. All the information has originated with the schools and programs themselves.

The standard format for a complete entry is shown below:

Name (year founded)
Address
District, county
Contact person, phone number, FAX number
Type, if boarding, if nonprofit; tuition, if scholarships
Number of teachers, assistants; students, predominant student population, age range; grade levels
Entrance requirements, procedures, and restrictions
Affiliations; accreditation
Governance
Teacher qualifications
Special features/philosophy, location, if there is childcare or transportation provided, features unique to the school, etc.

Notes on Selected Items

Address: is a mailing address, and not always the site of the school. Sometimes two locations are listed, separated by a slash.

District and County: You do not necessarily have to live within these geographic limits to participate. If there are residency requirements, we say so separately. For example, the "Pennsylvania Homeschool Education Network" may be located in Crawford County but it serves the entire state; likewise, many public choice (particularly *magnet*) schools are open to residents of several neighboring districts.

Number of Teachers, Students: We tried to determine the total number of *full-time* positions/attendants at any given time (and this was not always clear). Two half-time teachers would add up to one full-time position. The same goes for the number of students: Are they split between day and night classes, or several sessions?

Teacher Qualifications: This may describe the current staff (e.g., 22 years Montessori experience) and/or what is required of new staff applicants (e.g., CT certification).

Special features: Some entries conclude with a special features section. These last few lines are not necessarily meant to summarize the entry's focus. No entry can give a complete picture of what actually goes on. And schools may have features we don't mention; for instance, just because we don't say that a school is accredited does not necessarily mean it isn't. It may simply mean that we didn't receive that information.

In the interest of space we have sometimes given just one listing for schools with multiple sites. On the other hand, you might occasionally find a listing for a school or program that has closed. We decided that it was better to err on that side than to delete all entries for which we have not had a confirmation, in order to give the reader more possible choices.

"Choice," "at-risk," and "gifted"

The terms *choice, at-risk,* and *gifted* are widely used in the field of alternative education to distinguish different types of schools or programs and the students served in each case.

First, most public alternatives are listed as either *choice* or *at-risk*. This does not necessarily mean that the latter are mandatory (i.e., court-ordered, etc.). While at-risk alternatives are geared toward a specific population, enrollment is often by choice and frequently open to non-at-risk students as well.

Second, what puts someone "at-risk," and at-risk of what? The student *at-risk* is either in danger of falling behind or is already having trouble with school. This could be due to poverty, pregnancy, substance abuse, disability, etc. Often only the effects are known: poor performance, "discipline," attendance, etc. For students whose needs are not being met by regular school, *at-risk* alternatives are often the only thing that comes between failing and dropping out. Of course, there are many young people who decide to educate themselves, or otherwise lead lives outside of school, and are quite successful.

Finally, we believe that all people are gifted and talented, albeit in different and often unrecognized ways. There are public and private "magnet" schools that specialize in meeting the needs of the "gifted" or "talented" individual who excels in academics, the arts, public speaking, etc.

Definitions

Competency-based: student receives credit when they demonstrate proficiency in a given area.

Charter school: in certain states (including MN, CA, MA, and CO) private initiative and state funding can combine to set up schools with specific purposes and supported without many of the usual state regulations.

Childcare provided: either during school (for the children of teen and adult parents) or before/after school (for primary age students).

Contract: student and teacher make an agreement/commitment to each other

GED: General Education Diploma. Also called high school equivalency, offered to students who pass a competency test.

Glasser: advocates non-coercive education through behavior cards, level system.

Home-based: Programs controlled by parents for teaching their own children.

Homeschooling support groups: offer advice, support, get-togethers, legal and other information, and often go on field trips.

Independent: private, no part of a municipal or state system. However, independent schools sometimes contract with public systems to provide services.

International: multicultural, multiethnic; also used by Montessori schools to refer to first generation U.S. citizens, i.e., those who parents are immigrants—recent ones, in fact.

Open-entrance, open-exit: no rigid enrollment calendar.

Orff Shulwork: an approach to music used primarily in Montessori schools.

Public at-risk: programs geared for students with special needs who have experienced school problems.

Public choice: programs potentially open to all students in a given area, although there are sometimes lotteries or waiting lists.

Student-centered: an approach based on the interest of the student rather than an arbitrary curriculum.

Glossary: Abbreviations and Acronyms

General

N, S, E, W, NE, NW, SE, SW   north, south, east, west, etc.
E, J, M, S, Mag, H   Elementary, Junior, Middle, Senior, Magnet, High
S/P   School/Program
adt   adult
AE   alternative education
ALC   Area Learning Center
alt   Alternative
CC   Community College
Cont   Continuing
Ed   Education
Inc   Incorporated
Ind   Independent
ft, pt, ht   full-, part-, half-time
P/F   pass/fail (grading)
prog   program
req'd   required
SE   special education
St   Saint
tech   technology
V, voc   vocational
x   phone number extension (e.g., 444-5678 x129)

Postal

Ave, Blvd, Ct, Dr, Ln, Rd, St, Tr, PO, SR, RR   avenue, boulevard, court, drive, lane, road, street, trail, post office, state route, rural route

Titles

Adm   Administrator,–tive,–tion
Adms   Admissions
Assn   Association
Asst   Assistant
Chair   Chairman,–woman,–person
Comm   Community
Coord   Coordinator
CSW   Certified Social Worker
Dept   Department
Dev   Development
Dir   Director/Directress
Enrl   Enrollment
Fac   Faculty
Head   Head of School, Headmaster, Headmistress
LD   learning disability
Mgr   Manager

PPS   Pupil Personnel Services
Prin   Principal
Reg   Reglstrar
Sr   Sister
Supt   Superintendant
Tch   Teacher

Special Features

AIM   alternative instructional methods
ASL   American Sign Language
A/V   audio-visual
CAI   computer assisted instruction
cur   curriculum
ESL   English for speakers of other languages
HSED   HS Equivalency Diploma
IB   International Baccalaureate
IEP, ILP   individualized education/learning plan
gov   governance
home ec   home economics
JTPA   Federal Job Training and Partnership Act
lang   language
PASS   Portable Assisted Study Sequence
PE   physical education
voc   vocational

State Departments and Private Organizations

___   prefix or suffix (e.g., N for "National . . .")

AEE   Assn for Experiential Education
__AEYC   __ Assn for the Ed of Young Children
__ANS   __ Assn of Nonpublic Schools
__AANS,   __ Assn of Academic Nonpublic Schools
AC   Administrators Council
ACSI   Assn of Christian Schools, International
AECI   Assn for Early Childhood International
__AIS__   __ Assn of Independent Schools of . . .
AMI   Assn Montessori Internationale
AMITOT   AMI Teachers of Texas
__ASC   __ Assn of Schools and Colleges
ASN   Alternative Schools Network (Chicago)
AWSNA   Assn of Waldorf Schools of N. America
BE   Board of Education
BOCES   Board of Cooperative Educational Services
CAP   Community Action Program
CES   Coalition of Essential Schools
CIS   Council of Independent Schools

CME   Contemporary Montessori Education
CMF   Christian Montessori Fellowship
DE   Department of Education
DFS   Division of Family Services
DHR   Department of Human Resources
DSS   Department of Social Services
DHS   Department of Health Services
DL&E   Department of Labor and Education (SD)
__EA   __ Education Agency
FCOE   Friends Council on Education
FIS   Federation of Independent Schools
FOM   Friends of Montessori
FS   Family Services
FTP   Federation of Teaching Parents
HD   Health Department
HEA   Home Educators Association
HSGI   HS Graduation Incentive (MN)
ISA__   Independent Schools Assn of . . .
ISD   Independent School District
KC   Kindergarten Council
MA   Montessori Assn (also Massachusetts)
MAC   Montessori Administrators Council
MAEO   Michigan Alternative Education Organization
ME__   Montessori Educators of . . . (I: International)
MF   Montessori Foundation
MIA   Montessori Institute of America
__MS   __ Montessori Society
MS__   Montessori Schools of . . . (A: America)
MSA   Middle States Assn of Colleges and Schools
NAEYC   National Assn for the Ed of Young Children
NAECP   National Academy of Early Childhood Programs
NAEEC   National Academy for Ed of Early Childhood
NAMTA   North American Montessori Teachers Assn
NCME   National Center for Montessori Education
__NE   __ of New England
NIPSA   National Independent Private Schools Assn
NWASC   NW Assn of Schools and Colleges
OE   Office of Education
PAMS   Pan American MS
PIC   Private Industry Council
PNMA   Pacific Northwest MA
__PS   __ Public Schools
RSF   Religious Society of Friends
SACS   Southern Association of Colleges and Schools
SB   School Board
SNMC   St Nicholas' Montessori Centre/College
SNMTA   St Nicholas' Montessori Teachers Association
__SS   __ Social Services
USD   United/Unified Schools District
WASC   Western Assn of Schools and Colleges

Starting a New Educational Alternative

One of the options available in the United States is the right to start a new educational alternative. This option should not be taken lightly, because it is not available in all countries. In analyzing the data submitted to the *Handbook* we discovered alternative schools here today whose founding dates go all the way back to 1786. We also discovered another startling figure. When we plotted the founding dates filled in on questionnaires, it turned out that there has been a general gradual increase in the number of alternatives founded each year, starting with a low ebb in the early fifties. After reaching an initial peak in the late sixties and early seventies, there was a slight dip. But starting in the late seventies there has been a dramatic *increase* in foundings of educational alternatives, with over 60% of them founded since the early eighties. Without much fanfare, this movement has been growing much faster than many people would have believed.

Some of the forms of new alternatives being created today include parent cooperatives, homeschool resource centers, charter schools, public at-risk alternatives, public choice and magnet schools, Montessori and Waldorf Schools. Since education in the United States is primarily in the domain of the individual states, a first step would be to examine the education laws in your state. It might be more prudent to do that by first talking to the director of the type of new school or program in your state in which you are interested, to find what their experience has been in dealing with state regulations.

In organizing a group to found an alternative it is usually useful to have all segments of the proposed alternative represented, including potential parents, teachers, and students. Some of the most successful alternatives have initially as a leader or coordinator someone who embodies the values of the group, and who is a strong democratic empowerer. That person has the respect of the group, and the confidence and ability to empower the people around him or her to be involved with decision making and responsibility.

It seems that it is better to "strike while the iron is hot." Too much time studying and planning sometimes leads to no action. For example, we were invited to organize a group in Missoula, Montana in 1989. Within three days we had a large group meeting— a democratic meeting with potential students—named the school and established a working group. There was still no funding or school site, but its existence had been established. The school is now in its fourth year.

There is no definitive manual for starting a new alternative, and if there was, it might not be useful to all. Each situation is unique and calls for an approach to meet those particular needs. In some situations there are guidelines which can be followed. For example, in Toronto, the Board of Education has procedures by which a new public alternative can be established by interested students, parents, or teachers. When followed, the Board can provide space and teachers' salaries. Over 25 have been established since Seed School, the original one, in the early seventies. Sudbury Valley School has put out a "school starting kit," and dozens of independent alternatives have decided to follow that mode. Several states have passed new Charter School legislation, and have guidelines for their establishment. Montessori and Waldorf schools are being established with the help of any one of several national groups.

One fast growing phenomenon is the homeschool resource center. As the homeschool movement grows, groups of homeschoolers have been going beyond informal support groups toward centers which operate several days a week. They sometimes are able to sidestep cumbersome private school laws by the fact that all students are homeschooling. On the other hand, some public school systems, mostly in California, have created public school programs for homeschoolers, thus establishing homeschooling as a legitimate form of public education, and enabling the public system to receive state per-pupil funds, which assist with curriculum design and provide use of facilities.

An early step should be contacting the relevant groups described in the resource section of the *Handbook*. Through them you will get helpful advice, and they may lead you to additional resources.

Just keep in mind, all of the thousands of educational alternatives listed in this *Handbook* were originally founded by interested educators, parents, or students, some as recently as the past few months. Others are in process now. It is not necessary to think in terms of a large institution. If that new alternative helps only one child, it creates a living legacy.

Part Two

ALTERNATIVE EDUCATION VIEWPOINTS

The Research Record

Alternative schools have been studied more for their organizational arrangements and processes than for their outcomes. There are several important and related reasons for this. First, is the interest in making business and industrial organizations work well—as reflected in the corporate excellence literature of the last dozen years. Second, is the discovery in the early 1970s that the way a school is organized and structured may have as much to do with its success as do the quality of its program and instruction. Third, is that alternative schools offer the clearest extant example of organizational departure from the standard model of schools. Amid all the present talk of restructuring, it has been said, alternatives provide our most definitive example of what restructured schools might look like.

As the study of schools as organizations has developed over the past decade, one attribute after another has been identified as crucial: organizational climate, culture, downscaling and personalization, worker commitment and satisfaction, visionary leadership, shared decision-making. And as research came to focus on one of these components after another, some inquirers have looked at alternative schools to see whether and in what form these attributes were observable there. The findings have been positive and informative.

To cite a current example, one of the most recent emphases to emerge in organizational research on schools—a product of the last five or so years—has to do with the nature and extent of "professional community" within a school. It appears that the more developed the professional community, the greater the likelihood of success in dealing with students and helping them achieve. Research on professional community asks about the kind of relationships that exist among staff, the extent to which teachers work together and discuss their work, and the extent to which they share a common sense of the school's mission and goals.

Two national studies have recently found alternative schools outstanding in this regard. One, a study of sixteen high schools conducted by Stanford's Center for Research on the Context of Secondary School Teaching, found a Michigan alternative school to stand head and shoulders above the other fifteen on most of the indicators related to professional community. Indeed, they found Horizons High School to exceed national means by as much as two or three standard deviations on a number of the measures used. The study's final report indicated that teachers at Horizon have a greater influence on policy than at any other site, that teacher collaboration time is more extensive than at any other site; that they have high marks for their principal's leadership; and their job satisfaction is among the highest encountered in the study.[1]

A second study, conducted by the University of Wisconsin's Center on the Organization and Restructuring of Schools, took a longitudinal look at restructured schools. It found the alternative school in its study to be the most mature and effective example of professional community. Moreover, the alternative appeared to be the study's most successful example of a restructured school.[2]

Still another recent study which appears to offer substantial support for the organizational features of alternative schools is an extensive inquiry carried out in New York. It compared the impacts of two types of magnet schools on students: one type where the magnet students were not separated from others, save in their specialized courses, and were otherwise part of a standard comprehensive high school; and the other type where the students were grouped together in a school which operated separately, with its own students and teachers.[3] The second variety was found far more effective than the first with respect both to dropout prevention and student accomplishment. The study's authors attribute the success to the fact that the students in the second type of magnet program had the opportunity to take more courses in the magnet area. So there is a curricular rather than an organizational explanation. From what they have described, an organizational explanation of the advantage is at least equally plausible: the second type of program was able to change the daily experience of students, whereas the first one was not. The failure to separate students in the first type of magnet, from students outside the program, meant that not everybody was there by choice—and thus not everybody shared the interests that attracted the choosers. The result was that school climate and culture, and student sense of affiliation, had changed very little.

The study points to the importance of several factors that figure prominently in most alternative schools. The first is that alternative schools tend to elicit strong affiliation from those connected with them. They are, as some have called them "membership" schools or "communities" which students feel they have joined. Youngsters typically exhibit strong ties to the school, its teachers, and to one another.[4]

A second factor suggested by the New York Study (although not acknowledged there) is that curriculum may not occupy the sort of importance for students that it holds for adults in a school. One prominent researcher, Joan Goodlad, has said that even for the adults working there, as well as for the students, the most important thing about a school is not academics, but the way in which one's daily life unfolds and is lived there.[5] Alternative schools seem to acknowledge this in the spirit they bring to "doing" school, the climate that is carefully sustained in most, the activities they provide, and the way people—all people, students as well as staff—are treated within them.

The third thing the magnet school study suggests is the importance of choice—not only one's own choice, but the fact that *everyone* is there by choice. It makes for quite a different kind of setting than those to which some or all are assigned.

Both magnets and alternative schools have a record of trying to interest and genuinely engage youngsters in learning. At the secondary level, magnets tend to do so by featuring content in which students have a particular interest. Alternatives tend more often, though not exclusively, to attempt to engage students in the school environment and in the activities through which content is presented. One type of alternative that has been popular since the early days of public school alternatives, for instance, is the city-as-school concept that has students learning directly from observation (as in courtrooms) and participation (as in internships). Other activities that have been widely adopted have included independent study opportunities, mentorships, and service learning arrangements.[6]

Alternative schools are known for the dramatic turnarounds they often bring to the lives of individual youngsters whose previous school performance has ranged from poor to disastrous. It is not always the case by any means. But alternative school teachers can tell stories of kids who had hated schools and teachers, and who blossomed in the alternative. Yet such stories don't ordinarily impress researchers. They tend to look instead for hard, well-substantiated evidence, involving comparison groups and preferably, large numbers. This sort of evidence is harder to come by—and perhaps less important to alternative school audiences who are inclined to emphasize individuality and particularity anyway, over the typicality and generalizations researchers seek—but gradually the hard evidence is piling up.

One analysis summed up the situation this way:[7] Virtually all studies that compare magnet and non-magnet schools show that students in magnet schools have higher achievement, better attendance and dropout rates, and overall, better school performance. Increasingly, studies are ruling out such possible explanations as that the magnet students were smarter, or more accomplished to start, or more highly motivated. A study done in Montgomery County, MD, several years ago compared two sets of youngsters matched at the outset for their educational achievement and apparent potential, at the time when one group entered a magnet school and the other continued in the regular program. The investigators found that the magnet students accomplished more—and that the longer they remained in the magnet school, the greater the contrast became with the performance of their regular school counterparts[8] (Larson & Allen, 1988).

More recently, their findings were confirmed on a large scale by a study of 816 magnet school students in four cities. Long-term magnet students (for seven years or more) were matched with shorter term magnet students (under three years) as to sex, race, and entering achievement levels. The study found that the long-termers did better on all the indicators checked: grades, test scores, attendance, behavior, participation in extracurricular activities, and school awards. Moreover, it was ascertained that this was the case with weaker as well as stronger students, and irrespective of the theme of the magnet school.[9]

By virtue of their well-known holistic orientation, alternative schools are interested, however, in much more than academic achievement. They are concerned with the kind of experience school represents for students and how the students feel about their school. Here, too, the research is very positive. One large study that sought to determine how well schools respond to the needs of their students found alternative high schools to far surpass conventional ones on this count, in the eyes of both teachers and students. Indeed, even the *lowest* scoring alternative schools were judged to be far better at meeting student needs than were the *highest* scoring conventional ones![10] And constituent satisfaction rates associated with alternative schools—those of parents as well as of students and teachers—have long been known to outshine those of comparable traditional schools in the same locale.[11]

Follow-up studies show that these positive sentiments tend to prove long-lasting. Graduates don't later turn sour, and they don't conclude afterward that their school had not prepared them for what was to come.[12] For instance, a study of one famous alternative school—the Village School, in Great Neck, NY—polled all of its graduates, some from as long as ten and fifteen years earlier. It compared their views and sentiments regarding their high school with those of the graduates of one of the district's other high schools. After having graduated, the alternative school alumni were consistently more positive about their alma mater than were the graduates of the conventional high school.[13]

Another kind of follow-up study also testifies to the superiority of alternative schools. It has long been observed that a larger percentage of students from alternative schools than from other comparable local schools tend to go on to college—suggesting that they are more positively disposed toward education, and/or more convinced of their own capacity to handle higher education, than are other local youngsters. A study of the graduates of one of the nation's best-known high schools, which happens to be an alternative school—Central Park East Secondary School in New York City—showed that more than 90% of their students graduate in either four or five years (while on average only 55% of the city's students do so). Of these, 95% go on to college, and it appears that very few of those who start will fail to finish. CPESS has a dropout rate of only 5%[14]. To make clear the significance of such figures, it must be added that the school is in Spanish Harlem, an area where 96% of the students come from minority families and almost 80% of them qualify for free or reduced cost lunches. CPESS is a member, in fact a charter member, of the Coalition of Essential Schools, a much respected national network seeking to restructure schools. Ted Sizer, the Coalition's founder, reports that some of its most successful schools are alternatives.

Thus it would appear that the research record amassed by alternative schools may eventually come to equal that of progressive education, one of their ideological forebears. The famous Eight-Year Study, which examined the effects of 30 innovative Progressive high schools of the 1930s, concluded that the graduates of such schools had decided advantages over the graduates of conventional high schools. They were more likely to succeed in college than were their counterparts, and in fact, the more innovative their high schools and the farther they departed from the conventional, the greater the advantage of their students.[15] The carefully designed Eight-Year Study was widely acknowledged to have made the case for the innovative schools of its day. We may soon be approaching the place where studies like those cited here will, when taken collectively, be conceded to have documented the superiority of alternative schools.

Notes

[1] See Center for Research on the Context of Secondary School Teaching. "Report of Survey Findings to Horizon High School, Wyoming, Michigan." Stanford University and Michigan State University, March 1991; and M. W. McLaughlin & J.E. Talbert, "Contexts That Matter for Teaching and Learning." Stanford: Center for Research on the Context of Secondary School Teaching, March, 1993.

² M.A. Raywid, "Professional Community and Its Yield at Metro Academy," in "Professionalism in Schools: Communitarian Perspective," edited by K.S. Louis and S.D. Kruse. Madison, WI: National Center on the Organization and Restructuring of Schools.

³ R. L. Crain, A. Heebner, & Y. P. Si, *The Effectiveness of New York City's Career Magnet Schools. An Evaluation of Ninth Grade Performance Using an Experimental Design.* Berkeley: Center for Research in Vocational Education, 1992.

⁴ See G. A. Smith, ed., *Public Schools That Work: Creating Community.* New York: Routledge, 1993; and G. G. Wehlage, R. A. Rutter, G. A. Smith, N. Lesko, & R R. Fernandez, *Reducing the Risk: Schools as Communities of Support.* Philadelphia: Falmer, 1989.

⁵ J. I. Goodlad, *A Place Called School: Prospects for the Future.* New York, McGraw Hill, 1984

⁶ See M. A. Raywid, *The Current Status of Schools of Choice in Public Secondary Education.* Hempstead, NY: Project on Alternatives in Education, Hofstra University, 1982; and M.A. Raywid, "Synthesis of Research on Schools of Choice, *Educational Leadership,* April 1984, pp. 70–78.

⁷ M. Musumeci, & R. Szczypkowski, *New York State Magnet School Evaluation Study. Final Report.* Larchmont, NY: Magi Educational Services, 1991, p. 55.

⁸ J. Larson, & B. Allen, *A Microscope on Magnet Schools: 1983 to 1986,* Vol. 2: *Pupil and Parent Outcomes.* Rockville, MD: Montgomery County Public Schools, 1988.

⁹ Musumeci & Szczypkowski, *New York State Magnet School Evaluation Study.*

¹⁰ T. Gregory, & G. Smith, "School Climate Findings," *Changing Schools* 11(2) (Spring, 1983): 8–10.

¹¹ See M.A. Raywid, "The Mounting Case for Schools of Choice," in *Public Schools by Choice,* edited by J. Nathan. Distributed by Free Spirit Press of Minneapolis. 1989, pp. 13–40.

¹² See, e.g., J. Nathan, *Attitudes Toward High School Education Held by Graduates of a Traditional and an Alternative Public School in St. Paul, Minnesota.* Doctoral dissertation. University of Minnesota, 1981.

¹³ Clancy, P., "A Study of the Graduates of a Suburban Alternative High School." Hofstra University, 1988.

¹⁴ Paul Schwarz, "Dear Students, Parents and Staff," *Newsletter #31,* Central Park East Secondary School, May 17, 1993.

¹⁵ Aikin, W.M., *The Story of the Eight-Year Study.* New York: Harper & Bros., 1942.

— Mary Anne Raywid

Public Alternative Schools and Programs

Following the initial development of nonpublic, or "independent" alternative schools (typically called "free schools" in the beginning), which were so strongly tied to and reflective of the "counterculture" of the 1960s, "public" alternative schools have grown enormously in number since their beginnings in the late 1960s and early 1970s. In his excellent article "A History of Public Alternatives" (which appeared in the March 1976 *New Schools Exchange Newsletter,* the first major voice of the free and alternative schools), Joe Nathan, quoting Mario Fantini, described this important turning point as follows: ". . . the real impact of private free schools has not been to achieve radical reform outside the system of public schools, but rather to stimulate a more progressive, albeit moderate reform within the public schools."

These often have been (and are still today) alternative high schools to which students could (and can) choose to apply, such Philadelphia's Parkway Program and New York's City as School, which were designed to extend learning to the greater communities in which schools reside. Also in the early 1970s, the School of Education at the University of Massachusetts received a major U.S. government grant to develop a National Alternative Schools Program. During its five year history NASP produced a national directory, published a newsletter (*Applesauce*), issued a number of reports on such topics as the financing of public alternative schools, sponsored conferences, and helped start several public alternative high schools. At a similar time there were major funds from the National Institute for Education, given particularly to Minneapolis, Berkeley, and Seattle-Tacoma school districts to help them develop public alternative high schools. But, small groups of parents (and sometimes students) were also effective in getting public open schools or alternative schools in their communities, such as the St. Paul Open School, Louisville's Brown Open School, Cambridge Alternative School, Berkeley Other Ways School, Los Angeles Area Alternative School, and our own Ithaca (NY) Alternative Community School.

Then there have been the *magnet* schools, begun in the 1970s, more typically elementary schools, with their specific curricular themes or focus, drawing students from all sectors of a given community, and often designed to address new legal requirements for school desegregation. Other elementary public alternative schools were inspired by schools in England, among them the infant schools, or the integrated or open classroom schools. Also, there have been a number of *schools within schools*—a few classrooms and a handful of teachers in one wing or section of a larger building, usually a high school or junior high, typically with only a partial curriculum for which greater flexibility and freedom from the conventional curriculum is provided. And, more recently, there has been the development of public alternative schools for students with "behavioral problems"—sometimes referred to as "soft jails" and not often welcomed as part of the same alternative education movement—and those for students "at-risk," potential dropouts, for whom the alternative may involve one classroom and limited choice. All of these various types of public alternative schools or programs are found in this *Handbook*. Since 1970 teachers and administrators, and sometimes parents and students, of these various public alternatives have been meeting annually at conferences held throughout the country, early on under the aegis of the now defunct International Consortium for Options in Public Education (ICOPE) of the Department of Education at Indiana University. Currently such national gatherings are sponsored by the various statewide alternative education organizations (of which there presently are 21)—in 1992 the 22 annual conference was hosted by the Virginia Alternative Educators Association in Williamsburg, Virginia, and the 1993 conference in Colorado, hosted by the group Colorado Options in Education—and loosely affiliated through the editorial board of the *Changing Schools* publication which is a current national voice for alternative schools.

The effects of public alternatives have been analyzed by various people and through various studies throughout the most recent twenty- to thirty-year history of such schools. It is important to remember that these schools have their roots in the Progressive Education movement of the turn of the century, and that one of the most definitive studies which compared the college records of some 1500 students from non-traditional schools with those from traditional schools—finding the former group did as well as or better than the latter on all measures—was (and still is) *The Eight Year Study* published in 1942! In this 1976 article, Joe Nathan summarized these as follows:

1. They have made "life more bearable for thousands of young people, age 5 to 18, who are in them."

2. They have provided students with "the opportunity to learn from a variety of people, not just certified teachers."

3. Students have had "opportunities to spend more time out of the school building taking local or even cross-country field trips, and serving as interns at local community agencies or businesses."

4. "The feeling that someone other than their family really cares about them is a new experience for an astonishing number of students;" it has been the feeling of belonging that many have about their school.

5. Another "effect on many students has been to convince them that they can have more impact on both their own and the lives of others . . . alternative schools help them learn how participation in social action and service projects make them feel they can have a positive influence on their communities."

6. "Many public alternatives have helped increasing numbers of young people learn how to analyze community problems and deal with at least some of them."

7. Effectively served the needs of staff, "Alternative school teachers find different ways of using resources and greater flexibility . . . can spend more time on individual student evaluations because they don't have to fool with figuring grades . . . [and] have the opportunity to get a few copies of various materials, rather than having to accept class sets of required texts."

Similar findings have continued to be reported as described in the "highlights" of an extensive study of 1200 public alternative secondary schools published in 1982 by Mary Anne Raywid of Hofstra University, "The Current Status of Schools of Choice in Public

Secondary Education": staff morale high, better student-teacher relations, no greater cost, kids like alternatives, attendance goes up, and "the most outstanding features of alternative schools are human relationships and instructional activities—not equipment, nor facilities, nor curriculum . . . Alternative schools are pioneering new organizational structures, innovative forms of social control, and new varieties of learning activities." In his 1990 book *Public Alternative Education,* Central Washington University education professor Tim Young concludes, after a thorough analysis of the research to date, that: (1) Students have more positive attitudes toward school, (2) their school attendance improves, and (3) their achievement improves as the result of their attending public alternative schools.

Most importantly, throughout the past twenty-plus years, educators in these public alternative schools have all been doing things differently. The debate continues over the question of ". . . whether it was individual freedom or whether it was communitarian- ism and collective decision making instead, that is the real essence of alternative school- ing—or whether action learning takes precedence over curricular relevance as the more critical defining element," as Mary Anne Raywid recently explained in her article in the fall 1990 issue of *Changing Schools.* Raywid pointed out further ongoing debates over the mission of public alternative education: ". . . did it intend to institutionalize diver- sity by providing a mechanism enabling and inviting schools to differ from one another— or was alternative education the vanguard that would point the way, showing what *all* schools ought to be like?"

Perhaps Jonathan Kozol has captured the full meaning for those of us carrying on the struggle as public alternative educators in the closing of his Introduction to the republi- cation of his 1972 book originally entitled *Free Schools,* then in 1982 re-titled *Alterna- tive Schools: A Guide for Educators and Parents:*

> The Free School [or Alternative School] was conceived, not as an instrument by which to flee from history, but rather as a visible metaphor for many values, visions, and ideals that seemed to some of us to be essential in the struggle to assure the psy- chological and intellectual survival of our children."

Those of us in public alternative education are continuing to keep the metaphor alive!

— *Dave Lehman*

My Children Taught Me
How to Teach Them:

MONTESSORI SCHOOLS

The Montessori classroom is commonly referred to as a "prepared environment." This choice of words reflects the care and attention given to creating a learning environment that reinforces children's independence and intellectual development.

Dr. Maria Montessori spoke eloquently of the human potential and fundamental rights of the child. More importantly, she pointed the way to a practical implementation of humanistic and cognitive psychology in today's classroom. Hers is a holistic system, thorough and comprehensive in its design, from teacher training through the everyday bag of tricks that make real classrooms work.

Many practices in modern education have been adapted from Montessori's theories. She is credited with the development of the open classroom, individualized education, manipulative learning materials, teaching toys, and programmed instruction. Those who studied under her and went on to make their own contributions to child psychology include Anna Freud, Jean Piaget, Alfred Adler, and Erik Erikson. Even her critics generally acknowledge Montessori schools as places where children work and learn with quiet dignity and spontaneous enthusiasm. But only in the last twenty-five years have parents and educators in Europe and North America begun to recognize the consistency of the Montessori approach with what research teaches us about the way children learn.

No matter what age level the children are, certain characteristics will be found in all Montessori classes. First, the children are free to move about, working alone or with others at will. They may select any activity and work with it as long as they wish, so long as they do not disturb anyone or damage anything, and so long as they put things back where they belong. While the children work independently, their social skills and compassion are normally well-developed and discipline is rarely a problem. The class groups are always multiaged, normally covering a three-year span. The levels usually found in a Montessori classroom correspond to the developmental stages of childhood: birth to 2.6 years; 2.6 to age 6; age 6 to 8; age 9 to 11; age 12 to 14; and age 15 to 18. Each class is essentially a stable community, with only the oldest third moving on to the next level each year. At each level within a Montessori school, the curriculum and methods are logical and consistent extensions of what has come before.

Montessori's ideas have continued to evolve into a growing body of educational thought. Unlike her contemporaries and predecessors, Montessori offered less a philosophy of education than a specific set of strategies. Hence the name, "The Montessori

Method." It is not simple to implement, but it does come complete with specific strategies for the education of teachers, design of the learning environment, and methods of learning.

Montessori education is sometimes criticized for being too structured and academically demanding of young children, but she would have laughed at that idea. She often said, "I have studied my children, and they taught me how to teach them." She made a practice of paying close attention to their spontaneous behavior, arguing that only in this way could a teacher know how to teach. Traditionally schools pay little attention to children as individuals, other than to demand that they adapt to our standards. Montessori argued that the educator's job is to serve the child, determining what each one needs to make the greatest progress. To her, a child who "fails" in school should not be blamed any more than a patient who does not get well fast enough. After all it is the physician's job to help us find the way to cure ourselves in the same way as it is the educator's job to facilitate the natural process of learning.

Montessori evolved her method through trial and error, making educated guesses about the underlying meaning of the children's actions. She was quick to pick up on their cues, and constantly experimented with the class.

For example, she once told of the morning when the teacher of one of her "children's houses" came late to work. The children had crawled through a window and gone right to work. They had selected one material apiece from a tall cabinet and were working quietly. The teacher usually locked up the cabinet the night before, but this time had neglected to do so. The materials used by the students were costly to make and when Dr. Montessori arrived at the scene she found the teacher scolding the children for using them without permission. But Montessori recognized that the children's behavior showed that they were capable of selecting their own work. So she removed the cabinet and replaced it with low, open shelves, on which the activities were always available to the children. Today, this may sound like a minor change, but it contradicted all educational practice and theory of that period.

But the Montessori learning materials are not the method itself. Rather, they are simply tools that we use to stimulate the child into logical thought and discovery. They are provocative and simple, each carefully designed to appeal to children at a given level of development. Each material isolates and teaches one thing, or is used to present one skill at a time as the child becomes ready to learn them. Montessori carefully analyzed the skills and concepts involved in each subject, and noted the sequence in which children most easily master them. She proposed a specific sequence in which the materials are presented to the child. To facilitate the prepared order of the environment, the teacher arranges the materials on the shelf following their sequence in the curricular flowchart, from the most simple to complex, and from the most concrete to those that are most abstract.

The teacher's role is different from that commonly seen in many schools. She (or he) is not the center of attention, and spends little time addressing the class as a whole group. Her role centers around the preparation and organization of appropriate learning materials to meet the needs and interests of each child in the class. The Montessori teacher rarely presents a lesson to more than one or two children at a time, and limits them to a quick efficient presentation. The objective is to intrigue the child, so that he or she will come back on his or her own for further work with the material. Lessons center around the simplest information necessary for the child to do the work on her own: the name of the material, its place on the shelf, the ground rules for its use, and some of the possibilities inherent within it.

Montessori and Piaget together noted the inability of the young to learn from abstraction, as well as the need for concrete experience and direct interaction with the environment. Asking a child to sit back and watch us perform a process or experiment is like asking a one-year-old *not* to put everything in his mouth. The older child needs to manipulate and explore everything that catches his fancy. For this reason, Montessori, and later Piaget, emphasized the overriding importance of concrete learning apparatus. This is the rationale for the Montessori materials for mathematics, sensory development, language, science, history, and geography.

Montessori discovered that the environment itself was all-important in obtaining the results that she had observed. Not wanting to use school desks, she had carpenters build child-sized tables and chairs. She was the first to do so, recognizing the frustration that a little child experiences in an adult-sized world. Eventually, she learned to design entire schools around the size of the children. She had miniature pitchers and bowls prepared, and found knives that fit a child's tiny hand. The tables were light, allowing two children together to move them. She studied the traffic pattern of the rooms, arranging the furnishings and the activity area to minimize congestion and tripping. Over the years, Montessori schools carried this environmental engineering throughout the entire building and outside environment, designing child-sized toilets and low sinks, windows low to the ground, low shelves, and miniature hand and gardening tools of all sorts.

Dr. Montessori argued that the child's mind was not, as many believed, like an empty pitcher waiting to be filled in school. Rather, the child's mind was as different from that of an adult as a tadpole is different from an adult frog. Both belong to the same species, but one is at an earlier stage of development. Each successive stage is characterized by specific inclinations, interests, and ways of thinking. She noticed that as children pass from one stage to another they tend to become fascinated with certain kinds of experiences. If allowed to engage in the activities that fascinate them, their vigorous interaction with the environment leads to their full development, resulting in children with a much higher threshold for frustration, boredom, and a tendency to behave far more calmly than is normally associated with childhood.

Maria Montessori was in many ways a woman ahead of her time. Born in 1870 in Ancona, Italy, she pursued a scientific education against the considerable opposition of her father and teachers, and became Italy's first woman physician. It is ironic that she became famous for her contributions to the educational field, when originally she had rejected the occupation of teaching as the traditional refuge of most women at the time.

In its American resurgence over the last thirty years, Montessori schools tended to focus on the preschool age group, and only now are the elementary and secondary school levels being re-established. Over the past eighty-seven years, the Montessori approach has been successfully adapted by numerous schools around the world. Its effectiveness has been demonstrated with both poor and affluent children, and promising work is being done today with special children who have special needs.

— Tim Seldin

Reuniting Living and Learning:
THE APPEAL OF HOMESCHOOLING

"Why do I have to learn that stuff anyway Dad? I'm never going to use it."

"The kids make fun of me . . . I don't have any friends at school."

"Why can't I read this book for class? I already know the stuff the teacher is working on."

"I don't understand this stuff, the other kids seem to get it. Am I stupid, Mom?"

There is an admirable, though often unrecognized, awareness among children who ask such questions. These children are actually questioning if they might be better served in other learning situations. However, the seriousness of these statements is usually dismissed by adults with the standard reply: "School is for your own good. I had to go to school when I was a child."

Many people feel they have no choice but to send their children to traditional public or private school. But homeschooling is legal in every state of the U.S. Many parents tell their children to bite the bullet and get through school no matter how distasteful. Using school attendance as a primary example of teaching children to complete a distasteful task is pedagogically wrong because it sends a negative message to our children that learning and schooling are essentially coercive and unpleasant tasks. We learn to complete tasks we might not otherwise do for better, nobler reasons than someone making us do them by force or bribe. Self-motivation, pride in one's work, loyalty, a sense of responsibility, teamwork, and feeling connected to a larger community are but some of the reasons we all undertake unpleasant tasks. Further, you cannot "instruct" children on the reasons listed in the previous sentence in a classroom and expect them to become part of students' characters. These abstract virtues must be made concrete to have an impact on children, and they are best taught by example, by shared experiences, by real encounters with people, not through therapeutic "simulations" and "role-playing" games. Things like self-motivation and discipline are learned by being around adults and children who openly practice them, and this is the essence of homeschooling.

If you are aware of how much you have helped your children learn by your nurturing, example, and direct help, and how many truly difficult tasks children learn on their own before they reach school-age, such as learning to walk, talk, and socialize, you are well along the path toward homeschooling your children. Many families decide to homeschool simply because they enjoy being with their children, watching and helping them learn. Other families homeschool because of firm religious, political or pedagogical positions. But as happens to many people who decide to homeschool, it is some crisis in school, such as a terrible report card for an obviously smart child, sharp changes in behavior, or a suggestion that your child has "learning disabilities," that makes them consider finding an institution that fits their child, rather than fitting their child to the institution. Often the institution that fits the child best is the one they were in before they were sent to school: the family.

The last time the federal government tried to count the numbers of homeschooled children nationwide (1988) it arrived at an estimate of 300,000. Since that figure represents a significant increase in the numbers of homeschoolers in a decade (John Holt estimated about twenty thousand to thirty thousand children were being homeschooled in the early seventies) I think it is safe to propose that at least half a million children are being homeschooled now, if not more.

Thinking about learning and teaching before your children reach school-age not only helps clarify your ideas about children's learning, but also your role as teacher. Certainly the role of specific instructor creeps up now and then—such as how to solve a specific math problem or play a chord on the piano—but more often than not it is the role of the generalist that best suits homeschoolers. On any day you might have to be a facilitator, a travel agent, a librarian, a scientist, a referee, and a parent. Homeschool parents teach what they can, help their children find the information they need to learn on their own, and find tutors or apprentice/internships for areas in which they do not feel suited or in which they are not personally interested. There is no state that currently requires all parents of homeschoolers to have teaching certificates, and many states only require a high school diploma for the parents to homeschool. John Holt wrote in 1984, ". . . in my journal (*Growing Without Schooling*) you will hear from people without much schooling who are doing a wonderful job of helping their children, mostly because they have been able to discover from the children themselves what the schools have never been able to realize: It is the interest, ingenuity, and activity of the learner, not the teacher, that is primarily responsible for creating learning." Despite their "non-professional" status, homeschoolers get their children accepted in colleges and work places all over the world, from Harvard to Fort Wayne Bible School, from high-tech computer jobs to professional dogsled racing. Studies over the last twelve years have shown:

1. Homeschooled children perform academically as well as or better on standardized tests than children in school, regardless of how tightly or loosely structured their homeschooling experience is.

2. Homeschooled children are not socially deprived or social misfits. Homeschoolers find innumerable ways for their children to meet and play with other children, learn about different cultures, and befriend people of other races through homeschooling support groups, civic, church, and other social groups they participate in, as well as the less formal, and perhaps even more inclusive, areas of playgrounds, informal sports, and neighborhood friends. A researcher at the University of Florida, Dr. Larry Slyers, after examining his data on the socialization of homeschooled children, remarked that homeschoolers may have *better* social skills since they pick up their social skills primarily from adults, not their age-mates.

3. Homeschoolers face no special difficulty in gaining employment or college acceptance. While the big success stories of homeschoolers who never set foot in a classroom

until they got into Harvard, Cornell, Johns Hopkins, and so on get lots of media attention, there are thousands of other homeschoolers who enter college or work without
fanfare and do very well for themselves.

4. A recent study at the University of Michigan (done by Dr. Gary Knowles in 1991)
of adults who were homeschooled showed none of them to be on any form of government assistance: they were all employed, and 96% answered that they would be homeschooled again if they could.

By far the best way to get accurate information about rules, regulations, and what it
is like to homeschool is to talk to people in your area who are homeschooling. Contact
any of the homeschooling organizations listed in this book to find homeschoolers near
you. You can also look up the laws for your state under "Education" in a good-sized
public library, a law library, or at a friendly lawyer's office. The vast majority of homeschoolers do not need or use legal services, particularly if they are careful to make themselves aware of their rights and responsibilities before they start. There are two national
magazines which I can recommend: *Growing Without Schooling,* founded by John Holt
in 1977 and *Home Education Magazine,* founded in 1983.

Once you have decided to homeschool and found out the laws and regulations for
homeschooling in your state, you need to decide how you will homeschool. You have
many choices. Some states allow you to register as a private school each year and have
some year-end evaluation requirements; others let you register as a homeschool with the
Department of Education, subject to the state's laws or regulations pertaining to homeschooling. Other states require local education authorities to receive a homeschooling
curriculum for each school-age child each year, as well as written progress reports, standardized tests, or other forms of evaluation. So, you will have to give your homeschooling choice a certain degree of preparation before you can actually be "legal." For
states requiring a written educational plan, it is important to have an educational philosophy in your mind that guides your choice of materials and informs school officials
that what you are doing at home with your children is totally different than what they
do with children in school. You do not need to take a course in educational philosophy
to do this (it probably won't cover homeschooling anyway!). By reading a few homeschooling and education publications and books, you will be able to find what educational approaches match your family's learning style. It could be useful to quote from
these education writings throughout your proposal. You will also want to say how you
plan to direct, observe, and evaluate your child's learning; in *Growing Without Schooling* we print proposals and parents' letters to school officials that we feel are useful
models for others to use.

Certainly many people teach at home the way they were taught in school, but others
decide to loosen up and allow their children to learn without a preplanned curriculum.
Independent, self-initiated learning by children is a major reason parents continue to
homeschool. Some families decide in the beginning that this is an important reason for
them to homeschool. Other families, especially in the first few years, feel more comfortable purchasing a curriculum, enrolling their children in a correspondence school, or
setting their homes up as "satellite schools" of a larger private school to get them started;
some of the alternative schools listed in this book, such as Clonlara (MI), Upattinas (PA),
and Pinewood School (CO), offer these and other services to homeschoolers.

By imposing the structure of the school curriculum over the inherent structure of their families, many beginners simply duplicate school at home, with set times, grades, lesson plans, and so on. Many families find that as they homeschool they learn to trust themselves and one another to learn, and they use less and less prepackaged curricula.

Most homeschooling takes place during children's elementary school years, though there is an upswing in the number of teenage homeschoolers. Many teenagers seem to be attracted to the independent studies aspect of homeschooling, particularly for opportunities to work on a subject in depth, for apprenticeships, volunteering, interning at an office and other real-world encounters that develop their knowledge and skills. Learning without a curriculum allows children and teenagers not only the freedom to continue learning as they did before they went to school, but also to gain confidence and self-esteem by being able to lay claim to their own learning.

Homeschoolers can stop doing things that don't work. They don't need local, state, or federal approval to switch texts, take a day off, do chemistry experiments in the kitchen after dinner, or go on a field trip. Learning can be valued as it occurs during all hours of our daily lives. Homeschoolers get immediate feedback and demonstrable proof that their children have learned something and do not need to rely on third-party evaluations or standardized tests to know if their children can comprehend a reading passage or do long division.

Every state has laws or regulations that tell parents what their children ought to know in each grade, but the scope and sequence of that knowledge is completely in the family's hands. If during the year-end evaluation school officials feel certain objectives have not been met, homeschooling parents have the same options as if their children were in school: remediate the problem on their own, with a tutor, with a new approach, or come back to it at a later date. Chronic problems may arouse the attention of school officials, but as long as progress is being made in the area, and it can be shown that significant learning is taking place in other subjects, it would be very hard for a school official to force a family to stop homeschooling because of a perceived deficiency in one area.

Since it is your "school" you do not have to teach the material that is to be covered by tests as schools do, though if your child must take a standardized test it would be wise to practice test-taking at some point during the year. "Teaching to the test" is but one of the may school-created learning problems homeschoolers would do well to avoid! Homeschooling allows you to emphasize or de-emphasize elements in your studies as you and your child see fit. The important thing to remember is that you and your children are in control. If you decide your curriculum isn't holding your children's interest, then move directly to what does hold their interest. By working on your child's strengths you will discover that all knowledge is interconnected. Homeschooling allows plenty of time for an interdisciplinary approach to subjects, especially since the "lessons" do not stop when the bell rings or the weekend arrives. You can also alter or abandon your curriculum to take advantage of a sunny day, a special performance, or a sudden intense interest your child develops in, say, Indians. Should you decide to use the incidents of everyday life to enliven and direct learning, you should at least keep some notes and records of what it is your child is learning; this is often referred to as the portfolio method of evaluation. This will give you information that you can provide to any skeptical officials or relatives, as well as a record of your child's accomplishments that is far richer than grades on a report card. Videotapes and cassette tapes of your children's accomplishments and your own observations can also be used.

But the most important thing to do when you homeschool is make sure you and your children are enjoying and appreciating one another's company. Most parents love their children, but not too many enjoy their company all day long, every day. Of course, you are not really with your children *all the time* if you homeschool. Homeschoolers have support groups (this book is full of them), group activities (4-H, scouts, theater, Little League, etc.) classes (ballet, art, karate, etc.), individual lessons (music, religion, math, etc.) and blocks of time where children are engaged in independent projects that give parents time for themselves and for other siblings. Some families do not realize how much fun they can have together until they begin to homeschool; others, particularly those who find the homeschooling, household, and child-care burdens falling on one parent, typically the mother, have a hard time enjoying homeschooling. It is very important that parents enter homeschooling as partners; those who do not usually do not homeschool very long. It is also important for parents to be models of activity and learning for their children. This is done by pursuing your own interests, hobbies, and causes, and involving your children in them as much as possible. Your activities not only help satisfy your personal needs but provide a context for your children to understand why reading, writing and arithmetic are useful things to know, since they see you using them to accomplish your goals.

Homeschooling is not the sole province of two-parent, single-income families. Many families make homeschooling work for them in spite of both parents working full time jobs; this usually works when one has a day job, the other a night job or home business. (This is not easy, but many parents manage it.) Single parents, both men and women, have written about how they manage to homeschool their children and earn a living. Aunts, uncles, grandparents and friends have been known to help homeschool or supervise children in order to allow parents to work, go to the doctor, etc.

Every parent knows that juggling a family's schedule is a daily challenge. This is true whether the children are in daycare or school, and homeschooling is no different. While homeschooling can involve a series of tradeoffs of time and money, so do all your other educational options: if I want to send my daughter to private school I may have to work a second job and volunteer at the school; if I homeschool my child I may have to switch jobs or shifts and ferret out learning resources in my community. This book shows you that you and your children do have options, right now, that do not rely on the government providing you with "choice" somewhere down the line. One choice that may work for you is homeschooling, which you may do for a semester, a year, during a lengthy travel, or straight from kindergarten through college; the choice is yours.

— *Patrick Farenga*

The Waldorf Schools

The visionary ideas of Rudolf Steiner (1861–1925) inspired an international alternative education movement that today includes over 100 schools in the United States. Steiner was a philosopher and mystic who taught that Western materialist thinking is too narrow to encompass the full reality of the world; in his numerous writings he developed a "spiritual science" called Anthroposophy that explores the nonmaterial (psychic, archetypal, transpersonal) dimensions of reality. Steiner and his followers have applied this approach to medicine, agriculture, architecture, and other fields—including education.

In 1919, Steiner was asked by Emil Molt, owner of the Waldorf-Astoria company in Stuttgart, Germany, to inaugurate an adult education program for employees and a school for their children. Steiner developed a curriculum and prepared teachers for this first Waldorf school. He emphasized that education is an art requiring a teacher to be highly sensitive to each child's developing life energies. In a Waldorf school, a teacher takes a first grade class and remains with the same group of students for eight years in order to cultivate close relationships as well as a deeper understanding of their personalities.

Unlike many alternative school environments, the Waldorf classroom and curriculum are not "child-centered" in the sense that children plan or choose their own activities; rather, the environment is structured according to the educator's sensitive understanding of children's intellectual, emotional, and spiritual needs. Waldorf educators believe that young children require order, security and adult modelling as a foundation for their own freedom and autonomy. Steiner described, in great detail, the various spiritual "temperaments" of children and the developmental stages through which all children unfold; Waldorf education was designed in response to the characteristics.

The Waldorf curriculum is distinctive also for its extensive use of art, storytelling and mythology, and movement activities (such as eurhythmy, an expressive art from developed by Steiner). Waldorf educators emphasize the child's need to engage the world through physical activity and imagination rather than abstract, intellectual materials such as textbooks; this is especially true for young children, and Waldorf educators have consistently opposed our culture's push for earlier and earlier academic achievement.

In fact, Waldorf educators find themselves outside the public education mainstream in general. Steiner's notion of the "threefold social order" separates education and cultural pursuits from political and economic interests; consequently, Waldorf educators are concerned with the healthy, balanced development of children's personalities, not with the "competitiveness" of American corporations. The Waldorf approach is, in this sense, truly alternative.

— *Ron Miller*

Alternative Education:

CHALLENGING THE ASSUMPTIONS ABOUT SCHOOLS

As exemplified by the wonderful diversity of schools, programs, and approaches to teaching and learning featured in this book, the concept of "alternative education" has many meanings. From the democratic and libertarian impulses of homeschoolers and "free schools," to the delicately choreographed curriculum of Waldorf education, to special attention for troubled and failing youths in public schools, alternative education embraces a wide range of philosophical assumptions and educational methods. Yet there is an underlying commonality among these approaches—some core values and ideals that they all share.

Indeed, alternative education is a philosophically and historically significant social movement. As the progressive educational scholar Patrick Shannon has expressed it, "Those who seek alternatives are not odd, or negative, or necessarily modern; often unconsciously, they continue a deep tradition within the history of education in the United States."[1]

In this essay, I would like to explore why there is an alternative tradition in American education at all. I will suggest that "alternative" educators are those who substantially disagree with some of the core assumption underlying conventional schooling. These assumptions are deeply rooted cultural and political beliefs, and to oppose them is no small matter. Alternative education raises important questions that go beyond schooling.

Alternatives to What?

By examining the historical and cultural context of education, we can identify persistent themes underlying the formation of educational policy, decisions about curriculum, and school management. Though rarely articulated, these key themes or assumptions are tacitly accepted by most educators and policymakers.[2]

Assumption #1. Education is properly considered to be a political matter—i.e., the state has a legitimate interest in overseeing education policy and curriculum.

This assumption is taken for granted in almost every nation in the world. We too often forget that when modern public school systems were established in the 1830's, crusaders such as Horace Mann and Henry Barnard encountered significant opposition to their efforts to impose bureaucratic control over local schools; the notion of state-controlled schooling was abhorrent to many people. Religious leaders compared state schooling to state-controlled religion, which they considered to be "a strange doctrine in a free country."[3] In the mid-nineteenth century, social critic Orestes Brownson argued that

> the people do not look to the government for light, for instruction, but the government looks to the people. . . . To entrust, then, the government with the power of determining the education which our children shall receive is entrusting our servant with the power to be our master.[4]

In the twentieth century, philosopher Rudolf Steiner (who conceived the Waldorf school method) called for a "threefold social order" in which cultural life—with education at its heart—is kept autonomous rather than placed at the service of the political and economic domains of society. Steiner argued that a healthy cultural life requires freedom of thought and meaningful human relationships; schools should be responsible to children's developmental needs, not to political processes or bureaucratic rules.

This personal freedom and genuine community life are central characteristics of alternative education. While many alternative educators believe that the public system is the only way to assure all young people access to schools, even within that system alternative schools run on a human scale, involving honest, sensitive personal interaction within the context of a nurturing community. Educational processes in alternative schools are usually determined democratically, by the people most directly involved and affected.

Assumption #2. "Education's first duty is to make possible the survival of our country."[5]

If education is a state institution, then it serves the interests of society at large rather than the individuals who comprise it. From the very beginning, public schooling has been designed to mold the young generation into loyal citizens. As early as the 1790s, Benjamin Rush, a leading American intellectual, proposed the authoritarian goal of trying to "convert men into republican machines. This must be done if we expect them to perform their parts properly in the great machine of the government of the state." Rush seriously argued that the individual person "does not belong to himself," but is "public property."[6] This attitude has often been echoed by educational leaders; the historical literature contains numerous assertions such as this by Colin Scott of the Boston Normal (teacher training) School in 1908:

> It is not primarily for his own individual good that the child is taken from his free and wandering life of play. It is for what society can get out of him, whether of a material or spiritual kind, that he is sent to school.[7]

Most alternative educators, on the other hand, would hold that the interests of society are best served by cultivating *human* development through individuals' self-knowledge and meaningful relationships with each other and the world.

This means that education must respect the multitude of human differences that students bring to their learning—differences in learning style or intellectual interests, in language or ethnic background, in personal vision or ideals. Alternative educators do not seek to impose a homogeneous "cultural literacy" upon diverse persons and communities.

Assumption # 3. Education should primarily be concerned with our nation's economic growth.

It is very clear to historians that one major reason why the public school system emerged in the 1830s was to meet industry's need for trained employees. The United States had been an agrarian society, and workers were not used to the rhythms of mass production; the school would prepare them for it.[8] Throughout the nineteenth century and well into the twentieth, leading educators like William T. Harris and William Bagley emphasized the need for industrial-style discipline, and Harvard President Charles W. Eliot spoke for the nation's economic planners when he asserted that education should prepare children for their "probable destinies" in the workforce—i.e., white, upper middle-class children would become leaders and managers while nonwhite and working-class youths were *destined* to be laborers.[9]

Around the turn of the twentieth century, the public education establishment became dominated by the "scientific management" approach associated with the work of Frederick W. Taylor. Scholars and administrators set out to measure every possible behavior and endeavor, to strive for maximum "efficiency" according to the model established by American industry. Behaviorism and strictly empirical science set new standards for professional activity; school principals and superintendents became managers, accountants, and public relations professionals as much as educators.[10] Schooling would not only serve the corporate economy, but be completely integrated into it, until the whole system could accurately be described as an "educational-industrial complex" in which young people are to be trained, "that their skills are a product, and that the world is a vast marketplace where they should be prepared to compete, to create a demand, and eventually to sell for the best offer."[11]

Today's leaders of educational restructuring are primarily motivated by the demand to keep American industry "competitive," assuming that national economic success represents a common good above that of personal or community development. But alternative educators would ask whether such success can bring about a society in which all people have their basic needs for decent housing, nutrition, and health care adequately met, in which their work is fulfilling and their community life is healthy and nurturing. They have always resisted the cultural tendency to treat young human beings as economic units; the growing human being, they have argued consistently over the years, is too precious, too unique, too full of wonder and wondrous possibilities, to treat so crudely. The young person is far more than a future employee or manager, and needs to be educated accordingly.

Assumption #4. Educators are professionals who should control students and manage the learning process.

Along with industrial discipline, another primary goal of early public school crusaders was the moral discipline of working-class and immigrant families. In the historical literature we find many blatantly racist and nativist statements about the superiority of white, Protestant, middle-class values. For example, the Boston School Committee claimed in 1858 that immigrant children were characterized by "the inherent stupidity of centuries of ignorant ancestors" and needed to be disciplined "from animals into intellectual beings."[12] This moral self-righteousness set a tone for public education that has continued into the late twentieth century, even though it is no longer fashionable to insult ethnic subcultures. It is still commonly assumed that the specially trained and credentialed teacher and specially qualified administrator have the professional authority to intervene in the lives of families and children on behalf of society's interests.

This assumption was spelled out clearly at a symposium on education restructuring, featuring leading education scholars, in 1987. Two of these scholars explicitly define professionals as:

> those who through special training and socialization have gained a unique set of understandings that set them apart from nonprofessionals . . . The power of the professional is, in part, a function of their special knowledge and skills. If these are eroded and the mystery surrounding the professionals' work disappears, then the power of the professional is reduced.[13]

In this view the professional holds *power* over nonprofessionals. Like a priestly cult, there is an aura of "mystery" surrounding this power—it must not be examined too closely by ordinary people, and must not be questioned. The scholars quoted here recognize that such power is derived not only from technical expertise, but from the fact that professionalism serves the interests of "the larger society"—more specifically, the "dominant coalition" of decision-making "elites." Thus contemporary professionalism serves the same purpose of social control and cultural homogenization as the more explicit racism and nativism of the nineteenth century.

The professional educator is presumed to have the authority to "manage both the social relations of the classroom and the cognitive development of students."[14] Like a corporate manager, the educator is concerned with the *products* of the educational process (test scores) and the *products* of the school-factory (young people).

Alternative educators, conversely, see the teacher as a person intimately and mutually involved in a fluid, unfolding, social and moral endeavor with other persons. The teacher may have a great deal of experience to offer to young people, and may draw upon specialized knowledge about learning processes and tools. But alternative educators insist that adults engage students as whole, open, feeling *persons*—without letting techniques or credentials obstruct genuine human interaction. They see the student—even the young child—not as a passive client for their professional expertise, but as a deeply creative, self-unfolding being with his or her own unique path and destiny in life. Emerson said it well:

> The secret of Education lies in respecting the pupil. It is not for you to choose what he shall know, what he shall do. It is chosen and foreordained, and he only holds the key to his own secret. By your tampering and thwarting and too much governing he may be hindered from his end.[15]

Assumption # 5. The only valid knowledge is empirical, analytical, intellectual, and utilitarian.

Ever since the early seventeenth century, Western culture has demanded rational, scientific objectivity. The philosophical position of Bacon, Descartes, Galileo, and Newton—that the morally and emotionally detached knower can measure, evaluate, predict and control nature—has become an accepted foundation of modern thought. All our social institutions, our assumptions about knowledge, intelligence, professional expertise, and education, are permeated by this orientation toward reality. Until recent years, scientists, philosophers, and historians confidently asserted that this scientific objectivity (aptly called positivism) was the crowning achievement of the human mind, surpassing all superstition, faith, and dogma, and capable of solving moral and social problems as well as the riddles of nature.[16]

Schooling, then, has focused on giving students a command of positive, objective knowledge; "curriculum" has come to mean the repository of indisputable "facts" that people need to know in order to grasp reality. Education is considered successful when its graduates can find their proper niches in the social-economic order.

However, it should be obvious by now that rational, analytical knowing is only one, limited way of inhabiting the world, and the urge to manipulate nature and society is not necessarily the highest or noblest goal of human existence. Alternative education, for example, usually treasures the arts (which are, of course, always the first subjects to be dropped in conventional schools when budgets are tight) as means for self-discovery and self-expression; they tend to release creativity, spontaneity, intuition, and empathy; they usually encourage cooperative effort and a wider appreciation of personal uniqueness and cultural diversity. To alternative educators, such qualities are at least as vital as calculating intellect—if not *more* vital to a full and satisfying life.

In recent years, this insight of alternative educators has been gaining credibility through research in neuroscience, psychology, and learning theory. Scientists themselves now speak of the complementary "left" and "right" brain functions—rational intellect necessarily complemented by intuitive, holistic insight—and they are beginning to attend seriously to the reality of diverse learning styles and "multiple intelligences."

Varieties of Alternative Education

Today a growing number of alternative programs are being developed within the public school system. Whether they serve special populations, are designed as *magnet* schools, or in some states, are formed by teams of educators and parents as *charter* schools, most of these programs depart from some or all of the five assumptions outlined above. They represent an important shift in public policy, away from the nineteenth-century faith in "the one best system." Alternative education is more than a matter of "choice" however. I am arguing that alternative education is genuinely *countercultural*—it yearns to replace those values and assumptions that have dominated Western, particularly American, culture over the past two or three centuries. Its vision is profoundly humane, person-centered, democratic, and attuned to the deep human quest for meaning and purpose. For the most part, this vision has remained on the fringes of American education and society, but given the crisis in modern education, a progressive social and educational movement that draws inspiration and substance from its own rich heritage could have a profound impact on our thinking about schooling and learning.

Alternatives to mainstream educational thinking first appeared in the context of the Romantic movement toward the end of the eighteenth century. Jean-Jacques Rousseau's *Emile* (1762) advocated an education in harmony with the organic rhythms of nature, the self-guided unfolding of human development, and God's word "written in the secret heart" of every person. Although Rousseau was an eccentric man who wrote other books with more authoritarian social and political implications, *Emile* has exerted a profound influence on alternative educators for over two hundred years, being the first work to suggest that the growing, learning young person should be free from social and intellectual restraint because each person has a trustworthy inner urge to develop naturally.

The Swiss humanitarian Johann Heinrich Pestalozzi (1746–1827) is the best known, and most influential, of Rousseau's early disciples. In a series of schools he opened for poor and orphan children, Pestalozzi sought to provide a loving family-like community that would nourish the social, moral, and emotional development of young people, as well as their intellectual and vocational skills. Pestalozzi refused to use schooling to cast young people into the moral, intellectual, or economic molds dictated by the larger society, and trusted that their own inner nature would lead them to pursue fulfilling, meaningful lives within nature and society.

Pestalozzi influenced later generations of alternative educators, including two idealistic teachers who worked with him—Joseph Neef (1770–1854) and Friedrich Froebel (1782–1852). Neef came to the United States in 1806 and opened a school in Philadelphia, and later another at the New Harmony commune in Indiana; he also wrote a classic book on person-centered education, *Sketch of a Plan and Method of Education* (1808). Froebel became famous as the originator of the kindergarten, but it is not well known that he saw the kindergarten as part of an entire educational system devoted to raising the human being "into free, conscious obedience to the divine principle that lives in him," as he put it in *The Education of Man* (1826). Another Romantic educator of this time, A. Bronson Alcott (1799–1888)—the father of Louisa May Alcott and close friend of Emerson and Thoreau—was intuitively attuned to children's learning styles and repeatedly found himself in trouble for setting up child-centered schools; he found support in Pestalozzi's ideas.

What defines these educators as "Romantic" is their belief that an autonomous life force, creative energy, or divine power exists within the person, that the human being is not merely a rational animal nor a "republican machine" fitting mechanically into the social order. When alternative educators are called "child-centered," this refers to the fact that they take the young person's autonomous inner life seriously. The soul or authentic self is a delicate emerging identity that requires emotional nourishment, *which modern schooling does not generally provide.*

The early alternative educators worked alone—there was no alternative *movement* for over 130 years after the publication of Rousseau's *Emile*. But in the 1890s, building on the work of Francis W. Parker (1837–1902) and John Dewey (1859–1952), the progressive education movement began to take shape. Parker had been inspired by Pestalozzi's and Froebel's work, while Dewey was a brilliant and original thinker who complemented Romantic ideas with a solid philosophical and sociological critique of modern society.

Progressive education was the single most ambitious effort to transform schools in a humane, democratic, person-centered direction. Numerous creative and insightful educators—Margaret Naumburg, Harold Rugg, George Counts, Caroline Pratt, Boyd Bode, Carleton Washburne, William H. Kilpatrick, Helen Parkhurst, and Theodore Brameld, to name a few—sought to redefine the role of schooling and learning in modern society.

They came closer to success than any other alternative movement—in the 1920s the Progressive Education Association and its journal, *Progressive Education,* gained momentum and public attention—but ultimately they failed.

The Depression, World War II and the reactionary climate of the McCarthy era reinforced American culture's preference for an education concerned with social discipline. But meanwhile, two important educational movements were launched in Europe and brought to the U.S. Maria Montessori (1870–1952) was a physician who, treating disturbed children, found that intellectual and emotional deprivation in early life was a major source of their problems. She emphasized careful observation of children's developmental patterns and accordingly devised a "prepared environment" that would allow children to explore their world without undue adult interference. Her curriculum was integrated and interdisciplinary, oriented toward universal human themes rather than dry facts and skills. Thousands of Montessori schools now exist around the world as alternatives to conventional schooling. Rudolf Steiner (1861–1925) was another important innovator in education; his "Waldorf" school model has inspired over 400 schools in many parts of the world. Steiner called for a loving relationship between teacher and child; the class is a genuine community that remains with the same teacher from first through eighth grade. The Waldorf curriculum is built on the arts, myths, and legends of many cultures, and aims to appeal to the child's inner search for meaning and beauty. Steiner particularly emphasized the role of creative imagination.

In the 1960s, another sort of alternative education emerged as American culture came under intensive criticism from scholars, students, and activists in the civil rights, antiwar, and women's movements. By 1967–68, this criticism had extended to public education. Passionate educators including John Holt, George Dennison, Jonathan Kozol, Herbert Kohl, James Herndon and others rejected the education establishment and inspired the movement for "free schools" (run by teacher or parent cooperatives), "open classrooms," and even "deschooling" and homeschooling.

It is with this era that the phrase "alternative education" is most readily associated, for this was a serious rebellion against the assumptions underlying modern schooling. What is still called the "alternative education" movement today—the network of small democratic schools with which Jerry Mintz has been associated for twenty years—has its roots in this period. It is certainly a rich and diverse movement, with concerns ranging from interpersonal issues to radical social change, but at its heart it represents a *libertarian* orientation—the desire to free individuals and communities from ideological and bureaucratic authority. Libertarian education has a rich heritage of its own, going back to Tolstoy's school and the Modern School movement founded by Francisco Ferrer in Spain around the turn of the century.[17] (Over two hundred Ferrer "modern schools" were founded. Ferrer was executed on framed-up charges by the Spanish monarchy because his ideas were a threat to them.)

In the 1970s, another alternative movement emerged in conjunction with the larger "human potential" movement in American society. Basing their methods on the humanistic psychology of Abraham Maslow, Carl Rogers, Rollo May and Fritz Perls, these educators devised educational environments that would integrate intellectual and affective (emotional) experience, guide students through values-clarification exercises and introduce them to meditation and other paths to inner knowledge. By the early 1980s, the term "holistic education" was used to describe these approaches that sought to unify body, mind and spirit, including an ecological perspective. Inspired by various writers on these subjects and so-called new science (such as Willis Harman, Thomas Berry, Joanna Macy, Fritjof Capra, Marilyn Ferguson), a distinct holistic education movement emerged with the founding of GATE (the Global Alliance for Transforming Education) in 1990. This group reflects many of the countercultural themes historically represented by alternative educators, with an additional emphasis on "green" values such as global thinking and deep ecology.

Indeed, holistic education may well represent the tip of a "postmodern" iceberg. "Postmodern" thinking is a sophisticated, multifaceted critique of modern science, politics, and culture. Many of the foundational assumptions of modern education, like those discussed earlier, are now being critically examined by a growing number of theorists, including C.A. Bowers, Don Oliver, David Orr, Kathleen Kesson, Bill Pinar, and William E. Doll, among others. It may well be that for an "information age" in an increasingly global culture on an ecologically threatened planet, the present institution of schooling will prove to be obsolete.[18] Patrick Shannon would be correct, then, in saying that alternative educators "are not odd, or negative, or necessarily modern"; they may come to be seen as *postmodern* educators who were simply ahead of their time.

Notes

[1] Patrick Shannon, *The Struggle to Continue: Progressive Reading Instruction in the United States* (Portsmouth, NH: Heinemann, 1990).

[2] This discussion of the foundational assumptions of public schooling is based on a review I wrote of *Schooling for Tomorrow: Directing Reforms to Issues that Count,* edited by Thomas J. Sergiovanni and John H. Moore (Needham Heights, MA: Allyn & Bacon, 1989). My review appeared in *Holistic Education Review* vol. 4, no. 2 (Summer 1991).

[3] Quoted in Charles Leslie Glenn, Jr., *The Myth of the Common School* (Amherst, MA: University of Massachusetts Press, 1988), p. 183.

[4] Quoted in David Nasaw, *Schooled to Order: A Social History of Public Schooling in the United States* (New York: Oxford University Press, 1979), p. 64.

[5] Max Rafferty, *Suffer, Little Children* (New York: Devin, Adair, 1962).

[6] Frederick Rudolf, ed. *Essays on Education in the Early Republic* (Cambridge: Harvard University Press, 1965), pp. 9–23.

[7] Quoted in Joel Spring, *Education and the Rise of the Corporate State* (Boston: Beacon Press, 1972), pp. 56–7.

[8] See Paul G. Faler, *Mechanics and Manufacturers in the Early Industrial Revolution: Lynn Massachusetts 1780–1860* (Albany: State University of New York Press, 1981), Nasaw's *Schooled to Order* (note 4 above) and Herbert Gutman, *Work, Culture and Society in Industrializing America* (New York: Alfred A. Knopf, 1976).

[9] I have discussed these issues in more detail in *What Are Schools For? Holistic Education in American Culture* (Brandon, VT: Holistic Education Press, 1990).

[10] See Raymond E. Callahan, *Education and the Cult of Efficiency* (Chicago: University of Chicago Press, 1962); also Patrick Shannon, *Broken Promises: Reading Instruction in Twentieth Century America* (Westport, CT: Greenwood/Bergin & Garvey, 1989).

[11] The phrase "educational-industrial complex" was coined by James Moffet; see his *Coming on Center: Essays in English Education,* 2nd ed. (Portsmouth, NH: Heinemann, 1988) for a thoughtful critique of modern education. The other quotation is from Sandra Conn, "Education's Failure Stirs Small Business Ire" *Crain's Chicago Business,* Sept. 15, 1986.

[12] Quoted in Michael Katz, *The Irony of Early School Reform* (Cambridge: Harvard University Press, 1968), p. 120.

[13] Karl E. Weick & Reuben R. McDaniel, Jr., in Sergiovanni & Moore, *Schooling for Tomorrow* (see note 2 above) p. 137.

[14] Judith E. Lanier & Michael W. Sedlak, in Sergiovanni & Moore, *Schooling for Tomorrow,* p. 333.

[15] Ralph Waldo Emerson, "Education" in *Selected Writings,* edited by William H. Gilman (New York: New American Library, 1965), p. 430.

[16] See Morris Berman, *The Re-enchantment of the World* (Ithaca, NY: Cornell University Press, 1981); Fritjof Capra, *The Turning Point: Science, Society and the Rising Culture* (New York: Simon & Schuster, 1982); Rupert Sheldrake, *The Rebirth of Nature: The Greening of Science and God* (New York: Bantam Books, 1991); and Douglas Sloan, *Insight-Imagination: The Emancipation of Thought and the Modern World* (Brandon, VT: Resource Center for Redesigning Education, 1994) for important critiques of scientific positivism.

[17] See Paul Avrich, *The Modern School Movement: Anarchism and Education in the United States* (Princeton, NJ: Princeton University Press, 1980).

[18] This argument is very strongly articulated by Gregory A. Smith in *Education and the Environment: Learning to Live with Limits* (Albany: SUNY Press, 1992). Smith explicitly recognizes that already-existing alternative learning environments provide an important step toward a postmodern educational system. He describes some alternative programs in detail. This book, as well as other alternative and postmodern perspectives and Patrick Shannon's work quoted in this essay, are available through the catalog *Great Ideas in Education.* Contact the Resource Center for Redesigning Education, P.O. Box 298, Brandon, VT 05733 (phone 800-639-4122).

— Ron Miller

Part Three

DIRECTORY OF EDUCATIONAL ALTERNATIVES

Arranged alphabetically by state and by zip code within the state

UNITED STATES

Alabama

Fellowship of Christian Home Educators
PO Box 563, Alabaster, AL 35007
205-664-1633

EPIC Elementary
1000 Tenth Ave S, Birmingham, AL 35205
Louise Caskey, 205-581-5155
Type: magnet
K-5th grade
Philosophy.

Ramsay Alternative School
1800 Thirteenth Ave S, Birmingham, AL 35205
Robert Atkins Jr, 205-933-2420
Type: magnet
9-12th grade
Gifted and talented.

Creative Montessori, Inc (1968)
1650 28th Ct S, Birmingham, AL 35209
Barbara R. Spitzer, Dir, 205-879-3278
Non-profit; tuition: $225-355/mo
17 teachers, 200 students, ages 3-12
Affiliations: AMS, AMI, SNMC
Governance by board
French; PE; soccer field; gym; childcare; urban location.

St Theresa Montessori School
1800 Collier Dr, Midfield, AL 35228-2706

East Lake UMC Academy
1603 Great Pine Rd, Birmingham, AL 35235
Type: home-based

Joseph S. Bruno Montessori Academy (1982)
5509 Timber Hill Rd, Birmingham, AL 35242
Theresa B. Sprain, 205-995-8709
Non-profit; tuition: $195-285
11 teachers, 7 assistants, 206 students
Interview with director required
Affiliation: AMS
Governance by administrator
Extensive facilities and materials in (esp. physical and earth)
   science and biology; completely equipped classrooms in
   new buildings on 12 acres; rural location; transportation;
   interns accepted.

CHEF: Christian Home Education Fellowship of Alabama
3423 19th St, Tuscaloosa, AL 35401
Arné Williams or Wayne & Connie Atchinson, Pres
Type: state home-based
Database of AL contacts, schools and support groups.

University Place School
221 18th St, Tuscaloosa, AL 35401
Linda Albritton
Type: Montessori

Montessori School of Tuscaloosa
919 23rd Ave E, Tuscaloosa, AL 35404-3013

Tuscaloosa Academy
420 26th St N, Tuscaloosa, AL 35406-2722
Type: Montessori

Country Day Montessori School
4500 Crabbe Rd, Northport, AL 35476-2025

Fellowship Christian Support Group
PO Box 583, Double Springs, AL 35553
Rosemary Wright, 205-489-2636
Type: home-based

Crossroads Center
809 Church St NE, Decatur, AL 35601
Michael Ferguson, 205-552-3054
Type: public choice

Athens Support Group
16373 H'ville/Brownsville Ferry Rd, Athens, AL 35611
Randy & Dawn Wilson
Type: home-based
Way Home Christian School, area coordinator.

Children's House Montessori
PO Box 2237, Florence, AL 35630

Florence/Sheffield Area Support Group
1701 Lake Pickwick Dr, Sheffield, AL 35660
Joel Rainer, 205-381-6245
Type: home-based

The Country Day School (1987)
1930 Slaughter Road, Madison, AL 35758
Debby Clark, Admissions Dir, 205-772-8086
Type: Montessori; tuition: $250/400/mo.

15 teachers, 155 students, ages 3–12
Affiliations: NIPSA, NAYEC, Daycare Directors Assoc
Governance by an administrator
Hands-on approach; Mortenson Math; Spanish; whole language; computers; fine arts (art, music, classics); portfolio assessment; childcare; suburban location.

Anderson Montessori Academy
7887 Highway 72 W, Madison, AL 35758-9559

Montessori Learning Center (1990)
2334 Pansy, Huntsville, AL 35801
Brenda Tackett, Owner/Dir, 205-534-6296
Tuition: $190/330/mo
4 teachers, 1 assistant, 50 students, ages 3–6
Entrance requirement: toilet trained
Affiliation: AMS
Governance by an administrator
Childcare; urban location; interns accepted.

Mrs Rhonda's Montessori School
3102 Leeman Ferry Rd SW, Huntsville, AL 35801-5330
Rhonda Pennel

Children's House of Montessori
2605 Leeman Ferry Rd SW, Huntsville, AL 35801-5611

Montessori School of Huntsville (1965)
1220 Blevins Gap, Huntsville, AL 35802
Marcia Ramsey, Adm, 205-881-3790
Non-profit; tuition: $1,620/2,475/yr
5 teachers, 3 assistants; student ages 3–9
Affiliation: AMS
Governance by administrator, board
Childcare; suburban location; interns accepted.

Montessori Academy in Bailey Cove
1695 Shady Cove Cir SE, Huntsville, AL 35802-2753
Murty Vardhani

Lee High School
606 Forrest Circle, Huntsville, AL 35811
Tom Owens, 205-536-8136
Type: magnet
9–12th grade
Creative and performing arts and pre-engineering.

Homeschooling Network
PO Box 742, Tallahassee, AL 36078
205-283-5018

Tuskegee Institute Montessori School
School Of Education, Tuskegee Institute, AL 36088-1693

Montessori Academy
1025 S Hull St, Montgomery, AL 36104-5141

Carver Creative & Performing Arts Center
2001 W Fairview Ave, Montgomery, AL 36108
Cheryl Carter, 205-269-3813
Montgomery County
Type: magnet
10–12th grade
Creative & Performing Arts.

Covenant Academy
1147 Freemont St, Montgomery, AL 36111
Lauren Coats, 205-284-1574
Type: home-based
Umbrella.

Greengate Montessori School
3265 McGehee Rd, Montgomery, AL 36111-2301

Christian Educators at Home in Anniston (CHEAHA)
2044 Alexandria-Jacksonville Rd, Jacksonville, AL 36265
Dennis & Nancy Smith, 205-848-9944, 831-5355

Marietta Johnson School of Organic Education
8 Marietta Dr, Box 1555, Fairhope, AL 36532
Mary Bradshaw, 205-925-9347
Type: independent

Baldwin County Home Educators
PO Box 1645, Robertsdale, AL 36567
Gail Hinton

Child Day Care Association of Mobile
457 Conti St, Mobile, AL 36602-2407
Type: Montessori

Dunbar Magnet of the Performing Arts
500 St Anthony St, Mobile, AL 36603
Freddie Sigler, 205-690-8255
4–8th grade
Creative & Performing Arts.

Old Shell Rd Elementary
1705 Old Shell Rd, Mobile, AL 36604
Bobby Glenn Smith, 205-473-6571
Type: magnet
K–3rd grade
Creative and performing arts.

Montessori Academy (1973)
18 Pierpont Dr W, Mobile, AL 36606
Anne C. Brandon, Dir, 205-478-7219
Non-profit; tuition: $220-360/mo
3 teachers, 6 assistants, 84 students, ages 18 mo-6 yrs
Urban location.

Homeschool Advocates
5962 Chalet Dr N, Mobile, AL 36608
205-344-3239

Montessori Spring Hill Children's House
4307 Old Shell Rd, Mobile, AL 36608
Weinacker's Montessori School (1969)
227 Hillcrest Rd, Mobile, AL 36608
John P.B. Weinacker, 344-8755, FAX: 342-0712
Tuition: $150-285/mo
4 teachers, 4 assistants, 68 students, ages infant-9
Governance by administrator
Preschool Spanish; childcare; urban location; interns accepted.

The Sunshine House
Hwy 90 W, Mobile, AL 36609
Type: Montessori

Montessori Children's House
462 Yevonne Curve E, Mobile, AL 36609-2309

Southwest Alabama Home Educators
6721 Timbers Dr W, Mobile, AL 36695
Fred/Kathy Dryer, 205-639-9452

Auburn/Opelika Christian Home Educators
PO Box 2171, Auburn, AL 36830

Children's Montessori School
231 E Drake Ave, Auburn, AL 36830-3917

St Joseph School
General Delivery, Holy Trinity, AL 36859-9999
Type: Montessori

Chattahoochee Valley Homeschoolers Support Group
Phenix City, AL 36867
Bruce/Donna Potenza, 205-298-1229

Alaska

Chattah Central ABC Junior High
1405 E St, Anchorage, AK 99501
Keith Taton, 907-272-2581
7-8th grade

Chugach Optional
1205 E St, Anchorage, AK 99501
Nancy Wertzbaugher, 907-279-1531
Pre K-6th grade

Denali Elementary School
148 E 9th Ave, Anchorage, AK 99501-3699
Susan Moore
Type: Montessori

Northern Lights ABC Elementary
1705 W 32nd Ave, Anchorage, AK 99503
907-277-2439
K-6th grade

Stellar Secondary Alternative School (1992)
2508 Blueberry St, Anchorage, AK 99503
Donald Shackelford
Type: public choice
50 students

Steller Secondary School (1974)
2508 Blueberry, Anchorage, AK 99503
Donald Shackelford, 907-279-2541
Type: public choice
250 students, 9-12th grade
Governance by democratic school meeting
Seminar approach; community involvement; work
  experience.

McLaughlin Youth Center
2600 Providence Dr, Anchorage, AK 99508
Bernard Wesley, Prin, 907-561-1433
7-12th grade

SAVE
2650 E Northern Lights Blvd, Anchorage, AK 99508-0000
Benny Benson, 907-276-5535
9-12th grade

SEARCH
2650 E Northern Lights Blvd, Anchorage, AK 99508-0000
Barbara Garrison, 907-278-9631
7-10th grade

Anchorage Montessori School
1200 E 27th Ave, Anchorage, AK 99508-3303
Betsey Howard

King Career Center
2650 E Northern Lights Blvd, Anchorage, AK 99508-9631
Esther Cox

School Within a School
East HS, 4025 E 24th Ave, Anchorage, AK 99510
Type: public choice

Hillside Montessori
7340 Hillside Way, Anchorage, AK 99516
Lorrie Lundquist-Yeagle

SAVE
410 E 56th, Anchorage, AK 99518
Beverly Kirkbride, 907-561-1155
9-12th grade

Nikolaevsk School
PO Box 39010, Ninilshik, AK 99556
Kenneth Moore, Prin, 907-235-8972
K-12th grade

Aniak Vocational Technical Center
PO Box 49, Aniak, AK 99557
Bobette Bush, 907-675-4339, FAX: 907-675-4330

Homeschoolers of Cordova
PO Box 782, Cordova, AK 99574-0782
907-424-3943

Birchwood ABC Elementary
Birchwood Loop Rd, PO Box 400, Eagle River, AK 99577-0000
Frank Randazzo, 907-688-2549
Pre K-6th grade

Kodiak Island Correspondence
722 Mill Bay Rd, Kodiak, AK 99615
Christopher Provost, Teacher, 907-486-9251

Mat-Su Alternative High School
600 E Railroad Ave, Suite 6, Wasilla, AK 99654
Peter Burchell, 907-373-7775
9-12th grade

Mat-Su Correspondence
600 E Railroad Ave Suite 1, Wasilla, AK 99654
Peter Burchell, 907-746-9549
Pre K-12th grade

Independent and Distance Educators of Alaska
152 Park Ave, Soldotna, AK 99669
Judith McKinley, 907-262-6315

Kenai Alternative School
152 Park Ave, Soldotna, AK 99669
Rick Matiya, 907-262-6315
K-12th grade

Hermon Hutchens Special Ed School
PO Box 398, Valdez, AK 99686
907-835-4735
HS

Fairbanks Montessori School
2014 30th Ave, Fairbanks, AK 99701
Kristie Yunker

**Directory of Global Education Resources in North
  America**
(See Resource Appendix)

Hutchinson Career Center
3750 Geist, Fairbanks, AK 99709-3547
Don Verstrate, Principal, 907-479-8286
9-12th grade

Alternative Learning Center SAVE
PO Box 264, Kotzebue, AK 99752
Rolla Weber, Principal, 907-442-3341
Pre K-11th grade

Northwind School
PO Box 309, Nenana, AK 99760
Liz Boario, 907-832-5594
K-12th grade

Juneau Montessori Center
750 Saint Ann's Ave, Douglas, AK 99801
Deanna Claus

Centralized Correspondence School
3141 Channel Dr #100, Juneau, AK 99801-7897
Marylou Purvis, Prin, 907-465-2835, FAX: 465-2935
K-12th grade

Mt Edgecumbe High School
1330 Seward Ave, Sitka, AK 99835-9438
Tom Brown, Superintendent, 907-966-2201
9-12th grade

Ketchikan Correspondence
Pouch Z, Ketchikan, AK 99901
Anthony Kennedy, Asst Supt, 907-225-6226
K-12th grade

Revilla High School (1972)
3131 Baranof Ave, Ketchikan, AK 99901
Shelley Stallings, Educator, 907-225-6681
Type: public at-risk
4 teachers, 45–52 students, ages 14-21, 9-12th grade
Governance by teachers and principal
Teacher qualifications: AK Certification
Field study of forestry, archeology, karst, fisheries, wildlife
   biology; camping on remote island; multi-aged classes;
   non-compulsory class attendance; rural location; transportation; interns accepted.

Arizona

Khalsa School (1971)
346 E Coronado Rd, Phoenix, AZ 85004
Satwant Singh Khalsa, 602-252-3759
Type: Montessori, non-profit; tuition: $225/345/mo
6 teachers, 10 assistants, 100 students, ages infant-9
Affiliations: AZ Child Care Assn, FOM; accreditation: AZ DHS
Governance by teachers and administrators
Holistic education; Spanish; yoga; gymnastics; swimming;
   computers; creative dance; drama; art; childcare; urban
   location; interns accepted.

Reed Montessori School (1971)
1124 N 3rd St, Phoenix, AZ 85004
Rita Ramirez, Dir, 602-252-1953
Non-profit; tuition: $160-285/mo
1 teacher, 2 assistants, 30 students, mainly international, ages
   3-6
Affiliation: AMI
Governance by board
Childcare; interns accepted.

Sunrise Montessori Academy
844 North 9th Ave, Phoenix, AZ 85007-2316
Aleena Meyer

Arcadia Montessori Schools
5115 E Virginia Ave, Phoenix, AZ 85008-1628

Montessori Childrens Home
516 W Bethany Home Rd, Phoenix, AZ 85013-1554

North Central Montessori School
6730 N 7th St, Phoenix, AZ 85014-1003

Villa Montessori
4535 N 28th St, Phoenix, AZ 85016-4998
Marilyn Burbach

Phoenix Special Programs (1969)
3132 W Clarendon Ave, Phoenix, AZ 85017
Robert A. Dye, Supt; Eleanor Marine, Registrar, 602-263-2601,
   FAX: 602-265-7179
Maricopa County
Type: independent, non-profit; tuition: $80 per half credit
40 teachers, 3000 students, ages 11+, 7-12th grade
Affiliation: NCASC
Governance by principal and board
Teacher qualifications: AZ Certification
Correspondence courses; full curriculum available.

Montessori Day Schools (1981)
9215 N 14th St, Phoenix, AZ 85020
Margaret M. Huffman, 602-943-7672, FAX: 902-395-0271
Tuition: $260/375/mo
16 teachers, 9 assistants, 224 students, ages infant-18
Accreditation: AMS
Governance by an administrator
4 large campuses in Phoenix area; sports; music; dance;
   childcare; suburban location; interns accepted.

Montessori Center School
8625 N 19th Ave, Phoenix, AZ 85021

Phoenix Learning Alternatives Network (**PLAN**) (1989)
8835 N 4th Pl, Phoenix, AZ 85028
Nancy Sherr, 602-483-3381, FAX: 602-483-6299
Maricopa County
Type: home-based, non-profit; cost: $24/yr; $10/mo activity
   fee
Student ages infant-16
Weekly activities on yearly theme; hands-on approach; non-
   sectarian, eclectic; newsletter; suburban location.

Maryvale High School
3415 N 59th Ave, Phoenix, AZ 85033
Rene Diaz, 602-271-2503
District 210
Type: magnet
9-10th grade
Leadership education; community service.

South Phoenix Montessori
1300 S 10th St, Phoenix, AZ 85034-4516

South Mountain High School
5401 S 7th St, Phoenix, AZ 85040
Art Lebowitz, 602-271-2884
District 210
Type: magnet
9-12th grade
Visual and performing arts; law; aerospace.

Sigueme
PO Box 54171, Phoenix, AZ 85078
Type: Montessori

Good Earth Montessori (1978)
734 N Robson, Mesa, AZ 85201
Nelleke Van Savooyen, Dir, 602-833-2622

Tuition: $205/370
2 teachers, 3 assistants, 35 students, ages 3-6
Children must be 2 1/2 years old and toilet trained
Governance by an administrator
Located in small old house; suburban location; interns accepted.

Bethany Home Educators (1980)
2720 S Flint Circle, Mesa, AZ 85202
Lyn Codier, Secretary, 602-820-5050
Maricopa County
Cost: $15/yr membership fee
290 teachers, 1,000 students, ages 5-17, K-12th grade
Governance by board
Teacher qualifications: Affidavit; Iowa Test scores
Iowa Tests for ages 8+; resources; workshops; field trips; educational fairs; speech meets; spelling bees; urban location

Tempe Montessori School (1978)
410 S El Dorado Rd, Mesa, AZ 85202
Irma Letson, Adm, 602-966-7606
Tuition: $3,762/yr
10 teachers, 100 students, ages 2.5-12
Entrance requirement: toilet trained
Affiliation: AMI
Governance by teachers and principal
Teacher qualifications: AMI credential
Farm animal pets; German; French; optional religious ed; no letter grades; non-compulsory class attendance; multi-aged classes; extensive field trips; suburban location; interns accepted.

Mesa Montessori
2830 South Carriage Lane, Mesa, AZ 85202-7801
Lillian D Busch

Arizona Families for Home Education
639 E Kino Dr, Mesa, AZ 85203
602-964-7435
Type: state home-based

Montessori International School
1930 E Glencove St, Mesa, AZ 85203

Montessori Children's Centre
2834 E Southern Ave, Mesa, AZ 85204-5517
Tammy and Diane

Casa De Montessori
745 S Extension Rd, Mesa, AZ 85210-2212

Adobe Montessori School
1700 W Warner Rd, Chandler, AZ 85224-2676

Rainbow Montessori School (1980)
6520 E Cactus Rd, Scottsdale, AZ 85254
Doris or Robin Rasmussen, 602-998-0024
Tuition: $240-370/mo
5 teachers, 20 assistants, 151 students, ages infant-9
Affiliations: NAMTA, AMS
Governance by administrator
Computers; Spanish; Yamaha music; ethnic luncheons; international mix; childcare; urban location; interns accepted.

Families For Home Education
PO Box 4661, Scottsdale, AZ 85261
602-941-3938

Joyful Child
(See Resource Appendix)

Fountain Hills Montessori School
15055 N Fountain Hills Blvd, Fountain Hills, AZ 85268-2330
Carrie Jackson

Alpha Omega Institute (1991)
404 W 21st St, Tempe, AZ 85282
Trish Tackleson, VP of Finance, 602-731-9411, FAX: 602-438-2702
Maricopa County
Type: independent
175 students, ages 5-14, pre K-8th grade
Governance by board
Curriculum; service; supplies

Awakening Seed School
1130 W 23rd St, Tempe, AZ 85282
Bill Glover, 602-829-1479
Type: independent
Student ages 3-10
Student publishing; global responsibility; creative problem solving.

Sunrise Montessori School (1979)
14233 N 47th Ave, Glendale, AZ 85306
Mary Ellen Marion, Dir, 602-843-6053
Tuition: $155-310/mo
2 teachers, 5 assistants, 88 students, ages toddler-12
Entrance requirement: visit
Affiliation: NAMTA
Governance by an administrator
Complete traditional program; Spanish; childcare; suburban location.

SPICE (1992)
104-14 W Mulberry Dr, Avondale, AZ 85323
Susan Taniguchi, 602-877-3642
Type: home-based
Suburban location.

Pinal County Public Schools (1993)
PO Box 769, Florence, AZ 85323
Dr Peggy Roush, 602-868-6565, FAX: 602-868-4671
Type: public choice
400 students

Mountainside Montessori
29022 N 62nd St, Cave Creek, AZ 85331
Lucy Kastelic

World University (1967)
Box 2470, Desert Sanctuary Campus, Benson, AZ 85602
Dr. Howard John Zitko, President, 602-286-2985, FAX: 602-286-2985
Pima County
Type: higher education, non-profit
Governance by board
Consists of independent schools in the USA, Italy, Nigeria, Japan, and India; nontraditional; tutorial; experiential; soul oriented; parent institution, World University Roundtable, founded in 1947, has annual conference; interns accepted.

Wood Canyon School (1992)
PO Box 781; 54 Wood Canyon, Bisbee, AZ 85603
David Skinner, Dir, 602-432-3995
Cochise County
Type: independent, non-profit; tuition: shared expenses
2 teachers, 6 students, ages 6-18
Affiliations: NCACS, NALSAS, RGEA
Governance by faculty, student reps; parent cooperative
96 acres; seasonal streams; outdoor survival; fine arts; no letter grades; non-compulsory class attendance; multi-aged classes.

Cochise County Families for Home Education
PO Box 533, St David, AZ 85630
602-720-4134

Casas Adobess Montessori
665 W Roller Coaster Rd, Tucson, AZ 85704-3817

Carden School of Tucson (1980)
5260 N Royal Palm Dr, Tucson, AZ 85705
Nette F. Jeppson, Dir, 602-293-6661
Type: independent, non-profit; tuition: 1,750/yr
12 teachers, 95 students, ages 4–14, K-8th grade
Governance by principal
Teacher qualifications: Carden Ed Foundation training
Christian; language; arts; patriotism; urban location.

Montessori Schoolhouse
1127 N 6th Ave, Tucson, AZ 85705

Tucson High School
400 N Second Ave, Tucson, AZ 85705
John Hoge, 602-822-2480
Type: magnet
9–12th grade
Science, math, cumputers, and performing arts.

Reaching Their Highest Potential
430 S Essex Ln Dept N8a, Tucson, AZ 85711
Type: Montessori

New Morning Montessori
1135 N Craycroft Rd, Tucson, AZ 85712

Holladay Elementary
1110 E 33rd St, Tucson, AZ 85713
Nora Grig, 602-798-2737
Type: magnet
4–6th grade
Visual and performing arts.

Senior High Accomodations (1971)
115 N Fremont, Tucson, AZ 85716
Fred McConnell, 602-798-8663
Pima County
Type: public at-risk
2 teachers; student ages 15–22, 9–12th grade
For district resident dropouts only
Governance by faculty and student representatives, demo-
    cratic school meeting
Contracts; experiential; community use; multi-aged classes;
    extensive field trips; non-compulsory class attendance;
    urban location

Kino Learning Center
6625 N First Ave, Tucson, AZ 85718
602-297-7278
Type: independent

Highland Free School (1970)
510 S Highland St, Tucson, AZ 85719
Nicholas Sofka, Director, 602-623-0104
Pima County
Type: independent, non-profit; tuition: $340/mo,
    scholarships
3 teachers, 30 students, ages 4.5–12, ungraded
Entrance requirements: parent participation
Governance by parent advisory committee open to all
Teacher qualifications: certified teachers
Holistic approach; computer center; creative audio and video
    activities; music; Spanish; innovative adventure play-
    grounds; goats, ducks, geese; no letter grades; multi-aged
    classes; extensive field trips; urban location; interns
    accepted.

Project MORE (1973)
440 S Park Ave, Tucson, AZ 85719
Robert J Mackey, Dir, 602-798-2806
Pima County
Type: public choice/at-risk
8 teachers, 200 students, partly at-risk, ages 14–22, 9–12th
    grade
Entrance requires orientation, residency; waiting list
Affiliation: NCASC
Governance by teachers, principal, board

Teacher qualifications: AZ Certification
Multi-aged classes; field trips required; academic probation;
    urban location; limited transportaion; interns accepted.

Zephyr Press (1979)
(See Resource Appendix)

Tucson Home Education Network (THEN)
7521 E Lurlene Dr, Tucson, AZ 85730

Arches (1987)
PO Box 11482, Tucson, AZ 85746
Sarah Evans, 602-883-7436
Type: home-based, non-profit; cost: $20/yr
Emphasizes spiritual knowledge.

Hands-On Science
(See Resource Appendix)

Hermosa Montessori School (1978)
12051 E Fort Lowell/ 8800 E 22nd St, Tucson, AZ 85749/ 85710
Sheila Stolov, Dir, 602-749-5518, 296-9537
Tuition: $220-345/mo
8 teachers, 6 assistants, 160 students, ages 3–12
Governance by an administrator and democratic school
    meeting
Teacher qualifications: certification
Two 10-acre campuses; authentic Montessori program;
    nature studies; art; music; movement; Spanish; childcare; ·
    urban & rural locations; interns accepted.

Sunrise
PO Box 190, Whiteriver, AZ 85941
Dave Jones, 602-338-4844
Whiteriver USD
Type: public choice
20 students, HS
Community service; vocational; school-developed business;
    childcare.

Flagstaff Junior Academy
2401 W Hwy 66 #10, Flagstaff, AZ 86001
Type: Montessori

Twin Peaks Montessori School
2717 N Center St, Flagstaff, AZ 86001

Home School Advantage
(See Resource Appendix)

Prescott College
220 Grove Ave, Prescott, AZ 86301
Derk Janssen, 602-778-2090
Type: higher education

Primavera School
1410 Copper Basin Rd, Prescott, AZ 86301
Carol Darrow, 602-445-5382

The Garden Street Learning Center
134 Garden St, Prescott, AZ 86301
Marilyn King
Type: Montessori

Parents Association of Christian Home Schools
HC 63 Box 5530, Mayer, AZ 86333-9712

Wind, Sand and Stars Sedona Montessori
90 Deer Trail Dr, Sedona, AZ 86336-5120
Claudine Mohoney

Circle of Angels (1988)
PO Box 3452, West Sedona, AZ 86340
Leia & Douglas Stinnett, Dirs, 602-282-0580
Yavapai County
Type: home-based
Students mainly spiritually focused/gifted
Spiritual education; ready-to-use manual of lesson plans;
    teacher-training; no letter grades.

Veade Valley School (1948)
3511 Veade Valley School Rd, Sedona, AZ 86351
Roy E. Grimm, Head, 602-284-2272, FAX: 284-0432
Type: independent, boarding, non-profit; tuition: $17,325/yr,
    scholarships
24 teachers, 125 students, ages 13-18, 9-12th grade
Entrance restrictions: no significant psychological, drug,
    alcohol problems
Affiliations: NAIS, AEE
Governance by board
Teacher qualifications: prefer BA/MA
Emphasis on anthropology, intercultural understanding, envi-
    ronmental stewardship; classical college prep; experiential
    pedagogy; multi-aged classes; extensive field trips; rural
    location; interns accepted.

Montessori Schoolhouse
1325 Ramar Rd, Bullhead City, AZ 86442
Lynn Zubrick

Window Rock Alternative Education
PO Box 559, Ft Defiance, AZ 86504
Tom Hatch, Director, 602-729-5705 x479
Type: public at-risk
4 teachers, 53 students, mainly at-risk, ages 14-20, HS
Entrance requirements: HS counselor approval, residency
Governance by board
Teacher qualifications: state certification
Focus on Navajo culture; computer lab; self-paced; multi-
    aged classes; extensive field trips; rural location; trans-
    portation; interns accepted.

Arkansas

Lakeside Montessori School
609 W 15th St, Pine Bluff, AR 71601
Mark Willett

Montessori School of Pine Bluff
611 W 23rd Ave, Pine Bluff, AR 71601

El Dorado Watson Educational Center
1401 E Center St, El Dorado, AR 71730
Sue Castleberry, 501-864-5091
Students mainly at-risk
Experiential; community service required

South Conway County Alternative Education Program
2220 Prince St, Conway, AR 72032
Raymond Simon, Supt, 501-329-8849
Entrance by assignment
Ten day alternative to suspension; addresses affective and
    cognitive skills; interpersonal relations; parent involvement;
    community resources

Arkansas Christian Home Education Association
PO Box 4410, North Little Rock, AR 72116-2110
501-753-9164
Type: state home-based

Crystal Hill Elementary Magnet
5001 Doyle Venable Dr, N Little Rock, AR 72118
Wanda Ruffins, 501-753-4323
Student ages 4+,-6th grade
Written, oral, visual communications.

Montessori School of North Little Rock, Inc
Kierre & Perin Rd, N Little Rock, AR 72118

Hilltop Montessori School
3 Kierre Dr, North Little Rock, AR 72118-2303

Children's House Montessori School (1973)
4023 Lee Ave, Little Rock, AR 72205
Nancy Hall, Dir, 501-664-5993
Tuition: $125-205/mo
5 teachers, 4 assistants, 77 students, ages infant-9
Affiliation: AMS; accreditation: AMI
Governance by administrator
Homey; spacious grounds; multi-cultural; music; dance;
    childcare; urban location; interns accepted.

Dunbar Junior High School
1100 Wright Ave, Little Rock, AR 72206
Nancy Volsen, 501-324-2440
Type: magnet
7-9th grade
Gifted and talented; international.

Mann Arts & Math Junior High School
1000 E Roosevelt, Little Rock, AR 72206
Marian Lacey, 501-228-2450
Type: magnet
7-9th grade

Montessori Cooperative School
2101 Main St, Little Rock, AR 72206-1573

Infant Toddler Montessori School (1978)
1509 N Pierce, Little Rock, AR 72207
Jyothi R. McMinn, Dir/Owner, 501-666-7249, FAX: 501-664-
    8847
Tuition: $9-18/day
3 teachers, 3 assistants, 54 students, ages infant-6
Affiliations: AMI, AMS, NCME, AAWS; accreditation: NAEYC
Governance by an administrator
International and peace studies; visiting international faculty;
    interns accepted.

Tanglewood Montessori School
7217 Ohio St, Little Rock, AR 72207-5023

Little Rock Montessori School
3704 Woodland Hts, Little Rock, AR 72212
John Harris, Bd Pres, 501-225-2428
Non-profit; tuition: $195/240/mo
4 teachers, 7 assistants, 78 students, ages infant-6
Affiliation: AMI
Governance by parent cooperative
Childcare.

Joseph Pfeifer Kiwanis Camp (1929)
5512 Ferndale Cutoff, Little Rock, AR 72216
Sanford Tollette, 501-821-3714
Students mainly at-risk, ages 9-13, 4-6th grade
Enrollment restricted to underpriviliged children
Summer program; year-round alternative classroom

Children's House Montessori
PO Box 5105, Little Rock, AR 72225

Forrest City
334 Graham St, Forrest City, AR 72335
Emerson Hall, Supt, 501-633-1485
Students mainly at-risk
Low ratio; GED classes; specialized individual instruction
addresses special needs; childcare

Madison Montessori School
PO Box 170, Madison, AR 72359-0170
Vhaness W Chambers

Lee County Alternative Education Program
55 N Carolina St, Marianna, AR 72360
James Davis, Supt, 501-295-7100
7-12th grade
Enrollment restricted to students removed from regular
class
Behavior modification; social adjustment; supervision;
intense instruction in core subjects

Crowley's Ridge Christian Parent Education Association
4303 Brenda, Jonesboro, AR 72401
501-972-0243
Type: home-based

Jonesboro Alternative Education Program
1307 S Flint St, Jonesboro, AR 72401
Bill Beasley, Supt, 501-933-5800
ES
Enrollment restricted to academic underachievers, social/
emotional problems, family dysfunction, or disturbed pat-
terns of behavior
Intensive, positive, individualized academic, social services.

The Children's House
300 E Nettleton Ave, Jonesboro, AR 72401-4123
Type: Montessori

Batesville Montessori School, Inc
PO Box 2595, Batesville, AR 72503-2595

Montessori Children's Schoolhouse (1979)
415 N 2nd, Harrison, AR 72601
Karen Shrum, Adm, 501-741-1141
Non-profit; tuition: $160-200/mo
6 teachers, 6 assistants, 128 students, ages infant-12
Affiliation: NAMTA
Governance by board
French activities; custom designed facilities; childcare; rural
location; interns accepted.

Clear Spring School (1974)
Box 142, Eureka Springs, AR 72632
Molly Seeligson, Dir, 501-253-7888, FAX: 253-7590
Carroll County
Type: independent, non-profit
6 teachers, 4 assistants, 56 students, ages 3-12, pre K-6th
grade
Governance by board
Teacher qualifications: college degree
One on one learning; computer use beginning in first grade;
German; handbells; in a 12-acre wooded area, close to
downtown; no letter grades; multi-aged classes; extensive
field trips; rural location; interns accepted.

Fayetteville High School Within a School
1001 Stone, Fayetteville, AR 72701
Mr Wistry
Type: public

S-W-S (1993)
1001 Stone St, Fayetteville, AR 72701
Wisty Rorabacher or Gilda Pierce, 501-444-3050
Washington County

Type: public choice
2 teachers, 50 students, ages 15–19, 10-12th grade
Entrance requirements: interview, acceptance by team of
students, parents, teachers, residency
Governance by democratic school meeting
Design own course work; freedom to identify, pursue personal interests; multi-aged classes; non-compulsory class
attendance; extensive field trips

Uptown School (1972)
108 N West Ave, Fayetteville, AR 72701
501-444-3042
Washington County
Students mainly at-risk
Entrance requirements: referral, district residency
Governance by administrators
Teacher qualifications: AR Certification
Separate campus; graduation credits; multi-aged classes;
interns accepted.

Montessori Children's House
57 E Township St, Fayetteville, AR 72703-2814

Headwater School (1976)
Rt 1, Pettigrew, AR 72752
Kate Kuff, President, Board of Directors, 501-861-5613
Madison County
Type: independent, home-based, non-profit; cost: $6/day,
scholarships
5 teachers, 40 students, ages 2-17
Governance by democratic school meeting, parent
cooperative
Located in Ozark Mountains; outdoor education; cooperative
games; multi-disciplinary projects; with 1, 2, or 3 day attendance, combines home education with group experience;
global and environmental awareness; no letter grades;
non-compulsory class attendance; multi-aged classes;
extensive field trips; interns accepted.

Springdale Learning Center & "Nite" School (1989)
1103 Emma Ave, Springdale, AR 72764
John Dollarhide, 501-750-8832, FAX: 750-8811
Washington County
Type: public at-risk
8 teachers, 175 students, mainly at-risk, ages 15-50, 9-12th
grade
Residency required
Governance by principal
Teacher qualifications: BA, state certification
Urban location.

Comprehensive Health Education Program
PO Box 645, Paris, AR 72855
Ann Sneed, Dir, 501-963-6531
Student ages 7-18
Social skills development

Ft Smith Montessori School (1968)
3908 Jenny Lind, Ft Smith, AR 72903
Jacqie Mollenhauer, Dir, 501-646-7225
Non-profit; tuition: $1350/2250
6 teachers, 93 students, ages 3-12
Children must be at least age 2 3/4 yrs and toilet trained
Affiliations: AMS, NAMS
Governance by an administrator and board of trustees
Childcare; urban location.

St Scholastica Montessori
PO Box 3489, Fort Smith, AR 72913-3489

4-A School
PO Box 9050, Texarkana, AR 75505-9050
Robert McDonald, Dir, 501-772-4792
Students mainly at-risk
Social skills; counseling; resource speakers; field tours

California

Huntington Beach Alternative
16666 Tunstall Lane, Huntington Beach, CA

Drew Junior High School
8511 Compton Ave, Los Angeles, CA 90001
213-583-6961
Type: magnet
7–9th grade
Gifted and high ability.

Russell Elementary School
1263 E Firestone Blvd, Los Angeles, CA 90001
213-582-5034
Type: magnet
1–6th grade
Gifted and high ability.

Simon Rodia High School (1965)
2315 E 103rd St, Los Angeles, CA 90002
Michael Wardlow, Prin, 213-567-3804, FAX: 213-567-4346
Type: public at-risk
3 teachers, 110 students, mainly at-risk, ages 15–18, 9–12th
   grade
No residency requirement
Governance by principal
Teacher qualifications: CA secondary credential, LA USD
   teacher pool
Multi-aged classes; urban location.

Thomas Riley High School (1971)
1524 E 103rd St, Los Angeles, CA 90002
Mary Ann Shiner, Prin, 213-563-6692, FAX: 566-6379
Los Angeles USD
Type: public at-risk
15 teachers; student ages 13–18, 7–12th grade
Enrollment restricted to pregnant students; no residency
   requirement
Governance by teachers and principal
Teacher qualifications: secondary certification
3 locations; academics; child birth and parenting skills; multi-
   aged classes; urban location; transportation.

Jessie Owens Opportunity Center
8222 S San Pedro, Los Angeles, CA 90003

Burroughs Junior High School
600 S McCadden Pl, Los Angeles, CA 90005
213-938-9146
Type: magnet
7–9th grade
Gifted and high ability.

32nd St USC School
822 W 32nd St, Los Angeles, CA 90007
213-748-8007
Type: magnet
1–9th grade
Performing and visual arts.

Adams Junior High School
151W 30th St, Los Angeles, CA 90007
213-744-1502
Type: magnet
7–9th grade
Gifted and high ability.

Audobon Junior High School
4120 11th Ave, Los Angeles, CA 90008
213-299-2882
Type: magnet
7–9th grade
Gifted and high ability.

Hillcrest Elementary
4041 Hillcrest Dr, Los Angeles, CA 90008
213-296-6867
Type: magnet
1–6th grade
Enriched studies; music.

David Roberti Child Development Center
1156 East Vernon Ave, Los Angeles, CA 90011-3719
Type: Montessori

Los Angeles Unified Alternative Education
450 N Grand Ave, Los Angeles, CA 90012

Tri-C Opportunity
644 W 17th St, Los Angeles, CA 90015

Baldwin Hills Elementary
5421 Rodeo Rd, Los Angeles, CA 90016
213-937-7223
Los Angeles USD
Type: magnet
1–6th grade
Gifted and high ability.

Alternative Education and Work Center (AEWC) (1987)
1320 W Third St, Los Angeles, CA 90017
Wendy Reddish, 213-625-6649
Type: public at-risk; scholarships
62 teachers, 2,300 students, ages 14–19, HS
Enrollment restricted to HS dropouts; no residency
   requirement
Affiliation: LAUSD/Adult Division
Governance by school-based shared decision making
Teacher qualifications: ability to work with high-risk youth
23 locations; lab approach; voc training; competency-based;
   independent study; multi-aged classes; urban location.

Mid City Alternative School
3100 W Adams Blvd, Los Angeles, CA 90018
213-731-9346
Type: magnet
K–12th grade

Euclid Elementary
806 Euclid Ave, Los Angeles, CA 90023
213-263-6792
Type: magnet
1–6th grade
Gifted and high ability.

Stevenson Junior High School
725 S Indiana St, Los Angeles, CA 90023
213-262-4101
Type: magnet
7–9th grade
Gifted and high ability.

Southern California Montessori School
1430 S Centinela Ave, Los Angeles, CA 90025-2501

Hollywood High School
1521 N Highland Ave, Hollywood, CA 90028
213-461-7139
Los Angeles USD District
Type: magnet
9-12th grade
Performing arts.

El Sereno Junior High School
2839 N Eastern Ave, Los Angeles, CA 90032
213-223-2441
Type: magnet
7-9th grade
Gifted and high ability.

Los Angeles County High School for the Arts
5151 State University Dr, Los Angeles, CA 90032
Bo Vitolo, Prin; Alistair Hunter, Asst Prin, 213-343-2787,
    FAX:-2549
Type: public choice
485 students, ages 15-18, 10-12th grade
Entrance requirements: audition, portfolio review, 2.0 GPA,
    no F's
Affiliation: ALCOE/CSULA
Governance by shared decision making committees, princi-
    pal, faculty and student representatives, board
On CSULA campus; CSULA courses; performance; exhibits;
    extensive field trips; interns accepted.

Multnomah St Elementary
2101 N Indiana Ave, Los Angeles, CA 90032
213-224-8098
Type: magnet
1-6th grade
Highly gifted.

Hamilton High School
2955 Robertson Blvd, Los Angeles, CA 90034
310-836-1262
Type: magnet
10-12th grade
Humanities.

Palms Junior High School
10860 Woodbine St, Los Angeles, CA 90034
310-837-5001
Type: magnet
6-8th grade
Gifted and high ability.

Play Mountain Place (1948)
6063 Hargis St, Los Angeles, CA 90034
Gaile Price, Director, 213-870-4381
Type: independent, non-profit; tuition: call, scholarships
10 teachers, 84 students, ages 2-13
Entrance requirements: must share humanistic education
    philosophy
Governance by teachers and principal, board; student input is
    encouraged, expected; final decision by board
Teacher qualifications: experience in humanistic educational
    techniques
A "country school in the city"; non-authoritarian consensus
    based problem-solving, decision-making, communication
    skills; student body reflects the community, culturally and
    economically; no letter grades, non-compulsory class
    attendance; multi-aged classes; urban location; interns
    accepted.

Acacia Montessori School
10520 Regent St, Los Angeles, CA 90034-6304
Also at 2820 Ponce Ave, Belmont.

Community Elementary
5954 Airdrome St, Los Angeles, CA 90035
213-935-7288
Type: magnet
K-6th grade
Humanities; social sciences.

Los Angeles Center For Enrichment
5931 W 18th St, Los Angeles, CA 90035

Open School
6085 Airdrome St, Los Angeles, CA 90035
213-937-6249
Type: magnet
1-6th grade
Individualized.

Bancroft Junior High School
929 N Las Palmas Ave, Los Angeles, CA 90038
213-464-3174
Type: magnet
7-9th grade
Television; theater; fine arts.

Eagle Rock Elementary
2057 Fair Park Ave, Los Angeles, CA 90041
213-258-5342
Type: magnet
3-6th grade
Gifted and high ability.

Eagle Rock High School
1750 Yosemite Dr, Los Angeles, CA 90041
213-254-7767
Type: magnet
7-9th grade
Highly gifted.

Eagle Rock Montessori School
1439 W Colorado Blvd, Los Angeles, CA 90041-2320

Arroyo Seco Alternative School (1972)
4805 Sycamore Tr, Los Angeles, CA 90042
J. Sherrard, Asst Prin, 213-254-5141, FAX: 344-0235
Type: public choice
22 teachers, 500 students, ages 5-14, K-8th grade
Entrance requirements: application; no residency
    requirement
Teacher qualifications: state credential
Open structure; dedicated to academic excellence and multi-
    cultural education; students must be able to work inde-
    pendently; community-based learning; parents, students,
    teachers participate in decision-making; multi-aged
    classes; extensive field trips; urban location; transporta-
    tion; interns accepted.

Crenshaw High School
5010 11th Ave, Los Angeles, CA 90043
213-296-5370
Type: magnet
10-12th grade
Gifted and high ability.

Loyola Village Elementary/LMU
8821 Villanova Ave, Los Angeles, CA 90045
310-670-0480
Type: magnet
1-6th grade
Performing and visual arts.

Fairfax High School
7850 Merose Ave, Los Angeles, CA 90046
213-651-5200
Type: magnet
10-12th grade
Visual arts.

West Hollywood Opportunity
1049 N Fairfax Ave, Los Angeles, CA 90046

Wonderland Ave Elementary
8510 Wonderland Ave, Los Angeles, CA 90046
213-654-4914
Type: magnet

1-6th grade
Gifted and high ability.

74th St Elementary
2112 W 75th St, Los Angeles, CA 90047
213-753-2338
Type: magnet
1-6th grade
Gifted and high ability.

Pluralistic School
851 Wellsley, Los Angeles, CA 90049
Joel Pelcyger, Director

Westland School (1949)
16200 Mulholland Dr, Los Angeles, CA 90049
Janie Lou Hirsch, Dir, 310-472-5544, FAX: 310-472-5807
Type: independent, non-profit; tuition: $7,400/yr,
  scholarships
16 teachers, 130 students, ages 5–12, K–6th grade
Entrance by application
Governance by board
Integrated; social studies-based; experiential; block building;
  no letter grades; extensive field trip; interns accepted.

Montessori of West Los Angeles
PO Box 49325, Los Angeles, CA 90049-0325

Turningpoint School
1300 North Sepulveda Blvd, Los Angeles, CA 90049-1656
Deborah Richman
Type: Montessori

Ramona Opportunity High Alternative Education
231 S Alma Ave, Los Angeles, CA 90063

Home Education League of Parents (HELP) (1989)
3208 Cahuenga Blvd W, Suite 131, Los Angeles, CA 90068
Terri Endsley, Exec Dir, 800-582-9061
Supports affiliated, autonomous chapters; newsletter;
  unschooling philosophy.

Horizons High School (1991)
6740 E Suva St, Bell Gardens, CA 90201
Paul F. McKernan, Tch in charge, 213-726-1225 x 6191, FAX:
  213-887-7837
Type: public choice
2 teachers, 24 students, ages 15–18, HS
Entrance by student choice; residency
Affiliation: Montebello USD
Governance by teachers and principal
Teacher qualifications: credential
Site-based decision-making; outcome-based activities; pro-
  jects; work experience; post graduation assistance; subur-
  ban location.

Moreno High School (1971)
241 Moreno Dr, Beverly Hills, CA 90212
Joseph S. Wianecki, Dir, 310-201-0661 x456, FAX: 556-4319
Los Angeles County
Type: public at-risk
2 teachers, 40 students, ages 15–18, 9–12th grade
Entrance requirements: HS referral, residency
Governance by board
Counseling; no letter grades; multi-aged classes; urban
  location.

Compton Unified Alternative/Opportunity
1104 E 148th St, Compton, CA 90220

Compton Lynwood Child Development Center
530 W Alondra Blvd, Compton, CA 90221
Type: Montessori

Culver City Independent Study
11450 Port Rd, Culver City, CA 90230

Montessori School of Downey
11822 Downey Ave, Downey, CA 90240

Montessori Children's Academy
9062 Firestone Blvd, Downey, CA 90241-5318
Janet Morton

Ameston Elementary
1048 W 149th St, Gardena, CA 90247
310-327-3716
Los Angeles USD District
Type: magnet
1-6th grade
Television; theater; fine arts.

Moneta High School (1972)
1230 W 177th St, Gardena, CA 90248
Adele Bloom, Prin, 310-329-4139, FAX: 310-352-4027
Los Angeles County
Non-profit
3–4 teachers, 85–97 students, mainly at-risk, ages 16–20
Entrance requirements: referral, lacking credits, residency
Affiliation: Los Angeles USD
Governance by teachers, principal
Teacher qualifications: CA certification
Contract-based; self-paced; computers; diploma program;
  some SE services; multi-aged classes; interns accepted.

Lynwood Unified Alternative Education
4020 Imperial Hwy, Lynwood, CA 90262

Santa Monica Montessori Institute
27473 Pacific Coast Hwy, Malibu, CA 90265
Type: Montessori teacher education

Independent Study Program (1982)
1301 Artesia Blvd, Manhattan Beach, CA 90266
Judi James, Coord, 372-1730
Los Angeles County
Type: public at-risk
13 teachers, 440 students, ages 14+, 9–12th grade
Entrance requirements: 7th grade reading level, meeting, no
  residency requirement
Governance by teachers, principal
Interns accepted.

Manhattan Academy (1975)
1740 Mahattan Beach Blvd, Manhattan Beach, CA 90266
Gail Burch, 310-374-1804
Type: Montessori; tuition: $425-745/mo
6 teachers, 5 assistants, 102 students, ages infant–12
Accreditation: AMI
Governance by administrator
Self-concept, creativity; childcare; suburban location; interns
  accepted.

Temescal Canyon High School (1976)
777 Temescal Cyn Rd, Pacific Palisades, CA 90272
Kay Lachter, Prin, 310-454-0315, FAX: 310-459-8560
Los Angeles County
Type: public at-risk
3 teachers, 81 students, ages 15–18, 9–12th grade
Entrance requirements: referral, residency
Governance by leadership council, Principal, teachers, classi-
  fied member, parent member
Teacher qualifications: CA credential
Work experience; poet conducts literary sessions, has pub-
  lished students' work; counseling group for girls in abusive
  relationships; extensive field trips; multi-aged classes

Redondo Shores High School (1993)
1000 Del Amo Blvd, Redondo Beach, CA 90277
Judi James, Coord, 213-798-8690
Los Angeles County
Type: public at-risk
5 teachers, 134 students, ages 16–19, 10–12th grade
Entrance requirements: age 16, meeting, residency
Governance by teachers, principal

Redondo Beach Alternative Program (1993)
1401 Inglewood Ave, Redondo Beach, CA 90278
Sandy Clifton, 310-379-5449, FAX: 310-798-8659
Los Angeles County
Non-profit
Suburban location.

State St Elementary School
3211 Santa Ana St, South Gate, CA 90280-2305
Type: Montessori

Morning Glory School
2522 Lincoln Blvd, Marina Del Rey, CA 90291
Zarina Paroo
Type: Montessori

Westside Alternative School
104 Anchorage St, Marina del Rey, CA 90292
310-821-2019
Los Angeles USD District
Type: magnet
K-12th grade

Independent Study
401 S Inglewood Ave, Inglewood, CA 90301

The University of Children (1986)
1518 Centinela Ave, Inglewood, CA 90302
Lore Geissler, Adm, 310-677-4406
Type: Montessori; tuition: $275-520/mo
4 teachers, 7 assistants, 107 students, ages infant-9
Affiliations: NCME, AMS, AMI, PACE, NAEYC
Governance by administrator
Childcare; urban location.

Montessori Institute of Los Angeles
2918 Santa Monica Blvd #D, Santa Monica, CA 90404
Type: Montessori teacher education

Thoreau Montessori School
1508 17th St, Santa Monica, CA 90404-3402

Santa Monica Montessori School
1619 20th St, Santa Monica, CA 90404-3817

Santa Monica Alternative School House (SMASH) (1973)
2802 4th St, Santa Monica, CA 90405
Jim Cantor, Teaching Prin, 310-396-2640, FAX: 452-4353
Los Angeles County
Type: public choice
6 teachers, 180 students, ages 5-14, K-8th grade
Residency required
Affiliation: SMM USD
Governance by teachers, principal, parents, students
Teacher qualifications: CA credential
Community of learners; no letter grades; extensive field trips;
   multi-aged classe; interns accepted.

Santa Monica Waldorf School (1988)
1512 Pearl St, Santa Monica, CA 90405
Beth Resch, 310-450-0349
Non-profit; tuition: $6,400-7,200/yr, scholarships
5 teachers, 4 assistants, 47 students, ages 3-10, pre K-4th
   grade
Entrance requirements: mutual agreement; teacher deter-
   mines acceptability
Affiliation: AWSNA
Governance by board of trustees
Teacher qualifications: Waldorf teacher training
Emphasizes imaginition, creativity in all areas; each subject
   pursued intensively for several weeks; no letter grades;
   suburban location; interns accepted.

Montessori Institute of Los Angeles, Inc (1968)
PO Box 265, Santa Monica, CA 90406
Estela C. Palmieri, Dir of Training, 310-395-5676
Type: higher education, non-profit; tuition: $4,800/course

20 students, mainly International
Entrance requirements: college degree or 2 years college and
   experience with children.
Accreditations: AMI, MACTE
Governance by board
AMI 3-6 Primary Diploma summer course; approved by CA
   Supervisor of Public Instruction; urban location.

GreenMeadows Montessori
4627 Greenmeadows Ave, Torrance, CA 90505-5505

Peninsula Montessori School
3646 Newton St, Torrance, CA 90505-6635
Claudia Krikorian

Whittier Friends School (1974)
6726 S Washington Ave, Whittier, CA 90601
Sharon G. Rollins, 310-945-1654
Los Angeles County
Type: Quaker, non-profit; tuition: $3,400/yr, scholarships
1 teacher, 30 students, ages 6-13, 7th grade
Affiliation: Friends Council on Education
Governance by administrator, board
Teacher qualifications: credential
Latest technology; whole classroom learning; conflict man-
   agement-based approach; extensive field trips; multi-aged
   classes; urban location.

Primente Montessori School
10947 South Valley Home Ave, Whittier, CA 90603-3041
Millie Primanti

East Whittier City School District
14535 E Whittier Blvd, Whittier, CA 90605
Dr Ron Oliver
Type: Montessori

Sierra Vista High Alternative Education
9401 S Painter Ave, Whittier, CA 90605

Franklin Community School
5777 S Lockleed Ave, Whittier, CA 90606
Marsha A Brown, Prin, 310-692-1497, FAX: 908-0332
Los Angeles County
Type: public at-risk
2 teachers, 1 assistant, max 34 students, mainly at-risk, ages
   11-14, 6-9th grade
Serves Little Lake, South Whittier districts or Whittier city residents; referral required
Governance by teachers, principal, student reps.
Multi-aged classes; counselor; max 17/class; JTPA; parenting
   classes; suburban location; transportation; interns
   accepted.

HCL (1980)
PO Box 4643, Whittier, CA 90607
Susan Jordan, Dir, 310-696-4696
Los Angeles County
Type: home-based; cost: $196/family
600 students, ages 5-18, K-12th grade
Affiliations: NCACS, NHA, NALSAS
Governance by principal
Administrative unit.

Children's House
8271 Gay St, Cyprus, CA 90630
Ann Perrah, 714-995-2054
Type: independent

Contract Independent Study
123 S Montebello Blvd, Montebello, CA 90640

Fremont Elementary (1991)
200 W Madison Ave, Montibello, CA 90640
213-721-2435
Los Angeles County
Type: public choice

23 teachers, 700 students, mainly at-risk, ages 5–10, K–4th grade
Residency required
Governance by teachers, principal.
No letter grades; multi-aged classes; suburban location; transportation.

PASS Program (1990)
12820 Pioneer Blvd, Norwalk, CA 90650
Jerry McCamly, Team Leader, 310-868-0431 x5209, FAX: 802-1596
Los Angeles County
Type: public at-risk; scholarships
11 teachers, 550 students, ages 13–20, HS
Enrollment restricted to dropout residents; parent conference required
Governance by teachers and principal
Teacher qualifications: state certification
CAI; independent study; suburban location.

Home And Independent Study
9333 Los Lomas Ave, Pico Rivera, CA 90660

Ruben Salazar Continuation (1968)
9515 Haney St, Pico Rivera, CA 90660
Anne Eichman, Dir of Alt Ed, 310-801-5128
Los Angeles County
Type: public at-risk
7 teachers, 170 students, ages 16–18, 10–12th grade
Entrance requirements: age 16+, residency
Governance by teachers and principal
Teacher qualifications: BA
Self-paced; job development; multi-aged classes; suburban location; interns accepted.

ABC Secondary Independent Study
16534 S Carmenita Rd, Cerritos, CA 90701
Type: public choice

Montessori Center
12914 Wolverton Ln, Cerritos, CA 90701
Hasmita Parekh

Tracy High School
12222 Cuesta, Cerritos, CA 90701
George Hershey, Prin, 310-926-7136
Los Angeles County
Type: public at-risk
20 teachers, 350 students, ages 16–19, 10–12th grade
Governance by teachers and principal
Thematic instruction; student, family services; career ed; suburban location.

Bellflower Unified Alternative Education
9242 E Laurel St, Bellflower, CA 90706

Montessori School of Bell Flower
5840 Premiere Ave, Lakewood, CA 90712
Deborah Zampa

J. F. Cooper High Alternative Education
2210 Taper Ave, San Pedro, CA 90731

Dodson Junior High School
28014 Montereina, San Pedro, CA 90732
310-833-4877
Los Angeles USD District
Type: magnet
7–9th grade
Gifted and high ability.

Harbor Math & Science Elementary
1214 Park Western Pl, San Pedro, CA 90732
310-831-3253
Los Angeles USD District
Type: magnet
1–6th grade
Gifted and high ability.

South Shores/CSUDH
2060 W 35th St, San Pedro, CA 90732
310-832-6596
Los Angeles USD District
Type: magnet
1–6th grade
Performing and visual arts.

Brighter Days Montessori
1903 W Summerland St, San Pedro, CA 90732-2526

Ambler Ave Elementary
319 E Sherman Dr, Carson, CA 90746
310-532-4090
Los Angeles USD District
Type: magnet
1–6th grade
Gifted and high ability.

Stevenson Elementary
515 Lime Ave, Long Beach, CA 90802
Julie Mendell, 310-437-0407
Type: magnet
K–5th grade
Performing arts.

Bay Shore School
PO Box 13038, Long Beach, CA 90803
310-434-3940
Type: home-based
Entrance restricted to south CA residents.
Independent study.

Hamilton Middle School
1060 E 70th St, Long Beach, CA 90805
Ross Shickler, 310-602-0302
Type: magnet
6–8th grade
Visual arts and technology.

Lindberg Middle School
1022 E Market St, Long Beach, CA 90805
Dennis Lyman, 310-424-2845
Type: magnet
6–8th grade
Visual and performing arts.

Hughes Middle School
3846 California Ave, Long Beach, CA 90807
Gary Graves, 310-595-0831
Type: magnet
6–8th grade
Talent achievement program.

Butler Elementary
1890 Orange Ave, Long Beach, CA 90808
Charlotte Smith, 310-591-7477
Type: magnet
3–8th grade
Creative and performing arts.

Montessori School-Eureka
5306 E Arbor Rd, Long Beach, CA 90808
Leonard F. Pijpaert, 310-421-5505
Tuition: $300–330/mo
4 teachers, 10 assistants, 135 students, ages 3–12
Entrance requirements: toilet trained; test
Affiliation: AMI; accreditations: CA DSS, PACE
Governance by administrator
Support activities in piano, computers, sports, gymnastics, dance and karate; childcare; suburban location; interns accepted.

Audio Memory Publishing
(See Resource Appendix)

Long Beach Educational Partnership High School (1988)
125 E 8th St, Long Beach, CA 90813
Frederick Kimbrel, Asst Prin, 310-495-1397
Los Angeles County
Type: public choice
9 teachers, 500 students, mainly at-risk, ages 15–18, 9–12th
   grade
Enrollment restricted to residents out of school 45 days
Governance by board
Teacher qualifications: state credential
Cooperative effort between Long Beach USD and Ultimate
   Resources Inc. to recover youths who have dropped out of
   the regular comprehensive HS; modified independent
   study; urban location.

Fremont Elementary
4000 E 4th St, Long Beach, CA 90814
Jacquelyn Dodge, 310-439-6873
Type: magnet
K–5th grade
Conservatory of music.

Bixby Elementary
5251 E Stearns St, Long Beach, CA 90815
Naomi Blackmore, 310-498-3794
Type: magnet
K–5th grade
Structure of the intellect.

Montessori at Long Beach
2301 Ximeno Ave, Long Beach, CA 90815-1839
Barbara McClean

Montessori Children's House
5550 E Atherton St, Long Beach, CA 90815-4008

Pasadena Waldorf School (1979)
209 E Mariposa St, Altadena, CA 91001
Nancy Thurlbeck, Enrl Dir, 810-494-9564
Los Angeles County
Non-profit; tuition: $4,378-5,379/yr, scholarships
22 teachers, 162 students, ages 4.9–12, K–8th grade
Affiliation: AWSNA
Governance by faculty and board
Teacher qualifications: Waldorf training
Classical curriculum; suburban location.

Walden School
1999 Mar Vista Ave, Altadena, CA 91001-3127
Type: Montessori

Rancho High Independent Study
150 S 3rd Ave, Arcadia, CA 91006

Wonder Years Montessori School
141 W Las Tumas Dr, Arcadia, CA 91007
Sandhya Ray

Alternative Education Work Center
1620 Huntington Dr, Duarte, CA 91010

Monrovia Unified Alternative Education
325 E Huntington Dr, Monrovia, CA 91016

Park Alternative Center (1984)
c/o Monrovia USD, 325 E Huntington Dr, Monrovia, CA 91016
Dr Ellen A. Lavin, 818-357-0320
Los Angeles County
Type: public home-based choice
3 teachers, 80 students, mainly at-risk, ages 5–18, K–12th
   grade
Governance by teachers and principal
Teacher qualifications: state certification
Independent study for HS; homeschooling; suburban
   location.

Montrose Christian Montessori
2710 Piedmont Ave, Montrose, CA 91020
Linda Di Giovanni

Arcadia Montessori School
PO Box 767, Arcadia, CA 91066-0767

Pasadena Unified Alternative
1520 N Raymond Ave, Pasadena, CA 91103

Pacific Oaks Children's School (1945)
714 W California Blvd, Pasadena, CA 91105
Margaret Heritage, Dir
Los Angeles County
Type: Quaker, non-profit; tuition: $1,080-8,100/yr
45 teachers, 225 students, ages infant–9, pre K–3rd grade
Balance of genders, ages, and ethnicities sought
Affiliation: Pacific Oaks College
Governance by principal, faculty and student representatives,
   and board
Teacher qualifications: MA for faculty, BA for head teachers in
   ECE or CD
Anti-bias; emphasis on environment, self-esteem, choice
   making; parental involvement; arts; special needs; human-
   istic; Pacific Oaks College students work with children; two
   campuses, located in Cultural Heritage neighborhoods; no
   letter grades; multi-aged classes; childcare; suburban;
   interns accepted.

Sequoyah School (1958)
535 S Pasadena Ave, Pasadena, CA 91105
Hannah Maclaren, 818-795-4351, FAX: 818-795-8773
Los Angeles County
Type: independent, non-profit; tuition: $5400, scholarships
17 teachers, 166 students, ages 5–14, K–8th grade
Entrance requirements: no severely emotionally disturbed
Governance by democratic school meeting
Teacher qualifications: BA/BS, certification; open ed, Montessori, alt ed experience preferred
23,000 volume library; integrated curriculum; arts, science,
   camping/field studies; computers in all classrooms; science
   lab facility; no letter grades; multi-aged classes; extensive
   field trips; childcare; urban location; interns accepted.

Pasadena Alternative
2600 Paloma St, Pasadena, CA 91107

Victory Montessori Schools
444 S Sierra Madre Blvd, Pasadena, CA 91107

Glendale Montessori Elementary
1212 N Pacific Ave, Glendale, CA 91202
Nina O'Brian and Marta Tyler

St Anne Montessori School
1479 E Broadway, Glendale, CA 91205

Glendale Unified Alternative Education
223 N Jackson St, Glendale, CA 91206

Charter Oak Alternative Education
Box 9, Covina, CA 91273-5356

Oak View High School (1982)
5701 E Conifer St, Oak Park, CA 91301
Larry Misel, Dir of Alt Ed Progs, 818-707-7919
Ventura County
Type: public at-risk
4 teachers, 50 students, mainly at-risk, ages 14–19, 9–12th
   grade
Entrance requirements: must be approved by school district
Governance by teachers and principal
Teacher qualifications: state credential
A California Model School; college and non-college paths;
   suburban location; interns accepted.

Montessori School of Agoura
28124 Driver Ave, Agoura, CA 91301-2643

Welby Way Elementary
23456 Welby Way, West Hills, CA 91307
818-992-8229

Los Angeles USD District
Type: magnet
1–6th grade
Gifted and high ability.

Beginning Montessori Children's House
7475 Fallbrook Ave, West Hills, CA 91307-1502

Aggeler (William Tell) Opportunity
21050 Plummer St, Chatsworth, CA 91311

Santa Susana School
22280 Devonshire St, Chatsworth, CA 91311
Dr Marilyn Lucky
Type: Montessori

Region B Opportunity
15530 Hesby St, Encino, CA 91316

Montessori Children's House of Newbury Park (1986)
1360 S Wendy Dr, Newbury Park, CA 91320-5532
Pam Nelson, Dir, 805-499-7495
Non-profit; tuition: $275-315/mo
4 teachers, 3 assistants, 44 students, ages 3-9
Entrance requirements: age 2.5; toilet trained; visit
Quiet, natural setting; across from Santa Monica Rec. Area;
     interns accepted.

Balboa Blvd Elementary
17020 Labrador St, Northridge, CA 91325
818-349-4801
Los Angeles USD District
Type: magnet
1–6th grade
Gifted and high ability.

Highland Hall School
17100 Superior St, Northridge, CA 91325
Christine Meyer
Type: Waldorf

Casa Montessori
17633 Lassen St, Northridge, CA 91325-1400
Sakura Long

Vena Ave Elementary
9377 Vena Ave, Arleta, CA 91331
818-896-9551
Los Angeles USD District
Type: magnet
1–6th grade
Gifted and high ability.

Pacoima Junior High School
9919 Laurel Canyon Blvd, Pacoima, CA 91331
818-899-5291
Los Angeles USD District
Type: magnet
7–9th grade
Television; theater; fine arts.

Canterbury Ave Elementary
13670 Montague St, Pacolma, CA 91331
818-892-1104
Los Angeles USD District
Type: magnet
1–6th grade
Gifted and high ability.

Cleveland High School
8140 Vanalden Ave, Reseda, CA 91335
818-349-8410
Los Angeles USD District
Type: magnet
9–12th grade
Humanities.

Sherman Oaks Center for Enriched Studies
18605 Erwin St, Reseda, CA 91335

Park Montessori
13130 Herrick Ave, Sylmar, CA 91342
Grace Park

Sepulveda Junior High School
15330 Plummer St, Sepulveda, CA 91343
818-891-5859
Los Angeles USD District
Type: magnet
7–9th grade
Gifted and high ability.

Porter Junior High School
15960 Kingsbury St, Granada Hills, CA 91344
818-891-1807
Los Angeles USD District
Type: magnet
7–9th grade
Gifted and high ability.

San Jose St Elementary
14928 Clymer St, Mission Hills, CA 91345
818-361-4325
Los Angeles USD District
Type: magnet
1–6th grade
Highly gifted.

Rivendell Montessori School
10651 Vinedale St, Sun Valley, CA 91352-2825

Learning Post High Independent Study
23007 W Dalbey Dr, Valencia, CA 91355

Portola Junior High School
18720 Linnet St, Los Angeles, CA 91356
818-708-2865
Type: magnet
7–9th grade
Highly gifted.

Montessori World
2685 Calle Abedul, Thousand Oaks, CA 91360
David Browne

Little Oaks Montessori
101 N Skyline Dr, Thousand Oaks, CA 91361

International Association of Progressive Montessorians
2509 E Thousand Oaks Blvd #340, Thousand Oaks, CA 91362
Lori and Lowell Byrne

JFK School Within a School
27845 Beacon St, Castaic, CA 91384
Jane Lopez
Type: public choice

Valley Alternative Magnet (1973)
6701 Balboa Ave, Van Nuys, CA 91406
Terry Morton, Prin, 818-342-6133
Los Angeles County
Type: public choice
20 teachers, 540 students, ages 5-18, K–12th grade
Entrance by application
Affiliation: LA USD
Governance by principal, teachers, parents, students
Community service; career internships; concurrent enroll-
     ment in community colleges; speakers bureau; extensive
     field trip; interns accepted.

Fairfield School
16945 Sherman Way, Van Nuys, CA 91406-3614
Howard Spike
Type: Montessori

Kester Ave Elementary
5353 Kester Ave, Van Nuys, CA 91411
818-787-3026
Los Angeles USD District
Type: magnet
1-6th grade
Gifted and high ability.

Van Nuys High School
6535 Cedros Ave, Van Nuys, CA 91411
818-781-2371
Los Angeles USD District
Type: magnet
10-12th grade
Performing arts.

Tripod Montessori School
2901 Keystone St, Burbank, CA 91504

Earhart High School
5355 Colfax Ave, N Hollywood, CA 91601
Susan Allen, Prin, 818-769-4877, FAX: 818-980-1794
LA USD District
Type: public at-risk
4 teachers, 120 students, mainly at-risk, ages 15–19, 10–12th
  grade
No residency requirement
Governance by teachers, principal, and clerical rep
Teacher qualifications: CA Credential
Structured and individualized classes; special ed; student vol-
  unteer program; multi-aged classes.

North Hollywood High School
5231 Colfax Ave, N Hollywood, CA 91601
818-769-8510
Los Angeles USD District
Type: magnet
10-12th grade
Highly gifted.

Baldwin Park Unified Alternative Education
Box 3699, Baldwin Park, CA 91706

GoodEarth Montessori School (1991)
2593 Chino Hills Pkwy, Chino Hills, CA 91709
Sofi Kasubhai, Adm, 909-393-0998
Tuition: $285-330/mo
6 teachers, 11 assistants, 156 students, ages 2.5–6
Entrance requirements: immunization record; enrollment,
  emergency packets; change of clothing, blanket; county
  residency
Affiliation: NCME
Governance by administrator
Teacher qualifications: Montessori training
Individualized education; childcare; suburban location;
  interns accepted.

Buena Vista High School (1965)
13509 Ramona Ave, Chino, CA 91710
Jon L. Sweat, Prin, 909-628-9903
San Bernardino County
Type: public choice
11 teachers, 270 students, partly at-risk, ages 14–19, 9–12th
  grade
Residency required
Governance by board
Student advisory groups meet weekly with staff to set cur-
  riculum and goals; model teen parenting program; multi-
  aged classes; childcare; interns accepted.

Montessori Academy of Claremont
PO Box 1150, Claremont, CA 91711
Sandra Schmidt

Montessori Children's Center
4066 Las Casas Ave, Claremont, CA 91711-2323

Riverside Area Home Learners
c/o Gibson, 13171 Spur Branch Cir, Corona, CA 91719
909-245-0902

Children's Montessori Center
2791 Green River Rd # 112, Corona, CA 91720
Misreen A Firdjy

Montessori School of Pai Plaza (1991)
1400 W 6th St, #112, Corona, CA 91720
Mina Patel, Dir, 909-734-0555
Tuition: $250/350/mo
2 teachers, 4 assistants, 50 students, mainly international,
  ages 3–6
Entrance requirements: age 2.5; toilet trained
Governance by administrator
Safe environment; plentiful materials; computer; music;
  gymnastics; dance; childcare; urban location; interns
  accepted.

Ramona Community School
3548 Doe Springs, Carona, CA 91720-3603
Cheri Spies Havens
Type: Montessori

Ranger High Independent Study
Box 269, Covina, CA 91723

ET2 Eductional Clinic (1986)
15540 E Fairgrove Ave, La Puente, CA 91744
Michael Keith, Coord, 818-855-3132
Los Angeles County
Type: public at-risk
23 teachers, 400 students, ages 13–18, 8–12th grade
Must be 45+ days out of school; minors enroll with parent
Governance by teachers, principal
Teacher qualifications: CA credential
Assessment based; individualized; goal setting; job place-
  ment, readiness; HS completion; urban location.

Valley Alternative High School (1993)
14162 E Lomitac Ave, La Puente, CA 91744
Rob Arias, Prin, 818-855-3855, FAX: 818-855-3719
Los Angeles County
Type: public/independent choice/at-risk
13 teachers, 450 students, ages 13–19, 7–12th grade
Residency required
Governance by teachers and principal
Open school concept; technology-driven curriculum; subur-
  ban location; transportation; interns accepted.

Montessori Child Development Center (1974)
15207 Los Robles Ave, Hacienda Heights, CA 91745
Carolyn S. Mueller, Exec Adm, 968-8207
8 teachers, 4 assistants, 184 students, ages infant-12
Affiliation: AMI
Governance by administrator
Air conditioning; year-round swimming lessons; field trips;
  French; Spanish; music; keyboard; arts; suburban location;
  interns accepted.

Genesis Program (1989)
904 N Willow Ave, La Puente, CA 91746
Rita Leroux, Director, 818-918-3266, FAX: 918-3491
Bassett USD District
Type: public at-risk
2 teachers, 33 students, ages 14–19, 7–12th grade
Enrollment restricted to pregnant or parenting teens
Affiliations: Cal Poly, Pomona, Azusa Pacific College, Girl
  Scouts, United Way, JTPA
Governance by teachers and principal
Teacher qualifications: state certification
Multi-aged classes; urban location; transportation; interns
  accepted.

Rowland Heights Montessori Institute
18760 E Solima Rd, Rowland Heights, CA 91748
Dora Nedic

Meher Montessori School (1972)
2009 S Garfield Ave, Monterey Park, CA 91754
Gail Shaeffer, Dir, 213-724-0683
Tuition: $430/mo
5 teachers, 12 assistants, 130 students, ages 3–12
Affiliation: NAMTA; accreditation: AMI
Governance by administrator
Teacher qualifications: 20 years experience
Multi-cultural; childcare; suburban location; interns accepted.

Mujeres Y Hombres Nobles (1992)
1260 S Monterey Pass Rd, Monterey Park, CA 91754
Annie Cabrera, Asst Prin, 213-262-2263, FAX: 213-262-4043
Los Angeles County
Type: public at-risk
10 teachers, 150 students, ages 10–18, 7–12th grade
For youths involved in gangs and/or drugs; no residency
   requirements
Affiliation: LA Co Office of Ed
Governance by consortium model, including community-
   based organizations, parents, faculty and students
Teacher qualifications: multiple subject state credential
Community services homebase; counseling; health and
   welfare services, referrals; urban location.

Village Montessori Academy (1985)
23431 Golden Springs Dr, Diamond Bar, CA 91765
Sofi Kasubhai, Adm, 909-860-4001
Tuition: $285/330/mo
5 teachers, 6 assistants, 100 students, mainly international,
   ages infant–6
Affiliations: AMS, NAEYC, SCAEYC, NCME
Governance by an administrator
Interns accepted.

Pomona Alternative Secondary
800 S Garey Ave, Pomona, CA 91766

Bonita Unified Alternative Education
115 W Allen Ave, San Dimas, CA 91773

Pacific Ackworth Friends School
6210 Temple City Blvd, Temple City, CA 91780
Nancy Blomeyer, Dir, 818-287-6880
Type: Quaker

Del Paso High School
476 S Lemon Ave, Walnut, CA 91789
Dr Richard Stevens, Prin, 909-594-0776
Los Angeles County
Type: public choice/at-risk
11 teachers, 200 students, ages 15–18, 9–12th grade
District residency required
Affiliations: WASC, CCEA
Governance by board
Teacher qualifications: credentials
Continuation; CA model school; no letter grades; multi-aged
   classes; suburban location; transportation; interns
   accepted.

Independent Study
1717 W Merced, W Covina, CA 91790

Century High School (1932)
20 Marengo Ave, Alhambra, CA 91801
Jacqueline Coulette, Prin, 818-308-2250, FAX:-2597
Los Angeles County
Type: public at-risk
8 teachers, 250 students, ages 16–18, 9–12th grade
Affiliation: WASC
Governance by teachers, principal
Teacher qualifications: CA credential
Up to 30 advisees per teacher/advisor; model drug/alcohol
   program; petting zoo

Independence High Alternative
15 W Alhambra Rd, Alhambra, CA 91801

Oneonta Montessori School
2221 W Poplar Blvd, Alhambra, CA 91801

Alpine Union Alternative Education
1850 Alpine Blvd, Alpine, CA 91901

Friendly Foreign Language Learning
(See Resource Appendix)

Hilltop Learning Center (1991)
555 Claire Ave, Chula Vista, CA 91910
Anita Minor, 619-425-4593
San Diego County
Type: public at-risk
4 teachers, 180 students, ages 14–19, 9–12th grade
Residency required
Governance by teachers, principal
Flexible; client-centered; business-like environment; com-
   puter-based; independent study; JTPA outreach; service
   learning; counseling; multi-aged classes; interns accepted.

Castle Park Learning Center (1988)
1395 Hilltop Drive, Chula Vista, CA 91911
Jim Finnerty, 619-691-6205
San Diego County
Type: public at-risk
5 teachers, 240 students, ages 14–19, 9–12th grade
Residency required
Governance by teachers, principal
Flexible; client-centered; business-like environment; com-
   puter-based; independent study; JTPA outreach; service
   learning; counseling; multi-aged classes; interns accepted.

Chula Vista/Del Ray Learning Center (1992/1986)
1034 4th Ave, Chula Vista, CA 91911
Patrick Judd, Coord, 619-691-5801
San Diego County
Type: public at-risk
5 teachers, 100 students, ages 14–19, 9–12th grade
Residency required
Governance by teachers, principal
Flexible; client-centered; business-like environment; com-
   puter-based; independent study; JTPA outreach; service
   learning; counseling; multi-aged classes; tech-prep course;
   interns accepted.

Job Training Partnership Act (1991)
467 1/2 Moss St, Chula Vista, CA 91911
Dedra Wilson, Mgr, 619-691-5824
San Diego County
Type: public at-risk
1 teacher, 104 students, ages 14–18, 9–12th grade
Entrance requirements: JTPA Federal guidelines eligibility, low
   income with 10% high income window; no residency
   requirement
Teacher qualifications: certification
3 locations; partnerships, apprenticeships, internships;
   support services; school to work transition; paid work
   experience, training; pre-employment skills; work maturity;
   multi-aged classes; childcare

Centro de Ensenanza Montessori
PO Box 7818, Chula Vista, CA 91912
Norma Callado

Bonita Vista Learning Center (1993)
751 Otay Lakes Rd, Bonita, CA 91913
David Ashley, Coord, 619-691-6111
San Diego County
Type: public at-risk
2 teachers, 80 students, ages 14–19, 9–12th grade
Residency required
Governance by teachers, principal
Flexible; client-centered; business-like environment; com-
   puter-based; independent study; JTPA outreach; service
   learning; counseling; multi-aged classes; interns accepted.

Mar Vista Learning Center (1987)
505 Elm Ave, Imperial Beach, CA 91932
Nancy Cummins-Slovic, 619-691-5849
Type: public at-risk
5 teachers, 240 students, ages 14–19, 9–12th grade
Residency required
Governance by teachers, principal
Flexible; client-centered; business-like environment; computer-based; independent study; JTPA outreach; service learning; counseling; multi-aged classes; interns accepted.

Taproot Montessori School
5173 Guava Ave, La Mesa, CA 91941-3614
Ann Katzenmeyer

Lemon Grove Elementary Alternative Education
1750 Madera St, Lemon Grove, CA 91945

Sweetwater Learning Center (1986)
2900 Highland Ave, National City, CA 91950
Andy Sanchez, 619-691-5430
San Diego County
Type: public at-risk
8 teachers, 320 students, ages 14–19, 9–12th grade
Residency required
Governance by teachers, principal
Flexible; client-centered; business-like environment; computer-based; independent study; JTPA outreach; service learning; counseling; multi-aged classes; interns accepted.

Waldorf School of San Diego (1981)
3327 Kenora Dr, Spring Valley, CA 91977
Charlotte Dukich, Adm, 619-589-6404
Non-profit; tuition: $4,000/yr, scholarships
14 teachers, 75 students, ages 3.5–11, pre K–5th grade
Affiliation: AWSNA
Governance by faculty and board
Teacher qualifications: college degree, Waldorf training
Unhurried, stress-free; age-appropriate; no letter grades; suburban location; interns accepted.

Carlsbad Montessori School
740 Pine Ave, Carlsbad, CA 92008-2427
Pam Crisman

Casa Montessori de Carlsbad
3470 Madison St, Carlsbad, CA 92008-5032
Pamela Crisman

Cajon Valley Junior High School
395 Ballantyne St, El Cajon, CA 92020
Linda Fisher, 619-588-3092
Type: magnet
7–8th grade
Fine arts (FAME).

Chaparral High School (1959)
1600 N Cuyamaca St, El Cajon, CA 92020
Dr Barbara A. Stanley, Prin, 619-448-1401, FAX: 596-2815
Grossmont Union District, San Diego County
Type: public at-risk
22 teachers, 450 students, mainly at-risk, ages 14–17, 9–12th grade
Entrance requirements: referral, district residency
Governance by teachers and principal
Teacher qualifications: same as comprehensive high schools in district
Non-competitive; self-directed; self-paced; success-oriented, positive environment; transportation for SE students; multi-aged classes; suburban location; interns accepted.

Cooperative Home Education Program Center
750 E Main St Bldg 2, El Cajon, CA 92020

Flying Hills Elementary
1251 Finch St, El Cajon, CA 92020
Richard Pangborn, 619-588-3132

Type: magnet
3–6th grade
Fine arts (FAME).

Phoenix High Independent Study
181 Fletcher Parkway, El Cajon, CA 92020

San Dieguito Union Alternative
625 N Vulcan Ave, Encinitas, CA 92024

Sunset High School (1966)
684 Requeza, Encinitas, CA 92024
Terry Hendlin, 619-753-3860, FAX: 619-753-8469
San Diego County
Type: public at-risk
8 teachers, 182 students, ages 13–19, 9–12th grade
Entrance requirements: principal approval, residency
Governance by principal and board
Teacher qualifications: CA Credential
Support groups; multi-aged classes; suburban location; interns accepted.

Encinitas Migrant Infant-Toddler
915 Capri Rd, Encinitas, CA 92024-1214
Type: Montessori

Montessori Children's House
616 N Highway 101, Leucadia, CA 92024-2042

North Coast Montessori Center, Inc (1983)
2122 Encinitas Blvd, Encinitas, CA 92024-4304
Linda Campbell, Owner-Administrator, 619-753-9400
Tuition: $2,750/4,200/yr
4 teachers, 2 assistants, 50–60 students, ages 3–6
Governance by administrator
Teacher qualifications: AMS credential
Childcare; suburban location; interns accepted.

Montessori Children's Nest
1170 Arcadia Rd, Encinitas, CA 92024-4602

Masters Academy Montessori
275 Santa Fe Dr, Encinitas, CA 92024-5130

Escondido Union Alternative/Opportunity
240 S Maple St, Escondido, CA 92025

South Bay Union Alternative
601 Elm Ave, Imperial Beach, CA 92032

Montessori School of La Jolla
7427 Fay Ave, La Jolla, CA 92037-5041
Carol Sherlock

Lakeside Union Alternative Education
Box 578, Lakeside, CA 92040

Learning Forum/Supercamp
1725 South Hill St, Oceanside, CA 92054
Bobbi Deporter
Type: independent

Plato High Independent Study
2111 Mission Ave (Annex), Oceanside, CA 92054

Ocean Shores High School (1972)
3131 Oceanside Blvd, Oceanside, CA 92056
Dr R.J. Williamson, Coord, 619-439-3142, FAX: -5588
San Diego County
Type: public at-risk
12 teachers, 270 students, ages 15–18
Entrance via placement committee, district residency required
Governance by board
Interns accepted.

Old Mission Montessori School
4070 Mission Ave, Oceanside, CA 92057-6402
Debbie Cisneros and Maggie Sullivan

Abraxas High School (1972)
12450 Glen Oak, Poway, CA 92064
Andy Patapow, Prin, 619-748-5900, FAX: 679-1739
Poway USD District, San Diego County
Type: public at-risk; scholarships
18 teachers, 250 students, ages 16-19, 9-12th grade
Entrance requirements: age 16+, district residency
Affiliation: PUSD
Governance by principal, board
Teacher qualifications: multi-subject credential
Self-paced; support groups; frequent reviews; multi-aged classes; contracts; urban location; transportation; interns accepted.

Montessori Child Development Center (1978)
14911 Espola Rd, Poway, CA 92064
Marijane Sattler, 619-748-1727, FAX: 619-748-8995
Non-profit; tuition: $359/427/mo
4 teachers, 4 assistants, 60 students, ages 3-6
Affiliations: AMS, NAEYC
Governance by a board of trustees
In converted old farm house; outdoor education includes farm animals and gardens; childcare; rural location; interns accepted.

Poway Unified Alternative Education
13626 Twin Peaks Road, Poway, CA 92064

Country Montessori School
12642 Monte Vista Rd, Poway, CA 92064-2522
Elizabeth Bahn

Montessori Children's House
703 9th St, Ramona, CA 92065
Allison Welch

Ramona Alternative Education
1710 Montecito Road, Ramona, CA 92065-2207

Montessori at Fairbanks Country Day
PO Box 8953, Rancho Santa Fe, CA 92067

Foothills High School (1983)
158 Cassou Rd, San Marcos, CA 92069
Bob Henricks, Prin, 619-591-4134
San Diego County
Type: public choice/at-risk, boarding
3 teachers, 180 students, mainly at-risk, ages 14-18, 9-12th grade
District residency required
Governance by principal, board
Teacher qualifications: CA credential
Independent study; teen parenting/pregnancy; childcare; rural location.

San Marcos Unified Alternative- Foothills High
1995 N Twin Oaks Valley Rd, San Marcos, CA 92069

Santee Elementary Alternative Education
Box 719007, Santee, CA 92072

Santa Fe Montessori School
1010 Solana Dr; PO Box 745, Solana Beach, CA 92075
Nancy Sager and Connie Zylstra

Chinaberry Book Service
(See Resource Appendix)

Casa Montessori Schools (1982)
1930 Sunset Dr, Vista, CA 92083
Avril Warthen, 619-758-2434
Tuition: $2,500-4,150/yr
6 teachers, 4 assistants, 100 students, ages 3-12
Governance by administrator
Two locations, one with sports field; music; Spanish; German; computer; suburban location; interns accepted.

Cooperative Learning Center (1993)
454 Papaya St, Vista, CA 92083
Alonna Farrar, Educational Adm, 619-726-3020
San Diego County
Type: home-based
16 teachers, 24 students, mainly curious learners, ages 6-15
Enrollment restricted to residents of San Diego Co
Governance by parent cooperative
Teacher qualifications: Parents who want one-on-one learning experience with their children
Interest-centered; skills/knowledge exchange; field trip; interns accepted.

Memorial Christian School
1830 Anna Ln, Vista, CA 92083
Annette Brown
Type: Montessori

Vista Academy of the Performing Arts
600 N Santa Fe, Vista, CA 92084
Rodney Goldenberg, 619-941-0880
Type: magnet
K-5th grade
Performing Arts.

Vista Unified Alternative Education
1234 Arcadia Ave, Vista, CA 92084

Ivy High School (1974)
PO Box 368, Fallbrook, CA 92088
Marc Steffler, Prin, 619-723-6395, FAX: 619-723-6392
San Diego County
Type: public at-risk
5 teachers, 130 students, ages 14-19, 10-12th grade
Entrance requirements: age 16+, reading proficiency, district residency
Governance by principal, teachers, board
Full service continuation HS; flexible schedule, programs; individualized; close teacher/student/parent relationship; rural location; transportation; interns accepted.

Kids' Edition of Continental Newstime (1992)
341 W Broadway, Suite 265, San Diego, CA 92101
Gary P. Salamone, Editor-in-Chief, 619-492-8696, 202-452-7453
San Diego County
Daily fax-only educational aid; brief courses; distributed to ages 6-12; children's daily newspaper.

St Vincent de Paul Life Skills
1501 Imperial Ave, San Diego, CA 92101
Nadean Burinton, Literary Specialist, 619-233-8500 x1500-1, FAX: 235-9707
San Diego County
Type: independent, non-profit
5 teachers; students mainly at-risk
Enrollment restricted to low income adults only
Governance by life skills staff, village adm
Teacher qualifications: ABE credential; ESL, employment certificate
Multi-sensory, multi-dimensional interactive teaching; content-based goals; social services; referrals; multi-aged classes; no letter grades; non-compulsory class attendance; interns accepted.

San Diego City Alternative Education
4100 Normal St #3107, San Diego, CA 92103

Montessori School of San Diego
1323 W Spruce St, San Diego, CA 92103-5328

Futures High School (1990)
1450 Frazee Rd #301, San Diego, CA 92108
Sarita Bland, Dir, 619-297-5311, FAX: 619-297-5313
Type: independent; tuition: $3,700/yr
8 teachers, 30 students, ages 12-19, 7-12th grade

Governance by teachers and principal
Teacher qualifications: credential preferred
Independent study; suburban location; interns accepted.

Institute for Mutual Instruction (1993)
(See Resource Appendix)

Muir Alternative School
3390 Armstrong, San Diego, CA 92111
Samuel Wong, 619-268-1954
Type: magnet
K–12th grade
Humanistic studies.

Baker School
4041 T Steet, San Diego, CA 92113
Maria Garcia, 619-264-3139
Type: magnet
K–6th grade
Music conservatory.

Youth Opportunities Unlimited
2716 Marcy Ave, San Diego, CA 92113

Bethune School
6835 Benjamin Holt Rd, San Diego, CA 92114
Michael Giafaglione, 619-267-2271
Type: magnet
K–6th grade
Structure of the intellect.

National Center for Montessori Education
Elementary Course, 4454 Pocahontas, San Diego, CA 92117
Type: Montessori teacher education

Montessori School of San Diego at Coronado
901 C Ave, Coronado, CA 92118-2607

Mission Bay Montessori Academy (1968)
2640 Soderblom Ave, San Diego, CA 92122
Mary Gaber, Dir, 619-457-5895
24 teachers, 10 assistants, 380 students, ages 3–12
Affiliations: NAMTA, AMI, AMS
Governance by an administrator
On 18 secluded acres; computers; Spanish; extracurriculars; active parent involvement; suburban location; interns accepted.

Montessori School of Mira Mesa
11167 Westonhill Dr, San Diego, CA 92126
Sandra Manning

Priority Montessori Materials
(See Resource Appendix)

Albert Einstien School
PO Box 434136, San Ysidro, CA 92143
Christina A De Leon
Type: Montessori

Centro de Education Montessori
PO Box 434915, San Ysidro, CA 92143
Claudia Mondaca

Pinocho
PO Box 430172, San Ysidro, CA 92143-0172
Adriana Martinez
Type: Montessori

Montgomery Learning Center (1986)
3250 Palm Ave, San Diego, CA 92154
Lee Beca, 619-691-5489
San Diego County
Type: public at-risk
6 teachers, 260 students, ages 14–19, 9–12th grade
Residency required
Governance by teachers, principal
Flexible; client-centered; business-like environment; com-

puter-based; independent study; JTPA outreach; service learning; counseling; multi-aged classes; interns accepted.

Southwest Learning Center (1990)
1685 Hollister St, San Diego, CA 92154
Mike Pineda, 619-691-6230
San Diego County
Type: public at-risk
4 teachers, 180 students, ages 14–19, 9–12th grade
Residency required
Governance by teachers, principal
Flexible; client-centered; business-like environment; computer-based; independent study; JTPA outreach; service learning; counseling; multi-aged classes; interns accepted.

The Cheerful Cherub
(See Resource Appendix)

Twin Palms High School (1970)
190 N Fifth St, Blythe, CA 92225
Dave Distel, Prin, 619-922-4884, FAX: 619-922-1177
Palo Verde USD District, Riverside County
Type: public at-risk
4 teachers, 88 students, ages 16–18, 10–12th grade
Residency required
Governance by teachers and principal
Teacher qualifications: Experience, teaching area flexibility
Continuation HS; variable credits; no letter grades; rural location; interns accepted.

Midway High School (1979)
601 W Main St, Calipatria, CA 92233
Homer Stiff, Prin, 619-348-2430, FAX: 619-344-8926
Imperial County
Type: public at-risk
1 teacher, 20 students, mainly at-risk, ages 16–20, 9–12th grade
Enrollment restricted to age 16+ unless board-placed; residency required
Accreditation: WASC
Governance by principal and board
Teacher qualifications: high school multiple subject credential or higher
Contracts; tutorial; diploma; multi-aged classes; urban location; transportation.

Mt San Jacinto High School
30-800 Landau Blvd, Cathedral City, CA 92234
V. Richard Savarese, Prin, 619-324-7199
Riverside County
Type: public at-risk
18 teachers, 450 students, 9–12th grade
Entrance requirement: min age 16
Governance by principal
Teacher qualifications: CA credential
CA model school; multi-aged classes; extensive field trips

Montessori School of the Valley
43250 Warner Trail, Palm Desert, CA 92260-8245
Elaine Maloney

Independent Study (1977)
1555 Alejo, Palm Springs, CA 92262
Donald T. Aikens, Adm, 619-323-8047
Riverside County
Type: public choice
5 teachers, 150 students, mainly at-risk, ages 5–19, K–12th grade
Entrance requirements: voluntary request, residency
Governance by principal and board
Teacher qualifications: Elementary and secondary experience
Parent involvement required; suburban location.

Central High School (1969)
405 N 2nd Ave, Barstow, CA 92311
Richard L. Brown, Prin, 619-256-0611, FAX: 619-256-1436
San Bernardino County

Type: public at-risk; scholarships
7 teachers, 150 students, ages 16–18, 9–12th grade
Residency required
Governance by informal student body

Independent Study Program
1000 Armory, Barstow, CA 92311

Independent Study Program (1984)
551 S Ave "H", Barstow, CA 92312
Martelle Huff, Coord, 619-256-6517
Type: independent, non-profit
6 teachers, 170 students, partly at-risk, ages 5–53, K–12th grade
Residency required
Governance by principal, district coordinator
Teacher qualifications: CA Certification, non-emergency
Individualized; urban location.

Washington High Alternative
900 E C St, Colton, CA 92324-2603

CC-PALS (CA Coalition of People for Alternative Learning Situations) (1982)
PO Box 291786, Phelan, CA 92329
Debbie Bartle, State Dir, 619-868-2860
Los Angeles County
Regional and bi-annual state meetings; newsletter.

Desert View Independent Study
Box 296000, Phelan, CA 92329

Fontana Unified Alternative Education
9820 Citrus Ave, Fontana, CA 92335

International Montessori Institute
38395 Trifone Rd, Sage, CA 92343-9693
Type: Montessori teacher education

Hesperia Unified Alternative Education
9144 3rd Ave, Hesperia, CA 92345

Cole Elementary
1331 Cole Ave, San Bernardino, CA 92346
Rosalyn Doug, 714-862-5611
Type: magnet
K–6th grade
Music intensives; reading clinic.

Mountain High School (1979)
PO Box 430, Lake Arrowhead, CA 92352
Flo Mullendore, Prin, 909-337-0842
San Bernardino County
Type: public at-risk
4 teachers, 100 students, mainly at-risk, ages 16–20, 9–12th grade
Enrollment restricted to residents age 16+
Governance by board
Teacher qualifications: CA Credential
Extended family atmosphere; 94% average daily attendance; multi-media art programs; incentive grants; no letter grades; interns accepted.

Needles Unified Alternative Education
1900 Erin Drive, Needles, CA 92363-2699

Burke Montessori School (1985)
524 Via Vista Dr, Redlands, CA 92373
Dee Burke, Adm, 909-793-7065
Tuition: $248/mo
1 teacher, 12 students, ages 3–6
Governance by administrator

Montessori in Redlands (1976)
1890 Orange Ave, Redlands, CA 92373
Margie J. Armantrout, Dir, 909-793-6989
Non-profit; tuition: $340-520/mo
11 teachers, 13 assistants, 242 students, ages infant-12

Accreditation: AMI
Governance by board of trustees
In grapefruit grove adjacent to park, historic district; one hour to mountains, desert or ocean; childcare; rural location; interns accepted.

Johnson Center at University of Redlands (1969)
PO Box 3080 1200 E Colton Ave, Redlands, CA 92373-0999
Yasuyuki Awada, Dir, 909-335-4071, FAX: 909-793-2029
San Bernardino County
Type: higher education, boarding, non-profit; tuition: $15,760/yr, scholarships
140 students
Entrance requirements: HS diploma, SAT/ACT scores.
Accreditation: WASC
Governance by community consensus
Teacher qualifications: PhD, ABD
Students negotiate learning contracts with faculty; no letter grades; student designed curriculum and majors; suburban location.

Charles Zupanic High Alternative Education
182 E Walnut Ave, Rialto, CA 92376-3598

Mojave High School (1987)
16633 Lemon St, Hesperia, CA 92392
Arlene Gluck, 619-948-3999
San Bernardino County
Type: public at-risk
12 teachers, 240 students, ages 16–22, 9–12th grade
Residency required
Governance by principal
Teacher qualifications: certification
Incentives for attendance, achievement; self-esteem programs; rap groups; speaker program; designated model school by CA DE in 1993; no letter grades; multi-aged classes; extensive field trip; interns accepted.

High Desert Alternative Education Center (1988)
15733 First St, Victorville, CA 92392
Susan Wells-Massengale, Dir, 619-955-3440, FAX: 245-3512
San Bernardino County
Type: home-based, non-profit
13 teachers, 300 students, mainly at-risk, ages 13–20, 7–12th grade
No residency requirement
Governance by principal, teachers, board and student reps
Continuation; SB65 dropout clinic; GED prep; open entry/exit; no letter grades; multi-aged classes; suburban location; interns accepted.

California Elementary
2699 California St, San Bernardino, CA 92405
Manuel Salinas, 714-887-2501
Type: magnet
K–5th grade
Creative and performing arts; vanguard.

Marshall Elementary
3288 G St, San Bernardino, CA 92405
Alvina Pawlik, 714-882-3376
Type: magnet
K–6th grade
Multi-cultural.

Burbank Elementary
198 W Mill St, San Bernardino, CA 92408
Susan Vargas, 714-884-9404
Type: magnet
K–6th grade
Junior journalists.

9th Street Elementary
555 E Olive St, San Bernardino, CA 92410
Paul Shirk, 714-381-0889
Type: magnet
K–6th grade
Music intensives.

San Bernardino Unified Alternative Education
777 N F St, San Bernardino, CA 92410

Alessandro Elementary
670 Ramona Ave, San Bernardino, CA 92411
Tom Crist, 714-885-3281
Type: magnet
K–5th grade
Single track year-round; vanguard-gifted and talented.

Rio Vista Elementary
1451 California, San Bernardino, CA 92411
Carolyn Livingson, 714-884-3281
Type: magnet
K–5th grade
Vanguard; artists in residence.

The Weaver Curriculum (1986)
2752 Scarborough, Riverside, CA 92503
909-688-3126, FAX: 909-351-9625
For Christian and home schools.

Arachi Montessori Children's House
4174 Mobley Ave, Riverside, CA 92505-1732
Pat Arachi

Riverside Unified Independent Study
6735 Magnolia Ave, Riverside, CA 92506
Type: public choice

Helen Hunt Jackson Alternative School/
  Alessandro High School (1970)
26866 San Jacinto St, Hemet, CA 92544
Jim Smith, Prin, 909-765-5193,-5182, FAX: 765-5195
Riverside County
Type: public choice; scholarships
11 teachers, 200/400 students, mainly at-risk, ages 12–19,
  7–12th grade
Accreditation: WASC
Governance by principal, board
Teacher qualifications: credential
HHJ: independent study; small classes; computer lab; bilin-
  gual program; non-compulsory class attendance; AHS:
  model continuation school; work experience; applied business; SE inclusion; no letter grades; multi-aged classes;
  interns accepted.

March Mountain High School (1968)
24551 Dralaca Ave, Moreno Valley, CA 92553
Jon Gaffney, Prin, 909-485-5700, FAX: 909-485-5652
Riverside County
Type: public choice/at-risk
26 teachers, 900 students, ages 14–19, 9–12th grade
Entrance requirements: district residency
Governance by school council, principal
Teacher qualifications: CA credential
Continuation; independent study; GED prep; multi-aged
  classes; variable credits; suburban location.

Creekside (1992)
24105 Washington Ave, Murrieta, CA 92562
Dr Albert Ross, Prin, 909-696-1409, FAX: 909-696-1455
Riverside County
Type: public at-risk
4 teachers, 120 students, ages 15–19, 9–12th grade
Entrance requirements: credit deficient
Governance by principal, faculty, student representatives
Teacher qualifications: fully credentialed
Tailored to each student; alternative content, delivery and
  time frame; pregnant/parenting teens component; subur-
  ban location; transportation; interns accepted.

Temecula Valley Unified Independent Study High
31340 Rancho Vista Rd, Temecula, CA 92592

University Montessori
17 Calabria Lane, Foothill Ranch, CA 92610
Wendy Metrakos

Valley View High School (1990)
689 Wildcat Way, Brea, CA 92621
Katie Plass, Coord, 714-990-7559, FAX: 714-529-2137
Orange County
Type: public choice
2 teachers, 50 students, mainly teen parents, ages 15–19
Enrollment restricted to public school enrollees
Teacher qualifications: CA credential
Independent study; accelerated learning; parenting;
  employment

Montessori Universe of the Child
400 West Fir St, Brea, CA 92621-6422

Shekinah Curriculum Cellar
(See Resource Appendix)

Alternative Education Center, Monte Vista High School
390 Monte Vista Ave, Cost Mesa, CA 92627
Carole Castaldo, Prin, 714-760-3450, FAX: 760-3426
Orange County
Type: public choice
10 teachers, 350 students, ages 14–19, 9–12th grade
Residency required
Governance by board
Non-compulsory class attendance; suburban location; interns
  accepted.

Alternative Education Center, Back Bay High School
300 Monte Vista Ave, Costa Mesa, CA 92627
Carole Castaldo, Prin, 714-760-3450, FAX: 760-3426
Orange County
Type: public at-risk
4 teachers, 100 students, mainly at-risk, ages 14–19, 9–12th
  grade
Residency required
Governance by board
Suburban location; interns accepted.

The Sycamore Tree
(See Resource Appendix)

Montessori on the Lake (1987)
23311 Muirlands, Lake Forest, CA 92630
Sue Matsu, 714-855-5630
Tuition: $330-470/mo
25 teachers, 40 assistants, 432 students, mainly international,
  ages toddler–15
Affiliation: NCME
Governance by teachers and administrators
Suburban location; interns accepted.

Casa dei Bambini Montessori School
25435 Trabuco Rd # C5, El Toro, CA 92630-2738

Aliso Montessori
24291 Muirlands Blvd # 1/#2, El Toro, CA 92630-3000

North Orange County Community College District/Adult
  Education (1965)
1000 North Lemon St, Fullerton, CA 92632
Nilo Lipiz, ESL Coord, 714-871-4030, FAX: 738-7853
Type: public choice
55 teachers, 34,000 students, mainly multi-ethnic, ages 18+
No residency requirement
Governance by administration
Teacher qualifications: bachelor's degree
Adult ed: ESL, ABE, HS/GED, DSPS, Seniors, Medical, vocational,
  etc; tuition-based programs: computer, foreign language,
  others; no letter grades; urban location; interns accepted.

Arborland Montessori Children's Academy (1988)
1700 W Valencia Dr, Fullerton, CA 92633
Sueling Chen, Prin, 714-871-2311, FAX: 714-773-1532
Tuition: $310-385/mo
5 teachers, 5 assistants, 122 students, ages 3–12
Accreditation: AMI

Governance by administrator
Small class size; hands-on activities; computer; Spanish; piano; music; choir; gymnastics; swimming; dance; martial arts; optional hot lunches; childcare; urban location; interns accepted.

Alternative and Continuing Education Program
780 Beechwood 1, Fullerton, CA 92635
Jean Klinghoffer, 714-870-3775
Fullerton HS District
Type: public choice
730 students, ages 14+

Rainbow PreSchool
12914 Hazel Ave, Garden Grove, CA 92641
Sunja Oak
Type: Montessori

Montessori School
6921 Belgrave Ave, Garden Grove, CA 92645
Noreen Begole

Montessori Greenhouse School
5856 Belgrave Ave, Garden Grove, CA 92645-1729
Charles and Joy Turner

Montessori Child Development Center
16692 Landau Lane, Huntington Beach, CA 92651
Ellen Goodman

Community Learning Center
21601 Tree Top La, Laguna Beach, CA 92651
Kathie Reynolds or Libley Coleman, 714-497-7793
Type: independent

Montessori School of Laguna Beach
340 St Ann Dr, Laguna Beach, CA 92651
Ishwar Chainani

Home Study Alternative School
PO Box 10356, Newport Beach, CA 92658
Gaylen McGee, Dir
Cost: $100-150/sem
K-8th grade
Designed by certified teachers; comprehensive; lesson instructions; assistance always available; students placed according to ability; multidisciplinary

Waldorf School of Orange County
2627 Vista Del Oro, Newport Beach, CA 92660-3548
Mechtild Howard

Montessori of Orange
2261 N Orange Olive Rd, Orange, CA 92665-2746
Kathleen Glassman

Orange Unified Alternative Education
370 N Glassell St, Orange, CA 92666

Marygrove Montessori
419 S Glassell St, Orange, CA 92666-1905

Primanti Montessori Schools
5003 E Chapman Ave, Orange, CA 92669-4211
Lisa Koch

El Camino Real High School (1976)
1351 E Orangethorpe, Placentia, CA 92670
Glen Collard, Prin, 714-996-1971
Orange County
Type: public at-risk
15 teachers, 280 students, ages 16-18, 9-12th grade
Residency required
Affiliation: WASC
Governance by principal
Teacher qualifications: CA credential
Office practices; community service required; flexible scheduling; suburban location; interns accepted.

La Entrada High School (1989)
1351 E Orangethorpe Ave, Placentia, CA 92670
Glen Callard, Prin, 996-1971
Orange County
Type: public at-risk
2 teachers, 80 students, ages 16-18, 10-12th grade
Residency required
Governance by principal
Teacher qualifications: CA Certification
Independent study strategies; suburban location.

Montessori Children's World
431 E Palm Dr, Placentia, CA 92670-3296

Academia Montessori
3415 S El Camino Real, San Clemente, CA 92672

Kagan's Cooperative Learning
(See Resource Appendix)

Montessori School of Tustin
PO Box 15791, Tustin, CA 92681

Rancho Santa Margarita Montessori
30075 Comercio, Rancho Santa Margarita, CA 92688
Anne Munz

Silverado High School (1973)
25632 Diseno Dr, Mission Viejo, CA 92691
Dr Barry Lietz, 714-586-8800
Orange County
Type: public at-risk
14 teachers, 250 students, ages 14-19, 9-12th grade
Enrollment through committee, residency
Affiliation: Saddleback Valley USD
Governance by principal, teachers, board
State computer academy; multi-aged classe; interns accepted.

Appletree Montessori
25542 Jeronimo Rd, Mission Viejo, CA 92691-2724

Pathfinder High School of Independent Study
26440 La Alameda #350, Mission Viejo, CA 92691-6319
Terry & Margaret Ann Mccarty
Type: independent

Horizon Education (1983)
848 N Parton, Santa Ana, CA 92701
Ellen Wilson, 714-547-2423, FAX: 714-547-2344
Orange County
Type: public at-risk
75 teachers, 2000 students, ages 12-19, 7-12th grade
Entrance requirements: parole status or referral; no residency requirement
Governance by Adm of Alt Ed, Principal
Teacher qualifications: CA credential
Community-based; career education; counseling; teen parenting; mobile outreach classroom; state-of-the-art technology; multi-aged classe; interns accepted.

Teen Parent Program
1629 S Center St, Santa Ana, CA 92704

Foothill Montessori School
18692 E 17th St, Santa Ana, CA 92705-2700

Valley Vista High School (1968)
9600 Dolphin St, Fountain Valley, CA 92708
Richard Maynard, Prin, 714-964-7760, FAX: 964-3045
Orange County
Type: public at-risk
15 teachers, 265 students, ages 14-18, 10-12th grade
Residency required
Governance by teachers, principal and board
ESL; SE; school-centered curricula; safe environment; urban location.

Fountain Valley Christian Montessori
18110 Magnolia St, Fountain Valley, CA 92708-5605

Backyard Scientist
(See Resource Appendix)

IUSD, Montessori Early Childhood Education (1986)
31 West Yale Loop, Irvine, CA 92714
Feland L. Meadows, PhD, Coord, 714-551-1647/643-8174, FAX: 714-786-7521/831-7786
Non-profit; tuition: 0-$420/mo
13 teachers, 14 assistants, 255 students, mainly International, ages 3-9
Entrance requirements: ages 3-4, 1 month trial; ages 6-9, Montessori experience.
Accreditations: PAMS, Nat'l U, OBEMLA, CA DE, Irvine USD
Governance by teachers and administrators
Serve Chinese, Japanese, Hispanic, Vietnamese, Korean, Persian and English-speaking students in their home language and English; childcare; suburban location; interns accepted.

San Joaquin High School (1990)
311 W Yale Loop, Irvine, CA 92714
Ann Beirne, 714-857-2682
Type: public choice
10 students

Irvine Unified Alternative Education
5050 Barrana Pkwy, Irvine, CA 92714-4698

Village Montessori School
4552 Sandburg Way, Irvine, CA 92715-2735

University Montessori School
101 Russell Pl, Irvine, CA 92715-4052

Santiago Hills Elementary School
29 Christamon, Irvine, CA 92720
Type: Montessori

Montessori Child Develoment Center
1692 Landau Lane, Hunting Beach, CA 92749

Christian Home Educators of California
PO Box 28644, Santa Ana, CA 92799-8644
714-537-5121
Type: state home-based

Polaris High-Independent Study
501 Crescent Way, Anaheim, CA 92803

Beavercreek Montessori School
632 S Andover Dr, Anaheim, CA 92807-4608

Montessori Children's House (1988)
559 Aliso St, Ventura, CA 93001
Bonnie M. Gordon, 805-653-5759
Tuition: $225/255/mo
1 teacher, 1 assistant, 14 students, mainly international, ages 3-6
Affiliations: NCME, Orff Shulwork
Governance by an administrator
Spanish; art; childcare; suburban location; interns accepted.

Community Alliance Program (1990)
5109 Loma Vista Rd, Ventura, CA 93003
Lawrence Keegan, 805-654-2602, FAX: 805-658-0853
Type: public choice
15 students

Ventura Unified Alternative Education
3777 Dean Dr, Ventura, CA 93003

Ventura Montessori School
PO Box 3719, Ventura, CA 93006-3719

Bedford Open School (1976)
1199 Bedford Dr, Camarillo, CA 93010
Julie Cavaliere, Principal, 805 484-5116

Ventura County
Type: public choice
11 teachers, 223 students, ages 5-12, K-6th grade
Governance by principal, teachers, parents, students
Teacher qualifications: CA credential
Enrichment courses; learning lab; hands-on experiences; artist-in-residence for music, art, dance; perceptual motor lab; Education Through Music; no letter grades.

Fillmore Community High School (1980)
Box 697, Fillmore, CA 93016
Phil Catalano, 805-524-2271, FAX: 805-524-4625
Ventura County
Type: public at-risk
150 students, ages 12+, 7-12th grade
District residency required
Affiliation: WASC
Governance by board
Independent study; adult diploma; GED; ESL; no letter grades; multi-aged classes; rural location.

Landmark
(See Resource Appendix)

Laurel Springs School (1990)
PO Box 1440, Ojai, CA 93023
JoAnn LeClere, Registrar, 805-646-2473, FAX: 805-646-0186
Type: home-based
21 teachers, 250 students, ages 5-18, K-12th grade
Governance by principal
Teacher qualifications: BA or BS
Parent as primary teacher; students assigned to correspondence teacher

Oak Grove School
220 W Lomita, Ojai, CA 93023
Issa Ainsworth
Type: Montessori

Ojai Valley Children's House (1973)
806 W Baldwin Rd, Ojai, CA 93023
Rosemary Stone, Reg/Office Mgr, 805-649-2525, FAX: 646-1543
Type: Montessori; tuition: $2,000-4,070/yr
6 teachers, 6 assistants, 115 students, ages toddler-12
Accreditation: Montessori World Ed Inst
Ten acres of oak- and garden-studded grounds; concerts and field trips an integral part of varied curriculum; childcare; rural location.

Independent Studies
309 S K St, Oxnard, CA 93030

Rose Ave Elementary
220 S Driskill Ave, Oxnard, CA 93030
Dennis Johnson, 805-487-3918
Oakland USD District
Type: magnet
K-6th grade
Gifted and talented.

Simi Valley Alternative Education
3150 School St, Simi Valley, CA 93065

Santa Barbara Alternative Education
905 Nopal St, Santa Barbara, CA 93101

Oratory School
112 E De La Guerra St #44, Santa Barbara, CA 93101-2205
Marian Galvin
Type: independent

Santa Barbara Montessori
1500 State St, Santa Barbara, CA 93101-2514

Montessori Public School Systems
518 Casitas Rd, Canta Barbara, CA 93103
Nancy Williams

Jodi House Montessori School
916 Garcia Rd, Santa Barbara, CA 93103-2124
Jane Granite

Waldorf School of Santa Barbara
2300-B Garden St, Santa Barbara, CA 93105
Gita Labrentz

Montessori Center School (1965)
3970 La Colina Rd, Santa Barbara, CA 93110
Carla Mathieu, Dir, 805-682-5648
Non-profit; tuition: $4,800-5,900/yr
18 teachers, 18 assistants, 295 students, ages infant-12
Governance by teachers and administrators, board
8 acres; library; auditorium; music and art studios; childcare; suburban location; interns accepted.

Open Alternative School
4025 Foothill Rd, Santa Barbara, CA 93110-1209
Carol Preston, 805-962-3826
Type: public choice

Sunrise/Adelante High School (1982)
209 N Park Ave, Avenal, CA 93204
Richard L. Swanson, PhD, 209-386-4162, FAX:-5303
Type: public at-risk
4 teachers, 65 students, ages 13-18, 7-12th grade
Entrance by referral
Affiliation: Reef Sunset USD
Governance by teachers, principal
Teacher qualifications: CA credential
Multi-aged classes; interns accepted.

BEST Educational Systems
PO Box 1128, Ojai, CA 93204
Rene Martinez
Type: Montessori

Ygnacio Valencia High School (1979)
1925 Randolph, Delano, CA 93215
Dr Efrain Rodriguez, Prin, 805-725-4000, FAX: 721-9390
Kern County
Type: public choice
9 teachers, 230 students, mainly at-risk, ages 14-18, 9-12th grade
Entrance requirements: parent permission; no residency requirement
Governance by principal
Teacher qualifications: CA Credential, BA or BS
Work at home under contract; multi-aged classes; rural location.

Exeter Independent Study/Alternative Education
233 E Maple, Exeter, CA 93221

Summit Continuation High School (1983)
3284 Erskine Creek Rd; PO Box 3797, Lake Isabella, CA 93240
Vickie Johnston, Site Supervisor, 619-379-3997, FAX:-6234
Kern County
Type: public at-risk
2 teachers, 45 students, ages 16-19, 10-12th grade
Residency required
Governance by teachers and principal
Teacher qualifications: credential
Independent study; rural location; transportation; interns accepted.

Oak View High School (1989)
6449 De Woody, Caton, CA 93242
Thomas Kent, Prin, 209-923-4000
Type: public at-risk
1 teacher, 16 students, ages 14-19, 9-12th grade
Enrollment restricted to non-expelled students, residency
Governance by principal, board
Teacher qualifications: CA credential
Individualized; multiple intelligences programs; multi-aged classes

Laton Unified Alternative Education
Box 278, Laton, CA 93242

Lindsay Adult School (1980)
519 E Honolulu, Lindsay, CA 93247
Kent Stinson, Instructor, 209-562-2224,-8550
Tulare County
Type: public at-risk
2 teachers, 45 students, ages 18-55
Residency required
Affiliation: GAIN/ABE
Governance by principal and board
Teacher qualifications: state adult ed certification
ESL; diploma; multi-aged classes; rural location.

McFarland Independent School (1980)
5899 Fifth St, McFarland, CA 93250
Kathleen J. Heisey, Adm, 805-792-6312, FAX:-2447
Kern County
Type: independent at-risk, non-profit
6 teachers, 140 students, mainly at-risk, ages 13+, 9-12th grade
Entrance requirements: reading proficiency, interview, residency
Affiliation: McFarland USD
Governance by teachers, principal, board
Teacher qualifications: secondary credential, voluntary assignment
Electives; multi-aged classes; rural location.

San Joaquin High School (1980)
599 Fifth St, McFarland, CA 93250
Kathleen J. Heisey, Prin, 805-792-3178, FAX:-2447
McFarland District, Kern County
Type: public at-risk
6 teachers, 75 students, ages 13-20, 9-12th grade
Entrance requirements: graduated grade 8; residents age 15+
Governance by teachers, principal, board
Teacher qualifications: secondary teaching credential
Self-paced; small groups; vocational; multi-aged classes; rural location.

Tulare Tech Prep (1993)
426 N Blackstone, Tulare, CA 93274
Dr William Pendleton, 209-688-1815, FAX: 685-8286
Tulare County
Type: public at-risk
4 teachers, 51 students, mainly at-risk, ages 14-18, 9-12th grade
No residency requirement
Governance by board
Teacher qualifications: CA teaching credential in subject area
1-room classroom; 4-teacher team teaching, tech-based with CORD applied academic cur; job shadowing/work exp; college and specialty classes at regular HS available; multi-aged classes; rural location; interns accepted.

Greenhouse Montessori School- Chinowth
4143 S Dans St, Visalia, CA 93277-7901

Visilia Independent Study
315 E Acequia St, Visilia, CA 93291

Vista East High School (1979)
815 Eureka St, Bakersfield, CA 93305
Fuchsia Ward, Asst Prin, 805-323-9006, FAX: 805-631-0559
Kern County
Type: public at-risk
16 teachers, 300 students, ages 14-18, 9-12th grade
No residency requirement
Governance by principal
Teacher qualifications: credential
Personalized; counseling; model drug intervention program; community service; multi-aged classes; interns accepted.

Thorner Elementary
5501 Thorner, Bakersfield, CA 93306
Shirley Walston, 805-631-5490
Type: magnet
K-6th grade
Creative and performing arts.

Bessie Owens Junior High School
815 Potomac Ave, Bakersfield, CA 93307
Dennis Patrick, 805-631-5420
Type: magnet
K-6th grade
Gifted and talented education.

Mt Vernon Elementary
2161 Potomac Ave, Bakersfield, CA 93307
Lillian Tafoya, 805-631-5380
Type: magnet
K-6th grade
Creative and performing arts.

Friends School
7300 Ming Ave, Bakersfield, CA 93309
Katie Jennings, 805-833-6860
Type: Quaker

PBVUSD
3100 Actis St, Bakersfield, CA 93309
Lydia Zimmerman
Type: Montessori

Montessori Children's Center
3234 Belle Terrace, Bakersfield, CA 93309-4102
Anjali Sinha

Montessori Children's School (1983)
4200 S Higuera St, San Luis Obispo, CA 93401
Mary Kern, Adm, 805-544-6691
Tuition: $2,750/3,250/yr
3 teachers, 2 assistants, 56 students, ages 3-9
Entrance requirements: age 2.5
Affiliations: NAMTA, MWEI
Governance by administrator
Drama; art; music; puppetry; excursions to local perfor-
  mances; woodworking; Spanish; French; yoga; Native
  American study; summer programs; childcare; suburban
  location; interns accepted.

The New Dawn
1768 14th St, Los Osos, CA 93402
Ranae Turner
Type: Montessori

Pacific Beach High School (1967)
11950 Los Osos Valley Rd, San Luis Obispo, CA 93405
R D Christensen, Prin, 805-541-1216
Type: public choice
4 teachers, 80-100 students, ages 16-18, 10-12th grade
Entrance requirements: credit deficiency
Governance by principal
Teacher qualifications: CA certification
Rural location; interns accepted.

Lucia Mar Independent Study Center (1983)
227 E Bridge St, Arroyo Grande, CA 93420
Karen Mork, Tch, 805-473-4238
San Luis Obispo County
Type: public choice/at-risk
2 teachers, 60 students, partly at-risk, ages 13-18, 9-12th
  grade
Entrance requirements: grade 7 reading ability, district
  residency
Governance by principal
Teacher qualifications: multi-subject certification
Multi-aged classes; non-compulsory class attendance; no
  letter grades; rural location.

Arroyo Grande School
275 N Halcyon Rd, Arroyo Grande, CA 93420-2524
Type: Montessori

Central Coast Homeschoolers (1990)
7600 Marchant Ave, Atascadero, CA 93422
Barbara Alward, 462-0726
San Luis Obispo County
Non-profit
2 teachers, 2 students, ages 7-10
Affiliation: Homeschool Assn of CA
Governance by teachers; Prin
Student-centered; no preset curriculum; rural location.

West Mall Alternative
5601 W Mall, Atascadero, CA 93422

Children's House Montessori School
3025 Monterey Rd, Atascadero, CA 93422-1849

El Puente Community School in Lompoc
1100 W Laurel, Suite C, Lompoc, CA 93436

Clarence Ruth Elementary School
501 N W St, Lompoc, CA 93436-5099
Type: Montessori

Maple High School (1967)
Carob St, Vandenberg AFB, CA 93437
Hector Samaniego, Prin, 805-734-5666
Santa Barbara County
Non-profit
7 teachers, 100 students, mainly pregnant minors
Entrance requirements: as prescribed by CA Ed Code, age 16,
  residency
Affiliation: Lompoc USD
Governance by teachers, principal
Teacher qualifications: CA credential
Competency-based; no letter grades; multi-aged classes;
  childcare; interns accepted.

Children's Montessori School of Lompoc, Inc (1981)
PO Box 3510, Lompoc, CA 93438
Jim Murphy, Dir, 805-733-2290
Non-profit; tuition: 1,925/3,410/yr
2 teachers, 1 assistant, 35 students, ages 3-12
Affiliation: AMI
Governance by board of trustees
After-school art, dance, piano, voice, computer; choir;
  marine biology; childcare; suburban location.

El Puente Community School in Santa Maria
402 Farnel Rd, Suite M, Santa Maria, CA 93454-4960

Community Education Center (1983)
251 E Clark Ave, Santa Maria, CA 93455
Fred Miller, Prin, 805-937-6358, FAX: 805-934-4743
Santa Barbara County
Type: public choice
35 teachers, 1500 students, mainly at-risk, ages 13+, 9-12th
  grade
No residency requirement
Affiliation: CSU
Governance by shared decision making
Teacher qualifications: California certification
Delta program; teen parenting; concurrent adult education;
  wilderness trip; alternative ed work center; GAIN; work
  study; RECAP; BICEP; SAW; unscheduled school day; non-
  compulsory class attendance; interns accepted.

Santa Maria-Bonita Alternative Education
Box 460, Santa Maria, CA 93456

West Mall Alternative School
6495 Lewis Ave, Atascadero, CA 93465
Dan Ross, Prin, 805-462-0309, FAX: 805-466-2941
Atascadero District, San Luis Obispo County

Type: public/independent home-based at-risk
7 teachers, 125 students, mainly at-risk, ages 5–19, K–12th grade
Entrance requirements: average to above average academic skills, district residency
Governance by principal
Independent study; teachers assist parents in home-lesson planning, teaching; rural location.

Eagle Canyon High School (1993)
964 Old County Rd, Templeton, CA 93465
Douglas Nix, Prin, 805-434-1528
San Luis Obispo County
Type: public at-risk
4 teachers, 25 students, ages 14–18
Residency required
Governance by teachers and principal
Teacher qualifications: CA credential
Rural location.

Douglas High Alternative Education
3228 Douglas Ave, Mojave, CA 93501

Palisade Glacier High School (1972)
PO Box 938, Big Pine, CA 93513
John K. Helmbold, Prin, 619-938-2001
Inyo County
Type: public at-risk
3 teachers, 45 students, ages 16–19, 9–12th grade
Residency required
Affiliation: Bishop Joint Union HS District
Governance by principal
Teacher qualifications: CA certification, experience
Independent study; teen parenting; counseling; child development classes; career guidance; multi-aged classes

Lancaster Alternative Education
44711 N Cedar Ave, Lancaster, CA 93534-3210

Desert Montessori Academy
44503 North Fern Ave, Lancaster, CA 93534-3408
Sharon Davis

Independent Study
45024 3rd St, Lancaster, CA 93535

Heritage Montessori School
934 N Heritage Dr, Ridgecrest, CA 93555-5517
Helen DeVere

Rare Earth High School (1986)
PO Drawer CC, Rosamond, CA 93560
Dr Lawrence Jones, Prin, 805-256-5095, FAX: 256-1247
Kern County
Type: public at-risk
7 teachers; students mainly at-risk, ages 8–18, 3–12th grade
Entrance requirements: referral, no residency requirement
Governance by principal
Teacher qualifications: CA certification
Continuing education with behavior modification; no letter grades; interns accepted.

Summit High Alternative
400 S Robinson, Tehachapi, CA 93561

Caruthers Union High Alternative Education
Box 545, Caruthers, CA 93609

Clovis Unified Alternative Education
1450 Herndon Ave, Clovis, CA 93612

Enterprise Alternative Independent Study
1550 Herndon, Clovis, CA 93612

Sierra Vista High School (1984)
1327 E El Monte, Dinuba, CA 93618
Maryann Boylan, Prin, 209-591-5732, FAX: 209-591-3334
Tulare County

Type: public at-risk
3 teachers, 120 students, ages 13–18, 9–12th grade
Residency required
Governance by board
Teacher qualifications: CA certification
National drug-free school; model continuation HS; multi-aged classes; interns accepted.

Riverview Alternative Education
1976 Morris Kyle Dr, Firebaugh, CA 93622

Kerman Unified Alternative Education
151 S 1st St, Kerman, CA 93630

Kingsburg Jt High Alternative Education
1415 Marion St, Kingsburg, CA 93631

San Luis High School
125 7th St, Los Banos, CA 93635
M.E. Barr, Prin, 209-826-8410, FAX: 826-2252
Merced County
Type: public at-risk
6 teachers, 172 students, ages 16–18
Residency required
Governance by principal, board
Teacher qualifications: CA credential
Multi-aged classes; interns accepted.

Duane E. Furman High School
1903 Modoc, Madera, CA 93637
Kim Logan, 209-675-4482
Type: public choice

Mendota Unified Community Alternative Education
115 Mccabe Ave, Mendota, CA 93640

Chawanakee Home School/Independent Study (1988)
PO Box 707, North Fork, CA 93643
Doug Waltner, Mgr, 209-877-2215, FAX: 209-877-2377
Madera County
Type: public choice
2 teachers, 30 students, K–8th grade
Affiliation: CCIS
Governance by board
Teacher qualifications: CA credential
Homeschoolers participate in band, sports, science classes; monthly art activities; parent meetings; no letter grades; non-compulsory class attendance; extensive field trips

Oakhurst High Independent Study
49980 Rd 427, Oakhurst, CA 93644

Raymond Granite High Alternative Education
50200 Rd 427, Oakhurst, CA 93644

Parlier Alternative Education Center
Box 546, Parlier, CA 93648

Kings Canyon Alternative Education
477 W Manning Ave, Reedley, CA 93654

Taft High Alternative Education
1801 Seventh St, Sanger, CA 93657

El Portal High Independent Study
Box 210, San Joaquin, CA 93660

Cutler-Drosi Alternative Programs (1989)
41855 Rd 128, Drosi, CA 93674
Carolyn Kehrli, 209-528-4703, FAX: 209-528-3132
Tulare County
Type: public at-risk
12 teachers, 195 students, ages 14–18, 9–12th grade
No residency requirement
Governance by teachers, principal
Extensive field trips; multi-aged classes; interns accepted.

Roosevelt High School
4240 E Twarf, Fresno, CA 93702
Jane Hammaker, 209-441-3777
Type: magnet
9–12th grade
Visual and performing arts.

George M. DeWolf High School (1959)
2021 N Clark St, Fresno, CA 93703
Gerry Catanzarite, EdD, Prin, 209-441-3233, FAX: 209-323-7400
Fresno County
Type: public at-risk
16 teachers, 325 students, ages 15–19, HS
Affiliation: Fresno USD
Governance by principal
Teacher qualifications: California credential
Adventure-based education program; ropes course; in cooperation with Fresno City College; urban location.

Bullard Talent Elementary
4950 N Harrison, Fresno, CA 93704
Clytee Ramsey, 209-441-6831
Type: magnet
K–8th grade
Performing arts.

Whole Language Umbrella
(See Resource Appendix)

Fresno Valley High School
1540 M St, Fresno, CA 93721
Kelly Martin, 209-237-7215
Type: independent; tuition: $2500/yr, scholarships
12 students, mainly at-risk, ages 15–20, 9–12th grade
For those who "fall between the cracks" in PS; emphasis on community, critical thinking, accountability.

Central Unified Alternative Opportunity
4186 W Swift #103, Fresno, CA 93722

Manchester GATE Elementary
2307 E Dakota, Fresno, CA 93726
Nancy Hensel, 209-441-6741
Type: magnet
K–6th grade
Gifted and talented.

Pioneer Christian Academy (1991)
5533 E Swift Ave, Fresno, CA 93727
Marshall Fritz, President, 209-292-1776, FAX: 209-292-7582
Fresno County
Type: independent; tuition: sliding scale
Student ages 5–19, K–12th grade
Affiliation: Quality Schools Consortium
Governance by democratic school meeting
Multi-denominational; Christ chosen virtues, student chosen academics; an extension of home, assisting parents in raising their children; no letter grades; non-compulsory class attendance; multi-aged classes; extensive field trips; suburban location; interns accepted.

Children's Place Montessori School
5094 E Tulare Ave, Fresno, CA 93727-3929

Creative Teaching Materials
(See Resource Appendix)

Ala Carte, International School
1030 Kentfield Dr, Salinas, CA 93901-1064
Type: independent

Pacific Montessori Association
PO Box 2051, Salinas, CA 93902-2051

Marina Education Center (1993)
390 Caronel Ave, Marina, CA 93908
Ron Breding, Prin, 384-3305

Monterey County
Type: public choice/at-risk
20 teachers, 250 students, mainly at-risk, ages 6–25, 5–12th grade
Governance by principal, faculty and student reps
Teacher qualifications: CA credential
Multi-aged classes; continuing ed; suburban location; interns accepted.

Montessori Learning Center, Inc
30 Hitchcock Rd, Salinas, CA 93908-9341

Waldorf School of Monterey
PO Box 221057, Carmel, CA 93922
Victoria Lohman

Alternative Education Center at King City Joint Union High School
505 N Third Street, King City, CA 93930
Ed Bullard, Prin, 408-385-4661, FAX: 408-385-0695
Type: public choice/at-risk
15 teachers, 600 students, mainly at-risk, ages 15–60, 9–12th grade
Enrollment restricted to: voluntary placement for under age 16; limited involuntary placement for ages 16+; residency required
Governance by principal, faculty and student representatives, board
Teacher qualifications: secondary credential & voluntary placement
Independent study; CAI; competency-based; multi-aged classes; rural location; transportation.

Kinderhaus Montessori School
501 El Dorado St, Monterey, CA 93940-4608

Cypress High School (1965)
PO Box 1031, Monterey, CA 93942-1031
Vicki Phillips, Prin, 408-899-7026, FAX: 408-899-0628
Monterey District, Monterey County
Type: public at-risk
9 teachers, 150 students, ages 14–18, 9–12th grade
Governance by teachers and principal
Self-esteem; goal setting; decision making; responsibility; named CA model school in 1992; multi-aged classes; suburban location; transportation.

Critical Thinking Press
(See Resource Appendix)

P. G. Center for Independent Study (1984)
555 Sinex Ave, Pacific Grove, CA 93950
Bruce H. Henderson, Dir/Supervisor, 408-646-6512, FAX: -6500
Type: public choice, Home-based
1 teacher, 25 students, ages 6–20, K–12th grade
Enrollment restricted to students with no SE needs, residency
Affiliation: Pacific Grove USD
Governance by teachers; Principal; board
Teacher qualifications: certified
Access to Monterey Bay Aquarium, ocean environments, language institutes, Naval Library, historical museums, galleries.

Gonzales Union HSD Alternative Education (1979)
690 Main St, Soledad, CA 93960
Linda Coyne, Prin, 408-678-3066, FAX: 408-678-0162
Monterey County
Type: public choice, at-risk; scholarships
15 teachers, 1,000 students, ages 13+
Residency required
Teacher qualifications: Credential
Pinnacles Continuation HS; independent study; adult ed; Regional Occupation Programs; CAI; rural location; transportation; interns accepted.

College of Notre Dame Early Learning Center
1500 Ralston Ave, Belmont, CA 94002-1908
Adyllia Linka
Type: Montessori

Peninsula Montessori
1151 Vancouver Ave # A, Burlingame, CA 94010-5674
JoAnne Bailey

Burlingame Montessori School
2109 Broadway, Burlingame, CA 94010-5675
Lynette Muhlc

Jefferson Union Alternative
115 1st Ave, Daly City, CA 94014

Kinderlings
978 Highland Cir, Los Altos, CA 94022
Carolyn Courture
Type: Montessori

Montessori School of Los Altos
201 Covington Rd, Los Altos, CA 94022

Waldorf School of the Peninsula (1984)
401 Rosita Ave, Los Altos, CA 94022
Brenda Aronow, Business Mgr, 415-948-8433
Non-profit; tuition: $4,200-16,000/yr, scholarships
8 teachers, 101 students, ages 4.9-13, K-7th grade
Entrance requirements: interview
Affiliation: AWSNA
Teacher qualifications: Waldorf certification preferred
Suburban location.

Peninsula School (1925)
Peninsula Way, Menlo Park, CA 94025
Carol Young-Holt, Director, 415-325-1584
San Mateo County
Type: independent; tuition: $3530-5470, scholarships
19 teachers, 21 assistants, 254 students, ages 3-14, K-8th grade
Entrance requirements: holistic education philosophy
Governance by staff/parent cooperative with board of directors
Teacher qualifications: foundation in child development, CA credential or equivalent
Emphasis on the arts, with afternoon choices of weaving, clay, fine arts, wood shop, jewelry-making; play is highly valued; ETV video, "Why do These Kids Love School?" based on school; no letter grades; multi-aged classes; extensive field trips; suburban location; interns accepted.

Saint Joseph's Montessori School
150 Valparaiso Ave, Menlo Park, CA 94025
Janet Wildey

Green Oaks Montessori
490 Willow Rd, Menlo Park, CA 94025-2716
Kathy Hassan

Menlo Montessori
3300 Alpine Rd, Menlo Park, CA 94028-7525

Millbrae Montessori School
797 Santa Margarita Ave, Millbrae, CA 94030-1164

Montessori Gardens
1120 Rose Ave, Mountain View, CA 94040-4058

Nienhuis Montessori USA
(See Resource Appendix)

Western Montessori School
323 Moorpark Way, Mountain View, CA 94041-1621

Edison Montessori School
750 Dartmouth Ave, San Carlos, CA 94070

Math Products Plus
(See Resource Appendix)

Early Learning Institute Second Generation
850 Gateway Blvd, South San Francisco, CA 94080-7021
Dr Charles Bernstein
Type: Montessori

Sunnyvale School District Montessori Program
830 W McKinley, Sunnyvale, CA 94086
Betsy Reeves

Rainbow Montessori
790 E Duane Ave Bldg # 5, Sunnyvale, CA 94086-3359

Montessori School
622 Old San Francisco Rd, Sunnyvale, CA 94086-7960

Fremont Union Alternative Education
589 W Fremont Ave, Sunnyvale, CA 94087

Santa Clara Valley Homeschoolers
795 Sheraton Dr, Sunnyvale, CA 94087

Lakewood School
750 Lakechime Dr, Sunnyvale, CA 94089
Donna Myers
Type: Montessori

John Swett Elementary
727 Golden Gate Ave, San Francisco, CA 94102
Kay Nomura, 415-241-6320
Type: magnet
K-5th grade
Visual and performing arts.

Tenderloin Community Children's Center
302 Eddy St, San Francisco, CA 94102-2607
Type: Montessori

Sand Paths Academy
525 Bryant St, San Francisco, CA 94107-1222
Type: Montessori

Binet Montessori
1715 Octavia St, San Francisco, CA 94109
Daniel Binet, 415-567-4000
Tuition: $400-550/mo
5 teachers, 5 assistants, 125 students, ages 3-9
Accreditation: AMS
Governance by administrator
50 weeks/year; childcare; urban location; interns accepted.

Royal Day School
1 Daniel Burnham Ct, San Francisco, CA 94109-5455
Type: Montessori

Montessori House of Children
1187 Franklin St, San Francisco, CA 94109-6813

Global Voice Education Project for C Band Satellite (1993)
(See Resource Appendix)

Hilltop High Alternative Education
1325 Florida St, San Francisco, CA 94110

New College of California (1971)
766 Valencia St, San Francisco, CA 94110
Katrina Fullman, Adms Coord, 415-626-0884
Type: higher education
260 students, adult ages
School of Humanities; Public Interest Law School; Graduate School of Psychology; Weekend College; seminars; undergraduate thesis; journal work; credit for life experience.

Center For Independent Study
1000 Cuyuga Ave, San Francisco, CA 94112

Rivendell School
4512 Irving St, San Francisco, CA 94112
Li Moon
Type: independent

S. F. Community Elementary
125 Excelsior St, San Francisco, CA 94112
Paul Reinhertz, 415-469-4739
Type: magnet
K-8th grade

Newcomer High
2340 Jackson St, San Francisco, CA 94115

San Francisco Waldorf School
2938 Washington St, San Francisco, CA 94115
Monique Grund

Royal Montessori School
1550 Eddy St, San Francisco, CA 94115-4165

California Institute of Integral Studies
765 Ashbury St, San Francisco, CA 94117
Type: higher education
Has on-campus and on-line programs.

Synergy School (1973)
975 Grove, San Francisco, CA 94117
Elena Dillon, Adms Dir, 415-567-6177
Type: independent, non-profit; tuition: $4,700/yr,
    scholarships
8 teachers, 94 students, ages 5-12, K-6th grade
Governance by teacher cooperative
Teacher qualifications: elementary credential, experience
Empowers students to become self-confident, creative
    learners; no letter grades; multi-aged classes; extensive
    field trips; urban location; interns accepted.

Multicultural Education c/o Caddo Gap Press
(See Resource Appendix)

Montessori Children's House
25 Lake St, San Francisco, CA 94118-1422

Children's School of San Francisco
420 9th Ave, San Francisco, CA 94118-2913
Type: Montessori

Big City Montessori School
240 Industrial St, San Francisco, CA 94124-1917
Meighan Tideman

Maria Montessori School (1972)
678 Portola Dr, San Francisco, CA 94127
Ursula Thrush, Head, 415-731-8188, FAX: 415-566-4311
Non-profit; tuition: $350/470/mo
6 teachers, 2 assistants, 74 students, mainly international,
    ages 3-15
Affiliations: MACTE, NAMTA
Governance by administrator
Traditional Montessori with emphasis on peace ed; childcare;
    suburban location; interns accepted.

School of the Arts Alternative High School
700 Font Blvd, San Francisco, CA 94132
Yvonne McClung, 415-469-4027
Type: magnet
9-12th grade
Performing Arts.

Montessori Children's Center
755 Font Blvd, San Francisco, CA 94132-1795

Saybrook Institute Graduate School (1971)
450 Pacific, 3rd Fl, San Francisco, CA 94133
J. Bruce Francis, PhD, Pres, 415-433-9200, FAX: 415-433-9271
San Francisco County

Type: higher education, non-profit; tuition: $9,500/yr,
    scholarships
80 teachers, 300 students, mainly adult professionals, ages
    35-63
BA in psychology/humanities required
Governance by board
Psychology; human science; distance learning format taught
    by internationally known scholars.

San Francisco Montessori School
300 Gaven St, San Francisco, CA 94134-1113

The Learning Community at Los Altos HS (1971)
201 Almond Ave, Los Altos, CA 94301
Gary Bacon, Coord, 415-960-8869
Santa Clara County
Type: public choice
1 teacher, 25 students, ages 14-18, 9-12th grade
Residency required
Governance by board
Balanced, whole-person approach; student-centered; per-
    sonal and group experience; students participate in cur-
    riculum development; strong service component;
    multi-aged classes; interns accepted.

Ohlone
950 Amarillo, Palo Alto, CA 94303
415-856-1726

Creative Montessori Learning Center
1425 Bay Rd, Palo Alto, CA 94303-1109

Chrystie's Creche
3711 Ross Rd, Palo Alto, CA 94303-4551
Chrystie Tzugaris
Type: Montessori

Horrall Elementary School
949 Ocean View Ave, San Mateo, CA 94401-3462
Type: Montessori

Little Montessori School
27 10th Ave, San Mateo, CA 94401-4304

Neighborhood Montessori School
1333 Rosewood, Belmont, CA 94402

Bright Beginnings Montessori School
30 Hobart Ave, San Mateo, CA 94402
Joanne Adan

Meadow Heights Elementary School
PO Box K, San Mateo, CA 94402-0058
Type: Montessori

San Mateo Montessori
15 14th Ave, San Mateo, CA 94402-2407
Eleanor Spare

Hillsborough Montessori Children's House
315 Tulane Dr, San Mateo, CA 94402-3237
Eleanor Spare

Parkside Elementary School
1685 Eisenhower St, San Mateo, CA 94403-1098
Type: Montessori

Discovery Montessori School
1601 Oakwood Dr, San Mateo, CA 94403-3918
Bonnie Mathisen

Child Unique Montessori School
2226 Encinal Ave, Alameda, CA 94501
Cindy Acker

Island High School (1967)
2437 Eagle Ave, Alameda, CA 94501
Ed Tucker, Prin, 510-748-4024, FAX: 510-769-7417
Alameda County

Type: public at-risk
10 teachers, 170 students, ages 15–19, 9–12th grade
Entrance requirements: referral, proof of residency, age 16
Governance by principal
Teacher qualifications: credential
Teen parenting; ROP food service program; mainstreamed

Bayside Montessori Association
1523 Willow St, Alameda, CA 94501-2716

Rising Star Montessori School
770 Santa Clara Ave, Alameda, CA 94501-3102
Ann Gavey

Montessori School of Alameda
1247 Park Ave, Alameda, CA 94501-5235
Dr Pamela Lanaro

Prospects High Alternative Education
625 W 4th St, Antioch, CA 94509
Type: public choice

La Paloma High School (1974)
6651 Lone Tree Way, Brentwood, CA 94513
Jerry Hardt, Prin, 510-634-2888, FAX: 510-634-1687
Contra Costa County
Type: public at-risk
8 teachers, 130 students, ages 15–18, 9–12th grade
District residency required
Governance by board
1993 CA DE Continuation Model HS Excellence Award; interns
    accepted.

Alhambra Montessori
2771 Treat Blvd, Concord, CA 94518

Crossroads High School
1266 San Carlos Ave, Concord, CA 94518
Betty Potts, Adm, 510-933-1123
Contra Costa County
Type: public at-risk
2 teachers, 40 students, mainly at-risk, ages 14–19, 9–12th
    grade
Enrollment restricted to parenting and pregnant teens; resi-
    dency required
Governance by principal, faculty and student representatives
Teacher qualifications: secondary credential
Parenting, pre/post-natal health, childbirth, survival skills,
    career orientation; multi-aged classes; suburban location.

Nueva Vista High School (1991)
1101 Alberta Way, Concord, CA 94518
Julie Hernandez, Adm, 510-689-1487
Contra Costa County
Type: public choice/at-risk
2 teachers, 40 students, mainly at-risk, ages 13–19, 9–12th
    grade
Residency required
Governance by principal, faculty and student representatives,
    democratic school meeting
Community service, vocational, aviation programs; individual-
    ized and group learning; multi-aged classes; extensive field
    trips; suburban location.

Concordia School
2353 5th Ave, Concord, CA 94518-1112
Alice Marshall
Type: Montessori

Horizons School
2730 Salvio St, Concord, CA 94519
Doug Cook, Adm, 510-687-0374
Contica Costa County
Type: independent, non-profit
9 teachers, 235 students, mainly at-risk, ages 12–18, 7–12th
    grade
Governance by principal
Teacher qualifications: CA certification

Adelante High School (1992)
2450 Grant St, Concord, CA 94520
Marti Howell, Adm, 510-798-1168
Contra Costa County
Type: public at-risk
5 teachers, 85 students, mainly at-risk, ages 14–17, 9–12th
    grade
Residency required
Governance by teachers and principal
Teacher qualifications: expertise in subject areas
Necessary Small High School; "On Location" program com-
    bines classwork with off-campus projects; "On Campus" is
    more traditional; multi-aged classes; suburban location;
    interns accepted.

Myrtle Farm Montessori School
4980 Myrtle Dr, Concord, CA 94521-1436
Krista Ericson

Prospect High School (1991)
3100 Oak Park Blvd, Pleasant Hill, CA 94523
Noreen Doyle, Adm, 510-945-7902
Contra Costa County
Type: public at-risk
2 teachers, 40 students, ages 14–18, 9–12th grade
No provisions for SE; residency required
Governance by teachers and principal
Teacher qualifications: must teach multiple subjects
Counselor-trained faculty; self-esteem; productive hour
    concept; cooperative learning; computers; no letter
    grades; multi-aged classes; suburban location; interns
    accepted.

Willow High School (1970)
PO Box 816; 1650 Crockett Blvd, Crockett, CA 94525
Darlene Rourke, Lead Tch, 510-787-1286
Contra Costa County
Type: public at-risk
1 teacher, 20 students, ages 16–18, 9–12th grade
Residency required
Governance by teachers, principal
Teacher qualifications: CA certification
Flexible learning format; teen parenting; working students;
    no letter grades; multi-aged classes

Fountainhead Montessori (1973)
115 Estates Dr, Danville, CA 94526
Sarah Zimmerman, Pres/Adm, 510-820-1343
Non-profit; tuition: $3,050-6,050/yr
20 teachers, 27 assistants, 447 students, ages infant-9
Affiliations: AMS, NAEYC
Governance by administrator
Childcare; suburban location; interns accepted.

Das Montessori Kinderhaus
101 Sonora Ave, Danville, CA 94526-3833

Bright Star Montessori
7140 Gladys Ave, El Cerrito, CA 94530
Swarna Matz, Dir, 233-5330
Non-profit; tuition: $3,600-5,100/yr
9 teachers, 10 assistants, 139 students, mainly international,
    ages infant-15
Accreditation: AMS
Governance by administrator
Childcare; suburban location; interns accepted.

Sem Yeto High School (1967)
421 Madison St, Fairfield, CA 94533
Edward E. Welsh, Prin, 707-421-4271
Solano County
Type: public choice/at-risk
12 teachers, 290 students, ages 16–19, 9–12th grade
Entrance requirements: age 16 by end of placement semes-
    ter, district residency
Affiliation: WASC

Governance by board
Teacher qualifications: CA secondary credential
Close supervision; multi-aged classes; suburban location; interns accepted.

Vista Alternative School (1985)
4455 Seneca Park Ave, Fremont, CA 94536
Mary Douglass, 510-657-7028, FAX: 510-657-5535
Alameda County
Type: public choice
11 teachers, 260 students, ages 5-21, K-12th grade
Entrance requirements: ability to read for grades 7-12; residency
Affiliations: Fremont USD, CCIS
Governance by teachers and principal
Teacher qualifications: CA credential
Homeschooling component with certificated guidance of parents as teachers; independent study; JHSers meet in small groups; SHSers work individually; suburban location.

Vista Alternative (1985)
4455 Seneca Park, Fremont, CA 94538
Mary Douglass, 510-687-9155, FAX: 510-657-5535
Alameda County
Type: public choice/at-risk
9 teachers, 250 students, ages 5-21, K-12th grade
Entrance requirements: ability to read, grades 7-12, residency
Governance by teachers and principal
Teacher qualifications: CA credential
Independent study; tutorial; suburban location; interns accepted.

Montessori School of Fremont (1975)
1901 Washington Blvd, Fremont, CA 94539
Tess Buenaventura, Dir, 510-490-0919, FAX: 510-489-3913
Tuition: $250-395/mo
4 teachers, 5 assistants, 89 students, mainly international, ages toddler-6
Affiliations: AMI, NAMTA, MAC-USA
Governance by teachers and administrators
Rich cultural resources; computer ed; extensive ESL, parent ed; childcare; suburban location; interns accepted.

Hayward Unified Alternative Education
24411 Amador St, Hayward, CA 94540-5000
Type: public choice

Montessori School of Hayward
1101 Walpert St, Hayward, CA 94541
Dr Pamela Lanaro

Montessori Children's School
1620 East Ave, Hayward, CA 94541-5315

Montessori School of Castro Valley
19234 Lake Chabot Rd, Castro Valley, CA 94546-2902
Dr Pamela Lanaro

Montessori Children's House
915 Colina Ct, Lafayette, CA 94549

Diablo Valley Montessori
3390 Deer Hill Rd, Lafayette, CA 94549-3258
Barbara Grillo

Montessori Children's House of Lafayette
955A Moraga Rd, Lafayette, CA 94549-4524
Naome Dragstedt

Marshall
4602 Almond Cir, Livermore, CA 94550
Type: Montessori

Vineyard High Independent Study
685 Las Positas Blvd, Livermore, CA 94550
Type: public choice home-based

Valley Montessori School
460 North Livermore Ave, Livermore, CA 94550-2929
Mary Ellen Cordiss

Montessori School & Educational Foundation
5966 Greenridge Rd, Castro Valley, CA 94552-1818

Martinez Independent Study (1980)
600 F St, Martinez, CA 94553
Kathy Prout, Asst Dir, 510-228-5156, FAX: 510-228-6989
Contra Costa County
Type: public choice
4 teachers, 115 students, ages 5+, K-12th grade
Enrollment restricted to students without special needs; no residency requirement
Affiliation: CA Consortium
Governance by principal
Homeschooling support; multi-aged classes; extensive field trips

Montessori Children's Center
33170 Lake Meade Dr, Fremont, CA 94555
Naseem Meer

Montessori House of Children
22 Wakefield Dr, Moraga, CA 94556-1216
Vera Depass

Napa Valley Alternative Education
2425 Jefferson St, Napa, CA 94558

Sunrise Montessori of Napa Valley (1978)
PO Box 4077, Napa, CA 94558
Janice Tres, Co-owner/Adm, 707-253-1105
Tuition: $225-335/mo
8 teachers, 7 assistants, 110 students, ages infant-9
Two campuses; childcare; suburban and rural locations.

Temescal High School
2447 Old Sonoma Rd, Napa, CA 94558
Darlene Lance, Prin, 707-253-3791
Napa County
Type: public at-risk
5 teachers, 100 students, partly at-risk, ages 16-18, 10-12th grade
District residency required
Governance by teachers, principal
Teacher qualifications: credential
Integrated, project approach; varied schedule; art; adopted by Sunrise Rotary Club; no letter grades; multi-aged classes; interns accepted.

Crossroads High Independent Study
Box 385, Newark, CA 94560
Type: public choice home-based

Newark Independent Study
5715 Musick Ave, Newark, CA 94560

Newark Opportunity
6201 Lafayette Ave, Newark, CA 94560

Contra Costa Alternative High School
10 Irwin Way, Orinda, CA 94563
Joel Weber, 510-254-0199
Type: independent; tuition: $400-600/mo, scholarships
40 students, 9-12th grade
Focuses on social awareness, self-exploration; multi-cultural; wide variety of electives; suburban location.

Montessori Children's House of Pinole
2281 Johanna Ct, Pinole, CA 94564-1816

Grasp Independent Study
809 Black Diamond St, Pittsburg, CA 94565
Type: public choice

Amadora Valley Adult School
4659 Bernal Ave, Pleasanton, CA 94566
Jean Kaput, Asst Dir, 510-426-4280, FAX: 510-846-5317
Alameda County
Type: public choice
Governance by principal, board
Teacher qualifications: CA credential
Interns accepted.

River Delta Unified Alternative
500 Elm Way, Rio Vista, CA 94571

YMCA Child Development Center
200 Lake Ave, Rodeo, CA 94572
Sandra Farmer
Type: Montessori

Montessori Children's House of Rodeo
355 Parker Ave, Rodeo, CA 94572-1124
Johanna Lowe

St Helena Montessori School (1971)
1328 Spring St, St Helena, CA 94574
Ms Heil, Adm, 707-963-7642
Non-profit; tuition: $2,200-3,550/yr
3 teachers, 3 assistants, 58 students, ages 3-12
Affiliations: AMI, NAMTA
Governance by administrator, board
Catholic; Catechesis of the Good Shepherd; French; computer; art; Orff-Shulwerk music; gymnastics; suburban location.

Montessori Family Center
960 Dowdell Ln, St Helena, CA 94574-1452
Patricia Goldstein

Lincoln High
2600 Teagarden St, San Leandro, CA 94577
Janet McCarthy, Prin, 510-667-3594
Alameda County
Type: public at-risk
6 teachers, 90 students, ages 16-18, 9-12th grade
Enrollment restrictions: credit deficient, truant, no serious discipline problems, residency
Governance by teachers, principal
Teacher qualifications: CA credential
Volunteer service; regional occupational programs connection; personal, group counseling; variable credit

Montessori School at Washington Ave
14795 Washington Ave, San Leandro, CA 94578
Dr Pamela Lanaro

Montessori School of San Leandro
16292 Foothill Blvd, San Leandro, CA 94578-2105
Dr Pamela Lanaro

Independent Study
820 Bockman Rd, San Lorenzo, CA 94580

Venture School (1978)
3280 E Crow Canyon Rd, San Ramon, CA 94583
Norman Abraham, Prin, 510-275-0402, FAX: 510-275-0171
Contra Costa County
Type: public choice; Home-based
19 teachers, 504 students, mainly at-risk, ages 5-53, K-12th grade
No residency requirement
Governance by principal, board
Teacher qualifications: California credential
Independent study; individualized goals; extensive field trips; interns accepted.

Hacienda Child Development
4671 Chabot Dr, Pleasanton, CA 94588
Type: Montessori

Vallejo City Unified Alternative Education
211 Valle Vista, Vallejo, CA 94590

Parkmead Alternative Learning School
1920 Magnolia, Parkmead, CA 94595
510-939-2900
Type: public choice
6 teachers, 175 students, K-5th grade
5 hrs/mo parent participation required.

Oakland Montessori School
3636 Dimond Ave, Oakland, CA 94602-2213

Casa Montessori School
5062 Dublin Ave, Oakland, CA 94602-2605

Cole Elementary
1011 Union St, Oakland, CA 94607
Jaqueline Phillips, 510-444-7733
Type: magnet
4-6th grade
Performing arts.

East Bay Waldorf School
1275 61st St, Emeryville, CA 94608
Sherry McCarthy

Pacific Rim International School (1989)
5521 Doyle St, Emeryville, CA 94608
Christinia Cheung, Dir, 510-849-1889
Type: Montessori; tuition: $385-505/mo
5 teachers, 1 assistant, 48 students, mainly international, ages 2-8
Affiliations: NAEYC, IRA, NAMTA, NCME, AMS
Governance by an administrator
English-Mandarin bilingual and multicultural program; childcare; urban location; interns accepted.

Jardin Montessori School
3239 Elm St, Oakland, CA 94609

Park Day School (1976)
368 42nd St, Oakland, CA 94609
Tom Little, Dir, 510-653-0317, FAX: 510-653-0637
Type: independent, non-profit; tuition: $5,600/yr, scholarships
12 teachers, 200 students, ages 5-12, K-6th grade
Governance by consensus of staff and board
Teacher qualifications: experience in alternative school settings
Cloistered garden setting; activities-based curriculum; emphasis on multi-cultural, diversity elements in diverse population; central teacher involvement in long-range planning; no letter grades; extensive field trips; urban location; interns accepted.

St Academy Senior High Alternative
417 29th St, Oakland, CA 94609

Grand Lake Montessori
723 Santa Ray Ave, Oakland, CA 94610-1722

Casa Dei Bambini Montessori School
281 Santa Clara Ave, Oakland, CA 94610-2623
Helen Sears

Oakland High School
1023 MacArthur Blvd, Oakland, CA 94611
Joanne Grimm, 510-451-1208
Type: magnet
10-12th grade
Visual arts.

Piedmont Independent Learning High School (1981)
760 Magnolia Ave, Piedmont, CA 94611
Tra Holloway Boxer, Prin, 510-420-3702, FAX: 654-7374
Alameda County
Non-profit

5 teachers, 32 students, mainly at-risk, ages 15–19, 9–12th grade
Entrance requirements: interview, district residency
Governance by principal
Flexible; mastery-based; open entry/exit; individual assessments, contracts; multi-aged classes; interns accepted.

Applegarden Montessori School
5667 Thornhill Dr, Oakland, CA 94611-2156
Naome Dragstedt

Arts School
5263 Broadway Ter, Oakland, CA 94618
Type: public choice

My Own Montessori (1986)
5723 Oak Grove Ave, Oakland, CA 94618
Gena K. Lawrence, Adm, 510-652-5979
Non-profit; tuition: $400-620/mo
2 teachers, 2 assistants, 28 students, ages 3–6
Accreditation: AMS
Governance by board
Childcare; urban location; interns accepted.

Rockridge Montessori School
6118 Harwood Ave, Oakland, CA 94618-1340

Mountain Boulevard Preschool (1983)
4432 Mountain Blvd, Oakland, CA 94619
Dennis or Eleni Wanken, 510-482-2850, FAX: 510-482-0326
Type: Montessori; tuition: $695/mo
3 teachers, 4 assistants, 45 students, ages 3–6
Affiliations: PACE, NAEYC; accreditation: AMS
Childcare; transportation; interns accepted.

Skyline High School
12250 Skyline Blvd, Oakland, CA 94619
Thomas Lorch, 510-531-9161
Type: magnet
10–12th grade
Performing arts.

Cedar Creek Montessori Day Care (1979)
1600 Sacramento St, Berkeley, CA 94702
Kerry Woodward, Dir, 510-525-1377
Tuition: $590/mo
2 teachers, 2 assistants, 38 students, ages 3–6
Accreditation: AMS
Governance by administrator
Art; nature studies; interns accepted.

Encampment for Citzenship (1946)
2530 San Pablo Ave, Suite B-10, Berkeley, CA 94702
Doug Harkness, 415-548-8908
Type: independent, non-profit; tuition: $2,400/yr, scholarships
50 students, ages 16–19
Six-week summer camp; focus on current social, political issues; workshops; community service; arts and politics.

Montessori Family School (1981)
1850 Scenic Ave, Berkeley, CA 94703
Jane Wechsler, Dir, 510-848-2322
Non-profit; tuition: $3,700-6,250/yr, scholarships
12 teachers, 8 assistants, 123 students, ages 2–12
Affiliation: AMS; accreditations: NAEYC, PACE
Governance by teachers and administrators
Borders UC Berkeley; cultural diversity; summer program; parent involvement required; childcare; urban location; interns accepted.

Family Forum
1035 Pablo Ave #5, Albany, CA 94706
Grace Orenstein
Type: Montessori

Montessori Children's School
661 San Luis Rd, Berkeley, CA 94707

Montessori School of Kensington
52 Arlington, Kensington, CA 94707
510-527-1278
Tuition: $405/555/mo
4 teachers, 5 assistants, 52 students, ages infant–9
Affiliations: AMS, PACE
Governance by administrator
Adjacent to University of California gardens, local library, recreation center, park, and tennis courts; childcare; suburban location; interns accepted.

Northern Alameda/Western Contra Costa Homeschool Support Group (1988)
1090 Miller Ave, Berkeley, CA 94708
Ann Kositsky-Haiman, 510-527-5091
Alameda County
Regular meetings.

Concepts to Go
Dept M, PO Box 10043, Berkley, CA 94709
Ruth Ingram
Type: Montessori

Berkeley Montessori School
2030 Francisco St, Berkeley, CA 94709-2198
Curt Chamberlain

West County Montessori
716 Appian Way, El Sabrante, CA 94803

Keystone Montessori
801 Park Central St, Richmond, CA 94803-1225
Linda Shehabi

El Sobrante School
1060 Manor Rd, El Sobrante, CA 94803-1398
Type: Montessori

Kappa High School (1992)
4300 Cutting Blvd, Richmond, CA 94804
Dr Richard B. Blaettler, Prin, 510-234-0281
Contra Costa County
Type: public at-risk
4 teachers, 100 students, ages 15–18, 9–12th grade
Enrollment restrictions: no discipline problems, residency
Governance by principal
Tutoring; portfolios; computer labs; TAP; role model speakers; job shadowing/mentoring; breakfast program; multi-aged classes; interns accepted.

Montessori Kinderhaus
5638 Bayview Ave, Richmond, CA 94804-4827

Vista High Independent Study
2625 Barnard Rd, Richmond, CA 94806
Type: public choice

Middle College High School (1993)
2600 Mission Bell Dr, San Pablo, CA 94806
Myra Silverman, Prin, 510-235-7800 x411
Type: public choice
80 students

Seaview School
2000 Southwood Dr, San Pablo, CA 94806-1039
Type: Montessori

Columbia Pacific University
1415 3rd St, San Rafael, CA 94901
Cynthia Sirkin, 800-227-0119
Non-residential programs for BA, MA, PhD; credit for life experience; no letter grades.

Montessori School of Central Marin
317 Auburn St, San Rafael, CA 94901-5209
Dr Pamela Lanaro

Marin Waldorf School
755 Idylberry Dr, San Rafael, CA 94903
Karen Rivers

Montessori Special Education Institute
PO Box 6633, San Rafael, CA 94903

Montessori de Terra Linda
620 Del Ganado Rd, San Rafael, CA 94903-2306
Jim Cummesky

Creekside Montessori School
PO Box 570, Bolinas, CA 94924-0570

Marin Montessori School (1963)
5200 Paradise Dr, Corte Madera, CA 94925-2107
Jane Calbreath, Off Coord, 415-924-5388, FAX: 415-924-5305
Non-profit; tuition: $3,480-4,990/yr
8 teachers, 7 assistants, 179 students, mainly international,
    ages infant-12
Affiliations: NAMTA, ISBMA; accreditation: AMI
Governance by board of directors
Natural bayfront environment; childcare; suburban location.

Cascade Canyon School
2626 Drake Rd, Fairfax, CA 94930-0879
Anne Evans, Director, 415-459-3464, FAX: 415-459-1189
Marin County
Type: independent, non-profit; tuition: $4500-5500,
    scholarships
3 teachers, 36 students, ages 5-14, K-8th grade
Entrance requirements: family observation and interview
Affiliation: NCACS
Governance by parent cooperative, board
International education with several foreign languages, multi-
    cultural community service, sister school program via E
    mail and visits overseas; no letter grades; non-compulsory
    class attendance; multi-aged classes; extensive field trips;
    suburban location; interns accepted.

Rainbow Bridge Montessori School
21 William St, Cotati, CA 94931-4235
Juli Inman

San Andreas High Alternative/Opportunity
Doherty Dr, Larkspur, CA 94939

Tamiscal High School (1990)
599 William Ave, Larkspur, CA 94939
Debrah Stewart, 415-927-3465
Type: public choice
100 students, partly at-risk, ages 14-19, 9-12th grade
Residency required
Governance by teachers, principal
College prep; independent study

Ross Academy Montessori (1966)
7 Thomas Dr, Mill Valley, CA 94941
Claire Haeger, 415-383-5777
Tuition: $230-420/mo
5 teachers, 2 assistants, 75 students, ages infant-6
Entrance requirements: min age 2
Affiliation: NAMS; accreditation: AMS
Governance by administrator
Gymnastics, dance, music optional; childcare; suburban loca-
    tion; interns accepted.

Penngrove Montessori
11201 Main St, Penngrove, CA 94941

Marin Horizon School
305 Montford Ave, Mill Valley, CA 94941-3388
Type: Montessori

Montessori School of Novato (1985)
1915 Novato Blvd, Novato, CA 94947
Susan Young, Adm, 415-892-2228
Tuition: $290/380
2 teachers, 44 students, ages infant-6

Affiliation: AMI
Governance by an administrator
Childcare.

Nova Independent Studies (1990)
720 Diablo, Novato, CA 94947
Tom Ovens, Lead Tch; Jim Campagna, Prin, 415-897-7653
Marin County
Type: public choice
5 teachers, 135 students, ages 5-18, K-12th grade
Screening required
Affiliation: Novato Unified Schools
Governance by teachers, principal
Teacher qualifications: district requirements
Weekly individual student/teacher meetings; contract learn-
    ing; community service; no letter grades; interns accepted.

Carpe Diem High School (1992)
201 Fair St, Petaluma, CA 94952
Susan Rodkin, Prin, 707-778-4796
Petaluma HS District, Sonoma County
Type: public at-risk
3 teachers, 30 students, ages 14-18, 9-12th grade
No SE or 1st semester students; no residency requirement
Governance by teachers and principal
Mini-field trips: 3-4 students, one teacher for career explo-
    ration, community involvement; multi-aged classes; subur-
    ban location.

Montessori Schools of Petaluma (1975)
825 Middlefield Dr, Petaluma, CA 94952
Tom Sipes, Dir, 707-763-9222
Non-profit; tuition: $260-474/mo
7 teachers, 7 assistants, 135 students, ages infant-12
Governance by teachers and administrators
Childcare; suburban location; interns accepted.

Homeschool Association of California
PO Box 431, Petaluma, CA 94953
Type: state home-based

Marin School
PO Box 504, Petaluma, CA 94953-0504
Type: Montessori

Sonoma Mountain High School (1992)
333 Casa Grande Rd, Petaluma, CA 94954
Marilyn Stratford, Prin, 707-778-4738
Sonoma County
Type: public at-risk
3 teachers, 30 students, ages 14-17, 9-12th grade
Governance by teachers, principal
Integrated block curriculum; mini field trips; high level of
    technology; personal student-staff connections; multi-
    aged classes

Early Work
(See Resource Appendix)

San Anselmo Montessori School
100 Shaw Dr, San Anselmo, CA 94960-1904

Slide Ranch
2025 Shoreline Hwy, Muir Beach, CA 94965
Suzanne Connolly, Dir, 414-381-6155
Type: independent, non-profit; tuition: variable, scholarships
50 students, K-12th grade
Principles of ecology; farm, wild lands, ocean environments;
    1 day and overnight; experiential.

Sparrow Creek Montessori School (1973)
304 Caledonia St, Sausalito, CA 94965
Judith Bang-Kolb, 415-332-9595
Non-profit; tuition: $390/mo, scholarships
3-4 teachers, 22 students, ages 3-6
Governance by board of trustees
Art; year-round garden; childcare; suburban location; interns
    accepted.

Children's Cultural Center of Marin (1971)
620 Drake Ave, Sausalito, CA 94965-1107
Elice Webster, 415-332-1044, FAX: 332-1058
Type: Montessori; tuition: $595/mo
5 teachers, 8 assistants; student ages infant–9
Affiliation: NAMTA; accreditation: AMS
Daily French; extensive computer ed; Japanese; global
　　studies; suburban location; transportation; interns
　　accepted.

Liedloff Continuum Network
(See Resource Appendix)

Santa Cruz Montessori School (1964)
6230 Soquel Dr, Aptos, CA 95003
James M. Moore, Head, 408-476-1646, FAX: 408-476-2703
Non-profit; tuition: $3,200-4,650/yr
10 teachers, 15 assistants, 258 students, ages infant–15
Entrance requirements: interview; $250 enrollment fee
Affiliations: NAMTA, AMI, MAC; accreditation: AMI/USA
Governance by teachers, administrators, board
2-acres with access to Monterey Bay; creative conflict resolu-
　　tion; Great Books literature; Central Coast Writer's Work-
　　shop; childcare; suburban location; interns accepted.

Fawnhaven Montessori Pre-School
6401 Freedom Blvd, Aptos, CA 95003-9607
Barbara Hendricks

South Street Centre (1987)
PO Box 227, Boulder Creek, CA 95006
Betsy Herbert; Estelle Fein, Co-Dirs, 408-338-2540
Santa Cruz County
Type: home-based; cost: variable
7 teachers, 60 students, ages 5–16, K–12th grade
Residency required for some programs
Affiliation: San Lorenzo Valley SD
Governance by teachers and prin
Teacher qualifications: interest in learning process
Workshops; conferences; link for developing community-
　　based education; contracted by local SD for some service;
　　suburban location; interns accepted.

AMI Montessori House of Children
124 W Latimer Ave, Campbell, CA 95008-1105

San Jose Montessori School
564 Hawthorne Ave, Campbell, CA 95008-2117

Central Bay High School (1991)
13994 Castroville Blvd, Castroville, CA 95012
Rich Castello, Prin, 408-633-4790
Type: public at-risk
2 teachers, 24 students, mainly teen parents, ages 14–18
Residency required
Affiliation: NMCUSD
Governance by teachers, principal, board
Childcare.

North Monterey County Alternative Education
13390 Castroville Blvd, Castroville, CA 95012

Villa Montessori, Inc (1964)
20900 Stevens Creek Blvd, Cupertino, CA 95014
Renee Davis, Dir/Adm, 408-257-3374
Non-profit; tuition: $2,350/yr
2 teachers, 2 assistants, 60 students, mainly international,
　　ages 3–6
Entrance requirements: toilet trained
Affiliation: AMS
Governance by board of trustees
Mandarin, Spanish, Croatian, Russian, German, French, and
　　Dutch speaking staff; suburban location.

One World Montessori School, Inc (1979)
20220 Suisun Dr, Cupertino, CA 95014-4428
Pascale Marion, Office Manager, 408-255-3770

Tuition: $325-670/mo
11 teachers, 12 assistants, 203 students, mainly international,
　　ages infant–12
Affiliations: AMI, AMS
Governance by board
Emphasis on cultural subjects; multicultural student body
　　and teaching staff; childcare; suburban location; interns
　　accepted.

Monarch Montessori Christian
11700 Upland Way, Cupertino, CA 95014-5106

Quality Education Resources
(See Resource Appendix)

Natural Alternative
328 Redwood Dr, Felton, CA 95018
Susan Morin, 408-335-0765
Type: home-based
Student ages 2–6
Positive enrichment through play; home/outdoor environ-
　　ment; emphasis on natural rhythms and personality
　　development.

San Lorenzo Valley Alternative Education
6134 Highway Nine, Felton, CA 95018

South Valley Homeschoolers Association
7273 Carr Pl, Gilroy, CA 95020
Sheri Russell

Casa Di Mir Montessori Ele School
200 Prospect Ave, Los Gatos, CA 95030
Wanda Whitehead

Los Gatos–Saratoga Alternative Education
17421 Farley Road W, Los Gatos, CA 95030

Casa Maria Montessori School
PO Box 1906, Los Gatos, CA 95031-1906

Milpitas Independent Study
1500 Escuela Parkway, Milpitas, CA 95035

Home Educator's Almanac
(See Resource Appendix)

Wilson High School (1992)
1840 Benton Ave, Santa Clara, CA 95050
Dr Daniene Marciano, Vice Prin, 408-984-6442, FAX:-8250
40 students

Rainbow Montessori
1725 De La Cruz Blvd # 6, Santa Clara, CA 95050-3011

Pioneer Montessori
400 N Winchester Blvd, Santa Clara, CA 95050-6317

Bayside Children's College
609 Pacific Ave #102, Santa Cruz, CA 95060
Karen Ancic, Director, 408-454-0370

Global Youth Academy (1972)
819 1/2 Pacific Ave, Santa Cruz, CA 95060
Steve Myers, 408-423-4451, FAX: 408-423-3081
Type: independent, non-profit; tuition: $5,700/yr,
　　scholarships
6 teachers, 37 students, ages 12–18, 6–12th grade
Affiliation: CAN
Governance by principal, democratic school meeting, board
Teacher qualifications: varies by subject
Year-round; emphasis on world-citizenship, creativity, per-
　　sonal growth; extensive international travel; 3 Golden Bell
　　awards won; optional letter grades; multi-aged classes;
　　interns accepted.

Santa Cruz Waldorf School (1976)
2190 Empire Grade, Santa Cruz, CA 95060
Stephen Spitalny, Chair, 408-425-0519

Santa Cruz County
Non-profit; tuition: $4,500-4,800/yr, scholarships
180 students, ages 4.75-14, K-8th grade
Entrance requirements: teacher interview
Affiliation: ASWNA
Governance by faculty
Teacher qualifications: Waldorf training
Multi-cultural emphasis; community service; suburban/rural location; transportation; interns accepted.

The ARK School (1979)
313 Swift St, Santa Cruz, CA 95060
Leonard Cowan, Counselor; Joan Thompson, Secretary, 408-429-3434
Santa Cruz County
Type: public choice/at-risk
10 teachers, 210 students, mainly at-risk, ages 14-19, 9-12th grade
Governance by teachers and principal
Teacher qualifications: CA Certification
Community involvement; no letter grades; multi-aged classes; extensive field trips; suburban location; interns accepted.

International Association for the Study of Cooperation in Education
(See Resource Appendix)

Alternative Family Education Home Studies (1991)
300 La Fonda, Santa Cruz, CA 95062
Dr Terry Jones, 408-429-3052, FAX: 408-429-3303
5 teachers, 125 students, K-12th grade
Governance by teachers, principal, parent cooperative
Teacher qualifications: state certification
Non-compulsory class attendance; extensive field trips; urban location.

Children's Art Foundation, Stone Soup Magazine (1973)
(See Resource Appendix)

The Vineyard School
2317 Vine Hill Rd, Santa Cruz, CA 95065
JoAnn King, Director, 408-438-7320

Agape Montessori Children's Home
19732 Solana Dr, Saratoga, CA 95070

Notre Dame Montessori (1966)
15100 Norton Rd, Saratoga, CA 95070
Kathy Genereux, Adm, 408-867-1663
Non-profit; tuition: $215/mo
7 teachers, 64 students, ages 3-6
Accreditation: AMS
Governance by administrator
Rural location; interns accepted.

Pajaro Valley Unified Alternative Education
165 Blackbum St, Watsonville, CA 95076

Horace Mann Elementary
55 N Seventh St, San Jose, CA 95112
Milly Powell, 408-988-6237
Type: magnet
K-5th grade
Student-centered.

Campbell Union High Alternative Education-Blackford
3800 Blackford Ave, San Jose, CA 95117

Pioneer Plus High School (1992)
1290 Blossom Hill Rd, San Jose, CA 95118
Bob Heinrich, Counselor, 408-264-4428
Santa Clara County
Type: public at-risk
2 teachers, 40 students, ages 14-19, 9-12th grade
Entrance requirements: referral by mainstream school, low credits
Affiliation: San Jose USD

Governance by teachers and principal
Variable credit; individual studies classes available.

American Montessori School
19950 McKean Rd, San Jose, CA 95120

Castillero Middle School
6384 Leyland Park Dr, San Jose, CA 95120
E. Orta-Camilleri, 408-998-6385
Type: magnet
6-8th grade
Visual and performing arts.

Broadway High School (1982)
1088 Broadway Ave, San Jose, CA 95125
Kerm Hartley, Prin, 408-998-6215, FAX: 408-288-8039
Santa Clara County
Type: public at-risk
15 teachers, 300 students, ages 13-19, HS
Residency required
Governance by principal
Teacher qualifications: CA credential
Teen parenting; GED prep; work experience; drug/alcohol day treatment; ESL; urban location; transportation.

Willow Glen Plus (1992)
2001 Cottle Ave, San Jose, CA 95125
Fred Morales, Counselor, 408-264-4422
Santa Clara County
Type: public at-risk
2 teachers, 40 students, ages 15.5-18, 10-12th grade
Residency required
Governance by principal
Teacher qualifications: CA secondary credential
Focus on changing failure behaviors; close parent contact; multi-aged classes; field trips; counseling; suburban location; transportation; interns accepted.

Educational Options (1962)
1671 Park Negles, San José, CA 95126
Susan Truitt-Valdez, 408-998-6127, FAX: 408-998-8814
Santa Clara County
Type: public at-risk
43 teachers, 4000 students, ages 5-19, K-12th grade
Residency required
Affiliation: San José USD
Governance by principal
Teacher qualifications: certification
Business, college partnerships; independent study; no letter grades

Herbert Hoover Middle School
1635 Park Ave, San Jose, CA 95126
Patti Gregory, 408-998-6274
Type: magnet
6-8th grade
Visual and performing arts.

Lincoln High School
555 Dana Ave, San Jose, CA 95126
Oreen Gernreich, 408-998-6300
Type: magnet
9-12th grade
Visual and performing arts.

San Jose Unified School District
1605 Park Ave, San Jose, CA 95126
Norris Hill, Magnets Mgr
Type: Montessori

Trace Elementary
651 Dana Ave, San Jose, CA 95126
Rosanne Adona, 408-998-6257
Type: magnet
3-5th grade
Visual and performing arts.

Cory Elementary
2280 Kenwood Ave, San Jose, CA 95128
Mei Kamenik, 408-998-6219
Type: magnet
K–2nd grade
Visual and performing arts.

Peninsula Homeschoolers
4795 Lage Dr, San Jose, CA 95130
408-379-6835

Berryessa Union Elementary Alternative Education
1376 Piedmont Rd, San Jose, CA 95132-2498

Pegasus High School (1991)
1776 Educational Park Dr, San Jose, CA 95133
Tim McDonough, Prin, 408-729-3967, FAX: 926-6785
Santa Clara County
Type: public at-risk
6 teachers, 120 students, mainly at-risk, ages 16–20, 10–12th
    grade
Entrance requirements: interview with parent, residency
Governance by teachers and principal
Self-contained facility; 1:20 ratio; 3.5 hour day; in-class and
    independent study; earn credits toward graduation or
    transfer back to comprehensive HS; urban location; interns
    accepted.

HeadsUp! Child Development Centers
2841 Junction Ave, Suite 100, San Jose, CA 95134
Type: Montessori

Capitol High School Program (1990)
760 Hillsdale Ave, San Jose, CA 95136
Kathie Hodges, Coord, 408-723-6550, FAX: 266-6531
Santa Clara County
Type: public at-risk
3 teachers, 72 students, mainly at-risk, ages 16–19, 11–12th
    grade
Residency required.
Independent study; voc training; extensive field trips; urban
    location.

Casa Di Mir Montessori Elementary School
PO Box 4804, San Jose, CA 95150-4804
Nancy Curran

West Valley Montessori School
PO Box 611686, San Jose, CA 95161

Kohl Open Elementary
6325 N Alturas, Stockton, CA 95205
Bud West, 209-953-3020
Type: magnet
K–6th grade
Open School.

Stockton School Magnet Assistance
1144 E Channel St, Stockton, CA 95205
Joanne Miller, Dir
Type: Montessori

Hamilton Middle School
2245 E 11th St, Stockton, CA 95206
Edna Romos, 209-953-4701
Type: magnet
7–8th grade
Creative and performing arts; pre-IB.

Hazelton Elementary
535 W Jefferson St, Stockton, CA 95206
Petrina Romo, 209-953-4212
Type: magnet
4–6th grade
Gifted and talented.

James Monroe Elementary
2236 E 11th St, Stockton, CA 95206

Barbara Chan, 209-953-4271
Type: magnet
4–6th grade
Creative and performing arts.

Taft Elementary
419 Downing, Stockton, CA 95206
Margarita Ortega, 209-953-2011
Type: magnet
Student ages 3+,–6th grade
Montessori.

Creative Beginnings Montessori (1986)
6002 Plymouth Rd, Stockton, CA 95207
Sarah Wentworth, Owner/Dir, 209-474-8711
Tuition: $205/mo
1 teacher, 1 assistant, 21 students, mainly international, ages
    3–6
Entrance requirements: age 2.75; toilet trained
Affiliations: AMS, NAYEC
Governance by an administrator
Diverse, both ethnically and financially; urban location;
    interns accepted.

Independent Study Center
2010 W Swain Road, Stockton, CA 95207

Alternative Cluster (1992)
22 S Van Buren, Stockton, CA 95209
Andres Torres, Acting Prin, 209-953-4306
San Joaquin County
Type: public at-risk
25 teachers, 625 students, ages 14–18, 9–12th grade
Entrance requirements: referral, residency
Governance by teachers and principal
Multi-aged classes; urban location.

New World Montessori (1980)
2367 Waudman Ave, Stockton, CA 95209
Shirley Garey, Owner, 209-952-8854
Tuition: $115–400/mo
3 teachers, 25 students, ages infant–6
Affiliations: NCME, NAMTA; accreditation: NCME
Governance by administrator
Childcare; suburban location; interns accepted.

Adelita Migrant Child Development Center
14320 E Harney Lane, Lodi, CA 95230
Type: Montessori

Sue Brock Migrant Infant Center
333 W Mathews Rd, French Camp, CA 95231
Margarita Cervantes
Type: Montessori

Artesi II Child Development Center
777 W Mathews Rd, French Camp, CA 95231-9764
Type: Montessori

Independent Study
815 W Lockeford St, Lodi, CA 95240

Independent Study K-8 Program (1983)
420 S Pleasant Ave, Lodi, CA 95240
Pamela Loechler, Tch, 209-331-7245
San Joaquin County
Non-profit
3 teachers, 76–90 students, ages 5–14
Entrance requirements: parent/designee must be available to
    teach, approval by principal, interview, residency
Governance by board
Teacher qualifications: credential
Monthly teacher visits; field trips; newsletter; art class; weekly
    computer lab; non-compulsory class attendance; extensive
    field trips

Calaveras Unified Alterative Education- Sierra Hills
Box 178, San Andreas, CA 95249
Type: public choice

Escalon Independent Study Center
1520 E Yosemite Ave, Escalon, CA 95320

The Eagle's Nest
(See Resource Appendix)

Irwin High School (1990)
20384 Geer Ave, Hilmar, CA 95324
John C. Johnson, Teaching Principal, 209-667-0276
Hilmar USD District, Merced County
Type: public at-risk
3 teachers, 50 students, ages 15-19, 9-12th grade
No residency requirement
Governance by board
4-hour day; remedial; individualized; childcare; rural location; transportation.

Sierra Waldorf School
19234 Rawhide Rd, Jamestown, CA 95327
Karen Brock

Le Grand Union High Alternative Education
Box 67, Le Grand, CA 95333

Lindberg Educational Center (1987)
311 E North St, Manteca, CA 95336
Debbie Houck, 209-825-3100, FAX: same
Type: public choice
500 students

County Unified Alternative Education
Box 5001, Mariposa, CA 95338

Alexander Street Montessori (1982)
21 E Alexander St, Merced, CA 95340
Jan Child, Head, 209-383-1232
Non-profit; tuition: $1,980/4,180/yr
1 teacher, 2 assistants, 30 students, ages 3-6
Entrance requirements: ages 2.75-4; toilet trained
Governance by board
Large yard with flower and vegetable gardens; arbor; swimming pool; nature activities; pets; seasonal celebrations; childcare.

Independent Study
Box 2187, Merced, CA 95344

Homeschoolers For Peace
Box 74, Midpines, CA 95345
Pam & Craig Gingold, 209-742-6802

Yosemite Area Homeschoolers/ Homeschoolers for Peace
PO Box 74, Midpines, CA 95345

Elliot Alternative Education
1440 Sunrise Ave, Modesto, CA 95350

Oakdale Jt Unified High Alternative
200 Hinkley Ave, Oakdale, CA 95361

Sonora Union High Alternative
251 S Baretta St, Sonora, CA 95370

Duncan-Russell High School (1969)
164 W Grantiline Rd, Tracy, CA 95376
Cynthia Johannes, Prin, 209-831-5220
San Joaquin County
Type: public at-risk
7 teachers, 135 students, ages 16-18, 9-12th grade
Residency required
Governance by principal, board
Teacher qualifications: certification
Teachers are counselors; weekly academic, attendance reports; parent contacts; no letter grade; interns accepted.

Excel High School (1992)
315 E 11th St, Tracy, CA 95376
Barbara Shreve, lead teacher, 209-831-5135, FAX: 209-836-3347

San Joaquin County
Type: public at-risk
2 teachers, 40 students, ages 14-18, 9-12th grade
Enrollment restricted to non-special ed functioning at 6th grade level or higher
Affiliation: Tracy High School
Governance by teachers and principal
Abbreviated school day; self-paced; hands-on learning; urban location.

Montessori Services
(See Resource Appendix)

Santa Rosa High Alternative Education
325 Ridgway Ave, Santa Rosa, CA 95401

Summerfield Waldorf School (1974)
155 Willowside Rd, Santa Rosa, CA 95401
Leslie Sheldon, Office Mgr, 707-575-7194
Sonoma County
Non-profit; tuition: $3,800-5,230/yr, scholarships
31 teachers, 365 students, ages 5-18, K-12th grade
Entrance requirements: interview and application
Affiliation: AWSNA
Governance by teachers
Teacher qualifications: 2-yr Waldorf training
32 acres; working organic farm; wildlife preserve; farming, gardening integrated into curriculum; extensive field trips; rural location; interns accepted.

College Oak Montessori School
1925 W College Ave, Santa Rosa, CA 95401-4440

Consensus Classroom, Inc (1991)
7899 St Helena Rd, Santa Rosa, CA 95404
Linda Sartor, Facilitator/Consultant, 707-538-5123
Sonoma County
Non-profit
Publicizes, instructs in consensus decision making model.

Montessori Elementary School
1569 Brush Creek Rd, Santa Rosa, CA 95404-2099
Peggy Colgan

Montessori Visions
1625 Franklin Ave, Santa Rosa, CA 95404-2506

Paxundr Corp
1270 Franquette, Santa Rosa, CA 95405
Gayle Cavender
Type: Montessori

Rancheria High School (1978)
Box 457, Boonville, CA 95415
Val Muchowski, 707-895-3543, FAX: 707-895-2665
Mendocino County
Type: public at-risk
2 teachers, 16 students, ages 14-34, 9-12th grade
Governance by principal
Teacher qualifications: certification
Individualized; multi-aged classes; rural location.

Waldorf School of Mendocino County (1972)
6280 3rd St, Box 349, Calpella, CA 95418
Star Gilley, Office Mgr, 707-485-8719
Non-profit
135 students, K-8th grade
Governance by teachers and Board of Directors
Hebrew; woodworking; gardening; band; chorus; eurythmy; no letter grades; extensive field trips; rural location.

R.H. Lewis Independent Study
Box 6630, Clearlake, CA 95422
Type: public choice

Richard H. Lewis School (1982)
PO Box 6630; S Center Dr, Clearlake, CA 95422
Mary Ann Penson, Dir, 707-994-2045

Lake County
Type: public choice
5 teachers, 80 students, mainly at-risk, ages 5–18, K–12th
    grade
Enrollment restricted to grade-level proficient students; no
    residency requirement
Governance by director
Teacher qualifications: CA Credentials
Students attend weekly, work at home; rural location.

Osprey Learning Center Independent Study
Box 129, Garberville, CA 95440
Type: public choice

**Mountain View High School/ Center for Independent
Study**
1024 Prince St, Healdsburg, CA 95448
Elizabeth Burmudez, 707-431-3449
Type: public choice

Laytonville High School (1992)
PO Box 868, Laytonville, CA 95454
Mark Iacuaniello
Type: public choice
18 students

Leggett Valley Unified Alternative Education
Box 186, Leggett, CA 95455

Acorn School
PO Box 387, Point Arena, CA 95468
Ellen Lockwood, 707-882-2274
Type: public choice

Nonesuch School
4004 Bones Rd, Sebastopol, CA 95472
Type: independent

Montessori Children's House
500 N Main St, Sebastopol, CA 95472-3407

Pleasant Hill Montessori School
789 Pleasant Hill Rd, Sebastopol, CA 95472-4027

Family English Literacy Program (1991)
3273 Airway Dr, Santa Rosa, CA 95473
4 teachers, 2 assistants, 85–120 students, mainly at-risk
Families only
Governance by director
Teacher qualifications: experience in adult ESL or in working
    with children, multi-cultural sensitivity
Adult ESL at 2 sites: Woodland for Mexicans, W. Sacramento
    for Russians; intergenerational activities; Social Service
    referrals; interns accepted.

Hearthsong
(See Resource Appendix)

Mandala Montessori School
960 Lark Ave, Sonoma, CA 95476

NCME
4043 Pepperwood Ct, Sonoma, CA 95476
Karen Lecy
Type: Montessori

Sonoma Valley Waldorf School (1987)
PO Box 2063, Sonoma, CA 95476
Tiare Newport Wicklund, 707-996-0996
Non-profit; tuition: $4,080-5,220/yr, scholarships
3 teachers, 45 students, ages 3–8, pre K–2nd grade
Governance by teachers, board, and administrator
Teacher qualifications: Waldorf Institute training
Multi-aged classes; urban location.

Vintage Country Day School (1985)
PO Box 1514, Sonoma, CA 95476
Penny B. Aguer, Prin, 996-6560

Type: Montessori, non-profit; tuition: $230-355/mo
3 teachers, 3 assistants, 48 students, ages 3–12
Affiliation: AMS
Governance by administrator, board
Suburban location; interns accepted.

Montessori School of Sonoma
PO Box 760, Sonoma, CA 95476-0760

Young School
180 East Napa St, Sonoma, CA 95476-6710
Anthony Bell
Type: Montessori

Mariposa School (1969)
Box 387, Ukiah, CA 95482
Hannah Wild, 707-462-1016
Type: independent; tuition: $2000-3400, sliding scale
45 students, ages K–5
Hands-on approach, teaches students to experience nature
    in their everyday lives; conflict resolution part of curricu-
    lum; active parent involvement; rural location.

New School of Ukiah
433 N State St, Box 296, Ukiah, CA 95482
King Collins, 707-468-5537
6–12th grade

Ukiah Unified Alternative Education
1056 N Bush St, Ukiah, CA 95482
Type: public choice

Whale Gulch Elementary Independent Study
76811 Usal Rd, Whitethorn, CA 95489

Independent Study
249 N Main, Willits, CA 95490
Type: public choice

New Horizons/ Community as Classroom
371 E Commercial St, Willits, CA 95490
Thayer Craig, 707-459-6521
Type: public choice
Also houses City-as-School program.

Mistwood Montessori (1980)
1801 10th St, Eureka, CA 95501
Patti Frink, Owner, 444-8100
Tuition: $175/285/mo
3 teachers, 3 assistants, 75 students, ages 3–6
Entrance requirements: toilet trained
Governance by administrator
Music; Spanish immersion; childcare; suburban location.

Equinox School
470 Union St, Arcata, CA 95521
707-822-4845

Gateway Community School (1982)
1464 Spear Ave, Arcata, CA 95521
Duke Cairns, Teacher, 707-822-4721
Type: independent; tuition: $2000/yr
4 teachers, 29 students, ages 5–11, K–5th grade
Entrance requirements: visit, interview, application.
Governance by parent cooperative, democratic school
    meeting, board
Focuses on self-esteem, empowerment with responsibility,
    cooperation, community involvement, and environmental
    awareness; no letter grades; multi-aged classes; extensive
    field trips; interns accepted.

Mad River Montessori (1980)
PO Box 4334, Arcata, CA 95521
Robin Renshaw, 707-822-4027
Non-profit; tuition: $150/250/mo
1 teacher, 2 assistants, 36 students, ages 3–6
Governance by board
Rural location; interns accepted.

Michael Olaf Company
(See Resource Appendix)

Northern Humboldt Adult School (1971)
2755 McKinleyville Ave, McKinleyville, CA 95521
Kenny Richards, Prin; Jackie Hammer, Coord, 707-839-1613
Humboldt County
Type: public choice
5 teachers, 600 students
Entrance requirements: min age 18, orientation; no residency requirement
Affiliation: N Humboldt Union HS District
Governance by principal
Teacher qualifications: CA credential, CBEST
3 locations; GED prep; enrichment classes; independent study; multi-aged classes

Petrolia High School (1983)
Box 197, Petrolia, CA 95558
Seth Zuckerman, Director, 707-629-3509
Humboldt County
Type: independent, boarding, non-profit
10 teachers, 24 students, ages 14-18, 9-12th grade
Governance by teachers and principal, democratic school meeting, board
Year starts with 2 week backpacking; 6 week intercultural trip with home stay, often in Mexico; involvement in local environmental restoration efforts; individually designed project month; extensive field trips; rural location.

Humboldt Homeschoolers
688 S Whaven Dr, Trinidad, CA 95570
Paige Smith, 707-677-3290
Humboldt County
Inclusive; loosely organized; newsletter; rural location.

Placer Union High Alternative Education
322 Finley St, Auburn, CA 95603

Quest Independent Learning Center (1986)
332 Finley St, Auburn, CA 95603
Robert Klein, Counselor, 916-885-2401, FAX: 916-885-9371
Placer County
Type: public choice
10 teachers, 206 students, ages 14-19, 9-12th grade
Entrance requirements: application, ability to be self-directed, no residency requirement
Affiliation: WASC
Governance by teachers; Principal
Teacher qualifications: CA credential
Community-based; Trees for Mother Earth project on Navajo Reservation; interns accepted.

Village Faire for Educators
10594 Combie Rd #106515, Auburn, CA 95603
Lorna Wood
Type: Montessori

Village Montessori Schools
5033 Fair Oaks Blvd, Carmichael, CA 95608-6039
Karen Arnold

Valley Oak Montessori Children's House
7545 Tad Lane, Citrus Heights, CA 95610

Countryside Montessori
7416 Northlea Way, Citrus Heights, CA 95610-6525

Isabel S. Naranjo Migrant Child Development Center
180 Sequoia Ave, Courtland, CA 95615
Type: Montessori

Davis Montessori School (1989)
2907 Portage Bay W, Davis, CA 95616
Karen Fejta, Owner, 916-753-2030, FAX: 916-756-1210
Tuition: $3,250/3,500/yr
5 teachers, 2 assistants, 80 students, ages 3-12

Affiliation: AMS
Governance by an administrator
Spanish and computer enrichment for ages 4+; music weekly; parent participation welcome; childcare; suburban location; interns accepted.

Davis Waldorf School (1986)
3100 Sycamore Ln, Davis, CA 95616
Kathy Zablan, Adm, 916-753-1651
Non-profit; tuition: $4,675/yr, scholarships
10 teachers, 95 students, ages 4.75-13, K-7th grade
Entrance requirements: interview and application; may not be able to meet special needs
Affiliation: AWSNA
Teacher qualifications: completion of R. Steiner's teacher training courses
Rigorous academics; language arts; history; Spanish; German; handwork; woodwork; music; gardening in biodynamic farm; rural location.

Independent Study Program (1990)
526 B St, Davis, CA 95616
Katie Goetzinger, Prin, 916-757-5333
Type: public choice
6 teachers, 120 students, mainly at-risk, ages 5-18, K-12th grade
Governance by teachers, principal, board
Teacher qualifications: CA certification
Includes home schooling program.

LaRue Park Children's House
50 Atrium Way, Davis, CA 95616
Karen Fejta
Type: Montessori

Montessori Country Day
1811 Renoir Ave, Davis, CA 95616-0508

PLENTY (1974)
PO Box 2306, Davis, CA 95617
Charles Haren, Program Dir, 916-753-0731, FAX: 916-762-0731
Type: higher education, non-profit
Student ages 20+
Affiliation: York University
Governance by board of directors and staff
Teacher qualifications: Successful community development facilitators
Community education, development; overriding concern for indigenous people, environment; students participate in disaster relief, alternative energy, micro-economic development, reforestation, health care, agriculture; no letter grades; interns accepted.

Redbud Montessori
PO Box 1562, Davis, CA 95617-1562

Independent Learning Centers
Box 426, Diamond Springs, CA 95619

Elk Grove Montessori School
8842 Williamson Dr, Elk Grove, CA 95624
Norman Lorenz

Little London Montessori
9132 Elk Grove Blvd, Elk Grove, CA 95624

Transitions at Elk Grove High School (1992)
9800 Elk Grove-Florin Rd, Elk Grove, CA 95624
Patty Jungkeit, Tch-In-Charge, 916-686-7741
Sacramento County
Type: public at-risk
4 teachers, 60 students, ages 14-16, 9-10th grade
Entrance requirements: recommendations
Governance by teachers, principal, board
Teacher qualifications: CA credential
Weekly teacher conference; bi-weekly parent contact; counseling support groups; community service project; interns accepted.

Esparto Child Development Center
705 Omega St, Esparto, CA 95627
Type: Montessori

Esparto Homeschoolers
PO Box 305, Esparto, CA 95627
916-787-3613

Madison High (1980)
Box 69, Esparto, CA 95627
Barbara Evans, Prin, 916-787-3907
Yolo County
Type: public choice
3 teachers, 35–40 students, ages 15–19, 9–12th grade
Governance by teachers, principal

Rudolf Steiner College
9200 Fair Oaks Blvd, Fair Oaks, CA 95628
Gayle Davis
Type: Waldorf

Sacramento Valley School
9341 Fair Oaks Blvd; PO Box 1123, Fair Oaks, CA 95628
Kaye Lynn Peterson, Admissions Clerk, 916-962-3681
Sacramento County
Type: independent, non-profit; tuition: $2,700/yr
3 teachers, 14 students, ages 5–19, K–12th grade
Entrance requirements: family interview
Governance by democratic school meeting
Teacher qualifications: first volunteer, then be elected by
   school meeting
Based on Sudbury Valley School model; self-directed, free
   interaction in safe community environment; exchanges;
   apprenticeships; non-compulsory class attendance; multi-
   aged classes; extensive field trips; no letter grades; suburban location.

Sacramento Waldorf School
3750 Bannister Rd, Fair Oaks, CA 95628
Patrick McMahon

Association of Waldorf Schools
(See Resource Appendix)

Village Montessori Schools
4305 Bannister Rd, Fair Oaks, CA 95628-6918

Folsom Montessori School
502 Riley St, Folsom, CA 95630-3029
Lise Witthaus

Steward Ship
(See Resource Appendix)

Mountain Home Alternative
Box 395, Oakhurst, CA 95644

Lincoln High North (1991)
1081 7th St, Lincoln, CA 95648
Dale Pence, Prin, 916-645-6360
Placer County
Type: public at-risk
2 teachers, 25 students, ages 16–18, 10–12th grade
Min age 16
Governance by board
Teacher qualifications: CA credential
School within school; rural location.

Phoenix High School (1978)
870 J St, Lincoln, CA 95648
Bob Noyes, Prin, 916-645-6395, FAX: 916-645-6356
Placer County
Type: public at-risk; scholarships
3 teachers, 60 students, ages 16–18, 10–12th grade
Residency required
Governance by principal
Teacher qualifications: credential
Competency-based; variable credit; extensive field trips;
   multi-aged classes; interns accepted.

Sunrise Montessori School
8449 Sunrise Blvd, Roseville, CA 95661-5349

San Juan Unified Alternative Education
5843 Almond Ave, Orangevale, CA 95662

Cedar Springs Waldorf School (1989)
6029 Gold Meadows Rd, Placerville, CA 95667
Lauren Cushman, Administrator, 916-642-9903
El Dorado County
Non-profit; tuition: $3,100-3,600/yr, scholarships
19 teachers, 80 students, ages 4–11, K–4th grade
Entrance requirement: acceptance by entire faculty
Affiliation: AWSNA
Governance by faculty and board consensus
Teacher qualifications: BA/BS+ 2 yrs Waldorf training
Working toward becoming a working farm school; hands-on,
   minds-on approach; Spanish; Japanese; multi-aged classes;
   rural location; interns accepted.

Montessori of Placerville (1974)
100 Placerville Dr/PO Box 87, Placerville, CA 95667
Nancy A. Weddle, Owner/Dir, 916-626-5330
Tuition: $170–225/mo
3 teachers, 1 assistant, 40 students, ages 3–6
Entrance requirements: toilet trained; understands verbal
   communications
Affiliations: CH ADD, NAEYC
Governance by administrator
Peace education; movement area; rural location; interns
   accepted.

Bluestocking Press
(See Resource Appendix)

Folsom Cordova Unified Alternative Education
10850 Gadsten Way, Rancho Cordova, CA 95670

Independence High
600 Tahoe Ave, Roseville, CA 95678

American Montessori Academy
1050 Douglas Blvd, Roseville, CA 95678-2714

Cameron Park Montessori School (1974)
4645 Buckeye Rd, Shingle Springs, CA 95682
Deanna Gardner, Owner/Dir, 916-677-1776
Tuition: $175/250/mo
5 teachers, 6 assistants, 102 students, ages 3–9
Entrance requirements: age 2.75; toilet trained
Affiliations: NCME, NBA
Governance by administrator
Teacher qualifications: Montessori training
Montessori materials; childcare; rural location; interns
   accepted.

ACE at Markham (1991)
101 Markham Ave, Vacaville, CA 95688
Ricki Gaudie, 707-453-6230
Solano County
Type: public choice
4 teachers, 120 students, ages 5–12, K–6th grade
Residency required
Governance by parent cooperative
Parent participation required; lifelong research skills; cooper-
   ative learning; no letter grades; multi-aged classes; subur-
   ban location; interns accepted.

Country High School
343 Brown St, Vacaville, CA 95688
Muzetta M. Thrower, Prin, 707-453-6215
Solano County
Type: public at-risk
9 teachers, 185 students, mainly at-risk, ages 15–19, 9–12th
   grade
Residency required
Governance by democratic school meeting
Teacher qualifications: state credential

Teen mothers program with nursery; catering through Foods/Economics classes; computer lab; multi-media art classes; multi-aged classes; urban location; interns accepted.

Montessori Children's School
201 Beard St, Vacaville, CA 95688
Debbie Challburg

Vacaville Unified Alternative Education
751 School St, Vacaville, CA 95688

West Sacramento School for Independent Study
1712 Evergreen St, W Sacramento, CA 95691

Wheatland Alternative Education
Box 398, Wheatland, CA 95692

SPICE Homeschool Support Group
PO Box 282, Wilton, CA 95693
Bonnie Sellstrom or Loni Rossbach, 916-687-7053
Gatherings; no formal rules or elected leaders.

Winters Child Development Center
100 Myrtle Ave, Winters, CA 95694
Type: Montessori

Independent Learning Center (1988)
1016 1st St, Woodland, CA 95695
Sandi Redenbach, Coord, 916-666-0264, FAX: 916-756-5537
Yolo County
Type: public at-risk; scholarships
2 teachers, 50 students, ages 14-18, 9-12th grade
Entrance requirements: no SE students, adequate reading skills, residency
Affiliation: Woodland Joint Unified
Governance by coordinator/teacher
Self-esteem building; responsibility training; community service; career counseling; student contracts; law-related education; independent study; interns accepted.

Yolo Parent Child Center
1285 Lemen Ave, Woodland, CA 95695-3311
Type: Montessori

Woodland Montessori Children's House
1738 Cottonwood St, Woodland, CA 95695-5137
Pamela Barrow-Lynn

Contract Independent Study
Box 14429, S Lake Tahoe, CA 95702
Type: public choice

Live Oak Waldorf School
410 Crother Rd; PO Box 57, Applegate, CA 95703
Ellyn Hilliard, Coord, 916-878-8720
Placer County
Non-profit; tuition: $3,800/yr, scholarships
12 teachers, 190 students, ages 4-13, K-8th grade
Entrance requirements: interview with class teacher
Affiliation: AWSNA
Governance by board, faculty and student representatives
Teacher qualifications: prefer Waldorf training
1st Waldorf in US with pledge contribution funding; no one denied due to financial limitations; rural location; interns accepted.

Pondorado Alternative Education
Box 556, Camino, CA 95709

Auburn Discovery Montessori School
PO Box 5019, Auburn, CA 95713
Mariann Lokvig, Owner, 916-823-9577
Tuition: $238/364/mo
7 teachers, 4 assistants; student ages 3-12
Entrance requirements: toilet trained
Affiliation: NCME
Governance by administrator
Childcare; interns accepted.

Little London Montessori School
9124 Bruceville Rd, Elk Grove, CA 95757
Savi Godamunne

Educational Futures Project (1976)
(See Resource Appendix)

Mankato Wilson Campus School Remembered: Video (1968)
(See Resource Appendix)

Visual and Performing Arts Centre (1984)
2315 34th St, Sacramento, CA 95817
Connie Mockenhaupt, Coord, 916-454-6238, FAX:-6270
Type: public choice
14 teachers, 500 students, ages 14-18, 9-12th grade
Governance by principal, coordinator assists
Teacher qualifications: Specialized training, experience
Extensive field trips; interns accepted.

C.K. McClatchy High School
3066 Freeport Blvd, Sacramento, CA 95818
William Dionisio, 916-553-4400
Type: magnet
9-12th grade
Humanities.

Discovery Montessori School (1973)
5613 G St, Sacramento, CA 95819
Shirley Skadar-Smith, MEd, Exec Dir, 916-739-1462
Non-profit; tuition: $230-420/mo
2 teachers, 4 assistants, 32 students, mainly international, ages 3-6
Entrance requirements: toilet trained; parents commit to work 12 hrs/yr
Affiliations: AMS, NCME, NAEYC; accreditation: PACE
Governance by an administrator and a board of trustees
Spanish and culture part of curriculum; childcare; urban location; interns accepted.

Camellia Waldorf School (1989)
5701 Freeport Blvd, Sacramento, CA 95822
Meredith Johnson, Business Mgr, 916-427-5022
Sacramento County
Non-profit; tuition: $3,200-4,700/yr, scholarships
5 teachers, 42 students, ages 4-9, K-3rd grade
Affiliation: AWSNA
Governance by faculty and board
Urban location; interns accepted.

Edward Kemble Elementary
7495 29th St, Sacramento, CA 95822
Rovida Mott, 916-399-5025
Type: magnet
K-6th grade
GATE: gifted and talented education.

South Land Park Montessori School, Inc (1973)
6400 Freeport Blvd, Sacramento, CA 95822-5904
Steve Hempel, Office Mgr, 916-391-5380, FAX: 916-391-2678
Tuition: $2,400-3,950/yr
9 teachers, 9 assistants, 160 students, ages 3-15
Affiliation: AMS
Governance by an administrator
Childcare; suburban location; interns accepted.

Home School Association of California (1987)
PO Box 231236, Sacramento, CA 95823
Mary Griffith, Editor, CA Homeschooler, 707-765-5375
Type: state home-based, non-profit
Newsletter.

Las Flores High School (1987)
5900 Bamford Dr, Sacramento, CA 95823
Barbara Hyatt, 916-422-5604
Type: public choice
10 students

Rio Cazadero High School
7825 Grandstaff Dr, Sacramento, CA 95823
Ron Rule, Prin, 916-422-3058
Sacramento County
Type: public at-risk
10 teachers, 252 students, ages 14–19, 9–12th grade
Governance by teachers and principal
Teacher qualifications: CA certification
Classes (3 hrs/day) change quarterly; collegiate schedule; suburban location; interns accepted.

William Daylor
6131 Orange Ave, Sacramento, CA 95823
James Ross, Prin, 916-427-5428
Sacramento County
Type: public at-risk
Residency required
Governance by teachers, principal
Interns accepted.

Jonas Salk Alternative Middle School
2950 Hurley Way, Sacramento, CA 95825

Sunny Knoll Learning Center
10239 Sunol Way, Sacramento, CA 95827

Calvine High School (1991)
8833 Vintage Park Dr, Sacramento, CA 95828
Dale Dodson, Prin, 916-686-7760, FAX: 916-689-7546
Sacramento County
Type: public at-risk
10 teachers, 266 students, ages 14–20, 9–12th grade
Entrance requirements: under 16, referral by Office of Child Welfare, school, residency
Governance by democratic school meeting
Teacher qualifications: secondary credential
Focus on student success, overcoming learning problems, family difficulties, truancy; collegiate and block scheduling.

Insights (1992)
7956 Cottonwood Ln, Sacramento, CA 95828
Priscilla Marsh, 916-689-8600
Sacramento County
Type: public at-risk
5 teachers, 60 students, ages 14–16, 9–10th grade
Governance by teachers and principal
No F's given if no credit earned; urban location.

Montessori Country Day at Riverlake (1991)
7575 Rush River Dr, Sacramento, CA 95831
Pam Barrow-Lynn, Owner/Adm, 916-427-1900
Tuition: $31/day-335/mo
4 teachers, 20 assistants, 110 students, mainly international, ages infant–6
Accreditation: AMS
Governance by administrator
Modern classrooms and materials; childcare; interns accepted.

John Still Creative Center
2250 John Still Dr, Sacramento, CA 95832
Rachel Wallin, 916-399-5375
Type: magnet
K–8th grade

Countryside Montessori School
5590 Madison Ave, Sacramento, CA 95841-3114

Marysville Jt Unified Alternative
1919 B St, Marysville, CA 95901

Mariposa Waldorf School (1980)
12833 Colfax Hwy; PO Box 1210, Cedar Ridge, CA 95924
Patricia Montijo, Adm, 916-272-8411
Nevada County
Non-profit; tuition: $2,895-3,095/yr, scholarships
14 teachers, 105 students, ages 4–11, K–5th grade

Entrance requirements: teacher interview
Affiliation: AWSNA
Governance by faculty and board
2-5 week alternating subject blocks; school festivals; rural location.

Whiz Kidz (1992)
277 East Ave, Chico, CA 95926
Norman Rose, PhD, 916-898-8446
Type: home-based; cost: $55/mo
2 teachers, 55 students, ages 4–14
CAI; games; art; music; publishing

Montessori Children's Center
3105 Esplanade, Chico, CA 95926-0202
Paula Kenyon

Chico Montessori Children's House
814 Glenn St, Chico, CA 95928-4001

Colusa Unified Alternative Education
817 Colus Ave, Colusa, CA 95932
Type: public choice

Sierra-Plumas Jt Unified Alternative Education
PO Drawer E, Downieville, CA 95936

Grass Valley Charter School (1990)
10840 Gilmore Way, Grass Valley, CA 95945
Susan Byerrum, Coord, 916-273-8723
Nevada County
Type: public choice
5 teachers, 110 students, ages 5–13, K–8th grade
Entrance requirements: contract, residency
Governance by teachers, principal
Teacher qualifications: CA credential
Home school support; textbooks; supplies; enrichment classes; field trips; parent education workshops; no letter grades; non-compulsory class attendance; multi-aged classes; extensive field trips.

Sierra Mountain High (1980)
140 Park Ave, Grass Valley, CA 95945-7202
Earle Conway, Principal, 916-272-2635
Nevada County
Type: public choice, at-risk
12 teachers, 220 students, mainly at-risk, ages 14–18, 9–12th grade
No residency requirement
Governance by principal, staff, with input by students
Teacher qualifications: CA credential
Alternative calendar; has 9th and 10th grade in daytime, independent study school for adolescents and adults in evening; emphasis on four A's: acceptance, appreciation, affection, and attention; multi-aged classes, extensive field trips; rural location; interns accepted.

Ready Springs Union Elementary Alternative Education
10862 Spenceville Rd, Penn Valley, CA 95946

Indian Valley High School (1980)
Box 743, Greenville, CA 95947
Loana Gakle, Prin, 916-284-6099
Type: public at-risk
1 teacher, 15 students, ages 15–19, 10–12th grade
Residency required
For unit deficient students; rural location

Sierra Mountain High School (1988)
12338 McCourtney Rd, Grass Valley, CA 95949
Russ Jones, 916-273-4431
Type: public choice
100 students

Live Oak Alternative Education Center (1988)
2207 Pennington Rd, Live Oak, CA 95953
Joy Allingham, Prin, 707-695-1835
Sutter County

Non-profit
4 teachers, 136 students, ages 5+, K–12th grade
Governance by board
Opportunity education; Valley Oak Continuation HS; independent study; adult education; Even Start Family Literacy; gifted-talented education

Ananda School
14616 Tyler Foote Rd, Nevada City, CA 95959
Bruce Malinor or Susan Dermand, 916-292-3775
Type: independent; tuition: $195/mo.
60 students, ages 14+
Affiliations: Foundation for Life, Sharing Nature Assn
Education for Life Workshops; teaching math; children's literature.

Global Friends School Program
13075 Woolman Lane, Nevada City, CA 95959
Eric Joy, 916-477-1277
Type: Quaker, non-profit; tuition: flexible
Student ages 14–19, 9–12th grade
Entrance requirements: personal interview
Affiliation: Friends Council on Education
Governance by friends meeting
Academics within context of real life issues, experiences; learning with heart and hands as well as head; travel, service within diverse cultural settings; multi-aged classes; extensive field trips; rural location; interns accepted.

John Woolman School (1963)
13075 Woolman Ln, Nevada City, CA 95959
916-273-3183, FAX: 916-273-9028
Type: Quaker, boarding; tuition: $14,900/yr, scholarships
35 students, ages 14–17, 9–12th grade
Affiliation: NAIS
Governance by teachers, principal, board
Teacher qualifications: credentials, experience
Emphasizes truthfulness, simplicity, non-violence, respect, listening to the Spirit Within; nurtures inquiry, creativity, physical work, service; multi-aged classes; rural location.

Nevada City Elementary Alternative Education
700 Hoover Lane, Nevada City, CA 95959

Magic Meadow School
PO Box 29, N San Juan, CA 95960
Type: home-based

Pathfinder (1984)
PO Box 445, N San Juan, CA 95960
Keith Alpaugh, Dir, 916-292-3623, FAX: 916-292-3558
Nevada County
Type: independent, non-profit; tuition: $280/mo, scholarships
2 teachers, 12 students, ages 8–12
Entrance requirements: family's understanding of philosophy
Governance by board
Teacher qualifications: working knowledge of Natural Rhythms developmental theory
Student-directed; family involvement; wholistic; environmental; no letter grades; multi-aged classes; non-compulsory class attendance; extensive field trips; rural location; interns accepted.

Twin Ridges Elementary Alternative Education
Box 529, N San Juan, CA 95960
Chris Dach, 916-265-9051
Type: public choice home-based

Lewis Carroll Montessori
9391 Rices Texas Hill Rd, Oregon House, CA 95962
Janet Carter

Prospect Alternative Center for Education (1968)
2060 2nd St, Oroville, CA 95965
Dorence Young, Tch, 916-538-2330
Butte County

Type: public at-risk
10 teachers, 240 students, mainly at-risk, ages 14–18, 9–12th grade
Entrance requirements: referrals; no residency requirement
Governance by teachers, principal, board
Teacher qualifications: credential
Continuation; independent study; teen parenting; opportunity school; work-study; no letter grades; multi-aged classes; childcare; interns accepted.

Great Explorations (1993)
2085 E Main St, Quincy, CA 95971
Gloria Potvin, 916-283-1553
Type: independent; tuition: $100/mo, scholarships
1 teacher, 12–25 students, ages 5+, K+
Governance by parent cooperative
Teacher qualifications: MA, language literacy, 12 years experience
Based on GATE principals: holistic, experiential; educational enrichment program; no letter grades; multi-aged classes; rural location; interns accepted.

Plumas Alternative Education
Box 10330, Quincy, CA 95971

Albert Powell Continuation High School
1875 Clark Ave, Yuba City, CA 95991
Mike Hogan, Counselor, 916-741-5210
Yuba City USD District, Sutter County
Type: public at-risk
10 teachers, 240 students, mainly at-risk, ages 16–19, 10–12th grade
District residency required
Governance by teachers and principal
Individualized; multi-aged classes.

Churn Creek High School (1993)
3411 Churn Creek Rd, Redding, CA 96002
Allen Eggleston, Prin, 223-5177
Shasta County
Type: public at-risk
3 teachers, 70 students, ages 16–19, 10–12th grade
Enrollment restrictions: no provisions for special needs students, residency required
Governance by principal
Teacher qualifications: CA credential
Operates afternoons and evenings.

Shady Oaks Montessori School
1410 Victor Ave, Redding, CA 96003-4819

Anderson Union High Alternative Education
20083 Olinda Rd, Anderson, CA 96007

Mountain View High School (1984)
37579 Mountain View Rd, Burney, CA 96013
Max A. Best, Prin/Dir, 335-3852
Shasta County
Type: public at-risk
4 teachers, 75 students, ages 6–18, K–12th grade
Entrance by student request or assignment; residency required
Governance by principal, board
Multi-aged classes

Fall River Jt Unified Alternative Education
Box 89, Callel, CA 96016

Gateway Unified Alternative Education
Box 818, Central Valley, CA 96019

Mt Lakes High School (1992)
PO Box 818, Shasta Lake, CA 96019
Dr Mario Johnson, Prin, 916-275-7000, FAX: -7006
Shasta County
Type: public at-risk

9 teachers, 150 students, ages 16–18+, 10–12th grade
Residency required
Governance by principal, board
Teacher qualifications: Multiple or single subject CA credential
Pregnant minor/teen parenting program; rural location; transportation.

Sandhill Crane School (1989)
PO Box 160, Fall River, CA 96028
916-336-6582
Shasta County
Type: independent, boarding; tuition: $5,000/yr
2 teachers, 3 students, ages 9–15
Entrance requirements: independent-thinking, athletic, health-conscious
Affiliations: Kempo International, Ch'uan Tao Assn
Governance by benevolent director
Teacher qualifications: outstanding athlete, min 7 yrs training in Chinese martial arts
Does not advocate material gain, ego enhancement; vehicle is mind-body training of Chinese martial arts; no letter grades; multi-aged classes; extensive field trips; rural location; interns accepted.

Jefferson High School (1992)
720 Rockfellow Dr, Mt Shasta, CA 96067
Richard C Holmes, Prin, 916-926-0425
Siskiyou County
Type: public at-risk
3 teachers, 50 students, mainly at-risk, ages 15–18, 9–12th grade
Entrance by referral; min age 15; no residency requirement
Governance by principal.
Individualized; self-paced; interns accepted.

Kids Art
(See Resource Appendix)

Even Start
1135 Lincoln St, Red Bluff, CA 96080
Phil Hopkins, Dir, 916-527-5811
Corning District, Tehama County
Non-profit
9 teachers, 140 students

Enrollment restricted to parents with children age 7 and younger
Affiliation: Head Start
Governance by teachers and director
Teacher qualifications: C Best Test
GED prep; ESL; no letter grades; childcare; rural location; transportation.

Salisbury Continuation High School (1970)
1415 Burkcley St, Rcd Bluff, CA 96080
Dick Garcia, Prin, 916-529-8766, FAX: 916-529-8840
Tehama County
Type: public at-risk
4 teachers, 80 students, ages 16–18, 10–12th grade
Governance by teachers, principal, board
No letter grades; rural location; transportation; interns accepted.

Yreka Union High Alternative Education
431 Knapp St, Yreka, CA 96097

Alta Montessori
PO Box 2527, Kings Beach, CA 96143-2527

Tahoe Montessori House
848 Glorene Ave, South Lake Tahoe, CA 96158
Susan Ward

Santan High School (1971)
1006 Otterbein St, Rowland Heights, CA 96748
Lucario de Sylva, Prin, 818-965-5971
Los Angeles County
Type: independent choice/at-risk
14 teachers, 300 students, ages 15–18, 9–12th grade
Residency required
Affiliation: WASC
Governance by principal
Teacher qualifications: CA credential, dedication to students and profession
Competency-based; continuous progress; individualized; interactive technology based on staff-designed instruction; counseling/guidance; advanced courses; dropout recovery; pregnant teens program; transportation; suburban location; interns accepted.

Colorado

Allendale Elementary
5900 Oak St, Arvada, CO 80004
Nancy Sommers, Prin, 303-421-5157
Jefferson County

Jefferson County Adolescent Pregnancy and Parenting Program (JCAPPP) (1972)
6214 Johnson Way, Arvada, CO 80004
Tita Jergensen, Coord/Tch, 303-422-8520
Type: public choice
3 teachers, 150 students, ages 13–20, 8–12th grade
County residency required
Governance by teachers and principal
Teacher qualifications: certification
Interdisciplinary classes; independent study; multi-aged classes; childcare; interns accepted.

Arvada New Child Montessori School
6454 Simms St, Arvada, CO 80004-2650

Catholic Home Educators
556 Oakland Ct, Aurora, CO 80010
Laura Franceschi, 303-367-9317
Denver County

Teen Mothers Program
1585 Kingston, Aurora, CO 80010
Vera Scrivens, 303-341-1557
Aurora District 28J

Carousel Academy for Children
1440 Elmira St, Aurora, CO 80010-3217
Type: Montessori

Aurora Evening High School
1085 Peoria, Aurora, CO 80011
Kathleen Kirkpatrick, 303-344-8060 x253

East Academy
1275 Frazier St, Aurora, CO 80011
Linda Fenstermacher, 303-340-0630
Aurora 28J-East MS District

Homeschoolers of Central Aurora
3049 Wheeling St, Aurora, CO 80011
Michele Fox, 303-360-6653
Denver County

Independent Network of Creative Homeschoolers
c/o Woodhouse, 724 Victor St, Aurora, CO 80011
303-340-3185, 751-6421

I-Team Manor-OHS
1820 S Joliet, Aurora, CO 80012
Jim Wagle, 303-750-0203
Cherry Creek District

Independent Network of Creative Homeschoolers
1499 S Lima St, Aurora, CO 80012
303-751-6421

Overland High School Teen Parent Program
12400 E Jewell Ave, Aurora, CO 80012
Barb Pagano, 303-696-3700
Cherry Creek District

Over the Rainbow Child Care
16750 E Iliff Ave, Aurora, CO 80013-1135
Type: Montessori

"I" Team Estate (1968)
4360 S Pitkin, Aurora, CO 80015
John McCluskey, Teacher/Coordinator, 303-690-2594
Arapahoe County
Type: public at-risk
4 teachers, 65 students, ages 16–21, 11–12th grade
Enrollment restricted to SE students; no residency
    requirement
Affiliation: Cherry Creek Schools
Governance by teachers and principal
Teacher qualifications: SE/VE certification
Cooperative ed; classes culminate in outings; community
    climate essential; no letter grades; multi-aged classes;
    extensive field trips; suburban location; interns accepted.

A Child's Adventure Land Montessori House
7205 W 120th Ave, Broomfield, CO 80020-2358

Christian Single Home Educators' Network
5560 E 60th Ave #256, Commerce City, CO 80022
Marci Groblebe, 303-288-9581
Denver County

CIS/Burger King Academy
4451 E 72nd Ave, Commerce City, CO 80022
Karen Lewis, 303-288-3007
Adams County District 14
6–8th grade

Lester Arnold High School (1972)
6500 72nd Ave, Commerce City, CO 80022
Larry Nichols, 303-289-2983, FAX: 303-289-7167
Adams County
Type: public choice
18 teachers, 410 students, mainly at-risk, ages 16–21, 9–12th
    grade
No residency requirement
Governance by principal
Teacher qualifications: CO certification
Individualized; outcome-based; comprehensive integrated
    approach; no letter grades; interns accepted.

Teen Parent Program
4625 E 68th Ave, Commerce City, CO 80022
Mary Sampsel, Coord, 303-289-3111
Adams County District 14

Louisville Montessori School
461 Tyler Ave, Louisville, CO 80027-2700
Judith Cole

Alternative Center for Education
3455 W 72nd Ave, Westminster, CO 80030
Carole Bieshaar, Asst Prin, 303-428-2575, FAX:-2142 (CEP)
Adams County
Type: public at-risk

11 teachers; students mainly at-risk, ages 14–21, 9–12th
    grade
Enrollment restricted to those enrolled at home school,
    social worker approval and residency required
Governance by board and principal
Teacher qualifications: state certification
Enrichment days, flexible scheduling, 18-day grading
    periods/attendance contracts; outcome-based; experi-
    ence-based; small classes; multi-aged classes; extensive
    field trips; suburban location; transportation; interns
    accepted.

Colorado Home Educator's Association
3371 W 94th Ave, Westminster, CO 80030
Clark Echols
Adams County
Type: state home-based

Foothills Academy
4725 Miller St, Wheatridge, CO 80033
Mary Faddick, 303-431-0920
Type: independent; tuition: $4350, scholarships
131 students, ages K-8
Academic and social achievements are celebrated; basic skills,
    art, music, foreign language, outdoor ed program;
    monthly "mini-society" marketplace; visiting artists; exten-
    sive field trips.

Full Circle School
PO Box 217, Bennett, CO 80102
Daniel Plavney, Terri Inloes

Academy Charter School
794-A S Briscoe St, Castle Rock, CO 80104
303-660-4881
Douglas County

Christian Homes Educating for Excellent Results
Castle Rock, CO 80104
303-688-2286
Douglas County

Oakes Academy (1988)
4233 N Home St, Castle Rock, CO 80104
Ann Pearce, Adm, 303-688-2472
Douglas County
Type: public at-risk
64 students

Elizabeth High School (ORJT)
PO Box 520, Elizabeth, CO 80107
Cindy Nunneele, Coord, 303-688-3734
Elbert District C-1

William Smith High School
875 Peoria St, Aurora, CO 80110
Linda Ingram, 303-364-8715
Aurora District 28J

Colorado's Finest Alternative High School (1980)
2323 W Baker Ave, Englewood, CO 80110
Tom Synnott, Prin, 303-934-5786
Englewood District 1, Arapahoe County
Type: public choice
774 students

Montessori at Denver Tech Center (1990)
5460 DTC Pkwy, Englewood, CO 80111
Patrice K. Plainbeck, 290-8843
Tuition: $380-470/mo
3 teachers, 4 assistants, 56 students, ages 3-12
Entrance requirements: Montessori experience.
Accreditations: AMS, CO DSS
2 acres; library; computer lab; cooking; Orff music; childcare;
    suburban location; transportation; interns accepted.

Options-Littleton Public Schools (1992)
6558 S Acoma St, Littleton, CO 80120

303-387-3580, FAX: 303-347-3590
Arapahoe County
Type: public at-risk
Entrance requirements: age 16+, residency
Governance by teachers and principal
Small classes; community; wilderness experiences; extensive field trips; suburban location; interns accepted.

Hillcroft Academy, Ltd
7018 S Prince St, Littleton, CO 80120-3536
Type: Montessori

Montessori Children's House Of Littleton
71 E Panama Dr, Littleton, CO 80121-2333
Marjorie Ewing

Academy of Choice
9201 W Columbine Dr, Littleton, CO 80123
Tom Thompson, 303-978-1662
Jefferson County

Montessori Children's Academy
2819 W Belleview, Littleton, CO 80123
Linda Hurja and Kathy Porter

Columbine Montessori Preschool
6653 W Chatfield Ave, Littleton, CO 80123-5834

Montessori School at Lone Tree (1985)
9396 Ermindale Dr, Littleton, CO 80124
Jean Pilon, Adm, 303-799-8540
Tuition: $274-528/mo
5 teachers, 11 assistants, 120 students, ages 3-6
Entrance requirements: min age 2.8; toilet trained
Affiliation: AMS
Governance by administrator
Summer program with full science and nature study; extensive field trips; suburban location; interns accepted.

Montessori School of Douglas County
9396 Erminedale Dr, Littleton, CO 80124-8939
Jean Pilon

Front Range Eclectic Educators
5732 Stetson Ct, Parker, CO 80134
Pat Mason, 303-841-9494
Douglas County
Type: home-based

Parker Montessori Educational Institute
10750 E Victorian Dr, Parker, CO 80134
Jami Boarman, Prin, 303-841-4325, FAX: 303-841-5878
Non-profit; tuition: $2,100-5,700/yr
15 teachers, 12 assistants, 144 students, ages infant-12
Affiliations: AMS, ASCD, AMI, NAMTA, NAEYC
Governance by board
Childcare; suburban location; interns accepted.

Colorado Home Schooling Network
7490 W Apache, Sedalia, CO 80135
303-688-4136
Type: state home-based

Colorado Home Educators Association
1616 17th St Suite 372, Denver, CO 80202
303-441-9938
Type: state home-based

Montessori at Greenwood
5670 Greenwood Plaza Blvd, Englewood, CO 80202

Colorado Options
201 E Colfax Ave, Denver, CO 80203
Type: Montessori

SAFE School (1994)
1925 Blake St, Denver, CO 80203
Mike Clem, 303-295-3164

Type: public choice
5 teachers, 90 students, ages 11-21, 6-12th grade
Governance by faculty & student reps, board
Teacher qualifications: CO cert
Charter; formerly HS Redirection; no letter grades; non-compulsary class attendance; multi-aged classes; extensive field trips; transportation.

Center for International Studies (1985)
West High School
951 Elati St, Denver, CO 80204
Dr Daniel P Lutz, Prog Mgr, 303-620-5364, FAX: 303-620-5412
Denver Public Schools District, Denver County
Type: public choice
11 teachers, 200 students, ages 14-18, 9-12th grade
Entrance requirements: C average, performance contract
Governance by teachers and principal
Teacher qualifications: international experience, international studies academic background
Project and experiential learning; focus on international affairs, cross cultural communication skills; interdisciplinary projects; languages; volunteer service; high academic standards; urban location; interns accepted.

Colorado Community College & Occupational Education Systems
1391 N Speer Blvd, Suite 600, Denver, CO 80204
Lindsey Antle, 303-620-4079

Emily Griffith Opportunity School (1985)
1250 Welton St, Denver, CO 80204
Mary Ann Parthum, Prin, 303-572-8218
Denver County
1576 students, mainly at risk, ages 17-21
Open-entry/exit; individualized; competency-based; self-paced; vocational skills.

Florence Crittenton School
2880 W Holden Pl, Denver, CO 80204
Mikki Galiz, 303-825-9696

Mitchell Elementary
1350 E 33rd Ave, Denver, CO 80204
Dr Martha Urioste, 303-296-8412
Type: magnet
Student ages 3+,-6th grade
Montessori.

Second Chance Program (1986)
1250 Welton St, Denver, CO 80204
George F. Adian, PhD, Asst Prin, 303-575-4738, FAX: 303-575-4840
Type: public choice
16 teachers, 307 students, ages 17-21, HS
Entrance requirements: withdrawn from home school for min of 4 mos; grade 7 reading level; residency
Governance by teachers, principal, board
Teacher qualifications: state certification
Open-entry/exit; outcome-based; GED; vocational; multi-aged classes; urban location.

Barrett Elementary
2900 Richard Allen Ct, Denver, CO 80205
Daphne Hunter, 303-388-5841
Type: magnet
1-2nd grade
Highly gifted.

British Primary School
410 23rd St, Denver, CO 80205
Paul Biwer, Prin, 303-295-7869

Cole Center for Performing Arts
3240 Humboldt St, Denver, CO 80205
Barbara Batey, 303-296-8421
6-12th grade

Denver School of the Arts (1991)
3240 Humboldt, Denver, CO 80205
303-764-6817, FAX: 303-294-9049
Type: public choice
7 teachers, 410 students, ages 11–18, 6–12th grade
Entrance requirements: audition; no residency requirement
Affiliation: Network Performing Arts
Governance by teachers, principal, democratic school meeting
Teacher qualifications: degree in subject area, professional experience
Two art forms per year: writing, dance, vocal music, instrumental music, theater, technical theater/design, visual arts; process emphasized over performance; special ed; multi-aged classes; extensive field trips; urban location; transportation; interns accepted.

East Alternative High School
3800 York St-Unit B, Denver, CO 80205

Gilpin Elementary School
2949 California St, Denver, CO 80205
Joseph Langley, Prin, 303-297-0315

Harrington Elementary
3230 E 38th Ave, Denver, CO 80205
Sally Edwards, 303-333-4293
Type: magnet
K–5th grade
Highly gifted.

Mitchell Montessori Elementary (1986)
1350 E 33rd Ave, Denver, CO 80205
Dr Martha Urioste, 303-296-8912, FAX: 303-292-5349
Type: public choice Montessori
25 teachers, 560 students, ages 3–15
Enrollment restricted to 40% from outside neighborhood; entrance requirement: prior Montessori experience
Affiliations: AMS, AMI
Governance by committee
Teacher qualifications: Montessori training
Strong parent participation; supportive community partnership; no letter grades; multi-aged classes; urban location; transportation; interns accepted.

Garfield Montessori School
1557 Garfield St, Denver, CO 80206-1912

Academic Achievement Centers
150 S Pearl St, Denver, CO 80209
Ron McIrvin, 303-837-1000 x2556
Denver District

Christian Home Educators of Colorado
1015 S Gaylord #226, Denver, CO 80209
303-777-1022
Type: state home-based

Knight Fundamental Academy
3245 E Exposition Ave, Denver, CO 80209
Cora Redden, Prin, 303-722-4681
K–6th grade

Montessori School of Washington Park
320 S Sherman St, Denver, CO 80209
Sharon Wolf

Denver Waldorf School
735 E Florida, Denver, CO 80210
Ina Jaehnig

St Anne's Episcopal School
2701 South York St, Denver, CO 80210-6032
John Comfort
Type: Montessori

Fred N. Thomas Career Education Center (1976)
2650 Eliot St, Denver, CO 80211
Bill Smith, Prin, 303-964-3000, FAX: 303-964-3004

Denver County
Type: public choice
66 teachers, 800-1,000 students, ages 14–18, 9–12th grade
Residency required
Affiliation: Denver PS
Governance by collaborative decision making committee
Teacher qualifications: certified, vocationally licensed
30 career prep programs; career interest surveys, assessments; interns accepted.

Zuni Alternative High School
2417 W 29th Ave, Denver, CO 80211
Alfonso Jaquez, 303-433-8751

The Montessori Connection
2413 W 32nd Ave, Denver, CO 80211-3321

Jefferson County Open School
7655 W 10th Ave, Lakewood, CO 80215
Principal, 303-233-4878
Type: public choice
620 students, pre K–12th grade
Governance by democratic school meeting
Self-directed learning; team teaching; active parental involvement; evaluations and continuous progress; "Walkabout Program," a series of passages completed for graduation; multi-aged classes; no letter grades; extensive field trips; suburban location.

McLain High School Alternative Cooperative Education (1970)
2001 Hoyt St, Lakewood, CO 80215
Patricia Mishler, Head, 303-238-8171, FAX: 303-233-6875
Type: public at-risk; scholarships
9 teachers, 190 students, ages 16-20, 9–12th grade
Entrance requirements: application, interview, age 16, no residency requirement
Affiliation: Jefferson County Schools
Yearly river raft trip; no letter grades; multi-aged classes; interns accepted.

Pinyon Court School
(See Resource Appendix)

Garden Place Academy
4425 Lincoln St, Denver, CO 80216
Stan Reynolds, Prin, 303-295-7785
International Baccalaureate.

Wyman Elementary
1690 Williams St, Denver, CO 80218
Wanda Lenox, 303-320-1632
Type: magnet
1–5th grade
Highly gifted.

Byers Alternative High School
150 S Pearl St, Denver, CO 80219
Betty Emerson, Coord, 303-344-1915

Gust Elementary
3440 W Yale Ave, Denver, CO 80219
Joy Wilson, 303-935-4613
Type: magnet
1–5th grade
Highly gifted.

LAMP Lincoln High School
2285 S Federal Blvd, Denver, CO 80219
303-936-7291 x56

Southwest Montessori Preschool
3805 W Walsh Pl, Denver, CO 80219-3241

Eclipse Program at Denver Children's Home
1501 Albion St, Denver, CO 80220
David Dunn or Linda Lindsay, 303-399-4890
Type: independent, boarding, non-profit

15 teachers, 60 students, mainly at-risk, ages 11-18, 7-12th grade
Governance by teachers and principal
Integrated; thematic; internships; community service, placement; experiential; multi-aged classes; extensive field trips; urban location; interns accepted.

Eclipse/Independent Redirection
1501 Albion, Denver, CO 80220
Linda Lindsay, Dir, 303-399-4890, FAX: 303-399-9846
Type: public at-risk, boarding
24 teachers, 135 students
Governance by teachers, principal, students, parents
Emotional support; community-based and therapeutic day programs; multi-cultural; extensive field trips; multi-aged classes; interns accepted.

Gove Montessori Middle School (1993)
4050 E 14th Ave, Denver, CO 80220
Pauline McBeth, Principal, 303-355-1676
Type: public choice
2 teachers, 35 students, ages 11-13, 7th grade
No residency requirement
Governance by collaborative decision making committee
Teacher qualifications: Montessori training
No letter grades; multi-aged classes; extensive field trips; urban location; transportation; interns accepted.

Montessori Children's House of Denver (1991)
1467 Birch St, Denver, CO 80220
Gina Abegg, Dir, 303-322-8324
Tuition: $250/385/mo
2 teachers, 10 assistants, 47 students, ages 3-6
Entrance requirements: Montessori experience for ages 4.5+
Affiliation: AMS
Governance by teachers and administrators
Organic gardening; inner-city nature study; multi-cultural; cultural studies; ecology and peace education; childcare; urban location; interns accepted.

Cottage "I" Team (1968)
6444 E Floyd Ave, Denver, CO 80222
Orvin Breningstall, Team Leader, 303-757-6213
Arapaho County
Type: public at-risk
4 teachers, 5 students, ages 16-21, 11-12th grade
Enrollment restricted to emotionally disturbed or learning disabled, residency required
Affiliation: Cherry Creek HS
Governance by team of teachers with student input
Teacher qualifications: MA in behavior disorders
Experiential; student need/interest-based; outdoor ed; community involvement; extensive field trips; no letter grades; interns accepted.

Ellis Elementary
1651 S Dahlia, Denver, CO 80222
Tony Knight, 303-756-8363
Type: magnet
1-2nd grade
Highly gifted.

Montessori School of Denver
1460 S Holly St, Denver, CO 80222-3510
Sonnie McFarland or Karen Middleton

Post Oak School
83 W Archer Pl, Denver, CO 80223-1617
Type: Montessori

George Washington Computer Magnet High School and International Baccalaureate Program
655 S Monaco Pkwy, Denver, CO 80224
Ted Brucker; Suzanne Geimer, 303-394-8705; 399-2214

Changing Schools Newsletter
(See Resource Appendix)

Dennison Elementary/Junior High School
401 Independence, Lakewood, CO 80226
Lloyd Carlton, Prin, 303-233-4648
Jefferson County

Traylor Fundamental Academy
2900 S Ivan Way, Denver, CO 80227
Leo Goettelman, Prin, 303-985-1535
K-6th grade

Bear Creek Elementary
3125 S Kipling, Lakewood, CO 80227
Margaret Doll, Prin, 303-985-4461
Jefferson County

Montessori Child Discovery Center
1975 S Garrison St, Lakewood, CO 80227-2204

Montessori Academy of Bear Creek
9300 W Dartmouth Place, Lakewood, CO 80227-4407
Ann Bell

Alternative #1 High School (1980)
1200 E 78th Ave, Denver, CO 80229
Toni Finley, Secretary, 303-287-9400, FAX:-1864
Type: public at-risk
9 teachers, 150 students, ages 16-21, 9-12th grade
Entrance requirements: age 16+; no residency requirement
Governance by principal
Teacher qualifications: certification
Graduation by demonstration; multi-aged classes; urban location; transportation.

High Plains Adult High School (1986)
9451 N Washington, Thornton, CO 80229
Tom Mordue, 303-457-9107
Adams 12 District, Adams County
68 students
Evening classes; credit for life experiences; GED testing.

North Suburban Homeschoolers
9156 N Clermont, Thornton, CO 80229
Teri Daniel, 303-287-9878
Adams County

Cherry Creek Alternative High School
9659 E Mississippi Ave, Denver, CO 80231
Pam Allen, 303-341-2938

Expeditionary School
3750 S Magnolia Way, Denver, CO 80237
Barbara Volpe, 303-861-8661

McGlone Elementary Montessori ECE
4500 Crown Blvd, Denver, CO 80239
Dr J Maalis Hagen

Media Pride House at Montbello High School
5000 Crown Blvd, Denver, CO 80239
Willard Smith, Prin, 303-371-2050

Mapleton Montessori school (1979)
700 Highland Ave, Boulder, CO 80302
Dede Coogan Beardsley, Adm, 303-449-4499
Non-profit; tuition: $1,840-4,000/yr
3 teachers, 4 assistants, 60 students, ages 3-6
Governance by administrator
Childcare; interns accepted.

Naropa Institute (1974)
2130 Arapahoe Ave, Boulder, CO 80302
Marta Shaman, Adms Counselor, 303-444-0202, FAX:-0410
Type: higher education, non-profit; tuition: $8,000/yr
803 students
Governance by board
Accredited; Buddhist contemplative tradition; arts; writing; literature; contemplative and transpersonal psychology; environmental studies; religion; gerontology and long-term mgmt; education; dance; suburban location.

Naropa Institute-Early Education BA (1990)
2130 Arapahoe Ave, Boulder, CO 80302
Marta Shaman, Adms Counselor, 303-444-0202
Type: higher education, non-profit; tuition: $265/cr,
   scholarships
6 teachers, 15 students
Entrance requirements: completion of sophomore year
Governance by board
Joins Buddhist and holistic approaches in movement, medi-
   tation, arts, child development, parenting, contemplative
   teaching; Waldorf, Montessori, Shambhala; internship at
   Alaya Preschool; urban location.

September School
1902 Walnut St, Boulder, CO 80302
Brus Westby, Principal, 303-443-9933
Type: independent, non-profit; tuition: $4275/yr, scholarships
19 teachers, 96 students, partly at-risk, ages 14-19, 9-12th
   grade
Governance by teachers and principal, board
Teacher qualifications: 75% of teachers certified
Integrates academics with performing and visual arts; wilderness training; group and individual counseling; strong
   family-oriented evaluation conferences; multi-aged
   classes; extensive field trips; interns accepted.

The New High School (1993)
889 17th St, Boulder, CO 80302
Rona Wilensky, Prin, 303-447-5401, FAX: 303-938-1742
Boulder County
Type: public choice
400 students, ages 14-19
District residency required
Teacher qualifications: CO certification
Graduation by exhibition; multiple entry points; community
   service required; teaching for understanding; integrated
   learning; suburban location; interns accepted.

University Hill Elementary
956 16th St, Boulder, CO 80302
Jo Ann Trujillo Hays & Jeannie Jacobson, Leadership Team,
   303-442-6735, FAX: 303-939-9439
Boulder County
Type: public choice
22 teachers, 380 students, mainly multi-ethnic, K-5th grade
Non-residents of Boulder Valley are charged tuition
Governance by teachers and parents with student
   involvement
Teacher qualifications: experience-based philosophy; bilingual
Experience-based philosophy (Dewey); integrated curriculum
   built on student's interests and strengths; anti-bias; Family
   Resource School; bilingual program (half of school); training and internships for Univ of CO students; no letter
   grades; multi-aged classes; extensive field trips; urban
   location; interns accepted.

Boulder Valley Alternative Middle School
6096 Baseline Rd, Boulder, CO 80303
303-499-6800

Boulder Valley Schools Teen Parenting Program (1980)
1515 Greenbriar Blvd, Boulder, CO 80303
Gloria Parmerlee-Greiner, Coord, 303-447-5346, FAX: -5353
Non-profit
2 teachers, 50 students, ages 13-21, 9-12th grade
Residency required
Governance by teachers, principal, faculty and student reps
Teacher qualifications: vocational certification in consumer
   homemaking
Vocational training; employment, support, health care, pro-
   grammatic services; academic support; interns accepted.

Countryside Montessori
5524 Baseline Rd, Boulder, CO 80303
Nancy Ahlstrand, Dir, 303-494-3100
Non-profit; tuition: $500/mo

4 teachers, 4 assistants, 36 students, partly at-risk, ages 2.5-6
Accreditation: AMS
Governance by administrator
Emphasis on cultural studies; suburban location; interns
   accepted.

Friends' School (1987)
5465 Pennsylvania, Boulder, CO 80303
Marjorie Larner, Program Dir, 303-666-8886
Boulder County
Type: Quaker, non-profit; tuition: $2,200-5,500/yr,
   scholarships
12 teachers, 97 students, ages 2-11, pre K-5th grade
Governance by teachers and principal
Whole-person; interest-based; conflict resolution; student-
   directed, teacher-guided; environmental focus; no letter
   grades; extensive field trips; interns accepted.

Montessori Education Center of the Rockies (1978)
3440 Longwood Ave, Boulder, CO 80303
Virginia H. Hennes, Dir, 303-494-3002
non-profit; tuition: $3,000/yr
10 teachers, 20-30 students
Entrance requirements: age 21+; ability and desire to work
   with young children
Affiliation: AMS
Governance by a board of trustees
One-year teacher education program, preschool and toddler
   level: 8 wks of academics in the summer followed by 9
   mos of student teaching; no letter grades; suburban
   location.

Mountain Shadows Montessori (1976)
4154 N 63rd, Boulder, CO 80303
Marlene Skovsted, Adm, 303-530-5353
Non-profit; tuition: $2,832-4,512/yr
6 teachers, 7 assistants, 135 students, ages 3-12
Affiliations: NAMTA, MTAC; accreditation: AMI
Governance by teachers and administrators
Childcare; rural location; interns accepted.

Paddock Alternative School (1991)
805 Gillaspie Dr, Boulder, CO 80303
Ann Kane, Lead Tch, 303-447-5580
Boulder County
Type: public choice
10 teachers, 128 students, ages 5-12, K-5th grade
Enrollment by lottery
Governance by council of teachers and parents
Teacher qualifications: CO certification
Small classes; Spanish; no letter grades; extensive field trips;
   multi-aged classes; interns accepted.

Association for Experiential Education
(See Resource Appendix)

Boulder Montessori School
3300 Redstone Rd, Boulder, CO 80303-7139
Karen Olson

In Other Words
(See Resource Appendix)

Shining Mountain Waldorf School (1982)
987 Locust Ave, Boulder, CO 80304
Nancy Jane, Enrl Coord, 303-444-7697, FAX: 444-7701
Boarding, non-profit; tuition: $3,500-5,850/yr, scholarships
25 teachers, 326 students, ages 4-18, K-12th grade
Affiliation: AWSNA
Governance by teachers, principal, and board
Teacher qualifications: Waldorf training, certification
8 acres; extensive field trips; summer school; rural location;
   interns accepted.

Washington Bilingual Alternative Elementary
1215 Cedar Ave, Boulder, CO 80304
Tony Vigil, 303-449-6618
Boulder Valley District

Jarrow Montessori School
3900 Orange Ct, Boulder, CO 80304-0753
Marguerite Humphrey

Bitsy Montessori Day Care Center
1937 Upland Ave, Boulder, CO 80304-0934
Christine Adams

Kids Discover Magazine
(See Resource Appendix)

Montessori School of Lakewood (1978)
5925 W 1st Ave, Lakewood, CO 80401
Janice Norton Kruse, 303-232-7030
Tuition: $1850-3200/yr
4 teachers, 7 assistants, 115 students, ages infant-12
Governance by administrator
Childcare; suburban location; interns accepted.

Children's World Learning Center
573 Park Point Dr, Golden, CO 80401-5737
Type: Montessori

Montessori School of Golden Head
714 Cheyenne St, Golden, CO 80401-5834

Summit County Home Schoolers
Dillon, CO 80435
303-468-9412

Montessori Children's House of Evergreen
PO Box 2468, Evergreen, CO 80439-2468
Betsy Hohe

Summit Alternative School (1986)
Frisco, CO 80443
Demi Garner, 303-668-3522
Summit County
Type: public choice
2 teachers, 35 students, partly at-risk, ages 14-20, 9-12th
   grade
Entrance requirements: application and interview; no resi-
   dency requirement
Governance by principal and democratic school meeting
Within traditional HS; student-directed; extensive field trips;
   rural location; transportation; interns accepted.

Idaho Springs Home Educators
Idaho Springs, CO 80452
303-567-4800
Clear Creek County

Pinewood School
(See Resource Appendix)

Olde Columbine High School (1982)
1200 Sunset, Longmont, CO 80501
William R. Blick, Prin, 303-772-3333, FAX: 651-7446
St Vrain Valley District, Boulder County
Type: public at-risk
5 teachers, 85 students, ages 14-20, 9-12th grade
Entrance requirements: completed grade 8; orientation; no
   residency requirement
Governance by students
Teacher qualifications: CO Certification
Urban location; transportation; interns accepted.

Pleasant Hill Academy (1988)
1130 Francis St #7045, Longmont, CO 80501
Linda Kreibick, Reg, 303-772-8828
Boulder County
Type: home-based, non-profit; cost: $35/family
Student ages 5-90, K-12th grade
Governance by board
Family designed and taught; use of community resources;
   diversity in evaluation; state-wide branches.

St Vrain Valley Alternative Middle School
820 Main St, Longmont, CO 80501
Ken Poppe, 303-682-9377

Gateway Montessori School
1500 9th Ave, Longmont, CO 80501-4228

Eagle Rock School (1993)
Box 1770, Estes Park, CO 80517
Robert Burkhardt, Head, 303-588-0600, FAX: 586-4805
Larimer County
Type: independent, boarding, non-profit; tuition: free
20 teachers, 96 students, partly at-risk, ages 15-18, HS
Affiliation: Honda
Governance by teachers, principal, democratic school
   meeting, board
650 acres; 1 mile from Rocky Mountain National Park; integrated; stresses service learning, outdoor ed, environmental stewardship, cross-cultural understanding; no letter
   grades; multi-aged classes; extensive field trips; interns
   accepted.

Wyoming Homeschoolers
615 S Loomis, Ft. Collins, CO 80521
Type: state home-based

Children's House Montessori School
113 N Shields St, Fort Collins, CO 80521-2418

Centennial High School (1976)
330 E Laurel St, Fort Collins, CO 80524
Dr Bill Lamperes, Prin, 303-493-4129
Type: public at-risk
14 teachers, 180 students, mainly at-risk, ages 14-21,
   10-12th grade
Enrollment restricted to non-handicapped residents
Governance by principal, faculty, students, parents
Teacher qualifications: CO License/Certification
Students must maintain commitment to pledge card; multi-
   aged classes; urban location; interns accepted.

Ft Collins Teen Parent Program
330 E Laurel, Ft Collins, CO 80524
Barbara Loy, 303-484-4959
Poudre R-1 District

Harris Bilingual Alternative Elementary
501 E Elizabeth, Ft. Collins, CO 80524
303-482-7902
Poudre R-1 District
K-5th grade

Homeschoolers Under God
1749 Hastings Dr, Fort Collins, CO 80526
Larimer County

Northern Colorado Home School Association
4633 Skyline Dr, Fort Collins, CO 80526
303-493-2243; 669-6234
Larimer County

Ferguson High School (1972)
804 E Eisenhower, Loveland, CO 80537
Howard C. Wenger, Prin, 303-667-5881, FAX: 669-0772
Larimer County
Type: continuation, non-profit
7 teachers, 105 students, ages 25-50, 9-12th grade
Entrance requirements: application, transcript, orientation,
   testing; no residency requirement
Governance by democratic school meeting
Teacher qualifications: CO certification
Special 1-wk classes; daily leadership; college schedule; after-
   noon, night classes; multi-aged classes; suburban location;
   interns accepted.

Agape Family Schools
5108 Edgewood Ct, Loveland, CO 80538
303-669-2581
Larimer County
Type: home-based

Mary Blain Elementary Key School (1991)
860 E 29th St, Loveland, CO 80538
Randy Zila, Prin, 303-669-2973, FAX: 303-669-1785
Type: public choice
35 teachers, 485 students, ages 5–11, K–5th grade
No residency requirement
Governance by shared decision making
Class rotation with single aged class and teacher; multi-aged
  classes; interns accepted.

Brighton Alternative High School
270 S 8th Ave, Brighton, CO 80601
Paul Bettger, 303-659-4820
Adams District 27J

We Are Teaching Our Children At Home
Brighton, CO 80601
303-659-9282
Adams County

Brighton Montessori School
203 South 3rd Ave, Brighton, CO 80601-2011
Joyce Acre

Eastlake Campus Alternative School (1974)
12323 Claude Ct, Eastlake, CO 80614
Tom Mordue, Prin, 303-452-1617
Adams District 12
Type: public at-risk
386 students, 7–12th grade
student-centered; success oriented; 1:15–20 ratio; multi-
  aged classes.

EastLake Montessori School
12585 Third St, Eastlake, CO 80614

Sunrise Alternative at Ft Lupton High School
305 Reynolds St, Ft Lupton, CO 80621
Debbie Huerta, Dir, 303-857-4304

Orange Peel Education Clinic
6001 W 12th St, Greeley, CO 80631
Don and Annie Heiman, 303-353-6132

Trademark Learning Center
811 15th St, Greeley, CO 80631
Virginia Guzman, 303-352-1543 x243
Weld District Re-6

Weld Opportunity School (1987)
1112 9th Ave, Greeley, CO 80631
Bonnie Peterson, Dir, 303-351-7472
Weld County
Type: public at-risk
5 teachers, 65 students, ages 15–19, 9–12th grade
Entrance requirements: interview, enrollment papers,
  residency
Governance by teachers, principal
Teacher qualifications: CO certification
Work experience; pregnancy prevention; teen parenting;
  peer support; counseling; career exploration; life skills;
  multi-aged classes; interns accepted.

Montessori Early Learning Center
529 22nd St, Greeley, CO 80631-7134

University of Northern Colorado Laboratory School
Greeley, CO 80639
303-351-2321

South Platte Valley BOCES Alternative High School
110 Main St, Ft Morgan, CO 80701
Tim George, Prin, 303-867-8297

Brush Re-2(J) District Second Chance
PO Box 585, Brush, CO 80723
Ron Prascher, 303-842-5176

Morgan County Homeschoolers Network
Brush, CO 80723
303-867-4461

Sterling Alternative High School (1982)
201 S 11th Ave, Sterling, CO 80751
Darrell Smith, Prin, 303-522-5079, FAX: 303-522-5084
Logan County
Type: public at-risk
3 teachers, 32 students, ages 15–19, 9–12th grade
Interview required
Governance by teachers, principal
Shared decision making; monthly review of academic, per-
  sonal development; parent involvement; multi-aged
  classes; interns accepted.

Yuma High School Alternative Cooperative Education
1000 S Albany, Yuma, CO 80759
Bill Kalb, 303-848-5488

Community Learning Center (1990)
425 W Alabama, Fountain, CO 80817
Robert Vise, Dir, 719-382-7429, FAX: 719-382-7338
El Paso County
Type: public at-risk
2 teachers, 35 students, ages 16–12, 9–12th grade
Entrance requirements: age 16, interview, district residency
Governance by principal; board
Vocational; counseling; portfolios; work/study; multi-aged
  classes; suburban location; transportation; interns
  accepted.

Teller County Home Education Association
Woodland Park, CO 80863
719-687-8676

Teller District RE-2 Alternative High School
PO Box 99, Woodland Park, CO 80863
Rose Martin, 719-687-6800

Alternative Education Program (1981)
Box 99, Woodland Park, CO 80866
Rose Martin, 719-687-8450, FAX: 719-687-3880
Teller County
Type: public at-risk
1 teacher, 25–40 students, ages 16–19, 10–12th grade
Residency required
Governance by student gov't, democratic school meeting
Support groups; work-study; no letter grades; multi-aged
  classes

Palmer Night School (1981)
301 N Nevada Ave, Colorado Springs, CO 80903
Jack Terry, Dir, 303-520-2850
El Paso County
Type: public choice/at-risk
6 teachers, 120–300 students, ages 16–20, 9–12th grade
Entrance requirements: age 16+, district residency
Governance by principal and board
Teacher qualifications: CO Certification
For pregnant teens/mothers and students who work days;
  multi-aged classes; urban location; interns accepted.

Educational Opportunity Program (1970)
730 N Walnut, Colorado Springs, CO 80905
Pete Freeman, Prin, 719-630-0240, FAX: 719-630-0243
El Paso County
Type: public choice
14 teachers, 250 students, mainly at-risk, ages 16–20, HS
No SE provided
Affiliation: School District #11
Governance by principal

Teacher qualifications: CO certification
Personalized, small group instruction; personal, academic goal setting; flexible schedule; urban location; interns accepted.

Harrison Second Chance (1988)
2755 Janitell Rd, Colorado Springs, CO 80906
Jim Reid, Coord/Prin, 719-576-8226, FAX: 576-6980
Harrison School District 2, El Paso County
Type: public choice/at-risk
1 ft, 10 pt teachers, 80 students, mainly at-risk, ages 14-21, 9-12th grade
Entrance requirements: age 14-21, not enrolled in other program, district residency
Governance by teachers and principal
Teacher qualifications: current employment in district, interview
Volunteer tutors from local colleges; required work and/or community service; no SE; suburban location.

The Golden Mountain Schools (1975)
306 W Brookside, Colorado Springs, CO 80906
Rai Christiansen, Dir, 729-632-0872
Type: Montessori; tuition: $2,100-4,000/yr
6 teachers, 6 assistants, 100 students, ages 3-9
Affiliations: MTAC, AMS
Governance by administrator
Teacher qualifications: 30 yrs experience
French 4 times/wk an integral part of curriculum; peace, music ed in preschool; childcare; urban location; interns accepted.

Born to the Golden Mountain Montessori Child Center
306 W Brookside St, Colorado Springs, CO 80906-2156
Rae Christiansen

Belleau Montessori School
3131 Pennsylvania, Colorado Springs, CO 80907

A Montessori School
6480 Coolwell Dr, Colorado Springs, CO 80908-3324

Colorado Springs Homeschoolers
2906 Marilyn Rd, Colorado Springs, CO 80909
719-598-8444

Widefield Alternative High School (1987)
615 Widefield Dr, Colorado Springs, CO 80911
Dave Turner, Dean, 719-392-3481, FAX: 719-390-4372
El Paso County
Type: public at-risk
4 teachers, 60 students, ages 16-21, 10-12th grade
Enrollment restricted to dropout residents
Governance by board
Teacher qualifications: state certification
Credit per class; work/study; 20-day sessions; community environment; suburban location.

Woodland Hills Montessori School (1984)
3215 Woodland Hills Dr, Colorado Springs, CO 80918
Dr Jackie Howell, 719-594-0611
Tuition: $190/330/mo
13 teachers, 75 students, ages 3-9
Entrance requirements: age 3; toilet trained
Governance by board
Teacher qualifications: CO Certification
Childcare.

Woodman Montessori School
6985 Blackhawk Pl, Colorado Springs, CO 80919-1124

Colorado Springs Homeschool Support Group
PO Box 26117, Colorado Springs, CO 80936-6117
719-598-2636

Keating Education Center (1982)
215 E Orman Ave, Pueblo, CO 81003
Jim Wessely, 719-549-7371

Pueblo District 60, Pueblo County
346 students
Second chance; evening classes; work study for teen mothers, out of school students.

Pueblo Home School Association
2616 Lambert, Pueblo, CO 81003
MaryLou Greene, 719-545-5649

Pueblo Montessori Center
110 Calla Ave, Pueblo, CO 81005-1205
Leslie Kelham and Becky Chaussen

Arkansas Valley Attendendance Center
PO Box 1128, La Junta, CO 81050
Chris Gramstorff, 719-384-9482

Project Acquire
210 W Pearl, Lamar, CO 81052
Phil McDowell, 719-336-3251

Sonshine Support Group
Lamar, CO 81052
719-336-7990
Prowers County
Type: home-based

Alamosa Community Open School (1985)
216 Victoria St, Alamosa, CO 81101
Daryl Nyquist, Dir, 719-589-9011
Alamosa County
Type: public at-risk
104 students, 7-12th grade
Tutorials; CAI; vocational; community improvement; work experience.

Ignacio Second Chance (1986)
PO Box 460, Ignacio, CO 81137
Paulette Giambattista, Dir, 303-563-9417, FAX:-4524
Type: public at-risk
3 teachers, 60 students, ages 15-21, 9-12th grade
No residency requirement
Governance by teachers and principal
Individual guided study; multi-aged classes; rural location.

New Horizons (Second Chance) High School (1986)
PO Box 72, La Jara, CO 81140
Jean Kelley, 719-274-4220
North Conejos District Re-1J, Conejos County
50 students, mainly out of school, HS
Individual study; cont ed; health, career ed required.

Monte Vista Community School (1973)
345 E Prospect Ave, Monte Vista, CO 81144
719-852-2212, FAX: 719-852-6184
Rio Grande County
Type: public choice/at-risk
1 teacher, 20 students, mainly at-risk, ages 15-53
Residency required
Accreditation: Colorado State
Governance by director
Teacher qualifications: CO certification
Competency-based; GED prep; self-directed; field trips; rural location; transportation; interns accepted.

Chaffee County High School (1989)
PO Box 2027, Buena Vista, CO 81211
Dick Couch, Dir, 719-395-4064
Type: public at-risk
3 teachers, 40 students, ages 16-23, 10-12th grade
Enrollment restricted to age 16+ w/o learning difficulties
Governance by principal, faculty and student reps
Teacher qualifications: CO Certification
Point, attendance contract; 80 hrs service learning required; no letter grades; rural location.

Collegiate Peaks Home Educators
Buena Vista, CO 81211
719-395-2069
Chaffee County

Exploratory School-Lincoln Elementary
420 Myrtle, Canon City, CO 81212
Molly Merry, 719-275-7445

The Exploratory School (1992)
420 Myrtle Ave, Canon City, CO 81212
Molly Merry, Tch, 719-269-3785
Fremont County
Type: public choice
2 teachers, 60 students, 5-6th grade
Entrance requirements: application, parent commitment, not
for emotionally disturbed; no residency requirement
Governance by teachers, principal
Project-based learning; traditional and alternative experi-
ences; student-directed; experiential

Gunnison High School Alternative Program (1988)
800 W Ohio, Gunnison, CO 81230
Don and Gay Willson, 303-641-0063
Gunnison Watershed RE-1J District, Gunnison County
Type: public at-risk
18 students
Self-motivated; outcome-based; vocational awareness.

Gunnison Valley Homeschoolers
Gunnison, CO 81230
303-641-0870

Christian Parents Who Are Teaching at Home
Durango, CO 81301
303-884-4122
La Plata County

Home Education for Excellence in Durango (HEED)
917 CR 216, Durango, CO 81301
Maureen Clerici, 303-247-2725
La Plata County

La Plata Montessori School
2899 Holly Ave, Durango, CO 81301-4416

Adult Education Center (1986)
PO Box 1345, Durango, CO 81302
Mimi Frenette, Dir, 303-385-4354
La Plata County
Type: independent, non-profit
7 teachers, 101 students, mainly at-risk, ages 16-75
Governance by board
Teacher qualifications: CO certification preferred
Student-centered; students set goals and pace, participate
on Board of Directors and committees, evaluate instruc-
tion; rural location; interns accepted.

Durango Alternative Education (1982)
2390 N Main, Durango, CO 81302
Kurt Zeiner, 303-259-1632 x441
La Plata County
Type: public at-risk
83 students

Southwest Open High School (1985)
PO Box 1420, Cortez, CO 81321
Richard Fulton, Prin, 303-565-1150, FAX: 303-565-1203
Montezuma County
Type: public choice/at-risk
6 teachers, 80 students, mainly at-risk, ages 15-21, 9-12th
grade
District residency required
Governance by principal, faculty, student reps, board, demo-
cratic school meeting
Teacher qualifications: CO Certification

Experiential; community-based; mentorships; outdoor ed;
teen parenting; no letter grades; non-compulsory class
attendance; multi-aged classes; rural location; interns
accepted.

Dolores Re-4A District Second Chance
P O Box 757, Dolores, CO 81323
Greg Conway, 303-882-7255

Mancos Re-6 District Second Chance
P O Box 420, Mancos, CO 81328
Jack Curran, 303-533-7748

San Juan Home Educators
Montrose, CO 81401
303-249-6765
Montrose County

Vista Adult High School (1986)
PO Box 1483, 8 S 5th St, Montrose, CO 81402
Roger H. Lake, Prin, 303-249-4470, FAX: 303-249-1172
Montrose County
Type: public choice/at-risk
2 teachers, 60 students, mainly at-risk, ages 16+, 9-12th
grade
Entrance requirements: age 16+, residency
Governance by principal, board
Teacher qualifications: CO certification
Self-paced, individualized; computer; rural location.

Delta Alternative HS/**Area Vocational Tech Center**
1765 US Hwy 50, Delta, CO 81416
Frank Klein, 303-874-7671

Delta County Support Group
Paonia, CO 81428
303-527-4323
Type: home-based

Lamborn Valley School
1559 4110 Dr, Paonia, CO 81428
Addie Cranson, 303-527-3165
Type: independent, home-based; cost: variable
16 students, ages 3-18
Part of intentional community with some outside boarding
students; learning related to student experience and interest; organic farm and orchard; work projects; travel-study
trips; $120/yr for homeschoolers.

The Children's Cooperative Homeschool (1992)
PO Box 335, Ridgway, CO 81432
Jeanne Stewart, Dir/Tch, 303-626-5279
Ouray County
Non-profit; cost: $200/mo, scholarships
1 teacher, 9 students, ages 5-6, ES
Family must contribute 10 hrs/mo; 3 mo probation period,
residency required
Affiliation: NCACS
Governance by parent co-op and teacher
Teacher qualifications: CO Certification; MA in Teaching Elem
Ed
Field trips; rural location

Grand Junction Night School
1400 N 5th St, Grand Junction, CO 81501
Dale Schoenbeck, 303-242-7496
Mesa District 51

R-5 High School (1970)
310 N 7th St, Grand Junction, CO 81501
303-242-4350, FAX: 303-242-4465
Mesa County
Type: public at-risk
12 teachers, 235 students, ages 16-21, 10-12th grade
Entrance requirements: age 16, job working 15-20 hrs/wk
Affiliation: Mesa SD #51

Governance by teachers and principal
Teacher qualifications: degree, vocational certification
Multi-aged classes; extensive field trips; interns accepted.

The Children's Cottage
441 Kennedy Ave, Grand Junction, CO 81501
Type: Montessori

Home Education League of Parents
PO Box 4865, Grand Junction, CO 81502
Kara Lanctot, Coord
Mesa County
Non-profit
Governance by coordinators directed through national level
14 family membership; inclusive; suburban location.

National Association of Private Nontraditional Schools and Colleges
(See Resource Appendix)

Schools Without Walls (1988)
1405 Wellington, Grand Junction, CO 81506
Greg Cope, Coord, 303-243-4130
Mesa District 51, Mesa County
Type: public at-risk
110 students
Outdoor education; student-centered; self-directed; support system; networking.

Montessori School of Grand Junction
2405 Apricot Ct, Grand Junction, CO 81506-8450
Beth Long

Yampah Mountain High School
701 Midland, Glenwood Springs, CO 81601
Bob Breeden, 303-945-9463
Mountain BOCES District

Aspen Children Center
315 C Ave, Aspen, CO 81611
Type: Montessori

Aspen Sprouts
315 A A B C, Aspen, CO 81611
Type: Montessori

Aspen Waldorf School (1991)
PO Box 1563, Aspen, CO 81612
Patty Fox, 303-925-7938
Pitkin County

Non-profit; tuition: $3,500/yr, scholarships
3 teachers, 27 students, ages 3–12, pre K-4th grade
Affiliation: AWSNA
Governance by faculty and student representatives and board
Teacher qualifications: BA, Waldorf training
Extensive field trips; suburban location; transportation; interns accepted.

Mountain Sage School
PO Box 1241, Carbondale, CO 81623
Pricilla Dickinson, 303-963-9647
Type: independent; tuition: $2,680/yr, scholarships
12 students, ages K–2
Affiliation: NCACS
Will add a grade each year; individualized; Friday field trips, overnights, ski trips.

Mt Sopris Montessori School
PO Box 366, Carbondale, CO 81623-0366
Mark Ross

Grand Mesa High School (1987)
Rt 1, Box 26, Collbran, CO 81624
John Henderson, 303-487-3576
Plateau Valley District 50, Mesa County
Type: public at-risk
411 students
Self-paced; world of work; vocational training.

Aspen Community School (1970)
1199 Lenado Rd; PO Box 336, Woody Creek, CO 81656
George Stranahan, Head, 303-923-4080, FAX: 303-923-6207
Pitkin County
Type: independent, non-profit; tuition: up to $6900/yr, scholarships
14 teachers, 106 students, ages 2.5-14, pre K-8th grade
Affiliation: NCACS
Governance by board and parent cooperative
Log schoolhouse on mesa overlooking Rocky Mtns; rooted in community; fluid curriculum; respect for differences; apprenticeships with artist and woodworker in residence; multi-aged classes; extensive field trips; no letter grades; rural location; transportation; interns accepted.

Connecticut

The Educational Association of Christian Homeschoolers (TEACH)
(See Resource Appendix)

Alternative Education School (1986)
240 Stafford Ave, Bristol, CT 06010
Edward Mongeon, Dept Chair, 203-584-7709
Type: public choice
5 teachers, 48 students, mainly at-risk, 7-10th grade
Entrance requirements: referral, interview
At Bristol Community Center; individualized; experiential; life skills, awareness; field trips.

Wilderness School (1974)
PO Box 298, E Hartland, CT 06027
Tom Dyer, Dir; Dorothy Soden, Business Mgr, 203-491-3528, 566-4761

Type: public
Student ages 13.5-16
Entrance requirements: referral
Base camp/courses in natural settings; 20-day wilderness course.

The Alternative School (1981)
Housatonic Valley Regional HS, Falls Village, CT 06031
William DeVoti, Tch/Coord, 203-824-5123
Type: public choice
2 teachers, 14 students, mainly at-risk, 9-12th grade
Experiential; outdoor adventure; community shadowing; magazine.

ABLE (Alternative Behavioral Learning Environment) (1982)
134 W Middle Tpk, Manchester, CT 06040

Marilyn Fabian, Judith Spicker, Tchs, 203-647-3521
Type: public choice
2 teachers, 15 students, mainly at-risk, 10-12th grade
Entrance requirements: PPT and staff evaluation
In-house; short-term intervention.

Porter Street ADT Program (1984)
45 N School St, Manchester, CT 06040
Richard Cormier, PPS Dir; Joseph Fallacaro, Dir, 203-647-
   3448,-3442
Type: public at-risk
5 teachers, 24 students, 8-12th grade
Enrollment restricted to referred SE students
For very emotionally disturbed students; individualized;
   highly structured; voc; individual and group therapy;
   parent support group.

Vertices at Manchester High School (1976)
134 E Middle Tpk, Manchester, CT 06040
Sue Hardy, John Stedman, Tchs, 203-647-3509
Type: public choice
2 teachers, 30-35 students, mainly at-risk, 10-12th grade
Entrance requirements: referral
In-house; mainstream re-entry program.

Hans Christian Anderson Montessori
212 Bolton Center Rd; PO Box 9218, Bolton, CT 06043-7637
Kathy Hoyt

Alternative Vocational Education (AVE)
   New Britain High School
110 Mill St, New Britain, CT 06051
Paul N. Eshoo, Coord, 203-225-6351
Type: public choice
10 teachers, 30-38 students, mainly at-risk, 11-12th grade
In-house; machine tech; drafting and blueprint;
   telecommunications.

Montessori Children's House, c/o Ethel Walker School
Bushy Hill Rd, Simsbury, CT 06070

Freeman's Montessori Schoool
895 Main St, South Glastonbury, CT 06073-2218
Alberta Freeman

Resource Center at Suffield High School
350 Mountain Rd, Suffield, CT 06078
Robin Sorensen, Tch; Nora Lusignan, Psych, 203-668-7328
Type: public at-risk
2 teachers, 2 assistants, 30-45 students, 9-12th grade
Enrollment restricted to SE students
In-house.

Enfield Montessori
1370 Enfield St, Enfield, CT 06082
Sr Mary Anastasia, Prin, 203-745-5847
Non-profit; tuition: $1,400-1,600
5 teachers, 5 assistants, 122 students, ages 3-12
Entrance requirements: space availability; toilet trained
Affiliation: NAMTA; accreditation: CT
Governance by board
Suburban location; interns accepted.

Montesorri Children's House
PO Box 194, West Simsbury, CT 06092-0194
Type: Montessori

Alternate Learning Center at Sage Park Middle School
   (1980)
25 Sage Park Rd, Windsor, CT 06095
Anita W. Baten, Tch, 203-688-6415
Type: public choice
1 teacher, 1 assistant, 30-35 students, mainly at-risk, 7-8th
   grade
Study and organizational skills; peer counseling.

Alternative Center for Education (ACE)
Windsor High School, Windsor, CT 06095

Thomas G. Martin, Jr, Vice Prin, 203-688-8334
Type: public choice
2 teachers, 15 students, mainly at-risk, 9-10th grade
In-house; individualized; tutorial; human relations; career
   planning.

Windsor Montessori (1983)
114 Palisado Ave, Windsor, CT 06095-2531
Darlene Dulchinos, Dir, 203-285-1426
Non-profit; tuition: $290/320/634/mo
4 teachers, 1 assistant, 38 students, ages infant-6
Affiliation: AMS; accreditation: NAECP
Large building; gym; 2 playgrounds; childcare; suburban loca-
   tion; interns accepted.

Small Group Instruction
Windsor Locks HS, Windsor Locks, CT 06096
Edgar J. Gorman, Spec Serv Dir, 203-627-1480
Type: public choice
Students mainly at-risk, HS
Entrance requirements: PPT referral, SE classification
In-house; early graduation for potential dropouts; voc; modi-
   fied work experience.

TMR Program at Regional School #7 (1976)
Central Ave Ext, Winsted, CT 06098
Pat Keener, SE Dept Chair, 203-379-8525
Type: public choice
1 teacher, 2 assistants, 7 students, mainly at-risk, ages 13-21
In middle school; individualized; voc; perf arts; life skills.

Winchester Alternate High School (1977)
79 Gay St, Winsted, CT 06098
Marilyn P. Celadon, Prin, 203-379-5921
Type: public at-risk
3 teachers, 21 students, mainly at-risk, 7-12th grade
Enrollment restricted to at-risk and SE students
Vocational classes or work study.

Hartford Board of Education
249 High St, Hartford, CT 06103
Alice A Davis
Type: Montessori

Watkinson School (1881)
180 Bloomfield Ave, Hartford, CT 06105
Kay Montgomery, Adms Dir, 203-236-5618, FAX: 233-8295
Type: independent, non-profit; tuition: $13,550/yr,
   scholarships
36 teachers, 175 students, ages 10-19, grades 6-12+
Entrance requirements: teacher recommendations, SAT or
   PSAT
Affiliation: CES
Governance by board
Teacher qualifications: BS minimum, compatible philosophy
Special support for gifted, LD; early college courses at U of
   Hartford; pre-professional arts program; independent
   study; suburban location; interns accepted.

Synergy Alternative High School Program (1973)
110 Long Hill Dr, E Hartford, CT 06108
Dr Betti Colli, Coord, 203-282-3160
Type: public choice
6 teachers, 1 assistant, 80 students, mainly at-risk, 9-12th
   grade
Entrance requirements: interview
Informal; cooperative work experience; survival-type
   encampments; reality-therapy peer support; daily contract; weekly all-school meeting; student/staff discipline
   committee.

Alternate Day Program (1977)
51 Willow St, Wethersfield, CT 06109
Francis H. Stuart, PPS/SE Dir, 203-563-8181 x214
Type: public choice
3 teachers, 1 assistant, 20 students, mainly at-risk, 9-12th
   grade

Entrance requirements: staff observes student, interviews parents.
Daily peer counseling; psychiatric consultation; checklist level system.

Newington High Alternative Program (1978)
605 Willard Ave, Newington, CT 06111
Robert Pitocco, 203-666-5611
Type: public at-risk
3 teachers, 20 students, HS
Enrollment restricted to at-risk and SE students
In-house facility; individualized; independent studies.

ASK Program at Hall High School (1975)
975 N Main St, W Hartford, CT 06117
James Solomon, Coord, 203-232-4561
Type: public choice
2 teachers, 50 students, mainly at-risk, 10–12th grade
Entrance requirements: recommendation, interview
In-house; team taught English and social studies classes only; informal academic and personal counseling.

Montessori School of Greater Hartford (1964)
64 St. James St, West Hartford, CT 06119
Carol Kuszik, 203-236-4565, FAX: 203-233-1070
Non-profit; tuition: $3090/6890
6 teachers, 9 assistants, 110 students, mainly international, ages 3–9
Students must be 3 years old and toilet-trained
Governance by a board of trustees
Childcare; suburban location.

Alternative Learning Center (1977)
21 Valley St, Willimantic, CT 06226
Roz Rosen, Dir, 203-423-0233
Type: public choice
5 teachers, 2 assistants, 55 students, mainly at-risk, 7–12th grade
Enrollment restricted to Windham HS students
Small, flexible and intimate environment; student-operated bakery business.

Alternative Learning Program for Students (1983)
610 Wauregan Rd, Danielson, CT 06239
Mike Vose or Bill Scalise, Co-Chairs, 203-774-7836
Type: public choice
2 teachers, 1 assistant, 25 students, mainly at-risk, 9–12th grade
Enrollment restricted to Killingly HS students
Dropout intervention; emphasis on independent study, self-direction; computers.

Natchaug Democratic School (1993)
164 Main St, Hampton, CT 06247
Jed Katch, 203-455-0505
Windham County
Type: independent, non-profit; tuition: $3500, 2500 second, 1500 3rd
2 teachers, 10 students, ages 5–19, 1–12th grade
Governance by democratic school meeting
Teacher qualifications: expertise in one or more areas; certification not necessary
Students choose what they want to learn, when, how, and with whom; larger community used through visitations and apprenticeships with businesses, universities; no letter grades; non-compulsory class attendance; multi-aged classes; rural location.

Mount Hope Montessori School (1961)
48 Bassetts Bridge Rd, Mansfield Center, CT 06250
Florence Caillard, Dir, 203-423-1070
Non-profit; tuition: $4,000/yr
3 teachers, 5 assistants, 72 students, mainly international, ages 3–6
Entrance requirements: age 3 by Dec
Governance by board
Rural location.

Oak Grove Montessori School (1981)
132 Pleasant Valley Rd, Mansfield Center, CT 06250
Karen Drazen, Dir, 203-456-1031
Non-profit; tuition: $3,996-4,140/yr
5 teachers, 2 assistants, 72 students, ages 3–12
Affiliations: AMS, MSCT
Governance by board
Whole language program; passive solar, earth berm building; childcare; interns accepted.

Study Circles Resource Center (1990)
(See Resource Appendix)

Montessori Discovery School
218 Dudley St, Norwich, CT 06360
Patrice Champeigne

Norwich High School (1984)
Mahan Dr, Norwich, CT 06360
Nancy Elizabeth Young, Dir, 203-823-4213
Type: public choice
4 teachers, 50 students, mainly at-risk, 9–12th grade
Individualized; school gov and leadership opportunities; voc.

Montville Alternative High School (1977)
300 Norwich/New London Tpk, Uncasville, CT 06382
Richard Bilda, Prin, 203-848-7816
Type: public choice
3 teachers, 1 assistant, 35 students, mainly at-risk, 9–12th grade
Silk screening and chair caning subsidize field trips.

Waterford High School Satellite Program (1981)
15 Rope Ferry Rd, Waterford, CT 06385
Kate Novatto, Burke Reagan, Co-Tchs, 203-442-9401 x46
Type: public choice
2 teachers, 1 assistant, 20 students, mainly at-risk, 9–12th grade
Entrance requirements: PPT meeting
In-house; individualized; highly structured; small groups; voc; work experience; counseling; behavior modification.

Horizons: Branford High School (1990)
185 E Main St, Branford, CT 06405
Robert C Gaiser, Adm, 203-488-7291
New Haven County
Type: public choice/at-risk
8 teachers, 65 students, mainly at-risk, ages 14–20, 9–12th grade
Entrance requirements: contract, application, interview, residency
Affiliation: CT Assn of Alt Schs & Progs
Governance by teachers, administrator, students
Teacher qualifications: CT Certification
Interns accepted.

Wightwood School
56 Stony Creek Rd, Branford, CT 06405
Bill Kaplan, Head, 203-481-0363
Type: independent, non-profit; tuition: $5,595-7,195/yr, scholarships
100 students, pre K–8th grade
Integrated; topic-centered; experiential; family-oriented; art; Spanish; overnight, week-long trips; problem solving; environmental science.

Shoreline School of Montessori
675 East Main St, Branford, CT 06405-2934
Robin Barron

Boulder Knoll Montessori School
660 Boulder Rd, Cheshire, CT 06410-3216

Clinton Elementary Schools Integrated Day (1981)
c/o Joel School, Glenwood Circle, Clinton, CT 06413
Daniel Hesford, Coord; Kopi Saltman, Jim Snow, Prins, 203-669-5768

Type: public choice
14 teachers, 325 students, K–5th grade
In-house; multi-grade groups; students stay with teacher for more than 1 yr; no letter grades.

Connecticut Home Educators Association (1983)
PO Box 250, Middletown, CT 06414
Linda Schroth, Pres, 203-267-4240
Middlesex County
Type: state home-based

Programmed Alternative Learning (PAL)
Fairfield Public Schools (1978)
760 Stillson Rd, Fairfield, CT 06430
Mary Michael, Housemaster, 203-255-8308
Type: public choice
5 teachers, 1 assistant, 25 students, mainly at-risk, 6–12th grade
Enrollment restricted to SE students
For very emotionally disturbed students; extensive student, parent counseling; work experience.

Hunt Ridge Montessori
4670 Congress St, Fairfield, CT 06430-1721

Montessori Center for Early Learning
148 Beach Rd, Fairfield, CT 06430-6002
Belen Orejas Fernandez

Fairfield Montessori School
100 Mona Ter, Fairfield, CT 06430-6422

The Learning Cooperative at Fairfield High School (1978)
755 Melville Ave, Fairfield, CT 06432
Kenneth Tavares, Adm, 203-255-8350, FAX: 366-1371
Type: public at-risk
3 teachers, 30 students, mainly at-risk, ages 14–19, 9–12th grade
Entrance requirements: counselor recommendation, visit, interview, residency; no SE
Governance by board
In-house; individualized; small classes; family-like environment; work experience; community service required; multi-aged classes; suburban location.

Montessori School of Madison
213 Green Hill Rd, Madison, CT 06443-2103
Sharon Timek

Integrated Day at Memorial Middle School (1977)
Hubbard St, Middlefield, CT 06455
Maureen Hamilton, Judith O'Hare, Tchs, 203-349-3489
Type: public choice
5 teachers, 100 students, 5–6th grade
In-house; individualized; experiential; individual project research; vertical age grouping; cooperative group work; narrative evaluations or letter grades.

Center for Creative Youth
Wesleyan University, Middletown, CT 06459
Joan Hickey, Dir, 203-347-9411 x2684
Type: public choice
25 teachers, 22 assistants, 200 students
Entrance requirements: teacher/peer nominations, autobiographical essay, audition, interview
Residential summer program; music; creative writing; theater; dance; visual arts; technical theater.

Newtown Montessori School
40 Dodgingtown Rd, Newtown, CT 06470
Myriam Woods, Head
Non-profit; tuition: $3,050/5,000/yr
3 teachers, 3 assistants, 90 students, ages 3–9
Affiliations: AMS, NAEYC; accreditation: CAIS
Governance by board
Childcare; suburban location; transportation; interns accepted.

Alternative Education Program at North Branford High School (1977)
49 Caputo Rd, N Branford, CT 06471
John DeCaprio, Prin, 203-484-0421
Type: public
3 teachers, 15 students, 9–12th grade
Entrance requirements: referral, application, review meeting
In-house; work experience; individualized.

Oxford Alternative Program at Great Oak Middle School (1982)
222 Governor's Hill Rd, Oxford, CT 06483
Donna Fusco, Tch, 203-888-5418
Type: public choice
1 teacher, 7 students, mainly at-risk, 7–8th grade
In-house; experiential; individual or small group setting.

Seymour High School Alternative Education (1978)
2 Botsford Rd, Seymour, CT 06483
Edward Rostowsky, Asst Prin, 203-888-2561
Type: public choice
1 teacher, 10–15 students, mainly at-risk, 9–12th grade
Entrance requirement: referral
In-house; small groups; work-study.

Alternative Education Program (1988)
N Summit St, Southington, CT 06489
Michael Donahue, Lead Tch, 203-628-3223
Type: public choice
7 teachers, 25–40 students, mainly at-risk, 9–12th grade
Entrance requirements: in depth application and interview
For current or potential dropouts; small classes; computer, food service, marketing and retail studies.

ROPE at Southington High School (1971)
720 Pleasant St, Southington, CT 06489
Joel Davis, Dir of Secondary Ed, 203-628-0331
Type: public choice
2 teachers, 35 students, mainly at-risk, 10–12th grade
For dropouts and youths working full-time.

Parents Place and Kids Connection
420 Center St, Wallingford, CT 06492
Nancy Freyberg, Dir, 203-265-1253
Type: independent
Spiritually centered; parents, students, teachers develop integrated programs based on collaboration, inclusion, democratic decision-making, peaceful conflict resolution, care for others and the earth.

SAFE/SA Program (1979)
490 Chapel St, Stratford, CT 06497
Wayne Theriault, 203-385-4298
Type: public choice
3 teachers, 40 students, mainly at-risk, 9–12th grade
Conference required.
Work/study; independent study; volunteer work.

Career High School (1983)
21 Wooster Pl, New Haven, CT 06511
Charles J Williams, 203-787-8400
Type: public choice
36 teachers, 385 students, 9–12th grade
Enrollment by lottery
Affiliation: NEASC
Emphasis on business/computers and allied health; internships; partnership with Yale-New Haven Hospital.

Cooperative High School (1980)
800 Dixwell Ave, New Haven, CT 06511
Edward Linehan, Coord, 203-777-5923, -5924
Type: public choice
17 teachers, 240 students, 9–12th grade
Enrollment by lottery
Visual arts; vocal music; creative writing; theatre; dance; ind study; career planning; thematic approach; team teaching.

Educational Center for the Arts/ACES (1972)
55 Audubon St, New Haven, CT 06511
Robert D. Parker, Dir, 203-777-5451
Type: public choice
20 teachers, 165 students, 9–12th grade
Entrance requirements: portfolio, audition
Dance; music; visual arts; theatre; poetry/prose; letter grades
   or narrative evaluations.

High School in the Community (HSC) (1970)
45 Nash St, New Haven, CT 06511
Patricia Morgillo, Facilitator, 203-787-8635,-8636
Type: public choice
13 teachers, 230 students, 9–12th grade
Enrollment by lottery
Team teaching; inter-disciplinary courses; experiential; intensive guidance; peer support group; advocacy policy;
   student/parent/staff policy council.

Betsy Ross Arts Elementary
185 Barnes Ave, New Haven, CT 06513
Brenda Hollard, 203-787-8974
Type: magnet
5–8th grade

Cold Spring School
263 Chapel St, New Haven, CT 06513
Irene Fiss, Director, 203-787-1584
Type: independent; tuition: $6700–8500/yr, scholarships
110 students, ages 5–12, K–6th grade
Multicultural, diverse student body; active participation in
   community affairs; optional long-day program; Spanish
   language and culture program.

Jepson Non-Graded School
375 Quinnipiac Ave, New Haven, CT 06513
Johanna Wilson, 203-787-6077
Type: magnet
Ungraded
Cooperative learning technology.

Children's House Of Montessori
351 Mckinley Ave, New Haven, CT 06515-2026
C Patricia Totalo

Alternative Educational Program-Day Session (1977)
One Circle St, W Haven, CT 06516
Bert Siclari, Dir, 203-932-5701 x36
Type: public choice
3 teachers, 1 assistant, 70 students, mainly at-risk, 10–12th
   grade
Entrance requirements: student and parent interviews
In-house.

Polly T. McCabe Center (1966)
390 Columbus Ave, New Haven, CT 06519
Elizabeth S. Celotto, Coord, 203-787-8758,-6423
Type: public choice
14 teachers, 150–200 students, mainly at-risk, 6–12th grade
For pregnant/parenting students and dropouts; pre- and
   post-natal exercises; social/emotional, medical, and career
   counseling.

Sound School (1981)
60 S Water St, New Haven, CT 06519
George E. Foote, Coord, 203-787-6937
Type: public choice
11 teachers, 200 students, 9–12th grade
Enrollment by lottery
Oceanography; marine biology; ecology; field research; mer-
   chant marine history; boat building/maintenance; naviga-
   tion; boat shop; 66-foot ketch.

West Hills Elementary & Middle School
311 Valley St, New Haven, CT 06519
Janice Romo, 203-787-8613
Type: magnet

K–8th grade
Individualized.

Alternative Placement Program
Amity Regional SD 5, Woodbridge, CT 06525
Patricia A. Varanelli, PPS Dir, 203-397-4819
Type: public at-risk
3 teachers, 1 assistant, 20 students, 9–12th grade
Enrollment restricted to SE students
Behavioral emphasis on social/emotional goals; support
   groups include parents, teachers, and students; contracts.

Free-To-Be-Me! Montessori Early Development Center
PO Box 216, Bridgeport, CT 06601-0216

Park City Alternative (1973)
135 Park Ave, Bridgeport, CT 06602
Cliff Scheinkman, Coord, 203-576-8245
Type: public choice
5 teachers, 60 students, mainly at-risk, 10–12th grade
Entrance requirements: application, interview
At U. Bridgeport; internships; liaison with CT National Bank.

Center for Interim Education (1967)
115 Highland Ave, Bridgeport, CT 06604
Carla Corrigan, Coord, 203-576-7890
Type: public choice
7 teachers, 30–40 students, mainly at-risk, 6–12th grade
Entrance requirements: referral; must be under doctor's care
Located in Wheeler Community Center; education during
   pregnancy; prenatal care; parenting skills.

Bridgeport Montessori Center
210 Congress St, Bridgeport, CT 06604-4007

Paddy Bear Montessori Infant Toddler School
790 Central Ave, Bridgeport, CT 06607-1705

Bridgeport Montessori School
165 Logan St, Bridgeport, CT 06607-1931

Harding Prep (1973)
389 Kossuth St, Bridgeport, CT 06608
Clifford Scheinkman, Coord; Richard Sakowitz, Head Tch, 203-
   576-7178
Type: public choice
5 teachers, 50 students, mainly at-risk, 9–10th grade
Dropout intervention; in Benjamin Franklin Center.

Hall Neighborhood House
52 Green St, Bridgeport, CT 06608-2425
Patricia Howell
Type: Montessori

Trumbull Alternate School (TAS) (1972)
6254 Main St, Trumbull, CT 06611
Anthony Minotti, SE Dir, 203-268-1595
Type: public choice
2 teachers, 15–20 students, mainly at-risk, 9–12th grade
Enrollment restricted to SE students
Progress monitored through daily point system checksheet;
   career ed; work experience.

Alternate Education Program at Ledyard High School
24 Gallup Hill Rd, Ledyard, CT 06634
Anne A. Park, Dir, 203-464-9600
Type: public choice
13 teachers, 85 students, mainly at-risk, ages 16+, 9–12th
   grade
Entrance requirement: referral
In-house; evening diploma program.

Alternate School
201 Birch St, Waterbury, CT 06704-3808
Therese P. Guay, Prin, 203-574-8029
Type: public choice
12 teachers; students mainly at-risk, 7–12th grade
Entrance requirements: referral
Vocational.

Alternative Learning Program at Long River Middle School (1986)
Columbia Ave, Prospect, CT 06712
Holly Norton, Tch or Gary Gombar, Prin, 203-758-4421
Type: public choice
1 teacher, 1 assistant, 10 students, mainly at-risk, 6–8th grade
Entrance requirements: referral, parent conference
In-house; individualized; highly structured; small groups; community service.

Wolcott High School Alternative Program (1985)
457 Bound Line Rd, Wolcott, CT 06716
Joseph DiLeo, SHAPE Coord, 203-879-1434
Type: public choice
1 teacher, 25 students, mainly at-risk, 9–12th grade
Entrance requirements: recommendation, interview
In-house; for potential dropouts; point system rates behavior; credited counsel class.

Beatrice Ayer Patton School
Skyline Ridge Rd, Bridgewater, CT 06752
Mother Catarina Boyer
Type: Montessori

Alternative Education at Mary I. Johnson School
Whittemore Rd, Middlebury, CT 06762
Joan M. Quilter, PhD, Student Serv Dir, 203-758-1729
Type: public choice
4 teachers, 1 assistant, 20 students, mainly at-risk, 9–12th grade
Entrance requirements: referral, PPT recommendations, student contract
Small group structured environment.

Washington Montessori School
16 Church St, New Preston, CT 06777-1599
Patricia Werner

Montessori School Of Northwestern Conneticut
5 Knife Shop Rd, Northfield, CT 06778-2603

Southeast School Center for Alternative Learning (1979)
196 Oak Ave, Torrington, CT 06790
Gary Lambour, Prin, 203-489-2298
Type: public choice
5 teachers, 4 assistants, 35–40 students, mainly at-risk, 7–12th grade
Enrollment restricted to SE students
Intensive, highly motivational; counseling and guidance; voc; career exploration; adventure/experiential ed.

Watertown Alternative School (1977)
324 French St, Watertown, CT 06795
Colleen Spieler, Dept Head, 203-274-5411 x344
Type: public choice
4 teachers, 3 assistants, 42 students, mainly at-risk, 9–12th grade
Entrance requirement: interview
In-house; individualized; mainstream re-entry or graduation.

Nonnewaug Alternative High School Program (1975)
Five Minortown Rd, Woodbury, CT 06795
Nancy Saggese, Alt Dir, 203-263-2186
Type: public at-risk
3 teachers, 20 students, 9–12th grade
Enrollment restricted to at-risk and SE students
In-house; small classes; number and P/F grades; quarterly narrative progress reports.

Carden Education Foundation
(See Resource Appendix)

Alternative Center for Education (1977)
Locust Ave, Danbury, CT 06810
Joseph Pepin, Dir, 203-797-4762
Type: public choice
8 teachers, 90+ students, mainly at-risk, 9–12th grade
Individualized; emphasis on community service.

Anderson Montessori
PO Box 122, Danbury, CT 06813-0122

Alternate Learning Program at Darien High School (1975)
High School Lane, Darien, CT 06820
William Devlin, Team Leader, 203-655-3981 x13
Type: public choice
3 teachers, 25 students, mainly at-risk, 10–12th grade
Entrance requirements: counselor recommendation
In-house; small classes; contracts; class meetings; student ethics council; community service required.

Town & Country Montessori School
Florida Rd Box 127, Georgetown, CT 06829

Community Learning Program at Greenwich High School (1977)
10 Hillside Rd, Greenwich, CT 06830
Jane Carlin, Senior Tch, 203-625-8010, FAX: 203-863-8888
Fairfield County
Type: public choice/at-risk
2 teachers, 25 students, mainly at-risk, ages 15–21, 10–12th grade
Interview required
Governance by teachers, principal; democratic school meeting
Outdoor adventure; responsibility for self, others; college prep; internships; community service; ethnic, economic diversity; multi-aged classes; suburban location.

Montessori School
52 Brookside Dr, Greenwich, CT 06830

The Whitby School
969 Lake Ave, Greenwich, CT 06831-3095
Betsy Benham
Type: Montessori

Mead School (1969)
Box 1517, Greenwich, CT 06836
Norman Barron, 203-637-3800, FAX: 203-637-5917
Fairfield County
Type: independent, non-profit; tuition: $8,000/yr, scholarships
50 teachers, 230 students, ages 6–15
Entrance requirements: interview
Affiliations: CAIS, NAIS
Governance by principal, board
Recognizes various types of intelligence equally; high parental involvement; supports physical, emotional and cognitive; exchanges with inner city schools; no letter grades; non-compulsory class attendance; multi-aged classes; extensive field trips; suburban location; transportation.

Briggs Center for Vocational Arts (BCVA)
350 Main St, Norwalk, CT 06851
John H. Henshall, Dir, 203-847-7137
Type: public choice
20 teachers, 200 students, mainly at-risk
Individualized; self-paced; voc; counseling; teen parent program.

Montessori School of Redding
25 Cross Hwy, Redding, CT 06875
Ingrid Moe

Montessori Academy of Abingdon
5 Taporneck Ct, Ridgefield, CT 06877
Rhonda Kindig

Priyamont Montessori School
21 King Lane, Ridgefield, CT 06877-4404

Ridgefield Montessori School
40 Florida Rd # 185, Ridgefield, CT 06877-6111

Educational Reform Group (1993)
(See Resource Appendix)

Helen Gander Friends Nursery School
317 New Canaan Rd, Wilton, CT 06897
Marjorie Walton, 203-762-5669
Type: Quaker

The Montessori School (1963)
34 Whipple Rd, Wilton, CT 06897
203-834-0440, FAX: 203-761-9386
Non-profit; tuition: $3,736-6,800
11 teachers, 6 assistants, 217 students, ages infant-12
Entrance requirements: must begin before age 3.5 or trans-
    fer from another Montessori school.
Accreditation: AMI; CT AIS
Governance by board
Childcare; suburban location.

Tri-Town Alternative at Middlebrook Middle School (1985)
131 School Rd, Wilton, CT 06897
Robert Feldkircher, Dir, 203-762-8388
Type: public choice
10 teachers, 25 students, mainly at-risk, ages 16+
Evenings for students working full-time.

Wilton Montessori
345 Belden Hill Rd, Wilton, CT 06897

AIMS Program (1991)
61 Adams Ave, Stamford, CT 06902
Teresa Magistro, 203-977-5225
10 students

Learning Counseling Center at Stamford High School
    (1972)
55 Strawberry Hill, Stamford, CT 06902
Dr Michael F. Intrieri, Facilitator, 203-977-4761
Type: public at-risk
1 teacher, 9 assistants; students mainly at-risk, 9-12th grade

In-house intervention and suspension; individual, group
    counseling; career guidance.

LF Community Learning Program
37 Cascade Rd, Stamford, CT 06903
Jane Carlin, 203-329-0869
Type: public choice

Youth Employment & Education Program (1978)
137 Henry St, PO Box 929, Stamford, CT 06904
Kras Hristoff-Carlucci, Dir, 203-323-2171, 359-3524
Type: public
HS
In-house; career planning; job placement; voc; counseling;
    tutoring; teen parent program; P/F grading; contracts.

Executive High School Internship Program
Schewberry Hill Ave, Stamford, CT 06905
Frances L. Howes, Coord, 203-977-4265,-4531
Type: public choice
25-30 students, 11-12th grade
Entrance requirements: counselor, principal,
    recommendation
In-house; semester-long internships in public and private
    organizations; management theory; peer support; P/F
    contracts; career counselors.

The Vicarage School of Montessori
40 London Dr, Hamden, CT 26517
Donna Fronte, Dir, 288-2116
Tuition: $96-160/mo
2 teachers, 8 assistants, 80 students, ages infant-9
Affiliations: IMS, NAEYC
Governance by administrator
Science; geography; musical instruments; community activi-
    ties; childcare; suburban location; transportation; interns
    accepted.

Delaware

Paul M. Hodgson Vocational-Technical High School
2575 Summit Bridge Rd, Newark, DE 19702
Steven Godowsky, Prin, 302-834-0993, FAX: 834-0598
New Castle County
Type: public choice
986 students, ages 13-21, 9-12th grade
Residency required
Affiliation: CES
Governance by board/district
Teacher qualifications: state qualifications/certification
Senior Project: An Exhibition of Achievement; core interdisci-
    plinary teams; school management team; employability
    rating with grades; academic/vocational integration;
    common planning time-school-wide teams; suburban
    location; transportation; interns accepted.

Intensive Learning Center
3401 Green St, Claymont, DE 19703-2000
Type: public at-risk

CACC Montessori School
Little Baltimore & Valley Rds, Hockessin, DE 19707
Dorothy Conte, Dir, 302-239-2917, FAX: 302-239-0432
Non-profit; tuition: variable
5 teachers, 11 assistants, 125 students, mainly international,
    ages infant-6
Affiliation: AMS; accreditation: NAEYC
Governance by an administrator and a board of trustees
Suburban location; interns accepted.

Hockessin Friends Preschool
PO Box 192, Hockessin, DE 19707
Nancy Blockilinger, 302-239-2223
Type: Quaker

Hockessin Montessori School
7200 Lancaster Pike; PO Box 580, Hockessin, DE 19707-0565
Gina Reeves

The Children's House
175 Sawin Lane, Hockessin, DE 19707-9713
Fred and Elinore Barney
Type: Montessori

Christina School District
83 E Main St, Newark, DE 19711
Iris Metts, Supt of Schools
Type: Montessori

Newark Center For Creative Learning (1971)
401 Phillips Ave, Newark, DE 19711
Ann L. Brown, Director, 302-368-7772
New Castle County
Type: independent, non-profit; tuition: $3,951/yr (siblings
    80%), scholarships
11 teachers, 92 students, ages 5-14, K-8th grade
Entrance requirements: visit, accepted if program is
    appropriate
Governance by parent cooperative

Teacher qualifications: none required; parents like ed or grad degree

Oldest students spend week at outdoor skills center, apprentice one afternoon a week at local businesses; many outside visitors; no letter grades; multi-aged classes; extensive field trips; suburban location; interns accepted.

Delaware Home Education Association
11 Bristol Knoll Rd, Newark, DE 19711-2122
302-368-3427

Independence School
1300 Paper Mill Rd, Newark, DE 19711-3408
Type: independent

Alternative Program
1532 Capitol Tr, Newark, DE 19711-5716
Type: public at-risk

Tri-State Homeschoolers Association
PO Box 7193, Newark, DE 19714-7193

Elementary Workshop (1971)
502 Pine St, Wilmington, DE 19801
Lillian A. Shah, Dir, 302-656-1498, FAX: 302-656-1485
Type: Montessori, non-profit; tuition: $4,100/yr, scholarships
10 teachers, 105 students, ages 3-12
Entrance requirement: interview
Affiliation: AMS
Governance by principal, teachers, board
Model school; active parent co-op; scholarship program insures multi-racial/cultural student population; no letter grades; multi-aged classes; urban location; interns accepted.

Red Clay Consolidated School District
1400 Washington St, Wilmington, DE 19801
Patricia Reinbold
Type: Montessori

People's Settlement Preschool
408 E 8th St, Wilmington, DE 19801-3699
Type: independent

Willmington Friends School
101 School Rd, Wilmington, DE 19803
Carol Ramsey, 302-576-2900
Type: Quaker

Pilot School, Inc (1957)
100 Garden of Eden Rd, Wilmington, DE 19803-1599
Doris LeStourgeon, Dir, 302-478-1740, FAX: 302-478-1746
New Castle County
Type: independent, non-profit; tuition: $11,524/yr, scholarships
37 teachers, 159 students mainly at-risk, ages 5-14, ungraded
For average or above students with learning problems; testing series required
Affiliations: NAIS, DAIS, NAPSEC, CEC
Governance by principal and board
Teacher qualifications: degree
Individualized; psychologist; language therapist; music therapist; educational diagnostician; eclectic approach; no letter grades; suburban location; interns accepted.

Educational Enrichment Center, Inc
730 Halstead Rd, Wilmington, DE 19803-2228
Type: independent

Montessori Learning Centre
2313 Concord Park, Wilmington, DE 19803-2911
Gilda De Berardinis

Oakwood Clonlara School
228 Waverly Rd, Wilmington, DE 19803-3135
Type: independent

Design-A-Study
(See Resource Appendix)

The Children's House, Inc (1974)
2400 W 17th St, Wilmington, DE 19806
Elinore and Frederick Barney, Owners, 302-429-9244
Type: Montessori, tuition: $3,130-3,990/yr
3 teachers, 3 assistants, 41 students, ages Infant-9
Affiliations: AMS, NKAD, DAEYC
Governance by administrator, parent cooperative
Safe setting; childcare; urban location; interns accepted.

Children's House
5 Yale Rd/Cooper Farm, Wilmington, DE 19808-2205
Ardeth Savage
Type: Montessori

EUREKA! Learning Community, Inc
6 Ridgewood Circle, Wilmington, DE 19809-2813
Type: independent

Wilmington Montessori School
1400 Harvey Rd, Wilmington, DE 19810-4200
Marie Dugan

Alfred I. Du Pont Institute
PO Box 269, Wilmington, DE 19899-0269
Type: public at-risk

Early Childhood Laboratory School
1200 N Du Pont Hwy, Dover, DE 19901-2277
Type: independent

The Little School, Inc
308 N Queen St, Dover, DE 19901-3026
Type: independent

Dover Montessori Country Day School
1 Dover Air Park, Dover, DE 19901-9236

Rose Valley School
160 Rose Valley Rd, Dover, DE 19901-9713
Type: independent

Caesar Rodney Junior High Intensive Learning Center
25 E Camden-Wyoming Ave, Camden-Wyoming, DE 19934

Simpson Elementary Intensive Learning Center
5 Old North Rd, Camden-Wyoming, DE 19934-1247
Type: public at-risk

Joshua's Choice School
RD 1, Box 418, Ellendale, DE 19941-9617
Type: independent

King's Kids Academy
RD #5, Gox 130, Georgetown, DE 19947-9426
Type: independent

Community Learning Institute, Inc
RD #1, Box 307-P, Hartly, DE 19953-9511
Type: independent

The Child Craft Company
1307 Laurel Hwy, Seaford, DE 19973
Type: independent

The Idea Patch
451 Clayton Blvd, Smyma, DE 19977-1207
Type: independent

Florida

Gibbs High School
850 34 St S, St Petersburg, FL 22711
Barbara Shorter, 813-893-5452
Type: magnet
9–12th grade
Performing arts.

Amelia Island Montessori (1974)
Amelia Island Plantation, Amelia Island, FL 32034
Dr Jim Morgan, Adm, 904-261-6610
Non-profit; tuition: $1,275-3,320/yr
6 teachers, 6 assistants, 124 students, ages infant-9
Affiliation: AMS; accreditation: FLKC
Governance by a board of trustees
Heavily wooded area; language, music, arts and crafts;
childcare; suburban location.

Nassau Halfway House
1781 Lisa Ave, Fernandina Beach, FL 32034-2058
Vernon Ferguson, 904-261-6141
Type: public at-risk

Douglass Center
617 Ontario Ave SW, Live Oak, FL 32060-2947
Nancy Roberts, 904-364-2900
Type: public at-risk

Citizen's High School
188 College Dr, Box 1929, Orange Park, FL 32067-1929
904-276-1700
Type: public choice

Montessori School of Ormond Beach
50 Coolidge Ave, Ormond Beach, FL 32074
Susie White

Discovery School
413 Ponte Vedra Blvd, Pontevedra Beach, FL 32082
Suzy Dalt
Type: Montessori

Evelyn Hamblen Dropout Center
16 Isabel St, St Augustine, FL 32095-4002
Type: public at-risk

Stonesoup School (1979)
Star Rt 1, Box 127, Crescent City, FL 32112
Deborah Rogers, 904-698-2516
Type: independent, boarding, non-profit; tuition: $700/mo,
scholarships
3 teachers, 10 students, ages 8-18,-12th grade
Entrance requirements: interview, telephone or in person
Affiliation: NCACS
Governance by democratic school meeting
Free school approach to learning and living; freedom tempered with responsibility and independence, cooperation;
encourages self-reliance, character development; self
paced tutorials; on 50 acres with lake; no letter grades;
non-compulsory class attendance; multi-aged classes;
extensive field trips; rural location; interns accepted.

Riverview Learning Center
801 N Wild Olive Ave, Daytona Beach, FL 32118-3726
Michael A. Osborne, 904-255-3201

Florida Parent Education Association
Rt 4, PO Box 60-H, Interlachen, FL 32148
904-684-4940

Seaside Montessori School
264 Division St, Ormond Beach, FL 32174-6208

Halifax Montessori School
51 Coolidge Ave, Ormond Beach, FL 32174-6247

Pierson Montessori Center (1990)
592 S Volusia Ave, Pierson, FL 32180
David Cipolloni, 904-749-4420, FAX: 904-749-1002
Non-profit; tuition: $60-70/wk
3 teachers, 20 assistants, 80 students, mainly International,
ages infant-6
Affiliations: AMS, Comite de Hispano
Governance by administrator
Primarily serving Mexican farmworker community; bilingual
curriculum; rural location; interns accepted.

Fishweir Elementary
3977 Herschel St, Jacksonville, FL 32205
Josephine Fiveash, 904-389-2230
Type: magnet
K–5th grade
Creative arts.

Normandy Elementary
6803 Arques Rd, Jacksonville, FL 32205
Anoola Lott, 904-781-0511
Type: magnet
Student ages 4+,-5th grade
Community outreach.

J. Allen Axsen Elementary
1221 E 16th St, Jacksonville, FL 32206
Janice Hunter, 904-353-7225
Type: magnet
K–5th grade
Montessori.

Mattie V. Rutherford Alternative Education Center
1514 Hubbard St, Jacksonville, FL 32206-4536
Lee Marshall, 904-791-9688
Type: public at-risk

Duval County Public Schools
1701 Prudential Dr, Jacksonville, FL 32207
Betty White
Type: Montessori

Pine Forest Elementary
3929 Grandt Rd, Jacksonville, FL 32207
Margaret McCaughey, 904-398-7181
Type: magnet
K–5th grade
Performing arts.

Martin Luther King Elementary
8801 Lake Placid Dr, Jacksonville, FL 32208
Constance Hall, 904-768-8239
Type: magnet
K–5th grade
Gifted and talented; college prep.

James Weldon Johnson Middle School
1840 W 9th St, Jacksonville, FL 32209
Mary Brown, 904-630-6640
Type: magnet
6-8th grade
Gifted and talented.

Stanton College Prep High School
1149 W 13th St, Jacksonville, FL 32209
Jerry Gugel, 904-630-6760
Type: magnet
9-12th grade
Gifted and talented.

A Child's Place (1988)
3718 Salisbury Rd/3105 Southside Blvd, Jacksonville, FL 32216
Catherine Selhoust, 904-733-5797
Type: Montessori; tuition: $370-470
94 students, ages infant-6
Affiliations: NAMTA, N FL MTA; accreditation: NAEYC
Governance by administrator
Teacher qualifications: AMS, AMI, SNMC
Serves children of professional working parents; involved with local corporate community; Reed Grants for specific program expansion; childcare; urban location; interns accepted.

Hogan Spring Glen Elementary
6736 Beach Blvd, Jacksonville, FL 32216
Susan Schandelmaker, 904-725-1044
Type: magnet
K-5th grade
Community outreach.

San Mateo Elementary
600 Baisden Rd, Jacksonville, FL 32218
Marilyn Myrick, 904-757-4766
Type: magnet
K-5th grade
Gifted and talented.

Jacksonville Marine Institute
13375 Beach Blvd, Jacksonville, FL 32224
William J.Knigh, Exec Dir, 904-223-1121
Type: public at-risk

Discovery Montessori School (1990)
485 6th Ave N, Jacksonville Beach, FL 32233
Karin Clark, Adm, 904-247-4577
Non-profit; tuition: $930/3200
3 teachers, 3 assistants, 53 students, ages infant-toddler & 6-9
Montessori preschool required for elem students
Affiliation: AMS
Governance by board of directors
Neighborhood setting; outstanding materials; Atlantic Ocean beach nearby; childcare; suburban location.

Oakwood Country Day
PO Box 23950, Jacksonville, FL 32241-3950
Type: Montessori

Montessori Tides (1986)
533 2nd Ave N, Jacksonville Beach, FL 32250
Kathy Graham, Dir, 904-241-1139
Tuition: $1,820/yr
2 teachers, 4 assistants, 54 students, ages 3-6
Entrance requirements: toilet trained
Affiliation: AMS; accreditation: FKC
Governance by administrator
Quiet beach location; suburban location; interns accepted.

Crown Point Elementary
3800 Crown Point Rd, Jacksonville, FL 32257
Sherry Adams, 904-262-0960
Type: magnet
K-5th grade
Creative and expressive arts.

Schluck School
3221 Apalachee Pkwy, Tallahassee, FL 32301
Carolyn Schluck

Teenage Parent Program (1973)
438 W Brevard St, Tallahassee, FL 32301
Joan Wimberly, Prog Dir, 904-487-2525, FAX: 922-8483
Leon County
Type: public choice
10 teachers, 120 students, mainly at-risk, ages 13-19, 6-12th grade
No residency requirement
Governance by teachers, principal, board
Teacher qualifications: certification
Nursery; clinic; prenatal care; urban location; interns accepted.

Hurricane Island Outward Bound (1964)
Tallahassee, FL 32303
J. M. Howard, Staff Specialist, 904-224-2752, FAX: 904-922-6721
Type: independent, non-profit
10 teachers, 1,000 students, mainly at-risk, ages 13-18, 6-12th grade
Entrance by referral from FL HRS
Governance by board, administrators, staff specialists, director
Teacher qualifications: FL DE requirements, 1st aid, experience in alternative setting
One of four programs nationally; wilderness, urban, service expeditions; credit for peer counseling, outdoor ed, life mgmt skills, environmental science, reading, history; 28-80 day courses; multi-aged classes; rural location.

Magnolia School
2705 W Thorpe St, Tallahassee, FL 32303
Susan Smith, 904-385-3834
Type: independent; scholarships
35-40 students, ages 5-11

School for Applied Individualized Learning (SAIL) (1975)
725 N Macomb St, Tallahassee, FL 32303
Rosanne Wood, 904-488-2468, FAX: 904-922-8483
Leon County
Type: public choice; scholarships
17 teachers, 218 students, ages 14-19, 9-12th grade
Affiliation: FAASE
Governance by democratic school meeting
Teacher qualifications: FL certification
Environmental science magnet program; Spanish/Latin American history; computer applications; video productions; student court; college dual enrollment; multi-aged classes; extensive field trips; interns accepted.

Montessori School Of Tallahassee
1212 Stone Rd, Tallahassee, FL 32303-3626

Children's House Montessori School
5072 Easy St, Tallahassee, FL 32303-7912

Florida Association for Schools at Home
1000 Devil's Dip, Tallahassee, FL 32308
904-878-2793

Full Flower Education Center (1987)
1816 Mahan Dr, Box 2493, Tallahassee, FL 32308
Irwin Friedman, Director, 904-878-8476
Type: independent, non-profit
4 teachers, 27 students, ages 5-13, K-8th grade
Enrollment restricted to students who want to be in an environment that allows freedom
Governance by teachers and principal
Teacher qualifications: love to teach and love children
Intent is to establish a safe environment in which students discover what they truly love to do with their lives; no letter grades; multi-aged classes; extensive field trips; suburban location; interns accepted.

Huckleberry School
RR 3, Box 705A, Tallahassee, FL 32308
Laura Wharton
Type: independent

Montessori Cooperative Early School
2521 Mahan Dr, Tallahassee, FL 32308-5405

Grassroots Free School (1972)
2458 Grassroots Way, Tallahassee, FL 32311-9012
Patrick Seery, Coord, 904-656-3629
Type: independent, non-profit; tuition: sliding scale,
    scholarships
6 teachers, 40 students, ages 5-18
Affiliations: NCACS, AERO
Governance by democratic school meeting & parent
    cooperative
Based on Summerhill model; 20 min from Capitol; theater
    productions; whole language; integrated, interest-based
    curricula; independent study; cooperative learning; no
    letter grades; non-compulsory class attendance; multi-
    aged classes; extensive field trips; rural location; interns
    accepted.

A. D. Harris (1977)
819 E 11th St, Panama, FL 32401
Anita Goodman, Prin, 904-872-4590
Bay County
Type: public at-risk
24 teachers, 300 students, ages 12-21, 6-12th grade
Entrance requirements: referral, residency; no SE
Governance by teachers, principal, board
Teacher qualifications: certification
Performance based; work experience; small classes; school-
    within-a-school; extensive field trips; transportation;
    interns accepted.

Dozier School
Hwy 276, Marianna, FL 32446-8955
Billy Baxter, 904-482-9181
Type: public at-risk

Creative Learning Center
3151 Hyde Park, Pensacola, FL 32503
Mary Lee Porter
Type: Montessori

Petree Pre-K Center
916 E Fairfield Dr, Pensacola, FL 32503-2817
Type: Montessori

O.J. Semmes Elementary School
1250 E Texar Dr, Pensacola, FL 32503-4073
Type: Montessori

Spencer Bibbs Elementary School
2005 N 6th Ave, Pensacola, FL 32503-4521
Gena Keszthelyi
Type: Montessori

Learning Skills Center (1985)
5000 W Mobile Hwy, Pensacola, FL 32506
Hetty Krucke, 904-457-1627
Type: independent, home-based, non-profit; cost: $275/mo,
    scholarships
5 teachers, 35 students, mainly at-risk, ages 10-18, 4-12th
    grade
Entrance requirements: no prior juvenile delinquency record
Governance by board
Totally individualized instruction; grades by request; accred-
    ited HS; teachers and students work on having a relation-
    ship that counts in their lives; extensive field trips;
    suburban location.

Montessori Early School (1977)
20 Jamison St/1010 N 12th Ave, Pensacola, FL 32507
Mary Gaudet, Adm, 904-456-8735
Tuition: $1,930-2,880/yr

7 teachers, 8 assistants, 155 students, ages infant-12
Affiliation: AMS
Governance by co-owners and teachers
Accomodates students with special needs; childcare; subur-
    ban location; interns accepted.

Florida Parent Education Associaton
9245 Woodrun Rd, Pensacola, FL 32514
Dr. Larry Walker

A BEKA Correspondence School
(See Resource Appendix)

West Florida Home Education Support League
PO Box 11720, Pensacola, FL 32524
904-477-0333

Montessori Children's House
RR 3 Box 476, Crestview, FL 32536

Montessori Learning Center of Ft Walton
204 Hospital Dr NE, Ft Walton Beach, FL 32548-5067

Montessori Children's Schoolhouse
8 Pfeiffer St, Gulf Breeze, FL 32561-4410
Karen Blake

Waldorf School of Gainesville (1979)
921 SW Depot Ave, Gainesville, FL 32601
Kathleen Katz, Adm, 904-375-6291
Non-profit; tuition: $2,300-3,200/yr, scholarships
10 teachers, 60 students, ages 3-10, 1-4th grade
Governance by faculty and board
German, Spanish; ESL; after school care; festivals; urban
    location.

Alachua County Home Schoolers
1929 NW 42nd Pl, Gainesville, FL 32605
Kim Hooie, 904-372-8260

Flowers Montessori School
3111 NW 31st Ave, Gainesville, FL 32605-2125

Millhopper Montessori (1977)
8505 NW 39th Ave, Gainesville, FL 32606
Christine Miller, 904-375-6773
Tuition: $290-350/mo
4 teachers, 4 assistants, 940 students, ages infant-9
Accreditations: FL CIS, FL KC
Governance by administrator
State of the art facility; childcare; suburban location; interns
    accepted.

Community Home School
6715 NW 63rd Ave, Ocala, FL 32606
Bob & Nora Whitcomb

Alachua Home School Group
512 Forest St, Alachua, FL 32615
904-462-3930

Hogtown Homeschoolers
180 SW 21-A Rd, Archer, FL 32618
904-622-9735

Jordan Glen School (1974)
12425 SW 154th St, Archer, FL 32618
Jeff Davis, Director, 904-495-2728
Alachua County
Type: independent; tuition: $2700/yr, scholarships
8 teachers, 84 students, ages 5-14, K-8th grade
Governance by board made up of parents, teachers, principal
Teacher qualifications: education degree, masters in some
    areas
Values individual differences; believes that the joy of living
    and love of learning need never be separated; encourages
    process of exploration and discovery; meaningful academic
    study; multi-aged classes; suburban location; interns
    accepted.

Family Learning Center
(See Resource Appendix)

Homeschooling Today
(See Resource Appendix)

ABCD
PO Box 9093, Ocala, FL 32670
904-694-2223

Families For Excellence
3441 S Pine Ave #29, Ocala, FL 32671
LeRae McBroom

Florida Parent Education Association
2901 SW 41st St, Ocala, FL 32674
Gary Regoli, Director

Altamonte Montessori School
482 Osceola St, Altamonte Springs, FL 32701-7845
Muriel Owens

Grace Home Schoolers
115 Wolf Trail, Casselberry, FL 32707
407-695-3270
Seminole County

School Within A School
Apopka HS, 555 W Martin St, Apopka, FL 32712
Type: public

Euclid Avenue Learning Center
409 W Euclid Ave, Deland, FL 32720-6855
Michael A. Osborne, 904-734-2189
Type: public at-risk

Children's House
509 E Pennsylvania Ave, Deland, FL 32724-3616
Type: Montessori

Twinkle Stars Montessori School
238 S Amelia Ave, Deland, FL 32724-5914
Virginia Harris-Myrie

Deltona Group
350 Blythville Ave, Deltona, FL 32725
407-860-2318
Volusia County
Type: home-based

Family Centered Learning of Central Florida
1091 Ridge Rd, Longwood, FL 32725
407-332-8502
Seminole County
Type: home-based

North Lake Education Center (1990)
42630 State Rd 19, Altoona, FL 32726
Dorothy McCoo, Prin, 904-669-7979
Lake County
Type: public at-risk
10 teachers, 130 students, ages 10–14, 6-8th grade
Residency required
Governance by teachers and principal
Teacher qualifications: FL certification
Students may progress to the next teacher and unit every 21
   days; multi-aged classes; rural location; transportation;
   interns accepted.

Maitland Preparatory
1221 Trinity Woods Ln, Maitland, FL 32751-3159
Type: Montessori

Wymore Career Education Center
100 E Kennedy Blvd, Eatonville, FL 32751-5348
407-644-7518
Type: public choice

La-Amistad
201 Alpine Dr, Maitland, FL 32751-6505
Iris Anderson, 407-647-0660
Type: public at-risk

Family Learning Exchange
2020 Turpentine Rd, Mims, FL 32754
Type: home-based

Chuluota First Home Schoolers
2060 Miracle Ln, Chuluota, FL 32766
305-366-3270
Sanford County

Crooms School of Choice
2200 W 13th St, Sanford, FL 32771-1636
407-322-6022
Type: public choice

Lake Fern Montessori Academy (1981)
257 Aquinaldo Ave, Titusville, FL 32780
Roxanne L. Richards, 407-268-3365
Tuition: $115/220/230/mo
1 teacher, 4 assistants, 71 students, ages 3–9
Entrance requirement: toilet trained
Affiliations: NAMTA, AMS
Governance by an administrator
Teacher qualifications: FL certification
2.5 acres of natural habitat; nature studies; vegetable garden;
   fruit trees and plants; childcare; urban location; interns
   accepted.

HETE: Home Educators Teaching for Eternity
7853 Clarcona Ocoee Rd, Orlando, FL 32792
407-578-6251

Parkland Home Educators
517 Roughbeard Rd, Winter Park, FL 32792
Beth Girard, Co-Dir, 407-657-7560
Polk County
50+ families registered; field trips; math/science fair; spelling
   bee; family game night; variety show; worlds fair; monthly
   parent meetings.

YES Program at Astronaut High School
800 War Eagle Blvd, Titusville, FL 32796-2398
Sherry M Johnson, Dir, 407-264-3000
Type: public at-risk
3 teachers, 45 students, ages 16+, 10–12th grade
Competency-based; CAI.

Beeman Park Montessori School
2300 Ridge Ave, Orlando, FL 32803-1636

Montessori Children's House of St James
505 E Ridgewood St, Orlando, FL 32803-5620

Florida at Home
(See Resource Appendix)

Smith Alternative Center
434 Tampa Ave, Bldg 200, Orlando, FL 32805-1217
Henry Wright, 407-849-3244
Type: public at-risk

Paramore Center
445 S Paramore Ave, Orlando, FL 32805-2662
Henry Wright, 407-246-2526
Type: public at-risk

Village School
1718 E Michigan St, Orlando, FL 32806-4935
Henry Wright, 407-836-7627
Type: public at-risk

Montessori Casa dei Bambini
2500 S Bumby Ave, Orlando, FL 32806-5013

Beta School
4680 Lake Underhill Rd, Orlando, FL 32807-1182
Henry Wright, 407-277-1942
Type: public at-risk

Orange House Learning Center
5275 S Orange Blossom Tr, Orlando, FL 32809
Henry Wright, 407-849-3244
Type: public at-risk

Discovery Days Montessori
5304 Alpha Dr # 10, Orlando, FL 32810-4422

Plaza Educational Center
6520 Carrier Dr, Orlando, FL 32819
Henry Wright
Type: public at-risk

Glenbeigh Center
7450 Sandlake Commons Blvd, Orlando, FL 32819-8033
Henry Wright, 407-647-0660
Type: public at-risk

Oak Leaf Alternative School
6601 Central Florida Pkwy, Orlando, FL 32821-8091
407-345-5000
Type: public at-risk

Alpha Center
8433 Caetwyler, Orlando, FL 32827-5016
Henry Wright, 407-859-4780
Type: public at-risk

Family Training Fellowship
6828 W Livingston, Orlando, FL 32835
407-332-8502
Type: home-based

Buena Vista Academy (1990)
11601 Ruby Lake Rd, Orlando, FL 32836
Jean Cross, Adm, 407-238-0014
Non-profit; tuition: $3,100/yr
61 students, mainly International, ages 6–15
Governance by administrator, parent cooperative, board
Fosters creative thinking and learning; suburban location.

Montessori World School (1981)
11693 Ruby Lake Dr, Orlando, FL 32836
W. Nora Yee, Adm, 407-239-6027
Tuition: 1,800/3,375/yr
6 teachers, 3 assistants, 106 students, ages 3–6
Affiliations: AMS, NAMTA
Governance by administrator
Quiet wooded setting; field trips to area attractions; child-
    care; suburban location; interns accepted.

Florida Parent Educators Association (1984)
406 Dartmouth Ave, Melbourne, FL 32901
Monte F. Hancock, MS, Chair, 407-723-1714
Brevard County
4,000 member families.

Children's House of Montessori (1986)
1340 Wickham Rd S, W Melbourne, FL 32904
Sue King, 404-724-2740, FAX: 407-725-7463
Tuition: $170/220/mo
1 teacher, 1 assistant; students mainly International, ages 3–6
Entrance requirements: age 3
Governance by administrator
Interns accepted.

Country Day Montessori School
365 East Dr, Indian Harbor Beach, FL 32937
Cynthia Thomas

Especially for Children
1230 Banana River Dr, Indian Harbor Beach, FL 32937-4162
Cynthia Thomas
Type: Montessori

Suntree Montessori School
2990 Business Center Blvd, Melbourne, FL 32940
Cynthia Thomas

Rockledge Montessori School
3000 S Fistie, Rockledge, FL 32940
Cynthia Thomas

Montessori School of Frederick
210 Carib Dr, Merritt Island, FL 32952-3647

Island Montessori School
655 Oleander St, Merritt Island, FL 32952-3747

Vero Beach Support Group
1016 21st Ct, Vero Beach, FL 32960
407-562-4380
Indian River County
Type: home-based

J.W. Johnson School
735 W 23rd St, Hialeah, FL 33010-2141
Ms J Molina
Type: Montessori

Montessori Children's House of Miami Lakes
6381 Miami Lakeway NE, Miami Lakes, FL 33014
Charlene Thibodeau

Joella C. Good Elementary
6350 NW 188 Tr, Miami, FL 33015
Rosemarie Jaworski, 305-625-2008
Type: magnet
Student ages 4+,–K
Montessori.

Apple Tree Montessori
7755 NW 178th St, Miami, FL 33015-3859
Susan Levine

Sunrise Montessori Holistic School
2360 W 68th St # 10, Hialeah, FL 33016-5501
Armando Elias

Rainbow Montessori School
3351 N SR 7, Hollywood, FL 33021-2708
Gila Burke

Hollywood Hills Private School
5516 Hollywood Blvd, Hollywood, FL 33021-6458
Type: Montessori

Hilltop Montessori Elementary
2921 SW 56th Ave, Hollywood, FL 33023-5301

Avocado Elementary
16969 SW 294 St, Homestead, FL 33030
Carol S. Bernstein, 305-247-4942
Dade County
Type: magnet
K-2nd grade
Gifted program.

Kingswood Montessori Academy (1968)
20130 SW 304th St, Homestead, FL 33030
Elizabeth Calabrese, 305-248-2308, FAX: same
Tuition: $2,300/3,300/3,700/yr
4 teachers, 6 assistants, 106 students, ages infant-12
Affiliation: Dade ANS; accreditation: AISFL
Governance by an administrator
5 wooded acres in the Redlands; childcare; rural location;
    interns accepted.

Naranja Elementary School
13990 SW 264 St, Naranja, FL 33032
Johanna Teague, 305-258-3401
Dade County
Type: magnet
4-5th grade
Gifted program.

Ocean Reef Schoolhouse
Plaza Bldg Box B-108, 31 Ocean Reef Dr, Key Largo, FL 33037
Type: Montessori

Montessori Childrens House
99341 Overseas Hwy, Key Largo, FL 33037-4246
Carol Hilton

Montessori Children's School of Key West, Inc
1214 Varela St, Key West, FL 33040-3314
Elizabeth Shewan

Nathan Young School
14120 NW 24th Ave, Opa Locka, FL 33054
Ms E Pace
Type: Montessori

Opa-Locka Elementary
600 Ahmad St, Opa-Locka, FL 33054
Dr S. Frank McKoy, 305-688-4605
Type: magnet
2-5th grade
Gifted program.

Rainbow Park Elementary
15355 NW 19 Ave, Opa-Locka, FL 33054
Henry Haddon, 305-688-4631
Type: magnet
4-6th grade
Expressive arts.

Golden Glades School
16520 NW 28th Ave, Opa Locka, FL 33054-6493
Ms A Jackson
Type: Montessori

Parkway Middle School
2349 NW 175 St, Miami, FL 33055
Robert Edwards, 305-624-9613
Type: magnet
7-8th grade
Humanities.

North Carol City Elementary
19010 NW 37 Ave, Opa-Locka, FL 33056
Barbara Hawkins, 305-624-2615
Dade County
Type: magnet
K-6th grade
Gifted program.

Off Campus Alternative Programs
1400 NE 6th St #8, Pompano Beach, FL 33060-6536
Charles Hilgenfeldt, 305-786-7818
Type: public at-risk

North Broward School
3701 NE 22nd Ave, Lighthouse Point, FL 33064-3934
Type: Montessori

Coral Springs Montessori Preschool (1991)
11380 W Sample Rd, Coral Springs, FL 33065
John Freda, Dir, 305-344-0027
3 teachers, 3 assistants, 68 students, mainly international,
   ages 3-6
Affiliation: AMS
Interns accepted.

The Learning Experience of Coral Springs
3811 Coral Springs Dr, Coral Springs, FL 33065-2399
Type: Montessori

Dade County Division Of Magnet Schools/Programs
1444 Biscayne Blvd #303, Miami, FL 33132
Miriam Stoudt

New World School of Arts
300 NE 2 Ave, Miami, FL 33132

Dr Mandy Offerle, 305-237-3135
Type: magnet
10-12th grade

Southern Montessori Institute
3060 Orange St, Coconut Grove, FL 33133
Type: Montessori teacher education

Charles R. Drew Elementary
1775 NW 60 St, Miami, FL 33133
Frederick Morley, 305-624-1495
Type: magnet
4-6th grade
Expressive arts.

Crestview Elementary
2201 NW 187 St, Opa-Locka, FL 33133
Jill Witlin, 305-624-1395
Dade County
Type: magnet
1-5th grade
Writing.

Carrollton School of the Sacred Heart
3747 Main Hwy, Miami, FL 33133-5907
Type: Montessori

Sheandoah School
1023 SW 21st Ave, Miami, FL 33135-5049
Ms M Elias
Type: Montessori

Phyllis Wheatley School
1801 NW 1st Pl, Miami, FL 33136-1795
Ms D Pascal
Type: Montessori

Design & Architecture High School
4001 NE 2 Ave, Miami, FL 33137
Jacq. Hinchey-Sipes, 305-573-7135
Type: magnet
7-12th grade

Montessori School of Miami Beach
7141 Indian Creek Dr, Miami Beach, FL 33141-3030

Allapattah Middle School
1331 NW 46 St, Miami, FL 33142
Maria Jerkins, 305-634-9787
Type: magnet
6-8th grade
Media arts.

Charles Drew Middle School
1801 NW 60 St, Miami, FL 33142
Gail Senita, 305-633-6057
Type: magnet
7-8th grade
Visual and performing arts.

Olinda Elementary
5536 NW 2l Ave, Miami, FL 33142
Lenora Smith, 305-633-0308
Dade County
Type: magnet
1-6th grade
Gifted program.

Orchard Villa School
5720 NW 13th Ave, Miami, FL 33142-2699
Ms C McCalla
Type: Montessori

Alexander School, Inc
6050 SW 57th Ave, Miami, FL 33143
James R. McGhee, Adm, 305-665-6274, FAX: 305-665-7726
Type: Montessori; tuition: $3,850-7,310/yr
17 teachers, 30 assistants, 477 students, mainly International,
   ages infant-12

Entrance requirements: performance and maturity test
Accreditations: FCIS, FKC, AISF, AMS
Governance by administrator
State of the art computer lab; childcare; suburban location; near Bob; transportation; interns accepted.

Ludlam Elementary
6639 SW 74 St, S Miami, FL 33143
Donald Schwartz, 305-667-5551
Type: magnet
K-6th grade
Gifted program.

South Miami Elementary
6800 SW 60 St, S Miami, FL 33143
Rexford Darrow, 305-667-8847
Type: magnet
4-6th grade
Expressive arts.

South Miami Middle School
6750 SW 60 St, S Miami, FL 33143
Ms Ivery or Ms Valdez, 305-661-3481
Type: magnet
7-9th grade
Center for the arts.

The Children's House
7701 SW 76th Ave, Miami, FL 33143-4125
Susan Menendez
Type: Montessori

Sunset Montessori School
7430 Sunset Dr, Miami, FL 33143-4130
Janet Haigney

Lillie C Evans (1990)
1891 NW 75th St, Miami, FL 33147
Geraldine W. Tisdol, 305-691-4973
Type: public choice Montessori
2 teachers, 2 assistants, 56 students, mainly at-risk, ages 3-9
Entrance requirement: test scores
Governance by a teachers, administrators, democratic school meeting
Urban location; interns accepted.

St Christopher's Montessori School
95 Harbor Dr, Key Biscayne, FL 33149-1499
Catherine Hubbell

Miami Northwestern High School
7007 NW 12 Ave, Miami, FL 33150
Dr James Monroe, 305-836-0991
Type: magnet
9-12th grade
Visual and performing arts.

Martin Luther King School
7124 NW 12th Ave, Miami, FL 33150-3693
Ms B Nixon
Type: Montessori

Holmes School
1175 NW 67th St, Miami, FL 33150-4198
Ms J Goa
Type: Montessori

Everglades Elementary
8375 SW 16 St, Miami, FL 33155
Dr Stanley Dansky, 305-264-4154
Type: magnet
K-5th grade
Gifted program.

South Miami High School
6856 SW 53 St, Miami, FL 33155
Judith Weiner, 305-666-5871
Type: magnet

9-12th grade
Media arts.

Wagner Montessori School (1989)
6330 SW 40th St, Miami, FL 33155
Andrew K. Wagner, Adm, 305-661-6434, FAX: 305-663-9274
Tuition: $2,965/2,965/4,995/yr
3 teachers, 4 assistants, 71 students, ages infant-9
Affiliations: AMS, NAEYC
Governance by an administrator
CAI; childcare; suburban location; interns accepted.

Killian Montessori School
8640 SW 112th St, Miami, FL 33156-4325
Janice Kimrey

Perrine Elementary
8851 SW 168 St, Perrine, FL 33157
Rosemary Fuller, 305-235-2442
Dade County
Type: magnet
K-4th grade
Creative arts.

R.R. Moton Elementary
l8050 Homestead Ave, Perrine, FL 33157
Yvonne Hinson, 305-235-3612
Dade County
Type: magnet
5-6th grade
Expressive arts.

Winhold Montessori School
17700 Old Cutler Rd, Miami, FL 33157-6326
Eleanor Winhold

Star Bright Child Development
1253 NE 112th St, Miami, FL 33161
Type: Montessori

Barry University
11300 NE 2nd Ave, Miami Shores, FL 33161
Dr Ijya C. Tulloss, Dir, 305-899-3714, FAX: 899-3630
Type: higher education
Affiliation: AMS; accreditation: MACTE
Governance by board of trustees
Master's awarded with teaching certificate; computer lab; bookstore.

Von Wedel Montessori School (1968)
11820 NE 13th Ave, N Miami, FL 33161
R. A. or Tamara Von Wedel, 305-893-9876
Tuition: $2,350-3,700/yr
4 teachers, 1 assistant; student ages 3-9
Accreditation: AMS
Governance by an administrator
Traditional Montessori program; 2 acres of greenery; swimming pool; 2 large preschool classrooms; childcare; no letter grades; suburban location; interns accepted.

Montessori Children's House
9718 Bird Rd, Miami, FL 33165-4032

Scotts Lake Montessori Magnet (1988)
1160 NW 175th St, Miami, FL 33169
Dr Linda Levene, Head Tch; Christell Rocach, Prin, 305-624-1493, FAX: 305-625-2567
18 teachers, 3 assistants, 265 students, mainly international, ages 4-11
Entrance requirement: age 4 by Sept 1st
Governance by an administrator
Teacher qualifications: FL certification
Childcare; transportation; interns accepted.

Pine Villa Elementary
21799 SW 117 Ct, Goulds, FL 33170
Melvin Dennis, 305-258-5366
Type: magnet

Student ages 4+,-4th grade
Montessori.

Mays Middle School
11700 Hainlin Mill Dr, Miami, FL 33170
Robert Stinson, 305-233-2300
Type: magnet
6-8th grade
Visual and performing arts; humanities.

F.C. Martin Elementary
14250 Boggs Dr, Richmond Hghts, FL 33176
Ossie Hollis, 305-238-3688
Type: magnet
5-6th grade
Gifted program.

Caribbean Elementary
11990 SW 200 St, Miami, FL 33177
Carmen Suarez, 305-233-7131
Type: magnet
K-4th grade
Gifted program.

Montessori School Of Kendall
11860 SW 80th St, Miami, FL 33183-4821

Florida Association of Alternative School Educators
(See Resource Appendix)

Bethune Elementary
2400 Meade St, Hollywood, FL 33220
Linda Arnold, 305-926-0860
Broward County
Type: magnet
K-5th grade
Visual and performing arts.

Norland Middle School
1235 NW l92 Tr, Miami, FL 33269
John F. Gilbert, 305-653-1210
Type: magnet
7-9th grade
Center for the arts.

Parkway Middle School
3600 NW 5th Ct, Ft Lauderdale, FL 33311
Willie Dudley, 305-797-4550
Type: magnet
6-8th grade
Visual and performing arts; computers; high technology.

Summit Private School (1981)
1725 Davie Blvd, Ft Lauderdale, FL 33312
Judy Dempsey, 305-523-9489
Type: Montessori; tuition: $295-395/mo
9 teachers, 4 assistants, 123 students, ages infant-12
Affiliation: AMS
Governance by administrator
Swimming; gymnastics; dance; drama; karate; computer;
    childcare; urban location; interns accepted.

Blake School
7001 W Sunrise Blvd, Plantation, FL 33313-4427
Type: Montessori

Nova Blanche Forman Elementary School (1965)
3521 SW Davie Rd, Fort Lauderdale, FL 33314
Margaret Underhill, Prin, 305-370-1788, FAX:-1655
Type: public choice
57 teachers, 960 students, ages 5-11, K-5th grade
Enrollment restricted by county racial/ethnic guidelines;
    county residency required
Governance by School Improvement Team (including parents)
Teacher qualifications: BA, certification in elem ed
A Research and Development Center that has piloted many
    county projects, e.g., the original ESOL, Saludos and
    GOTCHA programs, Behavior Change Program, Study-

Travel, and primary multi-age classes; urban location; transportation; interns accepted.

Montessori Children's House
6590 SW 39th St, Fort Lauderdale, FL 33314-2416

Jacaranda School
8250 Peters Rd, Plantation, FL 33324-3298
Type: Montessori

Three Village Montessori
1400 Indian Ter, Fort Lauderdale, FL 33326-2771
Cheri Kaplan

North Andrews Gardens
345 NE 56 St, Ft Lauderdale, FL 33334
Sidney Ditkowsky, 305-928-0370
Type: magnet
K-5th grade
Visual and performing arts.

Walker Elementary
1001 NW 4th St, Ft Lauderdale, FL 33334
Lucy Thomas, 305-765-6878
Type: magnet
K-5th grade
Visual and performing arts.

Children's Garden Montessori
201 E Commercial Blvd, Fort Lauderdale, FL 33334-1625

Little Flower Montessori
533 E Oakland Park Blvd, Fort Lauderdale, FL 33334-2151
Mary Cronin Byrd

Children's House of the Palm Beaches
211 Trinity Place, West Palm Beach, FL 33401
Dr Helena Valldejuli-ButlerLois Carter
Type: Montessori

Little School of Rosarian Academy
807 North Flagler Dr, West Palm Beach, FL 33401-3705
Marie Schultz
Type: Montessori

Wee Wisdom Montessori School
1957 S Flagler Dr, West Palm Beach, FL 33401-7715

Village Montessori
21 W 21st St, Riviera Beach, FL 33404-5501

South Olive Elementary School
7101 S Olive Ave, West Palm Beach, FL 33405-4769
Type: Montessori

Hillwood Private School-Montessori
1366 Victory Dr, West Palm Beach, FL 33406

Palm Beach County Public Schools (1993)
3314 Forest Hill Blvd, A-210, West Palm Beach, FL 33406-5813
Patricia M. Hollings, Coord, 407-434-8347
Type: public choice
160 students

School of the Arts, Middle & High
3701 N Shore Dr, W Palm Beach, FL 33407
Edward Duhy, 407-881-4698
Type: magnet
7-11th grade
Dance/Music/Theatre/Visual & Performing Arts/Communica-
tions.

Sabal Palm School
4400 N Australian Ave, West Palm Beach, FL 33407-3699
Joanne R. Cochran, Prin, 407-881-4797
Type: public at-risk
9 teachers, 250 students, ages 10-16, 4-10th grade
County residency required
Affiliation: Palm Beach City Commissioners

Governance by teachers and principal

Teacher qualifications: In-field academic, vocational certification

Level system; rewards and incentives for appropriate behavior; tutoring; multi-aged classes; urban location; interns accepted.

Childrens Montessori House
4015 Spruce Ave, West Palm Beach, FL 33407-4215

Palm Beach Marine Institute
4260 Westgate Ave, West Palm Beach, FL 33409-4728
Daniel Alfonso, 407-640-5091

Montessori Unlimited
10277 Allamanda Blvd, Palm Beach Gardens, FL 33410
Elisabeth Goossens

Holland Northlake Day School
8788 N Military Trail, Palm Beach Gardens, FL 33410-6240
Diann Holland
Type: Montessori

Montessori Children's Center (1989)
353 Hiatt Dr, Palm Beach Gardens, FL 33418-7106
Mary C. Sandrini, Adm, 407-626-9222, FAX: 407-626-0418
Tuition: $375/425/450/mo.
2 teachers, 10 assistants, 65 students, ages infant-6
Affiliation: IMS
Governance by administrator
Custom designed facilities equipped with Nienhuis Montessori teaching materials; childcare; suburban location; interns accepted.

Montessori Academy
12532 Cobblestone Way, Boca Raton, FL 33428-2419

Claremont Montessori School (1985)
2450 NW 5th Ave, Boca Raton, FL 33431
Nancy Hallenberg, Dir, 407-394-7674
Non-profit; tuition: $4,800/yr
2 teachers, 1 assistant, 22 students, ages 6-12
Montessori preschool experience preferred
Affiliation: AMS
Governance by board
Montessori apparatus; camping skills taught from age 6-HS; new 8,000 sq-ft facility; suburban location.

Summit Private School of Boca Raton (1985)
3881 NW 3rd Ave, Boca Raton, FL 33431
Jeanne Hudlett, Adm, 407-338-5020, FAX: 407-338-5021
Type: Montessori; tuition: $330-435/mo
10 teachers, 6 assistants, 172 students, ages infant-9
Affiliations: AMS, NCME
Governance by an administrator
Children's garden; fish and turtle ponds; American History studied in authentic tipi; childcare; urban location; interns accepted.

Children's House of Boca Raton (1988)
100 Pine Circle, Boca Raton, FL 33432
Dr Kathleen L. Bowser, Dir, 407-391-0074
Type: Montessori; tuition: $3,100/4,500/yr
6 teachers, 2 assistants, 50 students, ages 3-6
Entrance requirements: age 2.5; toilet trained
Affiliations: NAMTA, NAEYC, SACUS; accreditation: AMS
Governance by an administrator
Multi-aged classes; no letter grades; urban location; interns accepted.

Addison Academy
19860 Jog Rd, Boca Raton, FL 33434-4454
Type: Montessori

Deerfield Park Elementary
627 SW 3nd Ave, Deerfield Beach, FL 33441
Carolyn Eggelletion, 305-481-5777
Broward County

Type: magnet
K-5th grade
Visual and performing arts.

S.D. Spady Elementary
330 NW 8th Ave, Palm Beach, FL 33444
Mavis Allred, 407-243-1558
Type: magnet
K-5th grade
Montessori.

Alternative Education Stop Camp
15450 SE Federal Hwy, Hobe Sound, FL 33455
407-546-3900
Type: public at-risk

South Area High School (1984)
716 S K St, Lake Worth, FL 33460
Ed Foley, Prin, 407-533-6364, FAX: 407-533-6417
Palm Beach County
Type: public at-risk; scholarships
13 teachers, 150 students, mainly at-risk and SE, ages 14-20, 9-12th grade
County residency required
Affiliation: Palm Beach City SB
Governance by principal and board
Teacher qualifications: state certification
2 courses/period; multi-aged classes; urban location; transportation; interns accepted.

Unity Wee Wisdom Montessori School
624 N H St, Lake Worth, FL 33460-2946

Northern Private Schools
1822 High Ridge Rd, Lake Worth, FL 33461-6172
Type: Montessori

Guardian Angels Montessori School
1325 Cardinal Ln, Lantana, FL 33462-4205

Oliver's Academy
PO Box 4041, Tequesta, FL 33469
Laura Ingman, Secretary, 407-340-0759
Type: independent; tuition: variable
19 students, pre K-12th grade
Bible-based; family oriented; cooperative; emphasizes self-teaching.

Dropout Prevention/Youth Services
PO Box 949, Moore Haven, FL 33471-0949
Mazie T. Ford, 813-946-0323
Type: public at-risk

Okeechobee Boys School
Rt 7, Box 250, Okeechobee, FL 33472
Ken Johnson, 904-763-2174
Type: public at-risk

School of Choice
541 Rardin Ave, Pahokee, FL 33476-2399
407-924-6470
Type: public choice

Gulf Stream School
3600 Gulf Stream Rd, Gulf Stream, FL 33483-7499
Nancy Froio
Type: Montessori

Montessori Unlimited/West Glades Montessori
20400 Cain Blvd, Boca Raton, FL 33498-6746
Elisabeth Goossens

Holy Name Academy
12117 Wichers Rd, Dade City, FL 33525
Sr Roberta Bailey
Type: Montessori

Countryside Montessori Academy
16720 Tobacco Rd, Lutz, FL 33549

Priory Early Childhood Center
Drawer H, St Leo, FL 33574-4002
Type: Montessori

Sarasota Public Schools Montessori Program
Booker MS, 2250 Myrtle St, Sarasota, FL 33580
Diane Riva

Alternative Education
901 E Kennedy Blvd, Tampa, FL 33602-3507
Kelly Lyles, 813-272-4809
Type: public at-risk

The Learning Tree Montessori School
305 S Melville Ave, Tampa, FL 33606

Beach Park Private School
4200 W North A St, Tampa, FL 33609-2269
Ann and Dick Winkler
Type: Montessori

Montessori Country Day School (1983)
5705 Interbay, Tampa, FL 33611
Polly Nelson, Dir, 813-831-4378
Tuition: $1,800/2,300/3,400/yr
3 teachers, 3 assistants, 55 students, ages infant-6
Accreditation: AMI
Governance by an administrator
Large yard includes gardens, swings, tree houses, chicken
    coops, rabbit hutches, large deck; convenient to Hyde
    Park, Davis Islands, Palma Ceia and South Tampa; urban
    location; interns accepted.

The Montessori House Day School (1970)
7010 Hanley Rd, Tampa, FL 33614
Kay H. Murrell, Head Dir, 813-884-7220, FAX: 813-961-8639
Tuition: $2,350/3,500/yr
1 teacher, 1 assistant, 30 students, ages 3-6
Entrance requirements: toilet trained; interview and visit
Affiliations: NAMTA, HAANS; accreditations: AMS, FL CIS, FL KC
Governance by administrator
MTTI satellite site; trees; grass; basketball court; fitness mate-
    rials; childcare; suburban location; interns accepted.

Under the Rainbow Montessori Learning Center
7916 N Himes Ave, Tampa, FL 33614

Montessori Academy of Temple Terrace
5804 Gibson Ave, Temple Terrace, FL 33617-1252
Sonia Johnson

Lake Fern Academy (1975)
4940 Northdale Blvd, Tampa, FL 33624
Nettie Rossi, Owner, 813-264-5362
Type: Montessori; tuition: $2,730-4,410/yr
7 teachers, 4 assistants, 122 students, ages infant-12
Affiliation: AMS
Governance by an administrator
Year-round; quarterly breaks; "camps" during breaks enhance
    special areas of study; childcare; suburban location; interns
    accepted.

Montessori Early Learning Institute
3823 W Hudson Ln, Tampa, FL 33624
Sonia Johnson

The Montessori House Day School (1980)
5117 Ehrlich Rd, Tampa, FL 33624
Kay H. Murrell, Head Dir, 813-961-9295, FAX: 813-961-8639
Tuition: $2,430-3,870/yr
9 teachers, 5 assistants, 142 students, ages 3-12
Entrance requirements: toilet trained; interview; visit
Affiliations: NAMTA, HAANS; accreditations: AMS, FL CIS, FL KC
Governance by administrator
Full complement of Montessori materials; faculty develop-
    ment; 3 acres; outdoor equipment; gardens; basketball
    court; aerobics court; childcare; suburban location; interns
    accepted.

Montessori In The City
3218 W Bay To Bay Blvd, Tampa, FL 33629-7106
Ann and Dick Winkler

Montessori Children's House of Tampa Palms
15347 Amberly Dr, Tampa, FL 33647-2144
Yvonne Kuhn

Ibis-South: North Ward
327 11th Ave N, St Petersburg, FL 33701-1745
Mary M. Rasor, Coord, 813-893-2930
Type: public at-risk

Montessori By The Sea
1603 Gulf Way, Saint Petersburg Beach, FL 33706-4237
Sue Haynie

Sunflower School
5313 27th Ave S, Gulfport, FL 33707
Molly Barnes, 813-321-7657
Type: independent; tuition: $2,850/yr, scholarships
50 students, ages 4-12
Environmental, community emphasis; art; music; drama;
    Spanish; computers; homeschooler advice, materials,
    books; no letter grades.

PTEC-St Petersburg-Goals
901 34th St S, St Petersburg, FL 33711-2209
Tom Maas, 813-323-1727

St Petersburg Challenge School
2350 22nd Ave S, St Petersburg, FL 33712-3020
Sandra S. Leanes, 813-893-2114
Type: public at-risk

Harris Center
4600 Haines Rd N, St Petersburg, FL 33714-3339
813-627-6552
Type: public at-risk

Lealman Discovery School
4100 35th St N, St Petersburg, FL 33714-3706
Marshall L. Brown, 813-527-7271
Type: public at-risk

De Soto Opportunity School
530 Lasalona Ave, Arcadia, FL 33821-4911
Dr Katherine Tracey, 813-494-4222
Type: public at-risk

George H. Gause Career Development Center
1395 Polk St, Bartow, FL 33830-3428
Scott Norton, 813-534-7425
Type: public at-risk

Tri-County Coordinated Child Care
PO Box 1269, Highland City, FL 33846-1269
Type: Montessori

Lifetime Books and Gifts
(See Resource Appendix)

Edison Learning Center
3243 Clifford St, Ft Myers, FL 33901-3514
Type: independent

Gulf Coast Homeschool
2454 Burton Ave, Ft Myers, FL 33907
813-936-5182

Montessori School of Ft Myers (1969)
2151 Crystal Dr, Ft Myers, FL 33907
Charlie or Linda Touton, Adms, 813-936-4515
Tuition: $2,150/3,400/yr
3 teachers, 3 assistants, 60 students, ages 3-12
Affiliation: AMS; accreditations: FLKC, NIPSA
Governance by administrator
Multi-cultural staff, students; childcare; urban location;
    interns accepted.

Wright Montessori Academy
37 Barkley Cir, Fort Myers, FL 33907-7531

Lee County Alternative Learning Center
3750 Michigan Ave, Fort Myers, FL 33916
Harold V. Springer, 813-334-4726
Type: public at-risk

Lee County Schools
3800 Michigan Ave, Fort Myers, FL 33916
Beth Godwin, Dropout Prev Coord, 813-334-6221, FAX: 332-4839
Type: public choice/at-risk
120 teachers, 1400 students, mainly at-risk, ages 10-23, 4-12th grade
Teacher qualifications: FL Certification
Teen parenting; accelerated credit; no letter grades; extensive field trips; urban, suburban and rural locations; transportation; interns accepted.

Bonita Montessori School
27040 Imperial St, Bonita Springs, FL 33923
Kathy Leitch, Dir, 813-992-5138, FAX: 813-481-5413
Tuition: $2,250-2,565/yr
2 teachers, 2 assistants, 30 students, ages 3-6
Affiliations: AMS, NAEYC
Governance by administrator
Private wooded location; active parent involvement; inclusive; peace curriculum; childcare; suburban location; interns accepted.

Florida Parent Education Association
609 Greenwood, Lehigh Acres, FL 33936
Steve Shelfer, Director

Central Sun Montessori Inc
1291 Hilltop Dr, Naples, FL 33940-3323

Cedar Montessori School (1983)
10904 Winterview Dr, Naples, FL 33942
Roy Marshall, Administrator, 813-597-7190
Non-profit; tuition: $2,530-3,700/yr
5 teachers, 7 assistants, 136 students, ages infant-12
Non-discriminatory; childcare.

New Challenge School (1990)
16529 Joppa Ave, Port Charlotte, FL 33948
Gregg Sinner, Prin, 813-625-0080, FAX: 813-625-3409
Charlotte County
Type: public at-risk
10 teachers, 180 students, ages 14-20, HS
Enrollment restricted to at-risk students
Governance by prin; faculty, student reps; democratic school meeting; board; parent coop; county office
Teacher qualifications: Florida certification-any field/level
Raywid Type I ed alt for teen parents, others; multi-aged classes; suburban location; transportation; interns accepted.

Montessori School of Charlotte County, Inc (1979)
4344 Pinnacle St, Punta Gorda, FL 33980
Maja B. Wolfe, Head, 813-629-7710
Tuition: $285/mo
2 teachers, 1 assistant, 25 students, ages 3-9
Entrance requirements: not hyperactive
Governance by administrator
Extra Spanish lessons; gymnastics; pre-ballet; childcare; suburban location; interns accepted.

Panama Support Group at Ft Amador
PSC Box 1578, APO Miami, FL 34001
Type: home-based

Center for Education (1976)
6024 26th St W, Bradenton, FL 34207
Janice Mattina, 813-753-4987
Type: Montessori; tuition: $2,200-3,245/yr

7 teachers, 4 assistants, 136 students, ages 3-12
Governance by administrator
Words in Color reading program; childcare; suburban location; interns accepted.

Gulf Coast Marine Institute
301 7th St E, Bradenton, FL 34208-1139
Janice Norrie, 813-741-3102
Type: public at-risk

Countryside Montessori School (1984)
5237 Ashton Rd, Sarasota, FL 34233
Kitty Williams, Dir, 904-922-4949
Tuition: $4,400/yr
9 teachers, 150 students, ages 3-12
Entrance requirements: no behavior problems; interview; trial days
Affiliation: AMS
Governance by board of trustees
Teacher qualifications: Montessori Certification
Located on organic farm; environmental principles; foreign language; music; art; creative movement; no letter grades; extensive field trips; non-compulsory class attendance; multi-aged classes; suburban location; interns accepted.

King Academy/Cyesis
4650 Beneva Rd, Sarasota, FL 34233-1808
813-361-6420
Type: public at-risk

New Directions
4409 Sawyer Rd, Sarasota, FL 34233-1808
813-361-6580
Type: public choice

New College
5700 N Tamiami Tr, Sarasota, FL 34243-2197
Jim Feeney, 813-359-4200

Ideal High School
1130 Indian Hill Blvd, Venice, FL 34293
813-486-2131
Type: public at-risk

Cornerstone School (1982)
2313 SE Lake Weir St, Ocala, FL 34471
Carol Montag, Dir, 904-351-8840
Type: independent, non-profit; tuition: $1,750/yr, scholarships
12 teachers, 118 students, ages 3-10, pre K-5th grade
Entrance requirements: approval of philosophy
Affiliations: FCIS, NPE
Governance by principal, parent cooperative, board
Whole language; literature-based reading; curriculum suspended for 5 day, thematic mini-courses with mixed groups; no letter grades; extensive field trips; rural location; interns accepted.

Phoenix Center of Marion County
2091 NE 35th St, Ocala, FL 34479-2900
904-732-6542
Type: public choice

Wider Horizons School (1986)
4060 Castle Ave, Spring Hill, FL 34609
Dr Domenick or Julie Maglio, 904-686-1934
Type: Montessori; tuition: $7.50-17/day
5 teachers, 150 students, ages infant-15
Accreditation: NIPSA
Governance by administrator
Research curriculum approach; childcare; suburban location; transportation.

The Home School Shopper
(See Resource Appendix)

Samuel L. Robinson Challenge School
1101 Marshall St, Clearwater, FL 34615-2644

Cavid C. Schmitt, 813-443-3222
Type: public at-risk

Clearwater Discovery School
1220 Palmetto St, Clearwater, FL 34615-4333
Scott East, 813-441-2281
Type: public at-risk

Belleair Montessori School
905 Ponce De Leon Blvd, Clearwater, FL 34616-1019

Florida Parent Education Association
14739 Mocking Bird Ln E, Clearwater, FL 34620

PTEC-Clearwater-Goals
6100 154th Ave N, Clearwater, FL 34620-2140
Don Bitting, 813-530-9149
Type: public at-risk

Ainsworth Montessori Academy
5990 142nd Ave N, Clearwater, FL 34620-2806

ESP Publishers, Inc
(See Resource Appendix)

Montessori Learning Circle
9618 Denton Ave, Hudson, FL 34667-4339
Mary Bowman

Palm Harbor Montessori School
2313 Nebraska Ave, Palm Harbor, FL 34683-3944
Christine Norbom

World of Knowledge: A Montessori School
1935 Abacus Rd, Holiday, FL 34690-5540
Rene Womelsdorf

Ibis-North: Safety Harbor Center
675 Elm St, Safety Harbor, FL 34695-2822
Keith A. Davis, 813-725-7965
Type: public at-risk

Open Door Private School of Pinellas Co, Inc
710 Scotland St, Dunedin, FL 34698
Lucy N. Basso Smith, 813-733-8202
Type: home-based; cost: $100/yr
50 students, K-12th grade
Administrative/record keeping office for homeschoolers; info
    on resources, scholarships, field trips, testing.

Dunedin Montessori Academy
637 Michigan Blvd, Dunedin, FL 34698-2618
Lydia Banome

Lee Education Center (1988)
207 N Lee St, Leesburg, FL 34748
Dr Joyce Driver, 904-787-0043
Lake County
Type: public at-risk
10 teachers, 150 students, ages 12–19, 6–12th grade
Enrollment restricted to potential dropouts; residency
    required
Governance by teachers and principal
Teacher qualifications: FL certification
Competency-based; multi-aged classes; suburban location;
    interns accepted.

Leesburg Montessori School
415 Lee St, Leesburg, FL 34748-5082

Montessori NEST
608 S 9th St # D, Leesburg, FL 34748-6378
Merry Hadden

Woodlands Academy
1805 Panther Ln, Fort Pierce, FL 34947-7021
407-468-5273
Type: public at-risk

Alternative Education Center
703 SW 6th St, Okeechobee, FL 34974-4288
Cathleen Blair, 813-357-1161

Sun Grove Montessori School (1978)
5610 Oleander Ave, Ft Pierce, FL 34982
Barbara Scott, Adm, 407-464-5436
Non-profit; tuition: $200-335/mo
4 teachers, 4 assistants, 75 students, mainly international,
    ages 3–9
Affiliations: NAMTA, MTA, NCME
Governance by administrator, board of trustees
Complete Montessori; gardening project with UF Coop Ext;
    Edu-Kinestetics; effective parenting classes; ungraded;
    childcare; suburban location; interns accepted.

Martin Downs Montessori
3001 SW Mill Creek Way, Palm City, FL 34990-3155

Georgia

Bibb County Alternative School
2064 Vineville Ave Box 6157, Macon, GA 21313
W. E. Bell, 912-741-8507
Type: public at-risk
7-12th grade
Small classes; individualized with CAI, A/V.

Avendale High School
1192 Clarendon Rd, Avendale Estate, GA 30002
Amers Kitchens, 404-289-6766
DeKalb County
Type: magnet
8-12th grade
Center for performing arts.

Challenge & Higher Order Thinking Skills (HOTS)
    Programs
320 N McDonough St, Decatur, GA 30030
Julie Freeman, 404-370-4405

Type: public at-risk
3-7th grade
CP: basic skills; HOTS: extensive CAI.

Day Care Center, 8th Grade at Decatur High School
310 N McDonough St, Decatur, GA 30030
Jenna Black, Karen Davenport, 404-370-4424
Type: public at-risk

Friends School of Atlanta (1991)
112 Adair St, Decatur, GA 30030
Waman W. French, Head, 404-373-8746
Type: Quaker, non-profit; tuition: $5,000/yr
15 teachers, 92 students, ages 4.5–11, K-6th grade
Affiliation: Friends Council on Education
Governance by board
Developmental approach; manipulatives, experiences build
    concepts for learning; philosophy of peace, justice, sim-
    plicity, diversity, community; no letter grades; multi-aged
    classes.

Lullwater School (1973)
705 S Candler St, Decatur, GA 30030
Dr Joan K Teach, 404-378-6643, FAX: 404-377-0879
DeKalb County
Type: independent, non-profit; tuition: $5900/yr, scholarships
9 teachers, 60 students, mainly at-risk, ages 4.5–14, K–9th grade
Entrance requirements: screening & previous testing
Affiliations: AIGE, CEC
Governance by board
Teacher qualifications: BS, certification; specialization, MS preferred
Confluent education, interrelated curriculum; continuous progress; multi-racial, holistic; supportive of ADD and LD students; multi-aged classes; extensive field trips; urban location.

TAPS Program
320 N McDonough St, Decatur, GA 30030
George Hickman, 404-370-4438
Type: public choice
For students who fall just below gifted classification; 1 day/week; identical to state's program; transportation.

The Oakhurst Project
320 N McDonough St, Decatur, GA 30030
Gloria Lee, 404-370-4403
Type: public at-risk
ES
Cracker Jacks Latchkey, Tutorial, Homework Help, and Read-On-My-Lap/Read-At-Home programs at Oakhurst and 5th Ave ES.

DeKalb County Magnet Programs
3770 N Decatur Rd, Decatur, GA 30032
Charles Hutcheson, Exec Dir, 404-297-2307
Type: public choice
Atherton Writing Academy (4th grade; computer literacy); Clifton Computer Education (4–7th grade; one workstation/student); Avondale ES Academy for Performing Arts (K–7th grade); Avondale HS Center for Performing Arts (5-year); Kittridge MagS for High Achievers (emphasis on creativity, critical thinking, independence, communication); Browns Mill MagP for High Achievers (emphasis on global ed, foreign language, and computer technology); Hooper Alexander Spanish MagP; Towers HS Foreign Language MagP (3 hrs/day earns 2 yrs credit in 1); Canby Lane Academy of Mathematics, Science, and Technology (4–7th grade, lab settings); Snapfinger Academy of Mathematics, Science, and Technology (4–7th grade, lab settings).

Story Book School, Inc
3471 Glenwood Rd, Decatur, GA 30032-4407
Type: Montessori

Northwoods Montessori World of Children
1879 Columbia Dr, Decatur, GA 30032-5908

Atlanta Alternative Education Network
c/o Paymer, 1158 McConnell Dr, Decatur, GA 30033
Type: home-based

Arbor Montessori School
2998 Lavista Rd, Decatur, GA 30033-1308

Occupational Education Center-South
3303 Panthersville Rd, Decatur, GA 30034
Larry Ladner, 404-241-9400
DeKalb County
Type: public choice
500 students

A Child's Campus
2780 Flat Shoals Rd, Decatur, GA 30034-1034
Type: Montessori

Atherton Elementary
1674 Atherton Dr, Atlanta, GA 30035
Paul Warner, 404-284-6662
Type: magnet
K–7th grade
Arts; writing academy.

Clayton County Alternative Program
5277 Ash St, Forest Park, GA 30050
Frank Brandon, 404-473-2700
Type: public at-risk

Progressive School System
2637 Panola Rd, Lithonia, GA 30058
Type: Montessori

Montessori Education Center #2
81 Bankhead Hwy SW, Mableton, GA 30059-2509

Marietta Alternative School
350-B Lemon St, Marietta, GA 30060
Susan H Newman, 404-427-7911
Type: public at-risk
6–12th grade
Small, self-contained environment.

Oakwood High School
1560 Joyner Ave, Marietta, GA 30060
Carla Northcutt, 404-424-7950
Cobb County
Type: public at-risk
HS
Open-campus.

The Hands-On Math
353 Lemon St, Marietta, GA 30060
JoAnn Crimm, 404-424-3674
Type: public choice
ES

Casa DiBambini Montessori
4010 Lower Roswell Rd, Marietta, GA 30068-4058

Country Brook Montessori School (1987)
2175 Norcross Tucker Rd, Norcross, GA 30071
Leroy Moffitt, 404-446-2397, FAX: 404-448-2805
Tuition: $250-375/mo
6 teachers, 6 assistants, 98 students, mainly international, ages 2-12
Affiliations: AMS, NAMTA, MACTE; accreditation: NCME
Governance by an administrator
Spanish; computers; multi-cultural enrollment; located in high-tech area in fast growing county; teacher training facility for NCME; childcare; urban location; interns accepted.

The Hammond School
11273 Elkins Rd, Roswell, GA 30076-1202
Type: Montessori

High Meadows
PO Box 859, Roswell, GA 30077
Sheryl Smith, 404-993-2940
Tuition: $4,140/yr
275 students, pre K–12th grade

National Center for Montessori Education
(See Resource Appendix)

DeKalb Alternative School
3262 Glendale Rd, Scottdale, GA 30079
Sam Black, 404-292-7315
DeKalb County
Type: public at-risk
For temporarily expelled students; highly structured; counseling.

Covered Bridge Montessori School (1981)
3941 Covered Bridge Rd, Smyrna, GA 30082
Barbara Moffitt, 404-434-3181, FAX: 404-434-1128
Tuition: $230-375/mo
7 teachers, 14 assistants, 136 students, ages infant-9
Entrance requirements: application/enrollment fees; speech,
    language, vision, hearing, and cognitive skills screening
Affiliation: MACTE-MEG; accreditation: NCME
Governance by an administrator
On 3 acres in wooded subdivision; pool; childcare; suburban
    location; interns accepted.

NCME Atlanta / National Reporter
3951 Covered Bridge Rd, Smyrna, GA 30082
Barbara Moffitt, Dir
Type: Montessori

Stone Mountain Montessori
4700 E Ponce De Leon Ave, Stone Mountain, GA 30083-1230

Rockbridge Montessori School
4733 Rockbridge Rd, Stone Mountain, GA 30083-4248

Aurora Montessori Academy
4451 Hugh Howell Hwy, Tucker, GA 30084

Open Campus High School
1300 Red Plum Rd, Norcross, GA 30093
Robert Campbell, 404-921-5395
Type: public at-risk
Evenings; mini-semesters for Green and Gwinnet County stu-
    dents; fee.

Montessori School at Brookstone
1680 Brookstone Walk, Acworth, GA 30101-4572
Tudy Cook

Open Campus/Night School
113 Central Rd, Carrollton, GA 30117
David Wiggins, 404-830-6045
Carroll County
Type: public at-risk
HS
Mini-semesters; co-op w/CC VHS.

Star Student Program
123 Brown St, Carrollton, GA 30117
Patricia Stokes, 404-834-1868
Carroll County
Students mainly at-risk, 5-6th grade
Enrollment restricted to students in the bottom quartile on
    the Iowa Test of Basic Skills
Weekly tutorial; emphasis on rewarding success.

Douglas County Programs
9030 Hwy 5, PO Box 1077, Douglasville, GA 30133
Randy Brittain, 404-920-4000
Gifted; vocational; co-op; JTPA; evening HS; joint HS/college
    enrollment; adult ed.

Montessori School of Douglas County Inc
8014 Duralee Ln, Douglasville, GA 30134-2539

International Academy
4160 Vansant Rd, Douglasville, GA 30135
Aghdas Kashi
Type: Montessori

Duluth Montessori School
2997 N Peachtree St, Duluth, GA 30136-2745

Cobb County Homeschoolers
813 Wyntuck Dr, Kennesaw, GA 30144

Montessori Children's House of Cobb Academy
2871 Cherokee St, Kennesaw, GA 30144-2823

Montessori Children's House of Kennesaw
3238 Cherokee St, Kennesaw, GA 30144-2901

Alternative Graduation Completion Program
171 Riverside Pkwy NE, Rome, GA 30161
Richard Ingram, 404-243-1031
Floyd County
Type: public at-risk
HS-credit-earning independent study at the Adult Education
    Center for students who have left school.

Night High School
4203 Martha Berry Hwy NW, Rome, GA 30161
Gary Kilgore, 404-236-1884
Floyd County
Type: public choice, at-risk
Students mainly at-risk, HS
Diploma prep; enrichment.

Overaged Students Instructional Service (OASIS)
508 E Second St, Rome, GA 30161
Gayland Cooper, 404-236-5050
Type: public at-risk
5-6th grade
Summer prep for special 7th grade.

Rome Montessori, Inc
PO Box 807, Rome, GA 30161

Montessori School of Rome (1982)
1499 Dodd Blvd, Rome, GA 30161-6643
Swarna Kumar, 706-232-7744
Tuition: $210/275/mo
4 teachers, 7 assistants, 72 students, ages infant-6
Governance by administrator
Childcare.

Sunshine Montessori School
1110 N 5th Ave, Rome, GA 30165-2604

Blackstock Montessori (1980)
87 Blackstock Rd, Villa Rica, GA 30180
R. O'Neil Duffy, Adm, 404-459-6797
Non-profit; tuition: $2,250-3,260/yr
6 teachers, 4 assistants, 98 students, ages infant-12
Affiliation: AMS
Governance by administrator
Custom designed building; 10 wooded acres; pilot study for
    AMS/SAC; childcare; rural location; transportation; interns
    accepted.

Herbst Homeschool (1983)
6473 Hickory Flat Hwy, Woodstock, GA 30188
Jill Herbst, 404-516-4826
Cherokee County
Non-profit
1-2 teachers, 3 students, ages 5-15, K-9th grade
Non-regimented; suburban location.

Park View Montessori (1989)
6689 Bells Ferry Rd, Woodstock, GA 30188
Kathy Faircloth, Owner/Dir, 404-926-0044
Tuition: $53.50-99.50/wk
5 teachers, 132 students, ages infant-6
Affiliation: MEGA
Governance by administrator
Childcare; suburban location; interns accepted.

REACH
617 Colony Ct, Woodstock, GA 30188
Vicki Scott
Type: home-based

Medlock Bridge Montessori School
10100 Medlock Bridge Pky, Alpharetta, GA 30201
Robin Hanson

Montessori Internationale
10250 Haynes Bridge Rd, Alpharetta, GA 30202
Cindy Savage

Preston Ridge Montessori (1988)
3800 N Point Pkwy, Alpharetta, GA 30202
Dolores R. Gang, 404-751-9510
Tuition: $3,195-5,265/yr
7 teachers, 7 assistants, 109 students, ages 3–12
Affiliations: AMI, NAMTA; accreditation: MIA
Governance by an administrator and a board of trustees
Childcare; transportation; interns accepted.

Nesbit Ferry Montessori
9330 Nesbit Ferry Rd, Alpharetta, GA 30202-5345

Lamar County Alternative School
204 Gordon Rd, Barnesville, GA 30204
E H Harris or William E Cook, 404-358-1159 or 404-647-9621
Type: public at-risk
K–12th grade
Affiliation: Lamar and Upson County Schools
Students establish contractual agreements with teachers for work to be accomplished; goal is to decrease student dropout rate.

Georgia Home Education Association
245 Buckeye Ln, Fayetteville, GA 30214
404-461-3657
Type: state home-based

Lee Crest Academy, Inc
402 Bates Ave, Fayetteville, GA 30214-1906
Type: Montessori

Montessori Woods
1305 Cone Circle, Grayson, GA 30221
John Long

Cities-in-Schools at Flynt St, Kelsey Ave, and Taylor St Middle Schools
PO Box 866, Griffin, GA 30224
Eddie Whitlock, 404-412-0435
Spalding County
Type: public at-risk
240 students, JH
Staffed by public and private specialists (counselors, health workers, and employers).

First Presbyterian Montessori Kindergarten
120 Broad St, La Grange, GA 30240-2704

Cities-in-Schools at LaGrange High School and Gardner-Newman Middle School
PO Box 2797, LaGrange, GA 30241
Russ Walker, 404-845-7145
Type: public at-risk
Staffed by public and private specialists (counselors, health workers, and employers).

Gwinnett Vocational Center at Oakland
990 McElvaney Lane, Lawrenceville, GA 30244
Roger Sarter, 404-963-7936
Gwinnett County
Type: public choice
HS

Homebound Teacher/Tele-classes
950 McElvaney Lane, Lawrenceville, GA 30244
Roberta Heron, 404-963-6713
Gwinnett County
Type: public at-risk
For severely ill.

Educating Speakers of Other Languages
52 Gwinnett Dr, Lawrenceville, GA 30245
Liz Rieken, 404-513-6641
Gwinnett County
Type: public choice

Gwinnett Vocational Center at Parkview
1000 Cole Dr, Lilburn, GA 30247

Roy Rucks, 404-921-4592
Gwinnett County
Type: public choice
HS

Teaching Our Peers (TOP)
166 Holly Smith Dr, McDonough, GA 30253
Andrea L Green, 404-957-3945
Henry County
Type: public at-risk
MS
Parental involvement; cooperation.

Georgians for Freedom in Education (1983)
209 Cobb St, Palmetto, GA 30268
Billie Jean Bryant, Coord, 404-463-3719 or 463-1073
Fulton County
Non-profit
Non-sectarian; newsletter; monitors legislation; promotes grassroots lobbying; seminars; workshops.

Peachtree City Montessori
232 Stevens Entry, Peachtree City, GA 30269-3320
Leslie Bryan

Montessori Education Center of Gwinnett
PO Box 692, Snellville, GA 30278
Trudy Friar

The Children's House
2350 Wisteria Dr, Snellville, GA 30278-2658
Type: Montessori

Montessori Children's Hall
2123 Easy St, Snellville, GA 30278-2839

Montessori Institute of Atlanta
2355 Virginia Pl NE, Atlanta, GA 30305
Type: Montessori teacher education

North Atlanta High School
2875 Northside Dr NE, Atlanta, GA 30305
Judith Rogers, 404-842-3108
Type: magnet
9–12th grade
International studies; arts.

Downtown Learning Center
1080 Euclid Ave, Atlanta, GA 30307
Robert Morrison, 404-330-4161
Type: public choice
HS
Traditional curriculum; contracts.

Fernbank Science Center
(See Resource Appendix)

Horizons School
1900 Dekalb Ave, Atlanta, GA 30307
Dr. Lorraine Wilson, Co-administrator, 404-378-2219, FAX: 404-373-3650
Type: independent, boarding, non-profit; tuition: $3800-8000/yr, scholarships: work, need
14 teachers, 145 students, ages 4–18, pre K–12th grade
Affiliation: NCACS
Governance by democratic school meeting; some decisions by administration +
Students and staff designed and built new campus; alternative evaluation methods in some classes; college prep program; wholistic approach; multi-aged classes; extensive field trips; urban location; interns accepted.

The Children's Garden (1987)
2089 Ponce de Leon Ave, Atlanta, GA 30307
Susan Jones, Grade II Tch, 404-371-9470
DeKalb County
Type: Waldorf, non-profit; tuition: $2,000-4,000/yr, scholarships

8 teachers, 44 students, ages 3–9, nursery, K, II
Entrance requirements: interview, application
Affiliation: AWSNA
Governance by faculty and board
Teacher qualifications: Waldorf training and/or experience
Only school in Atlanta with play kindergarten, nursery school, and arts daily; urban location; interns accepted.

Exodus
96 Pine St NE, Atlanta, GA 30308
Neil Shorthouse, Cities-in-School, Inc, 404-873-3979
Type: public at-risk
9–12th grade
Staffed by public and private specialists (counselors, health workers, and employers, etc.).

North Avenue Academy
27 North Ave NE, Atlanta, GA 30308
Keith Parsons, Dir, 404-888-5779
Type: public at-risk
HS
Cities-in-Schools program, staffed by public and private specialists (counselors, health workers, and employers, etc).

Gate City Heritage School
491 Ontario Ave, Atlanta, GA 30310

West End Academy
1325 Gordon St SW, Atlanta, GA 30310
Bobby Garrett, Dir, 404-755-7754
Type: public at-risk
HS
Cities-in-Schools program, staffed by public and private specialists (counselors, health workers, and employers, etc.).

Southwest Montessori
2407 Cascade Rd SW, Atlanta, GA 30311-3225

B.T. Washington High School
45 Whitehouse Dr SW, Atlanta, GA 30314
Robert Lowe, 404-752-0728
Type: magnet
9–12th grade
Health professions; multi-cultural; humanities.

Jessie Mae Jones Middle School
1255 Capitol Ave SW, Atlanta, GA 30315
Turner Sibley, 404-330-5600
Type: public at-risk
Enrollment restricted to overaged students who have been retained several times
Contracts; emphasis on self-concept.

Southside Comprehensive High School
801 Glenwood Ave SE, Atlanta, GA 30317
Joseph Carpenter, 404-624-2064
Type: magnet
9–12th grade
Information process and decision making.

Atlanta Northeast Montessori School Inc
2193 Johnson Ferry Rd NE, Atlanta, GA 30319-2503

Ben Franklin Academy
Clifton Rd, Atlanta, GA 30322

Creative Learning Montessori
1108 Heatherstone Dr, NE, Atlanta, GA 30324-4642

First Montessori School of Atlanta
5750 Long Island Dr NW, Atlanta, GA 30327-4844

East Cobb Montessori, Inc
5730 Pinebrook Rd NE, Atlanta, GA 30328-5224

Benjamin Franklin Academy (1987)
1585 Clifton Rd, NE, Atlanta, GA 30329
Wood Stonehurst, Head, 404-633-7404, FAX: 321-0610

Type: independent, non-profit; tuition: $11,800/yr, scholarships
60 students, mainly at-risk
Affiliations: GAIS, AAIS, SAIS, CES
Governance by board
Teacher qualifications: GA certificate
For those who are "out of step with conventional schools"; consensus decision-making; urban location.

Open Campus High School
2145-A N Druid Hills Rd, NE, Atlanta, GA 30329
William Hightower, 404-321-6989
DeKalb County
Type: public at-risk
Student ages 16+
Flexible schedule; full or part-time.

Montessori Child Dev Centers
PO Box 15281, Atlanta, GA 30333

South Fulton Alternative School
3605 NW Main St, College Park, GA 30337
Olin Presley, 404-669-8080
Fulton County
Type: public at-risk
For out-of-school youth; individualized, cooperative, experiential.

Occupational Education Center–North
1995 Womack Rd, Dunwoody, GA 30338
Frank Hall, 404-394-0321
DeKalb County
Type: public choice
450 students

Montessori Children's House of NE Atlanta
2635 Fairlane Dr, Doraville, GA 30340-3225

Northwoods Montessori School (1971)
3340 Chestnut Dr, Atlanta, GA 30340-3239
Elizabeth Samples, Executive Director, 404-457-7261
Non-profit; tuition: $2,985/4,170/yr
9 teachers, 9 assistants, 157 students, ages 3–12
Affiliations: NAMTA, MAC; accreditation: AMI
Governance by administrator
Traditional Montessori program; childcare; urban location.

Occupational Education Center–Central
3075 Alton Rd, Chamblee, GA 30341
Robert Burns, 404-457-3393
DeKalb County
Type: public at-risk

Four Seasons School
2459 Dresden Dr NE, Chamblee, GA 30341-5218
Type: Montessori

Atlanta Montessori International Teacher Training Center
820 Loridans Dr, Atlanta, GA 30342
Type: Montessori teacher education

North Side Atlanta Homeschoolers
c/o Jane Kelley, 4141 Wieuca Rd NE, Atlanta, GA 30342

Montessori Center of Buckhead, Ltd
3725 Powers Ferry Rd NW, Atlanta, GA 30342-4422

Tri-Cities High School
2575 Harris St, Atlanta, GA 30344
Hershel Robinson, 404-669-8200
Type: magnet
9–12th grade
Visual and performing arts.

Georgia Home Educators
PO Box 88775, Dunwoody, GA 30356
404-451-4130
Gwinnett County

Emanuel County Alternative Program
PO Box 130, Swainsboro, GA 30401
Jamie Lawrence, 912-237-6674
Type: public at-risk

Bulloch County Alternative Classroom
500 Northside Dr E, Statesboro, GA 30458
Seth Portwood, 912-764-6201
Type: public at-risk
HS
Short-term; individual schedules.

Dawson County Alternative Program
PO Box 280, Dawsonville, GA 30534
Kay Collins, 706-265-3245
Type: public at-risk
48 students, 8-12th grade
Vocational; life-skills.

Regional Evening High School
Box 820, 1668 Winder Hwy, Jefferson, GA 30549
Janet Adams, Dir, 706-367-5003
Jackson County
Type: public at-risk
HS
Acceleration program for 7th graders retained at least twice.

Foxfire Teacher Outreach (1975)
(See Resource Appendix)

Free to Learn at Home
4439 Lake Forest Dr, Oakwood, GA 30566
404-536-8077

Hall County Home Educators
PO Box 1283, Oakwood, GA 30566

Clarke County Alternative School
1000 Barber St, Athens, GA 30603-1708
Mark Argo, 706-543-8865
Type: public at-risk
5 teachers, 35–40 students
Small; structured; individualized.

Athens Montessori School
3145 Barnett Shoals, Athens, GA 30605-4327
Warren McPherson

Early Morning Classes/ Night School/ Community Education; Calhoun High School
700 W Line St PO Box 785, Calhoun, GA 30701
Jim Holloway, 404-629-2900
Type: public choice, at-risk; tuition: $100/115 (NS)
HS
Credit/diploma/GED earning; comm ed: college courses, after-school childcare, tutorial.

Evening High School
213 College Dr, Dalton, GA 30720
Kathryn Floyd, 404-272-4450
Whitfield County
Type: public at-risk
HS
Diploma-earning.

Individualized Language Arts (ILA) Project
501 Central Ave, Dalton, GA 30720
Barbara S. Rous, 706-226-6369
K–12th grade
"Writing-across-the-curriculum."

Christians Concerned for Education / Still Waters
330 Concord Ln, LaFayette, GA 30728
706-397-2941
Walker County
Type: state home-based

Cities-in-Schools at Norris Middle School; JTPA GED;Early Childhood Summer Parental Involvement
PO Box 957, Thomson, GA 30824
James Hutcheson, 404-595-1918
McDuffie County
Type: public at-risk
MS, Pre K
CS: staffed by public and private specialists (counselors, health workers, and employers, etc.); EC: accelerated learning for upcoming fall kindergarteners.

Innovative Program Center
(See Resource Appendix)

Partnership and Student Success (PASS) Project
PO Box 957, Thomson, GA 30824
Lynne Entrekin, 404-595-4452
McDuffie County
Type: public at-risk
3rd grade
At-home packet/computer/CAI for up to 2 wks.

Thomson's Optional Program for Success (TOPS)
PO Box 1077, Thomson, GA 30824
Genelda McClain, 404-595-9393
McDuffie County
Type: public at-risk
HS

Briarwood Montessori School
3155 Thomson Hywy, Warrenton, GA 30828-6354

Opportunity Magnet
1000 Turpin St, Augusta, GA 30901
Rush Utley, 404-823-6942
Richmond County
Type: public at-risk
For 8th graders retained at least twice.

A. R. Johnson Health Science and Engineering HS, John S. Davidson Fine Arts School (5–12th grade)
3146 Lake Forest Dr, Augusta, GA 30909
Bert Thomas, 404-737-7150
Richmond County
Type: public choice
HS

Self-Esteem Achievement Training (SEAT)
3146 Lake Forest Dr, Augusta, GA 30909
Fred Stallings, 404-737-7129
Richmond County
Type: public at-risk
MS
7-wk summer prep for tutoring third graders in reading.

Walden Hall Christian Montessori
3615 Wheeler Rd, Augusta, GA 30909-1825

Project Promoting Academic Success for Students (PASS)
PO Box 516 E Dykes St, Cochran, GA 31014
Linda Wood, 912-934-2821
Bleckley County
Type: public at-risk
ES, MS
Parent involvement.

The Co-op School
PO Box 1198 117 N Jackson, Dublin, GA 31040
John Deamer, 912-272-3440
Laurens County
Type: public at-risk
9-12th grade

Telfair Alternative Center
210-B E Parsonage St, Box 240, McRae, GA 31055
Wayne Crafton, 912-868-5661

Telfair County
Type: public at-risk
5–12th grade

GAIA Permaculture Community (1978)
Rt 1 Box 74, Mauk, GA 31058
Alton Deville, Founder, 912-649-7700
Non-profit
2 teachers, 7 students, mainly at-risk, ages 22–40
Two week visit required
Governance by community leader and students
Tending garden, poultry, goats; designing solar homes; building straw bale cottages; aquifer conservation; erosion prevention; group decision making; cooperation with surrounding community.

The Alternative School of Baldwin County
115 Hwy 49 W, Milledgeville, GA 31061
Joe Owens, 912-453-4176
Type: public at-risk
HS
Extensive CAI; individualized.

The Elberta Center
Reid St, Warner Robins, GA 31088
Danny Carpenter or Bud Meeks, 912-929-7898
Houston County
Type: public at-risk
HS
Vocational co-op, GED, JTPA, drug prevention, teen parenting; childcare available.

Bloomindage Elementary
Main St, Bloomingdale, GA 31302
Amelia Poppell, 912-748-4403
Type: magnet
K–5th grade
Learning styles; performing and fine arts.

ASAP
100 Pafford St, Hinesville, GA 31313
Johnny Riles, Dir
Liberty County
Type: public at-risk
7th grade
Acceleration program for 7th graders retained at least twice.

Liberty Educational Alternatives Division (LEAD)
5 Shipman Ave, Hinesville, GA 31313
Chris Chalker, 912-876-3795
Liberty County

Bartow Elementary
1804 Stratford St, Savannah, GA 31401
Dora Myles, 912-651-7331
Type: magnet
K–5th grade
Gifted and talented.

Optional Program with Training (OPT)
208 Bull St, Savannah, GA 31401
Edward G. Miller, 912-651-7000
Chatham County
Students mainly at-risk
Tutorial; CAI; self-paced; competency-based; GED/diploma prep.

Savannah-Chatham Cty Magnet Schools
208 Bull St, Savannah, GA 31401
Lillie Ellis, 912-651-7233
Type: public choice
The Biological Sciences Academy at Downtown W ES; The Business, Legal, Financial and Performing Arts Academy at SHS; The Gifted and Talented Academy at Bartow ES; The Computer Science and Video Technology Academy at E Broad St ES; The Charles Ellis Montessori Academy (K–5, no letter grades); The Academy of Performing and Fine Arts at Gadsden ES (partnership with the Savannah College of Art and Design and Savannah Symphony Orchestra); The Sciences and Mathematics Academy at Haven ES (astronomy, rocketry, space and environmental science, long-term research projects, Math-a-thon, Young Astronauts Club (works with Coastal Rocketry Association to design and launch model rockets), and a permanent greenhouse and weather station; extensive field trips); The Computer Science Academy at Hodge ES; The Honors, International Studies, and Foreign Language Academy at Spencer ES (Japan, Germany, Spain, and France); The Computer Science Academy at Hubert MS (modems, satellite dish); The Biological and Medical Professions Academy at Beach HS; Gould ES (Olympic theme; nature trail); Hesse ES (computers, video); Howard ES (individualized; CAI); Pooler ES (extensive CAI); Windsor Forest ES (curriculum integrates music, poems, rhymes, games, songs, and dances; performances); Jenkins HS (nationally recognized robotics, with lasers and lithograph; emphasis on physical sciences; technicians and engineers from Gulfstream Aerospace Corp); transportation.

Shuman Middle School
415 Goebel Ave, Savannah, GA 31404
Roland James, 912-651-7085
Type: magnet
6–8th grade
Performing arts; communications.

Parent & Child Montessori Learning Center
1407 E 41st St, Savannah, GA 31404-3525
Paula Washburn

Charles Ellis Elementary
220 E 49th St, Savannah, GA 31405
Anne Monaghan, 912-651-7250
Type: magnet
K–5th grade
Montessori academy.

Savannah Montessori School
6610 Abercorn St, Savannah, GA 31405-5827

Green Heart School
2611 Salcedo Ave, Savannah, GA 31406
Type: Montessori

Montessori Academy
8415 Cresthill Ave, Savannah, GA 31406-6113

Seminole Montessori School
2499 Seminole Trail, Waycross, GA 31501

OPT-ED
Rt 1 PO Box 712-A, Blackshear, GA 31516
Pat Park, 912-449-2057
Pierce County
Type: public at-risk
GED prep.

Children's Montessori School
810 Newcastle St, Brunswick, GA 31520

Risley Alternative Learning Center
1800 Albany St, Brunswick, GA 31520
Jonathan Williams, Dir, 912-267-4165
Glynn County
Type: public at-risk
Allows severly ill students to study at home through televised classes and/or actual teacher visits.

OP-ED Program
1313 Egmont St PO Box 1677, Brunswick, GA 31521
L. E. McDowell, 912-267-4220
Glynn County
Type: public at-risk
Student ages 16–18, HS
GED prep.

Montessori Guidance Center
136 Dunbarton Dr, St Simons Island, GA 31522-1015
Susan Williamson

Coffee County Alternative School
1303 S Peterson St, Douglas, GA 31533
C. Mathis, Dir, 912-384-2086
1 teacher, 2 assistants; MS, HS

Good Start
PO Box 1227, Valdosta, GA 31601
Mary Ethridge McRae, 912-245-2250
Lowndes County
Type: public at-risk
Pre K

Lowndes County Alternative Program
1112 N St Augustine Rd, Valdosta, GA 31601
Dennis Tipton, 912-245-2250
Type: public choice
HS
After school credit classes.

Dougherty County Alternative School
600 S Madison St, Albany, GA 31702
John R. Strong or Walter Judge, 912-431-1218 or 912-431-1212
Type: public at-risk
75 students

Americus/Sumter County Alternative School
802 Ashby St, Americus, GA 31709
Connie Caruthers, Dir, 912-924-3605,-6045
Student age 4, pre K
Individualized.

GED Preparation Program
PO Box 847, Americus, GA 31709
Ronnie Williams, 912-924-3605
Type: public at-risk
Jointly sponsored by South Georgia Technical Institute; CAI; small classes.

Alternative Opportunity (ALT-O) at Bainbridge HS
1301 E College St, Bainbridge, GA 31717

Richard Johnson, 912-248-2230
Decatur County
Type: public at-risk
HS
Allows 7th graders retained at least twice to enter 9th or 10th grade; rigorous, self-paced, "catch up" program.

The Opportunity Program (TOP)
413 Columbia Rd, Blakely, GA 31723
Chesley Wiger, 912-723-3746
Early County
Type: public at-risk
5-7th grade
Rigorous curriculum helps referred students retained at least twice.

Vocational Office Training (VOT) and Diversified Cooperative Training (DCT)
439 Firetower Rd, Leesburg, GA 31763
Marie Wright and Larry Murkerson, 912-759-6264
Lee County
Type: public choice
HS

Colquitt County Alternative School
5th St SW, Moultrie, GA 31768
Richard Warren, Dir, 912-890-6206
Diploma-earning; evenings.

The Fun Factory
PO Box 225, Ocilla, GA 31774
Rhonda Walters, 912-468-7485
Irwin County
Type: public at-risk
K-5th grade
Latchkey, summer; focus on substance abuse.

Muscogee County Intervention
1112 29th St, Columbus, GA 31904
George Casion, 404-323-4123
Type: public at-risk
MS
Accelerated, 9th grade prep for students retained at least twice.

Hawaii

Hawaii Military Families in Home Education
113 Nijmegen Rd, Fort Ord, HI 93941-1524
Gail Thomas
Type: state home-based
Other contact: Mary Lyons; 183 20th Ave, Honolulu, HI; 808-422-7949.

Aiea High School
98-1276 Ulune St, Aiea, HI 96701
Earnest Tamayose

Aiea Intermediate School
99-600 Kulaea St, Aiea, HI 96701
Karen Shinjo

Pali-uli Waldorf School (1988)
PO Box 1338, Kealakekua, HI 96704
Shelley Hoose, Adm, 808-322-3316
Tuition: $3,600-4,000/yr, scholarships
5 teachers, 65 students, ages 3-12, pre K-6th grade

Affiliation: AWSNA
Governance by board and faculty through administrator
Teacher qualifications: college degree, Waldorf training
Traditional Waldorf curriculum; Hawaiian studies; multi-aged classes; rural location; interns accepted.

Hale O Ulu
91-1841 D Ft Weaver Rd, Ewa, HI 96706
Ann Kawahara

Christian Homeschoolers of Hawaii
91-824 Oama St, Ewa Beach, HI 96706
Arleen Alejado, 808-689-6398
Type: state home-based

Ilima Intermediate School
91-884 Ft Weaver Rd, Ewa Beach, HI 96706
Scott Yamada

CORAL Ohana O Maui (1993)
4150 Hana Hwy, Haiku, HI 96708

Elizabeth Werthiem, 808-573-0978
Type: independent, non-profit; tuition: $225-450/mo
5 teachers, 48 students, ages 4-15, ungraded
Governance by democratic school meeting
Teacher qualifications: staff chosen by students and staff
On rural Maui; student motivated activities; outdoor explorations to waterfalls, beaches; drumming, dance, song; school is new and evolving; no letter grades; non-compulsory class attendance; multi-aged classes; rural location.

Ohana Community Center
880 Hana Hwy, Haiku, HI 96708
Type: home-based

Tropical Homeschooler Newsletter (1992)
(See Resource Appendix)

Hana High School & Elementary
PO Box 128, Hana, HI 96713
Betty Lou Kala

Compensatory Education
480 Waianuenue Ave, Bldg C, Hilo, HI 96720
Miriam Agcaoili

St Joseph's Montessori Preschool (1991)
999 Ululani St, Hilo, HI 96720
Nancy Graber, Dir, 808-961-0424
Non-profit; tuition: $300/350/mo
2 teachers, 4 assistants, 45 students, ages 3-6
Entrance requirements: toilet trained
Affiliations: NCEA, AMS
Governance by administrator
Large classrooms; in heart of Hilo; childcare; interns accepted.

Christ Lutheran Montessori (1964)
595 Kapiolani St, Hilo, HI 96720-3997
Christa Murufas, Dir, 808-935-6468
Tuition: $250/330/345/mo
3 teachers, 2 assistants, 52 students, mainly international, ages 3-9
Governance by an administrator and a board of trustees
Childcare; suburban location; interns accepted.

Hale O Kamali'l Montessori School
326 Desha Ave, Hilo, HI 96720-4817
Marie Roberts

Hale 'O Ho' oponopono (1972)
PO Box 376, Honaunau, HI 96726
Pat Bento, Site Mgr, 808-328-9166, FAX: 808-328-8917
Type: public at-risk
6 teachers, 30 students, ages 14-19, 9-12th grade
For at-risk only; no residency requirement
Teacher qualifications: BA, experience with at-risk
Vocational; counseling; HS curriculum; multi-aged classes; rural location; transportation; interns accepted.

Molokai High School
PO Box 158, Hoolehua, HI 96729
Kenneth Nakayama

Maui High School
660 S Lono Ave, Kahului, HI 96732
Ramson Wong

Kalaheo High School
730 Iliaina St, Kailua, HI 96734
Patricia Middleworth

Carey School
260 N Kainalu Dr, Kailua, HI 96734-2396
Type: Montessori

Kamuela & Kona Montessori Schools (1980)
PO Box 1604, Kamuela, HI 96743
Virginia Hammon, Head, 808-885-4141, FAX: 808-885-4994

Non-profit; tuition: $3,040-5,600/yr
14 teachers, 9 assistants, 166 students, ages infant-12
Affiliations: AMS, NAEYC, GATE
Governance by board, teachers, administrators
Peace ed by nurturing self-esteem, self-discipline, independence, self-motivation, responsibility; childcare; interns accepted.

Kohala Montessori
PO Box 1793, Kumuela, HI 96743
Cheri Spies Havens

Haiku Hale O'Keiki Montessori School
46-283 Kahuhipa St, Honolulu, HI 96744
Patricia Gooch

Castle High School
45-386 Kaneohe Bay Dr, Kaneohe, HI 96744
Nelson Maeda

Key Project
47-200 Waihee Rd, Kaneohe, HI 96744
Nancy Ravelo

Kapaa Elementary School
4886 Kawaihau Rd, Kapaa, HI 96746
Joan Sahw, Staff Facilitator
Type: Montessori

St Catherine's School
5021 Kawaihau Rd, Kapaa, HI 96746-2097
Carol West
Type: Montessori

Ka Papa Honua O Keawanui (1979)
HC-01 Box 471, Kaunakakai, HI 96748
Rose L. Moreno, Site Mgr, 808-558-8945, FAX:-8979
Maui County
Type: public at-risk
3 teachers, 25 students, ages 14-18, 7-12th grade
For at-risk only; no residency requirement
Teacher qualifications: BA, experience with at-risk
Vocational; counseling; HS curriculum; multi-aged classes; rural location; transportation.

Malamalama School
HCR2 13031, Keaau, HI 96749
Office Mgr
Type: Waldorf

Montessori Hale O Keiki (1991)
PO Box 2348, Kihei, HI 96753
Elaine O'Colmain, Dir, 808-874-7441, FAX: same
Non-profit; tuition: $3,720/3,900/yr
3 teachers, 3 assistants, 48 students, mainly international, ages 3-6
Entrance requirements: visit; orientation; interview
Affiliations: AMS, NAEYC, HAEYC, Kinei Comm Assn, Chaminade U; accreditation: HIDHS
Governance by board
Gymnastics; Kindermusik; Hawaiian studies; computers; childcare; suburban location; interns accepted.

Kanai Waldorf School (1986)
PO Box 818; 4480 Hookui Rd, Kilauea, HI 96754
Ann Simpson, Adm Dir, 808-828-1144, FAX: 825-1110
Kauai County
Non-profit; tuition: $4,000/yr
10 teachers, 94 students, ages 3-12, pre K-6th grade
Governance by board
Form drawing; modeling; German; Music; Hawaiian Studies; handwork; multi-aged classes; rural location.

Ka'Imi Naaua'O Montessori School
PO Box 1419, Kapaau, HI 96755-1419

Kalama Intermediate School
120 Makani Rd, Makawao, HI 96768
Ione Isobe

Montessori School of Maui (1978)
PO Box 1435, Makawao, HI 96768
Jing Wong, 808-871-2682, FAX: same
Non-profit; tuition: $3,630-4,100/yr
5 teachers, 4 assistants, 121 students, mainly international,
    ages 3-12
Governance by administrator, board of trustees
Hawaiian and Japanese cultural resource teachers; childcare;
    rural location; interns accepted.

Hawaii Island Home Educators
PO Box 851, Mountain View, HI 96771
Connie Siler, 808-968-8076; 968-8434
Type: state home-based

Kids Lib News
(See Resource Appendix)

Kalani Honua
RR 2, Box 4500, Pahoa, HI 96778
Cynthia Albers
Type: independent

Open Sky Home Education (1985)
(See Resource Appendix)

Open Sky HOME Education (1985)
PO Box 915, Alaili Rd, Pahoa, HI 96778
Michael Sunanda, Dir, 808-936-2561
Big Island County
Type: home-based resource, non-profit
3 teachers, 5 students, ages 3-10
Entrance requirements: trusting agreements
Governance by parent grouping
Teacher qualifications: sensitive, playful, aware, honest
Rooted in natural bonding, trust, cooperation; self-directed;
    artwork; natural games; Kids Lib Newsletter; non-
    compulsory class attendance; rural location.

Marti Jones
PO Box 1490, Pahoe, HI 96778
Marti Jones
Type: Montessori

Montessori Country School
PO Box 1203, Pahoa, HI 96778-1203
Marie Rieck

Montessori of Maui
Baldwin Ave, Paia, HI 96779
Jing Wong

Highlands Intermediate
1460 Hoolaulea St, Pearl City, HI 96782
Douglas Chow Hoy

Mililani Montessori Center
Wahiawa Site 11679, California Ave, Wahiawa, HI 96786

Central District Superintendent
300 Kahelu Ave, Leilehua #50, Mililani, HI 96789
Robert B. Lee

Friends Learning at Home
PO Box 3476, Mililani, HI 96789
Linda Inouye, 808-625-0445

St John's Mililani Montessori Center
95-370 Kuahelani Ave, Mililani, HI 96789-1103
Linda Durocher

Haleakala Waldorf School
RR 2 Box 790, Kula, HI 96790
Rosemary K. Moore, Adm Dir, 808-878-2511, FAX:-3341
Maui County
Non-profit; tuition: $4,850/yr
16 teachers, 175 students, ages 4-13, pre K-8th grade
Affiliation: WANA

Governance by board and teachers
Teacher qualifications: experience, Waldorf training, BA
Ecology; community service; exchanges with sister schools
    world-wide; extensive field trips; suburban location; trans-
    portation; interns accepted.

Maui Alternative Learning Center (1977)
c/o Baldwin HS, 1650 Kaahumanu Ave, Wailuka, HI 96790
Sydney Jamison, Teacher
Maui County
Type: public at-risk
1 teacher, 18 students, ages 14-19, HS
District residency required
Affiliation: HI DE
Governance by teachers and principal
Teacher qualifications: state certification
7 networked computers; Josten's Life Skills program; state
    funded work-study; multi-aged classes; extensive field
    trips; suburban location; transportation.

Hawaii Homeschool Association
66960 Kuewa Dr, Waialua, HI 96791
Type: state home-based

Nanakuli High School
89-980 Nanakuli Ave, Waianae, HI 96792
Skip Lopes

Baldwin High School
1650 Kaahumanu Ave, Wailuku, HI 96793
Craig Yatsushiro

**HAPPY (Homeschool Adventures: Program for Parents
and Youngsters)** (1989)
777 Kolani St, Wailuku, HI 96793
Gail Nagasako, Founder, 808-242-8225, FAX: 808-242-7020
Weekly field trips.

Maui District Superintendent
54 High St, 4th Flr, Wailuku, HI 96793
Ralph Murakami

Cities in Schools
94-366 Pupupani St #209, Waipahu, HI 96797
Fay Uyeda

JOBS: Department of Human Services
PO Box 339, Honolulu, HI 96809
Glenn China

Employment Training Office
33 S King St #300, Honolulu, HI 96813
Anne Koide

Kawaiahao Child Care Center
872 Mission Lane, Honolulu, HI 96813-5051
Wendy Lagreta
Type: Montessori

Marimed Foundation
1050 Ala Moana Blvd, Honolulu, HI 96814
Bob Bonar

Chaminade U Montessori Teacher Education Program
3140 Waialae Ave, Honolulu, HI 96816
Louise Bogart
Type: Montessori teacher education

Distance Learning
3645 Waialae Ave, Honolulu, HI 96816
Vicki Kajioka

DOE-OIS
2530 10th Ave, Honolulu, HI 96816
Carl Takeshita

Kaimuki High School
2705 Kaimuki Ave, Honolulu, HI 96816
Daryl Loo

Kaimuki Intermediate
631 18th Ave, Honolulu, HI 96816
Karen Tsubata

L Robert Allen Montessori Center (1982)
1365 Kaminaka Dr, Honolulu, HI 96816
Sylvia Carey, 808-735-4875, FAX: 808-735-4870
Non-profit; tuition: $3,300/3,800/yr
3 teachers, 4 assistants, 36 students, ages 3-6
Affiliation: AMS; accreditations: MACTE, WASC, HIDE
Governance by a board of trustees
Multi-ethnic; view of Diamond Head; Japanese; Orff and
  Suzuki instruction; childcare; urban location; interns
  accepted.

Elementary School Guidance Program (1987)
1887 Makuakane St, Honolulu, HI 96817
Wally Lau, Dir, 808-842-8627, FAX:-0080
Oahu County
Non-profit
2 teachers, 400 students, ages 5-12, K-6th grade
Teacher qualifications: BA, experience
Promotion of school success; prevention; guidance; hetero-
  geneous grouping; minimal labeling of at-risk; rural
  location.

Malama o ke Ola (Caring for Life) (1978)
1850 Makuakane St, Bldg C, Honolulu, HI 96817
Rick Campbell, Program Mgr, 808-842-8632, FAX:-8515
Type: public at-risk
7 teachers, 300 students, ages 12-16, 7-11th grade
Enrollment restricted to at-risk Hawaiian (part-Hawaiians pre-
  ferred) residents
Governance by principal
Teacher qualifications: BA
Hawaiian culture; self-awareness; communication, school sur-
  vival skills; experiential; suburban location.

Moanalua High School
2825 Ala Ilima St, Honolulu, HI 96818
Etuale V. Suafoa

St Philomena's Child Center
3300 Ala Laulani St, Honolulu, HI 96818-2837
Type: Montessori

Montessori Center of Pearl Harbor
45 Makalapa Dr, Honolulu, HI 96818-3110

Dole Intermediate School
1803 Kam IV Rd, Honolulu, HI 96819
Lesile Opuiauoho

Calvary by the Sea School
5339 Kalanianaole Hwy, Honolulu, HI 96821
Jane Stegmaier
Type: Montessori

Star of the Sea Early Learning Center
4449 Malia St, Honolulu, HI 96821-1138
Lisa Foster
Type: Montessori

Kilohana United Methodist Pre-school
5829 Mahimahi St, Honolulu, HI 96821-2120
Type: Montessori

Hawaii Nature Center
2131 Makiki Heights Dr, Honolulu, HI 96822
Diana King

Montessori Community School
1515 Liholiho St, Honolulu, HI 96822
Patsy Tom

Montessori Elementary
3225 Pakanu St, Honolulu, HI 96822

Maryknoll Elementary School-Montessori Center
1722 Dole St, Honolulu, HI 96822-4997

DOE Community Education Section
595 Pepeekeo, Bldg H, 2nd Flr, Honolulu, HI 96825
Gladys Naitoh

Honolulu Waldorf School (1961)
350 Ulua St, Honolulu, HI 96825
Michael Preston, Faculty Chair, 808-377-5471
Tuition: $4,000-5,500/yr, scholarships
25 teachers, 226 students, ages 3-14, pre K-8th grade
Entrance requirements: age appropriate competence
Affiliation: AWSNA
Governance by college of teachers and board
Languages; non-academic kindergarten; comprehensive,
  non-elective curriculum; suburban location; interns
  accepted.

Kaiser High School
511 Lunalilo Home Rd, Honolulu, HI 96825
Jimmy Hutcherson

Idaho

Sandpoint Montessori School
1004 Ruth Ave, Sandpoint, ID
Heidi Gonzales

Alternative Junior High School (1978)
252 Pershing St, Pocatello, ID 83201
Paul Matthews, 208-233-1161
Type: public at-risk
4 teachers, 30 students, mainly at-risk, ages 12-15, 7-9th
  grade
Placement through district discipline review committee
Governance by teachers, principal and board
Teacher qualifications: BS, ID Certification, ability

Highly structured; students required to complete 4 levels of
  responsibility; min 10 weeks; rural location; transportation;
  interns accepted.

Teen Parent Center (1989)
240 E Maple, Pocatello, ID 83201
Sheryl Brockett, Prin, 208-232-2994
Bannock County
Type: public at-risk
5 teachers, 60 students, mainly at-risk, ages 12-21, 7-12th
  grade
Enrollment restricted to pregnant or parenting students
Governance by teachers, principal, and board

Teacher qualifications: certified in subject area
Support services integrated with Health and Welfare, Job Service and Health Department; childcare; multi-aged classes; urban location; transportation.

Bonneville School
320 N 8th Ave, Pocatello, ID 83201-5713
Type: Montessori

Second Chance Alternative High School
270 E Bridge St, Blackfoot, ID 83221
Guy Gladden, Dir, 208-785-8825
Type: public at-risk

Second Chance High School
1328 S Meridian, Blackfoot, ID 83221
Guy Gladden, Dir, 208-785-8825, FAX:-8893
Bingham County
Type: public at-risk
7 teachers, 130 students, mainly at-risk, ages 14–21, 9–12th grade
Entrance requirements: age 14–21, at-risk; no residency requirement
Governance by teachers, principal, board
Teacher qualifications: ID Certification
Strong voc; 1:18 ratio; extensive community support; multi-aged classes; childcare; suburban location; transportation; interns accepted.

Magic Valley Alternative High School
Box 523, Twin Falls, ID 83303-0523
Joyce Houstan, Prin, 208-733-8823

Montessori Place
775 Lincoln Dr, Idaho Falls, ID 83401-4920

Continuation High School (1974)
1767 Blue Sky Dr, Idaho Falls, ID 83402
Aaron L Maybon, Prin, 208-525-7795, FAX: same
Bonnevile County
Type: public choice
20 teachers, 300 students, ages 16–24, 9–12th grade
Entrance requirements: age 16–21; non-enrollee status
Governance by principal, board
Teacher qualifications: ID Certification
Teen parenting; childcare; counseling; college rep; multi-aged classes; 90% attendance rule; urban location.

Alternative High School 9
134 Madison Ave, Rexburg, ID 83440
Michael Johnson, Dir, 208-359-3305

Alternative High School
135 N Bridge, St Anthony, ID 83445
Richard Law, Dir, 208-624-3416

Bridgeview Alternative High School
PO Box 790, Salmon, ID 83467
Jay Skeen, Head Tch, 208-756-6277

Lewiston High School
1114 9th St, Lewiston, ID 83501
Jim Wilund, Prin, 208-746-2331
Type: public

Alternative High School
714 Jefferson, Box 430, Grangeville, ID 83530
Janice Ingrahm, Clerk, 208-983-0940

Alternative Education Center
1114 Arthur, Caldwell, ID 83605
Gary Tuttle, Head Tch, 208-455-3325

Caldwell Alternative High School (1981)
1117 Arthur St, Caldwell, ID 83605
Michele Travis, Adm Asst, 208-455-3325, FAX: 455-3341
Lanyon County
Type: public at-risk
7 teachers, 120 students, mainly at-risk, ages 14–21, 9–12th grade
Entrance requirements: interview, testing, meet state definition of at-risk to attend for free or tuition is $90/sem
Governance by principal
Teacher qualifications: ID Certification
Multi-aged classes; open entry; individualized; self-paced; mastery learning; no homework; art; homeless student assistance; rural location; transportation; interns accepted.

Black Canyon Alternative (1990)
315 S Johns, Emmett, ID 83617
Amy Linville, Head Tch, 208-365-5552, FAX:-5085
Gem County
Type: public choice
5 teachers, 65 students, mainly at-risk, ages 16–21, 9–12th grade
Governance by teachers and principal
Interns accepted.

Academy 2000 Elmore Alternative Center
470 N 3rd E Suite 4, Mountain Home, ID 83617
Larry Slade, Dir, 208-587-2593

Heartland Alternative Education Center (1991)
PO Box 967, 411 South Hwy 55, McCall, ID 83638
Ralph Colton, PhD, Dir, 208-634-3686
Valley County
Type: public at-risk
1 teacher, 12–18 students, ages 14–21, HS
Residency required
Affiliation: SW ID PIC
Governance by board with student assistance
Teacher qualifications: certification
100% attendance policy; urban location.

Heartland Alternative Education Center
120 Idaho St, Mccall, ID 83638
Ralph E. Colton, 208-634-2161

Meridian Academy (1989)
2311 E Lanark, Boise, ID 83642
Marilyn Renolds, Superviser, 208-887-4759
Ada County
Type: public choice, at-risk
12 teachers, 150 students, mainly at-risk, HS
Governance by principal, faculty and student reps
Rural location; interns accepted.

Cloverdale Montessori
4765 Goldenrod, Meridian, ID 83642
Ron Dingwall

Meridian Alternative School
2311E Lanark, Meridian, ID 83642
Marilyn Renolds, Superviser, 208-887-4888

Northside Alternative Night School
4 N 100 E, Jerome, ID 83644
Karen Fraley, Dir, 208-324-8528

Middleton Evening School
511 W Maine, Middleton, ID 83644
John Beckwith, Prog Adm, 208-585-3027

Canyon Alternative Education Center
2407 Cadwell Blvd, Nampa, ID 83651
Dr Terry Haws, Prin, 208-467-5725

Alternative High School
PO Box 349, Payette, ID 83661
Pat Townsend, Dir, 208-642-4765

Teen Parent Alternative School
8444 Dearborn Rd, Nampa, ID 83686
Shirley Vendrell, Prin, 208-466-6921
Type: public at-risk

Boise Montessori Center
2999 Moore St, Boise, ID 83702-2140

Idaho Home Educators (1980)
Box 4022, Boise, ID 83703
Ada County
Type: state home-based, non-profit
Governance by parents
Resource store for help in choosing curriculum; no letter
   grades; extensive field trips; suburban location.

Scientific Wizardry Educational Products
(See Resource Appendix)

Elementary Montessori School
1004 Shoshone St, Boise, ID 83705-2340
Christel Nordhausen

Boise Evening High School (1975)
6001 Caggia, Boise, ID 83709
Bob Nisbett, Prin, 208-322-3723
Boise District, Ada County
Type: public choice
12 teachers, 300+ students, mainly at-risk, ages 16+, 9-12th
   grade
Entrance requirements: age 16+, seeking HS diploma; no resi-
   dency requirement
Governance by principal and board
Teacher qualifications: certification
Multi-aged classes; urban location.

Home Educators of Idaho
3618 Pine Hill Dr, Coeur d'Alene, ID 83814
208-667-2778
Type: state home-based

Project CDA (Creating Dropout Alternatives) (1978)
725 Hazel Ave, Coeur d'Alene, ID 83814
Roger Hansen, 208-667-7460
Kootenai County
Type: public at-risk
16 teachers, 234 students, ages 14-20, 8-12th grade
Entrance requirements: have failed 2 or more core courses
Governance by principal, faculty and student representatives
Teacher qualifications: ID certification
Emphasizes student responsibility; student/staff/parent part-
   nerships; self-governing school community; rural location;
   interns accepted.

Mortenson Company
PO Box 98, Hayden Lake, ID 83835
Jerry Mortensen
Type: Montessori

Alternative Education Program
402 E Fifth St, Moscow, ID 83843
Dr K.C. Albright, Prog Adm, 208-882-2591

Homeschooling on the Polouse (1993)
802 White Ave, Moscow, ID 83843
Peg Harver-Marose, 208-882-1593
Latah County
See WA listing of same name.

New Vision Alternative High School (1990)
Box 40, Post Falls, ID 83854
Colleen Kelsey, Head Tch, 208-773-3941, FAX:-3218
Kootenai County
6 teachers, 65 students, ages 14-21, 9-12th grade
Entrance requirements: meet state at-risk criteria; no resi-
   dency requirement
Governance by head teacher, faculty and student representa-
   tives, and democratic school meeting
Teacher qualifications: experience with at-risk
outcome-based; family atmosphere; rural location

Snow Valley Academy
HCR 5 Box 76F, Priest River, ID 83856
Marnie Mason, 208-448-1869

Echo Springs
105 N 1st Ave #229, Sand Point, ID 83864

Sandpoint Waldorf School
PO Box 95, Sand Point, ID 83864
Andrea Lyman

Echo Springs Transition Studies Center (1993)
105 N 1st Ave, Suite 229, Sandpoint, ID 83864
208-265-0208, FAX: 208-263-6908
Type: higher education
Student ages 18-24
Empower, assist students in identifying their interests and
   assessing their strengths and weaknesses.

Lake Pend Oreille High School (1989)
1005 N Boyer, Sandpoint, ID 83864
Leonard Parenteau, Prin, 208-263-6121, FAX: 265-5734
Bonner County
Type: public at-risk
7 teachers, 70 students, mainly at-risk, ages 15-19, 9-12th
   grade
Enrollment restricted to those who meet state guidelines; no
   residency requirement
Governance by teachers and principal
Teacher qualifications: certification, experience with at-risk
   youth
Vocational, technology programs competency-based; group,
   individual counseling; community involvement; multi-aged
   classes; rural location; transportation; interns accepted.

Alternative High School
PO Box 500, Wallace, ID 83873
George Heaton, Dir, 208-753-4515

Illinois

Montessori Learning Center
15 E Palatine Rd, Arlington Heights, IL 60004

Northwest Suburban Montessori School (1964)
800 N Fernandez, Arlington Heights, IL 60004
Rosemary Kreuser, 708-259-6044
Non-profit; tuition: $190–465/mo
5 teachers, 16 assistants, 182 students, ages infant-6
Governance by administrator, board
3-year modern art program; weekly arts/crafts and gymnastics for a fee; suburban location; interns accepted.

Christian Liberty Academy Satellite Schools (1968)
(See Resource Appendix)

Arlington Heights Little Peoples Montessori School
1234 N Arlington Heights Rd, Arlington Heights, IL 60004-4741

Creative Care Children's Center
415 N Hough St, Barrington, IL 60010-3028
Type: Montessori

Crystal Lake Montessori
8617 Ridgefield Rd, Crystal Lake, IL 60014

Deerfield Montessori School (1966)
760 North Ave, Deerfield, IL 60015
Lisa Kambich, Assoc Dir, 708-945-7580, FAX: 708-948-5136
Non-profit
Students mainly international, ages infant-6
Affiliations: AMS, ILMS
Governance by an administrator and a board of trustees
4 sites: Deerfield (2), Riverwoods, Glenview; ponds; woods; nature trails; small animals; gardens; music; dance; foreign language; summer program; childcare; suburban location; interns accepted.

Westminster School
824 Waukegan Rd, Deerfield, IL 60015-3206
Type: Montessori

Children's Learning World Montessori School
PO Box 1231, Des Plaines, IL 60017-1231
Rosemary Fish

Glencoe Montessori School
395 Jefferson Ave, Glencoe, IL 60022-1877
Dr James Tulloss

Country Meadows Montessori (1981)
100 S Cemetery Rd, Gurnee, IL 60031-4439
Catherine Ozark, Owner, 708-244-9352
Non-profit; tuition: $230–400/mo
6 teachers, 14 assistants; student ages 3–12
Entrance requirements: toilet trained
Affiliation: AMS
Governance by a board of trustees
On 3.8 acres in restored barn; childcare; rural location; interns accepted.

Montessori Center of Highland Park
1731 Deerfield Rd, Highland Park, IL 60035-3704

Highland Park Montessori School
1301 Clavey Rd, Highland Park, IL 60035-4539
Carol Lee

Forest Bluff School
121 E Sheridan Pl, Lake Bluff, IL 60044-2632
Type: Montessori

Montessori School of Lake Forest (1965)
13700 W Laurel, Lake Forest, IL 60045
Lissa Hektor, Adm, 708-918-1000, FAX: 907-918-1304
Non-profit; tuition: $184/wk-5,564/yr
16 teachers, 10 assistants, 190 students, ages infant-12
Affiliation: AMI; accreditations: AMS, ILBE
Governance by administrator, board
Orff music; Spanish; after-school German, French, drama, art, gymnastics; childcare; suburban location; interns accepted.

Steppingstone Montessori School
101 S Beck Rd, Lindenhurst, IL 60046-9655

Montessori School of Long Grove
Box 1115 RFD, Long Grove, IL 60047
Kris Mills

Montessori World of Discovery
1660 Checker Rd, Long Grove, IL 60047

Children's Corner Developmental Center (1992)
888 E Belvidere Rd #107, Grayslake, IL 60048
June Glogovsky and Lorna Collar, Owners, 708-548-2880
Type: Montessori; tuition: $185–370/mo
140 students, ages 3-6
Affiliation: AMS
Governed by owner partnership
Gymnastics; foreign language; suburban location.

Libertyville Montessori
PO Box 654, Libertyville, IL 60048-0654
Marjorie Cramer

Progressive Path School
510 Broadway, McHenry, IL 60050
Liz Berg, 312-497-3647
Type: independent
16 students, pre K-ES

Alexander Graham Bell Montessori School
2020 E Camp McDonald Rd, Mount Prospect, IL 60056-1727
Barbara Harris

Park View Montessori School
805 N Burning Bush Ln, Mount Prospect, IL 60056-1913

Career Publishing Inc
(See Resource Appendix)

Montessori Country Day School
200 W Maple Ave, Mundelein, IL 60060-1739

Children's House of the North Shore
1220 S Lake St, Mundelein, IL 60060-3706
Irene Voros
Type: Montessori

New Beginnings Montessori School
1401 S Lake St, Mundelein, IL 60060-4208
Carol Cossitt

Countryside Montessori School
1985 Pfingsten Rd, Northbrook, IL 60062-5853
Annette B Kulle

Barrington Montessori School
140 Patricia Ln, Palatine, IL 60067
Norma J Cicci

Dawn Gate- A Montessori School
728 S Wilke Rd, Palatine, IL 60067-7629

Montessori Edu-Care Centers
1004 N Cumberland Ave, Park Ridge, IL 60068-2047

Montessori Adventure to Learning Center
304 S Palatine Rd, Prospect Hts, IL 60070

Anatomical Chart Company
(See Resource Appendix)

Shimer College (1853)
PO Box A 500, Waukegan, IL 60079
David B. Buchanon, Adms Dir, 708-623-8400, FAX: 249-7171
Lake County
Type: higher education, boarding, non-profit; tuition:
    $12,000/yr, scholarships
20 teachers, 120 students, ages 15+
Governance by democratic school meeting
Small classes; no lectures or textbooks; early entrance option;
    weekend adult program; many homeschoolers accepted;
    suburban location.

Carman Elementary
520 Helmholz, Waukegan, IL 60085
Isabelle Buckner, 708-336-3100
Type: magnet
K-5th grade
Concerned citizen leadership; service.

Glenwood Elementary
2500 Northmoor, Waukegan, IL 60085
Robert Moran, 708-336-3100
Type: magnet
K-5th grade
Individually challenging.

North Elementary
410 Franklin, Waukegan, IL 60085
Sylvia Zon, 708-336-3100
Type: magnet
K-5th grade
Learning resource academy.

Robert E. Abbott Elementary
1319 Washington, Waukegan, IL 60085
Rita Melius, 708-336-3100
Type: magnet
6-8th grade
Project Discovery; gifted.

Thomas Jefferson Elementary
600 S Lewis, Waukegan, IL 60085
Allan Mismash, 708-336-3100
Type: magnet
6-8th grade
Gifted program.

Washington Elementary
110 S Orchard, Waukegan, IL 60085
Barbara Prendergast, 708-336-3100
Type: magnet
K-5th grade
Citizenship; community involvement.

Waukegan Montessori School
PO Box 133, Waukegan, IL 60085

Whittier Elementary
801 N Lewis Ave, Waukegan, IL 60085
Laurie Rickerd, 708-336-3100
Type: magnet
K-5th grade
Early childhood center; activity based learning.

Clark Elementary
601 Blanchard, Waukegan, IL 60087
Bernice Gehris, 708-336-3100
Type: magnet
K-5th grade
Global understanding through continental studies.

Oakdale Elementary
2230 McAree Rd, Waukegan, IL 60087
David Mackie, 708-336-3100
Type: magnet
K-5th grade
Global education.

Buffalo Grove Montessori School
950 Ellen Dr, Buffalo Grove, IL 60089-3707
Deborah LaPorte

Ronald Knox Montessori (1963)
2031 Elmwood Ave, Wilmette, IL 60091
Usha Bala, Ed Adm, 708-256-2922
Non-profit; tuition: $1,020-2,120/yr
8 teachers, 10 assistants, 199 students, ages infant-6
Entrance requirements: age 2 or 3 by Sept 1
Affiliations: AMS, ILMS, AMT, NAMTA, NAEYC
Suburban location; interns accepted.

Rose Hall Montessori School
1140 Wilmette Ave, Wilmette, IL 60091-2604

St Francis Xavier's Little Children's House
808 Linden Ave, Wilmette, IL 60091-2711
Type: Montessori

Forest Bluff Montessori School
1063 Cherry St, Winnetka, IL 60093
Haley C Nate

Montessori Childrens House
525 Sunset Ridge Rd, Northfield, IL 60093-1025

**Transitional Care program at Northwest Coonen High
    School** (1982)
101 S Jefferson St, Woodstock, IL 60098
Joyce A Gallery, Coord, 815-338-7360, FAX: 337-5510
McHenry County
Type: independent at-risk, non-profit; tuition: $125/sem
4 teachers, 20-30 students, ages 14-18, 9-12th grade
Must have at least a secondary diagnosis of substance abuse
Governance by teachers, principal, student reps
Teacher qualifications: flexibility, high tolerance level, team
    worker
Clinically based; daily group life skills class; therapeutic recre-
    ation; counseling; multi-aged classes; levels/privileges;
    rural location; interns accepted.

Community Montessori School
640 McHenry Ave, Woodstock, IL 60098-2923

Crystal Lake Montessori School
8700 Crystal Springs Rd, Woodstock, IL 60098-8058
Pamela Zirko

Illinois Christian Home Educators
PO Box 261, Zion, IL 60099
Type: state home-based

Discovery Montessori Center
PO Box 6, Bloomingdale, IL 60108-0006

Montessori School of DeKalb
321 Oak St, DeKalb, IL 60115-3369
Beverly Ann Smith

Children's House Montessori School
417 W Main St, West Dundee, IL 60118
Elizabeth Maliska

Forest Park Montessori School
16 Lathrop Ave, Forest Park, IL 60130-1009
Karla Ozima

La Leche League International
(See Resource Appendix)

Geneva Board of Education School District #304
400 McKinley Ave, Geneva, IL 60134
Adm Office, Dist 304
Type: Montessori

Mansio Mens
102 Howard St, Geneva, IL 60134-2318
Carolee Watts
Type: Montessori

Hansel & Gretel Haus
1 N 450 Park Blvd, Glen Ellyn, IL 60137
Annie Carlson
Type: Montessori

New Morning Children's House
400 N Walnut St, Itasca, IL 60143-1735
Joyce Czerwinskyyj
Type: Montessori

Creative Montessori Learning Center
550 S Edgewood St, Lombard, IL 60148-2822
Soumini Pillai

Alpha Montessori School
1625 S Mannheim Rd, Westchester, IL 60154-4318
Leanoore Dean

St Charles Board of Education School District 303
1304 Rongheimer Rd, St Charles, IL 60174
Child Study Office
Type: Montessori

Montessori Children's Academy (1981)
706 E Park Blvd, Villa Park, IL 60181
Chibi Lu Teng, Owner, 708-832-4423
Tuition: $15-35/day
3 teachers, 4 assistants, 45 students, ages infant-6
Affiliation: AMS; accreditation: ILBE
Governance by teachers and administrators
Childcare; interns accepted.

Seton Academy
350 N Westmore Ave, Villa Park, IL 60181
Type: Montessori

Wheaton Montessori Children's House
1970 Gary Ave, Wheaton, IL 60187-3029
Ms Vicks

Montessori Learning Center
1015 W Golf Rd, Hoffman Estates, IL 60194-1339
Rochelle Gutstadt

Montessori School of North Hoffman (1988)
1200 Freeman Rd, Hoffman Estates, IL 60195
Mrs Motlagh, PhD, Dir, 708-705-1234
Non-profit; tuition: $170-650/mo
7 teachers, 5 assistants, 129 students, ages infant-12
Affiliation: AMS
Governance by administrator
Specifically designed environment features lofts and fixtures
    at child's level; foreign language, art, music, Suzuki violin;
    childcare; suburban location; interns accepted.

Acarath Montessori School
22 Kristin Dr, Schaumburg, IL 60195-3302

Chiaravalle Montessori (1965)
425 Dempster St, Evanston, IL 60201
Linda Dolnick, Dir. of Admissions, 708-864-2190, FAX: 708-864-
    2206

Non-profit; tuition: $1,260-10,370/yr
30 teachers, 30 assistants, 381 students, ages infant-15
Affiliations: NAMTA, NAEYC, IL BE; accreditations: AMS, ISACS
Governance by administrator, board
In national historic landmark building; large gym; auditorium;
    art studio; music room; near Lake Michigan, public trans-
    portation, city playground; childcare; suburban location;
    interns accepted.

Child Care Center of Evanston
1840 Asbury Ave, Evanston, IL 60201'
Blair Grumman
Type: Montessori

Feltre School
518 Davis St, Suite 213, Evanston, IL 60201
Robert J. Ultima, Director, 708-733-0190
Type: public at-risk
Student ages 18+, HS
Affiliation: ASN

American Science and Surplus
(See Resource Appendix)

Grasp Adult Learning Center
835 Chicago Ave, 2nd Floor, Evanston, IL 60202
Cheryl Judice, 708-328-4420
350 students, ages 16+
Affiliation: ASN
Comprehensive GED; adult basic ed; ESL; survival skills.

Network of Progressive Educators (1989)
(See Resource Appendix)

HOUSE
806 Oakton, Evansville, IL 60202
Ann Wasserman, 708-328-6323
Cook County
Type: state home-based
Urban location

Intercultura Foreign Language Immersion Montessori
1145 Westgate St, Oak Park, IL 60301-1029
Dr Michael Rosanova

Children's Garden (1980)
165 N Lombard Ave, Oak Park, IL 60302
Roshan Mawani, Dir, 708-383-6570
Type: Montessori; tuition: $2,650-4,620/yr
2 teachers, 5 assistants, 40 students, ages 3-6
Affiliations: NAEYC, CAEYC, AMS
Governance by administrator
Spanish; Math Their Way; childcare; suburban location;
    interns accepted.

West Suburban Montessori School
1039 S East Ave, Oak Park, IL 60304

Alcuin Montessori School (1961)
7970 Washington Blvd, River Forest, IL 60305
Marianne Dunlap, Ed Dir, 708-366-1882
Type: Montessori, non-profit; tuition: $1,540-4,015/yr
13 teachers, 12 assistants, 273 students, ages infant-15
Affiliations: NAMTA, MAC/USA, AMI/EAA, AMI/USA; accreditation:
    IL DE
Governance by board
Classic Montessori school; childcare; suburban location;
    interns accepted.

Woodlite Design
PO Box 385, Elmwood, IL 60421-0385
Type: Montessori

Flossmoor Montessori (1966)
740 Western Ave, Flossmoor, IL 60422
Lawrence Lewis, Adm, 708-798-4600
Non-profit
Affiliation: ILMS; accreditation: AMI

Governance by administrator, board
Suburban location; interns accepted.

St Joseph's Earth Child School
925 Braemar Rd, Flossmoor, IL 60422-2205
Type: Montessori

Casa Montessori
3344 Knollwood Ln, Homewood, IL 60430-2710

Joliet Montessori School
1600 Root St; 3113 Heritage Dr, Joliet, IL 60435

Montessori West School
1711 Burry Circle, Joliet, IL 60435-2079

Suburban Lithuanian Montessori (1983)
14911 127th St, Lemont, IL 60439
Dana Dirvonis, 708-257-8891
Non-profit; tuition: 1,200/yr
1 teacher, 2 assistants, 30 students, ages 3–6
Affiliations: Lithuanian MS of America, Inc
Governance by board of trustees
Language and culture; interns accepted.

New Beginnings Christian Montessori Preschool
151 E Briarcliff Rd, Bolingbrook, IL 60440-3070
Patricia Stephens

St Dennis Montessori School
229 E 12th St, Lockport, IL 60441-3502

Education Service Network (1978)
1320 Union St, Morris, IL 60450
Jeffrey A, May, Dir, 815-941-3231, FAX: 815-942-5384
Type: public choice
10 teachers, 400 students, mainly at-risk, ages 14–21, 9–12th
   grade
Enrollment restricted to dropouts residents
Governance by director of vocational education
Teacher qualifications: state certification
Evenings; small classes; emphasis on student's culture; sub-
   urban location.

Oaklawn Montessori School
8901 S 52nd Ave, Oak Lawn, IL 60453-1307
Norma De La Cruz Froio

Garden Gates Montessori School
91st & 82nd Ave, Hickory Hills, IL 60457

Hands-On History
(See Resource Appendix)

Hickory House Montessori
8222 W 95th St, Hickory Hills, IL 60457-1942

Montessori Schools, Inc
7926 W 103rd Ave, Palos Hills, IL 60464

S W Suburban Montessori School
12219 86th Ave, Palos Park, IL 60464

Southwest Suburban Montessori (1970)
8800 W 119th St, Palos Park, IL 60464
Kathy Williams, Ed Adm, 708-448-5332
Non-profit; tuition: $632/1,714/2,370/yr
6 teachers, 9 assistants, 157 students, ages toddler-6
Entrance requirements: application; $45 fee
Affiliations: AMS, IMS; accreditation: NAEYC
Governance by an administrator and a board of trustees
Spanish instruction weekly; gym; handicap accessible; com-
   puters; testing available; parent rap sessions and work-
   shops; rural location; interns accepted.

Illinois Montessori Children's House
303 Illinois St, Park Forest, IL 60466
Ms Piunti

Laren Montessori School
425 E 164th St, South Holland, IL 60473-2216
Susan Considine

Palos-Worth Montessori School
7100 W 112th Ave, Worth, IL 60482

Creative Art Work
27 S Calumet, Aurora, IL 60506
Regina Barnett
Type: Montessori

Fox Valley Montessori School (1968)
850 N Commonwealth, Aurora, IL 60506
Robert Bates, Exec Dir, 708-896-7557
Non-profit; tuition: $35/day
18 teachers, 147 students, ages 2–12
Affiliation: AMS
Governance by a board of trustees
Teacher qualifications: Montessori certification
Guided by respect for each individual; focus on real life skills;
   no letter grades; non-compulsory class attendance; multi-
   aged classes; suburban location; interns accepted.

Illinois Mathematics and Science Academy (1986)
1500 W Sullivan Rd, Aurora, IL 60506-1039
708-801-6000
Type: magnet, boarding
Student ages 13–18, 10–12th grade
State-funded; mentorships; near Fermi Accelerator Lab.

Batavia Board of Education School Dist 101
12 W Wilson, Batavia, IL 60510
Adm Office
Type: Montessori

Carmel Montessori Academy & Children's House
595 S River Rd, Batavia, IL 60510
Arthur Basler

Montessori Academy (1971)
595 S River St, Batavia, IL 60510
Mary Yahnke, Dir, 708-879-2586
Non-profit; tuition: $250-513/mo
3 teachers, 6 assistants; student ages 3–12
Affiliation: AMS; accreditation: IMS
Governance by administrator
6 acres; 3 buildings; gym/auditorium; childcare; suburban
   location; interns accepted.

Seton Little People's School
5728 Virginia Ave, Clarendon Hills, IL 60514-1607
Sue Buntrock
Type: Montessori

Precious Child Montessori School
3910 Highland Ave, Downers Grove, IL 60515

Montessori of Woodridge
6953 Woodridge Dr, Woodridge, IL 60517-2009
Patricia Whyte

Montessori School of Hinsdale
302 S Grant, Hinsdale, IL 60521
Desmond Perry

MECA-SETON Montessori Teacher Education Program
302 S Grant St, Hinsdale, IL 60521-4053
Celma Pinho Perry or Desmond Perry
Type: Montessori teacher education

Montessori Children's House
8532 Wedgewood Dr, Burr Ridge, IL 60521-6353

Creative World Montessori
Edgewood & Goodman, La Grange, IL 60525
Gundrun Olson

Edgewood Children's Academy
1515 W Ogden Ave, La Grange Park, IL 60525-1721
Type: Montessori

Du Page Montessori School
23 W 600 Warrenville Rd, Lisle, IL 60532
Robert Breen

Woodridge Montessori
4510 River Dr, Lisle, IL 60532

Rosehill Children's Academy
1910 Maple Ave, Lisle, IL 60532-2164
Type: Montessori

Oakview Montessori Children's House
5325 Oakview Dr, Lisle, IL 60532-2357
Alice Sosnowski

Montessori School of Lisle
23 W 550 Hobson Rd, Naperville, IL 60540
Barbara Gleespen

Carmel Montessori Academy
3 S 238 Rt 59, Warrenville, IL 60555
Carmen LaFranzo

Montessori Children's House
238 Rt 59, Warrenville, IL 60555

Montessori School of Western Springs
4601 Franklin Ave, Western Springs, IL 60558-1572
Elizabeth Steves

Downers Grove Montessori School
909 Oakwood Dr, Westmont, IL 60559-1073

New Morning Montessori Children's House
234 S Adams St, Westmont, IL 60559-1904

Montessori Moppet Centre
25 W 530 75th St, Naperville, IL 60565
Judith Hojnackie

Wilcox & Follett
(See Resource Appendix)

Notre Dame De Chicago Academy
1338 W Flournoy St, Chicago, IL 60607-3328
Type: Montessori

Montessori of Holy Family
1019 S May St, Chicago, IL 60607-4232

First Immanuel Lutheran Montessori
1124 S Ashland Ave, Chicago, IL 60607-4604
Concetta McCartney

Carole Robertson Center for Learning
2020 W Roosevelt Rd, Chicago, IL 60608
312-243-7300, FAX: 312-243-4881
Affiliation: ASN

Institute for Latino Progress
2570 S Blue Island, Chicago, IL 60608
Gabriela Perez, 312-890-0055, FAX: 312-890-1537
700 students, ages 18+, HS
Affiliation: ASN
Adult ed; diploma/GED prep; college prep, bilingual, and voc classes; leadership development.

Garfield Alternative High School
220 W 45th Place, Chicago, IL 60609
Oye Khale, 312-924-0543, FAX: 312-924-0546
160 students
Affiliation: ASN
Vocational training; language arts; college prep.

Franklin Magnet Elementary & Middle School
225 W Evergreen Ave, Chicago, IL 60610

Alice M. Maresh, 312-534-8510
District 2
K–8th grade
Performing and creative arts.

Holy Trinity Montessori
1900 W Taylor St, Chicago, IL 60612-3732
Patricia Litberg

Disney Magnet Elementary
4140 N Marine Dr, Chicago, IL 60613
Raphael Guajardo, 312-534-5840
District 2
Student ages 4+,–8th grade
Open classroom.

Greenrose Elementary School
1446 W Montrose, Chicago, IL 60613
Margret Tucker, 312-477-2895, FAX: 312-477-2996
Student ages 4–11
Affiliation: ASN

Jane Addams Resource Corporation
1800 W Cuyler, Chicago, IL 60613
Mary LaPorte, 312-871-1151
Student ages 16–21
Affiliation: ASN
Learning program for out-of-school youth; GED and college prep; career awareness; employment; metal-worker training.

Lake View Academy
716 W Addison, Chicago, IL 60613
Deborah Bayly, 312-281-3065
Tuition: $750-4,500/yr
20 students
Affiliation: ASN
Whole-person emphasis.

Latino Youth Alternative High School
2200 S Marshall Blvd, Chicago, IL 60613
312-281-3065
Entrance requirement: interview
Affiliation: ASN
Emphasis on community and cultural awareness.

Search School
640 W Irving Pk, 3rd Flr East, Chicago, IL 60613
Audrey Giske
Type: Montessori

The Southern School (1969)
1447 W Montrose, Chicago, IL 60613
Margaret Tucker, Exec Dir or Betty Luckey, Dir, 312-477-2895, FAX: 477-2996
Type: independent at-risk/SE, non-profit
8 teachers, 50 students, mainly with behavior problems, ages 12–21
Governance by principal, board
Teacher qualifications: Certified Type 10 in SE
Therapeutic day school, combining social services and academics; urban location; interns accepted.

Chicago Waldorf School (1974)
1651 W Diversey, Chicago, IL 60614
Connie Starzynski, Adms Dir, 312-327-0079, FAX:-4544
Cook County
Non-profit; tuition: $4,800/yr, scholarships
26 teachers, 300 students, ages 3.5–14, pre K–8th grade
Entrance requirements: teacher recommendation
Affiliation: AWSNA
Governance by college of teachers
Teacher qualifications: Waldorf training
Full Waldorf curriculum; strong parent-community support; urban location.

The Ancona School
4770 S Dorchester, Chicago, IL 60615
Bonnie L. Wishne, 312-924-2356, FAX: 312-924-8905
Type: Montessori; tuition: $2,800-5,500/yr
Affiliation: ASN
Governance by parent cooperative
Spanish; arts; computers; multi-cultural emphasis; urban
    location.

Urban Life Center
5004 S Blackstone, Chicago, IL 60615
Scott E. Chesebro, 312-523-2333
Affiliation: ASN
Field placements.

Children's House at Harper Square
4800 S Lake Park Ave, Chicago, IL 60615-2044
Joan Alofs
Type: Montessori

South Harper Montessori
8358 S Stony Island Ave, Chicago, IL 60617-1759

Bobby Hebert Montessori School
33 E 83rd St, Chicago, IL 60619

South Harper Montessori School
9029 S Harper Ave, Chicago, IL 60619-7901   •

Accounters Community Center
1155 W 81st St, Chicago, IL 60620
Dr. Reggie McClinton, PhD, 312-602-2050
Type: public at-risk
Student ages 2-14, pre K-9th grade
Affiliation: ASN
Comprehensive, community-based youth services; crisis
    intervention; temporary living arrangements; foster care;
    drug and alcohol services; emergency food pantry; urban
    location.

Montessori School
9421 S Longwood Dr, Chicago, IL 60620-5643

Benjamin E. Mays Academy (1963)
6800 S Wentworth Ave, Chicago, IL 60621
Judith A. Starks, Dir, 312-602-5466, FAX: 312-602-5243
Cook County
Type: public at-risk; tuition: variable
10 teachers, 325 students, ages 16+, HS
Entrance requirements: age 16; standardized reading and
    math tests; no residency requirement
Affiliation: City Colleges of Chicago
Teacher qualifications: Bachelor's degree minimum
Multi-aged classes; urban location.

DeDiego Community Acadamy
1313 N Claremont Ave, Chicago, IL 60622
Lawrence McDougald, 312-534-4451
District 3
Type: magnet
K-8th grade
Fine and performing arts.

Near North Montessori School
1434 W Division, Chicago, IL 60622
Jacqueline Bergen, 312-384-1434
Tuition: $4535/yr
400 students, ages 3-13, pre K-8th grade
Affiliation: ASN

Bethel School
4215 West End, Chicago, IL 60624
Hazel Nelson, 312-533-3636, FAX: 302-533-3635
Type: public choice; tuition: $1250/yr
200 students, ages 3-13, K-8th grade
Entrance requirements: reading and math testing
Affiliation: ASN

Flower Vocational–Essential School (1911)
3545 W Fulton Blvd, Chicago, IL 60624
Bettie D.Stewart, Essential Coord, 312-534-6756, FAX: 312-
    534-6938
Cook County
Type: public choice
57 teachers, 720 students, partly at-risk, ages 14-20, HS
Entrance requirements: 5.5+ reading, math levels; no resi-
    dency requirement
Affiliations: U of I, DePaul
Governance by local school council, teachers, principal
Teacher qualifications: IL Certification
College prep; hands-on training in one of 7 on-site, student-
    run businesses; entrepreneurial training; urban location;
    interns accepted.

Lawndale Community School
3400 W Grenshaw, Chicago, IL 60624
Linda Berg, 312-826-6330
51 students
Affiliation: ASN

Delano Child-Parent Center
3905 W Wilcox St, Chicago, IL 60624-2833
Type: Montessori

Good News Educational Workshop
7645 N Paulina, Chicago, IL 60626
Linda Ballas, 312-764-2228, FAX: 312-262-2293
scholarships
60 students, ages 3-13
Affiliation: ASN
Racially and economically diverse population; computers;
    arts; Spanish; field trips and camping; hands-on; emphasis
    on problem solving and non-violent conflict resolution.

North Shore Academy for Children
6711 N Sheridan Rd, Chicago, IL 60626-4532
Type: Montessori

Christian Montessori School
10 W 110th St, Chicago, IL 60628

Lindblom Technical High School (1919)
6130 S Wolcott Ave, Chicago, IL 60628
Betty J. Miller, CES Coord, 312-535-9300, FAX:-9314
Cook County
Type: public choice
40 teachers, 680 students, ages 13-17, 9-12th grade
Entrance requirements: exam, math/reading series = 9.0+,
    residency
Governance by local school council
Teacher qualifications: bachelor's degree
Portfolio assessment; freshman portfolio exhibitions; team
    teaching; interdisciplinary instruction; socratic seminars;
    cooperative learning; student as worker, teacher as coach;
    urban location; interns accepted.

Tiny Tots Montessori School
901 E 104th St, Chicago, IL 60628
Mildred Bradley

Florence Foster Montessori Academy
11023 S Halstead St, Chicago, IL 60628-3908

Lithuanian Montessori Children's Center (1963)
2743 W 69th St, Chicago, IL 60629
Liuda Germanas, 312-476-4999
Non-profit; tuition: 1,200/yr
1 teacher, 1 assistant, 18 students, ages 3-6
Affiliations: Lithuanian MS of America, Inc
Language and culture; urban location; interns accepted.

Varnas Montessori Center
3038 W 59th St, Chicago, IL 60629-2542

Brickton Montessori (1986)
8622 W Catalpa, Chicago, IL 60630
Deborah A. Kelley, Prin, 312-714-0646
Non-profit; tuition: $3,340-5,490
10 teachers, 20 assistants, 172 students, ages infant-12
Affiliations: ISBE, IACNPS, IMS; accreditations: AMS, IL BE
Governance by board
Open year-round; childcare; urban location; interns accepted.

Curie Metropolitan High School
4959 S Archer Ave, Chicago, IL 60632
Robert B. Schneider, 312-535-2100
District 11
Type: magnet
9-12th grade
Performing and creative arts.

Chicago Urban Day School
1248 W 69th St, Chicago, IL 60636-3599
Georgia Jordan
Type: Montessori

American School
(See Resource Appendix)

Parkway Community House
500 E 67th St, Chicago, IL 60637
Laura Holmes, 312-493-1306, FAX: 312-493-9392
Affiliation: ASN
Governance by principal
Adult basic ed; GED prep; literacy.

The Blue Gargoyle Youth Service Center
5655 S University Ave, Chicago, IL 60637
Barbara Cramer, 312-955-4108
Affiliation: ASN
Vocational services; computer assistance; counseling; adult
   literacy; GED; U of C volunteers.

Serendipity Children's House
2625 N Laramie Ave, Chicago, IL 60639-1625
Type: Montessori

Alternative Schools Network
(See Resource Appendix)

Prologue Learning Center
1105 W Lawrence, Chicago, IL 60640
Nancy Jackson, 312-728-7221, FAX: 312-728-3865
60 students, ages 16+
Entrance requirements: interview, testing
Affiliation: ASN
Emphasis on basic skills, realistic life planning; GED prep;
   career assessment; job placement.

Uptown Community Learning Center
4409 N Broadway, Chicago, IL 60640
312-769-2085
Affiliation: ASN

St Bartholomew Montessori Preschool
4941 W Patterson Ave, Chicago, IL 60641-3512

Montessori Elementary School (1979)
10149 Utica Ave, Evergreen Park, IL 60642
Norine Colby, Head, 708-499-3238
Non-profit; tuition: $2,000-3,600/yr
3 teachers, 3 assistants, 52 students, ages 3-12
Entrance requirements: age 3-4; Montessori experience for
   older
Affiliations: NAMTA, MF, MAC/USA; accreditations: AMS, ASN
Governance by teachers and administrators
German; French; interns accepted.

Montessori Elementary and Preschool (1979)
14911 W 127th, Lemont, IL 60642
Norine Colby, Head of School, 708-257-1110
Non-profit; tuition: $4,000/4,600/yr (ages 6-12); varies for
   younger children

3 teachers, 3 assistants, 59 students, ages 3-12
A Montessori background and foundation are required for
   admission
Affiliations: AMS, NAMTA, MAC, ASN
Governance by teachers and administrators
German and French for ages 6-12;
   interns accepted.

Beverly Montessori School (1967)
9916 S Walden Pkwy, Chicago, IL 60643
Virginia Maciulis, Dir, 312-239-7635
Non-profit; tuition: 1,360/yr
6 teachers, 9 assistants, 152 students, ages 3-6
Entrance requirements: toilet-trained
Affiliation: AMS
Governance by an administrator
Urban location; interns accepted.

Clissold Elementary School
2350 W 110th Pl, Chicago, IL 60643
Nicki Ruiz
Type: Montessori

Vanderpoel Magnet Elementary & Middle School
9510 S Prospect Ave, Chicago, IL 60643
E. Robert Olson, 312-535-2690
District 10
K-8th grade
Humanities.

Council Oak Montessori School
11030 S Longwood Dr, Chicago, IL 60643-4042
Marsha Enright

Academy of Scholastic Achievement
4651 W Madison St, Chicago, IL 60644
Gladys Simpson, 312-921-1315, FAX: 312-921-1121
Affiliation: ASN
Open entry; college prep; child/parent center; voc;
   counseling.

Aspira Alternative High School
2555 N Kimball, Chicago, IL 60644
Robb Michael, 312-772-0950, FAX: 312-486-9280
60 students, ages 16-20, HS
Affiliation: ASN
Dropout retrieval; transition to "regular" HS; basic academic
   and social skills stressed; job placement; counseling.

Learning Network
5911 W Midway Park, Chicago, IL 60644
Luther Syas, 312-378-7076, FAX: 312-378-8190
1-8th grade
Affiliation: ASN
Basic skills; single and teen parent family counseling; adult
   ed; computer literacy; word processing.

Edgebrook-Wildwood Montessori Preschool
6736 N Loleta Ave, Chicago, IL 60646-1424

Casa Infantil Day Care Center
2222 N Kedzie, Chicago, IL 60647
Type: Montessori

Centro Latino Universidad Popular
2750 W North Ave, Chicago, IL 60647
Olivia Flores Godinez, 312-772-0836
Affiliation: ASN

Dr Pedro Albizu Campos High School (1972)
1671 N Claremont, Chicago, IL 60647
Marvin Garcia, Dir, 312-342-8022, FAX: 342-6609
Cook County
Type: independent, non-profit; tuition: $500/yr, scholarships
8 teachers, 60 students, mainly Puerto Rican-Latino, ages
   14-18, 9-12th grade
Entrance requirements: interview
Affiliation: ASN

Governance by faculty/student/parent board

Intensive; community-oriented; emphasis on Puerto Rican history and culture; extensive field trips; urban location; interns accepted; also has Consuelo Lee Corretjer Day Care Center.

Ruiz Belvis Cultural Center
1632 N Milwaukee Ave, Chicago, IL 60647
Rafael Arzuaga, 312-235-3988
Affiliation: ASN
Emphasis on Puerto Rican culture, history and community affairs; GED; ESL; Spanish literacy; plastic/graphic arts; salsa dance; musical instrument classes; counseling; after-school tutoring.

South Shore Montessori School
2555 E 73rd St, Chicago, IL 60649

Sullivan House High School (1970)
7305 S Clyde, Chicago, IL 60649
Meryl Domina, Prin, 312-324-5014
Cook County
Type: public at-risk
10 teachers, 60 students, mainly at-risk, ages 14–23, HS
Enrollment restricted to disadv youths from South Side
Affiliation: Alternative Schools Network
Governance by director with extensive input from faculty and students
Teacher qualifications: BA/BS, IL Certification or experience in AE
"Last chance" school; supportive services; career planning; literacy ed; no letter grades; extensive field trips; urban location; interns accepted.

The Neighborhood Institute's Career Education and Employment Center
2255 E 75th St, Chicago, IL 60649
Barbara Searles, 312-933-2040
Enrollment restricted to dropouts
Affiliation: ASN
GED prep; voc counseling; job placement.

Westside Holistic Family Center
4909 W Division, Chicago, IL 60651
Conna Blasingame, 312-921-8777, FAX: 312-921-1045
Affiliation: ASN
Adult ed; employment; GED tutoring; computer assistance; counseling.

Ted Lenart Regional Gifted Center
8445 S Kolin Ave, Chicago, IL 60652
William Harnedy, 312-535-2322
District 7
Type: magnet
1–8th grade
Regional Gifted Center.

Keller Gifted Elementary Magnet Center
3020 W 108th St, Chicago, IL 60655
Ruth Muth, 312-535-2636
District 10
1–6th grade
Regional Gifted Center.

World of Discovery Montessori School
12253 S McDaniel St, Alsip, IL 60658-2545
Mariam Fuillen

Kassers Childrens House
2449 W Peterson Ave, Chicago, IL 60659-4112
Kathleen Kasser
Type: Montessori

Alternatives, Inc
1126 W Granville, Chicago, IL 60660
Judy Gall, 312-973-0578
Affiliation: ASN

Individual, family, and group counseling; employment program; crisis intervention and advocacy; substance abuse prevention workshops.

Rogers Park Montessori School (1966)
1244 W Thorndale Ave, Chicago, IL 60660
Marsha Hahn, Adm, 312-271-1700
Non-profit; tuition: $2,400-5,720/yr
11 teachers, 7 assistants, 127 students, ages infant-9
Affiliation: AMS
Governance by board
Music; developmental gymnastics; childcare; urban location; interns accepted.

Kankakee Valley Montessori School
196 S Harrison Ave, Kankakee, IL 60901-4043
Tami Kacmar

Lincoln Cultural Center Montessori
240 Warren Ave, Kankakee, IL 60901-4319

Steuben Primary Center
520 S Wildwood Ave, Kankakee, IL 60901-5365
Type: Montessori

St Peter Montessori
320 Elmwood Ave, South Beloit, IL 61080-1929

Elmhurst- Lombard Montessori
550 S Edgewood, Rockford, IL 61102

Lathrop Elementary (1957)
2603 Clover Ave, Rockford, IL 61102
Jill Coffman, Principal, 815-966-3285
Type: public choice Montessori
5 teachers, 1 pt assistant, 478 students, ages 3–12
Enrollment for Montessori by lottery
Governance by administrator
Houses both traditional and Montessori classes; suburban location; transportation.

Montessori Learning Path (1983)
410 8th St, Rockford, IL 61104
Mary Schoembs, Adm, 815-964-1700
Non-profit; tuition: $160/404/mo
5 teachers, 2 assistants, 68 students, ages 3–6
Affiliations: Rockford Regional Daycare Dirs Assn, AMS
Governance by board of trustees
Parent cooperation; urban location; interns accepted.

Rockford Public Schools
201 S Madison St, Rockford, IL 61104
William Bowen
Type: Montessori

Montessori Children's House of Rockford
4700 Augustine Dr, Rockford, IL 61107

Montessori Learning Center of Rockford, Inc. (1984)
1390 N. Mulford Rd, Rockford, IL 61107
Emma Lou Mulnix, Adm, 815-226-0111
Non-profit; tuition: $1,625-2,700/yr
5 teachers, 7 assistants, 102 students, ages 3–15
Affiliation: AMS
Governance by board
Childcare; urban location; interns accepted.

Open Court Publishing
(See Resource Appendix)

Villa Montessori School (1979)
3010 26th Ave, Moline, IL 61265
Renee M. Detloff, Head, 309-764-7047, FAX: same
Non-profit; tuition: $3/hr-2,200/yr
12 teachers, 18 assistants, 180 students, ages infant-9
Affiliations: AMS, QCAEYC, NAEYC; accreditation: ISACS
Governance by administrator
Spanish and Japanese studies for all; childcare; suburban location; interns accepted.

Rainbow Re-Source Center
(See Resource Appendix)

Farm Country General Store
(See Resource Appendix)

Montessori School of Peoria
200 S Church St, Washington, IL 61571-2717

Montessori School of Bloomington-Normal
5 Kensignton Circle, Bloomington, IL 61704-7602

Pontiac Montessori School
102 E Michigan Ave #E, Pontiac, IL 61764-1158
Dorothy Rodgers

The Montessori School of Champaign-Urbana (1963)
1403 Regency Dr E, Savoy, IL 61874
Rita Young, Adm, 217-356-1818
Tuition: $210-414/mo
5 teachers, 5 assistants; student ages 3-6
Entrance requirements: age 3
Affiliations: AMS, IL BE
Governance by board
New facility; Spanish; ASL; music lessons available; interns
    accepted.

Montessori Children's House of Alton
5800 Godfrey Rd, Godfrey, IL 62035-2426
Laurie Milnor or Parents Assn

Edwardsville Montessori School
4401 Hwy 162, Granite City, IL 62040
Mary Beth McGivern

Children's House- St Clair
400 Joseph Dr, Belleville, IL 62221-1632
Type: Montessori

Belleville Alternative Night School (1976)
2600 W Main, Belleville, IL 62223
618-233-5094, FAX: 618-233-7586
St Clair County
Type: public at-risk
33 teachers, 195 students, mainly at-risk, ages 15-21, 9-12th
    grade
Residency required
Governance by teachers, principal, parent advisory board
Voc, community, parenting ed; work transition; counseling;
    multi-aged classes; suburban location.

Beck Optional Education Program (1985)
6137 Beck Rd, Red Bud, IL 62278
James W. Heil, Dir, 618-473-2222, FAX: 618-473-2292
Monroe County
Type: public at-risk
7 teachers, 60 students, ages 15.5-21, 9-12th grade
Entrance requirements: interview; no residency requirement
Affiliations: North Central, ISBE
Governance by teachers, principal, board
Teacher qualifications: IL Certification
Vocational; small classes; on-on-one instruction; community
    service; multi-aged classes; rural location; transportation;
    interns accepted.

Fearon Teacher Aids
(See Resource Appendix)

Futures Unlimited (1977)
250 E William St, Decatur, IL 62523
Randall Taylor, Director, 217-429-1054
Type: public at-risk
8 teachers, 120 students, mainly at-risk, ages 13-19, 7-12th
    grade
Entrance requirements: referral from home school, residency

Affiliation: Macon Co Ed Service Region
Governance by teachers and principal
Teacher qualifications: state certification
Parenting; family living; sociology; traditional academics; MS
    completion; multi-aged classes; urban location.

Montessori Ganderfeather's Children's House (1990)
6758 Minder Rd, Rochester, IL 62563
Jill Persinos, Adm, 217-498-8609
Tuition: $110-350/mo
2 teachers, 1 assistant, 45 students, ages infant-12
Affiliation: AMS
Governance by an administrator
Located on a rural farm; barnyard animals; Earth education;
    childcare; interns accepted.

Children's Village
860 S Main St, Jacksonville, IL 62650-3012
Type: Montessori

Montessori Children's of Springfield
4147 Sandhill Rd, Springfield, IL 62702-1114

John Hay Montessori Children's House
200 N 11th St, Springfield, IL 62703-1004

Montessori Schoolhouse (1987)
717 Rickard Rd, Springfield, IL 62704
Gail Parker, Owner/Adm, 217-787-5505
4 teachers, 3 assistants, 56 students, ages infant-15
Affiliation: AMS
Governance by administrator
Spanish; swimming pool; multi-cultural staff; childcare; urban
    location; interns accepted.

St Nicholas Montessori Preschool
326 S Douglas Ave, Springfield, IL 62704-1725

**Springfield Public Schools Alternative Education
    Program** (1976)
2530 E Ash St, Springfield, IL 62707
Dr. Linda W. Seltzer, Supervisor, 217-525-3275
Sangamon County
Type: public at-risk
25 teachers, 700 students, mainly at-risk, ages 11-21, 5-12th
    grade
Entrance requirements: school referral; no residency
    requirement
Governance by teachers and principal
Teacher qualifications: state SE certification
Individualized, integrated; whole person approach with com-
    munity agencies' support; urban location; transportation;
    interns accepted.

Matrix Institute
PO Box 4487, Springfield, IL 62708-4487
Type: Montessori

Carbondale New School
RR 5 Pleasant Hill Rd, Carbondale, IL 62901
Linda M. Rohling, Dir
Type: independent; tuition: $2,250/yr, scholarships
54 students, pre K-8th grade
Parental involvement.

Cairo Montessori Pre-School
PO Box 521, Cairo, IL 62914-0521

Emerson Elementary School
3101 Elm St, Cairo, IL 62914-1399
Dr Elaine Bonifield
Type: Montessori

Montessori School of Southern Illinois
507 N 9th St, Murphysboro, IL 62966-1841

Indiana

Anderson Community Alternative Education Program
30 W 11th St, Anderson, IN 46016
Sheila Decaroli, 317-641-2157
Type: public at-risk
6-12th grade
Entrance by referral.
Career planning; goal setting; action plans.

Countryside Learning Center
PO Box 3030, Anderson, IN 46018-3030
Type: Montessori

Montessori Academy
620 Kinzer Ave, Carmel, IN 46032-2311

Frankfort Community Alternative Education Program
1 S Marsh Rd, Frankfort, IN 46041
Michael Kelley, 317-654-8545
2-5 students, 6-12th grade
For expelled students.

Noblesville Montessori House
954 Mulberry St, Noblesville, IN 46060

Country Children's House
2225 Dakota Dr, Noblesville, IN 46060-9075
Type: Montessori

I Can! Montessori School
14506 Crystal Creek Dr, Noblesville, IN 46060-9506
Mr or Ms Rhodes

Montessori Children's House
222 S 4th Ave, Beech Grove, IN 46107-1915

Hancock-S. Madison Joint Services (1993)
820 N Broadway, Greenfield, IN 46140
Fritz Kolmerton, 317-462-9527
Type: public choice
150 students

Child's World Montessori Pre-School
199 W Pearl St, Greenwood, IN 46142-3534
Joyce Probst

Greenwood Montessori School
824 N Madison Ave, Greenwood, IN 46142-4127

Indiana Association of Home Educators
1000 N Madison Ave Suite S2, Greenwood, IN 46142-4158
317-865-3013
Type: state home-based

Foreign Language Magnet (1984)
1500 E Michigan St, Indianapolis, IN 46201
David Banks, Dir, 317-226-3964, FAX: 317-226-3932
Marion County
Type: public choice
160 teachers, 2100 students, ages 14-18, HS
Entrance requirements: reading and aptitude scores,
   residency
Affiliation: North Central
Governance by principal
Teacher qualifications: Degree, IN certification
Six instruction levels; companion history courses; immersion;
   language maintenance; college credit courses; travel and
   study abroad; foreign teaching; multi-aged classes; exten-
   sive field trips; interns accepted.

Key Renaissance Middle School
1401 E 10th St, Indianapolis, IN 46201
Patricia Bolanos, 317-226-4297
Type: magnet
6-8th grade
Theme-based.

Francis Parker Montessori School (1979)
2353 Columbia Ave, Indianapolis, IN 46205
Jean Harrell, Principal, 317-226-4256, FAX: 226-3370
Marion County
Type: public choice
30 teachers, 470 students, ages 3-12, pre K-5th grade
Enrollment by lottery; residency required
Affiliation: I PS
Governance by principal
Teacher qualifications: state certification, IPS Montessori
   training
Outdoor learning lab; close student-teacher partnership;
   strong parent organization; self-paced; no letter grades;
   multi-aged classes; 9 week grading periods; urban location;
   interns accepted.

Rousseau McClellan IPS #91
5111 N Evanston Ave, Indianapolis, IN 46205
Melissa Keller, Principal, 317-226-4291
Marion County
Type: public choice Montessori
24 teachers, 364 students, ages 5-11, K-5th grade
Entrance requirements: parents must attend Montessori
   information meeting, residency
Governance by principal, board
Teacher qualifications: state certification; system-based
   Montessori training.
Multi-aged classes; extensive field trips; no letter grades;
   urban location; transportation; interns accepted.

Montessori Activity Center
3819 N Delaware St, Indianapolis, IN 46205-2647

A Children's Habitat (1972)
4550 N Ilinois St, Indianapolis, IN 46208
Judy Weingartner, teacher, 317-283-7525
Type: Montessori, non-profit
3 teachers, 1 assistant, 45 students, ages 3-6
Entrance requirements: age 2.5 by Wed after Labor Day
Governance by parent cooperative
Childcare; suburban location; interns accepted.

Montessori Centres, Inc (1964)
563 W Westfield Blvd, Indianapolis, IN 46208
Evelyn Froehlich, Pres, 317-257-2224
2 teachers, 3 assistants, 45 students, mainly International,
   ages 3-9
Affiliation: CIMTA
Governance by board
Spanish speakers; near Children's Museum and Butler U;
   Kolbe resources for gifted.

Shortridge Middle School
3401 N Meridian St, Indianapolis, IN 46208
Al Finnell, 317-226-4010
Type: magnet
6-8th grade
Arts; mulitcultural; humanities.

Children's House
2401 W 39th St, Indianapolis, IN 46208-3271
Type: Montessori

Ben Davis High School Evening School
1200 N Girsl School Rd, Indianapolis, IN 46214
Dan Carrington, 317-244-7691
Type: public at-risk

Horizon Middle School
2310 E 30th St, Indianapolis, IN 46218
Sharon Wilkins, 317-226-4350
Type: public
65 students, mainly expelled, at-risk, 7-8th grade
Entrance requirements: referral
Community involvement.

Broad Ripple High School
1115 Broad Ripple Ave, Indianapolis, IN 46220
Larry McCoud, 317-226-3784
Type: magnet
9-12th grade
Humanities; performing and visual arts.

Little Friends Child Care (1985)
3030 E Kessler Blvd, Indianapolis, IN 46220
Karen Kosoglov, Dir, 317-251-5690
Marion County
Type: independent, non-profit; tuition: $89-111/wk
11 teachers, 73 students, ages 1-6
Must be walking and eating at the table
Governance by board
Teacher qualifications: teaching degree or child care
    experience
State licensed; parent advisory group; extensive field trips;
    suburban location; interns accepted.

Decatur Vocational Enrichment Center (1984)
5251 Kentucky Ave, Indianapolis, IN 46221
Elizabeth A. Gut, 317-856-7511
Marion County
Type: public at-risk
4 teachers, 50 students, ages 14-19, 9-12th grade
Enrollment restricted to adolescent residents referred for
    discipline
Affiliation: Decatur Central HS
Governance by teachers and principal
No letter grades; suburban location.

New Beginning High School
1902 W Morris St, Indianapolis, IN 46221
Sharon Wilkens, 317-226-4350
Type: public at-risk
65 students, 9-12th grade
Entrance requirements: referral
Goal-oriented; life skills.

Roberts Academy
1002 W Morris St, Indianapolis, IN 46221
Sharon Wilkins, 317-226-4350
Type: public at-risk
100 students, 9-12th grade
Entrance requirement: referral
Experiential/relevant learning.

Stephen Foster #67 Elementary
553 N Somerset Ave, Indianapolis, IN 46222
John Airola, 317-226-4267
Type: magnet
K-5th grade
Montessori.

**MSD of Warren Township Center for Personalized
    Achievement**
9039 E 10th St, Indianapolis, IN 46229
Charles Pfluger, 317-895-2145
Type: public at-risk

4 teachers, 28 students, 7-9th grade
Individualized need assistance.

Wayne Township Alternative Junior High (1986)
2001 Bridgeport Rd, Indianapolis, IN 46231
Jerry Stephens, Dept Chair, 317-243-5507
Marion County
Type: public at-risk
3 teachers, 45 students, ages 12-16
District residency required
Governance by teachers and principal
Teacher qualifications: IN license
Alternative to expulsion; multi-aged classes; transportation.

Discovery at Indian Creek (1986)
10833 E 56th St, Indianapolis, IN 46236
Dr Karen Gould, Prin, 317-823-4497, FAX: 823-0973
Type: public choice
29 teachers, 541 students, ages 6-11, 1-5th grade
District residency required
Governance by teachers, principal, parents, board
Teacher qualifications: Bachelor's
Science themes; integrated curriculum; use of technology;
    parental involvement; university collaboration as profes-
    sional development school; nature center; active learning;
    alternative assessments; extensive field trips; interns
    accepted.

Learning Unlimited (1976)
1801 E 86th St, Indianapolis, IN 46240
Jay Hill, EdD, Dir, 317-259-5301, FAX: 317-259-5369
Marion County
Type: public choice
14 teachers, 325 students, ages 15-18, 9-12th grade
Entrance requirements: application, teacher
    recommendation
Governance by principal, faculty and student reps, board
Humanities-based school-within-a-school; semester long
    community projects; contracts with community resource
    persons and teachers; projects integrated into academic
    classes; suburban location; interns accepted.

MSD of Wayne Township Demerit Program
1220 S High School Rd, Indianapolis, IN 46241
Dr Nancy J. Moller, Asst Supt, 317-243-8251
Type: public at-risk
Incorporates notification and intervention strategies for
    minor infractions.

Wayne Enrichment Center (1976)
5248 W Raymond, Indianapolis, IN 46260
Ellen Jose, Chair, 317-248-8685, FAX: 317-243-5537
Marion County
Type: public at-risk
6 teachers, 150 students, ages 14-19, 9-12th grade
Entrance requirements: referral by Vice Principal or Coun-
    selor, district residency
Affiliation: Indianapolis Dept of Empoyment & Training
Governance by teachers and principal
Teacher qualifications: state certification
Integrates employment/life skills; work-study; community
    service; no letter grades; suburban location; interns
    accepted.

Montessori Learning Center
11056 Westfield Blvd, Indianapolis, IN 46280

Lake County Christian Home School Association
11202 Parrish, Cedar Lake, IN 46303
219-365-5267

Chesterton Montessori School
270 E Burdick Rd, Chesterton, IN 46304-9303
Terry Cavollo

Montessori Children's Schoolhouse
5935 Hohman Ave, Hammond, IN 46320-2425
Kathleen Hill, Principal-Administrator, 219-932-5666

8 teachers, 15 assistants, 231 students, ages infant-9
Affiliation: ILMS; accreditation: AMS
Governance by board
Urban location; interns accepted.

Montessori Children
1814 Bluebird Ln, Munster, IN 46321-3427

Montessori School at Woodmar Church of God
1421 173rd St, Hammond, IN 46324-2860

Calumet Region Montessori
2109 57th St, Hobart, IN 46342-5629

Park Middle School Alternative Program
1921 A St, LaPorte, IN 46350
Dr William Patterson, 219-362-7056
Type: public at-risk
Integrated; individualized; counseling through local Youth
    Services Bureau.

Michigan City Area Alternative School
817 Lafayette St, Michigan City, IN 46360
Micki Webb, 219-873-2123
Type: public at-risk
50 students, 7-12th grade
Entrance by referral

Montessori School of Michigan City
5388 N Bleck Rd, Michigan City, IN 46360
Pamela K Smith

Portage Township Adult Education Center
5391 Central Ave, Portage, IN 46368
Linda O'Brien, Dir, 219-762-6113
Type: public at-risk
Student ages 16+
Entrance by referral
Alternative to expulsion.

Portage Township Alternative School
6450 Hwy 6, Portage, IN 46368
Lowell Johnson, 219-763-8106
Type: public at-risk
Work study for credit.

Lake Central Alternative Classroom
8260 Wicker, St John, IN 46373
Janet Emerick, 219-365-8507
Type: public·at-risk
6-12 students, MS, HS
Teacher qualifications: certification
Orientation program for Hoosier Boys Town residents; review
    of school rules; study skills; coping skills.

Montessori School of Porter Country
505 Marquette St, Valparaiso, IN 46383-2598

Porter County Career Center
1005 N Franklin St, Valparaiso, IN 46391
Kathy Spears, Prin, 219-531-3170, FAX: 219-531-3173
Non-profit; tuition: variable
5 teachers, 100-150 students, ages 16-19, 9-12th grade
Entrance by referral; county residency required
Governance by superintendent and principal
Credit for work; max 10 students/class; independent study;
    no letter grades; non-compulsory class attendance; multi-
    aged classes; urban location.

Montessori School of Elkhart
416 E Crawford St, Elkhart, IN 46514-2764

Montessori School House
58433 City Rd 105, Elkhart, IN 46517-9452

Discovery House Preschool
419 S 5th St, Goshen, IN 46526-3925
Type: Montessori

Youth Educational Service Program (YES) (1986)
c/o Starke Circuit Ct, Knox, IN 46534
John Baldwin, 219-772-9151
Knox-Judson District
3 teachers, 12 students
For expelled students under court jurisdiction; group
    counseling.

The Montessori Academy (1969)
15767 Day Rd, Mishawaka, IN 46565
Donna Durish, Head, 219-256-5313, FAX: 219-256-5499
Non-profit; tuition: $620-4,265/yr
13 teachers, 14 assistants, 314 students, ages infant-15
Entrance requirement: interview of students ages 5-14
Affiliation: NAMTA; accreditations: AMS, MACTE
Governance by a board of trustees
Extracurriculars; computer lab; PE; childcare; suburban loca-
    tion; interns accepted.

**Wawasee Community Substance Abuse Outreach
    Program**
#1 Warrior Path, Syracuse, IN 46567
Karen Parr, 219-457-3147
1 teacher, 4-5 students, 6-12th grade
Alternative to expulsion; counseling; job or volunteer work
    required.

Warsaw Alternative Instructional Methods (AIM) School
1802 E Winona Ave, Warsaw, IN 46580
Dave McGuire, 219-269-3721
Type: public at-risk
Students mainly disruptive, ages 14-21
Half day 'world of work' format; modified Glasser
    environment.

Whitko Community AIM School
2043 N Detroit St, Warsaw, IN 46580
Dave McGuire, 219-267-8875
Type: public at-risk
8 students
Staff function as counselors/advocates; open exit; SE.

Montessori Child Development Center
601 E Smith St, Warsaw, IN 46580-4540

The Montessori Center (1982)
1236 Lincoln Way E, South Bend, IN 46601
Marianne Surges, Adm, 812-289-1222
Non-profit; tuition: $1,450-2,500/yr
2 teachers, 3 assistants, 50 students, ages 3-6
Entrance requirements: toilet trained
Affiliation: AMS
Governance by administrator
Flexible program; childcare; urban location; interns accepted.

Montessori School of South Bend, Inc
1302 E Indiana Ave, South Bend, IN 46613-3230

Little Flower Montessori School
624 N Notre Dame Ave, South Bend, IN 46617

Montessori School
3002 S Michigan, South Bend, IN 46618

Countryside Montessori
53287 Ironwood Rd, South Bend, IN 46635-1385

Home BASE-Clay High School
19131 Darden Rd, S Bend, IN 46637
William Baldwin, 219-272-3400
South Bend District

Hamilton Community Educational Opportunity Center
400 S Martha St, Angola, IN 46703
Lisa Ulrey, 219-665-1360
Type: public at-risk
51 students, ages 13-18
Enrollment Requirements: testing; interview

Steuben County MSD Alternative School
400 S Martha, Angola, IN 46703
Lisa Ulery, 219-665-1360
Students mainly expelled, left school, ages 15–22, 9–12th
   grade
Half-day of work assisting social worker, teacher, etc.

Wells County Alternative School (1992)
120-22 LaMar St, Bluffton, IN 46714
Ron Harnish, Dir/Tch, 824-0474
Type: public at-risk
4 teachers, 32 students, ages 16–21, 9–12th grade
Entrance requirements: good MS record, residency
Governance by teachers and principal
Teacher qualifications: IN license
Teachers are tutors; self-paced; rural location.

Adams County Center for Educational Success
654 N 12th St, Decatur, IN 46733
Barbara Baker, Dir, 219-724-4434
Type: public choice
3 teachers; students mainly involved in special life challenges
Afternoons of work, community service, or childcare.

Alternative to Expulsion Program
1000 Prospect Ave, New Haven, IN 46774
Barbara Ahlersmeyer, 219-493-3761
East Allen County
Type: public at-risk
50 students, 6–12th grade
Entry based on disciplinary hearing.

Wells County Alternative Educatíonal Center
PO Box 386, Ossian, IN 46777
Dr Michael Sailsbery, 219-622-4125
Bluffton-Harrison MSD District
Type: public at-risk
7–12th grade
Entrance requirements: referral, out of school min 1 yr
Individualized; max 10/class.

Ft Wayne Community Alternative Learning Program
203 E Douglas St, Ft Wayne, IN 46802
Timon Kendall, Sharon Reynolds, or Thomas Smith, 219-425-
   7363
Type: public at-risk
38 teachers, 275 students, 4–12th grade
Short-term; counseling.

Ralph Bunche Elementary
1111 Green St, Fort Wayne, IN 46803
Connie Murphy, 219-425-7323
Type: magnet
Student ages 4+,–5th grade
Montessori.

Montessori Academy of Fort Wayne
2726 Lynn Ave, Fort Wayne, IN 46805-3842

Weisser Park-Whitney Young ES Fine Arts Magnet (1978)
902 Colerick St, Ft Wayne, IN 46806
Daniel A. Bickel, Prin, 219-425-7483
Allen County
Non-profit
47 teachers, 750 students, ages 4–12, pre K–5th grade
Entrance requirements: age 4 by June 1
Affiliation: Ft Wayne Comm. Schools
Governance by teachers, principal
Teacher qualifications: IN certification
Enriched basics program; extensive use of technology; inte-
   grated multicultural emphasis; extensive field trips; multi-
   aged classes; interns accepted.

Children's Cottage
2820 Reed St, Ft Wayne, IN 46806-1204
Type: Montessori

Martin Luther King Montessori School
326 E Wayne, Ft Wayne, IN 46807
Cathy Cullen

Franke Park Biological Science Magnet (1988)
828 Mildred Ave, Ft Wayne, IN 46808
Jean Linville, Prin, 219-425-7336
Allen County
Type: public choice
24 teachers, 514 students, ages 5–11, K–5th grade
Governance by principal
Large outdoor education area; hands-on-science lab; green-
   house; gardens; ampitheater; wetland; adjacent to
   park/zoo; extensive field trip; interns accepted.

Three Rivers Montessori (1967)
724 W 4th St, Ft Wayne, IN 46808-2609
Starr Watts, Joan Hayden, Co-Dir, 219-426-6143
Non-profit; tuition: $187/200/315/mo
5 teachers, 7 assistants, 92 students, ages infant-6
Affiliation: AMS
Governance by a board of trustees
Computer education; foreign languages; Oalcroze Euryth-
   mics; gymnastics; childcare; urban location.

Fort Wayne Area Home Schools
13428 Old Auburn Rd, Fort Wayne, IN 46816
Ron & Sharon Hoot
Fayette County

Montessori Children's House of Kokomo, Inc
PO Box 4052, Kokomo, IN 46904-4052

Logansport Alternative School
847 S Cicott St, Logansport, IN 46947
Susan Swartz, 219-753-3267
Type: public at-risk
15 students, ages 11–17, 6–12th grade
County-wide.

Pioneer Regional Co-op Alternative School
2829 George St, Logansport, IN 46947
Susan Swartz, Dir, 219-722-2911
Type: public at-risk
2 teachers, 1 assistant, 20 students, ages 14–18
Entrance by referral
Substance abuse counseling; living skills; learning without
   peer pressure.

Allen School Alternative Program
1240 S Adams St, Marion, IN 46952
Susan Bove, 317-662-2546
Type: public
Students mainly disruptive, K–4th grade
Intervention model; behavior modification in-service; struc-
   tured time-out room.

Wabash City Alternative Program
1101 Colerain St, Wabash, IN 46992
Connie Squires, 219-563-2151
Type: public at-risk
3–7 students, 5–12th grade
Court referrals accepted
Last chance before expulsion.

Eastern Pulaski Community Mini-Alternative School
711 School Dr, Winamac, IN 46996
Mike Miller, 219-946-4010
Type: public at-risk
8 students, partly mildly disruptive, 6–8th grade

Switzerland County Alternative Program
305 Seminary St, Vevay, IN 47043
Ron Connors, 812-427-2705
Type: public at-risk
Student ages 5–21, K–12th grade
Alternative to suspension or incarceration by courts; counsel-
   ing required.

Scott County Alternative Class
Hwy 31 S, Austin, IN 47102
Bill Comer, 812-794-8450
Type: public at-risk
10-12 students, mainly disruptive, 8th grade
Same teacher all day, all year.

River Falls Christian Association of Home Educators
PO Box 482, Charlestown, IN 47111
812-256-6446
Clark County

Ready for Life
2813 Grantline Rd, New Albany, IN 47150
Diane Muller, Dennis Renshaw, or Bill Chilton, 812-949-4200
New Albany-Floyd County
Type: public at-risk
20 students, mainly expelled, left school, ages 16-19
Entrance by referral
In cooperation with local Youth Services Bureau; year-round;
GED prep; vocational services; life skills; substance abuse
counseling; work program for suspended students.

Jefferson Education Center
1209 Sycamore St, Columbus, IN 47201
William Barton, 812-376-4428
Bartholomew Consolidated District
Type: public at-risk
Individualized.

McDowell Education Center (1972)
2700 McKinley Ave, Columbus, IN 47201
Paul G. Riddle, Dir, 812-376-4451, FAX: 376-4512
Bartholomew County
Type: public at-risk
45 teachers, 450-500 students, ages 16-20, 9-12th grade
Residency required
Governance by teachers, principal, democratic school
meeting
Teacher qualifications: IN certification
Vocational; multi-aged classes; extensive field trips; outcome
based; rural location.

Madison Consolidated Alternative Classroom
701 8th St, Madison, IN 47250
Larry D. Cummins, 812-265-6756
Type: public at-risk
15 students, ages 12-16, 7-9th grade
Entrance requirement: referral

Jackson County Christian Home Educators
528 E 16th St, Seymour, IN 47274
812-523-1532

Positive Alternatives for Student Success (PASS)
2nd & Community Dr, Seymour, IN 47274
Libby Roberts, 812-522-4384
Type: public at-risk
1 teacher, 75 students, 9-12th grade
Entrance by referral
Affective Skills Development.

Montessori House for Children
313 N Chinquapin Way, Muncie, IN 47304-3642

Friends Preschool
418 W Adams St, Muncie, IN 47305
Shelly Stewart, Head Tch, 317-288-5133
Type: Quaker

ACE Program (1986)
1300 Spartan Dr, Connersville, IN 47331
Kathy McCarty, Coord, 317-825-4110, FAX: 827-0836
Fayette County

Type: public at-risk
5 teachers, 72 students, ages 15-19, 8-12th grade
Entrance requirements: exam, referral, grade 4 reading profi-
ciency; no residency requirement
Governance by teachers and principal
Teacher qualifications: IN certification
Individual curriculum plans; self-directed; credit for work
completed; suburban location; transportation.

FATE: Fayette Alternative to Expulsion
1900 Grand Ave, Connersville, IN 47331
Dennis Metzger, 317-825-1139
Fayette County
Type: public at-risk
Students mainly behavior disordered, ages 11-14

Blackford County Alternative Learning Program
2392 State Rd 3 N, Hartford City, IN 47348
Dr John Hill, 317-348-7560
Type: public at-risk
2 teachers, 8-12 students, ages 15-18, 9-12th grade
Short-term intervention and correction.

New Castle Alternative School
522 Elliott Dr, New Castle, IN 47362
Ted Tibbits, 317-521-7223
Type: public at-risk
9-12th grade
Entrance by referral

North Campus Alternative School (1975)
80 Glenwood St, New Castle, IN 47362
Karen P. Marcum, Dir, 317-521-7237, FAX: 317-521-7268
Henry County
Type: public at-risk
11 teachers, 170 students, mainly IDEA handicapped, ages
12-21, 7-12th grade
Residency required
Governance by teachers; Principal
Teacher qualifications: IN SE License
Competency-based; psychologist; counselor; no letter
grades; multi-aged classes; level system; rural location;
transportation; interns accepted.

Children's School (1971)
607 W Main St, Richmond, IN 47374
Laurence Boggess, Head Tch, 317-966-5767
Type: Quaker, non-profit; tuition: 1,800/yr, scholarships
5 teachers, 50 students, ages 4-11, K-5th grade
Entrance requirements: interview, visit
Affiliation: Friends Council on Education
Teacher qualifications: BA or higher
No letter grades; multi-aged classes; suburban location;
interns accepted.

Meramec Montessori Children's Center
PO Box 64, Yorktown, IN 47396-0064

Bloomington Montessori (1968)
1835 S Highland Ave, Bloomington, IN 47401
Jeanne G. Jerden, Exec Asst, 812-336-2800
Non-profit; tuition: $165-370/mo
4 teachers, 11 assistants, 147 students, ages 3-12
Affiliation: AMS
Governance by board
Suburban location; interns accepted.

Harmony School (1974)
Box 1787, Bloomington, IN 47402
Steve Boncheck, Director, 812-334-8349, FAX: 812-334-8349
Monroe County
Type: independent, non-profit; tuition: sliding scale, 80% on
scholarships
17 teachers, 200 students, ages 3-21, pre K-12th grade

Entrance requirements: application; interview
Affiliations: Coalition of Essential Schools, NCACS
Governance by democratic school meeting
Teacher qualifications: all have BA-PhD, 60% certified, no specific qualifications
Based on the principal that the role of education in a democracy is to sensitize young people to the delicate balance between individual growth and community responsibility; no letter grades; multi-aged classes; extensive field trips; suburban location; interns accepted.

School of Education, Alternative Teacher Education
Indiana University, Bloomington, IN 47405
Tom Gregory, 812-876-9362
Type: higher education

North Lawrence Community Behavior Consultant Service
1401 15th St, Bedford, IN 47421
Barbara Miller, 812-279-6651
Type: public at-risk
75-100 students, K-12th grade
Entrance by referral.
Alternative to expulsion.

Paoli Community Alternative School
501 Elm St, Paoli, IN 47454
Roger Fisher, 812-723-4717
Type: public at-risk
15-20 students, ages 13-16, 7-9th grade
Field experiences; guest speakers; parent/student activities.

LEARN
7633 Shilo Rd, Unionville, IN 47468
Type: home-based

Padanaram Village School (1972)
RR 1, Box 478, Williams In, IN 47470
Steven Fuson, Schoolmaster, 812-262-7252
Martin County
Type: independent, boarding, non-profit; no tuition
9 teachers, 60 students, ages 5-18, K-12th grade
Enrollment restricted to members of the community
Governance by teachers and principal, parent cooperative
Community shares goods communally; 3 R's and strong curricula are blended with arts, hands-on learning, community life; no letter grades; multi-aged classes; extensive field trips.

Vincennes Community Alternative Education
300 N 6th St, Vincennes, IN 47591
Dr Joan Beckman, Asst Supt, 812-882-3668
MS, HS
Alternative to suspension/expulsion.

Early School Day
943 S Franklin, Oakland City, IN 47660
Roger Benson, 812-749-4755
East Gibson District
Type: public at-risk
Starts at 7:10 am.

Southern Indiana Support Group
PO Box 388, Princeton, IN 47670
812-385-4176
Gibson County
Type: home-based

Richmond Community Out of School Option
300 Hab Etchison Blvd, Richmond, IN 47674
Dr Karen Montgomery, 317-973-3300
6-8th grade
Enrollment voluntary or by recommendation
Short-term, intensive intervention as alternative to expulsion.

Christa McAuliffe Alternative Middle School
401 E Columbia St, Evansville, IN 47711
Greg Brown, 812-421-8508
Evansville-Vanderburgh District
Type: public at-risk
Combines assertive discipline with Glasser's theories of non-coercive ed through behavior cards, level system.

McCutchanville Montessori
8100 Petersburg Rd, Evansville, IN 47711-1777

Stanley Hall Enrichment Center (1988)
800 S Evans, Evansville, IN 47713
Patricia C. Cato, Prin, 812-465-8281
Vanderburgh County
Type: public at-risk
5 teachers, 110 students, ages 15-21, 10-12th grade
Entrance requirements: HS recommendation, district residency
Governance by teachers; Principal
Teacher qualifications: Licensed and/or endorsed
Student-centered; self-paced; multi-aged classes; life skills; career awareness; community service; urban location; interns accepted.

Montessori Academy
4611 Adams Ave, Evansville, IN 47714
Roxanne Crouch

Washington High School
1201 S 13th St, Terre Haute, IN 47802
Lieselotte Maher, Prin, 812-232-3142
Type: public at-risk
145 students, HS
Interview required.
Educational, vocational, personal counseling; childcare; transportation.

Terre Haute Montessori School
4310 S 11th St, Terre Haute, IN 47802-4318
Frances Murphy

Vigo County Juvenile Center Educational Services
961 Lafayette Ave, Terre Haute, IN 47804
Beverly Spear, 812-462-4224
Students mainly detained
Tutoring; counseling.

Wabash Valley Homeschool Association (1984)
2515 E Quinn Ave, Terre Haute, IN 47805
Barbara Palmer, 466-9467
Vigo County
Governance by parent cooperative

Montessori School at St Mary of Woods College
St Mary Of The Woods, IN 47876-1001

West Lafayette Community Learning Center
2300 Cason St, Lafayette, IN 47904
Jim Sands, 317-449-3200
Type: public at-risk
Students mainly disruptive

Elston Community Education Center
Tippecanoe School Corp
21 Elston Rd, Lafayette, IN 47905
June Hirschinger, 317-474-2481
HS

Rising Star Montessori School
413 Teal Rd, Lafayette, IN 47905-2311

Montessori School of Greater Lafayette
PO Box 2311, W Lafayette, IN 47906
Anita McKinney

Montessori School of Crawfordsville
1850 Ladoga Rd, Crawfordsville, IN 47933-3743

Indian Trials Career Center (1987)
807 N 6th St, Monticello, IN 47960
Carl Van Meter, Director, 219-583-9639
White County
Type: public at-risk
2 teachers, 30 students, ages 11-21, 6-12th grade
Residency required

Affiliation: Twin Lakes School Corp
Governance by teachers, principal, board
Teacher qualifications: state certification
Individualized; CAI; outcome-based; multi-aged classes; no
   letter grades; non-compulsory class attendance; rural loca-
   tion; transportation; interns accepted.

Upbeat Alternative School
RR 1, Oxford, IN 47977
Dale Jones, 317-884-1600
Benton CSD District
Students mainly teen parents, pregnant, other special needs,
   7-12th grade
Individualized entry/exit criteria.

Iowa

SHEEP
9400 NE 46th Ave, Altoona, IA 50009
Angela Sweiter
Des Moines County
Type: home-based

Project Success (1991)
20th & Ridgewood, Ames, IA 50010
Dr Clemmye Jackson, 515-232-8440
Type: public at-risk
5 teachers, 198 students, HS
Enrollment restricted to referred, district students
Cooperative learning; computers; learning packets; remediation; contracting; peer tutoring; vocational; GED; urban
   location.

Laurel Tree Montessori Preschool
3727 Calhoun Ave, Ames, IA 50010-4104

Bondurant-Farrar Summer School (1984)
300 Garfield, Bondurant, IA 50035
Warren Kyer, 515-967-7819
1 teacher, 15 students, JH
Enrollment restricted to referred, district students
Half-day; self-paced; remediation; rural location.

DMACC Academic Achievement Center (1972)
1125 Hancock Dr, Boone, IA 50036
Jinny Silberhorn, Dir, 515-432-7203 x 1020
Type: public at-risk
7 teachers; students partly at-risk, ages 17+, HS
Min age 17
Teacher qualifications: BA
Urban location.

Carlisle Learning Center (1991)
430 School St, Carlisle, IA 50047
Liz Brown, 515-989-0833
Type: public at-risk
2 teachers, 45 students, JH, HS
Enrollment restricted to referred, district students
In Carlisle HS; remediation; correspondence courses from Des
   Moines Area CC make up credit deficiencies; parent
   involvement; suburban location.

Indianola Learning Center (1992)
1301 E 2nd Ave, Indianola, IA 50125
Michael A. Baethke, 515-961-9580
Type: public choice
5 teachers, 60-65 students, HS
Entrance requirement: referral; quarterly enrollment

Vocational; teen parenting; student-based discipline; community involvement; competency-based; self-paced;
   urban location.

Caring Connection (1988)
1602 S 2nd Ave, Marshalltown, IA 50158
Anne Peglow, 515-752-4535
Type: public choice
13 teachers, 600 students, all ages
Entrance requirement: referral; no residency required
Independent and home study; contracting; mentoring; childcare; ESL; self-evaluation; pass/fail, no-grade options;
   special ed; vocational; teen parenting; urban location.

SAFE-Student Alternative Formula Education (1989)
216 Sherman, Murray, IA 50174
James F. Rhoads, 515-447-2517
Type: public choice
4 teachers, 50 students, mainly Native American, JH, HS
Entrance requirement: referral; no residency required
Competency-based; self-paced; independent study; GED;
   remediation; contracting; special ed; vocational; rural
   location.

Basics & Beyond Alternative School (1991)
600 N 2nd Ave W, Newton, IA 50208
James Fenton, 515-791-0700 x1700
Type: public choice
8 teachers, 80 students, HS
No residency requirement
Competency-based; self-paced; independent study; teen
   parenting; community studies, contracting; childcare;
   career/vocational; no letter grades; urban location.

Jasper County Support Group
1510 S 8th Ave, Newton, IA 50208
Pastor Jim Black
Type: home-based

Reading Recovery, Reading/Writing Lab, Math Lab
1800 Grand Ave, Des Moines, IA 50211
Sharon Castelda, Chap 1 Supervisor, 515-242-7731, FAX: 515-
   242-7550
Polk County
Type: public at-risk
78 teachers, 3000 students, ages 6-12, 1-6th grade
Enrollment restricted to low income, educational need
Teacher qualifications: reading endorsements
Urban location.

CAP (Clarke Alternative Program) (1985)
800 N Jackson, Osceola, IA 50213
Joe Shelton, 515-342-6505
Type: public choice
1 teacher, 30-35 students, HS
Entrance requirement: referral; one semester waiting period;
   no residency required
Flexible schedule; site-based; individualized study; 2 diploma
   types; arranged, regular school, and correspondence
   courses; work/study; childcare.

PASS Perry High School (1989)
18th & Lucinda, Perry, IA 50220
Kirk Waggie, 515-465-4656
1 teacher, 63 students, mainly at-risk, HS
Enrollment restricted to referred, district students
Teen parenting; independent study; computer-based; personalized; peer tutoring; pass/fail option; career/voca-
   tional; urban location.

Perry Learning Center (1993)
1200 18th St, Perry, IA 50220
Eugene Brady, Prin, 515-465-2997, FAX: 515-465-2426
Dallas County
Type: public at-risk
1 teacher, 20 students, mainly at-risk, ages 16-20, 10-12th
   grade
Residency required
Governance by principal
Multi-aged classes; rural location.

Story County Support Group
Roland, IA 50236
Claudia Nielsen, 515-388-4677
Type: home-based
Meets 1st Tuesday of month.

Roland-Story Elementary
900 Hillcrest Dr, Story City, IA 50248
Jane A. Todey, 515-733-4386
1 teacher, 10 students, mainly Asian, ES-HS
Student volunteers/assistants; mentoring; peer tutoring; ESL;
   personalized program.

Sayre Elementary and Middle School
1700 Vine St, West Des Moines, IA 50265
Barbara Sayre
Type: Montessori

Montessori Children's House
1025 28th St, West Des Moines, IA 50265-2124

New Horizons Program (1970)
1800 Grand Ave, Rm 450, Des Moines, IA 50309
C. Ronald Sallade, 515-242-7698
Type: public at-risk
1,500 students
Enrollment restricted to referred district students
At 5 HS's; self-paced; independent study; computers; mentoring; work experience; support services; home visits;
   peer tutoring; pass/fail option; self-evaluation; career/
   vocational; GED; urban location.

Montessori Learning Center
4533 University Ave #E, Des Moines, IA 50311-3359

Des Moines Alternative High School-North (1993)
1801 16th St, Des Moines, IA 50314
Vince Lewis, Prin, 515-244-0448, FAX: 244-0448
Polk County
Type: public choice
200 students, mainly at-risk, ages 15-20, 9-12th grade
Entrance requirements: 10 day orientation, residency
Governance by principal, teachers
Work experience credit; support groups; multi-aged classes;
   childcare; interns accepted.

Des Moines South Alternative High School (1969)
1000 SW Porter, Des Moines, IA 50315
Vince Scavo, 515-285-3323
Type: public choice
44 teachers, 350 students, pre-K, HS
Enrollment restricted to district students.
Separate building; computers; independent study; contracting; teen parenting; mentoring; childcare; self-evaluation;
   vocational; urban location.

Phillips Traditional School
1701 Lay St, Des Moines, IA 50317
Linda Hansen, Prin, 515-265-3406
Polk County
Type: public choice
23 teachers; student ages 5-12, K-5th grade
No residency requirement
Governance by principal
Teacher qualifications: excellent service
No letter grades; interns accepted.

**Bureau of Federal School Improvement, Dept of
   Education**
(See Resource Appendix)

Montessori Children's Center
8509 Alice Ave, Des Moines, IA 50325-7111

Cerro Cordo County Support Group
626 10th NE, Mason City, IA 50401
Dennis or Nancy Erickson
Type: home-based

Mason City Alternative School (1975)
19 N Illinois, Mason City, IA 50401
David A. Ciccetti, 515-421-4427
Type: public choice
7 teachers, 80-100 students, HS
Enrollment restricted to referred, district students; thirty-day
   waiting period required
Competency-based; independent study; computers;
   teaming; contracting; peer tutoring; Share-Time Program;
   childcare; special ed; vocational; teen parenting; urban
   location.

St Ansgar ABE/GED (1976)
206 E 8th St, St Ansgar, IA 50472
Larry Pheggenkuhle, 515-736-4329
1 teacher, 3-5 students, JH, HS
Entrance requirement: referral
Evening GED prep; no letter grades.

Gordon Willard Alternative Education Center
104 S 17th St, Fort Dodge, IA 50501
Jerry Einwalter, Coord/Tch, 515-576-7305, FAX:-1988
Webster County
Type: public choice
5 teachers, 65 students, mainly at-risk, ages 15-21, 9-12th
   grade
Entrance requirements: age 15, interview, testing, residency
Affiliation: IA AE Assn
Governance by advisory board of students, parents,
   community
Teacher qualifications: IA Certification
Individual education plans; self-paced; on-site work/study;
   social skills; 80% attendance required; rural location; trans-
   portation; interns accepted.

**Student Support Services-Iowa Lakes Community
   College** (1972?)
3200 College Dr, Emmetsburg, IA 50536
Melba Byrkeland, 712-852-3554, FAX: 712-852-2152
Palo Alto County
Type: public at-risk; tuition: $76/wk
3 teachers; student ages 17+, grades 12+
Governance by board

Teacher qualifications: certification
Psycho-social approach; supervised housing; rural location; interns accepted.

Storm Lake Senior High School (1989)
621 Tornado Dr, Storm Lake, IA 50588
Steve Berry, 712-732-8065
2 teachers, 49 students, JH, HS
Enrollment restricted to district students
Independent study; computer-based work; teaming; peer tutoring; ESL; self-evaluation; special ed; urban location.

Webster City Alternative School (1973)
1000 Des Moines St, Webster City, IA 50595
Mary Crystal, 515-832-2648
2 teachers, 2-26 students, JH, HS
After-school M-Th; credits toward graduation at Webster City HS; teen parenting; independent study; computers; self-paced; urban location.

Casa Montessori School, Inc (1982)
9204 University Ave, Cedar Falls, IA 50613
Patricia Poage, Dir, 319-277-8121
Non-profit; tuition: $230-295/mo
2 teachers, 2 assistants, 36 students, ages 3-9
Entrance requirements: age 2.5; toilet trained
Governance by administrator

Malcolm Price Laboratory School (1986)
19th & Campus St, Cedar Falls, IA 50613-3593
Linda Fernandez, 319-273-2202
Type: independent
95 teachers, 600 students, all ages
No residency requirement
Affiliation: Univ of N Iowa
Competency-based; special ed; performing arts; self-paced; cooperative learning; computers; learning packets; teaming; non-graded through grade 8; teen parenting; urban location.

Expo II (1973)
PO Box 848, Waverly, IA 50677
Jean Klunder, 319-352-2630
1 teacher, 20 students, HS
Enrollment restricted to district students; thirty day waiting period required
Academic instruction; independent study; self-paced.

Independent Learning Center (1968)
844 W 4th St, Waterloo, IA 50702
Charmaine Carney, 319-234-5745
6 teachers, 315 students, HS
Affiliation: Hawkeye CC
School year and summer drop-in center, 13 hrs/day, M-F; independent study; computer-based work; self-paced; home study; GED; urban location.

EXPO High School (1975)
927 Franklin St, Waterloo, IA 50703
W. Ray Richardson, Dir, 319-291-4842
Black Hawk County
Type: public at-risk
16 teachers, 245 students, ages 14-21
No residency requirement
Affiliation: NCA
Governance by teachers, principal, board
No letter grades; extensive field trips; multi-aged classes; interns accepted.

Creston Alternative School (1981)
107 N Maple, Creston, IA 50801
Angela Scallon, 515-782-4375
Type: public choice
1 teacher, 15 students, HS
Entrance requirement: referral, residency
Storefront; personalized program; contracting; urban location.

LeMars Community/WIT-ILC (1990)
410 5th Ave SW, LeMars, IA 51031
Jim Patera, 712-546-4153
Type: public choice
2 teachers, 50 students, HS
No residency requirement
Affiliation: W Iowa Tech
In printing business building; half-day; competency-based; self-paced; contracting; peer tutoring; urban location.

Whiting Community School (1988)
Whiting, IA 51063
Gary Funkhouser, 712-458-2468
2 teachers, 10 students, ages 3-4, pre-K
Afternoon program; student volunteers; special ed; urban location.

Central Campus Individual Learning Center (1971)
1121 Jackson St, Sioux City, IA 51105
Dr Paul VanderWiel, 712-279-6073
12 teachers, 450-550 students, HS
Entrance requirement: referral
Affiliation: W Iowa Tech
Competency-based; self-paced; independent study; teen parenting; special ed; vocational; GED; ESL; urban location.

Carroll Alternative School (1992)
2809 N Grant Rd, Carroll, IA 51401
Gary D. Currie, 712-792-8010
Type: public choice; tuition: if outside district
3 teachers, 17 students, HS
Entrance requirement: referral; no residency required
Pre-employment training; independent study; computers; learning packets; 1/3 credit every 30 school days; no letter grades; suburban location.

Ida County Support Group
Ida Grove, IA 51445
Sue Goodenow, 712-364-2209
Type: home-based
Meets 3rd Monday of month.

Independent Learning Center (1979)
Lewis Central H S, Hwy 275, Council Bluffs, IA 51503
Curt Peterson, 712-366-8240
Type: public choice
1 teacher, 24 students, HS
Enrollment restricted to district students; waiting period required; vacancies filled every 18 days
Competency-based; self-paced; independent study; urban location.

Iowa Western Community College Adult Learning Center (1972)
620 N 8th St, Council Bluffs, IA 51503
Margot Fetrow, Coord, 712-325-3266, FAX: 325-3424
Pott County
Type: public choice
13 pt teachers, 900 students, mainly at-risk, ages 16+
Enrollment restricted to age 16+ not enrolled in public school; no residency requirement
Governance by teachers and principal
Teacher qualifications: college grad
GED prep; ESL; ABE; self-paced; skills improvement in reading, writing, math at all levels; no letter grades; non-compulsory class attendance; multi-aged classes; suburban location.

Kanesville High School (1974)
807 Ave G, Council Bluffs, IA 51503
Romola Fritz, 712-328-6510
Type: public choice
14 teachers, 275 students, HS
Entrance requires application, district residency or open-enrolled out-of-district students.
Computers; SE; teen parenting; childcare; no letter grades; vocational; urban location.

Harlan Flexible Education Center (1991)
2712 12th St, Harlan, IA 51537
Amy Stallman, Adm; Kent Klinkefus, Prin, 712-755-3568, FAX:
    712-755-7413
Shelby County
Type: public at-risk
1 teacher, 1 assistant, 18 students, ages 16–21, 9–12th grade
Enrollment restricted to non-special ed students
Affiliation: IA Western CC
Governance by teachers and principal
Teacher qualifications: secondary education certification
Require 80% mastery; independent study; self paced; work-
    and volunteer-for-credit programs; rural location.

Iowa Families for Christian Education
RR 3 Box 143, Missouri Valley, IA 51555
Type: state home-based

Central Alternative High School (1973)
39 Bluff St, Dubuque, IA 52001
David Olson, 319-588-8395
Type: public choice
17 teachers, 275 students, JH, HS
Entrance requirement: waiting period; enrollment is quar-
    terly with exception; no residency required
Separate building; service learning; expeditionary learning;
    teaming; contracting; teen parenting; weekly visits by
    mental health and social work specialists; special ed; urban
    location.

Dubuque Montessori School, Inc Slattery Center
Flora Park, Dubuque, IA 52001

**MAC: Maquoketa Alternative Classroom
PAR: Prevention & Retention Program** (1973)
600 Washington, Maquoketa, IA 52060
Debbra J. Carson, Dir, 319-652-2451 x39
Type: public choice; tuition: if outside district
3 teachers, 40 students, mainly at-risk, HS
OBE, structured, individualized instruction; mentorships; On-
    The-Job training; business partnerships help student tran-
    sition from school-to-work; self-evaluation; rural location.

Allamakee Community District
1105 3rd Ave NW, Waukon, IA 52172
Dr Joe Schmitz
Type: Montessori

CEC Alternative Schools (1978)
509 S Dubuque, Iowa City, IA 52240
Diana Paulina, 319-339-6809, FAX: 319-339-5702
Johnson County
Type: public at-risk
8 teachers, 100 students, ages 13–21, 7–12th grade
Residency required
Governance by democratic school meeting
Teacher qualifications: state certification
Work-study; video/art studios; art museums; leaders in dis-
    trict tech; shared decision making; no letter grades; multi-
    aged classes; extensive field trips; transportation; interns
    accepted.

Johnson County Support Group
Iowa City, IA 52240
Diana Brahn; Leslie Johnson, 319-645-2918, 338-4522
Type: home-based
Meets 1st Monday of month, 8–9 pm.

Willowind School
226 S. Johnson, Iowa City, IA 52240-5146
Ruth Manna
Type: independent

Little Shadow Montessori School
416 Fairchild St, Iowa City, IA 52245-2822

Montessori School of Iowa City
502 Reno St, Iowa City, IA 52245-3039
Patricia Hanick

Cedar Valley Montessori School
3rd Ave & 23rd St, Marion, IA 52302

Marion Learning Center (1978)
600 10th Ave, Marion, IA 52302
Jerry Hora or Jacquie Oster, 319-377-2216
2 teachers, 220 students, ages 14+, HS
Self-paced; GED; HS diploma; serves Linn-Mar, Marion, Central
    City, North Linn, Springville, Alburnett, Center Point
    districts.

Lincoln Alternative School (1990)
102 E North, Stanwood, IA 52337
Lou Grimm, 319-945-3341
Lincoln Community District
Type: public choice
1 teacher, 9 students, JH, HS
Entrance requirement: waiting period; no residency required
Academic curriculum; self-paced; independent study; rural
    location.

STC Partnership Center (1990)
205 W 3rd St, Tama, IA 52339
Donna Downs Hempy, Proj Mgr, 515-484-3085, FAX: 515-484-
    3924
Tama County
Type: public at-risk
4 teachers, 45 students, ages 12+, 6–12th grade
Entrance requirements: approval of S Tama Co Sch officials
Affiliation: S Tama Co Schools
Governance by board
Teacher qualifications: certification
Tutoring; GED; ESL; learning lab; employment, recreational,
    and supportive human services; rural location; interns
    accepted.

Kirkwood Learning Center (1974)
111 Westview Dr, Washington, IA 52353
Sandy Weller, 653-4655, FAX: 653-6243
Washington County
Type: public choice/at-risk
1 teacher, 175–200 students, partly at-risk, ages 15–74
Residency required.
No letter grades; multi-aged classes; rural location.

West Campus (1981)
Hwy 22E, PO Box 150, Wellman, IA 52356
Valli Domsic, 319-646-2093
Type: public choice
1 teacher, 20 students, HS
Enrollment restricted to district students
Competency-based; independent and home study; voca-
    tional; teen parenting; GED; no letter grades; urban
    location.

Metro High School (1974)
1212 7th St SE, Cedar Rapids, IA 52401
Dr Mary Wilcynski, Prin, 319-398-2193
Linn County
Type: public at-risk
36 teachers, 620 students, mainly at-risk, ages 14–21, 9–12th
    grade
Students must have completed grade 8, dropped out of con-
    ventional school or be referred by previous school adm or
    advisor; residency required
Affiliation: NCA
Governance by teachers and principal
Teacher qualifications: BA in education
Academics, electives, Vocademics (e.g., food service, on-site
    daycare, laundry, recycling center, bike repair shop); credit
    awarded via a narrative evaluation by attendance, work

performance and behavior; twice cited by US DOE as Blue Ribbon School; no letter grades; multi-aged classes; extensive field trips; urban location; interns accepted.

Kirkwood Lincoln Learning Center (1985)
9th St & 18th Ave SW, Cedar Rapids, IA 52404
Jan McBurney, 319-366-0142
Type: public choice
5 teachers, 20–40 students, HS
Entrance requirement: referral; no residency required
Affiliations: Prairie HS, Kirkwood Adult HS
Separate building; flexible hours; ESL; correspondence courses; independent and home study; GED; computers; community studies; career/vocational; urban location.

Kirkwood Adult High School
6301 Kirkwood Blvd NW, Cedar Rapids, IA 52405
Jan McBurney, 319-366-0142
25 students, HS
Entrance requirement: referral
Affiliation: Kirkwood Lrng Ctr
GED/alternative diplomas; students referred to Kirkwood Learning Ctr; independent and home study; computers; childcare; career/vocational; urban location.

Monroe County Support Group
Albia, IA 52531
Erlene Gangsted; Bonnie Hall, 515-923-7912, 932-5680
Type: home-based
Meets 3rd Friday of month.

Davis County Alternative School (1990)
102 High St, Bloomfield, IA 52537-1738
Dee Altheide, 515-664-2200 x156
Type: public choice
2 teachers, 20 students, mainly Native American, HS
Enrollment restricted to referred, district students
Affiliation: Davis Cty HS
Flexible hours; summer courses; academic assistance; no letter grades; independent study; rural location.

Mahaishi International University
Fairfield, IA 52556

University Alternative High (1985)
1200 Market, Burlington, IA 52601
Raymond Eilenstine, 319-753-2701
8 teachers, 135–150 students, HS
Entrance by referral.
Independent study; career/voc; self-paced; in separate building; childcare.

Creative Learning Center (1974)
1733 Ave I, Fort Madison, IA 52627
Beverly Link, 319-372-8093
Type: public choice
4 teachers, 85 students, HS
Entrance requirement: referral; no residency required
In two-story frame house; self-paced; independent study; community studies; teen parenting; urban location.

Montessori Country School
835 Ave A, Fort Madison, IA 52627-2859

Learning Center (1978)
2285 Middle Rd, Keokuk, IA 52632
Barb Harrison, Dir, 319-524-2542
Lee County
Type: public at-risk

2 teachers, 50 students, mainly at-risk, ages 14–21, 9–12th grade
Entrance requirements: counselor recommendation, residency
Affiliation: Keokuk Community School
Governance by teachers and principal
Teacher qualifications: Iowa subject area certification
The program offers independent study, correspondence courses, career/vocational classes, and personalized educational programs; urban location.

Lincoln Alternative High School
732 11th Ave S, Clinton, IA 52732
Richard Grugin, Prin, 319-242-4073, FAX: 243-2415
Clinton Comm SD District
Type: public at-risk
10 teachers, 120 students, mainly at-risk, ages 14–21, 9–12th grade
Enrollment restricted to dropout or referred residents
Governance by teachers and principal
Teacher qualifications: state secondary certification
Teacher considered a "family leader"; emphasis on self-growth and positive social values; support groups on young parenting, substance abuse, sexual abuse, and children of alcoholics; multi-aged classes; urban location; transportation; interns accepted.

CEP (Continuing Education Program) (1988)
152 Colorado St, Muscatine, IA 52761
R. L. Casini, 319-263-6141
Type: public choice
1 teacher, 150 students, HS
Enrollment restricted to referred, district students
Affiliations: Muscatine CC, Muscatine HS
Self-paced; independent study; diploma.

Muscatine High School Evening Program (1988)
2705 Cedar St, Muscatine, IA 52761
Mary L. Wildermuth, 319-263-6141
Type: public choice
9 teachers, 200 students, HS
Entrance requirement: referral; no residency required
Transitional program; cooperative learning; computer-based work; teaming; childcare; ESL; urban location.

Kirkwood Education Center
N Cedar St, Tipton, IA 52772
HS
Entrance requirement: referral
Affiliation: Kirkwood CC
GED, Kirkwood Adult Ed diploma, or Tipton Comm School diploma; flexible hours.

Montessori House of Children
1918 W 16th St, Davenport, IA 52804
Margaret A Callett

2001 Alternative Program (1990)
1002 W Kimberly Rd, Davenport, IA 52806
Roger Fuerstenberg, 319-386-5840, 391-9161
Type: public choice
11 teachers, 275 students, HS
Entrance requirement: referral; one quarter waiting period for dropouts; no residency required
11 am-9 pm; traditional class structure with cooperative learning; remediation; computer-based work; urban location.

Kansas

Montessori Children's House of Lawrence
1900 University Dr, Lawrence, KS 66044-4554

Sunshine Acres Preschool
2141 Maple Ln, Lawrence, KS 66046-3299
Type: Montessori

Lawrence Alternative High School Program
2600 W 25th St; c/o 3705 Clinton Pkwy, Lawrence, KS 66047
Judith A. Juneau, Dir, 913-832-5940
Type: public at-risk
9 teachers, 70-75 students
Individualized instruction; diagnostic prescriptive teaching;
   flexible scheduling; JTPA, on-the-job training; support
   groups; individual, peer counseling; group activities.

Raintree Montessori School
4545 Clinton Pky, Lawrence, KS 66047-1913

Project STAY (Second Time Around for Youth)
1620 Rose, Leavenworth, KS 66048
Cynthia Bixby, Dir, 913-684-1580
3 teachers, 88 students
Entrance requirement: referral
Individualized learning contracts; work/study; community
   service; group studies.

Phase V Alternative Education Program (1972)
1800 W Dennis, Olathe, KS 66061
Jim Houghton, Dir, 913-780-7250
250-300 students, mainly at-risk
Entrance requirement: referral
Night classes; min. attendance, productive work required.

Children's House
1024 W Fairwood Ln, Olathe, KS 66061-2414
Type: Montessori

BaSE (Basic Skills Education)
15100 W 127th, Olathe, KS 66062
Paige May, 913-780-7270
1 teacher, 56 students
Teacher qualifications: certification
9 week study skills curriculum; daily monitor required;
   monthly parent meetings; independent study.

Final Focus at Olathe South High School
1640 E 151st St, Olathe, KS 66062
Zeny Schmidt, 913-780-7160
11 students, 11th grade
Affiliation: Olathe AVTS
Career education; vocational training; guest speakers; field
   trips; simulations; weekly grade, attendance reviews.

Student HELP Clinic
315 N Lindenwood, Olathe, KS 66062
Walter Carter, 913-780-7002
Students mainly at-risk, ES-HS
Study, social skills; self-concept class; evaluation services;
   tutoring; parenting class.

Lawrence Area Unaffiliated Group of Homeschoolers
   (LAUGH) (1992)
RR 1, Box 496, Perry, KS 66073
Barbara J. Michener, 913-597-5579
Jefferson County
Non-sectarian.

Kansans for Alternative Education
19985 Renner Rd, Spring Hill, KS 66083
913-686-2310
Type: state home-based

Career Learning Center (1980)
3016 N 9th St, Kansas City, KS 66101
Charles Knapp, Coord, 913-551-3635
USD #500
Type: public at-risk
9 teachers, 110 students, HS
Half days at Area Vocational Tech School or 15+ hrs/wk of
   supervised work-study; small class size; environmental,
   community projects; ethnic dinner; yearbook; prom.

Louisa May Alcott High School
1809 Bunker, Kansas City, KS 66102
Lindsey Cegelis, Prin, 913-551-3525,-3526
Type: public at-risk
10 teachers, 75-100 students
Vocational training; outcomes based; art; PE; individualized;
   computers; guest speakers; field trips; counseling; Teen
   Mother program for USD 500; childcare.

Associated Youth Services, Inc
3111 Strong, PO Box 6145, Kansas City, KS 66106
Pamela Wiens, Dir of Ed & Employment Training, 913-831-
   2820
Type: independent, non-profit
5 teachers, 2 assistants, 80 students, mainly at-risk, ages
   13-21, 6-12th grade
Affiliations: KSBE, KS City, JTPA
Summer, night courses; individualized; pre-employment
   skills; job placement assistance; on-staff social worker.

Career Opportunity Center
800 S 55th St, 2nd Flr, Kansas City, KS 66106
Carolyn Conklin, Dir, 913-596-1534
USD #202
4 teachers, 300 students, ages 16+, HS
Open entry/exit; individualized instruction; contracts; self-
   paced; no letter grades.

Center for International Studies
6649 Lamar, Shawnee Mission, KS 66202
David W. Wolfe, Dir, 913-384-6800
5 teachers, 2 assistants, 114 students, HS
Language, culture, geopolitical studies in Arabic, Chinese,
   Japanese, Russian; study at multinational corporations, art
   galleries, museums; summer program; cabaret concerts,
   festivals; evening courses; International Marketplace.

Shawnee Mission Alternative Education Program
5900 Lamar, Shawnee Mission, KS 66202
Dr Charles Jackard; Ron Bates, 913-789-3520
50 teachers, 600 students, mainly at-risk, 7-12th grade
Group counseling; personalized instruction; max 15 students/
   class; day and night classes; teen mothers required 1
   hr/day nursery care; RN on staff; childcare.

Christian Home Educators Confederation of Kansas
PO Box 3564, Shawnee Mission, KS 66203
Type: state home-based

Discovery Montessori
5603 Neiman, Shawnee Mission, KS 66203

Johnson City Preschool
6810 W 80th St, Overland Park, KS 66204
Type: Montessori

Overland Park Montessori
8029 Overland Park Dr, Shawnee Mission, KS 66204-3779

The Phoenix Montessori School (1992)
2013 W 104th St, Leawood, KS 66206
Alice Blackford, Dir, 381-1250
Non-profit; tuition: $255-305/mo
1 teacher, 1 assistant, 20 students, ages 3-6
Entrance requirements: toilet trained
Affiliation: AMI
Governance by board
Full range of Montessori materials; custom designed build-
ing; large outdoor play area; interns accepted.

Belmont Schools
PO Box 6212, Leawood, KS 66206-0212
Hal Swanson
Type: Montessori

Highlawn Montessori
3531 Somerset, Prairie Village, KS 66208
Carolyn Godfrey, Adm, 913-649-6160
Non-profit; tuition: $2,295/yr
4 teachers, 5 assistants, 93 students, ages 3-6
Governance by administrator, board
Teacher qualifications: AMI Certification
Traditional Montessori setting; extended day for ages 4.5-6;
childcare; multi-aged classes; suburban location; interns
accepted.

La Petite Academy
14 Corp Woods, 8717 W 110th St #300, Overland Park, KS
66210
Marketing Dept
Type: Montessori

Pre-Vocational Careers Class at Valley Heights Jr-Sr HS
(1983)
Rt 1, Blue Rapids, KS 66411
Ann Walter, 913-363-2508
1 teacher, 4 students, mainly learning disabled, JH, HS
Learning strategies and remediation class; 9-mo job; life skills
class; job placement and training; post graduation support
services.

School of Success
1st & Kickapoo, Hiawatha, KS 66434
Rosemary Schooler, 913-742-2119,-3312
Type: public choice
1 teacher, max 10 students, adult ages
Individualized; work/study; goal is employment or higher ed;
counseling; time clocks record attendance; contracts; HS
diploma.

K S Haugh Alternative Education Center (1981)
1833 Elmdale Ave, Junction City, KS 66441
Bernice Bullard, 913-762-3698
Type: public at-risk
2 teachers, 1 assistant, 100-150 students, ages 13+, HS
Entrance requirements: no behavior disorders or SE; Principal's referral
Individualized instruction; flexible attendance, if age 16+;
extensive curriculum.

Manhattan Parent Educators
1002 Houston, Manhattan, KS 66502
913-539-3641
Type: home-based

Rock Creek High School Alternative Education Program
9355 Flush Rd, St George, KS 66535
Chris Zerger, 913-494-8591
285 students, mainly at-risk

Here to Encourage the Learning Process (HELP)
Wamego High School
801 Lincoln, Wamego, KS 66547
Carol Wyatt, Dir, 913-456-2214
45 students
Resource room; study, career skills; trained peer tutors
receive credit.

Topeka Alternative Education Program
1900 Hope, Topeka, KS 66604
James Dodge, 913-271-6813
USD 501
20 teachers, 130 students, mainly at-risk
Individualized instruction; small class size; open entry;
support programs; child development courses; comprehensive intervention program; childcare.

Topeka West High School Alternative Education
Program
2001 Fairlawn, Topeka, KS 66604
Dr Robert McFrazier, Prin, 913-272-1643
Students mainly at-risk
Individualized instruction.

Discovery School
1701 SW Collins Ave, Topeka, KS 66604-3218
Jan Schiesser
Type: Montessori

Highland Park High School Alternative Education
Program
2424 California, Topeka, KS 66605
Dr Susan Rogers, 913-266-7616
1 teacher, max 36 students, mainly at-risk
Entrance requirement: referral
Individualized, small group instruction.

STARS at Topeka High School (1990)
800 W 10th St, Topeka, KS 66612
Bill Bagshaw, 913-232-0483 x29
60 students
Social work; video production; newspaper; mentorships; con-
sultations; social worker; volunteer tutors; interns
accepted.

Topeka High School Alternative Education Program
800 W 10th, Topeka, KS 66612
William Bagshaw, 913-232-0483
2 teachers, 27 students, mainly at-risk
Develops personal, academic skills.

Windows Reading Program at Topeka High School
800 W 10th, Topeka, KS 66612
Mary McGinty, 913-232-0483
Students mainly at-risk
Program as independent study or enrichment; personalized
reading list; required oral, written reports.

Emporia Alternative High School
1001 Commercial, Emporia, KS 66801
Carolyn Koch, Instructor, 316-341-2251
Type: public at-risk
4 teachers, 35 students, HS
Entrance requirements: no SE; sponsorship by accredited HS
Credit-earning; competency-based; open entry/exit; min 2
hrs/day; teen mothers in child development class may
bring infants; no letter grades.

Campus Center
620 Constitution St, Emporia, KS 66801-2847
Dr Wesley C. Jones
4 teachers, 18 students, ages 10-18
Enrollment restricted to the severely emotionally disturbed
Mental Health Ctr of E Central KS, Flint Hills Special Co-op
staff; family nights; individual case managers; summer
program; runs 11 months/year with abbreviated school
schedule in summer.

Work/Study Behavior Tracking Program at Burlington HS
830 Cross St, Burlington, KS 66839
Judy Hutson, Voc Facilitator, 316-364-2853
Type: public at-risk
2 teachers; HS
Enrollment restricted to KS DE at-risk
Affiliation: JTPA
Competency-based; credit-earning; vocational; work study; behavior tracking.

Renwick Secondary Extended Learning Program
PO Box 68, Andale, KS 67001
Carmen May, Coord of Gifted Ed, 316-445-2521
Renwick District #267
1 teacher, 21 students, HS
Independent projects; career shadowing; mentorships; advanced literature; Odyssey of the Mind; Stock Market Game; Citizen Bee; scholars' bowls; drama productions; film festival; college counseling; ACT/SAT prep.

Academic Enrichment
715 E Madison, Derby, KS 67037
Nancy L. Bolz, Coord, 316-788-8580
5 teachers, 60 students
Entrance requirement: teacher's referral
7 week minimum; tutorial assistance; grades monitored weekly; self esteem, goal setting, decision making, and responsibility are stressed; individual attention is paramount.

Derby Alternative High School (1988)
724 E Market, Derby, KS 67037
Don Taylor, Prin, 316-788-8515
Type: public at-risk
5 teachers, 86 students, ages 16–19
Affiliations: KDHR, JTPA
Part of DHS; LEAP (Let's Employ Alternative Pupils) job training and assistance.

BCCC Community Resource Center Alternative School
613 N Main, El Dorado, KS 67042
Sue Choens, Coor/Instructor, 316-321-4030
Tuition: variable
4 teachers; HS
Entrance requirement: Principal's referral
Affiliations: Butler Cty CC, Local District
3 locations; partly self-directed; one-room school programs; smoking area.

First Step Industries
900 W 12th, Newton, KS 67114
Dr Bill Harrington, 316-284-6280
2 teachers, 46 students, mainly differently abled, HS
Shop work; construction; daily evaluation determines school credit and paycheck amount through system of profit-sharing.

Newton Alternative Learning Center
218 E 7th St, Newton, KS 67114
Marlin Frey, Prin, 316-284-6231
2 teachers, 70–75 students, mainly at-risk, ages 16+
Flexible scheduling; individualized instruction.

Webster Community School
900 E 12th St, Winfield, KS 67156
Kathy Rogers, 316-221-5170
3 teachers, 66 students, 3–5th grade
Focus on community; research projects, activities; field trips; family involvement; hands-on learning; group interactions, cooperation.

Teaching Parents Association (1980)
PO Box 3968, Wichita, KS 67201
Jim Farthings, Pres, 316-945-0810, FAX: 316-685-1617
Sedowick County
Type: home-based, non-profit
Governance by parent cooperative and board
Mostly conservative Christian; open to all; newsletter; meetings; regular activities.

Downtown Law, Public and Social Service Magnet High School
455 N Main, 9th Flr, Wichita, KS 67202
Clare Korst, Prin, 316-833-4265
7 teachers, 100 students, 11–12th grade
Located in City Hall; internships; case studies; community service; mentorships; stresses good citizenship.

Emerson Elementary
2330 W 25th, Wichita, KS 67203
Marilyn Tilton, 316-833-3565
Type: magnet
K–5th grade
Open learning.

Rounds Montessori School
Box 8245, Wichita, KS 67206

Wichita Collegiate School
9115 E 13th St N, Wichita, KS 67206-1298
Type: Montessori

Celebration Montessori Center, Inc (1983)
2711 E Douglas, Wichita, KS 67211
Margaret W. Sandlin, Adm, 316-683-3149
Tuition: $155/mo
1 teacher, 3 assistants, 75 students, ages 3–6
Governance by administrator
Montessori math approach: bead cabinet and decimal system; urban location; interns accepted.

Metropolitan Boulevard Alternative High School
751 George Washington Blvd, Wichita, KS 67211
Dr Clarence H. Horn, 316-833-2500
11 teachers, 200 students
Individualized instruction; small classes; flexible attendence policies, scheduling; business; industrial technology.

Mayberry Middle Magnet School
207 S Sheridan, Wichita, KS 67213
Linda S. Wilson, 316-833-3500
600 students
Emphasis on Global Education; technology; foreign language required.

Metro-Meridian Alternative High School
301 S Meridian, Wichita, KS 67213
Mary J. Whiteside, Prin, 316-833-3535
200 students, mainly at-risk
Individualized instruction; self-paced; no failing grades given.

Northeast Magnet High School
1847 N Chautauqua, Wichita, KS 67214
Jim McNiece, 316-833-2300
415 students, 9–12th grade
Focus on science technology and visual arts; computers; interdisciplinary team-taught approach; humanities core; foreign language required.

Wells Alternative Middle School
3601 S Pattie, Wichita, KS 67216
Karen Cahow, 316-833-2995
100 students, mainly special needs

Lewis Elementary
3030 S Osage, Wichita, KS 67217
Eileen Copple, 316-833-3860
Type: magnet
K–5th grade
Open learning.

Brooks Middle Magnet
3802 E 27th St N, Wichita, KS 67220
Brenda E. Moore, Prin, 316-833-2345

825 students
Global Education; Science Technology; foreign language; parent, community involvement; tutoring; parent-teacher-student conferences; goal setting.

Buckner Elementary
3530 E 27th St N, Wichita, KS 67220
Nancy Roth, 316-833-2365
Type: magnet
1-5th grade
Performing arts.

Wichita Friends School, Inc (1991)
PO Box 9584, Wichita, KS 67277
Shelli Kodel, Head, 316-729-0303
Type: Quaker, non-profit; tuition: $2,300, scholarships
4 teachers, 44 students, ages 5-11, K-5th grade
Governance by board
Teacher qualifications: certification
Interdenominational; hands-on; class size limited to 20; multi-aged classes; suburban location; interns accepted.

Salina Alternative School
2640 Scanlan Ave, Salina, KS 67401
Gary White, Prin, 913-826-4680
6 teachers, 40+ students, 7-12th grade

Abilene High School's A+ Program
1300 N Cedar, Abilene, KS 67410
Dave Looysen, 913-263-1260
Type: public at-risk
1 teacher; HS
High expectations for student achievement and attendance.

Hesston/Canton Home Educators Association
Rt 1 Box 136, Canton, KS 67428
Connie Bunn, 316-367-8205

Ellsworth High School Individual Improvement Program
PO Box 46, Ellsworth, KS 67439
Sondra Rohr, 913-472-4471
1 teacher, 25-30 students, mainly at-risk

EXCEL (Extra-Curricular Educational Learning)
5056 E K-4 Hwy, Gypsum, KS 67448
Jackie Frevert, Coord, 913-536-4286
Type: public choice
6 teachers, 65 students, 5-12th grade
After-school tutorial program; 1:4-7 ratio; focus on academic skills, self-confidence, motivation.

Opportunity Hour
5056 E K-4 Hwy, Gypsum, KS 67448
Mike Garretson, Coord, 913-536-4286
Type: public at-risk
1 teacher, 30 students, 7-12th grade
Participants earn one semester credit.

Kanopolis Middle School Individual Improvement Program
PO Box 37, Kanopolis, KS 67454
Paula Bigham, 913-472-4477
1 teacher; 5-8th grade
Entrance by referral for grade 8.
Tutorial program; weekly study skills class required for grades 5-7.

Lincoln High School Secondary Tutoring
4th and College, Lincoln, KS 67455
Steve Seneff, Prin, 913-524-4193
2 teachers, 202 students, mainly at-risk, 7-12th grade
Entrance requirement: referral

Student Tutorial Assistance Program
400 N Walnut, Solomon, KS 67480

Joe Wiggins, Prin, 913-655-2560
Type: public at-risk
18 students, ES-HS
During, after school; credit given to day peer tutors; self-esteem course; study skills.

Alternate School of Hutchinson High
1401 N Severance, Hutchinson, KS 67501
Jim Harshbarger, Dir, 316-665-4563
Reno County
Type: public at-risk
11 teachers, 80 students
Serves entire county including private schools; night classes; diploma-earning; non-punitive attendance policy; open entry/exit; personalized instruction.

Montessori Children's House
PO Box 1791, Hutchinson, KS 67501

Central Kansas Home Educators
Route 1, PO Box 130, Lyons, KS 67554
Mike and Elaine Williamson

Community Based Education at Lyons High School
601 American Rd, Lyons, KS 67554
Larry Walker, Coord, 316-257-5114
10-12 students, mainly special needs
Work-study program.

Kathryn O'Loughlin McCarthy Elementary School
1401 Hall, Hays, KS 67601
Tanya Channell, Prin, 913-623-2510
USD #489
Type: public choice
20 teachers, 288 students, K-5th grade
Affiliation: Fort Hays State Univ
Emphasis on technology, computers, research; multimedia CAI; hands-on, non-textbook math; same teacher for 2 years; parent involvement; no letter grades; childcare.

Project SOS (Second Opportunity for Students) (1977)
1900 1st Ave, PO Box 460, Dodge City, KS 67801
Betty Allen, 316-227-1617
USD #443
2 teachers, 75 students, HS
Affiliation: DC HS
Self-paced; credit-earning; extensive CAI; work experience; support group meetings; childcare.

Garden City High School Alternative Center
1401 W Jones, Garden City, KS 67846
Gena Stanley, Prin, 316-276-5370
Type: public at-risk
14 teachers, 150-175 students, 6-12th grade
Enrollment restricted to at-risk (day program)
Night HS diploma program; small classes; credit given as earned; flexible schedule; materials and instruction adjusted to match learning styles.

Ti In
PO Box 99, Ingalls, KS 67853
John O'Brien, 316-335-5136
1 teacher, 28 students
Foreign language; marine science; psychology; astronomy; sociology; anatomy; physiology.

Tutoring Program
205 E 6th, Hugoton, KS 67951
Dr Nelson Bryant, 316-544-4397
USD #210
Type: public at-risk
60 students, ES-HS
Teacher qualifications: KS certification, 1.5 FTE certification
During school day for grades 7-12; before, after school and Saturdays for elementary.

Kentucky

Creative Education Center (1985)
110 N 5th St; PO Box 154, Bardstown, KY 40004
Janet MacLean, Dir, 502-348-6022
Nelson County
Type: independent, non-profit; tuition: $2,000/yr,
    scholarships
6 teachers, 46 students, ages 6-18, 1-12th grade
Entrance requirements: interview, test
Governance by teachers, principal, parent cooperative, board
School without failure; self-paced; individualized; multi-ability,
    multi-aged classes; extensive field trips; rural location;
    interns accepted.

Children's House Montessori
6710 Wolf Pen Branch Rd, Harrods Creek, KY 40027

Lagrange Montessori
5th St, Oldham County, KY 40031

Nazareth Montessori Children's Center
PO Box 44, Nazareth, KY 40048-0044
Pat Hill, SCN

Kentucky Christian Home School Association
1301 Bridget Dr, Fairdale, KY 40118
502-363-5104
Type: state home-based

Fairdale High School
1001 Fairdale Rd, Louisville, KY 40118
Marilyn M. Hohmann, 502-473-8248
Type: magnet
9-12th grade
Magnet career academy.

Saint Martin Montessori
639 S Shelby St, Louisville, KY 40202-1657

Central High School
1130 W Chestnut St, Louisville, KY 40203
Harold E. Fenderson, 502-473-8226
Type: magnet
9-12th grade
Magnet career academy.

Coleridge Taylor Elementary School
1115 W Chestnut St, Louisville, KY 40203-2090
Type: Montessori

Louisville Montessori Center
2316 Bonnycastle Ave, Louisville, KY 40205
Kaki Robinson

Hayfield Montessori School
2000 Tyler Ln, Louisville, KY 40205-2922

Mercy Montessori School
2181 Tyler Ln, Louisville, KY 40205-2953

Ursuline Montessori
3105 Lexington Rd, Louisville, KY 40206-3061

Waggener High School
330 S Hubbards lane, Louisville, KY 40207
Kathy Hopper, 502-473-8340
Type: magnet
9-12th grade
Magnet career academy.

DuPont Manual High School
120 W Lee St, Louisville, KY 40208
Beverly Keepers, 502-473-8241
Type: magnet
9-12th grade
Magnet career academy.

Noe Middle School
121 W Lee St, Louisville, KY 40208
Ron Crutcher, 502-473-8307
Jefferson County
Type: magnet
6-8th grade
Visual and performing arts.

Youth Performing Arts High School
1517 S Second St, Louisville, KY 40208
Beverly Keepers, 502-473-8355
Type: magnet
9-12th grade

Saint Columba Montessori
2208 Dixie Hwy, Louisville, KY 40210-2244

St Charles Montessori
2708 W Chestnut St, Louisville, KY 40211

John F. Kennedy Elementary School
3807 Young Ave, Louisville, KY 40211-2340
Jacqueline Austin
Type: Montessori

JCPS/Gheens Professional Development Academy
4425 Preston Hwy, Louisville, KY 40213
Ann Bruce
Type: Montessori

Kentucky Home Schoolers
3310 Illinois Ave, Louisville, KY 40213
502-636-3804
Type: state home-based

Doss High School
7601 St Andrews Church Rd, Louisville, KY 40214
Gordon E. Milby, 502-473-8239
Type: magnet
9-12th grade
Magnet career academy.

Kenwood Montessori School
4601 S 6th St, Louisville, KY 40214-1405

Iroquois Middle & High School
4615 Taylor Blvd, Louisville, KY 40215
James Decker, 502-473-8269
Jefferson County
Type: magnet
6-12th grade
Initiative program.

Southern High School
8620 Preston Hwy, Louisville, KY 40219
Steven D. Stallings, 502-473-8330
Type: magnet
9-12th grade
Magnet career academy.

Seneca/Binet High School
3510 Goldsmith Lane, Louisville, KY 40220
Charles Hill (Binet), 502-473-8209
Type: magnet
9-12th grade
Magnet career academy.

Moore High School
6415 Outer Loop, Louisville, KY 40228
Warren Shelton, 502-473-8304
Type: magnet
9-12th grade
Magnet career academy.

Westport Middle School
8100 Westport Rd, Louisville, KY 40242
Jim Stone, 502-473-8346
Jefferson County
Type: magnet
6-8th grade
Humanities; fine art.

Pleasure Ridge Park High
5901 Greenwood Rd, Louisville, KY 40258
Charles Miller, 502-473-8311
Type: magnet
9-12th grade
Magnet career academy.

Fern Creek High School
9115 Fern Creek Rd, Louisville, KY 40291
John Sizemore, 502-473-8251
Type: magnet
9-12th grade
Magnet career academy.

Jeffersontown High School
9600 Old Six Mile Lane, Louisville, KY 40299
Harold Russell, 502-473-8275
Type: magnet
9-12th grade
Magnet career academy.

Visitation Montessori School of Cardome
PO Box 594, Georgetown, KY 40324

Children's Montessori School
PO Box 545, Georgetown, KY 40324-0545

Montessori's House of Children
109 Berry Ave, Versailles, KY 40383-1454
Tony and Rene Guagliardo

Kentucky Home Education Association
PO Box 81, Winchester, KY 40392-0081
Type: state home-based

Boyle County Alternative Program (1991)
PO Box 520; PO Box 189, Danville, KY 40423
Kathy Belcher or Mike Swain, 606-236-6634, 238-1300
Type: public at-risk
1 teacher, 2 assistants, 15-20 students, ES, MS, HS
Enrollment restricted to potential drop outs.
Credit for community projects; JTPA; VOC; evenings; elementary SAFE program.

Danville Montessori School
PO Box 651, Danville, KY 40423-0651

Fayette County Public School
701 E Main St, Lexington, KY 40502
Carol Hiler
Type: Montessori

Southern Hills Montessori
2356 Harrodsburg Rd, Lexington, KY 40503-1795

Community Montessori School
166 Crestwood Dr, Lexington, KY 40503-2690
Janet Ashby

Wellington Academy
628 Wellington Way, Lexington, KY 40503-2734
Type: Montessori

The Lexington School
1050 Lane Allen Rd, Lexington, KY 40504-2099
Type: Montessori

Bluegrass Elementary & Middle School
475 Price Rd, Lexington, KY 40508
Ed Brand, 606-251-9497
Type: magnet
4-8th grade
Performing arts.

St Peter Claver Montessori
485 W 4th St, Lexington, KY 40508-1366

Providence Montessori School
1209 Texaco St, Lexington, KY 40508-2026

Children's House Kindergarten
135 Walton Ave, Lexington, KY 40508-2315
Type: Montessori

Montessori School of Frankfort (1978)
104 Cove Spring Rd, Frankfort, KY 40601
Cindy McKee, 502-875-3331
Non-profit; tuition: $145/205/mo
2 teachers, 1 assistant, 37 students, ages 3-9
Governance by administrator
4.5 park-like acres; swimming and gymnastics at YMCA; childcare; rural location; interns accepted.

St Camillus Montessori (1992)
709 E Center St, Corbin, KY 40701
Sr Mary Bezold, Dir, 606-528-9501
Non-profit; tuition: $950-1,450
1 teacher, 2 assistants, 30 students, mainly international, ages 3-6
Affiliations: NAMTA, NCEA
School within a school of 320 students, pre-school-HS; Spanish; accelerated program; AP classes; rural location; interns accepted.

Covington Children's House
1044 Scott St, Covington, KY 41011-3159
Type: Montessori

Northern Kentucky Montessori Center, Inc (1967)
232 Beechwood Rd, Ft Mitchell, KY 41017
Kitty K. Salter, Ed Dir, 606-331-3725, FAX: 606-282-4705
Non-profit; tuition: $1,900/yr
11 teachers, 30 students, ages 3-6
Affiliation: AMS; accreditation: KYDE
Governance by administrator, board
4 acres; individualized approach emphasizes self-development, self-confidence; suburban location; interns accepted.

Villa Early Learning Center
2402 Amsterdam, Villa Hills, KY 41017
Sr Mary Peter
Type: Montessori

Martha Arnett's Montessori Center
PO Box 18317, Erlanger, KY 41018-0317

St Anne Montessori School
River Rd Rt 8, Melbourne, KY 41059

Pikeville Independent
PO Box 2010, Pikeville, KY 41502
Anne Keene, Supervisor, 606-432-8161
Type: public at-risk
12th grade
Remedial; tutorial; flexible hours.

Speedwell Montessori School
1907 Ky Ave, Paducah, KY 42001

Murray Montessori School
212 N 15th St, Murray, KY 42071-1844

Brighten Green Montessori School
436 Plum Springs Rd, Bowling Green, KY 42101-9165

Montessori Children's House
2800 Bill Dedmon Rd, Bowling Green, KY 42101-9421

Community Montessori School
PO Box 422, Glasgow, KY 42142-0422
Kathy Khatib

Alternative Learning Center
PO Box 248, Morgantown, KY 42261
Kenneth Reed, 502-526-2204
Type: public at-risk

Triplett School
801 Old Hartford Rd, Owensboro, KY 42301
Rick Triplett
Type: Montessori

The Montessori Method
405 N Main St, Somerset, KY 42501-1408

Cumberland Alternative School
346 Steve Dr, Russell Springs, KY 42642
Al Sullivan, 502-866-2150
Type: public at-risk

Project Second Chance
110 S Main St, Elizabethtown, KY 42701
Dr Ernest G. Thro, Asst Supt, 502-769-8851
9–12th grade

LORD/Elizabethtown Montessori School
(See Resource Appendix)

Grayson County MS Alternative Classroom
726 Mill St, Leitchfield, KY 42754
Gary Gibson, Prin, 502-259-4175
Type: public at-risk
MS
No SE.

Louisiana

Montessori of the Riverlands
3601 River Rd, Destrehan, LA
Cynthia Pastor, Head, 504-785-8733
Tuition: $200–300/mo
2 teachers, 2 assistants, 45 students, ages 3–6
Entrance requirements: toilet trained
Accreditation: Board of Elementary and Secondary Education
Governance by administrator
Childcare; rural location; interns accepted.

Montessori School of Metarie
5220 Irving, Metarie, LA 70003

Montessori Learning Center
6220 Hodgson St, Metairie, LA 70003-4261

Alpha Montessori
301 Canal St, Metairie, LA 70005-3632

Family Resource Head Start Center
4219 N Rampart, New Orleans, LA 70017
Jeannine Thomas
Type: Montessori

Career Opportunity Preparation Education (COPE)
67 E Chalmette Circle, Chalmette, LA 70043
Marilyn Kimball, 504-271-2533
St Bernard Parish
Entrance requirement: retained at least twice
Remedial; vocational technology courses; career counseling; exit to regular HS or GED prep.

GED Preparation Alternative Program
67 E Chalmette Circle, Chalmette, LA 70043
Marilyn Kimball, 504-271-2533
St Bernard Parish
Entrance requirement: 15 or fewer Carnegie units earned
Students must earn a grade equivalent score of 8.5+ on the CAT in reading, language, and mathematics; class max 25 students.

Montessori West
3520 Claire Ave, Gretna, LA 70053

Stepping Stones Montessori
552 Terry Pkwy, Gretna, LA 70056-4047

Realizing Educational Achievement for Life (REAL)
501 Manhatten Blvd, Harvey, LA 70058
Dianna Dyer, 504-367-3120
Jefferson Parish
ES-HS
Remedial program; GED; Career Center.

Eight and 1/2 & Performance-Based Diploma Programs
PO Box 46, Luling, LA 70070
Dr James Taylor, Carolyn Woods, 504-785-6289
St Charles Parish
12 teachers, 140 students, 9–12th grade
Entrance requirement (8 1/2): retained at least twice
Affiliation: Destrehan HS and Hahnville HS
8 1/2: computers; counseling; mainstreamed for health, PE, elective; exit to regular HS; PBD: basic academic and vocational skills; comparative eval; CAI; counseling.

Plaquemines Parish Alternative School
PO Box 70, Port Sulphur, LA 70083
Louise Danielson, Phoenix HS, 504-564-2743
Students mainly at-risk, MS
Entrance requirement: overaged; repeated retention
Develops self-esteem, job skills; basic subjects at parish HS; vocational courses at Port Sulphur Vo-Tech.

Urban League Street Academy
1806 Canal St, New Orleans, LA 70112
Murphy Sanchez, Program Mgr, 504-523-3560
Student ages 16+, HS
Program open to all, but directed towards young male dropouts who are public housing residents; GED; values ed; counseling.

New Orleans Free School (1971)
3601 Camp St, New Orleans, LA 70115
Dr. Robert Ferris, Principal, 504-896-4065, FAX: 504-896-4065
Type: public choice
12 teachers, 325 students, ages 5-15, K-8th grade
Enrollment restricted to residents of Orleans Parish, and if
   there is room
Affiliation: Teach for America
Governance by teachers and principal
Teacher qualifications: certification, or alternative LA
   certification
Offers a progressive education to mostly low income students; based on meaningfulness, connections, engage-
   ment, inquiry, creativity, increased experience; no letter
   grades; multi-aged classes; extensive field trips; urban
   location; interns accepted.

New Child Montessori School
3915 Perrier St, New Orleans, LA 70115-3730

Our Lady of the Elms
1938 General Pershing St, New Orleans, LA 70115-5434
Type: Montessori

Audubon Montessori School
428 Broadway, New Orleans, LA 70118
Jill Otis

St Francis of Assisi
611 State St, New Orleans, LA 70118
Sr M Joanne Ladwig
Type: Montessori

University Montessori School
7508 Burthic Rt, New Orleans, LA 70118

Happy Times Nursery
1602 S Carrollton Ave, New Orleans, LA 70118-2826
Type: Montessori

Children's House Montessori School
3800 Eagle St, New Orleans, LA 70118-3404

Lake Vista Montessori School
6645 Spanish Fort Blvd, New Orleans, LA 70122

St Joseph Alpha
1200 Mirabeau Ave, New Orleans, LA 70122-1945
Type: Montessori

Hoadley School
475 Oak Ave, New Orleans, LA 70123
Type: Montessori

**Educational Success Through Alternative to Suspension
(ESTAS) Program**
5931 Milne Blvd, New Orleans, LA 70124
Mary Thompson, 504-483-6492
7-8th grade
Individualized instruction; max 1:15 ratio.

New Orleans Montessori School
6432 Bellaire Dr, New Orleans, LA 70124-1442

New Orleans Science and Mathematics High School
980 Navarre Ave, New Orleans, LA 70124-2710
Dr Barbara MacPhee, Prin, 504-483-4145
HS
Activity-based; integrated math, science; half-day program.

Children's Place
6317 Argonne Blvd, New Orleans, LA 70124-3901
Type: Montessori

Uptown Montessori School
6213 1/2 S Tonti St, New Orleans, LA 70125-4226

Lake Forest Montessori
8258 Lake Forest Blvd, New Orleans, LA 70126-3318

Lafourche Parish Alternative School
PO Box 879, Thibodaux, LA 70302
Lorene S. Watkins, 504-446-5631
Lafourche Parish
Students mainly at-risk, HS
At Central and North Vocational Training Centers; GED.

Ascension Parish Alternative Program
PO Box 189, Donaldsonville, LA 70346
Roy W. Stern, Brd Member, 504-473-7981
Ascension Parish
Students mainly at-risk, ages 16+, HS
Enrollment restricted to dropouts
4 academic courses; special ed resource course.

Eighth Grade Transitional Program
PO Box 189, Donaldsonville, LA 70346
Shelby Robert, Asst Supt, 504-621-2300
Ascension Parish
Entrance requirement: retained at least twice in ES
Teacher qualifications: LA certification
Reading; math; life-coping skills; PE; electives; exit to regular
   HS or GED program.

Curriculum Alternative Track
PO Box 5097, Houma, LA 70361
Bill Simons, 504-876-7400
Terrebonne Parish
Student ages 16-21
Entrance requirement: have not met graduation
   requirements
HS diploma or GED.

Genesis
PO Box 5097, Houma, LA 70361
Bill Simons, 504-876-7400
Terrebonne Parish
Students mainly at-risk, 9-12th grade
For students having difficulty in school, or dropouts; regular
   curriculum for 5 hours; supervised study/tutorial for 30
   min/day.

Alternative Diploma Program
PO Drawer B, Napoleonville, LA 70390
James D. Blanchard, Supervisor, 504-369-7251
Assumption Parish
Student ages 16+
Entrance requirement: failed at least twice
GED; elective courses; PE.

Tangipahoa Parish Magnet High School
111 J W Davis Dr, Hammond, LA 70401
Karl R. Ingram, Prin, 504-542-5634
Student ages 16+
Entrance requirement: 3+ credits short of graduation
Evening classes.

University Montessori of Hammond
702 N Magnolia St, Hammond, LA 70401-2526

Oak St Montessori
312 N Oak St, Hammond, LA 70401-3217

PM Senior High School
PO Box 310, Bogalusa, LA 70429
Chip Conerly, 504-735-1392
Students mainly adults and potential dropouts
HS diploma; refreshers in English, math, arts, humanities, for
   those pursuing postsecondary education.

Montessori Children's House
10 Karen Dr, Covington, LA 70433

Covington Montessori School
116 N Monroe St, Covington, LA 70433-2656
Colleen Ryan

Three Rivers Academy
14253 Highway 190, Covington, LA 70433-7307
Art Williams, 504-892-3126
St Tammany Parish
For those with learning or emotional problems to function as
  students and citizens; day and resident options; group,
  individual therapy.

Career Opportunity Preparation Education
PO Box 940, Covington, LA 70434
Dr Maria Guilott, 504-892-2276
St Tammany Parish
Students mainly at-risk
Vocational training; Carnegie units; GED and trade/industry
  certificate option.

Alternative to Suspension, Expulsion, Absenteeism, and Dropout (SEAD)
PO Box 540, Greensburg, LA 70441
Mary B. Smith, 504-222-4349
St Helena Parish
Students mainly at-risk, 6–12th grade
Increased self-esteem; close coordination with regular
  teacher; exit to regular school; guidance.

New Covenant Weekday School
4375 Hwy 22, Mandeville, LA 70448
Diane Ferguson, Dir, 504-626-5988
Type: Montessori, non-profit; tuition: $230/mo
2 teachers, 2 assistants, 38 students, ages 3–6
Affiliation: AMS
Governance by church session

Magnolia Montessori
170 N 7th St, Ponchatoula, LA 70454-3305
Terry Ann McMahon

Montessori Chateau
40804 Chinchas Creek Rd, Slidell, LA 70461
Neil J. Songy, Adm, 504-643-8507
Tuition: $160–220/mo
5 teachers, 5 assistants, 92 students, ages infant-6
Affiliations: AMS, LMS
Governance by administrator

Lafayette Parish Middle School Transitional Program
PO Drawer 2158, Lafayette, LA 70502-2158
Tammy Frey, 318-232-0681
Lafayette Parish
Student ages 15+, 5–8th grade
Remedial reading, mathematics, language arts; GED.

The Children's Community School
211 J.B. Rd, Lafayette, LA 70506
Cheryl Fell
Type: independent

Melody Montessori Tiny Tot School
620 Saint Louis St, Lafayette, LA 70506-4416

Vermilion Parish GED Preparation Alternative Program
2200 S Jefferson St, Abbeville, LA 70510
Susan V. Richard, 318-898-5722
5 hours of GED prep; elective courses; exit to adult ed.

JTPA Alternative Program
220 S Jefferson St, Abbeville, LA 70511
Dr Jane Abshire, 318-898-5770
Vermilion Parish
Entrance requirements: meet JTPA eligibility; retained at least
  twice; referral
Counseling; educational support; GED; career ed; class max:
  15; health; PE; vocational; Carnegie credit.

Children's House Acadiana
3725 Pinhook Rd, Broussard, LA 70518-5551
Type: Montessori

Alternative Program for GED Preparation
PO Box 170, Centerville, LA 70522
Amar Lancon, 318-836-9661
St Mary Parish
Student ages 15+
Entrance requirement: must have been promoted to 9th
  grade
Computer-assisted; counseling; GED; vocational; exit to
  regular HS or adult ed.

Jefferson Davis Parish Alternative Program
PO Box 640, Jennings, LA 70546
Johnnie Adams, 318-824-1834
20 students, 7–8th grade
At Lake Arthur HS and Fenton HS; reading; mathematics.

Alternative Curriculum to Success
1204 LeMaire St, New Iberia, LA 70560
Judith Guidry, Dale Henderson, 318-364-7641
Iberia Parish
Entrance requirement: retained at least twice
4 academic classes; 2-hour vocational block; GED.

Project Completion
PO Box 859, St Martinville, LA 70582
Elizabeth Judice, 318-394-6261
Student ages 16+, HS
Enrollment restricted to students who have failed 2+ sub-
  jects in 9th grade, scored 5.0+ on the CAT, and are poten-
  tial dropouts; or JH AE program participants
At Breaux Bridge, St Martinville, Cecilia; basic work skills; per-
  sonal, career counseling; health, PE, electives at HS.

Alternative Center for Education (ACE)
1101 Te Mamou Rd, Ville Platte, LA 70586
Fannie Soileau, 318-363-6651
Evangeline Parish
Students mainly at risk, ages 14+
Academic instruction; vocational and pre-employment skills
  training; counseling; GED.

GED Program for At-Risk Students
PO Box 438, Washington, LA 70589
Andrew C. Leon, 318-826-7360
St Landry Parish
Students mainly at risk, JH, HS
Vocational training.

Calcasieu PM High School
PO Box 800, Lake Charles, LA 70602
Garland Hamic, Jr, Asst Supt, 318-491-1670
Calcasieu Parish
Students mainly at-risk
HS diploma; M-Th 5-9 pm.

GED Alternative Program
PO Box W, Cameron, LA 70631
Adam Conner, 318-775-7393
Students mainly at-risk
Regular (Carnegie units) and GED classes.

Academic/Disciplinary Alternative Placement (ADAP)
PO Box 1090, DeRidder, LA 70634
J. R. Hickman, Asst Prin, 318-463-3266
Beauregard Parish
Students mainly at-risk
At DeRidder HS; for expelled, suspended students; tutorials;
  make up work, tests; Carnegie units; exit to regular HS.

Little Learners Montessori (1978)
73 Center Circle, Sulphur, LA 70663
318-625-9357
Tuition: $60–235/mo

3 teachers, 1 assistant, 42 students, ages infant-6
Affiliations: AMI, AMS, NAMTA
Governance by an administrator
Childcare; suburban location.

Louisiana Citizens for Home Education
3404 Van Buren, Baker, LA 70714
504-775-5472
Type: state home-based

Alternative Program for At-Risk Public School Students
PO Box 1130, Livingston, LA 70754
Raiford Leader
Livingston Parish
Students mainly at-risk, ages 14+, 6–12th grade
Entrance requirements: failed at least twice; referral
GED; individual, group counseling; job development and peer
  facilitation training.

West Feliciana High Pre-GED and GED Alternative/ Dropout Prevention Program
PO Box 580, St Francisville, LA 70775
Rodney A. Lemoine, 504-635-4561
Students mainly at-risk, ages 15+, JH, HS
Entrance requirement: retained at least twice
After 1-year readiness curriculum, JH students go to regular
  HS or GED prep.

St Francisville Montessori
PO Box 118, Saint Francisville, LA 70775-0118

Scotlandville Magnet High School
9870 Scotlandville Ave, Baton Rouge, LA 70801
Freddie Williams, 504-775-3715
Academic prep; engineering program.

Northdale Magnet Academy
1555 Madison Ave, Baton Rouge, LA 70802
Leroy Helire, Prin, 504-383-1812
Type: public at-risk
3 programs: traditional, competency-based proficiency, or
  GED; all have academic, vocational classes; counseling.

Office of Youth Development
504 Mayflower, Bldg 6, Baton Rouge, LA 70802
Gail Rambin, 504-342-2655
Students mainly at-risk
GED prep at correctional facilities in Monroe, Baton Rouge,
  Bridge City.

Polk Elementary School
408 E Polk St, Baton Rouge, LA 70802-7272
Type: Montessori

Howell Park Elementary School
6125 Winbourne Ave, Baton Rouge, LA 70805-6200
Type: Montessori

Baton Rouge Magnet High School
2825 Government St, Baton Rouge, LA 70806
Lois Anne Sumrall, Prin, 504-383-0520
Type: public choice
College prep; visual and performing arts.

La Printaniere Montessori School
5064 Perkins Rd, Baton Rouge, LA 70808-3441

Montessori Children's House
5640 Highland Rd, Baton Rouge, LA 70808-6554

Montessori School of Baton Rouge (1965)
8227 Wimbledon Ave, Baton Rouge, LA 70810
Leanne Smith, Adm, 504-766-9942
Non-profit; tuition: $1,610-2,905/yr
4 teachers, 2 assistants, 59 students, ages 3–6
Entrance requirements: over age 2.5; toilet trained.
Accreditations: LADE, LAMA
Governance by board

French; Orff music; culture studies involve parents and community; childcare; urban location; interns accepted.

Howell Park Elementary Montessori Parent Organization
4615 Dickens Dr, Baton Rouge, LA 70812
c/o Susan B Albin

Montessori NEST School
124 McGehee Dr, Baton Rouge, LA 70815
Shirley Maughan

Michele's Nursery
12380 Old Hammond Hwy, Baton Rouge, LA 70816-1020
Type: Montessori

Tanglewood Elementary School
9352 Rustling Oaks Dr, Baton Rouge, LA 70818-4799
Type: Montessori

Baton Rouge Marine Institute
PO Box 2950, Baton Rouge, LA 70821
Mary Ellen Jordan, 504-922-5400
6 teachers, 42 students, mainly adjudicated, ages 14–18
Entrance requirement: referral by Juvenile Srvc, Dept of Corr
Goals: reduced or eliminated criminal involvement, rehabilita-
  tion, increased academic levels and skills; exit to regular
  school, vocational training, job, military.

Juvenile Continuing Education Program
1050 S Foster Dr, Baton Rouge, LA 70821
Audrey Hampton, 504-922-5518
Students mainly at-risk, 6–10th grade
Entrance requirement: referral; top priority given to expelled
  students
Instruction individualized according to entrance test results;
  exit to regular HS or adult ed.

PM School
PO Box 2950, Baton Rouge, LA 70821
Mary Ellen Jordan, 504-922-5406
Students mainly at-risk, ages 17+
At Glen Oaks HS and Capitol HS; evening classes; diploma.

Christian Home Educators Fellowship of Louisiana
PO Box 14421, Baton Rouge, LA 70898
504-642-2059
Type: state home-based

Kinder Haus Montessori (1984)
5201 W Napoleon Ave, Metairie, LA 71001
Pat Lacoste, Dir of Ed, 504-454-2424
Tuition: $80-95/wk
6 teachers, 9 assistants, 71 students, ages infant-6
Governance by administrator, democratic school meeting
Childcare; suburban location; interns accepted.

Herndon Magnet Elementary
11845 Gamm Rd, Belceher, LA 71004
Dean Washam, 318-221-7676
Caddo County
K–5th grade
Fine and performing arts.

Bossier Achievement Center
PO Box 2000, Bossier City, LA 71006-2000
Dominic Salinas, Supervisor, 318-965-2281
Students mainly at-risk
Self-paced; teacher-directed; computers; independent study;
  academic; vocational; 12-month program.

Montessori Farm School
5111 US Hwy 80 E, Haughton, LA 71037-7921

Webster Parish Alternative School
209 Clerk, Minden, LA 71055
West Moses, 318-377-7052
Students mainly at-risk, JH, HS
Individual counseling; diploma or exit to adult ed.

Caddo Parish Magnet High School
1601 Viking Dr, Shreveport, LA 71101
Ascension Smith, 318-221-2501
9–12th grade
Fine and performing arts.

Hamilton Terrace Learning Center/Caddo PM School
1105 Louisiana Ave, Shreveport, LA 71101
John Baldwin, 318-222-4518
Affiliation: Caddo Career Ctr
HS courses; counseling; community service; cultural enrich-
    ment; pre-vocational training; GED; Adult Basic Ed.

Central Elementary
1627 Weinstock St, Shreveport, LA 71103-3063
Type: Montessori

Montessori School for Shreveport (1964)
2605 C E Galloway Blvd, Shreveport, LA 71104
Therese Misra, Adm, 318-861-6777
Non-profit; tuition: $1,850-2,800/yr
9 teachers, 171 students, ages toddler-12
Entrance requirements: max age 4, with exceptions
Affiliation: AMS
Governance by board
Childcare; interns accepted.

Klenter Montessori School
3452 Broadmoor Blvd, Shreveport, LA 71105-2026

Caddo Parish Middle School
7635 Cornelious Dr, Shreveport, LA 71106
Lel McCullough, 318-868-6588
Caddo Parish
Type: magnet
6–8th grade
Fine and performing arts.

South Highlands Magnet Elementary
831 Erie St, Shreveport, LA 71106
Pamela Byrd, 318-865-5119
Caddo County
K–5th grade
Fine and performing arts.

Christian Center School
207 Idema St, Shreveport, LA 71106-6557
Type: Montessori

J B Harville Alternative School
6660 Quilen Rd, Shreveport, LA 71108
Margaret A. Brown, 318-621-9724
Students mainly at-risk
7 sites for MS and HS: 5 offer academic/vocational courses,
    exit with diploma or return to regular HS; 2 sites for adjudi-
    cated students.

New Life Montessori
4445 Meriwether Rd, Shreveport, LA 71109-8409

Montessori Children's House
1959 Airline Dr, Bossier City, LA 71112-2407

Children's House of Monroe
2102 Valencia Ave, Monroe, LA 71201-2547
Type: Montessori

Children's House
1201 Stubbs Ave, Monroe, LA 71201-5621
Type: Montessori

A Performance-Based Diploma Program
PO Box 4180, Monroe, LA 71211
Maria Maggio, 318-325-0601
Students mainly at-risk
Dropout prevention/retrieval; alternative to college prep; GED.

Opportunity Learning Center
PO Box 4180, Monroe, LA 71211
Maria Maggio, 318-325-0601
Students mainly at-risk, 6–9th grade
Carnegie units; exit to regular HS or GED program.

Morehouse Parish Alternative Program
PO Box 872, Bastrop, LA 71220
Jimmy Sistrunk, Supervisor, 318-281-5784
Morehouse Parish
Students mainly at-risk
Academic, pre-vocational instruction for 13 year-old potential
    dropouts;14–15 year-olds prep for 9th grade; GED prep,
    career training for 16+.

Good Shepherd Early Childhood Dev Center
Box 442, 1404 1st St, Lake Providence, LA 71254-0442
Type: Montessori

West Carroll Parish Alternative Educational Program
PO Drawer 1318, Oak Grove, LA 71263
John Mercer, Supt, 318-428-2378
Student ages 16+, HS
Entrance requirements: retained at least twice; referral by
    local school selection committee; student/parent interview
GED; health; PE; vocational; electives; exit to regular HS, adult
    ed, postsecondary ed, or job; placement assistance.

Wildflower Montessori School
700 W Woodward Ave, Ruston, LA 71270
Rene Hunt

Woodland Hills Hospital School
6200 Cypress St, W Monroe, LA 71294
Patricia Johnson, Ed Coord, 318-396-5900
Ouachita Parish
7–12th grade
Enrollment restricted to adolescent treatment program
    patients
Classes limited to 10; individualized instruction; flexible
    schedule; counseling; medical treatment.

High School GED Program
PO Box 1230, Alexandria, LA 71301
Tommy Smith, 318-487-0888
Rapides Parish
HS
Enrollment restricted to 16 year-olds with up to three
    Carnegie units
Expanded vocational, elective and academic experiences;
    individualized and pre-GED instruction.

PM High School
PO Box 1230, Alexandria, LA 71301
Tommy Smith, 318-487-0888
Rapides Parish
Student ages 17+, HS
HS diploma; evenings; refresher courses.

Montessori Learning Center
1304 Beech St, Alexandria, LA 71301-6001

Montessori Educational Center (1978)
1717 Jackson St, Alexandria, LA 71301-6433
Rosemary Robertson-Smith, 318-445-0138
Non-profit; tuition: $1,170/1,980/yr
6 teachers, 108 students, ages 3-12
Entrance requirement: parents' full understanding of philos-
    ophy and methods
Affiliations: AMS, IMS, NCME; accreditations: LADE, LAMA
Governance by teachers, administrators, board
Childcare; urban location; transportation; interns accepted.

Ewell Aiken Optional School
3443 Prescott Rd, Alexandria, LA 71303
Richard Bushnell, Prin, 318-442-1846
Rapides Parish

Student ages 14+, 5-12th grade
Entrance requirement: assessment
Individualized instruction; computer-assisted; self-paced.

Alternative Secondary Curriculum Program
PO Box 308, Jonesville, LA 71343
Norma White, Supervisor, 318-339-9505
Catahoula Parish
Entrance requirement: retained at least twice
Reading; GED; health; PE; 3-hour vocational block.

Alternative Vocational Curriculum (AVC) Program
PO Box 308, Jonesville, LA 71343
Norma White, Mary Gene Trunzler, 318-339-9505, -9579
Catahoula Parish
Students mainly at-risk
Entrance requirement: interest in, and aptitude for, vocational training
Carnegie credits; vocational courses; exit to regular HS, GED program, another AVC program, employment.

Eight and 1/2 Program
PO Box 338, Lutcher, LA 71343
Caldonia S. Ceasar, 504-869-5375
St James Parish
7-8th grade
Entrance requirement: failed at least twice
Mainstreamed for health, PE, one elective; daily counseling; reading instruction.

Alternative Learning Experiences Reshape Thinking (ALERT)
201 Tunica Dr W, Marksville, LA 71351
John H. Wyatt, 318-253-5982
Avoyelles Parish
Students mainly at-risk, ages 16+
Affiliation: Avoyelles Vo-Tech School
Educational, support services for expelled students; vocational, diploma, and GED programs; exit to homebase school.

Grant Parish High School GED Program
PO Box 208, Colfax, LA 71417
Kenneth E. Deen, 318-627-3274
Grant Parish
Student ages 16+
Entrance requirement: retained at least twice

GED; academic or vocational courses for Carnegie credit; exit to regular HS or adult ed.

Beauregard/Vernon Home School Association
714 Tilley Rd, Leesville, LA 71446
Burwell, 318-535-9102
Vernon County
Inclusive.

Vernon Parish Alternative School
502 Berry Ave, Leesville, LA 71446
J. W. Pope, 318-239-3401
Students mainly at-risk, HS
Enrollment restricted to potential dropouts or students facing severe disciplinary consequences; entrance requirements: parental consent; principal/counselor recommendation; application; committee approval
Computer-assisted; small group instruction; personal, academic, vocational counseling.

Alternative High School Program
200 Hwy 3110, S By-Pass, Natchitoches, LA 71457
Julia Hildebrand, 318-352-2358
Natchitoches Parish
GED; vocational training.

Louisiana School for Mathematics, Science and the Arts
715 College Ave, Natchitoches, LA 71457
Dr Art Williams, 318-357-3176
Natchitoches County
Instruction via telecommunications to local schools throughout LA.

Natchitoches Parish Alternative School
1016 Keyser Ave, Natchitoches, LA 71457
Trudy Howell, Brd Member, 318-352-2358
Student ages 16+
Entrance requirement: failed at least twice
Vocational training; individualized instruction.

Winn Parish High School Alternative Program
PO Box 430, Winnfield, LA 71483
Jerry Bamburgh, 318-628-6936
Student ages 16+
Entrance requirements: retained at least twice; parental consent
Carnegie units; GED.

Maine

Experiential Education Alternative (1990)
Noble High School, Berwick, ME 03904
Jon Appleby or Thomas Ledue, Tchs, 207-698-1320
York County
Type: public choice
3 teachers, 30 students, mainly at-risk, ages 13-18, 8-12th grade
Entrance requirements: poor performance/behaviors; residency primarily for grades 9, 10
Governance by teachers and principal
Rural location.

BEAT (1986)
23 Maplewood ave, Biddeford, ME 04005
Harry Strother, Head Tch
Type: public at-risk
1 teacher, 2 assistants, 15 students, ages 12-15, 6-8th grade
No SE
Governance by teachers, principal

Teacher qualifications: ME Certification
3 classes; films; PE; suburban location.

Alternative Education Program Brunswick Junior High School
Barrows St, Brunswick, ME 04011
Linda Blakeman, 207-729-1669
Type: public at-risk
6-8th grade

Union Street Alternative Education (1985)
35 Union St, Brunswick, ME 04011
Beth Schultz, Lead Tchr, 207-729-0001
Cumberland County
Type: public at-risk
2 teachers, 1 assistant, 28 students, ages 14-19, 9-12th grade
Enrollment restricted to Brunswick HS students
Affiliations: AEA of ME, NCACS

Governance by teachers and principal
Teacher qualifications: MA in Ed or working toward one
Individualized; trust/community building field trips; Outward Bound component; interdisciplinary; alternative assessments; respect, accountability, tolerance emphasized; suburban location; interns accepted.

Cooperative Alternative School (1989)
340 Foreside Rd, Falmouth, ME 04011
Steve Gargiulo, Dir, 207-729-6609
Type: public choice
2 teachers, 18 students, partly at-risk, ages 14–18, 7–12th grade
Entrance requirements: interview, residency
Governance by supervisory council
Teacher qualifications: teaching and alternative experience
Work-study; film-making; Outward Bound; Project Adventure; occupational, career study; earned "personal days"; multi-aged classes; extensive field trips; suburban location; transportation; interns accepted.

Alternative Learning Center (1980)
Main St, Cumberland Center, ME 04021
Doreen Thompson, Coord, 207-829-4836
Cumberland County
Type: public at-risk
1 teacher, 1 assistant, 45 students, mainly at-risk, ages 12–20, 7–12th grade
Entrance requirements: parent permission, district residency
Governance by principal, board, superintendent
Teacher qualifications: ME Certification
In house near JHS and HS; partial day program; work-study community service; independent study; support groups; experiential activities; peer tutoring; CAI; creative visualization for learning; creativity, relaxation, transformation of anger; multi-aged classes; suburban location; interns accepted.

Pequawket Valley Alternative Program (1991)
152 Main St, Fryeburg, ME 04037
Dave Sturdevant or Dede Frost, Dirs, 207-935-3344
Oxford County
Type: public at-risk
4 teachers, 15 students, ages 15–21, HS
Residency required
Affiliation: Fryeburg Academy
Governance by faculty and student reps
Experiential; east coast ecology and community service projects; competency-based; no letter grades; non-compulsory class attendance; interns accepted.

Gorham High School
41 Morrill Ave, Gorham, ME 04038
Robert Bond, 207-839-5004
Type: public at-risk
9–11th grade
Entrance requirements: recommendation, interview.

Gray-New Gloucester High School
Libby Hill Rd, Gray, ME 04039
John Zeludancz, 207-657-3323
Type: public at-risk
HS
Entrance requirements: referral, team review.
Industrial arts shop; hands-on projects on school grounds and buildings.

The School Around Us (1970)
RR 1, Box 1912 Log Cabin Rd, Kennebunkport, ME 04046
Claudia Berman, 207-967-3143
York County
Type: independent, non-profit; tuition: $2200, scholarships
4 teachers, 34 students, ages 4–12, pre K–6th grade
Entrance requirements: visit school, attend business meeting
Affiliation: NCACS; accreditation: state of ME
Governance by parent cooperative
Teacher qualifications: excitement, commitment to self-growth

School meeting uses consensus model; developmental approach; interdisciplinary curriculum; 4-acre wooded location; emphasis on outdoors, community involvement, the arts, real work; concern for the environment and world community; no letter grades; non-compulsory class attendance; multi-aged classes; extensive field trips; rural location; interns accepted.

Windham Real School (1984)
55 High St, Windham, ME 04062
Arthur DiRocco, PhD, Dir, 207-892-4462
Cumberland County
Type: public at-risk; tuition: $17,500/yr
5 teachers, 42 students, ages 13–20, 7–12th grade
Affiliation: Boy Scouts
Governance by board
Teacher qualifications: state certification
Adventure based counseling; experiential education; rural location; transportation; interns accepted.

Sanford Alternative School (1986)
2R Main St, Sanford, ME 04073
Michael Fallon, 207-940-5135
York County
Type: public at-risk
2 teachers, 20 students, ages 13–17, 8–10th grade
Governance by teachers and principal
Teacher qualifications: ME certification
Experiential; community based; rural location.

Alternative Education at Scarborough High School
PO Box 370, Scarborough, ME 04074
Bill Haskell, 702-883-4315
Type: public at-risk
8–12th grade

Southern Maine Home Education Support Network (1985)
76 Beech Ridge Rd, Scarborough, ME 04074
207-883-9621
Cumberland County
Non-profit
Family activities, events; nonsectarian, diverse group; about 100 member families.

Sebago Lake Homeschoolers Support Group
RR 2 Box 54, Sebago Lake, ME 04075
207-642-4368

The Merriconeag School (1984)
PO Box 336; S Freeport Rd, South Freeport, ME 04078
Tricia Tonks, Business Mgr, 207-865-3900
Cumberland County
Type: Waldorf, non-profit; tuition: $2,400-6,500/yr, scholarships
17 teachers, 98 students, ages 3.5–11, K–4th grade
Affiliation: AWSNA
Governance by faculty
Teacher qualifications: Waldorf training
Suburban location; interns accepted.

Bonny Eagle Alternative Education (1988)
700 Saco Rd, Standish, ME 04084
Sam Jordan/Diane Beringer, Teachers, 207-929-3831
County
Type: public at-risk
2 teachers, 25 students, ages 14–17, 8–10th grade
Affiliation: ME Alt Ed Assoc
Governance by teachers and principal
Teacher qualifications: ME certification
Four mandatory components: individualized academics, community service, experiential (Outward Bound type), counseling (individual/group); suburban location; interns accepted.

Mount Ararat High School
122 Main St, Topsham, ME 04086
Jeff Davison, 207-729-5444

Type: public at-risk, HS
Entrance requirements: pre-screening, interview, 3 week trial
period.

New Country School (1972)
RR1, Box 6, West Baldwin, ME 04091
Jennifer Frick, Director, 207-625-4962
Type: independent, non-profit; scholarships
4 teachers, 29 students, ages 3-12, pre K-6th grade
Governance by parent cooperative
Teacher qualifications: Experience
Fifty acres of wood and bogland used for nature and land
study; Japanese intern teaches language and culture; ski
program; students help at local food pantry; five mini-
group projects per semester; no letter grades; non-
compulsory class attendance; multi-aged classes; extensive
field trips; interns accepted.

West School Prep Program (1968)
57 Douglas St, Portland, ME 04102
William C Shuttleworth, Dir, 207-874-8225, FAX: 207-874-8154
Type: public at-risk
10 teachers, 50 students, ages 9-19, 4-12th grade
Entrance requirements: referral
Governance by teachers and principal
Teacher qualifications: ME certification
Work opportunities; individualized; experiential; extensive
field trips; urban location; interns accepted.

Deering High School
370 Stevels Ave, Portland, ME 04103
Bruce Koharian, 207-874-8260
Type: public at-risk
HS
Entrance by referral.

Portland Alternative Credit Option
196 Allen Ave, Portland, ME 04103
David Shapiro, 207-874-8160
9-12th grade

Alternative Education Association of Maine
25 Granite St, Apt 12, Portland, ME 04104
Tina Clark
Type: state home-based

Maine Homeschool Association (1987)
PO Box 9715-199, Portland, ME 04104
207-353-3588
Cumberland County
Type: state home-based
Nonsectarian; membership-supported.

Cooperative Alternative Program
  Falmouth/Freeport/Yarmouth School
340 Foreside Rd, Falmouth, ME 04105
Steve Garguilo, 207-781-5013
8-11th grade

Pine Grove Child Development Center (1986)
32 Foreside Rd, Falmouth, ME 04105
B.J. Fifield, 207-781-3441
Type: Montessori; tuition: $351-499/mo
3 teachers, 3 assistants, 91 students, ages 3-6
Entrance requirements: age 3; toilet trained
Affiliations: NAEYC, AMS
Governance by an administrator
Childcare; suburban location; interns accepted.

South Portland Alternatives (1989)
637 Highland Ave, South Portland, ME 04106
Tom Hyland, Dir, 207-767-7729, FAX: 207-767-7713
Cumberland County
Type: public choice
1 teacher, 1 assistant, 30 students, mainly at-risk, ages 14-20,
9-12th grade
Entrance at discretion of Dir and Screening Committee; residency required

Governance by democratic school meeting (program);
faculty/students/adm (high school)
Maine Studies of Native Cultures includes building a kayak;
interdisciplinary courses; work with satellite imagery technology; multi-aged classes; urban location; transportation;
interns accepted.

Casco Bay Montessori School
440 Ocean St, South Portland, ME 04106-6612

Fairview School
Minot Ave, Auburn, ME 04210
Donn Marcus
Type: Montessori

Franklin Alternative High School (1978)
Pine St, Auburn, ME 04210
David T. Eretzian, Prin, 207-782-3242
Androscoggin County
Type: public at-risk
6 teachers, 90 students, mainly at-risk, ages 15-20, 9-12th
grade
No SE; residency required
Governance by teachers, principal, democratic school
meeting
Teacher qualifications: ME Certification
Rural location; transportation; interns accepted.

Homeschool Associates of New England
(See Resource Appendix)

Steven Mills Alternative School
Minot Ave, Auburn, ME 04210
Dave Eretzian, 207-783-0197
Type: public at-risk
HS
Entrance requirements: referral, selection committee deci-
sion, orientation.
Separate facility; fine arts lab.

Lewiston High School
156 East Ave, Lewiston, ME 04240
Phil Downs, 207-795-4190
Type: public at-risk
17 students, HS
Entrance requirements: referral, interview.
One-year program.

Poland Community School
HCR Box 20, Poland, ME 04273
Donald McGlauflin, 702-998-4934
5-8th grade

Center for Alternative Learning (1991)
59 Congress St, Rumford, ME 04276
Zebunnisa Weidler, John Schoen, teachers, 207-364-5604
District 43, Oxford County
Type: public at-risk
2 teachers, 20 students, mainly at-risk, ages 14-18, 9-12th
grade
MSAD #43 referral and interview required
Governance by teachers and principal
Teacher qualifications: secondary certificate, experience with
at-risk youth
1.5 room school with traditional and innovative courses; students must meet attendance, credit and behavior guidelines; multi-aged classes; extensive field trips; special
integrated classes; urban location; interns accepted.

River Valley Alternative School (1987)
RR 1, PO Box 1220, Turner, ME 04282
Ric French, Supervisor, 207-225-3478
Andro County
Type: public choice
3 teachers, 55 students, mainly at-risk, ages 14-20, 9-12th
grade
Entrance requirements: one yr of HS; non-special ed
students

Governance by teachers and principal
Teacher qualifications: BS, certification
Rural location; transportation; interns accepted.

Gardiner Regional Middle School (1989)
Cobbossee Ave, Gardiner, ME 04345
Alan R. Smith, 207-582-1326
Type: public choice
54 teachers, 630 students, ages 11–14, 6–8th grade
No residency requirements
Governance by principal

National Audubon Society Expedition Institute (1981)
PO Box 365, Belfast, ME 04352
Karen Woodsum, Office Mgr, 207-338-5859
Type: independent, higher education, boarding; tuition: $9300/yr, scholarships
4 staff & 20 students/bus, HS, college, graduate school
Affiliation: Leslie College
Governance by consensus
Explores 1 region of US & Canada each sem; environmental ed degrees; values-based, holistic approach; non-authoritarian; self-paced, directed and evaluated; camping, hiking, canoeing.

Adult Education at Maranacook Community School
PO Box 177, Readfield, ME 04355
Martha Thorton, 702-685-4732
10–12th grade

Bangor Montessori School
30 Otis St, Bangor, ME 04401
Amy Peterson-Roper

Penobscot Job Corps (1979)
1375 Union St, Bangor, ME 04401
207-990-3000, FAX: 942-9829
Penobscot County
Type: public at-risk, boarding; scholarships
23 teachers, 330 students, mainly at-risk, ages 16–24
Enrollment restricted by income verification; for age 16–24; no residency requirement
Governance by Training & Development Corp and Dept of Labor
Teacher qualifications: bachelor's degree
College prep; ESL; vocational training; remedial studies; community resources; culturally diverse staff with educational hands-on experience; opportunity for one-on-one attention; multi-aged classes; rural location; interns accepted.

Reach School, Inc (1987)
PO Box 1366, Bucksport, ME 04416
Richard W Crampton, Dir, 207-469-7147
Type: independent, non-profit
2 teachers, 21 students, mainly at-risk, ages 13–19, 7–12th grade
Governance by board
Teacher qualifications: ME certification
Students responsible for own education; point systems; accountability; family atmosphere; rural location; transportation; interns accepted.

Hampton Academy Alternative Education
Box 279, Hamden, ME 04444
Ellen Pariser, Alt Ed Teacher, 207-862-6249
Penobscot County
Type: public at-risk
1 teacher, 1 assistant, 16 students, mainly at-risk, ages 14–21, 9–12th grade
Apply through Hampden Academy Guidance; residency required
Governance by teachers and principal
Personal growth; credit for work; fine arts, including photography; course credit through fulfilling competency-based objectives; small classes; based on Glasser's Reality Therapy; students take responsibility for attendance; multi-aged classes; extensive field trips; rural location; interns accepted.

Stillwater Montessori School
RFD 2, Box 1300, Old Town, ME 04468-2165
Joe and Joanne Alex

Rural Education Program, HOME Coop
PO Box 10, Orland, ME 04472
Karen Saum, 207-469-7961
Type: higher education
4-year program offers baccalaureate-equivalent certificate in community economic development; designed for and by students.

Chewonki Foundation
RR 2 Box 1200, Wiscasset, ME 04578
Don Hudson, 207-882-7323
Environmental education; summer camp; wilderness trips; residential program; traveling natural science lessons; academic study for 11th grade

The Center
RR 1, Box 665, Woodwich, ME 04579
Sam Selby

College of the Atlantic
105 Eden St, Bar Harbor, ME 04609
Hancock, 207-288-5015
Type: higher education
Goal is to increase awareness of environmental problems and teach skills of human ecology necessary to solve them.

The Bay School
PO Box 269, Blue Hill, ME 04614
Michaela Colquhoun
Type: Waldorf

Peninsula Area Homeschooling Association
PO Box 235, Deer Isle, ME 04627

Gentle Wind School
(See Resource Appendix)

Mount Desert Island Homeschoolers (1992)
c/o Box 189A Richmond Rd, West Tremont, ME 04690
Kathy Van Gorder, 207-244-3615
Hancock County
24 students, ages 1–7

SAVE, Southern Aroostook County
PO Box 307, Houlton, ME 04730
Arthur Wittine, 207-532-9541
9–12th grade

Brook Farm Books
(See Resource Appendix)

Caribou Alternative High School
75 Bennett Dr, Caribou, ME 04736
Alan Morris, 207-493-4266
Type: public at-risk
HS
Entrance requirements: application, interview.

Presque Isle High School
377A Main St, Presque Isle, ME 04769
Wayne Harper, Dir, 207-764-8100
Type: public at-risk
HS
Entrance requirements: referral, meeting.

Madawaska Learning Center
St John Valley Technical Center
PO Box E, Upper Frenchville, ME 04784
Robin Jackson-Elbridge, 207-728-4833
9–12th grade

Van Buren District Secondary School
321 Main St, Van Buren, ME 04785
Bette Thibeault, 207-868-5274
Type: public at-risk

7-12th grade
Entrance requirements: referral; additional help on student's initiative.

Hurricane Island Outward Bound (1964)
PO Box 429, Rockland, ME 04841
Peals Wrobel, Dir, 207-594-1401, FAX: 594-9425
Knox County
Type: independent, non-profit; tuition: variable, scholarships
120 teachers, 1,000 students
Entrance requirements: medical screening
Affiliations: Outward Bound, Inc
Governance by board
Develops self-esteem, self-reliance, concern for others and for environment; sailing, kayaking, rock-climbing, ropes courses; 4 programs nationally; no letter grades; non-compulsory class attendance.

Children's House
63 Pearl St, Camden, ME 04843
Martha Monahan
Type: Montessori

The Community School (1973)
Box 555-79 Washington St, Camden, ME 04843
Emanual Pariser, Dora Lievow, Co-Directors, 207-763-3000
Knox County
Type: independent, boarding, non-profit; tuition: $17,000/yr, scholarships
6 teachers, 8 students, mainly at-risk, ages 16-21, HS
No untreated addicts; 6 gr+ reading level
Affiliations: NCACS, Nat Dropout Prev Net
Governance by democratic school meeting; faculty determines inalterable rules
"Real world" preparation includes work in community, maintenance of the facility, and meeting room and board costs; applied home economics; conflict resolution and anger management; competency-based academic program; new book: Changing Lives: Voices From a School that Works; no letter grades; multi-aged classes; extensive field trips; rural location; interns accepted.

Riley School (1972)
Box 91, Glen Cove, ME 04846
Glenna W. Plaisted, Director, 207-596-6405
Knox County
Type: independent, non-profit; tuition: $3700-5200, scholarships
11 teachers, 63 students, ages 4-14, ungraded
Entrance requirements: children spend 5 days evaluating process
Affiliations: NEAS&C, ISANNE
Governance by principal, board
Teacher qualifications: strong background in child development; experience
Integrated curriculum; interest-based; community service; independent study; narrative evaluations; team teachiing; environmental studies; no letter grades; multi-aged classes; extensive field trips; interns accepted.

Homeschoolers of Maine
HC 62, PO Box 24, Hope, ME 04847
207-763-4251

Northeast Montessori Institute
PO Box 68, Rockport, ME 04856
Helen DeVere
Type: Montessori teacher education

Georges Valley High School (1978)
PO Box 192, Thomaston, ME 04861-0192
Celeste Frisbee, 207-354-2502, FAX: 354-2369
Knox County
Type: public choice
33 teachers, 300 students, ages 13-19, 9-12th grade
Governance by board

Client-oriented; work-study; community service; modified school schedule; contracts; independent study; adult ed; Outward Bound; rural location; transportation; interns accepted.

Ashwood School (1986)
PO Box 129, West Rockport, ME 04865
Sarah McBrian, Pres Board of Trustees, 207-236-8021
Knox County
Type: Waldorf, non-profit; scholarships
7 teachers, 56 students, ages 4-10, K-4th grade
Governance by faculty and board of trustees
Teacher qualifications: Waldorf training
Rural location.

Kennebec Montessori School
PO Box 866, Waterville, ME 04901
Adele Carey

Waterville Alternative (1987)
21 Gilman St, Waterville, ME 04901
Bernard Peatman, Dir, 207-873-5595
Kenebec County
Type: public at-risk
5 teachers, 40 students, mainly at-risk, ages 13-19, 6-12th grade
Enrollment restricted to counselor-referred residents
Governance by principal
Teacher qualifications: state certification
Students may avail themselves of all activities, courses and facilities of regular HS; self-esteem and goal-setting programs; multi-aged classes; rural location; transportation.

Toddy Pond School
217 High St, Belfast, ME 04915
Andrea Stark, 207-525-4495
Type: independent; tuition: $2000/yr, scholarships
22 students, ages 5-12
Governance by parent cooperative
Thematic approach with independent study; rural location.

Options at Dexter Regional High School
Abbott Hill Rd, Dexter, ME 04930
Albert Worden, 207-924-5113
8-12th grade

PASS at Lawrence Junior High School
School St, Fairfield, ME 04937
Stephen Cottrel, 207-453-4200
8-12th grade

Madison High School
RFD #1 Box 229, Madison, ME 04950
Joseph Testa, 207-696-3395
Type: public at-risk
10-12th grade

TRANET: Transnational Network for Alternative/ Appropriate Technologies
(See Resource Appendix)

Crossroads Learning Center (1984)
63 Water St, Skowhegan, ME 04976
Penny McGovern, Dir, 207-474-7175
District 54, Somerset County
Type: public at-risk
7 teachers, 54 students, mainly at-risk, ages 14-20, 9-12th grade
Enrollment restricted to at-risk residents
Governance by principal, faculty and student representatives
Teacher qualifications: ME Certification
Competency-based and traditional classes; toward diploma or GED; focus on the needs of the whole student; multi-aged classes; rural location; transportation; interns accepted.

Maryland

Henry Ferguson
14600 Berry Rd, Accokeek, MD 20607
John Dade, 301-292-5000
Prince George County
Type: magnet
2-5th grade
Talented and gifted.

Alternative School
Radio Station Rd, La Plata, MD 20646
William G. McCall, 932-1855
Charles County
Type: public choice

Evening High School
1000 Radio Station Rd, Rte 5, La Plata, MD 20646
Jack Brown, 932-1003
Charles County
Type: public choice

St Mary's Community School
441 Autumnwood Dr, Mechanicsville, MD 20659
Lynn Erwin
Type: Montessori

Parents for Home Education
13020 Blairmore St, Beltsville, MD 20705
301-572-5827

Glenarden Woods
Echols Ave, Lanham, MD 20706
Oretha Bridgwaters, 301-772-6611
Prince George County
Type: magnet
2-6th grade
Talented and gifted.

Thomas Johnson Middle School (1993)
5401 Barker Pl, Lanham, MD 20706
John Robinson, Prin; Susan Wilkerson, Specialist, 301-459-5800
Type: public choice Montessori
1 teacher, 19 students, ages 12–15
Entrance requirement: Montessori experience
Accreditation: MDBE
Governance by an administrator
Urban location; transportation; interns accepted.

Cristian Family Montessori School (1982)
3628 Rhode Island Ave, Mt Rainier, MD 20712
Vernice W. Townsend, Adm, 201-927-7122
Tuition: $1,540/2,2120/yr
4 teachers, 4 assistants, 84 students, ages toddler-12
Entrance requirements: age 2.5; toilet trained; interview
Affiliation: Catechesis of the Good Shepherd
Governance by administrator, board
Full Montessori program; Catachist of the Good Shepherd; urban location; interns accepted.

Little Friends for Peace
4405 29th St, Mt Rainier, MD 20712
Mary Joan Park
Type: Montessori

Bowie Montessori Children's House (1967)
5004 Randonstone Ln, Bowie, MD 20715
Anne Byron-Riley, 301-262-3566
Non-profit

7 teachers; students mainly International, ages 3–15
Affiliation: AMI
Governance by board
Childcare; suburban location; interns accepted.

Heather Hills
12605 Heming Lane, Bowie, MD 20716
Patricia Brooks, 301-262-3013
Prince George County
Type: magnet
2-6th grade
Talented and gifted.

Tall Oaks Vocational High School (1988)
2112 Church Rd, Bowie, MD 20716
Burt Poulis, 301-249-2900
Type: public choice
200 students

Mitchelville Children's School
12112 Central Ave, Mitchelville, MD 20721
Ms Harvey
Type: Montessori

Julia Brown Montessori School (1967)
9450 Madison Ave, Laurel, MD 20723
Adm, 301-498-0604
4 teachers, 6 assistants, 115 students, mainly international, ages 3–12
Entrance requirements: age 2.5; toilet trained
Affiliation: AMS; accreditations: MDBE, DHR
Governance by an administrator
Traditional Montessori school; extracurriculars; childcare; suburban location; interns accepted.

Friends Community School (1986)
4601 Calvert Rd, College Park, MD 20740
Jane Manring, Tch-Dir, 301-699-6086
Type: Quaker, non-profit
10 teachers, 120 students, ages 5–11, K-6th grade
Affiliation: Adelphi Friends Meeting
Governance by friends meeting
Teacher qualifications: values consistent with Friends, experience.
Conflict resolution; portfolio assessment; multi-disciplinary, long-term projects; flexible teaching assignments; service projects; Math Their Way; no letter grades; multi-aged classes; extensive field trips; suburban location; interns accepted.

Doswell E Brooks Elementary (1986)
1301 Brooks Rd, Capital Hts, MD 20743
Margaret Williams, Prin; Susan Wilkerson, Specialist, 301-735-0470
Type: public choice Montessori; tuition: $1,400 (ages 3-4)
11 teachers, 4 assistants, 275 students, ages 3–12
Entrance requirement: Montessori experience for K+
Accreditation: MDBE
Governance by an administrator
Urban location; transportation; interns accepted.

Capitol Heights
601 Suffolk Ave, Capitol Height, MD 20743
Thelma Butler, 301-420-3430
Prince George County
Type: magnet
2-6th grade
Talented and gifted.

Central
200 Cabin Branch Rd, Capitol Height, MD 20743
William Watkins, 301-336-8200
Prince George County
Type: magnet
9-12th grade
Humanities; international studies.

Walker Mill
800 Karen Blvd, Capitol Height, MD 20743
Joan Brown, 301-366-8855
Prince George County
Type: magnet
7-8th grade
Talented and gifted.

Beddow School
8600 Loughran Rd, Fort Washington, MD 20744
Trudy Beddow
Type: Montessori

Flintstone Elementary (1986)
800 Comanche Dr, Oxon Hill, MD 20745
Dr Delores Smith, Prin; Susan Wilkerson, Specialist, 301-567-
3142
Type: public choice Montessori; tuition: $1,400 (ages 3-4)
11 teachers, 4 assistants, 275 students, ages 3-12
Entrance requirement: Montessori experience for K+
Accreditation: MDBE
Governance by an administrator
Urban location; transportation; interns accepted.

Valley View
5500 Danby Ave, Oxon Hill, MD 20745
Inez Sadler, 301-839-3444
Prince George County
Type: magnet
2-6th grade
Talented and gifted.

Andrew Jackson
3500 Regency Parkway, Forestville, MD 20747
William Simmons, 301-736-9700
Prince George County
Type: magnet
7-8th grade
French immersion; humanities; international studies.

Longfields
3300 Newkirk Ave, Forestville, MD 20747
Yvonne Crawford, 301-736-6671
Prince George County
Type: magnet
2-6th grade
Talented and gifted.

Suitland
5200 Silver Hill Rd, Suitland, MD 20747
Sterling Marshall, 301-568-7770
Prince George County
Type: magnet
9-12th grade
University HS; visual and performing arts.

Henson Valley Montessori School
7007 Allentown Rd, Temple Hills, MD 20748
Robin Knight, HVMS

Œkos
PO Box 10, Glenn Dale, MD 20769
Paul Epstein and Teresita Leimer
Type: Montessori

Glenn Dale Early Childhood Education Center
6700 Glenn Dale Rd, Glenn Dale, MD 20769-9407
Judy Hoyer
Type: Montessori

Blue Mountain Book Peddler
(See Resource Appendix)

Prince George's Board of Ed Montessori Magnet Office
14201 School Ln, Upper Marlboro, MD 20772
Susan Wilkerson

New City Montessori School (1968)
3120 Nicholson St, Hyattsville, MD 20782
Shirley Windsor, Adm, 301-559-8488
Non-profit; tuition: $2,625-3,800/yr
3 teachers, 2 assistants, 60 students, ages 3-9
Entrance requirements: min age 2.5; toilet trained
Affiliation: AMI
Governance by board
Between U of MD, Catholic U; near two subway stations;
childcare; suburban location; interns accepted.

Paint Branch Montessori School (1975)
3215 Powder Mill Rd, Adelphi, MD 20783
Patricia Barshay, 301-937-2244
Tuition: $2,648-4,142/yr
7 teachers, 5 assistants, 95 students, ages 3-12
Affiliations: NAMTA, Elementary Teachers of Classics
Governance by administrator
Wooded area; nature trails; PE; art; music; ASL; childcare; sub-
urban location; interns accepted.

Willowbrook Children's House
8151 15th Ave, Hyattsville, MD 20783-3501
Gloria Harvey
Type: Montessori

Kenmoor
3211 82nd Ave, Landover, MD 20785
Peter Bray, 301-722-1040
Prince George County
Type: magnet
2-6th grade
Talented and gifted.

Matthew Henson Elementary/Montessori (1986)
7910 Scott Rd, Landover, MD 20785
Sherra Chappelle, Prin, or Susan Wilkerson, Coord, 301-772-
1922
Type: public choice; tuition: $1,000
11 teachers, 3 assistants, 275 students, ages 3-12
Entrance requirements: lottery for waiting list; Montessori
experience for ages 5+
Governance by administrator, board
Computer lab; nearby woods; access to DC museums; suburban location; transportation; interns accepted.

Oakcrest
929 Hill Rd, Landover, MD 20786
James Chase, 301-336-8020
Prince George County
Type: magnet
2-6th grade
Talented and gifted.

Thomas G. Pullen
700 Brightseat Rd, Landover, MD 20786
Kathy Kurtz, 301-808-1260
Prince George County
Type: magnet
K-8th grade
Creative and performing arts.

Bethesda Montessori School (1982)
7611 Clarendon Rd, Bethesda, MD 20814
Gertrude A. Burr, Dir, 301-986-1260
Tuition: $4,250/yr
3 teachers, 4 assistants; student ages 2.5-6
Entrance requirements: toilet trained
Affiliation: AMI; accreditation: MD DE
Governance by an administrator
Childcare; suburban location.

Lone Oak Montessori School
10100 Old Georgetown Rd, Bethesda, MD 20814
Patricia Swann

World Future Society
(See Resource Appendix)

Oneness Family Peace School
6701 Wisconsin Ave, Chevy Chase, MD 20815
Andy Kutt
Type: Montessori

Holden Montessori Day School
5450 Massachusetts Ave, Bethesda, MD 20816
Mary Ann Atwell

New Age Montessori School
4728 Western Ave, Bethesda, MD 20816

Washington Waldorf School
4800 Sangamore Rd, Bethesda, MD 20816
Ann Finucane

Abingdon Montessori School
5144 Massachusetts Ave, Bethesda, MD 20816-2740

Farrell Montessori School
6601 Bradley Blvd, Bethesda, MD 20817
Maureen van Emmerik

Walden Montessori Academy (1987)
7730 Bradley Blvd, Bethesda, MD 20817
Linda Grodin, Dir, 301-469-8123
Tuition: $3,300-5,500/yr
2 teachers, 3 assistants, 62 students, ages infant-6
Affiliation: AMS
Governance by an administrator
Childcare; suburban location; interns accepted.

Triune Teaching Program (1992)
5206 Wissioming Rd, Bethesda, MD 20846
Mardy Burgess, 301-229-9577, FAX: 301-229-9578
Montgomery County
Type: public at-risk
2 teachers, 16 students, ages 13-16, 8th grade
Enrollment restricted to remedial reading needs; no resi-
    dency requirement
Governance by principal
Multicultural; Triune Brain Model; cooperative learning; class-
    room management; higher order mentoring; urban
    location.

Franklin Montessori School
10500 Darnestown Rd, Rockville, MD 20850
Pamela Trumble

Regional Institute for Children and Adolescents
15000 Broschart Rd, Rockville, MD 20850
Joan Benz, 251-6900
Montgomery County
Type: public choice

Green Acres School
11701 Canville, Rockville, MD 20852
Type: independent

Norbeck Montessori School
4500 Muncaster Mill Rd, Rockville, MD 20853
Elizabeth Bissett

Apple Montessori School
11815 Seven Locks Rd, Potomac, MD 20854
Lynn Oboler and Marian Pepper

Anchor Montessori School
11204 Tara Rd, Potomac, MD 20854-1348
Linda Grodin

Manor Montessori School
10500 Oaklyn Dr, Potomac, MD 20854-3936
Marie Fonseca and Kathy Damico

Sandy Spring Friends School
16923 Norwood Rd, Sandy Spring, MD 20860
Stephen Gessner, 301-774-7455
Type: independent

Mater Amoris Montessori School
18501 Mink Hollow Rd, PO Box 97, Ashton, MD 20861-0097
Charlottee Kovach

Gaithersburg Internationalle Montessori School
429 W Diamond Ave, Gaithersburg, MD 20877

Flower Hill Country Day
8507 Emory Grove Rd, Gaithersburg, MD 20877-3731
Type: Montessori

Gerber Children's Center
1199 Quince Orchard Blvd, Gaithersburg, MD 20878
Kathy Fletcher
Type: Montessori

Butler School
15120 Turkey Foot Rd, Gaithersburg, MD 20878-3960
Rila Spellman
Type: Montessori

Village Montessori Schools
20301 Fulks Farms Rd, Gaithersburg, MD 20879
Jeanne MacDougall

Good Shepherd Montessori School
8921 Warfield Rd, Gaithersburg, MD 20882

Evergreen Montessori School
10101 Connecticut Ave, Kensington, MD 20895-3803
Lynn Pellaton

Casa De Montessori
709 Hobbs, Silver Spring, MD 20904

Home Study International
12501 Old Columbia Pike, Silver Spring, MD 20904
Robert Burnette, Dir of Student Services, 800-782-4769, FAX:
    301-680-6577
Type: national home-based, non-profit; scholarships
62 teachers, 2,200 students, ages 4+, pre K-college
Affiliation: Columbia Union College
Governance by board
State approved; accredited by National Home Study Council.

Thornton Friends School (1973)
13925 New Hampshire Ave, Silver Spring, MD 20904
Douglas R. Price, Head, 301-384-0320
Montgomery County
Type: Quaker, non-profit; tuition: $8,745/yr, scholarships
12 teachers, 74 students, ages 13-18, 6-12th grade
Entrance requirements: interview, application, references
Affiliation: Friends Council on Education
Governance by faculty members, board
Socratic pedagogy; drama; co-ed interscholastic soccer, bas-
    ketball, softball; extensive field trips; multi-aged classes;
    middle school (gr 6-8) opening in Fall '94 for 20-30 addt'l
    students; interns accepted.

The Barrie School (1932)
13500 Layhill Rd, Silver Spring, MD 20905
Judy Yormick, 301-894-6200, FAX: 301-871-6406
Type: Montessori; tuition: $5,045-7,430/yr
54 teachers, 474 students, ages toddler-18
Governance by board of trustees, administrator
45 wooded acres; strong humanities; hands-on; foreign
    travel; community service; childcare; suburban location;
    transportation; interns accepted.

The Institute for Advanced Montessori Studies
13500 Layhill Rd, Silver Spring, MD 20906
Judy Yormick
Type: Montessori teacher education

Aspen Hill Montessori School
3820 Aspen Hill Rd, Wheaton, MD 20906-2904
Lance Gilbert

International Montessori Society
(See Resource Appendix)

Spring Bilingual Montessori School
2010 Linden Ln, Silver Spring, MD 20910-1703
Anne Neri

Home Study Institute
(See Resource Appendix)

South River Evening High School
201 Central Ave E, Edgewater, MD 21037
John McCorkill, 956-5600
Anne Arundel County
Type: public choice

Ellicott City Children's House
3604 Chatham Rd, Ellicott City, MD 21042-3920
Geri Herber
Type: Montessori

Children's Manor Montessori School
10495 Fair Oaks, Columbia, MD 21044
Dr Pradeep Ghosh

Columbia Montessori School (1972)
10518 Marble Faun Ln, Columbia, MD 21044
Maria E Garcia, Dir, 410-995-0337
Tuition: $320-560/mo
4 teachers, 4 assistants, 60 students, mainly international,
   ages infant-6
Affiliation: AMS
Governance by administrator
Traditional; childcare; interns accepted.

Love of Learning Montessori (1983)
10840 Little Patuxent Parkway, Columbia, MD 21044
Anulda Torres, Dir, 301-596-4412, FAX: same
Tuition: $385-523/mo
6 teachers, 65 students, mainly international
Affiliations: DHR, MDDE
Governance by an administrator
Multi-cultural staff; childcare; suburban location.

Bryant Woods Montessori
10449 Green Mountain Circle, Columbia, MD 21044-2457
Penny Friedberg

Julia Brown Montessori (1974)
9760 Owen Brown, Columbia, MD 21045
Adm, 410-730-5056
4 teachers, 7 assistants, 100 students, mainly international,
   ages 3-6
Entrance requirements: age 2.5; toilet trained
Affiliation: AMS; accreditations: MDBE, DHR
Governance by an administrator
Traditional Montessori school; extracurriculars; childcare; sub-
   urban location; interns accepted.

Maryland Home Education Association
9085 Flamepool Way, Columbia, MD 21045
410-730-0073
Type: state home-based

Children's House Montessori
9660 Basket Ring Rd, Columbia, MD 21045-3421
Mildred Stovall

Pretty Boy Elementary School
19810 Middleton Rd, Freeland, MD 21053
Dr Sue Rathbone
Type: Montessori

Glen Burnie Evening High School
505 Baltimore/Annapolis Blvd SE, Glen Burnie, MD 21061

Nelson Horine, Adm, 761-8950
Anne Arundel County
Type: public choice

The Glen Burnie Homeschool Support Group
6514 Dolphin Ct, Glen Burnie, MD 21061
301-850-4496
Anne Arundel County

The Montessory Society of Central Maryland (1962)
10807 Tony Dr, Lutherville, MD 21093
Marcia A. Hettinger, Adm, 410-321-8555, FAX: 410-321-8566
Type: Montessori, non-profit; tuition: $3,780-6,825/yr
22 teachers, 22 assistants, 371 students, mainly International,
   ages Infant-12
Affiliation: NAMTA; accreditations: MSA, AMS
Governance by administrator
Childcare; suburban location; interns accepted.

Towson Children's House
1710 Dulanly Valley Rd, Lutherville, MD 21093
Marcia Hettinger
Type: Montessori

Arlington Echo Outdoor Education Center
975 Indian Landing Rd, Millersville, MD 21108
Russell Heyde, 222-3822
Anne Arundel County
Type: public choice

Montessori Foundation
(See Resource Appendix)

North Country Home Educators (1992)
1688 Belhaven Ct, Pasadena, MD 21122-3722
Nancy Greer, Resource Librarian, 410-437-5109
Anne Arundel County
Inclusive; parent meetings; social activities; monthly newslet-
   ter; free membership.

Severna Park Evening High School
60 Robinson Rd, Severna Park, MD 21146
James Sledge
Anne Arundel County
Type: public choice

Montessori Society of Westminster
c/o St Benjamin's Church, Krider's Cemetary Rd, Westminster,
   MD 21157
Kathy Grout

Westminster Alternative Programs (1991)
125 Airport Dr, Suite 18, Westminster, MD 21157
Peg Kulow, 410-848-4441, FAX: 410-848-5058
Type: public choice
9 students

School For the Arts #415
706–712 Cathedral St, Baltimore, MD 21201
David Simon, 410-396-1185
Type: magnet
9–12th grade

Willow Country Day School
233 E Rodwood St, Baltimore, MD 21202
Type: Montessori

Odong Ridge Montessori School
2118 Pine Ave, Baltimore, MD 21207-2826
Fred Eustis

Waldorf School of Baltimore
4701 Yellowwood Ave, Baltimore, MD 21209
Jo Karp

Calvert School Home Instruction Department (1987)
105 Tuscany Rd, Baltimore, MD 21210
Susan Weiss, Prin, 410-243-6030, FAX: 410-366-0674
Type: non-profit; cost: $250-700/yr, scholarships
55 teachers, 10,000 students, ages 5–14, K–8th grade

English speakers only; placement test for grades 4+
Governance by board of trustees, head master, principal
Students world-wide; Day School as experimental lab for
   course development; professional guidance; integrated
   curriculum; French; music; art; classical lit.

Friends School
5114 N Charles St, Baltimore, MD 21210
W. Byron Forbush, Head, 410-435-2800
Type: Quaker

Francis M. Wood Alternative Secondary Center
100 N Calhoun St, Baltimore, MD 21223
John R. Nauright, Jr, 396-1290
Type: public choice

Harbor City Learning Center
1001 W Saratoga St, Baltimore, MD 21223
Gary Unfried, 396-1513
Type: public choice

Community Career Center in Catonsville
16 Bloomsbury Ave, Baltimore, MD 21228
Robert L. Cullison, 887-0934
Type: public choice

Community Career Center in Rosedale
Old Philadelphia Rd, Baltimore, MD 21228
Robert L. Cullison, 887-0934
Type: public choice

George F. Bragg Nature Study Center
6601 Baltimore National Pike, Baltimore, MD 21228
Benjamin Wallace, Naturalist, 747-8336
Type: public choice

Montessori School
1532 E Fort Ave, Baltimore, MD 21230

Inner Harbor Children's House
100 W Henrietta St, Baltimore, MD 21230-3610
Marcia Hettinger
Type: Montessori

Heritage Montessori School (1981)
9515 Belair Rd, Baltimore, MD 21236
Catherine Szeto, Owner/Dir, 410-529-0374
Tuition: $2,675-3,600/yr
3 teachers, 3 assistants, 67 students, ages infant-9
Affiliation: AMS
Governance by administrator
Childcare; suburban location; interns accepted.

Anne Arundel County Learning Center
600 Adams Park, Annapolis, MD 21401
James Lyons, 222-1639
Type: public choice

Chesapeake Montessori School
30 Old Mill Bottom Rd N, Annapolis, MD 21401
Anne Locke or Paula Shipley

Montessori International Children's House
1641 N Winchester Rd, Annapolis, MD 21401-5850
Jean Burgess, Dir

Easton Montessori School
2 Martin Ct #3, Easton, MD 21601
Susan Pugh, Head, 410-822-7827
Non-profit; tuition: $3250/4375
1 teacher, 1 assistant, 25 students, ages 3-6
Children must be toilet trained
Affiliation: AMI
Governance by an administrator and board of trustees
Rural location; interns accepted.

Cambridge Montessori School
309 Glenburn Ave, Cambridge, MD 21613-1531
Beth Lynch

Friendship Montessori School, Inc
25528 Worton/Lynch Rd, Worton, MD 21678

Evening High School
1501 Market St, Frederick, MD 21701
Richard Ramsburg, 694-1807
Frederick County
Type: public choice

Banner School
1730-A North Market Ave, Fredrick, MD 21701
Type: Montessori

Alpha Plus
(See Resource Appendix)

Eagle Voice Center
(See Resource Appendix)

Willow Country Day School
1134 Long Corner Rd, Mt Airy, MD 21771
Karen Plaskow
Type: Montessori

Massachusetts

Amherst Montessori School
27 Pomeroy Ln, Amherst, MA 01002
Bruce Marbin, Dir, 413-253-3101
Non-profit; tuition: $320-441/mo
3 teachers, 4 assistants, 52 students, ages 3-6
Entrance requirements: age 2.75
Affiliation: MSMA; accreditation: AMI
Governance by board
Student-centered; nature studies; childcare; rural location;
   interns accepted.

Hampshire College
Amherst, MA 01002
Admissions Office, 413-582-5471, FAX: 413-582-5631
Hampshire County
Type: higher education, boarding, non-profit; tuition:
   $19,490/yr, scholarships

100 teachers, 1079 students, ages 16-45
Entrance requirements: fee, transcripts, essays,
   recommendations.
Close collaboration between students and faculty; multidisciplinary learning; emphasis on independent research and
   creative work; member of Five Colleges Consortium; no
   letter grades; rural location.

The Common School
521 S Pleasant St Box 52, Amherst, MA 01004
Mark Segar, 413-256-8989
Type: independent

The Learning Cooperative (1993)
6 University Dr #240, Amherst, MA 01004-6000
Caroline Adams, 413-253-0444
Type: home-based

Hartsbrook School (1981)
94 Bay Rd, Hadley, MA 01035
Catherine Hopkins, Faculty Chair, 413-586-1908
Type: Waldorf; tuition: $3,625-4,650/yr, scholarships
22 teachers, 200 students, ages 4-14, pre K-8th grade
Affiliation: AWSNA
Governance by teachers, board
Teacher qualifications: BA, Waldorf teacher training and/or
   expertise in specific subject
Balances humanities, sciences, arts; foreign language, begin-
   ning grade 1; no letter grades; suburban location; interns
   accepted.

Holyoke Street School
130 Race St, Holyoke, MA 01040
413-536-2160
Type: independent
Students mainly at-risk

Magnet Middle School for Arts
325 Pine St, Holyoke, MA 01040
Selicita Elghadi, 413-534-2132
6-8th grade
Visual & performing arts.

Morgan Elementary
596 S Bridge, Holyoke, MA 01040
413-534-2083
Type: magnet
K-2nd grade
Pre-k Piaget; Montessori ungraded.

Morgan Montessori Kindergarten Program
596 S Bridge St, Holyoke, MA 01040-5953

Children's House Montessori
929 Northampton Hwy, Holyoke, MA 01040-9660

Folk Education Association of America
(See Resource Appendix)

Montessori Children's House
118 Riverdale St, W Springfield, MA 01089-4603

Experiment With Travel
Box 4884, Springfield, MA 01101-4884
Type: independent

Springfield Public Schools
195 State St, Box 1410, Springfield, MA 01102-1410
Teresa Regina
Type: Montessori

Montessori Internationale
56 Hopkins Pl, Longmeadow, MA 01106-1943

Elias Brookings Elementary
367 Hancock St, Springfield, MA 01107
Mary Anne Herron, 413-787-7200
Type: magnet
K-8th grade
Whole student approach.

Lincoln Elementary School
732 Chestnut St, Springfield, MA 01107
Enrique Figueredo, 413-787-7314
Type: magnet
K-5th grade

Frank H. Freedman Elementary
90 Cherokee Dr, Springfield, MA 01109
Beverly A. Brown, 413-787-7443
Zone 6 District
Type: magnet
K-5th grade
Whole student approach.

Homer Street Elementary
43 Homer St, Springfield, MA 01109
Robert Brown Jr, 413-787-7526
Type: magnet
K-5th grade
Whole student approach.

William N. DeBerry Elementary
670 Union St, Springfield, MA 01109
Barbara Jefferson, 413-787-7582
Type: magnet
K-5th grade
Education Today for Tomorrow.

Massasoit Montessori School
455 Island Pond Rd, Springfield, MA 01118

Montessori School of Springfield
1644 Allen St, Springfield, MA 01118-1818

Pioneer Valley Montessori School (1964)
1524 Parker St, Springfield, MA 01129
Laura Geryk, Head/Dir, 413-547-0342
Non-profit; tuition: $2,256-4,252/yr
4 teachers, 4 assistants, 98 students, ages 3-12
Affiliations: MSMA, NAEYC; accreditations: AISNE, AMS
Governance by administrator, board
Childcare; suburban location; transportation; interns
   accepted.

Hibbard Alternative
280 Newell St, Pittsfield, MA 01201
Laurie Bell
Type: home-based

Home Education Resource Center
505 East St, Pittsfield, MA 01201
Cindy Chandler, 413-499-5836
25 students, ages 2-16
Community guest lecturers; resource list; field trips; books
   and materials.

Berkshire Homeschoolers Group (1980)
217 Old State Rd, Berkshire, MA 01224
Judith A. Coons, 413-443-1770
Berkshire County
Non-profit
Testing; proposal writing; field trips; rural location.

Rudolf Steiner School of Great Barrington
35 W Plain Rd, Great Barrington, MA 01230
Virginia Flynn
Type: Waldorf

Montessori Berkshire (1979)
32 Pixley Hill Rd, Housatonic, MA 01236
Bonny Campbell, Dir, 413-274-3407
Non-profit; tuition: $3,000/yr
1 teacher, 2 assistants, 27 students, ages 3-6
Affiliations: AMS, MSMA
Governance by a board of trustees
Rural location; interns accepted.

Massachusetts Home Learning Association (1987)
PO Box 1976, Lenox, MA 01240-4976
Maggie Sadoway, 413-637-2169
Type: state home-based
Newsletter; legal fact sheet for MA ($1); homeschooling infor-
   mation packet ($5).

Ashley Falls Program
PO Box 339, Sheffield, MA 01257
Eileen Brennan, Tch, 413-229-8778, FAX: 413-229-2913
Southern Berkshire Regional District
Type: public choice
1 teacher, 22 students, ages 8-10, 3-4th grade

Entrance requirements: visit, application, lottery; no residency requirement
Affiliation: Undermountain Elementary
Governance by teachers, principal
Student ombudsman is arbiter of classroom conflicts; 2 students cook lunch each day; groupings vary; daily parent assistance; no letter grades, multi-aged classes; extensive field trips; rural location; transportation; interns accepted.

SALE: Specialized Alternative Learning Environment
PO Box 339, Sheffield, MA 01257
413-229-8778, FAX: 413-229-2913
Southern Berkshire Regional District
Type: public choice
1,100 students, ages 3–22, pre K–12th grade
Governance by faculty, student reps, parent co-op, teachers, principal
Comprehensive; therapeutic; integrated; multi-aged classes; rural location; transportation; interns accepted.

Buxton School (1928)
PO Box 646, Williamstown, MA 01267
C. William Bennett, 413-458-3919, FAX: 413-458-9427
Berkshire County
Type: independent, boarding, non-profit; tuition: $19,500/yr, scholarships
16 teachers, 80 students, ages 14–18, 9–12th grade
Entrance requirements: interview
Governance by teachers and principal
Teacher qualifications: Bachelor's
Work program; students maintain school; entire school travels to major city for research projects and to perform touring play; no letter grades; extensive field trips; multi-aged classes; rural location.

Institute for International Cooperation and Development (1986)
PO Box 103, Williamstown, MA 01267
Josefin Jonsson, Adm Dir, 413-458-9828, FAX: 413-458-3323
Berkshire County
Type: public choice; tuition: $3,200-4,300/yr, scholarships
6 teachers, 60 students, ages 18+
Residency required
Affiliation: Scandinavian folk HS's
Organizes 6–12 mo travel, study and solidarity courses; street-children school in Zimbabwe; treeplanting in Mozambique; rural construction projects in Nicaragua, Brazil; rural location.

NE Foundation For Children
(See Resource Appendix)

Full Circle School (1973)
Box 45410, 21 Parmenter Rd, Bernardston, MA 01337
Michael Muir-Harmony, Teacher/Director, 413-648-9842
Franklin County
Type: independent, non-profit; tuition: $5,000/yr, scholarships
5 teachers, 60 students, ages 2.9–12, ungraded
Governance by board
Teacher qualifications: similar philosophical beliefs
Libertarian school where liberty is viewed not as a byproduct, but as an essential ingredient of education; integrity of childhood is respected; no letter grades;non-compulsory class attendance; multi-aged classes; extensive field trips; rural location.

Assumption Montessori School
N Main St, Box 128, Petersham, MA 01366

Apple Country Homeschooling Association
PO Box 246, Harvard, MA 01451
508-456-8515

Harvard Elementary School Kindergarten
27 Massachusetts Ave, Harvard, MA 01451
Type: Montessori

Montessori Children's House of Auburn
135 Bryn Mawr Ave, Auburn, MA 01501-1605

Douglas Middle/High School
21 Davis St, E Douglas, MA 01516
Michael Masny, Dir, Spec Serv, 508-476-7026, FAX:-7901
Type: public at-risk
1 teacher, 8 students, ages 15–19, 9–12th grade
No residency requirement
Governance by teachers, principal
CAI; pre-vocational, student survival skills; community service; work/study; no letter grades; multi-aged classes; rural location; transportation.

Touchstone Community School
54 Leland St, Grafton, MA 01519
Dick Zajchowski
Type: independent

Maria Montessori School
21 Grove St, Millbury, MA 01527-2623

The Montessori Center of Shrewsbury
55 Oak St, Shrewsbury, MA 01545-2733
Nancy Corkum

Montessori Children's House (1976)
370 Worcester St, Southbridge, MA 01550
508-764-4032
Non-profit; tuition: $1,360-3,000/yr
11 teachers, 11 assistants, 35 students, ages 3–6
Accreditation: AMS
Governance by parent cooperative
Suburban location.

Treetops Montessori School
Baker Pond Rd, Dudley, MA 01571
Nancy Corkum

Worcester Area Homeschooling Organization
246 May St #2, Worcester, MA 01602
617-755-9553

City View Elementary
80 Prospect St, Worcester, MA 01605
Donald Shea, 508-799-3670
Type: magnet
K–6th grade
Discovery of self and world.

Burncoat Senior High School
179 Burncoat St, Worcester, MA 01606
William Hynes, 508-799-3300
Type: magnet
9–12th grade
Performing arts.

Burncoat St Elementary
526 Burncoat St, Worcester, MA 01606
Joseph Monfredo, 508-799-3537
Type: magnet
K–6th grade
Fine and performing arts.

Worcester Arts Magnet Elementary
315 St Nicholas Ave, Worcester, MA 01606
Margaret Vinditti, 508-799-3575
4–6th grade
Performing arts.

Metro West Homeschoolers
25 Carter Dr, Framingham, MA 01701
508-877-6536

Sudbury Valley School (1968)
2 Winch St, Framingham, MA 01701
Mimsy Sadofsky, 508-877-3030, FAX: 508-788-0674
Middlesex County

Type: independent, non-profit; tuition: $3600/2575/1550, 2nd, third child
11 teachers, 140 students, ages 4–20
Affiliation: NEASC
Governance by democratic school meeting
Teacher qualifications: students select staff invited to return each year
Students initiate; staff and equipment answer their needs; all ages mix freely; each staff and student has one vote at weekly meeting; offers school-starting kit; no letter grades; non-compulsory class attendance; multi-aged classes; suburban location.

Oak Meadow Montessori School
723 Massachusetts Ave, Boxborough, MA 01719-1413

Pincushion Hill Montessori School (1961)
30 Green St, Ashland, MA 01721
Christine Kovago, Dir, 508-881-2123
Non-profit; tuition: $2,750-5,500/yr
3 teachers, 3 assistants, 70 students, ages 3–9
Affiliations: AMI, AMS, MA Assn
Governance by administrator
Childcare; suburban location.

Concord Montessori (1975)
61 Birch Dr, Concord, MA 01742-2626
508-369-1455
Non-profit; tuition: $960-2,400/yr
5 teachers, 5 assistants, 78 students, ages infant-6
Affiliation: NAMTA
Governance by administrator
Suburban location; interns accepted.

Miller Elementary School (1973)
Woodland St, Holliston, MA 01746
Marcia Pinkham or Dr Anne Toule, Prin, 429-0668
Holliston Public Schools District
Type: public choice Montessori
10 teachers, 268 students, ages 3–12
Governance by administration
French Immersion; parents choose Montessori or traditional; transportation; interns accepted.

St Anne Montessori
720 Boston Post Rd E, Marlboro, MA 01752-3799
Sr Marie Joseph

Eliot Montessori School
5 Auburn St, South Natick, MA 01760-6064
Maggie Bryant or Bonnie James

The Life Experience School (1972)
2 N Main St, Sherborn, MA 01770
Lewis M. Randa, Dir, 508-655-2143, FAX: 655-5031
Type: Quaker; tuition: $18,000/yr
5 teachers, 15 students, mainly at-risk, ages 8–22
Entrance requirements: devoted to social justice, peace and non-violence
Affiliation: UN U for Peace; Harvard Div School
Governance by faculty and student representatives, board
Teacher qualifications: BS in SE or related field
No letter grades; extensive field trips; interns accepted.

Apple Valley Montessori School
80 Woodside Rd, Sudbury, MA 01776-3430
Audrey Newton

Barat Montessori School
5 Damon St, Cochituate, MA 01778-4807

Julie Billiart's Children's House
8 Summer St, Woburn, MA 01801
Type: Montessori

Woburn Montessori School
7 Kosciusko St, Woburn, MA 01801-3863

Merrimack Montessori School
55 Saltonstall Rd, Haverhill, MA 01830-4189

Georgetown School Department
1 Library St, Georgetown, MA 01833
Larry S. Borin, Supt, 508-352-5777, FAX: 508-352-5778
Type: public/independent choice
90 teachers, 1100 students, ages 5–19, K–12th grade
Entrance requirements: age 5 by Sept 1, no residency requirement
Governance by board
Comprehensive computer lab; 65 stations linked with Novell Network.

Presentation of Mary
209 Lawrence St, Methuen, MA 01844-3884
Type: Montessori

Andover School of Montessori (1975)
180 Main St, N Andover, MA 01845
Michelle B. DuBois, 508-688-1086
Tuition: $2,420/4,760/yr
4 teachers, 4 assistants, 75 students, ages 3–6
Affiliations: AMS, MSM, ISAM
Governance by board, administrator
Life skills; childcare; suburban location; interns accepted.

Greater Boston Home Educators
16 Hawthorne St, Wakefield, MA 01880
617-246-2059

Kitchen School Group
PO Box 96, W Boxford, MA 01885
617-352-2023
Type: home-based

Massachusetts Homeschool Organization of Parent Educators
15 Ohio St, Wilmington, MA 01887
508-658-8970
Type: state home-based

Children's Own School, Inc
86 Main St, Winchester, MA 01890-3928
Type: Montessori

Cape Ann Waldorf School
668 Hale St, Beverly Farms, MA 01915
Elizabeth Trocki

The Harborlight Montessori
243 Essex St, Beverly, MA 01915-1958
Susan McDonough

North Shore Homeschool Support Group
62 Matthies St, Beverly, MA 01915-2448
Marci Anthony, 508-927-8383
Essex County

Danvers Alternative High School (1978)
57 Conant St, Danvers, MA 01923
Dane Hamilton, Dir, 508-887-9567
Type: public at-risk
5 teachers, 25 students, mainly at risk, ages 14–18, 9–12th grade
Enrollment restricted to special needs/emotionally disturbed
Governance by teachers, principal, democratic school meeting
Teacher qualifications: certification in moderate special needs
Therapeutic milieu; extensive field trips; multi-aged classes; no letter grades; non-compulsory class attendance; suburban location; interns accepted.

Cape Ann Homeschoolers (1992)
6 Emily La, Magnolia, MA 01930
Judith A. Humbert, Dir, 508-525-3061
Essex County
Non-profit

12 teachers, 25 students, ages 5-12, K-6th grade
Governance by parent cooperative
Monthly meetings; non-sectarian; suburban location.

Gloucester Alternative School (1983)
48 Magnolia Ave, Magnolia, MA 01930
Cynthia Smith, Team Chair, 508-525-3572
Type: public at-risk
5 teachers, 24 students, ages 14-19, HS
Entrance requirements: average- above average IQ; IEP; no
    residency requirement
Governance by teachers and principal
Teacher qualifications: SE certification
Multi-aged classes; suburban location; interns accepted.

Ipswich Montessori (1976)
PO Box 612, Ipswich, MA 01938
Jame Brissette, 508-356-5698
Tuition: $1,575/3,500/yr
2 teachers, 2 assistants, 35 students, ages 3-6
Governance by an administrator
Extensive nature studies in woods.

Children's Montessori School
PO Box 681, Ipswich, MA 01938-0681

Don Bosco, Sacred Heart
RR 1 A, Ipswich, MA 01938-9801
Type: Montessori

Newburyport Montessori School
23 Pleasant St, Newburyport, MA 01950-2622

Salem Montessori School, Inc
4 Holly St, Salem, MA 01970-4611

Notre Dame Children's Class
74 Grapevine Rd, Wenham, MA 01984-1712
Type: Montessori

Bellingham Alternative Jr/Sr High School
387 Hartford Ave; mailing: 60 Harpin St, Bellingham, MA 02019
John Bonin, Dir, 508-966-1622, FAX: 508-966-4050
Type: public at-risk; tuition: $10,000 out of district
4 teachers, 33 students, ages 12-19, 7-12th grade
No residency requirement
Governance by teachers, principal
Teacher qualifications: SE certification
Problem solving; mainstream re-entry; multi-aged classes;
    suburban location; transportation; interns accepted.

Blue Hill Montessori School
163 Turnpike St, Canton, MA 02021-1300
Patricia Lukos

Dover Montessori School (1969)
16 Sherbrooke Dr, Dover, MA 02030
Terry Brown or Debbie Egan, 508-785-1387
Tuition: $2,795-5,200/yr
2 teachers, 5 assistants, 75 students, ages 3-6
Entrance requirements: $50 registration fee; application
Affiliations: NAMTA, NAEYC, BAEYC, AMI, AMS; accreditation:
    SNMC
Governance by administrator
Small group lessons in Spanish and science; large playground
    facility; special needs training; childcare; suburban location;
    interns accepted.

King's Wood Montessori (1968)
12 Gilmore St, Foxboro, MA 02035
Kathleen Dunn, 508-543-6391
Non-profit; tuition: $1,960-3,120/yr
2 teachers, 3 assistants, 58 students, ages 3-6
Affiliation: MSMA
Governance by administrator, parent cooperative
Childcare; suburban location; interns accepted.

**Seacoast Center Montessori Teacher Education
    Program**
PO Box 185, Scituate, MA 02040
Gary Davidson

Old Colony Montessori School
20 Derby St, Hingham, MA 02043-3707

Woodside Montessori School (1985)
350 Village St, Millis, MA 02054
Raui Kaur Khalsa, 508-376-5320
Tuition: $1,800-5,650/yr
4 teachers, 3 assistants, 72 students, ages 3-9
Governance by administrator
Low-ropes course built to scale; special needs accommo-
    dated; childcare; suburban location; interns accepted.

Harborside Montessori, Inc (1988)
188 First Parish Rd, Scituate, MA 02066
Shirley Carpenter, Adm/Dir, 617-545-2626
Tuition: $2,600/yr
1 teacher, 1 assistant, 24 students, ages 3-6
Affiliations: NAMTA, MSMA
Governance by administrator
French-speaking assistant; Kodaly music; professional gym-
    nastics; after-school French, recorder, piano for fee;
    childcare.

The Montessori Community School (1973)
136 Cornet Stetson Rd, Scituate, MA 02066
Charles Terranova, Head, 617-545-5544, FAX: 612-545-6522
Non-profit; tuition: $4,150-7,050/yr
10 teachers, 186 students, ages infant-12
Affiliations: AMS, MSMA
Governance by board
Childcare; suburban location; interns accepted.

Jewish Home Educator's Network (1991)
2 Webb Rd, Sharon, MA 02067
Marc Ernstoff, Treasurer, 617-784-9091
Type: national home-based

Transition Demonstration Programs
43 Mt Vernon St, Boston, MA 02108
David Robinson, EdD, Dir of Research, 617-227-2280
Type: public choice
K-3rd grade
Developmentally appropriate practices; family, health
    services.

Kingsley Montessori School (1986)
30 Fairfield St, Boston, MA 02116
Carole Forbes, Head, 617-536-5984, FAX: 617-536-7507
Non-profit; tuition: $2470/6370/yr
8 teachers, 7 assistants, 108 students, mainly international,
    ages infant-12
Affiliation: AMS; accreditation: AISNE
Governance by administrator, board of trustees
Childcare; urban location; interns accepted.

National Coalition of Advocates For Students
(See Resource Appendix)

Martin Luther King Middle School
77 Lawrence Ave, Dorchester, MA 02121
Steven Leonard, 617-445-4120
Type: magnet
6-8th grade
Communication; writing; arts.

Dorchester Youth Alternative School (1983)
1514A Dorchester Ave, Dorchester, MA 02122
Mary Lou O'Neill, Ed Dir, 617-288-1748, FAX:-2136
Type: public at-risk
3 teachers, 18 students, ages 12-16, 6-10th grade
Enrollment restricted to residents of Boston, CHINS of Boston
    Juvenile Court

Affiliation: Dept of Social Services/BPS
Governance by faculty, student reps, board
Individualized; flexible; accommodates different learning
 styles; multi-aged classes; extensive field trips; urban location; transportation; interns accepted.

The Log School (1975)
225 Bowdoin St, Dorchester, MA 02122
Gilbert Waytes, Dir, 617-288-6683
Type: public at-risk
3 teachers, 35 students, ages 12-15, 6-8th grade
Residency required
Affiliation: Boston Public Schools
Governance by principal
Teacher qualifications: state certification
Extensive field trips; urban location.

Dorchester High School
9 Peacevale Rd, Dorchester, MA 02124
Christopher Lane, 617-436-2065
Type: magnet
9-12th grade
Public service.

Notre Dame Montessori School
263/265 Mt Vernon St, Dorchester, MA 02125
Sr Elizabeth Calcagni

Julie's Children's House
230 W 6th St, South Boston, MA 02127-2635
Type: Montessori

Barron Assessment & Counseling Center (1986)
25 Walk Hill St, Jamaica Plain, MA 02130
Franklin A Tucker, Dir, 617-635-8123, FAX: 617-635-8117
Type: public at-risk
3 teachers, 550 students, ages 4-22, K-12th grade
No residency requirement
Affiliations: courts, community agencies
Governance by director
Teacher qualifications: state certification (Bilingual, SE)
For students involved with weapons, drugs, assaults; conflict
 resolution; Violence Prevention Counseling; psychological,
 educational testing; jail program; law student interns;
 building row boats, etc; urban location.

Creative Building Association Inc
54 Kenrick St, Brighton, MA 02135
Brad Harson
Type: Montessori

Pilot School
459 Broadway, Cambridge, MA 02138
617-349-6674
Type: public choice
An school within Cambridge Rindge and Latin.

Educator's Publishing Service (EPS)
(See Resource Appendix)

Cambridge Montessori School
161 Garden St, Cambridge, MA 02138-1240

Lesley College
29 Everett St, Cambridge, MA 02138-2790
Type: higher education
Gives credit support to Audubon Exploration Institute, other
 alternative programs.

Graham and Parks Alternative Public School (1972)
15 Upton St, Cambridge, MA 02139
Len Solo, Principal, 617-349-6613, FAX: 617-349-6615
Type: public choice
19 teachers, 370 students, ages 4.5-14, K-8th grade
Entrance requirements: application, lottery within racial cate-
 gories; 3 applications for each space, residency
Governance by parent and staff shared decision-making

Teacher qualifications: certified, experienced in urban ed,
 curriculum developer, high energy
Self-contained, multi-graded, open classrooms in K-6; flexible, student-centered program for grades 7-8; teacher
 developed, multi-cultural curriculum; extensive parent
 involvement; no letter grades; multi-aged classes; urban
 location; interns accepted.

National Center for Fair and Open Testing (FairTest)
(See Resource Appendix)

Cambridge Friends School (1961)
5 Cadbury Rd, Cambridge, MA 02140
Mary L. Johnson, Head, 617-354-3880, FAX: 617-876-1815
Type: Quaker, non-profit; tuition: $8,180-8,980/yr,
 scholarships
22 teachers, 200 students, ages 5-14, K-8th grade
Entrance requirements: interview and testing
Affiliations: FCOE, NAIS
Governance by principal, teachers, and board
Teacher qualifications: experience, agreement with mission
Multi-cultural, anti-racist, anti-homophobic; no letter grades;
 multi-aged classes; urban location; interns accepted.

Growing Without Schooling
(See Resource Appendix)

Holt Associates
(See Resource Appendix)

Full Circle High School
165 Broadway, Somerville, MA 02145
Type: independent

School Within a School (1970)
115 Greenough St, Brookline, MA 02146
Ellen Kaplovitz, Coord, 617-730-2747
Type: public choice
4 teachers, 100 students, ages 14-18, 10-12th grade
Entrance requirements: attendance at Brookline HS, parent
 permission, lottery, residency
Teacher qualifications: state certification
Democratic school with town meeting; student-directed
 activities; suburban location.

The Apple Orchard School (1971)
282D Newton St, Brookline, MA 02146
Lee Albright, Dir, 617-731-6463
Type: independent
80 students, ages 3-6
Located in renovated barn on farm; fields; woods; ponds;
 animals; environmental emphasis.

Hatsoff! Development Corp
42 Greenleaf St, Walden, MA 02148
Paul DuPont
Type: Montessori

Waltham Transition High School
100 Summer St, Waltham, MA 02154
William A Nolan, Prin, 617-647-0309, FAX: 617-647-9316
Type: public at-risk
6 teachers, 30 students, ages 14-18, 8-12th grade
Enrollment by recommendation of Transition Committee;
 residency required
Affiliation: Waltham Public Schools
Governance by teachers, principal
Teacher qualifications: state certification, Academic and
 Occupational
Living & learning skills; health/PE; career exploration
 sequence; multi-aged classes; suburban location.

Walnut Park Montessori School
47 Walnut Park, Newton, MA 02158-1442

Montessori Educare Inc
80 Crescent Ave, Newton, MA 02159-2102

Homeschoolers of Massachusetts Education Club
60 Parkway Rd, Newton, MA 02160
617-489-3275

Winthrop House at Brookline High School (1983)
490 Heath St, Brookline, MA 02167
Cathy Heller, Dir, 617-730-2507
Type: public at-risk
2 teachers, 1 assistant, 20 students, ages 14–22, 9–12th
   grade
Entrance requirements: no major assaultive behaviors,
   average to above-average intelligence, IEP meeting,
   residency
Governance by teachers, director, administrators
Teacher qualifications: SE certification
Cooperative; hands-on; life skills; conflict resolution; therapeutic intervention; multi-aged classes; suburban location;
   transportation.

Lexington Montessori School
130 Pleasant St, Lexington, MA 02173-8257
Peter Burleigh

Learning Things, Inc
(See Resource Appendix)

Waldorf School (1971)
739 Massachusetts Ave, Lexington, MA 02174
Susan Morris, Adms Coord, 617-863-1062
Non-profit; tuition: $4,500-6,700/yr, scholarships
30 teachers, 210 students, ages 3.5–14, pre K-8th grade
Entrance requirements: ability to learn in group setting
Affiliations: AWSNA, AISNE
Governance by faculty committee
Teacher qualifications: college degree, Waldorf certification
Special subject teachers; suburban location; interns accepted.

Wellesley Montessori School
79 Denton Rd, Wellesley, MA 02181-6404
Ida Friedman

**Alternative Education Program at Braintree High
   School**
128 Town St, Braintree, MA 02184
David M Swanton, Coord, 617-848-4000
Type: public at-risk
4 teachers, 30 students, ages 14–21, 9–12th grade
Entrance requirements: observation, residency
Governance by teachers, prin, coord, democratic school
   meeting
Teacher qualifications: special ed or social sciences
   certification
School within a school model; team teaching; counseling;
   behavior management system; daily group meetings;
   graduation credit; job training; multi-aged classes; extensive field trips; suburban location; interns accepted.

Thacher Montessori School
1425 Blue Hill Ave, Milton, MA 02186-2349
Maureen Coughlin

Institute for Responsive Education
(See Resource Appendix)

Munchkin Montessori Inc
145 Loring St, Duxbury, MA 02332-4823
Pam Malbouf

Pinewood Montessori
Federal Furnace Rd, Plymouth, MA 02360

South Shore Home Schoolers
163 Hingham St, Rockland, MA 02370
Plymouth County

READS Academy
70 Howard St, W Bridgewater, MA 02379
Deirdre Dowd-Pizzuto, LICSW, 508-587-6862

Type: public at-risk
4 teachers, 4 assistants, 25–40 students, ages 5–22, K–12th
   grade
Governance by board
Teacher qualifications: certification in moderate special needs
Basic interpersonal, social skills; counseling; behavior management; multi-aged classes; rural location; interns
   accepted.

Small World Children's House (1976)
395 West St, West Bridgewater, MA 02379-1014
Helena Bolster Marcotte, 508-584-0222
Type: Montessori; tuition: $355/mo
2 teachers, 6 assistants, 40 students, mainly international,
   ages 3–6
Entrance requirements: visit, interview
Affiliations: MSMA, NAEYC; accreditation: MA
Governance by administrator
Many student observers from nearby Bridgewater State and
   Stonehill Colleges; childcare.

South Shore Homeschoolers
87 Snell Av, Brockton, MA 02402
508-588-1529

Waldorf School of Cape Cod (1984)
85 Cotuit Rd, PO Box 3212, Bourne, MA 02532
Susan Joslin, Dev Dir, 508-759-7499
Barnstable County
Non-profit; tuition: $2,400-5,250/yr, scholarships
14 teachers, 98 students, ages 3–13, nursery-8th grade
No special needs
Affiliation: AWSNA
Governance by faculty and board of directors
Teacher qualifications: Waldorf certification preferred
Values-based; suburban location; interns accepted.

Center of Independent Learning, Inc (1989)
Box 619, 5 Depot Rd, Cataumet, MA 02534
Linda M. Zuern, Dir, 508-564-4875
Barnstable County
Type: independent, non-profit; tuition: $140/session
1 teacher, 10–20 students, ages 5–13, K–8th grade
Governance by board; dir
Teacher qualifications: BS or MS in Education
Small group classes; students, parents help set goals for each
   session; rural location.

Barnstable Montessori School
PO Box 832, East Sandwich, MA 02537-0832

Children's House of Nantucket
Pheasant Way, Nantucket, MA 02554
Type: Montessori

Nantucket New School
45 Surfside Rd, Nantucket, MA 02554
Linda Zola, Dir, 508-228-8569
Type: independent, non-profit; tuition: $0-5,000/yr, tuition-
   replacement jobs available
2 teachers, 21 students, ages 4–13, pre K-7th grade
Governance by teachers, principal
Equal emphasis on left and right brain functions; behavior
   modification; quiet classes; broad socioeconomic range;
   high CAT scores; 4-5 yr olds read and write; multi-aged
   classes; art; drama; suburban location.

Vineyard Montessori School
Main & Tashmoo Sts, PO Box 994, Vineyard Haven, MA 02568-
   0994
Debra Polucci

Abbington Academy (1983)
Box 330, Wareham, MA 02571-3303
Kristen Heisler, School Liaison, 508-291-1229
Plymouth County

Type: home-based, non-profit; cost: $300/yr/family,
  scholarships
25 students, ages 6-18, 1-12th grade
Entrance requirements: must live in reasonable driving
  distance
Governance by parent cooperative
Self-directed, community, and home-based learning; strong
  parental involvement in planning and activities; descriptive
  assessments and portfolios; apprenticeships, community
  service; no letter grades; multi-aged classes; extensive field
  trips; non-compulsory class attendance; suburban
  location.

Country Day Montessori School
1643 Hyannis Rd, Barnstable, MA 02630
Lynn Heslinga

Barnstable Country Day School
240 Flint St, Marstons Mills, MA 02648
Type: Montessori

Montessori School of the Angels
PO Box 360, Fall River, MA 02724-0360

St Joseph Montessori School
2501 S Main St, Fall River, MA 02724-2015

West Side Jr/Sr High School
181 Hillman St, New Bedford, MA 02740
508-997-4511 x2372
Type: public at-risk
11 teachers, 60 students, ages 14-20, 7-12th grade
Enrollment restricted to 502.4i special needs, residency
  required
Governance by principal
Teacher qualifications: state certification
Culinary, woodwork, art, pottery, photography shops; CCP
  computer lab; student operated restaurant; multi-aged
  classes; extensive field trips; urban location; transportation; interns accepted.

Michigan

Novi Worthville Montessori
6561 Tamerlane, Novi, MI 18375
Geetha Rao, Adm, 313-348-3033
Tuition: $200/336/mo
3 teachers, 8 assistants, 77 students, mainly international,
  ages 3-6
Children must be 2 1/2 years old and toilet trained
Affiliation: Social Services
Governance by an administrator
Highly academic and structured program includes music,
  gym, and art; childcare; suburban location.

Birmingham Community Montessori (1979)
2225 Fourteen Mile Rd, Birmingham, MI 48009
Arlene Ross, Administrator, 313-646-1535
Tuition: $2,260/yr
2 teachers, 2 assistants, 44 students, ages 3-6
Affiliation: MIMS
Governance by administrator, democratic school meeting
Weekly music; suburban location; interns accepted.

Halfway II
15501 Couzens, E Detroit, MI 48021
George Cairo, 313-445-4494
E Detroit District

Gateway Montessori School
32605 W Bellvine Tr, Bervery Hills, MI 48025
Mary Jo Meagher

Breakfast Club
45 E Pearl, Hazel Park, MI 48030
Ira Lax, 313-398-6568
Hazel Park District

Huron Valley Alternative High School
5061 Duck Lake Rd, Highland, MI 48031
Eldon Vanspybrook, 313-684-8298
Huron Valley District

Novi Northville Montessori (1984)
6561 Tamerlane, W Bloomfield, MI 48033
Geetha Rao, Adm, 810-348-3033
Tuition: $200/365/wk

3 teachers, 8 assistants, 70 students, mainly international,
  ages 3-6
Accreditation: AMS
Governance by an administrator and democratic school
  meeting
Language; math; geography; science; music; art; French;
  childcare; interns accepted.

Dropout Prevention Program
35200 Little Mack, Mt Clemens, MI 48043
Stephanie Majid, 313-553-0175
Clintondale District
Type: public at-risk

Montessori Stepping Stones
19 Byron Ct, Mount Clemens, MI 48043-5518

Chippewa Valley Adult Education
42755 Romeo Plank, Mt Clemens, MI 48044
Bonita Myrand, 313-286-7638
Chippewa Valley District

Alternative Education Program
24062 Taft, Novi, MI 48050
Dennis Lampron, 313-344-8300
Novi District

Upland Hills School (1971)
2575 Indian Lake Road, Oxford, MI 48051
Phillip Moore, Director, 313-693-2878, FAX: 313-693-1021
Oakland County
Type: independent, non-profit; tuition: $4020
9 teachers, 75 students, ages 4-14, K-8th grade
Governance by teachers and principal, board
Encourages students to develop the tools of self-awareness;
  celebrates the natural world; places emphasis on creative
  and performing arts; attempts to promote, foster, nurture
  and defend childhood; multi-aged classes; extensive field
  trips; rural location; interns accepted.

Kennedy Center
1541 N Saginaw, Flint, MI 48053
Susan Richvalsky, 313-760-1371
Flint District

Perdue High School
25 S Sanford, Pontiac, MI 48058
Rosevelt Daniel, 313-857-8376
Pontiac District

Secondary Alternative Program
600 Motor St, Pontiac, MI 48058
Linda Phillips, 313-857-8321
Pontiac District

Alternative Center for Education
1440 John Rd, Rochester, MI 48063
Rob Roy, 313-652-6799
Rochester District

Enterprise High School (1983)
175 Croswell, Romeo, MI 48065
Mary Tewksbury, Coord, 810-752-0312, FAX:-0228
Macomb County
Type: public choice
4 teachers, 50 students, mainly former dropouts, ages 16–21
No residency requirement
Governance by teachers, principal
Teacher qualifications: certification
Classes run like small businesses; students decide on products, prices, profits; multi-aged classes

Romeo Montessori Center (1977)
PO Box 414, Romeo, MI 48065
Susan Parker, 313-752-4411
Tuition: $165-385/mo
4 teachers, 4 assistants, 80 students, ages 3–6
Affiliations: AMS, MI MS
Childcare; interns accepted.

Holy Innocents
226200 Ridgemont, Roseville, MI 48066
Type: Montessori

Project IDEAL
16221 Frazho, Roseville, MI 48066
Richard Rinnan, 313-445-5711
Roseville District

Montessori Children's Center
18720 E 13 Mile Rd, Roseville, MI 48066-1326

Opportunity Center
739 S Washington, Royal Oak, MI 48067
Jonathan Young, 313-398-8603
Royal Oak District

Little Learners' Montessori Center
814 N Campbell Rd, Royal Oak, MI 48067-2125

At Risk-Addams Junior High
1123 Lexington, Royal Oak, MI 48073
Stan Pikos, 313-288-3100
Royal Oak District

Royal Oak Teen Parent Program (1987)
1123 Lexington Blvd, Royal Oak, MI 48073
Sue Beyerlein, 810-288-1411
Oakland County
Type: public at-risk
5 teachers, 24 students, ages 15–19, 9–12th grade
No residency requirement
Governance by principal
Living room area; kitchen; nursery; parent spends time with baby daily; suburban location; interns accepted.

Sterling Heights High School-ISS/Re-Entry
12901 Fifteen Mile Rd, Sterling Hts, MI 48077
Daniel Schafer, 313-939-5900
Warren District

Montessori School of St Clair
955 Fred Moore Hywy, St Clair, MI 48079
Diane Judson

Little Learners Montessori
22418 Grove Pointe St, St Clair Shores, MI 48081-1626

Born Alternative High School
23340 Elmira, St Clair Shores, MI 48082
313-296-8350
Lakeshore District

Enterprise High School
23055 Masonic, St Clair Shores, MI 48082
Laurie Kinch, 313-296-8219
St Clair Shores District

REACH (1983)
28500 Alden St, Madison Hts, MI 48083
Ruth Turner, Coord, 313-545-5585, FAX: 545-0112
Oakland County
Type: public at-risk
4 teachers, 70-80 students, ages 16-20, 10–12th grade
Entrance requirements: age 16, interview, recommendation; no residency requirement
Governance by teachers, principal
Teacher qualifications: certification
Community service agencies networking; team-building; cooperative learning; problem-solving activities; initiatives course; camping experience; multi-aged classes; interns accepted.

Troy Montessori
3950 Livernois Rd, Troy, MI 48083-5036

Maria Montessori Center
3813 Finch Rd, Troy, MI 48084-1670

Northgrove Academy
3423 Auburn Rd, Utica, MI 48087
George Cole, 313-254-8390
Utica District

New Potentials Alternative High School
615 N Pontiac, Walled Lake, MI 48088
V Gibbons, 313-624-0202
Walled Lake District

Mott High School-ISS Program
3131 12 Mile Rd, Warren, MI 48092
Margaret Kekovich, 313-751-2110
Warren District

Troy Adult-Community Education
201 W Square Lake, Troy, MI 48098
Cathy Pello, 313-879-7582
Troy District

Montessori Children's Learning Center
4141 Laurence, Allen Park, MI 48101
Jeannette B Vickery, 313-382-2777
7 teachers, 16 assistants, 165 students, ages 3–9
Affiliations: AMS, MI MS
Governance by administrator
Basic skills; art; music; gym; Spanish; choir; private and group music lessons available; childcare; interns accepted.

Rudolf Steiner School of Ann Arbor (1980)
2775 Newport Rd, Ann Arbor, MI 48103
Sha W. Buikema, Adm, 313-995-4141
Washtenaw County
Type: Waldorf, non-profit; tuition: $4,500-4,600/yr, scholarships
30 teachers; student ages 4-14, pre K-8th grade
Entrance requirements: interview
Affiliations: AWSNA, AIMS
Governance by faculty, administrators, parents, community members board
Teacher qualifications: college degree, Waldorf training
Global understanding; suburban location; interns accepted.

Peach Tree Montessori Preschool Workshop
319 N Ashley St, Ann Arbor, MI 48103-3305

Clonlara School (1967)
1289 Jewett St, Ann Arbor, MI 48104
Barb Maling, Campus School Coordinator, 313-769-4511, FAX:
   313-769-9629
Washtenaw County
Type: independent, non-profit; tuition: $3000/yr
4 teachers, 40 students, ages 4-19, pre K-12th grade
Affiliations: NCACS, Clonlara HBEP
Governance by democratic school meeting
Teacher qualifications: love of young people; willingness to
   work on self; creative.
Classes are formed only by mutual agreement among equal
   parties; teachers are models, resources, more than instructors; community built among free, autonomous individuals of all ages; no letter grades; non-compulsory class
   attendance; multi-aged classes; extensive field trips; urban
   location; interns accepted.

Clonlara School Home Based Education Program (1967)
(See Resource Appendix)

Community High School (1992)
401 N Division St, Ann Arbor, MI 48104
Robert A. Galardi, Dean, 313-994-2021, FAX:-0042
Washtenaw County
Type: public choice
30 teachers, 388 students, ages 14-18, 9-12th grade
Governance by principal
Creative curriculum; community based; student support;
   student input; extensive field trips; multi-aged classe;
   interns accepted.

Family Consultation Services
201 N Ashley #2, Ann Arbor, MI 48104
Sally E Wisotzkey, 313-747-9191

Plymouth Salem High School
46181 Joy Rd, Canton, MI 48104
Debby Cocoros, 313-451-6600
Plymouth-Canton District

Gay-Jay Montessori School
1128 White St, Ann Arbor, MI 48104-3741

Michelle Norris Montessori School
1122-1128 White St, Ann Arbor, MI 48104-3741

Law Montessori School
1150 Rosewood St, Ann Arbor, MI 48104-6227

Daycroft Montessori
100 Oakbrook Dr, Ann Arbor, MI 48104-6703

Go Like the Wind! Montessori School (1987)
3540 Dixboro Ln, Ann Arbor, MI 48105
Karl W. Young, Prin, 313-747-7422
Tuition: $2,185-3,795/yr
4 teachers, 3 assistants, 90 students, ages 3-12
Accreditation: AMS
Governance by administrator
Custom designed Montessori CAI; one computer/3 students;
   moral environment; childcare; rural location; transporta-
   tion; interns accepted.

Oak Trails School and Children's House (1956)
6561 Warren Rd, Ann Arbor, MI 48105
Kathryn Cote, Adm Asst, 313-662-8016
Type: Montessori, non-profit
3 teachers, 57 students, ages 2.5-13, pre K-8th grade
Entrance requirements: min age 2.5 and toilet trained
Affiliation: AMS
Teacher qualifications: Montessori or state certification
44 acres of old-growth hardwood; weekly field trips to
   YM/YWCA for swimming; suburban location; transporta-
   tion; interns accepted.

Modern Montessori & Nursery School
2250-60 Nixon Rd, Ann Arbor, MI 48105-1418

Aristoplay, Ltd
(See Resource Appendix)

Livingston Montessori Center
1381 S Old US 23, Brighton, MI 48116

Phoenix High School
7380 Teahen Rd, Brighton, MI 48116
Bill Lymangrover, 313-231-1810
Brighton District

Brighton Montessori School
1385 S Old US 23, Brighton, MI 48116-7608
Marge Arnott

Dearborn Heights Montessori Center (1972)
4950 Madison, Dearborn Heights, MI 48125
Kay Neff, Adm, 313-291-3200, FAX: 313-562-2239
Non-profit; tuition: $2,325-4,500/yr
9 teachers, 20 assistants, 250 students, ages 3-12
Affiliation: AMS
Governance by teachers and administrators
Classic Montessori approach; French; music; art; PE; child-
   care; suburban location; interns accepted.

Altra
4824 Lois, Dearborn, MI 48126
Terrence Campbell, 313-582-4075
Dearborn District

Dundee Alternative High School
144 1/2 Main St, Dundee, MI 48131
Janet Smith, 313-529-3916
Dundee District

Garden City Alternative Education
1333 Radcliff, Garden City, MI 48135
Mark H Gutman, 313-425-4900
Garden City District

Cherry Hill Alternative
28500 Avondale, Inkster, MI 48141
Bill Richardson, 313-722-1662
Wayne-Westland District

Montessori Center of Our Lady
36800 Schoolcraft Rd, Livonia, MI 48150-1115

Oasis
20155 Middlebelt, Livonia, MI 48152
Rose Govig, Cont Ed Mgr, 313-473-8933, FAX:-8932
Wayne County
Type: public choice
4 teachers, 40 students, mainly at-risk, ages 16-20, 9-12th
   grade
Entrance requirements: referral, age 16+, no residency
   requirement
Governance by teachers, principal
Teacher qualifications: certified, experienced
Self-paced; individualized; team teaching; behavioral and aca-
   demic contract; multi-aged classes

Livonia Montessori Center (1972)
32765 Lyndon St, Livonia, MI 48154
Kay Neff, Adm, 313-427-8255, FAX: 313-562-2239
Non-profit; tuition: $2,325-4,250/yr
3 teachers, 6 assistants, 90 students, ages 2.5-6
Affiliation: AMS
Governance by teachers and administrators
Classic Montessori approach; French, music specialists; child-
   care; suburban location; interns accepted.

Jefferson Schools
2400 N Dixie Hwy, Monroe, MI 48161
T Fitzpatrick, Asst Supt
Type: Montessori

Meadow Montessori School
502 W Elm Ave, Monroe, MI 48161-2833
Meg Fedorowicz

Montessori Children's House
PO Box 155, Monroe, MI 48166

Hines Park Montessori School
45801 W Ann Arbor Rd, Plymouth, MI 48170

New Morning School (1973)
14501 Haggerty Rd, Plymouth, MI 48170
Elaine Yagiela, Exec Dir, 313-420-3331
Wayne County
Type: independent, non-profit
10 teachers, 108 students, ages 3-14, pre K-8th grade
Entrance requirements: classroom visit, meeting
Governance by parent cooperative and executive director
Teacher qualifications: state certification
Individual child's needs come first; responsibility. self esteem, positive relationships encouraged; students learn to evaluate information, problem-solve, set and attain goals; multi-aged classes; suburban location; interns accepted.

Northville Montessori Center
15709 Haggerty Rd, Plymouth, MI 48170
Lynn Gall, Adm, 313-420-0924
4 teachers, 79 students, ages 3-12
Affiliations: MIMS, AMS
Governance by an administrator
Large campus; nature study; Japanese; childcare; suburban location; interns accepted.

West Middle School Alternative Education
44401 W Ann Arbor Trail, Plymouth, MI 48170
Renee Eley, 313-451-6573
Plymouth-Canton District

Michigan Montessori Society, c/o Northville Montessori Center
15709 N Haggerty Rd, Plymouth, MI 48170-4861
Anne Carson

Cory Elementary
35200 Smith Rd, Romulus, MI 48174-1604
Type: Montessori

South Lyon High School
1000 N Lafayette, S Lyon, MI 48178
Kerry Pendell, 313-437-2031
S Lyon District

Titan Alternative Program
9551 Westlake, Taylor, MI 48180
Dale Avery, 313-295-5738
Taylor District

Plymouth Canton Montessori School
45245 Joy Rd, Canton, MI 48187-1772

Wyandotte Alternative Education
4460 18th St, Wyandotte, MI 48192
Angela Pascuzzi, 313-246-8366
Wyandotte District

Montessori Children's Learning Center
17188 Fordline St, Riverview, MI 48192-7543

Creative Montessori Center
15500 Howard St, Southgate, MI 48195-1610

Montessori Center of Downriver
14151 Trenton Rd, Southgate, MI 48195-1936

Roberto Clemente Student Development Center (1974)
4377 Textile Rd, Ypsilanti, MI 48197
Joseph Dulin, Prin, 313-434-4611
Washtenaw County
Type: public at-risk

7 teachers, 60-80 students, ages 14-19, 8-12th grade
Entrance requirements: committee screening, interview, district residency
Affiliation: Ann Arbor Public Schools
Teacher qualifications: MI certification
Weekly rap sessions; teacher visits home; breakfast daily; six mandatory classes; no letter grades; multi-aged classe; interns accepted.

Spencer Home Learning Center
1717 Gregory, Ypsilanti, MI 48197
313-485-3548
Washtenaw County
Student ages 4-10
Certified teacher; consulting; informal assessments; private tutoring; resource center; program planning; suburban location.

New Center Montessori School
8007 2nd Ave, Detroit, MI 48202-2403

Highland Park Alternative High School
13321 Hamilton, Highland Park, MI 48203
Glenn A Holman, 313-252-0492
Highland Park District

Montessori Children's House of Martyrs of Uganda County
4317 Blaine St, Detroit, MI 48204-2301

Childhood Center, Inc
20210 Schoenherr St, Detroit, MI 48205-1108
Type: Montessori

Friends School in Detroit
1100 S Aubin Blvd, Detroit, MI 48207
Gail Thomas, Head, 313-259-6722, FAX: 313-259-8066
Type: Quaker, non-profit; tuition: $5,000/yr, scholarships
18 teachers, 125 students, ages 4-14, pre K-8th grade
Affiliation: Quaker
Governance by principal
Teacher qualifications: MI certification
Whole language; experiential; thematic studies; cooperation and peaceful conflict resolution; no letter grades; interns accepted.

Greater Detroit Montessori Center
900 North Ave, Detroit, MI 48207

Sunshine Montessori School
1519 Martin Luther King Jr Blvd, Detroit, MI 48208-2867

Rose Open School
5830 Field, Detroit, MI 48213
Joan Nagrant, 313-245-3673
Type: magnet
Pre K-5th grade
Open School.

Area E Open Magnet Middle School
2301 Van Dyke, Detroit, MI 48214
Michael Bartley, 313-245-3932
6-8th grade
Open Magnet Middle.

Bates Academy
Detroit, MI 48214
Beverly Gibson, 313-494-7000
Type: magnet
Pre K-8th grade
Gifted and talented.

Detroit Waldorf School
2555 Burns Ave, Detroit, MI 48214
Francina Graef

Detroit Open School
24601 Frisbee, Detroit, MI 48219
Laurajean Milligan, 313-533-1525
Type: magnet
K-8th grade

Alternative Education
162 W Hazelhurst, Ferndale, MI 48220
Gary Diehl, 313-546-6832
Ferndale/Oak Park District

Ferndale Montessori Center
400 W Marshall St, Ferndale, MI 48220-2419

Giving Tree Montessori School
4351 Marseilles St, Detroit, MI 48224-1481

Greater Grace Education Center
18940 Schaefer Hwy, Detroit, MI 48235-1763
Type: Montessori

Grosse Pointe Academy, Early and Lower Schools
171 Lake Shore Rd, Grosse Pointe Farms, MI 48236-3793
Camille DeMario
Type: Montessori

Deror Montessori Center
24061 Coolidge Hwy, Oak Park, MI 48237-1654

Acadia Montessori (1980)
1515 S Woodward, Bloomfield Hills, MI 48302
Delvita DiMichele, Adm, 335-7070
Tuition: $1,900-3,975/yr
64 students, ages Infant-9
Entrance requirements: application; $50 fee; $100 tuition
    deposit.
Accreditation: AMS
Governance by administrator
Music; gymnastics; French; computers; childcare; urban loca-
    tion; interns accepted.

Oakland Steiner School (1989)
1050 Square Lake Rd, Bloomfield Hills, MI 48304
Noemi Schaffa, Adm, 313-646-2540, FAX: 313-643-8316
Oakland County
Type: Waldorf, non-profit; tuition: $5,075/yr, scholarships
8 teachers, 84 students, ages 3-12, pre K-6th grade
Entrance requirements: teacher's acceptance
Affiliation: AWSNA
Governance by faculty and board
Teacher qualifications: MI, Waldorf certification or equivalent
Suburban location; interns accepted.

Kensington Academy Montessori Program
1020 E Square Lake Rd, Bloomfield Hills, MI 48304-1957
Sherry Bass

Bloomfield Hills Montessori Center (1972)
2101 Opdyke Rd, Bloomfield Hills, MI 48304-2216
Dot Feaheny, Laura Plotchan, Adm, 313-338-1166
Tuition: $2,991-4,882/yr
5 teachers, 9 assistants, 65 students, ages infant-12
Entrance requirement: parental interest in understanding
    Montessori
Affiliation: AMS
Governance by an administrator
Childcare; suburban location; interns accepted.

Avon Montessori Center
596 Willard Ave, Rochester Hills, MI 48307-2360

Daffodils Montessori & Day Care
879 W Auburn Rd, Rochester Hills, MI 48307-4901

Meadowbrook Montessori Center
151 Grosse Pines Dr, Rochester, MI 48309-1829

Messmore Education Center
8742 Dill Dr, Sterling Heights, MI 48312-1235
Ms Stacherski
Type: Montessori

Walsh Elementary School
38901 Dodge Park Rd, Sterling Heights, MI 48312-1323
Type: Montessori

Utica Montessori Program
53800 Mound Rd, Utica, MI 48316-1727

Ward Homeschool Fellowship
6734 Edinborough, W Bloomfield, MI 48322
Gene & Robin Newman, 313-626-8431
Livonia County

Bloomfield Maples Montessori
6201 W Maple Rd, West Bloomfield, MI 48322-2171
Usha Mangrulkar

Brookfield Academy
2965 Walnut Lake Rd, West Bloomfield, MI 48323-3757
Judith Scott
Type: Montessori

Mrs Mary's Montessori School
6350 Commerce Rd, West Bloomfield, MI 48324-2710

Avondale Adult Alternative Education
2950 Waukegan, Auburn Hills, MI 48326
Claire Collins, 313-852-5303
Avondale District

Discovery 21 (1989)
1415 Crescent Lake Rd, Waterford, MI 48327
Wayne Malin, Prin, 313-673-1241
Oakland County
Type: public choice
4 teachers, 75-100 students, ages 17-21, 9-12th grade
Governance by teachers and principal
Teacher qualifications: MI certification
HS completion; internships with local businesses; self-
    esteem; teen parenting; student-operated store.

Laurel Montessori School
2490 Airport Rd, Waterford, MI 48327-1210

Montessori Center of Farmington Hills
29001 W 13 Mile Rd, Farmington, MI 48334-2504

Farmington Alternative Academy
33000 Thomas, Farmington, MI 48336
Diane Duthie, 313-489-3827
Farmington District

Marillac
30415 Shiawassee, Farmington, MI 48336
Terry Klenczar, 313-489-3333
Farmington District

STRIVE Alternative High School (1983)
5275 Maybee Rd, Clarkston, MI 48346
Kathryn Larkin, CSW, 810-674-0993
Oakland County
Type: public choice/at-risk
6 teachers, 100 students, mainly at-risk, ages 16-19, 10-12th
    grade
Entrance requirements: interview, recommendation, no resi-
    dency requirement
Governance by teachers and principal
Teacher qualifications: certification
Suburban location.

Oxford TLCA Options
105 Pontiac St, Oxford, MI 48371
Karen J Eckert, 313-628-9220
Oxford District

Oxford Montessori Center
775 E Drahner Rd #167, Oxford, MI 48371-5315

Highland Montessori School
4501 Highland Rd, Milford, MI 48380
Lee Johnson

Milford Montessori School
2700 W Commerce Rd, Milford, MI 48380-3208

Middle School Alternative Education
8500 Commerce Rd, Commerce Twp, MI 48382
Judith G Leggett, 313-363-8189
Walled Lake District

Lakes Area Montessori
8605 Richardson Rd, Walled Lake, MI 48390-1362

SAFE (Sanilac Alternative for Education)
4290 Second St, Brown City, MI 48416
Daniel Reardon, 313-346-2781
Brown City District

Clio's BEST Alternative Education (1988)
430 N Mill St, Clio, MI 48420
Brenda S. May, Supervisor, 810-687-8198
Genesee County
Type: public at-risk
9 teachers, 70 students, mainly teen parents, ages 13-19,
   9-12th grade
Entrance requirements: referral, interview
Governance by teachers, principal, parent cooperative
Teacher qualifications: MI certification
Applied math for industries; journalism class produces bi-
   monthly newsletter, yearbook; prom; community service
   requirement; fund raiser; multi-aged classes; extensive
   field trips; childcare; interns accepted.

Montessori Academy
PO Box 52, Davison, MI 48423-0052

Durand Success Bound
310 N Saginaw, Durand, MI 48429
Ralph Kohn, 517-288-4245
Durand District

Owosso Alternative Education (1990)
120 Michigan Ave, Owosso, MI 48429
Shirley McNier, Coord, ?-723-5598
Shiawassee County
Type: public choice, boarding
7 teachers, 65 students, mainly at-risk, ages 16-18
Enrollment restricted to resident HS dropouts age 16+;
   limited SE services
Affiliation: MAEO
Governance by principal, faculty, student reps, board
Teacher qualifications: secondary certification
Electives; Glasser's control theory; reality therapy for behavior
   control; hands-on projects; volunteer work; suburban loca-
   tion; interns accepted.

Goodrich/Grand Blanc Community Education
11920 S Saginaw St, Grand Blanc, MI 48439
Kay Reed, 313-695-8534
Grand Blanc District

Grand Blanc MS Alternative Education
11920 S Saginaw St, Grand Blanc, MI 48439
Jim Gregory, 313-694-8211
Grand Blanc District

Mid-Michigan Homeschoolers
6109 Pebbleshire, Grand Blanc, MI 48439
313-695-0904
Genesee County

Heritage Home Educators (1989)
c/o Kander, 2122 Houser Rd, Holly, MI 48442
Lisa Hodge-Kander, Newsletter Editor, 313-634-4337
Oakland County
Non-profit
Parent meetings; family enrichment activities; children's pro-
   grams; newsletter.

Holly Alternative Education
111 College St, Holly, MI 48442
Dan Rolls, 313-634-4431
Holly District

East LaPeer County Alternative School
634 Borland Rd, Imlay City, MI 48444
Nick Johnson, 313-724-2200
Imlay City District

LaPeer Educational Alternatives Program (LEAP)
1025 W Nepessing St, LaPeer, MI 48446
Anthony Strump, 313-667-0115
LaPeer District

Montessori Children's Center
1100 W Newark Rd, Lapeer, MI 48446-9449

Montrose Alternative (1989)
300 Nanita Dr, Montrose, MI 48457
Mark W. Sands, 313-639-6131, FAX: 313-238-3864
Genesee County
Type: public at-risk
2 teachers, 25 students, ages 16-20, 9-12th grade
No residency requirement
Governance by teachers and principal
Teacher qualifications: Certification, experience
Flexible block schedule; multi-aged classes; rural location.

Mt Morris Alternative High School
8041 Neff Rd, Mt Morris, MI 48458
Lisa Revall, 313-687-0460
Mt Morris District

Lakeville/Millington Community Education
G-11107 Washburn Rd, Otisville, MI 48463-9731
Edward D Stone, 313-793-4843
Lakeville District

Sanilac Alternative for Education
147 Aitken, Peck, MI 48466
Juanita Clark, Coord, ?-648-4700
Sanilac County
Type: public choice
2 teachers, 14 students, 9-12th grade
Enrollment restricted to ages 16-20; no residency
   requirement
Governance by board and Community Ed Dir
Multi-aged classes; rural location.

Alpha Montessori School
701 Church St, Flint, MI 48502-1107

Schools of Choice
571 E Fifth St, Flint, MI 48503
Ed Thorne, 313-762-1390
Flint District

Montessori Children's House
1805 W Court St, Flint, MI 48503-3577
Ms Pitts

Forest Hill Montessori
2200 Forest Hill, Flint, MI 48504

Charity Day Care Center & Montessori School
4601 Clio Rd, Flint, MI 48504-1885

Kearsley Alternative High School
5340 N Genesee Rd, Flint, MI 48506
Terry Dawson, 313-736-1355
Kearsley District

Under 18 Program
1181 W Scottwood Ave, Flint, MI 48507
Denny Pickard, 313-235-2555
Bendle/Carman-Ainsworth District

Weston Early Childhood Education Center
2499 Cashin St, Burton, MI 48509-1123
Type: Montessori

Heritage High School/ Pass Program
3465 N Center Rd, Saginaw, MI 48603
Mary Jo Zuziak, 517-799-5790
Saginaw Township District

FORCE
440 S Ross, Beaverton, MI 48612
Rick Rees, 517-435-4148
Beaverton District

AIM Program
609 Summit St, Breckenridge, MI 48615
Jill Maylee, 517-842-3182
Breckenridge Schools District

MS Learning Center
431 N 4th St, Chesaning, MI 48616
Janet Emmendorfer, 517-845-3726
Chesaning Union District

Success Express (1987)
820 Vine St, Chesaning, MI 48616
Thomas Tihof, Comm Ed Dir, 517-845-7020, FAX:-3722
Saginaw County
Type: public at-risk
5 teachers, 43 students, ages 15–20, 9–12th grade
Entrance requirements: out of school or referral, residency
Governance by teachers, principal
Teacher qualifications: MI certification
Interns accepted.

Clare Alternative Education
306 Schoolcrest, Clare, MI 48617
Vaughn White, 517-386-3067
Clare District

COOL School
1400 N Bowery, Gladwin, MI 48624
Linda Northrop, 517-426-5491
Gladwin District

Harrison Alternative Education
224 W Main St, Harrison, MI 48625
Michele Sandro, 517-539-7194
Harrison District

Gateway Alternative Education
179 Cloverleaf Ln, Houghton Lake, MI 48629
Sue Milner, 517-422-6161
Houghton Lake District

Merrill Alternative Program
755 W Alice, Merrill, MI 48637
Cindy Komblevitz, 517-643-7093
Merrill District

Windover Enterprise High School
32 Homer Rd, Midland, MI 48640
517-832-0852
Midland County ISD District

Midland Montessori School
5709 Eastman Ave, Midland, MI 48640-2516

Montessori Children's House
5200 Jefferson Ave, Midland, MI 48640-2907

COOR Independent School District
11051 N Cut Rd, Roscommon, MI 48653
Jan Keith Farmer, 517-275-5137

Meridian Adult Education
3303 N M-30, Sanford, MI 48657
Dean Havelka, 517-687-7356
Meridian District

FORCE
960 S M-33, W Branch, MI 48661
Maryann North, 517-345-2855
W Branch District

Bay City Homeschooling Support Group
401 W Jenny, Bay City, MI 48706
517-893-7608

Bay-Arenac Alternative High School
1608 Hudson St, Essexville, MI 48732
Shelley Kennedy, 517-893-8811
Bay-Arenac ISD District

Whittemore-Prescott Alternative Connection
8970 Prescott Rd, Whittemore, MI 48770
Denise A Braun, 517-756-3530
Whittemore-Prescott District

Alternative Choices in Education (1981)
300 Republic Ave, Alma, MI 48801
Jan Gooding, Principal, 517-463-2488
Gratiot County
Type: public at-risk; tuition: $4,000/yr
4 teachers, 55 students, ages 15–22, 9–12th grade
Enrollment restricted to dropouts or referrals; no residency
   requirement
Affiliation: MAEO
Governance by faculty and student representatives
Teacher qualifications: state certification
School-operated silk screening business; multi-aged classes;
   rural location; transportation; interns accepted.

BASE (Belding Alternative School of Education)
300 Covered Village, Belding, MI 48809
Karen Barker, 616-794-0811
Belding District

Teen Age Parent Program (TAPP) (1984)
300 Covered Village Mall, Belding, MI 48809
Karen Barker, Prin, 616-794-1976 x319
Ionia County
Type: public at-risk
1 teacher, 20 students, ages 14–21, 9–12th grade
Governance by teachers, principal and board
Teacher qualifications: MI Certification
Nursery; rural location; transportation.

Alternative Education
115 E Main, Carson City, MI 48811
Greg Shook, 517-584-3300
Carson City-Crystal District

Corunna Alternative Education
106 S Shiawassee St, Corunna, MI 48817
D. Michael Haggerty, 517-743-4151
Corunna District

East Lansing High School (1905)
509 Burcham Dr, E Lansing, MI 48823
Celeste M. Crouch, Reading Consultant, 517-332-2545
Ingham County
Type: public choice
75 teachers, 1150 students, ages 13–18, 9–12th grade
Entrance requirements: completed 8th grade, residency
Governance by teachers, principal

Teacher qualifications: MI certification
On-going monitoring of interpersonal skills; individual, group
and teacher evaluations; evening classes; team teaching;
collaborative learning; multi-aged classes; interns
accepted.

The Montessori Center (1982)
469 N Hagadorn Rd, E Lansing, MI 48823
Loraine Friedl, Adm, 517-337-0674
Non-profit; tuition: $1,610/2,345/yr
2 teachers, 3 assistants, 55 students, mainly international,
ages 3-6
Affiliation: MIMS
Governance by an administrator and a board of trustees
Childcare; suburban location; interns accepted.

Haslett Alternative Education (1982)
6157 Rutherford, East Lansing, MI 48823
Susan Doneson, Supervisor, 517-337-1722
Ingham County
Type: public choice
8 teachers, 50 students, ages 14-19, 9-12th grade
Intended for pregnant, parenting teens
Governance by district community ed component
Teacher qualifications: MI certification
Teen parent support group; community referrals and net-
working; multi-aged classes; extensive field trips; childcare.

Eaton Rapids Alternative Education
208 King St, Eaton Rapids, MI 48827
Devin Pringle, 517-663-3510
Eaton Rapids District

Enterprise High School
2045 Bradley Rd, Fowlerville, MI 48836
Linwood Hibbard, Dir, 517-223-9556, FAX: 223-8754
Fowlerville District
Type: public at-risk
4 teachers, 60 students, mainly at-risk, ages 16-20, 9-12th
grade
No residency requirement
Governance by teachers, principal, democratic school
meeting, board
Teacher qualifications: certification or annual authorization
No letter grades; multi-aged classes; non-compulsory atten-
dance; school-to-work program; employability skills; men-
torships; community service; rural location.

Grand Ledge Alternative Education
112 W Scott, Grand Ledge, MI 48837
Laura Wyble, Sam Ortiz, 517-627-4702
Grand Ledge District
Type: public at-risk
2 teachers, 30 students, ages 16-18, 9-12th grade
students must agree with expectations, screening committee, residency required
Governance by faculty and student representatives
Teachers qualifications: MI cert
Family atmosphere; individual scheduling; computer facilities;
combined day care with student co-op; tutoring-mentor-
ing services.

Greenville Alternative Education
11691 S Greenville Rd, Greenville, MI 48838
Nancy Chambers, 616-794-1724
Greenville District

Alternative School
1509 Franklin Ave, Haslett, MI 48840
Dr Todd Dowrick, 517-339-2665
Haslett District

Holt Alternative Education
2169 N Cedar, Holt, MI 48842
J R Rauschert, 517-694-5780
Holt District, Ingham County
4 teachers, 60 students, ages 15-19, 9-12th grade
Referral; residency required
Affiliation: MAEO

School-Age Parent Program (1984)
415 N Barnard, Howell, MI 48843
Mari Docusen, Dir, 517-548-6348
Type: public at-risk
5 teachers, 12-15 students, ages 13-18, 7-12th grade
County residency required
Governance by advisory board and director
Teacher qualifications: BA in secondary education
Health class geared toward pregnancy issues; support group;
multi-aged classes; childcare; rural location.

Ionia Alternative Education
438 Union, Ionia, MI 48846
Mary Foy, 616-527-3530
Ionia District

Mason Alternative High School (1985)
1001 S Barnes St, Mason, MI 48854
Joe Kelly, 517-676-6498
Ingham County
Type: public choice
2 teachers, 20 students, mainly at-risk, ages 15-19, 9-12th
grade
Governance by faculty and student representatives
Teacher qualifications: MI certification
Suburban location.

Fulton Schools
8060 Ely Hwy, Middleton, MI 48856
Philip Garcia, 517-236-5130
Fulton District

Oasis High School (1986)
310 W Michigan, Mt Pleasant, MI 48858
Carol Meixner, 517-773-1383
Isabella County
Type: public at-risk
6 teachers, 160 students, ages 15-22, 9-12th grade
Entrance requirements: interview, residency
Governance by faculty and student representatives
Teacher qualifications: certification at secondary level
Personalized, family atmosphere; competency-based credit
every 3-wks; independent study; job shadowing/experi-
ence; interdisciplinary units; team teaching; mentorships;
non-compulsory class attendance; multi-aged classes;
urban location; interns accepted.

Odyssey High School (1988)
3441 S Wise Rd, Mt Pleasant, MI 48858
Raymond Yaklin, Lead Tch, 773-9473
Isabella County
Non-profit
5 teachers, 60 students, partly at-risk, ages 12-20, 7-12th
grade
Entrance requirements: referrals, residency
Affiliation: Shepherd PS
Teacher qualifications: MI certification
80 acres; multi-aged classes; extensive field trips; childcare
provided; interns accepted.

Binoojiinh Montessori
7070 E Broadway Rd, Mount Pleasant, MI 48858-8970
Leanne Barton

Okemos Montessori
2745 E Mount Hope, Okemos, MI 48864
Susan Cavanaugh

Michigan Montessori Internationale
2745 Mount Hope Rd, Okemos, MI 48864-2418

School Within A School
765 E North St, Owosso, MI 48867
Roger Elford, 517-723-8231
Owosso District

St Johns Alternative High School/Middle School
106 N Traver, St Johns, MI 48879
Ruth Wineman, 517-224-2224
St Johns District

Saranac Alternative Education (1986)
150 Pleasant St, Saranac, MI 48881
Susan Dunfee, Comm Ed Coord, ?-642-9232, FAX:-6850
Type: public choice/at-risk
1 teacher, 18 students, mainly at-risk, ages 16–21, 9–12th
   grade
Entrance requirements: application, interview; no residency
   requirement
Governance by teachers and principal
Teacher qualifications: secondary education certified
Social, personal, academic rehab; multi-aged classes; rural
   location; interns accepted.

Six Lakes Discovery Program
107 E Vota PO Box 148, Six Lakes, MI 48886
Terry Evanish, Dir, 517-365-3887, FAX:-3845
Montcalm County
Type: public at-risk
4 teachers, 62 students, ages 12–18, 7–12th grade
District residency required
Affiliation: MAEO
Governance by principal
Teacher qualifications: majors in subject area
Skill development; self-esteem; motivation; rural location;
   transportation; interns accepted.

Capitol Alternative School
1030 S Holmes, Lansing, MI 48912
Mike Hunter, 517-374-4223
Lansing District

Montessori Children's House of Lansing
2100 W St Joseph, Lansing, MI 48915
Suzanne M Husband

NEC Alternative
3131 W Michigan Ave, Lansing, MI 48917
Jane Rudisell, 517-484-1751
Potterville District

Waverly High School Alternative Education
5027 W Michigan, Lansing, MI 48917
Glenn Gross, 517-323-3831
Lansing District

Intensive Learning Center
1424 Gull Rd, Kalamazoo, MI 49001
Tom Noblet, 616-385-8523
Kalamazoo Valley ISD District

Youth Center School
1424 Gull Rd, Kalamazoo, MI 49001
Cathy Ampey, 616-385-8549
Kalamazoo Valley ISD District

Portage Alternative High School (1986)
1010 W Milham, Portage, MI 49002
Sarah Sult, 616-381-0393
Kalamazoo County
Type: public choice
30 teachers, 250 students, ages 16–19, 9–12th grade
Entrance requirements: application, interview; no residency
   requirement
Governance by teachers, principal, faculty and student reps
Teacher qualifications: MI certification
Critical thinking; parenting classes; "C" lowest grade assigned;
   multi-aged classes; extensive field trips; interns accepted.

Shamrock Montessori Center
7025 Rockford St, Portage, MI 49002-4119

Adventure Center at Pretty Lake
9301 W "R" Ave, Kalamazoo, MI 49007
Susan Brennan-Barnes, 616-375-1664

The Montessori School (1972)
750 Howard St, Kalamazoo, MI 49008
Pamela Boudreau, Head, 616-349-3248
Non-profit; tuition: $2,333-3,612/yr
6 teachers, 14 assistants, 144 students, ages 3–12
Affiliations: MAC, NAMTA, MIMS; accreditations: MIDSS, MIDE,
   MSS
Governance by administrator, board
Urban location; interns accepted.

Vine Street Alternative High School (1983)
604 W Vine St, Kalamazoo, MI 49008
Robert Horton, Prin, 616-337-0760
Kalamazoo County
Type: public at-risk
13 teachers, 180 students, ages 14–18, 7–12th grade
Enrollment restrictions: no SE; residency required
Affiliation: MAEO
Governance by teachers and principal
Multi-aged classes; urban location; transportation; interns
   accepted.

Kazoo School
1401 Cherry St, Kalamazoo, MI 49008-2278
616-345-3239
Type: public choice

Montessori Children's House
2424 Glenwood Dr, Kalamazoo, MI 49008-2406
Gertrude Palm Girr

South Ward School (1981)
550 Fifth St, Allegan, MI 49010
Ken Ebersole, Dir, 616-673-5433
Type: public choice
7 teachers, 75–100 students, mainly at-risk, ages 14+, 9–12th
   grade
Governance by teachers, principal
Teacher qualifications: MI certification
"Essential" school philosophy; performance exhibitions;
   interns accepted.

Bangor Alternative High School (1986)
309 S Walnut, Bangor, MI 49013
Patrick J. Conroy, Coord, 616-427-6861, FAX: 616-427-8274
Van Buren County
Type: public at-risk
8 teachers, 110 students, 9–12th grade
Enrollment restriction: no SE certified students
Affiliation: MI Alt Ed Org
Governance by teachers, principal
Teacher qualifications: MI certification
Emphasis on student preferences, teamwork, self-help; inte-
   grated alternative and adult HS; specialized classes;
   women's issues group; Aikido; computer, science lab;
   interns accepted.

Boynton Montessori School
1700 E Britain Ave, Benton Harbor, MI 49022-1604

**Benton Harbor Area Schools Montessori Magnet
  Program**
636 Pipestone St, Benton Harbor, MI 49022-4152

Brookview School
501 Zollar Dr, Benton Harbor, MI 49022-6429
Type: Montessori

Centreville Alternative Education
190 Hogan St, Centreville, MI 49032
John Hume, 616-467-5215
Centreville District

LaPetite Learning Center
86 S Clay St, Coldwater, MI 49036-1853
Matilda Hindbaugh
Type: Montessori

Coloma High School Alternative Education
PO Box 550, Coloma, MI 49038
Frances Pough, 616-468-2400
Coloma District

Comstock Adult Education
301 N 26th St, Comstock, MI 49041
Larry P Dopp, 616-388-9477
Comstock District

Enterprise Alternative School
PO Box 369, Comstock, MI 49041
Cam Davis, 616-388-9481
Comstock/Parchment District

Sundown Alternative High School
327 N Grove St, Delton, MI 49046
Louise Angelo, 616-623-9200
Delton Kellogg District

Dowagiac Schools Alternative Education (1986)
206 Main St, Dowagiac, MI 49047
Max Sala, Dir, 616-782-4470, FAX: 616-782-9748
Cass County
Type: public at-risk
3 teachers, 15 students, ages 14-18, 9-12th grade
Residency required
Governance by teachers and principal
Teacher qualifications: MI Certification
Multi-aged classes; rural location.

Otsego Alternative High School
538 Washington St, Otsego, MI 49078
Connie Pearson, 616-694-6333
Otsego District

Paw Paw Teenage Parent Program (1987)
313 W Michigan Ave, Paw Paw, MI 49079
Leslie Hainrihar, Coord, 616-657-8831
Van Buren County
Type: public choice
9 teachers, 50-65 students, ages 13-19, 7-12th grade
No residency requirement
Governance by discipline committee, coordinator, adult ed director
Teacher qualifications: certification
Food program; parenting; SE; vocational; agency referrals; open enrollment; diploma; childcare; rural location; transportation; interns accepted.

The Learning Corporation
101 S Main, Plainwell, MI 49080
Marvin G Simon, 616-685-8468
Plainwell District

Alternative Achievement Center
2214 S State St, St Joseph, MI 49085
Marge Camelet, 616-982-4624
St Joseph District

St Joseph Alternative Education (1989)
2521 Stadium Dr, St Joseph, MI 49085
Marjorie Camelet, 982-4622 x40
Berrien County
Type: public at-risk
2 teachers, 1 assistant, 26 students, ages 14-19, 9-12th grade
Residency required
Affiliation: MI Assn Ed Options
Governance by teachers; Principal
Re-designed each semester to meet students' needs; intra/interpersonal skills; multi-aged classes

South Haven Alternative Education (1978)
600 Elkenburg St, South Haven, MI 49090
Scott Raue or Cindy Liscow, Instructors, 616-637-0591
Van Buren County
Type: public at-risk
2 teachers, 25 students, ages 14-19, 9-12th grade
Entrance requirements: HS age; reports from all regular teachers, counselors, administrators, residency
Governance by teachers and principal
Teacher qualifications: certification in core curriculum offered
Self-contained classroom; contracts; independent study; team teaching; multi-aged classes; rural location; transportation; interns accepted.

Cooperative Learning Center (1989)
216 Vinewood, Sturgis, MI 49091
Lance Goodlock, Tch/Coord, 616-659-1586
St Joseph County
Type: public at-risk
3 teachers, 30 students, ages 14-19, 9-12th grade
Entrance requirements: interview, residency
Governance by teachers and principal
Rural location; transportation; interns accepted.

Three Rivers Adult Education (U-18)
1008 Eighth St, Three Rivers, MI 49093
Mimi Blake, 616-279-9581
Three Rivers District

Watervliet Alternative High School
E Red Arrow Hwy, Watervliet, MI 49098
Harry Borchert, 616-463-7173
Watervliet District

Bridgman Elementary School
3891 Lake St, Bridgman, MI 49106-9709
C Garbuschewski
Type: Montessori

Bass-Buchanan Alternative School System
401 W Chicago St, Buchanan, MI 49107
Monty D Bishop, 616-695-7711
Buchanan District

Brandywine Alternative School
1620 LaSalle, Niles, MI 49120
Dudley Garcia, 616-683-8805
Brandywine District

Cedar Lane Alternative Education (1989)
2301 Niles-Buchanan Rd, Niles, MI 49120
Jeneen Conway, Dir, 616-684-9554
Berrien County
Type: public choice and at-risk
4 teachers, 100 students, mainly at-risk, ages 14-19, 9-12th grade
Entrance requirements: director approval, not equipped for SE, district residency
Affiliation: Niles Community Schools
Governance by board
Teacher qualifications: certification
Self-esteem; goals; problem solving; development of socially acceptable behavior; cooperative learning; discipline with dignity; multi-aged classes; extensive field trip; interns accepted.

The Home School Manual, from Gazelle Publications (1976)
(See Resource Appendix)

Mid-High Option
4340 Walz Rd, Jackson, MI 49201
Debbie Osborne, 517-764-6010
E Jackson District

Northwest Adult/Community Education
6900 Rives Junction Rd, Jackson, MI 49201
Nancy Hay, 517-569-2240
Northwest District

Jackson Alternative School (1971)
766 Park Rd, Jackson, MI 49203
Donald R. Tassie, Prin, 517-784-3144
Jackson County
Type: public at-risk
10 teachers, 180 students, ages 12-20, 7-12th grade
No residency requirement
Governance by teachers and principal
Highly structured; clear expectations; multi-aged classes;
    urban location.

Maple City High School
410 E Maumee, Adrian, MI 49221
Lynn Hollosy, 517-265-4040
Adrian District

Montessori Children's House
1267 E Siena Heights Dr, Adrian, MI 49221-1755
Linda Salenbien

Starr Commonwealth Alternative Education
13725 Starr Commonwealth Rd, Albion, MI 49224
Herman J McCall, 517-629-5591
Calhoun ISD District

Columbia Options High School
4460 Northlake Rd, Clark Lake, MI 49234
Ralph B Piepkow, 517-524-9400
Columbia District

Hillsdale High School Alternative School
40 McCollum St, Hillsdale, MI 49242
Jerry Double, 517-439-1504
Hillsdale District

Homer Alternative Education
403 S Hillsdale, Homer, MI 49245
Rosemary Hahn, 517-568-4318
Homer District

Phoenix Alternative Secondary School
401 E Chicago St, Jonesville, MI 49250
Dennis Deeg, 517-849-7304

Family Learning Center
400 Kimball St, Leslie, MI 49251
Jean Ekins, 517-589-9102
Leslie District

Western Options Center
1400 S Dearing Rd, Parma, MI 49269
Richard Kalahar, 517-750-1009
Jackson Co Western District

Exceptional Training System
9960 Matthews Hwy, Tecumseh, MI 49286
Judy Edwards, 517-423-5982
Consulting to alternative schools.

Mecosta-Osceola Alternative High School
15760 190th Ave, Big Rapids, MI 49307
Bonnie Jacoby, 616-796-4410
Mecosta-Osceola District

Caledonia Options High School (1987)
330 Johnson, Caledonia, MI 49316
Jon Swets, Dir/Head Tch, ?-891-0236
Kent County
Type: public choice/at-risk
3 teachers, 70 students, ages 14-20, 9-12th grade
Enrollment restricted to SE; no residency requirement
Affiliation: MAEO
Governance by teachers and principal

Teacher qualifications: college, experience
Variety of learning styles; student-run restaurant; technol-
    ogy; languages; sports; field trips; suburban location;
    transportation; interns accepted.

Young Adult Program
204 E Muskegon St, Cedar Springs, MI 49319
Sandy Vanwingen, 616-696-1203
Cedar Springs District

North Kent Alternative High School
475 Six Mile Rd, Comstock Park, MI 49321
Diana M Trimberger, 616-784-9502
Comstock Park District

Northkent Learning Center
100 Betty St, Comstock Park, MI 49321
Debra Warwick, 616-361-7396
Northkent Consortium District

Loomis High School (1981)
360 S Mill St, Newaygo, MI 49337
Dick Smith, Prin, 616-652-6333
Type: public at-risk
6 teachers, 60-70 students, ages 14-21, 8-12th grade
Entrance requirements: interview, residency
Governance by faculty and student reps
Teacher qualifications: MI certificate
Utilizes area natural resources; mastery concept; interns
    accepted.

Genesis
PO Box 215, Remus, MI 49340
Martha Pety/Shelley Steele, 517-967-8471
Chippewa Hills District

Englishville High School
8285 Vinton NW, Sparta, MI 49345
Ken Willison, 616-887-7316
Sparta District

New Directions
1053 Aster St, Wayland, MI 49348
Coleen Young, 616-792-3072
Wayland Union District

Fennville Alternative Education
Memorial Dr, Fennville, MI 49408
Marc Zigterman, 616-543-3081
Fennville District

Hansen Montessori Child Development Center
5511 130th Ave, Fennville, MI 49408-9477

Fruitport Alternative Education
305 Pontaluna Rd, Fruitport, MI 49415
Annette Oleszczuk, 616-865-3114
Fruitport District

Lakeshore Alternative Education
300 N 6th, Grand Haven, MI 49417
Patricia Kratt, 616-847-4720
Grand Haven District

Options Alternative Education
6633 Lake Michigan Dr, Allendale, MI 49418
Dave Kail, 616-895-4353
Allendale District

Phoenix/Goals Alternative Schools (1980)
96 W 15th St, Holland, MI 49423
Jan Dalman, Assoc Dir/Adult Ed, 616-393-7600, FAX:-7615
Ottawa County
Type: public choice/at-risk
4 teachers, 75 students, mainly at-risk, ages 16-18, 9-12th
    grade
Entrance requirements: age 16, interview, screening for SE;
    no residency requirement

Governance by teachers and principal
Teacher qualifications: MI Certification, affective skills
Outcome Based Education; teen parenting; childcare; problem solving; caring for self/others; urban location; interns accepted.

Learning Tree Montessori School
370 Country Club Rd, Holland, MI 49423-7447

GOALS Teen Parent Program
411 Butternut Dr, Holland, MI 49424
Melissa Ramirez, 616-392-7818
Holland District

Holland Homeschool Group
17217 Riley, Holland, MI 49424
Sarah Aitken

Lakeside Montessori (1993)
411 Butternut, Holland, MI 49424
Ronan Young, 616-392-7009
Tuition: $2,700/yr
1 teacher, 20 students, ages 5–8
Governance by democratic school meeting
Multi-aged classes; urban location; interns accepted.

Dear Run Alternative
PO Box 186, Ludington, MI 49431
Thomas R McGill, 616-845-1213
Mason County Central District

Michigan Dunes Montessori (1981)
5248 Henry St, Muskegon, MI 49441
Claire Chiasson, Adm, 616-798-7293
Non-profit; tuition: $1,850-4,000/yr
5 teachers, 15 assistants, 145 students, ages infant-12
Affiliations: AMS, MIMS, NAEYC
Governance by an administrator
French instruction at all levels; nature trail constructed and maintained by 6-12 year-olds; childcare; suburban location; interns accepted.

Muskegon Alternative Center
417 Jackson, Muskegon, MI 49442
Greg Hazard, 616-726-5954
Muskegon District

Orchard View Alternative High School
2310 Marquette St, Muskegon, MI 49442
Bill Young, 616-744-5197
Orchard View District

Ravenna Alternative Education
2700 S Ravenna Rd, Ravenna, MI 49451
Susan J Sharp, 616-853-2228
Ravenna District

Blue Lake Fine Arts Camp
RR 2, Twin Lake, MI 49457
Type: Montessori

New Life Center
11 Cherry SE, Grand Rapids, MI 49503
Jim Botts, 616-771-2375

Vandenberg Creative Arts Academy
406 Lafayette SE, Grand Rapids, MI 49503
Sharon Altena, 616-456-4900
Type: magnet
Student ages 4+,-6th grade
Creative Arts.

Stepping Stones Montessori
1110 College Ave NE, Grand Rapids, MI 49503-1123

Grand Rapids Elementary School
143 Bostwick Ave NE, Grand Rapids, MI 49503-3201
Type: Montessori

Alternative Education
3950 Hendershot NW, Grand Rapids, MI 49504
Sandra K Greene, 616-784-2400
Kenowa Hills District

Excalibur Prep (1992)
1138 Pine NW, Grand Rapids, MI 49504
Janet Van Deusen, Prin, 616-771-2702
Kent County
Type: public at-risk
8 teachers, 150 students, ages 13-18, 8-12th grade
Entrance requirements: agency referral, immunizations, county residency
Affiliation: Grand Rapids Public Schools
Governance by teachers, principal
Teacher qualifications: MI teaching license
Special trips and activities; community volunteer activities; accomodates SE and special needs students; multi-aged classe; interns accepted.

Westbridge Academy
615 Turner NW, Grand Rapids, MI 49504
Walter Smith, 616-771-3240
Grand Rapids District

Northview Alternative High School
3801 E Beltline NE, Grand Rapids, MI 49505
Debra Warwick, 616-361-7396
Northview District

Wellerwood Montessori Academy
800 Wellerwood Ave, Grand Rapids, MI 49505
Carol Davis, 616-364-6763
Type: magnet
Student ages 4+,-K

Greenhouse Montessori (1989)
2023 E Fulton, Grand Rapids, MI 49506
Susan K. Brondyk, Adm, 459-3923
Non-profit; tuition: $1,800/yr
2 teachers, 1 assistant, 40 students, ages 3-6
Affiliations: AMS, MIMS
Governance by board
Children in Worship; urban location; interns accepted.

Congress Park Montessori Academy
940 Baldwin St SE, Grand Rapids, MI 49506-1429
Gordon Griffen

Ottawa Montessori
1515 Fisk Rd SE, Grand Rapids, MI 49506-6545

Climbing Tree School (1971)
256 Alger SE, Grand Rapids, MI 49507
Hildi Paulson, Director, 616-243-4763
Kent County
Type: independent, non-profit; tuition: $2,400/yr, scholarships
6 teachers, 85 students, ages 3-11, pre K-5th grade
Governance by board
Teacher qualifications: experience in similar program
Multi-cultural and environmental ed; parent participation required; hands-on; conflict resolution; Spanish; no letter grades; multi-aged classes; extensive field trips; urban location; transportation; interns accepted.

Young Adult Alternative High School-Godfrey Lee
1530 Grandville Ave, Grand Rapids, MI 49508
Gail Piland, 616-241-5600
Southkent Community Education District

Vision Quest High School (1983)
1324 Burton St, Wyoming, MI 49509
Susan Meyer, Dir of Adult & Comm Ed, 616-241-2661, FAX: 616-241-2664
Southkent Community Education District, Kent County
Type: public at-risk

8 teachers, 70 students, ages 15-19, 9-12th grade
Entrance requirements: must be 16 unless court referred, interview
Affiliation: none
Governance by board
Teacher qualifications: appropriate certification required
Basic knowledge and social skills; students learn to make informed decisions about political issues, lifestyles, and career planning; suburban location; transportation; interns accepted.

Wyoming Community Education
4334 Byron Ctr SW, Wyoming, MI 49509
Dan Diedrich, 616-530-7535
Type: public choice

Discovery High School (1979)
173 54th St SW, Wyoming, MI 49548
Sandra Wilkinson, Coordinator, 616-531-7433
Kent County
Type: public at-risk; tuition: for students under 16 yrs
6 teachers, 120 students, ages 15-18, 9-12th grade
Entrance requirements: referral by home district, residency
Affiliation: Southkent Comm Ed; Godfrey-Lee PS
Governance by principal, faculty, and student representatives
Teacher qualifications: subject area certification, experience with adolescents
Teacher serves as academic advisor/advocate; student board; fund-raising for yearly senior trip; cooperative learning; independent study; suburban location.

Pathfinders High School (1989)
3333 S Division, Wyoming, MI 49548
Susan Meyer, Dir of Adult & Comm Ed; Ila Dillinger, Program Supervisor, 616-241-2661, FAX: 616-241-2664
Kent County
Type: public at-risk
4 teachers, 90 students, ages 16-21, 9-12th grade
Entrance requirements: non-English speaking, interview, agency referral
Governance by board
Teacher qualifications: state certification
For immigrant/refugee students; ESL; basic skills; HS completion courses; suburban location; transportation; interns accepted.

Cooley Alternative School
221 Granite St, Cadillac, MI 49601
John Horrigan, 616-779-9380
Wexford-Missaugee ISD District

WMACTC
9901 E 36 Rd, Cadillac, MI 49601
Jim Sandborn, 616-779-8500
Wexford-Missaugee ISD District

Benzie Home Educators
PO Box 208, Benzonia, MI 49616

Crossroads Alternative High School
52 E Northern, Barryton, MI 49631
Jean Hartsell, 517-382-7285
Evart-Chippewa Hills District

Quest Alternative High School
101 1/2 S Main, Evart, MI 49631
Carol Wozcek, 616-734-3051
Evart-Chippewa Hills District

Mid-town Alternative
7741 Shippy Rd, Fife Lake, MI 49633
Mary Guy, 616-258-5140
Forest Area District

Umoja*Unidad*Unity (Homeschoolers of Color)
(See Resource Appendix)

Reed City Alternative Education (1990)
202 W Slosson, Reed City, MI 49677
Louis Stieg, Dir, ?-832-5517
Osceola County
Type: public at-risk
2 teachers, 24 students, ages 14-19, 8-12th grade
Residency required
Governance by teachers and principal
Community service; self-paced; outcomes based; no fail; job-readiness; behavior mod; self-esteem; multi-aged classes; outdoor adventure; rural location; interns accepted.

Montessori Children's House
PO Box 54, Suttons Bay, MI 49682
Gretchen Modrall, Adm, 616-271-3291
Non-profit; tuition: $2,350-3,100/yr
6 teachers, 6 assistants, 113 students, ages infant-6
Affiliations: NAMTA, MAC, AMI
Wooded setting; trout stream; gardens; wildlife; childcare; urban location; interns accepted.

Montessori Indian Preschool
1200 Ramsdell Rd, Traverse City, MI 49684-1451

Montessori Children's Center
6105 Center Rd, Traverse City, MI 49684-1923

Cheboygan Montessori East Elementary
PO Box 100, Cheboygan, MI 49721-0100

Presque Isle Children's House
719 N Bradley Hwy, Rogers City, MI 49779-1512
Type: Montessori

Sault Alternative High School
400 W Spruce St, Sault Ste Marie, MI 49783
Sault Ste Marie District

Amidon Alternative Programs
503 Norway St, Iron Mtn, MI 49801
Glady Nienstaedt, 906-779-2660
Iron Mtn District

James R. Fitz Harris High School (1979)
408 N 9th St, Gladstone, MI 49837
R Bruce Carlson, Dir, 906-428-3146, FAX: 786-9318
Type: public at-risk
6 teachers, 50-63 students, ages 15-21, 9-12th grade
Affiliation: MAEO; accreditation: NCASC
Governance by teachers, principal, democratic school meeting, board
Teacher qualifications: MI Certification
Multi-aged classes; outcome based; student input to curriculum; placement testing; rural location; interns accepted.

Bi County High School
111 E Ridge St, Marquette, MI 49855
J Howard Tamminen, 906-225-4323
Marquette District

Menominee Alternative School
2101 18th St, Menominee, MI 49858
Thomas Pichette, 906-863-5415
Menominee District

Learning Tree Resource Center
S Superior Rd RR 1 Box 80-B, Atlantic Mine, MI 49905
906-482-6393
Type: home-based·

Sunnyridge Alternative Learning Center
HCO 1 Box 134, Pelkie, MI 49958
Type: home-based

Minnesota

Center for Youth Development and Training
215 E 9th, St Paul, MN 55101
Phil Caliguiri, 612-228-3284
Type: public at-risk
Job skills; individualized; technology; counseling; childcare; transportation.

Southside Family School (1972)
2740 1st Ave S, Minneapolis, MN 35408
Flo Golod, 612-872-8322
Type: independent, non-profit
6 teachers, 52 students, ages 5–13, K–6th grade
Governance by board
Social justice; individualized; volunteer service; student advocacy; model for area educators; no letter grades; multi-aged classes; extensive field trips; interns accepted.

Home-Based Educators Accrediting Association
Rt 1 Box 381, Cambridge, MN 55008
Type: national home-based

Oak Land Area Learning Center
303 7th Lane NE, Cambridge, MN 55008-1269
Stephen G. Allen, 612-689-3344
Type: public at-risk
Holistic; evenings; middle level program at ALC, Braham, Cambridge, Princeton, St Francis: support services; parent involvement, education; individualized; advisors.

Montessori School of Cottage Grove
8177 S Hillside Tr, Cottage Grove, MN 55016

Faribault Alternative Evening High School
330 SW 9th Ave, Faribault, MN 55021
Jeffrey Selberg, 507-334-5527
Type: public at-risk
Students mainly employed, ages 16+
Mastery of math, reading required; accelerated learning; chemical dependency support groups.

Forest Lake Alternative Learning Center
6106 Scandia Trail N, Forest Lake, MN 55025
Dr Janet Palmer, 612-464-9343
Type: public at-risk
120 students, ages 13+
Emphasize self-esteem; different learning styles.

Minnesota Home School Network
9669 E 123rd, Hastings, MN 55033
612-437-3049
Type: state home-based

Montessori School of Hastings
1314 W 15th St, Hastings, MN 55033

Homeward
(See Resource Appendix)

Minnesota Valley Adult Diploma Program
17741 Juniper Path, Lakeville, MN 55044
Faith McCaghy, 612-469-7116
Type: public at-risk
Student ages 16+
Experiential; community based; flexible schedules; job shadowing; mentorships; career counseling.

Chisago Lakes Area Learning Center
29400 Olivda Trail, Lindstrom, MN 55045
Catherine Tschida, 612-257-1130
Type: public at-risk
Laubach Literacy tutoring; middle level program: support services; parent involvement; outcome based.

Forest Lake Montessori School
17126 Manning Tr, Marine on St Croix, MN 55047
Jane Norbin

Country Haven Montessori School
14878 Saint Croix Trail N, Marine on St Croix, MN 55047-9791

Mora Alternative Program
400 E Maple Ave, Mora, MN 55051
Kathy Koch, 612-679-2060
Type: public at-risk
Student ages 16+
Primarily independent study; work experience; job skills, business electives.

Intermediate School
320 Main St, North Branch, MN 55056
Lyle Koski, 612-674-7001
District 138
Type: magnet
4–5th grade
Creative arts; global studies; environment.

North Branch Area Lab School
North Branch, MN 55056
Mark Wolak, 612-674-5226
Type: public at-risk
Outcome based; issue-centered; middle level program: support services; parent involvement; youth service; personal, social skills; individualized; advisors.

Primary School
1108 1st, North Branch, MN 55056
Janice Fisher, 612-674-5270
District 138
Type: magnet
K–3rd grade
Creative arts; global studies; environment.

Northfield Alternative Learning Center
2nd and Orchard Streets, Northfield, MN 55057
David Bly or Karen Pownell, 507-633-0602
Type: public at-risk
100+ students, ages 16+
Independent study; work experience; teen parenting.

Prairie Creek Community School (1983)
27695 Denmark Ave, Northfield, MN 55057
Joanne Esser, teacher, 507-645-9640
Dakota County
Type: independent, non-profit
6 teachers, 100 students, ages 5–11, K–5th grade
Governance by teachers and principal, board
Teacher qualifications: strong foundation in child development
Thematic curriculum; cooperative learning; whole language; holistic assessment, including portfolios; strong parental participation through consensus model; no letter grades; multi-aged classes; extensive field trips; rural location; transportation; interns accepted.

Owatonna Alternative School
333 E School St, Owatonna, MN 55060
Ruth Russell, 507-451-4710
Type: public at-risk
Student ages 16+
Small groups; career counseling; tutoring; art; life, consumer skills; PE; nutrition/health; parenting; auto mechanics; wood shop.

St Mary's Montessori Center
122 E McKinley St, Owatonna, MN 55060-3326

Pine City Area Learning Center
1100 4th Ave, Pine City, MN 55063
Mary Jo Wittman, 612-629-3571
Type: public at-risk
Government studies; Laubach Literacy; middle level program: support services; parent involvement; youth service; personal, social skills; individualized; experiential.

Goodhue County DAC
1618 W 3rd, Red Wing, MN 55066
Type: Montessori

Montessori Preschool
240 Mississippi Ave, Red Wing, MN 55066

**Tower View Opportunity Program
Red Wing Technical College**
Highways 61 & 19, Red Wing, MN 55066
Robert L. Weir, 612-388-3595
Type: public at-risk
Student ages 16-20
Enrollment Requirement: passed grade 9 English, social studies.

Dakota County Area Learning Center (1989)
1400 E 145th St, Rosemount, MN 55068
Karen O'Brien, Dir, 612-423-8210, FAX: 612-423-1179
Type: public choice/at-risk
10 teachers, 92 students, ages 15-21, 10-12th grade
Entrance requirements: transfer, residency
Governance by board
Experiential; small classes; field trips; integration of vocational; multi-aged classes; rural location; interns accepted.

Rosemount Alternative Learning Center
14555 S Robert Tr, Rosemount, MN 55068
Shirley Gilmore, 612-423-7660
Type: public at-risk
Student ages 16-20
Affiliation: Dakota County Tech College
Student input into program; workshops on conflict resolution, goals, family issues; attendance incentives; intergenerational classes; community service; experiential.

South St Paul Area Learning Center
201 N Concord Exchange, South St Paul, MN 55075
Bill Zimniewicz, 612-450-9966
Type: public at-risk
Individualized; middle level program: support services; youth service; personal, social skills.

Providence School
785 17th Ave N, S St Paul, MN 55075-1429
Type: Montessori

New Heights Schools, Inc (1993)
614 W Mulberry St, Stillwater, MN 55082
Karen Garley, 612-439-1962
Type: public at-risk
200 students, ages 16-20, K-12th grade
Charter school.

Stonebridge
900 N Owens, Stillwater, MN 55082
John Johnson, Principal, 612-430-8386

Downtown Kindergarten Magnet School
Pioneer Building, 336 Robert, St Paul, MN 55101
Anne Rosten, 612-290-8372
ISD 625
Student ages 4+,-K
Work-place magnet.

Saturn School of Tomorrow
65 E Kellogg, St Paul, MN 55101
Paul Leverenty, 612-290-8354
District 625
Type: magnet
4-8th grade
Technology-based; personal groth; ungraded; community.

Jefferson Alternative
90 S Western Ave, St Paul, MN 55102
Don Sonsaela
Type: public choice

Cathedral Montessori
328 6th St W, Saint Paul, MN 55102-1997

MacDonald Montessori Childcare Center
175 Western Ave S, Saint Paul, MN 55102-2997

AGAPE
360 Colborne, St Paul, MN 55102-3299
612-228-7746
Career exploration; health and counseling services; vocational experience; personal skills; childcare.

Adams Montessori Magnet School
615 Chatsworth St S, Saint Paul, MN 55102-4038

Capital Hill Magnet School
560 Condordia Ave, St Paul, MN 55103
Robert Miller, 612-293-5918
ISD District 625
1-8th grade
Gifted and talented.

Jackson Preparatory Magnet School
437 Edmund Ave, St Paul, MN 55103
Louis Mariucri, 612-293-8650
ISD 625
K-6th grade
Life Long Learning.

Red School House
643 Virginia St, St Paul, MN 55103
Anne R. Mitchell, 612-488-6626
Students mainly Native American, all ages
Culture-based curriculum.

St Paul Area Learning Centers
590 University Ave, St Paul, MN 55103
Mary K. Boyd, 612-293-5900
Type: public at-risk
Student ages 12+
26 sites; vocational, career, work experience; CAI; independent study; community service; coop learning; outcome based; parent involvement.

Designs for Learning
(See Resource Appendix)

Evening High School Area Learning Center
275 N Lexington, St. Paul, MN 55104
Kenneth Taté, 612-293-5355
Student ages 16+
Evening classes; career exploration; work experience; personal skills; independent study.

EXPO Middle School
631 N Albert St, St Paul, MN 55104
Joan Sorenson, 612-293-5970
District 625

Type: magnet
6-8th grade
Learning theatre; ungraded.

Longfellow Humanities Magnet School
318 Moore St, St Paul, MN 55104
Juanita Morgan, 612-293-8725
ISD 625
K-6th grade
Humanities.

St Paul Expo Schools
449 Desnoyer, St Paul, MN 55104
Joan Sorenson, 612-644-2805

J. J. Hill Montessori Magnet (1986–87)
998 Selby Ave, St. Paul, MN 55104-6532
Dr Maria Calderon, Principal, 612-293-8720
Type: public
18 teachers, 6 assistants, 465 students, partly at-risk, ages
     3–12
Enrollment in upper grades requires prior Montessori
     experience
Affiliations: AMS, AMI, NAMTA
Governance by teachers and administrators, democratic
     school meeting
Urban location; transportation; interns accepted.

A Children's Place
1820 St Clair Ave, St Paul, MN 55105
Type: Montessori

Open School
1023 Osceola Ave, St Paul, MN 55105
Brad Manor, 612-293-8670
ISD 625
Type: magnet
K-12th grade
Open education.

Ramsey Junior High School
1700 Summit, St Paul, MN 55105
Dorothy LeGault, 612-293-8860
ISD 625
Type: magnet
7-8th grade
Gifted and talented; humanities.

St Catherine's Montessori (1931)
2004 Randolph Ave, St Paul, MN 55105
Cindy Scalia, Adm, 612-690-6608
Non-profit
Student ages 3–6
Affiliation: AMS
Governance by an administrator
Complete Montessori materials; 1:20 ratio; lab school; parents
     welcome; childcare; urban location; interns accepted.

American Indian Magnet School
1075 E 3rd St, St Paul, MN 55106
Cornel Pewewardy, 612-293-5938
ISD 625
K-8th grade
Native American Culture.

Cleveland Quality School
1000 Walsh St, St Paul, MN 55106
Larry Gallatin, 612-293-8880
District 625
Type: magnet
6-8th grade
Work with parents and students; success for all.

Face to Face Academy
1165 Arcade, St Paul, MN 55106
Leigh Anderson, 612-772-2539
Type: public at-risk

Student ages 12-20
Small classes; personal skills; support services; career explo-
     ration; challenge ed; health, prenatal care; mentors.

Cherokee Heights Pangea Ed Comm
694 Charlton St, St Paul, MN 55107
Christopher Canelake, 612-293-8610
District 625
Type: magnet
4-6th grade
PANGEA Educational Community.

Guadalupe Area Project
381 E Robie St, St. Paul, MN 55107
Allen Selinski, 612-222-0757
Students mainly at-risk, HS
Multi-cultural; individualized instruction.

Panger Educational Community School
160 E Isabel St, St Paul, MN 55107
Joan Rourke, 612-293-8655
District 625
Type: magnet
K-3rd grade
Part of cluster.

Riverview Panger Educational Center
271 E Belvidere, St Paul, MN 55107
Joan Schlen, 612-293-8665
District 625
Type: magnet
K-1st grade
PANGEA Educational Community.

Transition Plus
251 Starkey St, St Paul, MN 55107
Vernon Schultz, 612-293-5420
Students mainly SE needs, ages 18-21
Case managers; individualized plans focus on home living,
     community participation, leisure, world of work, post sec-
     ondary exploration.

622 Alternative High School (1972)
1945 Manton St, Maplewood, MN 55109
William R. Postiglione, Coord, 612-770-4745, FAX: 612-779-
     5845
Ramsey County
Type: public choice
11 teachers, 120 students, mainly at-risk, ages 16-21
Governance by board
Teacher qualifications: MN certification
Career counseling; no letter grades; interns accepted.

Growing Room
2555 Hazelwood, Maplewood, MN 55109
Type: Montessori

Little School of Montessori
1390 Larpenteur Ave E, St Paul, MN 55109-4524

Roseville Adult High School
1910 W County Road B, Roseville, MN 55110
Dorothy Henriksen, 612-631-2809
Students mainly out of school, ages 16+
Independent study model; self-paced; life experience credit;
     JTPA counseling; life skills; support groups; ELS; GED;
     childcare

LaPepiniere Montessori School, Inc
PO Box 11245, St Paul, MN 55111

Catholic Home School Newsletter
(See Resource Appendix)

Harbon Montessori School
2349 NW 15th St, New Brighton, MN 55112

Minnesota Waldorf School (1981)
2129 Fairview Ave N, Roseville, MN 55113
Carol-Jean Swanson; Jean Nelson, PR Coords, 612-636-6577
Ramsey County
Non-profit; tuition: $3,770-4,990/yr, scholarships
21 teachers; student ages 4-14, K-8th grade
Entrance requirements: visit, parent interview
Affiliation: AWSNA
Governance by faculty, parent council, board
Teacher qualifications: BA and 2-yr Waldorf training
Suburban location; interns accepted.

Kinderhaus Montessori School
3115 Victoria St N, Roseville, MN 55113-1935

States Educational Alternatives League (SEAL)
(See Resource Appendix)

Expo Excellence Magnet School
540 Warwick St, St Paul, MN 55116
Diana Swanson, 612-290-8384
ISD 625
K-6th grade
Ungraded; family; theatres of learning.

Highland Park Montessori School
1287 Ford Pkwy, St Paul, MN 55116-2259

NE Metro Area Learning Center
70 W County Rd B-2, Little Canada, MN 55117
Vernon Vick/Mike Donohue, 612-483-4427
Intermediate District #916
Type: public at-risk
Action-oriented; learning visuals; family units; student inter-
dependence; middle level program at ALC, Roseville MS:
support services; parent involvement; youth service.

Mississippi Creative Arts Magnet
1575 L'Orient St, St Paul, MN 55117
612-293-8840
ISD 625
K-6th grade
Creative Arts.

St Paul High School Evening Programs
Como High School, 740 Rose, St Paul, MN 55117
612-293-8800
Also located at Harding, 1540 E 6th St, 293-8900; Highland,
1015 S Snelling, 293-8940; Humboldt, 30 E Baker; Johnson,
1349 Arcade, 293-8990; Open School, 1023 Osceola, 293-
8670; individualized; counseling; vocational classes; work
experience; career exploration.

Twin Pines Montessori School
1919 Knob Rd, Mendota Heights, MN 55118

Mississippi Valley Montessori
1575 Charlton, St Paul, MN 55118

Creative Playhouse
1588 S Victoria Rd, Mendota Heights, MN 55118-3658
Type: Montessori

Families Nurturing Lifelong Learners
2452 Southcrest Av, Maplewood, MN 55119
Type: home-based

Woodbury Montessori School, Inc
1220 McKnight Rd, Maplewood, MN 55119

Boys Totem Town
398 Totem Rd, St Paul, MN 55119
Dave Ardoff, 612-292-6295
Boarding
Career exploration; work experience; year-round.

East Side Montessori
2019 Case Ave, St Paul, MN 55119

Nokomis Montessori/Developmental
985 Ruth St, St Paul, MN 55119
Elnore Battle, 612-293-8857
ISD 625
Type: magnet
Student ages 4+,-3rd grade
Childcare.

Highwood Hills School
2188 Londin Ln, Saint Paul, MN 55119-5393
Type: Montessori

Convent of the Vistation Montessori
2455 Visitation Dr, Mendota Heights, MN 55120-1696

Eagan Montessori & Child Care Center
1250 Lone Oak Rd, Saint Paul, MN 55121-2103

Cedar Alternative Center (1987)
2140 Diffley Rd, Eagan, MN 55122
Beverly Brucciani, Coord, 612-895-7429, FAX: 612-895-7297
Dakota County
Type: public choice/at-risk
7 teachers, 84 students, mainly at-risk, ages 16-21, 10-12th
grade
Entrance requirements: application; interview
Affiliation: ISD #191
Governance by faculty and student representatives, site
council
Teacher qualifications: secondary certification
Informal setting; parenting program; results oriented; small
group instruction; diploma program; suburban location.

Tesseract School
3800 Tesseract Pl, Eagan, MN 55122
Richard Dick, Executive Director, 612-454-0604
Pre K-6th grade

Sunny Hollow Montessori (1981)
225 Cleveland Ave S, St. Paul, MN 55122
Jeanette Meyer, Dir, 612-690-2307
Non-profit; tuition: $190-455/mo
3 teachers, 3 assistants, 70 students, ages 3-6
Affiliation: NAMTA
Governance by administrator, board
Childcare.

Lanka Trading
9129 Sequoia Bay, Woodbury, MN 55125
Bart Ratnayake
Type: Montessori

Woodview Terrace Montessori
6255 Upper Afton Rd, Woodbury, MN 55125

Mounds View Area Learning Center
4182 N Lexington Ave, Shoreview, MN 55126
Howard Dahl
Type: public at-risk
100 students
Communications; job, life skills; parent involvement; independent study; postsecondary scholarship; middle level
program: support services; individual skill learning.

Independence Montessori
850 South St, Anoka, MN 55303
Carol Landkamer, Adm; Charlotte Cushman, Dir, 612-427-3976
Tuition: $160/mo
1 teacher, 1 assistant, 50 students, ages 3-6
Entrance requirements: age 2-2.5; toilet trained
Accreditations: AMI, AMS
Suburban location; interns accepted.

Minnesota Association of Christian Home Educators
PO Box 188, Anoka, MN 55303
612-753-2370

Northern Lights School
3450 152nd Ln NW, Andover, MN 55304-3003
Type: Montessori

Wright Technical Area Learning Center
1400 Hwy 25 N, Buffalo, MN 55313
Julie Warner
Type: public at-risk
Open entry; teen parenting; 17 vocational programs; middle
    level program: support services; parent involvement; indi-
    vidualized; hands-on exploration.

Jonathon Montessori House of Children, Inc. (1968)
112050 Hundertmark Rd, Chaska, MN 55318
Randi Shapiro, Dir, 612-448-5232
Non-profit; tuition: $220-437/mo
3 teachers, 4 assistants, 48 students, ages 3-6
Entrance requirements: age 2.5-4
Governance by administrator, board
3 acres in semi-rural area; nature trails; committed parents
    and staff; childcare; interns accepted.

Scott County Area Learning Center
401 E 4th St, Chaska, MN 55318
Jeff Theis, 612-448-5787
Type: public at-risk
Holistic; vocational; mental health services; middle level
    program: support services; parent involvement; personal,
    social skills; home, independent study; work experience.

Elk River Area Learning Center
251 8th St, Elk River, MN 55330
Lynn Salisbury, 612-441-1003
Type: public at-risk
Independent study; CCP; middle level program at ALC, Salk
    JHS, VandenBerge JHS: support services; parent involve-
    ment; personal, social skills; individualized; advisors.

Hopkins High School Alternative Program
2400 Lindbergh Dr, Minnetonka, MN 55343
Scott Neiman, 612-593-3208
Hopkins School District 270, Hennepin County
Type: public at-risk
10-12th grade
Small group instruction; personal development focus; regular
    high school setting; core academic subjects; work experi-
    ence internship; vocational training.

Hopkins Montessori
3500 Willison Rd, Minnetonka, MN 55343

Prairie Center Alternative (PCA)
250 Prairie Center Dr, Suite 100, Eden Prairie, MN 55344
Doug Andrus, 612-941-7860
Intermediate District #287, Hennepin County
Student ages 16+
Independent study; extended year; community resources.

The International School of Minnesota
6385 Beach Rd, Eden Prairie, MN 55344
Nadia Reda, Head, 612-941-3500

High Point Montessori
9051 High Point Circle, Eden Priarie, MN 55344

Minnetonka Mini-School (1970)
18301 Hwy 7, Minnetonka, MN 55345
612-470-3574
Type: public at-risk
10-12th grade
Holistic; life, career, job skills; SE; men's, women's, and social
    issues groups; 3-18-day canoeing, bicycling, hiking; skiing;
    winter camping trips.

Ombudsman Educational Services, Ltd
6585 Edenvale Blvd #170, Eden Prairie, MN 55346
Laura Hauler, Director, 612-934-9791

Activities for Learning
(See Resource Appendix)

Crow River Area Learning Center
1200 Roberts Rd, Hutchinson, MN 55350
Jim Mills, 612-587-5939
Type: public at-risk
60 students
Open entry; attendance incentives; middle level program:
    support services; parent involvement; individualized.

Minnesota Homeschool Alliance
PO Box 281, Maple Plain, MN 55359
612-491-2828
Type: state home-based

Monticello High School Alternative Program
PO Box 897, Monticello, MN 55362
Robert Voecks, 612-295-2913
Type: public at-risk
10 students, ages 16-20
Outcome based.

Westonka Alternative Programs
5600 Lynwood Blvd, Mound, MN 55364
Larry Litman, 612-472-0280
Intermediate District #287, Hennepin County
Type: public at-risk
Student ages 12-20
Independent study; flex schedule; personal, career skills.

Student on a Rebound (SOAR) (1985)
317 2nd Ave NW, Osseo, MN 55369
LeRoy Putman, Prog Coord, 612-425-2323, FAX:-2702
Hennipen County
Type: public at-risk
9 teachers, 60 students, ages 16-21, 10-12th grade
No residency requirement
Affiliation: MN DE
Governance by teachers and principal
Teacher qualifications: BA/BS degree
No letter grades; childcare; multi-aged classes; suburban
    location; interns accepted.

Connections
County Rd 50, Box 70, Rockford, MN 55373
Peter Logas, 612-477-5846
Type: public at-risk
Student ages 12-20
Independent study; mentorships; individualized instruction;
    peer tutoring; conflict mgmt; drug ed; jobs; required com-
    munity service; parent involvement; accommodates
    behavior disorder students.

Dorothy's Daily Discoveries
1035 Bluff Ave E, Shakopee, MN 55379
Type: Montessori

Spring Hill Waldorf School
865 N Ferndale Rd, Wayzata, MN 55391
Brenda Fleisher, Tch, 612-473-2262
Hennepin County
Non-profit; tuition: 1,120-2,500/yr
2 teachers, 20 students, ages 3-6, pre K
Governance by parent cooperative and board.
Natural and handmade play materials; storytelling; nature
    activities; sewing; cooking; gardening; outdoor adventures;
    suburban location.

Deephaven Montessori School
18325 Minnetonka Blvd, Wayzata, MN 55391-3231

Loring Nicollet Alternative School
1925 Nicollet Ave, Minneapolis, MN 55403
Marin Peplinski, 612-871-2031
45 students, mainly at-risk, HS
10-12 students/class.

Urban League Street Academy
1911 Nicollet Ave S, Minneapolis, MN 55403
Marge Freeman or Richard Dillard, 612-874-9667
70 students, mainly at-risk, ages 16-21
City residency required.
HS diploma; computer programming; health; teen parenting;
    PE; urban location.

Child Garden Total Environment Montessori
1900 Nicollet Ave, Minneapolis, MN 55403-3746

Bryant Glenwood Montessori
4300 Bryant Ave N, Minneapolis, MN 55404

Center School, Inc
2421 Bloomington Ave S, Minneapolis, MN 55404
Paul Hegre, 612-721-1655
7-12th grade
Accredited
Small classes; counseling: individual, family, chemical depen-
    dency, career; student leadership; urban location.

Minneapolis Education & Employment Resource Center
2539 Pleasant Ave S, Minneapolis, MN 55404
Tyria Taylor Cobb, 612-872-8811
max 45 students, mainly at-risk, ages 15-21
Accredited
Emphasis on job-related skills, maintaining employment.

Harrison Open School
1500 4th Ave N, Minneapolis, MN 55405-1105
Type: Montessori

Jefferson Elementary
1200 W 26th St, Minneapolis, MN 55405-3541
Type: Montessori

Dowling School School
3900 W River Pkwy, Minneapolis, MN 55406
Jeffrey Ralson, 612-627-2732
District 1
Type: magnet
K-6th grade
Urban environment.

Minnesota Alliance of Montessorians
914 Franklin Ter, Minneapolis, MN 55406
Cameron Gordon

Seward Montessori School
2309 28th Ave S, Minneapolis, MN 55406-1397

Friends School of Minnesota (1988)
3244 34th Ave S, Minneapolis, MN 55406-2185
Mark Niedermier, Dir, 612-722-2046
Hennepin County
Type: Quaker, non-profit; tuition: $4,050/yr, scholarships
11 teachers, 73 students, ages 5-13, K-6th grade
Affiliation: FCOE
Governance by board
Hands-on, integrated cur; global, environmental, multi-
    cultural topics; conflict resolution; anti-sexist, racist, and
    homophobic; no letter grades; multi-aged classes; urban
    location; transportation; interns accepted.

Northrap Elementary
1611 E 46th St, Minneapolis, MN 55407
Sylvia Adams, 612-627-2810
District 1
Type: magnet
K-6th grade
Urban environment.

South High School
3131 19th Ave S, Minneapolis, MN 55407
Hubert Denny, 612-627-2508
District 1
Type: magnet
9-12th grade
Liberal arts; open; all Native American nations.

Public School Montessorian
(See Resource Appendix)

Montessori Day Care Center
2608 Blaisdell, Minneapolis, MN 55408

Superlearning
3028 Emerson Ave S, Minneapolis, MN 55408
Libyan Labiosa, 612-827-4856
Type: independent

Work Opportunity Center
2908 Colfax Ave S, Minneapolis, MN 55408
Dr R. C. Johnson, Prin, 612-627-2908
Type: public at-risk
Student ages 16-20
Small groups; continuous progress; voc; apprenticeships.

Center for Public Montessori Programs
(See Resource Appendix)

Little Red Hen Montessori School
4225 3rd Ave S, Minneapolis, MN 55409

Ramsey International Fine Arts Center
1 W 49th St, Minneapolis, MN 55409
Doris Zachary, 612-627 2540
District 1
Type: magnet
K-8th grade
International Studies/Fine Arts.

Lake Country School
3755 Pleasant Ave, Minneapolis, MN 55409-1282
Larry Shafer
Type: Montessori

Lake Harriet Montessori
4501 Colfax Ave S, Minneapolis, MN 55409-1736

WOLF School (1994)
c/o 5535 Richmond Curve, Minneapolis, MN 55410
Karen Locke, Co-Founder, 612-925-9819
Henn County
Type: home-based, non-profit
7+ students, ages 4-14, K-12th grade
Governance by democratic school meeting.
Student-centered and directed; urban location.

North High School
1500 James Ave N, Minneapolis, MN 55411
Harlan Anderson, 612-627-2778
District 1
Type: magnet
9-12th grade
Arts; communications.

Plymouth Youth Center Alternative Schools
2519 Lyndale Ave N / 2301 Oliver Ave N, Minneapolis, MN
    55411
Nancy Semler / Maureen Walsh, 612-522-1584, 522-6501
Type: public at-risk
JH, HS
Entrance requirements: referral by counselor, social worker
    or principal.
Short courses with clear objectives; vocational, career train-
    ing; post-secondary planning; urban location.

Bethune Elementary School
919 Emerson Ave N, Minneapolis, MN 55411-4199
Type: Montessori

City School-Northside/Southside
1315 12th Ave N / 1545 E Lake St, Minneapolis, MN
  55411/55407
Bobby Hickman or Ron Simmons / Terry Tendle, 612-377-
  7559, 724-3689
Students mainly at-risk from inner city, 7-12th grade
Affiliations: The City, Inc; accreditation: yes
Employment; recreation; individual, family counseling; childcare; urban location.

Afrocentric Educational Academy
1015 Olson Memorial Hwy, Minneapolis, MN 55412
Nell Collier or Birch Jones, 612-377-1556
Student ages 11-15
History; language arts; tutoring; mentoring; small classes;
  outcome-based; coop learning; multi-media technology.

Minneapolis Area Learning Center
2020 43rd Ave N, Minneapolis, MN 55412
Robert Jibben, 612-627-2716
Type: public at-risk
Multiple sites; serves homeless youth, returning Native American students; evening classes; middle level program;
  support services; parent involvement.

Minneapolis Junior High Alternative School
1006 W Lake St, Minneapolis, MN 55412
Harvey Winston or R. C. Johnson, 612-627-2850
Student ages 12-15
Transitional; support services; career exploration; parent
  support groups; summer program.

New Visions School
3820 Emerson Ave N, Minneapolis, MN 55412
Bob DeBoer, 612-521-2266
1-6th grade
Entrance requirements: for reading difficulties.
Developmental problems; whole optometric brain services;
  whole language; physical movement.

PM High School
1415 Hennepin Ave, Minneapolis, MN 55412
Ron Eikaas or Willarene Beasley, 612-627-2269
Type: public at-risk
Student ages 16+
CAI; counseling; career planning; safe atmosphere.

Pregnant Adolescent Continuing Education (PACE)
1201 Hennepin, Minneapolis, MN 55412
Lois Gehrman or Barbara Bellair, 612-339-6712
Student ages 12-20
Individualized; SE assessments; health screening; prenatal
  education; crisis counseling; career planning.

The Connection Center
25 N 16th St, Minneapolis, MN 55412
Dr Willarene Beasley, Prin or Mary Wise, Coord, 612-627-2265
Type: public at-risk
Student ages 14-25
Individualized; CAI; work experience; vocational, career explo-
  ration; counseling; life skills; childcare.

Heart of the Earth Survival School
1209 4th St SE, Minneapolis, MN 55414
Edward Benton-Benai or Mark Aquash, 612-331-8862,
  FAX:-1747
55 teachers, 250 students, mainly Native American, K-12th
  grade
Native American culture-based; parent, community support.

Marcy Open School (1971)
415 4th Ave SE, Minneapolis, MN 55414
Jay Scoggin, Tch/Leadership Council Co-Chair, 612-627-7474

Type: public choice
27 teachers, 630 students, ages 5-14, K-8th grade
Affiliation: Minneapolis Public Schools
Governance by teacher, administration, community, student
  leadership council
Family, community involvement; self-directed; student-
  centered; environmental education; volunteer program;
  Higher Order Thinking Skills; no letter grades; multi-aged
  classes; extensive field trips; interns accepted.

Peace Academy/Holos Foundation
601 13th Ave SE, Minneapolis, MN 55414
Barbara Schmidt, 612-377-8109
Holistic, interdisciplinary; competency-based; credit by self/
  staff evaluation; multi-aged classes; urban location.

Second Foundation School
1219 University Ave SE, Minneapolis, MN 55414
Bob Vincent, Director, 612-378-1014
Hennepin County
Type: independent, non-profit; tuition: $20-500/mo, sliding
  scale
4 teachers, 32 students, ages 5-18, K-12th grade
Entrance requirements: interview
Governance by democratic school meeting
Based on idea that people have good inner motivation,
  unique styles; students follow natural interests, work at
  their own pace; cooperation between students fostered;
  no letter grades; non-compulsory class attendance; multi-
  aged classes; urban location; transportation.

Children's Village Child Care Center
2812 University Ave SE, Minneapolis, MN 55414-3212
Type: Montessori

Operation deNovo
251 Portland Ave S, Minneapolis, MN 55415
Ralph Davies, 612-348-4805
Entrance requirements: by court order.
Education contract; monthly evaluation by student, staff,
  probation officer, parent/guardian; failure results in correctional facility placement; urban location.

Discoveries for Children
4100 Vernon Ave S, Saint Louis Park, MN 55416-3199
Heidi Dorfmeister
Type: Montessori

Menlo Park Alternative School
1929 2nd St NE, Minneapolis, MN 55418
Patricia A. Lobash, 612-781-6011
1:10 ratio; teen parent workers; violence/abuse education;
  youth work; computer; urban location.

Kenny Elementary School
57th & Emerson, Minneapolis, MN 55419
Type: Montessori

Mrs Liiste's Montessori School
8036 Lyndale Ave S, Bloomington, MN 55420

Project Re-Entry at Kennedy Senior High School
9701 Nicollet Ave S, Bloomington, MN 55420
Alan Fasching or Judy McDonald, 612-888-7786
Intermediate District #287, Hennepin County
Type: public at-risk
Student ages 16-20
Evening program; life skills; business; vocational classes, work
  experience; independent study; counseling.

Raamalynn Montessori Academy
9600 3rd Ave S, Bloomington, MN 55420

Rainbow Montessori
8736 Nicollet Ave, Bloomington, MN 55420

South Hennepin Adult Programs in Education (SHAPE)
8900 Portland Ave S, Bloomington, MN 55420
Kevin Byrne, 612-885-8550
Type: public at-risk
Student ages 17+
Outcome-based; evenings; job skills, experience; tutoring;
college prep; career counseling; parenting; childcare.

Marianna Montessori Day Care
8000 Portland Ave, Minneapolis, MN 55420

Little Voyageurs Montessori School
1515 44th Ave NE, Columbia Heights, MN 55421

Breck Montessori
123 Ottawa Ave N, Golden Valley, MN 55422

Minnesota High School for the Arts
6125 Olson Memorial Hwy, Golden Valley, MN 55422
Jim Undercofler, 612-591-4700
Type: public choice

TEACH Institute
4350 Lakeland Ave N, N Robbinsdale, MN 55422
Type: state home-based
Accrediting association for Christian home educators; consulting services available nationwide.

**Community Education Center/Program for Pregnant
Teens and Teen-age Parents** (CEC/PIE)
4139 Regent Ave N, Robbinsdale, MN 55422
Connie Harrison, 612-535-9190
Intermediate District #287, Hennepin County
Student ages 13-20
Other locations: 7440 Penn Ave S, Richfield 55423; 10902
Greenbrier, Minnetonka 55343; contact Nancy Bengston at
612-866-9780; childcare; transportation.

MN Homeschoolers Alliance
Box 23072, Richfield, MN 55423
Shari Henry
Type: state home-based

Edina Montessori School
5701 Normandale, Edina, MN 55424
Sunil Aiyadurai

Trinity School at River Ridge
2300 E 88th St, Bloomington, MN 55425-2185
William C. Wacker, Head Teacher, 612-854-0008
100 students, 7-12th grade

Ridgedale Alternative Program (RAP)
7400 Laurel Ave N, Golden Valley, MN 55426
Denny Gormley or Lola Vedders, 612-545-6502
Intermediate District #287, Hennepin County
Type: public at-risk
Student ages 16+
HS diploma; career, vocational exploration; community
involvement; peer help.

City of Lakes Waldorf School (1989)
3450 Irving Ave S, Minneapolis, MN 55426
Carol Jean Swanson, Adms Coord, 612-822-1092
Hennepin County
Non-profit; tuition: $4,740/yr, scholarships
20 teachers, 165 students, ages 3-14, pre K-8th grade
Affiliation: AWSNA
Governance by faculty and student representatives, board
Teacher qualifications: college, Waldorf training or equivalent
Urban location; transportation; interns accepted.

Intermediate District #287 Area Learning Center
7400 Laurel Ave, Golden Valley, MN 55426
Robert Papas or Chuck Komschlies, 612-540-0190
Type: public at-risk
Coordinates 18 programs at 47 locations in Hennepin County;
high school and middle level programs.

Knollwood Montessori
8115 Hwy 7, Minneapolis, MN 55426

Learning Through Music
3503 Sumter Ave S, St Louis Park, MN 55426
Hestia Abeyesekera
Type: Montessori

Senior High Options
6425 W 33rd St, St Louis Park, MN 55426
Carol Thompson, 612-928-6749
Type: public at-risk
6 teachers; student ages 16-20
Supportive; coordinated group, class and independent work.

West Metro Education Centers (WMEC)
6800 Cedar Lake Rd, St Louis Park, MN 55426
Missy Holbrook, 612-593-1181
Intermediate District #287, Hennepin County
Type: public at-risk
Student ages 5-20, K-12th grade
For emotionally/behaviorally disordered; academic, voca-
tional programs; mental health services, LD, adaptive PE.

70,001 WAVE
715 Florida Ave; 71145 Harriet Ave, Golden Valley; Richfield,
MN 55426; 55423
John Jones, 612-595-9717, 861-7481
Intermediate District #287, Hennepin County
Type: public at-risk
Student ages 16-20
Vocational education, work experience; pre-employment
training; career exploration; evening classes.

Golden Valley Montessori School
PO Box 27321, Golden Valley, MN 55427-0321

Highview Alternative Program
4701 Zealand Ave, New Hope, MN 55428
Cherryl Kachenmeister, 612-536-0243
Intermediate District #287, Hennepin County
Type: public at-risk
Student ages 16+
Self-directed; individualized; small groups; job seeking skills;
career planning.

Brookdale Montessori School
5827 Humboldt Ave N, Minneapolis, MN 55430-2637

Mariana Montessori
2501 W 84th St, Bloomington, MN 55431
Marie Dias

Ramalynn Montessori Academy
8800 Queen Ave S, Bloomington, MN 55431

Interaction Book Company
(See Resource Appendix)

La Pepiniere Montessori School
6515 Barrie Rd, Edina, MN 55435-2305

ABC/International Montessori Academy, Inc (1974)
10801 Normandale Blvd S, Bloomington, MN 55437
Dr Vijay B Gupta, Dir, 612-881-1717
Non-profit; tuition: $300-450/mo
12 teachers, 6 assistants, 143 students, mainly international,
ages 3-15
Entrance requirement: interview
Affiliations: AMI, MF MN; accreditation: MF MN
Governed by administrator
Modern Montessori building; ballet; Spanish; theatre; piano;
cosmic curriculum; childcare; urban location.

Sobriety High
5250 W 73rd St #A, Edina, MN 55439-2215
Judi Hanson, 612-925-5472
Type: public at-risk

Student ages 12–21, 8–12th grade
Alcohol and drug-free environment; group meetings; small classes; daily goals; AA group; summer program.

New Vistas School
2701 4th Ave S, Minneapolis, MN 55440
Gladys Randle, 612-870-6219
10–12th grade
For pregnant, parenting students; residency required
Affiliation: Honeywell
Outcome-based; CAI; coop learning; inductive thinking; mentoring; work experience; vocational courses; childcare, health, social services; urban location; transportation.

Armstrong HS, Alternative Program
10635 36th Ave N, Plymouth, MN 55441
John Lloyd, 612-546-3266
Type: public choice

Montessori School of Wayzata Bay
13501 Cty Rd 15, Plymouth, MN 55441

College of St Catherine, St Mary's Campus (1985)
2500 S 6th St, Minneapolis, MN 55454
Michael Dorer, Prog Dir, 612-690-7779, FAX: 612-690-7849
Type: Montessori teacher education
10–18 teachers, 33 students, ages infant-12/adult
Accreditations: AMS, MACTE
Governance by administrator
Urban location.

West Bank Community Development
1808 Riverside Ave #206, Minneapolis, MN 55454
Kathryn Hartman, 612-339-5767, FAX: 612-673-0379

Anwatin Middle School
256 Upton Ave S, Minneapolis, MN 55455
612-627-3150
Type: public choice
6–8th grade
Accomodates special needs
Affiliations: Dain Bosworth, Inc
Governance by principal, council
Student council; community service; computers; A/V; conflict mediation training; environmental learning center; Pre-IB Magnet Program; multi-aged classes; parent center.

Bethune Public School Academy
919 Emerson Ave N, Minneapolis, MN 55455
612-627-2685
Type: public choice
K–6th grade
Governance by teachers, principal
1:14 ratio; cooperative learning; parent involvement; in-class telephones, answering machines; partnership with General Mills.

Chiron Middle School
25 N 16th St, Minneapolis, MN 55455
612-627-3250
Type: public choice
6–8th grade
Governance by parents, staff, students
Hands-on, cooperative learning; whole-language; arts, government, science, technology; mentorships; community service; multi-aged classes; annual August festivities.

Downtown Open
730 2nd Ave S, Minneapolis, MN 55455
612-627-7145
Type: public choice
K–4th grade
Affiliations: NSP, IDS, Augsburg College
Governance by principal
Student-centered; cooperative learning; community interaction; individualized; whole language; Spanish-English bilingual; non-competitive evaluations; tutors; multi-aged classes; childcare; interns accepted.

Emerson Spanish Immersion Learning Center
1421 Spruce Place, Minneapolis, MN 55455
612-627-7452
Type: public choice
K–8th grade
Governance by parents, teachers, principal
Teacher qualifications: ESL specialty
Technology instruction; choir; band; computer lab; stage.

Four Winds Native American and French Language School
2300 Chicago Ave, Minneapolis, MN 55455
612-627-7160
Type: public choice
K–8th grade
Governance by principal
Cooperative learning; French immersion for grades 1–5; Dakota, Ojibwe language; community service; parent involvement; tutors; drum and dance group; community ed; preschool; childcare.

Franklin Middle School
1501 Aldrich Ave N, Minneapolis, MN 55455
612-627-2869
Type: magnet
6–8th grade
Governance by principal
Math/science/tech; small classes; computers; A/V; piano lab; cooperative learning; team teaching; interdisciplinary; parent involvement; peer groups; support services.

Hall Montessori School
1601 Aldrich Ave N, Minneapolis, MN 55455
612-627-2339
K–6th grade
Governance by principal
Teacher qualifications: Montessori training
Continue with same teacher for consecutive years; emphasis on global interrelatedness; practical life experiences; environmental and peace education; multi-aged classes.

Mill City Montessori
219 S 4th St, Minneapolis, MN 55455
612-338-5765
Type: public choice
K–5th grade
Serves Minneapolis Target employees
Governance by teachers, principal, parents
Teacher qualifications: Montessori, MN Certification
Student-centered; cooperative learning; computers; multi-aged classes; childcare.

Native American Program at Andersen Open School
1098 Andersen Ln, Minneapolis, MN 55455
612-627-2295
Type: public choice
K–8th grade
Governance by teachers and principal
Self-directed; student-centered; Student Leadership Councils; individual projects; thematic instruction; tutoring; team teaching; elder on staff; parent involvement; Ojibway language; multi-aged classes; childcare; multi-cultural gender fair and disability-aware lab demo site.

Northeast Middle School
2955 Hayes St NE, Minneapolis, MN 55455
612-627-3042
Type: public choice
6–8th grade
Governance by principal
Cooperative learning; mentorships; integrated curriculum; computers; peer tutoring, coaching; conflict mgmt; artist in residence; pre-IB; career exploration; multi-aged classes; parent involvement.

Pillsbury Math/Science/Technology School
2250 Garfield St NE, Minneapolis, MN 55455
612-627-2822
Type: public choice
K-6th grade
Governance by principal
School-wide theme projects; cooperative learning; parent involvement; computers; mentors; preschool and early childhood SE; multi-aged classes; childcare.

Sanford Middle School
3524 42nd Ave S, Minneapolis, MN 55455
612-627-2720
Type: public choice
6-8th grade
Governance by principal
Cooperative learning; interdisciplinary; environmental science; social skills; parent involvement.

Sheridan International/Fine Arts
1201 University Ave NE, Minneapolis, MN 55455
612-627-2348
Type: public choice
K-6th grade
Governance by principal
Individualized; whole language; Math Their Way; cooperative learning; learning centers; thematic instruction; parent involvement; weekly classroom newsletter; string instruments; Russian language, culture.

Shingle Creek Urban Environmental Center
5034 Oliver Ave N, Minneapolis, MN 55455
612-627-2673
Type: public choice
K-6th grade
Governance by principal
Individualized; along creek banks, adjacent to park; parent involvement.

Webster Open School
425 5th St NE, Minneapolis, MN 55455
612-627-2312
K-8th grade
Community, parent involvement; self-directed; Spanish; arts specialist; CAI; thematic learning; multi-cultural.

Willard Math/Science/Technology Magnet
1615 Queen Ave N, Minneapolis, MN 55455
612-627-2529
K-6th grade
Governance by council
Cooperative, experiential learning; whole language; role models; CAI; A/V; parent involvement; take-home family science kits; partnerships with Cray Research and Augsburg College; extensive field trips; yearly camping trip.

Northshore Children's House
PO Box 535, Grand Marais, MN 55604-0535
Type: Montessori

Carlton County Area Learning Center
302 14th St, Cloquet, MN 55720
Steven Syrett, 218-879-0115
Type: public at-risk
Independent study; multi-media approach; focus on health, sexuality, self-concept; middle level program: support services; parent involvement; youth service; personal, social skills; small classes.

Fond du Lac Reservation
105 University Rd, Clouet, MN 55720
Tom Peacock, Supt, 218-879-0241, FAX: 218-879-0007

Teaching Effective Curriculum, Citizenship and Communication
PO Box 520, Coleraine, MN 55722-0520
Mary Anderson, Student Service Dir, 218-245-1050

Type: public at-risk
Student ages 12+
Career exploration; individualized instruction; cooperative learning; computers; use of community resources; parent, community involvement; counseling; social services.

Pine County Area Learning Center
6495 Lake St, Finlayson, MN 55735
Jan Kurhajetz, 612-233-7231
Type: public at-risk
Demo center for Great Brain curriculum development; middle level program at Finlayson School; support services; parent involvement; personal, social skills.

District 318 Learning Center at Itasca Community College
Bailey Hall, 1851 Hwy 169 E, Grand Rapids, MN 55744
Dwight Grose, 218-327-4346
Type: public at-risk
Access to media center, computer lab.

Hibbing Area Learning Center
8th Ave E & 21st St, Hibbing, MN 55746
Michael Sushoreba, 218-263-3670
Type: public at-risk
Multimedia, outcome-based; middle level program: support; parent involvement; CAI; study skills; small classes.

Toivola-Meadowlands School
7705 Western Ave, Meadowlands, MN 55765
218-427-2311

Duluth Area Learning Center
2 E 2nd St, Duluth, MN 55802
Beth Tamminen, 218-727-4804
Type: public at-risk
Independent study; special group; college skills; middle level program: support services; integrated curriculum; parent involvement; personal, social skills.

New Moon Publishing (1992)
(See Resource Appendix)

Montessori School of Duluth, Inc
1215 Rice Lake Rd, Duluth, MN 55811-2160

Rochester Montessori School
400 5th Ave SW, Rochester, MN 55903
Chace Anderson, RMS

Franklin School
1801 SE 9th Ave, Rochester, MN 55904
Robert Funk
Type: Montessori

Rochester Area Learning Center
1420 11th Ave SE, Rochester, MN 55904
Roger Klimpel, 507-285-8813
Type: public at-risk
250 students
Outcome-based; no letter grades; middle level program at 3901 Marion Rd SE, contact Marcia Hockert, 507-287-1930; support services; parent involvement; youth service; social, personal skills; team teaching; coop learning; multicultural.

Austin Area Learning Center
301 3rd St NW, Austin, MN 55912
Royce R Helmbrecht, 507-433-0408
Student ages 12+
Open entry/exit; support services; parent involvement; youth service; personal/social skills; teen parenting; competency-based; childcare.

Bluffview Montessori (1988)
101 E Wabasha St, Winona, MN 55987
Haine Crown, Adm Asst, 507-452-2807
Type: public choice Montessori; tuition: $150/250 for ages 3-6
4 teachers, 4 assistants, 99 students, ages 3-12

Entrance requirement: open window application in March or
   April
Affiliations: AMI/USA, NAMTA
Governance by administration and staff
Minnesota's first charter public school; nation's first Montes-
   sori charter school; childcare; suburban/rural location;
   transportation; interns accepted.

Winona Area Learning Center
926 W 5th St, Winona, MN 55987
Scott Hannon, 507-454-9573
Type: public at-risk
Childcare; chemical counseling; psychological services; self-
   paced; independent study; job skills; middle level program:
   parent involvement; individualized.

Montessori School of Winona
PO Box 991, Winonaa, MN 55987

Bluffview Montessori School
101 E 7th St, Winona, MN 55987-3594

Good Counsel Montessori School
512 Mulberry St, Mankato, MN 56001

Mankato Alternative High School
110 Fulton St, Mankato, MN 56001
Roger Stoufer, 507-387-3047
Type: public at-risk
Student ages 16+
Teen parent program; childcare; interns accepted.

Albert Lea Area Learning Center
504 W Clark St, Albert Lea, MN 56007
Rob Esse, 507-377-6540
90–110 students
Evening classes; middle level program at SW JHS, Brookside
   MS: support services; parent involvement; youth service,
   personal/social skills; individualized.

Blue Earth Alternative Learning Center
315 E 6th St, Blue Earth, MN 56013
Randy Paulsen, 507-526-4123
Type: public at-risk
Student ages 16–20
Life skills.

Martin County Area Learning Center
115 S Park St, Fairmont, MN 56031
John Schuld, 507-235-6151
Type: public at-risk
Outcome based; conflict resolution; middle level program:
   support services; parent involvement; family sessions.

Southwest Area Learning Center
1400 17th St, Fairmont, MN 56031
Jerry Sorenson, 507-831-4881
Type: public at-risk
Outcome based; conflict resolution; middle level program:
   support services; parent involvement; family sessions; day
   treatment.

New Ulm Alternative Program
414 S Payne St, New Ulm, MN 56073
George Wagner, 507-359-8420
Type: public at-risk
Student ages 16–20, 10–12th grade

Waseca Alternative High School
501 E Elm Ave, Waseca, MN 56093
Gary Hawkins, 507-835-5628
Type: public at-risk
20 students, ages 16+
Word processing, spreadsheet, database; art; home ec;
   health/PE; personal, career counseling; childcare.

Pipestone High School Diploma Program
400 2nd Ave SW, Pipestone, MN 56164
Donna Berg, 507-825-5861
Type: public at-risk
Student ages 16+
Individualized instruction; self-paced; independent study;
   non-compulsory class attendance.

Worthington Area Learning Center
1211 Clary St, Worthington, MN 56187
Marlys Knuth, 507-376-6121
Type: public at-risk
Small classes; cultural diversity; support groups; independent
   study; interdisciplinary; life skills; middle level program:
   parent involvement; individualized.

Worthington Montessori School (1971)
Box 434, Worthington, MN 56187
Sally-Anne Benson, Dir, 507-376-3669
Non-profit; tuition: $110/mo
1 teacher, 1 assistant, 20 students, ages 3–6
Accreditations: AMS, MN DHS
Governance by parent-run board
Childcare.

Willmar Area Learning Center
PO Box 1097, Willmar, MN 56201
Bill Gulbrandsen, 612-235-5114 x204
Type: public at-risk
students mainly Hispanic
Satellite program at Prairie Lakes Detention Ctr for ages 12+;
   competency based; culturally diverse curriculum; middle
   level program: contact Patricia Thompson at 612-235-5114
   x143; support services; parent involvement.

Benson Area Learning Center
1400 Montana Ave, Benson, MN 56215
Doug Manzke or Gary Williams, 612-843-2710
Type: public at-risk
Community resources; middle level program at Benson JHS:
   support services; parent involvement; youth service;
   outcome-based; individualized.

Family Learning Center
344 W Main, Marshall, MN 56258
Wanda Ochocki, 507-537-6790
Type: public at-risk
40 students, ages 16+
Completely independent study; individualized learning.

Minnesota Valley Area Learning Center
301 N 1st St, Montevideo, MN 56265
John D. Johnson, 612-269-7131
Type: public at-risk
Flexible schedule; individualized; support services; middle
   level program: parent involvement; youth service.

Montessori School of St Cloud (1968)
302 S 5th Ave, St Cloud, MN 56301
Mary Theresa Anderson, Prin, 612-253-4719
Tuition: $195/390/mo
4 teachers, 7 assistants, 75 students, ages 3–6
Entrance requirements: toilet trained
Governance by administrator
Christian; non-denominational; language development; child-
   care; urban location; interns accepted.

Learning Day Montessori School
3124 Southway Dr, Saint Cloud, MN 56301-9589

St Cloud Area Learning Center
9th Ave & 12th St N, St Cloud, MN 56303
Mark Lindquist, 612-251-4963
Type: public at-risk
Competency-based; career; middle level program: support

services; parent involvement; youth service; independent study; personal, social skills; max 15/class; highly structured.

Runestone Regional Learning Center
1224 N Nokomis, Alexandria, MN 56308
Katy Mohabir, 612-762-0627
Life skills; evening classes; middle level program: holistic; support services; parent involvement; youth service.

Rocori Alternative Program
534 5th Ave N, Cold Spring, MN 56320
Rick Theisen, 612-685-8683
Type: public at-risk
Student ages 16–20

Continuing Education Center
109 NE 2nd Ave, Little Falls, MN 56345
John Russell, 612-632-5417
Type: public at-risk
Student ages 16+
Evenings; teen parenting; health, job placement support; informal, multi-aged classes; interns accepted.

W.C. Education District ALC
518 E 2nd St, Melrose, MN 56352
Jerome Beddow, 612-352-3819, 612-256-7836
Type: public at-risk
Comprehensive Competencies curriculum; middle level program: support service; parent involvement; individualized.

Milaca Evening Alternative Program
500 NW 4th St, Milaca, MN 56353
William Makinen
Type: public at-risk
20 students, ages 16+
Independent study option; work study; multi-aged classes.

Onamia Alternative Program
Evergreen Lane, Onamia, MN 56359
Guy Kokesh, 612-532-4673
Type: public at-risk
Student ages 16+
Completely independent study.

Camphill Village MN
Rt 3, Box 249, Sauk Centre, MN 56378
Debbie Leighton, 612-732-6365
Type: Waldorf

Brainerd Area Education Center
1102 Willow St, Brainerd, MN 56401
Arlo Renschler, 218-829-2915
Independent study; CAI; mentorships; middle level program at ALC, Franklin JHS, Washington MS: support services; youth service; personal/social skills; technology.

Minnesota Association of Alternative Programs (MAAP) Area Education Center
(See Resource Appendix)

Headwaters Educational Learning Program (HELP)
N Huntsinger Ave, Park Rapids, MN 56470
Bruce Gravalin, 218-732-3333
Type: public at-risk
Student ages 16–20
Individualized learning; trade, vocational skills training; post-secondary, career exploration.

Freshwater Area Learning Center
HCR #3, Box 15-1, Staples, MN 56479
Sue Boehland or Mark Wolhart, 218-894-2439, 894-2501
Freshwater District
Type: public at-risk

Accelerated Learning/Outcome Based Ed state demo site; Comprehensive Competency; Great Brain curriculum; middle level programs at ALC, Staples JHS, Eagle Bend JHS; support services; parent involvement.

Leaf River Alternative Program
PO Box 644; 418 N Jefferson, Wadena, MN 56482
Helen Allenson, 218-631-2281
Type: public at-risk
Student ages 16+
Required prep for work station placement; support services; PE; home ec.

Detroit Lakes Alternative Learning Center
1301 Rosevelt Ave, Detroit Lakes, MN 56501
Robert Soukup, 218-847-4491
Type: home-based
100+ students, ages 16+
100% independent study; multi-aged classes.

Fergus Falls Alternative Education Center
410 W Fir Ave, Fergus Falls, MN 56537
Norvin R. Rueckert, 218-739-2360
Type: public at-risk
Student ages 16+
Individualized instruction; special consideration for pregnant students, teen parents; mentoring mom program; extended year services; multi-aged classes.

Mahnomen Area Learning Center
PO Box 319, Mahnomen, MN 56557
Ron Liebel, 218-935-2211
Type: public at-risk
Outcome based; middle level program: support services; personal/social skills; parent involvement; ethnic sensitivity.

Fargo-Moorehead Homeschool Association
1909-8th St S, Moorehead, MN 56560

Youth Educational Services
2215 12th Ave S, Moorhead, MN 56560
Bob Wiltsey, 218-233-0924
Type: public at-risk
250 students
Independent study; childcare arranged; self-directed; middle level program: support services; parent involvement; youth service; personal, social skills; individualized.

Perham Alternative Learning Program
200 5th St NE, Perham, MN 56573
Jan Turgeon, 218-346-6502
Students mainly out of school, ages 16+
Home ec; PE; teen parenting; career planning.

Rothsay ISD #850
PO Box 247; 123 2nd St NW, Rothsay, MN 56579
Tom Fosse, 218-867-2735, FAX: 218-867-2376

Bemidji Area Learning Center
201 15th St NW, Bemidji, MN 56601
Dave Bucher, 218-759-3119
Experiential learning; individualized; life, job skills; middle level program: support services; parent involvement; youth service; personal/social skills; self-directed.

Riverside Schoolhouse
(See Resource Appendix)

Bagley Alternative High School
202 Bagley Ave NW, Bagley, MN 56621
Gary Bratvold, 218-694-6184
Type: public at-risk
Student ages 16+
Childcare in cooperation with Clearwater County SS; Pine to Prairie Teen Parent program; evening classes.

Cass Lake Area Learning Center
Rt 3, Box 4, Cass Lake, MN 56633
Patti Haasch, 218-335-6529
Type: public at-risk
200 students, ages 12+, 7-12th grade
Governance by local school board
Job, postsecondary skills; experiential; Indian studies; middle
    level program: support services; parent involvement;
    youth service; learning managers.

Montessori PreSchool
518 10th Ave W, International Falls, MN 56649-2238

Four Winds Alternative at Red Lake High School
Red Lake, MN 56671
Leo Soukup, 218-679-3899
Type: public at-risk

50-60 students, ages 16+
Computer; outcome based; video disc technology.

Northwest Area Learning Center
230 LaBree Ave, Thief River Falls, MN 56701
Wayne Johaneson, 218-681-8676
Type: public at-risk
CCP; tutoring; independent study; middle level program:
    support; parent involvement; individualized.

Crookston Area Learning Center
415 Jackson, Crookston, MN 56716
Marilyn Harris, 218-281-6363
Type: public at-risk
40-50 students
Personalized Education Management System; middle level
    program: support services; parent involvement.

Mississippi

Clarksdale City School
301 Washington St, Clarksdale, MS 38614
Bueford O. Spain, Principal, 601-627-8573
Coahoma County
Type: public at-risk
6 teachers, 20 students, ages 14-18, 9-11th grade
Entrance requirements: 2 yrs or more below grade level; no
    residency requirement
Governance by principal
Teacher qualifications: certification
Urban location; interns accepted.

Tate County Alternative School (1990)
PO Box CC, Coldwater, MS 38618
William Kelvin Knox, Dir, 601-622-0130
Type: public choice/at-risk
7 teachers; students mainly at-risk, ages 13+, 7-12th grade
Enrollment restricted to students with severe disciplinary
    infractions; no residency requirement
Governance by board
Teacher qualifications: certification
Part-time retired academics teachers; SE; counselor; enrich-
    ment teacher; no letter grades; multi-aged classes; subur-
    ban location.

Center of Attention
2047 Clifton Rd, Hernando, MS 38632
Type: Montessori

Cadet Child Care Center
PO Box 610, Holly Springs, MS 38635
Type: Montessori

Olive Branch Elementary School
9459 Pigeon Roost Rd, Olive Branch, MS 38654-2608
Type: Montessori

The Children's House of Tupelo
2225 W Main St, Tupelo, MS 38801-3143
Type: Montessori

NE Mississippi Regional Alternative Education Co-op
    (1993)
PO Box 247, Booneville, MS 38829
Lisa Wigginton, Dir, 601-728-7144, FAX: 601-728-7104

Type: public at-risk
6 teachers, 71 students, ages 10-21, 5-12th grade
Admission through due process by individual school boards;
    no residency requirement
Governance by board
Teacher qualifications: must meet MTAI guidelines
4 counties; for repeatedly suspended, expelled students;
    social, academic skills; behavior mod; multi-aged classes;
    interns accepted.

The Children's House, Inc
1710 Magnolia Rd, Corinth, MS 38834
Type: Montessori

Debbie Walker
RR 1, Plantersville, MS 38862-9801
Type: Montessori

T. Y. Fleming Alternative School (1993)
1901 Highway 82 W, Greenwood, MS 38930
Irvin L. Whittaker, Supt, 601-453-8566, FAX: 459-7250
Leflore County
Type: public at-risk
3 teachers, 30 students, ages 12-18, 6-12th grade
Governance by teachers, principal, security officials
Social science; life, job skills; multi-aged classes; rural location;
    transportation.

The Learning Tree
211 W Pres Ave, Greenwood, MS 38930-3545
Type: Montessori

Alternative Learning Center of Montgomery County
    (1993)
PO Box 687, Winona, MS 38967
W. P. Williamson, Coord, 601-283-1696
Type: public choice
1 teacher, 10-12 students, mainly at-risk, ages 13-17, 7-10th
    grade
County residency required
Governance by ALC committee, teacher; coord;
    superintendent
Multi-aged classes

Cotton Boll Learning Center (1993)
301 Fairground St, Winona, MS 38967
Eddie Hamilton, 601-283-1244, FAX: 601-283-1003
Montgomery County
Type: public at-risk
3 teachers, 15 students, ages 11–18, 5–12th grade
Enrollment restricted to at-risk residents
Governance by teachers and principal
Teacher qualifications: elementary and secondary
    qualifications
GED; multi-aged classes; urban location; transportation;
    interns accepted.

Yazoo County High School Alternative Program (1993)
PO Box 288, Benton, MS 39039
John P. Smith, Prin, 601-673-9777
Type: public at-risk
4 teachers, 12 students, ages 15–20, 9–12th grade
Entrance by recommendation
Governance by principal
Teacher qualifications: certification
No letter grades; rural location; transportation.

Simpson County Schools (1993)
101 Court St, Mendenhall, MS 39114
Lillie L. Hardy, Asst Supt, 601-847-1890, FAX:-8003
Type: public at-risk
1 teacher, 15 students, ages 12–20, 6–12th grade
Entrance requirements: school committee recommendation
Governance by teachers and principal
Teacher qualifications: certification
No letter grades; multi-aged classes; transportation.

Natchez Adams School District
1089 Commerce St, Natchez, MS 39120
Etta Mae Swalm
Type: Montessori

Home Educators of Central Mississippi
c/o McDonald, 109 W Willow Ct, Ridgeland, MS 39157
601-366-9218

Center for Alternative Programs (1992)
Vicksburg, MS 39180
Morris Richards, Dir, 601-631-5126
Vicksburg Warren District, Warren County
Type: public choice/at-risk
61 students, mainly at-risk, ages 8–17, 1–9th grade
Entrance requirements: referral, residency
Governance by teachers, principal, board
Day treatment; joint effort of SD, mental health agency;
    counseling; social skills; multi-aged classes; urban location;
    interns accepted.

Davis Magnet School
750 N Congress St, Jackson, MS 39202
Paula Keller, 601-960-5333
K–5th grade
Open education with emphasis on arts.

APEC at Chastain Middle School
4650 Manhattan Rd, Jackson, MS 39206
Jack Rice, 601-987-3550
Type: magnet
6–8th grade
Fine and performing arts.

APEC at Murrah High School
1120 Riverside Dr, Jackson, MS 39206
Linda Dick, 601-960-5380
Type: magnet
9–12th grade
Fine and performing arts.

APEC at Power Elementary
1120 Riverside Dr, Jackson, MS 39206
Linda Dick, 601-960-5387
Type: magnet
K–5th grade
Fine and performing arts.

Children's House Montessori School
PO Box 16011, Jackson, MS 39206

Educational Services Center (1993)
475 Parkway Drive; PO Box 5750, Pearl, MS 39208
Betty B. Wilson, Dir, 601-933-2461, FAX: 601-933-2462
Pearl District, Rankin County
Type: public at-risk
4 teachers, 20 students, ages 10–16, 3–8th grade
Residency required
Governance by teachers and principal
Teacher qualifications: MS Certification
One behavior targeted per student; incentives; positive
    reductive techniques; modified report cards; field trips;
    multi-aged classes; suburban location; transportation;
    interns accepted.

APEC at Powell Middle School
3655 Livingston Rd, Jackson, MS 39213
John Wicks, 601-987-3580
Type: magnet
6–8th grade
Fine and performing arts.

The Children's House Montessori School
2700 Davis St, Meridian, MS 39301-5707

Noxubee County Alternative School (1993)
PO Box 540, Macon, MS 39341
Murphy R. Greer, Head Adm, 601-726-4288, FAX:-2800
Type: public at-risk
4 teachers, 60 students, ages 13–21, 6–12th grade
No residency requirement
Governance by board
Multi-aged classes; rural location; transportation; interns
    accepted.

Hattiesburg Montessori Children's House (1982)
323 S 23rd Ave, Hattiesburg, MS 39401
Erlene Welden, Owner/Dir, 601-545-1944
Tuition: $155-225/mo
3 teachers, 4 assistants, 52 students, ages infant-9
Accreditation: MSMA
Governance by administrator
Modern dance; ballet; Spanish; private piano; childcare;
    transportation.

Pine Belt Education Service Center (1990)
923-B Sawmill Rd; PO Box 6441, Laurel, MS 39441
Dewey Blackledge, 601-649-4141, FAX: 601-649-4150
Jones County
Type: public at-risk
12 teachers, 177 students, ages 13–21, 5–12th grade
Entrance requirements: age 13, district residency and referral
Governance by board, Supt, teachers and principal
Teacher qualifications: MS Certification
Serves 8 districts; pilot for alt ed designated by MS DE; behav-
    ioral modification; rural location; transportation.

First Baptist Church Daycare
2105 14th St, Gulfport, MS 39501-2004
Type: Montessori

The Learning Center (1993)
1215 Church St, Gulfport, MS 39507
Charlotte Taylor, Building Prin, 601-897-6045

Harrison County
Type: public at-risk
8 teachers, 52 students, ages 12-18, 7-12th grade
Entrance requirements: school or court referral
Affiliation: MAAAE
Governance by board
Teacher qualifications: MS Certification
No textbooks; hands-on activities; computers; self-esteem; multi-aged classes; extensive field trips; urban location; interns accepted.

Westminister Academy
5003 Lawson Ave, Gulfport, MS 39507-4498
Type: Montessori

Project New Start (1993)
750 Blue Meadow Rd, Bay St Louis, MS 39520
Jo-Dell Beckham, Alt Tch, 601-467-6611
Hancock County
Type: public at-risk
1 teacher, 19 students, ages 13-18, 7-12th grade
Governance by principal
Teacher qualifications: certified, with at risk experience
Vocational skills; behavior modification; community, work ethics; in-school suspension program; drug education; multi-aged classes; urban location.

Kinderlearn
310 Delrays Ave, Biloxi, MS 39530
Type: Montessori

Kessler AFB Montessori/Thelma Miller
1299 Kensington Dr, Biloxi, MS 39530-1623

Creative Learning Center
2140 Pass Rd, Biloxi, MS 39531-4002
Type: Montessori

Holy Angels
PO Box 523, Biloxi, MS 39533-0523
Type: Montessori

Montessori Special Preschool (1969)
Keesler AFB, Biloxi, MS 39534
Thelma Miller, Dir, 601-432-5109
Non-profit; tuition: Variable
1 teacher, 5 assistants, 40 students, ages 3-6
Enrollment restricted to Dept of Defense dependents
Governance by administrator
Urban location.

Loving Care Learning Center
644 E RailRd St, Long Beach, MS 39560
Type: Montessori

St Thomas School
712 E Beach Blvd, Long Beach, MS 39560-6298
Type: Montessori

Moss Point Alternative School (1986)
4924 Church St, Moss Point, MS 39563
Burton W. Hoitt, Coord, 601-769-1309
Jackson County
Type: public at-risk
5 teachers, 2 assistants, 40 students, ages 13-21, 7-12th grade
Residency required
Governance by principal
Teacher qualifications: certification

Behavior modification; Glasser's Quality School; central theory taught and practiced; computer; multi-aged classes; urban location; transportation; interns accepted.

St Martin Elementary
Rose Farm Rd, Ocean Springs, MS 39564
Type: Montessori

Children's House Montessori
PO Box 668, Ocean Springs, MS 39564-0668

Alpha Montessori School
PO Box 698, Ocean Springs, MS 39564-0698

Montessori Schools & Day Care
2221 Government St, Ocean Springs, MS 39564-3957

Jackson County Alternative Program (1993)
PO Box 5069, Vancleave, MS 39565-5069
Ernest L. Rivers, Asst Supt, 601-826-1757, FAX:-1765
Type: public at-risk
4 teachers, 18 students, ages 12-18, 7-12th grade
Entrance requirements: placement by school board; no residency requirement
Governance by board
Teacher qualifications: MS Certification
Alternative to expulsion; rural location.

Hancock County School for Success (1993)
6069 Cueras Town Rd, Pass Christian, MS 39571
Elaine Lizana, Prin, 601-255-6626
Type: public at-risk
3 teachers, 30 students, mainly at-risk, ages 13-19, 9-12th grade
Residency required
Governance by teachers, principal, board.
CYBIS computer-based system; no letter grades; multi-aged classes; rural location; transportation.

Pineville School
5192 Menge Ave, Pass Christian, MS 39571
Type: Montessori

Alternative Education Program of Amite County (1990)
PO Box 378, Liberty, MS 39645
Dale Bailey, Dir of Psych Serv, 601-657-4361, FAX:-4291
Type: public choice
15 teachers, 68 students, partly at-risk, ages 12-20, 8-12th grade
County residency required
Governance by director and principal
Teacher qualifications: BA
Field trips; rural location; interns accepted.

Columbus Alternative (1993)
2217 7th St N, Columbus, MS 39701
Donnie E. Gross, Prin, 601-243-7601
Lowndes County
Type: public at-risk
6 teachers, 51 students, mainly at-risk, ages 6-17, 1-12th grade
Entrance requirements: behavioral/academic, residency
Governance by teachers and principal
Teacher qualifications: certification
Separate facilities from regular students; multi-aged classes; transportation.

The Children's House Montessori School
923 6th Ave N, Columbus, MS 39701-4621

Missouri

Free State Montessori (1980)
2018 Rock Spring Rd, Forest Hill, MO 21050
Claire J Salkowski, Head, 410-879-2132
Non-profit
3 teachers, 60 students
Affiliation: AMS
Elementary camping; school-wide community service; suburban location; interns accepted.

Linda Vista Catholic School
1633 Kehrs Mill Rd, Chesterfield, MO 63005-4310
Type: Montessori

Hope Montessori West
48 Strecker Rd, Ellisville, MO 63011-1904
Serena Shelton-Dodge

Montessori Children's House (1981)
14000 Ladue Rd, Chesterfield, MO 63017
Anita Chastain
Tuition: $3,852-7,704/yr
6 teachers, 8 assistants, 91 students, ages infant-9
Previous Montessori required for elementary students
Affiliation: AMI
Governance by administrator
Classic Montessori; student-centered; self-paced; childcare; suburban location; interns accepted.

Chesterfield Day School (1963)
1100 White Rd, Chesterfield, MO 63021
Dr Barbara Fulton, Head, 314-469-6622, FAX: 314-469-7889
Type: Montessori, non-profit
22 teachers, 5 assistants, 274 students, ages infant-12
Affiliations: NAIS, AMS; accreditation: ISACS
Governance by board
Traditional approach in grades 2-3; accelerated, departmentalized program in grades 4-6; parental involvement; childcare; suburban location; interns accepted.

Progressive Results
(See Resource Appendix)

Practical Homeschooling
(See Resource Appendix)

Midwest Montessori School
13775 New Halls Ferry Rd #A, Florissant, MO 63033-3028

Children of Promise Christian Montessori (1984)
11339 St Charles Rock Rd, Bridgetown, MO 63043
314-878-1534
Tuition: $50-200/mo
2 teachers, 3 assistants, 36 students, mainly International, ages Infant-6
Entrance requirements: interview and visit
Affiliation: MMA; accreditation: AMI
Governance by administrator
German.

Positive School
2497 Creve Coeur Mill Rd, Maryland Hgts, MO 63043-1199
Mike Black, 314-291-2035

Washington Montessori School (1978)
4 W 12th St, Washington, MO 63090
Nancy Schwartz, Owner/Adm, 314-239-5144
Non-profit
2 teachers, 2 assistants, 25 students, ages 3-6
Accreditation: AMS
Governance by administrator

Humbolt Visual & Performing Arts
2516 S 9th St, St Louis, MO 63104
James Strughold, 314-772-3164
Type: magnet
6-8th grade

A Growing Place Montessori School (1975)
6800 Wydown Blvd, St Louis, MO 63105
Laurie H. Kleen, Owner/Dir, 314-863-9493
Tuition: $200-300/mo
3 teachers, 2 assistants, 27 students, mainly International, ages 3-6
Affiliation: NAMTA; accreditations: MMA, SNMC
Governance by administrator
Enclosed courtyard; adjoining woods; ecological classroom; urban location.

Ames Visual & Performing Arts School
2900 Hadley, St Louis, MO 63107
David Bird, 314-241-7165
Type: magnet
Student ages 4+,-5th grade

Central Visual & Performing Arts
3616 N Garrison Ave, St Louis, MO 63107
Carl Landis, 314-371-1046
Type: magnet
9-12th grade

Marquette Visual & Performing Art
4015 McPherson Ave, St Louis, MO 63108
Alice Roach, 314-531-6233
Type: magnet
6-8th grade

Enright Classical Junior Academy
5351 Enright Ave, St Louis, MO 63112
Mary Beth Purdy, 314-367-0555
Type: magnet
6-8th grade
Gifted education.

Nursery Foundation of St Louis
1916 N Euclid Ave, Saint Louis, MO 63113-1701
Type: Montessori

Euclid Montessori School
1131 N Euclid Ave, St Louis, MO 63113-2009
Bessy Mosley

Visitation Holy Ghost
4515 Evans Ave, Saint Louis, MO 63113-2390
Type: Montessori

Christy Park Academy Montessori
5800 Christy Blvd, Saint Louis, MO 63116-2211

A.B. Green Middle School (1992)
1313 Boland, Richmond Heights, MO 63117
Arline Kalishman, Prin, 314-644-4406
St. Louis County
Type: public choice
19 teachers, 207 students, ages 11-16, 7-8th grade
Residency required
Governance by teachers and principal
Teacher qualifications: state certification
Only US school to combine philosophy of Ted Sizer's CES and Henry Levin's Accelerated Schools Project; no D or F grades; 8 block schedule (4 85-min classes one day, 4 others next day); suburban location; transportation; interns accepted.

Society for Utopian Studies (1975)
(See Resource Appendix)

Kirkwood High Alternative
801 W Essex, Kirkwood, MO 63122
Deborah Coco, Assoc Prin, 314-984-4407
St Louis County
Type: public at-risk
110 teachers, 1500 students, ages 14–19, HS
Entrance requirements: application process, residency
Governance by board
Teacher qualifications: MO Certification
Independent study; small groups; language arts; pre-
    vocational skills; special services; GED; teaming; sometimes
    no letter grades; multi-aged classes; suburban location;
    transportation; interns accepted.

Villa di Maria Montessori Center
1280 Simmons Ave, Saint Louis, MO 63122-1113

Kirkwood Children's House
11232 Big Bend Blvd, Saint Louis, MO 63122-5719
Type: Montessori

Home Schooling Network
47 Clermont Ln, St Louis, MO 63124

Montessori Learning Center
3612 Union Rd, Saint Louis, MO 63125-4315

South County Montessori School
12016 Tesson Ferry Rd, St Louis, MO 63128-1727

Casa Cia Montessori Teacher Training
610 Kinswood Ln, St Louis, MO 63129
Type: Montessori teacher education

Child of Nazareth Lutheran School (1975)
1401 N Hanley Rd, St Louis, MO 63130
Ruth Hummel, Dir, 314-863-0520
Type: Montessori; tuition: $300/350/mo
2 teachers, 3 assistants, 52 students, ages infant-6
Affiliation: Lutheran School System
Governance by administrator, board
Mainstreams deaf students in both classes; childcare; subur-
    ban location; interns accepted.

Montessori Institute for the Deaf (1990)
1417 Anna Ave, St Louis, MO 63130
Emilie McArthur, 314-863-0520
Non-profit; tuition: $208/340/430/mo
2 teachers, 1 assistant, 14 students, mainly at-risk, ages 3–9
Governance by an administrator
Sign language and speech taught; childcare; transportation.

Des Peres Montessori School
11155 Clayton Rd, St Louis, MO 63131

Sherwood Montessori School
12292 Clayton Rd, St Louis, MO 63131

The Principia
13201 Clayton Rd, St. Louis, MO 63131
Type: independent

Academy of the Visitation Montessori School
3020 N Ballas Rd, Saint Louis, MO 63131-2316

Logos High School
9137 Old Bonhomme, St Louis, MO 63132
314-997-7002
Type: public at-risk

Ferguson-Florissant Education Center (1972)
200 Church St, Ferguson, MO 63135
Jeffrey Spiegel, Adm, 314-522-0867
St Louis County
Type: public at-risk
25 teachers, 525 students, all ages, K–12th grade
Entrance requirements: referral, residency
Governance by teachers; Principal
Teacher qualifications: MO certification

Aggression replacement training; drug education; contracts;
    social, SE, psychological, support services; adult education;
    ESL; multi-aged classes; parenting; childcare; senior citi-
    zens' center

L'Academie Montessori
9859 Halls Ferry Rd, Saint Louis, MO 63136-4048

Kennard Classical Junior Academy
5031 Potomac, St Louis, MO 63139
Frances Gooden, 314-353-8875
Type: magnet
Student ages 4+,–5th grade
Gifted education.

Shaw Visual & Performing Arts School
5329 Columbia, St Louis, MO 63139
Robert Lewis, 314-776-5091
Type: magnet
K–5th grade

Fern Ridge High School (1992)
13157 N Olive Spur Rd, Creve Coeur, MO 63141
Beth Plunkett, Prin, 542-0042, FAX: 542-0695
St Louis County
Type: public choice
9 teachers, 100 students, mainly at-risk, ages 15–19, 9–12th
    grade
Entrance requirements: attempted 1 full year of HS, district
    residency
Governance by principal
Teacher qualifications: MO certification

Countryside Montessori School (1964)
12226 Ladue Rd, St Louis, MO 63141
Rita Zimny, Dir, 314-434-2821
Tuition: $255–495/mo
2 teachers, 6 assistants, 90 students, ages 2.5–6
Affiliation: AMS
Governance by administrator
Art; French; spacious playground; vegetable garden; wooded
    valley for nature walks, study; two resident ponies; child-
    care; suburban location; interns accepted.

Hope Montessori Academy–Central
900 Mason Rd N, Creve Coeur, MO 63141-6308
Susan Shelton-Dodge

Saint Charles Montessori Academy
1250 Hawks Nest Dr, Saint Charles, MO 63303-3670

Eastern Jackson County Alternative High School (1988)
205 NW 16th St, Blue Springs, MO 64015
Dr Glenn A. Berry, Prin, 816-224-4388, FAX: 224-1374
Type: public at-risk
4 teachers, 120 students, ages 14–20, 9–12th grade
Entrance requires application, district residency
Governance by teachers, principal, board
Science weather station; garden; newspaper; yearbook;
    hands-on projects; multi-aged classes; suburban location;
    transportation; interns accepted.

C.R. Anderson Alternative School
9701 E 35th St, Independence, MO 64052-1131
Clarence Cole, 816-435-4722

Families for Home Education
4400 Woods Rd, Sibley, MO 64088

Woodland Elementary
711 Woodland, Kansas City, MO 64106
Marcella Clay, 816-871-7950
Type: magnet
K–5th grade
Classical Greek.

Phillips Elementary
1619 E 24th Terrace, Kansas City, MO 64108
Marilyn Cowthran, 816-871-1660
Type: magnet

K–5th grade
Visual and performing arts.

De La Salle Education Center (1971)
3740 Forest, Kansas City, MO 64109
Jim Dougherty, Exec Dir, 816-561-3312, FAX:-6106
Jackson County
Type: independent, non-profit
34 teachers, 530 students, mainly at-risk, ages 13–21, HS
Governance by board
Teacher qualifications: certification
Nationally recognized; comprehensive; individualized; vocational instruction; intensive counseling; no letter grades; interns accepted.

Discovery Montessori School
5603 Nieman Rd, Kansas City, MO 64109

Faxon Montessori School
1320 E 32nd Terrace, Kansas City, MO 64109
Frank Vincent, 816-871-6450
Type: magnet
Student ages 3+,-5th grade
Montessori.

Longfellow Elementary
2830 Holmes, Kansas City, MO 64109
Gayle Bradshaw, 816-871-7050
Type: magnet
K–5th grade
Visual and performing arts.

Notre Dame DeSion Grande
3823 Locust St, Kansas City, MO 64109-2697
Type: Montessori

KC Middle School of the Arts
4848 Woodland, Kansas City, MO 64110
Roger Williams, 816-871-0550
Type: magnet
6–8th grade
Visual & Performing Arts.

Paseo Academy
4747 Flora, Kansas City, MO 64110
Patti Bippus, 816-871-0500
Type: magnet
9–12th grade
Fine and performing arts.

Forest Jones & Company
3130 Broadway, Kansas City, MO 64111
G Jan Pacey
Type: Montessori

St Paul's Episcopal School
4005 Main St, Kansas City, MO 64111-2312
Type: Montessori

Global Montessori Academy (1984)
707 W 47th St, Kansas City, MO 64112
Ellen Hamilton, Exec Dir, 816-561-4533
Non-profit; tuition: $264-323/mo
4 teachers, 5 assistants, 62 students, ages infant-9
Accreditation: MIA
Governance by parent cooperative
Robert Muller's Global Peace Curriculum; Lessons in Living: values, character development, self-esteem; childcare; urban location; interns accepted.

The Belmont Schools
6900 Ward Pky, Kansas City, MO 64113-2018
Type: Montessori

Hartman Elementary
8111 Oak, Kansas City, MO 64114
Elinor Etterling, 816-871-4950
Type: magnet
K–1st grade
Montessori.

St Peter's Episcopal School
100 E Red Bridge Rd, Kansas City, MO 64114-5499
Type: Montessori

Gracemor Accelerated School
5125 N Sycamore, Kansas City, MO 64119
Lewis Gowin, 816-453-0353
Type: public at-risk

Kansas City Center Montessori Teacher Education
5026 N Brighton Ave, Kansas City, MO 64119

Civic Center Children's House
Holmes at 13th, Kansas City, MO 64120-1089
Type: Montessori

Gladstone Academy
335 N Elmwood, Kansas City, MO 64123
Diana Kolen, 816-871-6800
Type: magnet
K–5th grade
Visual and performing arts; science and math.

Northeast Middle School
4904 Independence Ave, Kansas City, MO 64124
Lloyd Seales, 816-871-6830
Type: magnet
6–8th grade
Global studies.

Oliver Montessori School
4206 E 9th St, Kansas City, MO 64124-2822

Paul Robeson Middle School
4610 E 24th St, Kansas City, MO 64127
Cleo Washington, 816-871-6950
Type: magnet
6–8th grade
Classical Greek.

Central High School
3211 Indiana, Kansas City, MO 64128
Emmerson Payne, 816-871-8900
Type: magnet
9–12th grade
Computers Unlimited; classical Greek.

Genesis School Inc (1975)
3831 E 43rd St, Kansas City, MO 64130
Mamie Isler, Dir, 816-921-0775, FAX: 921-6248
Jackson County
Type: public/independent at-risk
7 teachers, 85 students, mainly at-risk, ages 11–21, 6–11th grade
No residency requirement
Governance by faculty and student reps, parent cooperative, board
Teacher qualifications: MO certification
Holistic approach; multi-ethnic curriculum; counseling; community outreach; multi-aged classes; urban location; interns accepted.

Harold Holliday Montessori School
5015 Garfield, Kansas City, MO 64130
Douglas Becker, 816-871-0200
Type: magnet
Student ages 3+,-2nd grade

Meservey Elementary
4210 E 45th St, Kansas City, MO 64130
Carole Ladd, 816-871-0240
Type: magnet
K–5th grade
Visual and performing arts.

Bishop Helmsing Early Childhood Center
1221 E Meyer Blvd, Kansas City, MO 64131
Type: Montessori

Center Alternative School
85th & Paseo, Kansas City, MO 64131-2616
816-822-1242

Satchel Paige Elementary
3301 E 75th St, Kansas City, MO 64132
Herman Gant, 816-871-5320
Type: magnet
K-5th grade
Classical Greek.

Little Red School House
10029 E 63rd Terr, Kansas City, MO 64133
Type: Montessori

Pitcher Elementary
9915 E 38th Tr, Kansas City, MO 64133
Deborah Kelly, 816-871-0400
Type: magnet
K-5th grade
Classical Greek.

Bright Beginnings, Inc. (1983)
9812 E 66 St, Raytown, MO 64133
Mary Catalano, Owner/Dir, 816-356-3514
Type: Montessori; tuition: $10/14/day
3 teachers, 7 assistants, 60 students, ages infant-6
Admission by interview with Directress
Affiliation: AEYC-GKC & MO. Vol. Accreditation
Governance by an administrator
Language, math, cultural arts, social studies, science, Spanish;
    childcare; interns accepted.

Small World Montessori
5301 Blue Ridge Blvd, Raytown, MO 64133-3062

The Children's Center
11327 Hickman Mills Dr, Kansas City, MO 64134-4206
Type: Montessori

Children's Center
325 E Gundell, Kansas City, MO 64141
Type: Montessori

Highlands Montessori School
8050 Mission Blvd, Kansas City, MO 64141

Avila Montessori School
11901 Wornall Rd, Kansas City, MO 64145
Carol Frevert, 816-942-8400 x2268
Tuition: $90-195/mo
2 teachers, 1 assistant, 45 students, ages 3-6
Entrance requirements: toilet-trained
Affiliation: NAEYC; accreditation: MIA
Governance by teachers, administrators
Teacher qualifications: BS in Ed, Montessori certification
Computers; childcare; suburban location; interns accepted.

Academy Montessori Internationals
12501 State Line Rd, Kansas City, MO 64145-1149

L'Ecole Montessori
3 Woodbridge Ln, Kansas City, MO 64145-1325

Clay Platte Children's House
5901 NW Waukomis Dr, Kansas City, MO 64151
Larry Merriman, Owner/Adm, 816-741-6940
Type: Montessori; tuition: $165-340/mo
21 teachers, 5 assistants, 211 students, ages infant-12
Affiliation: MIA
Governance by an administrator
10-acre campus; childcare; suburban location; interns
    accepted.

Montessori Institute of America
(See Resource Appendix)

Learning Academy, Hilyard Vo-Tech
3424 Faraon, St Joseph, MO 64506
Jim Cornett, 816-232-5459
Type: public at-risk

Satellite Alternative School
2nd & School Sts, Joplin, MO 64801
417-625-5293
Type: public choice

Neosho Evening Alternative School (1987)
511 Neosho Blvd, Neosho, MO 64850
Robin D. Montz, Coord, 417-451-8662, FAX:-8694
Neosho R-5 District, Newton County
Type: public at-risk
12 teachers, 36 students, ages 15-20, 9-12th grade
District residency required
Governance by teachers and principal
Teacher qualifications: MO certification
Parenting education; self-esteem; vocational; multi-aged
    classes; variable credit; rural location.

Eldon Montessori Children's House
Rt Box 361, Eldon, MO 65026

Jefferson City Children's House
1212 East High, Jefferson City, MO 65101
Type: Montessori

Scholastic Book Clubs, Inc
(See Resource Appendix)

Children's House Montessori
524 Schumate Chapel Rd, Jefferson City, MO 65109-4915

Children's House of Columbia, Inc (1972)
915 Maryland Ave, Columbia, MO 65201
Mary-Angela Johnson, 314-443-2825, FAX: 314-442-4134
Type: Montessori, non-profit; tuition: $250-380/mo
4 teachers, 5 assistants; student ages 2-8
Affiliation: AMS; accreditation: NAEYC
Governance by board
Straightforward, assertive, non-violent conflict resolution;
    independent study; cooperative; urban location.

Golden Moment Montessori Center
300 Saint James St, Columbia, MO 65201-4952

Columbia Montessori School (1967)
3 Anderson Ave, Columbia, MO 65203
Rebecca Melton, Dir, 314-449-5418
Non-profit; tuition: $270-460/mo
4 teachers, 16 assistants, 101 students, mainly International,
    ages infant-9
Accreditations: MIA, MO DFS
Governance by administrator
Multi-cultural; inclusive; childcare; suburban location.

Douglas School
310 N Providence, Columbia, MO 65203-4399
Tim Travers, 314-886-2645

Phoenix International School for Peace
Box 336, Birch Tree, MO 65438
John Staniloiu, Dir, 314-292-3880
Type: independent, boarding
Student ages 8-16
320 acres; animals, rivers, caves; hands-on experiences.

Little Piney Schoolhouse
Rt 1, Box 20, Newburg, MO 65550
314-762-2036
Type: independent

Ozark Lore Society (LORE) (1990)
c/o Resource Center, Brixey, MO 65618
Debra Eisenmann, Founder/Organizer, 417-679-4773,-3391
Homeschooling support network founded on principles of
    bioregionalism; newsletter; bioregional programs.

East Wind Community
Rfd 682, Tecumseh, MO 65761
Type: independent

Fairview Alternative
3850 Pittman Rd, Kansas City, MO 65802
Curtis Rogers, 417-831-0979

Bailey Education Center (1987)
501 W Central, Springfield, MO 65802
Dr Gloria Creed, Prin, 417-831-0979
Type: public at-risk
7 teachers, 100 students, ages 14-20, 9-12th grade
Entrance requirements: interview, district residency

Governance by teachers and principal
Teacher qualifications: MO Certification
Interdisciplinary; thematic; teaming; cooperative learning;
   community service; nursery; multi-aged classes; urban
   location; interns accepted.

Children's House Montessori
1461 E Seminole, Springfield, MO 65804

Springfield Area Homeschoolers
1730 W Winchester Rd, Springfield, MO 65807-448

Montana

Gardiner's Homeschoolers
PO Box 201, Gardiner, MT 59030
406-848-7226

Crazy Mountains Montessori
PO Box E, Harlowton, MT 59036-0905

Pan American Montessori
PO Box A, Corwin Springs, MT 59047
Mary Ellen Mautz

Billings Montessori School
2316 Rehberg Ln, Billings, MT 59102-2044
Nancy Jo McElroy

New Child Montessori School
1241 Crawford Dr, Billings, MT 59102-2442

Great Falls Montessori School
1521 1st Ave N, Great Falls, MT 59401-3206
Sally Heard

Little Flower Montessori
1625 Central Ave, Great Falls, MT 59401-3837

Shining Mountain Elementary
423 W Montana, Leviston, MT 59457

Helena Area Christian Home Educators
1263 Bighorn Rd, Helena, MT 59601
406-442-9510

Valley Montessori
1041 Leslie, Helena, MT 59601
Michele Webster, Dir, 406-449-3726
Tuition: $150/275/mo
1 teacher, 2 assistants, 20 students, ages 3-6
Entrance requirements: age 2.5, toilet trained
Affiliation: AMI
Governance by an administrator
Director is AMI trained; childcare; rural location.

Central Elementary
402 N Warren St, Helena, MT 59601-4047
Type: Montessori

Rocky Mountain Montessori Neighborhood Center
201 S Main St, Helena, MT 59601-4136

Bryant School
1529 Boulder Ave, Helena, MT 59624

Project for Alternative Living
815 Front, Helena, MT 59624

Homeschoolers of Montana
PO Box 654, Helena, MT 59624-0654
Type: state home-based

Prisbliz Pear Co-op
306 E Main, East Helena, MT 59635

Butte Home Education Association
2950 Bayard, Butte, MT 59701
Melda Freeman, 406-494-7949

Silver Bow Montessori School
1416 W Gold St, Butte, MT 59701-2114

Headwaters
216 W Wallace Ave, Bozeman, MT 59715
TimTate, 406-586-8158

Headwaters Academy (1990)
418 Garfield, Box 7258, Bozeman, MT 59715
Shawn Gant, Headmaster, 406-585-9997
Gallatin County
Type: independent, boarding, non-profit; tuition: $4850/yr,
   scholarships
7 teachers, 23 students, ages 12-18, 7-12th grade
Entrance requirements: interview, references, essay
Governance by faculty and student representatives, board
Teacher qualifications: certification of advanced degree
No formal grade levels; group work, art, music, adventure
   considered as important as academics; travel to Baja, Spain,
   Guatemala; grades given are A, B, C, in progress, not com-
   plete; multi-aged classes; field trips; urban location.

The Learning Circle Montessori
516 W Cleveland, Bozeman, MT 59715
Nancy Characklis, Dir, 406-587-2672
Tuition: $250-310/mo
7 teachers, 50 students, ages 3-8
Entrance requirements: age 3; toilet trained
Affiliations: AMS, ECEA
Governance by administrator
No letter grades; multi-aged classes; urban location; interns
   accepted.

World Family
120 E Story, Bozeman, MT 59715

Learning Circle
516 W Cleveland St, Bozeman, MT 59715-5122
Type: Montessori

Great Beginnings Montessori (1986)
PO Box 1794, Bozeman, MT 59771
Phyllis White, Adm, 406-587-0132
Non-profit; tuition: $200/360/mo
3 teachers, 1 assistant, 35 students, ages 3-6
Affiliations: AMS, AMI, NAEYC
Governance by board of directors elected by current parent-
   owners
Childcare; suburban location; interns accepted.

Sussex School
1800 S 2nd West, Missoula, MT 59801
Beth Loehnen, 406-721-1696
Type: independent
66 students, K-8th grade

Swann Beckwith Montessori
715 E Beckwith Ave, Missoula, MT 59801-4420

Clark Fork School (1983)
432 E Pine, Missoula, MT 59802
Ann Ford, Administrator, 406-728-3395
Type: independent, non-profit; tuition: $1000-4000/yr, scholarships
8 teachers, 2 assistants, 44 students, ages 3-10, pre K-3rd grade
Enrollment restricted to waiting list
Governance by parent cooperative
Teacher qualifications: creativity and respect for students; must meet formal requirements
Theme oriented, environmental emphasis; no letter grades; non-compulsory class attendance; multi-aged classes; extensive field trips; urban location; interns accepted.

Avalon School (1989)
Box 5676, Missoula, MT 59806
Dr. Louise Bell, Administrator, 406-543-1976
Type: independent, non-profit; tuition: $125-220/mo, scholarships
3 teachers, 17 students, ages 3-10, pre K-6th grade
Will not accept remedial students
Governance by board
Teacher qualifications: teacher certification
For students who were bored in public schools; process approach to writing; literature-based reading; computer programs; hands-on approach to science; no letter grades; multi-aged classes; extensive field trips; urban location.

Missoula Homeschoolers Association
PO Box 3228, Missoula, MT 59806
Pascal & Mona Redfern, 406-273-2430
Other contacts: Lyle & Debbie Kline, 406-721-1714; Kevin Rognstad, 406-542-1222.

Primrose Montessori
600 S Ave E/PO Box 3354, Missoula, MT 59806
Nancy Deskins

Shining Mountain School (1989)
Box 4402, Missoula, MT 59806
406-721-6303
Type: independent, non-profit

Mission Mountain School
Guest Ranch Rd, Condon, MT 59862

Homeschool Information
PO Box 960, Seeley Lake, MT 59868

The Grapevine (Montana Homeschool News)
(See Resource Appendix)

Kalispell Montessori School (1977)
5 Park Hill Rd, Kalispell, MT 59901
Sally Black Welder, Adm, 406-755-3824
Non-profit; tuition: $150-240/mo
8 teachers, 10 assistants, 130 students, ages 3-12
Affiliation: AMS
Governance by administrator, teachers, board
Strong bond with community; childcare; interns accepted.

Garden
985 N Meridan Rd, Kalispel, MT 59903

Sugar N Spice
255 Summit Ridge Dr, Kalispel, MT 59903

Flathead Homeschool Association
360 One Way, Columbia Falls, MT 59912
406-892-4052

Nebraska

Coney High Alternative Program for Students (CHAPS) (1986)
104 Coney St, Augusta, NE 04330
Nancy Ruark, 402-626-2460
Kennebec County
Type: public choice
4 teachers, 45 students, mainly at-risk, ages 14-19, HS
Entrance requirements: application, interview, enrolled in Coney HS
Governance by principal
Teacher qualifications: ME Certification
Employment for credit; point reward system; opportunities to explore areas of special interest; work portfolios; urban location.

Nebraska Home School Contact
1208 Robin Dr, Bellevue, NE 68005
Doug and Cindy Nurss, 402-292-0962

Alternative Learning Center (1974)
957 N Pierce, Fremont, NE 68025
Cindy Diers, Head Tch, 402-727-3180
Dodge County
Type: public choice/at-risk
4 teachers, 50 students, mainly at-risk, ages 13-21, 7-12th grade
Residency required
Governance by teachers and principal
Graduation or exit to home school; contracts; voc, social skills; multi-aged classes; rural location; transportation.

Fremont Learning Center
957 North Pl, Fremont, NE 68025
Cindy Diers, 402-721-2865
Type: public at-risk
100 students
Entrance requirements: recommendation, conference, review, district residency.
Guidance; counseling; remotivation; diagnostic individualized instruction; small controlled group work; vocational awareness.

Nebraska Home School Contact
Rt 1 Box 142, Herman, NE 68029
Nancy Boswell, 402-456-7733
Washington (Blair) County

COPE: Curriculum Options Program for Education
Papillion-LaVista Senior High
402 Centennial Rd, Papillion, NE 68046
Kathy Roehrig, 402-339-0405
Type: public at-risk
225 students, HS
Students involved in program/curriculum planning; individual counseling; HS diploma or GED; minimal attendance policy.

Montessori Children's Room
5405 Franklin St, Omaha, NE 68104
Mary Boden

Jackson Alternative Center
620 S 31st St, Omaha, NE 68105
402-978-7241

Child's World
7101 Mercy Rd, Omaha, NE 68106-2619
Type: Montessori

King Science Center
3720 Florence Blvd, Omaha, NE 68110
402-554-6063

Competency Center for Occupational Education #3
4224 N 30th St, Omaha, NE 68111
Yvonne Steinbach, 402-554-6291
Type: public at-risk
Self-paced.

Druid Hill Math & Computer Center
3030 Spaulding St, Omaha, NE 68111
Elmer Crumbley, 402-554-6084
Type: magnet
4-6th grade
Communications; arts.

Individualized Study Center #2
Building 17 Fort Omaha (1968)
30th & Fort, Omaha, NE 68111
Shirley Simmons, 402-554-6184
Type: public at-risk
Weekly progress reports; classroom for behavior-impaired;
  drug/chemical counseling; pre-natal and childcare;
  problem solving.

Westside Alternative School
1414 Robertson Dr, Omaha, NE 68114
Suzann Morin, Dir, 402-390-8214
Type: public choice
100 students, mainly at-risk, 10-12th grade
Individualized; social skills; vocational.

Montessori School of Omaha
PO Box 24211, Omaha, NE 68124

Father Flanagan High School (1986)
2606 Hamilton, Omaha, NE 68131
Father Jim Gilg, 402-341-1833
Type: independent
27 teachers, 300 students, mainly at-risk, ages 14–21
Success-oriented; social services; self-paced; vocational,
  group, individual counseling; sports; plays; yearbook;
  newspaper; childcare.

Individualized Study Center #1A (1968)
3025 Farnam, Omaha, NE 68131
Judith Fisher, Lead Tch, 402-978-7383
Type: public at-risk
Weekly progress reports; behavior-impaired classroom; drug/
  chemical counseling; pre-natal and child care; problem
  solving.

Omaha Magnet Center
3230 Burt St, Omaha, NE 68131
402-554-6738

Montessori Parent's Co-Op for Children
3869 Webster St, Omaha, NE 68131-1809

House of Montessori
400 S 39th St, Omaha, NE 68131-3711

Montessori Academy for Children (1983)
7828 MapleSt, Omaha, NE 68134
Peggy A. Klausen, Dir, 402-393-2035
Tuition: $303/mo
2 teachers, 1 assistant, 22 students, mainly international,
  ages 3-6
Affiliations: AMS, NAEYC
Governance by administrator

Fully equipped Montessori environment fosters individual initiative and growth; suburban location.

Sandor Elementary
5959 Oak Hills Dr, Omaha, NE 68137-3319
Type: Montessori

Montclair Elementary School
2405 S 138th St, Omaha, NE 68144-2498
Barbara Junes
Type: Montessori

OPEN
7930 Raven Oaks Dr, Omaha, NE 68152
402-572-8515
Type: home-based

Great Plains Montessori
12610 Pacific, Omaha, NE 68154

Millard Public Schools
1010 S 144th St, Omaha, NE 68154
Dr Tom Nenneman
Type: Montessori

Montessori Educational Centers
12504 Pacific St, Omaha, NE 68154-3599
Lavonne Plambeck

Nebraska Home School Contact
Rt 1 Box 115, Firth, NE 68358
Bonnie Paschold, 402-791-5717
Holland County

Nebraska Home School Contact
RR 1, Johson, NE 68378
Nancy Baltensperger, 402-868-6765
Auburn County

Nebraska Home School Contact
Rt 2 Box 129A, Milford, NE 68405
Arlyn and Cindy Hanseling, 402-761-2225
Seward County

Nebraska Home School Contact
Rt 3 Box 222, Nebraska City, NE 68410
Mike and Garcia Binder, 402-873-4627

Prairie Hill Learning Center
RR 1 Box 17, Roca, NE 68430-9708
Type: Montessori

Weeping Water Schools Resource Room
Weeping Water, NE 68463
Heidi Goodenkauf, 402-267-2435
Type: public at-risk
15-20 students, 7-12th grade
Entrance by referral only.
Vocational and individual counseling; personal, social transi-
  tion adjustments.

Howard Dougherty Learning Center at Epworth Village
21st & Divion Ave, York, NE 68467
George Young, 402-362-3353
Type: independent
Students mainly at-risk, K-12th grade
Holistic treatment; work experience; small groups;
  individualized.

The Villare Pre-School
1328 Plum St, Lincoln, NE 68502-2342
Type: Montessori

Nebraska Center for Children & Youth: Whitehall School
5701 Walker, Lincoln, NE 68504
402-471-3305
Type: public at-risk, boarding
K-12th grade
Enrollment restricted to wards of the state.
Work experience; cooperative programs; behavior modifica-
  tion, contracts; vocational, group, individual counseling.

LEARN
7741 E Avon Ln, Lincoln, NE 68505
402-488-7741
Type: home-based

Nebraska Home Educators Association
PO Box 57041, Lincoln, NE 68505
Type: state home-based

Children's Circle Montessori
121 Skyway Rd, Lincoln, NE 68505-2627

Bryan Extension Center (1970)
1801 S 40th, Lincoln, NE 68506
Ted McCartney, 402-489-8659
Type: public at-risk
400 students, partly at-risk, 7-12th grade
Learning activity packets; students involved in program/curriculum planning; dual enrollment; career exploration; individual, vocational counseling; minimal attendance policy.

Montessori School for Young Children (1977)
4727 A St, Lincoln, NE 68506
Debbie Nugara, Suzanne Wolford or Chris Dregalla, 402-489-4366
Non-profit; tuition: $170-185/wk
2 teachers, 4 assistants; students mainly international, ages infant-6
Affiliations: AMS, AMI
Governance by teachers, administrators, parent cooperative; urban location; interns accepted.

Nebraska Independent Homeschoolers Network
8010 Lillibridge St, Lincoln, NE 68506
Type: state home-based

Lincoln East High Optional School
1000 S 70th St, Lincoln, NE 68510
D. C. Salesteom, 402-489-7121
Type: public at-risk
14 students, HS
Entrance by referral.
Counseling.

Nebraska Home School Contact
2610 Winchester S, Lincoln, NE 68512
Kathleen Lenzen, 402-423-4297

Lincoln Independent Study High School
University of Nebraska (1929)
269 NCCE, Lincoln, NE 68583-9800
James E. Schiefelbein, EdD, Prin, 402-472-1926, FAX: 404-472-1901
Lancaster County
Type: independent, non-profit; tuition: $81/course
12 teachers, 4,000 students, ages 13-19, HS
Accreditation: NCACS; NE
Governance by principal
Teacher qualifications: NE Certification
Complete college prep; urban location

Columbus High School Alternative Program
2200 26th St, Columbus, NE 68601
402-564-3224 x47
Type: public at-risk
35 students
Entrance by referral.
Vocational, individual counseling; behavior contracts; vocational training, placement.

Nebraska Home School Contact
1601 Clark St, Norfolk, NE 68701
Walt and Kathy Steinke, 402-371-8089

Nebraska Home School Contact
PO Box 576, Dakota, NE 68731
Ed Reising, 402-987-3827
Lewis and Clark (S Sioux City) County

Progress School Alternative Education Center
615 N Elm, Grand Island, NE 68801
308-382-4467
Type: public at-risk
100 students, HS
Entrance requirements: determined by executive board
One semester course; open, non-scheduled classes; community-based; dual enrollment; vocational, group, individual counseling; individual learning packets; minimal attendance policy.

The Children's Place
504 W 10th St, Grand Island, NE 68801-4045
Type: Montessori

Kearney High School Alternative Education (1977)
3610 6th Ave, Kearney, NE 68847
308-234-1720 x9
Type: public at-risk
HS
Entrance by referral.
Tutorials; attitudinal adjustment; career exploration; vocational training; minimal attendance policy.

Nebraska Home School Contact
Rt 3 Box 238, Kearney, NE 68847
Bill and Robin Phipps, 308-237-3783

Nebraska Home School Contact
Rt 1 Box 116, Merna, NE 68856
Martin and Karen Bredthauer, 308-643-2591
Broken Row County

Nebraska Home School Contact
Rt 3 Box 73, Ord, NE 68862
Duane and Kathy Lange, 308-728-3217

Hastings Junior High Alternative Program
505 N Hastings, Hastings, NE 68901
Dr John Ewing, 402-462-5196
Type: public at-risk
10 students, JH
Entrance by referral.
Individual counseling; behavior modification, contracts; self-paced; minimal attendance policy.

Nebraska Home School Contact
1323 7th Ave, Holdrege, NE 68949
Linda Rodenbaugh, 308-995-2485

Nebraska Home School Contact
212 Water Ave, Holdrege, NE 68949
Lee and Carol Sanders, 308-995-6933

Nebraska Home School Contact
RR1 Box 23, Oxford, NE 68967
Robert and Martha Bergquist, 308-824-3452
South Central County

Nebraska Home School Contact
R1 Box 159, Indianola, NE 69034
Jim and Marilyn Gaster, 308-364-2528
McCook County

Nebraska Home School Contact
1404 Burlington, North Platte, NE 69101
Walt and Jolene Catlett, 308-728-3217

Haskell Hill Montessori
1600 Ash St, Sidney, NE 69162-1122
Wendy Lou Jacons

Nebraska Home School Contact
Rt 2 Box 210, Miniature, NE 69359
Rod and Lori McCoy, 308-783-2208
Valley (Scottsbluff) County

Nevada

Clark County Alternative Education Program
1941 Jefferson St, N Las Vegas, NV 89030
Bill Rohnkohl
Type: public

Montessori Academy of Southern Nevada
6000 W Oakey Blvd, Las Vegas, NV 89102-1253
Connie Mormon

Clark Cty Alternative Education
2201 E St. Louis Ave, Las Vegas, NV 89104
Steve Mudery
Type: public choice

Christian Home Educators of Nevada
1576 Del Almo Dr, Las Vegas, NV 89104-5009
Joleen Hatfield
Type: state home-based

Our Lady of Las Vegas Montessori School
3036 Alta Dr, Las Vegas, NV 89107-3202

Home Schools United/Vegas Valley
PO Box 93564, Las Vegas, NV 89121
702-870-9566

Trinity Montessori School
PO Box 2246, Reno, NV 89505-2246

Cambridge School
1330 Foster Dr #A, Reno, NV 89509-1200
Type: Montessori

Nevada Home Schools, Inc
PO Box 21323, Reno, NV 89515
702-972-4126

New Hampshire

Souhegan High School
Boston Post Rd, Amherst, NH 03031
Dr Robert McKin, Prin, 603-673-9940
Type: public; tuition: $7,200/yr
60 teachers, 675 students, ages 14-18, HS
Affiliation: CES
Governance by school-based community council, board,
   faculty and student reps
Teacher qualifications: NH Certification
Interdisciplinary; team structures; outcomes-based; exit exhi-
   bitions, portfolios; inclusive; rural location; interns
   accepted.

Derry Montessori School (1982)
65 E Broadway, Derry, NH 03038
Donna J. Ouellette, Adm, 603-432-8345
Tuition: $2,200-2,700/yr
5 teachers, 2 assistants, 50 students, ages 3-6
Affiliation: AMS
Governance by administrator, board
Music; computer programs; summer program includes arts,
   swim instruction, science; childcare; interns accepted.

New England Montessori Teacher Education Center
   (1977)
30 Moose Club Rd, Goffstown, NH 03045
Bonne LaMothe, 603-641-5156, FAX: 603-641-1339
Type: Montessori higher education
Student adult ages
Affiliation: AMS; accreditation: MALTE
AMS training in Boston area.

Clearway Alternative High School (1977)
40 Arlington St, Nashua, NH 03060
Keith Howard, Prin, 603-598-8303, FAX: 603-882-0069
Hillsborough County

Type: independent, non-profit; tuition: $7,558/yr
8 teachers, 60 students, mainly at-risk, ages 15-19
Entrance requirements: interview by principal and students
Governance by principal, teachers
Teacher qualifications: Learning disabilities, emotional handi-
   caps, subject certification
Improvisational theater; 160+ performances nationwide; no
   letter grades; non-compulsory class attendance; multi-
   aged classes; interns accepted.

New Hampshire Home Education Association
9 Mizoras Dr, Nashua, NH
Type: state home-based

Materials Company of Boston
(See Resource Appendix)

New England Montessori Children's Center
223 Main St, Salem, NH 03079

Geocommons College (1991)
RR 2 Box 793 Derbyshire Farm, Temple, NH 03084
Bruce Kantner, Dir, 603-654-6705
Hillsboro County
Type: higher education, boarding, non-profit; tuition: vari-
   able, scholarships
4 teachers, 5-15 students
Entrance requirements: must be able to travel, live simply in
   rural India
Affiliations: UNH, Gaia Educational Outreach Institute
Governance by consensus
Teacher qualifications: background, skills, goals in harmony
   with program
Sustainable community; ecological literacy; bioregional, world
   studies; compassionate, mindful living; visits exemplary
   communities in USA, Europe, India; partial UNH credit;
   interns accepted.

High Mowing School (1942)
PO Box 850, Abbot Hill Rd, Wilton, NH 03086
Virginia R. Buhr, Adms Dir, 603-654-2391
Hillsborough County
Type: Waldorf, boarding, non-profit; tuition: $9,950-10,500
    day, $16,250-18,000 boarding/yr, scholarships
20 teachers, 85 students, ages 13–19, 9–12th grade
Entrance requirements: application, transcripts, tch recs,
    interview
Affiliations: NEASC, NAIS, ISANNE, AWSNA, SATB
Governance by faculty
Teacher qualifications: BA, Waldorf interest/training, love
    teenagers
College prep; extensive arts; social responsibility; interna-
    tional community; multi-aged classes; rural location;
    interns accepted.

Pine Hill Waldorf School (1972)
PO Box 668, Abbot Hill Rd, Wilton, NH 03086
Catherine Weld, Adm, 603-654-6003, FAX: 603-654-2662
Hillsborough County
Non-profit; tuition: $5,000/yr, scholarships
215 students, ages 4.5–14, K–8th grade
Affiliation: NAWS
Governance by teachers, principal, board
Teacher qualifications: Waldorf certification
Extensive field trips; rural location; interns accepted.

New Hampshire Alliance for Home Education
16 Winter Circle #RFD3, Manchester, NH 03103-1008
Type: state home-based

Christian Home Educators of New Hampshire
PO Box 961, Manchester, NH 03105
Type: state home-based

Bedford Montessori School (1984)
24 Tirrell Hill Rd, Bedford, NH 03110-5208
Gail R. Bannon, Adm, 603-627-9545
Tuition: $2,200/yr
5 teachers, 4 assistants, 65 students, ages 3–6
Affiliations: AMS, NAMTA, NAEYC
Governance by an administrator
Foreign language; private and group music lessons; gymnas-
    tics; interns accepted.

Montessori Learning Center (1977)
389 Pembroke St, Pembroke, NH 03275
Myrta Bergevin, Adm, 603-485-8550
Non-profit; tuition: $4,100-4,200/yr
3 teachers, 3 assistants, 59 students, ages 3–12
Governance by democratic school meeting, board
Childcare; rural location; interns accepted.

Second Start (1979)
19 Knight St, Concord, NH 03301
Jim Snodgrass, Caroline Durr, 603-225-3318
Merrimack County
Type: public at-risk
4 teachers, 40 students, ages 14–19, 8–12th grade
Referral by sending school
Governance by principal, board
Some students identified as having learning or emotional
    handicaps; structured, highly individualized program; no
    letter grades; multi-aged classes; also located at 450 N
    State St; interns accepted.

New Hampshire Homeschooling Coalition
PO Box 2224, Concord, NH 03302
Abbey Lawrence, Coord, 603-539-7233
Type: state home-based
$15/yr membership fee; bi-monthly newsletter; guidebook.

Monadnock Waldorf School (1976)
98 S Lincoln St, Keene, NH 03431
Hanneke Van Riel, Admission Dir, 603-357-4442, FAX:-2955
Cheshire County

Non-profit; tuition: $2,500-4,850/yr, scholarships
20 teachers, 150 students, ages 3.5–14, pre K–8th grade
Entrance requirements: application, transcripts, health
    forms, interview
Affiliation: AWSNA
Governance by college of teachers and board
Teacher qualifications: Waldorf training, experience
Largest independent ES in region; 2 sites; student experi-
    ences self as musician, painter, craftsperson, scholar, actor,
    writer, citizen; urban & rural location; interns accepted.

Montessori Schoolhouse of Cheshire County
259 Summit Rd, Keene, NH 03431-1581

Keene Montessori School
91 West St, Keene, NH 03431-3374
Diane Lucas Plotczyk

Antioch New England Graduate School (1964)
40 Avon St, Keene, NH 03431-3516
Torin Finser, Dir, Waldorf; David Sobel, Heidi Watts, Ed Dept,
    603-357-3122, FAX: 603-357-0718
Cheshire County
Tuition: Waldorf cert $7725 masters $12300, scholarships
Entrance requirements: BA or equivalent, studies in
    Anthroposophy.
Fully accredited
Governance by board
MA, MEd, MHSA, MS programs in Waldorf training, integrated
    day, science and env ed, counseling psychology, dance,
    therapy, administration; Waldorf Program limited to 20
    new students/yr; the arts and internship are essential parts
    of program; no letter grades

The Well School
360 Middle Hancock Rd, Peterboro, NH 03458
Jay Garland, 603-924-6908
Type: independent

Cobblestone Publishing
(See Resource Appendix)

The Meeting School (1957)
Thomas Rd, Rindge, NH 03461-9781
Ed Miller, Admissions Director, 603-899-3366
Cheshire County
Type: independent, boarding, non-profit; tuition: $15,000,
    scholarships
12 teachers, 27 students, ages 13–19, 9–12th grade
Entrance requirements: willingness on part of student; won't
    take extreme at-risk
Affiliations: NCACS, ISEANNE
Governance by faculty consensus for some decisions; whole
    community or board for some
Students live in cooperative households with faculty, sharing
    cooking, cleaning; 4-hr work study: farm, childcare, office;
    4 week intersession project-travel; apprenticeships, peace
    studies; student-run radio station, post graduates; no
    letter grades; multi-aged classes; extensive field trips; rural
    location; interns accepted.

Montessori Childcare Center
58 South St, Littleton, NH 03561-1818

The Children's House
30 Bronson St, Littleton, NH 03561-1826
Type: Montessori

Claremont Kindergarten Center
10 Vine St, Claremont, NH 03743
Peg Lyon
Type: Montessori

Dartmouth College Area Montessori School
10 Barrett Rd, Hanover, NH 03755-2421
Moira Ripley

Boynton School (1964)
RR 1, Box 31B, Orford, NH 03777
Arthur Boynton Jr, Director, 603-353-4874
Type: independent, boarding; tuition: $5000
2 teachers; 7-12+
Governance by cooperative
Individualized help with languages, music, athletics; multi-aged classes; no letter grades; rural location; interns accepted.

Heinemann Educational Books
(See Resource Appendix)

Lancaster Children's House
RFD 1 Box 156, Conway, NH 03818
Type: Montessori

Green Fields Montessori School
PO Box 259, Dover, NH 03820-0259

Montessori School of Exeter (1979)
2 Newfields Rd, Exeter, NH 03833
603-772-5558
Tuition: $3,500-4,600/yr
78 students, ages infant-9
Affiliations: AMI, AMS
Governance by administrator

Montessori School for the Arts and Sciences
13 School St, Exeter, NH 03833-3207

Rockingham County Montessori School, Inc (1983)
144 East Rd, Hampstead, NH 03841-2230
Sara A. Covell, Owner/Adm, 603-329-8041
Tuition: $1,250/1,975/4,100/yr
3 teachers, 4 assistants, 77 students, ages infant-9
Affiliations: AMS, NHDE
Governance by an administrator
Drama; arts; childcare; suburban location; interns accepted.

Support Alternative Family Education (SAFE) (1992)
PO Box 15, Plaistow, NH 03865
Sandra Maida, 603-382-3839

Rockingham County
Non-profit
Non-sectarian; monthly meetings; weekly gatherings for children.

The Children's House Montessori School (1988)
80 Sagamore Rd, Rye, NH 03870-2025
Rebecca Varner, 603-436-5074
Tuition: $2,314-4,819/yr
3 teachers, 4 assistants, 80 students, ages infant-6
Affiliations: NAMTA, NAEYC
Governance by an administrator
French; music; childcare; suburban location; interns accepted.

Community School (1989)
Perkins Farm Rd Box B, S Tamworth, NH 03883
Martha Carlson, Dir, 603-323-7000
Type: independent, non-profit; tuition: $4,300/yr, scholarships
4 teachers, 7 assistants, 28 students, ages 12-18, 6-12th grade
Governance by democratic school meeting, board, faculty and student representatives
Non-competitive atmosphere; traditional academics; community service; hands-on problem solving; environmental education; no letter grades; multi-aged classes; extensive field trips; rural location; interns accepted.

The Cornerstone School (1985)
146 High St, Stratham, NH 03885
Margaret Rice, Adm, 603-772-4349
Type: Montessori, non-profit
14 teachers, 125 students, ages 3-15
Affiliation: AMS
Governance by administrator, board
In pilot program by MAS for NAIS; childcare; rural location; interns accepted.

The Book Cellar
(See Resource Appendix)

New Jersey

Project Achievement at Memorial High School
5501 Park Ave, West New York, NJ
Lillian J. Cave, Dir of Guidance, 902-1140
Type: public at-risk
10 students, ages 15+, 7-8th grade

Project ALIVE at Avenel Learning Center
Woodbine Ave, Avenel, NJ 07001
John F. O'Malley, Prin or Dr Carole Brown, Dir, 201-388-9594
Type: public at-risk
58 students, 7-12th grade
Departmentalized; vocational emphasis.

Bayonne High School Alternative Education
30th St & Ave A, Bayonne, NJ 07002
Donald Ahern, Dir, 201-858-5884
Type: public at-risk
50 ES, 100 HS students

Children's House/Children's World Magazines
(See Resource Appendix)

Children's House
437 Pompton Ave, Cedar Grove, NJ 07009-1802
Type: Montessori

Small World Montessori School
777 Anderson Ave, Cliffside Park, NJ 07010-2121

Rainbow Montessori School
43 Clifton Ave, Clifton, NJ 07011

Project Rebound at Clifton High School
333 Colfax Ave, Clifton, NJ 07013
Bill Cannici, Vice Prin, 201-470-2455
5 teachers, 21 students, mainly at risk
Volunteer staff, students.

Cranford Alternative Program at Lincoln School
Cranford, NJ 07016
Gary Sorrentino, 272-9100 x277
Type: public at-risk
50 students, 7-12th grade
Behavior management system.

Montessori School of Cranford
110 Eastman St, Cranford, NJ 07016-2122

Middle College High School at Union County College
1033 Springfield Ave, Cranford, NJ 07018
Barbara H. Wilson, Coord, 201-709-7082, 709-7084

Type: public at-risk
65 students, mainly at-risk, 9–12th grade

Fort Lee Preschool
449 Anderson Ave, Fort Lee, NJ 07024
Type: Montessori

Early Education Centre
326 Guntzer St, Fort Lee, NJ 07024-4709
Type: Montessori

St Anthony Montessori School
672 Passaic Ave, Kearny, NJ 07032
Sr Bernadette

Project ASPIRE (1989)
Monmouth Court Community Center, Livingston, NJ 07039
Rosemary McGuinness, Dir, 535-8179
Type: public choice
5 teachers, 40 students, 10–12th grade
For LHS students
Tutorial; cooperative; small groups; flexible schedule; con-
    tracts; CAI; interdisciplinary; independent study; team
    teaching; field trips.

Montessori School of Millburn
19 Main St, Millburn, NJ 07041-1301

Edgemont Elementary
20 Edgemont Rd, Montclair, NJ 07042
Adunni Anderson, 201-509-4162
Type: magnet
Student ages 4+,-5th grade
Montessori.

Glenfield Middle School
25 Maple Ave, Montclair, NJ 07042
David Gidich, 201-509-4171
Type: magnet
6–8th grade
Gifted and talented; performing arts.

Montclair Cooperative School
65 Chestnut St, Montclair, NJ 07042
Lauretta Freeman
Type: independent

Montclair High School Alternative Programs
Rand Bldg, 176 N Fullerton Ave, Montclair, NJ 07042
Frank Rennie, Prin, 201-783-8957
35 students, mainly at-risk
Separate facility on campus; community service; guidance;
    work study.

Nishuane Primary
32 Cedar Ave, Montclair, NJ 07042
Frank Alvarez, 201-509-4222
Type: magnet
Student ages 4+,-2nd grade
Gifted and talented.

Maria Montessori Early Learning
90 Christopher St, Montclair, NJ 07042-4228

George Innes Annex
141 Park St, Montclair, NJ 07043
Roger Scales, 201-509-4004
Type: magnet
9–12th grade
Performing arts.

Montclair High School
1000 Chestnut St, Montclair, NJ 07043
Roger Scales, 201-509-4100
Type: magnet
9–12th grade
Performing arts.

Montessori Pre-School
43 Watchung Ave, Montclair, NJ 07043-1337

The Children's House, Inc
26 Montrose Ave, Verona, NJ 07044-1813
Type: Montessori

Mustard Seed Montessori
PO Box 261, Montville, NJ 07045-0261

St Elizabeth's Montessori
499 Park Rd, Parsippany, NJ 07054-1736
Sr Anna Maria

Children's Place
PO Box 1272, Plainfield, NJ 07061-1272
Type: Montessori

Project ACE
1138 Kline Pl, Rahway, NJ 07065
Paul R. DiGiano, 908-396-1023
45 students, mainly at-risk, 9–12th grade

Rutherford Alternative Program
56 Passaic Ave, Rutherford, NJ 07070
Marilyn Gillio, Dir, 201-933-2671
10 students, mainly at risk, 7–8th grade
Community experiences; individualized; interest based.

Phoenix School
144 Boiling Springs, East Rutherford, NJ 07073
Melinda Miller
Type: Montessori

The Christopher Academy (1986)
1390 Terrill Rd, Scotch Plains, NJ 07076
Amelia McTamaney, Evelyn Hagman, 908-322-4652, FAX: 908-
    322-4616
Type: Montessori, non-profit; tuition: $1,430-5,940/yr
100 students, ages infant-6
Affiliations: AMS, NJAC, NAEYC
Governance by an administrator and a board of trustees
On-site teacher training program associated with SNMC;
    workshop site for SNMC correspondence students;
    summer camp with swimming; childcare; suburban loca-
    tion; interns accepted.

L'Academy Montessori
1171 Terrill Rd, Scotch Plains, NJ 07076-2227

South Orange Country Day School
461 Vose Ave, South Orange, NJ 07079-3018
Type: Montessori

Children's Academy of Springfield (1977)
37 Church Mall, Springfield, NJ 07081
Susan Weller, Dir/Owner, 201-379-3524
Type: Montessori; tuition: $2,350-5,600/yr
6 teachers, 1 assistant, 120 students, ages toddler-6
Governance by administrator
Computer; French; dance; piano; storytelling and book sign-
    ings by well-known children's authors; suburban location.

**Union City Student Awareness of Substance Abuse
    Program**
3912 Bergen Tpk, Union City, NJ 07087
Tom Kelly, Dir, 201-392-3642
K–12th grade
City-wide programs; Here's Looking at You-2000; peer
    groups;counseling; linked with Project Fresh and UCPD
    Dare Program.

The Christopher Academy (1963)
510 Hillcrest Ave, Westfield, NJ 07090
Amelia McTamaney or Cathy Maravetz, Dir, 908-233-7414, FAX:
    908-322-4616
Type: Montessori
4 teachers, 6 assistants, 100 students, ages infant-6

Affiliations: AMS, NJMAC; accreditations: SNMC, NAEEC
Governance by administrator
Teacher training program associated with SNMC; workshop
    site for SNMC correspondence students; summer program;
    childcare; suburban location; interns accepted.

Arts High School
550 Dr Martin L. King Blvd, Newark, NJ 07102
Eleta J. Caldwell, Prin, 201-733-6757
Type: public choice
500 students, 9–12th grade
Entrance requirements: competitive exam and audition.

University High School
55 Clinton Pl, Newark, NJ 07108
Doris Culver, 201-374-3190
Type: magnet
9–12th grade
Humanities.

Frank H. Morrell
1253 Clinton Ave, Irvington, NJ 07111
Anthony Pilone, 201-399-6893
Type: magnet
9–12th grade
Musically and artistically talented.

Irvington Alternative High School
1253 Clinton Ave, Irvington, NJ 07111
Richard Graves, Asst Prin, 399-6956
7 teachers, 75 students, mainly truants, 9–11th grade

Madison Ave School
163 Madison Ave, Irvington, NJ 07111
Franklin Saunders, 201-399-6871
Type: magnet
K–6th grade
Gifted.

Mt Vernon Ave School
36 Mt Wernon Ave, Irvington, NJ 07111
Priscella Butts, 201-399-6875
Type: magnet
K–8th grade
Gifted.

Union Ave School
427 Union Ave, Irvington, NJ 07111
Walter Rusak, 201-399-6885
Type: magnet
K–8th grade
Musically and artistically talented.

Mont-Vail Day Care Center
871 Sanford Ave, Irvington, NJ 07111-1511
Type: Montessori

Storms-Street School Juvenile Diversion Project
1 Canal St, Jersey City, NJ 07302
Major Smith, Dir, 201-915-6773, 915-6774
20 students, mainly truants; disruptive

Teenage Expectant Mothers' Program (TEMP)
30 Baldwin Ave, 10th Flr, Clinic Bldg, Jersey City, NJ 07305
Jennifer C. Figurelli, PhD, Dir, 201-915-6431
145 students, 7–12th grade
Pre, post-natal instruction; child bearing, rearing, parenting
    concepts; guidance program.

Apple Montessori
104 Boonton Ave, Kennelong, NJ 07405

Kinnelon Montessori School
Maple Ln, Kinnelon, NJ 07405

Pride Alternative School at Fairlawn High School
Berdan Ave, Fair Lawn, NJ 07410
Peter J. Natale, Dir, 794-5457

15-45 students, mainly at-risk
Off-campus facility.

Young World Day School (1972)
585 Wyckoff Ave, Mahwah, NJ 07430
Janet D. Jaarsma, 201-327-3888
Type: Montessori, non-profit; tuition: $810-6,000/yr
17 teachers, 7 assistants, 230 students, ages infant-12
Affiliations: AMS, NCCAA; accreditation: NAEYC
Governance by administrator
Ungraded classrooms; max 2:18 ratio/class; traditional
    Montessori preschool, K; childcare; suburban location;
    transportation; interns accepted.

Friends' Neighborhood School (1953)
224 Highwood Ave, Ridgewood, NJ 07450
Penny Dalto, Dir, 201-445-0681
Bergen County
Type: public/independent choice; scholarships
6 teachers, 55-63 students, partly at-risk, ages 2.5-5, pre-K
Governance by board
Teacher qualifications: BA in early childhood
Developmentally appropriate curriculum; conflict resolution;
    problem solving; no letter grades; suburban location;
    interns accepted.

Montessori Learning Center
169 Fairmont Rd, Ridgewood, NJ 07450
Patricia Janson

Ridgewood Friends Neighborhood Nursery
224 Highwood, Ridgewood, NJ 07450
Penny Dalto
Type: Quaker

Ridgwood Montessori School (1989)
52 Passaic St, Ridgewood, NJ 07450
Evelyn Moshier, Dir, 201-447-5989
Tuition: $175-575/mo
3 teachers, 3 assistants, 52 students, ages infant-6
Entrance requirement: min age 2.5
Affiliation: AMS
Governance by administrator
Computer ed; drama; art; childcare; suburban location; trans-
    portation; interns accepted.

The Village School for Children (1977)
660 E Glen Ave, Ridgewood, NJ 07450
Marilyn Larkin, 201-445-6160
Type: Montessori, non-profit; tuition: $3,024-7,100/yr
10 teachers, 7 assistants, 138 students, ages infant-9
Entrance requirements: interview
Affiliation: AMS
Governance by board of trustees
Childcare; suburban location; interns accepted.

Lakeland Regional High School Alternative Program
205 Conklintown Rd, Wanaque, NJ 07465
Ann Badia, Dir, 201-835-1900
Passaic County
20-30 students, mainly emotionally disturbed, 7–12th grade
Departmentalized curriculum; counseling; work study;
    behavior modification system; computers.

Apple Montessori
Church Ln, Wayne, NJ 07470

Rainbow Montessori Schools
970 Black Oak Ridge Rd, Wayne, NJ 07470
Cheryl Trutt

Hackensack High School Alternative Program
1st & Beech St, Hackensack, NJ 07601
Greg Esposito, Head Teacher, 201-646-7903 or 646-0722
30-40 students, mainly at-risk, 9–12th grade

New World Montessori School
165 Burton Ave, Hasbrouck Heights, NJ 07604-1923
Susan Fleming

Maywood Montessori Learning Center (1981)
39 E Pleasant Ave, Maywood, NJ 07607
Barbara Pilipie, Dir, 201-843-4466
Tuition: $2,600-4,000/yr
4 teachers, 3 assistants, 75 students, mainly international,
    ages 3–6
Entrance requirements: toilet trained
Affiliations: AMS, NCCA, NAMTA,NEA, NJMAC, NJAEYC, NJCCA
Governance by administrator
Inclusive; flexibility for working parents; computer program;
    convenient location; childcare; rural location; interns
    accepted.

Center for Design Studies
154 St Nicholas Ave, Englewood, NJ 07631
Michael J Shannon, Dir, 201-568-5528, FAX: 201-568-9341
Non-profit
Interdisciplinary; hands-on; project and community-based.

Institute of General Semantics (1938)
(See Resource Appendix)

Bede School
255 Walnut, Englewood, NJ 07631-3104
D Lilly
Type: Montessori

The Spring School (1970)
276 Haworth Ave, Haworth, NJ 07641
Dr Deborah Knapp, Dir, 201-384-2444, FAX:-0590
Type: Montessori, non-profit; tuition: 1,800-5,700/yr
4 teachers, 4 assistants, 47–92 students, ages infant-12
Entrance requirements: interview; transfers accepted
Affiliation: AMS; accreditations: AMS, NJ
Governance by administrator, board of trustees
History of science curriculum includes experiments; whole
    language; phonics; suburban location; interns accepted.

North Jersey Home Schoolers Association (1987)
c/o 44 Oak St, Hillsdale, NJ 07642
Christa Grajcar, New Member Coord, 666-6025
Bergen County
Type: state home-based, non-profit
Student ages 4-18, pre K-12th grade
Christian; classes; special events; newsletter; bi-annual kids'
    newsletter; all faiths, backgrounds supported.

Creative Learning, Inc
465 Westminister Pl, Lodi, NJ 07644
Donna Jemas
Type: Montessori

Paramus Community School Transitional Class
145 Spring Valley Rd, Paramus, NJ 07652
Richard Piazza, Dir, 201-261-7800
18 students, mainly at risk, 9–12th grade

Montessori Learning Center (1974)
65 Pascack Rd, Park Ridge, NJ 07656
Helen M. O'Brien, Adm, 201-573-0898
Tuition: $1,750-$6,000/yr
4 teachers, 2 assistants, 41 students, ages infant-6
Affiliations: AMS, NJMAC, MI
Governance by administrator
Teacher qualifications: average 13 yrs Montessori experience
Music; PE; computers; suburban location; interns accepted.

Teaneck High School Alternative II
100 Elizabeth Ave, Teaneck, NJ 07666
Joseph O. White, Dir, 201-833-5406
4 teachers, 1 assistant, 50-70 students, mainly at risk, 9–12th
    grade

Early Learning Center
1234 Teaneck Rd, Teaneck, NJ 07666-4929
Type: Montessori

Chrismont Academy (1986)
701 D St, Belmar, NJ 07719
Patricia Fosdick, Dir, 908-681-2572
Type: Montessori; tuition: $2,000/yr
1 teacher, 1 assistant, 40 students, ages 3–6
Entrance requirements: toilet trained
Affiliations: NAMTA, NJMAC
Governance by administrator
French; dance/movement; suburban location.

Wall Township Educational Improvement Program
PO Box 1199, Wall, NJ 07719
Raymond Steelman, Dir, 201-449-3070, 681-9772
20 students, mainly at-risk, 9–12th grade
Individualized; Lifeskills curriculum.

New Jersey Unschoolers
2 Smith Rd, Farmingdale, NJ 07727
Nancy Plent, 908-938-2473
Type: state home-based

Montessori Enrichment Center (1979)
29 Newbury Rd, Howell, NJ 07731
Joanne Lister or Maureene Peruzzi, Co-Dirs, 908-364-2244
Tuition: $150-300/mo
5 teachers, 5 assistants, 150 students, ages infant-6
Affiliations: NAMPTA, NJMAC; accreditation: AMS
Governance by board
New building; intro to French; childcare; suburban location;
    interns accepted.

The New School of Monmouth County (1969)
301 Middle Rd, Holmdel, NJ 07733
Jay Smith, Dir, 201-787-7900
50 students, K-8th grade
Based on philosophies of Dewey, Piaget, British Integrated
    Day; family involvement; individualized; ungraded;
    student-centered; Spanish; drama; piano; music.

Vincent S. Mastro Montessori
36 Birch Ave, Little Silver, NJ 07739-1194

**Education Network of Christian Homeschoolers of New
    Jersey, Inc. (ENOCH)**
65 Middlesex Rd, Matawan, NJ 07747-3030

Montessori Academy of New Jersey
3504 Asbury Ave, Neptune, NJ 07753-2504
Chari Torello

Roots and Wings
8 Landing Trl, Denville, NJ 07834-1004
Type: home-based

Deer Path Montessori School
24 Main St, Flanders, NJ 07836-9112
Cindy Meyer

Rockaway Township Board of Education
School Rd, Hibernia, NJ 07842
Dr Fanning
Type: Montessori

Hilltop Montessori School
32 Lafayette Rd, Sparta, NJ 07871-3599
Laraine Kensicki

Eisenhower Middle School Alternative Program
47 Eyland Ave, Succasunna, NJ 07876
Owen Toale or Penny Sharp, 201-584-2973
8-12 students, mainly at-risk, 8th grade

New Jersey Family Schools Association
RD 3 Box 208, Washington, NJ 07882

Project Excel
PO Box 451, Washington, NJ 07882
Robert Fluck, Dir, 201-689-2193, 689-2199

40-45 students, mainly at risk, 9-12th grade
Small classes; inter-agency support; pre-employment skills; on-the-job experience.

The Albrook School (1979)
PO Box 352, 361A Somerville Rd, Basking Ridge, NJ 07920
Anita Albers, Dir, 908-580-0661, FAX: 908-580-0785
Type: Montessori, non-profit; tuition: $1,675-6,750/yr
12 teachers, 3 assistants, 207 students, ages toddler-12
Affiliations: AMS, NJMAC, NAEYC
Governance by administrator
6.5 acres; heated pool; summer program; art; music; foreign language; childcare; rural location; interns accepted.

Somerset Montessori School
173 Madisonville Rd, Basking Ridge, NJ 07920-0109
Anneliese Gliese

Albrook School
PO Box 352, Basking Ridge, NJ 07920-0352
Type: Montessori

Montessori School
190 Lord Stirling Rd, Basking Ridge, NJ 07920-1329

Sprout House
200 Main St, Chatham, NJ 07928
Joanne Lockwood-White, 201-635-9658
Morris County
Type: independent, non-profit; tuition: $350/mo, scholarships
4 teachers, 38 students, ages 5-12, ungraded
Entrance requirements: interview
Affiliation: NAEYC
Governance by teachers and principal
Teacher qualifications: certification
Focus for younger students on science, children's literature, for older students, social studies; family-type closeness; natural food; strong environmental committment; no letter grades; multi-aged classes; extensive field trips; suburban location; interns accepted.

Madison Montessori School (1981)
19 Green Ave, Madison, NJ 07940
Teresa A Armstrong or Kathy Jenco, 201-966-9544
Non-profit; tuition: $2,400-3,275/yr
7 teachers, 4 assistants, 68 students, ages infant-6
Entrance requirements: application, interview
Affiliation: AMS
Year-long study of one country; small classes; suburban location; interns accepted.

Rainbow Montessori
53 Central Ave, Madison, NJ 07940-1848

Montessori Children's House of Morristown (1965)
21 Cutler St, Morristown, NJ 07960
Brenda Mizel, Exec Dir, 201-539-7853, FAX: 201-539-5182
Non-profit; tuition: $3,250-5,600/yr
9 teachers, 5 assistants, 146 students, ages 3-12
Entrance requirement: Montessori experience for elementary
Affiliations: NAMPTA, NJAIS; accreditations: AMS, MSA, NAEYC
Governance by board
Hands-on workshops, forums in visual, music, performing arts at Children's Cultural Arts Center; childcare; suburban location; interns accepted.

Environmental Montessori School
40 St Joseph Dr, Stirling, NJ 07980
Ms Walsh

Montessori Ceneter for Early Learning
304 Berkshire Ave, Cherry Hill, NJ 08002
Eydie Cohen

Montessori Children's House (1970)
1825 Garden Ave, Cherry Hill, NJ 08003-2303
Caryl Founds, Director, 609-424-0077

Tuition: $2,600/3,800/yr
4 teachers, 7 assistants, 107 students, mainly international, ages 2.5-6
Entrance requirements: toilet trained
Governance by administrator
Gymnastics, music and Tiny Tumbles optional; suburban location; transportation; interns accepted.

Coles Program at Malberg School
Ranoldo Terr, Cherry Hill, NJ 08034
Seymour J. Wallach, 609-429-7283
Cherry Hill District
60 students, mainly emotionally handicapped, 9-12th grade

Unschoolers Support Group for Central NJ
150 Folwell Station Rd, Jobstown, NJ 08041
Karen Mende-Fridkis
Burlington County
Weekly activities; writers workshop; science; music; field trips; art; play; suburban location.

LaHara Steele Productions
705 Downing Ct, Willingboro, NJ 08046
Joe Steele, Dir, 609-871-3318
Write, produce, perform educational music about dangers of substance abuse.

Montessori Child Development Center
PO Box 231, Marlton, NJ 08053

Naudain Academy
RD 1 School Ln, Marlton, NJ 08053
Leddy Naudain
Type: Montessori

Moorestown Friends School
110 E Main St, Moorestown, NJ 08057
Alan Craig, Head, 609-235-2900
Type: Quaker

Burlington County Special Services School District
PO Box 775, Woodlane Rd, Mt Holly, NJ 08060
Dr Carmine DeSopo, Supt, 609-261-5600
800 students, ages-21
For multiply-handicapped, trainable mentally retarded and emotionally disturbed students.

Friends School (1969)
15 High St; Box 488, Mullica Hill, NJ 08062
Hanshi Deshbandhu, Tch/Adm, 609-478-2908, FAX:-0263
Gloucester County
Type: Quaker, non-profit; tuition: $5,550-6,250/yr, scholarships
23 teachers, 218 students, ages 4-14, pre K-8th grade
Entrance requirements: screening, testing
Affiliation: FCOE-MS Ac. S
Governance by head of school
Teacher qualifications: college degree
Ethnically diverse; languages; sports; word processing; community service; extensive field trips; childcare.

Rancocas Friends School
1 E Main St, Rancocas, NJ 08073
Constance Beetle, 609-267-8198
Type: Quaker

Infanta Montessori School
Conrow Rd, Delran, NJ 08075
Accreditation: AMI

Montessori Academy
Conrow Rd, Delran, NJ 08075
Ellen Fox Tronco, 609-461-2121
Non-profit; tuition: $2,955-6,030/yr
3 teachers, 3 assistants, 78 students, ages infant-12
Accreditations: AMI, MTA, AMS
Governance by administrator
Childcare.

Project ADVANCE
172 Salem-Woodstown Rd, Salem, NJ 08079
Raymond J. Bielicki, Dir, 609-935-7363
24 students, mainly severely emotionally disturbed, ages 11-21
Behavior mod; individualized; (pre)vocational training.

Homeschoolers of South Jersey
Rt 2 Burnt House Rd, Vincentown, NJ 08088

Children's Montessori Schoolhouse (1986)
730 Barlow Ave, Woodbury, NJ 08096
Ritamarie Akins, Owner/Adm, 609-848-0922, FAX: 609-848-1623
Tuition: $1,695-2,730/yr
2 teachers, 2 assistants, 40 students, ages 3-6
Entrance requirements: age 2.5-3.75; toilet trained; interview
Governance by administrator
Custom designed facility; 4 large child-height windows/class-
    room; yearly nature camp; weekly enrichment in science/
    nature study; creative movement/music; theatre; dance;
    art; childcare; suburban location; interns accepted.

Atlantic County New School
1021 South Main St, Pleasantville, NJ 08232
Type: independent

PACE II (Pregnant Adolescents Continuing Education)
W Decatur Ave, Pleasantville, NJ 08232
Harriett Devlin, Dir, 609-383-6800 x281
9-12th grade
Childbirth, nutrition, parenting classes; counseling; adaptive PE.

Atlantic County Alternative High School
Atlantic CC, 5100 Black Horse Pike, Mays Landing, NJ 08330
John Kellmayer, Prin, 609-343-5004
Type: public choice
80 students, mainly at-risk, 10-12th grade
For chronically disruptive and disaffective students.
County-wide; behavior mod; job skills; access to college
    resources; counseling; learning contracts.

Millville Alternative High School
200 Wade Blvd, Millville, NJ 08332
Charles J. Brett, Jr, Prin, 609-825-2341
9 teachers, 110 students, mainly at-risk, 8-12th grade
Small, evening classes; counseling.

The Tutor (1989)
1239 Whitaker Ave, Millville, NJ 08332
Rose Sias, Dir, 609-327-1224
Cumberland County
Type: home-based
1 teacher, 4 students, ages 4-14, pre K-12th grade
Residency required.
Supplies textbooks; extensive field trips; suburban location

Upper Freehold Regional Alternative School
27 High St, Allentown, NJ 08501
Joe Jakubowski, Dir, 609-259-0300
max 20 students, mainly at risk, 10-12th grade
Off-campus; individualized; small groups.

Jackson Memorial High School Alternative Program
Don Connor Blvd, Jackson, NJ 08527
201-928-1400, 928-5959
Type: public at-risk
Individualized; community-centered human services.

Project RISE at Hopewell Valley Central High School
Pennington-Titusville Rd, Pennington, NJ 08534
Diane Paul, Dir, 609-737-1411
19 students, mainly at risk, 9-10th grade
Individualized; parent contracts; counseling specialists.

Pennington Montessori School
102 W Franklin Ave, Pennington, NJ 08534-1483
Maria O'Connell

Lakeside Montessori Center
39 Magnolia Ln, Princeton, NJ 08540

Princeton Friends School (1987)
470 Quaker Rd, Princeton, NJ 08540
Bonnie Benbow, Adm Coord, 609-683-1194, FAX: 292-0686
Mercer County
Type: Quaker, non-profit; tuition: $3-6,700/yr, scholarships
14 teachers, 80 students, ages 4-14, pre K-8th grade
Affiliations: RSF, NAYS
Governance by teachers and principal
Community service; integrated curriculum; foreign language;
    art; music; dance; exchange with Katzenback School for
    the Deaf; weekly worship; suburban location.

Princeton Montessori School (1968)
487 Cherry Valley Rd, Princeton, NJ 08540
Anita Corzano, Admissions Dir, 609-924-4591, FAX: 609-924-
    2216
Non-profit
315 students, ages infant-15
Affiliations: AMS, NAIS, NJAIS; accreditation: MSA
Governance by a board of trustees
Serves as lab school for Princeton Center for Teacher Educa-
    tion; childcare; suburban location; interns accepted.

Waldorf School of Princeton (1983)
1062 Cherry Hill Rd, Princeton, NJ 08540
Patricia Cuyler, Adm, 609-466-1970
Somerset County
Non-profit; tuition: $6,300/yr, scholarships
27 teachers, 180 students, ages 3.5-14, pre K-8th grade
Entrance requirements: interview and records
Affiliations: AWSNA, NJAIS
Governance by board, college of teachers and administrative
    staff
Teacher qualifications: Waldorf certificate or Masters in
    Waldorf ed
Historic farmstead on 20 acres; field studies; rural location;
    interns accepted.

Holland Middle School
1001 W State St, Trenton, NJ 08618
Morris Kimble, 609-989-2730
Type: magnet
6-8th grade
Fine and performing arts.

LIFT, Inc
225 N Warren St, Trenton, NJ 08618
Alma J. Hill, Exec Dir, 609-392-8688
Students mainly pregnant
GED prep; counseling; emergency assistance.

Hedgepeth/Williams Middle School
301 Gladstone Ave, Trenton, NJ 08629
Michael Rothstein, 609-989-2780
Type: magnet
6-8th grade
Fine and performing arts.

Independence Montessori
2157 Pennington Rd, Trenton, NJ 08638-1429

Pathways at Laurelton School
1819 Rt 88, Brick, NJ 08724
Jane Kohlrenken, 477-2800 x304
Students mainly emotionally disturbed, ages 8-18
Counseling; educational services.

Seeds of Learning (1988)
1138 Concord Dr, Brick, NJ 08724-1015
Maria Hidaldo Dolan, Esq, Founder, 908-458-5435
Ocean County
Type: home-based, non-profit
1 teacher, 2 students, ages 1-5, pre K
Residency required

Governance by parent cooperative
Teacher qualifications: parent
No letter grades; non-compulsory class attendance; multi-aged classes; extensive field trips; multi-cultural.

Woodmansee at Lacey High School
PO Box 206, Haines St, Lanopa Harbor, NJ 08734
William Kaskow, 609-971-1391
9-16 students, mainly classified ED, 9-12th grade
Vocational; life skills; behavior mod model; counseling; bi-weekly parent conferences; parent workshops.

Toms River Alternative Learning Center
1 Drake Ln S, Toms River, NJ 08757
Stephen Finkelstein, Dir, 908-505-5770, FAX: 908-341-1853
70-80 students, mainly at risk, 8-10th grade

Twilight Program
PO Box 6350; N Bridge St & Vogt Dr, Bridgewater, NJ 08807
Sherman Harris, Dir, 201-526-8900
60 students, ages 14-21
Vocational training; career counseling; job orientation.

Dunellen High School Pupil Improvement Program (PIP)
1st St & Lincoln Ave, Dunellen, NJ 08812
John A. Feldman, EdD, Prin, Marybeth Connolly or Cota Kania, 908-968-0885
1 teacher, 30-35 students, mainly at-risk, 7-12th grade
Social worker on staff.

Unitarian Montessori (1985)
176 Tices La, East Brunswick, NJ 08816
Mary Ann Keller, Dir, 908-246-0606
Non-profit; tuition: $400
2 teachers, 5 assistants, 50 students, ages 3-6
Affiliation: AMS
Governance by an administrator and a committee of parents and Unitarian Society members
Near Rutgers U; childcare; suburban location; interns accepted.

East Brunswick Montessori
176 Tices Ln, East Brunswick, NJ 08816-1345
Mary Ann Keller

Acorn Montessori School (1984)
1222 Route 31, Lebanon, NJ 08833

Beverly Peutz, 908-730-8986
Non-profit; tuition: $2,525-5,100/yr
3 teachers, 4 assistants; student ages 3-6
Affiliation: AMS
Governance by administrator, board
Childcare; rural location; interns accepted.

Peppermint Tree Child Care
165 Fieldcrest Ave, Edison, NJ 08837-3622
Type: Montessori

Montessori Children's House of Kendall Park
N Main & E Church St, Milltown, NJ 08850

ACE (Alternative Classroom Experience)
800 Washington Rd, Parlin, NJ 08859
Chuck Faust or Jerry Carney, 201-727-8200 x43,44,45
12 students, mainly at-risk, 7-8th grade

Phillipsburg Adolescent Pregnancy Program
Warren Hospital, Fairview Ave, Phillipsburg, NJ 08865
Office of Special Services, 454-3400 x288
15 students, MS, HS

Raritan Valley Montessori
880 S Branch River Rd, Somerville, NJ 08876-4047
Leslie Meldrum

Charlotte Mason Research & Supply
(See Resource Appendix)

Children's House Montessori School
115 Commercial Ave, New Brunswick, NJ 08901-2748
Sandra Murgall

Lipman-Stern
341-C Crowell's Rd, Highland Park, NJ 08904
Type: home-based
Rituals for Solstice, Rosh Hoshanah, Kwanza, etc.

Westmont Montessori School (1964)
577 Rte 24, Mendham, NJ 09745
Enid Lattner, 908-879-6355, FAX: 908-879-8127
Non-profit; tuition: $2,400-4,500/yr
6 teachers, 6 assistants, 144 students, ages infant-6
Affiliation: AMS
Governance by administrator, board
Interns accepted.

New Mexico

Montessori Learning Center
PO Box 2720, Corrales, NM 87048
Woodcock

Career Enrichment Center
807 Mountain Rd NE, Albuquerque, NM 87102
Jim Simpson, 505-247-3658
Type: public at-risk

Evening High School
800 Odelia Rd NE, Albuquerque, NM 87102
Milton Sanchez, 505-247-4200
Type: public at-risk

Recovery High School
2700 Yale Blvd SE, Albuquerque, NM 87102

Albuquerque Friends School (1992)
1600 5th St NW, Albuquerque, NM 87102-1302

Beverly Booth McCauley, Head, 505-242-8092
Type: Quaker, non-profit; tuition: $4,500/yr, scholarships
2 teachers, 7 students, ages 5-8, K-3rd grade
Affiliation: Friends Council on Education
Governance by board
Teacher qualifications: share values, competent, creative, energetic
Whole child approach; multiple intelligences; conflict resolution skills; strong in Spanish; no letter grades; multi-aged classes; extensive field trips; urban location.

Escuela Del Sol Montessori (1968)
1315 Mountain Rd NW, Albuquerque, NM 87104
Friedje van Gils, Head, 505-242-9817
Non-profit; tuition: $1,617-4,000/yr, scholarships
8 teachers, 6 assistants, 111 students, ages 3-12
Affiliation: AMS

Governance by administrator, faculty/student representatives, board of trustees
Modern approach to Montessori; parental involvement; multi-cultural; childcare; multi-aged classes; suburban location; interns accepted.

School On Wheels
129 Hartline SW, Albuquerque, NM 87105
Felipe Perea, 505-247-0489
Type: public at-risk

Albuquerque Family School (1989)
3211 Monte Vista Blvd NE, Albuquerque, NM 87106
Gael Keyes, Coord, 505-268-0252
Bernalillo County
Non-profit
8 teachers, 160 students, ages 6-13, 1-8th grade
Governance by teachers; principal; parent cooperative
Half day public school, half day home school; parent-taught class once a week; no letter grades; interns accepted.

Adobe Rose Montessori
333 Osuna NW, Albuquerque, NM 87107

Hogares
1218 Griegos NW, Albuquerque, NM 87107
Susan Vandekerkhove, 505-345-8471
Type: public at-risk

The Montessori School
3821 Singer Blvd NE, Albuquerque, NM 87109-5804
Dan Herrick

New Futures School (1973)
5400 Cutler NE, Albuquerque, NM 87110
Dr. Sandy Dixon, Prin, 505-883-5680, FAX: 880-3977
Bernalillo County
Type: public at-risk
30 teachers, 380 students, ages 12-20, 7-12th grade
Enrollment restricted to pregnant/parenting students
Governance by principal
Teacher qualifications: state certification
Works with community health and social services; prenatal and child health clinics; infant daycare; mentorships; comprehensive counseling; parent support groups; multi-aged classes; urban location; transportation; interns accepted.

Freedom High School
2332 San Mateo Pl NE, Albuqurque, NM 87110
Mary Sullivan, 505-884-6012
Type: public at-risk

Montessori of the Southwest
3111 Eubank NE, Albuquerque, NM 87111
Roxanne Checchini

Sunset Mesa Schools
3020 Morris St NE, Albuquerque, NM 87111-4900
Type: Montessori

Academy Montessori School
11216 Phoenix NE, Albuquerque, NM 87112
Indu Kaushal

Albuquerque Montessori School
1334 Wyoming NE, Albuquerque, NM 87112

Sandia Montessori
2433 Chelwood NE, Albuquerque, NM 87112
Mindy Montes, 505-293-6614

New Mexico Christian Home Education
5749 Paradise NW, Albuquerque, NM 87114

New Mexico Family Educators
PO Box 92276, Albuquerque, NM 87199-2276

Aztec Montessori
PO Box 3103, Gallup, NM 87301
Sherry Haskins, Dir, 505-863-4430

Night High School
406 Airport Dr, Farmington, NM 87401
Robert Rank, Lead Tch, 503-599-8627
Type: public at-risk

Rocky Mountain High Academy
PO Box 418, Flora Vista, NM 87415
Type: home-based

Shiprock Alternative School
PO Box 1799, Shiprock, NM 87420
Karen Bates, Exec Dir, 505-368-4904
Type: public choice

Devon's Montessori
844 Old Santa Fe Tr, Santa Fe, NM 87501
Devon Stokhof de Jong

Nizhoni School for Global Consciousness
1304 Old Pecos Trail, Santa Fe, NM 87501
Alex Petofi, 505-982-8293
Type: independent; tuition: $15,000/yr, scholarships
40 students, ages 14-21
Spirituality classes; world travel; diplomas and certificates in arts, ecology, business; students from 12 countries; 2 one-month trips abroad.

Santa Fe SER: Jobs for Progress
1337 Acequia Borrada, Santa Fe, NM 87501

Teen Action Program
1101 Camino de la Cruz Blanca, Santa Fe, NM 87501

Camel Tracks Montessori
10 E Wildflower Dr, Santa Fe, NM 87501-8501

Academy of Communication
21200 Yucca Rd, Santa Fe, NM 87503-5498

Little Earth School (1978)
321 West Zia Rd, Santa Fe, NM 87505
Ellen Souberman, Administrator, 505-988-1968
Type: independent, non-profit; tuition: $4300-4700, scholarships
10 teachers, 52 students, ages 4-8, pre K-3rd grade
Entrance requirements: interview and visit
Governance by teachers and principal, board
Teacher qualifications: state certification
Integrated, multicultural, hands-on, developmentally appropriate curriculum; story telling, music, Spanish, visual and performing arts; cooperative and individual learning; diverse student body and staff; large outdoor learning environment; no letter grades; multi-aged classes; extensive field trips; rural location; interns accepted.

Odyssey Montessori
2638 Via Caballero del Norte, Santa Fe, NM 87505
Shelly Bailey

Santa Fe Learning Cooperative
2463 Camino Capitan, Santa Fe, NM 87505
Type: home-based

Santa Fe Waldorf School (1983)
Rt 9, PO Box 50-B3, Santa Fe, NM 87505
Marline Marquez Scally, Dev & Events Coord, 505-983-9727, FAX:-0486
Non-profit; tuition: $4,900+/yr, scholarships
22 teachers, 183 students, ages 4-13, K-8th grade
Entrance requirement: parent/child interviews
Governance by faculty committees, college, and board
Teacher qualifications: Waldorf training
Spanish; German; instrumental & choral music; fall & spring camping/study trips; spring theater presentations; suburban location; interns accepted.

A Voice For Children
(See Resource Appendix)

Monte Vista Montessori School
1001 Avenida Vista Grande, Santa Fe, NM 87505-8796
Teresa Seamster

National Coalition of Alternative Community Schools
(1976)
(See Resource Appendix)

Chamisa Mesa High School
PO Box 220, El Prado, NM 87529
Maritza Vega, Adm, 505-751-0943
Taos County
Type: independent, non-profit; tuition: $3200/yr, 10 $1000
scholarships
8 teachers, 50 students, ages 14–18, 9-12th grade
Entrance requirements: Application, reading and math
competency
Governance by faculty board
Teacher qualifications: MA, credential or unique subject
qualification
Classical liberal arts program; evaluation by demonstration;
emphasis on critical thinking and problem solving; college
type schedule; coached seminars; interns accepted.

Glorieta Family Educators
Star Rt 1 Box 404, Glorieta, NM 87535
Type: home-based

Canyoncito Montessori
PO Box 1261, 2525 Canyon Rd, Los Alamos, NM 87544
Mary Ann Schnedler, 505-662-2910

Los Alamos Montessori
2400 Canyon Rd, Los Alamos, NM 87544

Sage Montessori School (1972)
304 Rover Blvd, Los Alamos, NM 87544
Connie Hayden, Owner, 505-672-3189, FAX: 505-672-9218
Tuition: $431/445/mo
130 students, ages 3–10
Affiliation: NCME
Governance by principal
Complete Montessori curriculum; no letter grades; multi-
aged classes; suburban location; interns accepted.

School of the North Star
627 North Star Route, Questa, NM 87556
Connie Long, Pres, 505-586-0112; 586-1392
Type: independent, non-profit
6 students, ages 5–14
Individualized; group experience, cooperation; creative
problem solving; artistic, creative expression encouraged.

Vista Grande Preparatory School (1978)
PO Box 1656, Taos, NM 87571
Carolyn Lake, Dir, 505-758-9306
Type: independent; tuition: $250/mo, scholarships
55 students, K–6th grade
Accreditations: Rio Grande Ed Assn, NM Assn of Non-Public
Schools
Low ratio; parent involvement.

GRADS Program
5th & Friedman, Las Vegas, NM 87701

Armand Hammer United World College (1982)
Box 248, Montezuma, NM 87731
Dan Tyson, Dir of Admissions, 505-454-4248, FAX: 505-454-4274
San Miguel County
Type: independent, boarding, non-profit; tuition: $16,500/yr,
scholarships
24 teachers, 200 students, ages 16–19
Entrance requirements: strong academic record, leadership,
interest in world community; max 27 US residents/year
Affiliation: United World Colleges
Governance by teachers; principal
Teacher qualifications: Masters in teaching field, international
experience

IB curriculum, 6th form; equivalent to grades 12–13; students
enter into UK 3-yr undergraduate programs or as sopho-
mores in the US; extensive field trips; community service;
rural location; transportation; interns accepted.

Twin Buttes High School
PO Box 680, Zuni, NM 87752

Socorro Alternative High School
Hwy 60 PO Box 1367, Socorro, NM 87801

Excel Career Program
410 W Court, Las Cruces, NM 88001
John Krause, 505-524-8561
Type: public at-risk

San Andres High School/Las Cruces Night High School
Hwy 28, Mesilla, NM 88001

Mesilla Valley Montessori
1809 El Paseo St, Las Cruces, NM 88001-6009
Carolann Staley

Mount Cristo Rey Challenge High School (1991)
PO Drawer 899, Santa Teresa, NM 88008
Russell E. Phipps, Administrator, 505-589-5350
Gadsdeti ISD District, Dona Ana County
Type: public at-risk
8 teachers, 180 students, ages 16–27, 9-12th grade
Entrance requirements: interview, residency
Governance by teachers, principal, board
Teacher qualifications: BS, state certification
Day care; drug/alcohol intervention; mastery learning; no
letter grades; non-compulsory class attendance; multi-
aged classes; rural location; transportation; interns
accepted.

Mount Cristo Rey High School
PO Box 899, Santa Teresa, NM 88008

Animas Elementary School
PO Box 85, Animas, NM 88020-0085
Type: Montessori

Night High School
Hwy 28, Mesilla, NM 88046
Mike Dobbyn, 505-526-2125
Type: public at-risk

National Homeschool Service
(See Resource Appendix)

Down to Earth School (1988)
112 E 11th St, Silver City, NM 88061
Linda Egge, Dir, 505-388-2902
Grant County
Type: independent; tuition: $160/mo, scholarships
16 teachers, 33 students, ages 11–19, 7-12th grade
Entrance requirements: acceptance of 5 basic rules
Governance by co-directors
Teacher qualifications: student acceptance, knowledge of
subject
Specialist teachers from community; overnight camping
trips; Latin; German; Spanish; mechanics; mountain biking;
student-created electives; multi-aged classes; urban loca-
tion; interns accepted.

Guadalupe Montessori School (1979)
1731 N Alabama St, Silver City, NM 88061
Kathy Dahl-Bredine, 505-388-3343
Tuition: $1,380-1,836/yr, scholarships
4 teachers, 4 assistants, 91 students, ages 3–12
Entrance requirements: age 2.5; toilet trained.
Accreditation: AMI
Governance by administrator
Spanish bilingual program; Catechesis of the Good Shepherd;
parent involvement; family diversity; childcare.

Clovis Evening School
1900 Thronton Ave, Clovis, NM 88101

Broad Horizons Educational Center (1992)
1034 Community Way, Portales, NM 88130
Betty Johnson, Project Dir, 505-356-4254, FAX:-4303
Roosevelt County
Type: public at-risk
100 students, mainly at-risk, ages 15–50, 8-12th grade
Entrance requirements: application, interview, residency.
Outcome-based; social services; work-study; open entry/
open exit; self-paced; learning style assessment; multi-
aged classes; no letter grades; rural location; interns
accepted.

Artesia High School
1006 W Richardson Ave, Artesia, NM 88210
Mike Phipps, 505-746-9816
Type: public at-risk

Alternative School Program
801 N 8th St, Carlsbad, NM 88220
Tom F. Hansen, 505-887-0006

Walter Craft AWARE Program
3000 W. Church St, Carlsbad, NM 88220

Hobbs Alternative High School
800 N Jefferson, Hobbs, NM 88240
Bruce Hardison, 505-397-3241
Type: public at-risk

CHAPS Alternative Junior High School (1989)
1401 College Ave, Alamogordo, NM 88310

505-439-3350, FAX: 505-439-3354
Otero County
Type: public choice
4 teachers, 60 students, mainly at-risk, ages 12–15
Governance by teachers and coordinator
Cooperative learning; integrated instruction; extended day;
natural-logical consequences discipline; field trips; rural
location; interns accepted.

**Montessori Learning Center/Alamogordo Montessori
Academy**
1012 Cuba Ave, Alamogordo, NM 88310
Laurie A. Roth, Dir; Cindy Crouch, Asst Dir, 505-437-0993
Tuition: $190/320/mo
65 students, mainly international, ages 1–12
Affiliation: AMS
Governance by teachers and principal
Manipulative materials for all ages in all academic areas;
extensive field trips; non-compulsory class attendance; no
letter grades; suburban location; transportation; interns
accepted.

Wilderness Experiences School
PO Box 871, Capitan, NM 88310
Tom Tracey, Director, 505-354-2472

Montessori's Little Red School House
PO Box 1977, Ruidoso, NM 88345-1977
Kortney Lee Hall, 505-258-4945

Starlite Montessori School
407 Mechem Dr, Ruidoso, NM 88345-6811

New York

Hawthorne Valley School (1973)
Rd 2 Box 225, Ghent, NY
Patrick Stolfo, College Chair, 518-672-7120, FAX:-0181
Columbia County
Type: Waldorf, non-profit; tuition: $5,300-5,800, scholarships
32 teachers, 305 students, ages 4–18, pre K-12th grade
Affiliation: R. Steiner Ed & Farming Assn
Governance by college faculty with mandated committees
Teacher qualifications: college degree, prefer Waldorf training
Specialist teachers; near working farm; rural location; trans-
portation; interns accepted.

Apple Montessori
8 Adelaide Pl, Edgewater, NY 07020
R Bailey

Institute for Secondary Education (1993)
127 E 22 St, New York, NY 10001
John Pettinato, Dir, 212-475-7972
Type: public choice
6 teachers, 75 students, ages 12–15, 7-9th grade
Entrance requirements: interview; no residency requirement
Affiliation: CES
Governance by director, teachers, parents, students
Teacher qualifications: Masters- min 12 ed credits
For college bound; cultivates college collaborations; urban
location; transportation; interns accepted.

Phoenix Learning Resources
12 W 31st St, New York, NY 10001
Nancy Woodruff
Type: Montessori

Eugene Lang College
65 W 11th St, NY, NY 10001
Jenifer Gill Fondiller, Admissions, 212-229-5665
Type: higher education
350 students
Seminar approach; maximum 15 students/class; emphasis on
discussion and participation; no texts or core curriculum;
interdisciplinary; internships.

West Chelsea Learning Center
330 W 28th St, New York, NY 10001-4722
Type: Montessori

Auxiliary Services for High Schools (1969)
198 Forsyth St, New York, NY 10002
Margaret Bing-Wade, Dir, IA, 212-673-8254, FAX: 260-2617
Type: public at-risk
300 teachers, 14,500 students, mainly GED, ages 16+, 9-12th
grade
Entrance requirements: age 16+, proof of immunization
Affiliation: NYC BE
Governance by principal, School-Based Planning Committee
Teacher qualifications: NYC BE License
92 sites throughout NYC; GED prep; career services, counseling; individual, whole group, collaborative self-paced
instruction in 7 languages; community-based job training;
day and evening classes; ongoing admission, graduation;
multicultural, student-centered; ongoing personalized
assessment; no letter grades; extensive field trips; multi-
aged classes; urban location; interns accepted.

Florence Nightingale Elementary
285 Delancey St, New York, NY 10002
Alex Tare, 718-674-2690
District 1
Type: magnet
Student ages 4+,-6th grade
Gifted and talented.

John Burroughs Elementary
442 E Houston St, New York, NY 10002
George Fener, 718-677-5710
District 1
Type: magnet
Student ages 4+,-6th grade
Communication; arts.

Lower East Side Preparatory School (1970)
145 Stanton St, 4th Floor, NY, NY 10002
John W Lee, Principal, 212-505-6366
Manhattan District
Type: public choice
575 students, 9-12th grade
Full academic program; serves emotional, socio-economic, and academic needs of students.

East Manhattan School for Bright and Gifted Children
(1968)
208 E 18th St, New York, NY 10003
Irina Pigott, MA, 212-475-8671
Non-profit; tuition: $6,000-8,000/yr
113 students, ages infant-12
Entrance requirements: >130 IQ for ages over 5
Affiliations: NAEYC, Parents League; accreditation: NY HD
Governance by board
Based on premise that giftedness depends on early stimulation and encouragement; childcare; urban location; transportation; interns accepted.

Friends Seminary (1786)
222 E 16 St, New York, NY 10003
Richard Eldridge, 212-979-5030, FAX: 212-979-5035
New York County
Type: Quaker, non-profit; tuition: $12,000/yr, scholarships
7 teachers, 570 students, ages 5-18, K-12th grade
Entrance requirements: interview, testing, previous grades
Affiliations: FCOE, NAIS
Governance by board
Teacher qualifications: BA
Community service required; daily meeting for worship; wilderness program; integrated cur; no letter grades for K-8; multi-aged classes; extensive field trips; urban location; interns accepted.

New York U Montessori Teacher Education Center
200 E Building, Washington Sq, New York, NY 10003
Marleen Barron

PS 40 Professional Development Lab
319 E 19th St, New York, NY 10003
Bea Ramirez-Epstein, 212-475-5500
Type: magnet
K-6th grade
Integrated multi-cultural.

Village Montessori School
7 E 14th St, New York, NY 10003
Dr Ruth Selman

Manhattan Comprehensive Night and Day HS (1989)
240 2nd Ave, NY, NY 10003
Stanley L Gordon, Dir Community Affairs, 212-353-2010
Type: public choice
500 students, ages 17-21, 9-12th grade
Certified, accredited night and day high school; diploma program; emphasis on nurturing and flexibility; services students with adult responsibilities and new immigrants.

New York City Home Educators Alliance (1988)
341 E 5th St #1R, NY, NY 10003
Theresa Morris, 212-505-9884
Support group; info on laws; help with education plans; social activities; monthly meetings; field trips; library; newsletter.

Independence School at PS 234
292 Greenwich St, New York, NY 10007
Anne Switzer, Prin, 212-233-6034
Type: public choice
ES
Affiliations: NYC Public School, Center for Collaborative Education
Governance by staff and parents
Collaboratively designed building; social studies core of integrated curriculum; interactive learning; urban location.

Satellite Academy High School (1972)
51 Chambers St, New York City, NY 10007
Alan Dichter, Prin, 212-349-5350, FAX: 212-964-5587
Type: public at-risk
60 teachers, 800 students, ages 15-21, 9-12th grade
Affiliation: Coalition of Essential Schools
Governance by staff with student/parent input
Portfolios; urban location; interns accepted.

The Odysseus Group
(See Resource Appendix)

East Side Community High School
420 E 12th St, NY, NY 10009
Jill Herman, Director

Lower East Side School (LESS)
333 E 4th, NY, NY 10009
Barbara Goldman, 212-982-0682
Type: public choice
7 teachers, 100 students, ages 4-12, pre K-6th grade
Affiliation: CCE
Governance by democratic meeting, with parents having decision making power.
Started by parents; small classes, student-centered, developmentally appropriate, individualized program; whole language approach; arts enrichment; multicultural population and curriculum.

Escuela Hispana Montessori
12 Ave D, New York, NY 10009-7011

Institute for Democracy in Eastern Europe
(See Resource Appendix)

American Montessori Society
(See Resource Appendix)

Career Education Center (1986)
250 W 18th St, New York, NY 10011
212-727-7720
Type: public choice
HS
Entrance requirements vary; call for info
Affiliation: NYC Schools
Transitional programs for students in temporary housing; GED prep; counseling; computers; small classes; CAI; vocational.

City and Country (1914)
146 W 13th St, New York, NY 10011
Zoe Hauser, Adms, 212-242-7802, FAX: 212-242-7996
Type: independent, non-profit; tuition: $7,300-10,500/yr, scholarships
14 teachers, 12 assistants, 195 students, ages 2-13
Governance by board, teachers and principal
Relevant and developmentally appropriate learning; job program; school store, 100-yr-old print shop; creative block building; no letter grades; extensive field trips.

Clinton School
320 W 21st St, New York, NY 10011
Jill Myers, 212-255-8860
Type: magnet
6–8th grade
Visual arts.

Corlears School (1968)
324 W 15 St, New York, NY 10011
Marion Greenwood, Head, 212-741-2800, FAX: 807-1550
Type: independent, non-profit; tuition: $7,400-10,400/yr,
    scholarships
35 teachers, 115 students, ages 2.5–9
Entrance requirements: within normal range
Affiliations: NYSAIS, NYAEC, NAIS
Governance by board
Teacher qualifications: BA/MA in Ed
Real experiences; manipulative materials; parent and com-
    munity involvement; no letter grades; multi-aged classes;
    extensive field trips; interns accepted.

New York Foundlings
590 Ave of Americas, New York, NY 10011
Type: Montessori

NYC Lab School for Gifted Education (1989)
333 W 17 St, New York, NY 10011
Sheila Breslaw, Rob Menken, Co-Dirs, 212-691-6119, FAX: 212-
    691-6219
Type: public choice
16 teachers, 305 students, partly MISI SE, 6–9th grade
Entrance requirements: exam, interview, at or above grade-
    level performance, residency
Governance by teachers and principal
Interdisciplinary planning, study; strong student govt; weekly
    community service; cooperative learning; electives; peer-
    tutoring in math; chess team; computers, video, CD-ROM;
    urban location; interns accepted.

**Project BLEND: Building Learning Experiences in New
    Directions** (1990)
351 W 18th St, New York, NY 10011
212-206-0570
District 75
Type: public choice
HS
Entrance requirements: interview, orientation, residency
Affiliation: NYC Schools
Multi-sited; interdisciplinary; supportive; vocational; SE;
    student leadership; small classes; support services; family
    groups.

PS 11 Chelsea Primary
320 W 21st St, New York, NY 10011
Leslie Gordon, 212-929-1743
Type: magnet
Pre K–6th grade
School for peace; literacy curriculum.

School for the Physical City
333 W 17th St, New York, NY 10011
Mark Weiss
Type: magnet
6–12th grade
Urban Studies.

The American Montessori Society
150 Fifth Ave, New York, NY 10011
212-924-3209
Type: Montessori resource

Legacy School For Integrated Studies
14th St Armory, 125 W 14th St, 4th fl, NY, NY 10011
212-337-4429

Nazareth Nursery Montessori School (1901)
216 W 15th St, NY, NY 10011

Sister Lucy Sabatini, 212-243-1881
55 students, ages 2–6
Montessori philosophy, methods, and materials.

The Urban Academy (1986)
High School of the Humanities, 351 W 18th St, NY, NY 10011
Ann Cook or Herb Mack, Co-Directors, 212-220-6397
Type: public choice
100 students, HS
An outgrowth of "Inquiry Demonstration Project"; inquiry-
    based curriculum; independent research; external learning
    experiences.

Vanguard High School
14th St Armory, 125 W 14th St, 3rd fl, NY, NY 10011
Louis Delgado, 212-337-4445

Greenwich Village Neighborhood School
219 Sullivan St, New York, NY 10012
Type: Montessori

New York Open Center
83 Spring St, NY, NY 10012
212-219-2527
Type: higher education

**Unity Alternative High School at the Door Youth
    Agency** (1990)
555 Broome St, New York, NY 10013
212-941-9090
Type: public choice
HS
Residency required
Affiliations: NYC Schools, Citibank
Interdisciplinary; thematic; college prep; mentorships.

City-As-School High School (1971)
16 Clarkson St, New York, NY 10014
Robert Hubetsky, Prin, 212-691-7801, FAX: 212-675-2858
Type: public choice
70 teachers, 750 students, mainly at-risk, ages 16–19, 9–12th
    grade
Entrance requirements: completion of math and science
    credits, no residency requirement
Affiliation: NYC BE
Governance by SMB/SOM
Teacher qualifications: NYC or NY certification
Community learning experiences; student-centered Learning
    Experience Activities Packets; multi-aged classes; no letter
    grade; interns accepted.

Executive Internship Program (1980)
16 Clarkson St, New York, NY 10014
212-691-7801
Type: public choice
HS
Entrance requires application, residency
Affiliation: NYC Schools
Government, politics, community agencies, business and
    industry; weekly seminars; transportation.

PS3 Charrette School
490 Hudson St, New York, NY 10014
Donna Connelly, 212-691-1183
Type: magnet
K–6th grade
Open classroom; whole language.

School of Culture and Communication (1993)
490 Hudson St, New York, NY 10014
Kathy McCullagh, Dir, 212-647-9275
New York County
Type: public choice
3 teachers, 53 students, ages 11–14, 6–8th grade
Entrance requirements: interest, ability to work indepen-
    dently and cooperatively; no residency requirement
Affiliation: Center for Collaborative Ed

Governance by advisory council of administrators, parents and teachers

Teacher qualifications: experience with diverse urban pop. and integrated cur development, enjoy adolescents

Anthropological emphasis; photography; video; community service; integrated curr; advisory program; co-ed, multi-aged, cooperative groups; portfolio assessment; no letter grades; extensive field trips; non-compulsory class attendance; urban location; interns accepted.

The 15th Street School Foundation (1983)
(See Resource Appendix)

The School of the Future
210 East 33rd St, New York, NY 10016
Gwen Solomon, Dir, 212-679-0328
Type: public choice
7-8th grade
Affiliations: NYC Public Schools, Center for Collaborative Education
Integration of technology into all aspects of school life; interdisciplinary studies; diverse.

Family School (1975)
323 E 47th St, NY, NY 10017
Lesley Nan Haberman, Head, 212-688-5950
100 students, pre K-6th grade
Multi-cultural, socio-economic environment; individualized program; Montessori setting; eclectic classroom approach.

Landmark High School (1993)
220 W 58 St, New York, NY 10019
Sylvia Rabiner, Dir, 212-866-4450, FAX: 212-289-4195
Type: public choice
8 teachers, 85 students, ages 14-16, 9th grade
Priority to residents of district served by Julia Richmon HS; must have passed all grade 8 subjects; residency required
Affiliation: CES
Governance by teachers and principal
Teacher qualifications: extensive interview process
Small, heterogeneous classes; active/cooperative learning; advisory classes; individualized instruction; graduation by demonstration/performance; no letter grades; extensive field trips; urban location; interns accepted.

Public School Repertory Company c/o Park West HS
(1991)
525 W 50th St, New York, NY 10019
212-262-5860 x289
Type: public choice
HS
Entrance requirements: 15 credits, interview by students and administrators, orientation, residency
Affiliation: NYC Schools
Performing arts; small classes; interdisciplinary.

East Side Middle School
1458 York Ave, New York, NY 10021
Ann Hochman, 212-439-6278
Type: magnet
6-8th grade
Interdisciplinary.

Rudolf Steiner School (1928)
15 E 79 St, New York, NY 10021
Lucy Schneider, Fac Chair, 212-535-2130, FAX: 861-1378
New York County
Type: Waldorf, non-profit; tuition: $7,250-10,500, scholarships
24 ft, 7 pt teachers, 235 students, ages 3-18, pre K-12th grade
Entrance requirements: ISEE grades 7+
Affiliations: NYSAIS, NAIS, ISAAGNY, Guild of Ind. Schools NYC, AWSNA, Ind. Schools Athletic League
Governance by faculty and non-faculty board members
Teacher qualifications: pre-school: MA; primary: BA; secondary: MA min, PhD desirable

Block system allows focused concentration, multiple approaches; teacher stays with class for 8 yrs; professional music/art faculty; extensive field trips; urban location; interns accepted.

Caedmon School (1962)
416 E 80th St, NY, NY 10021
Carol G Devine, 212-879-2296
190 students, ages 2.5-10, pre K-5th grade
Modified Montessori school; mixed age groups, family environment; group work encouraged.

Resurrection Episcopal Day School (1990)
119 E 74th St, NY, NY 10021
Ruth Wiltshire, 212-535-9666
Type: Montessori
30 students, ages 2.6-6
Formerly Vera Gander School.

PS 59 United Nations Public School
228 E 57th St, New York, NY 10022
Galen Guberman, 212-722-2998
Type: magnet
K-6th grade
Interdisciplinary science and art program.

Manhattan Montessori School of NY
347 E 55th St, NY, NY 10022
Miss Lina, 212-223-4630
80 students, ages 2.5-14
Branches in Brooklyn and Queens.

Beacon School, c/o Fordham U (1993)
1213 W 60th St, New York, NY 10023
718-974-6096
District 3
Computer science; educational, cultural, community services; performance-based; shared decision-making.

Center School
270 W 70 St, New York, NY 10023
Elaine Schwartz, 212-678-2729
District 3
Type: magnet
5-8th grade
Drama.

PS 191
210 W 61 St, New York, NY 10023
Elena Nasereddin, 212-678-2810
District 3
Type: magnet
Pre K-5th grade
Media.

PS 44 W. Sherman Humanities School
160 W 78th St, New York, NY 10023
Jane Hind, 212-678-2826
CSD 3
Type: magnet
K-5th grade
Humanities.

Integrative Studies
242 W 76th St, NY, NY 10023
Dr. Fern Crowell, 212-838-5122
Type: independent

Beacon School (1993)
113 W 60 St, Room 1024, New York, NY 10024
212 636-7811, FAX: 636-7113
District 3
Computer science; educational, cultural, community services; performance-based; shared decision-making.

IS 44
100 W 77 St, New York, NY 10024
William Colavito, 212-678-2817

District 3
Type: magnet
6–8th grade
Science; art.

PS 166
132 W 89th St, New York, NY 10024
Jack Regan, 212-678-2829
District 3
Type: magnet
Pre K–5th grade
Arts.

DOME Project (1973)
486 Amsterdam Ave, NY, NY 10024
Joe Flax, 212-724-1780
Type: public at-risk
40 students, 6–8th grade
Small classes; part of 1200 student recreation and education agency; summer, college prep, prep school placement, after school and dance programs; community garden; juvenile justice assistance; truancy prevention services.

The Computer School
100 W 77th St, NY, NY 10024
Steve Seigelbaum, Director, 212-678-2785

Crossroads School (1990)
234 West 109th St, New York, NY 10025
Ann F. Wiener, Dir, 212-316-5256
Manhattan County
Type: public choice
6 teachers, 125 students, ages 10–14, 6–8th grade
Residency required
Governance by teachers and principal
Active parent involvement; small classes; diverse; teachers write curriculum; community service; writing and writing technologies; multi-aged classes; no letter grades; extensive field trips; urban location; interns accepted.

MS 54
103 W 107 St, New York, NY 10025
Jules Linden, 212-678-2902
District 3
Type: magnet
6–8th grade
Global education.

PS 145 Bloomingdale School
150 W 105th St, New York, NY 10025
Ann Budd, 212-678-2857
CSD 3
Type: magnet
Student ages 4+,–6th grade
Performing and creative arts.

PS 163
163 W 97 St, New York, NY 10025
Jorge Izquierdo, 212-678-2854
District 3
Type: magnet
Pre K–5th grade
Community ventures.

PS 84
32 W 92 St, New York, NY 10025
Sidney Morison, 212-678-2823
District 3
Type: magnet
Pre K–5th grade
Environmental arts and science.

West Side Montessori School (1963)
309 W 92nd St, New York, NY 10025
Marlene Barron, Head, 212-662-8000, FAX: 212-662-8323
Non-profit; tuition: $5,350-9,710/yr
15 teachers, 19 assistants, 200 students, ages 3–6

Affiliations: AMS, NYSAIS, ISAAGNY, ERB
Governance by board
Multi-cultural; family involvement; urban location; interns accepted.

Bank Street College
610 W 112th St, NY, NY 10025
Happy Byers
Type: higher education
Affiliated with Little Red Schoolhouse.

Holy Name School (1905)
202 W 97th St, NY, NY 10025
Deborah L Hurd, Asst Principal, 212-749-1240
Type: independent
600 students, pre K–8th grade
Multicultural student body; Montessori early childhood; computer technology; IBM writing to read; after school program; urban location.

Morningside Montessori School
251 W 100th St, NY, NY 10025
212-316-1555

School for Academic and Athletic Excellence
154 W 93rd St, NY, NY 10025
Olivia Lynch, 212-678-5847

St Michael's Montessori School
225 W 99th St, NY, NY 10025
Ramani Dealwis, 212-663-0555

West Side Alternative High School (1972)
140 W 102nd St, NY, NY 10025
Ed Reynolds, Principal, 212-865-3522
Type: public at-risk
650 students, ages 15–21, 9–12th grade
Governance by school-based management team
Family groups; day care; health clinic; court liaison; job counselor; 9 social workers; special education program; night school; adult education; urban location.

National Center for Restructuring Education (NCREST)
(See Resource Appendix)

Central Harlem Montessori School/Champ Morningside Children's Center (1968)
160 W 129th St, NY, NY 10027
Roslyn Williams, 212-864-0400
176 students, pre K–6th grade
Multicultural; parents help with some classes.

Manhattan New School
311 E 82nd St, New York, NY 10028
Shelley Harwayne, 212-734-7127
Type: magnet
K–6th grade
Student-centered; collaborative; multi-cultural; language.

Upper Lab
311 E 82nd St, New York, NY 10028
Shiela Brewslaw, 212-570-6880
Type: magnet
6–12th grade
Interdisciplinary; gifted.

East Harlem Performing Arts School
433 E 100 St, New York, NY 10029
Randy Soderman, 212-860-5958
District 4
Type: magnet
5–9th grade

Harbor Performing Arts Junior High School
240 E 109 St, New York, NY 10029
Victor Lopez, 212-860-8947
CSD 4
Type: magnet
7–9th grade

Manhattan West Center For Humanities
19 E 103rd St, New York, NY 10029
Karen Marino, 212-860-7953
CSD 4
Type: magnet
7-8th grade

Central Park East I/JHS 113 (1974)
1573 Madison Ave, NY, NY 10029
Lucy Matos, 212-860-5821
Type: public choice
K-6th grade
Informal, personalized program; model-making; scientific experimentation; sculpture; drama; library research; no workbooks; close family-school relationship required.

Central Park East II
215 E 99th St, NY, NY 10029
Kyle Haver, Director, 212-860-6010
Type: public choice
K-6th grade
"Hands-on" program; integrated curricular themes; two years with same teacher; close parent-student-teacher teamwork; field trips; visiting professionals; individual research.

Central Park East Secondary School (1985)
1573 Madison Avenue, NY, NY 10029
Deborah Meier, Principal; Paul Schwartz, Co-Director, 212 860-5871
Manhattan County
Type: public choice
450 students, 7-12th grade
Entrance requirements: visiting day, application
Affiliation: National Coalition of Essential Schools
Governance by principal and teachers
Preference to dist 4, but others may apply; grew out of success of Central Park East Alternative School; emphasizes learning how to learn, reason, work collaboratively; internships; mentorships; community service experience; demonstration-based diploma; urban location.

College for Human Services Junior High/PS 21
232 E 103 St, NY, NY 10029
Linda Hill, Director, 212-860-6044
Type: public choice
30 students, 7-8th grade
Combines academic learning with life experience in a service setting; internships at schools, daycare and senior settings, community offices.

Park East High School (1970)
230 E 105th St, NY, NY 10029
Jacqueline E Beverly, 212-831-1517
Manhattan District
Type: public choice
400 students, HS
Manhattan or Bronx residency required.
Founded by coalition of community groups; business education; college and career advisement; active student government; off site vocational training; computer literacy.

River East
116th St & FDR Dr, NY, NY 10029
Leslie Alexander, Director, 212-860-6033
Type: public choice
Pre k-6th grade
Part of Manhattan Center for Science and Mathematics; vertical grouping (students and teachers stay together for 2-3 years); active, interest-based learning.

The Bridge School (1977)
141 E 111th St, NY, NY 10029
Michael Friedman, Director, 212-860-5890
Type: public choice
230 students, 6-9th grade

Emphasizes mutual respect and responsibility; offers courses in criminal justice, human relations, consumer and career education; overnight trips to Washington, Boston, etc.

The Key School (1982)
240 E 109th St, NY, NY 10029
Iris Novak, Director, 212-860-6016
Type: public at-risk
Admission by recommendation only.
Individualized; interest-based curriculum; small supportive environment; for students who show consistent underachievement.

Center for Collaborative Education
1573 Madison Ave, Room 201, NY, NY 10029-3988
Heather Lewis, Priscilla Ellington, Co-Directors, 212-348-7821
Type: public choice
Joint project with 18 NYC public schools; focuses on thinking skills, personalizing teaching and learning, student participation, parental input, and evaluation based on performance.

Salome Urena Middle Academics
4600 Broadway, New York, NY 10034
Mark Kavakshy, 212-567-2322
District 6
Type: magnet
6-8th grade
Business studies; community service; technology; fine and performing arts.

Borough Academies (1992)
2005 Madison Ave, New York, NY 10035
212-423-0251
Type: public choice
HS
Entrance requirements: referral, interview, orientation
Affiliation: NYC Public Schools
Extended day; CAI; community service; enriched arts; creative conflict resolution; guidance; credit for continuous progress.

Barbara Taylor School (1986)
2032 Fifth Ave, NY, NY 10035
Dr. Lois Holzman, Director, 212-996-0339, FAX: 212-941-8340
Type: independent, non-profit; tuition: $3,000/yr, one scholarship
3 teachers, 17 students, mainly at-risk, ages 4-13, K-8th grade
Affiliation: East Side Inst for Short-term Psychotherapy
Governance by staff, students, parents
Approach based on Lev Vygotsky's work; students and staff create a learning environment where everyone goes "beyond themselves" the way infants do; no letter grades; non-compulsory class attendance; multi-aged classes; extensive field trips; urban location; interns accepted.

Children's Storefront Support Corporation (1966)
57 E 129th St, NY, NY 10035
Ned O'Gorman, 212-427-7900
Type: independent
115 students, ages 2.5-14, pre K-8th grade
Governance by director and staff
Non-tuition, private school in Harlem, with traditional academic program; goal is to heal, liberate, and teach the oppressed child.

Choir Academy of Harlem
2005 Madison Ave, NY, NY 10035
212-289-6227
Type: public choice
Entrance requirement: audition, academic record
Based at the Boys' Choir of Harlem; vocal training; college preparatory program; multicultural focus; concert performances.

Coalition School For Social Change (1993)
2005 Madison Ave, NY, NY 10035
Charlene Jordan, Director, 212-860-0212
Manhattan County
Type: public choice
10 teachers, 92 students, ages 14–15, 9th grade
NYC residency required
Affiliation: CES
Governance by teachers and principal
Essential school philosophy; project-based assessment; inter-
    disciplinary; urban location; interns accepted.

Northview Technical Junior High School
319 E 117th St, NY, NY 10035
Maria Bonet, Director, 212-860-7952
Type: public choice
130 students, 7–9th grade
Affiliation: Youth Alliance Program
Family-oriented, mentoring program; computers; internships
    in other schools.

Upper Manhattan Outreach (1980)
140 W 102nd St, NY, NY 10035
Marita Franzman, Center Administrator, 212-662-1000
Type: public at-risk
335 students, ages 17–21, 9–12th grade
NYC residency required.
Student internships; independent study; GED preparation;
    high school credit; college advisement; job referrals.

Urban Peace Academy
2351 First Ave, NY, NY 10035
212-987-1906

Midtown West
328 W 48th St, New York, NY 10036
Saudhi Vargas, 212-247-0208
Type: magnet
K–5th grade
Student-centered; multi-cultural.

Professional Performing Arts School (1990)
328 West 48 St, New York, NY 10036
Claudia DiSalvo, Dir, 212-247-8652, 246-7576, FAX: 212-247-
    7514
New York County
Type: public choice
25 teachers, 340 students, ages 10–18, 6–11th grade
Audition required
Governance by director
On-location academics program for students wherever they
    are in US or overseas.

Manhattan International High School
PS 126, 80 Catherine St, NY, NY 10038
212-964-2286

Community Service Academy (1992)
4600 Broadway, NY, NY 10040
Lydia Bassett, Asst Prin, 212-567-2589
18 teachers, 350 students, ages 11–15, 6–8th grade
Students attend by district zone plan
Affiliations: CCE, Bank St College, NCSL
Governance by teachers and principal
Teacher qualifications: NYC Bd of Ed License, community
    involvement
Builds on natural instincts of early adolescents to make the
    world a better place; school-community collaboration:
    teacher works with student advisory group and commu-
    nity organization to design service learning project; interns
    accepted.

Enterprise Foundation
888 7th Ave #402, New York, NY 10106
Margarita R Reynes
Type: Montessori

Cooperative Tech (1986)
321 E 96th St, New York, NY 10128
212-369-8800
Type: public choice
Student ages 16+, 11–12th grade
Residency required; admission on shared instruction basis
Affiliation: NYC Schools
Advanced, specialized training in 10 voc-tech areas; ESL
    support services; building construction/repair; daycare; job
    placement; occupational skills; transportation.

Lower Lab
1700 Third Ave, New York, NY 10128
Denise Levine, 212-427-2798
Type: magnet
K–6th grade
Inquiry-based; intergrated; gifted.

Partnership School
1763 First Ave, New York, NY 10128
Carole Mulligan, 212-876-7248
Type: magnet
K–6th grade
Multi-cultural whole language curriculum.

Primary Effective Program
1700 Third Ave, New York, NY 10128
Nancy Rodriguez, 212-427-6489
Type: magnet
K–6th grade
Multi-cultural creative arts curriculum.

PS 198 Multicultural School
1700 Third Ave, New York, NY 10128
Goria Buckery, 212-289-3702
Type: magnet
Pre K–6th grade
Whole language; literature-based curriculum.

The Dalton School
108 E 89th St, New York, NY 10128
Catherine Evedon
Type: Montessori

Manhattan Country School
7 E 96th St, NY, NY 10128
Gus Trowbridge, 212-348-0592
Type: independent; tuition: sliding scale, income dependent
50% white, 50% minority by design.

Seton Day Care Center
1675 3rd Ave #93RD, New York, NY 10128-3702
Maria Gravel
Type: Montessori

St Vartan Playgroup (1992)
PO Box 1073, NY, NY 10156-0604
Ellen Ellis, President, 212-447-6035
Type: public choice; tuition: $550
10 students, ages 2–5
Governance by parent cooperative
Extension of homeschooling; multi-aged classes; urban
    location.

Building Blocks Montessori School (1972)
55 Forest Ave, Staten Island, NY 10301
Gloria Friedman, Dir, 718-448-2992
Tuition: $2,400-4,800/yr
7 teachers, 13 assistants, 150 students, ages infant-12
Entrance requirements: interview.
Accreditations: NYS, NYC
Governance by board
Multi-cultural curriculum; Spanish education; childcare; trans-
    portation; interns accepted.

Children's Harbor Preschool
1000 Richmond Terr, Staten Island, NY 10301

Leanne Bernacki, Dir, 718-442-6112
Non-profit; tuition: $1,170-4,160/yr
3 teachers, 4 assistants, 60 students, ages infant-6
Accreditation: AMS
Governance by board
Art-based; at Snug Harbor Cultural Center; parent co-op; childcare; suburban location; transportation; interns accepted.

Concord High School (1976)
109 Rhine Ave, Staten Island, NY 10304
Mr. Contardo, Assistant Principal, 718-447-1274
Type: public at-risk
275 students, ages 14-21, 9-12th grade
Governance by teachers and principal
Student internships; independent study; individual, group and family guidance.

Tanglewood School (1983)
15 Tanglewood Dr, Staten Island, NY 10308
Fay Taranto, 718-967-2424
Type: Montessori
275 students, ages 2.5-6
Extensive materials.

Staten Island Montessori (1966)
500 Butler Blvd, Staten Island, NY 10309
Stephanie Whalen, 718-356-7833
150 students, pre K-5th grade
Multi-age grouping; 2-3 years in each class; students progress at their own rate.

Hostos-Lincoln Academy of Science (1986)
475 Grand Concourse, Bronx, NY 10451
Dr Michele Cataldi, Principal, 718-518-4333
Type: public at-risk
300 students, ages 14-18, 9-12th grade
Entrance requirements: recommendation and interview
Governance by principal, democratic school meeting
Student internships; independent study; college courses offered in partnership with Hostos Community College; designed to improve basic skills, reduce absenteeism and dropping out.

Youth Options Unlimited (YOU) (1987)
470 E 172nd St, Bronx, NY 10452
718-993-5350 x 209/210
JH
Residency required
Affiliation: NYC Schools
Peer group counseling; parental involvement; career exploration; small classes; individualized; continuous intake.

University Heights High School at Bronx Community College
University Ave & W 181st St, Bronx, NY 10456
Deborah L Harris, 212-220-6397
Type: public choice
375 students, ages 16+
Smaller, personalized program with support services to help students prepare for college/career.

Camelot Program (1971)
JHS 118, 577 E 79th St, Bronx, NY 10457
A. Goodstone, Coord, 212-220-8803
Type: public at-risk
85 students, ages 14-16, 8-9th grade
Governance by teachers and principal
For students who have not been successful because of absence, poor reading or math skills, socialization problems or lack of motivation.

Pace Academy Middle School 118 (1972)
577 E 179 St, Bronx, NY 10457
Joseph Landes, 718-584-2568
Bronx District 10
Type: public choice

James Baldwin Literacy Center (1984)
1010 Rev J Polite Ave, Bronx, NY 10459
Susan Weliky, 212-842-9200
Alternative Superintendency District
Type: public at-risk
140 students, 9-12th grade
Reading/writing skills program for students who read between 0 and 6th grade level.

Riverdale Academy (1982)
3333 Independence Ave, Bronx, NY 10463
Joseph F Sasiela, 212-796-8630
Bronx District
Type: public choice
186 students, 7-9th grade
Atmosphere of a small private school, but diversity of services of a comprehensive junior high school.

The Bronx New School
3200 Jerome Ave, Bronx, NY 10468
Esther Forrest, Principal, 212-584-8772
Type: public choice
225 students, K-6th grade

C S 152 School
1007 Evergreen Ave, Bronx, NY 10472
Ms Eidlin, 718-822-5029
District 8
Type: magnet
4-6th grade
Fine and performing arts.

Northeast Academy (1978)
750 Baychester Ave, Bronx, NY 10475
Harry Reiss, 212-671-7700
Type: public choice

Ardsley Alternative High School (1992)
300 Farm Rd, Ardsley, NY 10502
Jay Shaplou, Dir, 914-693-6300 x231, FAX: 914-693-0892
Westchester County
Type: public choice
1 teacher, 20 students, mainly at-risk, ages 15-18, 10-12th grade
Entrance requirements: application, interview, residency
Governance by democratic school meeting
First community-as-school in county; business partnerships; whole language; required evening parent meetings every 8 weeks; multi-aged classes; suburban location.

Alcott School (1968)
700 Ashford Ave/Crane Rd at Woodlands Pl, Ardsley/Scarsdale, NY 10502/10583
A. Donegan, 914-472-4404
Type: Montessori, non-profit; tuition: $2,575-7,000/yr
6 teachers, 18 assistants, 300 students, mainly International, ages infant-6
Entrance requirements: age 2 by Dec
Affiliation: AMS; accreditation: NAEYC
Governance by board
SE for ages 1.5-5; ESL; science; art; music; childcare; suburban location; interns accepted.

Montessori Children's Room (1970)
67 Old Route 22, Armonk, NY 10504
914-273-3291
Tuition: $430-935/mo
7 teachers, 5 assistants, 72 students, ages infant-6
Affiliation: AMI
Governance by administrator
Childcare.

Academic Community for Educational Success (1977)
200 Railroad Ave, Bedford Hills, NY 10507
Joan E. Barickman, Tch/Dir, 914-666-5983
Non-profit

2 teachers, 25 students, partly at-risk, ages 14–21, 9–12th grade
Residency required
Affiliation: Bedford Central Schools
Governance by democratic school meeting
Teacher qualifications: certification
Intensive core courses; adventure-based counseling; PE; government course; multi-aged classes; extensive field trips

Chappaqua Alternative High School (1977)
Horace Greeley High School, Chappaqua, NY 10514
William Huppuch, 914-238-3911
Type: public at-risk

Haldane Alternate Program (1982)
Craigside Dr, Cold Spring, NY 10516
Dennis Cairl, Tch, 914-265-9254 x18
Putnam County
Type: public choice
1 teacher, 24 students, mainly at-risk, ages 14–18, 9–12th grade
Governance by principal, teachers, board
Teacher qualifications: certification in secondary English and Social Studies
Success-oriented curriculum; structured; multi-aged classes; rural location.

Croton Montessori School (1968)
Box 84, Croton-on-Hudson, NY 10520
Elizabeth terPoorton, 914-271-6580
Tuition: $2100/4000
2 teachers, 3 assistants, 50 students, mainly international, ages 3–6
Affiliations: AMS, AMT
Governance by an administrator
Music, art, foreign languages; suburban location; interns accepted.

Alternative HS Program for Special Education
Mahopac Falls School, Mahopac, NY 10541
Corinne Bloomer, 914-628-3415
Type: public at-risk

Berjan School (1984)
145 New St, Mamaroneck, NY 10543
Jane Marsella Schumer, 914-698-4002
Type: Montessori; tuition: $2,550–6,200/yr
90 students, ages 2–7
Small classes; self-paced, wholistic curriculum.

Westchester Day School
856 Orienta Ave, Mamaroneck, NY 10543
Zeev Aviezer, 914-698-8900
Type: independent
370 students, pre K–8th grade
Pre-school is Montessori; combines English and Judaic studies.

Fox Lane Middle School
Route 172, Mount Kisko, NY 10549
Dennis Mcgrath, 914-241-6118
Type: public choice

Bronxville Montessori School (1977)
101 Pondfield Rd W, Bronxville, NY 10550
Jean Nelson, 914-793-2083, FAX: 914-793-2360
Non-profit; tuition: $3,075-6,500/yr
4 teachers, 10 assistants, 144 students, mainly International, ages infant-6
Affiliation: NAEYC; accreditations: AMS, NY DSS
Governance by administrator, board
Multi-cultural; movement; music; ESL; psychotherapist; large gym; play areas; childcare; suburban location; interns accepted.

Nelson Mandella School (1977)
47 S 11th Ave, Mt Vernon, NY 10550

Abishai Ben Reuben, Coodinator, 914-665-5159
Type: public at-risk
125 students, HS

The Fleetwood Montessori School (1969)
199 North Columbus Ave, Mount Vernon, NY 10553-1101
William B. Adams, Director, 914-668-5570
Tuition: 1,680/2,800/yr
1 teacher, 3 assistants, 35 students, ages infant-6
Affiliations: AMI, WAEYC
Governance by administrator
Suburban location.

PASS-Peekskill Alternative Secondary School (1986)
1432 Park St, Peekskill, NY 10566
Delores Jones, Dir; Sheldon Levine, Prin, 914-737-2088, FAX:-3912
Westchester County
Type: public at-risk
4 teachers, 64 students, ages 14–19, 9–12th grade
Entrance requirements: referral by SE committee or pupil personnel services, residency
Governance by director and principal
Teacher qualifications: NY Certification
Total inclusion classes; investigating a curriculum; multi-aged classes; urban location.

Alternative Education Program at Pleasantville HS (1985)
Romer Ave, Pleasantville, NY 10570
Vivian Owowski, 914-769-8102
Type: public choice

Resurrection School
116 Milton Rd, Rye, NY 10580
Alice Sweeney
Type: Montessori

Choice Program at Scarsdale Junior High School (1974)
Mamaroneck Rd, Scarsdale, NY 10583
Susan Taylor, 914-472-3478
Type: public choice
49 students, 7–8th grade
Governance by teachers and principal
Some ungraded classes; model United Nations; community meeting.

Our Lady of Fatima School
963 Scarsdale Rd, Scarsdale, NY 10583
Type: Montessori

Scarsdale Alternative School (1972)
45 Wayside Ln, Scarsdale, NY 10583
Tony Arenella, Dir, 914-721-2590
Westchester County
Type: public choice
5 teachers, 75 students, ages 14–18, 10–12th grade
Enrollment by lottery; residency required
Affiliation: CES
Governance by democratic school meeting
Teacher qualifications: NY Certification
"Just Community" School promotes moral/social growth with democratic decision-making; 1-month community service internship; Senior Project demonstrates publicly important skills, knowledge; no letter grades; multi-aged classes; suburban location; interns accepted.

Scarsdale Friends Nursery School (1954)
133 Popham Rd, Scarsdale, NY 10583
Jeanette Livoti, Dir, 914-472-6550
Westchester County
Type: Quaker, non-profit; tuition: $1,300/yr, scholarships
3 teachers, 20 students
Governance by teachers, parents, Quaker board
Teacher qualifications: certification for director
Suburban location.

Lakeland Alternative High School (1982)
Rt 132, Shrub Oak, NY 10588
Marc Gessin, Principal, 914-245-3382, FAX: 914-245-4391
Westchester County
Type: public at-risk
4.4 teachers, 40 students, mainly at-risk, ages 15–21, 10–12th grade
Residency required
Governance by board
Teacher qualifications: state SE certification
Thematic instruction; cooperative learning; team teaching; Glasser's Ten-Step Approach to Discipline; parent support group; non-traditional counseling; work experience; project adventure challenge program; multi-aged classes; suburban location; transportation; interns accepted.

Phoenix Academy
PO Box 458 Stoney St, Shrub Oak, NY 10588
Joan Ahern, 914-962-2402
Type: public at-risk
350 students, HS
Enrollment restricted to students who have had drug abuse problems
Affiliation: Phoenix House
Self-contained BOCES program; part of Bronx HS District; peer tutoring; SAT, GED, job training; work/study.

Putnam-Westchester BOCES Alternative High School (1977)
Fox Meadow Rd, Yorktown, NY 10598
Robert Kelderhouse, 914-245-2700
Type: public choice

Our Montessori School (1972)
PO Box 72, Yorktown Heights, NY 10598
Werner H. Hengst, Adm, 914-962-9466, FAX: same
Tuition: $3,750-7,500/yr
11 teachers, 20 assistants, 204 students, ages infant-12
Entrance requirements: interview
Governance by administrator
Individualized instruction; music; dance; computer; French; Montessori teacher training course; childcare; suburban location; interns accepted.

Alt Education Program at Mildred E. Strang MS (1982)
2701 Crompond Rd, Yorktown Hts, NY 10598
Judy O'Toole, 914-243-8100
Type: public at-risk
30 students, 6–8th grade
Extra help in particular subjects.

Bright Beginnings Pre-school Learning Center
1974 Commerce St, Yorktown Hts, NY 10598
Mara Ziedins, 914-962-2929
Type: Montessori
100 students, ages 18 mo-5 yrs
Three locations: Yorktown, Amawalk, Granite Springs; summer programs.

The Learning Center (1980)
200 BOCES Dr., Yorktown Hts, NY 10598
David J Zurkhellen, Principal, 914-248-2270
Type: public at-risk
130 students, ages 5–21, K–12th grade
Governance by teachers and principal
Fewer than 12 students/class; serves Putnam and N Westchester counties; therapeutic environment and insight-oriented counseling.

The Walkabout (1977)
Pinesbridge Rd, Yorktown Hts, NY 10598
Eugene Lebwohl, 914-245-2700
Type: public choice
Affiliation: Putnam-Westchester BOCES

Caroline Montessori School
52 N Broadway, White Plains, NY 10603

Regional Alternative High School
666 Old Orchard St, N White Plains, NY 10604
David Chura
Type: public choice

Montessori Children's Center at Burke (1991)
785 Mamaroneck Ave, White Plains, NY 10605
Carole Wolfe Korngold, Exec Dir, 914-948-2501, FAX: 914-421-0779
Tuition: $8923/10,437
7 teachers, 8 assistants, 50 students, ages infant-6
Affiliation: AMS
Governance by an administrator
Happy, nurturing; park-like site; toddler, infant, early childhood classrooms; childcare; suburban location; interns accepted.

Community School (1972)
228 Fisher Ave, White Plains, NY 10606
John P Garcia, 914-997-2420
Type: public choice

Enrico Fermi School for Performing Arts
27 Poplar St, Yonkers, NY 10701
Edward DeFino, 914-376-8460
Type: magnet
Pre K–6th grade
Computers; Montessori.

Museum School of the Arts & Sciences
579 Warburton Ave, Yonkers, NY 10701
Robert Torp, 914-376-8450
Type: magnet
Pre K–6th grade

School 32
1 Montclair Pl, Yonkers, NY 10701
Jennifer Schulman, 914-376-8595
Type: magnet
Pre K–6th grade
Family school.

Emerson Junior High School
160 Bolmer Ave, Yonkers, NY 10703
Charles Whelan, 914-376-8300
Type: magnet
7–8th grade
Computer science; arts; scenery and display.

School 22
1408 Nepperhan, Yonkers, NY 10703
Marvin Feldberg, 914-376-8440
Type: magnet
K–6th grade
FLAME: foreign language and multi-cultural education.

School 9
53 Fairview St, Yonkers, NY 10703
Jacques Weaver, 914-376-8325
Type: magnet
K–6th grade
Humanities.

Mark Twain Junior High
160 Woodland Ave, Yonkers, NY 10704
Ivan Toper, 914-376-8540
Type: magnet
7–8th grade
Health related studies; humanities.

Burroughs Junior High School
150 Roackland Ave, Yonkers, NY 10705
Mary Lou Macdonald, 914-376-8200
Type: magnet
7–8th grade
Computers; business; human services; international studies.

Montessori at School 27 (1986)
132 Valentine Ln, Yonkers, NY 10705
Kathleen P. MacSweeney, 914-376-8455
Type: public choice Montessori
16 teachers, 16 assistants, 364 students, ages 3-12
Entrance requirement: Montessori experience
Affiliation: AMS
Governance by administrator
Italian; greenhouse studies; transportation.

Pearls Elementary
348 Hawthorne Ave, Yonkers, NY 10705
Sara Butler, 914-376-8253
Type: magnet
Pre K-6th grade
Gifted and talented.

School 21
100 Lee Ave, Yonkers, NY 10705
E. Cardona-Zuckerman, 914-376-8435
Type: magnet
K-6th grade
FLAME: foreign language and multi-cultural education.

Westchester Home Learners (1989)
190 Hollywood Ave, Crestwood, NY 10707
Beryl Polin, 914-337-5825
15-20 students, ages 2-13
Homeschooling support group for Westchester families;
    lending library, regular meetings, field trips and other
    activities.

Roosevelt High School
631 Tuckahoe Rd, Yonkers, NY 10710
Michael Yarzulo, 914-376-8519
Type: magnet
9-12th grade
Commercial illustration, photography; fine arts.

Yonkers Prep (1973)
7 Ravenswood Rd, Yonkers, NY 10710
Peggy Schwartz, Head Teacher, 914-376-8600
Type: public at-risk
60 students, ages 14-18, 9-12th grade

New Rochelle Prep (1978)
116 Guion Pl, New Rochelle, NY 10801
Helen McLaughlin, 914-235-2969
Type: public choice

Brain-Compatible Information
(See Resource Appendix)

Transitional Learning Center
19 2nd Ave, Pelham, NY 10803-1417
Type: Montessori

Hudson Country Montessori School (1972)
340 Quaker Ridge Rd, New Rochelle, NY 10804
Musya Meyer, Dir, 914-636-6202, FAX: 914-636-5139
Non-profit; tuition: $3,065-8,470/yr
14 teachers, 23 assistants, 315 students, ages infant-9
Affiliation: SNMC; accreditations: NAEYC, DSS
Governance by administrator, board
Also Hudson Institute for Teacher Education; childcare; sub-
    urban location; transportation; interns accepted.

New Rochelle Academy
80 Mount Tom Rd, New Rochelle, NY 10805
Type: Montessori

Suffern Montessori School (1984)
3 Church Rd, Suffern, NY 10901
Martha Hyams, 914-357-1410
30 students, ages 3-6, pre K-1st grade
Multi-aged classes.

Sugar Loaf Union Free School (1991)
PO Box 530, Gibson Hill Rd, Chester, NY 10918
Stephen Janove, 914-469-2136
Type: public choice
30 students

Thevenet Montessori School (1972)
Country Rd 105, Highland Hills, NY 10930
Sr Loretta Knapp, 914 -928-2213
120 students, pre K-1st grade
Student-centered approach.

Stepping Stones Montessori School (1984)
66 Bennett St, Middletown, NY 10940
Rose Moskowitz, 914-343-5774
64 students, ages 2.6-7, pre K-2nd grade
Teachers demonstrate, but neither interfere nor correct.

**STTAR (Saunders Trades and Technical Academic
    Response)** (1993)
181 Palmer Rd, Yonkers, NY 10956
Bernard Pierorazio, Principal, 914-376-8150, FAX:-8154
Type: public at-risk
3 teachers, 30 students, ages 14-18, 9th grade
Entrance requirements: poor record, interviews, contracts
Governance by teachers and principal
Individualized and cooperative learning; research, film, slide,
    video and computer work culminate in portfolios; multi-
    aged classes; suburban location; transportation.

Montessori Center of Nyack
77 Marion St, Nyack, NY 10960-2035

Rockland Learning Center (1971)
130 Concklin Rd, Pomona, NY 10970
Freyda Michelson, Dir, 914-354-5253
Non-profit; tuition: $243/486/mo
2 teachers, 1 assistant, 40 students, mainly International,
    ages 3-9
Accreditation: NY Chartered pre k-6
Governance by administrator, democratic school meeting,
    board
Teacher qualifications: taught together 22 years
Monthly units in science; music; childcare; suburban location;
    transportation; interns accepted.

Green Meadow Waldorf School (1950)
Hungry Hollow Rd, Chestnut Ridge, NY 10977
David Sloan, High School Chair, FAX: 914-356-2921
Non-profit; tuition: $4,225-7,110/yr, scholarships
418 students, ages 3-18, nursery, K-12th grade
Entrance requirements: grade level competence
Affiliations: NYSAIS, AWSNA
Governance by faculty
Teacher qualifications: college, Waldorf training
Exchange program with Waldorf in Europe, Australia, New
    Zealand; suburban location; transportation; interns
    accepted.

Waldorf Institute of Sunbridge College (1967)
260 Hungry Hollow Rd, Chestnut Ridge, NY 10977
Jonathan Hilton, Reg, 914-425-0055, FAX: 425-1413
Rockland County
Type: Waldorf higher education, non-profit; tuition: variable,
    scholarships
30 teachers, 125 students, adult ages
Entrance requirements: HS diploma, application, interview
Affiliations: AWSNA, Assn of Anthroposophical Colleges
Governance by faculty and board
Teacher qualifications: MSEd in early childhood, elem ed
Lectures; workshops; seasonal, special events; suburban
    location.

A+ Discount Distributors and Educational Warehouse
(See Resource Appendix)

QUEST (1982)
Vista Rd, Spring Valley, NY 10977
Larry Greenbush, Teacher-in-Charge, 914-577-6149
East Ramapo District
Type: public at-risk
75 students, ages 15-18, 10-12th grade
Governance by democratic school meeting, faculty and
    student representatives, parent cooperative.
Diploma program for above average students with perfo-
    mance below grade level; independent study; internships;
    highly personalized, self-governed, community atmos-
    phere; student-teacher advisory sessions; bi-weekly com-
    munity seminars.

Tri-County Homeschoolers
130 Blanchard Rd, Stoneypoint, NY 10980
914-429-5156

**Grade 9 Alternative Program at North Rockland High
    School** (1985)
Hammond Rd, Thiells, NY 10984
George F Jochum, 914-942-2700
Type: public choice

Blue Rock School (1987)
110 Demarest Mill Rd, W Nyack, NY 10994
Mary Guthrie, Administrator, 914-627-0234
Type: independent, non-profit; tuition: $3392-6254,
    scholarships
K-6th grade
Non-sectarian; whole language; philosophy: when student is
    wholly engaged, his/her work is his/her own.

Gemini (1987)
Demarest Mill Rd, W Nyack, NY 10994
Anne Gusmano, English Teacher, 914-624-3480
Clarkstown District, Rockland County
Type: public home-based at-risk
4 teachers, 50 students, mainly at-risk, ages 15-18, 10-12th
    grade
Entrance requirements: non-learning disabled, Child Study
    Team approval, residency
Governance by teachers and principal
Teacher qualifications: MA degree
Teachers serve as mentors/informal counselors; interdiscipli-
    nary projects; contracts; suburban location; interns
    accepted.

Rockland County BOCES City As School Program (1993)
61 Parrot Rd, W Nyack, NY 10994
Ron Tullock, Adm, 914-627-4794, FAX: 914-627-6124
Type: public choice
2 students

The Alternative School at H Frank Carey High School
    (1981)
230 Poppy Ave, Franklin Square, NY 11010
Lory P Gitter, 516-560-8680
Type: public at-risk
30 students, ages 16-21
Students receive a regular HS diploma through competency-
    based education and completion of 2 yr vocational course
    and/or 1500 hrs work experience.

Spirit of January
(See Resource Appendix)

Village School (1971)
614 Middle Neck Rd, Great Neck, NY 11023
Charles Piemonte, PhD, Dir, 516-773-1705
Nassau County
Type: public choice
6 teachers, 40 students, mainly at-risk, ages 14-18, 9-12th
    grade
Governance by teachers, principal

Student-directed; advisory system; Exhibition Studies; port-
    folio assessment techniques; multi-aged classes; extensive
    field trips; interns accepted.

Our Lady of Grace Montessori (1968)
29 Shelter Rock Rd, Manhasset, NY 11030
Sr Dorothy Kibler, Prin, 516-365-9832, FAX: 516-365-9329
Non-profit; tuition: $2,025-2,925/yr
8 teachers, 5 assistants, 190 students, ages 3-6
Affiliation: NCEA; accreditations: AMS, MSA
Governance by administrator
Suburban location; interns accepted.

Happy Montessori School (1970)
40 Pleasant Ave, Port Washington, NY 11050
Amrit Sethi, Director, 516-883-1131
55 students, nursery-K

International High School at LaGuardia CC (1985)
31-10 Thomson Ave, Long Island City, NY 11101
Eric Nadelstern, Prin, 718-482-5455
Queens County
Type: public choice/at-risk
35 teachers, 460 students, mainly at-risk, ages 14-21
Enrollment restricted to those with limited English profi-
    ciency; no residency requirement
Affiliations: CUNY, NYC BE
Governance by teachers and principal
Teacher qualifications: NYC License
Multilingual, multicultural; interdisciplinary; experiential; col-
    laborative; multi-aged classes; urban location; interns
    accepted.

Les Enfants Montessori
2921 Newtown Ave, Long Island City, NY 11102-2128

Institute for the Arts and Technology
31-51 21st St, Astoria, NY 11106
Terry Borne, Co-Director, 718-349-4009

Brooklyn Friends School (1867)
375 Pearl St, Brooklyn, NY 11201
718-852-1029, FAX: 718-643-4868
Type: Quaker, non-profit; tuition: $11,000/yr, scholarships
55 teachers, 440 students, ages toddler-18, pre K-12th
    grade
Affiliations: NAIS, NYSAIS
Governance by principal
Teacher qualifications: MA
Video-making; ceramics; wood shop; art studies; computer
    labs; strong science dept; community service; racially
    diverse; no letter grades; extensive field trips; interns
    accepted.

Brooklyn Heights Montessori School (1965)
185 Court St, Brooklyn, NY 11201
Marcia Gardere, Dir, 718-858-5100, FAX: 718-243-0261
Non-profit; tuition: $5,550-8,975/yr
12 teachers, 1 assistant, 156 students, ages 3-9
Affiliations: AMS, NAEYC, ASCD, AECI
Governance by administrator, board
The Little Room, preschool SE program; childcare; urban loca-
    tion; transportation; interns accepted.

Mary McDowell Center For Learning (1984)
110 Schermerhorn St, Brooklyn, NY 11201
Debbie Zlotowitz, Head, 718-625-3939
Kings County
Type: Quaker, non-profit; tuition: $15,600/yr, scholarships
8 teachers, 32 students, mainly at-risk, ages 5-11, ungraded
Entrance requirements: learning disability, testing, interview
Affiliation: FCOE
Governance by principal, board
Teacher qualifications: head teacher: MA Special Ed; asst
    teacher: BA/BS
Responsibility, recognition of individual worth; individualized;
    multi-aged classes; urban location; interns accepted.

The New Program at PS 261 (1988)
314 Pacific St, Brooklyn, NY 11201
Arthur Foresta, Prin or Ann Powers, Dir, 718-330-9275
Type: public choice
Affiliations: NYC Public Schools, Center for Collaborative
　Education
Open classrooms; hands-on experience; individual work;
　small groups; developmentally-based social studies;
　includes thematic units; active parent participation.

IS 285
5909 Beverly Rd, Brooklyn, NY 11203
Anthony Raziano, 718-451-2200
CSD 18
Type: magnet
6-8th grade
Careers in the performing arts.

P 235
525 Lenox Rd, Brooklyn, NY 11203
Mitchel Levine, 718-773-4869
CSD 18
Type: magnet
Pre K-5th grade
Gifted students; early learning center.

Mercy Montessori School
1397 Brooklyn Ave, Brooklyn, NY 11203-5518
Sr Mary Harvey

Mapleton School
6015 18th Ave, Brooklyn, NY 11204
Joseph Maiello, 718-232-3880
CSD 20
Type: magnet
K-5th grade
Visions: community activists and ambassadors.

PS 192
4715 18th Ave, Brooklyn, NY 11204
Gennaro DeMarco, 718-633-3061
CSD 20
Type: magnet
K-5th grade
Environmental arts.

East New York Family Academy (1993)
2057 Linden Blvd, Brooklyn, NY 11207
718-927-0012
Type: public choice
HS
Priority to Districts 19, 23 residents
Affiliation: NYC Schools
College prep; vocational; internships; community service;
　personalized.

IS 296
125 Covert St, Brooklyn, NY 11207
N. Letow, 718-574-0288
CSD 32
Type: magnet
6-8th grade
Business careers; theater technology.

Brooklyn College Academy (1986)
1311 James Hall, 2900 Bedford Ave, Brooklyn, NY 11210
Madeline Lumachi, 718-951-9541
NYBE/HS Div District
Type: public choice, at-risk
HS
Enrollment restricted to Brooklyn residents.
Located at Brooklyn College campus; uses college facilities;
　interest-related internships; college preparatory courses;
　taught by college professors; students can earn high
　school or college credit.

Midwood Montessori
2825 Bedford Ave, Brooklyn, NY 11210
Harriet Safran

High School Redirection (1969)
226 Bristol St, Brooklyn, NY 11212
Sharyn Wetjen, Prin, 718-498-2605
Type: public choice
35 teachers, 500 students, mainly at-risk, ages 17-21
Residency required
Governance by teachers, principal
Teacher qualifications: NYC credential
Intense guidance; no letter grades; multi-aged classes.

IS 281
8787 24th Ave, Brooklyn, NY 11214
Rose Molinelli, 718-996-6706
CSD 21
Type: magnet
6-8th grade
Media and communication arts.

Brooklyn New School (1987)
330 18th Street, Brooklyn, NY 11215
Mary Ellen Bosch, Director, 718 330-9288
Type: public choice
15 teachers, 250 students, ages 5-12, K-6th grade
No residency requirement
Affiliations: Center for Collaborative Education, Coalition of
　Essential Schools
Teacher qualifications: NY License
Shared decision-making; created by parents and teachers;
　hands-on curriculum for racially mixed population; no
　letter grades; multi-aged classes; extensive field trips;
　urban location; transportation; interns accepted.

The Children's House of Park Slope (1977)
421 7th St, Brooklyn, NY 11215
Gretchen Courage, Dir, 718-499-5667
Type: Montessori; tuition: $5,350-7,500/yr
3 teachers, 3 assistants, 48 students, ages 3-6
Affiliation: AMS
Governance by an administrator
Childcare; urban location; interns accepted.

Carroll Street School
712 Carroll St, Brooklyn, NY 11215-2101
Angela Apuzzi
Type: Montessori

Frederick Douglass Literacy Center (1982)
832 Marcy Ave, New York, NY 11216
Lois Rekosh, 718-636-5770, FAX: 718-398-4476
Kings County
Type: public at-risk
10 teachers, 180 students, ages 17-21, 10th grade
Entrance requirements: reading below fifth grade level
Affiliation: NYC Board of Ed
Governance by school based management/shared decision
　making
Literacy classes; computer lab; free meals available; urban
　location; transportation; interns accepted.

Street Academy High School (1971)
832 Marcy Ave, New York, NY 11216
718-622-4310
Type: public at-risk
250 students, 9-12th grade
NYC residency required
Family program; career development; external learning expe-
　riences; keyboarding and computer tech.

Metropolitan Corporate Academy (1990)
362 Schermerhorn St, Brooklyn, NY 11217
212-935-5911
Type: public choice
9-12th grade

Entrance requirements: grade 9, open house attendance
Affiliations: NYC BE, Goldman Sachs Inc
Interdisciplinary; school-based mgmt; internships; business ed; portfolio assessment; social services; college prep; parental involvement.

The Berkeley Caroll School
181 Lincoln Pl, Brooklyn, NY 11217
Joan Martin, 718-965-4166
Type: Montessori
635 students, pre K-12th grade
Three locations; lower school has Montessori approach.

YMCA Montessori Day School
30 3rd Ave, Brooklyn, NY 11217-1822

Peaceable School Montessori
33 7th Ave, Brooklyn, NY 11217-3439

New York City Vocational Training Center (1987)
1171 65th Street, Brooklyn, NY 11219
Alan Werner, Prin, 718-236-1661, FAX: 718-236-4340
Kings County
Type: public/independent
60 teachers, 2000 students, mainly at-risk, ages 17-21, ungraded
Entrance requirements: age 17; voluntary; no residency requirement
Affiliation: NYC BE
Governance by principal
Teacher qualifications: NYC License
Industrial work experience; on-site academic and voc training; diploma/GED; multi-aged classes; no letter grades; urban location.

Bay Ridge Montessori School
6301 12th Ave, Brooklyn, NY 11219-5213
June Grancio

J 126 School
424 Leanard, Brooklyn, NY 11222
Dr Toback, 718-782-2527
District 14
Type: magnet
7-9th grade
Creative arts.

PS 215
415 Ave S, Brooklyn, NY 11223
Gail Feuer, 718-339-2464
CSD 21
Type: magnet
K-1st grade
Gifted and talented.

PS 95
345 Van Sicklen St, Brooklyn, NY 11223
James Filatro, 718-449-5050
CSD 21
Type: magnet
K-5th grade
Multi-grade primary; open door.

IS 239
2401 Neptune Ave, Brooklyn, NY 11224
Gary Goldstein, 718-266-0814
CSD 21
Type: magnet
6-8th grade
Gifted and talented.

PS 188
3314 Neptune Ave, Brooklyn, NY 11224
Augusto Martinez, 718-266-6380
CSD 21
Type: magnet
K-5th grade
Gifted and talented.

PS 329
2929 W 30th St, Brooklyn, NY 11224
Stephen Levy, 718-996-3800
CSD 21
Type: magnet
K-5th grade
Gifted and talented.

Hawthorne Corners Preschool (1965)
1950 Bedford Ave, Brooklyn, NY 11225
Patricia Oduba, 718-282-7200
Type: Montessori
61 students, ages 3-6
Located in East Flatbush; population is mainly from the Caribbean and USA.

Lefferts Gardens Montessori (1982)
559 Rogers Ave, Brooklyn, NY 11225
Lenore Briggs, 718-773-0287
45 students, ages 2.5-8
Two locations.

Rosa Weatherless Alternative Middle School
797 Bushwick Ave, Brooklyn, NY 11227
S. Callari, 718-574-0148
CSD 32
Type: magnet
6-8th grade

Lefferts Park School
7115 15th Ave, Brooklyn, NY 11228
Alex Poehlemann, 718-232-0685
CSD 20
Type: magnet
K-5th grade
Global studies through literature, performing arts and media.

Windmill Montessori School
1317 Ave T, Brooklyn, NY 11229-3397
Liza Herzberg, Dir, 718-375-4277
Tuition: $3,200-5,800/yr
8 teachers, 8 assistants, 151 students, ages infant-15
Affiliation: AMS; accreditation: BH; NYS
Governance by an administrator
Outer-bound JHS; upper elementary is part of Newsday programs; urban location; interns accepted.

Pacific High School (1972)
112 Schermerhorn St, Brooklyn, NY 11230
Joan Ahern, Assistant Principal, 718-855-7155
Type: public at-risk
400 students, ages 16-21, 10-12th grade
Governance by principal
Student internships; independent study.

PS 99
1120 E 10th St, Brooklyn, NY 11230
Louis Galinsky, 718-338-9201
CSD 21
Type: magnet
K-7th grade
Gifted and talented.

The Alternative Program at PS 27 (1987)
Hicks St & Nelson St, Brooklyn, NY 11231
Paul Schwarz, 718-330-9345
Type: public choice

East Brooklyn Congregations High School for Public Service-Bushwick, East New York (1993)
1495 Herkimer St, Brooklyn, NY 11233
718-385-6071
Type: public choice
HS
Selection based on Educational Option criteria; priority to Districts 32, 23, 19 residents
Affiliation: NYC Public Schools
Mentorships; internships; inquiry-based; student-centered.

Montessori School of Mill Basin
6311 Avenue N, Brooklyn, NY 11234
Joan Indovino, Dir, 718-444-3200
Also has annex at 6301 Ave N, Brooklyn, 11234.

Montessori School of Mill Beach
6311 Ave N, Main Bldg, Brooklyn, NY 11234

P 276
1070 E 83 St, Brooklyn, NY 11236
Eileene Leibowitz, 718-241-5757
CSD 18
Type: magnet
Pre K–5th grade
Gifted and talented.

IS 162
1390 Willoughby Ave, Brooklyn, NY 11237
Aida Rivera, 718-821-4860
CSD 32
Type: magnet
6–8th grade
Bio-medical; performing arts.

IS 291
231 Palmetto St, Brooklyn, NY 11237
A. Bryan, 718-574-0361
CSD 32
Type: magnet
6–8th grade
Video technology; bilingual.

IS 383
1300 Greene Ave, Brooklyn, NY 11237
Mildred Boyce, 718-574-0390
CSD 32
Type: magnet
6–8th grade
Gifted and talented.

Tree of Life Montessori
810 Classen Ave, Brooklyn, NY 11238

Flushing Montessori School (1982)
147-08 Bayside Ave, Flushing, NY 11354
Mrs H Lucas, Director, 718-353-5544
30 students, ages 3–5, nursery-K
Governance by principal
Offers 2, 3 and 5 day schedules; environmental awareness in
   outdoor, parklike setting.

The House for Bright and Gifted Children (1989)
33-15 154th St, Flushing, NY 11354
718-461-6464
Type: independent
28 students, nursery-K
Everyone is gifted;"playing is learning, learning is playing";
   stress on English.

PS 29 School of Theater Arts
125-10 23 Ave, College Point, NY 11356
Theresa Harris, 718-886-5111
CSD 25
Type: magnet
K–6th grade

PS 193
152-20 11th Ave, Whitestone, NY 11357
Marc Rosenberg, 718-767-8810
CSD 25
Type: magnet
1–6th grade
Discovery.

**Early Education Program at St Mary's Hospital for
   Children** (1991)
29-01 216th St, Bayside, NY 11360

Sondra Friedman, Dir, 718-281-8841, FAX: 718-428-0531
Type: Montessori, non-profit
2 teachers, 3 assistants, 16 students, ages infant-5
Enrollment restricted to in-patients
Accreditation: AMS
Suburban location; interns accepted.

Linda Tagliaferro
248-44 Thebes Ave, Little Neck, NY 11362
718-423-0928
Type: home-based
Author, lecturer, long-time home educator.

MS 67
51-60 Marathon Pkwy, Little Neck, NY 11362
Mae Fong, 718-423-8138
District 26
Type: magnet
6–9th grade
Inquiry-based.

PS 162
201-02 53rd Ave, Bayside, NY 11364
Georgina Durando, 718-423-8621
District 26
Type: magnet
3–4th grade
Inquiry-based.

Parsons Junior High School 168
157-40 76th Rd, Flushing, NY 11366
Nat Blaivas, 718-591-9000
CSD 25
Type: magnet
7–9th grade
Performing arts.

PS 154
75-02 162 St, Flushing, NY 11366
Marjorie Richardson, 718-591-1500
CSD 25
Type: magnet
7–9th grade
Art and design.

IS 250
144-39 D Gravett Rd, Flushing, NY 11367
Jeffrey Ratner, 718-544-6912
CSD 25
Type: magnet
7–9th grade
Community campus school.

PS 164 School of Visual, Performing & Literary Arts
138-01 77 Ave, Flushing, NY 11367
Barbara Brown, 718-544-1083
CSD 25
Type: magnet
K–6th grade

PS 164 The Queens Valley
138-01 77th Ave, Flushing, NY 11367
Barbara Brown, 718-544-1083
CSD 25
Type: magnet
1–6th grade
Visual, performing and literary arts.

Kew Resources
(See Resource Appendix)

Rainbow Montessori School
15030 Union Tpke, Flushing, NY 11367-3977

Apple Montessori School
5938 Xenia St, Rego Park, NY 11368-3926

PS 92
99-01 34th Ave, Corona, NY 11370
Kathleen Murphy, 718-458-4580
CSD 30
Type: magnet
K-5th grade
Music; multi-cultural.

Island Academy (1986)
10-10 Hazen St, East Elmhurst, NY 11370
Timothy Lisante, Prin, 718-728-6774, FAX: 274-9541
Queens County
Type: public at-risk
22 teachers, 270 students, mainly at-risk, ages 16-21,
    ungraded
Students are incarcerated on Rikers Island
Affiliation: NYC BE
Governance by principal
Teacher qualifications: NYS/NYC certification
Comprehensive services for male adolescents while incarcer-
    ated; multi-aged classes; urban location; interns accepted.

JHS 141
37-11 21st Ave, Long Island, NY 11370
Carl Tomaselli, 718-278-6547
CSD 30
Type: magnet
7-9th grade
Humanities.

PS 112
35-05 37th Ave, Long Island, NY 11370
Daisy Martin, 718-784-5250
CSD 30
Type: magnet
K-6th grade
Social studies; multi-cultural.

PS 126
31-51 21st St, Long Island, NY 11370
Barbara Embriano, 718-274-8316
CSD 30
Type: magnet
6-9th grade
Visual and performing arts.

PS 171
14-14 29th Ave, Long Island, NY 11370
Anne Bussell, 718-932-0909
CSD 30
Type: magnet
K-5th grade
Media and telecommunications.

Montessori Progressive Learning
195-09 Linden Blvd, St Albans, NY 11412

Wise Memorial Montessori Learning Center
195-05 Linden Blvd, St Albans, NY 11412

PS 178
189-10 Radnor Rd, Jamaica, NY 11423
Joan Weingarten, 718-464-5763
District 26
Type: magnet
4-5th grade
Inquiry-based.

Ideal Montessori School (1982)
87-41 165th St, Jamaica, NY 11432
K P Chandu, Principal, 718-523-6237
140 students, ages 3-14, K-8th grade
Governance by principal
Montessori method and materials; special education class.

Montessori Tutoring & Pre-School
9001 Merrick Blvd, Jamaica, NY 11432-5244

Dover Publications, Inc
(See Resource Appendix)

Lawrence Evening High School (1984)
#2 Reilly Rd, Cedarhurst, NY 11516
Edward S. Erlich, 516-295-8027
Type: public choice
Students mainly at-risk, ages 16+, 10-12th grade
Work experience; accelerated diploma program; individual
    and group counseling.

Jack & Jill Montessori School
23 Front St, E Rockaway, NY 11518

Freeport Community Evening High School (1971)
235 N Ocean Ave, Freeport, NY 11520
Joseph L Cleary, 516-867-5300
Type: public choice

Kid's Place of Choice at South Nassau HS (1992)
186 E Ave, Freeport, NY 11520
Devorah Weinmann, 516-868-5766, FAX: 516-379-8435
Nassau County
Type: home-based, non-profit
15 students, ages 3-16
Governance by parent cooperative
Supervision by parents on rotating basis; member-generated
    activities

Long Island Growing at Home (LIGHT) (1990)
186 E Ave, Freeport, NY 11520
Devorah Weinmann, 516-868-5766, FAX: 516-379-8435
Governance by parent cooperative
Homeschool support group for Suffolk, Nassau, Queens;
    monthly meetings; 2-3 field trips/mo.

P S International Montessori School
228 S Ocean Ave, Freeport, NY 11520-4446
516-623-0716
Pre K-6th grade

The Waldorf School of Garden City (1947)
Cambridge Ave, Garden City, NY 11530
Marilyn Ruppart, Faculty Chair, 516-742-3434
Nassau County
Non-profit; tuition: $1,650-8,200/yr, scholarships
37 teachers, 270 students, ages 3-18, nursery-12th grade
Entrance requirements: must be at grade level
Governance by teachers and principal
Teacher qualifications: BA, Waldorf mentoring
1-wk/yr at New Hampshire campus; suburban location.

Another Way at North Shore High School (1990)
450 Glen Cove Ave, Glen Head, NY 11545
Jay Emmer, Coordinator, 516-671-5500
Nassau County
Type: public at-risk
2 teachers, 15 students, ages 14-18, 9-12th grade
Governance by teachers and principal
Teacher qualifications: state certification
Team teaching; narrative assessments; interdisciplinary; no
    letter grades; multi-aged classes; suburban location.

Hempstead High School
  City As School Program (1993)
185 Peninsula Blvd, Hempstead, NY 11550
Lisa Harris, 516-292-7052
Type: public choice
25 students

New Frontier Montessori School (1970)
35 Fulton St, Hempstead, NY 11550
Leona Budin, 516-678-2983
93 students, ages 2.5-11, pre K-6th grade
Affiliation: AMS

Long Beach High School
City As School Program (1993)
233 Lagoon Drive West, Lido Beach, NY 11561
Robert Dodes, 516-897-2036
Type: public choice
10 students

Harriet Eisman Community School (1972)
165 E Park Ave, Long Beach, NY 11561
Johanna Mathieson, 516-889-5575
Type: public at-risk
150 students, ages 16–21
Self-governing, supportive diploma program offers individual
   counseling, video production, college/career placement;
   informal setting.

Progressive School of Long Island (1985)
1425 Merrick Ave, Merrick, NY 11566
Eric Jacobson, Director, 516-868-6835
Nassau County
Type: independent, non-profit; tuition: $3750, scholarships
17 teachers, 105 students, ages 5–12, K–6th grade
Entrance requirements: interview, no special ed
Governance by teachers and principal, board
Philosophy of "neo-humanism," which embraces oneness of
   all things; 2 teachers per class; varied learning styles; yoga,
   computer, drama, social awareness, other electives; subur-
   ban location; transportation; interns accepted.

SWS (School Within A School) c/o The Wheatley School
   (1972)
11 Bacon Rd, Old Westbury, NY 11568
Bob Bernstein, Coordinator, 516-876-4700
Nassau County
Type: public choice
4 teachers, 76 students, ages 15–18, 10–12th grade
Entrance requirements: application, lottery; no residency
   requirement
Governance by democratic school meeting
Academically rigorous; honesty, integrity, and trust; student
   accepts responsibility for own education; constitution;
   supreme court; elected moderator; multi-aged classes;
   suburban location; interns accepted.

Ann Frank Montessori School
430 DeMott Ave, Rockville Centre, NY 11570
Carolyn Larcy, 516-678-5955
75 students, ages 3–8
Affiliation: AMI
Individualized program; advanced students transfer to Maria
   Montessori School in Levitown.

Greenhouse Alternative at South Side High School (1974)
Shepherd St, Rockville Centre, NY 11570
Richard Zodda, Coord, 516-255-8962
Nassau County
Type: public at-risk
3 teachers, 30 students, ages 15–18, 10–12th grade
Entrance requirements: application, residency
Governance by democratic school meeting
Comprehensive; career awareness; community resources;
   basic social skills; extensive field trips; multi-aged classes;
   suburban location; interns accepted.

Southside High School
City As School Program (1993)
140 Shepherd St, Rockville Centre, NY 11570
Robin Calitri, 516-255-8947
Type: public choice
34 students

Merle Avenue Program (1985)
Merle Ave School, Oceanside, NY 11572
Ira Sarison, 516-678-1200
Type: public choice

Extended Support Program (1986)
Roslyn High School, Roslyn, NY 11577
Dr Pat James Jordan, 516-625-6379
Nassau County
Type: public choice
2 teachers, 25 students, mainly at-risk, ages 14–19
District residency required
Governance by board
School-within-a-school; counseling; course work; behavior
   modification; suburban location.

Alternative Education Resource Organization (AERO)
(See Resource Appendix)

Valley Street Central High School (1987)
One Kent Rd, Valley Stream, NY 11582
Henry Cram, 516-561-7910
Type: public choice

Alternative School
W Tresper Clarke HS, Westbury, NY 11590
William J. Schaub, Asst Prin, 516-876-7416
Nassau County
Type: public at-risk
3 teachers, 30 students, ages 15–21, 10–12th grade
Residency required
Governance by teachers and principal
For potential dropouts; suburban location; transportation;
   interns accepted.

North Babylon Alternative High School (1985)
1 Phelps Ln, North Babylon, NY 11703
Carl A. Torrillo, Coord, 516-321-3279
N Babylon District, Suffolk County
Type: public at-risk
18 teachers, 50 students, ages 15–19, 10–12th grade
Entrance requirements: recommendation, principal approval,
   residency
Governance by principal
Teacher qualifications: NY Certification, experience
Diploma; contract; strict attendance policy; no letter grades;
   multi-aged classes; suburban location.

John F. Kennedy Elementary
175 Brookvale Ave, W Babylon, NY 11704
Emanuel Campisi, 516-321-3053
Type: magnet
4–5th grade
Cognitively gifted.

South Bay Elementary
160 Great E Neck Rd, W Babylon, NY 11704
Patricia Farrell, 516-321-3145
Type: magnet
3rd grade
Cognitively gifted.

Tooker Ave Elementary
855 Tooker Ave, W Babylon, NY 11704
Gary Loker, 516-321-3136
Type: magnet
K–5th grade
Cognitively gifted.

Bethpage Alternative for Success Curriculum (BASC)
   (1986)
Cherry Ave, Bethpage, NY 11714
Ira J. Kahn, Asst Prin, 516-733-3750
Nassau County
Type: public choice
9 teachers, 28 students, ages 14–17, 9–11th grade
Governance by board
Teacher qualifications: NY certification
Regents level education.

Bethpage Alternative Success Curriculum (1986)
Bethpage High School, Bethpage, NY 11714

Ira Kahn, Assistant Principal, 516-931-2900
Type: public at-risk
30 students, ages 14-17, 9-11th grade
Housed within the regular school; focuses on potential
    dropouts.

Grasso Homeschool (1993)
332 Brentwood Parkway, Brentwood, NY 11717
Alicia Grasso, 516-434-1117
Suffolk County
1 teacher, 1 student, age 8, 4th grade
Works with 2 PTAs, Council of PTAs, school improvement
    team, Brentwood Bd of Ed, to improve education for all
    children; suburban location.

Bellport PM High School (1985)
Beaver Dam Rd, Brookhaven, NY 11719
Bette E Errig, 516-286-4363
Type: public choice

Middle Country Performing Arts School (1985)
Unity Drive School, Centereach, NY 11720
Arthur Dermer, 516-588-1029
Type: public choice

American Open University (1955)
211 Carlton Ave, Central Islip, NY 11722
Dr Norma Talley, 516-348-3300
Tuition: $90/credit hour
Non-residential arm of NY Institute of Technology; courses by
    computer teleconferencing; credit for previous experi-
    ence; mentors.

Central Islip Alternative High School (1989)
Wheeler Rd, Central Islip, NY 11722
D. Meehan, Principal, 516-348-5065
Suffolk County
Type: public at-risk
4 teachers, 25-60 students, ages 15-21, 9-12th grade
Residency required
Governance by teachers, principal, and board
Daily counseling; suburban location; transportation; interns
    accepted.

**Operation: Setauket Approach to Interage Learning
    (OP-SAIL) at Setauket ES** (1976)
134 Main St, E Setauket, NY 11733
Dr Thomas DeBello, Prin, 516-474-7690
Suffolk County
Type: public choice
3 teachers, 70 students, ages 9-12, 4-6th grade
Entrance requirements: lottery system, district residency
Governance by principal, teachers, parent cooperative, board,
    democratic school meeting, faculty and student reps
Interns accepted.

Theatre Arts Option (1981)
134 Main St, Setauket, NY 11733-2867
Joseph Baldino, 516-474-7690, FAX: 516-474-7692
Suffolk County
Type: public choice
2 teachers, 50 students, ages 9-12, 5-6th grade
No residency requirement
Teacher qualifications: certification
Interns accepted.

PAGE at Farmingdale Senior High School (1983)
Lincoln & Midwood, Farmingdale, NY 11735
Eugene McSweeney, Coord, 516-752-6624
Type: public at-risk
5 teachers, 50-60 students, mainly at-risk, ages 15-18,
    10-12th grade
Entrance requirements: interview, residency
Governance by teachers and principal
Builds self-confidence; peer counseling; student council;
    yearbook; holiday dinners; fund raisers; suburban location;
    interns accepted.

Long Island School for the Gifted
Pigeon Hill Rd, Huntington, NY 11743
Carol Yilmez

The North Suffolk Montessori School (1965)
PO Box 525, Huntington, NY 11743
Patricia St Jean, Director, 516-449-0988, 516-331-5113
Non-profit; tuition: $2200-5400, scholarships
150 students, ages 2-12, pre K-6th grade
Governance by principal and teachers
Multisensory; multicultural; computer-aided, hands-on learn-
    ing; teaching teams; small classes; after school enrich-
    ment; summer sessions; student internship; 2 locations:
    North Huntington, Commack.

West Hills Montessori School (1968)
21 Sweet Hollow Rd, Huntington, NY 11743-6530
Sheldon Thompson, Director, 516-385-3342
Tuition: $1895 preK, 2250 K, 2800 Extended, scholarships
150 students, ages 3-9, pre K-3rd grade
Affiliation: AMS
Governance by teachers and principal
Full range of Montessori materials.

Center for Alternative Education (1987)
17 Westminster Ave, Dix Hills, NY 11746
Virginia Murchison, Administrator, 516-667-6000, ext 404
Type: public at-risk; tuition: $4450/yr
200 students, ages 14-21, 9-12th grade
Governance by principal and teachers, democratic school
    meeting, parents
Part of BOCES III, Suffolk County; offers GED and diploma pro-
    grams; includes pregnant and parenting teens; hours
    based on need; occupational education.

Suffolk 3, BOCES Alternative Education Program (1986)
507 Deer Park Rd, Dix Hills, NY 11746
Edward J Murphy, 516-549-4900
Type: public at-risk

Center for the Study of Educational Alternatives (1977)
(See Resource Appendix)

South Huntington Alternative High School (1988)
301 W Hills Rd, Huntington Station, NY 11746
Daniel Kalina, Dir, 516-673-1772
Suffolk County
Type: public at-risk
6 teachers, 24 students, ages 16-19, 11-12th grade
Residency required
Governance by principal
Teacher qualifications: NY certification
Small classes; life skills; academic prep; suburban location.

Early Childhood Center (1985)
Craig Gariepy Ave, Islip Terrace, NY 11752
Margaret Harper, 516-581-1600, FAX: 516-581-1617
Type: Montessori
2 teachers, 1 assistant, 60 students, ages 3-6
Entrance requirements: screening
Governance by administrator
Ameliorates entering kindergarteners' learning difficulties;
    childcare; suburban location.

East Islip Public Schools-Montessori Preschool
Graig B Gariepy Ave, Islip Terrace, NY 11752
Barbara Mead

Maria Montessori School (1964)
11 Laurel Lane, Levitown, NY 11756
Carolyn Larcy, 516-520-0301
100 students, ages 3-14
Affiliation: AMI
Four levels: 3-6, 6-9, 9-12, junior high; students ready for
    Regents by 8th grade.

Levittown Schools Alternative Program (1988)
Division Avenue HS, Division Ave, Levittown, NY 11756
Daniel K. Provost, 516-520-5719
Nassau County
Type: public at-risk
1 teacher, 14 students, mainly at-risk, ages 15–21, HS
Residency required
Governance by teachers, principal, and building chairman
Teacher qualifications: SE certification, experience with ED
    population
Half-day; contract-based; VOC; GED prep; multi-aged classes;
    suburban location.

Lindenhurst Alternative Learning Center (1986)
350 Daniel St, Lindenhurst, NY 11757
James Connolly, Asst Principal, 516-226-6562
Suffolk County
Type: public at-risk
4 teachers, 70 students, ages 13–19, 9–12th grade
Entrance requirements: referral, residency
Affiliation: Lindenhurst HS
Governance by teachers and principal
Teacher qualifications: patience and resourcefulness
Academic and social behavior modification; multi-aged
    classes; extensive field trips; suburban location;
    transportation.

Montessori School of Lindenhurst (1971)
1755 11th St, Lindenhurst, NY 11757
Maryellen Clark, Owner/Administrator, 516-226-3066
Affiliation: AMS

Alternative Learning Program at Plainedge HS (1986)
Wyngate Dr, Massapequa, NY 11758
Frank Caramanica, Team Coord, 516-797-4428
Nassau County
Type: public at-risk
2 teachers, 20 students, ages 14–20, 9–12th grade
Governance by team of teachers with student input
Teacher qualifications: certification
Breakfast program; daily school meeting; multi-aged classes;
    suburban location; interns accepted.

Montessori Children's School, Inc (1966)
Box 422, Central & Jerusalem Aves, Massapequa, NY 11758
Charlene Sherwin, 516-541-6365
120 students, ages 2 yrs 9 mo–8 yrs, pre K–3rd grade
Affiliation: AMS
Didactic materials used in all areas of curriculum.

Long Island Home Schoolers Association
4 Seville Pl, Massapequa Park, NY 11762
Lynn Rudin, 516-795-5554
12+ students
Information and resources for begining homeschoolers;
    non-sectarian support group; field trips.

Step by Step Early Learing Center
138 Radio Ave, Miller Place, NY 11764-3412
Type: Montessori

LMC Montessori Teacher Centre
Nantucket Way, Mt Sinai, Long Island, NY 11766
Type: Montessori teacher education

Suffolk 1 Regional Alternative High School (1984)
379 Locust Ave, Oakdale, NY 11769
Les Meneilly, 516-244-5975
Type: public at-risk
100 students, ages 14–21, 9–12th grade
Small classes; flexible scheduling; BOCES Occupational Educa-
    tion Classes and/or cooperative work study program.

Sachem (1978)
Sachem North HS, 212 Smith Rd, Lake Ronkonkoma, NY 11779
William Schmidt, Supervisor; John Heslin, Asst Supervisor,
    516-476-0417

Suffolk County
Type: public at-risk
15 teachers, 40 students, mainly at-risk, ages 14–21, 9–12+
Residency required
Governance by teachers and principal
Teacher qualifications: certifications
Student, parent sign an educational contract; low ratio;
    secure, structured classroom environment; counselors,
    psychologist address behavior, life problems; no letter
    grades; multi-aged classes; suburban location; interns
    accepted.

Suffolk Lutheran School-Montessori Program
Moriches & Woodlawn, St James, NY 11780

Children's Montessori Center
7 Flowerfield #32, Saint James, NY 11780-1514

Maria Montessori School
2025 Washington Ave, Seaford, NY 11783
Carolyn Larcy, 516-785-0372
Tuition: $2600–5000
120 students, K–8th grade
Experiential learning; extended field trips.

Montessori School of Selden (1976)
38 Adirondack Dr, PO Box 1028, Selden, NY 11784
Linda Beeccroft, Director, 516-736-2246
Tuition: $139–414/mo
72 students, ages 2.75–6, pre K–6th grade
Governance by principal
BOCES II.

Smithtown Alternative HS (1982)
100 Central Rd, Smithtown, NY 11787
Mr Collins, 516-361-2418
Type: public at-risk
25 students, 9–12th grade

North Shore Montessori School
218 Christian Ave, Stony Brook, NY 11790
Barbara Ende, 516-689-8273
Creative movement; drama; Spanish twice a week; library;
    music.

Wyandanch Memorial High School (1973)
32 St & Brooklyn Ave, Wyandanch, NY 11798
Anthony Fusco, 516-491-1022
Type: public choice

Hampton Day School (1966)
Butter Lane, Bridgehampton, NY 11932
Claud Okin, 516-537-1240
Type: independent; tuition: $2150–6500, scholarships
26 teachers, 164 students, pre K–8th grade
No letter grades; thematic approach; child-driven curriculum.

William Floyd HS Equivalent Attendance Program (1985)
240 Mastic Beach Rd, Mastic Beach, NY 11951
Jean Thoden, 516-281-3020
Type: public choice
40 students, 9–12th grade
For 16 and 17 year-olds with less than half the credits needed
    for age-appropriate school year; GED preparation program
    offered 2 1/2 hours/day for 1 year; work credit given.

Southampton Montessori School (1983)
135 St. Andrews Rd, Southampton, NY 11968
Irene Hope Gazza, Dir, 516-283-2223
Tuition: $3,400/yr
4 teachers; student ages 3–6
Entrance requirements: age 3 by Dec 31.
Accreditations: AMS, NY Charter
Governance by administrator, teachers, democratic school
    meeting
Suburban location; interns accepted.

Friends World Program of Long Island University (1965)
Southhampton Campus, Southhampton, NY 11968
Lewis Greenstein, Director, 516-287-8464, FAX: 616-283-4081
Type: Quaker higher education, boarding, non-profit; tuition:
$11,000, scholarships
23 teachers, 130 students, ages 17+
Governance by democratic school meeting
Teacher qualifications: PhD, MA/MS
Fully accredited BA program; experiential model; students
study in eight centers around the world: China, India,
Costa Rica, England, Israel, Japan, Kenya in US at
Southampton; student internships; independent study; no
letter grades; non-compulsory class attendance.

Averill Park High School Alternative Program (1984)
16 Gettle Rd, Averill Park, NY 12018
Gibson Bernard, 518-674-3826
Type: public at-risk
32 students, 9-12th grade
Self-contained classroom; students work at own pace; traditional curriculum; work-study program, 1200 hours; volunteer work, 600 hours for full credit.

Rensselaer Columbia Greene Boces High School (1984)
1550 Schuurman Rd, Castleton, NY 12033
Diane Keating, 518-477-8771
Type: public choice

The Alternative Learning Center (1991)
c/o Barnett-Mulligan, 143 Hudson Ave, Chatham, NY 12037
Wendy Barnett-Mulligan
Columbia County
Type: independent, non-profit; tuition: $25/half-year session
Governance by parent cooperative
Children/parent group; skills, interest sharing; workshops;
field trips; rural location.

Schoharie County Area Home Educators
RD 2, Box 759, Cobleskill, NY 12043
Amy G White

Montessori Center
75 Jordan Blvd, Delmar, NY 12054
Kathleen Hutter

Blossoms Montessori Learning Program
56 Hudson Ave, PO Box 223/56, Delmar, NY 12054-0121
Gaston Cadieux

Alliance for Parental Involvement in Education (1989)
PO Box 59, East Chatham, NY 12060
Katharine Houk, Exec Dir; Seth Rockmuller, Pres, 518-392-
6900
Columbia County
Non-profit
Affiliations: NCACS, NHA, ERIC, Parent Ed Network
Newsletter; book; resources catalog; mail-order lending
library; annual conference; workshops.

Alternative Program
Luther Road, East Greenbush, NY 12061
Gerald Elliott, Asst Prin, 518-477-4138
Rensselaer County
Type: public at-risk
30 students, mainly at-risk, ages 13-20, 9-12th grade
Residency required
Governance by principal and board
Teacher qualifications: NYS certification in subject area
Small classes; extra counseling; some older students exit to
mainstream; suburban location.

GALLAH (Green/Albany Learning At Home) (1991)
Rte 54, Hanacroix, NY 12087
Charlotte Carter, Sally Bogardus, 518-756-6120
20+ students, K-6th grade
Governance by parent cooperative
Group of homeschooling families; organizes peer workshops;
publishes newsletter with events and students' work.

**Gloversville High School, Lexington Center Alternative
Program** (1974)
465 N Perry St, Johnstown, NY 12095
Jack T Deweese, 518-725-0671
Type: public at-risk

Johnstown Alternative and Continuing Education (1991)
501 Glebe St, Johnstown, NY 12095
Laurie Bargstedt, Community Educator, 518-762-4769
Type: public choice
Student ages 16-60
GED, diploma and ESL programs; computer literacy; Adkins
Life Skills; conflict management; career development;
apprenticeships; personal interest courses; parenting and
financial education; counseling.

Montessori School of Albany
PO Box 245, Rensselaer, NY 12144-0245
Bernadine Starrs

Capital District Home Educators
Rd 2, Box 6A, Schaghticoke, NY 12154
Rebecca MacKenzie

Troy High School Alternate Learning Center (1976)
6 & Ingalls Ave, Troy, NY 12180
Christopher T Mahoney, 518-271-5200
Type: public at-risk

Robert C Parker School (1991)
141 Main Ave, Wyantskill, NY 12198
Susan Merrett, Director, 518-286-3449
Type: independent; tuition: $5600, scholarships
50 students, ages 8-13, 4-8th grade
Governance by principal
Self-paced, individualized curriculum; cooperative, hands-on
learning; small classes.

Montessori Magnet School, Albany Public Schools
75 Park Ave, Albany, NY 12202
Kathleen Mrozak or Maggie Fuller

The Free School (1971)
8 Elm St, Albany, NY 12202
Mary Leue, Director Emeritus, 518-434-3072, FAX: 518-432-
8984
Type: independent, non-profit; tuition: sliding scale
10 teachers, 42 students, ages 3 mo-14yrs, ungraded
Entrance requirements: consent by both parents, willingness
by student
Affiliation: NCACS
Governance by democratic school meeting, board; teachers
do long-range planning.
School has forest land in Taconic Mts, ancient homeland of
Mohicans; will be used as teaching resource for all students; apprenticeship and counseling training; no letter
grades; non-compulsory class attendance; multi-aged
classes; extensive field trips; childcare; urban location;
interns accepted.

SKOLE (1985)
(See Resource Appendix)

St Catherine's Center for Children
40 N Main Ave, Albany, NY 12203
Sr Dorothy Copson
Type: Montessori

Project Future
1015 Watervleit Shaker Rd, Albany, NY 12205
Virginia Ward, Coordinator, 518-456-9240
Type: public at-risk
100 students, partly at-risk, ages 14-21, 9-12th grade
Governance by coordinator, staff and students
Occupational, parenting, prenatal, and postpartum instruction; GED and diploma programs; linkage to three community colleges; field trips; Liberty Partnership Project.

Pine Hills Montessori Day Care
715 Morris St, Albany, NY 12208
Jean Dearstyne

Loving Education At Home
Box 12846, Albany, NY 12212-2846

Assistant Commissioner for Non-Public Schools
State Education Department, Albany, NY 12234
Rachel Smith, 518-474-3879
Type: state home-based
NY state does not require parents to be certified; individualized home instruction plan, quarterly progress reports,
annual assessment are submitted to local superintendent;
testing required in alternate years in grades 4-8 and every
year 9-12.

Albany Area Home Schoolers (1992)
46 Pershing Ave, Scotia, NY 12302
Jon or Sheila Stone, 518-346-3413, FAX: 518-399-3277
Schenectady County
Governance by board
Newsletter; support.

Graduation Achievement Program (1989)
2072 Curry Rd, Rotterdam, NY 12303
Niel Tebbano, Prin; Rosemarie Devoe, Tch/Coord, 518-356-
5010, FAX: 518-356-1518
Schenectady County
Type: public choice
1 teacher, 1 assistant, 25-30 students, mainly at-risk, ages
16-20, 10-12th grade
Residency required
Governance by teachers and principal
Teacher qualifications: secondary certification
Self-motivation is an essential goal; 3 hour academic sessions;
independent study; no letter grades; 100% parental
involvement; suburban location; transportation.

Cities as School Academy (1972)
Oakwood Ave, Schenectady, NY 12303
James Guedette, 518-370-8183
Type: public at-risk

Shalmont High School (1993)
1 Sabre Dr, Schenectady, NY 12306
Peter Rings, 518-355-6110
Type: independent, non-profit
1 teacher, 8 students, ages 15-19, 9-12th grade
Residency required
Governance by board
No letter grades; rural location.

Linton Ace Program (1985)
The Plaza Linton High School, Schenectady, NY 12308
Albert Aldi, 518-370-8190
Type: public choice

The Montessori School (1991)
2117 Union St, Niskayuna, NY 12309
Pam Slotsky, Dir/Tch, 518-374-4764
24 students, ages 3-6
Entrance requirements: toilet trained; visit; interview
Affiliations: AMS, NAMTA
Governance by an administrator
12/class max; traditional Montessori program; cooking; sign
language; Spanish; multi-aged classes; suburban location.

Open School at Howe School (1971)
Baker Ave, Schenectady, NY 12309
Jack D Hickey, 518-370-8295
Type: public choice

Villa Fusco Montessori School
955 Balltown Rd, Schenectady, NY 12309-6532

Alternative Education Evening
403 Broadway, Kingston, NY 12401
Carlton Bell, 914-331-1970
Type: public choice

Northern Catskill Alternative (1986)
PO Box 26, Grand Gorge, NY 12434
Dee or Emilio DaBramo, Coordinator, 607-588-6420
Delaware County
Type: public at-risk
2 teachers, 26 students, ages 14-19, 7-12th grade
Entrance requirements: interview, residency, referral
Affiliation: BOCES
Governance by principal, board
Teacher qualifications: state certification
Students referred to program to improve and maintain
strong academic performance and attendance, improve
self-esteem, return to home school, earn diploma; rural
location; transportation.

Woodstock Support Group
PO Box 34, Lake Hill, NY 12448
Mary Pustilnik
Type: home-based

Margaretville Central School (1991)
Margaretville, NY 12455
Michael D Benedette, 914-586-2647
Type: public at-risk
6-8th grade
Governance by teachers and principal
For students who have failed at least one grade and are cur-
rently failing; students choose classes in alternative
program and regular class; resource room.

Port Ewen Ed Ctr
Rt 9W, Box 1176, Port Ewen, NY 12466
Nancy Plummer, 914-339-8710
Type: public at-risk

Ulster County BOCES Alternative School (1985)
PO Box 1176, Port Ewen, NY 12466
Nancy Plumer, 914-339-8718
Type: public at-risk
110 students, 7-12th grade
Teen parent, GED, vocational and diploma programs; focus on
integration of arts in curriculum.

High Meadow School (1984)
PO Box 552, Stone Ridge, NY 12484
Hope S. Wootan, Adm, 914-681-4855
Ulster County
Type: independent, non-profit
14 teachers, 51 students, ages 4-12, K-7th grade
Governance by teachers, principal, democratic school
meeting, parent cooperative, board
Student-centered; self-directed; cooperative spirit; wholistic;
self-esteem; conflict resolution; no letter grades; multi-
aged classes; extensive field trips; rural location; trans-
portation; interns accepted.

Mountain Laurel Waldorf (1978)
PO Box 208, Tillson, NY 12486-0208
Julia Roig, Administrator, 914-658-3740
Tuition: $4500, scholarships
92 students, ages 4-14, K-7th grade
Affiliation: AWSNA
Governance by board/faculty with parent involvement
Regular Waldorf curriculum; German, Spanish; handwork,
woodworking.

Woodstock Montessori School
Rt 212, Woodstock, NY 12498

**Cornwall Central High School
City As School Program** (1992)
122 Main St, Cornwall, NY 12518

Robert Maher, Prin, 914-534-8908
Type: public choice
25 students

HELP Resource Center
RR1 Box 60-B, Elizaville, NY 12523
Barbara S. Calabrese, 914-756-3902
Type: home-based

Anthroposophic Press
(See Resource Appendix)

R-C-G BOCES (1985)
61 Union Tpk, Hudson, NY 12534
Fred Root, 518-828-4157, FAX: 518-828-0084
Columbia County
Type: public at-risk; tuition: $8000/yr, scholarships
7 teachers, 98 students, ages 13–21, 7–12th grade
Entrance requirements: 5th grade math and reading levels
Governance by teachers and principal
Teacher qualifications: NYS certification in subject area
Emphasis on affective education; thematic curriculum; coop-
    erative learning design; "Project Adventure" activities; rural
    location; transportation; interns accepted.

Haviland Junior High School Program (1983)
20 Haviland Rd, Hyde Park, NY 12538
Richard Kuralt, 914-229-2181
Type: public choice

Children's House (1982)
RD 1 Galle Lane, La Grangeville, NY 12540
Cathy Billone, 914-223-3783
Type: Montessori
50 students, ages 2–6
Three-year age groupings; student-centered environment;
    individual instruction.

Duane Lake Academy (1983)
Franklin Ave, Box 372, Millbrook, NY 12545
Cheryl Pogonowski, Administrator, 914-677-6845
Dutchess County
Type: independent/home-based, non-profit; cost: $3000
20 students, ages 4–20
Governance by parent cooperative, board
Teacher qualifications: must love children, be a good
    communicator
Classes on Monday and Wednesday; students home study
    other days; parents teach at school; progressive mastery
    learning; students can operate at different grade levels at
    once; multi-aged classes; rural location; interns accepted.

Valley Central High School
  City As School Program (1992)
1175 Route 17K, Montgomery, NY 12549-2210
Don Crispell, Asst Prin, 914-457-3122
Type: public choice
34 students

Evening High School at Newburgh Free Academy (1979)
201 Fullerton Ave, Newburgh, NY 12550
Anthony Marino, 914-563-7561
Type: public at-risk
Student ages 16–21, 9–12th grade
Courses offered for catching-up on credits or graduating; no
    charge for in-district students; small classes.

Fostertown ETC
216 Fostertown Rd, Newburgh, NY 12550
Peter Copeletti, 914-563-7337
Type: magnet
K–6th grade
Education through creativity.

Horizons-on-the-Hudson
137 Montgomery St, Newburgh, NY 12550
Mary Ann Joyce, 914-563-7373

Type: magnet
K–6th grade
Gifted; talented.

Meadow Hill GEM
50 Meadow Hill Rd, Newburgh, NY 12550
William Castellane, 914-563-7600
Type: magnet
K–6th grade
Global explorations.

Newburgh Middle School
191 Washington St, Newburgh, NY 12550
Louis Tullo, 914-563-7744
Type: magnet
6–8th grade
Interdisciplinary; black rock forest.

West Street Community
39 W St, Newburgh, NY 12550
Joan Goudy-Crosson, 914-563-7777
Type: magnet
K–6th grade
Micro community.

Creamery Kids Adventure Group
173 Huguenot St, New Paltz, NY 12561
Michelle Riddell, 914-255-5482
Type: home-based

New Paltz Area Home Educators Collective (1993)
415 Springtown Rd, New Paltz, NY 12561
Joanne Clark, 914-255-5032
Ulster County
Non-profit
40 students, ages 1–15, K–12th grade
Governance by parent cooperative
Weekly meetings; students may participate in planned activi-
    ties or create their own; outdoor play; suburban location;
    interns accepted.

The Threefold Review
(See Resource Appendix)

Omega Institute for Holistic Studies (1977)
260 Lake Dr, Rhinebeck, NY 12572
Kathleen Jespersen, Marketing Asst, 914-266-4444, FAX: 914-
    266-4828
Type: independent, non-profit; tuition: $130–350/course,
    scholarships
250–300 teachers, 10,000 students, ages 8+
Workshops; conferences; health, psychology, multicultural
    arts, spirituality; winter traveling programs.

National Coalition of Educational Activists (NCEA)
(See Resource Appendix)

Dutchess Alternative Education Program (1985)
RD 1, Box 369A, Salt Point Turnpike, Poughkeepsie, NY 12601
Frank J Falanga, 914-471-9200
Type: public at-risk

Montessori School of Dutchess
Bradley Court, Poughkeepsie, NY 12601

Oakwood School (1976)
515 South Rd, Poughkeepsie, NY 12601
Dexter S. Lewis, 914-462-4200
Type: Quaker
120 students, 9–12+
Governance by consensus of students and teachers
Boarding and day; 60-acre campus; strong emphasis on
    visual and performing arts; advanced placement courses;
    competitive sports.

Dutchess Alternative Middle/High School (1990)
350 Dutchess Turnpike, Poughkeepsie, NY 12603
Ruth A Klein, Coordinator of Alternative Education, 914-473-
    1190

Type: public at-risk; tuition: $10,200/yr
125 students, ages 13-21, 7-12th grade
Affiliation: Dutchess BOCES
Governance by parent cooperative with parent, teacher and
    student participation
Local or regents diploma; interdisciplinary classes; demon-
    strated mastery through specific applications of knowl-
    edge; daily student progress meetings.

Dutchess County Homeschoolers
24 Cramer Rd, Poughkeepsie, NY 12603
Tracey Covell

Poughkeepsie Evening High School (1984)
May & Forbus Sts, Poughkeepsie, NY 12603
Rosemarie Gardner, 914-454-9007
Type: public at-risk

Frost Valley Environmental Education (1968)
2000 Frost Valley Rd, Claryville, NY 12725
John Haskin, Dir, 914-985-2291, FAX: 914-985-0056
Ulster County
Type: independent, non-profit; tuition: variable, scholarships
25 teachers, 11,800 students, K-adult ages
Residency required
Affiliation: International YMCAs
Governance by teachers, principal and board
Teacher qualifications: BS
Resident program; discovery-based; urban location; interns
    accepted.

Homestead School
326 Hollow Rd, Glen Spey, NY 12737
Type: Montessori

Liberty Central High School (1987)
125 Buckley St, Liberty, NY 12754
Shirley Weigard, 914-292-5400
Type: public at-risk
10-15 students, ages 16-19
Governance by principal
GED, diploma, and entry level job skills programs; promotes
    realistic self-image.

Saratoga Independent School
Box 112, Gansevoort, NY 12831-0112
Julie Van Deusen, 518-583-0841
Type: independent, non-profit
3 teachers, 30 students, ages 5-8, K-3rd grade
Entrance requirements: no facilities for hamdicapped
Governance by board
Teacher qualifications: certification
Open classroom; developmental program, by needs, not age;
    hand-on, manipulative work; group and individualized
    instruction; no letter grades; non-compulsory class atten-
    dance; multi-aged classes; extensive field trips; rural
    location.

9th Grade Alternative Program at Hudson Falls Senior High School (1986)
E Labarge St, Hudson Falls, NY 12839
Lady Rucinski, 518-747-2121
Type: public at-risk

Alternative High School, Washington-Saratoga-Warren-Hamilton-Essex BOCES (1985)
10 La Crosse St, Hudson Falls, NY 12839
Keith Brown, 518-793-7721
Type: public at-risk

Saratoga Springs JHS Alternative (1979)
W Circular St, Saratoga Springs, NY 12866
J Michael Gonroff, 518-584-7510
Type: public choice

Spring Hill School (1981)
62-66 York Ave, Saratoga Springs, NY 12866

Virginia W Reamer, Office Coordinator, 518-584-7643
Type: Waldorf, non-profit; tuition: $675-4350, scholarships
119 students, ages 3-11, pre K-6th grade
Governance by faculty
Waldorf-trained staff; integration of material into rhythms of
    human growth and development; wholistic curriculum
    includes moral, artistic and intellectual aspects.

Schuyler Academy on the Hudson
Clarks Mill Rd, Schuylerville, NY 12871
Type: Montessori

Infant & Child Developmental Center
8 Coastland Dr, Plattsburgh, NY 12901-9504
Type: Montessori

North Country School (1938)
Box 187, Lake Placid, NY 12946
Christine Lefevre, Adms Dir, 518-523-9329, FAX:-4858
Essex County
Type: independent, boarding, non-profit; tuition: $22,000/yr,
    scholarships
30 teachers, 55 students, ages 9-14, 4-8th grade
Affiliation: Camp Treetops
Governance by board
Teacher qualifications: BA/BS and interest/experience
School-as-village model; outdoor ed; art; work program;
    greenhouse; organic gardens; farm animals; maple-
    sugaring; no letter grades; transportation; interns
    accepted.

Franklin Essex Hamilton BOCES Alt Ed Center (1985)
N Franklin Educational Ctr, Malone, NY 12953
Kathryn K Leavitt, 518-483-1390
Type: public at-risk
67 students, 8-10th grade
For potential dropouts; emphasis on academic/vocational
    credit.

Raymond Street Preschool
26 Raymond St, Malone, NY 12953-1626
Type: Montessori

Tri-Lakes Community Home Educators (1990)
PO Box 270, Raybrook, NY 12977
Lynn Waickman, 518-891-5657
Essex County
Rural location.

Prevocational Alt Ed Student System, Adirondack Educational Center (1986)
RD 1 Box 7A, Saranac Lake, NY 12983
Nancy Montevago, 518-891-1330
Type: public at-risk

Summit School (1985)
c/o YMCA, 27 Williams St, Auburn, NY 13021
Bill Speck, 315-253-5304 ext 32
Type: public at-risk
60 students, ages 13-17, 7-10th grade
Governance by teachers
Multi-dimensional, ecological approach to intervention ser-
    vices for students of average to above average intellect
    with academic/social failure in traditional school.

West Genesee Step Program (1968)
Sanderson Rd, Camillus, NY 13031
Marvin A Bodley, 315-487-4601
Type: public choice
9-12th grade

Families for Home Education (1991)
5458 Oxbow Rd, Cazenovia, NY 13035
Brynda Filkins, Coord, 315-655-3238
Madison County
Non-profit
Pre K-8th grade

Governance by parent cooperative
Group lessons; play groups; 20 families; suburban & rural.

The Eidos In-School Program (1975)
Town & County Plaza, Cazanovia, NY 13035-0455
Brian W Burns, Executive Director, 315-655-2704
Type: public at-risk
12-20 students, ages 12-19, 7-12th grade
Affiliation: The Idyllic Foundation
Governance by staff and student body cooperative
Counseling/education program for Madison Cty youth experiencing home, community, school and employment problems; student internships; community service and entrepreneurial projects; high school & GED, diploma preparation.

Discovery Montessori School
241 Seneca St, Chittenango, NY 13037-1638

Cortland Alternative High School
PO Box 2000, Cortland, NY 13045
607-753-4601
Type: public at-risk
5 teachers, 41 students, ages 15-19, 9-12th grade
Governance by principal and teachers, with parent and student participation
Strong "family group" counseling component; located on university campus; staff and students collaborate on curriculum and discipline policies.

Parents Instructing Challenged Children (1987)
615 Utica St, Fulton, NY 13069-1954
Allen and Barb Mulvey, 315-592-7257
Type: state home-based
Support group to inform and assist home schoolers who have special educational or physical needs in NY State; 100+ families; directory of PICC families.

The Academy (1990)
4 Burkle St, Oswego, NY 13126
Warren Shaw, Dir, 315-341-5992
Type: public at-risk
9 teachers, 80 students, ages 13-21, 7-12th grade
Entrance requirements: application, interview, residency
Governance by teachers and principal
Teacher qualifications: NY Certification
Mastery learning; technology, mentorships; students assigned to family groups; performance based; multi-aged classes; childcare; suburban location; transportation; interns accepted.

Homer/Cortland Home Educators
4211 Cuyler Rd, Truxton, NY 13158
Priscilla Colletto

The New School (1988)
1103 Burnet Ave, Syracuse, NY 13203
Lisa Saile, 315-475-6453
Type: independent
16 students, ages 5-11
Governance by parents' board.
Individualized curriculum; non-graded; team-teaching; students work independently on agreed contracts.

Blodgett Truancy Rehab Program (1979)
312 Oswego St, Syracuse, NY 13204
Winonn Ciota, 315-425-4386
Type: public at-risk

Occupational Learning Center at Fowler High School
(1986)
227 Magnolia St, Syracuse, NY 13204
Linda Cimusz, 315-425-4376
Type: public choice

Onondaga Alternative High School (1987)
LeMoyne College, Foery Hall, Syracuse, NY 13204

Daniel DeBona, Coordinator; Joseph Catalano, Team Leader, 315-445-4711
Type: public at-risk
25-30 students, ages 14-19, 9-12th grade
Family units; town meetings; team teaching; cooperative learning.

Loving Education at Home (LEAH) (1983)
PO Box 332, Syracuse, NY 13205
Onondaga County
Type: state home-based
Christian; 1,900 member families in 105 local chapters; quarterly newsletter; seminars; legislative info.

William R. Beard Alternative (1978)
220 W Kennedy St, Syracuse, NY 13205
Dr Joe D. Woods, Dir, 315-435-5855
Onondaga County
Type: public at-risk
21 teachers, 300 students, mainly at-risk, ages 11-21, 4-12th grade
Enrollment through Supt designee; restricted to non-ED residents
Governance by teachers, principal, democratic school meeting, and Supt designee
Teacher qualifications: state certification
Individual and group counseling; no diplomas; no letter grades; urban location; transportation; interns accepted.

Qualifying School at Henninger High School (1986)
600 Robinson St, Syracuse, NY 13206
Peter Kavanagh, 315-425-4343
Type: public choice

Occupational Learning Center at Corcoran High School
919 Glenwood Ave, Syracuse, NY 13207
Louis Georgiana, 315-435-4935
Type: public at-risk
Competency-based.

Onondaga-Cortland-Madison Alternative Junior High School (1980)
310 Lakeside Rd, Syracuse, NY 13209
Daniel Debona, 315-468-0406,-1352
Type: public at-risk
50 students, ages 13-16, 7-9th grade
Dropout intervention aimed at successfully returning students to home high school; focuses on whole child development, and social, academic, and personal skills.

Syracuse PS City As School Program (1993)
725 Harrison St, Syracuse, NY 13210
Richard List, 315-435-5842
Type: public choice
70 students

The Learning Co-op
522 Nottingham Rd, Syracuse, NY 13210
Barb Irvine
Type: home-based
Small group of homeschooling families who meet one morning a week to coordinate cooperative activities.

Upstate Homeschoolers
Rd 2, Box 104A, Earlville, NY 13332
Jim Goldstein

Alternative Ed Program at Herkimer/Fult/Mont BOCES
(1985)
Gros Blvd, Herkimer, NY 13350
Charles Schreiber, 315-867-2011
Type: public at-risk
100 students, ages 14-21
7th-11th grade curriculum; GED prep and Career Technology program for 16-21 year-olds.

EIDOS Alternative Education Program (1985)
221 Broad St, Oneida LC, Oneida, NY 13421
Krista Raineri, Site Coordinator, 315-363-4073
Type: Independent at-risk, non-profit
30 students, mainly at-risk, ages 16–21
Enrollment restricted to Job Training Partnership Act eligible
   dropouts.
GED, job, lifeskills education; work experience, counseling,
   and support available.

Project LINKS
Spring Rd, Verona, NY 13478
Thomas Schlueter, Principal, 315-368-8000 ext 227
Type: public at-risk
123 students, ages 14+, 9–12th grade
Affiliation: Madison-Oneida BOCES
Governance by teachers and principal
Students referred by application from school of origin; pro-
   grams designed to meet special needs of students unsuc-
   cessful in traditional setting.

Conkling Futures Academy
1115 Mohawk St, Utica, NY 13501
Karen Kunkel, 315-792-2180
Type: magnet
K–6th grade
Futures.

Watson Williams
107 Elmwood Place, Utica, NY 13501
John Scriber, 315-792-2167
Type: magnet
K–6th grade
Performing arts.

Jefferson Alternative High School (1986)
Arsenal Street Rd, Watertown, NY 13601
Kathleen Morris-Kortz, Teacher-coordinator, 315-785-8647
Type: public at-risk
20 students, ages 16–18, ungraded
Affiliation: Dr William Glasser's Quality School Consortium
Governance by democratic school meeting, teachers and
   principal
Student internships; independent study; outcome-based
   curriculum, focusing on portfolio completion; GED; work-
   study; vocational and community college courses.

Richville Opportunity Center (1985)
PO Box 57, Richville, NY 13617
Kimberly Hunt, Math/Science Coordinator, 315-287-2140
Type: public at-risk
40 students, ages 14–17, 9–10th grade
Governance by teachers and principal, democratic school
   meeting
Students alternate one week of in-school academics with one
   week of a worksite experience.

St Lawrence County Group
Christian Fellowship Academy, Box 5, Madrid, NY 13660
Debbie Marr
Type: home-based

Norwood-Norfolk ELP (1993)
Rt 56; Norwood Rd, Norwood, NY 13668
Jane S. Mott, 315-353-6631
Type: public at-risk
4 teachers, 10 students, ages 14–17, 9–11th grade
Entrance requirements: 6th grade reading level, acceptance
   by committee, residency
Governance by board
Teacher qualifications: BS in Education

Pinewood Alternative School
PO Box 225, Norwood, NY 13668
Dale Gordon, 315-229-2293
Type: public at-risk
9–12th grade

St. Lawrence-Lewis BOCES Comprehensive Youth (1985)
PO Box 236, Rt 56, Norwood, NY 13668
Bill Short, Prog Specialist; April Bender, Sr Prog Ldr, 315-353-
   6693, FAX: 315-353-8875
St. Lawrence County
Type: public at-risk
15 teachers, 200 students, mainly at-risk, ages 16–20
Enrollment restricted to age 16+, out of school, subject to
   eligibility or waiver from SED; no residency requirement
Governance by faculty and student representatives
Teacher qualifications: NY certification in any K–12 area
Customized mixes of basic, life and occupational skills education; support services as needed; sample program: occupational certificate program, paid work experience and/or
   community service, independent study academics, team
   learning life skills; no letter grades; multi-aged classes;
   extensive field trips; rural location; transportation; interns
   accepted.

The Opportunity Centers (1984)
c/o Pinewood Box 225, Norwood, NY 13668
David Lansford, 315-353-6643
Type: public choice

Mountain Tree
HCR 84, PO Box 60A, Potsdam, NY 13676
315-265-0621, FAX: 315-328-4129

Akwesasne Freedom School (1979)
Box 290, Rooseveltown, NY 13683
James Ransom, Parent Committee, 518-358-2073
Type: independent, non-profit; tuition: $500
6 teachers, 46 students, mainly Mohawk, ages 5–13, pre
   K–7th grade
New students accepted in preK and K
Governance by parent cooperative
Teacher qualifications: fluent in Mohawk language
Traditionalist school taught in the Mohawk language;
   designed to help preserve language and culture; curricu-
   lum reflects Iroquoian environmental philosophy; encour-
   ages cooperation rather than competitiveness; rural
   location.

Broome-Chenango Alternative High School (1986)
Cumber Rd, Harpursville, NY 13787
Dr Joyce O. Knapp, Prin, 607-693-3110
Broome County
Type: public at-risk; tuition: $4,591/yr
5 teachers, 105 students, ages 12–21, 7–12th grade
No classified students; no residency requirement
Affiliation: Broome-Tioga BOCES
Teacher qualifications: NY secondary certification
Work experience; apprenticeship; self-esteem; rural location.

Otsego Area Alternative School (1985)
130 East St, Oneonta, NY 13820
William J Nagle, 607-652-7531
Type: public at-risk

Day Care Center of Owego
228 Main St, Owego, NY 13827-1683
Type: Montessori

Christian Homesteading Movement (1961)
RD #2-G, Oxford, NY 13830-1580
Richard Fahey
Chenango County
Non-profit; tuition: $200/wk
5 teachers, 15 students, mainly Mature
Residency required
Governance by dir
Basic, intense study of farm animals, gardening, fruit trees,
   forestry, herbs, midwifery, hand tools, log building, Christ-
   ian celebration and spirituality; rural location.

Evergreen (1983)
201 Main St, Vestal, NY 13850
Alice Heier, Program Coord, 607-785-8216, FAX:-8218

Broome County
Type: public at-risk
4 teachers, 47 students, ages 16-21, 9-12th grade
Entrance requirements: average to above average ability, residency
Governance by teachers and principal
Independent study; community-based; performance-based; cooperative learning; town meetings; counseling; suburban location; transportation.

Home Education Exchange of the Southern Tier (1991)
59 Grippen Hill Rd, Vestal, NY 13850
Allison Mesnard, 607-754-9456
Broome County
Nonsectarian; support.

Genesee Wyoming Vocational Center (1985)
8250 State Street Rd, Batavia, NY 14020
Thomas Staekell, Principal, 716-343-1400
Type: public at-risk
30 students, ages 12-14, 6-8th grade
Governance by teachers and principal
For students with average or above average intelligence who are not academically successful in the mainstream; focus on basic skills, self-esteem, positive peer interaction; integrated learning approach.

9 & 12 Grade Alternative Learning, Terrace Educational Center
591 Terrace Blvd, Depew, NY 14043
Joseph Lazzaro, 716-684-0157
Type: public at-risk

East Aurora Montessori (1975)
591 Porterville Rd, East Aurora, NY 14052
Mary Jane Wesoloski or Sharon Lewis, 716-668-8211
Tuition: 1,220-2,120/yr
2 teachers, 2 assistants, 40 students, ages 3-6
Affiliation: NAMTA
Governance by administrators
Suburban location.

School to Employment Program (STEP) (1986)
Fredonia Central School, Fredonia, NY 14063
Terry Redman, District Prin, 679-1581
Chautauqua County
Type: public choice; tuition: $1,600/yr
5 teachers, 20 students, mainly at-risk, ages 15-16, 9-10th grade
Residency required
Governance by teachers and principal
All students go to paying jobs in afternoon; multi-aged classes; rural location; interns accepted.

Western NY Homeschooling Network
53 Maple Ave, Fredonia, NY 14063
Wendy Westwood

Gowanda Central School Alt Ed Program (1986)
Prospect St, Gowanda, NY 14070
M Althea Kester, 716-532-3325
Type: public at-risk

Montessori Early Childhood Education Center
Cattaraugus Reservation, Irving, NY 14081

Southtown's Children's Creative Center
6006 Old Lake Shore Rd, Lakeview, NY 14085-9525
Type: Montessori

Harrison/BOCES Coop Program (1985)
3181 Saunders Settlement Rd, Sanborn, NY 14132
Art Polychronis, Coord, 716-625-6811
Niagara-Orleans County
Type: public choice
Student ages 15-18, 11-12th grade
Entrance requirements: scholastic aptitude, maturity, self-discipline, interviews, county residency

Alternately work as apprentices for 2 weeks and attend school for 2 weeks; accelerated subjects; emphasis on science and math

Orleans-Niagara Alt Instructional-Middle School (1985)
3181 Saunders Settlement Rd, Sanborn, NY 14132
Fred Fierch, 716-731-4176
Type: public at-risk
25 students, ages 13-15
For students experiencing difficulty, program prepares them for return to the mainstream.

New Directions School (1985)
PO Box 160, 121 Savage Rd, Sardinia, NY 14134
John R Baronich Jr, Principal, 716-496-5002
Type: public at-risk
45 students, ages 14-18, 9-11th grade
Entrance requirement: no special ed
Affiliations: Cattaraugus, Allegany BOCES
Governance by teachers and principal
Teacher qualifications: certified
Alternating one week academic learning, one week on-the-job training; offers rock climbing, outdoor awareness, cross country skiing; extensive field trips; rural location; interns accepted.

Stella Niagara Education Park
4421 Lower River Rd, Stella Niagara, NY 14144-1001
Type: Montessori

Occupational Skills Program (1968)
333 Dexter Terrace, Tonawanda, NY 14150
Gerald J Ozimek, Principal, 716-694-6671
Type: public at-risk
200 students, ages 14-19, 9-12th grade
Governance by teachers and principal
Students earn credits toward diploma while developing social skills, responsibility, and improved self-image.

Kaleidoscope Montessori Center
1216 E Quaker St, East Aurora, NY 14152

Aurora Waldorf School
525 W Falls Rd, West Falls, NY 14170
Jeff Tunkey

City-As-School Satellite at D'Youville College (1992)
320 Porter Ave, Buffalo, NY 14201
716-888-7185
Type: public choice
50 students

Buffalo Alternative High School Bilingual Satellite (1975)
512 Pear St, Buffalo, NY 14202
Maria A Perea, 716-856-4736
Type: public at-risk

Buffalo Alternative High School (1974)
280 Oak St, Buffalo, NY 14203
Tom Hallett, 716 -851-3878
Type: public at-risk
80 teachers, 500 students, ages 12-19, 7-12th grade
Residency required
Governance by principal, board
Teacher qualifications: State certified
"City as school" program gives school credit for work; urban location; interns accepted.

Academic Challenge Center (1977)
S Division & Hickory Sts, Buffalo, NY 14204
Bernice T. Richardson, Prin, 716-851-3767, FAX: 716-851-3770
Erie County
Type: public choice
72 teachers; student ages 4-15, pre K-8th grade
Governance by board
Personalized; Project Advance; whole language; Push-Excel, motivates and supports student; interns accepted.

Bennett Park Montessori School
342 Clinton St, Buffalo, NY 14204

Northwest Community Center (1985)
155 Lawn Ave, Buffalo, NY 14207
Arty McKee, 716-876-4390
Type: public at-risk

Buffalo Montessori Teacher Education Program
453 Parker Ave, Buffalo, NY 14216
Eileen Buermann

7 & 8 Grade Alt Learning at Philip Sheridan School (1987)
3200 Elmwood Ave, Kenmore, NY 14217
Margaret Hollstein, 716-874-1619
Type: public at-risk

St Andrew's Country Day Montessori School
1545 Sheridan Dr, Kenmore, NY 14217-1211

Maplemere Elementary (1958)
236 E Maplemere Rd, Amherst, NY 14221
Michelle Kavanaugh, Prin, 716-634-6260
Erie County
Type: public choice
35 teachers, 435 students, ages 4–12, K–5th grade
Governance by school leadership team, values education
   committee
Partnership with U of Buffalo, Public Library; Geologo;
   authors, artists in residence; literary, cultural awareness;
   Creative Empowerment Model; cross-age peer partnering;
   parent involvement; no letter grade; interns accepted.

AIM Program (1984)
1595 Hopkins Rd, Williamsville, NY 14221
Samuel H. Gang, 716-626-8550
Type: public at-risk
40–60 students, ages 14–19, 9–12th grade
Governance by teachers and principal
Serves 3 school districts; emphasizes participation, respect,
   trust; small classes; individualized planning; group and individual counseling; cultural and community experiences.

Nardin Academy
135 Cleveland Ave, Buffalo, NY 14222-1699
Type: Montessori

Pine Hill Middle School (1980)
1635 E Delavan Ave, Cheektowaga, NY 14225
Frank A Cantie, 716-892-1033
Type: public choice

Union East Elementary School (1968)
3550 Union Rd, Cheektowaga, NY 14225
William E Koepf, 716-686-3620
Type: public choice

Alternate 7/8 Program at Albion Middle School (1985)
254 East Ave, Albion, NY 14411
Robert E Huyck, 716-589-7033
Type: public choice

Brockport Montessori School
472 West Ave, Brockport, NY 14420

Canandaigua Montessori School
11 Gibson St, Canadaigua, NY 14424-1309

Churchville Chili Central School (1986)
5786 Buffalo Rd, Churchville, NY 14428
William J O'Connell, 716-293-1800
Type: public choice

Trinity Montessori (1967)
501 S Garfield St, East Rochester, NY 14445
Sr Clare Francis Mogenhan, Adm, 716-586-1044
Non-profit; tuition: $920-2,840/yr
6 teachers, 5 assistants, 92 students, ages infant-7

Entrance requirements: age; Director's approval
Affiliation: AMS; accreditation: NYDE
Governance by administrator, board
Teacher qualifications: Montessori certification
Complete Montessori materials; childcare; suburban location;
   interns accepted.

MOVE (Make Our Vocations Educational)
BOCES # 1, 41 O'Connor Rd, Fairport, NY 14450
Gale Berger, Teacher, 716-377-4660
Type: public at-risk; tuition: $7500
HSED, job readiness training, vocational/technical skills and
   cooperative job placement.

Geneva Middle School Alternative Education (1993)
63 Pultney St, Geneva, NY 14456
Marlene Simizon, 716-781-0404
Ontario County
Type: public choice
1 teacher, 16-20 students, ages 12–16, 7–8th grade
Entrance requirements: pass 6th grade, residency
Governance by teachers, principal, board
Teacher qualifications: New York certified, experience
Organizational skills; stress reduction; cooperation; commu-
   nity involvement; volunteer projects; how to say "no" to
   negative peer pressure; extensive field trips; multi-aged
   classes; interns accepted.

SCORE at Rush-Henrietta Central School (1972)
1799 Lehigh Station Rd, Henrietta, NY 14467
James Hoagland, Mary Moss, 716-359-5265
Type: public at-risk
30 students, ages 15–21, 9–12th grade
Governance by faculty and student representatives
Independent study; blends traditional and nontraditional
   classes with community experience.

Occupational Skills Program
Charles G May Vocational Ctr, Lackawana Ave, Mt Morris, NY
   14510
Marilyn Gross, Assistant Principal, 716-658-2253
Type: public at-risk
2 teachers, 2 assistants, 20 students, ages 15–21, 9–12th
   grade
Affiliation: Livingston-Steuben-Wyoming BOCES
For students who have shown inappropriate social and emotional behaviors; integrates academic program in vocational setting; work study/experience and GED programs.

WAS (Work and Study Academy) (1985)
625 Peirson Ave, Newark, NY 14513
P. David Caccamise, Dir, 315-331-5150, FAX: 332-3567
Wayne County
Type: public at-risk
4 teachers, 6 students, mainly at-risk, ages 16–18, 9–12th
   grade
Enrollment restricted to HS dropout residents; assessment by
   evaluation committee required
Governance by teachers and principal
Teacher qualifications: state certification
No letter grades; suburban location.

Penn Yan Academy Alternative (1985)
305 Court St, Penn Yan, NY 14527
Linda G Shail, Coordinator, 315-536-4408
Type: public at-risk
10–16 students, ages 12–14, 7–9th grade
Goal is to break cycle of truancy and failure and return stu-
   dents to mainstream; uses Project Adventure and New
   Games; social skills program; high success rate.

Family Learning Center (1985)
30 Hart St, Rochester, NY 14605
Claire Miles, 716-262-8000
Type: public at-risk
Adult education program.

Josh M Lofton Junior High School (1985)
54 Oakman St, Rochester, NY 14605
Paul Moore, 716-325-2920
Type: public at-risk
100 students, 7-8th grade
Hands-on experiences; horticulture; sciences; small class size.

Cobblestone School (1983)
10 Prince St, Rochester, NY 14607
Jon Greenbaum, 716-271-2320
Monroe County
Type: independent, non-profit; tuition: $4385, scholarships
15 teachers, 175 students, ages 4-12, ungraded
Not wheelchair accessible
Governance by two co-directors and parent board, weekly
     student meeting
Integrated curriculum, based on children's questions, broad
     themes; progressive and open classroom tradition enables
     students to become independent and cooperative learn-
     ers; no letter grades; multi-aged classes; extensive field
     trips; rural & urban location; transportation; interns
     accepted.

School of the Arts
494 Averill Ave, Rochester, NY 14607
David Silver, 716-325-7594
Type: magnet
7-12th grade

Frederick Douglass Middle School
940 Fernwood Park, Rochester, NY 14609
Bert Alexander, 716-482-2000
Type: magnet
6-8th grade

Morgan Home School (1991)
1851 E Main St, Rochester, NY 14609
Linda Morgan, PhD, 716-654-9153
Monroe County
1 teacher, 1 student, age 18, 12th grade
Governance by democratic school meeting
Have homeschooled two boys (age 18 and 19) for a total of 9
     years; work-study (co-op); urban location.

Our School
220 S Winton Rd, Rochester, NY 14610
716-461-2639

Rochester Area Homeschoolers Association (1980)
275 Yarmouth Rd, Rochester, NY 14610
Amy Berkley Mantell, 716-482-8592
Monroe County
Child-led activities and clubs; extensive field trips; multi-aged
     activities; inclusive.

Lincoln Park School #44
820 Chili Ave, Rochester, NY 14611
Joan Miller, 716-328-5272
Type: magnet
2-6th grade
Multicultural studies.

Association Montessori Internationale
(See Resource Appendix)

School Without Walls (1971)
480 Broadway, Rochester, NY 14617
Dan Drmacich, 716-546-6732
Monroe County
Type: public choice
175 students, ages 13-19, 9-12th grade
For those who demonstrate enthusiasm for the goals and
     requirements of SWW
Affiliation: Coalition of Essential Schools
Governance by democratic school meeting, principal and
     teachers, school-based planning team
Teacher qualifications: support of school philosophy

Internships; independent study; creative problem solving;
     time management; portfolios; authentic assessment; com-
     munity service; evaluation as a learning experience;
     learner-centered curriculum; senior project; no letter
     grades; multi-aged classes; extensive field trips.

Brighton Montessori House of Children
2131 Elmwood Ave, Rochester, NY 14618-1021

Rochester Children's House
175 Allens Creek Rd, Rochester, NY 14618-3229
Type: Montessori

Lewis H. Morgan School #37
353 Congress Ave, Rochester, NY 14619
Miriam Vazques, 716-328-0037
Type: magnet
K-6th grade
Intercultural studies; PAL.

James P.B. Duffy School #12
999 S Ave, Rochester, NY 14620
Barbara Wagner, 716-461-3240
Type: magnet
K-6th grade
Inter-cultural studies center.

Pinnacle School #35
194 Field St, Rochester, NY 14620
Charles Moscato, 716-271-4583
Type: magnet
K-6th grade
Communication through performing arts; bilingual; multi-
     cultural.

Webster Montessori School (1967)
260 Embury Rd, Rochester, NY 14625
David F Boneham, Prin, 716-671-9269
Non-profit; tuition: $2,300-2,900/yr
2 teachers, 2 assistants, 60 students, mainly international,
     ages 3-6
Entrance requirement: min age 2 yr 10 mos
Affiliations: AMI, NAMTA
Governance by administrator, board of trustees
Traditional; child care; suburban location; transportation by
     local school district for 5 & 6 yr olds.

Greece Montessori School
200 Alcott Rd, Rochester, NY 14626-2424

Alternative Learning Program at South Western Central
     (1972)
600 Hunt Rd, Jamestown, NY 14701
D. Clifton Bowman, 716-664-6273
Chautauqua County
Type: public at-risk
1 teacher, 25 students, mainly at-risk, ages 14-18, HS
Residency required
Governance by principal
Self-examination and development of a personal value
     system; goal-setting, decision-making, vocational and sur-
     vival skills; cooperative learning; relaxed and supportive
     atmosphere; no letter grades; multi-aged classes; exten-
     sive field trips; suburban location; transportation.

Montessori Children House
120 Chandler, Jamestown, NY 14701

Ninth & Tenth Grade At Risk Program at Jamestown HS
     (1987)
350 E Second St, Jamestown, NY 14701
Ted Bilicki, 716-483-4392
Type: public at-risk

**Seventh & Eighth Grade At Risk Program at Jefferson
     School** (1983)
195 Martin Rd, Jamestown, NY 14701
Ted Bilicki, 716-483-4392
Type: public at-risk

Montessori Children' s House of Olean
1020 Reed St, Olean, NY 14760-2221
Brenda Snyder

Salamanca Alternative High School (1991)
50 Iroquois Dr, Salamanca, NY 14779
Paula Kenneson, Coord, 716-945-2405 x527, FAX:-5736
Type: public at-risk
6 teachers, 35 students, partly at-risk, ages 13-18
No residency requirement
Governance by teachers, principal, board
Teacher qualifications: certification
Work experience; School & Business Alliance and JTPA provide
  career experiences, skill training; outcomes based; rural
  location; interns accepted.

Seneca Nation of Indians Montessori
PO Box 231, Salamanca, NY 14779-0231

Alfred Montessori School
Openhym Dorm, Alfred Univ, Alfred, NY 14802

Steuben-Allegany BOCES (1985)
RD 1, Bath, NY 14810
Michael Bracy, 607-776-7631
Type: public choice

Valley Montessori (1976)
PO Box 198, Winters Rd, Big Flatts, NY 14814
Cynthia Raj, Administrator, 607-562-8754
Non-profit; tuition: $1600-3400
7 teachers, 6 assistants, 130 students, ages 2-12, pre K-6th
  grade
Governance by parent cooperative
Located on wooded acreage; Italian classes for students 6-12
  years.

Southern Tier Unschoolers
8033 Van Amburg Rd, Hammondsport, NY 14840
Lisa Treichler
Type: home-based

Alternative Community School (1974)
111 Chestnut St, Ithaca, NY 14850
Dave Lehman, Principal, 607-274-2183,-2263
Type: public choice
260 students, ages 11-19, 6-12th grade
Affiliations: CES, NYS Compact Partnership
Governance by democratic school meeting, teachers,
  principal
Internships; community & independent studies; small family
  groups; some services for homeschoolers; interdisciplinary; integrated studies.

Democratic School of the Finger Lakes (1994)
206 Muriel St, Ithaca, NY 14850
Kay Slentz Milling, Organizer, 607-257-4769
Tompkins County
Type: independent, non-profit
Student ages 5-19
Governance by democratic school meeting
Allows individual to pursue any investigations and activities of
  interest; student must respect the rights of others; pat-
  terned on Sudbury Valley School; no letter grades; non-
  compulsory class attendance; multi-aged classes; extensive
  field trips; rural location; interns accepted.

Fingerlakes Unschoolers Network (1988)
249 Coddington Rd, Ithaca, NY 14850
Linda Holzbaur, Coord, 607-277-6300, FAX: 607-277-6300
Tompkins County
Type: home-based
Directory; newsletter; workshops; field trips; referrals.

Hillside Children's Garden (1978)
26 Quarry St, Ithaca, NY 14850
Kundry Willwerth, Director, 607-277-6371
Type: Waldorf; tuition: $2620
25 students, ages 3-6, pre K-K
Affiliation: WKANA
Governance by teachers and principal
Stresses development through play and artistic activities,
  rather than academic learning, in the early years.

Montessori School of Ithaca (1979)
120 E King Rd, Ithaca, NY 14850
Andrea B. Coby, Adm, 607-277-7335
Non-profit; tuition: $2,875-4,235/yr
7 teachers, 3 assistants, 99 students, mainly International,
  ages 3-12
Entrance requirements: interview for ages 6-12.
Accreditations: AMS, NY
Governance by administrator, board
Childcare; rural location; interns accepted.

T-S-T Community School (1986)
555 Warren Rd, Ithaca, NY 14850
Dr Gerry Friedman, Principal, 607-273-9015, FAX: 607-275-
  9702
Tompkins County
Type: public at-risk
7 teachers, 100 students, ages 12-21, 6-12th grade
Governance by democratic school meeting, teachers, and
  principal
Program for pregnant/parenting teens in supportive, warm,
  demanding, democratic community; life skills; apprenticeships; family groups; childcare; multi-aged classes; extensive field trips; urban location; transportation; interns
  accepted.

Waldorf School of the Finger Lakes (1982)
855 Five Mile Dr, Ithaca, NY 14850
Maureen C. McKenna, Dir Adms, Dev, 607-273-4088
Tompkins County
Non-profit; tuition: $2,400-4,600/yr, scholarships
17 teachers, 98 students, ages 3.5-15, pre K-8th grade
Affiliation: AWSNA
Governance by board, faculty, parent council
Teacher qualifications: Waldorf training
Two sites; French; strings; before, after school care; trans-
  portation; interns accepted.

Schuyler-Cayuga, Tioga BOCES
179 Benjamin Rd, Newfield, NY 14867
Mary Hayes
Type: public at-risk

The Children's Room
Box 147, Van Etten, NY 14889
Type: Montessori

Crossroads Program (1980)
Madison & Maple, Wellsville, NY 14895
Phyllis Pascarella, 716-593-5387
Type: public at-risk
12-20 students
Diploma program for pregnant teen-agers and young
  fathers, now taken over by BOCES.

Schuyler-Chemung-Tioga Alternative HS **Program** (1984)
TEC Center, Elmira, NY 14903
Gail Orso, 607-739-3581
Type: public at-risk
200 students, 7-12th grade
Students earn HS diploma; also has teenage parent program.

North Carolina

Petree Middle School
3815 Old Greensboro Rd, Winston-Salem, NC 27101
Ben Henderson or Ron A. Caviness, 919-761-0868
Forsyth County
Type: public at-risk
13 teachers, 145 students, 6–8th grade
Governance by teachers, principal, board
Teacher qualifications: certification
Behavior management; banking; school store; academic indi-
    vidualization; Adler's Paideia approach; urban location;
    interns accepted.

Winston-Salem/Forsyth Elementary Alternative
    Program
Box 2513, Winston-Salem, NC 27102
C. Douglas Carter, 919-727-2816

Montessori Children's Center
3908 Old Vineyard Rd #3904, Winston-Salem, NC 27104-4740

Forsyth Montessori School
407 Petree Rd, Winston Salem, NC 27106-3502

Reynolds Montessori School
2130 Brookfield Dr, Winston Salem, NC 27106-5813

Montessori School
23 Banner Ave, Winston-Salem, NC 27107

The Jefferson Academy
PO Box 7383 Reynolds Sta, Winston-Salem, NC 27109
Type: Montessori

Magnum Opus Developmental Education Laboratory
    (MODEL) (1987)
607 S Park St, Asheboro, NC 27203
Gary L. Cameron, 919-625-1656
Type: home-based
6 students, ages 2–12
Enrollment restricted to family members
Governance by parent cooperative
Focus on developing the family; no letter grades; suburban
    location; interns accepted.

Randolph County Christian Home Educators
637 Allred St, Asheboro, NC 27203
Brenda Yelverton, 910-626-2751

High Point Area Home Educators
610 Monlieu Ave, High Point, NC 27262
Amy Gies, 919-882-4339

Our Greenhouse (1986)
610 Montlieu Ave, High Point, NC 27262
Amy Gies, Mother, 910-882-4339
Guilford County
Type: home-based, non-profit
1 teacher, 2 students, age 10 & 12, 5, 8th grade
Affiliation: Christian Home
Governance by parents under non-public school state office
Teacher qualifications: HS diploma or degree
History unit approach; extensive use of local library; multi-
    aged classes; no letter grades; urban location.

Brookside Montessori School (1981)
736 Piney Grove Rd, Kernsville, NC 27284
Marjorie Carson, Adm, 910-996-5351
Non-profit; tuition: $212/470/mo
2 teachers, 1 assistant, 30 students, ages 3–12
Affiliations: AMS, Montessori Assn. of the Carolinas
Governance by an administrator
Childcare; suburban location; interns accepted.

Eanes Alternative School
1010 Fair St, Lexington, NC 27292
Bobby R. Pope, 704-242-1527

A Discovery Place
PO Box 1471, Sanford, NC 27331-1471
Paula Rowland
Type: Montessori

Thomasville Home Educators
324 Walker St, Thomasville, NC 27360
Christi Crane, 919-643-7088

EDU*CARE Montessori School
40 Archie Rd, West End, NC 27376

Dudley High School
1200 Lincoln St, Greensboro, NC 27401
Lenwood Edwards, 919-370-8130
Type: magnet
9–12th grade
Science, math, technology; open education.

Guilford County Schools
120 Franklin Blvd, Greensboro, NC 27401
Gloria Ramsey, 919-271-0700

Peeler Elementary
2200 Randall St, Greensboro, NC 27401
Martha Hudson, 919-370-8270
Type: magnet
K–5th grade
Open education.

Greensboro Home Educators
PO Box 4213, Greensboro, NC 27404
910-548-5111

Erwin Elementary
3012 E Bessemer Ave, Greensboro, NC 27405
Dan Jones, 919-370-8150
Type: magnet
K–5th grade
Open education.

Gillespie Park Education Center Extended Day Program
1900 MLK, Jr Blvd, Greensboro, NC 27406
Leon F. Goolsby, 919-370-8160

Jones Elementary
502 S St, Greensboro, NC 27406
Edward Allred, 919-370-8230
Type: magnet
K–5th grade
Cultural arts; foreign language.

Global Studies Year-round School
1215 Westover Tr, Greensboro, NC 27408
Phillip Mobley, 919-370-8228
Type: magnet
K–4th grade
Global studies.

Hester's Creative Schools
2715 Pinedale Rd, Greensboro, NC 27408-4713
Type: Montessori

Greensboro Montessori
2856 Horse Pen Creek Rd, Greensboro, NC 27410
919-668-0119
12 teachers, 8 assistants; student ages infant-15
Affiliations: AMS, SACS
Governance by board
Childcare; suburban location; interns accepted.

New Garden Friends School (1971)
1128 New Garden Rd, Greensboro, NC 27410
David R. Tomlin, Co-Head, 919-299-0964
Guilford County
Type: Quaker, non-profit; tuition: $3,700/yr, scholarships
15 teachers, 110 students, ages 3–15, pre K–8th grade
Entrance requirement: interviews
Affiliation: FCOE
Governance by board
Whole language; integrated studies; community service; narrative evaluations; contracts; team teaching; cooperative learning; independent study; craft design tech; multi-aged classes; extensive field trips; no letter grades; suburban location; interns accepted.

Randolph County Home Educators
3606 Birchwood Ln, Greensboro, NC 27410-2802
Susan Pratt, 919-241-2399

International Alliance for Invitational Education
(See Resource Appendix)

Apex Elementary
700 Tingen Rd, Apex, NC 27502
Claude Willie III, 919-387-2150
Wake County
Type: magnet
K–5th grade
Gifted; talented.

Christian Home Education Association of Greater Durham
PO Box 3293, Durham, NC 27512-3293

Sas Institute Daycare Center
1 Sas Cir, Bldg K, Box 8000, Cary, NC 27512-8000
Type: Montessori

Chapel Hill Homeschoolers (1989)
PO Box 269, Chapel Hill, NC 27514
Dale Pratt-Wilson, 919-942-3300, FAX: 919-942-0700
Orange County
Non-profit
65 teachers; students all ages
Membership requires parental involvement
Governance by board
Field trips; special classes, events; clubs.

Montessori Day School
1165 Weaver Dairy Rd, Chapel Hill, NC 27514-1576

Chapel Hill/Carrboro City Alternative Program
Merritt Mill Rd, Chapel Hill, NC 27516
Lillian Lee or Mildred Jones, 919-967-8211

Lincoln-Heights Elementary
307 Bridge St, Fuquary-Varina, NC 27526
Marge Ronco, 919-557-2588
Wake County
Type: magnet
K–5th grade
Gifted; talented.

Pathfinders
5400 Lafayette Dr, Fuquay-Varina, NC 27526
Lucinda and Sharles Estill, 919-552-0578
Type: home-based

Wayne Christian Home Educators
607 Prince St, Goldsboro, NC 27530
Pat Wright, 919-734-4441

Wayne Montessori School
PO Box 10646, Goldsboro, NC 27532-0646

Harnett County Schools
700 Main St, Lilington, NC 27546
Jane Schumann, 919-893-8151

Cary Montessori School (1989)
201 High House Rd, Cary, NC 27573-4204
Andrea Uzzell, Dir, 919-469-9406
Tuition: $55–150/wk
8 teachers, 12 assistants, 144 students, ages infant-9
Affiliation: AMS
Governance by a board of trustees
47 wks/yr; childcare; suburban location; interns accepted.

Wake Forest Elementary
136 W Sycamore St, Wake Forest, NC 27587
C.W. Fisher, 919-554-8655
Wake County
Type: magnet
K–5th grade
Gifted; talented.

Carver Elementary
1 Morphus Bridge Rd, Box 769, Wendell, NC 27591
Alex Taylor, 919-365-2680
Wake County
Type: magnet
K–1st grade
Gifted; talented.

Wendell Elementary
212 W Wilson Ave Box 727, Wendell, NC 27591
Elizabeth Rountree, 919-365-2660
Wake County
Type: magnet
2–5th grade
Gifted; talented.

New Beginnings
Rt 3, Box 114-D, Zebulon, NC 27597
Evelyn and William Wesson, 919-269-6165
Type: home-based

Zebulon Elementary
700 Proctor St, Zebulon, NC 27597
Lewis Liles, 919-269-3680
Wake County
Type: magnet
K–5th grade
Gifted; talented.

Heart of Carolina
1523 Cellwood Rd, Raleigh, NC 27601
Janice and Lewis McKenzie, 919-787-3482
Type: home-based

Hunter Elementary
1018 E Davie St, Raleigh, NC 27601
Cecilia Lindsey, 919-856-7676
Type: magnet
K–5th grade
Gifted; talented.

Washington Elementary
1000 Fayetteville St, Raleigh, NC 27601
Del Burns, 919-856-7960
Type: magnet
K–5th grade
Gifted; talented.

North Carolinians for Home Education (1984)
419 N Boylan Ave, Raleigh, NC 27603-1211
Susan Van Dyke, Exec Adm, 919-834-6243, FAX: 919-834-6241
Wake County
Type: state home-based, non-profit
Governance by board
1,500 members; supported by contributions; newsletter;
   large annual conference and book fair.

Conn Elementary
1221 Brookside Ave, Raleigh, NC 27604
Lois Hart, 919-856-7637
Type: magnet
K–5th grade
Gifted; talented.

The "Y" Group
1012 Oberlin Rd, Raleigh, NC 27605
Beth Stevenson, 919-828-3205
Type: home-based

Martin Middle School
1701 Ridge Rd, Raleigh, NC 27607
David C. Coley, 919-881-4970
Type: magnet
6–8th grade
Gifted; talented.

Joyner Elementary
2300 Noble Rd, Raleigh, NC 27608
George L. Risinger, 919-856-7650
Type: magnet
K–5th grade
Language arts; communications; extended day.

New School Montessori Center for Children
1810 White Oak Rd, Raleigh, NC 27608
Ceres Schroer York

Underwood Elementary
1614 Glenwood Ave, Raleigh, NC 27608
Anne Doman, 919-856-7663
Type: magnet
K–5th grade
Gifted; talented.

National Society For Internships
(See Resource Appendix)

St Timothy's School
4523 Six Forks Rd, Raleigh, NC 27609-5759
Type: Montessori

Carnage Middle School
1425 Carnage Dr, Raleigh, NC 27610
William Crockett, Jr, 919-856-7600
Type: magnet
6–8th grade
Gifted; talented.

Central Wake Optional High School
1923 Milburnie Rd, Raleigh, NC 27610
Delores Revis, 919-856-7710

Enloe High School
128 Clarendon Crescent, Raleigh, NC 27610
Calvin Dobbins, 919-856-7860
Type: magnet
9–12th grade
Gifted; talented.

Islamic Home School Association of North America
   (1988)
1312 Plymouth Ct, Raleigh, NC 27610
Anisa Alzoubi, 919-832-1960
Type: national home-based
Bi-monthly newsletter; networking.

Fuller Elementary
806 Calloway Dr, Raliegh, NC 27610
Marlee Ray, 919-856-7625
Type: magnet
K–5th grade
Gifted; talented.

Powell Elementary
1130 Marlborough Rd, Raliegh, NC 27610
Joyce Faulkner, 919-856-7737
Type: magnet
K–5th grade
Gifted; talented.

Wake County Schools
3600 Wake Forest Rd, Raleigh, NC 27611
Pat Kinlaw, Magnets Dir
Type: Montessori

TEACH of NC
7804 Hemlock Ct, Raleigh, NC 27615
Sherry and Blake Talbott, 919-846-2556
Type: home-based

Montessori School of Raleigh
7005 Lead Mine Rd, Raleigh, NC 27615-5905
William Friday, Exec Dir

Duke University Talent Identification Program
(See Resource Appendix)

Carolina Friends School
4809 Friends School Rd, Durham, NC 27705
John Baird, Prin, 919-383-6602
Type: Quaker

Home Education Association
2934 Ridge Rd, Durham, NC 27705
Sarah Howe or Susan Dunathan, 919-490-6304

Montessori Community School (1980)
4512 Pope Rd, Durham, NC 27707
Barbara Crockett, Adm, 919-493-8541
Non-profit; tuition: $3,320-4,250/yr
6 teachers, 7 assistants, 132 students, ages 3–9
Affiliation: AMS
Governance by board; administrator
9 wooded acres; serves Chapel Hill, Durham, Raleigh; childcare; suburban location; interns accepted.

Montessori Children's House of Durham
2400 University Dr, Durham, NC 27707-2150

Park Montessori School
PO Box 12363, Research Triangle Park, NC 27709-2363

CHARM: Christian Homeschool Association of Rocky Mount
296 Creekridge Dr, Rocky Mount, NC 27804
Susan Stone, Pres, 919-937-8540
Cost: $10/yr
Inclusive membership, Christian leadership; about 55 families.

Families Learning Together (1989)
Rt 1, Box 219, Chocowinity, NC 27817
Jocelyn Butler or Feryl Masters, Membership Coords
Inclusive; non-sectarian; family directory; bi-annual meeting.

Down East Homeschoolers
717 W 2nd St, Washington, NC 27889
Jocelyn Butler, 919-975-2020

Profile
404 W Main St, Elizabeth City, NC 27909
Gladys Racette, 919-338-5905
Type: home-based

PATH
Rt 1 Box 25A, Manteo, NC 27954
Pat Rouckle, Co-Chair, 919-473-1301
Homeschoolers support group.

Stanly/Montgomery
2222 Monza Dr, Albemarle, NC 28001
Karen McAlister, 704-983-1559
Type: home-based

Children's House Montessori School
PO Box 1326, Bessemer City, NC 28016-1326

Montessori Community School of Bessemer City
119 W Pennsylvania Ave #A, Bessemer City, NC 28016-2635

Gaston County Homeschool Network
781 Niblick Dr, Gastonia, NC 28054
Lisa Carpenter, 704-853-1731

Monroe City Schools
Union Co Courthouse, 6th Flr, Monroe, NC 28110
Sandy Deskins, 704-392-0378

Cooperative Opportunity in Pursuit of Education
Drawer 989, Morganton, NC 28110
Danny Williams, 704-433-4300

Mooresville Optional Year-round Program (1990)
160 S Magnolia St, Mooresville, NC 28115
Carol Carroll, Prin, 704-664-9520, FAX: 704-663-3005
Iredell County
Type: public choice
47 teachers, 1,040 students, ages 5-14, K-8th grade
Application required
Governance by teachers and principal
Teacher qualifications: NC Certification
Remediation; enrichment; childcare; transportation; interns accepted.

Countryside Montessori School
PO Box 427, Newell, NC 28126

Rowan County Homeschoolers
333 Montrose Rd, Salisbury, NC 28146
Pam Ribelin, 704-633-0325

Irwin Avenue Open School
329 N Irwin, Charlotte, NC 28202
Type: public choice

Piedmont Open School
6000 Rose Valley Dr, Charlotte, NC 28210
Dan Faris
Type: public choice

Charlotte Montessori School (1971)
212 Boyce Rd, Charlotte, NC 28211
Maura Leahy-Tucker, Head, 704-366-5994
Tuition: $3,600-4,050/yr
12 teachers, 8 assistants, 189 students, ages toddler-12
Entrance requirements: interview; review of past records
Affiliation: London Montessori; accreditations: AMS, NC non-public schools
Governance by administrator
6 acres; new custom designed buildings; childcare; suburban location; interns accepted.

Imagination Times
(See Resource Appendix)

Concord Montessori School
7324 Cedarbrook Dr, Charlotte, NC 28215
Suzann Herrington

Brisbane Academy
5901 Statesville Rd, Charlotte, NC 28269
Geraldine Brisbane-White, 704-598-5208, FAX: same, call first
Type: Montessori; tuition: $2,500/yr
27 students, ages 3-12
Entrance requirement: testing
Governance by an administrator
Teacher qualifications: NC certification
Fosters love of self and the learning process; childcare; interns accepted.

Charlotte Home Educators Association
8600 Duck's Bill Dr, Charlotte, NC 28277
Debbie Mason, 704-541-5145

Omni Montessori (1984)
9536 Blakeney-Heath Rd, Charlotte, NC 28277
Cindy Boucherle, 704-541-1326
Tuition: $250-405/mo
6 teachers, 5 assistants, 101 students, ages 3-12
Accreditation: AMI
Governance by teachers, administrators, board
Parent participation encouraged; parent education program; childcare; rural location; interns accepted.

Montessori School of Fayetteville
1201 Cape Ct, Fayetteville, NC 28304-4404
Kerry Lydon

Home Offering Meaningful Education
2606 Phoenician Dr, Fayetteville, NC 28306
Dale Kozikowski, 919-323-0539

Sandhills Montessori School
205 S Pinehurst St, Aberdeen, NC 28315-2010

Children's House by Edu-Care
3150 McIntyre Rd Sta, Pinehurst, NC 28374
Type: Montessori

Wilmington Homeschool Organization
Box 6011, Hanover Center, Wilmington, NC 28403
Marty Grist, 919-251-9444

Pamlico County Schools
507 Anderson Dr, Bayboro, NC 28515
Ben Potter, 919-745-4171

Home Educators of Carteret
Rt 3 Box 241, Beaufort, NC 28516
Frances Arrington, 919-728-2809

New Bern Homeschoolers
PO Box 125, Ernul, NC 28527
Joan Cowell, 919-244-1912

Greenville Montessori School
21 Baywood Dr, Winterville, NC 28590-9615

Creekside School-A Montessori Middle School
Route 2, Box 545A, Boone, NC 28607
Elizabeth Howell

Mountain Pathways School
Route 5, Box 593 A, Boone, NC 28607
Cheryl M. Smith, Director, 704-262-5787
Watauga County
Type: Montessori; tuition: $2950, scholarships
5 teachers, 40 students, ages 3–9, pre K–3rd grade
Entrance requirements: application fee, interview
Governance by board
Teacher qualifications: NC teaching certificate, Montessori training
In 1992-3 all teachers had American Montessori Training; each year two teachers and director go to AMS conference; no letter grades; multi-aged classes; rural location; interns accepted.

SHARE
305 Maplewood Dr, Morganton, NC 28655
Bonnie Perkins, 704-437-1210
Type: home-based

The Children's School
105 W Concord St, Morganton, NC 28655
Joanna Young, 704-438-8835

Montessori Learning Center of Wilkes, Inc
601 Boston Ave, N Wilkesboro, NC 28659
Elizabeth Aversa, 919-667-4032
Non-profit; tuition: $320/mo
2 teachers, 3 assistants, 30 students, ages 3–6
Entrance requirements: age 3; toilet trained
Affiliations: AMS, NAMTA
Governance by administrator
Rural location; interns accepted.

Iredell County Home Educators
Rt 18, Box 227, Statesville, NC 28677
Donna and Roger Hames, 704-876-6516

Montessori Children's House
111 Hartness Rd, Statesville, NC 28677-3209

Fellowship & Instruction to Home Educators
1808 Chestnut Ave, Charlotte, NC 28705
Catheryn Pell, 704-376-5093

Camp Elliot Therapeutic Wilderness Program (1987)
601 Camp Elliot Rd, Black, NC 28711
Catherine Buie or Linda Tatsapaugh, 704-669-8639, FAX:–2521
Buncomb County
Type: independent, non-profit
2 teachers, 14-20 students, mainly at-risk boys, ages 12–17
Enrollment restricted to min IQ 95, good physical condition
Governance by exec committee, head staff
Teacher qualifications: special education
Construct and maintain buildings; SE; multi-aged classes; interns accepted.

Arthur Morgan School (1962)
1901 Hannah Branch Rd, Burnsville, NC 28714
Johno Zakelj & Joy Montagano, Co-clerks, 704-675-4262
Type: Quaker, boarding, non-profit; tuition: $5150-10500, scholarships
12 teachers, 24 students, ages 12-15, 7-9th grade
Entrance requirements: no severe mental, emotional problems, 2 day visit
Affiliations: NCACS, NAMTA, FEAA

Governance by staff, staff and student all-school meeting
Rare junior high boarding school, geared to meet their specific needs; challenging outdoor experiences; community service; daily work projects; caring community environment; based on Montessori's Erkinder model; no letter grades; multi-aged classes; extensive field trips; rural location; interns accepted.

CELO Community
816 Grindstaff Rd, Burnsville, NC 28714
Barbara Stuehling, 704-675-9590
Type: home-based

The Hampton School
PO Box 546, Cashiers, NC 28717-0546
Type: Montessori

Blue Ridge Waldorf Community
Rt 2, Box 2972, Columbus, NC 28722
Beth Love, 704-863-2775
Waldorf study group; play groups, festivals; children's learning days.

Carolina Superschoolers
Rt 2, PO Box 2972, Columbus, NC 28722
704-863-2775
Polk County
Type: home-based

Polk County Schools
PO Box 638, Columbus, NC 28722
Spencer Johnson

Cullowhee Montessori
Rt 66, Box 73-B, Cullowhee, NC 28723

Christian Home Education Association of Franklin
141 Harrison Ave, Franklin, NC 28734
Catherine Wright, 704-524-2208

ED-venturous Learning Families
68 Lakey Creek, Franklin, NC 28734
Trish Severin or Doug Woodward, 704-369-6491
Type: home-based

Montessori Center of Hendersonville
1306 Valmont Dr, Hendersonville, NC 28739

McDowell County School
320 S Main St, Marion, NC 28752
Dean Gouge, 704-652-4535

Statesville Montessori School, Inc (1989)
1012 Harmony Dr/ 111 Hartness Rd, Statesville, NC 28766-6080
Julia Sutton, Dir, 704-873-1092
Tuition: $1,950-3,650/yr
13 teachers, 5 assistants, 123 students, ages 3–12
Affiliation: AMS
Governance by an administrator
Childcare; urban location; interns accepted.

Carolina Mountain Montessori
28 Ridgeway St, Sylva, NC 28779-2946

Haywood County Home Educators
506 Oak St, Waynesville, NC 28786

Union Acres Alternative School
Rt 1, Box 61J, Whittier, NC 28789
Margaret Haun, 704-497-4964
Type: home-based

Claxton Elementary
241 Merrimon Ave, Asheville, NC 28801
Charles Cutshall, 201-255-5367
Type: magnet
K-5th grade
Arts; mulitcultural; humanities.

Issac Dickson Elementary
125 Hill St, Asheville, NC 28801
Bob McGrattan, 201-255-5376
Type: magnet
K-5th grade
Fox Fire School; experiential; continuous program.

Randoff Elementary
90 Montford Ave, Asheville, NC 28801
Barbara Lewis, 201-255-5359
Type: magnet
4-5th grade
Gifted and talented.

Asheville Montessori School
23 Congress St, Asheville, NC 28801-4342

St Genevieve-Biggons Hall School, Inc
103 Victoria Rd, Asheville, NC 28801-4811
Type: Montessori

The Robert Muller School
1875 Hendersonville Rd, Asheville, NC 28803
Barbara Darden, 704-274-0283

Jones Primary
544 Kimberly Ave, Asheville, NC 28804
Sue Harris, 201-255-5366
Type: magnet
K-3rd grade
Gifted and talented.

Children's Grammar School
10 Kidstown Rd, Asheville, NC 28806
Type: independent

Rainbow Mountain School
574 Haywood Rd, Asheville, NC 28806
Type: independent

Warren Wilson College (1984)
PO Box 9000, Asheville, NC 28815
Tom Weede, Dean of Admission, 704-298-3325, FAX: 704-299-3326
Non-profit; tuition: $12,917/yr, scholarships
47 teachers, 500 students, ages 18-25
Governance by democratic school meeting and board
Diverse; all students work 15 hrs/wk for College, do 20 hrs/yr community service; rural location.

Ligon Middle School
706 E Lenoir St, Raleigh, NC 62701
Dan Bowers, 919-856-7929
Type: magnet
6-8th grade
Gifted and talented.

North Dakota

Community High School
207 Main Ave W, West Fargo, ND 58071
John Peterson, Prin, 701-282-9703

Community High school
315 N University, Fargo, ND 58102
Jerry Hasche, Prin, 701-241-4856

Woodrow Wilson (1971)
315 N University Dr, Fargo, ND 58102
Jerry Hasche, Prin, 701 241-4889
Cass County
Type: public at-risk
7 teachers, 200 students, mainly at-risk, ages 16–19, 9–12th grade
Enrollment restricted to ages 16+; residency
Affiliation: Fargo Public Schools
Governance by teachers, principal, board
Urban location; interns accepted.

Academy for Children
20 S 8th St, Fargo, ND 58103-1805
701-232-7787
Type: Montessori; tuition: $145–340/mo
4 teachers, 3 assistants, 81 students, ages infant-9
Affiliation: NAEYC
Governance by an administrator
French and music for all ages; childcare; urban location; interns accepted.

Dakota Montessori School
1620 16th Ave S, Fargo, ND 58103-4055
Elizabeth Boyer

Community High School
911 Cottonwood St, Grand Forks, ND 58201
William O'Toole, Prin, 701-746-2425

Little Scholarship
1420 24th Ave S, Grand Forks, ND 58201-6735
Type: Montessori

Kinderhaus Montessori
PO Box 1284, Jamestown, ND 58402-1284

South Central Alternative School
222 W Bowen, Bismarck, ND 58501
Serenus Hofffner, Prin, 701-221-3790

Missouri Valley Montessori School
2600 Gateway Ave, Bismarck, ND 58501-0568
Laurie Langeliers

North Dakota Home School Association
PO Box 486, Mandan, ND 58554
701-663-2868

Souris River Campus
215 2nd St SE, Minot, ND 58701
Robert Kelly, 701-857-4496

Ohio

Delaware Montessori
117 Eaton St, Delaware, OH 43015

Dublin Montessori Academy (1987)
6055 Glick Rd, Powell, OH 43065
Mary Jill Roshon, Owner, 614-761-2020
Tuition: $1,800-4,392/yr
2 teachers, 2 assistants, 72 students, ages 3-6
Entrance requirements: toilet trained
Affiliation: AMS
Governance by administrator
Childcare; suburban location; interns accepted.

Shamrock Montessori Academy
PO Box 605, Powell, OH 43065-0605

Reynoldsburg High School
6699 E Livingston Ave, Reynoldsburg, OH 43068
Dan Hoffman, Prin, 614-866-6397, FAX: 614-575-3098
Type: public choice
65 teachers, 1100 students, 10-12th grade
District residency required
Affiliation: CES
Governance by teachers and principal
Employs CES research: reorganizes time, curriculum and the
    assignment of students to teachers; interdisciplinary work;
    double-blocked classes; inclusion strategies; suburban
    location; interns accepted.

Johnny Appleseed Montessori
PO Box 189, Urbana, OH 43078-0189

Lancaster Montessori Center
PO Box 52, Lancaster, OH 43130-0052

**Fifth Ave Alternative Elementary for International
    Studies**
1300 Forsythe Ave, Columbus, OH 43201
614-365-5564, FAX: 614-365-5564
Type: public choice
K-5th grade
Entrance by city-wide lottery or assignment.
Multi-age grouping; team teaching; whole language; litera-
    ture-based; integrated; open space/informal; flexible;
    culture studies; camping trips; educational tours.

Indianola Elementary
140 E 16th Ave, Columbus, OH 43201
614-365-5579
Type: public choice
K-5th grade
Enrollment by application and lottery
Self-directed; individualized.

Champion Middle School
1270 Hawthorne Ave, Columbus, OH 43203
Andrew Meilton, 614-365-6082
Type: magnet
6-8th grade

Hilltonia Alternative Middle School
2345 W Mound St, Columbus, OH 43204
Robert Jones, 614-365-5937
Type: magnet
6-8th grade
Regional Alternative.

**Westgate/Windsor Schools of Academic and Physical
    Excellence**
3080 Wicklow Rd/1219 E 12th Ave, Columbus, OH
    43204/43211
614-365-5971/365-5906
Type: public choice
K-5th grade
Fitness; nutrition; critical thinking; healthy lifestyles.

Open Space at Douglas Elementary
43 S Douglas St, Columbus, OH 43205
614-365-6087
Type: public choice
K-5th grade
Enrollment by application and lottery
Incorporates city institutions, activities; flex scheduling;
    multi-age grouping; cooperative teaching.

**IGE (Individually Guided Education)
    Fairwood/Linden Park Elementaries**
726 Fairwood Ave/1400 Myrtle Ave, Columbus, OH
    43205/43211
614-365-6111/365-6037
Type: public choice
K-5th grade

**Project Adventure at Cedarwood/Devonshire
    Elementaries**
775 Bartfield Dr/6286 Ambleside Dr, Columbus, OH
    43207/43229
614-365-5421/365-5335
Type: public choice
K-5th grade
Holistic; experiential.

Spanish Immersion at Gladstone Elementary
1965 Gladstone Ave, Columbus, OH 43211
614-365-5565
Type: public choice
K-5th grade
Enrollment by application and lottery, grades 2-5 must be
    approved by review panel

Columbus Montessori Center
5412 Malibu Dr, Columbus, OH 43213
Anne McCarrick, SND
teacher education

HELP: Home Education League of Parents (1992)
PO Box 14296, Columbus, OH 43214
Laurie Clark or Janet Attanasio, 614-268-5363
Franklin County
Non-profit
Student ages infant-18
Governance by parent cooperative
Inclusive; newsletter.

Mohawk Alternative Middle School
300 E Livingston Ave, Columbus, OH 43215
Lorenzo Hunt, 614-365-6517
Type: magnet
6-8th grade

St Joseph Montessori School
300 E Main St, Columbus, OH 43215

**Literature Based/Language Arts
  Franklinton/Olde Orchard Elementaries**
617 W State St/800 McNaughten Rd, Columbus, OH
  43215/43213
614-365-6525/365-5388
Type: public choice
K–5th grade
Enrollment by application and lottery
Magazines; newspapers; young authors' promotions.

Christian Home Educators of Ohio
PO Box 262, Columbus, OH 43216
800-274-2436
Type: state home-based

Brentnell Montessori School
1270 Brentnell Ave, Columbus, OH 43219
614-365-6079
Type: public choice
K–5th grade

Duxbury Park Elementary
1779 E Maynard Ave, Columbus, OH 43219
William Dwyer, 614-365-6023
Type: magnet
K–5th grade
Fine and performing arts.

St Mary of the Springs Montessori School (1962)
2320 Airport Dr, Columbus, OH 43219
Sr Marietta Miller, OP, Adm, 614-258-0024
Tuition: $215-375/mo
3 teachers, 4 assistants, 72 students, ages 3–6
Affiliation: AMS; accreditation: OHDHS
Governance by board
Spirituality of natural environment; foreign language; multi-
  cultural; newspaper; enrichment; parent participation;
  summer program; childcare; suburban location; interns
  accepted.

**IMPACT (Interdisciplinary Model Program in the Arts for
  Children and Teachers) at Duxberry Park/Fair
  Elementaries**
1779 E Maynard Ave/1395 Fair Ave, Columbus, OH
  43219/43205
614-365-6023/365-6107
Type: public choice
K–5th grade
Enrollment by application and lottery

French Immersion at Kenwood Elementary
3770 Shattuck Ave, Columbus, OH 43220
614-365-5502
Type: public choice
K–5th grade
Enrollment by application and lottery, grades 2-5 must be
  approved by review panel

Columbus Montessori Education Center
979 S James Rd, Columbus, OH 43227
Dottie Feldman, Mary Lee
Type: Montessori teacher education

**Science/Math/Environmental Studies
  Georgian Heights Elementary**
784 Georgian Dr, Columbus, OH 43228
614-365-5931
Type: public choice
K–5th grade
Experiential; math integrated into other subjects; other sites:
  Hamilton, 2047 Hamilton Ave, 43211, 365-5568; Cassady,
  2500 N Cassady Ave, 43219, 365-5456; Berwick, 2595
  Scottwood Rd, 43209, 365-6140 (lottery only).

Growing Together (1988)
1676 Tendril Ct, Columbus, OH 43229
Nancy McKibben, 614-890-3141

Franklin County
Type: home-based
Non-sectarian; bi-monthly learning co-op; newsletter; partici-
  pates in events such as National Geography Bee.

Occupational Work Adjustment
Room 912, 65 S Front St, Columbus, OH 43266-0308
David M. Wolfe, 614-292-5015
Type: public at-risk
Student ages 14–15

Montessori School of Bowling Green, Inc (1980)
630 S Maple St, Bowling Green, OH 43402
Dr Charlotte Scherer, Dir, 419-352-4203
Tuition: 1,365-3,100/yr
6 teachers, 4 assistants, 31+ students, ages 3–12
Affiliation: AMS; accreditation: OH Charter
Governance by board of trustees
2.5 wooded acres; outdoor ed; transportation for ages 3–6;
  childcare; rural location; interns accepted.

**Wood County Juvenile Detention, In-School and Out-of-
  School Youth Programs**
Courthouse Square, Bowling Green, OH 43402
Polli Balie/Deb Doup Bailey/Christy C. Spontelli, 419-354-9010
Job seeking and placement assistance; career counseling;
  financial assistance for support services.

Nazarene Montessori School
1291 Conneaut Ave, Bowling Green, OH 43402-2125

The Defiance College
701 N Clinton, Defiance, OH 43512
Philip A Griswold, Ed D
Type: Montessori

Together We Can!
419 Fernwood St, Delta, OH 43515
Jane Spurgeon, 419-822-3391
Type: public at-risk
Tutoring by peers and teachers; counseling.

Henry County Alternate Learning Center
PO Box 345, Haley St; 660 N Perry St, McClure, OH 43534
John Wilhelm, Co Supt or Rick Bailin, Dir, 419-592-1861, 748-
  8102
Serves handicapped, emotionally disturbed, severely behav-
  iorally handicapped students.

Montessori Children's House
840 Ashbury Dr, Perrysburg, OH 43551
Barbara Kaiser, 419-874-7030
Tuition: $2,000/4,000/yr
1 teacher, 3 assistants, 34 students, mainly international, ages
  3–6
Entrance requirements: age 2.5-3.75; toilet trained
Affiliation: AMS
Governance by administrator
French; cooking; baking; music; piano; language; parent
  study; Dreikurs Series discipline; childcare; suburban loca-
  tion; interns accepted.

Home Education League of Parents
PO Box 98, Perrysburg, OH 43552-0098
419-874-2148
Wood County

Lucas County Out of School Program
2025 Arlington Ave, Toledo, OH 43609
Robin Seifert, 419-473-2245, 245-4150
Type: public at-risk
Student ages 16–21
Enrollment restricted to low income, handicapped, foster
  child or substance abuse
Correspondence courses; GED prep; job placement assis-
  tance; transportation and childcare reimbursement; cash
  incentives for completion.

West Side Montessori Center
2105 N McCord Rd, Toledo, OH 43615-3001
Lynn Fisher

RSM Creative Services Inc
(See Resource Appendix)

Changes for Youth
1300 Jefferson Ave, Toledo, OH 43624
Sue Cochrell, 419-255-7196
Type: public at-risk
Student ages 17–21
GED, employment prep; work experience; childcare;
　transportation.

Toledo Public Schools Family Life Programs
Suite 235 of the Jefferson Center, Toledo, OH 43624
419-255-7196
Type: public at-risk
Career Transitions; Adult Job Training; Childcare Training
　Ohio's Parents for Success; Culinary Arts; Elder Care.

Olney Friends School (1837)
61830 Sandy Ridge Rd, Barnesville, OH 43713
Bonnie Irwin, Asst Head, 614-425-3655
Belmont County
Type: Quaker, boarding, non-profit; tuition: $13,230/yr,
　scholarships
12 teachers, 49 students, ages 13–19, 9–12th grade
Affiliations: ISACS, NAIS, FCOE
Teacher qualifications: BS with a major in subject to be taught
Whole-person approach; college prep; multi-aged classes;
　rural location; interns accepted.

Sandstone Montessori
400 Tenney Ave, Amherst, OH 44001
Kristine Huffman, 216-984-2729
Non-profit; tuition: $100/mo, 2700/yr
1 teacher, 4 assistants, 49 students, ages infant-6
Affiliation: AMS
Governance by democratic school meeting and a committee
　of teachers and parents
Childcare; suburban location; interns accepted.

Ohio Home Educators Network (Cleaveland-Akron area)
PO Box 23054, Chagrin Falls, OH 44023-0054
216-543-5644, 216-562-5173

Notre Dame Montessori
13000 Auburn Rd, Chardon, OH 44024-9331
Sr Mary Doloretta Coyne

Faith Montessori School
8665 Prescott Dr, Chesterland, OH 44026

Golden Crescent Montessori (1982)
266 Washington Ave, Elyria, OH 44035
Evelyn L. Miller, Adm, 216-323-6925
Non-profit; tuition: $990-1,550/yr
2 teachers, 2 assistants, 49 students, ages infant-6
Affiliation: AMS; accreditation: NAEYC
Governance by administrator, board
Suburban location; interns accepted.

Gilmour Academy Montessori School
34001 Cedar Rd, Gates Mills, OH 44040-9732
Sr Loretta May

Washington Continous Progress Academy
2700 Washington Ave, Lorain, OH 44052
Sam Coleman, 216-246-2187
Type: magnet
K-3rd grade
Continuous progress; fine arts.

Lorain City Schools Montessori Program
1020 W 7th St, Lorain, OH 44052-1459
Doug Mathews

Montessori Child Enrichment Center
3840 Kolbe Rd, Lorain, OH 44053

Lincoln Academy
E 31st St & Vine Ave, Lorain, OH 44055
Tim Dortch, 216-277-8188
Type: Montessori magnet
K-6th grade

Palm Academy
3330 Palm Ave, Lorain, OH 44055
Sylvia Cooper, 216-277-9226
Type: Montessori magnet
K-3rd grade

HELP-Oberlin (1993)
10915 Pyle-S Amherst Rd, Oberlin, OH 44074
Gina McKay Lodge, Coord, 774-2720, FAX: 775-1368
Lorain County
Type: home-based, non-profit
Resources; support; participation in adult work; field trips;
　suburban location.

Hershey Montessori School, Inc (1978)
10229 Prouty Rd, Concord Township, OH 44077
Michael Bagiackas, Head, 216-357-0918, FAX: 216-357-1505
Non-profit
7 teachers, 135 students, ages 1–12
Governance by a board of trustees
Custom designed building; parent-child program; 11+ acres;
　land lab; developing farmstead; integration of indoor and
　outdoor learning environments; no letter grades; multi-
　aged classes; suburban location.

Ohio Coalition of Educational Alternatives Now
PO Box 094, Thompson, OH 44086
Type: state home-based

Willoughby Montessori Dayschool
5543 Som Center Rd, Willoughby, OH 44094-4281

Max S Hayes Vocational High School
4600 Detroit Ave, Cleveland, OH 44102
Theodis Fipps, Prin, 216-631-1528
Type: public choice
HS
Autobody, diesel technician; construction; textiles; welding
　cutting; manufacturing; placement assistance.

Thomas Jefferson CompuTech Center
3145 W 46th St, Cleveland, OH 44102
Joseph Mueller, Prin, 216-631-5962
Type: public choice
6-8th grade
Instruction supported by electronic technology.

West Technical High School
2201 W 93rd St, Cleveland, OH 44102
Bobby McDowell, Prin, 216-281-9100
Type: public choice
HS
School of manufacturing, automotive and related technolo-
　gies; childcare; commercial art; drafting/graphics; con-
　struction; electronics; landscape; Project Smart
　apprenticeship program.

Marotta Montessori School
11450 Franklin Blvd, Cleveland, OH 44102-2310
Alcillia Clifford

East High Academy of Finance and Vocational Magnet
1349 E 79th St, Cleveland, OH 44103
Mary Stokes, Prin, 216-431-5361
Type: public choice
Childcare; commercial art; drafting/graphics; construction;
　cosmetology; electronics; landscape; small animal care.

Martin Luther King Jr Law and Public Service High School
1651 E 71st St, Cleveland, OH 44103
Melvin Jones, Prin, 216-431-6858
Type: public choice
Mediation and conflict management.

Alfred A Benesch Primary Achievement Program
5393 Quincy Ave, Cleveland, OH 44104
Allene Warren, Prin, 216-431-4132
Type: public choice
K-3rd grade
Ungraded; self-paced.

Anton Grdina Primary Achievement Program
3050 E 77th, Cleveland, OH 44104
Inez Powell, Prin, 216-641-7477
Type: public choice
K-3rd grade
Ungraded; self-paced.

Dike Montessori Center
2501 E 61st St, Cleveland, OH 44104
Carolyn Bridges-Graves, Prin, 216-361-0708
Type: public choice
K-4th grade
Cooperative learning; multi-aged classes.

East Technical High School Engineering/Technician Program and Vocational Magnet
2439 E 55th St, Cleveland, OH 44104
Terry Butler, Prin, 216-431-2626
Type: public choice
HS
Childcare; commercial art; computer-aided drafting, graphics; electronics; food service.

Harvey Rice Primary Achievement Program
11529 Buckeye Rd, Cleveland, OH 44104
Elizabeth Ward, Prin, 216-231-2411
Type: public choice
1-3rd grade
Ungraded; self-paced.

Corlett Primary Achievement Program
13013 Corlett Ave, Cleveland, OH 44105
David Keilin, Prin, 216-295-2590
Type: public choice
1-3rd grade
Ungraded; self-paced.

John Adams Classical Academy
3817 Martin Luther King Jr Dr, Cleveland, OH 44105
Darryl Smith, Prin, 216-561-2200
Type: public choice
HS
College prep.

Robert H Jamison CompuTech Center
13905 Harvard Ave, Cleveland, OH 44105
George J. Billingsley, Prin, 216-295-0655
Type: public choice
K-5th grade
Keyboarding; WP; computer programming.

South High School Sports and Health Management Program and Vocational Magnet
7415 Broadway Ave, Cleveland, OH 44105
Jerry T. Mitchell, Prin, 216-641-0410
Type: public choice
Childcare; commercial art; drafting/graphics; construction; cosmetology; electronics; landscape; small animal care.

Bolton Primary Achievement Program
9803 Quebec Ave, Cleveland, OH 44106
William Lodwick, Prin, 216-231-2585
Type: public choice
K-3rd grade
Ungraded; self-paced.

Cleveland School of the Arts
2064 Stearns Rd, Cleveland, OH 44106
Anthony Vitanza, Prin, 216-791-2496
Type: public choice
5-12th grade
Opportunities with Cleveland Inst of Music, Cleveland Inst of Art, Cleveland Ballet, Music School Settlement.

John Hay Medical/Biological Program
2075 E 107th St, Cleveland, OH 44106
Leroy L. Melton, Prin, 216-421-7700
Type: public choice
HS

North American Montessori Teachers' Association
(See Resource Appendix)

Forest Hill Montessori School
2419 Euclid Heights Blvd, Cleveland Heights, OH 44106-2707

Montessori Neighborhood School
2555 Euclid Hts Blvd, Cleveland Heights, OH 44106-2709

AMI Montessori Learning Center
12900 Lake Ave #1116, Cleveland, OH 44107-1552

Empire CompuTech Center
9113 Parmelee Ave, Cleveland, OH 44108
Lincoln Haughton, Prin, 216-268-6350
Type: public choice
K-5th grade
Keyboarding; WP; computer programming.

Glenville Vocational Magnet Program
650 E 113th St, Cleveland, OH 44108
Elbert Cobbs, Jr, Prin, 216-851-9400
Type: public choice
HS
Childcare; commercial art; drafting/graphics; construction; cosmetology; electronics; landscape; small animal care.

Louis Pasteur Primary Achievement Program
815 Linn Dr, Cleveland, OH 44108
Norma J. Murray, Prin, 216-541-5727
Type: public choice
1-3rd grade
Ungraded; self-paced.

Miles Standish Primary Achievement
1000 E 92nd St, Cleveland, OH 44108
James Eland, 216-451-7013
Type: magnet
1-3rd grade
Non-graded; continuous progress; individualized; Montessori.

Wm. C. Bryant Primary Achievement
3121 Oak Park Ave, Cleveland, OH 44109
Marilyn Kurnath, 216-351-6343
Type: magnet
1-3rd grade
Non-graded; continuous progress; individualized; Montessori.

East Clark Primary Achievement Program
885 E 146th St, Cleveland, OH 44110
Peggie Brown, Prin, 216-451-4973
Type: public choice
K-3rd grade
Ungraded; self-paced.

Margaret Spellacy CompuTech Center
655 E 162nd St, Cleveland, OH 44110
Henry Orr, Prin, 216-531-2872
Type: public choice
6-8th grade
Instruction supported by electronic technology.

Teaching Professions at Collinwood High School
15210 St Clair Ave, Cleveland, OH 44110
William Martin, Prin, 216-451-8782
Type: public choice

Garfield CompuTech Center
3800 W 140th St, Cleveland, OH 44111
Barbara Clark, Prin, 216-251-3876
Type: public choice
3-6th grade
Keyboarding; WP; computer programming.

Louis Agassiz
3595 Bosworth Rd, Cleveland, OH 44111
Kathleen Freilino, Prin, 216-251-7747
Type: public choice
1-3rd grade

Newton D Baker School of the Arts
3690 W 159th St, Cleveland, OH 44111
Marion E. Aguilera, Prin, 216-252-2131
Type: public choice
K-4th grade
Activities with various cultural institutions.

Garrett Morgan Cleveland School of Science
4016 Woodbine Ave, Cleveland, OH 44113
Patricia Oster, Prin, 216-281-6188
Type: public choice
6-12th grade
Experiential; computers.

Hicks Montessori School
2409 Bridge Ave, Cleveland, OH 44113
H. Barbara Booker, Prin, 216-621-2616
Type: public choice
K-4th grade
Cooperative learning; multi-aged classes.

Lincoln Contemporary Academy
1701 Castle Ave, Cleveland, OH 44113
James Joyner, Principal, 216-241-7440
Type: public choice
6-8th grade
Learning styles inventory; individualized instruction, learning
kits to fit student's learning style.

Aviation High School
4101 N Marginal Rd, Cleveland, OH 44114
Joseph Takacs, Prin, 216-621-1357
Type: public choice
Aircraft maintenance; avionics; marketing; air traffic control;
ground support equipment; FAA certification test.

Health Careers Center
1740 E 32nd St, Cleveland, OH 44114
Robert J. Black III, Prin, 216-579-9984
Type: public choice
HS
Dental/lab, medical/lab, OR, optical lab assistants; senior com-
munity health technician; mentorships.

Jane Addams Business Careers Center
2373 E 30th St, Cleveland, OH 44115
Gwendolyn Lynton, Prin, 216-621-2131
Type: public choice
11-12th grade
Computer business systems; finance/credit; legal, medical
secy; merchandising; computer repair; food service.

Ruffing Montessori School of Rocky River
1285 Orchard Park Dr, Rocky River, OH 44116
Tim Duax

Westshore Montessori Association
1101 Morewood Pky, Rocky River, OH 44116-1499

Montessori School of University Heights
2441 Fenwick Rd, Cleveland, OH 44118

Westshore Montessori
3249 E Monmouth Rd, Cleveland Heights, OH 44118
Ro Eugene

Lafayette Contemporary Academy
12416 Signet Ave, Cleveland, OH 44120
John Nairus, Prin, 216-561-2561
Type: public choice
K-5th grade
Individualized; learning kits.

Rainbow Bridge Montessori
3875 Monticello Blvd, Cleveland, OH 44121

Lillian Ratner Montessori School
4900 Anderson Rd, Lyndhurst, OH 44124-1000
Linda Shapiro

Emile B deSauze Contemporary Academy
4747 E 176th St, Cleveland, OH 44128
Patricia Faulkner, Prin, 216-587-2133
Type: public choice
K-5th grade
Individualized; learning kits.

**John F Kennedy Communications and Technology
Program**
17100 Harvard Ave, Cleveland, OH 44128
Wally Caleb, Prin, 216-921-1450
Type: public choice
HS

Moses Cleveland Primary Achievement
4092 E 146th St, Cleveland, OH 44128
Cynthia Evans, 216-295-3508
Type: magnet
1-3rd grade
Non-graded; continuous progress; individualized;
Montessori.

North Star Academy
6500 Emory Dr, Brook Park, OH 44130
Ernest Mason, Dir, 216-243-8660
Type: public at-risk
9-10th grade
Career education.

**Foreign Languages/International Studies Program
Robinson G Jones Elementary**
4550 W 150th St, Cleveland, OH 44135
Shirley McNair-Robinson, Prin, 216-267-6464
Type: public choice
K-5th grade
Heritage studies.

Valley View Community School
17200 Valley View Ave, Cleveland, OH 44135
Angela Zaccardelli, Prin, 216-251-5873
Type: public choice
K-5th grade
Radio station WCTC: We Celebrate the Children.

Berea Area Montessori School
19543 Lunn Rd, Cleveland, OH 44136-4915

Solon Creative Playrooms Montessori School
32800 Solon Rd, Solon, OH 44139

Bay Village Montessori
493 Forestview Rd, Bay Village, OH 44140-2757
Karen Cunningham

South Suburban Montessori School
23 Public Sq, Cleveland, OH 44141-1801

Westlake Montessori & Child Development Center
26830 Detroit Rd, Westlake, OH 44145-2368

Decker Family Development Center
633 Brady Ave, Barberton, OH 44203
Mary Frances Ahern, Dir; Dee Siegferth, Literacy Coord, 216-
   848-4264
Student ages infant-7
Educational, social and health services.

Hudson Montessori School
7545 Darrow Rd, Hudson, OH 44236-1399

Medina Children's House
425 Ridge Dr, Medina, OH 44256
Type: Montessori

Spring Garden Waldorf School (1981)
2141 Pickle Rd, Akron, OH 44312
Jennell A. Woodard, Coord, 216-644-1160
Summit County
Non-profit; tuition: $3,000/yr
16 teachers, 111 students, ages 4-14, pre K-8th grade
Affiliation: AWSNA; accreditation: State certified
Governance by faculty and board
Teacher qualifications: degree
Suburban location.

Margaret Park School
1413 Manchester, Akron, OH 44314
Barbara Nelson
Type: Montessori

Erie Island School
1532 Peckham Ave, Akron, OH 44320
Johnnette Curry
Type: Montessori

Lisbon Montessori School
P O Box 87, Lisbon, OH 44432

Childhood Manor Montessori School
North Rd, Warren, OH 44483

Blossom Montessori, Inc
2138 E Market St, Warren, OH 44483-6104

Natural Beginnings Preschool
1145 Turin Ave, Youngstown, OH 44510
Type: Montessori

St Anthony's Montessori School
1145 Turin St, Youngstown, OH 44510-1198

Montessori School of Mahoning Valley
2008 Lynn Ave, Youngstown, OH 44514-1123
216-788-4622
Non-profit
5 teachers, 3 assistants, 81 students, ages 3-12
Entrance requirements: toilet trained
Affiliations: AMS, IMS; accreditation: AMS
Governance by administrator
Wooded setting; nature studies; childcare; sub/urban loca-
   tion; interns accepted.

Children's House Montessori (1984)
637 College Ave, Wooster, OH 44691
Marge Thomas, Head, 216-264-5222, FAX: 216-262-6295
Non-profit; tuition: $1,800/2,650/yr
1 teacher, 1 assistant, 21 students, ages 3-6
Affiliations: AMS, NAEYC
Governance by a board of trustees
Low enrollment fosters teacher-parent-student relationships;
   kindergarten participates in archaeological dig; rural loca-
   tion; interns accepted.

Canton Montessori School
125 15th St NW, Canton, OH 44703-3207

La Escuela de Las Madras y Los Ninos
3500 Cleveland Ave NW, Canton, OH 44709-2749
Type: Montessori

Ashland City Schools Alternative High School
416 Arthur St, PO Box 156, Ashland, OH 44805
Carl B Roloff, 419-289-1117
Type: public at-risk
6-12th grade
Job training.

Ashland University Montessori Preschool (1981)
Jacobs Hall, Ashland, OH 44805
Sarah Telego, Dir, 419-289-5699
Tuition: $1,125-2,831/yr
1 teacher, 4 assistants, 50 students, ages 3-6
Affiliation: AMS; accreditations: NAEYC, OHDS
Governance by board
Swimming; university students read to, interact with stu-
   dents, conduct gym class; childcare; rural location; interns
   accepted.

Home Ed. League of Parents/HELP Unlimited
Box 93, Ashland, OH 44805
419-869-7916

Montessori Child Enrichment Center
710 Cleveland Rd E, Huron, OH 44839-1871
Mary Helen Kay

Home Educator's Resource Organization (1991)
4 Erie St, Norwalk, OH 44857
Jane Janovyak, Support Group Leader, 419-668-6480
Huron County
Non-profit; Pre-K to 9th grade.

Barker Alternative School
1925 Barker St, Sandusky, OH 44870
Robert M Beck, 419-627-8124
Type: public at-risk
Student ages 4-18, K-12th grade
For severe behavior disorders
Gradually integrates students back into regular classroom.

St Peter's Montessori Pre-School
63 Mulberry St S, Mansfield, OH 44902-1909
Tina Siegfried

Comprehensive Competencies Program (CCP)
c/o Human Resource Bureau
445 Bowman St, Mansfield, OH 44903
Joseph H. Mudra, 419-525-6375
Type: public at-risk
HS
Individualized; self-paced; competency-based; multi-media;
   CAI; tutorials; life skills.

Mansfield Teenage Pregnancy Program
Mansfield Human Resources Bureau
445 Bowman St, Mansfield, OH 44903
Joseph H. Mudra, 419-525-6375
Student ages 14-21
Guidance; work experience; community services referrals.

PALS (Principles of the Alphabet Literacy Program)
Mansfield Human Resource Bureau
445 Bowman St, Mansfield, OH 44903
Joseph H. Mudra, 419-525-6375
Type: public at-risk
Teens and adults
Computer based; two locations.

Project Prevent
445 Bowman St, Mansfield, OH 44903
Joseph H. Mudra, 419-525-6375
Type: public at-risk
Student ages 14-21
Affiliation: Mansfield PALS and CCP Programs
Individualized; year-round.

Project Renew at the D Russell Lee Career Center
3603 Hamilton-Middletown Rd, Hamilton, OH 45011

Antoinette Lipscomb, 513-868-6300
Butler County
Assists dropouts to attempt re-entry, GED or job training.

St Julie Billiart School
1206 Shuler Ave, Hamilton, OH 45011
Type: Montessori

St Mary School
610 High St, Hamilton, OH 45011
Type: Montessori

The Partnership Project at D Russell Lee Career Center
3603 Hamilton-Middletown Rd, Hamilton, OH 45011
Antoinette Lipscomb, 513-868-6300
Butler County
Type: public at-risk
500+ students, ages 14-18
9 participating districts; mentorships; volunteer tutors;
    parent and community agency involvement.

Homeschool Network of Greater Cincinnati
3470 Greenfield Ct, Maineville, OH 45039-9517
513-732-6455
Issues oriented; contact for info on new Association of OH
    Homeschoolers

The Child's Place-A Montessori Preschool, Inc (1987)
4936 Irwin-Simpson Rd, Mason, OH 45040-5004
Patricia M. Elder, Dir/Owner, 513-793-0569, 398-7773
Tuition: $2,225/yr
3 teachers, 2 assistants, 70 students, ages 3-6
Affiliation: AMS
Governance by an administrator
Custom designed facility; large outdoor area; geography/cul-
    tural program enriched by multi-ethnic student body;
    childcare; suburban location; interns accepted.

Garfield Alternative Education Center
1830 Yankee Rd, Middletown, OH 45044
Sally Williamson, 513-420-4593
Type: public at-risk
17 teachers; 9-12th grade
Vocational; team teaching; psychologist; nurse; Severe
    Behavior Handicap (SBH) unit.

Talawanda Adult High School
101 W Chestnut St, Oxford, OH 45056
Nancy L. Kane, 513-523-8686, 523-4137
19 teachers, 275 students, ages 18-80
Diploma; post-HS assistance; community ed; career prep.

Challenge Club at Lockland City Schools
7519 Keehner Rdg Ct, West Chester, OH 45069
Barbara Greiwe, Dir, 513-733-4991
Type: public at-risk

Children's Meeting House Montessori School (1972)
931 O'Bannonville Rd, Loveland, OH 45140
Barbara W. Collins, Director, 513-683-4757
Non-profit; tuition: $2,480/3,500/yr
7 teachers, 112 students, ages 3-12
Entrance requirements: $50 application fee; visit
Affiliation: AMS; accreditation: State of Ohio
Governance by administrator, board
5-acre eco-learning lab: pond, orchard, vegetable and flower
    gardens, pine forest and nature trail; suburban location;
    interns accepted.

Children's House
5878 Cook Rd, Milford, OH 45150-1506
Type: Montessori

Cincinnati Adult Basic Education Program
230 E 9th St, Cincinnati, OH 45202
Jo L. Frazier, 513-369-4018
Type: public at-risk
Retraining; client-centered; GED; ESL; US citizenship prep.

Peter H Clark Academy
2423 Eastern Ave, Cincinnati, OH 45202
Deborah B. Ullner, 513-961-0022
Type: public at-risk
HS

Montessori Center East
2505 Eastern Ave, Cincinnati, OH 45202-1815

Total Learning Center for Children
205 W 4th St, Cincinnati, OH 45202-2628
Jennifer Hartman
Type: Montessori

Downtown Montessori
318 E 4th St, Cincinnati, OH 45202-4202

Montessori School of Western Cincinnati (1987)
4431 Glenway Ave, Cincinnati, OH 45205
Eileen Hof, Dir, 513-471-6792
Non-profit; tuition: $1,475/yr
2 teachers, 1 assistant, 60 students, ages 3-6
Affiliation: Cincinnati MS; accreditation: AMS
Governance by board
Extensive science program; suburban location; interns
    accepted.

Western Hills Montessori
4125 St William Ave, Cincinnati, OH 45205

Union Institute (1964)
440 E McMillan St, Cincinatti, OH 45206
Anu M. Mitra, Director of Communications, 513-861-6400,
    FAX: 513-861-0779
Type: higher education, non-profit; tuition: $2175-2484/qrtr,
    scholarships
105 teachers, 1600 students, ages 20-75
Enrollment restricted to PhD candidates with Master's degree
Governance by board of trustees
Offers adult learners alternative approach to BA, BS, PhD; fully
    accredited; students study from where they live; interdisci-
    plinary arts and sciences; tutorials and independent study;
    no letter grades.

Walnut Hills Montessori Child Care Center
813 Beecher St, Cincinnati, OH 45206-1513

Mercy Montessori Center
2335 Grandview Ave, Cincinnati, OH 45206-2219
Sr Mary Jacinta Shay

Xavier University Montessori TEP
3800 Victory Pkwy, Cincinnati, OH 45207-7341
Elizabeth L Bronsil
Type: Montessori teacher education

Summit Country Day School
2161 Grandin Rd, Cincinnati, OH 45208-3300
Phyllis Schueler
Type: Montessori

Parents & Children
34 Green St, Cincinnati, OH 45210-1252
Type: Montessori

Montessori Discoveries International
3756 Carson Ave, Cincinnati, OH 45211-4610

Cincinnati Waldorf School (1973)
5411 Moeller Ave, Norwood, OH 45212
Brenda Roberts, Adm Coord, 513-531-5135
Hamilton County
Non-profit; tuition: $1,500-3,840/yr, scholarships
10 teachers, 53 students, ages 3-8, pre K-2nd grade
Entrance requirements: variable: interview; no special needs
Affiliation: AWSNA
Governance by faculty and parent representatives
Teacher qualifications: commitment to anthroposophy,
    Waldorf training, college degree

Foundation program in Anthroposophical Studies for adults; weekend and summer programs for students; urban location; interns accepted.

Kennedy Heights Montessori Center
6065 Red Bank Rd, Cincinnati, OH 45213
513-631-8135
Non-profit; tuition: $150/375/mo
4 teachers, 4 assistants, 96 students, ages 3-6
Affiliations: AMI, AMS
Governance by board of trustees
Suburban location.

Sands Montessori (1975)
940 Poplar St, Cincinnati, OH 45214
Rita Swegman, Principal, 357-4330, FAX: 357-4333
Type: public choice; tuition: $1,395
29 teachers, 27 assistants, 707 students, ages 3-12
Entrance requirements: alternative application process
Affiliation: AMS
Governance by administrator
Unique playground and auditorium; over 30 specialized programs; teacher trainers on staff; nation's first public Montessori school; childcare; urban location; transportation; interns accepted.

Montessori Creative Portfolio
PO Box 15132-L, Cincinnati, OH 45215
Judith A Berger

Montessori Matters
701 E Columbia Ave, Cincinnati, OH 45215
Sr Helen Denise Somers

Reading Hilltop Community School (1967)
2236 Bolser Dr, Reading, OH 45215
Arnol Elam, Prin, 513-733-4322
Type: Montessori; tuition: $800/yr
1 teacher, 1 assistant, 41 students, ages 3-6
Entering children must be age 3 by Sept 30
Affiliation: AMS
Governance by an administrator
Suburban location; interns accepted.

Terry's Montessori School
209 Wyoming Ave, Cincinnati, OH 45215-4307

National Homeschool Association
PO Box 157290, Cincinnati, OH 45215-7290
Sydney Mathis, Office Coord, 513-772-9580, FAX: same: call first
Type: national home-based, non-profit
Annual conference; Homeschoolers Travel Network.

Clifton Montessori Center
351 Volkert Ave, Cincinnati, OH 45219-1138

Montessori Learning Center
2147 Auburn Ave, Cincinnati, OH 45219-2906

Cincinnati Montessori Society
395 Terrace, Cincinnati, OH 45220
Rita Hoppert

Clifton Multi-Age Elementary
3645 Clifton Ave, Cincinnati, OH 45220
Jay Parks, 513-861-7640
Type: magnet
K-6th grade
Multi-Age.

St Mary Lisa Steigerwald
1768 Cedar Ave, Cincinnati, OH 45224-2802
Type: Montessori

Lotspeich Montessori Center
5400 Red Bank Rd, Cincinnati, OH 45227-1122

North Avandale Montessori School
615 Clinton Springs Ave, Cincinnati, OH 45229
Thomas Rothwell, 513-221-3478
Type: magnet
K-6th grade
Montessori.

The New School (1970)
3 Burton Woods Ln, Cincinnati, OH 45229
Robyn Breiman, Dir, 413-281-7999
Type: Montessori, non-profit
11 teachers, 4 assistants, 133 students, ages 3-12
Affiliations: AMS, OHAIS; accreditation: OH
Governance by board
In 101-year-old stone mansion; national historic site; childcare; urban location; interns accepted.

Apple Hill Montessori School
1009 Nimitz Ln, Cincinnati, OH 45230-3648

Children's Way Montessori School
8779 Winton Rd, Cincinnati, OH 45231-4821

Children's Montessori Center
7000 Hamilton Ave, Cincinnati, OH 45231-5240

McKie Montessori School
124 Zinn Pl, Cincinnati, OH 45233-1227

Bond Hill Child Development Center
1600 Carolina Ave, Cincinnati, OH 45237
Type: Montessori

Dayspring Children's Center
6831 Colerain Ave, Cincinnati, OH 45239
Type: Montessori

Child's Place, A Montessori Preschool
7745 Trailwind Dr, Cincinnati, OH 45242-5004

Cincinnati Country Day School
6905 Given Rd, Cincinnati, OH 45243-2898
Type: Montessori

Maple Knoll Child Center (1977)
11070 Springfield Pike, Springdale, OH 45246
Nancy Drobish Lloyd, Dir, 513-782-2450
Type: Montessori, non-profit; tuition: $3744/1953
5 teachers, 55 students
Affiliation: AMS
Located in retirement village; suburban location; interns accepted.

Garden Montessori School
8108 Beechmont Ave, Cincinnati, OH 45255-3154

Fifth & Walnut Montessori
600 Walnut St, Greenville, OH 45331-1944
Nancy Dean

Shepherd Program
8811 Career Dr, Piqua, OH 45356
Donna Monnier, Coord, 513-778-1980
Type: public at-risk
Tutoring; small group instruction; correspondence class/GED prep; vocational; support services.

Miami County Juvenile Court Alternative Education Program
201 W Main St, Troy, OH 45373
Diane Cline, Adm, 513-332-6993
1 teacher
Teacher qualifications: OH Certification
Serves probation or parole youths suspended or expelled from school; operates 3 hrs/day.

Miami Montessori School
86 Troy Town Rd, Troy, OH 45373-2328

Antioch School (1921)
1160 Corry St, Box 242, Yellow Springs, OH 45387
Gilah Rittenhouse, School Manager, 513-767-7642
Greene County
Type: independent, non-profit; tuition: $3275
5 teachers, 75 students, ages 3.5-11, pre K-6th grade
Entrance requirements: application, interview, no severe
    behavioral problems
Governance by faculty and board of parents, community
    members
Teacher qualifications: certification
All students learn to ride unicycles; school-wide art/science
    program; borders on 1000-acre nature preserve; founded
    by Arthur Morgan, who was President of Antioch Univer-
    sity; no letter grades; multi-aged classes; suburban
    location.

Antioch University
Admissions, Yellow Springs, OH 45387
Jimmy Williams, Dean of Adms, 800-543-9436
Type: higher education; tuition: $17,500/yr, scholarships
675 students
Pioneer in co-op ed, with six experience-based programs
    across US and abroad; scholarships for environmental and
    social action; no letter grades.

Community Service, Inc
(See Resource Appendix)

Home Education League of Parents (HELP)
Miami Valley Chapter (1993)
PO Box 63, Yellow Springs, OH 45387
Leslie Baynes, Coord, 513-767-2346
Greene County
Non profit
Inclusive; interest-based.

Montessori Nature School
1045 E Hyde Rd, Yellow Springs, OH 45387-9756

Lutheran School of Dayton
239 Wayne Ave, Dayton, OH 45402-2939
Type: Montessori

Stivers Middle School
1313 E Fifth St, Dayton, OH 45403
Timothy Nealon, 513-223-3175
Type: magnet
7-8th grade
Visual and performing arts.

Wilbur Wright Middle School
1361 Huffman Ave, Dayton, OH 45403
Dale Frederick, 513-253-2343
Type: magnet
7-8th grade
Individualized.

Franklin Montessori School (1989)
2617 E 5th St, Dayton, OH 45403-2696
Judith O'Ryan, 513-253-2138
Type: public choice
21 teachers, 19 assistants, 465 students, ages 3–12
Entrance requirements: magnet application process
Affiliation: AMS; accreditation: MACTE
Governance by teachers and administrators
Peace education; character education; cultural programs;
    extensive field trips; urban location; transportation; interns
    accepted.

Horace Mann Montessori (1979)
715 Krebs Ave, Dayton, OH 45403-2696
Theolauda Harewood, 278-0966
342 students, ages 3–12
Entrance requirements: apply through magnet application
    process
Affiliation: AMS

Governance by teachers and administrators
Transportation; interns accepted.

Charles H. Loos Elementary
45 Wampler Ave, Dayton, OH 45405
Winifred Lee, 513-278-0785
Type: magnet
1-6th grade
Environmental studies; museum studies.

Colonel White High School
501 Niagara Ave, Dayton, OH 45405
Craig William, 513-276-2107
Type: magnet
9-12th grade
Visual and performing arts.

E. J. Brown Elementary
48 W Parkwood Dr, Dayton, OH 45405
Jane Rafal, 513-276-2144
Type: magnet
K-6th grade
Individualized.

Van Cleve Elementary
45 W Helena St, Dayton, OH 45405
Lillian Walker, 513-228-4153
Type: magnet
1-6th grade
Visual and performing arts.

Longfellow Alternative Learning Center
245 Salem Ave, Dayton, OH 45406
Tom Webb, 513-223-7700
Type: public at-risk
Parenting; pre/postnatal care; childcare.

Jefferson Montessori, Campus 1
1231 N Euclid Ave, Dayton, OH 45407
Therman Sampson, 513-276-2147
Type: magnet
K-2nd grade
Montessori.

Lincoln Elementary School
401 Nassau St, Dayton, OH 45410
Grayee Toles, 513-252-9915
Type: magnet
K-6th grade
Individualized.

Gloria Dei Montessori School (1962)
615 Shiloh Dr, Dayton, OH 45415
Virginia Varga, Adm, 513-274-7195
Non-profit; tuition: $230-349/mo
7 teachers, 7 assistants, 118 students, ages infant-12
Affiliation: AMS; accreditation: OH DE
Governance by board
Childcare.

Dayton Public Schools
2013 W 3rd St #158, Dayton, OH 45417
Diane Sherman, Dir of Elem Ed
Type: Montessori

Jackson Elementary
3201 McCall St, Dayton, OH 45417
Kenneth Dixon, 513-268-6791
Type: magnet
1-6th grade
Environmental studies; museum studies.

Cleveland Elementary
1102 Pursell Ave, Dayton, OH 45420
Darlene Borgert, 513-253-2175
Type: magnet
1-6th grade
Visual and performing arts.

Alexandria Montessori School
2900 Acosta, Kettering, OH 45420
Carol Schwob

Montessori Children's Center (1978)
4369 Valley Pike, Dayton, OH 45424
Dianne Remmers, Head, 513-236-6805
Tuition: $145-250/mo
2 teachers, 3 assistants, 65 students, ages 3–9
Affiliation: NAMTA; accreditation: Chartered
Governance by administrator
Childcare; suburban location; interns accepted.

Cassidy and Nells
PO Box 24133, Huber Hts, OH 45424
800-453-6114
Montgomery County
Publishes Home Education, Answers for Ohio Parents; materials; free catalog.

Beavercreek Montessori School
2262 N Tulane Dr, Beavercreek, OH 45431

Discovery House Montessori School
2525 Obetz Dr, Beaver Creek, OH 45434-6956
Ardyce Powell

Effica School of Montessori
71 Marco Ln, Centerville, OH 45458-3818

Montessori School of Centerville (1977)
16 E Elmwood Dr, Centerville, OH 45459
Wende Delre, Dir, 513-435-4572
Non-profit; tuition: $1,750/3,800/yr
1 teacher, 2 assistants, 40 students, ages 3–6
Accreditations: AMS, OH DE
Governance by administrator, board
Student-centered curriculum; practical life skills; interpersonal skills; emphasis on independence and self-confidence; suburban location; interns accepted.

Springfield Adult and Community Education Department
Jefferson Ctr, 50 E McCreight Ave, Springfield, OH 45504
Randy Milner, 513-328-2147
Type: public at-risk
Wright State U Consortium for Professional Dvlpmt; Adult HS Completion, Basic Ed; GED; ESL; Adult/Youth Enrichment & Recreation.

Nightingale Montessori School
1106 E High St, Springfield, OH 45505
Nancy Schwab

Keifer Alternative
501 S Wittenberg Ave, Springfield, OH 45506
Hannah Dixon, 513-328-6875
Type: public at-risk
Counseling; individualized.

Ohio Alternative Education Organization
(See Resource Appendix)

Andis Alternative Education Center and Drift Creek Farm for Youth
2204 SR 217, Kitts Hill, OH 45645
Earl Hutchinson, Dir, 614-532-8882,-9068
Lawrence County
Boarding
81-acres; residential services available; voc; natural resources, agri. prod, work & family; lab work in forestry, soil conservation, hydroponic horticulture, food prep, nutrition; CAI.

Special Friends
Box 457, Winchester, OH 45647-0457
Ann Vanorio
Type: home-based

Institute for Democracy in Education
(See Resource Appendix)

River Valley Community School (1982)
8075 State Route 56, Athens, OH 45701-9206
Claudia Shultz, Director, 614-698-6154
Type: independent, non-profit
4 teachers, 67 students, ages 3–12, pre K-6th grade
Affiliations: NAEYC, IDE
Governance by board
Offers continuous developmentally appropriate program through all grades; integrates subject matter through theme; conflict resolution skills, foreign languages, fine arts, movement; no letter grades; multi-aged classes; extensive field trips; rural location; interns accepted.

Attention Alternate Learning Program
1850 Spenceville Rd, Lima, OH 45805
Sandra J Monfort, Dir, 419-227-5531
Type: public at-risk
6-12th grade
Entrance by court order
Affiliation: Allen Cty Juvenile Ct's Unruly Dept
One-room schoolhouse model; books and assignments from respective schools; urban location.

Ohio Alternative Education Association
49 E College Ave, Springfield, OH 54404
Nadine Koogler, State & Fed Prgms

Oklahoma

Project Connect (1989)
6505 E Highway 66, El Reno, OK 73036
Clark McCaskill, Dir, 405-422-2200, FAX: 405-422-2299
Canadian County
Type: public at-risk
3 teachers, 2 assistants, 60 students, ages 15–19, 9–12th grade
Enrollment restricted to potential or actual dropouts; district residency required
Affiliation: Canadian Valley Vo-Tech
Governance by teachers, principal, advisory committee
Teacher qualifications: OK certification
Learning packets; vocational; counseling; adaptive PE; community service; no letter grades; multi-aged classes; suburban location; transportation.

Guthrie Job Corps Center
PO Box 978, Guthrie, OK 73044-0978
Type: Montessori

Children's House of Norman (1971)
606 S Santa Fe, Norman, OK 73069
Marilyn Hammond, Adm, 405-321-1275
Type: Montessori, non-profit; tuition: $125/250/mo
3 teachers, 4 assistants, 80 students, ages 3–6
Affiliation: AMS
Governance by teachers and administrators
Teacher qualifications: Montessori certification
Student-centered environment; developmentally appropriate activities; childcare; suburban location; interns accepted.

Home Educators Resource Organization (1993)
475 College, Norman, OK 73069
Lynne M. Keller, Coord, 405-321-6423
Cleveland County
Non-profit
12 teachers, 26 students, ages infant-17, pre K–12th grade
Governance by parent cooperative
Student newspaper; resource center; field trips; urban location

Normal Public Schools ASE
110 Eufaula St, Norman, OK 73069
Rayma Massey, 405-366-5797

Saxon Publishers, Inc
(See Resource Appendix)

Southwind Montessori, Inc (1982)
1601 Imhoff, Norman, OK 73072
Carol Zerboni, Owner/Prin, 405-364-2772
3 teachers, 4 assistants, 50 students, ages 3-6
Governance by an administrator

Emerson School
715 N Walker, Oklahoma City, OK 73102
Ann Allen, 405-232-5273

Pathways Child Development Center
1901 N Douglas Ave, Oklahoma City, OK 73106-4263
Mary Ann Heard
Type: Montessori

Southwest Montessori Early Learn
5419 S Western Ave, Oklahoma City, OK 73109-4506

The Rainbow Fleet
4305 Meadow Oak, Oklahoma City, OK 73110
Alfreda Little
Type: Montessori

Westminster Day School
4400 N Shartel Ave, Oklahoma City, OK 73118-6400
Type: Montessori

Northwest Montessori Preschool
13417 Inverness Ave, Oklahoma City, OK 73120-8512

OK Central Home Educators Consociation
PO Box 270601, OKC, OK 73137

Casaday School-Primary Division
PO Box 20390, Oklahoma City, OK 73156-0390
Type: Montessori

Moore Public Schools
400 N Broadway, Moore, OK 73160
Earl Capps

Oak Hall Montessori (1971)
401 3rd St NW, Ardmore, OK 73401
Bettye Brown, Vicki Smith or Ginny Little, 405-223-1244
Non-profit; tuition: $120/mo
3 teachers, 3 assistants, 52 students, ages 3-9
Affiliation: Episcopal Diocese of OK; accreditation: AMS
Governance by administrator, board of trustees
In-depth geography study; art; cooking; childcare; urban location; interns accepted.

Take Two-AES (Alternative Education Services) (1993)
2600 Harris, PO Box 1709, Ardmore, OK 73401
Bob Haynes, Director, 405-226-7680
Carter County
Type: public at-risk
5 teachers, 36 students, ages 16-21, 9–12th grade
Entrance requirements by individual contract; residency required
Affiliation: PS I-19
Governance by teachers, principal, board
Teacher qualifications: state certification
Contracts; intensive core curriculum; multi-aged classes; interns accepted.

Montessori School of Ardmore
401 3rd Ave NW, Ardmore, OK 73401-6106

Cimarron School
419 W Maple, Enid, OK 73701
Amy Cromwell
Type: Montessori

Enid Public Schools
500 Independence, Enid, OK 73701-5693
405-234-5270

Springwater Children's House
4619 W Randolph Ave, Enid, OK 73703-3442
Type: Montessori

Woodward Public Schools
PO Box 668, Woodward, OK 73802-0668
Jim Hines, 405-256-6063

Montessori Academy
127 S Chickasaw Ave, Bartlesville, OK 74003-2810

Bartlesville Alternative High School
PO Box 1357, Bartlesville, OK 74005
Beverly Teague

Cornerstone
PO Box 2472, Broken Arrow, OK 74013-2472
Paulet Garrett, 918-481-6248
Type: home-based
Everyone welcome.

Alternative Learning
200 N Caves, Claremore, OK 74017
918 341 8292

Fail-Safe
PO Box 1609, Cushing, OK 74023
918-225-6622

Jenks Alternative Center
205 E B Street, Jenks, OK 74037
Ben Ferem, 918-299-4415

Bartlett Alternative School
1025 E Grayson, Sapulpa, OK 74066
Susan Wheeler, Prin, 918-224-7958, FAX: 918-227-3287
Creek County
Type: public choice
4 teachers, 30 students, ages 14-21, 9–12th grade
Residency required
Governance by board
Teacher qualifications: certification
Basic skills; emphasis on self-esteem, study skills, socially appropriate problem solving, conflict resolution; behavior management; extensive field trips; multi-aged classes; interns accepted.

Sapulpa Public Schools
1 S Mission, Sapulpa, OK 74066
Susan Wheeler, 918-224-3400

Lincoln Alternative School
215 E 12th, Stillwater, OK 74074
405-743-6331

Booker T. Washington High School
1631 E Woodrow Place, Tulsa, OK 74106
James Furch, 918-428-6000
ISD 1
Type: magnet
9–12th grade
Multi-cultural; IB.

Carver Middle School
624 E Oklahoma Place, Tulsa, OK 74106
Bobbie Johnson, 918-587-5583
ISD 1

Type: magnet
6-8th grade
Multi-cultural; multi-age grouping.

Emerson Elementary
909 N Boston, Tulsa, OK 74106
Catherine Frederick, 918-583-5808
ISD 1
Type: Montessori magnet
K-5th grade
Open classroom; ungraded; individualized.

Street School
1135 S Yale, Tulsa, OK 74112
Mitch Dittus, 918-834-4300
Type: independent; tuition: none
90 students, mainly at-risk, ages 13-19
Goal setting behavior modification; drug/alcohol prevention;
   life skills program.

Cornerstone
1148 S Owasso Av, Tulsa, OK 74120
Type: home-based

Margaret Hudson Program (1968)
1205 W Newton, Tulsa, OK 74127
Jan L. Figart, Exec Dir, 918-585-8163, FAX: 592-2368
Osage County
Type: public at-risk
13 teachers, 400 students, ages 11-21, 6-12th grade
Enrollment restricted to pregnant or parenting teens; resi-
   dency required
Governance by board
Teacher qualifications: OK Certification
Health, social services; 3 sites: Tulsa, Broken Arrow, Owano;
   multi-aged classes; interns accepted.

Pershing Center
1903A W Easton, Tulsa, OK 74127
Tom McGuire, 918-585-2065

Project 12 (1970)
1205 W Newton, Tulsa, OK 74127
Farryl Stokes, Coord, 918-587-8133
Tulsa County
Type: public choice
8 teachers, 150 students, ages 16-21, 9-12th grade
District residency required
Governance by teachers and principal
Teacher qualifications: OK Certification
HS diploma program for former dropouts; urban location;
   transportation; interns accepted.

Montessori Academy
4018 S Oswego Ave, Tulsa, OK 74135-2431
Judith Billings

Undercroft Montessori School (1964)
3745 S Huds, Tulsa, OK 74135-5604
M. LeAnn Huxall, Adm, 918-622-2890
Non-profit; tuition: $1,880-3,660/yr
6 teachers, 5 assistants, 111 students, ages 3-12
Entrance requirements: elementary, Montessori experience
Affiliation: AMS
Governance by administrator, board
Fine arts; located near major expressway; childcare; urban
   location; interns accepted.

STAR (Student Training and Re-entry) Program (1988)
3420 S Memorial, Tulsa, OK 74145
Dr Leslie Hale, Coord, 918-627-7200, FAX: 627-9499
Tulsa County
Type: public at-risk
1 teacher, 150 students, ages 14-21
County residency required; not under suspension
Affiliation: Tulsa Technology Center
Governance by principal
Teacher qualifications: MA, certification, experience
Follow up for 5 years; scholarships for vocational training;
   multi-aged classes; urban location; interns accepted.

Oklahoma Christian Home Educators Association
PO Box 471032, Tulsa, OK 74147-1032

Muskogee Public Schools
570 N 6th St, Muskogee, OK 74401-6009
918-684-3700

Talequah Public Schools
PO Box 517, Talequah, OK 74465
Mr Wilson, 918-458-4100

Wagoner Public Schools
PO Box 707, Wagoner, OK 74467
David Harlow, 918-485-9539

Washington Alternative School
326 N Union, Shawnee, OK 74801
John Wilson, 405-273-0653

Learning All Ways
(See Resource Appendix)

Wewoka Public Schools
PO Box 870, Wewoka, OK 74884
Bill Bentley, 405-257-6404

Sallisaw Public Schools
211 S Main, Sallisaw, OK 74955
918-775-9482

Oregon

SAGE School (1992)
19701 S Beavercreek Rd, Oregon City, OR 97004
Barbara Markwell or Ron McMurry, Tchs, 503-650-6600
Type: public at-risk
2 teachers, 60 students, ages 14-21, 9-12th grade
Entrance requirement: min 4th grade reading level
Affiliation: Oregon City District
Governance by faculty
Diploma; GED; outcome-based; portfolios; contracts for
   interdisciplinary projects; non-compulsory class atten-
   dance; multi-aged classes; suburban location; interns
   accepted.

Oregon Home Education Network (1991)
4470 SW Hall Blvd #286, Beaverton, OR 97005
Ann Lahrson, Coord, 503-321-5166

LUNO (Learning Unlimited Network of Oregon) (1985)
31960 SE Chin St, Boring, OR 97009
Gene Lehman, 503-663-5153
Clackamas County
Type: independent
Inclusive; Phonetic Fun for Everyone; non-compulsory
   ungoverned class attendance.

Alternative Choices in Education (1988)
721 SW 4th, Canby, OR 97013
Jim Gadberry, Prin or Marcia Parker, 503-266-7861
Type: public choice
1 teacher, 45–50 students, mainly at-risk, ages 14–18, 9–12th
    grade
Tutorial; study skills; self-esteem; rewards for grades and
    attendance.

Sunnyside Montessori Center
12011 SE Sunnyside Rd, Clackamas, OR 97015-9312
Durward Gurusinghe

Westport Alternative Program
Hwy 30, Clatskanie, OR 97016
Les Openlander, 503-455-2282
Columbia Co District
Type: public at-risk
1 teacher, 3 assistants, 15 students, ages 14–19, HS
Placement from 3 schools; each supplies curriculum.

North Columbia Learning Center (1989)
F.I. Tagg School, Hwy 30, Westport, OR 97016
Les Oppenlander, 503-455-2282
Columbia District, Columbia County
Type: public at-risk
1 teacher, 2 assistants, 25–30 students, ages 15–21, HS
Accreditation: NW Assn
Special needs; counseling; work-study; drug prevention,
    intervention; prevocational, vocational skills.

Colton Regional Learning Center (1993)
30205 S Wall St, Colton, OR 97017
Pat Gentry, Coord, 503-824-4495
Tuition: variable, scholarships
1 teacher, 35 students, ages 14+, 8th grade-college
Governance by input from all parties
Work experience; home study; credit options; multi-aged
    classes; non-compulsory class attendance; rural location;
    interns accepted.

Estacada District Secondary Alternative Program (1992)
PO Box 519, Estacada, OR 97023
Sharles M Smith, LSW, 503-630-8599
Type: public at-risk
1 teacher, 24 students, ages 14–19, 9–12th grade
GED; diploma; HS/CC transition; leadership, recovery, and
    management skills.

Timber Lake Job Corps CCC (1964)
59868 E Hwy 224, Estacada, OR 97023
Juanita Morin, Mgr, 503-834-2291
Type: public at-risk, boarding
7 teachers, 234 students, ages 16–21
Intensive; voc and life skills; GED/diploma.

Mt Hood Academy (1985)
PO Box 189, Government Camp, OR 97028
Mary M Gunesch, 503-272-3503
Type: independent, non-profit
4 teachers, 23 students, ages 14–18, 9–12th grade
College-prep for nationally-ranked ski racers; student-
    athletes travel 4–6 weeks each winter.

**ALPHA: Alternative Learning Program for High
    Achievement** (1980)
150 W Powell, Gresham, OR 97030
Mark L Sherman, Prin, 503-661-0422
E Multnomah County
Type: public at-risk
5 teachers, 75 students, ages 14–19
Enrollment restricted to referrals; county residency required
Governance by democratic school meeting, board
Teacher qualifications: state certification
Serves 7 districts; community-based work experience,
    diploma programs; suburban location.

Hall School Montessori (1984)
2505 NE 23rd, Gresham, OR 97030
Debra Clark, Doug Shivers and Diane Ingle, Teachers, 503-661-
    6330
Type: public choice
3 teachers, 100 students, ages 3–9
Enrollment by parental request
Affiliations: NEA, OEA
Governance by teachers and administrators
Suburban location; interns accepted.

Morningstar Montessori House
PO Box 401, Gresham, OR 97030-0075

Opportunity School (1977)
PO Box 920, Hood River, OR 97031
Blakely/Foster, 503-387-5025
Type: public at-risk
1 teacher, 22 students, ages 14–18
Entrance by recommendation.
Accreditation: NW Assn
Problem solving, communication, life skills; work experience;
    GED or regular diploma; students own, operate own
    company.

Waucoma School (1991)
2115 Avalon Way, Hood River, OR 97031
Linda Short, Assembly Member, 503-386-2038
Type: independent, non-profit
Student ages 5–19
Governance by democratic school meeting
Teacher qualifications: elected by school meeeting
Modeled after Sudbury Valley School; reorganizing; no letter
    grades; non-compulsory class attendance; multi-aged
    classes; extensive field trips; rural location.

Lakeridge HS Alternative Program (1975)
PO Box 739, Lake Oswego, OR 97034
Jack DePue, Coord, 503-635-0319, FAX: 503-635-9495
Clackamas County
Type: public choice
1 teacher, 30 students, mainly at-risk, ages 15–21, 10–12th
    grade
Entrance requirements: average or above IQ, HS reading level,
    no violent discipline problem, residency
Governance by principal, teachers
Teacher qualifications: OR certification
Democratic classroom; student-initiated; self-motivation

Molalla High School Alternative Education Program
    (1992)
413 Molalla Ave, PO Box 188, Molalla, OR 97038
Chris Nuffer, 503-829-2351 x37
U-4 District
Type: public at-risk
150 students, ages 14–20, 9–12th grade
Entrance requirements: referral, interview, district residency.
GED; HS credit, diploma; substance abuse counseling; work/
    study; career development.

Adult High School Diploma (1966)
19600 S Molalla Ave, Oregon City, OR 97045
Carol J Evans, 503-657-6958 x2444 or x2315
Type: public choice
8 teachers, 100 students, ages 16+
Affiliation: Clackamas CC
High school diploma earned on basis of transcripts, credits
    earned at college, and work/life experience.

**Alternative Programs Department
    Clackamas Community College** (1981)
19600 S Molalla Ave, Oregon City, OR 97045
Mary Craren, Dept Chair, 503-657-6958, FAX: 650-6659
Type: public at-risk
11 teachers, 150 students, ages 15–19
Entrance requirements: HS referral, 5th grade reading ability,
    residency

Governance by teachers, department chair, administration
Teacher qualifications: MA or BA, experience
Transitions GED, HS credit students to short-term training, HS, jobs, or CC; suburban location.

Crossroads Alternative School (1971)
724 Molalla Ave; PO Box 348, Oregon City, OR 97045
Jacy Zarosinski, 503-655-2755
Type: public choice
3 teachers, 35 students, 7-12th grade
Entrance requires referral.
Basic skills; self-esteem; problem solving; critical thinking; counseling.

Parrott Creek School/Canby Union Annex (1971)
22518 S Parrott Creek Rd, Oregon City, OR 97045
Bill Shapiro or Lonnie Shumaker, 503-655-9144
Type: independent, non-profit
1 teacher, 21 students, mainly at-risk, ages 14-18, 8-12th grade
Tutorial; GED prep.

Select Alternative Growth Experience (1992)
19701 S Beavercreek Rd, Oregon City, OR 97045
Barb Markwell or Jim Ryan, 503-657-6600
Type: public at-risk
2 teachers, 25 students, mainly at-risk, ages 15-21, 9-12th grade
Entrance requirements: interview, test, referral.
Diploma, voc; emphasis on self-esteem and community.

Tri-City Alternative Program (1980)
19600 S Molalla, Oregon City, OR 97045
Mary Craven, Dept Chair, 503-657-6958 x2414
Type: public at-risk
4 teachers, 250 students, ages 15-18, 9-12th grade
Entrance requirements: referral, interview.
Also at 19140 SE Saint Helens St, Clackamas, OR 97015. Basic skills; GED prep; HS credit; transition to other programs.

Vocational Options Program (1985)
701 John Adams, Oregon City, OR 97045
Michael Watkins, Instructor, 503-655-8220
Clackamas County
Type: public choice
3 teachers, 1 assistant, 40 students, ages 16-21, HS
Entrance requirements: referral, interview
Governance by Clackamas CC
Work experience; job placement.

Young Parent Opportunity Program (1990)
19600 S Molalla, Oregon City, OR 97045
Mary Craven, Coord, 503-657-6958 x2341
Clackamas County
Type: independent at-risk
30 students, mainly at-risk, ages 15-19, HS
Entrance requirements: referral, interviews, assessment, district residency
Governance by Clackamas CC
Employment skills; childcare; transportation.

Youth Adventures, Inc (1990)
15544 S Clackamas River Dr, Oregon City, OR 97045
Marcia McClocklin, Exec Dir, 503-656-8005
Clackamas County
Non-profit
1 teacher, 10 students, mainly at-risk, ages 13-18, 7-12th grade
Enrollment restricted to students referred by local school districts; interview
Accreditation: OR Alliance of Children
Intensive day treatment program.

South Columbia Learning Center (1987)
Deer Island School, Hwy 30, Deer Island, OR 97054
Virginia Mickel, 503-397-0226
Columbia District, Columbia County
Type: public at-risk

1 teacher, 2 assistants, 25-30 students, ages 15-21, HS
Special needs; counseling; work-study; drug prevention, intervention; prevocational, vocational skills.

Alternative Program at Vernonia High School (1982)
299 Bridge St, Vernonia, OR 97064
Ellis D. Mason, 503-429-5891
Vernonia 47J District, Columbia County
Type: public at-risk
6 students, ages 17-18, 10-12th grade
Accreditation: NW Assn
GED; vocational; transportation.

Sun Garden Montessori Center (1981)
2284 Long St, Westlinn, OR 97068
David Cannon, Adm, 508-655-2609
Non-profit; tuition: $240-360/mo
4 teachers, 4 assistants, 95 students, ages 3-9
Accreditation: AMI
Governance by administrator and board
Suburban location; interns accepted.

North Marion Alternative High School (1993)
120 E Lincoln, Woodburn, OR 97071
Mr MacDonald, Tch/Supervisor, 503-981-5331
Type: independent, non-profit
2 teachers, 29 students, mainly at-risk, ages 16-19, 10-12th grade
Min age 16
Affiliation: Chemeketa College
Governance by Chemeketa College, districts
Teacher qualifications: bilingual, certification, experience with at-risk students
Open entry; independent study; diploma; urban location.

Parents Education Association
PO Box 1482, Beaverton, OR 97075
503-693-0724
Type: home-based, PAC

Fire Mountain School (1983)
Box 96, 6505 Elk Flat Rd, Arch Cape, OR 97102
Barbara McLaughlin, Board President, 503-436-2610
Type: independent, non-profit; tuition: $3000, scholarships
3 teachers, 27 students, ages 5-12, K-6th grade
Governance by parent cooperative, board
Cooperative community setting; high priority on self-esteem, love of learning; integrated approach to all subjects; multi-aged classes; no letter grades; rural location.

Tongue Point Job Corps (1972)
Hwy 30, Astoria, OR 97103
Carol Puls, Academic Progs Mgr, 503-325-2131, FAX:-5365
Clatsop County
29 teachers, 530 students, mainly at-risk, ages 16-24
Residency required
Teacher qualifications: state certification
Voc, ed, GED, and diploma programs; no letter grades; rural location; interns accepted.

Forestry Education Assistance Program
Oregon Department of Forestry (1992)
(See Resource Appendix)

Hillsboro Alternative High School
1665 SE Enterprise Circle, Hillsboro, OR 97124
Carol Loughner, Lead Tch, 503-648-2344, FAX: 640-6053
Type: public at-risk
5 teachers, 225 students, ages 14-21, 9-12th grade
Governance by democratic school meeting
Credit make-up; diploma; multi-aged classes; suburban location.

CHOICES: Challenging Holistic Opportunities Individualized in a Cooperative Environment for Success (1992)
800 E 2nd St, McMinnville, OR 97128
Sandy Cameli, Instructor, 503-434-4358, FAX: 472-8778

Type: public at-risk
1 teacher, 30 students, ages 11-14, 6-8th grade
Entrance by district referral; no residency requirement
Governance by board, Educational Services District
Teacher qualifications: Experience with at-risk adolescents
Cooperative learning; heterogeneous grouping; multi-assessment; interdisciplinary; no letter grades; multi-aged classes; rural location; transportation; interns accepted.

Windson Learning Center
1101 Brooks, McMinnville, OR 97128
Karin Schockley, 503-472-4876
Also, homeschooler support.

McMinnville Montessori School
PO Box 372, McMinnville, OR 97128-0372

Tillamook Alternative Education Program
2605 12th St, Tillamook, OR 97141
Julie Widder, Alt Ed Tch, 503-842-2566
Type: public choice
2 teachers, 40 students, ages 14-19, 9-12th grade
District residency required
Governance by principal
Multi-subject classes; voluntary mentoring program; multi-aged classes; rural location.

Italic Handwriting Series
Portland State University
(See Resource Appendix)

North Willamette Homeschoolers
6501 SW Macadam, Portland, OR 97202
503-291-8493

New Deal at Roosevelt High School
6941 N Central, Portland, OR 97203
Diane Green, Coordinator, 503-280-5260
Type: public at-risk
15 students, ages 15-18, 9-12th grade
Enrollment restricted to freshman; recommendation, residency required
Affiliation: Portland Public Schools
Governance by teachers, principal
Teacher qualifications: extensive experience in alternative education environments
Students stay in same group for all classes; modified curriculum; urban location.

Open Meadow Learning Center (1971)
7654 N Crawford, Portland, OR 97203
Carole Smith, Dir, 503-285-0508
Type: independent, non-profit; tuition: by contracts
11 teachers, 84 students, mainly at-risk, ages 13-18, 7-12th grade
Governance by teachers, principal, board
Teacher qualifications: state certification & 4 yrs experience with high risk population
No letter grades; multi-aged classes; urban location.

Greenhouse Alternative High School (1990)
820 SW Oak, Portland, OR 97205
Jay Harris, Prin, 503-239-1247
Type: independent, non-profit
4 teachers, 200 students, mainly at-risk, ages 13-21, 7-12th grade
Restricted to homeless youth with no other academic options or support
Affiliations: Portland Public Schools, Salvation Army
Governance by faculty and student reps
Teacher qualifications: lots of patience and big heart
GED; diploma; emotional, employment skills; Freire, Ilyich, Bruner learning methodologies; youth crisis support: counseling, food, clothing; non-compulsory class attendance; multi-aged classes; extensive field trips; urban location; transportation; interns accepted.

Montessori School of Portland
6148 SE Holgate Blvd, Portland, OR 97206-4739

Metropolitan Learning Center
2033 NW Glisan St, Portland, OR 97209
Patrick Burk, 503-280-5737
Type: magnet
K-12th grade

Childpeace Montessori School
105 NW Park Ave, Portland, OR 97209-3315
Sue Pritzker

Oregon Christian Home Educators Association Network (OCEAN)
2515 NE 37th St, Portland, OR 97212
503-288-1285
Type: state home-based

Portland Night High School (1973)
2245 NE 36th Ave, Portland, OR 97212
David Mesirow, Dir, 503-280-6486, FAX: 503-280-5673
Type: public at-risk
5 teachers, 100 students, ages 16-20
Entrance requirements: working, close to graduation; no residency requirement
Governance by teachers, director
Teacher qualifications: state certification
Diploma; GED; staff/students determine appropriate course work; CAI; job preparation; no letter grades; multi-aged classes; urban location; interns accepted.

Montessori Education Center of Oregon
4370 NE Halsey #218, Portland, OR 97213
Type: Montessori teacher education

Portland Waldorf School
109 NE 50th Ave, Portland, OR 97213
John Miles, Administrator, 503-234-9660, FAX:-6206
Multnomah County
Non-profit; tuition: $4,620/yr, scholarships
25 teachers, 234 students, ages 3-15, pre K-8th grade
Entrance requirement: interviews
Affiliation: AWSNA; OFIS
Governance by college of teachers
Teacher qualifications: Waldorf training
Community enrichment courses; extensive field trips; urban location; interns accepted.

Providence Montessori School
830 NE 47th Ave, Portland, OR 97213-2212

Buckman Elementary
320 SE 16th Ave, Portland, OR 97214
Candice Beck, 503-280-6230
Type: magnet
K-5th grade
Arts.

Sunnyside Mennonite Montessori
1312 SE 35th Ave, Portland, OR 97214-4236

Jefferson High School
5210 N Kerby Ave, Portland, OR 97217
Alcena Boozer, 503-280-5180
Type: magnet
9-12th grade
Performing arts; TV production.

Child's View Montessori (1988)
4729 SW Taylors Ferry Rd, Portland, OR 97219
Tamara Lacey, 503-293-9422
Tuition: $210-415/mo
3 teachers, 3 assistants, 49 students, ages 3-6
Entrance requirements: min age 2.5, toilet-trained
Affiliations: NAEYC, NAMTA, OFIS, OMA
Governance by administrator

Strong emphasis on peace, acceptance/respect, caring for the world, and building self-esteem; suburban location; interns accepted.

West Hills Montessori School
4920 SW Vermont St, Portland, OR 97219
Anne Blickenstaff

Portland Community College
PO Box 19000, Portland, OR 97219-0990
Cathy Howard, Counselor/Advisor, 503-244-6111, FAX: 503-452-4947
Type: higher education, mainly at-risk, ages 16+
Residency required
Governance by college
Teacher qualifications: college degree, preferably Masters
Concurrent college, HS credits; students pay college tuition; multi-aged classes; suburban location.

The Teaching Home
(See Resource Appendix)

Raleigh Hills Montessori
4909 SW Shattuck Rd, Portland, OR 97221-2945

People Assisting the Challenge of Home-Study
PO Box 82415, Portland, OR 97282

SAIL Program (1980)
11300 SE 23rd Ave, Milwaukie, OR 97222
Lois Rutkin, 503-653-3754
North Clackamas 12 District
Type: public at-risk
15-20 students, ages 14-19, 9-12th grade
Entrance requirements: IEP, evaluation.
Weekly evaluation; daily group sessions, individual counseling.

Cascade Valley School
13515 A SE Rusk Rd, Portland, OR 97222-3230
Cary Brown, staff member, 503-653-8128
Clackamas County
Type: independent, non-profit; tuition: $3500/yr, $2700, $1500 subsequent
7 teachers, 24 students, ages 4-18, ungraded
Open enrollment ages 4-19.
Entire community is governed democratically; curriculum not pre-set, individually determined, with students experiencing the full consequences of making their own decisions; teachers elected by school meeting yearly; no letter grades; multi-aged classes; extensive field trips; non-compulsory class attendance; suburban location.

Montessori School of Beaverton (1977)
PO Box 25021, Portland, OR 97225
Peter Davidson, Adm, 503-645-5247
Non-profit; tuition: $2,100-3,650/yr
6 teachers, 6 assistants, 145 students, ages 3-12
Entrance requirements: ages 3-6, toilet trained; elementary, Montessori experience
Affiliations: ORMA, ORFIS; accreditation: AMI
Governance by a board of trustees
Environmental ed includes nature studies, conservation of daily resources, recycling, composting, student-led fundraising for old-growth forest preservation; suburban location; interns accepted.

Franciscan Montessori Earth School (1977)
14030 NE Sacramento St, Portland, OR 97230
M. Cardew
Tuition: $2,210-4,493/yr
22 teachers, 15 assistants, 366 students, ages 3-18
Previous Montessori required for ages 6+
Affiliations: AMI, FISA, ORDE; accreditation: AMI
Governance by administrator
Childcare; urban location; interns accepted.

Multnomah Elementary & Middle School (1984)
2508 NE Everett St, Portland, OR 97232
503-234-1363, FAX: 503-257-1519

Analyne Flanagan, Supervisor or Kevin LaVacque, Tch
Type: public at-risk
5 teachers, 44 students, ages 6-14, 1-8th grade
Enrollment restricted to Special Education, SED; county residency
Governance by special education/public school regulations
Teacher qualifications: OR Handicapped Learner's Certification
Highly structured; behavior constantly monitored, extensive rewards; individualized; no letter grades; multi-aged classes; urban location; transportation.

Centennial Learning Center
14750 SE Clinton, Portland, OR 97236
Darrel Dyer, 503-251-2202, FAX: 503-760-7990
Type: public at-risk
2 teachers, 26 students, 7-10th grade
Enrollment restricted to referrals
Governance by board
Teacher qualifications: state certification
Certificate of Initial Mastery; multi-aged classes; field trips; suburban location; transportation; interns accepted.

AIM High School (1976)
10822 SE Bush, Portland, OR 97266
Dr Don E O'Neill, Dir, 503-256-6530, 252-2900 x530
David Douglas District
Type: public at-risk; tuition: $15, or $601 out of district
12 teachers, 253 students, ages 13-20, 8-12th grade
Entrance requirements: application, screening, residency
Governance by teachers, principal
Teacher qualifications: state certification
Family approach; vocational; extensive sports; outdoor work experience; diploma; multi-aged classes; extensive field trips; suburban location; transportation.

Oliver P Lent Elementary School
5105 SE 97th Ave, Portland, OR 97266-3799
Type: Montessori

AIM (1979)
14211 SE Johnson Rd, Milwaukie, OR 97267
Roger Rolen, 503-653-3812
North Clackamas 12 District
Type: public at-risk
2 teachers, 100 students, ages 14-15, 9-10th grade
Entrance requirement: poor school attendance.
Two periods/day+classes at home HS.

Owen Sabin Occupational Skills Center (1982)
14211 SE Johnson Rd, Milwaukie, OR 97267
Ron Dextor, Dir, 503-653-3812
North Clackamas 12 District
Type: public choice
2 teachers, 45 students, ages 16-18, 9-10th grade
GED; AIM; CAI.

Putnam High School-SAIL Program (1981)
4950 SE Roethe, MIlwaukie, OR 97267
David Ware, 503-653-3794
N Clackamas District 2
Type: public at-risk
15-20 students, ages 14-19, 9-12th grade
Entrance requirements: IEP, team review and approval.
Weekly goal setting and evaluation; daily group sessions; counseling.

SAIL Program (1980)
13801 SE Webster Rd, Milwaukie, OR 97267
Paul Geller, 503-653-3732
Type: public at-risk
15-20 students, ages 14-19, 9-12th grade

People Assisting the Challenge of Home Study
PO Box 82415, Portland, OR 97282

Homeschooling in Oregon, the Handbook
(See Resource Appendix)

Montessori Children's House
600 State St, Salem, OR 97301-3848

National Home Education Research Institute
(See Resource Appendix)

HELP-Salem
2850 Vibbert St S, Salem, OR 97302
503-370-9534

The Downtown Learning Center (1987)
360 Commercial St, Salem, OR 97302
Jim Hindman, Mgr, 503-399-3421, FAX: 503-399-3407
Type: public at-risk
10 teachers, 250 students, ages 16+
Entrance requirements: referral, interview; no residency requirement
Governance by board
Teacher qualifications: state certification
Partnership between public school system, CC, JTPA; HS credit; GED; multi-aged classes; urban location.

Waldo Helping Everyone Experience Learning (WHEEL) at Waldo MS
2805 Lansing Ave NE, Salem, OR 97303
Anthony Stamper, Tch, 503-399-3215
Type: public choice
58 teachers, 1000+ students, ages 12-15, 7-8th grade
Entrance requirements: completed 6th grade, no residency requirement
Independent study skills; service learning projects; tutoring; camp cleanup; cooperative community activities

MECCA at McKay High School (1992)
2440 Lancaster Dr, Salem, OR 97305
John Neal, Asst Prin, 503-399-3080
Type: public choice
1 teacher, 37 students, mainly at-risk, ages 16-20, 11-12th grade
Entrance requirements: counselor's recommendation, residency
Governance by teachers, principal
Teacher qualifications: state certification
Self-paced; career research/job shadowing; no letter grades; urban location; transportation.

SERVE at McKay High School (1992)
2440 Lancaster Dr, Salem, OR 97305
John Neal, Asst Prin, 503-399-3080
Type: public choice
1 teacher, 20 students, mainly at-risk, ages 14-16, 9-10th grade
Entrance requirements: counselor's recommendation, residency
Governance by teachers, principal
Teacher qualifications: state certification
Self-paced; community service; no letter grades; extensive field trips; urban location; transportation.

Salem Emotional Growth Center
3780 Cavalier S, Salem, OR 97309
Steve Rosen, 503-399-3499
Type: public at-risk
40 students, HS
Social skills; coping with depression; emotional education; conflict resolution; relationships; psychology; student-run small business.

Community Services Consortium's Learning Opportunities Center (1980)
2225 Pacific Blvd SE, Republic Plaza #201, Albany, OR 97321
Pat Zsyett, Employment Specialist, 503-928-6335, FAX: 967-9307
Type: public at-risk
4 teachers, 60+ students, ages 14-21
Enrollment restricted to economically disadvantaged, basic skills deficient students; residency required
Affiliation: JTPA
Governance by board
Teacher qualifications: state certification.

Located in urban, suburban and rural settings; vocational, communication skills; non-compulsory class attendance; multi-aged classes; transportation; interns accepted.

Linn-Benton Community College Adult Basic Education/GED Program (1967)
6500 SW Pacific Blvd, Albany, OR 97321
Candy Johnson, 503-967-8836
Type: public choice
4 teachers, 1,800 students, ages 16+
Open-entry/exit; small groups; basic skills; ESL.

Albany Montessori School
PO Box 1844, Albany, OR 97321-0502

Philomath Montessori School (1984)
1123 Main St, Philomath, OR 97324
Pauline Tanaka, Adm, 503-929-2672
Tuition: $1,500-1,850/yr
1 teacher, 1 assistant, 24 students, ages 3-6
Entrance requirements: toilet trained
Affiliations: AMI, NAMTA, OR MA
Governance by an administrator
Rural location; interns accepted.

Cooperative Work Experience, Parenteen, Options in Education (1990)
836 NW 11th St, Corvallis, OR 97330
Cherie Baker, Facilitator, 503-757-5871
Corvallis 509J District
Type: public choice/at-risk
12 students, ages 14-20, 9-12th grade
District residency required
Affiliation: Corvallis HS
Supportive problem-solving; vocational exploration; parenting; community agency access; decision making; communication skills; stress management; work experience.

Corvallis Montessori School
1240 NW 27th St, Corvallis, OR 97330
Cathryn Kasper

Aleph Montessori Children's House
437 NW 6th St, Corvallis, OR 97330-6424

Options Plus/Positive Approach to Career and Education (1984)
545 SW 2nd St Suite A, Corvallis, OR 97333
Skybird, Instructor or Sarah Jordan, Adm, 503-752-1010
Corvallis 509J District
Type: public at-risk
1 teacher, 42 students, ages 14-21, 9-12th grade
Entrance requirements: referral, JTPA eligibility
Affiliation: Community Services Consortium
Pre-employment training; life skills; external experiences; individualized; GED; diploma.

OPTIONS (1981)
316 Main St, Dallas, OR 97338
Fred R Ott, Dir/Tch, 503-623-7889
Dallas District
Type: public at-risk
1 teacher, 50 students, ages 13-21, 7-12th grade
Residency required
Governance by teachers, principal, board
Teacher qualifications: prefer Master's (SE)
HS credits; GED; life, job hunting skills; counseling; multi-aged classes; urban location; transportation.

Lincoln City Montessori School
4094 NE Hwy 101, Lincoln City, OR 97367-5069

Philomath High School (1987)
2054 Applegate St, PO Box 391, Philomath, OR 97370
Nels Thompson, Prin or Marlene McDonald, Instructor, 503-929-3211
Type: public at-risk
1 teacher, 30-35 students, ages 14-18, 9-12th grade

Entrance requirements: credit-deficiency, inability to work in regular classroom.
Self-contained classroom with individual student courses; counseling; GED.

West Valley Academy
PO Box 127, Sheridan, OR 97378
Jan Davidson, Exec Dir, 503-843-4123, FAX: 503-843-2080
Type: public at-risk; tuition: $4,000/yr, scholarships
18 teachers, 85 students, partly at-risk, ages 5–19, K–12th grade
No residency requirement
Affiliations: OR DE, OR Mental Health Dept
Governance by teachers, principal
Teacher qualifications: Master's in specialized areas
Intervention; diversion; remediation; diagnostic testing; counseling; workshop; written evaluations; Intelligence Education Training; active parental participation; multi-aged classes; extensive field trips; rural location; transportation; interns accepted.

Santiam Montessori
171 W Locust St, Stayton, OR 97383-1667

Leonardo da Vinci Middle School (1987)
850 Howard Ave, Eugene, OR 97401
Michael Caley, Jill Heyerly or Tim Whitely, 503-687-3224
Type: public choice
6 teachers, 168 students, ages 11–14, 6–8th grade
Enrollment based on application, orientation, space available, lottery; residency required
Governance by teachers, principal
Teacher qualifications: state certification
Educational technology; committed to success of all; suburban location.

Looking Glass Educational Services
44 W Broadway Suite 501, Eugene, OR 97401
Galen Phipps, Dir, 503-686-2688
Type: independent
4 teachers, mainly at-risk, ages 11–18, 5–12th grade
For residents of Looking Glass Shelter and Crisis Center
Governance by teachers, principal
Teacher qualifications: state certification
Basic academics, psychology, sex ed and life skills; no letter grades; multi-aged classes; urban location; interns accepted.

Eugene Montessori School
2255 Oakmont Way, Eugene, OR 97401-5554
Ethel Barclay

Lane School
1200 Hwy 99 N, Eugene, OR 97402
Dr Michael George, Supervisor, 503-334-4796, FAX: 503-688-4015
Type: public at-risk
3 teachers, 28 students, ages 12–17, 6–12th grade
Entrance requirements: severe behavior problems and emotional disturbance, IEP, Lane Co district referral, residency
Governance by teachers, principal
Teacher qualifications: state certification (HLE)
Short-term; remedial; educational-behavioral model for teaching pro-social behaviors; urban location; interns accepted.

Patterson Family School
1510 W 15th, Eugene, OR 97402
Kay Mehas, 503-687-3406
Type: magnet
K–5th grade

Alternative Kindergarten
1150 E 29th Ave, Eugene, OR 97403
George Wilhelmr, 503-687-3286
Type: magnet

Pioneer Montessori Children's House
1639 E 19th Ave, Eugene, OR 97403-1902

Corridor Elementary Alternative School
250 Silver Ln, Eugene, OR 97404
Judy Sobba, Prin, 503-687-3165
4J District
Type: public choice
12 teachers, 240 students, ages 5–11, K–5th grade
Enrollment by lottery; district residency required
Governance by teachers, principal
Teacher qualifications: state certification
Team planning; thematic units; large group performance in community (drama, music, juggling); staff with special skill areas; parental involvement; multi-aged classes; suburban location; interns accepted.

Drinking Gourd Elementary School (1991)
2809 Shirley St, Eugene, OR 97404
Tricia Whitney, Dir, 503-461-4570
Type: independent; tuition: $300/mo, 2 half scholarships for minorities
1 teacher, 10 students, ages 5–8, ungraded
Director runs business and decides curriculum; students decide social concerns in consensus class meetings; success-based curriculum; anti-bias approach; conflict resolution skills; cooperative learning; no letter grades; multi-aged classes; suburban location; interns accepted.

Traditional Alternative School
950 W 22nd Ave, Eugene, OR 97404
Penny McDonlad, 503-687-3475
Type: magnet
K–5th grade

Eastside Alternative School
2855 Lincoln St, Eugene, OR 97405
Ted Calhoun, 503-687-3375
Type: magnet
1–5th grade
Non-graded; continuous progress.

Eugene Waldorf School (1980)
1350 McLean Blvd, Eugene, OR 97405
Holly Tracy, Business Mgr, 503-683-6951
Lane County
Non-profit; tuition: $2,850-3,900/yr, scholarships
33 teachers, 253 students, ages 4–17, K–12th grade
Entrance requirements: interview
Governance by college of teachers
Teacher qualifications: 2-yr Waldorf training
Suburban location; interns accepted.

Magnet Arts Alternative School
1620 W 22nd Ave, Eugene, OR 97405
Bob Bolden, 503-687-3331
K–5th grade

Willamette Homeschoolers (early 80s)
245 W 27th Ave, Eugene, OR 97405
Jill Hubbard, 503-344-4956
Lane County
Student ages infant-18
40 families; inclusive; activities; park days.

Children's House
585 Douglas Ave Box 1214, Bandon, OR 97411
Donna Leveridge-Campbell
Type: Montessori

BHHS Alternative Program (1992)
564 Fern Ave, Brookings, OR 97415
Don Bryant, 503-469-2108
Brookings-Harbor 17C District, Curry County
Type: public at-risk
55-95 students, ages 14–19, HS
Enrollment by approval of principal and counselor.
Accreditation: NW Assn
Night school; private training, educational service; home tutoring; work experience.

Camas Valley
PO Box 57, Camas Valley, OR 97416
Robert E. Kloss, 503-445-2131
Camas Valley 21 District, Douglas County
Type: public choice
6 teachers, 25 students, ages 18-21, HS
Entrance requirement: over age16
Accreditation: NW Assn
ND DE correspondence courses.

Eugene International High School (1984)
400 E 19th, Eugene, OR 97419
Jon Doornink, Head Tch, 503-687-3115
Type: public choice
25 teachers, 952 students, ages 14-18, 9-12th grade
Request enrollment prior to March 15; residency required
Affiliation: IB
Governance by site-based policy council
Teacher qualifications: state certification
School within a school; interdisciplinary; based on Socratic
    method; global perspective; option to earn IB; multi-aged
    classes; urban location; interns accepted.

Belloni on Campus (1978)
3599 3rd St, Coos Bay, OR 97420
Paul Huzefka, 503-269-5444
Type: public at-risk
1 teacher, 1 assistant, 18 students, ages 13-18, 7-12th grade
Accreditation: NW Assn
Close monitoring.

Bridge Program (1986)
10th & Ingersoll, Coos Bay, OR 97420
Joan Johnson, 503-267-3104 x281
Type: public at-risk
1 teacher, 1 assistant, 20 students, ages 14-17, 9th grade
Accreditation: NW Assn
Self-esteem; social skills; responsibility; school store.

Englewood Learning Center, CE 2
1400 Pennsylvania Ave, Coos Bay, OR 97420
Bob Lockridge, Adm, 503-267-3104 x228
Type: public at-risk
2 teachers, 1 assistant, 100 students, ages 16-19, HS
Entrance requirements: recommendation, interview, review
Accreditation: NW Assn; ODE Standardization
Individualized; workbooks; mini-courses; CAI; contracts.

Psychology of Success at Marshfield High School
10th & Ingersoll, Coos Bay, OR 97420
Les Engle, 503-267-3104 x265
Coos Bay District, Coos County
Type: public choice
1 teacher, 102 students, ages 14-19, HS
Required elective class.
Accreditation: NW Assn
Required elective class; making choices; positive attitudes;
    self-esteem; personal power.

The Upstairs School
  Alternative Youth Activities, Inc (1981)
575 S Main St, Coos Bay, OR 97420
Norman A. Welch, 503-888-2543
Coos County
Type: independent, non-profit
5 teachers, 2 assistants, 105 students, mainly at-risk, ages
    12-18, 7-12th grade
Counseling; self-paced; tutoring; life skills; nutrition instruc-
    tion for young parents.

Aprovecho Research Center (1978)
80574 Hazelton Rd, Cottage Grove, OR 97424
503-942-8198
Non-profit; tuition: $300/mo, scholarships
5 teachers, 6 students
Enrollment restricted to college students or graduates
Governance by board

Teacher qualifications: Experts in their field
Internships in appropriate technology, sustainable forestry,
    organic farming; interns accepted.

Willamette Valley Montessori School
PO Box 11470, Eugene, OR 97440-3670

Glendale Alternative Program School District 77 (1993)
PO Box E, Glendale, OR 97442
Robert C. Wallauer, 503-832-2171
Douglas County
Type: public at-risk; tuition: District funded
1 teacher, 20 students, ages 16-28, 11-12th grade
Enrollment restricted to ages 16+ and in 3rd year of HS; tran-
    scripts required
Tutorial program and/or project approach.

Glide High School (1992)
18990 N Umpqua Hwy, Glide, OR 97443
Sharon Briggs, 503-496-3554
Glide 12 District, Douglas County
Type: public at-risk
Student age 15, HS
Priority given to Glide HS students.
Accreditation: NW Assn
Learning packets; students meet with administrators for
    assistance, to turn in work.

Wolf Creek Job Corps (1965)
2010 Opportunity Ln, Glide, OR 97443
John Voltz, Prin, 503-496-3507
Douglas County
Type: public choice
15 teachers, 250 students, ages 16-22
Sign up through Job Corps screeners; must meet DOL
    program requirements.
Accreditation: NW Assn
Vocational training, union programs, and basic education for
    disadvantaged youth.

SOCRATES (1989)
PO Box 1485, Gold Beach, OR 97444
Rick Foertsch, 503-247-4140, 469-2650, 469-0873
Curry County
Type: independent, non-profit
2 teachers, 75-100 students, mainly at-risk, ages 14-21, HS
3 sites; open-entry; self-paced; occupational skills; parenting.

South Umpqua Alternative Center (1992)
140 SW Chadwick, Myrtle Creek, OR 97457
Carol Hilderbrand, 503-863-5896
South Umpqua District, Douglas County
Type: public at-risk
1 teacher, 40 students, ages 14-20, HS
Entrance requirements: application, interview
Accreditation: NW Assn
Develop positive skills, personal well-being, educational,
    career success.

The Opportunity Center
Myrtle Creek, OR 97457
Carol Hildebrand, Dir, 503-863-5846, FAX: 863-5486
Type: public at-risk; scholarships
1 teacher, 30 students, ages 16-21, 11-12th grade
Enrollment restricted to at-risk residents
Affiliation: S Umpqua HS
Governance by principal and board
Teacher qualifications: experience
GED; self-paced; classes and childcare for teen parents; career
    and employment planning and training; community con-
    nection; individualized; rural location; interns accepted.

Pacific Child Center, Inc (1972)
PO Box 987, North Bend, OR 97459
Dr Dale Helland, Dir, 503-756-2516
Coos County
Type: independent, non-profit
1 teacher, 1 assistant, 12 students, ages 5-13, K-6th grade

Accreditation: NW Association
Pacific Student Center program; resource room at Roosevelt ES.

Pacific High School (1992)
PO Box 8, Port Orford, OR 97465
Jon Bates, Prin, 503-332-3131
Port Orford-Langlois 2CJ District, Curry County
Type: public at-risk
1 teacher, 30 students, ages 13–18, HS
Accreditation: NW Assn
Student-centered; personal development; work experience.

Douglas County Homeschoolers Connection
4053 Hanna St, Roseburg, OR 97470

John C. Fremont Junior High (1992)
850 W Keady Ct, Roseburg, OR 97470
Dan Faught, Prin, 503-440-4055
Douglas Co SD 4
Type: public at-risk
10 students, ages 12–14, 7–8th grade
Accreditation: NW Assn
After-school courses, counseling, social skill building

Phoenix School
Roseburg Junior/Senior High Schools (1989)
704 SE Cass St; PO Box 2404, Roseburg, OR 97470
Ron Breyne; Tina Daily, 503-673-3036
Douglas County
Type: public at-risk
6 teachers, 2 assistants, 65 students, ages 13–19, 7–12th grade
Enrollment restricted to referrals from public school district.
Accreditation: NW Assn
Integrated curriculum; experiential; counseling; support services; communication skills

Umpqua Community College (1963)
PO Box 967, Roseburg, OR 97470
Doris A Johnson, Dir, 503-440-4603, FAX: same
non-profit; tuition: $20/term, scholarships
25 teachers, 1,800 students, ages 16–72, ungraded
Governance by board
Teacher qualifications: BA in Ed or equivalent
Progressive software for cognitive rehabilitation; individualized learning labs; transition classes; developmental studies; disability services; tutoring; GED Plus; no letter grades; multi-aged classes; non-compulsory class attendance; rural location.

Woolley Center (1955)
PO Box 967, Roseburg, OR 97470
Doris Johnson, 503-440-4603
Douglas County
Type: public choice
3 teachers, 75 students, ages 16+
Accreditation: NW Assn
Governance by Umpqua CC
GED prep; individualized learning labs; group work; lectures; computers.

The Learning Network (1985)
91913 Marcola Rd, Springfield, OR 97478
Bruce Gates, Prin, 503-933-2034
Lane County
Type: home-based; cost: $25/mo, scholarships
5 teachers; student ages infant–18
Affiliation: NCACS/NALSAS
Governance by democratic school meeting; board
Music; art; philosophy; language; human relations, potentials; creative movement; majic; non-compulsory class attendance; rural location; interns accepted.

NOVA at Sutherlin High School (1991)
500 E 4th St, Sutherlin, OR 97479
John Lahley; Ellie Tripp, Tch, 503-459-9551

Sutherlin SD 130, Douglas County
Type: public at-risk
30 students, HS
Entrance requirements: application, interview
Accreditation: NW Assn
Self-motivation; learning packets; career, personal counseling

Scotts Valley Alternative School
290 5th St, Yoncalla, OR 97499
Sharon, Director, 503-849-2175
Yoncalla SD#32
Type: public at-risk
1 teacher, 15 students, ages 16+, 9–12th grade
Adults enrolled on a space available basis
Governance by teachers and principal
GED/diploma; teen parenting; rural location.

Competency Development Center (1992)
500 Monroe St, Medford, OR 97501
Carolyn Hays, District At-Risk Supervisor, 503-776-8501
Type: public at-risk
30 students, ages 16–20, HS
Entrance by mutual agreement.
Accreditation: NW Assn
Individualized GED prep

Medford Center (1992)
W 4th & Oakdale, Medford, OR 97501
Ginna Neufeld, 503-770-5339
Type: public choice
36 students, ages 16+
ESL; ABE; GED/HS completion.

South Medford High School
815 S Oakdale Ave, Medford, OR 97501
Herb Beavers, 503-776-8661
Type: public at-risk
2 teachers, 68 students, ages 14–18, HS
Entrance requires IEP.
Accreditation: NW Assn
Integrated curriculum; co-op learning; authentic assessment; GED prep.

Students Together Achieving Results (1991)
500 Monroe St, Medford, OR 97501
Carolyn Hayes, District At-Risk Supervisor, 503-776-8501
Type: public at-risk
4 teachers, 153 students, ages 12–18, 7–12th grade
Entrance requires student and parent commitment.
Accreditation: NW Assn
Integrated

Teen Parent Program (1992)
500 Monroe St, Medford, OR 97501
Carolyn Hayes, 503-776-8501
Medford SD 549C, Jackson County
Type: public at-risk
1 teacher, 80 students, ages 13–20, HS
Accreditation: NW Assn
Self-esteem; personal growth; practical reasoning; child development; health; personal management

Youthworks Educational Services (1988)
1032 W Main, Medford, OR 97501
Michael Warner, 503-770-1270
Jackson County
Type: independent, non-profit
3 teachers, 40 students, mainly at-risk, ages 14–20, 7–12th grade
Entrance by referral.
Service center model; life skills; counseling; cooperative work experience; medical services; case management; childcare; transportation

Alternative Program at Crater High School (1987)
4410 N Rogue Valley Blvd, Central Point, OR 97502
Dave Gardner, Prin, 503-664-6611
Central Point SD 6, Jackson County
Type: public choice
2 teachers, 40 students, mainly at-risk, ages 14–19, HS
Entrance by referral.
Accreditation: NW Assn
Self-paced; tutoring.

Early Years Montessori School
3347 Old Stage Rd, Central Point, OR 97502-1132

Crossroads (1988)
1150 Knutsen #6, Medford, OR 97504
Michael Warner, Dir, 503-770-1270, FAX: 503-779-3317
Type: public at-risk
6 teachers, 60 students, mainly at risk, ages 14–21, 7-12th
    grade
Enrollment by district referral
Affiliation: Youthworks
Teacher qualifications: certification (any state)
CAI; outcome-based; GED; HS diploma; cooperative work
    experience; small groups; life skills; childcare; parenting;
    on-site clinic; no letter grades; multi-aged classes; exten-
    sive field trips; non-compulsory class attendance; subur-
    ban location; transportation; interns accepted.

Ashland Middle School (1992)
100 Walker Ave, Ashland, OR 97520
Jim Martin, 503-482-1611
Ashland District, Jackson County
Type: public at-risk
43 teachers, 750 students, ages 10–14
Communication; personal management

Lithia Springs School (1987)
540 YMCA Way, Ashland, OR 97520
Doug Shipley, Prin, 503-482-5818
Type: independent, non-profit
3 teachers, 22 students, mainly at-risk, ages 14–18, 9–12th
    grade
Enrollment by court order, or parents pay tuition; residency
    required
Affiliations: OAAE, NWASC
Governance by teachers, principal
Computer lab; vocational setting; multi-aged classes; exten-
    sive field trips; suburban location; transportation.

Rogue Community College, Ashland Center (1978)
455 Walker St, Ashland, OR 97520
Linda Renfro, 503-482-3868
Jackson County
Type: public choice
476 students, ages 16+
ABE; GED/HS completion.

The Waldorf School of the Rogue Valley (1979)
78 4th St, Ashland, OR 97520
Clista Perlle-Tworek, Co-Office Mgr, 503-482-9825
Jackson County
Non-profit; tuition: $3,500/yr
8 teachers, 150 students, ages 3+, pre K-8th grade
Affiliation: AWSNA
Governance by faculty and board
Teacher qualifications: BA, Waldorf training
Extensive field trips; rural location; interns accepted.

The Dome School (1976)
9367 Takilma Rd, Cave Junction, OR 97523
Oshana Emerald, 503-592-3911
Type: independent, non-profit; tuition: $50-135/mo,
    scholarships
6 teachers, 55 students, ages 3–11, pre K-5th grade
Governance by parent co-op, board

Teacher qualifications: experience, willing to work in coopera-
    tive environment.
Low ratios; team teaching; multi-cultural; mainstream enroll-
    ment for multi-handicapped community children; no
    letter grades; multi-aged classes; rural location; interns
    accepted.

Eagle Point High School (1984)
PO Box 198, Eagle Point, OR 97524
Deborah Dorn, Tch, 503-826-4939,-3364 x319
Eagle Point SD 9, Jackson County
Type: public at-risk
3 teachers, 36 students, ages 14–21, HS
Accreditation: NW Assn

Eagle Point Junior High School Nova Program
PO Box 218, Eagle Point, OR 97524
Deborah Dorn, Tch, 503-479-3001
Type: public at-risk
1 teacher, 18 students, ages 12–15, 7-8th grade
Governance by teachers, principal
Integrated; based on token system for rewards; rural
    location.

Education Exchange at Grants Pass High School
522 NE Olive St, Grants Pass, OR 97526
Dave Currie, Vice Prin GPHS, 503-474-5710
Grants Pass District, Josephine County
Type: public choice
1 teacher, 30 students, ages 14–16, 9–10th grade
Entrance requires screening process.
Accreditation: NW Assn

The Learning Connection
PO Box 1091 #196, Grants Pass, OR 97526
503-476-5686
Type: home-based

Josephine County Alternative Center
415 Murphy Creek Rd, Grants Pass, OR 97527
Jan Bonn, Dir, 503-862-2517
Type: independent
4 teachers, 30 students, mainly at-risk, ages 13–19, 7-12th
    grade
Must be referred by public school counselors
Teacher qualifications: credential and/or experience with at-
    risk teens
Democratic governance; students decide attendance and dis-
    cipline; small/large groups or individual instruction; multi-
    aged classes; rural location.

North Valley Alternative Center (1992)
6781 Monument Dr, Grants Pass, OR 97527
Stephen H Calkins, 503-476-8252
Type: public at-risk
1 teacher, 20-25 students, partly at-risk, ages 13–21, 7-12th
    grade
Residency required
Governance by teachers, principal, faculty, student reps, dis-
    trict personnel
Teacher qualifications: state certification
Life skills oriented; cooperative; independent study contracts;
    multi-aged classes; rural location; transportation; interns
    accepted.

Children's House Montessori
2175 Williams Hwy, Grants Pass, OR 97527-5686

Rogue Community College, Jackson County Center
    (1972)
PO Box 667, Phoenix, OR 97535
Carolyn Chancler, 503-535-7050; 772-7698
Type: public at-risk
3 teachers, 814 students, ages 16+
Must be over 18 or 16-18 with HS release.
ESL; ABE; GED/HS completion.

Rogue Community College, Rogue River Center
Rogue River High School, Rogue River, OR 97537
Vickie Reese
Type: public choice
Student ages 16+, HS
Accreditation: NW Assn
Basic skills; ABE; GED/HS completion.

Rogue River Middle School
Box 1045, 301 Pine St, Rogue River, OR 97537
Marie Reeder, 503-582-3233
Jackson County
Type: public at-risk
1 teacher, 8 students, ages 12-15
Token economy, daily feedback on behaviors; project oriented; cooperative work; self-paced; emphasis on technology, community involvement.

Horizon School (1981)
1960 E Fork Rd, Williams, OR 97544
503-846-6944
Josephine County
Type: independent, non-profit; scholarships
4 teachers, 24-30 students, ages 4-11, pre K-5th grade
Governance by parent-teacher cooperative
Teacher qualifications: credential, first aid/cpr
Parents actively involved; nearby creek, pond, fields, woods are extensions of classroom; cooperative games; 4 day week; multi-cultural curriculum; no letter grades; non-compulsory class attendance; multi-aged classes; extensive field trips; rural location; interns accepted.

Klamath Institute (1987)
3810 S 6th, Klamath Falls, OR 97603
Martha F. Christensen, Head teacher, 503-883-4719
Klamath Falls District
Type: public at-risk; tuition: if out of district
500 students, ages 14+, 9-12th grade
Enrollment restricted to credit deficient residents; counselor referral required
Affiliation: Rogue CC
Governance by staff
Teacher qualifications: state certification
Self-paced; academic work follows regular school; open entry, open exit; independent study; rural location.

Lake County Learning Center (1986)
8 N "F" St, Lakeview, OR 97630
Joyce Thayer, Learning Mgr, 503-947-4883
Type: independent
1 teacher, 5-12 students, mainly at-risk, ages 14+
Entrance requirements: FSA "Jobs" and JTPA eligibility, referral; residency
Affiliations: JTPA, FSA "Jobs"
Governance by learning manager
Teacher qualifications: state certification (Secondary Ed)
Self-paced; comprehensive; competency-based; job readiness training; diploma; GED; computer literacy; open entry/exit; multi-aged classes; rural location.

Bend High School Alternative School (1993)
230 NE 6th, Bend, OR 97701
Rusty Clemons; Patsy Smith; Gene Dusan, 503-383-6290
Bend-LaPine 1 District, Deschutes County
Type: public at-risk
1 teacher, 15 students, ages 15-17, HS
Entrance requirements: referral, review
Accreditation: NW Assn
Study skills; job search skills; self-image.

Hands On Schools (1993)
1072 NW Union, Bend, OR 97701
Glenn Young, Owner, 503-389-9238
Type: independent; tuition: $300/mo
1 teacher, 12 students, mainly at-risk, ages 10-15
Governance by owner

Teacher qualifications: empathy, business and occupational skills
Self-esteem; group cooperation; math; music; students develop business-for-profit activities, share in earned profits; no letter grades; multi-aged classes; rural location; interns accepted.

J Bar J Transitional Classroom (1988)
62895 Hamby Rd, Bend, OR 97701
Jan Hughes, ESC, 503-389-1409
Bend-LaPine 1 District, Deschutes County
Type: public at-risk
2 assistants, 16 students, ages 13-17, 7-12th grade
Located in residential treatment center for delinquent boys; academic, behavioral skills.

Mountain View High School (1985)
2755 NE 27th St, Bend, OR 97701
Tom Pannell, Judy Collett, 503-388-5479
Bend District, Deschutes County
Type: public at-risk
50 students, ages 14-17, HS
Entrance requirements: committee screening, GPA below 2.0, parental interest
Accreditation: NW Assn
Study, life skills; positive image.

Nomadic Tipi Makers
17671 Snow Creek Rd, Bend, OR 97701
Jeb Barton
Type: Montessori

Oregon Association of Alternatives in Education
(See Resource Appendix)

Westside Learning Center High School (1989)
1010 NW 14th St, Bend, OR 97701
Jan Hughes, ESC, 503-388-9019
Bend-LaPine 1 District, Deschutes County
Type: public choice
1 teacher, 30 students, mainly at-risk, ages 14-18, HS
Self-paced packet system.

Montessori Children's House of Bend
520 NW Wall St # 212, Bend, OR 97701-2608

Central Oregon Community College (1949)
2600 NW College Way, Bend, OR 97701-5998
Dianne Dean, 503-383-7277
Tuition: variable
4 teachers; student ages 16-18, HS
Governance by Central Oregon CC
HS completion; study skills.

Westsider Alternative at Cascade Middle School (1990)
19740 SW Century Dr, Bend, OR 97702
Tom Achterman, 503-388-5477
10 students, mainly at-risk, ages 11-14, 6-8th grade
Self-esteem; social skills.

Bend Homeschoolers
PO Box 9306, Bend, OR 97708
503-382-1547
Deschutes County

Burns High School Alternative Education (1986)
1100 Oregon Ave, Burns, OR 97720
Rod Folen, 503-573-5191
Harney Co SD 3
Type: public at-risk
1 teacher, 30-55 students, 7-12th grade
Entrance by referral.
Accreditation: NW Assn
Off campus; GED prep; work experience credit; home study.

LaPine Junior-Senior High, Opportunity Room (1991)
PO Box 306, LaPine, OR 97739
Joe Dolan, Dir, 503-536-1783

Bend-LaPine District, Deschutes County
Type: public at-risk
1 teacher, 1 assistant, 50 students, ages 12–20, 6–12th grade
Entrance by referral to CORE team.
Accreditation: NW Assn
Personal Education Plans; computers; Odyssey of the Mind; field trips; all-school support services.

Madras High School (1986)
390 SE 10th St, Madras, OR 97741
Dick Junge, 503-475-7265
Jefferson Co SD 509J
Type: public at-risk
4 teachers, 12 students, HS
Entrance by referral.
Accreditation: NW Assn
Learning packets; required courses, electives; PM class for seniors 1 credit short of graduation

COIC Skills Lab (1987)
411 W Third, Prineville, OR 97754
Ann Thomas; Meredith Junge; D. Tillinghast, 503-548-8163, 447-3119
Crook County
Type: public choice; tuition: Various grants
1 teacher, 88 students, ages 14+, HS
One of 4 sites; open to economically disadvantaged, dislocated, unemployed; Youth Conservation Corp for dropouts; diploma or skill improvement for adults.

Crook County Alternative School (1988)
430 W 4th St, Prineville, OR 97754
Dave McCourtney/Dave Doty, 503-447-1806
Type: public at-risk
2 teachers, 40 students, ages 14–18, 8–12th grade
Accreditation: NW Assn
Individualized; API.

Rimrock Trails ATC (1990)
1099 N Elm, Prineville, OR 97754
Steve Bucknum, 503-477-2631
Crook Co District
Type: public at-risk
1 teacher, 16 students, 6–12th grade
Enrollment restricted to clients of Rimrock Trails Adolescent Treatment Center.
Individual planning; core skills.

Alternative Education Program at Obsidian Junior High School (1991)
1335 SW Obsidian, Redmond, OR 97756
Margaret Goodman, AE Coord/Tch, 503-923-4900
Type: public at-risk
1 teacher, 17 students, ages 12–15, 7–8th grade
Entrance requirements: referral, student and parent approval of placement, residency
Governance by teachers, principal
Teacher qualifications: BA Elem Ed, Ed M Reading
Interest-based; students tutor daily in elementary classrooms; visits to businesses and job sites; adopted city park; multi-aged classes; weekly grades; rural location.

Sisters Flex High School (1992)
PO Box 3099, Sisters, OR 97759
Stan Shipley, 503-549-4045
Deschutes County
Type: public at-risk; tuition: Private community organizations
10 students, ages 16–20, HS
Enrollment restricted to HS dropouts and retained at least once
Accreditation: NW Assn
Coordinates support services, business involvement; 30 hrs/wk cooperative work required.

Baker Alternative School
2020 Church St, Baker City, OR 97814
Lori L Russell, 503-523-5091
5J District
Type: public at-risk
1 teacher, 1 assistant, 25 students, ages 14–21, 9–12th grade
Entrance requirements: referral, Review Team approval
Governance by teachers, principal, board
Teacher qualifications: TSPA certification
Half day work or volunteer position; rural location; transportation; interns accepted.

Baker County ESD HSC/Abe Program (1977)
2100 Main St, Baker City, OR 97814
Nola Whitley or Ruth Whitnah, 503-523-5801
Type: public at-risk
2 teachers, 45 students, ages 16+
Enrollment restricted to dropouts and credit deficient students released from compulsory attendance.
GED prep; urban location.

Blue Mountain Community College (1988)
PO Box 575, Condon, OR 97823
Candy Barnett, 503-384-6221
Gilliam and Wheeler County
Type: public choice
15 students, ages 19–59, HS
Accreditation: NW Assn
GED prep; adult HS completion; ESL; other location in Grant County, S Canyon Blvd, John Day, OR, 97845, contact Cindy Kimble at 503-575-1799.

Condon High School
PO Box 575, Condon, OR 97823
Rita Rattray, 503-384-2441
Gilliam County
Type: public choice
Student ages 14–18
Accreditation: NW Assn
Independent and/or guided instruction.

Grant Union High School (1989)
PO Box 129, John Day, OR 97845
Dorothy Piazza; Carl Lino, 503-575-1799
John Day SD 3, Grant County
Type: public choice
1 teacher, 60 students, ages 15–30+, HS
Entrance requirements: referral, MDT placement
Accreditation: NW Assn
Evenings; tutorial; GED prep; slower paced; makeup credit; work experience; independent study.

Union Alternative School
10100 N McAlister Rd, Island City, OR 97850
Lyle Mann, Dir, 503-963-4106, FAX: 503-963-7256
Union Education Service District
Type: public at-risk
4 teachers, 300 students, ages 14+, 9–12th grade
Residency required
Governance by board
Teacher qualifications: BA or BS
Self-paced; competency based; non-compulsory class attendance; rural location; interns accepted.

Harmony Lane School (1993)
932 Harmony Ln, Ashland, OR 99520
Peter Spring, Head, 503-482-6536
Jackson County
Type: independent, non-profit; tuition: $200/mo, scholarships
2 teachers, 8 students, ages 6–16
Governance by democratic school meeting
Emphasis on music; headmaster is former professional musician, flute-maker, piano tuner; students' rock band; no letter grades; non-compulsory class attendance; multi-aged classes; extensive field trips; suburban location; interns accepted.

Pennsylvania

Franklin Elementary School
Cheltenham & Rising Sun, Philadelphia, PA 10120
Type: Montessori

Beaver Montessori School
855 2nd St, Beaver, PA 15009-2600

St Agatha Montessori School
220 Station St, Bridgeville, PA 15017-1897

MonValley Montessori Preschool &K
550 Isabella Ave, Charleroi, PA 15022-2337

Bows 'n Arrows
28 Deer Park Dr, Cheswick, PA 15024
Louis Kress, 412-487-8422

Monessen Catholic Montessori Preschool
7th & Schnmaker Ave, Monessen, PA 15062

Parkway West Alternative Education Center
RD #1, PO Box 242, Oakdale, PA 15071

Southwestern Pennsylvania Home Education Network
Rd 3, PO Box 256 B, Tarentrum, PA 15084
412-922-8344

Northern Area Alternative High School (1978)
9600 Babcock Blvd, Allison Park, PA 15101
Dr Victor T. Zakowski, Prin, 412-366-2800, FAX: 412-366-9600
Allegheny County
Type: public at-risk
7 teachers, 76 students, ages 15–19, 9–12th grade
Governance by teachers and principal
Teacher qualifications: PA Certification
Vocational education; multi-aged classes; transportation.

Western PA Montessori School (1965)
2379 Wyland Ave, Allison Park, PA 15101
Carol Miskell, Adm, 487-2700
Non-profit; tuition: $1,990-4,240/yr
6 teachers, 5 assistants, 106 students, ages 3–6
Entrance requirements: age 3; toilet trained
Affiliation: PAEYC; accreditation: AMS
Governance by administrator, board
Childcare; suburban location; interns accepted.

Montesorri Childhood Center
5303 Madison Ave, Bethel Park, PA 15102-3631

Franklin Street Montessori
400 Franklin St, East Pittsburgh, PA 15112-1019

Montessori Centre Academy
1014 Wm Flynn Hwy, Glenshaw, PA 15116
Yolanda Glasso or Yolanda Sweenie

Mon Valley Education Consortium
3356 Shaw Ave, McKeesport, PA 15132

Glen Montessori School
RR 2, Sewickley, PA 15143-9802

East Suburban Montessori School
500 Laurel Dr, Monroeville, PA 15146-1136

Secondary Options Center City As School Program (1993)
Washington Education Bldg, 169 40th St, Pittsburgh, PA 15201

Georgia Vassilakis, Adm, 412-622-3490, FAX: 622-3489
Type: public choice
10 students

St Francis Montessori (1989)
45th St, Pittsburgh, PA 15201
Sister Mary Meyer, Director, 412-622-7128
Non-profit; tuition: $18/day
1 teacher, 2 assistants, 37 students, ages 3–6
Enrollment restricted to St. Francis Medical Center employ-
ees' children
Affiliation: Greater Pittsburgh M
Governance by administrator
In-hospital setting lets students see facility in action; child-
care; urban location; interns accepted.

The Village Montessori School
10 Walnut St, Pittsburgh, PA 15202-1541
John Crawford

Rogers Creative & Performing Arts School
5525 Columbo St, Pittsburgh, PA 15206
Neal Huguley, 412-665-2000
Type: magnet
6-12th grade

Pittsburgh Creative & Performing Arts
925 Brushton Ave, Pittsburgh, PA 15208
Harry Clark, 412-247-7860
Type: magnet
9-12th grade

Homewood Montessori (1980)
Hamilton and Lang St, Pittsburgh, PA 15208-1829
Dr Johnson Martin, 247-7855
Type: public choice
15 teachers, 2 assistants, 124 students, ages 3–9
Enrollment requires magnet school application.
Accreditation: MSA
Governance by teachers and administrators, parent coopera-
tive, school board

Alternative Education Vocational Program
200 N Dirthridge, Pittsburgh, PA 15213

Carlow Campus Montessori (1975)
3333 5th Ave, Pittsburgh, PA 15213
Billie Girard, Adms Dir, 412-578-6075
Non-profit; tuition: $3,550/5,000/yr
2 teachers, 2 assistants, 40 students, ages 3–6
Affiliation: AMS; accreditation: MSA
Governance by administrator
French; swimming; art; computer ed; librarian; transporta-
tion for K students; childcare; interns accepted.

Project Succeed at Keystone Oaks High School (1990)
1000 Kelton Ave, Pittsburgh, PA 15216
Joel Vanucci, Dir, 412-571-6066, FAX: 571-6006
Allegheny County
Type: public at-risk
5 teachers, 14 students, ages 19–55
Governance by director/Teachers
Teacher qualifications: PA certification
Night classes; HS diploma; community service required.

Hill House Association
1835 Center Ave, Pittsburgh, PA 15219

Letsche Alternative Learning Center
1530 Cliff, Pittsburgh, PA 15219

Camalt Elementary
1583 Breining St, Pittsburgh, PA 15226
Elmer Parks, 412-885-7760
Type: magnet
1–5th grade
Open space.

Allegheny Academy
900 Agnew Rd, Pittsburgh, PA 15227
Bridget Burns

Highland School
5250 Caste Dr, Pittsburgh, PA 15227
Dan Findley

Laural Learning Centers, Inc
2720 Custer Ave, Pittsburgh, PA 15227-2153
Type: Montessori

Mt. Lebanon Montessori School (1976)
550 Sleepy Hollow Rd, Mt Lebanon, PA 15228
Barbara Popchak, Dir, 412-563-2858
Non-profit; tuition: $600/2500
5 teachers, 7 assistants, 124 students, partly international,
   ages infant-9
Entrance requirements: toddlers must be age 2 by Sept
Affiliations: AMS, AMI, NAMTA
Governance by an administrator, board of trustees
Music; Orff & Kodaly philosophies; involved parent body; play
   area blends indoor, outdoor environments; gardening;
   childcare; suburban location; transportation; interns
   accepted.

Maria Montessori PreSchool
957 Connor Rd, Pittsburgh, PA 15234-1003
Bianca Nardei

Pittsburgh East Suburban Homeschoolers
238 1/2 Evaline St, Pittsburgh, PA 15235
Debbie Jackson, 412-247-4497

Montessori Early Childhood
407 Southvue Dr, Pittsburgh, PA 15236-2030

Holiday Farms Country Day School
1907 O'Block Rd, Pittsburgh, PA 15239-2333
Dorothy Lamuth
Type: Montessori

Washington County Alternative School (1988)
524 E Beau St, Washington, PA 15301
Herman J. Ross, Dir, 412-225-5505
Type: public at-risk
4 teachers, 55 students, ages 15-21, 9-12th grade
No residency requirement
Governance by board
Teacher qualifications: state certification
Drug, alcohol counseling; life skills; work exploration; com-
   munity service; GED prep; open-ended courses; suburban
   location; transportation.

Pressley Ridge School
RD #1, PO Box 25, Ophiopyle, PA 15470

Elizabeth Seton Montessori School
RR 7 Box 268, Greensburg, PA 15601-9569
Anita Schulte

Verna Montessori School
RD 2, Box 348, Mt Pleasant, PA 15666
Sr Margherita Ferrero

Adelphi Private School
354 Main St, Latrobe, PA 15670

Keys Montessori School, Inc
695 School St, Indiana, PA 15701-3076

AYS Day Treatment (1991)
115 S Marion St, Ebensburg, PA 15931
Thomas Prout, Exec Dir, 814-472-7874, FAX: 472-7920
Cambrie County
Type: independent, boarding, non-profit
8 teachers, 40 students, mainly at-risk, ages 11-18, 4-12th
   grade
Interview required
Governance by board
Very structured.

Central Area Pennsylvania Home Education Network
PO Box 191, Summerhill, PA 15958
Karen Leventry, 814-495-5651

Montessori Pre-School (1989)
One Benbrooke Pl, Butler, PA 16001
Maryanne Herbert Pribis, 412-482-4200
1 teacher, 3 assistants, 34 students, ages infant-6
Entrance requirements: interview; toilet trained
Affiliation: WMS of Pittsburgh; accreditations: AMI, PDOE
Governance by teachers and administrators
Rolling hills and valley; summer nature camp; childcare; rural
   location; interns accepted.

Montessori Day Academy
321A Benbrook Rd, Butler, PA 16001-7301

Butler Area Homeschoolers
145 Brose Rd, Marwood, PA 16023
412-352-2639

George Junior Republic
PO Box 471, Grove City, PA 16127

Sunflower School
Box 3732 Rd 3, Grove City, PA 16127
Joe Jenkins
Type: home-based

Pennsylvania Homeschoolers
RD 2 Box 117, Kittanning, PA 16201
Susan Richman, 412-783-6512
Type: state home-based

Armstrong County Area Homeschoolers
Rd 1, PO Box 221A, Templeton, PA 16259
Sandy Houston, 412-868-2331

Venanga Christian High School
1505 W First St, Oil City, PA 16301

Lakeland Home Educators (1986)
285 Allegheny St, Meadville, PA 16335
Jean Bartlett, Vicki Bocan, Brendra Van Matre, 814-333-2852
Crawford/Mercer County
Field trips; social activities; bi-monthly newsletter; phone
   tree.

Pennsylvania Home Education Network
285 Allegheny St, Meadville, PA 16335
Diana Baseman, 412-265-2734
Crawford County
non-profit; cost: $15/yr
Inclusive; newsletter.

Erie County Homeschoolers
9129 State Rd, Cranesville, PA 16410
Janet Preston, 814-774-8598

Homeworks
10730 Rt 98, Edinboro, PA 16412
Laurea Polo, 814-734-7180

Montessori Day School
1372 W 6th St, Erie, PA 16505-2596

Montessori School of Erie County
2910 Sterrettania Rd, Erie, PA 16506-2646
Martin Maly

Children's House of Erie Montessori School, Inc (1981)
4701 Old French Rd, Erie, PA 16509
S. Daniel Magoc, Exec Dir, 814-868-0615
Non-profit; tuition: $1,500/2,100/yr
2 teachers, 3 assistants, 53 students, ages 3-6
Affiliation: NAMTA
Governance by board
Teacher qualifications: AMI credential
Childcare; suburban location; interns accepted.

Pennsylvania Montessori Academy
439 Lotz Ave-Lakemont, Altoona, PA 16602-5643
Michelle Hartye

Parent-Child Press
(See Resource Appendix)

New Beginnings
Cove Forge, PO Box B; Route 1, PO Box 79, Williamsburg, PA
   16693

Delta Program (1973)
411 S Fraser St, State College, PA 16801
Kathy Kelly, Dir, 814-231-1000, FAX: 814-231-4103
Centre County
Type: public choice; tuition: $6,000/yr for non-residents
12 teachers, 120 students, ages 11-21, 7-12th grade
District residency required
Governance by shared decision making
Teacher qualifications: PA certification
Team planning; goal achievement support; no letter grades;
   extensive field trips; multi-aged classes; interns accepted.

State College Alternative Program
4011 S Fraser St, State College, PA 16801
Type: public choice

State College Friends School (1980)
611 E Prospect Ave, State College, PA 16801
Lee Quinby, Head, 814-237-8386
Centre County
Type: Quaker, non-profit; tuition: $3,700/yr
10 teachers, 90 students, ages 5-12, K-6th grade
Affiliation: Friends Meeting
Governance by teachers, principal
Parent involvement; non-violent conflict resolution; thematic
   studies; no letter grades; multi-aged classes; interns
   accepted.

STS Program, Penn State U
133 Willard, University Park, PA 16802
Lee Hoinacki

Park Forest Montessori School
1833 Park Forest Ave, State College, PA 16803-1403
Rose Park or Janet Dargitz

Our Children's Center
Corner of Mary & Mulberry Sts, Lemont, PA 16851
Martha Torrence
Type: Montessori

United Methodist Childrens Center
PO Box 531, Wellsboro, PA 16901-0531
Type: Montessori

Parallel Education Programs
8 Ruah St, Blossburg, PA 16912

Endless Mountains Homeschoolers
c/o Kellogg, RD 3 Box 80, Columbia Cross Rds, PA 16914
717-549-8179

Wilderness School
PO Box 10, 960 Century Dr, Mechanicsburg, PA 17007-0010

Alternative Education Center
#1 Cumberland & Ront Sts, Lebanon, PA 17042

Circle School (1984)
210 Oakleigh Ave, Harrisburg, PA 17111
Beth Stone, Comm Chair, 717-564-6700, FAX: 938-0190
Dauphin County
Type: independent, non-profit; tuition: $2900/yr, scholarships
9 teachers, 36 students, ages 3-16
Governed by democratic school meeting; students manage
   their own time; no letter grades; non-compulsory class
   attendance; multi-aged classes; extensive field trips; urban
   location; transportation; interns accepted.

Manito Inc (1979)
7564 Browns Mill Rd, Chambersburg, PA 17201
Robert C. Whitmore, EdD, Exec Dir, 717-375-4733, FAX: -4336
Franklin County
Type: public at-risk
14 teachers, 110 students, ages 12-18, 7-12th grade
Entrance requirements: referral by district or juvenile court;
   no residency requirement
Governance by board
Teacher qualifications: BS or MS
Integration of counseling, educational services; conflict reso-
   lution skills; 3 locations, urban and rural; transportation;
   interns accepted.

Montessori School of Chambersburg
2011 Scotland Ave, Chambersburg, PA 17201-1451
Mary Jane Bittle

Lincoln IU #12
PO Box 70, New Oxford, PA 17350

Lancaster Home Educators Association
c/o RR 6 Box 3335, Red Lion, PA 17356-9557
Kim Huber, 717-246-0188
Lancaster County

Circle of Children Co-op of Cornucopia Enterprises (1993)
PO Box 67, Shrewsbury, PA 17361
Eileen Stein, Pres, 717-993-3603
York County
Type: home-based; cost: $500-1,500/yr
2 teachers; student ages infant-18, pre K-12th grade
Parents must assume responsibility for child's education
Affiliation: NCACS
Governance by parent co-op and staff under guidance of
   pres
Teacher qualifications: 4 yr college degree or in process of
   acquiring; regard for children, humanity, nature
Holistic; Kids in Business; Creative Solutions for teens; parent
   co-op ECE; low ratio; real-life activities; extensive field trips;
   rural location; transportation; interns accepted.

DC Rise YCYDC
3564 Heindel Rd, York, PA 17402

Montessori Children's House of York
3417 E Market St, York, PA 17402-2623
Movair Chami

York County High School (1990)
W Manchester Mall; Box 8042, York, PA 17404
Donald Bohr, Dir, 717-767-4863, FAX: 717-767-4336
Type: public at-risk
6 teachers, 100 students, ages 16-45, 9-12th grade
Enrollment restricted to HS dropouts referred by district; no
   residency requirement
Governance by director, counselor, teachers
Teacher qualifications: PA Certification
Self-paced; competency-based; multi-aged classes; urban
   location.

Montessori Academy
PO Box 177, East Petersburg, PA 17520

Christian Homeschool Association of Pennsylvania
1464 Old Line Rd, Manheim, PA 17545
717-665-7091
Lancaster County
Type: state home-based

Susquehanna Waldorf School (1987)
15 W Walnut St, Marietta, PA 17547
Diana Ingraham, Faculty Chair, 717-426-4026
Lancaster County
Non-profit; tuition: $2,616-3,228/yr, scholarships
8 teachers, 105 students, ages 3.5-12, nursery-6th grade
Entrance at discretion of teacher
Affiliation: AWSNA
Suburban location; interns accepted.

Alternative Program at Willow St Vo-Tech (1988)
1730 Han Herr Dr, Willow St 1, PA 17584
Daniel Burkholder, 717-464-2771
Lancaster County
Type: public at-risk
3 teachers, 45 students, ages 15-20, 8-12th grade
County residency required
Affiliation: Intermediate Unit #13
Governance by teachers and principal
Support groups; community-based; extensive field trips;
    multi-aged classes; suburban location; transportation;
    interns accepted.

Montessori Academy of Lancaster (1982)
1460 Eden Rd, Lancaster, PA 17601
Mary E. Gerhart, Dir, 717-397-4617
Non-profit; tuition: $1,600-3,950/yr
5 teachers, 5 assistants, 70 students, ages toddler-9
Affiliation: MTA-PA; accreditation: AMS
Governance by a board of trustees
Weekly classes in Spanish, fine arts, music, PE, and library;
    childcare; suburban location; interns accepted.

Montessori Learning Center
700 Pleasure Rd, Lancaster, PA 17601-4438

The New School of Lancaster (1990)
2312 Marietta Ave, Lancaster, PA 17603
Beth M. Crosby, Dir, 717-397-7655
Type: Montessori, non-profit; tuition: 1,200-3,850/yr
7 teachers, 6 assistants, 141 students, ages infant-9
Accreditation: PA State Board of Private Academic Schools;
    day care license
Governance by board of trustees
Searching for new building to expand and include ages 9-16;
    childcare; suburban location; interns accepted.

West Branch School (1970)
755 Moore Ave, Williamsport, PA 17701
Carolyn Erickson, Coordinator, 717-323-5498
Type: independent; tuition: $2200/yr, scholarships
50 students, K-6th grade
Uses basic skills as tools; real experiences in solving problems,
    accepting responsibilities, making decisions.

Montessori School
320 Valley Rd, Bloomsburg, PA 17815-8441

Greenwood Friends School
PO Box 438, Millville, PA 17846
Sheila Lunger, Dir, 717-458-5532
Type: Quaker, non-profit; need-based scholarships
6 teachers, 50 students, ages 3-12, pre 6th grade
Affiliation: Friends Council on Education
Governance by board
Community of families and friends; student-centered; no
    letter grades; multi-aged classes; extensive field trips; rural
    location; transportation; interns accepted.

Center for Humanistic Change
7574 Beth-Bath Pike, Bath, PA 18014

Wiley House
1650 Broadway, Bethlehem, PA 18015-3998

TASHKA Directives/Alcott Montessori School
PO Box 148, Bethlehem, PA 18016

Datzyk Montessori School
3300 Broadway, Allentown, PA 18104-5927
Ruth Datzyk

Childrens Learning Center
PO Box 253, Hazleton, PA 18201-0253
Type: Montessori

Preschool House —Rush Elementary School
RD #2 Meadow Ave, Tamaqua, PA 18252
Type: Montessori

Crossroads Day Treatment (1994)
Rt 115 & Weir Lake Rd, Broadheadsville, PA 18322
Betty Jeanne Segear, Dir, 717-992-1473, FAX: 717-992-7490
Monroe County
Type: independent at-risk, non-profit
2 teachers, 1 assistant, 24 students, mainly at-risk, ES-HS
No residency requirement
Governance by multi-disciplinary team
Teacher qualifications: SE Degree
SE; socially/emotionally disturbed; LD; tutoring.

Growing Concern
515 Hemlock Dr, Mt Bethel, PA 18342
Type: Montessori

Montessori Childrens House of the Poconos
PO Box 667, Stroudsburg, PA 18360-0667
Stuart Scharf

Lourdesmount
537 Venard Rd, Clarks Summit, PA 18411

Harmony Home Educators
Rd 3 Waverly Rd, Dalton, PA 18414
Charlene Radman, 717-563-2368

Hamlin Elementary Center
Matthews & Ferraro, Hamlin, PA 18427
Type: Montessori

Montessori Elementary School of Scranton
134 School St, Scranton, PA 18508-2766

Children's Cornerstone (1986)
1759 Sanderson Ave, Scranton, PA 18509
Barbara Holzman, Owner/Director, 717-347-4450
Type: Montessori; tuition: $1,500/2,600/yr
1 teacher, 1 assistant, 30 students, ages 3-6
Entrance requirements: toilet trained
Affiliation: AMS
Converted old Victorian home; located in progressive city
    near the Poconos; interns accepted.

Early Learning Center Marywood College
2300 Adams Ave, Scranton, PA 18509
Sr Regina Barrett
Type: Montessori

Himalayan Institute Children's School
RR 1 Box 400, Honsdale, PA 18531
Irene Avlonitis
Type: Montessori

Crossroads
281 S Franklin St, Wilkes-Barre, PA 18701

Wyoming Valley Montessori
851 W Market St, Kingston, PA 18704
Jean Warrington, Adm, 717-288-3708
Non-profit
7 teachers, 8 assistants, 177 students, ages infant-12
Affiliation: AMS
Governance by board
Urban location; transportation; interns accepted.

Barclay Friends School
RD 1, Box 167-B, Towanda, PA 18848
Kathy White, Head Tch, 717-265-9620
Type: Quaker

Northern Tier Regional Planning & Development Commission (1983)
507 Main St, Towanda, PA 18848
James W. Gregory, Dir, 717-265-9103, FAX: 265-7585
Students mainly at-risk
Governance by board
Administers JTPA and Economic Dislocated Worker Assistance Act; serves Bradford, Sullivan, Susquehanna, Tioga, Wyoming; rural location.

Opportunity School
67 E Butler Ave, New Britain, PA 18901

Newton Friends School
Newtown Langhorne Rd, Newton, PA 18904
Type: Quaker

Creative Education Network (1993)
Star Route, Mechanicsville Rd, Carversville, PA 18913
Mary Lounsbury, 215-297-0642
Bucks County
Type: home-based, non-profit
Governance by parent cooperative
Workshops; 30 family membership; rural location.

Buckingham Friends School (1974)
Box 158, Lahaska, PA 18931
Peter Pearson, Prin, 215-794-7491, FAX: 215-794-7955
Bucks County
Type: Quaker, non-profit; tuition: $7,200/yr, scholarships
22 teachers, 176 students, ages 5-15, K-8th grade
Affiliation: Society of Friends
Governance by principal, board
Sense of community; meeting for worship; extensive field trips; rural location; interns accepted.

TLC Montessori Educational Preschool
5179 New Hope Rd, New Hope, PA 18938-5408

George School (1893)
Box 4000, Newtown, PA 18940
Karen S. Hallowell, Adms Dir, 215-579-6500, FAX:-6549
Type: Quaker, boarding, non-profit; tuition: res:$17,900/yr day:$11,650/yr, scholarships
70 teachers, 525 students, ages 13-18, 9-12th grade
Entrance requirements: grades, testing, recommendations, interview
Affiliation: Religious Society of Friends
Governance by consensus
Teacher qualifications: college degree
65 hours community service; work camps in developing countries; IB; suburban location.

Newtown Friends School
PO Box 978, Newtown, PA 18940
Joel Schmidt, Head, 215-968-2225
Type: Quaker

Wrightstown Friends Nursery School
Box 293, Penns Park, PA 18943
Martha Severn, 215-968-9900
Type: Quaker

Community Service Foundation
PO Box 262, Pipersville, PA 18947

Waldorf School Association of the Delaware River Valley (1991)
PO Box 112, Bridge Two Lane, Pt. Pleasant, PA 18950
Leslie Torkelson, Dev Coord, 215-297-5713, FAX:-8863
Bucks County
Non-profit
2 teachers, 20 students, ages 3.5-6, pre K-1st grade
Governance by board of parents, teachers, community
Rural location; interns accepted.

Country Gardens
4126 Axehandle Rd, Quakertown, PA 18951
Arlene Albright, 215-536-2703
Type: independent

United Friends School (1983)
20 S 10th St, Quakertown, PA 18951
Betty Sue Zellner, Head, 215-538-1733
Bucks County
Type: Quaker, non-profit; tuition: $3,900/yr, scholarships
10 teachers, 80 students, ages 5-12, K-6th grade
Entrance requirements: potential benefit, recommendations, records, interview
Affiliation: RSF
Governance by board
Teacher qualifications: college degree
Whole language; manipulative math; hands-on-science; extensive field trips; no letter grades; urban location.

Penn Foundation School
807 Lawn Ave, Sellersville, PA 18960

Childtowne Montessori School
348 Coldspring Rd, Southampton, PA 18966-3530

Satellite School
Willard & Twining, Ivyland, PA 18974

Middle Earth, Inc
299 Jacksonville Rd, Warminster, PA 18974
Elizabeth A Quigley, Dir of Ed Prog, 215-443-0280, FAX: 215-443-0245
Bucks County
Type: independent, non-profit; tuition: per diem
7 teachers, 60 students, mainly at-risk, ages 13-18, 9-12th grade
Entrance requirements: referrals by court and public schools
Governance by teachers and principal
Teacher qualifications: background in education, psychology, social work, or criminal justice
Democratic; small group and individualized instruction; therapeutic community; suburban location; interns accepted.

Abington Children's House
2350 Easton Rd, Roslyn, PA 19001
Type: Montessori

Bala House (1969)
PO Box 91/Conshohocket and St Asaphs Rd, Bala Cynwyd, PA 19004
Debbie Eastwood, 215-664-6767
Non-profit; tuition: $6,200/yr, scholarships
3 teachers, 3 assistants, 65 students, ages 3-6
Entrance requirements: toilet trained
Affiliations: AMS, NAEYC, DVAEYC
Governance by board
Right outside Philadelphia; multi-cultural; suburban location; interns accepted.

Montgomery Montessori School
1620 Pine Rd, Huntingdon Valley, PA 19006-7938

Delaware Valley Friends School (1987)
PO Box 71, Bryn Mawr, PA 19010
Irene McHenry, Head, 215-526-9595, FAX: 526-2756
Montgomery County
Type: Quaker, non-profit; tuition: $13,200/yr, scholarships
29 teachers, 102 students, ages 12–19, 7-12th grade
Enrollment restricted to those with learning differences and
    without primary emotional problems
Affiliation: RSF
Governance by board
Teacher qualifications: college degree, prefer certification
Multi-sensory; Orton-Gillingham approach; organizational,
    study skills; computer writing lab; adventure-based; effort
    grades; extensive field trips; suburban location; interns
    accepted.

Family Resource Center
312 Bryn Mawr Ave, Bryn Mawr, PA 19010
Peter Bergson, 215-527-1504, 527-4982
Type: home-based

Media Childrens House
24 Radio Park Ln, Brookhaven, PA 19015
Type: Montessori

De La Salle Vocational
PO Box 334, Street Rd & Bristol Pike, Bensalem, PA 19020

Delta School
Neshaminy Plaza II, Bristol Pike & Street Rd, Suite 101, Ben-
    salem, PA 19020

Ted DiRenzo Montessori School
709 Bartram Ave, Collingdale, PA 19023-3508

Children's House of Bucks County
840 Trenton Rd, Fairless Hills, PA 19030-2598
Virgina Cannon
Type: Montessori

Carson Valley School
Mill Rd, Flourtown, PA 19031

Montessori Children's House
200 Camp Hill Rd, Fort Washington, PA 19034

New Horizons Montessori School
PO Box 408; Madison & Prospect Aves, Fort Washington, PA
    19034
Maggi Funchiow

Wordsworth Academy
Pennsylvania Ave & Camp Hill, Fort Washington, PA 19034

Whitemarsh Montessori
7215 Sheaff Ln, Ft Washington, PA 19034

The Gladwyne Montessori School (1962)
920 Youngs Pond Rd, Gladwyne, PA 19035
Annmarie R. Torres, Head, 215-649-1761, FAX: 215-649-7178
Non-profit; tuition: $3,675-6,495/yr
10 teachers, 15 assistants; student ages infant-12
Entrance requirement: visit (primary level+)
Affiliations: NAMTA, MTA; accreditation: PAPAS
Governance by a board of trustees
Summer and after-school programs in art, music, drama,
    French and nature study; childcare; suburban location;
    interns accepted.

The Wetherill School
1321 Beaumont Dr, Gladwyne, PA 19035-1392
Type: Montessori

Sleighton School
Valley & Forge Rds, Lima, PA 19037

InPrint for Children
(See Resource Appendix)

The Quaker School at Horsham (1982)
318 Meetinghouse Rd, Horsham, PA 19044
William S. Hallowell, Head, 215-674-2875
Montgomery County
Type: Quaker, non-profit; tuition: $11,200/yr, scholarships
15 teachers, 50 students, mainly at-risk, ages 6–13, 1–7th
    grade
Entrance requirements: average to above-average IQ,
    psychological/educational testing
Governance by teachers, principal, board
Teacher qualifications: Masters in Special Ed
For students with ADD, ADHD, auditory and visual processing
    problems, dyslexia; auditory skills; speech therapy; study
    skills; woodshop; individualized, hands-on; multi-aged
    classes; no letter grades; suburban location; transporta-
    tion; interns accepted.

Abington Friends School
575 Washington Ln, Jenkintown, PA 19046
Bruce Stewart, Head, 215-886-4350
Type: Quaker

Meadowlane Montessori (1961)
616 Meetinghouse Rd, Jenkintown, PA 19046
JoAnne Hartsough, 215-887-1222
Non-profit; tuition: $298-616/mo
6 teachers, 3 assistants, 45 students, ages infant-6
Affiliations: MTA, AMS; accreditation: AMS
Governance by administrator
Childcare; interns accepted.

Woods School
Rt 413, Langhorne, PA 19047

Neshaminy Valley Montessori School
4951 Central Ave, Trevose, PA 19047

Lansdowne Friends School
110 N Lansdowne Ave, Lansdowne, PA 19050
Paul Seaton, Head, 215-623-2548
Type: Quaker

Bucks County Alternative School (1976)
280 Red Cedar Dr, Levittown, PA 19055
Dr Charles Miller, Supervisor, 215-547-0962
District 22
Type: public at-risk
4 teachers, 36 students, mainly SE, ages 12–19, 7-12th grade
Residency required
Teacher qualifications: state SE certification
Credit-earning coop ed (work exp) for age 16+; suburban
    location; transportation; interns accepted.

Media Providence Friends School
125 W 3rd St, Media, PA 19063
Stewart Bartow, Head, 215-565-1960
Type: Quaker

The School in Rose Valley (1929)
20 School Ln, Moylan, PA 19065
Paul Lindenmaier, Prin, 215-566-1088, FAX:-4640
Delaware County
Type: independent, non-profit; tuition: $6,375-6,750,
    scholarships
14 teachers, 100 students, ages 3–12, pre K-6th grade
Governance by principal
Several unique buildings; safe environmental setting; wood
    shop, art room, multi-purpose dome, music room, science
    room, library, kitchen, projects building; whole child
    approach; no letter grades; multi-aged classes; suburban
    location; interns accepted.

Mercy Montessori Center
513 Montgomery Ave, Merion, PA 19066-1214
Sr Mary Christella

Springton Lake Montessori School
3090 S Newtown St Rd, Newtown Square, PA 19073-3913

The Walden School (1967)
100 College Ave, Swarthmore, PA 19081
Cynthia K. Wein, 544-8970
Type: Montessori, non-profit; tuition: $2,175-3,885/yr
148 students, ages 3-15
Entrance requirements: application, interview
Affiliations: MTA-PA, ESR, ASCD
Governance by administrator, board
Environmental, peace education; literature enrichment;
   childcare; suburban location.

Stratford Friends School (1976)
5 Llandillo Rd, Havertown, PA 19083
215-446-3144
Delaware County
Type: Quaker, non-profit; tuition: $11,450/yr, scholarships
63 students, mainly SE, LD, ages 5-12
Affiliation: Papas
Enriched thematic curriculum; SE Masters Core Program in
   Multisensory Teaching; no letter grades; multi-aged
   classes; camping trip; Orton-Gillingham reading/writing for
   dyslexics; interns accepted.

Pendle Hill
338 Plush Rd, Wallingford, PA 19086
Daniel Seeger, Exec Sec, 215-742-3150, FAX: 566-4507
Type: Quaker higher education

Springfield Children's House
2 Chester Rd, Wallingford, PA 19086-6606
Type: Montessori

Montessori Children's House
600 Walker Rd, Wayne, PA 19087-1420
Mary Jane Chapman

Armenian Sisters Academy
440 Upper Gulph Rd, Radnor, PA 19087-4699
Type: Montessori

Lakeside School (1976)
Box L, Willow Grove, PA 19090
Brian Dager, Program Director, 215-542-7737, FAX: 215-657-
   3593
Montgomery County
Type: independent, non-profit; tuition: $51-61/day
41 teachers, 150 students, mainly at-risk, ages 10-21, 6-12th
   grade
Entrance requirements: no SE or extreme behavior disorders;
   interview
Governance by board
Integrated systematic approach involving all; 40-acre campus;
   intensive individual and group therapy; vo-tech programs;
   behavior managements built on rewards, recognition,
   problem resolution; funded by school districts; suburban
   location; interns accepted.

Vantage Program (1992)
PO Box L, Willow Grove, PA 19090
Kathy Van Horn, Dir of Alt Ed Prgms, 215-542-7737, FAX: 215-
   657-3593
Montgomery and Bucks County
Type: independent, non-profit; paid by district
7-10 teachers, 25-35 students, mainly At-risk, ages 12-21,
   7-12th grade
Entrance requirements: interview; residency
Affiliation: Lakeside Youth Service
Governance by board
Teacher qualifications: PA certification
Involves family, community; intensive counseling; conflict
   resolution, social skills; 8-12 students/class; transition to
   district classes; suburban location; interns accepted.

Friends Central School
1101 City Ave, Wynnewood, PA 19096
David Felsen, Head, 215-642-7575
Type: independent

Lane Montessori School
630 Clothier Rd, Wynnewood, PA 19096-2214

Friends Council on Education
(See Resource Appendix)

Center City Homeschoolers (1989)
2203 Spruce St, Philadelphia, PA 19103
Marion Cohen; Kitty Anderson, 215-732-7723, 482-7933
Philadelphia County
Non-profit

Friends Select School
17th & the Parkway, Philadelphia, PA 19103
Donald Billingsley, 215-561-5900
Type: Quaker

Greene Towne School
2013 Appletree St, Philadelphia, PA 19103-1409
Regina Delaney
Type: Montessori

Montessori Genesis II
631 N 39th St, Philadelphia, PA 19104

Schuylkill City Child Development
PO Box 302, Philadelphia, PA 19105-0302
Type: Montessori

The Bridge
8400 Pine Rd, Philadelphia, PA 19111
Robert Randall

**Wyndmoor Montessori School/AERCO Montessori
   Teacher Ed Program**
1400 E Willow Grove Ave, Philadelphia, PA 19118-1652
Barbara Pimental

Chestnut Hill College Montessori TEP
Germantown & Northwestern, Philadelphia, PA 19118-2695
Roseann Quinn, SSJ
Type: Montessori teacher education

Norwood-Fontbonne Academy
8891 Germantown Ave, Philadelphia, PA 19118-2777
Sr Roseann Quinn
Type: Montessori

Project Learn School (1969)
6525 Germantown Ave, Philadelphia, PA 19119
Robin Ann Ingram, Educational Coordinator, 215-438-3623
Type: independent, non-profit; tuition: $3,900/yr
8 teachers, 80 students, ages 5-14
Entrance requirements: fee and visit
Governance by parent cooperative
Staff/parent and student consensus decision-making;
   student narrative self-evaluation; extensive parent participation and teaching; no letter grades; multi-aged classes;
   extensive field trips; urban location; interns accepted.

Germantown Montessori School
6767 Germantown Ave, Philadelphia, PA 19119-2111

William Dick Head Start Program
2500 W Diamond St, Philadelphia, PA 19121-1202
Type: Montessori

Philadephia Schools Pre-K Headstart
Stevens Bldg, 13th & Spring Garden #301, Philadephia, PA
   19123
David Silberman, Asst Dir
Type: Montessori

Frankford Friends School
1500 Orthodox St, Philadelphia, PA 19124
J. Terrrence Farley, Prin, 215-533-5368
Type: Quaker

Young Horizons Learning Center
5024 Penn St, Philadelphia, PA 19124-2628
Type: Montessori

Bambino Gesu Nursery
1624 W 16th St, Philadelphia, PA 19130
Type: Montessori

New Path Montessori School
4953 N 10th St, Philadelphia, PA 19141
Ilona Shafer or Richard Chapman

Manna Head Start
4830 N 11th St, Philadelphia, PA 19141-3404
Type: Montessori

Morton School
63rd & Elmwood, Philadelphia, PA 19142
Type: Montessori

Philadelphia Community School
4625 Baltimore St, Philadelphia, PA 19143

Germantown Friends School
31 W Coulter St, Philadelphia, PA 19144
Richard Goldman, 215-951-2300
Type: Quaker

Greene Street Friends School
5511 Greene St, Philadelphia, PA 19144
Norma Vogel, Prin, 215-438-7545
Type: Quaker

William Penn Charter School
3000 W School House Ln, Philadelphia, PA 19144
Earl Ball, 215-844-3460
Type: independent

Aquarian Research Foundation (1970)
(See Resource Appendix)

JFK Education Center
734 Schuylkill Ave, Philadelphia, PA 19146

Philadelphia School (1972)
2501 Lombard St, Philadelphia, PA 19146
Sandra Dean, Prin, 215-545-5323, FAX: 215-546-1798
Type: independent, non-profit; scholarships
27 teachers, 239 students, ages 5-14, K-8th grade
Affiliations: PAPAS, NAIS
Governance by board
Interdisciplinary thematic curriculum; empasis on environ-
    mental education, urban studies and the arts; Spanish;
    team teaching; no letter grades; multi-aged classes; exten-
    sive field trips; interns accepted.

Creative and Performing Arts
11th and Catherine Sts, Philadelphia, PA 19147
Ellen Savitz, 215-351-7140
Type: magnet
9-12th grade

Homeschool Resource Center
7318 Castor Ave, Philadeophia, PA 19152

Learning Experiences, Inc
RD #3, Buck Run Rd, Coatesville, PA 19320

School of Living
(See Resource Appendix)

Concord Friends Nursery School (1963)
Box 23, Concordville, PA 19331
Noreen Gaynor, Dir
Delaware County
Type: Quaker, non-profit; tuition: $1,400/yr, scholarships
3 teachers, 17 students, ages 4-5, pre K
Entrance requirement: age 4 by Sept 1
Affiliation: Quaker
Governance by principal, board
Teacher qualifications: early childhood, elementary
    certification
Hands-on approach; environment and nature study.

PRIMAK Education Foundation
38 N Waterloo Rd, Devon, PA 19333

Chester County Homeschoolers (1985)
226 Llandovery Dr, Exton, PA 19341
Don & Claudia Joye; Pres, Secretary/Editor, 215-524-0296
Large group; newsletter; meetings; classes; workshops; clubs;
    field trips; project fairs.

NCACS Teacher Education Program (1991)
429 Greenridge Rd, Glenmoore, PA 19343
Sandra M. Hurst, Dir, 215-458-5138
Chester County
Entrance requirements: application and recommendation.
Individually designed mentorships; seminars; research or
    project; alternative month placement; certification.

Upattinas School (1971)
429 Greenridge Rd, Glenmoore, PA 19343
Sandra Hurst, Dir, 215-458-5138
Chester County
Type: independent/home-based, boarding, non-profit
11 teachers, 80 students, ages 5-19, K-12th grade
Entrance restriction: no Neo-Nazi students permitted;
    entrance requirements: application, visit
Governance by democratic school meeting
Teacher qualifications: individually decided by school
Enrollment, materials, support for homeschooling; interna-
    tional student placement; I-20 authorization; exchanges,
    part time programs; independent study; no letter grades;
    non-compulsory class attendance; multi-aged classes;
    extensive field trips; rural location; interns accepted.

Allshouse
88 E Thomas Ctd, Kennett Square, PA 19348-1852
Sara T Allshouse
Type: Montessori

Willistown Country Day School
Paoli Pike, Malvern, PA 19355
Marilyn Reeves
Type: Montessori

Fairville Early Learning Center
Box 189, Mendenhall, PA 19357
Barbara Rowe, 215-388-1268
Type: independent

Goshen Friends School (1959)
814 N Chester Rd, West Chester, PA 19380
Linda H. Traver-Neeld, Head, 215-696-8869
Type: Quaker, non-profit; tuition: $910-4300/yr, scholarships
15 teachers, 172 students, ages 3-10, pre K-5th grade
Affiliation: Society of Friends
Governance by school committee, Goshen Friends Meeting
Teacher qualifications: college degree, experience, ability to
    create programs
Eclectic approach; thematic; stresses community building;
    conflict resolution; suburban location.

West Chester Friends School
415 N High St, West Chester, PA 19380
Leslie Spangler, Dir of Adms, 610-696-293, FAX: 610-431-1457
Type: independent, non-profit; tuition: $5,600-5,900/yr,
    scholarships
24 teachers, 161 students, ages 5-12, K-6th grade
Admissions testing required
Affiliation: Religious Society of Friends
Governance by principal, board
On-site intergenerational service in adjacent boarding home
    for elderly; extensive field trips; suburban location; trans-
    portation; interns accepted.

Geode Educational Options
(See Resource Appendix)

Brandy Wine Children's House
4121 Ciderknoll Way, West Chester, PA 19382
Type: Montessori

Montessori Requisites–USA
(See Resource Appendix)

Shelter Educational Program
    Montgomery County Youth Center (1988)
540 Port Indian Rd, Norristown, PA 19403
Kevin Gentilcore, Lead Tch, 215-631-1893, FAX:-5394
Type: public at-risk
2 teachers, 12 students, ages 12-17, 6-12th grade
Enrollment restricted to court orders and dependency cases
Governance by lead teacher and exec dir
Teacher qualifications: PA Certification, 3 years experience
Law related curriculum; teens and tots program; guest
    speakers; field trips; art; multi-aged classes; suburban loca-
    tion; interns accepted.

Centre Square Montessori School
1775 Skippack Pike, Centre Square, PA 19422-1314
Patricia McNicholas

Gwynedd Friends Preschool (1943)
Rt 202 & Sumneytown Pke, Box 142, Gwynedd, PA 19436
Pam Callentine, Dir, 215-699-3055
Montgomery County
Type: Quaker, non-profit; tuition: $580-1,260/mo,
    scholarships
9 teachers, 100 students, ages 2.5-5
Affiliation: Religious Society of Friends
Governance by principal, board
Teacher qualifications: education degree preferred
Wholistic; suburban location.

Kimberton Waldorf School
W Seven Star Rd, Kimberton, PA 19442
Andy Dill

Learning Tree Montessori School
500 W Main St, Lansdale, PA 19446

Miquon School
Harts Lane, Miquon, PA 19452
Greg Williams, 215-828-1231
Type: independent

Plymouth Meeting Friends School
2150 Butler Pile, Plymouth Meeting, PA 19462
Anne Javsicas, Head, 215-828-2288
Type: Quaker

Alternatives Corporation of Pottstown
Beech & Warren Sts, Pottstown, PA 19464
Denise Bray

Children's House of Northern Chester County (1978)
RD #2 Old Rt 23, Pottstown, PA 19464
Caryl Ann Cooper, 215-469-0742
Type: Montessori, non-profit
1 teacher, 1 assistant, 30 students, ages 3-6
Governance by administrator
Music; aerobics; kinder-gym; one-way observation mirrors;
    parent volunteers accepted for various activities; childcare;
    suburban location.

Collegeville Montessori Academy
952 Bethel Church Rd, Spring City, PA 19475
Alisa Dooley

Montessori Academy of Pennsylvania
645 South Reading Ave, Boyertown, PA 19512-2017
Robin John

Alsace Montessori Day Care
RR 3 Box 3221, Fleetwood, PA 19522-9323

Montessori Childrens House
RR 2 Box 2403, Fleetwood, PA 19522-9422

Project STAY
RR 1, PO Box 7, Robesonia, PA 19551

Reed Shelter Alternative Education Program
RD #2, PO Box 96B, Womelsdorf, PA 19567
Alan B. Moyer

Winston Hall
2249 Fairview Ave, Reading, PA 19606-1823
Elaine Macey
Type: Montessori

Alvernia Montessori School
Mt Alvernia, Reading, PA 19607

Montessori Country Day School
2200 State Hill Rd, Wyomissing, PA 19610
Cindy Rusnak

Puerto Rico

Escuela Montessori del Caribe
PO Box 8607, Huaco, PR 00661

Puerto Rico Homeschooling Association
503 Barbe St, Santurce, PR 00912
Type: state home-based

Centro Pre-Escolar Montessori
622 Andalucia Ave, Puerto Nuevo, PR 00920

Centro de Estudios Montessori
Apartado 34155-Estación San Fernando,Calle Paraná, Río
    Piedras, PR 00926-4155
Type: Montessori teacher education

Escuela Montessori Mercedes Morales
Calle Eugenia 6A #1, Guaynabo, PR 00966
Mercedes Morales

Rhode Island

Rhode Island Guild of Home Teachers
97 Robin Hollow Rd, W. Greenwich, RI 02817

Frenchtown Learning Center
PO Box 252, East Greenwich, RI 02818-0252
Type: Montessori

Merlyn's Pen (1985)
(See Resource Appendix)

Parent Educators of Rhode Island
PO Box 782, Glendale, RI 02826
Type: state home-based

South County Montessori School
1239 Tower Hill Rd, N Kingstown, RI 02852
Marika Moosbrugger, 401-294-3575, FAX: 401-295-8444
Non-profit
6 teachers, 14 assistants, 98 students, mainly International, ages 3-6
Affiliation: NAEYC; accreditations: RI DE, DCYF
Governance by administrator, board
Childcare; rural location; interns accepted.

South Kingston High School
215 Columbia St, Wakefield, RI 02879
Community School
Type: public choice

Rhode Island Guild of Home Teachers
272 Pequot Av, Warwick, RI 02886
401-737-2265

Meadowbrook Waldorf School (1988)
PO Box 508, West Kingston, RI 02892
Patricia McGauran, Secretary, 401-782-1312
Washington County
Non-profit; tuition: $2,780-4,050/yr, scholarships
14 teachers, 117 students, ages 4-11, K-5th grade
Entrance requirements: application, parent interview
Affiliations: AWSNA, AEC, Waldorf Kindergarten Assn
Governance by faculty and staff
Teacher qualifications: college degree, Waldorf certificate
Rural location; interns accepted.

E. W. Flynn Elementary
220 Blackstone St, Providence, RI 02905
Robert Britto, 401-456-9373
Type: magnet
K-5th grade
Critical thinking; gifted.

Mary E. Fogarty Elementary
199 Oxford St, Providence, RI 02905
Lummer Jennings, 401-456-9381
Type: magnet
K-5th grade
Computers; multi-media; gifted.

Roger Williams Middle School
278 Thurbers Ave, Providence, RI 02905
Joseph Maguire, 401-456-9355
Type: magnet
6-8th grade
Science; visual, performing arts.

Wellspring Community School (1993)
155 Gordon Ave, Providence, RI 02905

Maria Sperduti, Dir, 401-941-3114
Type: independent; tuition: $4,200/yr, scholarships
2 teachers, 12 students, ages 5-7, K-3rd grade
Entrance requirements: visit
Governance by teachers, principal, board
Experiential; multi-disciplinary; encourages independent and cooperative work; empathy and respect; active and fun; no letter grades; multi-aged classes; extensive field trips; urban location.

Hope High School
424 Hope St, Providence, RI 02906
John Short, 401-456-9161
Type: magnet
9-12th grade
Arts; communications.

Lincoln School (1984)
301 Butler Ave, Providence, RI 02906
Hallie Sammartino, Marketing/PR Dir, 401-331-9696, FAX: 751-6670
Providence County
Type: Quaker, non-profit; tuition: $4,600-9,500/yr, scholarships
58 teachers, 305 students, ages 5-18, pre K-12th grade
Governance by administrative council, board
College prep; honors sections; AP courses; extensive field trips; interns accepted.

Moses Brown School
250 Lloyd Ave, Providence, RI 02906
David C. Burnham, Head
Type: independent

School One
75 John St, Providence, RI 02906
Type: independent

NEECA Childcare Program
343 Morris Ave, Providence, RI 02906-2610
Nancy Rose
Type: Montessori

Montessori Children's House
518 Lloyd Ave, Providence, RI 02906-5429

Educational Resource Center of Rhode Island
50 Rounds Avenue, Providence, RI 02907
Maria Sperduti, 401-941-4114
Type: home-based, non-profit

The Alternate Learning Project
582 Elmwood Ave, Providence, RI 02907
Anne Colannino, Coord, 401-456-9194
Type: public choice
HS

Curriculum Resource Center, Rhode Island College
600 Mt Pleasant Ave, Providence, RI 02908
Dr David C Woolman
Type: Montessori

Coalition of Essential Schools
(See Resource Appendix)

Montessori School, Inc
160 Orchard St, E Providence, RI 02914

South Carolina

Montessori Learning Center (1978)
190 Battleship Rd, Camden, SC 29020
Sheryl M. Sweet, Adm Dir, 803-432-6828
Non-profit; tuition: $1,650-2,650/yr
5 teachers, 5 assistants, 67 students, mainly international,
    ages infant-12
Accreditation: MIA
Governance by administrator, board
Childcare; suburban location; interns accepted.

Institute for Guided Studies (1990)
PO Box 13, Lugoff, SC 29020
Sheryl M. Sweet, Course Dir, 803-438-1797
Type: Montessori teacher education
Students mainly International
Entrance requirements: HS diploma
Affiliation: MIA
Governance by administrator
Seminars; workshops; consultants; on-site programs.

**South Carolina Association of Independent
    Homeschools**
PO Box 2104, Irmo, SC 29063
803-551-1003
Type: state home-based

South Carolina Home Educators Association
PO Box 612, Lexington, SC 29071
803-951-8960

College of Early Learning
PO Box 711, Columbia, SC 29202
Kathy Macedon, 803-772-3317
Type: Montessori
Student ages 2-14

Montessori Elementary School of Columbia (1983)
2807 Oleola St, Columbia, SC 29205
Nathan M. Crystal, Treasurer, 803-256-2823
Non-profit; tuition: $2,600/yr
2 teachers, 1 assistant, 39 students, ages 6-12
Accreditation: AMS
Governance by board
Spanish; arts; interns accepted.

Montessori Middle School of Columbia, Inc. (1989)
3504 Devine St, Columbia, SC 29205
Diane Buchanan, Dir, 803-254-6646
Non-profit; tuition: $2650/yr.
1 teacher, 15 students, ages 12-15
Affiliation: AMS
Governance by a board of trustees
Focus on full personal development.

Crystal Montessori Elementary School of Columbia
3949 Kenilworth Rd, Columbia, SC 29205-1503

Montessori Child Development Center
611 Holly St, Columbia, SC 29205-2513

Montessori Early Learning Center, Inc
1101 Balsam Rd, Columbia, SC 29210-7914

Wil Lou Gray Opportunity School (1921)
PO Drawer 280128, Columbia, SC 29228
Dr Mary Catherine Norwood, Superintendent, 803-822-5480,
    FAX: 803-822-8146

Lexington County
Type: public at-risk, boarding; scholarships
23 teachers, 170 students, ages 15+, 9-12th grade
Entrance requirements: school records, medical information,
    application
Governance by board
Case management teams; outdoor education; vocational
    training; college residential setting; individualized instruc-
    tion; suburban location; interns accepted.

Carolina Super Schoolers
777 Hillview St, Spartanburg, SC 29302
Merike Tamm, 803-583-4018

Hidden Vista Montessori
7500 Hwy 9, Inman, SC 29349-8030

Montessori Fountainhead School
PO Box 729, Bryn Athyn, SC 29401

Burke Academic High School
244 President St, Charleston, SC 29403
Leckyler Gaillard, 803-724-7290
District 20
Type: magnet
9-12th grade
School within school.

Ashlye River Elementary
1871 Wallace School Rd, Charleston, SC 29407
Rose Maree Myers, 803-723-1555
District 10
Type: magnet
K-5th grade
Arts-at-Heart.

Charles Towne Montessori School
56 Leinbach Dr, Charleston, SC 29407-6988
Esta Drr

Montessori School of Charleston
95 Folly Rd Blvd, Charleston, SC 29407-7532

Montessori Community School (1989)
2120 Wood Ave, Charleston, SC 29414
Eva Abbate, Dir, 803-763-8506, FAX: 803-763-5827 x51
Non-profit; tuition: $220-285/mo
3 teachers, 3 assistants, 39 students, ages 3-12
Affiliation: AMI
Governance by board
Childcare; suburban location; interns accepted.

Howard School
PO Box 609, Georgetown, SC 29440
Judy Engle, Director, 803-546-0219

Montessori School of Mount Pleasant
414 Whilden St, Mount Pleasant, SC 29464-5341

Central School
Greenwood School District 50, Greenwood, SC 29468
Gayle Fish, Principal

Compu-Educare BBS
(See Resource Appendix)

Montessori School of Florence
619 Gregg Ave, Florence, SC 29501
B. J. Warner

Pawleys Island Montessori
Hwy 17 S, PO Box 426, Pawleys Island, SC 29585
Pamela Mills

Bob Jones University Press
(See Resource Appendix)

Montessori School of Greenville
305 Pelham Rd, Greenville, SC 29615-3110

Montessori School of Anderson (1973)
280 Sam McGee Rd, Anderson, SC 29621
Karen R. Holt, Adm, 803-226-5344
Non-profit; tuition: $200-335/mo
6 teachers, 6 assistants, 175 students, ages infant-15
Affiliation: AMI; accreditation: AMS
Governance by administrator, board
Community outreach projects for grades 5-8; multi-cultural;
   childcare; rural location; interns accepted.

Clemson Montessori School (1976)
207 Pendleton Rd, Clemson, SC 29631
Gail Paul, Dir, 654-4483
Tuition: $1,300-3,350/yr
8 teachers, 4 assistants, 102 students, mainly International,
   ages infant-12
Governance by administrator
Emphasis on science and art; childcare; rural location; interns
   accepted.

Alpha Montessori School
211 Pendleton Rd, Clemson, SC 29631-2262

National Dropout Prevention Center
(See Resource Appendix)

Todd's Montessori School
109 Blakely St, Mauldin, SC 29662

Montessori Children's House
PO Box 743, Mauldin, SC 29662-0743
Mallika Vejay

Oconee County Target 2000 Project
PO Box 220, Walhalla, SC 29691
803-546-0219

Aiken Montessori Center
15 Hills Woodland Ln SW, Aiken, SC 29801-3383
Ellen Snyder

John de la Howe School
Route 1, PO Box 154, McCormick, SC 29835
803-391-2131

Walden Hall Christian Montessori
1896 Knobcone Ave, North Augusta, SC 29841-6027

Eleanor Christensen Montessori
PO Box 1438, Beaufort, SC 29901
Ellen Taylor

E. C. Montessori School (1973)
810 Duke St, Beaufort, SC 29902
Jeni C. Feeser, Admin Dir, 803-525-1141
Non-profit; tuition: $1710-2385/9 mo
5 teachers, 4 assistants, 15 students, ages infant-12
Affiliations: AMS, AMI
Governance by board
Urban location; interns accepted.

Sea Pines Montessori School (1968)
9 Fox Grape Rd, Hilton Head Island, SC 29928
Maxine, 803-785-2534, FAX: 803-785-9537
Non-profit; tuition: $950-2,990/yr
9 teachers, 17 assistants, 270 students, ages infant-6
Affiliations: AMS, SCAFYC
Governance by board
Teacher qualifications: AMS Certification
Cited by Ford Foundation as one of top 10 US preschools;
   interns accepted.

South Dakota

Aspire High
1109 W Cedar, Beresford, SD 57004
Dean Lindstrom, Dir

Select High
700 22nd Ave, Brookings, SD 57006
Fran Schoenfelder, Dir

STRIVE High Alternative School (1989)
513 E 8th St, Dell Rapids, SD 57022
Barb Resick, Coord, 605-428-5231
Minnehaha County
Type: public at-risk
2 teachers, 24 students, ages 14-21, 9-12th grade
District referral and residency required
Affiliation: DL&E
Governance by board, coordinator, staff, district
Teacher qualifications: certification
Training program; required attendance; students must have
   part-time job, work one subject at a time; rural location;
   interns accepted.

AIM High
102 N Egan, Madison, SD 57022-1199
Carol M. Stonefield, Dir

Zenith High
PO Box 430, Tyndall, SD 57066-0430
Rick Klawiter, Dir

Goal Achievement Program
PO Box 76, Yankton, SD 57078-0076
Kim Crossan, Dir

Alternative Learning Center
1900 Ferdig, Yankton, SD 57078-1858
David Bitter, Dir

South Dakota Homeschool Association
PO Box 882, Sioux Falls, SD 57101

Reach High
1001 W 11th, Sioux Falls, SD 57104
Teri Sheppard, Dir

Nova Alternative School
PO Box 81, Watertown, SD 57201-0081
Bob Nygaard, Dir

Alternative Education Program
PO Box 949, Huron, SD 57350-0949
Fred Kober, Dir

Montessori Center of Aberdeen
117 12th Ave NE, Aberdeen, SD 57401

George S. Mickelson Alternative Program
PO Box 560, Redfield, SD 57469-0560
Betty Williams, Dir

Right Turn
302 E Cakota Ave, Pierre, SD 57501-3133
Kay Gilsrud, Dir

Gutzon Borglum Alternative (1990)
2000 Mulberry, Yankton, SD 57580
Elaine Kauer, Coord, 605-665-1416, FAX: 605-665-8369
Yankton County

Type: public at-risk
3 teachers, 25 students, ages 16–21, 10–12th grade
Residency required
Governance by teachers and principal
Teacher qualifications: SD Certification
Urban location.

Program Project 2000
300 6th St, Rapid city, SD 57701-2723
Norma Denault, Dir

Nils A. Boe Youth Forestry Camp
HC 83 Box 69A, Custer, SD 57730
Brian Wallin, Dir

ACE
215 N 3rd St, Custer, SD 57730-1005
Gloria Schaffer

Red Cloud Indian School
Holy Rosary Mission, Pine Ridge, SD 57770
Type: Montessori

Tennessee

Overton High School
1770 Lanier, Memphis, TN 33117
Clark White, 901-684-2136
Type: magnet
9–12th grade
Creative and performing arts.

Hawkins County Alternative (1992)
Hwy 11 W, Surgoinsville, TN 33117
Gena Venable, 615-345-3506
Type: public at-risk
3 teachers, 50 students, ages 14–18, HS
Governance by principal
Multi-aged classes.

Montessori Academy (1967)
6021 Cloverland Dr, Brentwood, TN 37027
Eileen Bernstorf, 615-833-3610
Non-profit; tuition: $180–380/mo
11 teachers, 8 assistants, 240 students, ages 3–12
Entrance requirements: interview
Affiliation: AMS
Governance by administrator
24 acres; French; PE; music; extras include Suzuki violin and
piano, drama, Montessori singers; childcare; suburban
location; interns accepted.

Montessori School
121 Circle Hill Dr, Clarksville, TN 37042-6438

Harpeth Academy
150 Franklin Rd, Franklin, TN 37064-2216
Type: Montessori

Ithaka Montessori
1261 Columbia Ave, Franklin, TN 37064-3639
Merrie B King

Greenleaf Press
(See Resource Appendix)

Family Christian Academy
(See Resource Appendix)

Murfreesboro Montessori School
324 E College St, Murfreesboro, TN 37130-3825

Abintra Montessori School (1980)
914 Davidson Dr, Nashville, TN 37205
Francie Beard, Dir, 615-352-4317, FAX: 615-352-1529
Non-profit; tuition: $3,675-4,150/yr
6 teachers, 4 assistants, 100 students, ages 3–12
Affiliation: AMS; TNDHS License
Governance by board of trustees
4 wooded acres in residential area; visual arts, music and
drama artist in residence program; whole language, anti-
bias, multicultural specialist; childcare; interns accepted.

Overbrook School
4210 Harding Rd, Nashville, TN 37205-2088
Type: Montessori

Academy for Kiddies
1007 21st Ave N, Nashville, TN 37208-2911
Type: Montessori

Home Education Association of Tennessee (HEAT)
3677 Richbriar Ct, Nashville, TN 37211
Type: state home-based

Mercy Montessori School
2008 24th Ave S, Nashville, TN 37212-4202

HOT
3135 Lakeland Dr, Nashville, TN 37214-3312
Jacki Willard
Type: home-based

Children's House of Nashville
3404 Belmont Blvd, Nashville, TN 37215-1642
Type: Montessori

Montessori Centre (1967)
4608 Granny White Pike, Nashville, TN 37220
Harriette Derryberry, Owner/Dir, 615-373-0897
Tuition: $407-500/mo
3 teachers, 3 assistants, 64 students, ages infant-6
Affiliation: AMS
Governance by owner
Twelve month, full day; on 4 acres; urban location; interns
    accepted.

North Cleveland Alternative School (1991)
PO Box 399, Cleveland, TN 37364
John Driver, 2ndary Supervisor, 615-476-0620, FAX:-0485
Bradley County
Type: public at-risk
3 teachers, 25 students, ages 6-18, 1-12th grade
Enrollment restricted to SE or suspended county residents
Governance by board
Teacher qualifications: state license
SE, SED, BD, LD; urban location; interns accepted.

Montessori Children's House
302 Signal Mountain Blvd, Signal Mountain, TN 37377-1831

Alternative Classroom (1990)
Grundy County High School, Tracy City, TN 37387
Marshall Gilliam, Tch, 615-592-5741, FAX: 615-692-2188
Type: public at-risk
1 teacher, 10 students, ages 11-18, 7-12th grade
No residency requirement
Governance by teachers, principal, parent coop, board
Teacher qualifications: TN Certification
Rural location; transportation; interns accepted.

Ray's Montessori School
101 Bragg Circle, Tullahoma, TN 37388-2975

School Training At-Risk Students (STARS) (1988)
College St, Winchester, TN 37398
Juanita Syler, Attendance Supervisor, 615-967-5317, FAX: 615-
    967-7832
Franklin County
Type: public at-risk
2 teachers; students mainly at-risk, ages 12+, 7-12th grade
Entrance requirements: school referrals
Governance by Disciplinary Hearing Authority
Teacher qualifications: bachelor's degree/vocational skills
Mission: place students in the world of work, with skills for
    getting a job; emphasis on survival skills; rural location.

Training Learning Center (TLC) (1988)
Franklin County BE, PO Box 129, Winchester, TN 37398
Juanita Syler, Attendance Supervisor, 615-967-2574, FAX: 615-
    967-7832
Franklin County
Type: public choice/at-risk
1 teacher; students mainly at-risk, ages 12-17, 6-12th grade
Entrance requirements: school referrals; no residency
    requirement
Governance by board and Disciplinary Hearing Authority
Teacher qualifications: bachelor's degree/special ed
Mission: prepare students to return to regular classes to
    get regular or special diploma; emphasis on behavioral
    skills; individual attention; multi-aged classes; rural
    location.

Red Bank Middle and Central High (1990)
201 Broad St, Chattanooga, TN 37401-1089
Don Upton, 2ndary Ed Dir, 615-757-1730, FAX:-1777
Type: public at-risk
10 teachers, 40 students, ages 12-21
Entrance by referral for discipline problems
Governance by teachers and principal
Teacher qualifications: TN certification
Suburban location.

Montessori World of Children (1981)
1080 McCallie Ave, Chattanooga, TN 37404
Bobbe Spink, Dir, 615-622-6366
Tuition: $225-350/mo
5 teachers, 5 assistants, 105 students, ages infant-12
Governance by teachers and administrators
French (ages 5-12); computer programming (ages 6-12); girl
    and boy scouts (age 6-12); childcare; urban location.

Henry L. Barger School
4808 Brainerd Rd, Chattanooga, TN 37411
Christine Hicks
Type: Montessori

Johnson City Montessori School
1208 Timberlake Rd, Johnson City, TN 37601

Ashley Academy
816 Lacy St, Johnson City, TN 37604-3767
Type: Montessori

Johnson Academy (1993)
John Exum Pkwy, Johnson City, TN 37605
Frank Hill, Dir
Washington County
Type: public at-risk
7 teachers, 125 students
Entrance requirements: interview, residency
Governance by principal and democratic school meeting
Multiple handicapped preschoolers; grades 6-12, at risk; sub-
    urban location; interns accepted.

TN Homeschool Families
888 Shadden Rd, Gray, TN 37615
Margie Lesch
Type: state home-based

YMCA Children's House
400 Edgemont Ave, Bristol, TN 37620-2360
Type: Montessori

Kingsport Montessori School
1705 Orchard Ct, Kingsport, TN 37660-4521

Maryville Montessori School
1833 Wright Rd, Alcon, TN 37701

Alcon City Schools
524 Faraday St, Alcon, TN 37701
Bill Symon, 615-989-0531, FAX: 615-984-5830
Non-profit
1500 students, ages 5-20
Governance by principal
Multi-aged classes; extensive field trips; suburban location;
    interns accepted.

Alternative Vocational Program (1980)
Rt 4 Box 445, Harriman, TN 37748
Chester Silvers, 615-882-6815
Roane County
Type: public at-risk
3 teachers, 20 students, ages 14-18, 9-12th grade
Entrance requirements: committee referral, residency
Governance by faculty and student representatives
Glasser control theory; no letter grades; rural location.

Educational Choices
Rt 2, Box 224X, Harriman, TN 37748
Susan Thatcher
Type: home-based

New Horizon Montessori School (1978)
913 Cumberland Dr, Louisville, TN 37777
Aleta Ledendecker, 615-970-4322
Tuition: $225-310/mo

4 teachers, 2 assistants, 64 students, ages 3–15
Affiliations: NAMTA, AMI, TN; accreditation: MEI
Governance by administrator
Nursing home visits; student-directed Shakespearean and original plays; childcare; suburban location; interns accepted.

Montessori Center of Oak Ridge (1976)
100 Adams Ln, Suite C, Oak Ridge, TN 37830-4903
Susan Tull, Administrator, 615-482-5036
Non-profit; tuition: $200/260/mo
2 teachers, 2 assistants, 50 students, ages 3–6
Entrance requirements: age 2.5 and toilet trained
Affiliations: AMS, AMI
Governance by administrator, board
Childcare; urban location.

Tennessee Homeschooling Families (1986)
214 Park Lane, Oak Ridge, TN 37840
Lynn Kemper-Wallace, Managing Editor, 615-345-4375
Anderson County
Newsletter; promotes unschooling.

Homeschooling Families
214 Park Ln, Oliver Springs, TN 37840

Oneida Special School District (1915)
PO Box 4819, Oneida, TN 37841
L. Mayfield Brown, Supt, 615-569-8912, FAX: 569-2201
Scott County
Type: public choice
82 teachers, 1180 students, ages 4–22, pre K–12th grade
No residency requirement
Governance by school board, Supt
Teacher qualifications: certification
Flexible scheduling; mini-courses; low ratio; fine arts; whole language; manipulatives; cooperative learning; multi-aged classes; interns accepted.

Sevier County PS City As School Program (1993)
1150 Dolly Parton Pkwy, Sevierville, TN 37862
Scott Borah, 615-453-1077
Type: public choice
25 students

The Elijah Company
(See Resource Appendix)

Laurel High School
1539 Laurel Ave, Knoxville, TN 37914
Mary Oliver, 615-525-3885
Type: independent; tuition: $3478/yr, scholarships
5 teachers, 30 students
Governance by board, democratic school meeting
Wide range of classes and independent projects; considers that education goes on all the time and gives recognition for any constructive activity, in or out of school; non-compulsory class attendance; multi-aged classes; extensive field trips; urban location.

Nature's Way Montessori School
3225 Garden Dr, Knoxville, TN 37918
Mary Smith

Giving Tree Montessori School
4311 Kingston Pike, Knoxville, TN 37919-4077

Smoky Mountain Chapter, Tennessee Home Education Association
925 View Harbor, Knoxville, TN 37922
615-675-3073
Knox County

Crockett County Alternative School (1988)
Conley Rd, Rte 2, Alamo, TN 38001

Charles Williamson, Dir, 901-696-4778
Type: public at-risk
2 teachers, 5–15 students, ages 12–18, 5–12th grade
No residency requirement
Teacher qualifications: BS, TN license
Rural location; transportation.

Volunteer State Academy
PO Box 143, Brownsville, TN 38012
Type: Montessori

Lauderdale County Alternative High School (1989)
PO Box 350, Ripley, TN 38063
Louis Wheatley, 901-635-2941, FAX: 901-635-7985
Type: public at-risk
1 teacher, 15 students, ages 14–18, 7–12th grade
Enrollment restricted to residents assigned by Disciplinary Hearing Board
Governance by principal and board
Teacher qualifications: state certification
Rural location; interns accepted.

Idlewild Elementary
1950 Linden, Memphis, TN 38104
Dr James Luckey, 901-733-3440
Type: magnet
1–6th grade
Individualized.

Cendrillion Montessori School
1642 Poplar Ave, Memphis, TN 38104-2510

St Peter's DC
1805 Poplar Ave, Memphis, TN 38104-2650
Type: Montessori

First Class Montessori School
1336 Peabody Ave, Memphis, TN 38104-3500
Type: Montessori

Greater Community Day Care
PO Box 7271, Memphis, TN 38107
Type: Montessori

Vollentine Elementary
1682 Vollentine, Memphis, TN 38107
Nettye Hassan, 901-722-4632
Type: magnet
1–6th grade
Individualized.

Springdale/Memphis Magnet School
880 N Hollywood, Memphis, TN 38108
Mamie Foster, 901-325-3488
1–6th grade
Open education.

Double Tree Elementary
4500 Double Tree, Memphis, TN 38109
Dora Purdy, 901-789-8144
Type: magnet
K–6th grade
Montessori.

Center of Attention
150 Hayden Pl, Memphis, TN 38111-3506
Type: Montessori

Threshold-A Montessori School
581 Ellsworth St, Memphis, TN 38111-4331

Lipman Montessori School
3771 Poplar Ave, Memphis, TN 38111-6020

Optional Schools Project Room 106
2597 Avery Ave, Memphis, TN 38112
Marilyn Simmons, 901-454-5200
Type: public choice

Roselle Elementary
993 Roland, Memphis, TN 38112
Charlene Turner, 901-722-4612
Type: magnet
1-6th grade
Creative and performing arts.

Lamplighter (1967)
1021 Mosby Rd, Memphis, TN 38116
Kathy Roemer, Assoc Head, 901-332-7500
Type: Montessori; tuition: $2,808-5,643/yr
6 teachers, 3 assistants, 155 students, ages infant-12
Affiliation: Memphis Ind. Schools; accreditations: AMS, SACS
Governance by board
Field trips to area museums; History of the Universe; foreign
   languages; computers; childcare; sub/urban location;
   interns accepted.

First Montessori Mid-South School
1864 Janis Dr, Memphis, TN 38116-2008

The Frady School
951 McClure Rd, Memphis, TN 38116-7715
Type: Montessori

Colonial Junior High School
4778 Sea Isle Rd, Memphis, TN 38117
Donna Essary, 901-761-8980
Type: magnet
7-9th grade
Creative and performing arts.

LaPapillon Montessori School
3246 Raines Rd E, Memphis, TN 38118

Israel Preschool
1376 East Massey, Memphis, TN 38120
Type: Montessori

Lausanne Montessori School
1381 W Massey Rd, Memphis, TN 38120-3298

Maria Montessori School at St Michael
3848 Forrest Ave, Memphis, TN 38122-3808

Memphis Montessori School
2619 Tricia Dr #2, Memphis, TN 38127

St Elizabeth Montessori School
4780 Yale Rd, Memphis, TN 38128

Montessori School
7623 US Highway 64, Memphis, TN 38133-3905

Raleigh-Bartlett Montessori
6050 Hwy 70, Bartlett, TN 38134

Olivia's Montessori School (1990)
2755 Appling, Memphis, TN 38134
Olivia Flasdick, 901-377-3081
Non-profit; tuition: $300/mo
1 teacher, 2 assistants, 20 students, ages 3-6
Affiliations: AMS, NAEYC
Governance by an administrator, democratic school meeting
Non-sexist; non-racist; ASL; Orff music; childcare; suburban
   location; interns accepted.

Play Care Montessori
6634 US Hwy 70, Bartlett, TN 38134-4741

Middle College High School at Shelby State CC (1987)
737 Union Ave E-102, Memphis, TN 38174-0568
Joyce C. Mitchell, Prin, 901-544-5360, FAX: 901-544-5368
Shelby County
Non-profit
21 teachers, 300 students, mainly at-risk, ages 15-20,
   10-12th grade
Affiliations: Memphis City Schools, SACS/TBR
Governance by faculty, principal, parents, students
Interdisciplinary; dual credit/enrollment; internships; teacher-
   counselor concept; activities; community outreach; interns
   accepted.

Parkview Elementary (1992)
905 E Chester St, Jackson, TN 38301
Charles I. Mercer, Prin, 401-422-3116
Type: public choice Montessori
6 teachers, 6 assistants, 136 students, ages 3-9
Affiliation: AMS
Governance by administrator

University School of Jackson (1970)
1981 Hollywood Dr, Jackson, TN 38305
Sherry Tignor, Admissions Dir, 668-0444;664-0812, FAX: 668-
   6910
Type: Montessori, non-profit; tuition: $2,190-3,660/yr
8 teachers, 8 assistants, 805 students, ages 3-18
Entrance requirements: exam; interview
Affiliations: NAMTA, TNMA, NAEYC, TNAEYC, NAIS, TNAIS; accreditation: SACS
Governance by board
20 acres; nature studies; student-centered approach; childcare; rural location; transportation.

Montessori Center of Jackson
2732 N Highland Ave, Jackson, TN 38305-1764

Montessori Kinder Care
502 S High St, Trenton, TN 38382-2032

The Farm School
50 The Farm, Summertown, TN 38483
615-964-2325
Type: home-based, non-profit
20 students, ages 5-12
Serves community and some outside students.

Dry Valley Alternative School (1979)
3860 Phifer Mtn Rd, Cookeville, TN 38501
Marcus Durley, Prin, 615-528-1847, FAX: 372-0382
Putnam County
Type: public at-risk
4 teachers, 40 students, ages 10-17, 5-12th grade
Entrance requirements: conference, residency
Governance by principal, board
Teacher qualifications: BA or BS
Multi-aged classes; individualized; suburban location; trans-
   portation; interns accepted.

Montessori Children's House
122 E 12th St, Cookeville, TN 38501-1303

Early School Materials
Rt 2, Celina, TN 38551
Jake Rockwood
Type: Montessori

Southeast Educational Materials
(See Resource Appendix)

Texas

Pebblebrook Academy
612 Pebblebrook, Allen, TX 75002
Type: Montessori

Contemporary Montessori Education
PO Box 1036, Allen, TX 75002-1036
Carmen Sexton

Mary Grimes Education Center
1745 Hutton, Canutillo, TX 75006
Dr Frank Taylor, 214-323-6450

Carrollton Montessori at Midway (1988)
3225 Belmeade, Carrollton, TX 75006-2341
214-380-2395
Tuition: $325/435/mo
4 teachers, 8 assistants, 110 students, ages 3-6
Entrance requirements: age 3 and toilet trained
Affiliations: MACTE, NAMTA; accreditation: MIA
Governance by administrator
Breakfast and lunch served; childcare; suburban location;
    transportation; interns accepted.

A Child's Garden Montessori
1935 Old Denton Rd, Carrollton, TX 75006-3756
Patricia Bradford

West Plano Montessori School
3425 Ashington Ln, Plano, TX 75023-3930

Preston Meadow Montessori School
6912 Ohio Dr, Plano, TX 75024-2515

DeGroot Learning Centers, Inc (1968)
PO Box 260765, Plano, TX 75026
Patricia De Groot-Cowles, Pres, 214-422-2414, FAX: 214-732-
    0678
Type: Montessori
10 teachers, 16 assistants, 206 students, ages infant-12
Entrance requirements: conference with family
Affiliation: NAEYC
Governance by administrator
Mortensen math; childcare; suburban location; interns
    accepted.

Sing and Learn Curriculum Supplies
(See Resource Appendix)

The Helping Hand
(See Resource Appendix)

Westchester Montessori
290 Westchester Pkwy, Grand Prairie, TX 75052

Agape School
151 W Purnell St, Lewisville, TX 75057-3917
Pat Bottalico
Type: Montessori

MEGA/Union Bower Center
101 E Union Bower, Irving, TX 75061
Margaret Barnett

Amberwood Montessori Academy
804 W Pioneer Dr, Irving, TX 75061-7434

Montessori of Las Colinas School & Training Center (1988)
4961 N O'Connor Blvd, Irving, TX 75062
Gale Keppler, Exec Dir, 214-717-0417
Type: Montessori higher education; tuition: $350-505/mo
8 teachers, 12 assistants, 134 students, ages infant-6/adult
Entrance requirements: interview with family.
Accreditations: MIA, MACTE
Governance by administrator
Awards full Montessori certification; evening and weekend
    classes; childcare; urban location; interns accepted.

Redeemer Montessori School (1978)
120 E Rochelle Rd, Irving, TX 75062
Donna Hatter, 214-257-3517
Tuition: $270-360/mo
4 teachers, 3 assistants, 65 students, ages 3-9
Entrance requirements: trial day
Affiliation: AMS
Culturally diverse area; Spanish; art; music; PE; intern site for
    AMS; staff development; strong parent group; childcare;
    suburban location; interns accepted.

Lewisville Learning Center
1597 S Edmonds, Lewisville, TX 75067
Beverly Martin, 214-219-6900

Montessori Learning Center
1319 Monaco Dr, Lewisville, TX 75067-5613

North Texas Self Educators (1991)
150 Forest Ln, Double Oak, TX 75067
Sarah Jordan, 817-430-4835, FAX: 817-430-4311
Non-profit
Inclusive; John Holt's student-led approach; workshops.

LINC Center
1 Duvall, McKinney, TX 75069
Gene Helton, 214-569-6428

Holy Nativity Montessori
2200 18th St Box 467, Plano, TX 75074

Keystone Academy
701 E Plano Pkwy, Suite 414, Plano, TX 75074
214-422-0826

Montessori: New Beginnings Academy
1301 Custer Rd #703, Plano, TX 75075-7486
Laurann Sutton

Alternative School
506 Lockwood, Richardson, TX 75080
Thresa Colgin, 214-470-5340

Highland Academy (1981)
1231 W Belt Line Rd, Richardson, TX 75080
Faye E. Handlogten, Dir, 214-238-7568
Dallas County
Type: independent; tuition: $7,000/yr, scholarships
14 teachers, 65 students, mainly at-risk, ages 5-14
Evaluation required
Governance by principal, teachers, democratic school
    meeting
Teacher qualifications: Academic Language Therapy
    certification
No letter grades; interns accepted.

Weise Memorial Academy (1991)
801 Canyon Creek Sq, Richardson, TX 75080
Rita Weise, Dir, 214-497-9667, FAX: 497-9667
Collin County
Type: independent, non-profit; tuition: $6,500/yr,
    scholarships
8 teachers, 35 students, mainly at-risk, ages 12–19, 7–12th
    grade
Entrance requirements: testing, drug free, contract
Governance by board, director
Teacher qualifications: degree, certification
Close personal relationship between student and teacher;
    small groups; interns accepted.

Alexander School (1975)
409 Richardson Pkwy, Richardson, TX 75081
David B. Bowlin, Exec Dir, 214-690-9210, FAX:-9284
Dallas County
Type: independent; tuition: $12,000/yr
21 teachers, 50 students, ages 13–19
Entrance requirements: testing, interview, transcript
Affiliation: SACS
Governance by teachers and principal
Teacher qualifications: degree, min 24 semester hrs in field
One to one teaching; supervised study time; electives in small
    groups; free tutoring; science lab; urban location.

Dallas Learning Center (1990)
301 S Sherman, Suite 116, Richardson, TX 75081
Kathleen Herrin-Kinard, Dir, 231-3723
Dallas County
Type: independent; tuition: $7,000/yr
4 teachers, 20 students, mainly at-risk, ages 14–20, 9–12th
    grade
Entrance requirements: interview, visit
Governance by teachers, principal
Teacher qualifications: TX certification and/or Master's
Self-paced; tutorials; accelerated programs; credit make up;
    no letter grades; multi-aged classes; extensive field trips;
    interns accepted.

KONOS
(See Resource Appendix)

Kinderhaus
203 Woodpark Ln, Rockwall, TX 75087
Judith A Head
Type: Montessori

Ridge Road Montessori School
2306 Ridge Rd, Rockwall, TX 75087

Creative Learning Center
704 Ridgeview Dr, Rockwall, TX 75087-4137
Type: Montessori

Belden Street Montessori School
618 W Belden St, Sherman, TX 75090-3711
Scottie Johnson

Pace School (1993)
815 Fairlawn Dr, Duncanville, TX 75116
Ruth Richey, Prin, 214-298-9661, FAX: 298-9698
Dallas County
Type: public at-risk
4 teachers, 27 students, mainly at-risk, ages 16–19, 10–12th
    grade
Entrance requirements: max age 21, residency
Governance by faculty and student representatives
Teacher qualifications: state certification
Self-paced; individualized; flexible scheduling; suburban loca-
    tion; transportation.

Lancaster ISD
1105 Westridge, Lancaster, TX 75146
Kathlyn Williams
Type: Montessori

Meadowview School
2419 Franklin, Mesquite, TX 75150
214-289-1831

B.T. Washington High School
2501 Flora, Dallas, TX 75201
Robert Watkins, 214-720-7300
Type: magnet
9–12th grade
Visual and performing arts.

Comprehensive Evening School
2218 Bryan, Dallas, TX 75201
Barbara Manns, 214-720-7380

Metropolitan Education Center
912 S Irving, Dallas, TX 75201
Pearly Wallace, 214-746-2620

School Community Guidance Center (1986)
912 S Ervay, Dallas, TX 75201
Maurice E. Walker, Prin, 214-746-2650, FAX: 746-2655
Type: public at-risk
10 teachers, 125 students, ages 12–17, 7–12th grade
Enrollment restricted to referred expelled/suspended
    residents
Affiliation: TX EA
Governance by principal
Teacher qualifications: TEA certification
Intensive management system; focus on appropriate behav-
    ior; multi-aged classes; urban location.

Metropolitan Center
1403 S Corinth, Dallas, TX 75202
Donna Johnson, 214-565-6440

**Salesmanship ClubCenter for Youth and Family
    Education**
110 E 10th St, Dallas, TX 75203
214-941-9192

The Notre Dame of Dallas Schools, Inc
2018 Allen St, Dallas, TX 75204
214-720-3911

St Christopher's Montessori School
2600 Westminster Ave, Dallas, TX 75205-1503

Hillier School of Highland Park Presbyterian Church
3821 University Blvd, Dallas, TX 75205-1710
214-526-7457

White Rock Montessori School (1975)
3204 Skillman St, Dallas, TX 75206-5999
Sue Henry, Dir, 214-827-3220, FAX: 214-327-3229
Non-profit; tuition: $2,048-3,616/yr
7 teachers, 3 assistants, 94 students, ages 3–12
Entrance requirements: waiting list; visit; interview
Affiliations: AMS, NAMTA
Governance by an administrator and a board of trustees
Cultural studies; Spanish; cooking; music; art; drama;
    computer; PE; plant and animal care; after-school
    drama, violin, piano; childcare; urban location; interns
    accepted.

Sidney Lanier Expressive Arts Vang.
1400 Walmsley, Dallas, TX 75208
Miriam Kelley, 214-746-2670
Type: magnet
4–6th grade
Expressive Arts.

Shelton School and Evaluation Center
5002 W Lovers Ln, Dallas, TX 75209
214-352-1772

Montessori School Park Cities
4011 Inwood Rd, Dallas, TX 75209-5711
Cathy Rutherford

Amelia Earhart Montessori Vanguard School
3531 N Westmoreland Rd, Dallas, TX 75212-2358

Branch Schools
6144 Prospect Ave, Dallas, TX 75214
Hart Robinson
Type: Montessori

Texas Home School Coalition
PO Box 140944, Dallas, TX 75214
214-227-0333
Type: state home-based

Education & Social Services
1738 Gano, Dallas, TX 75215
Ruth Woodward, 214-565-6570
Type: magnet
9-12th grade

Lincoln Humanities/Communications
2826 Hatcher, Dallas, TX 75215
Napoleon Lewis, 214-421-7121
Type: magnet
9-12th grade

Harry Stone Elementary
4747 Veterans Dr, Dallas, TX 75216
Myrtle Walker, 214-302-2180
Type: magnet
Student ages 4+,-6th grade
Montessori.

Dallas Academy
950 Tiffany Way, Dallas, TX 75218
214-324-1418

White Rock Montessori School of the Good Samaritan
1522 Highland Rd, Dallas, TX 75218-4420

Sam Houston Elementary School
2827 Throckmorton St, Dallas, TX 75219-3447
Type: Montessori

Lakemont Academy (1976)
3993 W Northwest Hwy, Dallas, TX 75220
Edward Fidellow, Headmaster, 214-351-6404, FAX: 214-358-4510
Type: Montessori, non-profit; tuition: $3,960-5,880/yr
9 teachers, 3 assistants, 121 students, ages infant-18
Entrance requirements: exam and interview
Affiliations: CMF; ACSI, TX ANS; accreditation: SACS
Governance by board
Renaissance curriculum; formal dining room; etiquette; farm animals; garden; greenhouse; travel; sports; entrepreneurship; childcare; urban location; interns accepted.

East Dallas Community School
924 Wayne St, Dallas, TX 75223
Type: independent

Windsong Montessori School (1992)
4331 Allencrest Ln, Dallas, TX 75224
Mr or Ms Albanese, Dirs, 214-239-0537, FAX: 214-490-0427
Tuition: $4,000/4,500/yr
2 teachers, 3 assistants, 35 students, ages 6-12
Entrance requirements: testing and evaluation during visit
Affiliations: AMITOT, CME
Governance by administrator
Teacher qualifications: Directors: 20+ yrs experience
Suburban location; interns accepted.

Montessori Sunshine High School
11215 Ferguson Rd, Dallas, TX 75228-1953

Dallas Montessori Academy
7979 E R L Thornton Fwy, Dallas, TX 75228-6950
Dina Paulik

Meadowbrook School
5414 N W Highway, Dallas, TX 75229
Type: Montessori

Ursuline Montessori School
4900 Walnut Hill Ln, Dallas, TX 75229

Winston School
5705 Royal Ln, Dallas, TX 75229
214-691-6950

Academic Achievement Asssociates
12830 Hillcrest Rd, Suite 111, Dallas, TX 75230
214-490-6399

Montessori Center of Light
6525 Forest Ln, Dallas, TX 75230

St Alcuin Montessori School (1964)
6144 Churchill Way, Dallas, TX 75230
Ron Ackerman, Dir, 214-239-1745, FAX: 214-934-8727
Non-profit; tuition: $2,975-6,235/yr
19 teachers, 18 assistants, 437 students, ages infant-15
Entrance requirement: interview
Affiliations: NAMTA, AMITOT; accreditation: AMI/USA
Governance by a board of trustees
Childcare; suburban location; interns accepted.

The Robert Muller School, Whole Kids
5707 Caladeium, Dallas, TX 75230
Angie Levy, 214-987-1546

L.L. Hotchkiss Montessori Academy
6929 Town N Dr, Dallas, TX 75231
Torance Vandygriff, 214-553-4430
Type: magnet
7-8th grade
Montessori.

North Texas Montessori Center
6929 Town North Dr, Dallas, TX 75231
Marge Farmer
Type: Montessori teacher education

Montessori Children's House
7335 Abrams Rd, Dallas, TX 75231-4703

Dean Memorial Learning Center
8800 N Central Expy #300, Dallas, TX 75231-6421
Type: Montessori

Arbor Acre Preparatory School
8000 S Hampton Rd, Dallas, TX 75232
214-224-0511

Williams Montessori School
1030 Oak Park Dr, Dallas, TX 75232-1238

Advent Montessori School
6697 S Hampton Rd, Dallas, TX 75232-2917

St James Montessori School
9845 McCree Rd, Dallas, TX 75238-3444
Marie Maneley

Walden Preparatory School
14552 Monfort Dr, Dallas, TX 75240
214-233-6883

Hillcrest Academy Foundation
6930 Alpha Rd, Dallas, TX 75240-3602
Type: Montessori

Carillon Montessori
6411 LBJ Freeway, Dallas, TX 75240-6406

Bending Oaks High School (1985)
13777 N Central Expwy, Dallas, TX 75243
Dr Robert Costello, Prin, 214-669-0000, FAX: 669-8149
Type: independent; tuition: $8,000/yr
15 teachers, 70 students, ages 14-18, 9-12th grade
Entrance requirements: principal interview
Governance by teachers and principal
Teacher qualifications: TX Certification or MA
College schedule; open campus; for profit school; extensive
    field trips.

Bridgeway School
12250 Inwood Rd, Suite 10, Dallas, TX 75244
214-991-1699

Westwood Montessori School (1983)
13618 Gamma Rd, Dallas, TX 75244
Pamela A. Butler, Adm, 214-239-8598, FAX: 214-239-1028
Tuition: $2,450-4,750/yr
4 teachers, 1 assistant, 54 students, ages 3-12
Affiliation: NAEYC; accreditation: AMITOT
Governance by an administrator
Kumon math; science-by-mail; computer programming; ACP
    curriculum; transportation available to and from school,
    and to music, athletics, and art classes; childcare; urban
    location; interns accepted.

Fairhill School
16150 Preston Rd, Dallas, TX 75248
214-233-1026

Montessori School of North Dallas
18303 Davenport Rd, Dallas, TX 75252-5454

Basic Education
PO Box 610589, D/FW Airport, TX 75261
214-462-1909
Type: home-based

Oak Hill Academy
6464 E Lovers Ln, Dallas, TX 75314
214-368-0664

Summit Christian Academy
(See Resource Appendix)

The Children's House Montessori School of Commerce
1722 Park St, Commerce, TX 75428

Bowie County School of Success
Rt 11 Box 446, Texarkana, TX 75501
Gaylon Garrison, 903-831-5767

Carver Children's House
2300 Preston St, Texarkana, TX 75502-5762
Type: Montessori

Donna Hatter Three Candles School
c/o St Lukes Methodist 3500 Main St, Texarkana, TX 75503
Type: Montessori

TALK Center for Hearing-Impaired Children
PO Box 670805, Dallas, TX 755367-0805
214-373-4357

SAILS
711 N Longview St, Kilgore, TX 75662
Daniel Chadwick, 903-984-1239

Cullen Outdoor Center
Trinity, TX 75862
Carol King, 800-659-2733
Houston ISD District
Type: magnet
5th grade

Olympia Outdoor Center
Trinity, TX 75862
Tom Cosper, 800-729-6291
Houston ISD District
Type: magnet
5th grade

Rapid Advancement Program (1978)
1523 E Main St, Nacogdoches, TX 75961
Vicki Stephens, Exec Dir, 409-564-1222
Type: independent, non-profit; tuition: $200/mo,
    scholarships
5 teachers, 40-60 students, infant-8th grade
Governance by parent cooperative
Teacher qualifications: BS in Ed, teaching certificate
Extensive phonics training; humane education; summer
    enrichment; no letter grades; multi-aged classes; extensive
    field trips; urban location; interns accepted.

Venture
2315 Stonegate, Arlington, TX 76010
Lonnie Porter, 817-460-7841

Arlington Country Day School
1100 Roosevelt St, Arlington, TX 76011
Lenny Young
Type: Montessori

Children's House of Arlington Montessori
1400 S Cooper St, Arlington, TX 76013-2752
Pamela Watson and Bobbie Nelson

Arlington Cooperative Montessori School
2217 Michigan Ave #A, Arlington, TX 76013-5916

Montessori Academy
2111 Roosevelt Dr, Arlington, TX 76013-5920
Gail Corley
Also at 5 Kingston Ct, Bedford

Robert Muller School (1979)
6005 Royaloak Dr, Arlington, TX 76016
Gloria Crook, 817-654-1028
Tarrant County
Type: independent, non-profit
8 teachers, 17 students, ages 2-17, through 12th grade
Accreditation: Southern Association of Colleges and Schools
Governance by pupils, teachers, and parents
Teacher qualifications: certification or college degree
World Core Curriculum: our planetary home and place in the
    universe; our place in time; the human family; miracle of
    individual human life; no letter grades; non-compulsory
    class attendance; multi-aged classes; extensive field trips;
    suburban location; interns accepted.

Alternative Education Program
1849 Central Dr, Bedford, TX 76021
Lawrence Harville, 817-267-1462

Barbara Gordon Montessori (1971)
1513 Hall Johnson Road, Colleyville, TX 76034
Rosemarie Blais, 817-354-6670
Non-profit; tuition: $2950/4485
6 teachers, 6 assistants, 144 students, ages infant-9
Affiliation: AMI
Governance by a board of trustees
Well-equipped; supportive parents; Spanish, music, art, PE;
    after-school classes; summers; childcare; suburban loca-
    tion; interns accepted.

North Texas Self-Educators
3013 Hickory Hill, Colleyville, TX 76034
Barb Lundgren, 817-354-4305
Type: home-based
Monthly one-day workshop for beginners; unstructured,
    child-led approaches emphasized.

Crowley Alternative High School
PO Box 688, Crowley, TX 76036
Pat Findley, 817-297-5949

KEYS Learning Center
1100 Raider, Euless, TX 76040
Betty Cuncan-Coon, 817-354-3581

Happy Hill Farm Academy/Home
Star Route, Box 56, Grandbury, TX 76048

McGuffey Academy
2213 Spur Trail, Grapevine, TX 76051
Arlon A. Widder, PhD, Adm, 817-481-7008
Tarrant County
Type: independent
3 teachers, 400 students, ages 5–19
Complete correspondence school; variety of curricula; diag-
    nostic, achievement testing; complete administrative
    assistance.

NAM Enterprises
(See Resource Appendix)

PASS Campus
PO Drawer N, Weatherford, TX 76086
Steve Glenn, Sr, 817-598-2832

Highland Meadow Montessori Academy (1980)
1060 Highland St, Southlake, TX 76092
Pat McCormick, Adm, 817-488-2138
Non-profit; tuition: 1,800-4,400/yr
8 teachers, 4 assistants, 74 students, ages infant-12
Affiliation: AMS; accreditation: AMS
Governance by administrator, board of trustees
Childcare; interns accepted.

Clariden School
1325 N White Chapel Blvd, Grapevine, TX 76092-9017
Type: Montessori

Shelby Learning Center
300 Shelby Rd, Everman, TX 76104
Travis Winn, 817-568-3590

B.H. Carroll/New Lives
3908 McCart, Fort Worth, TX
Jody Wycoff, 817-922-6840

Carroll Peak Elementary
1212 Elmwood Ave, Fort Worth, TX 76104-5733
Type: Montessori

Morningside Elementary
2601 Evans Ave, Fort Worth, TX 76104-6898
Type: Montessori

Metro Opportunity School (1979)
215 NE 14th St, Fort Worth, TX 76106
Gladys Pettid, Prin, 817-740-5550, FAX: 817-740-5566
Fort Worth Ind. School District, Tarrant County
Type: public at-risk
11 teachers, 124 students, ages 14–21, HS
Enrollment restricted to students who are deficient in credits
    or referred by Central Hearing; residency required
Governance by principal; site based decision making team
Independent study; mentor program; career day; volunteer

tutors assigned for TAAS prep; multi-aged classes; commu-
    nity service; drama group; urban location; interns
    accepted.

Como Montessori Elementary
4001 Littlepage St, Fort Worth, TX 76107
Robert Vick, 817-377-7379
Type: magnet
K–6th grade

Oasis Learning Center
1850 White Settlement Rd #115, Fort Worth, TX 76107
Weldon Newton, 817-334-0819

Ft Worth Montessori School
1801 Ashland Ave, Fort Worth, TX 76107-3809
Denise Pulido

South Hi Mount
4101 Birchman Ave, Fort Worth, TX 76107-4396
Type: Montessori

Trinity Episcopal
3401 Bellaire Dr S, Fort Worth, TX 76109-2199
Type: Montessori

Daggett Middle School (1983)
1108 Carlock, Fort Worth, TX 76110
Attn: Adm Coord, 817-922-6550
Type: Montessori; tuition: none
9 teachers, 1 assistant, 180 students, mainly international
Montessori experience required
Affiliations: AMS, NAMTA, MSA, MSTX
Governance by administrator and democratic school meeting
Two years/same staff; environmental activites; childcare;
    urban location; transportation; interns accepted.

Essential Program at R.L. Paschal High School (1984)
3001 Forest Park Blvd, Fort Worth, TX 76110
Larry B. Barnes, Coord, 817-922-6600, FAX: 817-922-6661
Tarrant County
Type: public
15 teachers, 375 students, ages 12–18, HS
Governance by board
Collaborative; interdisciplinary; cross disciplinary; multi-aged
    classes; interns accepted.

New Lives School
3908 McCart, Fort Worth, TX 76110
Jody Wyckoff, 817-922-6840
Type: public at-risk

Daggett Elementary Montessori School
958 Page, Fort Worth, TX 76110-2627
Judy Seymour

Worth Heights Montessori
519 E Butler St, Fort Worth, TX 76110-5598

Montessori Children's House
3420 Clayton Rd E, Fort Worth, TX 76116-7342
Joy Sheffield

Shannon Learning Center
6010 Walker St, Fort Worth, TX 76117
Mike Fritz, 817-831-5866

Glen Park Elementary (1983)
3601 Pecos St, Ft Worth, TX 76119
Dr Pat Coemes, Prin, 531-6380
Type: public choice
3 teachers, 1 assistant, 66 students, ages 3–9
Affiliation: AMS
Governance by teachers and administrators
Urban location.

A.M. Pate Elementary School
3800 Anglin Dr, Fort Worth, TX 76119-2126
Type: Montessori

Event Montessori School
PO Box 921001, Fort Worth, TX 76121-0001

Sycamore School, Inc
3400 Charleston Ave, Fort Worth, TX 76123
817-292-3434

Benbrook Elementary
800 Mercedes St, Benbrook, TX 76126-2594
Type: Montessori

Middle Level Learning
3813 Valentine, Fort Worth, TX 76127
Steve Gay, 817-377-7350

Fort Worth Montessori School (1984)
6605 Dan Danciger Rd/ 1801 Ashland St, Ft Worth, TX 76133/76107
817-732-4276, 294-9850, FAX: 817-732-6502
Tuition: $164-293/mo
7 teachers, 7 assistants, 80 students, mainly international, ages infant-6
Governance by an administrator
Two campuses; childcare; suburban location; interns accepted.

Azlann Montessori School (1986)
2301 Hinkle Dr, Denton, TX 76201
Beverly Morey, 817-565-9330
Tuition: $2,600-3,600/yr
6 teachers, 2 assistants, students mainly international, ages 2.5-11
Affiliations: AMS, AMI, NAMTA
Governance by an administrator
Most staff are adjunct professors; childcare; suburban location; interns accepted.

Community School (1991)
2046 Scripture, Denton, TX 76201
Linda Lavendar, 817-387-0995
Type: independent, boarding, non-profit; tuition: $3,250
4 teachers, 2 assistants, 50 students
Governance by teachers and owners
Suburban location; interns accepted.

Evenhorn School
2301 Hinkle, Denton, TX 76201
Type: Montessori

Fred Moore Learning Center
815 Cross Timbers, Denton, TX 76201
Wade Lillie, 817-381-1806

R.E. Lee Elementary School
800 Mack Dr, Denton, TX 76201-6314
Type: Montessori

Selwyn School-Lower School
3333 W University Dr, Denton, TX 76201-7495
Alan Gibby
Type: Montessori

Borman Elementary School
1201 Parvin St, Denton, TX 76205-6799
Type: Montessori

Bright Ideas School (1985)
2507 Central Frwy E, Wichita Falls, TX 76302
Linda Plummer, Principal, 817-767-1561
Type: independent, non-profit
5 teachers, 28 students, ages 3-15, pre K-11th grade

Governance by teachers and principal
Interdisciplinary projects; history-based curriculum; gifted education approach; encourages responsibility and self-direction; multi-aged classes; extensive field trips; urban location; interns accepted.

Notre Dame Elementary
4060 York, Wichita Falls, TX 76309
Dr Bronte Gonsalzes
Type: Montessori

Harrell Alternative Learning Center (1992)
3115 5th St, Wichita Falls, TX 76310
R.J. Stone, Prin, 817-720-3144, FAX: 817-720-3228
Wichita Falls ISD District, Wichita County
Type: public at-risk
17 teachers, 192 students, ages 17-21
Entrance requirements: GED
Governance by teachers, principal, board
Open entry/exit; computers; work experience, job-search; no letter grades; multi-aged classes; suburban location; interns accepted.

Graham ISD Learning Center
701 Tennessee, Graham, TX 76450
Mary Humphries, 817-546-7526

Montessori Children's House
3119 Commerce Dr, Killeen, TX 76543-4012

Kileen Alternative Center
101 N 5th, Nolanville, TX 76559
Robert Hausmann, 817-698-4441

Waco Montessori School (1976)
1300 Austin Ave, Waco, TX 76701
Judy Schmeltekopf, Dir, 817-754-3966
Non-profit; tuition: $167-260/mo
5 teachers, 5 assistants, 88 students, ages infant-9
Affiliation: AMS
Governance by board
New facility; childcare; urban location; interns accepted.

Hillcrest Professional Development School
4225 Pine, Waco, TX 76703
Ronald McIntire, 817-772-4286
Type: magnet
Pre K-5th grade
Multi age; interdisciplinary.

J.H. Hines Elementary
1102 Paul Quinn St, Waco, TX 76704
Renee Garrett
Type: Montessori

Options Learning Center (1991)
2100 Fir, McAllen, TX 76850
Rosalinda S. Gonzalez, Prin, 210-632-3222
Hidalgo County
Type: public at-risk
13 teachers, 162 students, 9-12th grade
Entrance requirements: referral, recommendation, application, residency
Governance by principal
Teacher qualifications: certification
Cross-age tutoring; work/study; self-paced; contracts; self-esteem; community involvement; counseling; transportation; interns accepted.

First Baptist Church Child Development Center
37 E Harris Ave, San Angelo, TX 76903-5821
Type: Montessori

PAYS
1820 Knickerbocker, San Angelo, TX 76904
Mark Gesch, 915-947-3900

Cathedral House Montessori School
1100 Prairie St, Houston, TX 77002-3119

Dominican Montessori School
3617 Milam St, Houston, TX 77002-9535

Dodson Elementary
1808 Sampson, Houston, TX 77003
O. D. Curtis, 713-225-5624
Type: magnet
K–5th grade
Montessori.

Born to Explore, Inc (1992)
2625 San Jacinto St, Houston, TX 77004
Rosalba Ortiz Dow, Pres, 713-659-2425
Type: Montessori; tuition: $350–400/mo
2 teachers, 4 assistants, 45 students, ages infant-6
Entrance requirements: $50 registration fee; 30-day notice to
    withdraw; complete immunization record
Affiliation: HAAEYC
Governance by administrator
Bilingual; Hooked on Phonics; Spanish classes for ages 5–10
    on Saturdays; childcare.

Contemporary Learning Center
1906 Cleburne St, Houston, TX 77004
Marita Daniels, 713-526-3629

Ryan Middle School
2610 Elgin, Houston, TX 77004
Anita Ellis, 713-528-0922
Type: magnet
6–8th grade
Gifted and talented.

Turner Elementary
3200 Rosedale, Houston, TX 77004
Alma Allen, 713-523-3265
Type: magnet
People place center.

Montessori School of Downtown
4701 San Jacinto St, Houston, TX 77004-5045

The Sheridan School
5116 Caroline St, Houston, TX 77004-5802
Type: Montessori

St Mary's School
3002 Rosedale St, Houston, TX 77004-6128
Type: Montessori

Palmer Dev Center
5310 Greenbriar, Houston, TX 77005
Type: Montessori

Village Montessori School
2329 Bissonnet St, Houston, TX 77005-1511

Southampton Montessori School
5012 Morningside Dr, Houston, TX 77005-2592

Avalon Academy
1616 Indiana, Houston, TX 77006
Roseanne Sands, 713-524-1174

Montessori Country Day School
30 Oakdale St, Houston, TX 77006-6522
Marge Ellison

St Peter Pre-Kindergarten
1501 Houston Ave, Houston, TX 77007-4135
Type: Montessori

Hamilton Middle School
139 E 20th St, Houston, TX 77008
Diana Mulet, 713-861-9478
Type: magnet
6–8th grade
Gifted and talented.

Heights Montessori School (1981)
2028 Harvard St, Houston, TX 77008
Jennifer Bennett, Owner/Dir, 713-862-3792
Tuition: $255–460/mo
4 teachers, 7 assistants, 55 students, ages infant-6
Affiliation: AMS
Governance by administrator
Homey environment in historic area; urban location; interns
    accepted.

Travis Elementary
3311 Beauchamp, Houston, TX 77009
Helen Clingan, 713-862-1796
Type: magnet
K–3rd grade
Gifted and talented.

DeZavala Elementary
7521 Ave H, Houston, TX 77012
Mwerva Perez, 713-923-8669
Type: magnet
3–5th grade
Gifted and talented.

Northwood Montessori School
14901 Welcome Ln, Houston, TX 77014-1405

New Beginnings Montessori
335 Audrey Ln, Houston, TX 77015-2209

St Christopher School
8134 Park Place Blvd, Houston, TX 77017
Susan E Sanchez
Type: Montessori

Oak Forest Elementary
1401 W 43rd St, Houston, TX 77018
Sharon Koonce, 713-613-2536
Type: magnet
K–5th grade
Gifted and talented.

River Oaks Elementary
2008 Kirby Dr, Houston, TX 77019
Michele Pola, 713-528-7319
Type: magnet
K–5th grade
Gifted and talented.

Montessori Society of Houston
1800 Huldy St, Houston, TX 77019-5725

Whidby Elementary
7625 Springhill, Houston, TX 77021
Vivian Harrison, 713-747-1233
Type: magnet
K–5th grade
Montessori.

Burbank Middle School
315 Berry Rd, Houston, TX 77022
Glenda Alvarez, 713-694-2813
Type: magnet
6–8th grade
Gifted and talented.

Burrus Elementary
701 E 33rd St, Houston, TX 77022

Flossie Sylvester, 713-861-6938
Type: magnet
K–5th grade
Arts.

Roosevelt Elementary
6700 Fulton, Houston, TX 77022
Charlotte Parker, 713-695-2772
Type: magnet
K–5th grade
Gifted and talented.

Houston Montessori Center (1973)
9601 Katy Freeway, Suite 170, Houston, TX 77024
Elisabeth Coe, PhD, 713-465-7670
Type: Montessori higher education, non-profit; tuition:
   $1,475-3,250/yr
26 teachers, 1 assistant; students mainly international
Entrance requirements: application; interview; 4-year college
   equivalent
Affiliation: AMS; accreditations: MACTE, TX Ed Agency
Governance by administrator, board
Provides speakers and consultants to institutions across
   country; urban location; interns accepted.

Montessori Morning Glory School
737 Bunker Hill Rd, Houston, TX 77024-4405

Fleming Middle School
4910 Collingsworth, Houston, TX 77026
Chester Smith, 713-674-3415
Type: magnet
6–8th grade
Arts; physical development.

The Briarwood School
4811 San Felipe, Houston, TX 77027
Type: Montessori

The Wilhelm Schole
4242 Richmond, Houston, TX 77027
713-626-2532

River Oaks Baptist School
2300 Willowick Rd, Houston, TX 77027-3996
Type: Montessori

Holland Middle School
1600 Gellhorn, Houston, TX 77029
Adele Rogers, 713-675-3538
Type: magnet
6–8th grade
Gifted and talented.

Pleasantville Elementary
1431 Gellhorn, Houston, TX 77029
Linda Whitley, 713-673-2726
Type: magnet
K–5th grade
Gifted and talented.

Children's Hour Montessori
2227 Dorrington, Houston, TX 77030
Carolyn Mullen

Wildlife Discovery (Houston Zoo)
1513 Outer Belt Dr, Houston, TX 77030
Karyl Watz, 713-520-3265
Type: magnet
3rd grade

Jones High School
7414 St Louis, Houston, TX 77033
Arthur Pace, 713-733-1111
Type: magnet
9–12th grade
Gifted and talented.

Little Red Schoolhouse (1960)
611 Westbury Sq, Houston, TX 77035
Sheila Finch, Head, 713-723-2877
Type: Montessori; tuition: $2,000-3,730/yr
21 teachers, 4 assistants, 244 students, ages infant-15
Entrance requirements: report card, test scores for grades 1+
Affiliation: AMS
Governance by administrator
Computer lab; computers in every classroom; grades 6-8
   edit, format documents, use data base; childcare; subur-
   ban location; interns accepted.

Montessori Vistas
12138 Fondren Rd, Houston, TX 77035-4002

Southwest Teacher
7497 S W Frwy, Houston, TX 77036
Type: Montessori

Montessori Conservatory
10001 Westheimer Rd, Houston, TX 77042-3132

Sherwood Forest Montessori School
1331 Sherwood Forest St, Houston, TX 77043-4637

Magnet Schools of America
(See Resource Appendix)

Awty International School
7455 Awty School Ln, Houston, TX 77055
713 686 4830
Type: independent

School of the Woods (1962)
1321 Wirt, Houston, TX 77055
Sherry Herron, Dir, 713-686-8811, FAX: 713-686-1936
Type: Montessori, non-profit; tuition: $240-470/mo
17 teachers, 8 assistants, 295 students, ages 3-15
Entrance requirements: age 2.5; toilet trained
Affiliations: AMS, NAEYC, TXAEYC
Governance by a board of trustees
5-acre wooded site; cultivates respect, uniqueness and lifelong learning; childcare; suburban location; interns
   accepted.

T. H. Rogers Middle School
5840 San Felipe, Houston, TX 77057
Meredith Wedin, 713-783-6220
Type: magnet
6–8th grade
Gifted and talented.

Clear Lake Montessori (1973)
16300 Sealark Rd, Houston, TX 77062
Cheryl Cook, Prin, 713-486-4416, FAX: 713-486-7167
Tuition: $2,520-2,900/yr
11 teachers, 291 students, ages infant-12
Affiliations: SNMTA, NAMTA, MACTE; accreditation: SNMC
Governance by administrator
Extensive math materials; childcare; interns accepted.

Montessori & Day Care School
8644 Richmond Ave, Houston, TX 77063-5629

Montessori Child Development
11707 Huffmeister, Houston, TX 77065

Learn 'n Play- Montessori
11707 Huffmeister Rd, Houston, TX 77065-1047

Greystone House
6731 Apple Valley Ln, Houston, TX 77069
Brenda Berleith
Type: Montessori

Southeast Texas Homeschool Association
5620 FM 191960 W, PO Box 354, Houston, TX 77069
713-370-8787

Montessori Vistas Inc
7910 Deer Meadow Dr, Houston, TX 77071-2713

Martin Elementary School
11718 Hendon, Houston, TX 77072
Diane Stanky
Type: Montessori

Montessori Learning Institute
5701 Beechnut, Houston, TX 77074
Myle Yo

Askew Elementary
11200 Woodlodge, Houston, TX 77077
Elaine Allen, 713-497-5450
Type: magnet
3-5th grade
Gifted and talented.

Westside Montessori School, Inc
1570 S Dairy Ashford, Houston, TX 77077-3862

Wingate Montessori
14130 Westheimer Rd, Houston, TX 77077-5363

Smaller Scholars Montessori School
12280 Westheimer Rd #50, Houston, TX 77077-6050
Dot Ahuja

American Montessori School (1986)
14434 Bellaire Blvd, Houston, TX 77083
Mrs Trehan or Mrs Weiser, Dirs, 713-498-6000, FAX: 713-265-
  3147
Tuition: $215/405
5 teachers, 7 assistants, 82 students, ages 2.5-8
Governance by an administrator
Suburban location.

Windsor Village Elementary
14440 Polo, Houston, TX 77085
Sandra Satterwhite, 713-726-3542
Type: magnet
K-5th grade
Gifted and talented.

Penelope Vanderwerth-Carter
6308 Spindle, Houston, TX 77086
Type: Montessori

Montessori Children's Cottage/Inwood
4646 Victory Dr, Houston, TX 77088-7238

Montessori Adventure, Inc
10904 Scarsdale #256, Houston, TX 77089
Laura C Trellue

Brookwoods Montessori Elementary School
4107 Sherwood Ln, Houston, TX 77092
Cynthia Foster, Admissions Director, 713-686-5427, FAX: 713-
  686-8780
Tuition: $420/435/mo
5 teachers, 4 assistants, 97 students, ages 3-9
Entrance requirements: visit and interview
Affiliation: AMS
Governance by administrator
French daily; separate classroom for studies/experiments in
  nature, science, and art; greenhouse; 3+ acres; indoor
  pool; summer program; childcare; suburban location;
  interns accepted.

Montessori Children's Cottage/Copperfield (1970)
15703 Longenbaugh, Houston, TX 77092

Cynthia Foster, Admissions Coordinator, 713-550-1191, FAX:
  713-686-8780
Tuition: $280-585/mo
5 teachers, 8 assistants, 100 students
Entrance requirements: visit and interview
Affiliation: AMS
Governance by administrator
French lesson daily for students over 3 years; PE; dance;
  tumbling; piano; separate classroom for science, nature,
  and geography studies/experiments; summer program;
  childcare; suburban location; interns accepted.

Janice Newsum Montessori Preschool
6111 Del Rio, Houston, TX 77095

West Montessori School of Copperfield
15810 Longenbaugh Dr, Houston, TX 77095-1606

Cottage School System
7142 Cherry Park Dr, Houston, TX 77095-2713
Type: Montessori

Herod Elementary
5627 Jason, Houston, TX 77096
Nancy Nichols, 713-774-6972
Type: magnet
K-3rd grade
Gifted and talented.

United Orthodox Montessori
9001 Greenwillow St, Houston, TX 77096-3599
Hetty Perl

Lanier Middle School
2600 Woodhead, Houston, TX 77098
Brenda Lanclos, 713-529-5451
Type: magnet
6-8th grade
Gifted and talented.

St Stephen's Episcopal School
1805 Alabama, Houston, TX 77098
Type: Montessori

Children's Garden Montessori
2144 Kipling St, Houston, TX 77098-2304

Alief Westwood Montessori (1971)
11959 Bissonnet (at Kirkwood), Houston, TX 77099
Ms Selby, Dir, 713-933-6808
Tuition: $235-375/mo
3 teachers, 4 assistants, 53 students, ages infant-9
Governance by administrator
Individualized; childcare; interns accepted.

Southwest Montessori Center
12222 Bissonnet St #3, Houston, TX 77099-1439

St Catherine's Montessori
PO Box 20728, Houston, TX 77225-0728

Montessori Children's House
200 Ave J, Conroe, TX 77301-3779

The Pines Montessori
3059 Woodland Hills, Kingwood, TX 77339

Pines Montessori School
3535 Cedar Knolls Dr, Kingwood, TX 77339-2468
Maureen Peterson

Rustic Woods Montessori
3923 Rustic Woods Dr, Kingwood, TX 77339-2611

Kingwood Day School
Loop 494 at Memorial Dr, Porter, TX 77365
Type: Montessori

Northwest Montessori School
301 S Cherry St, Tomball, TX 77375-6614

Woodlands Montessori Schools
1201 Many Pines, Woodlands, TX 77380
Joni McEuen

Post Oak School (1963)
4600 Bissonnet, Houston, TX 77401
Suzanne Pugin, 912-661-6688, FAX: 912-661-4959
Type: Montessori; tuition: $4,100-7,00/yr
15 teachers, 15 assistants, 166 students, ages infant-15
Entrance requirements: max age 3.5 or Montessori
    experience
Affiliations: NAMTA, AMITOT; accreditation: AMI
Governance by administrator
Enrichment classes, specialists; art; music; PE; computers;
    dance; childcare; urban location; interns accepted.

Nature Discovery Center (1979)
PO Box 777, Bellaire, TX 77402
Melissa Geis, Dir, 713-667-6550, FAX: same
Type: Montessori, non-profit
1 teacher, 5 assistants
Accreditation: TX Ed Agency
Governance by board
Ecology approach; urban location.

Alief Children's House
4215 H St, PO Box 702, Alief, TX 77411
Type: Montessori

Cy-Fair Montessori (1980)
12815 Huffmeister Rd, Cypress, TX 77429
Rebecca Huebner, Dir, 713-890-3937
Non-profit; tuition: $160-290/mo
3 teachers, 2 assistants, 75 students, ages infant-6
Affiliation: Corporate Hands Network; accreditation: AMI
Governance by administrator, parent cooperative
4 wooded acres; childcare; rural location.

Houston Alternative Education Alliance
12811 Ivy Forest Dr, Cypress, TX 77429
Kay Crowley
Type: home-based

Montessori Child Development Center
11103 Mills Rd, Cypress, TX 77429-3008

Katy Montessori School
2437 N Fry Rd, Katy, TX 77449-6220

S.B. Burger King Corp Academy
9016 Westview, Houston, TX 77450
CLynthia Chai, 713-973-1793

The Cottage School
20201 Kingsland Blvd, Katy, TX 77450-3008
Niroo Somaya
Type: Montessori

Great Expectations Montessori Center
3420 Cartwright Rd, Missouri City, TX 77459-2434

Children's World Montessori Center
4010 Ave N, Rosenberg, TX 77471-4802

First Colony Montessori
2229 Settlers Way Blvd, Sugar Land, TX 77478-5231
Ruean Ulesee

Riverbend Montessori School (1976)
4225 Elkins St, Sugar Land, TX 77479
Barbara Crawford, Adm, 713-980-4123, FAX: 980-0120
Tuition: $235-385/mo
6 teachers, 7 assistants, 140 students, mainly international,
    ages infant-12
Affiliation: AMS
Governance by board of trustees
Childcare; suburban location; interns accepted.

Cedarwood School, Inc
311 Present St, Missouri City, TX 77489-1145
Type: Montessori

Opportunity Awareness Center
1732 Katyland Dr, Katy, TX 77493
Pete Dempsey, 713-391-6858

Montessori School of Pasadena
1033 Fairmont Pkwy, Pasadena, TX 77504
Joseph Manjos

ASSETS Learning Center (1993)
605 W House, Alvin, TX 77511
Sherry Goen, 713-388-1130
Brazoria County
Type: public at-risk
5 teachers, 60-75 students, ages 14-16, 7-8th grade
Enrollment restricted to residents below level academically
Governance by faculty and student representatives
Teacher qualifications: state certification
Boys Town social skills curriculum; cooperative learning;
    adventure based counseling; community service; town and
    parent meetings; mentor and advisory programs; com-
    puter lab; multi-aged classes; extensive field trips; subur-
    ban location.

Holy Comforter Episcopal School
227 S Chenango St, Angleton, TX 77515-6001
Type: Montessori

Alternative Learning Program
320 Wye Dr, Baytown, TX 77520
Peter Hyland, 713-420-4555

Wolters Learning Center
204 Ivy, Deer Park, TX 77536
Don Dean, 713-930-4656

Montessori Pre-School
7 Flounder Circle, Freeport, TX 77541-8910

Montessori School & Day Care
809 S Friendswood Dr, Friendswood, TX 77546-4556

Clear Creek Montessori School
1903 Carriage Creek Ln, Friendswood, TX 77546-5133

Island Montessori School
1520 Market St, Galveston, TX 77550

Alternative School
4116 Ave N 1/2, Galveston, TX 77553
Don Roy, 409-766-5859

Montessori Unlimited
10122 Carlow Ln, La Porte, TX 77571
Gail Morgan

South Shore Montessori School
201 S Shore Blvd, League City, TX 77573-4389

School of Montessori
1503 S 16th St, Nederland, TX 77627-4427

Central Catholic School
3611 Gulfway Dr, Port Arthur, TX 77642-3675
Type: Montessori

Children's House Montessori School
2510 N 11th St, Beaumont, TX 77703

Montessori School House (1979)
2509 Roundtree Dr, Bryan, TX 77801
Lydia Cumings, Owner, 409-822-5192
Tuition: $155-355/mo
3 teachers, 1 assistant, 68 students, ages 3-6
Affiliation: NAMTA; accreditation: AMI
Governance by administrator

ACE/Bryan High School
2200 Villa Maria, Bryan, TX 77802
Katie Pruitt, 409-361-9690

Aggieland Country School
1701 Brook Hollow Dr, Bryan, TX 77802-1122
Type: Montessori

Keystone Montessori School
2320 E Villa Maria Rd, Bryan, TX 77802-2549
Kim Oehme

Brenham Montessori School
1500 S Baylor, Brenham, TX 77833-4969

Alternative Academic Program (1993)
1812 Welsh St, College Station, TX 77840
Claude Cunningham, 2ndary Dir, 409-764-5481, FAX:-5492
College Station District, Brazos County
Type: public at-risk
2 teachers, 15 students, ages 17-20, 9-12th grade
Entrance requirements: 2 years over-age for grade
    placement
Teacher qualifications: Texas Certification
Self-paced; self-directed; career/technology credit; no letter
    grades; multi-aged classes; suburban location.

EAGLE Center
913 W Brown St, Hearne, TX 77859
409-279-9211

Dudley Elementary
3307 Callis St, Victoria, TX 77901
Armando Villarreal, 512-575-3477
Type: magnet
Pre K-5th grade
Gifted and talented.

Hill Country Montessori School, Inc (1981)
606 S School St, Boerne, TX 78006
Peggy Wallace, Financial Adm, 210-816-3819
Non-profit; tuition: $275-340/mo
4 teachers, 4 assistants, 57 students, ages infant-9
Affiliations: AMI, NAMTA; accreditation: AMITOT
Governance by teachers and administrators
Natural lighting; integrates indoors and outdoors; secure sur-
    rounding; childcare; suburban location.

Montessori Pre-School
517 B Wigham, Kerrville, TX 78028

Learning Asssistance Program
1702 Houston, Laredo, TX 78040
Carlos Vargas, 210-727-4401

Navarro Achievement Center
623 S Pecos, San Antonio, TX 78207
Joe Zatarain, 210-224-0328

The Circle School (1965)
217 Pershing, San Antonio, TX 78209
Mary Barton, Co-op Pres, 210-822-0461
Type: independent, non-profit; tuition: $300/mo
6 teachers, 50 students, ages 2.5-12, pre K-5th grade
Governance by parent cooperative
Teacher qualifications: long-term experience in alternative
    teaching, open-mindedness
Curriculum integrates Montessori, Waldorf, peace studies,
    Native American learning, oral traditions; story-telling used
    daily; no letter grades; non-compulsory class attendance;
    multi-aged classes; extensive field trips; urban location;
    interns accepted.

Kriterion Montessori School (1965)
611 W Ashby Pl, San Antonio, TX 78212
Andreas Laven, Business Mgr, 210-735-9778
Tuition: $380/400/mo
8 teachers, 4 assistants, 120 students, ages 3-15
Affiliations: AMS, AMI, NCME, IMS, NMSA
Governance by an administrator
Childcare; urban location.

Student Alternatives Program, Inc
PO Box 12724, San Antonio, TX 78212
Ed Gutierrez

Burger King Corp Academy
102 White, San Antonio, TX 78214
Warren Wagner, 210-924-7177

The Judson Montessori School (1974)
705 Trafalgar, San Antonio, TX 78216
James J. Judson, Dir, 210-344-3117, FAX: 210-344-1223
Non-profit; tuition: $3,735-5,400/yr
24 teachers, 8 assistants, 201 students, ages 3-15
Entrance requirements: developmental readiness
Affiliations: COE, TAN; accreditation: AMITOT
Governance by administrator, board
Junior Great Books; communications and debate; computers;
    science; library resource center; Orff & Kodaly music;
    Spanish; after-school sports and arts; chess; childcare; sub-
    urban location; interns accepted.

Mount Sacred Heart Montessori Society
619 Mount Sacred Heart Rd, San Antonio, TX 78216-6695
Pam Snow

St Mary's Hall Montessori (1968)
9401 Starcrest Dr, San Antonio, TX 78217
Vicki S. Raney, 210-655-7721, FAX: 210-655-6276
Non-profit; tuition: $3,320/4,735/yr
7 teachers, 7 assistants, 139 students, ages 3-6
Entrance requirements: application; developmental screen-
    ing; interview
Affiliation: AMS; accreditation: ISASW
Governance by an administrator and a board of trustees
Wooded 54-acre campus; feeds into traditional college prep,
    coed school, grades 1-12; students from TX, SW states,
    other countries; suburban location.

Academy of Creative Education
10333 Broadway St #XI, San Antonio, TX 78217-3809
Mary Jo McLaughlin, 210-377-2330

Children's House & Montessori School
4927 Evers Rd, San Antonio, TX 78228-2148

Bilingual Montessori School
3703 John Alden Ave, San Antonio, TX 78230-3203
Stephen Jackson

Competency Based High School
563 SW, San Antonio, TX 78237
David Chagoya, 210-436-1221

Challenge High School
66632 Bandera Rd, San Antonio, TX 78238
Irene Chavez, 210-522-8120

San Antonio Country Day School
4194 Jung Rd, San Antonio, TX 78247-2711
Type: Montessori

Southwest Enrichment Center
11914 Dragon Ln, San Antonio, TX 78252
Laura Yzaguirre, 210-622-5551

Open the Door to a Different Approach to Learning
(1991)
PO Box 871, Kingsville, TX 78363
Mary Ann Colin, Dir, 512-592-3368
Kleberg County
Type: public choice; scholarships
5 teachers, 100 students, mainly at-risk, ages 16–21, 9–12th
grade
Entrance requirements: application, residency
Governance by teachers, principal
Teacher qualifications: BS
Open entry/exit; outcome-based; mastery learning; inte-
grated instruction; career, technology training; support
services; cooperative education; multi-aged classes; exten-
sive field trips; childcare provided; interns accepted.

The Montessori School of Corpus Christi
2205 16th St, Corpus Christi, TX 78404

Incarnate Word Montessori
450 Chamberlain St, Corpus Christi, TX 78404-2442
Sr M Christina Bradley

Windsor Park Elementary
4525 S Alameda St, Corpus Christi, TX 78412
Ginger Harris, 512-994-3664
Type: magnet
1–5th grade
Gifted and talented.

The Living Classroom
2526 Flour Bluff Dr, Corpus Christi, TX 78418
Type: Montessori

McAllen Montessori School
2917 W US Hwy 83 #250, McAllen, TX 78501

Options in Education High School
1619 Galveston, McAllen, TX 78501
Rosalinda Gonzales, 210-630-1765

Discovery School
4601 N 2nd St, McAllen, TX 78504-2927
Ann Chambers and Patricia Deeren
Type: Montessori

Bowie School
Box 2514, Alamo, TX 78516
Type: Montessori

Franklin School
900 Brich St, Alamo, TX 78516
Type: Montessori

Kenmont —The Montessori School (1972)
2734 N Coria St, Brownsville, TX 78520
Donald G. Massey, Dir, 210-542-0500
Tuition: 1,950–2,730/yr

7 teachers, 6 assistants, 172 students, ages infant-12
Interview required for ages 6–12.
Accreditation: AMITOT
Governance by administrator
Childcare; suburban location.

Home Montessori School
925 E Los Ebanos Blvd, Brownsville, TX 78520-8726

Dropout Prevention Center
1900 Price, Brownsville, TX 78521
Raye Lokey, 210-548-8242

Gonzalez Elementary School
4450 Coffee Port, Brownsville, TX 78521
Janet R Schooley
Type: Montessori

Claire's House for Children
RR 4 Box 823, Edinburg, TX 78539-9418
Claire van der Put
Type: Montessori

KEYS Academy
216 N 21st, Harlingen, TX 78550
Blanca Hernandez, 210-427-3220

Montessori Academy of Harlingen
1806 Laurel, Harlingen, TX 78550
Ann Hall

Alternative Center
PO Box J, La Joya, TX 78560
Randy Bourland, 210-580-5041

Henry Ford Elementary School
PO Box JJ, Pharr, TX 78577-1236
Type: Montessori

Longoria School
400 E Rendon St, Pharr, TX 78577-1859
Type: Montessori

Napper School
903 N Flag St, Pharr, TX 78577-2999
Type: Montessori

Buell School
218 E Juarez St, Pharr, TX 78577-3990
Type: Montessori

Carnahan School
317 W Gore St, Pharr, TX 78577-5331
Type: Montessori

Palmer School
703 E Sam Houston St, Pharr, TX 78577-5599
Type: Montessori

Basic Skills Learning Center
195 W Adele, San Benito, TX 78586
Marie Helen Lara, 210-361-1070

Clover School
N San Juan Rd, San Juan, TX 78589
Type: Montessori

Garza-Pena Primary School
E Gasline Rd PO Box 1270, San Juan, TX 78589
Type: Montessori

Sorensen School
715 S Standard Ave, San Juan, TX 78589-2446
Type: Montessori

South Palm Gardens
PO Box 266, Weslaco, TX 78596
Alfredo Fernandez, 210-565-0404

Genesis High School
105 Loop 150 W, Suite J, Bastrop, TX 78602
Sheryl Hopper, 512-321-2593

Greenbriar School (1969)
Box 466, Elgin, TX 78621
Jose & Maria Garcia, 512-285-2661
Type: independent
25 students
Located on 171 acres of woodland; evolved into collective
    homeschooling in a cooperative intentional community;
    community members are volunteer staff; many are self
    employed craftsmen, etc, and involve students with work.

Kindernest Montessori (1990)
113 E San Antonio, Fredericksburg, TX 78624
Linda Muegge, Dir, 210-997-8939
Non-profit; tuition: $173/205
2 teachers, 2 assistants, 48 students, ages 3-9
Children must be 2 1/2 years old and toilet trained
Affiliation: NAMTA
Governance by a board of trustees
Music, art, aerobics, German; childcare; suburban location;
    interns accepted.

PRIDE Center
540 Staples Rd, San Marcos, TX 78666
Ana Lopez, 512-396-6864

Creative Learning
PO Box 1925, Wimberly, TX 78676

Old Town Elementary School
2001 Old Settlers Blvd, Round Rock, TX 78681-2160
Type: Montessori

Govalle Elementary School
3801 Govalle Ave, Austin, TX 78702
Type: Montessori

Casa Montessori Child Development Center
2201 W 1st St, Austin, TX 78703-4619

Town & Country Montessori House of Children
3801 Keats Dr, Austin, TX 78704

Montessori Center
605 Academy Dr, Austin, TX 78704-1816

Montessori House of Children of Austin
1601 Brackenridge, Austin, TX 78704-6741
Ginger Logan

TAFFIE
6502 Bradley Dr, Austin, TX 78723

Austin Children's House
8512 F M 969, Austin, TX 78724-5719
Type: Montessori

Jollyville Alternative Education Learning Center
13401 Pond Springs, Austin, TX 78729
Mike Mirelez, 513-331-5270

Case Montessori Child Development Centers
4025 Tealwood Dr, Austin, TX 78731

The Children's School, Inc (1979)
2825 Hancock Dr, Austin, TX 78731
Clay Wallin, Adm, 512-453-1126

Type: Montessori; tuition: $200-295/mo
6 teachers, 9 assistants, 130 students, ages infant-9
Affiliation: AMS; accreditation: AMITOT
Governance by administrator
Childcare; urban location; interns accepted.

Austin Waldorf School (1980)
8702 Southview Rd, Austin, TX 78737
Betsy Hanelius, Faculty Chair, 512-288-5942, FAX:-9578
Travis County
Non-profit; tuition: $4,000/yr, scholarships
18 teachers, 135 students, ages 4-12, K-6th grade
Entrance requirements: interview
Affiliation: AWSNA
Governance by teachers and board of trustees
Teacher qualifications: college, Waldorf training
Suburban location; interns accepted.

Austin Montessori School (1967)
5014 Sunset Trail, Austin, TX 78745
Donald C. Goertz, PhD, Exec Dir, 512-892-0253
Tuition: $2,100-3,700/yr
11 teachers, 11 assistants, 270 students, ages 3-12
Affiliation: NAMTA; accreditations: AMI, AMITOT
Governance by administrator, board
Classical curriculum; alternative methodology; emphasis on
    personal responsibility; childcare; rural location; transporta-
    tion; interns accepted.

Bay Area Montessori House
PO Box 891083, Austin, TX 78745

White Bird Montessori School
6305 Manchaca Rd, Austin, TX 78745-4945

The Montessori Center (1983)
4108 Ave H, Austin, TX 78751-4725
Jessica Salinas, Dir, 512-451-5081
Tuition: $255/370/mo
4 teachers, 5 assistants, 49 students, ages infant-6
Affiliation: AMS; accreditation: NAECP
Governance by teachers and administrators
Warm, loving, respectful environment fostered in school and
    at home; childcare; suburban location; interns accepted.

A Bar Z Pondersoa
Alief-Westwood, Austin, TX 78758
Type: Montessori

HOPE: Home-Oriented Private Education for Texas
PO Box 17755, Austin, TX 78760-7755
512-280-HOPE
Type: state home-based

Alternative School
PO Box 1409, Eagle Pass, TX 78852
Lynn Purcell, 210-757-5326

Gibko
808 Saunders, Round Rock, TX 78864
Type: Montessori

Children's Montessori House of Canyon
2523 5th Ave, Canyon, TX 79015
Martha Johnson

Pampa Learning Center
212 W Cook, Pampa, TX 79065
Pat Farmer, 806-669-4750

St Mary's Montessori Preschool
1200 S Washington St, Amarillo, TX 79102-1645

North Heights Alternative School
607 N Hugh, Amarillo, TX 79107
Lyon Lee, 806-354-4200

Amarillo Montessori Academy
3806 Bowie St, Amarillo, TX 79110-1235

PEP High School
Box 394, Morton, TX 79353
Fredda Schooler, 806-933-4499

Post Elementary School
200 W 8th St, Post, TX 79356-3217
Type: Montessori

Iles Elementary
2401 Date Ave, Lubbock, TX 79404
Suzanne Christopher, 806-766-1755
Type: magnet
K-6th grade
Creative and expressive arts.

Williams Elementary
4812 58th St, Lubbock, TX 79414
Carolyn Solomon, 806-766-0988
Type: magnet
K-6th grade
Self-esteem; cooperative learning.

Montessori School of the Plains
4600 48th St, Lubbock, TX 79414-3502

Texas Homeschool Coalition
Box 6982, Lubbock, TX 79493
806-797-4927

Hobbs Accelerated Education Co-op
Rt 1 Box 1086, Rotan, TX 79546
Dr Frank Cockrell, 915-735-2850

PASS: Project for Academic Success and Skills (1986)
342 Cockerell Dr, Abilene, TX 79601
Don Eiland, Principal, 915-672-6456
Taylor County
Type: public at-risk
8 teachers, 113 students, ages 13-17, 6-8th grade
Enrollment restricted to non-SE residents retained at least
    twice
Governance by teachers and principal
Teacher qualifications: selected from AISD
Accelerated option (two yrs in one); multi-aged classes; sub-
    urban location; interns accepted.

Coleman High School
1600 E Golf Course, Midland, TX 79701
Helen Lackey, 915-689-5003

Viola M. Coleman High School
1600 E Golf Course Rd, Midland, TX 79701
Helen B. Lackey, Prin, 915-689-5000, FAX: 689-5016
Midland County
Type: public at-risk
10 teachers, 300 students, ages 15-21, 9-12th grade
Teacher qualifications: certification
Computers; non-compulsory class attendance; childcare;
    urban location; transportation.

Milam Magnet Elementary
815 S Dixie, Odessa, TX 79761
Cindy Abel, 915-337-1561
Ector County
K-6th grade
Visual and performing arts.

Alpine Montessori School (1988)
Box 664 Marfa Hwy, Alpine, TX 79831
Liz Sibley, Bd Pres, 915-837-2173
Non-profit; tuition: $175-265/mo, scholarships
1 teacher, 4 assistants; students mainly Hispanic, ages 3-9
Entrance requirements: age 2.5; toilet trained
Governance by board
Near Big Bend Nat'l Park; bilingual teaching in pre-school;
    Spanish; childcare; rural location; interns accepted.

New Opportunities Learning Center
PO Box 100, Canutillo, TX 79835
Esther McLeod, 915-877-3726

The Xinachtli Project (1989)
8404 N Loop D4, El Paso, TX 79907
Carlos Aceves, 915-594-8683
El Paso County
Type: independent
3 teachers; students mainly Chicano, ages 5-18
Integrates MesoAmerican culture with holistic approaches;
    workshop presentations.

Wm Beaumont Army Medical Center
PO Box 70537, El Passo, TX 79920
Type: Montessori

Jardin de Ninos Montessori School
10476 Seawood Dr, El Paso, TX 79925
Erma Chandler

East Montessori Learning Center
3510 N Yarbrough Dr, El Paso, TX 79925-1626

El Paso Homeschoolers Association
PO Box 371676, El Paso, TX 79937
Mare Hohholt, 915-857-3487

U.S. Virgin Islands

Virgin Islands Montessori School
6936 Vessup Ln, St Thomas, USVI 00802
Shournagh McWeeney

The Manor School
4236 La Grande Princesse, Christiansted, St Croix, USVI 00820
Type: Montessori

Rattan Montessori School
3B East Rattan; Box 1798, Kingshill, USVI 00851
Jane Little

Utah

American Montessori Academy
215 N Center St, American Fork, UT 84003-1629

Gingerbread House Pre-School
867 W 3800 S, Bountiful, UT 84010-8433
Type: Montessori

Great Basin High School
PO Box 1388, Clearfield, UT 84016
Mary DeLaRosa, Prin, 801-774-4000
Davis District
100 students
Accreditation: NWASC
Residential, vocational ed.

Utah Home Education Association
1099 S 200 E, Farmington, UT 84025
801-488-3676

Wasatch Alternative High School
235 N 200 E, Heber City, UT 84032
Marilyn Baird, Prin or Vickie Todd, Dir, 801-654-4231
Wasatch District
1 teacher, 65 students

Davis District Young Parents School
264 S 500 E, Kaysville, UT 84037
Betty Brand, Prin, 801-546-7970
8 teachers, 122 students, ages 13-21

Mountain High School
490 S 500 E, Kaysville, UT 84037
Betty Brand, Prin, 801-546-7960
Davis District
Type: public at-risk
11 teachers, 240 students, 10-12th grade
Accreditation: NWASC
Evening classes; home study.

Montessori Learning Center
538 Monterey Dr, Orem, UT 84057-3926

Creative Beginnings/Creative Beginnings Too
2180 Sidewinder/1800 Prospector Ave, Park City, UT 84060
802-645-7315, FAX: 649-4097
Type: Montessori; tuition: $250-500/mo
1 teacher, 10 assistants, 111 students, ages infant-6
Affiliation: AMI
Governance by administrator
Childcare; transportation.

Adult High–Young Mothers
85 E 100 S, Pleasant Grove, UT 84062
Jennie Barber, Dir, 801-756-8457
Alpine District
2,700 students
3 other sites: American Fork HS, 510 N 600 E, American Fork, UT 84003, 801-756-8547; Mountain View HS, 665 W Center, Orem, UT 84057, 801-227-8759; UT Valley CC, 800 W 1200 S, Orem, UT 84058, 801-222-8000.

Thompsen School
Rt 2, Box 2148, Roosevelt, UT 84066
Carol Parrish, Prin, 801-722-5185

Duchesne District
8 teachers, 42 students, mainly behavioral handicapped, 1–12th grade

Valley High School
11020 S State, Sandy, UT 84070
Clyde Melberg, Prin or Michele Hendrickson, 801-565-7574
Jordan District
19 teachers, 600 students, 10-12th grade
Accreditation: NWASC
Evening classes; teen mothers program.

Tooele Valley High School
240 W 1st S, Tooele, UT 84074
Gary King, Lead Teacher, 801-833-1928
Sevier District
Type: public at-risk
3 teachers, 95 students
Young mothers program; home study.

Ashley Valley High School (1989)
650 N Vernal Ave, Vernal, UT 84078
Dr A. J. Pease, Prin, 801-781-3125, FAX: 801-781-3128
Uintah District, Uintah County
Type: public choice/at-risk
4 teachers, 145 students, ages 13+, 9-12th grade
Affiliation: NASC
Governance by faculty, student reps, democratic school meeting, board
Teacher qualifications: UT Certification
Application worth 1/2 credit; mentor/advisor for every student; Glasser's control theory; reality therapy; non-compulsory class attendance; multi-aged classes; rural location; interns accepted.

Salt Lake Community High School
180 N 300 W, Salt Lake City, UT 84103
James P. Andersen, Prin, 801-533-3015
Salt Lake City District
Type: public at-risk
60 teachers, 2,859 students, 7-12th grade
Accreditation: NWASC
Evening classes; teen parenting.

Montessori Children's House
1303 S 11th E, Salt Lake City, UT 84105-2420

Bonnyview High School
4984 S 300 W, Murray, UT 84107
Shauna Ballou, Prin, 801-264-7470
Murray School District
6 teachers, 150 students, 7-12th grade
Accreditation: NWASC
Night classes; home study.

Mount Vernon Academy
184 Vine St, Murray, UT 84107
Type: home-based

Hawthorne University
2965 East, 3435 South, Salt Lake City, UT 84109
Dr Alfred Munzert, 801-485-1801, FAX: 801-485-1563
Type: higher education
100 students

In addition to regular undergraduate, a program for last 2 years of high school and first two years of college at the same time.

Central High School (1973)
3031 S 200 E, Salt Lake City, UT 84115
Edward Campos, Prin, 801-481-7100, FAX: 801-481-7104
Type: public at-risk
18 teachers, 700 students, ages 13–19, 7–12th grade
Governance by principal, teachers
Teacher qualifications: UT Certification
Home study; intensive learning; high expectation in academics, behavior; urban location; interns accepted.

Granite District Coordinator for Alternative Education
340 E 3545 S, Salt Lake City, UT 84115
Shelley Iverson, Coord, 801-268-8560, 481-7105
Programs in each junior, senior high school.

Brighton Montessori Early Learning Center
2887 E 7000 S, Salt Lake City, UT 84121-3444

American Home Academy/Latter Day Saints Home Educators' Association (1989)
(See Resource Appendix)

National Association of Mormon Home Educators
2770 S 1000 W, Perry, UT 84302

Cache County High School
265 W 1400 N, Logan, UT 84321
Dean Phillips, Prin, 801-755-0716
Cache District
Type: public at-risk
5 teachers, 125 students, 9–12th grade
Accreditation: NWASC

Logan Alternative Programs
83 S 100 W, Logan, UT 84321
Larry Petersen, Dir, 801-755-2395
Cache County
Cache District Young Mothers Program: 2 teachers, 24 students; Logan North Campus: 42 students; Logan South Campus, 347 S 300 W, Logan, UT: 65 students.

Valley Montessori Preschool
1240 N 225 E, Logan, UT 84321

Vocational Incentive Program
1301 N 600 W, Logan, UT 84321
Robert O. Brems, Prin or Shirley Hammon, 801-723-5281
Box Elder District
80 students, HS

Washington High School
3279 Washington Blvd, Ogden, UT 84403
Craig Pace or Wilford Hale, 801-625-8935
Ogden and Weber Districts
Type: public at-risk
31 teachers, 450 students, 9–12th grade
Accreditation: NWASC
Young mothers program; afternoon classes.

Weber Basin High School
RFD #6, Ogden, UT 84405
Vern Brown, Prin, 801-479-9806
Davis District
Type: public at-risk

225 students, ages 16–22
Accreditation: NWASC
Residential, voc ed; group living, social skills; ungraded.

Canyon Country Homeschoolers
1605 W. Highland Dr, Moab, UT 84532
Donna Grah, 801-259-5864

HELP-Four Corners
Castle Valley Star Route, PO Box 1901, Moab, UT 84532
801-259-6968

FCLA Utah Spice Group
1510 W 500 N, Provo, UT 84601
801-377-4728
Type: home-based

Independence High School
636 N Zepher Ave, Provo, UT 84601
Gregory A. Hudnall, Prin, 801-374-4920
Provo District
Type: public at-risk
55 pt teachers, 250 students, 9–12th grade
Accreditation: NWASC
Evening classes; home study.

Brigham Young U—Dept of Independent Study
(See Resource Appendix)

Utah Home Education Association
PO Box 50565, Provo, UT 84605
Karl Pearson, Pres, 801-342-4027, 801-535-1533
Conventions; newsletter; bookstore; testing.

Delta High School ALC
351 S 100 E, Delta, UT 84624
Barbara Nelson, Prin, 801-864-2764
Millard District
Type: public at-risk
2 teachers, 27 students, 9–12th grade
Young mothers program; home study.

Home School Supply House
(See Resource Appendix)

Landmark High School
320 S Main, Spanish Fork, UT 84660
Don Jones, Prin, 801-798-4030
Nebo District
Type: public at-risk
7 teachers, 300+ students, 10–12th grade
Accreditation: NWASC
Evening classes; home study.

Cedar Ridge High School
50 N 650 W, Richfield, UT 84701
Randall E. Brown, Prin, 801-896-9464
Sevier District
5 teachers, 125+ students, ages 14+
Accreditation: NWASC
Night classes; home study.

Millcreek High School
25 E Telegraph, Washington, UT 84780
Terry G. Carr, Prin, 801-628-2462
Washington District
Type: public at-risk
15 teachers, 186+ students
Accreditation: NWASC
Night classes; home study.

Vermont

Pre-Vocational Program for At-Risk Youth (1980)
Oxbow Vocational Center, Bradford, VT 05033
Carolyn Roe, 802-222-5212
Type: public at-risk
10th grade
Family involvement; experiential; tutorials; school/community partnerships; behavior management; comprehensive planning.

Project Champ
Chelsea School, Chelsea, VT 05038
Melinda Turnbull, 802-685-4551
Type: public at-risk
HS
Work experience, placement; participation of local businesses.

Montessori School of the Upper Valley, Inc (1973)
PO Box 368 Main St, Norwich, VT 05055
Joyce Dion, Head Teacher, 802-649-2827
Non-profit; tuition: $2,350/yr
1 teacher, 1 assistant, 31 students, ages 3-6
Entrance requirements: age 3
Governance by board
Rural location; interns accepted.

Project Advance
Randolph Vocational Center, Randolph, VT 05060
Richard Flies, 802-728-9595
Type: public at-risk
Student ages 14-16, HS
Behavior management; vocational exploration; hands-on community projects.

Upper Valley Waldorf School (1991)
PO Box 15, Norwich, VT 05074
Phebe McCosker, Coord, 802-649-5729
Orange County
Tuition: $2,500-3,250/yr, scholarships
5 teachers, 32 students, ages 4-9, K-2nd grade
Affiliation: AWSNA
Governance by board
Teacher qualifications: college degree and Waldorf training
Rural location.

Blue Mountain Alternative Program
Thetford Academy, Thetford, VT 05074
Beverly Moody, 802-785-4805
Type: public at-risk
HS
Vocational; agricultural; behavior modification; counseling; transition to work.

Open Fields School
Academy Rd, Thetford, VT 05074
Jean Aull, 802-785-2077
Type: independent

Mtn. School Program of Milton Academy
RFD Box 123-F, Vershire, VT 05079
David Grant, 802-685-4520
Type: independent

Alternative Education at Windsor High School (1993)
Union St, Windsor, VT 05089
Martin Tewksbury, Tch/Coord

Windsor County
Type: public choice
1 teacher, 7 students, ages 12-16, 7-10th grade
Governance by principal
Teacher qualifications: VT certification
Opportunity to design course work, schedule and work experience wtih staff guidance, support; positive relationship development with peers, staff, public and home; multi-aged classes; interns accepted.

Gifted and Talented Program
Bellows Falls Union High School, Bellows Falls, VT 05101
Mark Kennedy, 802-463-3944
Type: public choice
HS
Newsletter; inclusive; self-selective; decompartmentalized.

Global Alliance for Transforming Education (1990)
(See Resource Appendix)

West River Montessori School
Box 171, South Londonderry, VT 05155
Kim Merrow

Alternative Community Experiences
S Stream Rd, Bennington, VT 05201
Edward Sanders, 802-447-8405

Bennington Program (1970)
Mount Anthony UHSD, Bennington, VT 05201
Ralph Wright, 802-442-2811
Type: public at-risk
7-12th grade
School/community partnerships; early intervention; vocational training; job placement; work transition; wilderness experience; HS diploma.

Bennington School, Inc
19 Fairview St, Bennington, VT 05201
Jeffrey La Bonte, 802-447-1557
Type: independent
Students mainly at-risk

Hiland Hall School (1991)
RR 2 Box 1700, Bennington, VT 05201
Jessica Howard, Prin, 802-442-3868
Bennington County
Type: independent, non-profit; tuition: $1,500-5,500/yr, scholarships
2 teachers, 28 students, ages 5-14
No residency requirement
Governance by principal, board
Teacher qualifications: Bachelor's, experience
Low ratio; individual attention; self-understanding; critical thinking; communication; skills mastery; no letter grades; multi-aged classes; extensive field trips; interns accepted.

Transitional Class of Bennington Elementory School
128 Park St, Bennington, VT 05201
Aldona Guilmette, 802-442-5256
Type: public at-risk
Pre-first grade, hands-on curriculum; non-stressful learning; manipulatives; whole language; early identification, intervention; behavior management; family involvement.

Central Vermont Homeschool Group
RR1, PO Box 2980, Manchester Center, VT 05255
802-362-4337

Southshire Community School
Box 634, N Bennington, VT 05257
Susan Lambert, Administrative Assistant, 802-442-4601
Bennington County
Type: independent, non-profit; tuition: $2875/yr, scholarships
3 teachers, 30 students, ages 4.5-12, K-6th grade
Governance primarily by parents
Located in a small village, family oriented, in tradition of one room schoolhouse; holds ideal that the inner world of the child is recognized, valued, guided; students pursue personal interests, create knowledge, master academic skills; no letter grades; multi-aged classes; interns accepted.

Hilltop Montessori School
118 Maple St, Brattleboro, VT 05301
Tonia LWheeler, 802-257-0500

Meadows School
75 Linden St Box 803, Brattleboro, VT 05301
Ruth MacDonald, 802-257-7785

School for International Training
Kipling Rd, Brattleboro, VT 05301
Bill Huff, 802-257-7751; 800-451-4465
Type: higher education; tuition: variable, scholarships
250 students
Senior college, graduate school, study abroad for international/intercultural education and language teaching.

The Neighborhood Schoolhouse (1980)
Box 119, Brattleboro, VT 05302
Norma Willingham, Prin, 802-257-5544
Windham County
Type: independent, non-profit; tuition: $3880, scholarships
68 students, ages 3-12, ungraded
Entrance requirement: commitment to philosophy
Affiliations: NCACS, NAEYC, VISA
Governance by consensus of principal/staff or board
Developmentally appropriate; experiential; student need and interest-based; no letter grades; multi-aged classes; rural location; interns accepted.

Marlboro College (1946)
PO Box A, Marlboro, VT 05344
Wayne R. Wood, Adms Dir, 802-257-4333, FAX:-4154
Type: Boarding, non-profit; tuition: $17,175/yr, scholarships
36 teachers, 270 students, ages 17-40
Entrance requirements: HS diploma
Governance by faculty and student reps
Self-designed curriculum; one to one tutorials; small classes; philosophy of self-governance, academic rigor.

Grammar School (1960)
RR4 Box 195, Hickory Ridge Rd, Putney, VT 05346
Marcia Leader, Adms Dir, 802-387-5364
Windham County
Type: independent, non-profit; tuition: $5,540-7,500/yr, scholarships
15 teachers, 99 students, ages 5-14, K-8th grade
Affiliations: NEASC, NAIS, AISNE, VISA, ERB
Governance by board
Science fairs; 9 yr French program; skiing; running; computer literacy; visual, performing arts; poetry; rural location; interns accepted.

Windham County Homeschool Group
RR 2, PO Box 1332, Putney, VT 05346
Julie Tamler, 802-387-5285

Rutland County Homeschoolers
PO Box 161, Pittsford, VT 05352
Liz Swift, 802-483-6296

Green Meadows Community School
Stowe Hill Rd, Wilminton, VT 05363
Steven Cohen, 802-464-8646

Advance at Burlington High School
52 Institute Rd, Burlington, VT 05401
Evelyn Carter, 802-864-8411
Type: public at-risk
25 students, 9-10th grade
CAI; team teaching in small groups; integrated curriculum; parent involvement; school/community partnerships; vocational; job placement.

Burlington College (1972)
95 North Ave, Burlington, VT 05401
Nancy Wilson, Adms Dir, 802-862-9616, FAX: 658-0071
Chittenden County
Non-profit; tuition: $250/cr, scholarships
75 teachers, 230 students
Entrance requirements: HS diploma/GED, interview
Governance by faculty and student reps
Accredited degrees in psychology, humanities, human services, feminist studies, fine arts or individualized major; external degree program; no letter grades; urban location.

Burlington Lighthouse Project
150 Colchester Ave, Burlington, VT 05401
Evelyn Carter, 802-864-8418
Type: public at-risk
Pre K-12th grade
Comprehensive team planning.

FOCUS
Burlington Area Voc-Tech Center, Burlington, VT 05401
Emile Cote, 802-863-8426
Type: public at-risk
JH+
Job matching activities; career exploration; attitudes and aptitude testing; workshops; support; GED.

Learning Materials Workshop
274 N Winiski Ave, Burlington, VT 05401
Karen Hewitt
Type: Montessori

ONTOP
14 S Williams, Burlington, VT 05401
Rick Ebel
Type: public at-risk
Residency required.

Rock Point School
Institute Rd, Burlington, VT 05401
Russell Ellis
Type: independent, boarding
Students mainly at-risk, HS
Low ratio; counseling; tutoring; self-image/motivation; substance abuse counseling; 24 hr/day supportive environment; positive peer culture.

Schoolhouse
99 Proctor Ave Ext, S Burlington, VT 05403
Joni Avritic, 802-658-4164
Chittenden County
Type: independent, non-profit; tuition: $2850/yr, scholarships
4 teachers, 39 students, ages 5-12, K-6th grade
Governance by parent cooperative
Teacher qualifications: VT license or degree and related experience
Thematic units; art; yearly all school play based on cultural study; peer conflict resolution; parent-taught mini-courses; no letter grades; multi-aged classes; suburban location; interns accepted.

International Children's School
1 Executive Dr, South Burlington, VT 05403
Sadie Khouri, 802-865-3347

Alternative Education Program at Mount Abraham J-SHS
7 Airport Dr, Bristol, VT 05443
Robert Rhein, 802-453-2347
Type: public at-risk
35 students, 7-12th grade
Early identification/intervention; community partnerships; vocational training; part-time job program.

Mount Abraham UHS Reading Center
Addison Northeast Supervisory Union, Bristol, VT 05443
Jan Willey, 802-453-5146
Type: public at-risk
JH
Integrated compensatory, special, regular education; break down barriers between interest groups.

Red Cedar School (1989)
PO Box 393, Bristol, VT 05443
Jackie Werner Gavrin, 802-453-5213
Addison County
Type: independent; tuition: $3600/yr, scholarships
2 teachers, 17 students, ages 4-12
Affiliation: Sudbury Valley School
Governance by democratic school meeting
Teacher qualifications: interest and ability to work with young people; commitment to philosophy of school.
Students initiate their own activities and are free to decide how they will use their time; the weekly meeting governs the school and rules are enforced by a judicial group; no letter grades; non-compulsory class attendance; multi-aged classes; extensive field trips; rural location; interns accepted.

Vermont Homeschoolers Association
Rd 2, PO Box 4440, Bristol, VT 05443
Type: state home-based

West Wind Montessori School
West Wind Farm, Charlotte, VT 05445

Pathfinders Alternative Education
Eronsburg Falls High School, Enosburg Falls, VT 05450
Judith de Rancourt, 802-933-5103
Type: public at-risk
7-12th grade
Comprehensive psychosocial services; integrated vocational/academic studies; job training, placement; community service; interagency cooperation; family involvement.

ACE: Alternative Center for Education
Essex Junction Ed Center, Essex Junction, VT 05452
Lars Baris, 802-878-1392
Type: public at-risk
Work experience; group activities; field trips; parent involvement; community partnerships; adventure-based counseling; pregnant, teen parenting support.

Climate Project
Summit School, Essex Junction, VT 05452
Marge Simmons, 802-878-1377
Type: public at-risk
K-2nd grade
Projects to foster sense of responsibility, belonging and fun; family involvement; early intervention; school and community partnerships.

Star Program
Fleming School, Essex Junction, VT 05452
Thomas Perry, 802-878-1381

Type: public at-risk
ES
Self-esteem building; interest-based; fun-shops.

Life Program
Champlain Valley High School, Hinesburg, VT 05461
Thomas Hart, 802-482-2109
Type: public at-risk
School/community partnerships; family involvement; support, transition to work, return to school; GED; vocational training; job placement.

EYEP: Exemplary Youth Employment Program
Mount Mansfield Union High School, Jericho, VT 05465
Jennifer Muncil, 802-899-2657
Type: public at-risk
Student ages 14-21, 7-12th grade
Placement; work transition; community/school partnerships; early intervention.

Saxon Hill School Inc
PO Box 68, Jericho, VT 05465
Ann Manning, 802-899-3832
Type: independent

New Beginnings
S Main St, St Albans, VT 05478
Neal Smith or Chuck Soule, 802-524-5818
Students mainly at-risk, HS
Behavior management; family involvement; social, emotional, vocational growth.

Lake Champlain Waldorf School (1983)
27 Harbor Rd, Shelborne, VT 05482
Pam Graham, Adm, 802-985-2827
Chittendyn County
Non-profit; tuition: $3,600-4,320/yr, scholarships
14 teachers, 116 students, ages 3-12, pre K-6th grade
Entrance requirements: interview, school records
Affiliation: AWSNA
Governance by faculty
Teacher qualifications: Waldorf certification
Suburban location; interns accepted.

Heartworks School
PO Box 835, Shelburne, VT 05482
Diane Rooney, 802-985-2153

Resource Center for Redesigning Education
(See Resource Appendix)

Alternative Program at Missisquoi Valley Union HS
RR 2 Box 268, Swanton, VT 05488
Robert McHugh, 802-868-2597

Project Wrap Around
Box 130, Swanton, VT 05488
James A. Marshall, 802-868-2441
Type: public at-risk
Pre K-12th grade
Enrollment restricted to severely emotionally disturbed.
Counseling; home support; services in mainstream settings.

Addison County Homeschool Group
Rd 2, PO Box 2850, Vergennes, VT 05491
802-877-3959

Homeschool Representative
RD 1, PO Box 1265, Belvidere, VT 05492
Denise Starkey, 802-644-2606

Pine Ridge School
1075 Williston Rd, Williston, VT 05495
Mary Jean Thielen, 802-434-2161
Type: independent
Students mainly at-risk

Insight Alternative Program
Vermont College, Box 240, Montpelier, VT 05602
Ann Burns, 802-223-8812
Type: public at-risk
Work experience, placement; affective education; community service; learning contracts; family involvement; school/community partnerships; vocational.

The Montpelier Waldorf Child's Garden (1991)
280 Main St, Montpelier, VT 05602
Susan Darrah, 802-223-5346
Non-profit; tuition: variable
Student ages 4-5
Governance by parent cooperative
Honor dignity, joy of nurturing, sustaining life; cooking, crafts, gardening, watercolors, ample play.

Turtle Island Children's Center
659 Elm St, Montpelier, VT 05602
Meg Baird, 802-229-4047

U 32 Jr-Sr High School
RR2 Box 3315, Gallison Hill Rd, Montpelier, VT 05602
Ann Burns, 802-229-0322, FAX: 802-229-2761
Washington County
Type: public choice

Vermont Home Schoolers
c/o Vermont Dept of Ed, Montpelier, VT 05602
Sue Lafavre, Sec or Natalie Casco, Dir, 802-828-3352
Type: state home-based
Also contact DeWes Guarnaccia, VT Homeschoolers Assn, 207-777-0077; interns accepted.

Home School Coordination—At Risk Youth
Spaulding High School, Barre, VT 05641
Linda Mailly, 802-476-6411
6-12th grade
Career, academic counseling; first Inter-Agency Collaboration Group in VT; behavioral, disciplinary modification; substance abuse counseling; pregnant teen/young parent support.

Laraway School
Box 618, Johnson, VT 05656
Scott Johnson, 802-635-7212
Type: independent
Students mainly at-risk

Upward Bound
Johnson State College, Johnson, VT 05656
Sally Ballin
Type: independent

Lamoille County Homeschool Group
RR2, PO Box 3344, Morrisville, VT 05661
Dena Keith, 802-888-3574

LINK: Lamoille Interagency Network for Kids
Lamoille Family Ceille, VT 05661, Morrisville, VT 05661
Jane Sanders, 802-885-5229
Type: public at-risk
7-12th grade
Behavior/disciplinary problem management; counseling; parent/student mediation; shelter for runaways.

The Regional Alternative Program-Aim High (1990)
PO Box 340, Morrisville, VT 05661
Richard F. Kovacs, Director, 802-888-6586
Chittenden County
Type: public at-risk
3 teachers, 20 students, ages 14-18, 9-12th grade
Entrance requirements: contract between student, parent and school; no residency requirement
Affiliation: Lamoille South Supervisory Union
Governance by teachers and principal

Teacher qualifications: alternative ed experience
Project-oriented; theme-based; hands-on; extensive forestry, conservation, and agricultural activities; transportation; interns accepted.

Student Assistance Program
31 Vine St, Northfield, VT 05663
Daniel Dilena, 802-485-5751
Type: public at-risk
7-12th grade
Enrollment restricted to potential dropout/suicide; substance abuse; neglect/abuse.
Case management; family involvement; early identification/intervention; behavior management; suicide prevention; teen parenting.

Goddard College
Plainfield, VT 05667
Peter Burns, Admissions Director, 802-434-8311
boarding, non-profit
450 students
Entrance requirements: personal statement, transcripts, references
Governance by collaborative models involving staff, faculty, students, administration
Encourages experiential learning; students design their own BA, MA, MFA; based on Dewey's educational theories; located on old farm estate in hills of Vermont; looks for indepenent, creative individuals who write well, read constantly; on campus and low residence programs; no letter grades; rural location.

Maplehilll Community School
POBox 248, Plainfield, VT 05667
Karen Heath, 802-454-7747
Type: independent
Students mainly at-risk

New School,Inc
PO Box 378, Plainfield, VT 05667
Susan Remington, 802-454-8534
Type: independent

Green Mount Valley School
RR1 Box 166, Waitsfield, VT 05673
Cavid Gavett, 802-496-2150
Type: independent

Vermont Home Schoolers (1985)
RD 2 Box 1775, Plainfield, VT 05677
Mary Harris, Secretary/Treasurer, 802-454-8555
Provides networking and information to all regional groups; assists in writing education plans, dealing with VT DE hearings; interns accepted.

Washington County Homeschool Group
PO Box 111, Waterbury Center, VT 05677
Anne Marie Parker, 802-244-5351

Green Mountain Waldorf School (1982)
RR 1 Box 4885, Wolcott, VT 05680
Karen Case Talbert, Adm, 802-888-2828
Lamoille County
Non-profit; tuition: $2,755/yr, scholarships
9 teachers, 76 students, ages 3-12, pre K-6th grade
Affiliation: AWSNA
Governance by faculty, board, administrator
Environment; oral tradition; extensive field trips; multi-aged classes; rural location; transportation.

Alternative Education Program
41 Merchants Row, Rutland, VT 05701
Paul Fenwick, 802-773-1955
Type: public at-risk
7-12th grade

Off campus; job skills; occupational interests; community service; family involvement; transition to work; discipline/behavioral assistance; pregnant/young parenting; extensive field trips.

Rutland Lcity Alternative Education Program
6 Church St, Rutland, VT 05701
Greg McClallen

Mountain View Community School
PO Box 202, Rutland, VT 05702
Teresa Miele, 802-775-4067
Type: independent; tuition: $2,100/yr, scholarships
40 students, pre K–2nd grade
Developmentally appropriate curriculum; childcare; multi-aged classes.

Holistic Education Press
(See Resource Appendix)

Smokey House Project (1974)
RFD Box 292, Danby, VT 05739
Lynn Bondurant, 802-293-5121
Type: independent
Students mainly at-risk, ages 14–19
Natural resource mgmt; trained adult crew leaders in forestry, agriculture; work experience; community partnerships; Benchmarking; work transition.

Students At Risk Team at Fair Haven Union HS
Mechanic St Ext, Fair Haven, VT 05743
Bruce Gee, 802-265-4966
Type: public at-risk
Family involvement; early intervention; behavior management.

Eckerd Wilderness
RR 2 Box 6800, Fair Haven, VT 05743-9112
Mike Kydd, 802-537-4101
Type: independent
Students mainly at-risk

Bridge School
PO Box 27, Midddlebury, VT 05753
Gerry Loney, 802-388-3498
Type: independent

Atrium Society
(See Resource Appendix)

Gailer School
19 Shannon St, Middlebury, VT 05753
Harry Chaucer, 802-388-0830
Type: independent

Middlebury Union High School AEP (1982)
Charles Ave, Middlebury, VT 05753
Rodney Morris, 802-388-4460
Addison County
Type: public choice
4 teachers, 25 students, mainly at-risk, ages 12–18, 9–12th grade
Residency required
Governance by principal and board
For potential dropouts; vocational training; job placement; case management; comprehensive planning; work/study; multi-aged classes; extensive field trips.

Vermont Homeschool Association
RR 1, Box 6680, Middletown Springs, VT 05757
Debbie Kniffin
Type: state home-based

North Hollow School
PO Box 358, Rochester, VT 05767
Judy Geller, 802-767-3580
Type: independent

Addison County Home Schoolers
RD 1, PO Box 150, Salisbury, VT 05769
Leigh Harder, 802-388-2005

Exemplary Youth Employment Program
7 Main St, St Johnsbury, VT 05819
Virginia Van Damm, 802-748-8171
Type: public at-risk
Student ages 14–21
Community partnerships; family involvement.

Project Rediscovery
25 Western Ave, St Johnsbury, VT 05819
D. James King or Howard Crawford, 802-748-8912, 748-8171
Type: public choice
JH
Career awareness; vocational; family involvement; behavior management; school/community partnerships; comprehensive planning process.

School of Human Service (1978)
PO Box 66 Emerson Falls Rd, St Johnsbury, VT 05819
800-444-1812, FAX: 802-748-5719
Type: higher education, non-profit; tuition: $6,000/yr, scholarships
12 teachers, 70 students, partly at-risk
Entrance requirements: HS diploma or GED, work experience
Affiliation: Springfield College
Teacher qualifications: MA/MS or equivalent
Work related; portfolio based; rural location; interns accepted.

Walden Farm School
Rd 1 Box 1520, East Hardwick, VT 05836
Kathryn Hull, 802-533-7095

Orleans Southwest Lighthouse Project (1988)
Main St, Hardwick, VT 05843
William Dunn, 802-472-6511
Type: public at-risk
Pre K–12th grade
Comprehensive team planning; long-term, multi-year approach; community resources.

Northeast Kingdom Homeschool Group
RD 1, PO Box 37, Irasburg, VT 05845
802-754-8780

Caledonia County Homeschool Group
PO Box 55, Lyndon Center, VT 05850
Colleen LaRiviere, 802-626-9503

At-Risk Program of the Canaan School System
PO Box 69, Canaan, VT 05903
Cynthia V. Mills, 802-266-8910
Type: public at-risk
K–12th grade
Counseling; employment resource; transition to work; HS diploma, GED.

Virginia

Northern Virginia Homeschoolers / LEARN
47756 Fathom Pl, Sterling, VA 20165
703-444-3455

Montessori School of Northern Virginia (1962)
6820 Pacific Ln, Annandale, VA 22003
Betsy Mitchell, 703-256-9577
Non-profit; tuition: $2,440-4,585/yr
5 teachers, 5 assistants, 129 students, mainly international,
   ages infant-9
Entrance requirement: interview
Affiliation: AMS
Governance by administrator, board of trustees
Custom built; in secluded area surrounded by parkland; child-
   care; suburban location; transportation; interns accepted.

Hope Montessori School
4614 Ravensworth Rd, Annandale, VA 22003-5641

Linton Hall
9535 Linton Hall Rd, Bristow, VA 22013
Glenna Smith
Type: Montessori

New School of Northern Virginia (1989)
9431 Silver King Court, Fairfax, VA 22031
John Potter, 703-691-3041
Type: independent, non-profit; tuition: $7700/yr, scholarships
9 teachers, 70 students, ages 5-18, K-12th grade
Affiliation: NCACS
Governance by republic form with head, staff, students.
Student ownership of education; community issues, Socratic,
   experiential; many Summerhillian values; uses Howard
   Gardner's multiple intelligences; no letter grades; multi-
   aged classes; extensive field trips; non-compulsory class
   attendance; suburban location; interns accepted.

Montessori School of Cedar Lane
3035 Cedar Ln, Fairfax, VA 22031-2100
Lance Gilbert

Montessori School of Holmes Run (1973)
3527 Gallows Road, Falls Church, VA 22042
Judith W. Clarke, Head, 703-573-7652
4 teachers, 2 assistants, 76 students, ages 3-12
Affiliation: AMS
Governance by principal
Strong parent participation; suburban location; interns
   accepted.

Falls Church Children's House of Montessori
3335 Annandale Rd, Falls Church, VA 22042-3721

Montessori Children's Center
6103 Arlington Blvd, Falls Church, VA 22044

Montessori Country School (1971)
621 Alabama Dr, Herndon, VA 22070
Pat Kretsch, Adm, 703-437-8285
Non-profit; tuition: $2,290/3,120/yr
8 teachers, 4 assistants, 115 students, mainly international,
   ages 3-6
Governance by board
Suburban location; interns accepted.

The Learning Community Inc
PO Box 5177, Herndon, VA 22070
Type: home-based

Montessori School of Herndon (1984)
840 Dranesville Rd, Herndon, VA 22070-3019
Nasim Mallick Khan, Dir, 703-437-8229
Tuition: Variable
8 teachers, 12 assistants; student ages 3-12
Affiliations: AMS, NAEYC
Governance by administrator and democratic school meeting
4-acres; computers in each class; daily French; after school
   clubs, music, dance, karate; strong PTA; childcare; suburban location.

Douglass Community School
407 E Market St, Leesburg, VA 22075
Laurraine G. Landolt, Prin

Reston Montessori School (1987)
1928 Isaac Newton Sq W, Reston, VA 22090
Kathleen Lanfear, Dir, 703-481-2922
Tuition: $300-840/mo
8 teachers, 150 students, ages 2.5-9
Affiliations: AMS, NAEYC, VAMA
Governance by administrator
Kindermusik/Orff; French for ages 2.5-6; French bilingual for
   ages 6-9; childcare; suburban location; interns accepted.

Montessori School of McLean (1973)
1711 Kirby Rd, McLean, VA 22101
Dorothy P. DiDio, Head, 703-790-1049, FAX: 703-790-1962
Non-profit; tuition: $3,400-4,100/yr
7 teachers, 7 assistants, 165 students, mainly international,
   ages 3-9
Entrance requirements: preschool, toilet trained; elementary,
   Montessori experience
Affiliation: AMS
Governance by board
Professional art program for ages 5+; near Washington, DC;
   suburban location; interns accepted.

**National-Louis University's Northern Virginia/
   Washington, DC Center** (1986)
8000 Westpart Dr Suite 125, McLean, VA 22101
Dr Robert Skenes, Assoc Prof, 703-749-3000
Type: higher education, non-profit; scholarships
Students mainly working adults, ages 22+
Entrance requirements: 2 yrs college credit
Governance by faculty and student reps
15 students/class; practical, applied learning; BS, Master's
   degrees; suburban location.

The Brooksfield School (1987)
1830 Kirby Rd, McLean, VA 22101
Mary Anne Duthis, 703-356-5437, FAX: same
Type: Montessori, non-profit; tuition: $3,900-15,500/yr
5 teachers, 4 assistants, 73 students, mainly international,
   ages 3-9
Affiliations: AMS, NAYEC
Governance by administrator
Cultural studies; individualized instruction; emphasis on language and arts; childcare; suburban location; interns
   accepted.

Ridgemont Montessori School
6519 Georgetown Pike, Mc Lean, VA 22101-2223
Mary Beth Humen

Alternative Education Center (1991)
8220 Conner Dr, Manassas, VA 22110
Dr. Ed Doyle, Prin, 703-361-9808, FAX: 703-361-2864
Prince William County Schools District
Type: public at-risk
70 students, ages 13–18, 7–12th grade
No residency requirement.
Partnership with George Mason U; mobile classroom; community outreach; suburban location; interns accepted.

Alternative Program at New Dominion School
8220 Conners Dr, Manassas, VA 22111
Edward Doyle, Supervisor

Elementary Montessori School of Oakton
PO Box 412, Oakton, VA 22124-0412

Montessori School of Oakton
12113 Vale Rd, Oakton, VA 22124-2222

Home School Legal Defense Association
(See Resource Appendix)

St Mark's Montessori School (1968)
5800 Backlick Rd, Springfield, VA 22150
Judith Carter-Sanford, Dir, 703-451-4470
Non-profit; tuition: $180/220/mo
3 teachers, 3 assistants, 71 students, mainly international,
   ages 3–6
Entrance requirement: toilet trained
Affiliation: AMI
Governance by an administrator and board of trustees
Childcare; suburban location.

The Springs School
5407 Backlick Rd, Springfield, VA 22151-3915
Cathy Shields
Type: Montessori

Home Instruction Support Group
217 Willow Terr, Sterling, VA 22170

Green Hedges School
415 Windover Ave NW, Vienna, VA 22180-4232
Type: Montessori

Cardinal Montessori (1992)
1424 G St, Woodbridge, VA 22191
Leneale A. Gallegos, Dir, 703-491-3810
Tuition: $2,250/3,500/yr
3 teachers, 1 assistant, 40 students, ages 3–9
Affiliation: AMS
Governance by administrator
Childcare; suburban location; interns accepted.

Edelen's Montessori Learning Center
1337 Horner Rd, Woodbridge, VA 22191-1722

Page Traditional School
1501 N Lincoln St, Arlington, VA 22201
Holly Hawthorne

Francis Scott Key School
2300 Key Blvd, Arlington, VA 22201-3415
Type: Montessori

Montessori Children's Creative Center, Inc
3809 Washington Blvd, Arlington, VA 22201-4514

Hoffman-Boston Public School
1415 S Queen St, Arlington, VA 22204-4739
Type: Montessori

Drew Model School (1971)
3500 S 24th St, Arlington, VA 22206
Dr Michael Grinder, Prin, 703-358-5825
Arlington County
Type: public choice Montessori
20 teachers, 410 students, ages 3–11, pre K–5th grade

Entrance requirements: birth certificate, immunizations,
   physical exam, proof of county residency
Governance by teachers, principal
Teacher qualifications: VA certification
Cooperative learning; no letter grades; multi-aged classes;
   interns accepted.

Chesterbrook Montessori School
3455 N Glebe Rd, Arlington, VA 22207
Judy Balcazar-Mercill, 703-241-8271
Tuition: $2,600/3,000/yr
3 teachers, 2 assistants, 60 students, mainly international,
   ages 3–6
Affiliation: AMS
Governance by administrator
Emphasis on music, singing; Spanish; suburban location;
   interns accepted.

H. B. Woodlawn High School
City As School Program (1987)
4100 Vacation Lane, Arlington, VA 22207
Deneen Snow, 703-358-6376
Type: public choice
10 students

H-B Woodlawn Program (1971)
4100 N Vacation Lane, Arlington, VA 22207
Ray Anderson, Prin, 703-358-6363, FAX: 703-358-6383
Type: public choice
41 teachers, 522 students, 6–12th grade
Entrance by student request
Governance by democratic school meeting
Students primarily responsible for use of time, behavior, goal
   setting, school governanc; interns accepted.

Key Elementary School-Partial Immersion
2300 Key Blvd, Arlington, VA 22207
Katharine G. Panfel, Prin, 703-358-4210
Arlington County
Type: public choice
58 teachers, 703 students, ages 3–12
Residency required
Affiliation: SACS
Governance by staff
Teacher qualifications: VA certification, bilingual
Spanish bilingual; extensive field trips; multi-aged classes;
   interns accepted.

Montessori Chesterbrook School
3455 N Glebe Rd, Arlington, VA 22207

Glebe School
1770 N Glebe Rd, Arlington, VA 22207-2098
Type: Montessori

STEP Center
3330 King St, Alexandria, VA 22302
Type: public at-risk

Aquinas Montessori School
8334 Mount Vernon Hwy, Alexandria, VA 22309-1998
Kathleen H Futrell

Gyldenlove School
3709 Colonial Ave, Alexandria, VA 22309-2546
Type: Montessori

Montessori School of Alexandria, Inc (1969)
6300 Florence Ln, Alexandria, VA 22310-2200
Jean Adolphi, Administrator, 703-960-3498, FAX: same
Non-profit; tuition: $3,150/4,250/4,995/yr
4 teachers, 4 assistants, 108 students, ages infant-12
Governance by board
Emphasis on students' independence, joy of learning, and
   choosing appropriate work; childcare.

Institute for Alternative Futures
(See Resource Appendix)

Old Town Montessori School
115 S Washington St, Alexandria, VA 22314-3028

Home Educators Network
3320 Waverly Dr, Fredericksburg, VA 22401

Fredericksburg Montessori
312 Sophia St, Fredericksburg, VA 22401-6057

Gates Alternative High School
6717 Smith Station Rd, Spotsylvania, VA 22553
Meghan O'Connor

Frederick County Middle School
441 Linden Dr, Winchester, VA 22601
Attn: Principal

Winchester Montessori School
1905 Henry Ave, Winchester, VA 22601-6309

Seton Home Study School (1975)
1350 Progress Dr, Front Royal, VA 22630
Dr Mary Kay Clark, 703-636-9990, FAX: 703-636-1602
Warren County
Boarding; cost: $500/yr, scholarships
35 teachers, 6300 students, K–12th grade
Placement test required
Governance by board
Catholic curriculum in all subject areas.

Home Educators Association of Virginia
PO Box 1810, Front Royal, VA 22630-1810
703-635-9322
Type: state home-based

Robert E. Ayler Middle School
PO Box 357, Stephens City, VA 22655
Attn: Principal

Children's Center Montessori
PO Box 184, Strasburg, VA 22657-0184

Core Knowledge Foundation
(See Resource Appendix)

Elementary Montessori
RR 13 Box 53, Charlottesville, VA 22901

Montessori Community School (1982)
Rt 13, PO Box 53, Charlottesville, VA 22901
Laurie Curtin, Adm, 804-979-8886
Non-profit
4 teachers, 3 assistants, 54 students, ages 3–12
Governance by teachers, administrators and a board of
    trustees
Rural location; interns accepted.

Montessori School of Charlottesville
631 Cutler Ln, Charlottesville, VA 22901-3901
Lindsey Schwab

Living Education Center for Ecology and the Arts (1993)
PO Box 2612, Charlottesville, VA 22902
Ernie & Sue Reed, Dirs, 804-971-1647
Type: home-based, non-profit; cost: variable
2 teachers, 15 students, ages 13–18
Affiliation: Oak Meadow School
Governance by directors
Individualized; student/parent responsibility for education
    emphasized; community resources; non-compulsory class
    attendance; multi-aged classes; urban location.

Children's Montessori School
109 E Jefferson St, Charlottesville, VA 22902-5103
Bliss Abbot or Penny Gorman

Elementary Montessori School of Charlottesville
1901 Thomson Rd, Charlottesville, VA 22903
Dan Roell

Murray High School
1200 Forest St, Charlottesville, VA 22903
Deborah E. Cooper, Prin
Type: public at-risk

University Montessori School (1978)
322 Monte Vista Ave, Charlottesville, VA 22903
Michele Mattioli, Dir, 804-977-0583
4 teachers, 3 assistants, 36 students, mainly international,
    ages infant-6
Affiliations: AMS, NAEYC
Governance by administrator
Actiive community of students, parents, teachers; childcare;
    suburban location; interns accepted.

Elementary School of Charlottesville
401 Alderman Rd, Charlottesville, VA 22903-2403
Type: Montessori

**BRANCH: Blue Ridge Area Network for Congenial
    Homeschoolers** (1991)
Rt 3, PO Box 602, Afton, VA 22920
Joan Cichon, Founder/Coordinator, 703-456-9822
Nelson County
Reconciling religious and secular groups; newsletter; 4-H;
    drama; writer's club; languages; arts and crafts; camping;
    no letter grades; multi-aged classes; extensive field trips;
    rural location.

North Branch School (1983)
Rt 1, Box 386, Afton, VA 22920
Charlotte Zinsser Booth, Head teacher, 703-456-8450
Type: independent, non-profit; tuition: $20–320/mo,
    scholarships
11 teachers, 95 students, ages 3–14, nursery-8th grade
Governance by teachers and principal, board; all students and
    parents are polled per issues, discuss solutions
Teacher qualifications: flexible, prefer alternative ed
    experience
11-acre site, woods, meadows, stream, mountain views;
    strong music, movement, drama; board works toward
    diversity of student body; extended-family context; no
    letter grades; multi-aged classes; extensive field trips; rural
    location.

Crossroads Waldorf School (1982)
Rt 3 Box 189, Crozet, VA 22932
Priscilla Friedberg, Coord, 804-823-6800
Albemarle County
Non-profit; tuition: $2,810-4,350/yr
21 teachers, 185 students, ages 3–13, pre K-7th grade
Entrance requirements: application and interview
Governance by teachers, principal, and board
Teacher qualifications: certification, higher ed degree,
    Waldorf training, experience
Rural location; interns accepted.

**Alpha Alternative Program at Nelson County High
    School**
Rt 1, Box 153, Lovingston, VA 22949
Sarah R. Spruill, Exec Dir

**Waynesboro High School Alternative Program
    Blue Ridge Community College**
Wayne Hills Center, Waynesboro, VA 22980
George Buzzard
Type: public choice

Virginia Randolph Community High School
2204 Mountain Rd, Glen Allen, VA 23060
Marti Collier, Prin

Project Star at Gloucester High School
Rt 4, Box 2155, Gloucester, VA 23061
Nancy Keenan
Type: public at-risk

Gloucester Montessori School
Business Rt 17, Gloucester, VA 23061-1506
Patricia Landau

To Kids-For Kids-By Kids Newsletter
(See Resource Appendix)

Powhatan High School
4135 Old Buckingham Rd, Powhatan, VA 23139
Sharon Poland

Sunrise Montessori
856-A Longhill Rd, Williamsburg, VA 23185

Williamsburg Montessori School (1982)
4214 Longhill Rd, Williamsburg, VA 23188
Carlotta P. Cundari, Adm, 804-565-0977
Non-profit; tuition: $2,550-5,472/yr
7 teachers, 4 assistants, 67 students, ages infant-6
Accreditation: AMS
Governance by administrator, board
Childcare; rural location; interns accepted.

Educate Program
100 W Baker St, Richmond, VA 23220
Hugo Thompson

Open Senior High School
600 S Pine St, Richmond, VA 23220
Brenda Drew, 804-780-4661
Type: magnet
9-12th grade
Community-based.

The Governor's School for International Studies (1991)
4100 W Grace St, Richmond, VA 23221
Dr Steven E. Ballowe, Dir, 510-780-6155, FAX:-6043
Type: public choice
47 teachers, 400 students, ages 11-17, 9-12th grade
Entrance requirements: grades, test scores, writing sample,
    letters of recommendation, residency
Governance by principal
Teacher qualifications: Master's, PhD, or in progress
Interdisciplinary; multi-aged classes; extensive field trips;
    interns accepted.

New Start Program of Henrico County Public Schools
PO Box 23120, Richmond, VA 23223
Cozette McIntyre, Adm

George Wythe High School
4314 Crutchfield St, Richmond, VA 23225
James Bynum, 904-780-5037
Type: magnet
9-12th grade
Visual and performing arts.

REACH
1805 N Junuluska Dr, Richmond, VA 23225

Southside Montessori School
7833 Brentford, Richmond, VA 23225
Pamela Ranson

Richmond Community High School
5800 Patterson Ave, Richmond, VA 23226
Pamela Trotter-Cornell

Thomas H. Henderson Model School
4319 Old Brook Rd, Richmond, VA 23227
Harold Fitrer, 804-780-8288
Type: magnet
6-8th grade
School within school.

Richmond Montessori School
499 Parham Rd, Richmond, VA 23229-7217
Nelda Nutter

Burger King Academy at Meadowbrook High School
4901 Cogbill Rd, Richmond, VA 23234
Jamie Accashian, Site Coord, 804-743-3675 x42
Chesterfield County
Type: public at-risk
3 teachers, 54 students, ages 14-20, 9-12th grade
Enrollment by application; for at-risk residents only
Affiliations: Burger King, City in Schools
Governance by site coord, principal, faculty and student reps
Teacher qualifications: current degree
Computers; degree program at night; extensive field trips;
    suburban location; transportation.

Virginia Commonwealth University TEP
School of Education, Richmond, VA 23284
Type: Montessori teacher education

Onancock Learning Center
6 College Ave, Onancock, VA 23317
Karen Lewis

The Robert Muller School
905 Clear Springs Ct, Chesapeake, VA 23320
Dr Catherine K Clark, 804-548-9030

Montessori School of Learning
2004 Dock Landing Rd, Chesapeake, VA 23321

Montessori Preparatory School
4032 Maple Dr, Chesapeake, VA 23321-1915
Marilyn Jennings

Montessori Harmony School
2100 Christopher Dr, Chesapeake, VA 23321-2004

Chesapeake Alternative (1975)
920 Minuteman Rd, Chesapeake, VA 23323
J.E. Thompkins, Principal, 804-494-7620
Type: public at-risk
17 teachers, 120 students, mainly at-risk, ages 12-18, 7-10th
    grade
Governance by principal
Individualized; clearly defined limits; strictly enforced conse-
    quences for inappropriate behavior; urban location; trans-
    portation; interns accepted.

Home Free
PO Box 562, Virginia Beach, VA 23451
JR DuBois

Virginia Beach Friends School
1537 Laskin Rd, Virginia Beach, VA 23451
Phyllis Sullivan, Head, 804-428-7534
Type: Quaker

The Literacy Center (1992)
3352 Virginia Beach Blvd, Virginia Beach, VA 23452
Gloria Harris, Principal
Type: public at-risk
15 teachers, 104 students, ages 15-16, 9th grade
Entrance requirements: failure of VA Literacy Test, residency
Governance by teachers, principal, parent cooperative
Teacher qualifications: state certification
Writers and readers workshop; mentorships; conflict resolu-
    tion; goal setting; study skills; extensive field trips; urban
    location; interns accepted.

Bayshore Learning Center
1608 Pleasure House Rd #112, Virginia Beach, VA 23455
Kinney Glascock
Type: Montessori

St Nicholas Montessori
4425 Monmouth Castle Rd, Virginia Beach, VA 23455
Nancy Guarnieri

Career Development Center
273 N Witchduck Rd, Virginia Beach, VA 23462
Lee Scarborough

Center for Effective Learning
233 N Witchduck Rd, Virginia Beach, VA 23462
Lee Brumfield, Prin

Open Campus High School
4400 Virginia Beach Blvd, Virginia Beach, VA 23462
Lillian J. Donnally, Prin

Montessori Children's House
700 Hillingdon Ct, Virginia Beach, VA 23462-6455

Beach Educators Association for Creative Homeschooling (BEACH)
1305 White Marlin Ln, Virginia Beach, VA 23464
804-474-0389

Summit School and Montessori Center
1100 Indian Lakes Blvd, Virginia Beach, VA 23464-6012
Louise Becerra

Ghent Montessori School (1978)
610 Mowbray Arch, Norfolk, VA 23507
Sarah Frost, Owner, 804-622-8174
Tuition: $1,625-4,220/yr
8 teachers, 6 assistants, 119 students, ages infant-12
Accreditation: AMS
Governance by administrator
Childcare; urban location; interns accepted.

Virginia Montessori School
818 Jacinth Cir, Newport News, VA 23602-3526

Hampton Roads Montessori School (1991)
12749 Nettles Dr, Newport News, VA 23606-1870
Carol Frieden, Business Dir, 804-930-9545
Non-profit
3 teachers, 3 assistants, 75 students, mainly international, ages 3-6
Entrance requirements: toilet trained; teacher/child interview
Affiliation: VAMA; accreditation: AMI
Governance by teachers and administrators, board
Childcare; interns accepted.

Peninsula Montessori School
372 Hiden Blvd, Newport News, VA 23606-2934
Mary McIntosh

Beachside Alternative School (1983)
710 Buckroe Ave, Hampton, VA 23664
Benjamin C. Rich, Prin, 804-850-5068, FAX: 804-850-5072
Type: public at-risk
23 teachers, 301 students, mainly at-risk, ages 13-18, 8-12th grade
Enrollment restricted to residents referred by regular school
Affiliations: Hampton Univ, Thomas Nelson CC
Governance by teachers and principal
Teacher qualifications: state certification
Alternative learning setting; five academic programs; multi-aged classes; urban location; transportation.

Montessori Harmony School
PO Box 3505, Portsmouth, VA 23701

Montessori School of Learning
PO Box 6102, Portsmouth, VA 23703-0102

Portsmouth Public Schools
3651 Hartford St, Portsmouth, VA 23707
Daisy Murphy
Type: Montessori

Greenville County High School
403 Hardine St, Emporia, VA 23847
Milton Featherston

School After School (1992)
403 Harding St, Emporia, VA 23847
Milton E. Featherston, Coord, 804-634-2195, FAX:-4021

Greensville County
Type: public at-risk
15 teachers, 50 students, ages 16+, HS
Enrollment restricted to dropouts; residency required.
Academic behavior contract; rural location.

S.P. Morton Middle School
300 Oak St, Franklin, VA 23851
George Marshall, Prin

Alternative Education Center (1992)
PO Box 190, Boydton, VA 23917
E.A. Lyons, Asst Supt or M.G. Walker, Dir of Student Support, 738-6111, FAX:-6679
Mecklenburg County
Type: public at-risk
3 teachers, 42 students, ages 11-21, 6-12th grade
Entrance requirements: recommendations, JTPA Cert, residency
Governance by teachers, principal, board
GED prep; multi-aged classes; rural location; transportation.

Highland Park Learning Center
1212 Fifth St SW, Roanoke, VA 24016
John Lensch, 703-981-2963
Type: magnet
K-5th grade
Continuous progress; experiential.

Forest Park New American School
2730 Melrose Ave NW, Roanoke, VA 24017
Judith Gorham, 703-981-2923
Type: magnet
K-5th grade
Cultures; commununications; problem solving.

Westside Elementary of Performing Arts
1441 Westside Blvd NW, Roanoke, VA 24017
Linda Wright, 703-981-2697
Type: magnet
K-5th grade

The Children's House
4515 Brandleton Rd, Roanoke, VA 24018
Judith Larson
Type: Montessori

Community School (1971)
7815 Williamson Rd, Roanoke, VA 24019
Tina Dawson, Director, 703-563-5036
Type: independent, home-based, non-profit; cost: $2750-3200, scholarships
20 teachers, 140 students, ages 3-14
Affiliation: NCACS
Governance by board
Builds on child's natural curiosity; teachers monitor mastery skills; relaxed atmosphere; diverse population; earth education program with organic farm; community ecological systems study; student internships; no letter grades; multi-aged classes; extensive field trips; suburban location; interns accepted.

Axton Middle School
PO Box 426, Axton, VA 24054
Jay Gilbert, Tch, 703-650-1193, FAX: 703-650-1462
Type: public at-risk
40 teachers, 451 students, ages 11-14, 6-8th grade
Parental consent required; restricted to failing students
Governance by principal
Teacher qualifications: degree, experience with at-risk
Teachers as Big Brother or Big Sister; small classroom atmosphere; rural location; transportation; interns accepted.

Blacksburg New School
1660 Whipple Dr, Blacksburg, VA 24060
Type: independent

Montessori Children's House of Blacksburg
703 Tall Oaks Dr, Blacksburg, VA 24060-4400

Oak Meadow School (1975)
PO Box 712, Blacksburg, VA 24063
Lawrence T. Williams, EdD, Dir, 703-552-3263, FAX: 703-552-9474
Montgomery County
scholarships
30 teachers, 1,000 students, ages 5–18, K–12th grade
Governance by teachers and prin
Teacher qualifications: BS or BA; completion of teacher training program
Home study only: curr materials, diploma programs; Waldorf inspired; telecommunications program for grades 5–12; interns accepted.

Blacksburg Montessori School
PO Box 684, Blacksburg, VA 24063-0684
Lynne Knox

Schwartz-Gralla Homeschool (1981)
Rt 1 Box 43, Check, VA 24072
Randye Schwartz, 703-651-3971
Floyd County
Boarding, non-profit
2 teachers, 2 students, ages 9–12
Governance by democratic school meeting
Teacher qualifications: Certified
Small homestead in Blue Ridge Mtns; family works on raising food, repairing and building projects, community service, travel; no letter grades

Independence Secondary/Alternative School
1180 N Franklin St, Christiansburg, VA 24073
Karen Pederson

Fieldale-Collinsville High School
415 Miles Rd, Collinsville, VA 24078
Hugh Tucker

Pulaski County High School Alternative Program
5414 Cougar Trail Rd, Dublin, VA 24084
Kelly Fitzpatrick, Coordinator, 703-674-8659
Type: public at-risk
6 teachers, 40 students, ages 13–17, 9–10th grade
Entrance requirements: referral from child study team; no residency requirement
Governance by teachers and principal
Teacher qualifications: state certification
Contracts; cooperative learning; volunteer college student tutor-assistants; rural location; transportation.

Botetourt Technical Education Center
Fincastle, VA 24090

Blue Mountain School (1981)
Rt 3, Box 211, Floyd, VA 24091
Chrys Bason, Administrator, 703-745-4234
Type: independent, non-profit; tuition: $125/mo, scholarships
3 teachers, 22 students, ages 3–12, pre K–7th grade
Governance by parent cooperative, council
On 8 wooded acres near town; offers variety of traditional, non-traditional educational opportunities; no letter grades; rural location; interns accepted.

Laurel Park High School
Rt 8, Box 67, Martinsville, VA 24112
Harriet Tharington

Project Achieve at Martinsville High School
351 Commonwealth Blvd, Martinsville, VA 24112
Dr Ralph Nelson, Prin

YES Program at G.W. Carver Middle School (1987)
Rt 4 Box 800, Martinsville, VA 24112
Fredrick Lockhart, Instructor, 703-957-2226
Henry County
Type: public at-risk
50 teachers, 460 students, ages 11–13, 6–8th grade
Enrollment restricted to at-risk residents with teacher referral
Governance by principal
Teacher qualifications: VA Certification
Basic life skills; incentives; rural location; transportation.

Drewry Mason Middle School
Rt 3, Ridgeway, VA 24148
Bill Farmer

Magna Vista High School
Rt 3, Magna Vista Dr, Ridgeway, VA 24148
Roger Spencer

Washington County Technical School
850 Thompson Dr, Abingdon, VA 24210
Carl McMurray, Prin

Alternative Education Program at Lee High School
Rt 2, Box 740, Jonesville, VA 24263
Lowell William, Prin

Wise County Vocational Center
PO Box 1218, Wise, VA 24293
Robert Raines, Prin

Grayson County Schools Alternative Program Fries Middle School
PO Box 446, Fries, VA 24330
Danny Edwards, Dir

Carroll County High School
PO Box 1328, Hillsville, VA 24343
Pat Sharp

Children's Circle (1986)
Rt 1, Box 132A, Mouth of Wilson, VA 24363
Deborah Greif, 703-579-4252
Type: home-based, non-profit
8 teachers; student ages 2–13
Governance by parent cooperative
Crafts, drama, puppets, science, nature projects; games; rural location.

Staunton Montessori School
Box 722, Staunton, VA 24402
Linda Grogan, Dir, 703-885-4301
Non-profit; tuition: $1,800/2,200/yr
1 teacher, 1 assistant, 28 students, ages 3–6
Entrance requirements: age 2.5; toilet trained; visit; interview
Affiliation: NAMTA; accreditation: AMI
Governance by board
Teacher qualifications: 21 years AMI experience
In historic Italianate house on Stuart Hall campus; rural location; interns accepted.

Alleghany High School Alternative Program, GED Prep
11 Mountainer Dr, Covington, VA 24426
Phillip B. Douglas, Prin

Regional Alternative Program (1993)
Rt 3 Boyshome, Covington, VA 24426
Dwayne Ross, Dir, 703-965-1118, FAX: 703-965-3445
Alleghany Highlands County
Type: public at-risk
7 teachers, 22 students, ages 17–19, 9–12th grade
Enrollment restricted to potential drop out residents
Governance by teachers and principal
GED prep; unstructured; hands-on; no letter grades; extensive field trips; multi-aged classes; transportation.

Montessori Center for Children (1992)
2 Dold Pl, Lexington, VA 24450
Shirley Ziegler, Dir, 703-463-6461, FAX: 703-463-1141
Non-profit; tuition: $2,000/2,700/yr
1 teacher, 1 assistant, 25 students, ages 3-6
Affiliations: AMI, AMS, NAMTA
Governance by an administrator and a board of trustees
Rural location; interns accepted.

Shenendoah Country Day School (1993)
Route 5 Box 394, Lexington, VA 24450
Tom McNalley, 703-463-7246
Type: independent
2 teachers, 15 students, ages 6-11
Integrated curriculum; French, German, musical instruments, hands-on science; whole language; no letter grades; non-compulsory class attendance; extensive field trips; multi-aged classes.

Snakefoot School (1989)
PO Box 189, Lexington, VA 24450
Lenna Ojure, Board Member, 703-463-9645
Type: home-based, non-profit; cost: $1,125/yr, scholarships
2 teachers, 14 students, ages 6-14, 1-7th grade
Entrance requirements: parents donate 3 hours of labor/week or pay higher tuition
Governance by parent cooperative, board
Teacher qualifications: state certification, experience, compatible philosophy
3 days/wk on-site; no letter grades; multi-aged classes; rural location; interns accepted.

National Consortium of Specialized Secondary Schools of Mathematics, Science and Technology
Governor's School, 3020 Ward's Ferry Rd, Lynchburg, VA 24502
Cheryl Lindeman, Pres, 804-582-1104
Resource
National group of several dozen schools.

Lynchburg Montessori School
PO Box 3061, Lynchburg, VA 24503-0061

Monroe Alternative School
Amherst County High School, Amherst, VA 24521
Karl Carter, Principal

Legacy
Rte 4 Box 265-MT, Bedford, VA 24523
Type: Montessori

Cherry Hill Montessori School
PO Box 2722, Danville, VA 24541-0722
Grace Thomas

Blue Ridge Montessori School (1982)
Rt 4 Box 47, Forest, VA 24551
Tom Taylor, Dir, 804-525-0061
Tuition: $1,450-1,800/yr
1 teacher, 1 assistant, 30 students, ages 3-6
Affiliation: AMS
Governance by administrator
Suburban location; interns accepted.

Alternative Education Program; Halifax-S Boston (1977)
PO Box 1849, Halifax, VA 24558
Charles C. Edwards, Jr, Coord, 804-476-3114, FAX:-1858
Type: public at-risk
9 teachers, 100 students, ages 14-21, 7-12th grade
No extremely violent students; residency required
Governance by teachers, principal, board
Teacher qualifications: Master of Ed, experience
Evenings; transferable credits; computers; low ratio; rural location; interns accepted.

VA Alternative Education Assn
(See Resource Appendix)

National Institute for Christian Home Education
(See Resource Appendix)

Washington

Auburn Alternative Junior High School (1974)
615 15th St SW, Auburn, WA 98001
Dr Largo Wales, Adm, 206-931-4992
Type: public choice
2 teachers, 40 students, ages 12-15
Entrance requirement: recommendation from JHS
Self-paced.

Creative Montessori
14904 Juanita Dr, Bothell, WA 98001
Alice B Evans

St Nicholas Montessori School
31015 Military Rd S, Auburn, WA 98001-3218
Susan Ennaro

West Auburn Senior High (1971)
401 W Main St, Auburn, WA 98002
Bob Wiley, Prin, 206-931-4990
10 teachers, 250 students, ages 14-21, 9-12th grade
Entrance requirements: referral, district residency (9th gr); release from home district, proof of immunization, orientation.
Social responsibility; vocational; contract night school; day care/teen parenting combination; self-paced JH class; Reading Lab.

Continuation High School (1970)
31455 28th Ave S, Federal Way, WA 98003
Larry Merlino, Prin, 206-838-1004, 927-4477
Federal Way District
Type: public at-risk
25 teachers, 220 students, ages 14-20
Entrance requirements: student must not be attending any other school; referral from Prin or designee; Continuation staff approval; drug/alcohol assessment
Self-directed; competency-based; teen parenting.

Contract Based Education (1981)
31455 28th Ave S, Federal Way, WA 98003
Bob Kohn, Coord, 206-941-8237,-9417
Type: public at-risk
25 teachers, 100 students, ages 14-21, 9-12th grade
Entrance requirements: assessment for chemical use; adherence to recommendations
Tutorials; self-paced; counseling; min 25 hrs/wk homestudy; guitar; computer programming; career ed; health; teen parenting; Student Assistance Program.

Spring Valley Montessori School
36605 Pacific Hwy S, Federal Way, WA 98003-7499
Gulsevin Kayihan

Bellevue Montessori School
2411–112th NE, Bellevue, WA 98004

Montessori Teacher College Northwest
2411 112th Ave NE, Bellevue, WA 98004

Puget Sound Community School
1715 112th Ave NE, Bellevue, WA 98004
Andy Smallman, 206-455-7617
Type: home-based
1 teacher, 10 students
Resource teacher; field trips; computer networking.

The Little School (1959)
2812 116th St NE, Bellevue, WA 98004
Lorna Greene, Director, 206-927-8708
Type: independent, non-profit
14 teachers, 170 students, ages 3–12, ungraded
Affiliations: NAIS, PNAIS, NAEYC
Governance by board with input from faculty and parents
Teacher qualifications: WA credential, experience
On an 11-acre site; self contained classroom developmental
    groups; emergent curriculum; whole language; multi-
    ethnic awareness; required parental observation; narrative
    evaluations. Teacher education program affiliated with
    Pacific Oaks College; no letter grades; multi-aged classes;
    suburban location.

Cougar Mountain Montessori (1978)
4442 158th Ave, SE, Bellevue, WA 98006
Eileen Peterson, 206-747-5029
Tuition: $285/450/mo
4 teachers, 4 assistants, 37 students, ages infant-6
Entrance requirements: toilet trained.
Accreditation: AMS
Governance by administrator
Large playground adjacent to woods; bunnies, gerbils, fish,
    birds, cat and goat; childcare; suburban location; interns
    accepted.

Off Campus High School (1970)
14200 SE 13th Pl, Bellevue, WA 98007
Phil Barber, 206-455-6183
Type: public choice
17 teachers, 255 students, ages 14–21, 9–12th grade
Entrance requirements: orientation; application; non-district
    students admitted on a space-available, tuition basis
Student-centered; individualized; competency-based;
    student input; self-paced; flexible schedule; year-round;
    open exit/entry; tutorials; teen parenting.

Absorbent Mind Montessori
15653 NE 6th, Bellevue, WA 98008
Henrietta Walker

Eton School (1978)
2701 Bel-Red Rd, Bellevue, WA 98008
Dr Patricia Feltin, 206-881-4230
Type: Montessori; tuition: $2,700-6,800/yr
16 teachers, 12 assistants, 324 students, ages 3–15
Affiliations: AMS, PNAIS, PNMA
Governance by administrator
National Blue Ribbon Award Winner, '91–92; Montessori Time-
    line approach; childcare; suburban location; interns
    accepted.

Olympus Northwest (1974)
16247 NE 24th St, Bellevue, WA 98008
Jan Fluter, Head Tch, 206-455-6152
Type: public choice
5 teachers, 110 students, ages 11–14, 6–8th grade
Entrance requirements: application, residency
Governance by council of students, parents, staff
Teacher qualifications: K-8 or 6-8 Certification
Non-traditional; liberal arts; home groups integral to process;
    no letter grades; multi-aged classes; extensive field trips;
    suburban location; interns accepted.

Lake Hills Montessori
114 157th Ave NE, Bellevue, WA 98008-4336

The International School (1991)
301 151st Pl NE, Bellevue, WA 98009-9010
Terry LaRussa Banton, 206-455-6266
Bellevue District
Type: public choice
6 teachers, 400 students, ages 11–18, 6–12th grade
Inclusive; interdisciplinary; team efforts; cooperative learning;
    independent study; mentorships; year-round; Bellevue
    Children's Theater; extensive field trips.

Evergreen Academy (1977)
16017 118th Pl NE, Bothell, WA 98011
Krista McKee, Head, 206-488-8000, FAX: 206-488-0994
Type: Montessori; tuition: $2,000-3,950/yr
4 teachers, 5 assistants, 75 students, ages 3–6
Entrance requirements: age 2.5, toilet trained
Affiliation: PNAIS; accreditations: NAEYC, NASC
Governance by administrator
French; computers; childcare; suburban location;
    transportation.

Homeschoolers Organized for Meaningful Education
10352 NE 141st St, Bothell, WA 98011

SAS-Secondary Alternative School (1970)
18603 Bothel Way NE, Bothell, WA 98011-1995
Dr Len Fellez, Prin, 206-489-6244
Northshore District
Type: public at-risk
11 teachers, 120 students, ages 14–19, 9–12th grade

Duvall Montessori School
217 Main St, Duvall, WA 98019

SnoValley Homeschool Association
PO Box 1244, Duvall, WA 98019
Connie Douvier, 206-788-0149

Madrona Elementary School (1985)
9300 236th SW, Edmonds, WA 98020
Joe Rice, Prin, 206-670-7980
Type: public choice
11 teachers, 280 students, ages 5–13
District residency required
Students stay in multi-aged units for three year periods with
    same teacher; competency-based; foreign language;
    school-based management; parent involvement.

Pacific Montessori Learning Center
23700 104th Ave W, Edmonds, WA 98020
Nancy Kesteek

Washington Homeschool Organization (WHO) (1986)
18130 Midvale Ave N Suite C, Seattle, WA 98020
206-546-9483, 298-8942, FAX: 206-546-1810
Non-profit
support group referral; non-sectarian; non-discriminating;
    convention.

Edmonds Horizon Montessori School (1982)
700 Main St, Edmonds, WA 98020-3032
Rick Schleicher, Administrator, 206-742-0344
Tuition: $140/mo
3 teachers, 48 students, ages 3–6
Entrance requirements: toilet trained
Affiliation: UMA; accreditation: WFIS
Governance by administrator
Ballet, gymnastics, tai kwan do and music enhancement
    optional (at Cultural Center); urban location; interns
    accepted.

Whole Earth Montessori
2930 228th St SE, Bothell, WA 98021-8927

Lockwood Elementary (1973)
24118 Lockwood Rd, Bothell, WA 98021-9499
Lew Dickert, Prin, 206-489-6328
Northshore District
Type: public at-risk
6 teachers, 145 students, ages 5-13, K-6th grade

Tower Montessori School
1606 SW Dash Point Rd, Federal Way, WA 98023-4530

Issaguah Montessori School
22601 SE 56th St, Issaquah, WA 98027
Conleth Grotob

Sequoia Montessori School
24611 SE Mirrormont Dr, Issaquah, WA 98027
Meg Wade

Tiger Mountain High School (1975)
565 NW Holly St, Issaquah, WA 98027
Jeanne Hanson, Prin, 206-392-0840
Type: public choice
17 teachers, 95 students, ages 14-21
District residency required
12-14 students/class; optional activities; pass/fail; computer-
     ized on network; community involvement; mini-courses;
     integrated SE; teen parenting; extensive field trips.

Clark Elementary School (1976)
565 NW Holly St, PO Box 7003, Issaquah, WA 98027-7003
Randy Fortenberry, Prin, 206-392-0813
Type: public choice
28 teachers, 425 students, ages 5-11, K-5th grade
Enrollment by lottery; district residency required
Parents commit min 40 hrs/student/yr, participate in curricu-
     lum development; computer literacy; cooperative learning;
     mathematical problem solving; integrated curriculum.

Big Sky Montessori
14800 245th Ave SE, Issaquah, WA 98027-7322
Maggie Worrix-Hosking

Montessori Plus School (1971)
3410 S 272nd St, Kent, WA 98032-7802
Sharlet J. McClurkin, Dir, 206-859-2262, FAX: 206-859-1737
Non-profit; tuition: $180/mo
3 teachers, 5 assistants, 50 students, ages 3-6
Affiliation: PNMA; accreditation: MIA
Governance by a board of trustees
International interns, primarily from Taiwan and Korea; subur-
     ban location; interns accepted.

BEST Alternative High School (1963)
6512 111th Ave NE, Kirkland, WA 98033
Lynn Shebilske, Prin, 206-828-3289
Lake Washington District
Type: public at-risk
9 teachers, 190 students, ages 15-20, 9-12th grade

Community Elementary (1960)
11133 NE 65th, Kirkland, WA 98033
Lynn Shebilske, Prin, 206-827-0735
Lake Washington District
Type: public choice
3 teachers, 78 students, 1-6th grade
Entrance requirement: application
Parents as instructional partners; multi-disciplinary; enriched
     discovery-type environment; whole child approach; split
     grades; fluid transition between grades; whole-school
     multi-age instruction and environment projects; partner-
     ship projects with JH and HS.

Blue Gables Montessori
11410 NE 124th St #349, Kirkland, WA 98034-4399

Montessori School
13446 NE 132nd St, Kirkland, WA 98034-5608

Brier Montessori Preschool & Kindergarten
24016 29 A West, Brier, WA 98036

Scriber Lake High School (1969)
19400 56th Ave W, Lynnwood, WA 98036
Karol L. Gadwa, Prin, 206-670-7270
Edmonds District
Type: public choice
16 teachers, 250 students, ages 14-19
Entrance requirements: information session, application,
     enrollment in 20-day entry program, district residency
CAI; self-paced; teen parenting integrated with day care;
     mini-courses; Resource Room; career center; support
     groups; GED prep; fire service training; carpentry; ESL.

**WALA, CLIP I-V (Contracted Learning for Individual
     Pacing)** (1984)
3800 196th SW, Lynnwood, WA 98036
Karol Gadwa, Coord, 206-670-7270
Edmonds District
8 teachers, 150 students, ages 14-20, 9-12th grade
Individualized; self-paced; flexible scheduling; competency-
     based; mentorships; community service; experiential learn-
     ing; independent study; tutorials; seminars.

Teaching Parents Association
14004 Jefferson Way, Lynnwood, WA 98037
Mary Ehrmin, 206-742-7033

Homeschoolers in FOCUS
17105 36th Ave W, Lynwood, WA 98037
Deane Schrader, 206-742-2521

Homeschoolers Support Association (1985)
PO Box 413, Maple Valley, WA 98038
Janice M. Hedin, 206-432-9805
King County
Non-profit
Governance by board

Maple Valley High School (1987)
23015 SE 216th Way, Maple Valley, WA 98038
Gary Morris, Dir/Head Tch, 206-432-5702
Tacoma District
Type: public at-risk
3 teachers, 45 students, ages 15-20, 9-12th grade

Lake Wilderness Elementary School
24216 Witte Rd SE, Maple Valley, WA 98038-6827
Type: Montessori

Crest Learning Center (1971)
4150 86th Ave SE, Mercer Island, WA 98040
Michael Hagen, Head Tch, 206-236-3390
Type: public choice
5 teachers, 2 assistants, 115 students, ages 14-21, 9-12th
     grade

Northwest Montessori-Mercer Island
4545 Island Crest Way, Mercer Island, WA 98040-4443

Two Rivers High School (1986)
1546 Boalch Ave, N Bend, WA 98045
Dennis Moroney, Dir, 206-888-4394
Snoqualmie Valley District
Type: public at-risk
12 teachers, 115-120 students, ages 14+, 9-12th grade

Snoqualmie Valley Homeschoolers Co-op
42512 SE 170th Ct, North Bend, WA 98045
Melode Brewer, 206-888-0461

Parent Cooperative Elementary Program (1983)
PO Box 1602, Lynnwood, WA 98046
Pam Hurst; Teresa Henrichs, 206-670-7086
Edmonds District
8 teachers, 180 students, ages 5-12
Required monthly meeting; min 90 hrs in-class time/yr/

student; mini-courses; fund raising; voluntary pledge system; Math Their Way; Weekly Readers; computers; French; Spanish; ASL; extensive field trips.

Builder Books
(See Resource Appendix)

Cascadia Montessori School (1977)
4259 162nd Ave NE, Redmond, WA 98052
Marilyn Franklin, Di, 881-1026
1 teacher, 2 assistants, 27 students, ages 6-9
Entrance requirements: interview and visit.
Accreditations: AMS, WA BE
Governance by administrator
Teacher-parent communication; childcare; suburban location.

Marymoor Montessori
4244 Bel Red Rd, Redmond, WA 98052

Sammamish Montessori School (1977)
17411 NE Union Hill Rd #150, Redmond, WA 98052
Joan M Starling, Dir, 206-869-0804
Tuition: $209-418/mo
7 teachers, 20 assistants, 275 students, ages 3-6
Affiliations: NAMTA, NCME, MWEI
Governance by administrator
Childcare; interns accepted.

Re-entry Program at Sartori School (1984)
315 Garden Ave N, Renton, WA 98055-1730
Diana Caple, Dir, 206-235-2480,-2103
Type: public at-risk
6 teachers, 3 assistants, 150 students, ages 16-21, 9-12th grade
GED; HS credit.

Cedar River School
15828 SE Jones Rd, Renton, WA 98058
Melissa Baker, Business Dir, 206-271-9614, FAX: same
Type: Montessori, non-profit; tuition: $270/495/mo
8 teachers, 4 assistants, 75 students, ages 3-15
Affiliation: NAMTA
Governance by board
16-acre farm with animals, garden; heated outdoor swimming pool; 12 month program; childcare; rural location; interns accepted.

Tillicum Options Program (1984)
15920 Vashon Hwy SW, Vashon, WA 98070
Lynn Dils, Tch, 206-567-4425
Vashon Island District
Type: public at-risk
2 teachers; student ages 6-12, 1-6th grade

Teaching Parents Association
16109 NE 169th Pl, Woodinville, WA 98072

Under the Apple Tree Magazine
  Apple Tree Press
(See Resource Appendix)

Woodinville Montessori
13965 NE 166th St, Woodinville, WA 98072-9085

The Drinking Gourd, Harambee
(See Resource Appendix)

Pacific First Montessori Children's Center
1420 5th Ave, Seattle, WA 98101-2333

American Indian Heritage School (1969)
1330 N 90th St, Seattle, WA 98103
Robert Eaglestaff, Prin, 206-298-7801
Seattle District
Type: public choice
6 teachers, 109 students, ages 10-20, 6-12th grade
Entrance requirements: interview, desire to be drug free and to learn about Indian Heritage.

Indian Heritage values and traditions; sports based on traditional Indian sports: cross-country, basketball, track & field, Indian Dancing.

B.F. Day Elementary School
3921 Linden Ave N, Seattle, WA 98103
Carole Williams, 206-281-6340
Type: magnet
K-5th grade
World culture center.

Gypsy Alternative School (1968)
7821 Stone Ave N, Seattle, WA 98103
Karen Watson, Head Tch, 206-281-6240
Type: public choice, at-risk
3 teachers, 16 students, ages 5-11, K-5th grade
Entrance requirements: must be of Gypsy race
Addresses special needs of students in the Gypsy community; gypsy staff person who speaks Romanes.

Small Planet Montessori (1988)
2125 N 51st St, Seattle, WA 98103
Lucie Ury, Dir, 206-632-3434
Tuition: $185/mo
2 teachers, 2 assistants, 24 students, ages 3-6
Affiliations: AMS, NAMTA
Governance by administrator
Urban location; interns accepted.

Pacific Crest Montessori School
5555 Phinney Ave N, Seattle, WA 98103-5853

Northwest Montessori-Woodland Park
4910 Phinney Ave N, Seattle, WA 98103-6347

Highland Park Elementary
1012 SW Trenton St, Seattle, WA 98106
Venus Place-Barber, 206-281-6480
District 1
Type: magnet
K-5th grade
World culture center.

Rainbow Way Homeschool Group
5004 20th Av NW, Seattle, WA 98107
206-782-3071,-9076
Holt oriented.

Concord Elementary
723 S Concord St, Seattle, WA 98108
Toby Gonzales, 206-281-6320
Type: magnet
K-5th grade
World culture center.

Maple Elementary
4925 Corson Ave S, Seattle, WA 98108
Lynn Fuller, 206-281-6960
Type: magnet
K-5th grade
World culture center.

New Option Middle School (1990)
411 Boston, Seattle, WA 98109
Barbara Kuznetz, 206-281-6226
Type: public choice
5 teachers, 11 students, ages 12-18, 6-9th grade
District residency required
Central theme is "Global Citizenship"; individual support; mutual trust; multi-cultural; parent participation.

BI/PATCH
7300 NE Bergman Rd, Bainbridge Is, WA 98110
Martha Young, 206-842-8582

Montessori Country School (1992)
10994 Arrow Pt Dr, Bainbridge Island, WA 98110
Patricia Christensen, Director, 842-4966

Non-profit; tuition: $800-3,750/yr
7 teachers, 95 students, ages infant-9
Affiliations: NAEYC, NW MA, NAMTA
Governance by board
2.5 acres; 35 minute ferry from Seattle; parent support; interns accepted.

Strawberry Hill Alternative School at Bainbridge High School (1970)
7560 NE High School Rd, Bainbridge Island, WA 98110
David Ellick, Prin; Sharon Bishop, 206-842-5063
Bainbridge Island District
Type: public at-risk
1 teacher, 1 assistant, 20 students, mainly at risk, ages 14-19, 9-12th grade
Enrollment restricted to at-risk; full day visit, application, referral required
Self-paced; group process skills; cooperative learning; individualized instruction; parent involvement; support networks.

Children's Montessori School on Bainbridge
PO Box 11127, Bainbridge Is, WA 98110-5127

Alternative Education II
1222 41st Ave E, Seattle, WA 98112

Minimax Montessori School
946 17th Ave E, Seattle, WA 98112

Montessori School of Seattle
720 18th E, Seattle, WA 98112
Steffani Mott, 206-325-0497
Tuition: $250-500/mo
3 teachers, 3 assistants, 70 students, ages 3-6
Entrance requirements: interview; toilet trained
Affiliation: NAMTA
Governance by administrator
Within large parochial school; dance; Spanish; music; interns accepted.

Montessori School
720 18th Ave E, Seattle, WA 98112-3928

Bryant Elementary
3311 NE 60th, Seattle, WA 98115
Terry Acena, 206-281-6290
Type: magnet
K-5th grade
World culture center.

Children's World Montessori
7711 43rd NE, Seattle, WA 98115
Suzanne Haggard

New Horizons For Learning (1980)
(See Resource Appendix)

Northwest Montessori School (1965)
7400 25th Ave NE, Seattle, WA 98115
Jan Thorslund, Dir, 524-4244
Non-profit; tuition: $2,422-3,753/yr
11 teachers, 14 assistants, 195 students, mainly International, ages 3-12
Affiliation: NAMTA; accreditation: AMI
Governance by board
Spanish; 'going out' opportunities for elementary; childcare; sub/urban location; interns accepted.

Seattle Evening High School (1970)
520 NE Ravenna Blvd, Seattle, WA 98115
Richard N. Erdman, Prin, 206-281-6146
Seattle District
Type: public at-risk
23 teachers, 500-600 students, 9-12th grade

Ballard Homeschoolers
7037 22nd Ave NW, Seattle, WA 98117
Marcy Ray, 206-789-1721

Cinquegranelli Montessori (1989)
3316 NW 68, Seattle, WA 98117
Gail Longo, 206-789-2942
Tuition: $250/390/mo
2 teachers, 22 students, ages 3-6
Completed forms, interview, and $75 deposit are required for admission
Affiliations: AMS, NAMTA, MIA
Governance by an administrator
Italian language, culture; outdoor ed; urban location; interns accepted.

Konos Around Puget Sound
7749 17th Ave NW, Seattle, WA 98117

Shine Bright Montessori School
8350 14th Ave NW, Seattle, WA 98117-4232

The Niche
1412 NW 67th St, Seattle, WA 98117-5240
Type: Montessori

Brighton Elementary
4425 S Holly St, Seattle, WA 98118
Beverly Raines, 206-281-6270
District 1
Type: magnet
K-5th grade
Global studies.

Cornerstone Montessori Academy
6027 S Roxbury, Seattle, WA 98118

Graham Hill Montessori (1990)
5149 S Graham St, Seattle, WA 98118
Gloria Etcheson, 206-281-6430
Type: public choice; tuition: 0-140/mo sliding scale
4 teachers, 2 assistants, 102 students, ages 3-12
Montessori experience preferred for grades 1+
Affiliation: PNMA
Inclusive; plans for expansion; childcare; urban location; transportation; interns accepted.

Jesse's Corner
5200 Wilson Ave S, Seattle, WA 98118
Susan Lenihan
Type: Montessori

ORCA at Columbia Elementary (1972)
3528 S Ferdinand St, Seattle, WA 98118
Larry Jacobs, Prin, 206-281-6310
Type: public choice
18 teachers, 240 students, ages 5-11, K-5th grade
Arts, dance, and environmental science; ethnically balanced community of staff and parents; team teaching; parent participation; multi-disciplinary; artists-in-residence; art resource teacher; computer lab; greenhouse; multi-aged classes; extensive field trips.

Seattle Alternative High-Sharples (1983)
3928 S Graham, Seattle, WA 98118
Roscoe B. Bass, Prin, 206-281-6910
Seattle District
Type: public at-risk
19 teachers, 228 students, ages 13-21, 9-12th grade

Sunnyside Montessori
3939 S Americus St, Seattle, WA 98118-1639

Montessori South Pre-School
4602 43rd Ave S, Seattle, WA 98118-1802

Children's House Montessori
6027 S Roxbury St, Seattle, WA 98118-5944
Andrea Skeel

O' Rainbow Support Group
511 W Lee St, Seattle, WA 98119
Debbie Hemingway, 206-283-4194

Garfield Alternative High School (1973)
400 23rd Ave, Seattle, WA 98122
Dr Jim Simmons, Prin, 206-281-6115
Seattle District
Type: public at-risk
47 teachers, 450 students, ages 12-21, 6-12th grade

Middle College High School (1990)
1701 Broadway, Seattle, WA 98122
Doug Danner, 206-281-6154
Seattle District
Type: public at-risk
10 teachers, 120 students, ages 15-20, 9-12th grade

Nova (1968)
2410 E Cherry, Seattle, WA 98122
Elaine S. Packard, Program Mgr, 206-281-6363
Seattle District
Type: public choice
5 teachers, 130 students, ages 14-21, 9-12th grade

The Learning Tree Montessori Childcare (1979)
1721 15th Ave, Seattle, WA 98122-2614
Laurie Ross, Director, 206-324-4788
Non-profit; tuition: $485/mo, scholarships
3 teachers, 5 assistants, 50 students, mainly international,
   ages 3-6
Affiliations: AMS, PNMA, NCME; accreditation: NAEYC
Governance by administrator
Multi-ethnic population; staff 1/2 male; very active parent
   involvement; childcare; urban location; interns accepted.

**Montessori Education Institute of the Pacific
   Northwest**
Seattle University, Seattle, WA 98122-4460
John Chattin-McNichols, PhD or Dora Lange
Type: Montessori teacher education

Alternative Elementary School #2 (1975)
7711 43rd Ave NE, Seattle, WA 98125
Zoe Jenkins, PhD, Prin, 206-281-6770
Seattle District
Type: public at-risk
25 teachers, 300 students, ages 5-12, K-6th grade

Alternative School #1 (1969)
11530 12th Ave NE, Seattle, WA 98125
Ron Snyder, Prin, 206-281-6970
Type: public choice
10 teachers, 158 students, ages 5-14, K-8th grade
Entrance requirements: orientation, interview, younger than
   grade 8, no residency requirement
Affiliation: Seattle Public Schools
Governance by principal, council of staff, parents, students
Teacher qualifications: WA certification, alternative
   endorsement
Experiential kinesthetic and visual teaching-learning center;
   extensive field trips; no letter grades; multi-aged classes;
   interns accepted.

SUMMIT K-12 (1978)
11051 34th Ave NE, Seattle, WA 98125
Catherine Hayes, Prin, 206-281-6880
Seattle District
Type: public choice
47 teachers, 606 students, ages 5-18, K-12th grade
District's only K-12 school; conflict resolution; multi-cultural;
   cross-age tutoring; cooperative problem-solving; artists-in-
   residence; family-oriented; extensive arts experiences;
   widespread use of community resources; multi-aged
   classes.

Proyecto Saber (1975)
2600 SW Thistle St, Seattle, WA 98126
Maria M. Ivarra, Head Tch, 206-281-6066
Seattle District
Type: public choice, at-risk

4 teachers, 450-500 students, ages 5-21, K-12th grade
Enrollment restricted to at-risk Chicano/Latino students; culturally relevant curriculum; home/school liaison; bilingual
   newsletter; bilingual/bicultural staff.

West Seattle Montessori School
4536 38th Ave SW, Seattle, WA 98126-2725

Montessori for Kids (1986)
14410 Greenwood Ave N, Seattle, WA 98133
Mary Louise Ellsworth, 206-361-2264
Tuition: $280/425/mo
6 teachers, 50 students, ages 3-6
Entrance requirements: toilet trained
Affiliation: PN MA; accreditations: MIA, AMI
Governance by administrator
Spanish; movement; computer; art; urban location; interns
   accepted.

Franklin High School
3013 S Mt Baker Blvd, Seattle, WA 98144
Sharon Green, 206-281-6030
District 1
Type: magnet
9-12th grade
Literary, visual and performing arts.

Montessori in Seattle Public Schools
3308 19th Ave S, Seattle, WA 98144
Frederica Merrell

Satellite Alternative High School (1969)
440 S 186th St, Seattle, WA 98148
Barbara Birch, Prin, 206-433-2574
Highline District
Type: public choice
27 teachers, 384 students, mainly at risk, ages 12-20
Entrance requirement: interview
Short-term intervention; tutorials; work experience; evening
   classes; individualized; GED prep; teen parenting; childcare.

Alta Vista Curriculum (1983)
PO Box 55535, Seattle, WA 98155
Susan Talbot, Curriculum Coordinator, 206-771-7740, 800-
   544-1397, FAX: 206-771-6861
Pre K-9th grade
Affiliation: Alta Vista College
Bible-based; hands-on approach to all activities including
   student texts and worksheets.

Lake Forest Park Montessori
19935 19th Ave NE, Seattle, WA 98155
Connie Falconer

Room Nine Program at Meridian Park Elementary (1974)
17077 Meridian Ave N, Seattle, WA 98155
Wendy Borton, Tch, 206-368-4127
Type: public choice
3 teachers, 72 students, ages 5-12, K-6th grade
Entrance requirements: parent involvement, residency
Governance by teachers, principal, democratic school
   meeting, parent cooperative
Hands-on curriculum; problem solving; arts; student self-
   assessment; multi-aged classes; extensive field trips;
   interns accepted.

Shorecrest Alternative Education Program
15343 25th Ave NE, Seattle, WA 98155
David Paul
Type: public choice

Shoreline Alternative Education Program (1972)
15343 25th Ave, Seattle, WA 98155
Linda Johnson, Adm; Dave Peterson, Dir, 206-368-4751
Shoreline District
Type: public at-risk
14 teachers, 130 students, ages 13-19, 7-12th grade

Shoreline Homeschoolers Co-op
1131 NE 187th, Seattle, WA 98155
Lyn Baxter, 206-367-4680

Newport Alternative/Continuation High School (1985)
PO Box 70, Newport, WA 98156
Linda Karr, Dir, 509-447-2482
Newport District
Type: public at-risk
3 teachers; student ages 15-21, 9-12th grade

Family Academy (1982)
146 SW 153rd #290, Seattle, WA 98166
Candice Oneschak, Adm, 206-246-9227, FAX: 785-4995
Type: independent, non-profit; tuition: $600-1,700/yr
40 teachers, 45 students, ages 5+, K-12th grade
Entrance requirements: interview, residency
Governance by board
Teacher qualifications: certification
Weekly learning activities for homeschoolers with local
    teacher; no letter grades; multi-aged classes; extensive
    field trips.

The Basic Skills Program (1988)
15820 6th Ave SW, Seattle, WA 98166
Jim Hopkins, Dir, 206-433-2266
Highline District
Type: public at-risk
9 teachers, 126 students, ages 14-20, 8-12th grade
Enrollment restricted to returning students
After-school extra-credit program for credit-deficient stu-
    dents; students who miss 10 days of school are put on
    probation and replaced by students on waiting list; located
    at Evergreen HS, Highline HS, former Maywood School;
    individualized; open entry; after-school remediation.

Burien Rainbow Montessori School
1005 SW 152nd St, Seattle, WA 98166-1845

Seattle Homeschool Group
1221 NW Norcross Way, Seattle, WA 98177
206-367-9440

Seattle Waldorf School (1980)
2728 NE 100th, Seattle, WA 98177
Elena Leonard, Office Mgr, 206-524-5320
King County
Non-profit; tuition: $3,830-5,300/yr, scholarships
18 teachers, 194 students, ages 4-14, pre K-8th grade
Affiliation: AWSNA
Governance by parent/faculty, board of trustees, and college
    of teachers
Teacher qualifications: Waldorf training
7 specialist teachers; urban location; interns accepted.

Renton Alternative High School (1969)
7800 S 132nd St, Seattle, WA 98178
John Rogers, Prin, 206-235-2272
Type: public at-risk
15 teachers, 185 students, ages 13-20, 9-12th grade

Valley View Alternative Elementary (1979)
17622 46th Ave S, Seattle, WA 98188
Janice E. Tietz, 206-433-2377
Highline District
Type: public choice
30 teachers, 258 students, ages 5-12
Entrance requirement: student requests transfer, is placed
    on list, and called as openings occur
Open concept building; team teaching; challenge program.

Kent Continuation High School (1970)
22420 Military Rd, Des Moines, WA 98198
Mark Weston, Prin, 206-859-7488
Kent District
Type: public at-risk
27 teachers, 195 students, ages 15-18, 9-12th grade

Discovery Montessori School (1983)
2836 34th Ave W, Seattle, WA 98199
Dee Hirsch, Dir, 206-282-3848
Non-profit; tuition: $210/270/mo
4-5 teachers, 1-2 assistants, 48 students, ages infant-6
Affiliations: NAMTA, PNMA, St Nicholas NCME
Governance by administrator
Science room; outdoor activity area; urban location; interns
    accepted.

Tuscany Montessori School
6801 Stanton Pl NW, Seattle, WA 98199
Stacia Kostuik

Contract Learning Opportunities Program (1991)
3516 Rucker Ave, Everett, WA 98201
Roy E. Morris, Jr, Prin, 206-339-4320
Everett District
Type: public choice
15 teachers, 30 students, ages 14-21, 9-12th grade
District residency required
Self-paced; conferences; seminars; flexible schedule; teen
    parenting; counseling; evening class.

Everett Alternatives (1979)
3516 Rucker Ave, Everett, WA 98201
Roy E. Morris, Jr, Prin, 206-339-4320
Type: public choice
25 teachers, 400 students, ages 14-20, 9-12th grade
Variable start times; vocational training; contracts; individual-
    ized; small classes; accelerated credit achievement; teen
    parenting, childcare.

YOU (Youth Options Unlimited) Center (1987)
3902 Broadway, Everett, WA 98201
Roy E. Morris, Jr, Prin; Mark Bigger, Mgr, 206-339-4359
Everett District
Type: public at-risk
10 teachers, 66 students, ages 13-19, 7-12th grade
County residency required
Educational, social, career, health assessment and placement;
    vocational training; CAI; GED prep.

Youth Resource Center (1975)
1509 California St, Everett, WA 98201
Roy E. Morris, Jr, Prin; Doug Corce, Mgr, 206-339-1909
Snohomish County
Type: public at-risk
15 teachers, 70 students, 9-12th grade
Enrollment restricted to court involved, adjudicated youth,
    former offenders, and students at high risk of offending.
SE; vocational skills center; job opportunities; GED prep; CAI;
    nurse services; nutrition; Mental Health Team; alcohol/drug
    intervention; parent support; teen parenting.

Middle College at Everett Community College (1991)
801 Wetmore Ave, Everett, WA 98203
Roy E. Morris, Jr; Karla Wilson, 206-338-9245
Type: public choice
2 teachers, 40 students, ages 16-21, 9-12th grade
Entrance requirements: evaluation; recommendation from
    District's YOU assessment center.
Self-paced; HS and/or college credit; counseling; support;
    teen parenting; childcare.

Montessori Schools
1804 Puget Dr, Everett, WA 98203-6600

ACES High School (1985)
9700 Holly Dr, Everett, WA 98204-2678
Marilyn Wiltz, Prin, 206-356-1300
Mukilteo District
Type: public at-risk
14 teachers, 170 students, ages 13-21, 9-12th grade

Trestle Homeschoolers
5305 131st SE, Everett, WA 98208
Bev Wendt, 206-337-0530

Learning Opportunity Center (1985)
2801 Commercial Ave, Suite A, Anacortes, WA 98221
Marge Setting, Program Dir, 206-293-1225
Anacortes District
Type: public at-risk
2 teachers, 30 students, ages 14-21, 6-12th grade
Entrance requirements: desire to attend school, application, considered "at-risk," credit deficient, or in need of strengthening basic skills, residency
Self-paced; open-entry/exit; competency-based; CAI; flexible scheduling.

Our Children's House
1308 7th St, Anacortes, WA 98221-1811
Type: Montessori

Arlington Alternative School (1984)
18722 59th Ave NE, Arlington, WA 98223
Deborah Borgens, Dir, 206-435-8375
Type: public choice
5 teachers, 115 students, ages 14-20, 9-12th grade
Entrance requirements: informational meeting, application, interview, testing, immunization record, transcript, district transfer request for out-of-district students.
Monthly Celebrations of Achievement; required participation in staff-facilitated discussion groups; contracts; extracurriculars; vocational; teen parenting; childcare.

The Home School
(See Resource Appendix)

Bellingham Cooperative School
2710 McKenzie, Bellingham, WA 98225
Scott Stodola, 206-733-1024
Type: independent

Campus Alternative Program at Sehome High School (1988)
2700 Bill McDonald Way, Bellingham, WA 98225
Jim Cozad, Dir, 206-676-2796
Bellingham District
Type: public at-risk
3-4 teachers, 100-120 students, ages 14-19, 9-12th grade
Enrollment restricted to students who have failed two+ classes, have chemical dependencies, and/or have serious academic problems
A/V; CAI; self-directed; life skills; counseling; competency-based; individualized; contracts based.

Center for Academic Skills at Bellingham High School (1988)
1916 Ellis St, Bellingham, WA 98225
Joe McAuliffe, Instr, 206-676-4988
Bellingham District
Type: public at-risk
2 teachers, 38 students, ages 15-18, 9-12th grade
Enrollment restricted to credit deficient students; two semester limit
Competency-based; CAI; weekly progress reports; community service required.

Fairhaven College (1967)
Western Washington U, Bellingham, WA 98225-9118
Marie Eaton, Dean, 206-650-3680, FAX: 206-650-3677
Type: higher education; tuition: $660-2,316/qtr, scholarships
15 teachers, 380 students, ages 17+
Entrance requires admission to WWU
Governance by faculty, students, dean
Students may design their majors; no letter grades; extensive field trips; urban location.

Whatcom Hills Waldorf School (1986)
941 Austin St, Bellingham, WA 98226
Pam Went, Adm, 206-671-1035
Non-profit; tuition: $2,100-4,100/yr, scholarships
10 teachers, 100 students, ages 4-14, K-8th grade
Governance by faculty, board, administrator

Teacher qualifications: Waldorf, WA certification
Botany, zoology, history, physics, physiology, chemistry, geography; suburban location; interns accepted.

Whatcom Homeschool Association
3851 Britton Rd, Bellingham, WA 98226
206-671-3689

Burlington Little School
207 S Gardener Rd, Burlington, WA 98233
Roberta Nelson, 206-757-8257

Visions-Parent Involved Program (1991)
PO Box 128, Clear Lake, WA 98235
Betsy Senff, Tch, 206-856-1026
Sedro Woolley District
Type: public at-risk
1 teacher, 22 students, ages 6-9, 1-3rd grade

Whidbey Island Waldorf School
Box 469, Clinton, WA 98236
Kendall Hubbard

Garden Isle Montessori School
207 NW Cloveland Box 1305, Coupeville, WA 98239
Darrellyn Currier

Orcas Homeschoolers
Rt 1, Box 10-G, Eastsound, WA 98245
Cheryl Dankin, 206-376-5396

Everson Homeschool Support Group
7107 Goodwin Rd, Everson, WA 98247
Rose Anne Featherston, 206-966-5005

Mt Pilchuck Homeschoolers
PO Box 1097, Granite Falls, WA 98252
Karen Rieger, 206-691-6066

PROVE High School (1979)
12708 20th St NE, Lake Stevens, WA 98258
Jack Hein, Prin, 206-335-1541
Lake Stevens District
Type: public at-risk
2 teachers, 40 students, ages 14-20, 9-12th grade

Re-Entry Program/South Whidbey High School (1987)
PO Box 390, Langley, WA 98260
Virginia Horner, Tch, 206-321-4300
Type: public at-risk
1 teacher, 20 students, ages 14-20, 9-12th grade

South Whidbey Homeschool Support Group
5410 S Coles Rd, Langley, WA 98260
206-321-6477

Lynden Home Learners
9856 Van Buren Rd, Lynden, WA 98264
Mark and Kathy Iblings, 206-988-4038

Marysville Alternative High School (1983)
4317 76th St NE, Marysville, WA 98270
Larry Wilson, Prin, 206-653-0628
Marysville District
Type: public at-risk
8 teachers, 140 students, ages 14-20, 9-12th grade

Project Salmon, c/o Tulalip Tribes (1984)
6700 Totem Beach Rd, Marysville, WA 98270
Arlen James, Mgr, 206-653-0229
Type: public at-risk
2 teachers, 18 students, ages 13-19, 8-12th grade

Children's House Montessori
202 S 9th, Mt Vernon, WA 98273
Arlene Forsyth

Skagit Alternative High School
2121 E College Way, PO Box 217, Mt Vernon, WA 98273

Pam Church, Coord, 206-428-4818
Burlington, Mt Vernon and LaConner Districts
Type: independent, non-profit
5 teachers, 65–70 students, mainly at risk, ages 13–21
Entrance requirement: referral by counselors/Adm
Independent study; self-paced; contract-based home study;
    teen parenting.

Skagit Valley Homeschool Association
1198 Farm to Market Rd, Mt Vernon, WA 98273
Mr. or Mrs. Peterson, 206-757-4170

Homeschoolers On Whidbey
1348 Western Dr, Oak Harbor, WA 98277
M. Mattson, 206-679-3150

Outreach
8616 800 Ave W, Oak Harbor, WA 98277
Alerd Johnson, Adm, 206-679-5835
Oak Harbor SD 201
Type: public at-risk
2 teachers, 30 students, ages 15–20, 9–12th grade
Dropout retrieval

Der Kinderhuis Inc
5096 50th St NW, Oak Harbor, WA 98277-4024
Jeanan Richter
Type: Montessori

State Street Educational Center (SSEC) (1986)
800 State St, Sedro Woolley, WA 98284
Carl Bruner, 206-855-1035
Sedro Woolley District
Type: public at-risk
8 teachers, 65 students, ages 14–21, 9–12th grade

Aim High School (1985)
800 2nd St, Snohomish, WA 98290
Mary Sherman, Dir, 206-568-0675
Type: public at-risk
2 teachers, 18 students, ages 15–19, 9–12th grade

MATCH
15200 Utley Rd, Snohomish, WA 98290
206-334-6550

Snohomish Re-entry High School (1974)
1316 5th St, Snohomish, WA 98290
June Shirey, Dir, 206-568-0646
Type: public at-risk
4 teachers, 60–80 students, ages 14–18, 9–12th grade

Valley View Middle School (1994)
14308 99th SE, Snohomish, WA 98290
Ken Knautz, Prin, 206-568-0671
Type: public at-risk
650 students, ages 12–14, 7–8th grade

Crown Hill Montessori School
13801 235th St SE, Snohomish, WA 98290-7871

CCS Program at Stanwood High School (1990)
7400 272nd NW, Stanwood, WA 98292-7410
Dan Follette, 206-629-2167
Stanwood #401 District
Type: public at-risk
1 teacher, 90 students, ages 14–19, 9–12th grade

Sky County Home Educators
31931 116th St SE, Sultan, WA 98294
Peggy Tuttle, 206-793-2445

TEAM School (1987)
5550 Tracyton Blvd NW, Bremerton, WA 98310
Marian Turgeon, 206-692-3137
Central Kitsap District
Type: public choice
4 teachers, 100 students, ages 6–12, 1–6th grade

District residency required
Inclusive; parent involvement; competency-based.

Montessori Country Schools
1547 Sheridan Rd, Bremerton, WA 98310-3423

Lakeside Montessori
7730 NW Wildcat Lake Rd, Bremerton, WA 98312
Lee Ann Powers, 206-830-4568
Tuition: $1,450/yr
2 teachers, 2 assistants, 38 students, ages 3–6
Governance by an administrator
Fully equipped; rural location; interns accepted.

Central Kitsap Montessori Program
6200 Dowell Rd, Bremerton, WA 98312-1895

Collins High School (1990)
PO Box G, 2160 Collins Rd, Buckley, WA 98321
Kathy Hillig, Dir, 206-829-1182
Enumclaw, Sumner and White River Districts
Type: public at-risk
7 teachers, 101 students, ages 14–21
Entrance requirements: at-risk status, visit, interview; coun-
    selor recommendations
Individualized; vocational electives; Learning Lab; conflict res-
    olution; problem solving; required community service;
    teen parenting.

Chimacum High School Alternative Program (1988)
91 W Valley Rd, PO Box 278, Chimacum, WA 98325
Trevor Gloor, Instr, 206-732-4481
Type: public at-risk
1 teacher, 25 students, ages 13–20
Entrance requiremenst: at-risk status, referral
Learning contracts; credit for work experience, community-
    based learning; GED prep.

Eatonville Area Homeschool Association
PO Box 430, Eatonville, WA 98328
Michelle Wilbur, 206-832-4568

Forks Alternative High School (1987)
PO Box 60, Forks, WA 98331
Linda Wells, Dir, 206-374-2475
Quillayute Valley District
Type: public choice
90 students, ages 12–21, 7–12th grade

Greater Gig Harbor Homeschool Support Group
PO Box 2041, Gig Harbor, WA 98335
206-265-8210

HALL Program (1992)
PO Box 2253, Gig Harbor, WA 98335
Tom Schneider, Liaison, 206-858-5574
Pierce County
Type: public choice, Home-based
2 teachers, 175 students, ages 5–18, K–12th grade
Parents required to teach their children on site 4 hrs/wk
Affiliation: Peninsula PSD
Overseen by administrator with parent input.
Extensive software for CAI; official transcripts and public
    school diploma for independent study, parent-taught sub-
    jects; non-compulsory class attendance; multi-aged
    classes; extensive field trips; suburban location.

Harbor Montessori
5414 68th St Ct NW, Gig Harbor, WA 98335

Graham Homeschool Fellowship
13915 240th L St E, Graham, WA 98339
Nowl Orton, 206-893-5392

North Kitap Support Group
34077 Pilot Pt Rd, Kingston, WA 98346
Cathy McDonald, 206-638-2272

Spectrum Community School (1984)
8998 NE West Kingston Rd, Kingston, WA 98346
Chris Wendelyn, Dir, 206-297-2132
N Kitsap District
Type: public choice
7 teachers, 100 students, ages 15–21, 9–12th grade
Daily classes & independent study; counseling; vocational; parenting classes; men's and women's groups; electives in art, media, music, computer graphics, and foreign languages; school-wide projects in human rights advocacy; foreign student exchanges.

National Challenged Homeschoolers Associated Network
5383 Alpine Rd SE, Olalla, WA 98359
Tom or Sherry Bushnell, 206-857-4257
Type: national home-based
Newsletter; family directory; lending library.

Choice High School
216 E 24th St, Port Angeles, WA 98362
Michelle Reid, 206-452-7602
District 121
Type: magnet
9–12th grade
Dropout retrieval.

Franklin Elementary (1980)
2505 S Washington St, Port Angeles, WA 98362
Ron Bellamy, Prin, 206-457-9111
Type: public choice
4 teachers, 100 students, ages 5–11, K–5th grade
District residency required
Numerous volunteers and supportive parents; independent learners; flexible groupings/room arrangements; weekly/daily contracts; multi-aged classes.

DISCOVERY PROGRAM (1971)
c/o District Office, 1962 Hoover Ave SE, Port Orchard, WA 98366
Doug Green, Prin, 206-876-7341
S Kitsap District
Type: public at-risk
6 teachers, 120 students, ages 14–21, 9–12th grade

Homeschooling and Other Parents Encouraged
7017 Knight Dr SE, Pt Orchard, WA 98366
Karen Jogerst, 206-871-7249

Mar-Vista Alternative (1993)
450 Fir St, Port Townsend, WA 98368
Penny Kelley or Trina Steel, Coords, 206-385-5737
Port Townsend District
Type: public at-risk
2 teachers, 62 students, ages 14–21, 9–12th grade

OPEPO (Optional Education Program) (1977)
1919 Blaine St, Port Townsend, WA 98368
Bob DeWeese, parent, 206-385-2124
Port Townsend District
Type: public choice
3 teachers, 60 students, ages 6–12, 1–6th grade
Updated one-room schoolhouse; self-paced, interest-directed learning; integrated curriculum emphasizing cooperative problem solving; group/individual projects; parent participation; 3-day camping trip.

Port Townsend Migrant Education Program (1978)
450 Fir St, Port Townsend, WA 98368
Penny Kelley, Coord, 206-385-5737
Port Townsend District
Type: public home-based
1 teacher, 41 students, ages 5–18, K–12th grade
Enrollment restricted to children of migrant fishing, horticulture or agriculture workers.
Correspondence; individualized; parents act as home-teachers.

Washington Alternative Learning Assn (WALA) (1975)
(See Resource Appendix)

The Montessori Farm
17197 Clear Creek Rd, Poulsbo, WA 98370
Barbara Rhoe or Marie Cable

Puyallup Alternative School (1975)
5715 Milwaukee Ave E, Puyallup, WA 98372
Earlene J. Bogrand, Prin, 206-841-8781, FAX: 206-841-6435
Puyallup District
Type: public at-risk
7 teachers, 160 students, ages 14–20, 9–12th grade

Puyallup Homeschool Fellowship
13023 126th Ave E, Puyallup, WA 98374
206-840-3834

Christian Home Educators
111 Bon Jon View Way, Sequim, WA 98382
Bonnie Baisotti, 206-683-8625

Homeschoolers in Sequim
178 Kirner Rd, Sequim, WA 98382
Diana Hay, 206-683-6731

North Olympic Homeschool Association
72 W Quail Ln, Sequim, WA 98382
Rose Marshall

Outreach Alternative Program (1988)
503 N Sequim Ave, Sequim, WA 98382
Rita Thatcher, Dir, 206-683-3336
Sequim District
Type: public at-risk
1 teacher, 22 students, ages 14–21, 9–12th grade

Central Kitsap Alternative High School (1988)
PO Box 8, Silverdale, WA 98383
Steve McAboy/Robert Morton, Co-Dirs, 206-692-3210
Central Kitsap District
Type: public at-risk
10 teachers, 160 students, ages 14–20
Enrollment restricted to at-risk
Independent study; contracts; work program for pregnant teens at off-site cooperative day care center; drug/alcohol counselor.

Silverwood School
8551 Dickey Pl NW, Silverdale, WA 98383
Jane Van Buecken
Type: Montessori

Brownsville Montessori School
PO Box 3510, Silverdale, WA 98383-0733
Diana Zegers

Olympic View Montessori
PO Box 733, Silverdale, WA 98383-0733

Challenger High School, Graham Campus (1990)
7311 Eustus Hunt Rd, Spanawax, WA 98387
Ande Chapman; John Zurfluh, 206-847-4768
Bethel District
Type: public choice
2 teachers, 50 students, ages 15–21, 9–12th grade
Enrollment restricted to returning students; district residents
In renovated farmhouse; small groups; life skills; health professions; career exploration; teen parenting; childcare; rural location.

Challenger High School (1974)
18020 E "B" St, Spanaway, WA 98387
Gary Mesick, Prin, 206-846-9734
Bethel District
Type: public choice
15 teachers, 205 students, mainly at risk, ages 16+, 10–12th grade

Entrance requirements: application; interview
Daily discussion groups for skills development, career planning; self-developed contracts; drug/alcohol counselor; social worker; teen parenting; multi-aged classes.

Discovery Preschool (1988)
18020 E "B" St, Spanaway, WA 98387
Gary Mesick, Coord, 206-847-0288
Bethel District
Type: public at-risk
3-4 teachers; student ages 1.5-6 yrs, infant-K
Enrollment restricted to high-risk preschool children of Challenger HS students

Explorer Elementary (1989)
18020 E "B" St, Spanaway, WA 98387
Gary Mesick, Prin, 206-846-9734
Bethel District
Type: public choice
3-4 teachers, 30 students, ages 6-12, 1-6th grade
Entrance requirements: parent participation 10 hrs/mo, district residency
Hands-on education; parent involvement required; independent learning; multi-aged classes.

Voyager Junior High (1984)
18020 E "B" St, Spanaway, WA 98387
Gary Mesick, Coord, 206-846-9734
Bethel District
Type: public choice
3 teachers, 36 students, ages 13-15
Entrance requirements: application, district residency
Modified contract system; peer tutoring; cooperative learning; teen parenting; drug/alcohol counselor; social worker; support groups.

Bonney Homeschool Support Group
5521 175th Ave Ct E, Sumner, WA 98390
Terri McCoy, 206-863-7266

Suquamish Options in Education (1990)
18950 Park Ave NE, Suquamish, WA 98392
Bruce Colley, Prin, 206-598-4219,-4164
N Kitsap District
Type: public choice
2 teachers, 50 students, ages 6-12, 1-6th grade
Multi-age groups; class meetings; parent involvement; field trips; family atmosphere.

CHOICE Program School (1987)
747 St Helens, Tacoma, WA 98402
206-627-4050
Tacoma District
Type: public at-risk
2 teachers, 18-20 students, ages 12-17, 7-12th grade
Enrollment restricted to homeless and runaway youth and those highly at risk of becoming street involved
Mental health groups.

St Patrick Montessori
1112 N G St, Tacoma, WA 98403-2518

Lister Elementary
2106 E 44th St, Tacoma, WA 98404
Leonoa Schmit, 206-596-2066
Type: magnet
K-5th grade
Arts; mulitcultural; humanities.

Tacoma Homeschool Fellowship
2017 E 35th St, Tacoma, WA 98404
Cheryl Hulsizer, 206-272-1498

Tacoma Urban League Learning Center (1985)
2550 S Yakima Ave, Tacoma, WA 98405
Sam Chandler, Mgr, 206-597-6435
Tacoma District

Type: public at-risk
6 teachers, 50 students, ages 16-21, 9-12th grade

Alternative Middle School (1988)
3110 S 43rd St, Tacoma, WA 98408
Kelly Kerrone, Tch, 206-596-1875
Tacoma District
Type: public at-risk
1 teacher, 12-15 students, ages 12-17, 6-8th grade

Continuous Progress Center (1990)
3110 S 43rd St, Tacoma, WA 98408
Michael Jankanish, 206-596-1875
Tacoma District
Type: public at-risk
4 teachers, 100 students, ages 14-21, 9-12th grade

Eugene Tone School (1987)
3110 S 43rd St, Tacoma, WA 98408
Connie Iverson, 206-596-1898
Tacoma District
Type: public at-risk
6 teachers, 45 students, ages 5-14, K-8th grade

Parent Assisted Learning Services (1992)
3110 S 43rd St, Tacoma, WA 98408
Dr Wanda Buckner, 206-596-1875
Tacoma District
Type: Home-based Public choice
1 teacher, 40 students, ages 6-14, 1-8th grade
Support for homeschoolers; certified teacher consults in establishing learning objectives, designing lessons, and documenting progress.

Oakland Alternative (1991)
3319 S Adams, Tacoma, WA 98409
Kelly Kerrone, Tch, 206-596-1387
Tacoma District
Type: public at-risk
1 teacher, 20 students, ages 14-15, 6-12th grade

Tacoma Re-Entry Program (1989)
3319 S Adams St, Tacoma, WA 98409
Butch Stallard, Counselor, 206-596-1470
Tacoma District
Type: public at-risk
2 teachers, 40 students, ages 14-19, 9-12th grade

Homeschool Support for Military Families
6380 Olive Way, Ft Lewis, WA 98433
Janet De Villars, 206-964-0572

Enriched Learning Institute
4039 Altluras L St W, Tacoma, WA 98444
Mrs. Arnold, 206-565-6789

GATES Secondary School (1978)
813 S 132nd St, Tacoma, WA 98444-3532
Frank Hewins, 206-535-9882
Franklin Pierce District
Type: public at-risk
20 teachers, 250-300 students, ages 15-19, 9-12th grade
Enrollment restricted to severe at-risk/returning students; entrance requirements: interview; evaluation of drug/alcohol usage and emotional development
Individualized; work experience credit for ages 16+; teen parenting; support groups; childcare.

Homeschool Support Association
9024 24th L Ave E, Tacoma, WA 98445
Barbara Atchison, 206-537-7192

Larchmont Elementary
8601 East B, Tacoma, WA 98445
Richard Klumpar, 206-596-2096
Type: magnet
K-5th grade
Technology; world cultures.

Spic N' Span
1314 Sherwood Ct E, Tacoma, WA 98445
Debra White, 206-537-5452

Montessori School of Tacoma
7727 40th St W, Tacoma, WA 98466-3146
Charlene Moffet

Lakewood Christian Home Educators
6305 78th St W, Tacoma, WA 98467
Joan Kozelman, 206-582-1751

Lincoln Elementary/Options (1984)
213 E 21st St, Olympia, WA 98501
Doug Gall, Prin, 206-753-8967
Olympia District
Type: public choice
7 teachers, 144 students, ages 5–12, K–5th grade
Entrance requirements: parental application; informational
    meeting; class visit; enrollment by lottery
Classrooms contain up to 3 grade levels each; required
    parent participation; individualized instruction; community
    is part of the school.

New Market Vocation Skills Center (1986)
7299 New Market St, Tumwater, WA 98501
James H. Taylor, Dir, 206-586-9375
Host Districts: Tumwater, N Thurston, Olympia, Shelton,
    Tenino, Yelm, Oakville
Type: public at-risk
29 teachers, 500 students, ages 16+, 11–12th grade

Adventures In Montessori
2010-A Blacklake Blvd SW, Olympia, WA 98502
Dixie Matthews

Olympia Home School Support Group
1616 Brawne Ave NE, Olympia, WA 98502
James Hall, 206-754-0375

Cathedral of Praise Home Education Support
5204 Brentwood Dr SE, Lacey, WA 98503
Cathleen Lamb, 206-456-4617

New Century High School (1989)
6120 Mullen Rd SE, Lacey, WA 98503
Gail McBride, Prin, 206-493-2992
N Thurston District
Type: public choice
15 teachers, 140 students, ages 16–19, 10–12th grade
Entrance requirements: C grade pt avg; good attendance,
    district residency
High-tech: data bases, word processing, and on-line
    searches; focus on building leadership and creating a link
    between school and community.

Schools for the 21st Century
(See Resource Appendix)

Evergreen State College
Olympia, WA 98505
Doug Skinner, 206-866-6824
Type: higher education

Capital Montessori
3604 Surrey Dr NE, Olympia, WA 98506
Mergene Noble

Puget Sound High School (1987)
5900 54th Ave SE, Lacey, WA 98513
Jim Slosson, Prin, 206-493-2977
N Thurston District
Type: public at-risk
11 teachers, 250 students, ages 15–21, 10–12th grade

Aberdeen Continuation High School (1972)
359 N Division St, Aberdeen, WA 98520
Mitch Rajcich, Prin, 206-532-7690

Aberdeen District
Type: public at-risk
2 teachers, 50 students, ages 14–20, 9–12th grade
Enrollment restricted to current/potential dropouts;
    entrance requirements: interview, district residency
Individual conferences; teen parenting; child development;
    adjustable hours; required self-concept development class.

**Grays Harbor Christian Homeschool Parent Support
Group**
PO Box 1163, Aberdeen, WA 98520
Linda Edwards, 206-533-6418

Olympia Waldorf School (1983)
8126 Normandy St SE; PO Box 638, E Olympia, WA 98540
Kathy Kelly, Board; Julie Barrett, Faculty Chair, 206-493-0906
Thurston County
Non-profit; tuition: $3,500-3,950/yr, scholarships
11 teachers, 90 students, ages 4–12, K–5th grade
Entrance requirements: faculty interview, residency
Governance by board, faculty, parent council
Teacher qualifications: Waldorf training
In circa 1914 wooden schoolhouse; all students learn knitting,
    crochet, wooden flute/lyre playing, singing, watercolor,
    ceramics, woodwork; ethnic dinners; Yuletide craft fairs;
    Maypole dancing; seasonal celebrations; multi-aged
    classes; rural location; interns accepted.

Aberdeen Support
828 N 7th, Montesano, WA 98563

Napavine High School (1989)
PO Box 357, Napavine, WA 98565
Connie Van Egdom, Coord, 206-262-3301
Napavine District
Type: public at-risk
1 teacher; student ages 15–21, 9–12th grade

Community Learning Opportunity Center (1990)
303 4th St, Raymond, WA 98577
Nina Jeffre, Prog Dir, 206-942-9721
Willapa Valley District, Pacific County
Type: public at-risk
1 teacher, 45 students, mainly at-risk, ages 16–20, 9–12th
    grade
Enrollment restricted to residents age 16 or 8th grade com-
    pletion, out of school 45 days and not on active IEP
Governance by teachers and principal
Teacher qualifications: state certification
Community service required; independent study; CAI; teen
    parent ed; environmental ed; community volunteers teach
    special interest subjects; student government; non-
    compulsory class attendance; multi-aged classes; extensive
    field trips; integrated curriculum; rural location.

Willapa Community School (1987)
656 Barnhart St, Raymond, WA 98577
Karen Good, Dir, 206-942-3212
Pacific County
Type: independent, non-profit
1 teacher, 8 students, ages 5–15, K–8th grade
Governance by faculty and student representatives
Teacher qualifications: MA
Highly experiential; holistic; independent study; thematic cur-
    riculum; in former church building adjacent to woods;
    music; art; pottery; computer; no letter grades; non-
    compulsory class attendance; multi-aged classes; extensive
    field trips; rural location; interns accepted.

CHOICE Continuation High (1984)
428 W Birch, Shelton, WA 98584
Ron Wright, Prin, 206-426-7664
Shelton District
Type: public at-risk
7 teachers, 165 students, ages 14–21, 9–12th grade

Timberdoodle
(See Resource Appendix)

Ocosta Continuation School (1990)
HCR 76, 2422 S Montesano St, Westport, WA 98595-9718
Dale Bowen, Tch, 206-268-9123
Ocosta District
Type: public at-risk
2 teachers, 10 students, ages 14–20, 9–12th grade

CARE
783 Rhoades Rd, Winlock, WA 98596
Lori Hail

Yelm Extension School (1979)
PO Box 476, Yelm, WA 98597
Billie J. Needham, Dir, 206-458-2002
Yelm District
Type: public at-risk
5 teachers, 130 students, ages 15–21, 9–12th grade

Battle Ground District Alternative Learning Program
(1990)
11104 NE 149 St/ 204 W Main, Brush Prairie, WA 98604
Vynnette Rettenmaier; Warren Reeves, 206-260-5331
5 teachers, 300 students, ages 14–21, 7–12th grade
Enrollment restricted to returning students willing to
commit to program's rules and regulations
Contracts; individualized.

Moore Academy
(See Resource Appendix)

TOUTLE RIVER Alternative Program (1984)
2232 S Silver Lake Rd, Castle Rock, WA 98611
Luella Paulson, Adm, 206-274-6611
Toutle Lake District
Type: public at-risk
2 teachers, 40 students, ages 14–19, 9–12th grade

New World Montessori Children's House
4035 Rosewood, Longview, WA 98632
DeAnne Lightfoot

Pride Program
2210 Olympia Way, Longview, WA 98632
Bob Misener, Prin
Longview District
Type: public at-risk
120/day students, ages 14–19, 9–12th grade
Transition program.

School Biz
1515 Baltimore, Longview, WA 98632
Madeline Loren, 206-636-3495

Family Centered Learning Alternatives
HCR 63 Box 713, Naselle, WA 98638
206-484-3252
Type: home-based

South Pacific County Homeschoolers
27010 U St, Ocean Park, WA 98640
Ariel Campbell, 206-665-6698

Lewis River Home Educators
33112 NW Lancaster Rd, Ridgefield, WA 98642
206-887-8050

Skinner School
400 E Evergreen Blvd, Vancouver, WA 98660-3263
Type: Montessori

Pan Terra Alternative Secondary (1974)
2800 Stapleton Rd, Vancouver, WA 98661
Steve Friebel, Prin, 206-696-7288
Vancouver District
Type: public at-risk
10 teachers, 250 students, ages 14–20, 9–12th grade
Individual education magnet.

Montessori Institute NW (1979)
10316 NE 14th St, Vancouver, WA 98664
M. Shannon Helfrich, Exec Dir, 206-260-0360
Type: teacher education, non-profit
2 teachers
Entrance requirements: Bachelor's degree
Affiliations: AMI, AMI/USA, NAMTA, NAEYC
Governance by board of trustees
Urban location.

Vancouver Montessori School
10316 NE 14th St, Vancouver, WA 98664-4304
Audreen Williams

Hazel Dell Montessori
76207 NE Hazel Dell Ave, Vancouver, WA 98665
Robin Matson

Clark County Christian Home Educators (1988)
PO Box 5941, Vancouver, WA 98668

Evergreen Alternative Learning Center (1976)
PO Box 8910, Vancouver, WA 98668-8910
Jeffrey Evans, Coord, 206-256-6015
Evergreen District
Type: public choice
22 teachers, 180 students, ages 14–21, 9–12th grade
6 programs: Quest: academically committed students;
Bridge: grade 9; Recovery Transition: after drug/alcohol
treatment; Independent Study/Contract; Teen Parenting;
Credit Recovery; childcare.

Hewitt Research Foundation (1964)
(See Resource Appendix)

View Point Alternative School (1986)
2349 "B" St, Washougal, WA 98671
Tom Hays, Tch, 206-835-8766
Washougal District
Type: public at-risk
4 teachers; student ages 14–21, 9–12th grade

Woodland High School (1987)
PO Box 370, Woodland, WA 98674
Lee Knight, Prin, 206-225-8201
Woodland District
Type: public at-risk
3 teachers, 78 students, ages 13–18, 9–12th grade

Woodland Homeschool Support Group
189 Dee Creek Rd, Woodland, WA 98674
Jim & Veronica Stult, 206-225-6173

Family Advocates in Teaching Homes
PO Box 326, Yacolt, WA 98675
Darlene Beatty

Westside High School (1984)
1521 9th St, Wenatchee, WA 98801
John M. Waldren, Prin, 509-663-7947
Wenatchee District
11 teachers, 300 students, ages 14–21, 9–12th grade

Valley Home Educators
209 Stull Ct, E Wenatchee, WA 98802
Kim Bartel, 509-884-7635

Children's Gate Montessori School
PO Box 4025, Wenatchee, WA 98807-4025

Chelan Alternative School (MAC) (1986)
428 Bradley St, Chelan, WA 98816
George Valison, Prin, 509-682-2537
Lake Chelan District
Type: public at-risk
4 teachers, 30 students, ages 13–20, 9–12th grade

Columbia Basin Alternative High (1984)
1318 W Ivy, Moses Lake, WA 98837
Patty Jo Austin, Dir, 509-766-2667
Moses Lake District
Type: public choice, at-risk
5 teachers, 5 assistants, 120 students, ages 15-21, 9-12th
   grade

Moses Lake/Warden Support Group
907 S Balsom, Moses Lake, WA 98837-2108
Roxanne Hall, 509-766-1462

Oroville Alternative High School (1989)
10th and Ironwood; 1117 Main St, Oroville, WA 98844
Harold Jensen, Tch, 509-476-2011
Oroville District
Type: public at-risk
2 teachers, 22 students, ages 14-21, 9-12th grade

Grant County Home Educators Association
730 Rd V NW, Quincy, WA 98848
Harriet Weber, 509-787-3757

**Quincy Training and Learning Center/Alternative High
   School** (1988)
614 5th Ave SE, Quincy, WA 98848
Sandra Shelton, Dir, 509-787-4449
Quincy District
Type: public at-risk
1 teacher, 2 assistants, 25 students, ages 14-21, 9-12th
   grade

Smokiam Alternative School (1989)
PO Box 158, Soap Lake, WA 98851
Noreen Dyer, Dir, 206-246-0770
Soap Lake District
Type: public at-risk
3 teachers, 32 students, ages 14-21, 9-12th grade

Home Education Press
(See Resource Appendix)

Little Star School-Montessori (1982)
PO Box 608, Winthrop, WA 98862
Rayma Hayes, Dir, 509-996-2797, FAX: 509-996-2889
Non-profit; tuition: 1,800-2,900/yr
4 teachers, 6 assistants, 65 students, ages infant-9
Affiliations: AMS, NCME, AMI, PNMA
Governance by teachers, administrators, democratic school
   meeting, board
Childcare; rural location.

Adams Elementary (1990)
723 S 8th St, Yakima, WA 98901
Marcia McGill, Coord, 509-575-3448
Type: public choice
14 teachers, 14 assistants, 350 students, mainly at-risk &
   International, ages 3-9
Accreditation: AMS
Governance by administrator
Childcare; urban location; transportation; interns accepted.

**Migrant Alternative School (MAS) at Southeast
   Community Center** (1985)
1211 S 7th St, Yakima, WA 98901
Lee West, Lead Tch, 509-454-3539
Yakima District
Type: public at-risk
4-6 teachers, 125 students, ages 15-21, 9-12th grade

OUTREACH (1978)
508 W "B" St, Yakima, WA 98901
Tom Mullen, Lead Tch, 509-575-2950
Yakima District
Type: public at-risk
2 teachers, 18 students, ages 15-20, 9-12th grade

PROJECT 107 (1984)
602 S 3rd St, Yakima, WA 98901
Greg Hurst, Lead Tch, 509-454-3509
Yakima District
Type: public at-risk
2 teachers, 40 students, ages 15-18, 9-12th grade

Stride at Southeast Community Center (1986)
1211 S 7th St, Yakima, WA 98901
Steve Mitchell, Lead Tch, 509-454-3540
Yakima District
Type: public at-risk
3 teachers, 50-60 students, ages 14-18, 9-12th grade

Yakima Alternative High School (1982)
602 S 3rd St, Yakima, WA 98901
Chris Hunter, Tch, 509-454-3509
Yakima District
Type: public at-risk
1 teacher; student ages 15-20, 9-12th grade

OIC/Key (1978)
815 Fruitvale Blvd, Yakima, WA 98902
Melanie Mitchell, Lead Tch, 509-575-2975
Yakima District
Type: public at-risk
2 teachers, 36 students, ages 15-20, 9-12th grade

Ridgeview Group Home (1978)
1728 Jerome Ave, Yakima, WA 98902
Lloyd Running, Dir or Don Dunham, Lead Tch, 509-575-2736
Yakima District
Type: public at-risk
16 students

Yakima Learning Center (The Place) (1971)
215A N 3rd Ave, Yakima, WA 98902
Craig Gilley, Coord, 509-575-2619
Yakima District
Type: public at-risk
8 teachers, 92 students, ages 15-20, 9-12th grade

**Stanton Alternative High School (formerly Upstairs
   School)** (1971)
901 Whitman, Yakima, WA 98903
Jesse Cox, Prin, 509-575-3492
Yakima District
Type: public at-risk
19 teachers, 190-200 students, ages 15-20, 9-12th grade
Entrance requirement: counselor/adm approval
"Umbrella" program for all the various alternative programs
   in Yakima; childcare.

Children's House Montessori
905 S 48th Ave, Yakima, WA 98907
Esther Closner

Montessori Society of Yakima (1928)
511 N 44th Ave, Yakima, WA 98908
Bonnie Eglin, Adm, 509-966-2768
Tuition: $150/260/mo
4 teachers, 4 assistants, 76 students, ages 3-6
Affiliations: NAMTA, OMA, PNMA
Urban location; interns accepted.

Ellensburg High School Alternative Education Program
   (1979)
Hogue Tech, Rm 197, Central WA U, Ellensburg, WA 98926
Jim Ayer, Coord, 509-925-6185
Ellensburg District
3 teachers, 25-35 students, ages 14-20, 9-12th grade
Enrollment restricted to district residents not enrolled in a
   public school.
Individualized; films; swimming; extensive field trips; re-entry
   into regular program

Ellensburg Homeschool Support Group
11 Frontier Rd, Ellensburg, WA 98926

Kittitas Valley Homeschool Association (1988)
PO Box 1492, Ellensburg, WA 98926
Debbie Williams, Communications Chair, 509-925-4033, FAX:
  same
Kittitas County
50 teachers, 200 students, ages 5-15, K-9th grade
Governance by parent cooperative
Teacher qualifications: 45 college credit-hours
Interns accepted.

REACH at Lincoln Elementary (1982)
200 S Sampson, Ellensburg, WA 98926
Rod Goosman, Prin, 509-925-9831
Ellensburg District
Type: public choice
5 teachers, 125 students, ages 6-11, 1-5th grade
Parent support team; arts; competency-based; team
  teaching.

PULSE Alternative School (1986)
105 W Bartlett, Selah, WA 98942
Lance Ostrom, Tch/Prin, 509-697-9164
Selah District
Type: public at-risk
9 teachers, 70-90 students, ages 13-21, 6-12th grade

Rainbow Valley School
1510 Freimuth Rd, Selah, WA 98942-9732
Marcia Williams
Type: Montessori

PRIDE (1993)
1110 S Sixth St, Sunnyside, WA 98944
Ruben Carrera, Asst Supt, 509-837-0560
Sunnyside District
Type: public at-risk
2 teachers, 40+ students, ages 14-20, 9-12th grade

TRIAD (1985)
1110 S Sixth, Sunnyside, WA 98944
Ruben Carrera, Asst Supt, 509-837-5851
Sunnyside District
Type: public at-risk
1 teacher, 30 students, ages 14-20, 8-12th grade
Entrance requirements: must be migrant eligible, severe
  at-risk or returning students; counselor/Adm must sign
  release
Individualized instruction.

Eagle Alternative School (1987)
106 Franklin Ave, Toppenish, WA 98948
Marion R. Licano, Prin, 509-865-3377
Toppenish District
Type: public at-risk
80 students, ages 14-21, 9-12th grade

PACE Alternative School (1977)
PO Box 38, Wapato, WA 98951
Terry N. Smith, Prin, 509-877-6138
Wapato District
Type: public at-risk
27 teachers, 300 students, ages 12+, 7-12th grade
GED; ESL.

Zillah Homeschoolers
PO Box 1277, Zillah, WA 98953
William J. & Rebecca Schenker

Riverside Alternative School (1986)
34515 N Newport Hwy, Chattaroy, WA 99003-9734
Janet Kemp, Dir, 509-292-0201
Riverside District
Type: public at-risk
10 teachers, 60 students, ages 14+

Cheney High School Parallel Education (1985)
460 N 6th St, Cheney, WA 99004
Roy A. Schmidt, Asst Prin, 509-235-9510
Cheney District
2 teachers, 84 students, ages 15-21, 9-12th grade
Entrance requirements: multi-disciplinary assessment team
  approval, district residency
Educational planning; CAI; GED prep.

Deer Park Alternative High School (1990)
PO Box 550, Deer Park, WA 99006
Mike Blair, Dir, 509-276-5466
Deer Park District
Type: public at-risk
5 teachers, 30+ students, ages 14-20
Enrollment based on need, waiting list
Inclusive; self-paced; individualized; Mentor, Peer Helper
  programs.

PATH
South 8715 Silver Lake Rd, Medical Lake, WA 99022

Woodinville Montessori School (1983)
13965 NE 166th St, Woodinville, WA 99072
Mary Schneider or Sheri Nick, 206-481-2300
Tuition: $1,750-4,000/yr
7 teachers, 9 assistants, 60 students, ages 6-12
Entrance requirements: Montessori experience
Affiliations: AMS, NAEYC, PNMA; accreditation: WA
Governance by administrator
In open valley with horses; traditional Montessori program
  with innovative touches; childcare; rural location; interns
  accepted.

Lake Roosevelt High School Alternative Program (1980)
Civic Way, Coulee Dam, WA 99116
Ian E. Wilder, 509-633-1089
Grand Coulee Dam District, Okanogan County
Type: public at-risk
2 teachers, 34 students, ages 14-21, 9-12th grade
Entrance requirements: at-risk status, referral
Teen parenting; students may assist in day care center.

Homeschooling on the Palouse
SE 405 Hill, Pullman, WA 99163
Susan McMinn Seefldt, 509-332-8127
Nonsectarian family support group; also based in Idaho.

Montessori School of Pullman (1968)
NW 115 State St, Pullman, WA 99163
Tanya Carper, Adm, 509-334-4114
Whitman County
Non-profit; tuition: $125/mo, scholarships
4 teachers, 4 assistants, 70 students, ages 3-6, pre K, K
Must be toilet trained
Affiliations: AMI, AMS, NAMTA, PNMA
Governance by parent-executive committee, non-profit board
Teacher qualifications: Montessori Certification
Daily French class; music; movement; daily circle activities,
  outdoor play; multi-aged classes; suburban location;
  interns accepted.

**Washington State University-High School Equivalency
  Program** (1967)
23 Cleveland Hall, Pullman, WA 99164-2131
Attn: Dir, 509-335-5652
Pullman District
Type: public at-risk
4 teachers, 100 students, ages 17+
GED for migrant/seasonal farmworkers

Mary Walker Alternative (1980)
PO Box 159, Springdale, WA 99173
Glen Brooke, Coord, 509-258-4533
Mary Walker District
Type: public at-risk
2 teachers, 10 students, ages 14-21, 9-12th grade

American Indian Community Center
E 905 Third Ave, Spokane, WA 99202
Judith Johnston, Coord, 509-535-0886
Spokane District
Type: public at-risk
2 teachers, 50+ students, ages 14+, 9–12th grade

St Aloysius School
611 E Mission Ave, Spokane, WA 99202-1917
Susan Boughton
Type: Montessori

EAGLES
E 429 27th Ave, Spokane, WA 99203

Little Way Montessori Services
2213 29th, Spokane, WA 99203
Barbara Templin

Montessori Central
S 2900 Bernard, Spokane, WA 99203
Beverley Burger

Montessori Schools of Washington
E 2213 29th Ave, Spokane, WA 99203
Brian Templin

Jefferson Elementary School
3612 S Grand Blvd, Spokane, WA 99203-2693
Type: Montessori

Sacred Heart (1984)
101 W 8th Ave, PCCA Unit, Spokane, WA 99204
Mary Brown, Supervisor, 509-455-3177
Spokane District
Type: public at-risk
2 teachers, 24 students, ages 5–18, K–12th grade

Spokane Montessori West
4040 W Wright Ave, Spokane, WA 99204
Hope Caprye-Boos

Woodland Montessori School
3404 W Woodland Blvd, Spokane, WA 99204-2240

Bridge Alternative School (1971)
2610 Northwest Blvd, Spokane, WA 99205
George Renner, Coord, 509-456-3250
Spokane District
Type: public at-risk
7 teachers, 40 students, ages 14–19, 9–12th grade

Montessori Central Preschool, Inc
W 2421 Garland Ave, Spokane, WA 99205
Beverly Burger

REAL (Regional Educational Alternative Laboratory)
(1974)
1300 W Knox Ave, Spokane, WA 99205
George Renner, Prin, 509-353-4502
Spokane District
Type: public at-risk
3 teachers, 60 students, 10–12th grade

Spokane Montessori Schools
W 1904 Glass Ave, Spokane, WA 99205

Transition (1991)
1300 W Knox, Spokane, WA 99205
Lyn Erickson, Coord, 509-353-5343
Spokane District
Type: public at-risk
5 teachers, 25–30 students, ages 12–18, 7–12th grade

4 Acres (Alternative Curriculum and Educational Support) (1989)
N 701 Pines Rd, Spokane, WA 99206
Nancy Dean, Coord, 509-922-6910
Central Valley District
Type: public at-risk; tuition: $85/course if already full-time
17 teachers, 85 students, ages 14–21, 9–12th grade
Enrollment intended for students whose graduation is in jeopardy, dropouts or potential dropouts; 9th grade to age 21.

Contract Based Education (1987)
S 123 Bowdish, Spokane, WA 99206
Bob Shill, Dir, 509-927-1100
Central Valley District
Type: public at-risk
15 teachers, 280–300 students, ages 12–21, 7–12th grade
Enrollment restricted to referred students from co-op HS/JH, and returning students
Individualized instruction; min 30 hrs/wk homestudy; counseling; SE; teen parenting.

Learning Opportunity Center (1988)
S 123 Bowdish, Spokane, WA 99206
Bob Shill, Dir, 509-927-1100
Central Valley District
2 teachers, 80 students, ages 12–20, 7–12th grade
Enrollment restricted to returning students
Individualized; self-paced; competency-based; A/V; CAI; 15–20 students/class; immediate feedback; life skills.

SPACE (Student Parent Alternative Classroom Experience) at South Pines Elementary (1988)
E 12021 24th Ave, Spokane, WA 99206
Ralph Larsen, Prin, 509-922-6760
Central Valley District
Type: public choice
14 teachers, 62 students, ages 6–12, 1–6th grade
Entrance requirement: written "Parent Involvement Contract"
Individualized; competency-based; attempts made to balance boys and girls, and home school and non-home school students; multi-aged classes.

Family Learning Center
Box 7256, Spokane, WA 99207-0256
Kathleen McCurdy, 509-467-2552
Type: home-based

Marian Heights School (1961)
3754 W Indian Trail Rd, Spokane, WA 99208
Michael B. Seubert, Head Tch, 509-353-5357
District 81
Type: public at-risk
10 teachers, 85 students, ages 10–18, 4–12th grade

SPICE at Seth Woodward Elementary (1985)
E 8508 Uprive Dr, Spokane, WA 99212
Sherri Wagemann, Tch, 509-921-2160
W Valley District
Type: public choice
3 teachers, 73 students, ages 5–11, 1–5th grade
Entrance requirements: family visit, application, understand philosophy/obligations, teacher conference, district residency
Student-centered; multi-aged; emphasizes parent, teacher, student, community interaction; intense parent participation; variety of instructional strategies.

Spokane Valley High School (1981)
E 8920 Valleyway, Spokane, WA 99212
Doug Grace, Prin, 509-922-5475
West Valley District
7 teachers, 140–150 students, mainly at risk, ages 14–20
Entrance requirement: must be released from home HS
Individualized; self-paced; small class size; SE; teen parenting; community activities; career/counseling center; hot lunches; childcare; transportation.

Valley Montessori
13900 E Mission Ave, Spokane, WA 99216-1932
Gwen Melcher

Mead Educational Alternative Department (1990)
W 529 Hastings Rd, Spokane, WA 99218
Steve M. Hogue, Prin, 509-468-3073
Mead District
Type: public at-risk
6 teachers, 96 students, ages 14-20, 9-12th grade

New Horizons High School (1968)
3110 W Argent Rd, Pasco, WA 99301
Connie Bailey, Prin, 509-547-7775
Pasco District
Type: public at-risk
7 teachers, 116 students, ages 14-21, 9-12th grade

Tri-Cities Homeschool Support Group
4355 Kahlotus Rd, Pasco, WA 99301
Kay Hayes, 509-547-6623

Wee Kare Korner
927 W Henry, Pasco, WA 99301
Terri Allen
Type: Montessori

Lower Valley Homeschool Support Group
PO Box 157, Bickleton, WA 99322
Kathy Juris, 509-896-2315

House of Children
6510 W Arrowhead, Kennewick, WA 99336
Lorretta Levno
Type: Montessori

The Rock (Youth Resources and Opportunity Center of Kennewick) (1992)
1701 S Washington, Kennewick, WA 99336
Jack Anderson, Adm, 509-736-2531
Kennewick District
Type: public at-risk
3 teachers, 50+ students, ages 14-20, 9-12th grade
Dropout retrieval.

St Joseph's Montessori
901 W 4th, Kennewick, WA 99337
Cherie Moll

New Horizons Support Group
2045 SW Road 26, Mattawa, WA 99344

Richland Alternative High School (1987)
975 Gillespie, Richland, WA 99352

Steven Witeck, Prin, 206-335-9355
Richland District
Type: public at-risk
6 teachers, 75-85 students, ages 15-21, 9-12th grade

Cathedral Montessori School
325 W Gage Blvd, Richland, WA 99352-9603
Shawna Boolen

Royal Middle School (1989)
PO Box 486, Royal City, WA 99357
Sandra Adams, Tch, 509-346-2268
Royal City District
Type: public at-risk
2 teachers, 38 students, ages 13+, 8-12th grade

Blue Mountain Homeschool Association
PO Box 13631, Walla Walla, WA 99362
509-525-2860

Paine Campus Alternative High School (1986)
S 4th St, Walla Walla, WA 99362
Jan Eyestone, Prin, 509-527-3083
Walla Walla District
Type: public at-risk
7 teachers, 100 students, ages 14-20, 9-12th grade

Clarkston High School Alternative Program (1988)
PO Box 370, Clarkston, WA 99403
Elece Lockridge, Dir, 509-758-5591
Clarkston District
Type: public at-risk
2 teachers, 110 students, ages 14-21
Entrance requirements: referral; interview
Individualized; attendance contract; after school classes; GED prep; teen parenting.

The Educational Opportunity Center (1993)
PO Box 665, Clarkston, WA 99403
Elece Lockridge, Dir, 509-758-5591
Clarkston District
Type: public at-risk
2 teachers, 2 assistants, 70 students, ages 14-21
Entrance requires referral and recommendations.
Individualized; CCP; independent contract; GED prep; GRADS; self esteem; community support, involvement.

Washington, DC

Benjamin Banneker Academic High School
800 Euclid St NW, Washington, DC 20001
Linette M. Adams, Prin, 202-673-7322
Type: public choice
9-12th grade
Rigorous; 270 hrs community service required.

M. M. Washington Career Senior High School
27 "O" St, NW, Washington, DC 20001
Alethia Spraggins, Prin, 202-673-7224
Type: public choice
10-12th grade
Health care, business-medical fields, culinary arts.

Pre-Engineering Program at Dunbar Senior High School
1301 New Jersey Ave, NW, Washington, DC 20001
Eva R. Rousseau, Prin, 202-673-7239

Type: public choice
10-12th grade
Enrollment in 9th or 10th grade

Midtown Montessori School
33 K St, NW, Washington, DC 20001-1369
Cheryl Harris

Academy of Integrated Media Studies (AIM), Public Safety Program at McKinley/Penn SHS
2nd & T Sts, NE, Washington, DC 20002
James Greene, Prin, 202-576-6011
Type: public choice
9-12th grade
Enrollment in 9th or 10th grade
AIM: media management, broadcast/print journalism, advertising/marketing, photography, publishing, broadcast engi-

neering; PSP: law enforcement, fire fighting, corrections; cadets earn hourly wage; post-grad employment options.

Institute for Independent Education (1984)
(See Resource Appendix)

Marsh Montessori School
300 G St NE, Washington, DC 20002

Phelps Career Senior High School
26th St & Benning Rd, NE, Washington, DC 20002
Earnest Johnson, Prin, 202-724-4516
Type: public choice
10-12th grade
Floriculture; agri-business; construction; transportation; post grad apprenticeships; Integrated Design and Electronics Acad: UDC-prep for JROTC students.

Pre-Architecture, Interior Design, and Landscape Architecture; Justice and Security Academy; STAY at Spingarn SHS
26th St & Benning Rd, NE, Washington, DC 20002
Elizabeth S. Smith, Prin, 202-724-4525
Type: public choice, at-risk
10-12th grade
PILA: enrollment in 9th/10th grade; computer-assisted design; strong business component. STAY: ages 16-21; individualized CAI; voc; childcare available.

Washington-Dix Street Academy
6th St & Brentwood Pkwy, NE, Washington, DC 20002
Jerome Shelton, Prin, 202-724-4562
Type: public at-risk
Student ages 16+

Chamberlain Career Development Center
14th St & Potomac Ave, SE, Washington, DC 20003
Waverly Jones, Prin, 202-724-4648
Type: public choice
10-12th grade

Health and Human Services Academy at Eastern SHS
17th & E Capitol Sts, NE, Washington, DC 20003
Ralph Neal, Prin, 202-724-4805,-8737
Type: public choice
9-12th grade

Watkins Elementary School
12th & E Sts, SE, Washington, DC 20003
Helen Flagg, Prin, 202-724-4714
Type: public choice Montessori
Pre K-4th grade

Capitol Hill Montessori School
701 5th St SE, Washington, DC 20003-4210
Brenda Neal

High School/College Internship Program
415 12th St NW, Washington, DC 20004
Guidance and Counseling Office, Rm 906
Dr Dorothy Jenkins, Dir, 202-724-4185
Type: public choice
12th grade
College courses for HS credit.

Ellington School of the Arts
35th & R Sts, NW, Washington, DC 20007
Carolyn Wilson, Acting Prin, 202-282-0123
Type: public choice
9-12th grade
Enrollment through audition only

Georgetown Montessori School
1301 35th St, NW, Washington, DC 20007
Lee Allard

Montessori School of Washington
1556 Wisconsin Ave NW, Washington, DC 20007

Second Renaissance Montessori School
3526 Garfield St, NW, Washington, DC 20007
Margaret Bethea Abourezk

The Children's House of Washington
3133 Dumbarton St, NW, Washington, DC 20007-3309
Patti Harburger
Type: Montessori

Academic Preparation Centers of Transemantics Inc
4301 Connecticut Ave NW, Washington, DC 20008
Type: Montessori

Mater Amoris Montessori School
3600 Ellicott St, NW, Washington, DC 20008
Charlottee Kovach

School For Friends
2121 Decatur Pl NW, Washington, DC 20008
James Clay, Director, 202-328-1789
Type: independent

Washington Montessori Institute
2119 S St NW, Washington, DC 20008
Type: Montessori teacher education

Home Study Directory/National Home Study Council
(See Resource Appendix)

TransTech Academy at Cardozo Senior High School
13th & Clifton Sts, NW, Washington, DC 20009
Bernard Lucas, Acting Prin, 202-673-7385
Type: public choice
10-12th grade
Transportation technology.

Mt Pleasant Montessori School
PO Box 21362, Washington, DC 20009-0862

Language Development, Career Specializations, and 2+2 Tech-Prep at Bell Multicultural SHS
3145 Hiatt Pl, NW, Washington, DC 20010
Maria Tukeva, Prin, 202-673-7314
Type: public choice

Lincoln Multicultural Middle School
16th & Irving Sts, NW, Washington, DC 20010
Roberto R. Butler, Prin, 202-673-7345
Type: public choice
6-8th grade
Stresses 5 geo-cultures of student population from over 35 ethnic groups.

Burdick Career Development Center
1300 Allison St, NW, Washington, DC 20011
Ruth Clauselle, Prin, 202-576-6241
Type: public choice
10-12th grade
Computer repair, cosmetology, hair and child care.

Coolidge High School for the Teaching Professions Program (1988)
Coolidge SHS, 5th & Tuckerman Sts, NW, Washington, DC 20011
Christine Easterling, 202-722-1656, 576-6143
Type: public choice
Students mainly African-American, 9-12th grade
Enrollment in 9th or 10th grade
Foreign language, government, physics, calculus, English, communication skills; professional practicum; work-study.

Travel and Tourism Program at Roosevelt SHS
13th & Upshur Sts, NW, Washington, DC 20011
Robert Gill, Acting Prin, 202-576-6130

Type: public choice
9–12th grade
Hotel and convention management.

Aiden Montessori School (1961)
3100 Military Rd NW, Washington, DC 20015
Jane Scheuermann, Admissions; Marsha Donnelly, Adm, 202-966-0360, FAX: 202-966-1878
Non-profit; tuition: $2,061-6,670/yr
8 teachers, 5 assistants, 120 students
Entrance requirement: age 4.5+, must transfer from another Montessori school
Affiliations: NAMTA, AISGW, MAC/USA; accreditation: AMI
Governance by a board of trustees
Childcare; urban location.

Montessori School Of Chevy Chase
5312 Connecticut Ave, NW, Washington, DC 20015-1804
Donna Tambornino

International Studies Program at W. Wilson SHS
Nebraska Ave & Chesapeake St, NW, Washington, DC 20016
Sherri Furlott, Coord, 202-282-0120
Type: public choice
9–12th grade
Enrollment in 9th or 10th grade
Social studies, languages; work-study; foreign exchange.

DC Street Academy Senior High School
10th & Monroe Sts NE, Washington, DC 20017
Dr Reginald B. Elliott, Prin, 202-576-7005
Type: public at-risk
Student ages 16-23, 9–12th grade
Diploma/GED prep; mentorships; internships; counseling.

Math, Science and Technology Magnet
Backus Middle School
S Dakota Ave & Hamilton St, NE, Washington, DC 20017
Ann Hilliard, Acting Prin, 202-576-6110
Type: public choice
6–8th grade

Trinity College School of Professional Studies
125 Michigan Ave, NE, Washington, DC 20017-1094
Type: Montessori teacher education

Fort Lincoln Elementary School
Fort Lincoln & Barney Drs, NE, Washington, DC 20018
Barbara Colston, Prin, 202-576-6900
Type: public choice Montessori
Pre K–7th grade

John Burroughs Montessori Program
18th & Monroe St NE, Washington, DC 20018

Montessori Avalon School
2814 Franklin NE, Washington, DC 20018

Montessori Memories
3137 24th St NE, Washington, DC 20018
Pam Bellino

Woodridge Elementary School
Carlton & Central Aves, NE, Washington, DC 20018
Claudia Thompson, Prin, 202-576-6042
Type: public choice Montessori
Pre K–6th grade

Business and Finance Program at H. D. Woodson SHS
55th & Eads Sts, NE, Washington, DC 20019
Lucile E. Christian, Prin, 202-724-4512
Type: public choice
10-12th grade
Enrollment in 9th or 10th grade by application

Kimball Elementary School
Minnesota Ave & Ely Pl, SE, Washington, DC 20019
Isaac Jackson, Acting Prin, 202-767-7011
Type: public choice Montessori
Pre K–6th grade

Math, Science and Technology Magnet
Roper Middle School
4800 Meade St, NE, Washington, DC 20019
Helena N. Jones, Acting Prin, 202-724-4632
Type: public choice
6–8th grade

Merritt Elementary School
50th & Hayes Sts, NE, Washington, DC 20019
Nancy Shannon, Prin, 202-724-4618
Type: public choice Montessori
Pre K–7th grade

Nalle Elementary School
50th & C Sts, SE, Washington, DC 20019
Shirley Williams, Prin, 202-767-7029
Type: public choice Montessori
Pre K–6th grade

Public Service Academy at Anacostia Senior High School
16th & R Sts, SE, Washington, DC 20020
Zavolia D. Willis, Prin, 202-767-7041, 7040
Type: public choice
9–12th grade

Ballou STAY Senior High School
4th & Trenton Sts, SE, Washington, DC 20032
Lloyd Williams, Dir, 202-767-7225
Type: public at-risk
Student ages 18+
Accelerated diploma/GED prep.

Douglass Junior High School
Douglas & Stanton Rds, SE, Washington, DC 20032
Louise Buckner, Prin, 202-767-7190
Type: public choice
7–9th grade
Focus on self-esteem and leadership.

School of Mathematics and Science
Ballou Senior High School
4th & Trenton St, SE, Washington, DC 20032
Richard Washington, Prin, 202-767-7071
Type: public choice
Educational partnerships with NASA, Naval Research Lab, Westinghouse, Smithsonian, etc.

Network of Educators on the Americas
(See Resource Appendix)

School Without Walls Senior High School
21st & G Sts, NW, Washington, DC 20037
Emily Crandall, Prin, 202-724-4889
Type: public choice
9–12th grade
Entrance requires interview and tests.
College prep; internships, apprenticeships, independent study in conjunction with GWU; concentrated humanities and integrative learning.

Magnet School Assistance Program
400 Maryland Ave SW #2056, Washington, DC 20202
Sylvia Wright, Branch Chief
Type: Montessori

West Virginia

Alternative Learning Center
105 Old Bluefield Rd, Princeton, WV 24740

Gesundheit Institute (1971)
HC 64 Box 167, Hillsboro, WV 24946
Dr. Patch Adams, Dir, 304-653-4338
Type: independent
Teacher qualifications: Looking for teachers interested in creating the school
Building a free hospital which will have an alternative school for children of staff, sick children, and children of sick parents, as well as local area children; staff will live at the hospital; 310-acre site.

Alternatives in Education
Rt 3 Box 305, Chloe, WV 25235
304-655-7232
Type: home-based

Cabell Alternative High School
1301 2nd Ave, Charleston, WV 25302

Laurelbrook Montessori
400 Swarthmore Ave #1, Charleston, WV 25302
Lori Ann Flanigan

Mountaineer Montessori (1978)
308 20th St SE, Charleston, WV 25304
Mary E. McKown, Dir, 304-342-7870
Tuition: $2,200-3,350/yr
98 students, ages 3-12
Affiliations: NCME, AMI, AMS
Governance by director, administrator, and parent board
Extensive field trips; multi-aged classes; no letter grades; urban location; interns accepted.

Montessori, Etc
869 Sherwood Rd, Charleston, WV 25314
Mary Esther McKown

West Virginia Home Educators Association, Inc
PO Box 3707, Charleston, WV 25337-3707
304-733-4735, 800-736-9843
Type: state home-based

Charleston Montessori School
PO Box 4443, Charleston, WV 25364
Eleanor Kawsek

Berkeley Springs Community Preschool
302 Warren St, Berkeley Springs, WV 25411
Type: Montessori

The Learning Tools Company
PO Box 657, Berkeley Springs, WV 25411
Ellen Gould
Type: Montessori

Tri-State Montessori School
773 Norway Ave, Huntington, WV 25705-3830
Judith Smith

Children's House
203 S Kanawha St, Beckley, WV 25801-5616
Type: Montessori

Mount de Chantal Montessori School
410 Washington Ave, Wheeling, WV 26003
Margaret Erickson

Salomi's Montessori School
35 G C & P Rd, Wheeling, WV 26003
Salomi Jayasekera

Alternative Learning Center
2606 Commerce St, Wellsburg, WV 26070

De Sales Hts Academy
37 Willowbrook Dr, Parkersburg, WV 26104-1002
Type: Montessori

Mid-Ohio Valley Montessori School
PO Box 4106, Parkersburg, WV 26104-4106

Alternative School
1400 S Davis Ave, Elkins, WV 26241

Montessori Early Learning Center (1979)
1002 S Davis Ave, Elkins, WV 26241-3528
Virginia Longtain Zuboy, 304-636-2075
Tuition: $1,278/2,655/yr
1 teacher, 4 assistants, 65 students, ages 3-6
Governance by teacher/owner
Interns accepted.

Tri-CountyAlternative High School
Rt 3, Box 43-C, Clarksburg, WV 26301

Highland School (1981)
Rt 83 Box 56, Highland, WV 26346
Dr. Charlotte Landvoigt, Director, 304-869-3250
Ritchie County
Type: independent, boarding, non-profit; tuition: day 60, bdg 560/mo
3 teachers, 14 students, ages 5-18
Entrance requirements: interview for children over 11
Governance by democratic school meeting
Teacher qualifications: BA min; willingness to be equal member of democratic community
Located on 480 acres: woods, pond, streams, fields, wildlife; international visitors and exchanges; stresses individual interests, responsibility; apprenticeship program: oil and gas, veterinary science, office skills; PSAT administered; no letter grades; non-compulsory class attendance; multi-aged classes; extensive field trips; rural location; interns accepted.

Barbour County Alternative School
Route 2, Philippi, WV 26416

Alternative Learning Center
417 Holland Ave, Morgantown, WV 26505

Saint Luke's Montessori School
RR 6 Box 145-CC, Morgantown, WV 26505-9806

White Alternative Learning Center
601 Locust Ave, Fairmount, WV 26554
Type: public at-risk

Wisconsin

Amy Montessori School
305 N Calhoun Rd, Brookfield, WI 53005-3403

Basic Academic Skills Increase Career Success (BASICS)
c/o Hartford School District
805 Cedar St, Hartford, WI 53027
Delores Rettler, Youth At Risk Coord, 414-673-8950
Type: public at-risk
9-12th grade
Individualized course; life skills, social, career development.

Arrowhead East
c/o Arrowhead High School
700 North Ave, Hartland, WI 53029
Tom Tallmadge, Coord, 414-367-3611
Arrowhead District
Type: public at-risk
Student ages 15-19, 11-12th grade
Goals to increase world awareness, learn how to learn,
  become valuable employees.

PREP
c/o Kiel Area School District
PO Box 201, Kiel, WI 53042
Bill Stadler, Dir, Student Services, 414-894-2266
Type: public at-risk
5-8th grade
Skill, self-esteem development; students, parents, teachers
  work together.

PACE
c/o New Holstein District
1715 Plymouth St, New Holstein, WI 53061
Jon Turnell, At Risk Coord, 414-898-4256
Type: public at-risk
10-12th grade
Set goals, values; work experience.

Prairie Hill Waldorf School (1987)
N 14 W 29143 Silvernail Rd, Pewaukee, WI 53072
Sally Sommer, Adm Coord, 414-691-8996
Waukesha County
Non-profit; tuition: $1,950-3,200/yr, scholarships
18 teachers, 142 students, ages 3.5-12, K-8th grade
Entrance requirements: student and family interview
Governance by faculty and board of trustees
Teacher qualifications: Waldorf training
Weekly French, German; clay modeling; written evaluations;
  suburban location; interns accepted.

Alternative Education at Port Washington High School
427 W Jackson St, Port Washington, WI 53074
Richard Rokus, Alt Ed Coord, 414-284-7712
Port Washington–Saukville District
Type: public at-risk/class
15 students, 9-12th grade
Educational, vocational goals set by student, parents, alt ed
  coord; resource/tutoring room; modified curriculum.

Alternative High School Program
c/o Sheboygan Area School District
830 Virginia Ave, Sheboygan, WI 53081
Dona Schwichtenberg, Alt Programs Coord, 414-459-3329
Type: public at-risk
85 students, 10-12th grade
Focus on learning, interpersonal and social skills; affective
  development has priority.

Alternative High School
W220 N6151 Town Line Rd, Sussex, WI 53089
Sharon Turner, Alt School Coord, 414-246-6471
Hamilton School District
Type: public at-risk
12th grade
Competency-based; computer education; career info.

Alternative Learning Environment (ALE)
c/o Watertown High School
505 S 8th St, Watertown, WI 53094
Bruce Fero, ALE Social Studies Instructor, 414-262-1470
Watertown Unified School District
Type: public at-risk
10-12th grade
Develops thinking skills through knowledge, comprehension,
  analysis, synthesis, evaluation.

Montessori Children's House
1701 Vogt Dr, West Bend, WI 53095

Guadalupe Montessori School
PO Box 368, Burlington, WI 53105-0368

Switch
(See Resource Appendix)

ACCESS Alternative High School
6801 Southway, Greendale, WI 53129
Raymond H. Petitpren, Prin, 414-423-0110
Greendale School District
Type: public at-risk
Student age 17, 9-12th grade
Signed contract between student, school, and parents.

At Risk
c/o Brighton #1 School District
1200-248th Ave, Kansasville, WI 53139
Laurie Wright, District Adm, 414-878-2191
Type: public at-risk
K-8th grade
One-on-one tutorial.

Kenosha Montessori School
5900 Seventh Ave, Kenosha, WI 53140

Reuther Central High School
913-57th St, Kenosha, WI 53140
Rochelle Henning, Prin, 414-653-6160
Kenosha Unified School District #1
Type: public choice, at-risk
9-12th grade
Awareness of global interdependence; critical/creative thinking; problem solving strategies; decision making; social
  responsibility; environmental concern.

Montessori Children's House of Kenosha
4601 8th Ave, Kenosha, WI 53140-3301
Marcia Ray

Rosehart Montessori School
1711 74th St, Kenosha, WI 53143-5379

Palmyra-Eagle Area School District
709 Maple St, Palmyra, WI 53156
Nick Niehausen, AODA Coord, 414-495-2136
Type: public at-risk

9-12th grade

Peer Facilitator Course: trains HS students to facilitate small group sessions with 7-8th graders on alcohol/drug abuse prevention; HSED: for ages 17-18, Individual Plan of Action developed to gain HSED; Effective Skills: personal, social responsibility, decision making, long-term goals.

Educational Crossroads: Contract to Encourage Learning (EX:CEL)

c/o South Milwaukee School District

1225 Memorial Dr, South Milwaukee, WI 53172

Robert E. Schmielau, Dir of Instruction, 414-768-6300

Type: public at-risk

9-12th grade

Contracts; overcome barriers of traditional school.

Futurebound Program

c/o Union Grove High School

3433 S Colony Ave, Union Grove, WI 53182

Anne Tobias-Becker, Social Worker/At Risk Coord, 414-878-2434

Type: public at-risk

9-12th grade

Social skills; group work; experiential; extensive community service projects; extra credit for improved attendance in other coursework; sponsors children's Very Special Arts Festival.

Montessori School of Waukesha (1964)

2600 Summit Ave, Waukesha, WI 53188

Jane Walrath, Adm, 414-547-2545

Non-profit; tuition: $2,127-2,860/yr

7 teachers, 5 assistants, 126 students, ages 3-9

Governance by administrator

Childcare; suburban location.

Lincoln Center Middle School

820 E Knapp St, Milwaukee, WI 53202

Hector Perez-LaBoy, 414-272-6060

Type: magnet

6-8th grade

Creative arts.

Waldorf School of Milwaukee (1977)

718 E Pleasant St, Milwaukee, WI 53202

Lucas G. Hendrickson, Teacher, 414-272-7727

Non-profit; tuition: $3,000-4,000/yr, scholarships

12 teachers, 96 students, ages 3.5-11, K-5th grade

Entrance requirements: teacher interview; toilet-trained

Affiliation: AWSNA

Governance by teachers and board

Teacher qualifications: openness to Anthroposophy, willingness to learn

Teachers show LOVE to the students daily; struggles shared openly; multi-cultural; no letter grades; urban location; interns accepted.

Kagel Elementary

1210 W Mineral St, Milwaukee, WI 53204

Rose Guajardo, 414-647-1552

Type: magnet

K-5th grade

Bilingual gifted and talented.

Brown St Academy

2029 N 20th St, Milwaukee, WI 53205

Mack Hughes, 414-933-4011

Type: magnet

Student ages 3+,-5th grade

Talent development.

Elm Elementary

900 W Walnut St, Milwaukee, WI 53205

Darrel Jacobs, 414-562-1000

Type: magnet

Student ages 4+,-5th grade

Creative arts.

Lloyd St Elementary

1228 W Lloyd St, Milwaukee, WI 53205

Helen Harris, 414-562-5893

Type: magnet

Student ages 4+,-5th grade

Multi-unit; individually guided.

Multilingual Elementary Academy

2035 N 25th St, Milwaukee, WI 53205

D. Guzman-Estevez, 414-933-7500

Type: magnet

Student ages 4+,-5th grade

NOVA (1993)

3718 W Lancaster Ave, Milwaukee, WI 53205

Felita Daniels, Dir, 414-438-8320, FAX: 414-438-8325

Milwaukee County

Type: independent at-risk, non-profit

8 teachers, 70 students, mainly at-risk, ages 12-17, 7-12th grade

Residency required

Affiliation: NCSG

Governance by teachers, principal, democratic school meeting

Teacher qualifications: BA, desire to work with at-risk

School-to-work; competency-based; extensive business community involvement; multi-aged classes; urban location; interns accepted.

Roosevelt Middle School

800 W Walnut St, Milwaukee, WI 53205

Michael Hickey, 414-263-2555

Type: magnet

6-8th grade

Creative arts.

Shalom High School (1973)

1749 N 16th St, Milwaukee, WI 53205

Gwendolyn Spencer, Dir, 414-933-5019, FAX:-5433

Milwaukee County

Type: independent at-risk, non-profit

80 students, mainly at-risk, ages 14-19, 9-12th grade

No residency requirement

Affiliation: NCSC

Governance by teachers, principal, democratic school meeting, board

Teacher qualifications: BA

Competency-based; at-risk students catch up to age group; multi-aged classes; urban location; interns accepted.

Urban Day School (1967)

1441 N 24th St, Milwaukee, WI 53205

Bob Rauh, Principal, 414-937-8400, FAX: 414-937-8406

Type: independent, non-profit; scholarships, state choice

28 teachers, 620 students, ages 3-14, K-8th grade

Entrance requirements: no learning disabled; funding source; parent contract

Governance by a board of staff, parents, community volunteers

Teacher qualifications: degree, certification

Solid basic education for high school readiness; many staff are parents; financing includes state public funds for Choice School District; urban location; interns accepted.

Urban Waldorf Elementary

2023 N 25th St, Milwaukee, WI 53205

Dorothy St Charles, 414-933-4400

Type: magnet

Student ages 4+,-5th grade

Educating the Heart, Hands and Mind.

Elm Creative Arts

900 W Walnut, Milwaukee, WI 53205-1099

Darrel Jacobs, 608-562-1000 x148

Multicultural Community HS
1645 N 25th St, Milwaukee, WI 53205-1435
Carl Hedman
Type: independent

Franklin Elementary
2308 W Nash St, Milwaukee, WI 53206
James Henry, 414-873-0771
Type: magnet
K-5th grade
Multi-age; multi-unit.

Clement Ave Elementary
3666 S Clement Ave, Milwaukee, WI 53207
Janetta Trotman, 414-482-2720
Type: magnet
K-5th grade
Individualized; ungraded.

Montessori Institute of Milwaukee (1989)
3195 S Superior St #L 428, Milwaukee, WI 53207
Allyn S. Travis, Adm, 414-481-5050
Type: Montessori higher education, non-profit; tuition:
    $4,500/yr
Student adult ages
Entrance requirements: BA degree
Affiliation: AMI; accreditation: MACTE
Governance by administrator
Elementary teacher training; one year full-time course; along
    Lake Michigan.

Tippecanoe Elementary
357 E Howard Ave, Milwaukee, WI 53207
Patricia Holmes, 414-769-3220
Type: magnet
K-5th grade
Humanities.

Highland Community School
2004 W Highland Blvd, Milwaukee, WI 53208
Tim Souers, Principal, 414-342-1412
Type: Montessori; tuition: ability to pay
6 teachers, 75 students, ages 2.5-10, pre K-3rd grade
Enrollment restricted to immediate neighborhood; parent
    contract
Governance by parent cooperative
Teacher qualifications: Montessori background, community
    involvement
Serves 15 sq. block area; focuses on empowerment and liber-
    ation through loving, supportive, politically active staff,
    parents, students; no letter grades; multi-aged classes;
    extensive field trips; urban location; interns accepted.

Hi-Mount Boulevard
4921 W Garfield Ave, Milwaukee, WI 53208-1197
Spencer Korte, 608-449-3314

Milwaukee Montessori School
4610 W State St, Milwaukee, WI 53208-3198

Thurston Woods Campus Elementary
5966 N 35th St, Milwaukee, WI 53209
Joyce Taylor, 414-536-8664
Type: magnet
Student ages 4+,-3rd grade
Ungraded.

38th St Elementary
2623 N 38th St, Milwaukee, WI 53210
Donna Zoble, 414-449-9624
Type: magnet
Student ages 4+,-5th grade
Open education.

Sherman Elementary
5110 W Locust St, Milwaukee, WI 53210
Dolores K. Jackson, 414-449-0918

Type: magnet
K-6th grade
Multi-cultural arts.

Family Montessori School
5806 W Burleigh St, Milwaukee, WI 53210-1516

Dr Martin Luther King, Jr Elementary
3275 N 3rd St, Milwaukee, WI 53212
Josephine Mosely, 414-562-4174
Type: magnet
K-5th grade
African-American immersion.

Meir Elementary
1555 N Martin Luther King, Milwaukee, WI 53212
Albin Kacsmarek, 414-271-6840
Type: magnet
3-5th grade
Gifted and talented.

Rethinking Schools
(See Resource Appendix)

Fratney Street
3255 N Fratney St, Milwaukee, WI 53212-2297
Carol Schmuhl, 608-264-4840 x182

Granville Elementary
9520 W Allyn St, Milwaukee, WI 53215
Debrorah Bent, 414-355-1230
Type: magnet
K-5th grade
Multi-aged, multi-unit; IGE.

Greenfield Elementary
1711 S 35th St, Milwaukee, WI 53215
Debra Jupka A/P, 414-647-2767
Type: magnet
Student ages 3+,-5th grade
Montessori.

65th St Elementary
6600 W Melvina St, Milwaukee, WI 53216
Kay Mantilla, 414-464-5005
Type: magnet
K-5th grade
Comprehensive; multi-cultural.

Alternative School Program
c/o Nicolet School District
6701 N Jean Nicolet Rd, Glendale, WI 53217
Jane Joyce, At Risk Coord, 414-352-7110
Type: public at-risk
10-12th grade
Extra structure, support; individualized instruction, students
    set up academic plan; job skills, goals, survival skills.

New World Montessori School
217 W Dunwood Rd, Milwaukee, WI 53217-3108

Turning Point School
5460 N 64 St, Milwaukee, WI 53218
Ellen Smith
Type: independent

Lowell Elementary
4360 S 20th St, Milwaukee, WI 53221
Claudette St. Clair, 414-282-6560
Type: magnet
K-5th grade
High achievement.

Victory Elementary
2222 W Henry Ave, Milwaukee, WI 53221
Estell Sprewer, 414-282-9050
Type: magnet
K-5th grade
Multi-aged; multi unit; IGE; ungraded.

Thoreau Elementary School
7878 N 60th St, Milwaukee, WI 53223
Judith Rick, 414-354-3650
Type: magnet
K–6th grade
Multi-age; multi-unit; IGE

Emerson Elementary
9025 W Lawrence Ave, Milwaukee, WI 53225
Roberta Wilkerson, 414-464-9550
Type: magnet
K–5th grade
Ungraded.

Morse Middle School
4601 N 84th St, Milwaukee, WI 53225
Rogers Onick, 414-466-9920
Type: magnet
6–8th grade
Gifted and talented.

River Trail Elementary
12021 W Florist Ave, Milwaukee, WI 53225
Barbara Birks, 414-353-0370
Type: magnet
K–5th grade
Multi-unit.

Grand Ave Middle School
2430 W Wisconsin Ave, Milwaukee, WI 53233
Thomas McGinnity, 414-933-9900
Type: magnet
6–8th grade
Global education; multiple intelligences.

MacDowell Elementary
1706 W Highland Blvd, Milwaukee, WI 53233
John Schmuhl, 414-933-0088
Type: magnet
Student ages 3+,–5th grade
Montessori.

Milwaukee High School of the Arts
2300 W Highland Ave, Milwaukee, WI 53233
Jo Alice Bender, 414-933-1500
Type: magnet
9–12th grade

Scott Middle School
1017 N 12th St, Milwaukee, WI 53233
James Townes, 414-344-6200
Type: magnet
6–8th grade
Individualized.

Red Apple Elementary
914 St Patrick St, Racine, WI 53402
Sheryl Esch, 414-637-5635
Type: magnet
K–5th grade

Bull Fine Arts Elementary
815 DeKoven Ave, Racine, WI 53403
Frank Germinaro, 414-632-8931
Type: magnet
1–5th grade

Lighthouse Gifted & Talented Elementary
1722 W 6th, Racine, WI 53403
Steve Miley, 414-632-5147
Type: magnet
K–5th grade
Gifted/Talented.

Racine Montessori School (1963)
520 21st St / DeKoven Foundation, Racine, WI 53403
Rita C. Lewis, Adm, 414-637-7892

Non-profit; tuition: $1,544-2,780/yr
9 teachers, 2 assistants, 130 students, ages 3-12
Accreditation: AMS
Governance by board
Historic buildings in park-like setting on Lake Michigan; child-
care; urban location; interns accepted.

Walden III (1972)
1012 Center St, Racine, WI 53403
Charles Kent, Prin, 633-1321
Type: public choice
30 teachers, 405 students, ages 11–18, 6–12th grade
District residency required
Affiliation: CES
Governance by democratic school meeting
One of the oldest alt schools in WI; member CES since 1986;
oldest comprehensive Portfolio Evaluation Program in US;
no exceptional education labeling; multi-aged classes;
urban location; transportation; interns accepted.

Burdge Elementary
321 Olympian Blvd, Beloit, WI 53511
Barbara Hickman, 608-364-6055
Racine USD District
Type: magnet
K–6th grade
Expressive arts.

Morgan Elementary
Lee Lane, Beloit, WI 53511
Anthony Beardsley, 608-364-6090
Type: magnet
K–6th grade
Expressive arts.

Project Succeed
c/o Cambridge District
PO Box 27, Cambridge, WI 53523
Jim Kneece, Dir, Student Services, 608-423-3261
Type: public at-risk
K–12th grade
Tutorial resource centers in each school; HS students assist
elem students under supervision.

**Alternative Class Scheduling and Individualization of
Instruction**
c/o Clinton High School
PO Box 566, Clinton, WI 53525
Stephen Cass, Prin, 608-676-2223
Clinton Community School District
Type: public at-risk
9–12th grade
Involves alternative courses, individualization of instruction,
and working with Blackhawk Technical College.

Families in Schools at Home (FISH)
4639 Conestoga Trail, Cottage Grove, WI 53527

LIFE (Learning is ForEver)
c/o Deforest Middle School
500 S Cleveland St, DeForest, WI 53532
Barb Forrum, At Risk Facilitator, 608-846-6560
DeForest Area School District
Type: public at-risk
6–8th grade
Parent participation; develops communication between
school, home, and student.

Phoenix Project/Bridge Program
DeForest High School, PO Box 399, DeForest, WI 53532
Mary Ellen Rieland, Coord, 608-846-6636
DeForest Area School District
Type: public at-risk
9–12th grade
School-within-a-school; career planning; employability; work
experience.

Edgerton High School Alternative Program
200 Elm High Dr, Edgerton, WI 53534
Jeffrey Gibson, Prin, 608-884-9402
Edgerton School District
Type: public at-risk
9–12th grade
Technical ed, music, art, computer, work programs.

Extended Kindergarten
c/o Rockwell Elementary School
821 Monroe St, Fort Atkinson, WI 53538
Pauline Nikolay, Prin, 414-563-7818
Fort AtkinsonSchool District
Type: public at-risk
12 students
Extend, enhance social, emotional, and cognitive skills.

Student At-Risk/High Risk Resource Rooms
c/o Fort Atkinson School District
317 S High St, Fort Atkinson, WI 53538
Joseph M. Overturf, Dir, Special Ed, 414-563-7804
Type: public at-risk
16 teachers; 6–12th grade
Intervention strategy; resource rooms; eclectic approach.

GED Prep
c/o Juda School District, Juda, WI 53550
Don Budde, District Adm, 608-934-5251
Type: public at-risk
11–12th grade
Classes by Blackhawk Tech College.

Little Friends Montessori
6273 University Ave, Middleton, WI 53562

Children's Community School (1976)
211 Parkway, Mt Horeb, WI 53572
Pence Revington, 608-437-4121
Type: Montessori, non-profit; tuition: $80–420/mo
2 teachers, 10 assistants, 85 students, ages infant-6
Affiliations: WECA, 4-C's; accreditations: AMS, WI
Governance by board
Creative use of natural resources in Practical Life, geography;
   childcare; rural location; transportation; interns accepted.

PASS (Parkview Alternative School for Success)
c/o Parkview High School
106 W Church St, Orfordville, WI 53576
Greg Fahrman, Assistant Prin, 608-879-2994
Parkview School District
Type: public at-risk
7–12th grade
Attendance committment; student is responsible for being
   prepared for class, adhering to school policies and com-
   pleting all assignments.

Extended Kindergarten with Home Trainer Component
c/o Kegonsa Elementary School
PO Box 189, Stoughton, WI 53589
Anne Wheiland, Extended Kindergarten/Home Trainer, 608-
   873-2754
Stoughton Area School District
Type: public at-risk
Individually tailored, supplemental support; home trainers
   work with parents, students to reinforce school learning.

Parent Place
c/o Stoughton Area School District
PO Box 189, Stoughton, WI 53589
Ellen Leggett, Coord, 608-873-2660
Type: public at-risk
Weekly meetings for parents of students at-risk.

Stoughton High School
PO Box 189, Stoughton, WI 53589
Mark R. Felix, Dir, Vocational Programs, 608-873-2712
Stoughton Area School District
Type: public at-risk
Alternative Learning Program in Stoughton (ALPS): ages
   16–21, 11–12th grade, individualized; voc; HS/GED credit;
   Work Experience Career Exploration Program (WECEP):
   ages 14-15, 9–10th grade, Individual Education Plans;
   employability, on-the-job training; Adult Passport Program:
   ages 16-21, 11–12th grade, dropout prevention; career
   planning, education for employment, developing options
   for at-risk, severely handicapped, etc; Single Parent
   Program: ages 14-18, 9–12th grade, course tutoring, economic self-sufficiency, childcare.

Wisconsin Parents Association
PO Box 2502, Madison, WI 53701
Type: state home-based

Countryside Montessori
721 Northport Dr, Madison, WI 53704
Deborah Nicholson

HOME (1983)
c/o 5745 Bittersweet Pl, Madison, WI 53705
Alison McKee, 608-238-3302
Dane County
2 teachers, 2 students
Governance by parents
Inclusive.

Madison Central Montessori
4337 W Beltline Hwy, Madison, WI 53711

Wingra School (1972)
3200 Monroe St, Madison, WI 53711
Ann Jarvella Wilson, Dir, 608-238-2525
Type: independent, non-profit; tuition: $4,500, scholarships
18 teachers, 146 students, ages 4–14, K–8th grade
Entrance requirements: interviews, records
Affiliations: NCACS, Network of Progressive Schools
Governance by principal, board
Teacher qualifications: teacher training programs of several
   area colleges
Thematic; integrated; problem-solving; communication skills;
   independent thinking; encourages interest in local and
   world communities; no letter grades; multi-aged classes;
   extensive field trips; urban location; interns accepted.

Quest Learning Center, Inc (1991)
PO Box 9174, Madison, WI 53715
Donna R. Mahr, Dir, 608-255-1080
Dane County
Type: independent, non-profit; tuition: $25/day, scholarships
6 teachers, 12 students, ages 6–16, K–12th grade
Family participation required
Governance by parent cooperative, board, democratic school
   meeting
Mini-classes; activities; tutoring; equipment; individual learn-
   ing plans; extensive field trips; no letter grades; multi-aged
   classes; interns accepted.

Woodland Montessori School
1124 Colby St, Madison, WI 53715-2008

Montessori Children's House
5530 Medical Cir, Madison, WI 53719-1202

Juneau County Adolescent Needs (JCAN)
PO Box 564, Portage, WI 53901
Ed Hawkinson, Dir, Special Ed, 608-742-8811
Type: public at-risk
7–12th grade
Serves emotionally disturbed students through joint efforts
   of school districts and county social service agencies.

Beaver Dam Unified School District
705 McKinley St, Beaver Dam, WI 53916
Emmet Weber, Curr Manager, 414-887-7131
Type: public at-risk

4 programs: Content Area Study Help (CASH): 7–12th grade, tutorial, small group review of academics; Community Service: 12th grade, credit for volunteering; Pre-Employment Skills Training I and II: 11–12th grade, employability skills, worker maturity, credit for work.

JTPA Remediation/Work Study
c/o Montello High School
222 Forest Ln, Montello, WI 53949
Jane Kronschnabel, Teacher, 608-297-2126
Montello School District
Type: public at-risk
9–12th grade
Job skills, placement in work program.

The Bike Farm (1993)
2780 230th St, Cushing, WI 54006
Steve Clark, Adm, 715-648-5519, FAX: same
Polk County
Type: home-based, non-profit
2 teachers, 3–12 students, mainly at-risk, ages 13–18, 7–12th grade
Enrollment restricted to referrals from Social Services; residency required
Governance by democratic school meeting
Work on Ice Age Trail and other community service; organic sustainable living; student-led; no letter grades; non-compulsory class attendance; multi-aged classes; extensive field trips; rural location; transportation; interns accepted.

Alternative High School Program
c/o Hudson School District
416 St. Croix St, Hudson, WI 54016
Sandra Griswold, At Risk Resource Coord, 715-386-4257
Type: public at-risk
9–12th grade
Individualized; small classes.

Latchkey At Risk Program
c/o Hudson School District
416 St. Croix St, Hudson, WI 54016
Don Kadidlo, At Risk Resource Coord, 715-386-4257
Type: public at-risk
1–6th grade
Retired teachers offer tutorials; parent education workshops.

Tutorial Assistance Program (TAP)
c/o Hudson School District
416 St. Croix St, Hudson, WI 54016
Don Kadidlo, At Risk Resource Coord, 715-386-4257
Type: public at-risk
8–9th grade
Media center; learning styles; study skills; conflict resolution; promotes family wellness.

Hudson Children's House
605 North End Rd N, Hudson, WI 54016-9570
Rebecca Janke and Noreen Teachout
Type: Montessori

Marinette County Alternative High School
c/o Coleman High School
PO Box 259, Coleman, WI 54112
Ted Verges, Prin, 414-897-3822
Coleman School District
Type: public at-risk
Student ages 17+
For students pursuing HS equivalency diploma.

Pass/ Mini Pass Program
c/o CESA #8
223 W Park St, Gillett, WI 54124-0320
Frank Kazmierczak, WI PASS Coord, 414-855-2114
Type: public at-risk
6–12th grade
Semi-independent semester competency-based courses for supplemental instruction; self-paced

Nicolet Elementary School (1981)
109 E 8th St, Kau Kauna, WI 54130
John P. Moore, Prin, 414-766-6124
Non-profit
18 teachers, 210 students, ages 5–9, K–3rd grade
Residency required
Governance by teachers, principal
Kagan cooperative learning strategies; Marie Clay reading recovery; no letter grade; interns accepted.

Kaukauna Area School District Programs
101 Oak St, Kaukauna, WI 54130
Joseph Lucas, Dir, Exceptional Ed, Pupil Services, 414-766-6100
Type: public at-risk
School Within a School: 11–12th grade, community service, job exploration, good citizenship; individual strengths, learning styles, interests; Learning Strategies: 9–10th grade, small classes, individualized academic, personal attention.

Freedom Alternative Education Program
c/o Freedom Area School District
PO Box 1008, Freedom, WI 54131
David Moscinski, Dir, Pupil Services, 414-788-7940
Type: public at-risk
9–12th grade
Small classes.

Seymour High School Alternative Education Plan
c/o Seymour High School
10 Circle Dr, Seymour, WI 54165
John R. Peterson, Prin, 414-833-2306
Seymour Community School District
Type: public at-risk
10–12th grade
Personalized instruction; career ed; family living.

Alternative School (1990)
c/o Shawano High School
1050 S Union St, Shawano, WI 54166
Gary Lindeman, Dir, 715-526-2175
Shawano-Gresham School District
Type: public at-risk
10–12th grade
Three components: Alternative Diploma Program, Return Program and High School Credit Program.

Children's House of Manitowoc
4020 Memorial Dr; PO Box 506, Manitowoc, WI 54220
Pam Eggebrecht
Type: Montessori

Alpha Project
c/o Manitowoc School District
PO Box 1657, Manitowoc, WI 54221
Lawrence N. Jones, Dir, Secondary Schools, 414-683-4777
Type: public at-risk
10–12th grade
Remedial ed, interaction with community, employment experiences.

Aim Toward Awareness
c/o Two Rivers School District
1500–27th St, Two Rivers, WI 54241
Frank Helquist, Asst Supt, 414-793-4560
Type: public at-risk
11–12th grade
Public education, private sector partnership; helps students be knowledgeable, responsible, productive citizens.

Children's House (1985)
4020 Memorial Dr, Two Rivers, WI 54241-3221
Janice Schaden, 414-793-2629
Type: Montessori, non-profit; tuition: 1,600/2,900/yr
2 teachers, 30 students, ages 3–6
Affiliation: AMS

Governance by board
Multi-aged classes; rural location; interns accepted.

Aldo Leopold Alternative Program at Allouez School
(1976)
116 W Allouez, Green Bay, WI 54301
Dr Margaret A. Hutchison, Prin, 414-448-2140
Brown County
Type: public choice
23 teachers, 400 students, ages 5–14, K–8th grade
Residency required; accomodates special needs
Governance by principal, district BE, parents, teachers
Teacher qualifications: WI Certification, MA
Experiential; whole language; cooperative learning; inte-
    grated curriculum; peer teaching; environmental issues; no
    letter grades; non-compulsory class attendance; multi-
    aged classes; extensive field trips; urban location.

WOW: World-of-Work
c/o Ashwaubenon School District
1055 Griffiths Ln, Green Bay, WI 54304
Lawrence Heyerdahl, PhD, Dist Adm, 414-492-2902
Ashwaubenon School District
Type: public at-risk
9–12th grade
Vocational/academic competencies; successful world of work
    attitudes; max 28 hours on-the-job training/week.

Montessori Children's Village, Inc (1990)
214 Sherman St, Wausau, WI 54401
Patricia Filak, Adm, 715-842-9540
Tuition: $220/315/325/mo
2 teachers, 3 assistants, 57 students, ages infant–9
Affiliations: AMS, NAEYC, WECA
Governance by an administrator
100-year-old school building; childcare; urban location;
    interns accepted.

Montessori School of Wausau Inc. (1970)
1921 Wagner Street, Wausau, WI 54401
Ursula Velm, 715-842-7917
Non-profit; tuition: $135/320/mo.
3 teachers, 3 assistants, 80 students, ages 3–6
Affiliations: IMS, CMNE
Governance by board, administrator

Project Reprieve, c/o Wausau District
PO Box 359, Wausau, WI 54402
David Damgaard, Dir, Pupil Services, 715-848-2934
Type: public at-risk
11–12th grade
At Northcentral Technical College; community work, service.

Edgar Consortium
c/o Abbotsford Middle/Senior High School
307-4th Ave N, Abbotsford, WI 54405
Phillip L. Cassata, Prin, 715-233-2386
Abbotsford School District
Type: public at-risk
10–12th grade
For working students; GED/HS diploma; credit for supervised
    work program.

Alternative Education
120 S Dorr St, Antigo, WI 54409
Joseph Sveda, District Adm, 715-627-4355
Antigo Unified School District
Type: public at-risk
Student ages 17+, 12th grade
HS diploma from home school board or an HSED.

SWIS (School Within a School) and VOICE (Vocational Orientation In Career Education)
c/o Marshfield School District
1010 E Fourth St, Marshfield, WI 54449
Tom Kongslien, Dir, Student Services, 715-387-1101
Type: public at-risk

7–12th grade
Tutorial, counseling, career services; teacher-student-parent
    understanding.

Alternative School
c/o Merrill Junior High School
North Sales St, Merrill, WI 54452
Strand Wedul, Prin, 715-536-9593
Merrill Area School District
Type: public at-risk
8 students, 8–10th grade
For chronically disruptive: academics, job and social skills.

PACE (Providing Alternative Credit Education)
c/o Mosinee High School
1000 High St, Mosinee, WI 54455
Steve Smolek, Assistant Prin, 715-693-2550
Mosinee School District
Type: public at-risk
11–12th grade
Self-paced; Northcentral Tech College prep for GED, HSED;
    work-study; vocational guidance.

At-Risk Program
c/o Rosholt School District
PO Box 310, Rosholt, WI 54473
Ann Kislove, At-Risk Coord, 715-677-4570
Type: public at-risk
9–10th grade
Weekly meetings with counselor, coord; contracts.

Spencer Alternative Program
c/o Spencer High School
300 School St, Spencer, WI 54479
Dean E. Sanders, Prin, 715-659-4211
Spencer School District
Type: public at-risk
10–12th grade
Self-paced.

International Institute
(See Resource Appendix)

Montessori Children's Center
445 Chestnut St, Wisconsin Rapids, WI 54494-4803

Guided Education (Enterprise, Forward)
c/o Rhinelander High School
665 Coolidge Ave, Rhinelander, WI 54501
Bob LeFebvre, At Risk Teacher, 715-362-6955
Rhinelander School District
Type: public at-risk
9–10th grade
Beginner level course applies contemporary technology to
    communication, manufacturing, construction; R&D, pro-
    duction, and marketing of a product.

Montessori North
PO Box 24, Rhinelander, WI 54501

Montessori of Rhinelander (1977)
121 N Stevens / PO Box 24, Rhinelander, WI 54501
Diane Reupert, Adm, 369-4830
Tuition: $10-17.50/day
1 teacher, 2 assistants, 23 students, ages 3–6
Accreditation: NAEYC
Governance by administrator, parent board
Emphasis on local and global peacekeeping; childcare.

KARE: (Kids At-Risk in Education)
c/o Crandon Middle/Senior High School
100 N Prospect Ave, Crandon, WI 54520
James Engebretson, At Risk Coord, 715-478-3583
Crandon School District
Type: public at-risk
7–12th grade
Self-paced; contracts; independent study; small classes.

CASE II (Care About Students Education)
c/o Hurley School District
PO Box 157, Hurley, WI 54534
Roger Myren, District Adm, 715-561-4900
Type: public at-risk
7-12th grade
Self-esteem; basic skills; employability; job shadowing; work
    experience; wellness program.

Alternative Education
c/o Lakeland High School
8669 Old Highway 70 West, Minocqua, WI 54548
John Eckardt, Youth At Risk Coord, 715-356-5252
Lakeland School District
Type: public at-risk
2 teachers; 9, 12th grade
School within a school; 1-room schoolhouse model; block
    scheduling, reduced student movement; skill streaming;
    developmental guidance; vocational; competency-based.

Alternative Education Program
c/o Phillips High School, Phillips, WI 54555
Scott A. Johnson, Prin, 715-339-2141
Phillips District
Type: public at-risk
2 teachers; 5-9, 11-12th grade
Self-contained classroom; HSED or GED prep; at-risk/chronic
    offenders in off-campus behavior modification.

Alternative Education Program
c/o Prentice School District
PO Box 110, Prentice, WI 54556
David Christoffersen, Guidance Dir, 715-428-2811
Type: public at-risk
9-12th grade
Entrance requirements: successful completion of employa-
    bility skills program.
Includes specialized instruction, personal counseling, career
    planning assistance, and work study.

La Crosse Montessori Preschool (1966)
1818 Redfield St, La Crosse, WI 54601
Peggy Parry or Georgia Maas, Co-Dir, 782-3320
Non-profit; tuition: $85-140/wk
2 teachers, 1 assistant, 49 students, ages 3-6
Entrance requirements: age 2.5; toilet trained.
Accreditation: AMS
Governance by democratic school meeting
Childcare; urban location.

Beach Alternative School (1989)
c/o Lincoln Middle/Senior High School
PO Box 38, Alma Center, WI 54611
Craig S. McIntosh, Prin, 715-964-5311
Type: public at-risk
2 teachers, 1 assistant, 22 students, 11-12th grade
Serves five Trempealeau Valley school districts.

Daytime GED
c/o Black River Falls High School
1200 Pierce St, Black River Falls, WI 54615
Dennis Lee, Counselor, 715-284-4324
Black River Falls School District
Type: public at-risk
Student ages 17+
In cooperation with Western Wisconsin Tech College.

Basic Skills Program
c/o Onalaska School District
612 Main St, Onalaska, WI 54650
Pamela J. Pager, Dir, Special Ed/Pupil Services, 608-783-4610
Type: public at-risk
9-12th grade
Vocational counseling; goals developed by student, teacher,
    parent; works with Private Industry Council, Community
    Action Program.

LEARN
W 6442 Schilling Rd, Onalaska, WI 54650
Chris Mayou

Kickapoo High School
Rt 2, Box 63, Viola, WI 54664
Brian Schroeder, Prin, 608-627-1494
Kickapoo Area School District
Type: public at-risk
Portable Assisted Study Sequence (PASS): 6-12th grade, for
    credit-deficient students, materials from CESA 8; GED: 12th
    grade, contracts with Western Wisconsin Tech College.

Pleasant Ridge Waldorf School (1979)
321 E Decker St, Viroqua, WI 54665
Kate Walter, Development, 608-634-2746
Vernon County
Non-profit; tuition: 1,250-2,400/yr, scholarships
15 teachers, 97 students, ages 4.5-11, K-5th grade
Entrance requirement: mutual decision of parents and
    faculty
Affiliations: AWSNA, WI ANS
Governance by faculty
Teacher qualifications: at discretion of faculty
No letter grades; rural location.

CACTUS
c/o Eau Claire Area School District
500 Main St, Eau Claire, WI 54701
Perry Smith, Dir, Special Ed, 715-833-3478
Type: public at-risk
6-12th grade
Proactive attempt to facilitate change in thinking patterns of
    students with severe behavior problems.

Eau Claire County Off-Campus School
c/o Eau Claire Area School District
500 Main St, Eau Claire, WI 54701
Holly Hart, Director, 715-834-2488 or 834-8104
Type: public at-risk
Student ages 16-21, 11-12th grade
Counseling; human services, job placement agency referral;
    exploring postsecondary ed; childcare; transportation.

Children's House Montessori School
510 S Farwell St, Eau Claire, WI 54701-3723

Dunn County Alternative Program
c/o Boyceville High School
RR 2, Box 500, Boyceville, WI 54725
Steve Olson, Dir, Pupil Services, 715-643-4321
Boyceville CSD District
Type: public at-risk
Student ages 16-21, 9-12th grade
For credit/basic skills remediation; individual ed planning.

Chippewa County Alternate High School (1984)
1130 Miles St, Chippewa Falls, WI 54729
Jay Wagner, Prin, 715-723-5542, x294
Bloomer, Chippewa Falls, Cornell, New Auburn and Stanley-
    Boyd Districts
Type: public at-risk
10 teachers, 3 assistants; 9-12th grade
Structured and independent study courses.

Osseo-Fairchild School District
PO Box 130, Osseo, WI 54758
Rosemary Twesme, At Risk Coord, 715-597-3141
Type: public at-risk
9-12th grade
Basic Skills Program: operates school year, summer school,
    work experience; PASS (Portable Assisted Study Sequence):
    credits from self-directed semester courses.

Alternative Education
120 E Main St, Ashland, WI 54806
Tim Foley, Dir of Curr/Instruction, 715-682-7080

Ashland School District
Type: public at-risk
9–12th grade
Equal chance and new beginning for all through belonging
and acceptance; vocational direction; develop positive
social/emotional attitudes, behaviors.

Barron County Alternative High School
c/o Barron Area School District
100 W River Ave, Barron, WI 54812
Scott Pfefferle, Coord, 715-537-3261
Type: public at-risk/session
1 teacher, 1 assistant, 20 students, 9–12th grade
Self-paced; vocational; JTPA; Private Industry Council.

Alternative Education-or Homebound
c/o Bayfield High School
PO Box 5001, Bayfield, WI 54814
Robert H. Lind, Prin, 715-779-5666
Bayfield School District
Type: public at-risk
11–12th grade
Part-time or 100% at home; evening tutoring required.

BIG MAC
c/o Bruce School District
PO Box 308, Bruce, WI 54819
Lee L. Paul, District Adm, 715-868-2533
Type: public at-risk
9–12th grade
For positive vision of students' futures, realistic career plan.

Lac Court Oreilles
RR #2, Hayward, WI 54843
Don Wiesen, Exec Dir, 715-634-8924, FAX:-6058

Jobs Target Program
c/o Northwestern High School
PO Box 188, Maple, WI 54854
Mary Frostman, JTPA Coord, 715-363-2431
Maple School District
Type: public at-risk
5–12th grade
Tutoring/remediation; Pregnancy Prevention; career plan,
preemployment skills, work experience; parent
involvement.

JOVA (Job Opportunity and Vocational Awareness)
c/o Roosevelt Junior High School
318 E Brewster St, Appleton, WI 54911
Mary Wiegand, Program Coord, 414-832-1645
Appleton Area School District
Type: public at-risk
9th grade
Work experience, in class and on the work site.

Siekman Alternative School
c/o Appleton Area School District
120 E Harris St, Appleton, WI 54911
Kenneth Kilgore, At-Risk Coord, 414-832-6149
Appleton Area School District
Type: public at-risk/yr
18–21 students, 10–12th grade
Under contract with Fox Valley Tech College.

Unschooling Families
1908 N. Clark St, Appleton, WI 54911
414-735-9832
Type: home-based

Columbia, c/o Appleton Area District
120 E Harris St, Appleton, WI 54913
Bonnie L Mayer, Coord, 414-832-6160
Type: public at-risk

Student ages 16–21, 9–12th grade
Job specific skills; pre-employment, work maturity skills; work
experience sites.

Accent
c/o West High School
610 N Badger Ave, Appleton, WI 54914
Sharon Brooker, Program Coord, 414-832-6219
Appleton Area School District
Type: public at-risk
10–12th grade
Traditional classroom and individualized opportunities; vocational component.

Montessori Adventure Schools, Inc
900 N Mason St, Appleton, WI 54914-3669

Patriot PLUS
c/o East High School
2121 Emmers Dr, Appleton, WI 54915
LuAnn Coenen, Program Coord, 414-832-6200
Appleton Area School District
Type: public at-risk
10–12th grade
Individualized opportunities; vocational component.

Alternative Education Program
c/o Clintonville Senior High School
255 N Main St, Clintonville, WI 54929
Lynn Schevers, Assistant Prin, 715-823-2174
Clintonville School District
Type: public at-risk
1 teacher, 15 students, 11–12th grade
Columbia Program: work skills, social issues for teens.

ALP (Alternative Learning Program)
c/o Lowell P. Goodrich High School
382 Linden St, Fond du Lac, WI 54935
Jon W. Kaiser, Prin, 414-929-2707
Fond du Lac School District
Type: public at-risk
10–12th grade
A controlled learning environment.

Learning Center c/o Menasha High School
420 7th St, Menasha, WI 54952
Terrence Shwonek, Coord, 414-751-4766
Menasha School District
Type: public at-risk
9–12th grade
Seminars, work experience, community service, career explo-
ration, tutorial assistance based on Copernican Plan and
Portable Assisted Study Sequence curriculum.

Neenah's Employment & Academic Training Program
(NEAT)
c/o Neenah High School
1275 Tullar Rd, Neenah, WI 54956
Larry Lewis, Prin, 414-751-6905
Neenah Joint School District
Type: public at-risk
10–12th grade
Personal success skills; community work experience.

Winneconne High School
400 N 9th Ave, Winneconne, WI 54986
Stephanie Forbes, At Risk Counselor, 414-582-4324
Winneconne Community School District
Type: public at-risk
9–12th grade
Personal Growth and Development: appropriate courses,
close monitoring, support, individual attention through
small groups, private conferences, developmental at-risk
curriculum; Peer Helper Program: peer counseling training.

Wyoming

High School III
2201 Morrie Ave, Cheyenne, WY 82001
Durla M. Cockley, Counselor, 307-771-2500, FAX:-2383
Laramie County
Type: public choice
17 teachers, 200 students, mainly at-risk, ages 14–21, 9–12th
    grade
Governance by principal
Teacher qualifications: WY certification
Outcome-based; technology-based vocational courses; com-
    munity-oriented; work programs, explorations; multi-aged
    classes; extensive field trips; outreach programs with
    college and adult learning center; interns accepted.

Montessori School of Cheyenne
3619 Evans Ave, Cheyenne, WY 82001-1427

The Village School
5307 Hynds Blvd, Cheyenne, WY 82009-4053
Type: Montessori

Whiting Alternative High School
509 S 9th St, Laramie, WY 82070
Judy Bruce

Riverton Alternative High
2002 W Sunset Dr, Riverton, WY 82501
Mike Kouris, Dir

Wyoming Unschoolers (1993)
23 Dance Hall Rd, Lander, WY 82520
Cynthia W. Howdyshell, 307-332-6941
Fremont County
Type: state home-based
Secular; support; open to all; connections to isolated
    homeschoolers.

Roosevelt Center
140 East K, Casper, WY 82601
Dr Carl Madzey

Roosevelt High School (1977)
140 E K St, Casper, WY 82601
Dr Carl Madzey, 307-577-4630, FAX: 307-577-4633
Natrona County
Type: public at-risk
15 teachers, 170 students, ages 14–21, 9–12th grade
Entrance requirements: referral, residency
Governance by teachers, principal, parent cooperative
Teacher qualifications: Behavioral MS

Whole-school activities; projects; multi-aged classes; exten-
    sive field trips; rural location; transportation; interns
    accepted.

Montessori School of Casper
224–226 S David; PO Box 684, Casper, WY 82602

Montessori Family Development Center
PO Box 684, Casper, WY 82602-0684

Alternative/Transitional Center
601 Pohan, Gillette, WY 82716-4160
Lee Hellevang, Prin

High School IV
411 Main PO Box 830, Sundance, WY 82729

Rock Springs Alternative High School (1978)
1600 College Dr; PO Box 1089, Rock Springs, WY 82901
Don White, Director, 307-382-4851
Sweetwater County
Type: public at-risk
7 teachers, 70 students, mainly at-risk, ages 16–21, 9–12th
    grade
Entrance requirements: completion of 8th grade, application,
    interview, references, screening, residency
Governance by teachers and principal
Teacher qualifications: state certification
Self-paced and directed; contracts; no letter grades; multi-
    aged classes; extensive field trips; rural location; interns
    accepted.

Rock Springs Alternative High
    Western Wyoming College Campus
Rock Springs, WY 82901
Robert L. Plant, Prin

Western Wyoming High School (1988)
Box 568, Jackson, WY 83001
Terry Roice, Prin/Tch, 307-733-9116, FAX: 307-733-6443
Teton County
Type: public choice
4 teachers, 23 students, 9–12th grade
Affiliation: Teton SD #1
Governance by advisory board; faculty and student reps
Teacher qualifications: WY certification
Outcome-based; performance assessment; portfolios; senior
    project; community service; expeditionary, experiential
    learning; flexible schedule; multi-aged classes; interns
    accepted.

CANADIAN ALTERNATIVES

Alternative High School
5003-20 St SW, Calgary, AB, Canada
Jim Hoeppner, Prin, 403-287-9500, FAX:-9500
Type: public at-risk
11 teachers, 120 students, 10-12th grade
Entrance requirements: no major LD; probation period.
Weekly democratic meeting
Flexible; first name basis with staff; "beyond the walls" com-
munity use; multi-aged classes; extensive field trips; urban
location; interns accepted.

Medicine Hat Montessori Society
410 6th St NE, Medicine Hat, AB, Canada T1A 5P1
Pres/Dir

Calgary Waldorf School
1915 36th Ave SW, Calgary, AB, Canada T2T 2G6
Faculty Chair

Calgary Alternative High School (1974)
5003 20th St SW, Calgary, AB, Canada T2T 5A5
Jim Hoeppner, Prin, 403-287-9500, FAX: 287-9485
Type: public choice; tuition: $140/mo
11 teachers, 120 students, ages 15-19, 10-12th grade
Entrance requirements: interview, 6-week probation, residency
Governance by democratic school meeting
Informal community atmosphere; extensive field trips; multi-
aged classes; interns accepted.

Bishop Carroll High School (1971)
4624 Richard Rd SW, Calgary, AB, Canada T3E 6L1
Gerald Fijal, Vice Prin, 403-249-6601, FAX: 403-240-1141
Type: public choice
52 teachers, 57 assistants, 1,180 students, ages 15-19
Entrance requires grade 9 completion
Affiliation: CES
Governance by principal
Teacher qualifications: Alberta certification
Completely individualized, self-directed study; holistic
teacher-advisory program; flexible class times; urban
location.

Bilingual Montessori Learning Centre
9003 168th St, Edmonton, AB, Canada T5R 2V7

Homeschoolers Association of Alberta
8754 Conners Rd, Edmonton, AB, Canada T6C 4B6
403-988-4652
Type: state home-based

**Alberta Home Education Association c/o Aine
Stasiewich**
Box 3451, Leduc, AB, Canada T9E 6M2
Type: state home-based

The Pembina Institute
(See Resource Appendix)

Plenty Valley Montessori School
315 Aqueduct Rd, Diamond Creek, Victoria, BC, Canada
Ms J P Puckey

Vancouver Public Schools
6330 Sophia St, Vancouver, BC, Canada U5W 2W6
Debbie Adams
Type: Montessori

Kelowna Waldorf School
Box 93, 429 Collett Rd, Okanaga Mission, BC, Canada V0H 1S0
Faculty Chair

Home Learning Resource Centre
Box 61, Quathiaski, BC, Canada V0P 1N0

Gabriola Homeschoolers
PO Box 223, Gabriola Island, BC, Canada V0R 1X0

Nelson Waldorf School (1983)
Box 165, 3468 Ymir Rd, Nelson, BC, Canada V1L 5P5
Deborah Kranenburg, Adm, 604-352-6919
Non-profit; tuition: $2,960/yr, scholarships
13 teachers, 135 students, ages 4-15, K-8th grade
Governance by college of teachers and faculty
Teacher qualifications: Waldorf training or experience, college
teaching certificate
35 mountainside acres; hiking, cross-country ski; French;
rural location; transportation.

Canadian Home Educators Association of BC
4684 Darin Ct, Kelowna, BC, Canada V1W 2B3
604-764-7462
Type: state home-based

Schoool District 27 Montessori Program
1894 9th Ave, Prince George, BC, Canada V2M 1L7
Don Reimer

High Glen Elementary School
290 Voyageur Dr, Prince George, BC, Canada V2M 4P2
Bonnie Addison
Type: Montessori

Montessori Elementary School Society
RR2 Site 23 Comp 32, Prince George, BC, Canada V2N2H9
Cynthia Christensen

East Canyon Springs Montessori School
2910 Walton Ave, Coquitlam, BC, Canada V3B 2W3
Halina Pisarski

Western Montessori
16-800 Egmont Ave, Coquitlam, BC, Canada V3J 4J8
Carol Scarratt

Strawberry Hill Annex
12028 75th Ave, Surrey, BC, Canada V3W 2S5
Type: Montessori

Boundary Bay Montessori House
PO Box 237, Delta, BC, Canada V4K 3N7
Montessori in Delta Society

Wondertree Educational Society
PO Box 38083, Vancouver, BC, Canada V52 4L9
604-739-5943, FAX: 604-739-6903

Wondertree Education Society
1940 Napier St, Vancouver, BC, Canada V5L 2N5
Karen Martin
Type: independent

Community Association of Montessori Parents
1461 E 19th Ave, Vancouver, BC, Canada V5N 2H9
Fran Tanner

Typee Elementary Montessori Alternative
3525 Dumfries St, Vancouver, BC, Canada V5N 3S5

Little Learners Preschool
2175 W 14th Ave, Vancouver, BC, Canada V6K 2V8
Rita deGraaf
Type: Montessori

Greater Vancouver Home Learners Support Group
Box 39009 Pt Grey RPO, Vancouver, BC, Canada V6R 4P1
Diana Sandberg, 604-228-1939, 298-6710

University Colleges
Head Office: 548 Beatty St, Vancouver, BC, Canada V6V2L3
604-685-7095
Type: Montessori higher education
Accreditations: MACTE, IMI
International consortium of institutions and programs;
    awards Montessori teaching degrees; correspondence
    courses.

Vancouver Waldorf School
2725 St Christopher's Rd, N Vancouver, BC, Canada V7K 2B6
Colin Price

Windsor House
714 Westmorland Crescent, North Vancouver, BC, Canada V7P
    2G7
Helen Hughs, 604-985-7315
Type: public/independent choice
3 teachers, 1 assistant, 80 students, ages 5-18
Entrance requirements: waiting list
Governance by democratic school meeting
Teacher qualifications: BC Ministry certification
Strong parent involvement; bicameral system for rule-
    making; community-oriented; public choice school is age
    5-12, 56 students; also has independent high school with
    25 students; no letter grades; non-compulsory class atten-
    dance; multi-aged classes; extensive field trips; urban loca-
    tion; interns accepted.

Education Advisory
2267 Kings Ave, W Vancouver, BC, Canada V7V 2C1
Type: home-based

Montessori Centre of Victoria
1530 Lionel St, Victoria, BC, Canada V8R 2X8
Karen Colussi

Sundance Elementary
1625 Bank St, Victoria, BC, Canada V8R 4V5
Type: public choice

IAPM
301-667 Head St, Victoria, BC, Canada V9A 5S9
Angela Martin, Pres
Type: Montessori

Maria Montessori Academy
637 Head St, Victoria, BC, Canada V9A 5S9
Milo Coldren

Cowichan Valley Christian Homelearners Support Group
1050 Marchmont Rd, Duncan, BC, Canada V9L 2M7

Cowichan Valley Trade School
81 Trunk Rd, Duncan, BC, Canada V9L 2N7
Joanne Pastor, Coord, 604-748-6255, FAX:-4997
Type: independent
4 teachers, 45 students, ages 20+
Affiliations: PCTA, Chamber of Commerce
Teacher qualifications: degree from recognized institute and
    6 mo experience
Job entry/re-entry; project-based training; no letter grades;
    multi-aged classes; urban location.

The Cowichan Valley Open
c/o SD #65, 2557 Beverly St, Duncan, BC, Canada V9L 2X3

Cowichan Valley Alternate
1843 Tzhouhalem Rd, RR #5, Duncan, BC, Canada V9L 4T6
G. Harvey, Principal
15-18 students, ages 13-19
Voc, emphasis on Cowichan Valley logging industry; monthly
    allowance based on academic/work performance.

Consulting in Free Range Learning and Deschooling
    (1987)
RR 7, Duncan, BC, Canada V9L 4W4
Juanita Haddad, 601-746-5129
Critical consciousness; reclaim parental responsibility, trust;
    heal from forced separation; rural location.

Sunrise Waldorf School (1979)
4344 Peters Rd, RR #7, Duncan, BC, Canada V9L 4W4
Lynda Curry, Adm, 604-743-7253
Non-profit; tuition: $250-300/mo, scholarships
132 students, ages 3.5-13, pre K-8th grade
Residency required
Governance by teacher/parent board
Teacher qualifications: BC certification, Waldorf training
Language; orchestra; PE; Bothmar; rural location.

Charles Hoey VC School
756 Castle Place, Duncan, BC, Canada V9L 4Y3
Students mainly developmentally disabled, ages 5-19
Self-directed.

Kootenay Home Educators (1989)
PO Box 814, Nelson, BC, Canada VIL 6A5
Sarah Sherk, 604-352-9496, FAX: 604-352-3400
Student all ages
Affiliation: Canadian HEA
Unstructured curriculum; art; skating; foreign languages.

Personal Power Press International, Inc
(See Resource Appendix)

Maxwell International Baha'i School
Bag 1000, 2371 E Shawnigan Lake Rd, Shawnigan Lake, BC,
    Canada VOR 2WO
multi-cultural
Whole-person approach.

Manitoba Education and Training
Office: 507-1181 Portage Ave, MB, Canada
Brian Hanson, Asst Dir, 204-948-2154, FAX: same
Type: public choice
Group of 9 secondary, vocational/technical, cooperative, and
    adult education schools.

Manitoba Association for Schooling at Home
89 Edkar Cres, Winnipeg, MB, Canada R2G 3H8
Type: state home-based

Manitoba Association for Schooling at Home (1982)
98 Baltimore Ave, Manitoba, MB, Canada R3L 1H1
Keith Michaelson, Pres
Winnipeg County
Type: state home-based
Non-violence; positive socialization.

New Brunswick Association of Christian Homeschoolers
RR 1 Site 11 Box 1, Hillsborough, NB, Canada EOA 1XO
506-734-2863
Type: state home-based

Francombe Place Research Associates
PO Box 2000 RR 1, Westfield, NB, Canada EOG 350

Schole (1985)
Box 10 RR #1, Margaree Valley, NS, Canada
Donald Knight, 902-248-0601
Type: Independent, home-based, boarding; cost: C$12,000/yr,
    scholarships

2-3 teachers, 4-6 students, ages 6-16, 1-12th grade
Student letter required
Governance by board
Wilderness setting; extensive travel, eg, to Latin America,
   1994-95 to Europe; no letter grade; interns accepted.

Nova Scotia Homeschool Support Group
c/o Laura Uhlman
RR 1, Pleasantville, NS, Canada B0R 1C0

Primavera Montessori School
5303 Tobin St, Halifax, NS, Canada B3H 1S3

Indian Way School
Box 732, Kahnawake Quebec, ON, Canada J0L 1B0
Dianne Delaronde, 514-632-3258
Type: independent

Alexander Montessori School
188 Billings Ave, Ottawa, ON, Canada K1H 5K9

Quest, The Home Educators' Journal
(See Resource Appendix)

Ottawa Waldorf School
10 Coral Ave, Nepean, ON, Canada K2E 5Z6
Paul Power

Canadian Montessori Academy
2 Peter St, Nepean, ON, Canada K2G 1K2
Sherie De Mel

Catholic Homeschoolers Association
(See Resource Appendix)

Kanata March Montessori School
355 Michael Cowpland Dr, Kanata, ON, Canada K2M 2C5
Erin Gailor, Principal

Rideau Valley Home Educators Association
Box 313 North Gorler, Ottawa, ON, Canada K0A 2T0
Ellen Hackett, 613-228-8145

Pinewood Alternative School (1986)
RR 3, Millbrook, ON, Canada L0A 1C0
Melisande Neal, Prin, 705-932-3129
Peterborough County
Type: home-based, non-profit
Student ages 6-16
Affiliations: Canadian Alliance of Homeschoolers, FTP
Rural location.

Halton Waldorf School
83 Campbellville Rd E, Campbellville, ON, Canada L0P 1B0
Helmut Krause

Orilla Homeschoolers Support Group
45 Albert St N, Orilla, ON, Canada L3V 5K3
M. Black, 705-326-5260

Pickering College (1842)
16945 Bayview Ave, Newmarket, ON, Canada L3Y 4X2
J. F. Lockyer, Dir of Devp, 416-895-1700, Fax: 905-895-9076
Type: Quaker
22 teachers, 200 students, ages 9-19, 4-13th grade
Governance by board
University preparatory; suburban location; interns accepted

Rudolf Steiner Centre
9100 Bathurst St #4, Thornhill, ON, Canada L4J 8C7
Diana Hughes
Type: Waldorf

Toronto Waldorf School (1968)
9100 Bathurst St #1, Thornhill, ON, Canada L4J 8C7
Brenda Kotras, Registrar, 905-881-1611, FAX: 881-6710

Non-profit; tuition: $6,815/yr
35 teachers, 370 students, ages 3-18, pre K-12th grade
Entrance requirements: interview
Governance by democratic school meeting
Teacher qualifications: Waldorf training
Two languages; suburban location.

Sheridan College Montessori
1430 Trafalgar Rd, Oakville, ON, Canada L6H 2L1
Vi Matheson

Dearcroft Montessori School
1167 Lakeshore Rd E, Oakville, ON, Canada L6J 1L3
Gordon Phippen

MUDPUDL
c/o 25 Magill St, Hamilton, ON, Canada L8R 2Y4
Lisa Weintraub, 416-577-9491
Type: home-based, non-profit; cost: max $18/wk
1 teacher, max 15 students, ages 5-12, K-6th grade
Governance by parent cooperative
Traditional curricula and student-directed environment;
   based on John Holt's "unschooling"; non-compulsory
   attendance; non-sectarian; urban location.

Beaches Alternative School at Kimberley PS
50 Swanick Ave, Toronto, ON, Canada M4E 1Z5
416-393-1451
Type: public choice
Pre K-6th grade
Field trips; individualized.

SOLE c/o Greenwood Secondary School
24 Mountjoy Ave, Toronto, ON, Canada M4J 1J6
416-393-0756
Type: public at-risk
Max 100 students, ages 16+, 9-OAC
Independent study.

Subway Academy One
c/o Eastern High School of Commerce
16 Phin Ave, Toronto, ON, Canada M4J 3T2
416-393-9466
Type: public at-risk
Max 70 students, ages 16+, 9-OAC
Independent study.

Quest Alternative Senior School at Withrow PS
25 Bain Ave, Toronto, ON, Canada M4K 1E5
416-393-9430
Type: public choice
7-8th grade
Interview required.
Individualized math, science; experiential; French exchange;
   extensive computer ed; 3 one-week field trips.

Our Schools Our Selves
(See Resource Appendix)

First Nations School of Toronto at Dundas PS
935 Dundas St E, Toronto, ON, Canada M4M 1R4
416-393-0555
Type: public choice
Pre K-8th grade
Governance by executive committee, parents, community
   support representatives
Instruction in Ojibwe and English; curriculum centered
   around four seasons; stress on spiritual and cultural heritage of Native Way of life; day care.

The Student School
c/o Eastdale C.I.
701 Gerrard St E, Toronto, ON, Canada M4M 1Y4
416-393-9639
Type: public at-risk

max 120 students, ages 16+, 11-OAC
Interview required.
Small classes; active student involvement in all decision-making.

Spectrum Alternative Senior School at Eglinton PS
223 Eglinton Ave E, Toronto, ON, Canada M4P 1L1
416-393-9311
Type: public choice
7-8th grade
Small classes; individualized goal-setting and evaluation; field trips; community-based projects; intensive research in areas of interest.

The Schoolhouse (1971)
243 St Clair Ave W, Toronto, ON, Canada M4V 1R3
Laura Schein, Prin, 416-920-0972
Type: independent, non-profit; tuition: $6,300/yr
3 teachers, 4 assistants, 50 students, ages 4-12, pre K-6th grade
Entrance requirements: interview
Governance by teachers and principal
Teacher qualifications: we train asst staff w/out certification
No letter grades; multi-aged classes; urban location; interns accepted.

CONTACT
410 Sherbourne St, Toronto, ON, Canada M4X 1K2
416-393-1455,-1457
Type: public at-risk
145 students, age 18 (avg), 9-12th grade
Community liaison; student-run nutrition program.

Inglenook School
19 Sackville St, Toronto, ON, Canada M5A 3E1
416-393-0560
Type: public choice
max 120 students, 10-OAC
Advanced level courses only; emphasis on community; parent involvement; outreach program 1 day/wk required.

SEED (1970)
22 College St Suite 500, Toronto, ON, Canada M5G 1K3
416-393-0564
Type: public choice
max 135 students, 10-OAC
Interview by committee of staff and students required.
Individualized; seminars; extensive resources and visiting staff from community.

Alternative Primary School at North Preparatory PS
1100 Spadina Ave, Toronto, ON, Canada M5N 2M6
416-393-9199
Type: public choice
Pre K-6th grade
Governance by parent cooperative, board, teachers, principal
Field trips; group projects; multi-age activities; day care.

Alan Howard Waldorf School (1987)
228 St George St, Toronto, ON, Canada M5R 2N9
Barbara Ackerman, Adm, 416-975-1349
Non-profit; tuition: variable, scholarships
15 teachers, 130 students, ages 3-12, nursery-8th grade
Entrance requirements: interview
Affiliation: AWSNA
Governance by faculty and board
Teacher qualifications: Waldorf certification
Urban location; interns accepted.

Green Teacher
(See Resource Appendix)

Subway Academy Two
304 Brunswick Ave, Toronto, ON, Canada M5S 2M7
416-393-1445

Type: public at-risk
max 75 students, 9-OAC
Credit earned on-site, at other Toronto schools, or through accredited community resources, eg, Conservatory of Music.

West End Alternative
70 D'Arcy St, Toronto, ON, Canada M5T 1K1
416-393-0660
Type: public at-risk
max 120 students, 9-12th grade
Individualized; work-study.

Horizon Alternative Senior School at Kensington PS
401 College St, Toronto, ON, Canada M5T 1S9
416-393-1298
Type: public choice
7-8th grade
Flexible grouping; individualized goal-setting and evaluation; field trips; integrated and term projects; extensive CAI; non-competitive PE.

Oasis Alternative
707 Dundas St W, Rm 3, Toronto, ON, Canada M5T 2W6
416-393-9830
Type: public at-risk
Max 75 students, 9-12th grade
Independent and work-study; Alexandra Park Outreach for adults.

Downtown Alternative Alpha School at Brant St School
20 Brant St, Toronto, ON, Canada M5V 2M1
416-393-1880,-1882
Type: public choice
Pre K-8th grade
Multi-age grouping; daily school meeting; problem solving; day care; families volunteer at least half-day/week, serve on committee; whole language; team-learning; hands-on math, science; peacemaking.

Reading Circles
c/o The Second Floor Community Library, 61 Humewood Dr, Toronto, ON, Canada M6C 2W3
Edmund P. Fowler, Coordinator, 416-651-9772
Type: independent; tuition: $50 for 5 sessions, scholarships
1 teacher, 10 students, adult ages
Small group discussion; no letter grades; non-compulsory class attendance; multi-aged classes; urban location.

Hawthorne II Bilingual School
50 Essex St, Toronto, ON, Canada M6G 1T4
416-393-0727
Type: public choice
Pre K-6th grade
Instruction in English and French; student-centered; experiential; field trips; extensive use of community resources; non-competitive PE; day care.

Delta Senior Alternative School at Montrose PS
301 Montrose Ave, Toronto, ON, Canada M6G 3G9
416-393-9730
Type: public choice
7-8th grade
Contracts; voluntary service; community; enriched lunchtime; extracurriculars.

Indoor Park (1985)
c/o 242 Havelock St, Toronto, ON, Canada M6H 3B9
Jutta Mason, 416-533-0153
Inclusive meeting place structured around food, free play, swapping, gardening, gossip.

City School
315 Osler St, Toronto, ON, Canada M6N 2Z4
416-393-1470
Type: public choice

max 113 students, 10-OAC
Interview required.
Consortiums with other alternative schools; interdisciplinary
   courses.

High Park Alternative School at Annette St PS
265 Annette St, Toronto, ON, Canada M6P 1R3
416-393-9050
Type: public choice
Pre K-6th grade
Governance by parent cooperative
Self-paced; activity-centered; multi-aged grouping; non-
   competitive evaluations.

Mountview Alternative School at Keele St PS
99 Mountview Ave, Toronto, ON, Canada M6P 2L5
416-393-9037
Type: public choice
Pre K-6th grade
Groupings based on needs, skills, interests; team teaching;
   themes; school paper; newsletter; field trips; day care.

Foundation for Montessori Education
3 Riverview Gardens, Toronto, ON, Canada M6S 4E4

Canadian Association of Montessori Teachers
#818-6 Humberline Dr, Etobicoke, ON, Canada M9W 6X8
Tracy Gilmour

The Rural Learning Association
PO Box 1588, Guelph, ON, Canada N1H 6R7

Montessori School of Cambridge
Box 56, Cambridge, ON, Canada N1R 5S9
Marilyn Herrriot

London Waldorf School
1697 Trafalgar Sq, London, ON, Canada N5W 1X2
Merwin Lewis

Gibbons Park Montessori School
29 Victoria St, London, ON, Canada N6A 2B1
Maia Burghardt

Lakeview Montessori School
13803 Riverside Dr E, St Clair Beach, ON, Canada N8N 1B5

Canadian Alliance of Home Schoolers (1979)
(See Resource Appendix)

Oneida Learning Center
RR 2, Southwold, ON, Canada N0L 2G0
Bruce Elijah, 519-652-6367, FAX: 519-652-9603
Type: independent
4 teachers, 38 students, ages pre K-14
Total immersion Oneida; oral tradition; agriculture; field expe-
   riences; rural location.

Institute for Bioregional Studies (1982)
PO Box 126, Charlottetown, PEI, Canada C1A 4P3
Phil Ferraro, Dir, 902-892-9578
Queens County
Type: higher education, boarding
1-6 teachers, 11 students, ages 17+
Application required
Affiliation: York University
Governance by faculty, student reps, board
Teacher qualifications: MA, licensed
Integrated resource management training; summer camp;
   apprenticeships; community resources include organic
   farms, eco land trust, Fundy Folk Society; interns accepted.

Immanuel Christian School
PO Box 1991, Charlottetown, PEI, Canada C1A 7N7
Type: independent

Grace Christian School
50 Kirkdale Rd, West Royalty, PEI, Canada C1E 1N6
Type: independent

Les Ecoles Montessori
1357 Van Horne, Montreal, PQ, Canada H2V 1K7
Ann Lendman

Montreal Homeschoolers' Support Group
5241 Jacques Grenier, Montreal, PQ, Canada H3W 2G8
514-481-8435

L'Ecole Rudolf Steiner de Montreal
8205 Rue Mackle, Cote St-Luc, PQ, Canada H4W 1B1
Sasha Manacas
Type: Waldorf

Montreal Home Schoolers (1989)
730 Pine Beach Blvd, Dorval, PQ, Canada H9P 2L5
Sheryl Farrell, 514-636-8534

Quebec Homeschool Association (1983)
(See Resource Appendix)

Survival School
Kahnawake, PQ, Canada J0L 1B0
Type: independent

Système Montessori Chez Denyse (1989)
548 Village, Morin Heights, PQ, Canada J0R 1H0
Denyse Richard, Dir, 514-226-8369
Tuition: variable
1 teacher, 2 assistants, 25 students, ages 3-6
Entrance requirement: toilet trained
Affiliation: AMI
Governance by an administrator
Situated in the Laurentian Mountains near ski resort areas;
   150 year-old building; nature study; geography; bilingual
   program; childcare; rural location; interns accepted.

Au Grand Bois (1980)
RR 1, Ladysmith, PQ, Canada J0X 2A0
A & L Prost, Co-Dirs, 819-647-3522
Type: independent, boarding, non-profit; scholarships
20 teachers, 50 students, ages 8-16
Governance by staff, co-directors, much input from campers.
Summer program; vegetarian, organic gardens; 565-acre
   semi-wilderness; non-competitive; campers choose activi-
   ties; promotes understanding and respect for self, others,
   natural environment; rural location.

Allegro Montessori School
2606 Broadway Ave, Saskatoon, SK, Canada 57J 026
Ursula Hodgson, Adm Dir

Community Folk Schools of Saskatchewan
Box 22114, Regina, SK, Canada S4S 7G7
Type: independent

Saskatoon Montessori School (1979)
432 10th St E, Saskatoon, SK, Canada S7N 0C9
Patricia Janetzki, 306-244-1027
Non-profit; tuition: $1850/2930
1 teacher, 2 assistants, 34 students, ages 3-6
Children must be toilet trained
Affiliations: NAMTA, CAMT
Governance by an administrator, board of trustees
Suburban location.

Montessori School of Regina
2935 Regina Ave, Regina, SK, Canada SHS 0G7
Maggie Volke

INTERNATIONAL ALTERNATIVES

Escuela Del Siglo Nuevo (1987)
Olleros 3855, Buenos Aires, Argentina 1427
Gabriella Roncoroni de Christeller, 553-4872,-9689, FAX:
5418145264
Also parent and teacher program.

CONNECT, The Newsletter of Youth Participation in Education (1979)
12 Brooke St, Northcote, Victoria, Australia 3070
Roger Holdsworth, 03 489-9052
Type: resource; cost: $10/yr (6 issues)

Schulproject Wienerwald (1988)
Nimmersdorf 27, 3041 Asperhofen, NO, Austria
Michael Pichler, 0277218444
Type: home-based
2 teachers, 19 students, ages 6-10
Governance by parent cooperative
Teacher qualifications: university study, Montessori
Student-centered, directed, and paced; rural location.

Colegio Bilingue "Jorge Emilio Gutierez"
Apdo Aereo 101634, Bogota, DE, Columbia SA
Alejandro Acero, 011571-2150051
Type: independent, boarding
60+ students, partly international, indigenous, K-12th grade
Summerhill philosophy; outdoor classes on mountainside;
exchange program.

La Casa de los Ninos Montessori
Apartado 1108-1250, Escazu, Costa Rica
Alexandra Franco de Olher

Global Personal Teachers' Transformation (1993)
Myslfkova 7, Prague 1, Czech Republic 100 00
Dr Miluse Kubfekova, 24913899, FAX: 295561
Type: higher education, non-profit
Affiliation: Pedagogika Fakulta Uk Praha
Governance by board
Improving pre/postgraduate teacher training based on
research of professional attitudes and personal needs.

Lib Ed
(See Resource Appendix)

Education Otherwise
36 Kinross Rd, Leamington Spa, England CV32 7EF
0926-886828
Type: home-based
For everyone who practices or supports the right of students
to learn without schooling.

Summerhill School (1921)
Leiston, Suffolk, England IP16 4HY
Zoe Redhead, 0728-830540
Type: independent, boarding; tuition: $£5,000/yr
12 teachers, 70 students, mainly international, ages 6-17
Entrance requirements: interview
Governance by democratic school meeting
Teacher qualifications: dictated by position
Founded by A.S. Neill as a pioneering free school and democ-
ratic community; 12 acres; no letter grades; non-
compulsory class attendance; multi-aged classes; rural
location; interns accepted.

Brockwood Park Krishnamurti Educational Centre (1969)
Bramdean, Hampshire, England SO24 OLQ
Scott Forbes, 962-771-744, FAX: 962-771-875
Type: independent, boarding, non-profit
30 teachers, 60 students, ages 14-19
Affiliation: Krishnamurti Schools
Governance by all faculty with school meeting
Holistic; in 1769 Georgian mansion and park; no letter grades;
multi-aged classes; extensive field trips; rural location.

Small School (1982)
Fore St, Hartland, Bideford, Devon, England EX39 5EA
Caroline Walker, Co-Head Tch, 0237441672, FAX: 0237441203
Type: independent, non-profit
6 teachers, 10 assistants, 36 students, ages 11-16
Entrance restrictions: for residents of catchment area of
Hartland
Affiliation: Human Scale Education
Governance by consensus in parent-teacher-pupil meeting
Teacher qualifications: willingness to work for little pay
Equal emphasis on creative, spiritual, practical, academic;
multi-aged classes; extensive field trips; rural location;
interns accepted.

Sands School (1987)
48 East St, Ashburton, Devon, England TQ13 TAX
Sean Bellemy, 0364 653666
Type: independent, non-profit; tuition: $£3,000/yr,
scholarships
6 teachers, 30 assistants, 10-18 students
Entrance requirements: interview; acceptance by school
meeting
Governance including staff selection by democratic school
meeting
Teacher qualifications: staff ranges from no degree to PhD
Minimum rules; no system of punishments; cooking, cleaning, gardening by students and staff; non-compulsory
class attendance; multi-aged classes; no letter grades;
urban location; transportation; interns accepted.

Park School
Park Road, Dartington, Totnes, Devon, England TQ9 6EQ
Chris Nichols, Coord Tch, 0803-864588, FAX:-866676
Type: independent, non-profit; tuition: £1,738/yr,
scholarships
5 teachers, 60 students, ages 3-11
Entrance requirements: children, parents feel at ease with
school
Governance by democratic school meeting, board
Teacher qualifications: degree, certification
Students-parents-teachers partnership for a broad, creative
education; no letter grades; multi-aged classes; extensive
field trips; rural location.

Theleme (1984)
3 Rue Des Chalets, Vernet, France 66820
Michel Ferre, Head, 68056585
Type: independent, non-profit
4 teachers, 25 students, ages 12-18
Governance by teachers and principal, democratic school
meeting, parent cooperative
Teacher qualifications: no official qualifications
"Learning space" approach; student-centered; multi-cultural
approach through international travel; deeply environmen-
tally oriented; no letter grades; multi-aged classes; non-
compulsory class attendance; rural location.

Agence Information Enfance
(See Resource Appendix)

European Forum for Freedom in Education (EFFE) (1989)
Annener Berg 15, Witten, Germany D 58454
Eginhard Fuchs, Speaker, 49-2303-699-442, FAX: 49-3202-
669-443
Type: teacher education, resource
Over 500 members from 30 countries; semi-annual confer-
ences; publications and surveys in English and German.

World List of Rudolf Steiner (Waldorf) Schools,
Herausgeben vom Bund der Freien Waldorfschulen
(See Resource Appendix)

Montessori School of Hong Kong (1977)
99 Caine Rd, 1st Flr, Hong Kong
Dr George E. Caruso, Dir, 852-559-0066, FAX: 852-547-7807
Tuition: $4,000/6,000/yr
175 students, mainly international, ages 3-6
Entrance requirement: visit; interview; orientation
Affiliations: MSHK, AMS, NAMTA; accreditations: AMI, AMS,
NAEYC, HKED, MSA of HK
Governance by a board of trustees
Bilingual program: English/Mandarin, English/Cantonese;
parent education program; cultural studies; childcare;
urban location; transportation; interns accepted.

Rogers Person Centered School Foundation
Szeher Ut 29, Budapest, Hungary
Dr. Anna Gador
Type: higher education

Budapest: Waldorf School (1989)
Kozseghaz St 8-10, Budapest, Hungary 1028
Tamas Vekerdy, 2120 Dunakeszi, Baratsag Str 21, Ph: 176-
5609, FAX: 201-2908
Non-profit; tuition: none
18 teachers, 187 students, ages 7-13, 1-6th grade
Governance by board
Bio-gardening; eurythmy; hand crafts; religious studies;
school under construction; no letter grades;
transportation.

Godolloi Waldoff Iskola (1990)
Godolloi Waldorf Pedagogiai Alap., Erzsebet Krt 27, Godollo,
Hungary 2100
Attilla Giecse, 06-28/320-495
Type: Waldorf; tuition: $2,500
4 teachers, 35 students, 3rd grade
Governance by college of teachers
Teacher qualifications: teacher's diploma
Urban location.

Montessori College at Mount St Mary's
Dundrum Rd, Milltown, Dublin, Ireland 14
Susan Goldman, Adm, 01-269-2499
Type: higher education; tuition: £1,675/1,780/yr
Entrance requirement: registration fee £100/yr
Affiliations: AMI, UNESCO
Governance by AMI
3-year AMI teacher training course; credit transfers accepted
from AMI centers in US, Mexico, Canada, Italy, Sweden,
Japan.

Democratic School of Hadera
Brandeis Grove, Hadera, Israel
Yakov Hecht
Type: public choice, teacher education
300 students, K-12th grade
2500 students on waiting list!
Governance by democratic school meeting
Computers, including Lego room; exchange program; drama;
networking; in eucalyptus grove; no letter grades; non-
compulsory class attendance; extensive field trips; multi-
aged classes.

Centre for Educational Technology
Man in His Environment Department (1975)
16 Klausner St, POB 39513, Ramat Aviv, Israel 61394
Ayala Yiftah, 03-6460160, FAX: 03-6422619
Type: resource, teacher education
Affiliations: Ministry of Ed, Trans, Labour; Inst for Occupa-
tional Safety & Health
Contracts; programs on safety, life stages/cycles, individual in
community; books and articles.

Adam Institute
(See Resource Appendix)

AMI Centro Internazionale Montessori
Via Abruzzi 2, Perugia, Italy 06100
Type: Montessori teacher education

AMI Montessori Institute of Tokyo
332-19 Unomori, Sagamihara-shi 228, Japan
Type: Montessori teacher education

Global School (1985)
(See Resource Appendix)

La Casa del Niño
Collegio 300, Pedregal San Angel, Mexico City, Mexico 01900
Type: Montessori

Centro de Estudios de Educacion
Canal de Miramontes Esquina y Estrolla Binaria, Prados de
Coyoacan, Mexico 04810DF
Type: Montessori Teacher Education

Instituto Montessori del Norte
Carbonel 4108 Ave, Chihuahua, CHI, Mexico
Zulema Ruiz or Josefina Espino
Type: Montessori Teacher Education

Colegio Waldorf de Cuernavaca (1988)
Jesus H Preciado 103 Col. San Anton, Cuernavaca, MOR,
Mexico 62020
Rosa Barocio, Faculty Chair or Martha Nanez, 18-85-76, FAX:
11-30-06
Type: Waldorf; Quaker, non-profit; scholarships
16 teachers, 140 students, ages 3-12, K-6th grade
Entrance requirements: interview, residency
Affiliation: AWSNA
Governance by faculty, college of teachers, board
No letter grades; interns accepted.

Montessori Sierra Madre School (1965)
Juarez 250 Sur, San Pedro Garza Garcia, NL, Mexico 66200
Adriana Vega, Dir, 83-338-0924, FAX: 83-338-5879
Non-profit; tuition: $2,990-5,500/yr
29 teachers, 10 assistants, 267 students, ages infant-15
Accreditation: AMS
Library; music; athletics; computer science; cafeteria; A/V
room; urban location.

Tamariki School (1967)
PO Box 19506, 83 Rutherford St, Christchurch, New Zealand
Pat Edwards, 00613-38490141
Type: independent, non-profit; tuition: 1,240
4 teachers, 55 students, ages 5-14, P1-F2nd grade
Enrollment 60 students maximum
Governance by democratic school meeting
Teacher qualifications: NZ certification, emotionally literate
Emphasis on basic emotional health; family and student-
centered; everyone (students & staff) learns; no letter
grades; non-compulsory class attendance; multi-aged
classes; urban location; interns accepted.

Ripple Educational Community (1989)
493 Manchester St, Christchurch, New Zealand 8001
Marsha Morgan; Pauline Matsis, 011-643-365-7770, FAX: 011-
643-379-2544
Type: home-based Montessori; cost: NZ$3,000/yr
2 teachers, 22 students, ages 5-11

Governance by teachers and prin
In Victorian house; working garden; parents teach, learn with
   students; no letter grades; field trips; urban location.

Eureka Free University (1989)
Novokosinskaya 27-151, Moscow, Russia 111672
Alexander Adamsky, 7095-350-3157, FAX: 7095-350-3157
Type: higher education, resource
Russia's first private university; on-site alternative teacher
   training thoughout former S.U.; seminars in England, US,
   and other countries; internships; see AERO for more info.

English Montessori Educational Group
Avda Alfonso XIIII 40, Madrid, Spain 28002
Maria Olaechea

AMI Montessori Primary Course at Uppsala University
Dept of Teacher Training, Box 2136-S750 02, Uppsala, Sweden
Type: Montessori teacher education

Leicester Montessori School (1990)
137 Loughborough Rd, Leicester, UK
Dr Dayah, 0533-610022, FAX: same
Tuition: variable
8 teachers, 15 assistants, 115 students, ages infant-12
Affiliations: LMC, MENSA; accreditation: CHI (support society
   for children of high intelligence)
Governance by administrator, board
Childcare; urban location; transportation.

Cherry Trees School (1982)
Flempton Rd, Risby, Bury St Edmunds, Suffolk, UK IP28 6QJ
Wendy E. S. Compson, 0284-760531
Type: Montessori; tuition: $£70-1,270/term
10 teachers, 4 assistants, 216 students, ages infant-15

Entrance requirements: interview and assessment for older
   children
Affiliation: ISIS; accreditations: MATS, ISAI
Governance by principal
French house in Normandy for ages 7+; childcare; rural loca-
   tion; interns accepted.

Stork Family School
Ul Stakhurskogo 62 Kv 40, Vinnitsa, Ukraine
70432265577
Type: independent; tuition: $5/mo
70 students, ages K-17
Family cooperative; emphasis on English language, crafts,
   fine arts, music; teacher education with Eureka Free
   University.

Scarborough Montessori Center (1985)
Glen Rd, Scarborough, Tobago, West Indies
Susan Sandiford, Principal, 639-5195
Tuition: $550/610
6 teachers, 1 assistant, 250 students, ages 3-12
Entrance requirements: toilet trained; report from previous
   school for older students
Affiliation: London M Center
Governance by administrator

Sacred Heart Montessori (1980)
Upper De Gannes Street, Arima, Trinidad, West Indies
Sister Jerome Boland, SJC, 667-4279
1 teacher, 5 assistants, 100 students, ages 3-6
Birth certificate, health record required for admission
Affiliation: London Montessori
Governance by an administrator

RESOURCES

General and Miscellaneous

A+ Discount Distributors and Educational Warehouse
Spring Valley, NY
800-443-7900
For K-12.

ABeka Catalog
800-874-BEKA
Curriculum; free catalog.

Activities for Learning
21161 York Rd, Dept BK, Hutchingson, MN 55350
612-587-9146

Adam Institute
Jerusalem Forest, POB 3353, Jerusalem, Israel 91033
Uki Maroshek-Klarman, Ed Dir, 2-419184
Promoting democracy in education; opening International
  Center for Education for Democracy in a Multicultural
  Society; '93 conference attended by 400 from 40 coun-
  tries; books and publications.

Agence Information Enfance
29 Rue Davy, Paris, France F 75011
Roger Auffrand
National ed alternatives clearinghouse; newsletter POSSIBLE;
  directory.

Alpha Omega
800-622-3070
Curriculum; free catalog.

Alpha Plus
PO Box 185, Chewsville, MD 21721
301-733-1456
Math counseling, advice, products; free brochure.

Alternative Education Resource Organization (AERO)
417 Roslyn Rd, Roslyn Hts, NY 11577
Jerry Mintz, Dir, 516-621-2195, FAX: 516-625-3257
Nassau County
Type: non-profit
Helped create Handbook of Alternative Education; sponsored
  by School of Living; helps people who want to homeschool, find or found alternative schools, restructure existing schools or programs; publishes networking newsletter,
  AERO-GRAMME, $15/yr; many videos; speaking and consult-
  ing services; interns accepted.

Alternative Schools Network
1807 W Sunnyside, Suite 1D, Chicago, IL 60640
Jack Wuest, 312-728-4030, FAX: 312-728-3335
Clearinghouse; support; assistance.

American Home Academy
Latter Day Saints Home Educators' Association (1989)
2770 S 1000 W St, Perry, UT 84302
Joyce Kinmont, founder, 801-723-5355
Materials including books, math manipulatives, Brite music,
  health products; LDS: quarterly newsletter; annual
  conference.

American Preparatory Institute
PO Box 1800, Kileen, TX 96540-9990
Darine Stabile, 800-792-3748
Provides curricula for alternative schools

American Science and Surplus
601 Linden Pl, Evanston, IL 60202
708-475-8440

Anatomical Chart Company
8221 Kimball Ave, Skokie, IL 60076
800-621-7500
Science books and kits.

Anthroposophic Press
RR 4 Box 94 A1, Hudson, NY 12534
518-851-2054
Books by Rudolf Steiner and others.

Aquarian Research Foundation (1970)
5620 Morton St, Philadelphia, PA 19144-1330
Art Rosenbloom, Dir, 215-849-3237
Type: non-profit
Promotes Earth's positive future through science, intuition,
  freedom; new social movements; computer networking;
  students may donate toward expenses and/or share
  poverty communally; newsletter, Aquarian Alternatives.

Aristoplay, Ltd
PO Box 7529, Ann Arbor, MI 48107
Educational games.

Association for Experiential Education
2885 Aurora Ave #28, Boulder, CO 80303-2252
Maria Riley, 303-440-8844
Sponsors regional, national conferences; publishes Journal of
  Experiential Education, Jobs Cearinghouse, other books,
  periodicals.

Association of Waldorf Schools
3750 Bannister Rd, Sacramento, CA 95628
David Alsop

Atrium Society
PO Box 816, Middlebury, VT 05753
802-388-0922, FAX: 802-388-1027
Type: non-profit
Education for Peace program focuses on creative, non-
  violent conflict resolution; publications; seminars; training;
  community events; open forums.

Audio Memory Publishing
1433 E 9th St, Long Beach, CA 90813
Learning tapes.

Backyard Scientist
Box 16966, Irvine, CA 92713
Jane Hoffman

Blue Mountain Book Peddler
15301 Grey Fox Rd, Upper Marlboro, MD 20772
Free catalog.

Bluestocking Press
PO Box 1014, Dept 5, Placerville, CA 95667-1014
American History learning materials.

Bob Jones University Press
Greenville, SC 29614
800-845-5731
Christian; for K-12; free catalog.

Brain-Compatable Information
Box 427, New Rochelle, NY 10802
Leslie Hart, 914-632-9029

Builder Books
PO Box 5291, Lynwood, WA 98046
Free catalog.

Bund der Freien Waldorfschulen
Heidhofstrasse 32, Stutgart 1, Germany D-7000
0711-21042-0, FAX: 0711-21042-19
World List of Rudolf Steiner (Waldorf) Schools

Bureau of Federal School Improvement, Dept of Education
Grimes State Office Bldg, Des Moins, IA 50319
Ray Morley

Carden Education Foundation
Box 659, Brookfield, CT 06804

Career Publishing Inc
905 Allanson Rd, Mundelein, IL 60060
Book/cassette phonics program.

Centre for Educational Technology
Man in His Environment Department (1975)
16 Klausner St, POB 39513, Ramat Aviv, Israel 61394
Ayala Yiftah, 03-6460160, FAX: 03-6422619
Type: teacher education
Affiliations: Ministry of Ed, Trans, Labour; Inst for Occupational Safety & Health
Contracts; programs on safety, life stages/cycles, individual in community; books and articles.

Center for the Study of Educational Alternatives (1977)
Hofstra University, Hempstead, NY 11746
Dr Mary Anne Raywid, Director, 516-463-5766, 516-271-0661
Type: non-profit
Undertakes research and evaluations related to alternative schools; clearinghouse, consulting.

Changing Schools Newsletter
c/o Colorado Options in Education
98 N Wadsworth Blvd #127 Box 191, Lakewood, CO 80226
Mary Ellen Sweeney, 303-331-9352

Charlotte Mason Research & Supply
PO Box 172, Stanton, NJ 08885
Newsletter.

Children's Art Foundation, Stone Soup Magazine (1973)
PO Box 83, Santa Cruz, CA 95063
Gerry Mandel, William Rubel, Editors, 408-426-5557
School; museum and national magazine of students' work.

Chinaberry Book Service
2830 Via Orange Way, Suite B, Spring Valley, CA 92078-1521

Coalition of Essential Schools
Brown U Ed Dept Box 1938, Providence, RI 02912
Theodore Sizer

Cobblestone Publishing
7 School St, Peterborough, NH 03458
800-821-0115
Cobblestone (US history), Calliope (world history), Faces (cultures) magazines.

Community Service, Inc
PO Box 243, Yellow Springs, OH 45387
Jane Morgan, 513-767-2161; 767-1461
Type: non-profit
Mail order book service; annual conference; newsletter; correspondence.

Compu-Educare BBS
RR #2 Box 324, Summerville, SC 29483
Brian Comstock, 803-873-1050
Computer bulletin board for Charleston area; games; download educational programs; part of nationwide group.

CONNECT, The Newsletter of Youth Participation in Education (1979)
12 Brooke St, Northcote, Victoria, Australia 3070
Roger Holdsworth, 03 489-9052
Cost: $10/yr (6 issues)

Core Knowledge Foundation
2012-B Morton Dr, Charlottesville, VA 22901
800-238-3233
What Your ** Grader Should Know books sequence and related materials.

Creative Teaching Materials
PO Box 7766, Fresno, CA 93747
800-767-4282
Catalog.

Critical Thinking Press
PO Box 448, Pacific Grove, CA 93950
800-458-4849
Books; software; secular; for K-12.

Design-A-Study
408 Victoria Ave, Wilmington, DE 19804
Books, including The Natural Speller; for K-8.

Designs for Learning
449 Desnoyer, St Paul, MN 55104
Wayne B Jennings, 612-645-0200

Directory of Global Education Resources in North America
PO Box 83916, Fairbanks, AK 99708
Lisa Brosseau, 907-479-9093
Descriptions of organizations which promote economic justice, environmental protection, racial and gender equity, human rights, media literacy, indiginous people, peace education, area studies; resources, curriculum, audiovisual.

Dover Publications, Inc
31 E 2nd St, Mineola, NY 11501
Coloring books; dioramas; classics; free catalog.

Duke University Talent Identification Program
1121 W Main St, Suite 100, Durham, NC 27701
Educational Opportunity Guide, Directory of Programs for the Gifted.

Eagle Voice Center
Box 44, Glenelg, MD 21737
Henry Niese, 301-531-6166

Educational Futures Project (1976)
Box 2977, Sacramento, CA 95812
Don Glines, 916-393-8701
Consulting group; workshops, articles, books on educational alternatives, human potential, year-round continuous learning.

Educational Reform Group (1993)
76 Glenview, Wilton, CT 06897
Linda Moore, 203-834-0144, FAX: 203-761-1479
Fairfield County
Publicizes, promotes and distributes video and audio tapes of select educational reformers.

Educator's Publishing Service (EPS)
75 Moulton St, Cambridge, MA 02138-1104
800-225-5750
Secular materials.

European Forum for Freedom in Education (EFFE) (1989)
Annener Berg 15, Witten, Germany D 58454
Eginhard Fuchs, Speaker, 49-2303-699-442, FAX: 49-3202-
    669-443
Over 500 members from 30 countries; semi-annual confer-
    ences; publications and surveys in English and German.

ESP Publishers, Inc
7163 123rd Circle N, Largo, FL 34643

Eureka Free University (1989)
Novokosinskaya 27-151, Moscow, Russia 111672
Alexander Adamsky, 7095-350-3157, FAX: 7095-350-3157
Type: higher education
Russia's first private university; on-site alternative teacher
    training thoughout former USSR; seminars in England, US,
    and other countries; internships; see AERO for more info.

Family Learning Center
Rt 2 Box 264, Hawthorne, FL 32640
904-574-5869
Learning Language Arts Through Literature series; Valerie
    Bendt's unit study books; free catalog.

Farm Country General Store
Rt 1 Box 63, Mctamora, IL 61548
800-551-FARM
Curriculum; kits; free catalog.

Fearon Teacher Aids
Box 280, Carthage, IL 62321
Secular; catalog.

Fernbank Science Center
156 Heaton Park Dr, Atlanta, GA 30307
Mary Hiers, 404-378-4311
DeKalb County
K-12th grade
Exhibition hall, forest, botanical gardens, greenhouse, plane-
    tarium, observatory, meteorological lab, electron
    microscopy lab, human development classroom, library.

Florida Association of Alternative School Educators
1201 NE 191st St, G117, N Miami Beach, FL 33197

Folk Education Association of America
107 Vernon St, Northampton, MA 01060
Christopher Spicer
Based on Scandinavian folk HSs; newsletters; journal; annual
    conference; networking; study tours; exchange programs.

Forestry Education Assistance Program
Oregon Department of Forestry (1992)
801 Gales Creek Rd, Forest Grove, OR 97116
Ric Balfour, Public Use Coord, 503-357-2199, FAX:-4548
Washington County
Students mainly at-risk
Access to 2-acre arboretum, 350,000-acre state forest; staff
    available, self-sufficiency encouraged.

Foxfire Teacher Outreach (1975)
PO Box 541, Mountain City, GA 30562-0541
Hilton Smith, 706-746-5318, FAX: 706-746-5829
Collaborative process; community-based; respect for elders
    and what they have to teach us; summer courses; net-
    working; workshops; also Urban Foxfire Network.

Friendly Foreign Language Learning
29481 Manzanita Dr, Campo, CA 91906
Newsletter/catalog; tapes; software; flashcards.

Friends Council on Education
1507 Cherry St, Philadelphia, PA 19102
Kay Edstone, Dir, 215-241-7245
Coordinates N. American Quaker schools; consultants; work-
    shops; referrals; newsletter; film library.

Geode Educational Options
PO Box 106, West Chester, PA 19381
Materials for teaching and parenting.

Global Alliance for Transforming Education (1990)
Box 21, Grafton, VT 05146
Phil Gang, Dir, 802-843-2382, FAX: 802-843-2300
Network of holistic educators, social change agents; pro-
    motes vision of education that fosters personal empower-
    ment, peace, social justice and sustainable living; Gateways
    newsletter.

Global School (1985)
525-3 Imazu-Machhi, Takasago-Cho, Takasago, Hyogo, Japan
    676
Kazuhiro Kojima, 0794-42-1473
Students all ages
Natural curiosity is starting point; references and info; con-
    ferences; non-compulsory class attendance.

Global Voice Education Project for C Band Satellite
(1993)
1017 Van Ness, San Francisco, CA 94110
Julie Ward, 415-647-6374
Creative learning broadcasts; emphasis on SE, home, alterna-
    tive, and rural schools.

Green Teacher
95 Robert St, Toronto, ON, Canada M5S 2K5
Tim Grant, 416-960-1244

Greenleaf Press
1570 Old LaGuardo Rd, Lebanon, TN 37087
615-449-1617
History units, books; free catalog.

Growing Without Schooling
2269 Massachusetts Ave, Cambridge, MA 02140
Magazine and group founded by John Holt.

Hands-On History
201 Constance Dr, New Lenox, IL 60457
Kits; books; study materials.

Hands-On Science
12642 E Calle Tatita, Tucson, AZ 85749
602-749-1263

Hearthsong
PO Box B, Sebastopol, CA 95473-0601
Materials include Waldorf items, toys, gifts.

Heinemann Educational Books
361 Hanover St, Portsmouth, NH 03801-3959
603-431-7894

Holistic Education Press
39 Pearl St, Brandon, VT 05733-1007
Charles Jakiela, 802-247-8312
Publishes Holistic Education Review and What Are Schools
    For? by Ron Miller.

Home School Supply House
PO Box 7, Fountain Green, UT 84632
800-772-3129
Secular; mainstream texts.

Imagination Times
1811 Tartan Court, Charlotte, NC 28212
Stories; fingerplays; recordings; games; crafts.

Innovative Program Center
526 Mt Pleasant Rd, Thomson, GA 30824
Lynne Entrekin, Coordinator, 404-595-9742
McDuffie County
Pre K–12th grade
State support.

Institute for Alternative Futures
108 N Alfred St, Alexandria, VA 22314
Chris Bui, 703-684-5880

Institute for Democracy In Eastern Europe
48 East 21st 3rd Floor, NY, NY 10010
Irena Lasota, 212-677-5801

Institute for Democracy in Education
119 McCracken Hall, Ohio U, Athens, OH 45701-2979
George Wood

Institute for Independent Education (1984)
1313 N Capitol St NE, Suite 200, Washington, DC 20002
Joan Ratteray, 202-745-0500
Technical assistance and policy development; works with
    community-based schools serving African-American, His-
    panic, Latin-American, Native American, and Asian Ameri-
    can communities, numbering over 350; located primarily in
    inner cities.

Institute for Mutual Instruction (1993)
4875 San Joaquin Dr, San Diego, CA 92109-2318
E.M. "Mac" Swengel, Founder/Pres, 619-272-1935, FAX: 619-
    272-1935
Type: non-profit
Comprehensive; focus on individual tutoring; students teach
    what they learn.

Institute for Responsive Education
605 Commonwealth Ave, Boston, MA 02215
Owen Heleen

Institute of General Semantics (1938)
163 Engle St, Englewood, NJ 07631
Marjorie Zelner, Exec Sec, 201-568-0551, FAX: 569-1793
Bergen County
Tuition: variable, scholarships
6 teachers
Governance by board, executive committee
Theory of evaluation based on scientific method and leading
    to critical evaluation; seminars on theory and its
    application.

Interaction Book Company
7208 Cornelia Dr, Edina, MN 55435
612-831-9500

International Alliance for Invitational Education
c/o School of Ed, UNC Greensboro, Greensboro, NC 27412
919-334-5100
Promotes humanistic, individualized, respectful approach.

**International Association for the Study of Cooperation
    in Education**
Box 1582, Santa Cruz, CA 95061
408-426-7926
Publishes Cooperative Learning Magazine.

Italic Handwriting Series
Portland State University
PO Box 1394, Portland, OR 97202
Tena Spears, 503-725-4846, FAX: 503-725-4840
Type: non-profit
Student K-adult ages
Small press; comprehensive, self-directed program; italic is
    logical, based on printing, easy to write and teach.

Joyful Child
Box 5506, Scottsdale, AZ 85261
Peggy Jenkins

Kagan's Cooperative Learning
27134 Paseo Espada, Suite 302, San Juan Capistrano, CA
    92675
800-933-2667

Kew Resources
79–12 154th St, Kew Gardens, NY 11367
Anthony Cardo, 718-969-3454

Kids Art
PO Box 274, Mt Shasta, CA 96067
916-926-5076
Arts and crafts books and projects; magazine $10/yr.

Kids Discover Magazine
PO Box 54205, Boulder, CO 80322-4205
Use for unit study.

KONOS
PO Box 1534, Richardson, TX 75083
214-669-8337
Christian unit studies/time line; free catalog.

La Leche League International
PO Box 1209, Franklin Park, IL 60131
Early child-raising, breastfeeding ed.

Learning Things, Inc
68A Broadway; PO Box 436, Arlington, MA 02174
Microscope viewers; slide sets; catalog $3.

Lib Ed
Phoenix House, 170 Wells Rd, Bristol, England BS4 2AG
Richard Musgrove, 0272–778453
Magazine (3/yr) & books for the liberation of learning, includ-
    ing No Master High or Low, Libertarian Education and
    Schooling; conferences.

Lifetime Books and Gifts
3900 Chalet Suzanne Dr, Lake Wales, FL 33853
Homeschoolers Complete Reference Guide; curriculum
    items.

Magnet Schools of America
2111 Holly Hall Suite 4203, Houston, TX 77054
Don Waldrip, 800-462-5526
11,000 members in over 300 schools; directory (2,452
    entries), $65; annual conference.

Mankato Wilson Campus School Remembered: Video
    (1968)
PO Box 2977, Sacramento, CA 95812
Don Glines, 916-393-8701
Featured completely individualized curriculum, student-
    selected facilitators, optional attendance, and no text-
    books or homework.

Math Products Plus
PO Box 64, San Carlos, CA 94070
415-593-2839

Merlyn's Pen (1985)
PO Box 1058, East Greenwich, RI 02818-0964
Valerie English, Assoc Ed, 800-247-2027, FAX: 401-885-5222
Student ages 11–18
National magazine; authors/artists submit original fiction,
    essays, poetry, book reviews, artwork; circulation 100,000;
    Parent's Choice Award recipient.

Minnesota Association of Alternative Programs (MAAP)
Area Education Center
1102 Willow St, Brainerd, MN 56401
Lorin Ellertson, 218-829-2915
Over 100 member programs; information; assistance; work-
    shops; meetings; tours; conferences; newsletter.

Multicultural Education c/o Caddo Gap Press
3145 Gaeary Blvd #275, San Francisco, CA 94118
415-750-9978
Quarterly journal addresses stereotypes, racism, democracy and diversity; reviews and extensive resource listings.

NAM Enterprises
PO Box 67, Keene, TX 76059
800-262-1069
Supplies.

National Association of Private Nontraditional Schools and Colleges
182 Thompson Rd, Grand Junction, CO 81503
Earl Heusser, 303-243-5441

National Center for Fair and Open Testing (FairTest)
342 Broadway, Cambridge, MA 02139
617-864-1410

National Center for Restructuring Education (NCREST)
Box 110, New York, NY 10027
212-678-3432
Major network and clearinghouse for new progressive, learner-centered approaches within public ed.

National Coalition of Advocates For Students
100 Boylston St, Suite 737, Boston, MA 02116

National Coalition of Educational Activists (NCEA)
PO Box 679, Rhinebeck, NY 12572-0679
Debi Dukc, 914 658 8115
Supports change within the public school system.

National Coaltion of Alternative Community Schools
(1976)
Box 15036, Santa Fe, NM 87506
Ed Nagel, Office Manager, 505-474-4312
Membership Requirements: must support organization's preamble.
Governance by board and annual membership meeting.
A national organization of educational alternatives; annual and regional conferences; publishes National Directory of Alternative Schools; quarterly newsletter; information on alternative schools; school accreditation program through NALSAS.

National Dropout Prevention Center
Clemson U, Clemson, SC 29634-5111
National Dropout Prevention Newsletter, 803-656-2599
A partnership between concerned business and education leaders and schools and communities throughout the United States; technical assistance for dropout prevention; database; consultant services, publications.

National Home Education Research Institute
5000 Deer Park Dr SE, Salem, OR 97301-9392
Brian D Ray, PhD, Pres, 503-375-7018
Type: non-profit
Clearinghouse; identifies effective educational approaches; lectures; quarterly journal, Home School Researcher; court testimony.

National Society For Internships
3509 Haworth Dr S 207, Raleigh, NC 27609
Sally Migliore, 919-787-3263

NE Foundation For Children
71 Montague City Rd, Greenfield, MA 01301
Chip Wood

Network of Educators on the Americas
1118 22nd St NW, Washington, DC 20037
Deborah Menkart, Dir, 202-429-0137, FAX: 202-429-9766
Works with schools, communities to develop, promote pedagogies, resources, cross-cultural understanding for social, economic justice in the Americas; books; workshops.

Network of Progressive Educators (1989)
PO Box 6028, Evanston, IL 60202
Carol Ouimette, Director, 708-869-1794
Cook County
Type: non-profit
Supports progressive principals, connects educators and organizations, both public and private, encourages progressive classroom practices and democratically organized schools; pursues diversity, equity, and inclusion for all children.

New Horizons For Learning (1980)
PO Box 15329, Seattle, WA. 98115
Dee Dickinson, CEO; Teri Howatt, Coordinator, 206-547-7936
$50/yr membership
Network of people, programs, products dedicated to innovative learning; synthesizes and communicates successful research; supports lifespan learning communities; has networking electronic "building" in Bitnet; newsletter: "New Horizons for Learning."

Ohio Alternative Education Organization
1512 Woodward Ave, Springfield, OH 45506
Ruth Chapman

Open Court Publishing
PO Box 599, Peru, IL 611354-0599
815-223-2520
Specify math and reading catalog.

Our Schools Our Selves
1698 Gerrard St, Toronto, ON, Canada M4L 2B2
George Martel, 416-463-2637, 563-3657

Personal Power Press International, Inc
Box V-49, Bowen Island, BC, Canada V0N 1G0
Terry Carruthers, 604-947-2739, FAX: 604-947-0706
Books by Dr Maurice Gibbons on self-directed learning, integration; how-to guidebooks for students and teachers; compatible with Education 2000 Guidelines.

Progressive Results
160 Old State Rd, Ballwin, MO 63021-5915
Walter A. De Anna, Pres, 314-394-7015, 800-966-1737, FAX: 314-394-2501
4-12th grade
Skills Bank home tutoring software for grades 4–12; lessons; word problems; quizzes; tests.

Quality Education Resources
PO Box 847, Cupertino, CA 95015-0847
408-252-2254
Free catalog.

Rainbow Re-Source Center
PO Box 491, Kewanee, IL 61443
New and used curricula.

Resource Center for Redesigning Education
Po Box 818, Shelburne, VT 05482
Ron Miller, 802-865-9752
Has hard-to-find books, videos, information on holistic education, change; publishes catalog; also see books written by Miller in bibliography.

Rethinking Schools
1001 E Keefe Ave, Milwaukee, WI 53212
414-964-9646
Independent journal published by Milwaukee area educators.

Riverside Schoolhouse
HCR 34 Box 181A, Bemidji, MN 56601
USBORNE books.

Saxon Publishers, Inc
1320 W Lindsey St #100, Norman, OK 73069-4310
405-329-7071
Math program for grades 4+.

Scholastic Book Clubs, Inc
PO Box 3745, Jefferson City, MO 65102
Teacher aids.

School of Living
Rd 1 Box 185 A, Cochranville, PA 19330
Ginny Green, 215-593-6988
Type: non-profit; membership: $20/yr
60 year old group founded by Ralph Borsodi; pioneer in environmental protection, consumer protection, land trust, home education, intentional communities, educational alternatives; newsletter: Green Revolution.

Schools for the 21st Century
Old Capitol Bldg FG-11, Olympia, WA 98504-3211
John Anderson, 206-586-4512

Scientific Wizardry Educational Products
9925 Fairview Ave, Boise, ID 83704
208-377-8575

Shekinah Curriculum Cellar
967 Junipero Dr, Costa Mesa, CA 92626
Catalog $1.

SKOLE (1985)
72 Philip St, Albany, NY 12202-1789
Mary Leue, 518-465-0241
A journal of writings on educational alternatives, primarily by the grassroots practitioners; $15/yr, two issues.

Society for Utopian Studies (1975)
U of MO, 8001 Natural Bridge Rd, St Louis, MO 63121
Lyman Sargent, Exec Dir

States Educational Alternatives League (SEAL)
2550 University Ave W, Suite 347 N, St Paul, MN 55114-1052
612-645-0200, FAX: 612-645-0240
Type: nonprofit
Affiliation: State Alternative Education Organizations
Governance by state organization presidents

Steward Ship
PO Box 164, Garden Valley, CA 95633
Makers of Choreganizers; send large SASE for brochure.

Study Circles Resource Center (1990)
PO Box 203, Pomfret, CT 06258
Phyllis Emigh, 203-928-2616, FAX: 206-928-3713
Windham County
Type: non-profit
Students mainly adult
Networking services; topical discussion programs.

The 15th Street School Foundation (1983)
4 Jane St, New York, NY 10014
Betta Ehrenfeld, Pres, 212-243-1387
Clearinghouse for those interested in Summerhill model.

The Book Cellar
87 Union Square, Milford, NH 06055
800-338-4257
Used curriculum.

The Cheerful Cherub
Box 262302-H, San Diego, CA 92196
Catholic catalog; magazine.

The Eagle's Nest
1539 Oakwood Dr, Escalon, CA 95320
Supplies; free catalog.

The Elijah Company
PO Box 12483, Knoxville, TN 37912-0483
615-475-7500
Educational programs; catalog.

The Helping Hand
5006 Barcelona Dr, Garland, TX 75043-5101
214-681-5161
Unit study curriculum for grades 3-6 based on children's classic literature; magazine.

The Home School
3131 Smokey Point Dr, Arlington, WA 98223
Huge inventory of materials.

The Home School Shopper
PO Box 11041, Spring Hill, FL 34610
813-856-5160
Used curriculum.

The Odysseus Group
295 8th St #3W, New York, NY 10009
John Taylor Gatto, 212-529-9327
1991 NY State Teacher of the Year; author of The Guerrilla Curriculum and Dumbing Us Down; goal that every student develops own learning style, interests, and needs.

The Pembina Institute
PO Box 7558, Drayton Valley, AB, Canada TOE OMO
403-542-6272, FAX: 542-6464
The Canadian Environmental Education Catalogue

The Threefold Review
PO Box 6, Philmont, NY 12565
518-392-5728
Promotes R. Steiner's idea that education and other cultural pursuits should be kept separate from government control; special report on "Real Choice in Education."

Timberdoodle
E 1610 Spencer Lake Rd, Shelton, WA 98584
Supplies and games.

To Kids-For Kids-By Kids Newsletter
11119 Pucket Pl, Midlothian, VA 23112
Sherri Raynor
$4/yr; kids ages 6-18.

TRANET: Transnational Network for Alternative/ Appropriate Technologies
PO Box 567, Rangeley, ME 04970
William Ellis, 207-864-2252
Assists grassroots workers and community developers through information distribution, meetings, conferences, and newsletter.

Under the Apple Tree Magazine
Apple Tree Press
PO Box 8, Woodinville, WA 98072
Crafts; projects; hands-on studies; $18/yr.

VA Alternative Education Assn
Box 310, Monroe, VA 24574
Ken Payne, 804-929-6931

Washington Alternative Learning Assn (WALA) (1975)
PO Box 795, Port Townsend, WA 98368
Jane B. Ansley, Exec Dir, 206-385-9252
Funds scholarships and projects; liaison with State Office of Public Instruction; Options in Education Newsletter; meetings; workshops; conferences.

Whole Language Umbrella
4848 N Fruit, Fresno, CA 93705
Debbie Manning

Wilcox & Follett
1000 W Washington Blvd, Chicago, IL 60607
Used curriculum; send request on school stationery.

World Future Society
7910 Woodmont Ave, Suite 450, Bethesda, MD 20814
Robert Schley, 301-656-8274, FAX: 951-0394

Zephyr Press (1979)
PO Box 66006, Tucson, AZ 85728
Amy Myers, 602-322-5090, FAX: 602-323-9402
Publisher; distributor; for K-12 teachers; student-centered curricula; multiple intelligence; multiculturalism; language arts; higher-core thinking skills.

Home-Based Education

A BEKA Correspondence School
Box 18000, Pensacola, FL 32523

A Voice For Children
7 Casa Del Oro Ct, Santa Fe, NM 87505-3718

American School
850 E 58th, Chicago, IL 60637

Brigham Young U—Dept of Independent Study
206 Harman Continuing Ed Building, Provo, UT 84602

Brook Farm Books
Box 246, Bridgewater, ME 04735
Donn Reed

Canadian Alliance of Home Schoolers (1979)
272 Hwy 5 RR 1, St George, ON, Canada NOE 1NO
Wendy Priesnitz, Coord, 519-448-4001, FAX: same
Resource, Home-based
Publishes Natural Life Magazine; coordinates info of homeschooling and alternative schools in Canada.

Catholic Home School Newsletter
688 11th Ave NW, New Brighton, MN 55112

Catholic Homeschoolers Association
PO Box 24145; 300 Eagleson Rd, Kanata, ON, Canada K2L 3M3

Christian Liberty Academy Satellite Schools (1968)
502 W Euclid Ave, Arlington Hgts, IL 60004
708-259-8736
Cook County
Type: non-profit
Student ages 4-60, K-12th grade
Governance by church board
Curriculum from 30 publishers; self-publications; flexible; comprehensive; suburban location.

Clonlara School Home Based Education Program (1967)
1289 Jewett, Ann Arbor, MI 48104
Barb Maling, Campus School Coord, 313-769-4515, FAX: 313-769-9629
Washtenaw County
Type: non-profit; cost: $450/yr per family
Student ages 5-19, K-12th grade
Guidance; assistance with completion of forms; upkeep of cumulative records; transfer reports; diplomas

Family Christian Academy
487 Myatt Dr, Madison, TN 37115
Robin Scarlata, 800-788-0840; 615-860-3000
Cost: $25
Umbrella school; newsletter; teacher training; testing; seminars; bookstore; unit studies; Bible-based books; Saxon math; Learning Language Through Literature; publications.

Florida at Home
4644 Adanson St, Orlando, FL 32804-2024
407-740-8877
Magazine by Circle Christian School

Gentle Wind School
Box 184, Surry, ME 04684

Hewitt Research Foundation (1964)
PO Box 9, 2103 B St, Washougal, WA 98671
Donna Fisher, Dir of Student Services, 800-348-1750
206-835-8708, FAX: 206-835-8697
Clark County
Type: non-profit
4 teachers, 1200 students, ages 5-18, K-12th grade
Governance by board
Services and products include testing for grades 3-8, phone counseling, evaluations, special needs dept.

Holt Associates
2269 Mass Ave, Cambridge, MA 02140
Pat Farenga, 617-864-3100
Books and materials for unschoolers and homeschoolers in general; beginners packets; publishes networking newsletter, Growing Without Schooling.

Home Education Press
PO Box 1083, Tonasket, WA 98855
509-486-1351
Publisher of Home Education Magazine; other publications include Alternatives in Education.

Home Educator's Almanac
18515 Murphy Springs Ct, Morgan Hill, CA 95037

Home School Advantage
Box 8190, Phoenix, AZ 86066-8190
Donna Hamill

Home School Legal Defense Association
PO Box 159, Paeonian Spgs, VA 22129
703-338-5600

Home Study Directory/National Home Study Council
1601 18th St NW, Washington, DC 20009

Home Study Institute
6940 Carroll Ave, Takoma Park, MD 20912
202-723-0800

Homeschool Associates of New England
116 Third Ave, Auburn, ME 04210
Steve Moitozo, 800-882-2828
Yearly homeschool conference; consultation service; radio show; books and resource materials.

Homeschooling in Oregon, the Handbook
PO Box 80214, Portland, OR 97280
Ann Lahrson, 503-244-9677
Cost: $14.95

Homeschooling Today
Box 1425, Melrose, FL 32666
Dale Simpson

Homeward
17020 Hamilton Dr, Lakeville, MN 55044
Joan Torkildson
South Metro Families for Home Education; newsletter.

International Institute
N6128 Sawyer Lake Rd, White Lake, WI 54491
715-484-5002, FAX: same

Kids Lib News
Box 28, Naalehu, HI 96772

Landmark
PO Box 849, Fillmore, CA 93016
Lori Harris, 805-524-2388, FAX: 805-524-7334
Governance by board
Materials for K-12; focus on ability to research, record, reason, relate the history of any subject; facilitates Master Teachers.

Learning All Ways
7 Canyon Oaks Dr, McLoud, OK 74851
Carol Tofani, 405-386-5979

Liedloff Continuum Network
PO Box 1634, Sausalito, CA 94966
415-332-1570
For people wanting to incorporate Continuum Concept into
    their lives; newsletter; members list; consultations with
    Jean Liedloff in Sausalito or by phone.

Moore Academy
Box 1, Camas, WA 98607
Dr Raymond S. Moore, Chair/CEO, 206-835-5500, FAX:-5392
Type: nonprofit; cost: $125-400/mo
Student ages 6-20, K-12th grade
Entrance Requirements: adherence to the "Moore Formula"
Affiliation: Dr. Moore affiliated with 6 universities
Governance by teachers and Principal
Balances study, work and service; students have never been
    rejected for college; no early formal school; interns
    accepted.

National Homeschool Service
PO Box 167, Rodeo, NM 88056
505-557-2250

National Institute for Christian Home Education
Rt 3 Box 543, Rustburg, VA 24588

New Moon Publishing (1992)
PO Box 3587, Duluth, MN 55803
Nancy Gruver, Publisher, 218-728-5507, FAX:-1812
St Louis County
Girls ages 8-15 and adults edit and produce bi-monthly inter-
    national magazine: New Moon, the Magazine for Girls and
    Their Dreams; interns accepted.

Open Sky HOME Education (1985)
PO Box 915, Alaili Rd, Pahoa, HI 96778
Michael Sunanda, Dir, 808-936-2561
Big Island County
Type: nonprofit
3 teachers, 5 students, ages 3-10
Entrance requirements: trusting agreements.
Governance by parent cooperative
Teacher qualifications: sensitive, playful, aware, honest
Rooted in natural bonding, trust, cooperation; self-directed;
    artwork; natural games; Kids Lib Newsletter; noncompul-
    sory class attendance; rural location.

Pinewood School
112 Road D, Pine, CO 80470
Olivia Loria, Director, 303-670-8180
Type: nonprofit; cost: $425 or 125
4 teachers, 200 students, ages 4-21, K-12th grade
Affiliations: NCACS, NHA, CHEA, NALSAS
Governance by annual general meeting
Teacher qualifications: teaching certificate, experience
Has individualized curriculum; units of study; diploma
    program; on-line computer service; educational resource
    center; serves families throughout United States and other
    countries; no letter grades; non-compulsory class atten-
    dance; multi-aged classes; extensive field trips; rural
    location.

Pinyon Court School
7215 West 8th Pl, Lakewood, CO 80215
Mary Rothfeld, 303-238-3254
Cost: $30/family/yr
16 students, K-12th grade
Flexible curriculum and evaluation for homeschoolers.

Practical Homeschooling
Box 1250, Fenton, MO 63026
Mary Pride, 314-225-9790, 800-346-6322, FAX: 314-225-0743
Magazine: Practical Homeschooling; Big Book of Home Learn-
    ing, other publications.

Quebec Homeschool Association (1983)
1002 Rose Marie Rd, Val David, PQ, Canada J0T 2N0

Elizabeth Edwards, Editor, 819-322-6495
Quarterly newsletter; advice/support phone line; small library
    of books, magazines, catalogs.

Quest, The Home Educators' Journal
1144 Byran Ave, Ottawa, ON, Canada K2B 6T4
Andre Dubuc, Editor, 800-668-5878, FAX: 613-729-0117
Cost: $35/yr (US), 26/yr (Can)
Quarterly.

Sing and Learn Curriculum Supplies
2626 Club Meadow, Garland, TX 75043
Sarah Cooper, 214-840-8342

Spirit of January
Box 234162, Great Neck, NY 11023
Asiba Tupahache, 516-877-1630
Newsletter for homeschoolers.

Summit Christian Academy
PO Box 802041, Dallas, TX 75380
Jan Bailey, Dir, 800-362-9180
Cost: $395/yr
1,000 students, K-12th grade
Alpha Omega curriculum; electives; educational games;
    achievement tests; diplomas; record keeping.

Switch
Box 403, Fontana, WI 53125
Alan Fiebig, 414-275-5497
Support group and magazine.

The Drinking Gourd, Harambee
PO Box 2557, Redmond, WA 98073
Donna Nichols-White, 836-0336
King County
Multicultural publication, support group; 75% African Ameri-
    can; Harambee means "Let's pull together."

**The Educational Association of Christian
    Homeschoolers (TEACH)**
PO Box 91, Bloomfield, CT 06002

The Grapevine (Montana Homeschool News)
1702 Hwy 83 N, Seeley Lake, MT 59868
406-754-2481

The Home School Manual, from Gazelle Publications
    (1976)
c/o 1906 Niles-Buchanan Rd, Niles, MI 49120
Ted Wade
Christian perspective, but with respect for all opinions; 55
    chapters, 26 appendices; forms; by Theodore E. Wade and
    38 others; $21.95 pp.

The Sycamore Tree
2179 Meyer Pl, Costa Mesa, CA 92627
Curriculum; umbrella school.

The Teaching Home
Box 20219, Portland, OR 97220-0219
503-253-9633

Tropical Homeschooler Newsletter (1992)
220 Waipalani Rd, Haiku, HI 96708
Ken and Adrienne Pinsky, Eds/Owners, 808-572-9289, FAX:
    808-572-0168
Maui County
Local, national topics; bookstore/catalog; rural location.

Umoja*Unidad*Unity (Homeschoolers of Color)
5621 S Lakeshore Dr, Idlewild, MI 49642
Kristin Cleage Williams, 616-745-3001
Lake County
2 teachers, 4 students, ages 6-17
Newsletter; forum and support group for Latina/o, Black,
    indigenous and other interested people of color; rural
    location.

Montessori

Association Montessori Internationale
170 W Scholfield Rd, Rochester, NY 14617
Virginia McHugh, 716-544-6709

Center for Public Montessori Programs
Box 8354, Minneapolis, MN 55408-0354
612-823-6348

Children's House/Children's World Magazines
PO Box 111, Caldwell, NJ 07006
Teaching materials

Early Work
PO Box 5635, Petaluma, CA 94955-5635
Resources for classrooms and parents.

In Other Words
2000 Floral Drive, Boulder, CO 80304
Spanish and French language curriculum materials.

InPrint for Children
2270 Mt Carmel Ave, Glenside, PA 19038-4610
Supplemental classroom materials.

International Montessori Society
912 Thayer Ave, Silver Spring, MD 20910
Lee Havis, 301-589-1127

LORD/Elizabethtown Montessori School
100 Gray St, Elizabethtown, KY 42701-2608
Montessori materials and classroom furniture.

Materials Company of Boston
PO Box 378, Salem, NH 03079
Ben Feldman and Bonnie LaMothe, 603-641-1339
American-made Montessori materials.

Michael Olaf Company
PO Box 1162, Arcata, CA 95521
Susan or Jim Stephenson, 707-826-1557
Supplies; publication.

Montessori Foundation
4157 Mountain Rd, Pasadena, MD 21122
Support to entire Montessori community; publishes Montessori parents' magazine, "Tomorrow's Child"; seminars; consultation; resource center for Montessori schools.

Montessori Institute of America
5901 NW Waukomis, Kansas City, MO 64151

Montessori Requisites–USA
314 West Main St, Norristown, PA 19401
800-365-0671
Montessori materials from Sri Lanka.

Montessori Services
228 S A St, Santa Rosa, CA 95401
Supplemental educational and practical life skills materials for the home and Montessori classroom.

National Center for Montessori Education
PO Box 1543, Roswell, GA 30077
404-434-1128

Nienhuis Montessori USA
320 Pioneer Way, Mountain View, CA 94041-1576
800-942-8697
Montessori materials from Holland.

North American Montessori Teachers' Association
11424 Bellflower Rd NE, Cleveland, OH 44106
216-421-1905
Videos and publications for staff development, administrators, and parent education.

Oregon Association of Alternatives in Education
1005 NW Galveston Ave #A, Bend, OR 97701

Parent-Child Press
PO Box 675, Hollidarpburg, PA 16648
Art appreciation curriculum; books and posters for parent education

Priority Montessori Materials
10141 Rookwood Dr, San Diego, CA 92131
619-271-7312
Supplemental materials for the Montessori classroom.

Public School Montessorian
127 W. Lake St, Suite 1, Minneaplois, MN 55408
Dennis Schapiro

RSM Creative Services Inc
2600 Navarre Ave, Oregon, OH 43616
Supplemental materials for the Montessori classroom.

Southeast Educational Materials
1149 Rocky Lane, Monterey, TN 38574
615-839-3822

The American Montessori Society
150 Fifth Ave, New York, NY 10011
212-924-3209

Part Four

VIGNETTES OF ALTERNATIVE SCHOOLS

Democratic to the Core:

LIFE IN SUDBURY VALLEY SCHOOL

Sudbury Valley is a school started in 1968 by a group of parents, teachers, and students who were deeply dissatisfied with the direction education was taking at that time.

The challenge was to create an environment where learning about democracy would be synonymous with learning about life, about the real world and growing up. The real life surroundings of the children had to be democratic in every respect, through and through, and down to the last detail. This means that in the whole school community each person has an equal input, makes all decisions—including budget, staff hiring, discipline, rules of behavior, and administration. All individuals in the school are endowed with a full set of rights, including freedom of expression, of belief, of thought, of assembly, and the right to full judicial process. This guarantee of rights has enormous, far-reaching consequences for the daily activities of the students. It means that the students are never placed in any groupings that they do not themselves form; that there are no classes, no tests, no curriculum imposed by others; that everyone has the freedom to pursue whatever interests one wishes to pursue, as far as one wishes to take them; and that one may control the use of one's time, and all can give full play to the rich roving of their imaginations. All persons attending the school have equal opportunity to pursue their goals and their dreams.

Whatever the time of day, and whatever their age, students in the school are all doing what they want to do. Usually that means that they are doing things not done in most other schools, and doing them with a very unusual intensity and concentration. Most often students are unconscious that "learning" is taking place. Doing what they choose to do is the common theme; learning is the by-product.

The school teems with activity. Adults and students mix freely. People can be seen talking, reading, and playing. They may be in the photo lab developing or printing pictures. They may be in a karate class or just playing on mats in the dance room. Someone may be building a bookshelf in the woodworking shop, or fashioning chain mail armor and discussing medieval history. There are almost always people making music of one kind or another, and others listening to music. You might find someone studying French, or Latin, or algebra. It would be most unusual if there were not people engaged in role-playing games; others rehearsing a play. People will be trading stickers and trading lunches. A group may be selling pizza that they made to raise money for an activity— perhaps they need to buy a new kiln, or want to go on a trip. In the art room people will be drawing; they might also be sewing, or painting, or working with clay, either on the wheel or by hand.

Always there are people playing happily and busily, indoors and outdoors, in all seasons and all weather. Always there are groups talking, and always there are individuals quietly reading here and there.

One of the things most adults notice first about Sudbury Valley is the ease of communication. *No matter what their age, people treat one another with easy respect.* There is a comfortable air of self-confidence—the confidence normal to individuals pursuing goals they set themselves. Things are almost never quiet, and there is an exhausting intensity, but the activity is not chaotic or frenetic.

The students at Sudbury Valley are doing what they want, but they are not necessarily choosing what comes easily. They are challenging themselves; they are acutely aware of their own weaknesses and strengths, and likely to be working hardest on their weaknesses. Along with the ebullient good spirits, there is an underlying seriousness—even the six-year-olds know that they, and only they, are responsible for their education. (They are acutely aware that very young people are not given this much freedom or this much responsibility almost anywhere in the world.)

Although the school has no curriculum, there are some certainties about what students learn. They learn to know themselves. They learn to ask for what they want, and see to it that they get it. They learn how to try something and relish success, and they learn how to try something and fail at it—and try again.

The weekly *School Meeting* is the core of our democratic community. It runs Sudbury Valley. The most momentous issues in the life of the school have been resolved there.

Rules of the school are proposed to the School Meeting, and passed by it. They are collected in the school's *Law Book*. Special interest groups are chartered by the School Meeting to pursue their day-to-day activities. Staff contracts are negotiated by it. Special expenditures are appropriated there. Private concessions are granted, or revoked, on the Meeting floor. The judicial system's administrative officers are elected there periodically.

Everyone, student or staff, votes. Attendance is optional. So what happens at school is just what happens everywhere else in a free democracy: when an issue is dear to someone's heart, that person comes. Democracy rests on universal *suffrage,* not on universal participation. What is essential is that each person *have access* to a full share in decision-making. After a while, you can guess at the agenda by looking at who is there. When a bunch of athletic youngsters suddenly show up *en bloc,* it's a good bet we're going to be asked for a special expenditure to buy some new sports equipment. When five nine- and ten-year-olds appear out of the blue, a concession to sell something is in the wind. There are some regulars of all ages, of course, who like being involved in running the school, just as there are in every town.

Sudbury Valley awards a high school diploma to students who are able to demonstrate that they are ready to function as responsible members of the community at large. Graduates have gone on to colleges and universities all over the country, and abroad. Most are admitted to schools of their first choice. Other graduates have entered directly into the world of business, trade, arts, crafts, and technical vocations.

Beyond the descriptions lies the reality of the school: a place where freedom is cherished, mutual respect is the norm, and where children and adults are comfortable with each other, where learning is integrated into life.

— *Daniel Greenberg*

A Day in the Life of

THE NEW SCHOOL OF NORTHERN VIRGINIA

Gyn is a New School first: the first student to move from the lower to the upper school at age 14. She's been a New School student for three years; when she was a middle schooler, she was an Old Timer.

Her Dad drops her off at 8:30—a little early, but she doesn't mind. She's happy to have time to grab a place on the sofa in the student lounge and relax. She's not alone. Other kids are mingling too, as are teachers.

She's talking to John—she doesn't know John's last name. There are four teachers named John. (Since they don't use last names, they could all have the same one and she wouldn't know.) Anyway, John the Revolutions teacher is showing her his book on paintings of Washington: Washington as Napoleon, Washington as Zeus, Washington as the man who resigned his commission.

She walks downstairs to pay a visit to a few old friends from middle school. Maril, one of the middle school teachers, and several students, are admiring the model pyramid and mummy Tim made for his Egypt project.

"Last year I tried to make the Parthenon out of sugar cubes," Gyn says, "but the glue made the cubes melt, so I made it out of cardboard instead." Everyone laughs. Gyn wishes she could stay a while longer, especially after seeing copies of *Tuck Everlasting* and *The Thief of Always* on the desk. Last year, Maril used to read them those stories every day at 10:40. Now—it's off to the upper school with a wave good-bye and an, "I'll see you at lunch."

The classes gather—although no bells announce a beginning. Gyn goes to Algebra, the largest class in the school—16 students. She grabs her book and moves to a corner. Other students move to different locations around the room; some take the high ground—a table by the wall. Moments later, her teacher, Lisa, makes eye contact and gives her work assignments for the day. (She will swing around later to check on her progress and to answer questions.) About midway through the class, Will and Jack from Sandy's lower school come in to take attendance. Lisa fills out the form and they leave smiling broadly.

At 9:55 morning meeting begins with Kathy going on and on about Cuddles the Guinea Pig. Gyn doesn't mind—she misses Cuddles, too. Little Elizabeth shows everyone the wonderful book she made last week with her upper school tutor, Doug. Everyone loves the story and applauds the accomplishment. After meeting she wants to go outside to enjoy the sun with her friend Lewis, but he has to miss break again.

This six-week period her morning module class is Freud and Literature; it starts miraculously at 10:20. A couple of kids meander in late. Michael reminds them of that fact. After a brief review of ego, id, and superego, Michael organizes the students in two groups of five. They proceed to design a scene demonstrating the Freudian principles. It's a bit strange, but she'll live. After all, last year when she was still in middle school, she played the part of the queen in the "Careless Astronaut," a play she and her classmates performed based on the ill-fated flight of Daedalus and Icarus. She also researched the costumes and got to design and wear her very own chiton.

About halfway through the improvisation, two students from Lisa's Physical Roots of Behavior class enter and take notes. Michael asks them what they're doing; everyone discovers they are studying the different learning styles and are now observing what type of style Michael's present assignment is appealing to. They seem puzzled, but amused by Gyn's skit.

At 12:15 the two vans go to the local shopping center to drop off those high school students who want to eat out for lunch. As they pull out of the parking lot, several middle schoolers play basketball. Gyn and Carol eat lunch with the middle schoolers so they can make popcorn and play with Mouse Jones and Indiana Mouse. While they are eating, Shannon pops in to see how the two mice she gave to the middle school are doing—she graduated last year but still visits occasionally to see if her protégé mice-keepers are living up to her standards. They are, and everyone is happy.

Outside, Sandy watches her crew of lower schoolers play on the slides. One of the vans returns early to deliver her kids to the swimming pool by 12:50. It'll bring the high schoolers back to the school by the desired 1:00.

Normally, after lunch Gyn has paleontology class. She's disappointed; yesterday, she got to touch the fossils from John's collection—again, she's not sure of his last name, but he's the "nice one." He collected them while looking at medicine wheels in Wyoming: arthropods and clams from the Miocene period mostly. Now, she's looking forward to her trip to Calvert Cliffs for her first real live fossil hunt.

Today, however, it's the all-school-meeting: what starts as a lackluster affair with one of the Johns—a completely different one this time—complaining about the condition the classrooms are left in, reminding the kids to clean up after themselves. Everyone nods in agreement, even Scott who then tosses his empty McDonald's cup on the floor. She thinks of saying something cute to him, but decides to leave well enough alone.

Right before the all-school-meeting is about to break up into a lower and an upper school meeting, Andrew, one of her old nemeses from Denise's class last year, brings up an all-school topic—the censorship of students by teachers. Apparently, in middle school that morning "where nothing exciting ever happens" he was "asked" by Maril to hide the writing on his Naked Co-Ed T-Shirt—something obscene about "hunting in the buff." He was told to cover it, but he doesn't think it's right; he wants the whole school to discuss it.

She still can't believe what these upper schoolers can get away with. Here, they are discussing with the teachers who has the right to decide what is appropriate language and what's not, and the high school kids are saying that the teachers have no right whatsoever to tell anyone what to wear. The teachers rebut those beliefs, of course; and in the end Andrew doesn't get to wear his T-Shirt, but students and teachers have come to an agreement that in the future if there is a problem with someone's apparel, the offended party will ask the offender to conceal the offense; but if the offender truly believes he could take the issue to the fairness committee or the meeting again.

That's how that goes, but she's adjusting to the upper school bravado thing. During the interview with John—the big John this time, Headmaster John—when he told her about this ownership stuff, about owning her education and her community, she had no idea that was what he meant.

The meeting continues, minus the lower school since Joan's Sex-Ed class has started their presentation on how to prevent STDs (Sexually Transmitted Diseases). Gyn recalls how at the earlier censorship meeting Rachel stood up and told the teachers that they were "dead wrong to tell Andrew to cover his shirt." She wishes she had used her tape recorder so she could listen to Rachel's passionate speech now, but unfortunately, she keeps the recorder in Freud class so she can tape Michael's lectures.

As the Sex-Ed presentation ends, Gyn moves on to her final stop of the day— Contemporary Issues.

This week's topic is animal rights. She is ready for a fiery debate, so when John the Revolutions teacher expresses his mystification about how people can say that they would rather save an injured animal than one of their fellow humans, she stands up to vehemently defend her position, but before she knows it, another day at the New School of Northern Virginia has come to an end. She says good-bye to her friends, scurries into her mother's Ventura, and leaves.

— *Michael Oliver*

A Day in the Life of

THE ACADEMIC COMMUNITY
FOR EDUCATIONAL SUCCESS

The minute you walk through the big double doors into the Academic Community, you sense friendliness and security. The building is a small church, and the room you've entered is flooded with multicolored lights from the stained glass windows. The beams of light strike twenty-five desks; and on each you see the students' own decor—pictures of their brothers and sisters, small figurines, and other personal treasures.

Tim, a tall, blond seventeen-year-old, walks forward to shake your hand. He and the students are genuinely pleased to greet you. As you go through the day, you'll continue to notice how open, respectful, and affectionate they are toward one another and their teachers. When you watch them work in class you'll see eager attention, hard work, and high academic achievement. However, back in the conventional schools many people would have labeled them "at-risk."

Right now, it is only eight in the morning; students are sitting around casually, talking with one another and the teachers eating a sandwich from the nearby deli, and listening to music. Tim introduces you to all twenty-five students and the two teachers, Joan and Jerry.

At 8:30 Marcos rings a bell. Dan walks up to a flip at the front of the room, writes that "Eleanor Roosevelt said, 'It's not fair to ask others what you are not willing to do yourself.' How does this statement apply to you?" All of the students then go to their desks and write answers in journal books. You look around for a teacher to ask what to do, but there is not one in the room; however, Dan hands you a piece of paper and a pencil and indicates that you should also write. (Later, you find out that students often monitor their own classes and activities.)

No one speaks for fifteen minutes. Then Joan, one of the teachers, walks into the room. She says, "epistemic." Everyone repeats "epistemic." Then she shows a five-by-eight card with the word on it, gives the root, definition and a sentence. She repeats this vocabulary ritual twice with other words. As you go through the day, you notice students using the words and initialing the cards taped on their desk. Pete, another student, tells you that this activity is one of many authentic "assignments." Students must use the words correctly instead of taking a written test.

Pete also tells you about the honor code. When students enter the Academic Community, they sign a contract pledging them to an honor system; they promise to always "volunteer the truth, without being asked." So students are not only responsible for signing their own card, but they also monitor their classes and other tests. There are no locks on doors; money lies on people's desks; and students can borrow equipment such as computers and video cameras.

The next two hours are "core" classes. At the Academic Community, English, social studies, and science are taught in three-week, intensive quarter "units." Each unit ends with a demonstration project directed toward the students' portfolios; each unit carries one-quarter credit in at least one of those subjects. Students at the Academic Community use portfolios as alternatives to the Regents Exams or Regents Competency Tests, and they can get local, regents, or honors credits for their courses.

Finally, at 11:15, the community starts gathering "on the stage," a slightly raised area in front of the room circled with old couches. On the way to the stage, each person does a small cleanup job (such as wash out the microwave); then Wayne runs a short community meeting. The Academic Community is run almost entirely by students like Wayne. The school government is modeled on the federal government. Wayne is the elected chief administrator (comparable to the president); since there is no school principal in the building, Wayne fulfills many aspects of that role, in this public school program.

In this particular community meeting, Kevin, the elected Speaker of the House, announces, "There will be a Congress meeting next Thursday, at 3:30; all proposals must be in the Congress box by this Thursday, at 3:30." Sarah, the Chief Justice of the Court also announces the results of the last Discipline Court meeting. The two teachers are simply participants in this meeting. At the end of announcements, Wayne asks each person to share what he appreciated in that day so far.

At 11:40, you see Jessica, another student, taking orders for the deli. There are two lunch periods; Jessica orders out for anyone who didn't bring lunch or cook it in the school kitchen. Some students go to work on math in the downstairs classrooms; others sit around in the big upstairs classroom, watching TV, doing homework, eating, playing chess, or talking. The second lunch/math period is similar.

From 1:30 to 3:30, there are small classes downstairs: music, art, ILTs (Independent Learning Time), and study halls. The music and art students work with teachers; ILT students and those who need study-time work in the kitchen silently. That room is always absolutely silent; there are no adult supervisors. Some students are downstairs for music, art, ILTs or study hall; some leave on the 1:30 bus; still others stay upstairs to finish work or talk with their friends.

The last bus leaves at 3:30, but that isn't the end of the day. Many students, and the two full-time teachers, stay until after five. Parents drop in, students get help, committees such as hospitality, attendance, and interview meet.

As you leave around 5:30, a student, Jay asks you for a ride to the train, just up the road. "Do you have a lot of homework?" you ask. "Just look," he says, and shows you his bulging backpack. "But it's not so bad. I'm finishing my writing and reading for book talks. Every spring, we all go to someone's home in groups of five or six; the cooking class fixes a fancy dinner, and we discuss a book with community members, sort of like an adult book club. Book talks are really fun." When he gets out, you thank him for letting you visit, and he says, "Sure, thanks for coming; we really like guests." And you know he means it.

— *Joan Estes Barickman*

A Day in the Life of a Montessori Student

It's dark at 7:05 on this midwinter's morning when Jeanne Saunders pulls up to the drop-off circle at Barrie, the Montessori school that her three children have attended since each was two years old. Jeanne has made this trip so often over the years that Barrie feels like her second home. Jeanne works downtown and typically cannot leave work until after five. Her husband, who teaches in the local public schools, is off much earlier. He'll pick the children up from the after-school program by 4:30, but if he's late, he knows that they'll be fine until he arrives.

Barrie prides itself on being a family-friendly school. Working families appreciate its extended day and summer camp.

Teddy, Josh, and Jennifer definitely think of Barrie as their second family. Jennifer is one of those children who, after ten years in Montessori, speaks about Montessori with affection and conviction. Visitors often find her coming up without a moment's hesitation to greet them and offer a cup of coffee or campus tour. When people ask her if she likes it in Montessori, she smiles and says, "Sure, how could anyone not love it here? Your teachers are your best friends, the work is really interesting, and the other kids are like my brothers and sisters. It's a family. You feel really close to everyone."

Jennifer walks Teddy, age four, and Josh, who's seven, up to morning supervision. After dropping them off, she walks down the hill to the upper school where she is a seventh grader. She joins two of her friends in the commons, and sits and talks quietly waiting for her first class to start at 8:00.

Teddy's morning supervision is in his normal classroom. After hanging up his coat, he walks over to Judy, the staff member in charge of his room until school officially begins at 8:30. He asks if there is anything ready to eat. Judy suggests that he help himself. He scoops out a bowl of cereal from a small bin, and adds milk. He takes his morning snack over to a table and eats. Children and parents drift in to the room every so often, and gradually the number of children in the early morning program grows to about 15.

Teddy meanders over to the easel and begins to paint with Teresa, a little girl just three who has only joined the class over the last few weeks. They paint quietly, talking back and forth about nothing in particular. Eventually Teddy tires of painting and cleans up. He is tempted for a moment just to walk away and leave the easel messy, but he carefully cleans up and puts his materials away as he has learned from more than two years in Montessori.

At 8:30, his two teachers arrive, along with several more children. Other follow over the next few minutes until all 30 students and two teachers quietly move about the room.

Montessori children work with hands-on learning materials that make abstract concepts clear and concrete. They allow young students to develop a good inner image of concepts in mathematics, such as how big is a thousand, what we mean when we refer to the "hundreds" column, and what is taking place when we divide one number by another. This approach makes sense to children. Through this foundation of concrete experiential learning, operations in mathematics, such as addition, become clear, allowing the child to internalize a picture of how the process works.

Teddy and another child have begun to work together to construct and solve a mathematical problem. Using sets of number cards, each decides how many units, tens, hundreds, and thousands will be in his addend. The cards showing the units 1 to 9 are printed in green, the cards showing the numbers from 10 to 90 are printed in blue, the hundreds from 100 to 900 are printed with red ink, and the cards showing the numbers 1000 to 9000 are printed in green again because they represent units of thousands.

As Teddy and his friend construct their numbers, they decide how many units they want, find the card showing that quantity, and place it at the upper right hand corner of their work space. Next they go to the bank, a central collection of golden bead material, and gather the number of unit beads that corresponds with the number card selected. This process is repeated with the tens, hundreds, and thousands. The two addends are combined in the process we call addition. Beginning with the units, the children count the combined quantities to determine the result of adding the two together. If the result is nine or less, they simply find the large number card that represents the answer. If the addition has resulted in a quantity of ten beads or more, the children stop at the count of ten and carry these unit beads to the bank to exchange them for a ten-bar: ten units equals one unit of ten. This process is repeated with the tens, hundreds, and thousands.

It's about ten o'clock now, and Teddy is a bit hungry. He wanders over to the snack table and prepares himself several pieces of celery stuffed with peanut butter. He pours himself a cup of apple juice, using a little pitcher that is just right for his small hands. When he is finished, Teddy wipes off his place mat. Clearing up his snack has put Teddy in the mood to really clean something, and he selects table washing. He gathers the bucket, little pitcher, sponge, scrub brush, towel and soap needed, and proceeds to slowly and methodically scrub down a small table. As he works, he is absorbed in the patterns that his brush and sponge made in the soap suds on the table's surface. Teddy returns everything to its storage place. When he is finished, the table is more or less clean and dry; a four-year-old washes a table for the sheer pleasure of the process—that it leads to a cleaner surface is incidental. What Teddy is learning above all else is an inner sense of order, a greater sense of independence, and a higher ability to concentrate and follow a complex sequence of steps.

Teddy moves freely around the class, selecting activities that capture his interest. In a very real sense, Teddy and his classmates are responsible for the care of this child-sized environment. When they are hungry they prepare their own snack and drink. They go to the bathroom without assistance. When something spills, they help each other carefully clean things up. We find children cutting raw fruit and vegetables, sweeping, dusting, washing windows. They set tables, tie their own shoes, polish silver, and steadily grow in their self-confidence and independence. Noticing that the plants need watering, Teddy carries the watering can from plant to plant, barely spilling a drop.

Now it's eleven o'clock, and one of his teachers, Ann, comes over and asks him how the morning has been going. They engage in conversation about his latest enthusiasms, which leads Ann to suggest another reading lesson.

She and Teddy sit down at a small rug with several wooden tablets on which the shapes of letters are traced in sandpaper. Ann selects a car and slowly traces out the letter *d*, carefully pronouncing the letter's phonetic sound: *duh, duh, duh*. Teddy traces the letter with his tiny hand and repeats the sound made by his teacher. Teddy doesn't know this as the letter *d;* for the next year or so, he will only call it by its phonetic sound: *duh*. This way, he never needs to learn the familiar process of converting from the letter name *d* to the sound it makes, *duh*. Continuing on with two or three additional letters, Ann slowly helps Teddy build up a collection of letters which he knows by their phonetic sounds.

Ann leads Teddy through a three-step process. "Teddy, this is *duh*. Can you say *duh?* Terrific! Now, this is a *buh* (the letter *b*). Teddy, can you show me the *duh?* Can you give me the *buh?* Fine. Okay, what is this? (holding up one of the sandpaper letters just introduced)." Teddy responds, and the process continues for another few minutes. The entire lesson is fairly brief; perhaps fifteen minutes or so. Before long Teddy will begin to put sounds together to form simple three-letter words.

Teddy's day continues just like the morning began. He eats his lunch with the class at 11:45, after which he goes outside with his friends to play in the snow. After lunch, the Spanish teacher comes into the room and begins to work with small groups of students. Eventually, she taps Teddy on the shoulder and asks him if he would like to join her for a lesson. He smiles, but graciously declines. He is too engaged in the project that he's chosen.

In the afternoon he does some more art, listens to selections from a recording of the "Nutcracker" ballet, works on his shape names with the geometry cabinet, and completes a puzzle map of the United States.

When the day is over, Teddy has probably completed twenty to thirty different activities, most representing curriculum content quite advanced for someone who after all just turned four two months ago. But when his dad picks him up at 4:50, his response to the usual question of "What did you do in school today?" is no different from the comments of many children, "Oh, I don't know. I guess I did a lot of stuff!"

—*Tim Seldin*

Snakefoot Educational Association

PARENT-COOPERATIVE ACADEMIC PROGRAM FOR HOMESCHOOLERS

Snakefoot Educational Association is a parent-cooperative program for homeschooled children ages five through fourteen. With plenty of educational and art materials, professional teachers and parent and community volunteers, the children get many unique experiences.

For five years Snakefoot has served homeschooled children with love and sensitivity. They learn with consideration for one another's differences in personality and academic development; without pressure and competition with one another; with the joy of accomplishing for themselves, in the way that best suits them and according to their own developmental time table.

A WEEK IN THE LIFE OF ADAM: ELEVEN-YEAR-OLD SEA STUDENT

MONDAY

After washing his cereal bowl, Adam works on his math; then begins writing a story about a Neanderthal family while reflecting on his research of early man. His dad is in his workshop and available if need arises.

TUESDAY

"Mom," says Adam, "will you call out my spelling words before we go?" At 7:45 they drive to the carpool pick-up point where Adam joins other children for the half-hour ride to the three-room country schoolhouse nestled in the trees and mountains south of Lexington, VA. After 15 students, ages six through fourteen, greet one another in morning circle—Adam volunteers to read his story to the other children. They readily offer appreciation and criticisms after he is finished.

WEDNESDAY

Adam and his classmates sit around a table creating bowls and sculpture from clay they gathered near the pond earlier during a biology lesson. While their hands are busy their teacher reads to them about the people of an African village.

With a full morning of academics, afternoons at Snakefoot are diverse and usually hands-on; painting with a local artist volunteer, writing and practicing the annual play, science experiments with a parent, math magic and logic games, native American survival skills training and primitive shelter building.

THURSDAY

The younger children find a big buddy to sit with. Little Levin sits on Adam's lap as they both answer questions in Spanish. Their teacher turns into a señora from Mexico for the daily Spanish lesson. At Snakefoot, older and younger children get opportunities to be together. "I like it," says six-year-old Emma, "I wish school was more than three days a week."

FRIDAY

The parents and Board of Directors have agreed to add a fourth day of instruction beginning in the fall of 1994. In order to finance the additional salaries and expenses, parents fundraise in various ways. Today Adam and Summer from the older group and Jimez, Trista, and Sunya of the younger group will help Trista's dad peddle environmental T-shirts on the local college campus. The children are exuberant as they approach each student explaining their enterprising venture.

"Wouldn't you like to have a shirt like this?" Adam queries one college senior. "I would but I have no money," she answers ruefully. "That's OK," replies Adam cheerfully. "We will take checks too!" The children are proud of the money they earn for their school. The experiences in fundraising, leadership, salesmanship and finance may go unnoticed, but the lessons our children learn are very valuable.

— *Katie McNeil*

A Community of Families, Parents, and School:

JEFFERSON COUNTY OPEN SCHOOL

Jefferson County Open School, located in Lakewood, is part of Colorado's largest school district. It is a pre-kindergarten through twelfth grade public school of choice for students throughout the district. Transportation is provided. There is a first come, first served waiting list. Depending on age, students have been known to wait from two to four years.

Students work in multiage groups based on interests, needs, and developmental levels. Staff members work in teams. Parental involvement is extensive. Evaluations, portfolios, and continuous progress assessment are used in place of credits or grades. To graduate, a student must demonstrate proficiency from adolescence to adulthood and write a narrative transcript that documents learning experiences and accomplishments.

The Community Learning Apprenticeship and Service Program provides opportunities for students from the upper elementary through the high school level to explore interests and learn in the community. Extended trips are integral parts of the curriculum. Students, parents, and staff participate in the decision-making and running of the school. The Shared Leadership Circle, the school's advisory board, is a consensus-based decision-making body with equal representation of students, parents, and staff.

Upon entry to the school building an observer might find preschool students choosing from an array of activities ranging from art to building; or engaged in guided activities, reading, or resolving a conflict with the aid of older students. Down the hall in the Early Learning Center students begin plans for organizing and articulating how they will spend the choice time they have throughout their day. Some students sort through folders of work to choose "Banana Split Work" to be shared with their advisors during personal conferencing time.

Later these students may be found working together in cooperative groups on murals for the hallway with a parent observing and mediating the process or out in the school yard measuring the capacity of a bucket with scoops of snow. Meanwhile, upstairs in the Intermediate Area a group of students sit on couches reading a novel together with a high school teacher. A contingent of students works on a huge ceramic tile mosaic with a student teacher. In another room students share a voyage project with an audience of parents, students and teachers on the game of chess using an assortment of visual aids.

Down the hall to the library a group of people gather for a debate on banned books, a controversy within the school district. The debate is run by Intermediate Area students and is being videotaped by the library aide. A small committee of parents, consultants and staff meet in an adjoining room to discus a grant proposal for automating the library and setting up an interactive classroom where classes from the local college can be brought into the school.

In the "pit," a central meeting area of the school, middle school and high school students of the leadership class discuss pros and cons of the media blitz on a young ex-gang member gone teenage role model. Up in the computer room, a continual buzz of activity momentarily subsides as students pause to hear someone read the dictionary definitions of *accept* vs. *except*. In the school cafeteria, students from the intermediate area through high school work with parents and the kitchen staff serving lunch. Students of all ages eat among staff members, parents with babies, and visitors.

The high school wing is relatively quiet today. It is Wednesday, Plaid Day, an experiential day for high school students. They are doing class or Passage projects, apprenticeships, and other learning activities outside of the school building. A student leaves a group meeting for the Museum of Natural History where she has an apprenticeship studying archeology and prepares to lead a class at the Mayan ruins of Tulum in Mexico on an upcoming school trip. A group of middle school students enter the building carrying shovels and bags of equipment from the third Missouri Mud Trip, made to aid the flood victims in the Midwest. Commendations to these middle school and high school students from both the Governor and Colorado's Commissioner of Education are displayed in a showcase down the hall.

Outside the building the yellow school buses pull up and students scramble and scuffle to board. This is a typical day at Jefferson County Open School. But it is much more than a school to many of the 600 students who spend their day here. It is a caring supportive, energized community of families where students feel connected to people of all ages.

— Joy Jensen

Learning from the Land
With Audubon's Traveling University

From the back of the room, hand after hand rose in the air, signaling the speaker to stop and clarify his statements. Craig Suggs was finishing a slide show presentation for a group from the Audubon Expedition Institute. Suggs is a public affairs representative for the U.S. Department of Energy's Waste Isolation Pilot Plant in New Mexico, known as WIPP. The controversial project is planned to be the nation's first permanent repository for radioactive waste created in nuclear weapons production. Suggs said that such a thorough cross-examination by visitors was atypical; for Institute students, it was a typical day at school.

The Audubon Expedition Institute is an alternative to traditional academic programs of study. From September to May, students travel throughout the United States and Canada by bus, camping wherever they go, and learning through on-site visits to places like WIPP. Three or four buses are filled every fall; each bus group decides by consensus where it will travel.

The Institute offers programs for undergraduate and graduate students. Undergraduate participants may spend a semester or a year with the Institute, while graduate students enroll for one or two years, earning an M.S. in Environmental Education in conjunction with Lesley College in Boston. Founded in 1978 as part of the Audubon Society's Education Department, the Institute is the only accredited degree program sponsored by an environmental organization.

My group of 23 graduate students, ages twenty-two to thirty-nine, and two staff camped and cooked out nightly. The outdoors was our home and classroom, and a yellow school bus—whose back half was converted into a library on one side and a kitchen on the other—was our means of transportation.

At the WIPP Site

Before the visit we watched a videotape about WIPP. Background literature on the site—both for and against—filled the bus files. Evening discussion sessions focused on nuclear waste issues. We were readying ourselves for the WIPP visit much as one prepares for an exam.

We visited the site early the next morning, first viewing a two-hour slide presentation given by three public affairs officials. At lunch we were expected to eat in a designated dining room, but some students lingered in the main cafeteria, trying to strike up conversations with employees.

After lunch, we took a shaft elevator 2000 feet down to the salt mines where the waste would be stored. We climbed into golf carts and drove down long, dimly lit passageways, looking at excavated rooms expected to hold six million cubic feet of radioactive waste.

The last segment of our visit was a tour of the waste handling building where waste will be brought before being stored underground. It was late afternoon by the time we reassembled for a wrap-up discussion. Taking off our hard hats, eye protectors and emergency gear, we sat cloaked in a thin layer of salt, writing notes and asking final questions.

An Alternative Education

The major objective of the Institute is to teach students to see the planet as a living organism. Students learn not only from other people, but also from the earth itself. To this end, they sleep outdoors and live as lightly as possible on the planet, recycling, conserving electricity, gas and water, and eating foods low on the food chain. Students maintain their own community based on interdependency, decision-making by consensus, and openness. They participate in group activities, share daily chores and responsibilities, and agree to refrain from alcohol and drugs during the program.

Course work is a combination of textbook and on-site learning. Students read and critique each other's papers, give seminars on their research projects, and prepare presentations on new subjects. The week before the WIPP visit, for example, one student gave a short lecture on the geologic formations and history of Carlsbad Caverns, which we were to visit the next day. "One of the best aspects of AEI is learning from your peers," said Richard Becker, a teacher from Massachusetts. "Everyone contributes to your education, not just one figure of authority. You are a teacher and a student at once."

As I boarded the bus to leave the WIPP site, I surveyed the seating options, trying to decide which WIPP conversation to join. One student seemed undaunted by the constant flow of questions and answers and sat enjoying the debates. What she said was already clear: "The people make the program what it is."

— Shelley Preston

Part Five

BIBLIOGRAPHY AND APPENDICES

Bibliography

This is a partial listing of mostly new books and periodicals that would be useful in studying educational alternatives.

Armstrong, Thomas. *Awakening Your Child's Natural Genius.* Los Angeles: Jeremy P. Tarcher, 1991.

Avrich, Paul. *The Modern School Movement.* NJ: Princeton University Press, 1980. History of the movement pioneered by Spanish Anarchist Francisco Ferrer, with a special emphasis on the Stelton Community.

Barickman, Joan Estes. *Schoolwise, Teaching Academic Patterns of Mind.* New Hampshire: Heinemann/Boynton/Cook Publishers, 1992.

Bear, John. *College Degrees by Mail.* Berkeley, CA: Ten Speed Press, 1991.

Loomis, Mildred Jensen, and Ralph Borsodi. *Reshaping Modern Culture; The Story of the School of Living and Its Founder.* Cochranville, PA: The School of Living, 1922.

Chattin-McNichols, John. *The Montessori Controversy.* Delmar Publishers, 1992.

Colfax, David and Micki. *Hard Times in Paradise.* New York: Warner Books, 1992. *Homeschooling for Excellence.* New York: Warner Books, 1988. Stories by a homeschool family whose children went to Harvard.

Dewey, John. *Experience and Education.* London: Collier-Macmillan, 1938. Dewey's philosophy is the basis for progressive education.

Fellowship for Intentional Communities. *Directory of Intentional Communities: A Guide to Cooperative Living.* Rutledge, MO: Communities Publications Cooperative, 1991.

Fliegel, Seymour. *Miracle in East Harlem: The Fight for Choice in Public Education.* New York: Times Books, 1992.

Gatto, John Taylor. *Dumbing Us Down.* Philadelphia, PA: New Society Publishers, 1992. A veteran, award-winning teacher gets fed up with the system.

Gribble, David. *Considering Children: A Parents' Guide to Progressive Education.* London, England: Dorling Kindserly Limited.

Glasser, William. *The Quality School: Managing Students Without Coercion.* New York: Harper & Row, 1990.

Goldman, Jenifer. *My Life as a Traveling Homeschooler.* Roslyn, NY: Solomon Press, 1991. An 11-year-old girl writes about her experiences.

Greenberg, Daniel. *Announcing a New School: A Personal Account of the Beginnings of the Sudbury Valley School.* Framingham, MA: Sudbury Valley Press, 1973. *The Sudbury Valley School Experience.* Framingham, MA: The Sudbury Valley School Press, 1987.

Hainstock, Elizabeth G. *Teaching Montessori in the Home: The Preschool Years.* Teaching Montessori in the Home: The School Years. New York: Random House, 1968, 1971.

Hart, Leslie A. *Human Brain and Human Learning.* Oak Creek, AZ: Books for Educators, 1983. The implications of brain research for education.

Hegener, Mark and Helen. *Home Education Magazine.* Tonasket, WA: Home Education Press. *Alternatives in Education.* Tonasket, WA: Home Education Press, 1993.

Holt, John. *How Children Learn,* 1967. *How Children Fail,* 1964. NY: Pitman. *Teach Your Own.* New York: Delta/Lawrence, 1981. Evolution from school criticism and change to homeschooling.

Lamb, Albert. *Friends of Summerhill Trust Journal.* Leiston, Suffolk, England: Summerhill School, 1992. *Summerhill School, A New View of Childhood.* New York: St. Martin's Press, 1993. New and more recent editing of A. S. Neill's writings.

Llewellen, Grace. *Teenage Liberation Handbook: How to Quit School and Get a Life and Education.* Eugene, OR: Lowry House, 1991.

O'Leary, Jenifer. *Write Your Own Curriculum.* Stevens Point, Wisconsin: Whole Life Publishing, 1993.

Leue, Mary. *SKOLE, The Journal of Alternative Education.* Albany, NY: Down to Earth Books, summer 1991.

McCullough, Virginia. *Testing and Your Child,* New York, NY: Penguin Books, 1992.

Miller, Ron. *What Are Schools For: Holistic Education in American Culture.* Brandon, VT: Holistic Education Press, 1990. *The Renewal of Meaning in Education: Responses to the Cultural and Ecological Crisis of Our Times.* Brandon, VT: Holistic Education Press, 1993.

Mintz, Jerry. *AERO-GRAMME: The Newsletter of the Alternative Education Resource Organization.* Roslyn, NY. Networks spectrum of educational alternatives world-wide.

Montessori, Maria. *The Secret of Childhood.* Ballantine Books, 1973.

Nagel, Ed. *National Coalition News.* Santa Fe, NM: NCACS Publications.

Nathan, Joe. *Public Schools by Choice.* St. Paul, MN: The Institute for Learning and Teaching, 1989.

Neill, A. S. *Summerhill, A Radical Approach to Child Rearing.* New York: Hart, 1960.

Sheffer, Susannah. *Growing Without Schooling.* Cambridge, MA: Holt Associates. Letters and reports from homeschoolers around the country.

Shotton, John. *No Master High or Low.* Bristol, England: Libertarian Education, 1993. History of libertarian education in England.

Sizer, Theodore R. *Horace's Compromise: The Dilemma of the American High School.* Boston: Houghton Mifflin, 1984.

Spring, Joel. *A Primer of Libertarian Education.* New York: Free Life Editions, 1977.

Trickett, Edison J. *Living an Idea: Empowerment and the Evolution of an Alternative High School.* Bookline Books, 1991.

Wade, Theodore E. *The Home School Manual.* Bridgman, MI: Gazelle Publications, 1993.

Wagner, Patricia. *Building Support Networks for Schools.* Santa Barbara, CA: ABC-Clio, 1992.

Weinstein, Miriam. *Making a Difference College Guide, Education for a Better World.* San Anselmo, CA: Sage Press, 1993. Selected descriptions of forward-looking colleges.

Wheelock, Anne. *Crossing the Tracks.* New York: The New Press, 1992.

Colleges That Have Accepted Alternative School Graduates

The following colleges and universities were listed in the questionnaires returned to us as having accepted students graduating from their alternative schools or homeschool programs. Of course, this is not a complete list, but it indicates the spectrum of colleges which welcomes graduates from educational alternatives.

Alabama State U
Allan Hancock College
Am. River College
American Institute of
    Business
American River
Antelope Valley CC
Antioch
Arapaho CC
Arizona
Army Academy
Art Center
Art Inst. of Chicago
Austin Peay U
Baker Business College
Baker College
Bakersfield CC
Ball State
Barstow CC
Boston College
Boston U
Brandeis
Brown
Butte CC
BYU
Cabot College
California Arts
California State Hayward
California State U
Carson Newman College
Central Michigan U
Central Washington U
Central Wyoming CC

Chabot
Chaffey College
Clarkson
Cleveland Inst. of Music
Colgate
College of Sequoias
College of the Desert
College of the Redwoods
Colling County CC
Colorado Aerotech
Colorado State U
Colorado U
Columbia
Contra Costa JC
Cooper Union
Cornell
Cosumnes River College
CSU
Cuesta JC
CUNY
Curry
CW Post
Cypress CC
Davenport CC
Del Mar Tech
Delta CC
Delta College
Denison
Des Moines Area CC
Diablo Valley College
Dickinson
Dowling
Duke

E. Tennessee State U
E. Texas
Earlham
Easter State U
El Camino JC
Evergreen
Ferris State U
Fort Lewis College
Fresno State
Front Rance CC
FSU
Ft. Lewis College
Fullerton CC
George Fox U
Georgetown U
Grand Valley Central
    Michigan U
Grandview College
Grossmant CC
Guilford
Hampshire
Hanover College
Harbor JC
Harvard
Hawkey CC
Hayward State U
Healds Business College
Hofstra
Humboldt State U
Indiana Tech
Indiana U
Irvine Valley
ITT Tech Inst.

JFK U
Juilliard
Kalamazoo Valley CC
Kendall School of Design
Kentucky State U
Kings County
Kirkwood CC
Lake Michigan College
Lakewood CC
Lansing CC
Laramie CC
Lawrence
LeMoyne-Owen College
Lincoln U
Loma Linda U
Long Beach State U
Los Angeles City College
Los Medanos College
Macomb CC
McAlister
McGill Merced College
Metro State College
Michigan State U
Michigan Tech
Mid-Michigan CC
Middle Tennessee State U
Mira Costa CC
Mott CC
Mount San Jacinto CC
Mt. Royal
Mt. Sac
Mt. San Antonio College
N. Texas State
Napa Valley College
Nassau CC
NE Technical College
New College
Northeastern
Northeastern JC
NYU
Oakland CC
Oakland U
Oberlin
Oneida Area Vocational
Oregon
Palomar
Peralta Colleges
Pikes Peak CC
Pima CC
Pomona
Portland School of Art

Pratt
Princeton
PSU
Pueblo CC
Purdue
Radcliffe
Red Rocks CC
Reed
Richland
RISD
RIT
Roane State CC
S. Maine Tech. College
Sacramento City College
Sacramento State
Saddleback JC
San Diego City College
San Diego State
San Francisco College of Art
San Francisco State U
San Jose State U
Santa Monica City College
Sarah Lawrence
Seattle Pacific U
Shelby State CC
Shimer
Sierra JC
Sierra Valley
Skadron Business College
Smith
SMU
Sonoma State
Southwestern
Southwestern Michigan
    College
St. Clair CC
St. Joseph's
Stanford
SUNY
Swarthmore
Syracuse
Tennessee State U
Tennessee Tech U
Texas A & I
Texas State Tech College
Tulane
U at New York
U Nacional Autonoma
U of Alabama
U of Arizona
U of Calgary

U of California
U of Colorado
U of Hawaii
U of Illinois
U of Lowell
U of Maine
U of Michigan
U of Missouri
U of N. Colorado
U of N. Iowa
U of New Hampshire
U of Northern Colorado
U of Pennsylvania
U of S. Maine
U of San Diego
U of Santa Clara
U of Tennessee
U of Victoria
U of Virginia
U of Washington
UC Berkeley
UC Irvine
UCLA
UC Santa Barbara
UC Santa Cruz
U of Louisville
U of N. Colorado UNH
Union College
UNLV
UNR
USC
Victor Valley College
Virginia Tech
Warren Wilson
Washington State U
Washington U
Wayne State U
Western
Western Michigan College
Western Michigan U
Western Washington U
Western Wyoming CC
Whitman College
William & Mary
Wisconsin CCs
Wooster
Worcester Polytech
Yale
Yuba City CC

Schools That Have Had Research and Publications

(Refer to comprehensive index for page reference of full listing)

Higher Education

Aprovecho Research Center, OR
Fairhaven College, WA
Global Personal Teachers' Transformation, Czech Republic
Institute for Bioregional Studies, PEI, Canada
PLENTY, CA
Portland Community College, OR
Saybrook Institute Graduate School, CA
School of Human Service, VT
Union Institute, OH
World University, AZ
University Colleges, BC, Canada

Home-Based

Abbington Academy, MA (1-12)
Albuquerque Family School, NM (1-8)
Arches, AZ
Bethany Home Educators, AZ (K-12)
Canadian Alliance of Home Schoolers, ON, Canada
Chapel Hill Homeschoolers, NC (all)
HALL Program, WA (K-12)
Home Education League of Parents (HELP) Columbus Chapter, OH
Home Study International, MD (pre K-college)
HOUSE, IL
Oak Meadow School, VA (K-12)
Our Greenhouse, NC (5, 8)
Moore Academy, WA (K-12)
New Moon Publishing, MN
Venture School, CA (K-12)
Vermont Home Schoolers, VT

Independent

Adult Education Center, CO
Alexander School, TX
Aprovecho Research Center, OR
Aspen Community School, CO (pre K-8)
Barbara Taylor School, NY (K-8)
Benjamin Franklin Academy, GA
Blue Mountain School, VA (pre K-7)
Boynton School, NH (7-12+)
Bright Ideas School, TX (pre K-11)

Brockwood Park Krishnamurti Educational Centre, England
Carden School of Tucson, AZ (K-8)
Cascade Valley School, OR (ungraded)
Clearway Alternative High School, NH
Community Service Academy, NY (6-8)
Corlears School, NY
Cowichan Valley Trade School, BC, Canada
De La Salle Education Center, MO (HS)
Eagle Rock School, CO (HS)
Eclipse Program at Denver Children's Home, CO (7-12)
Family English Literacy Program, CA
Frost Valley Environmental Education, NY
Genesis School Inc, MO (6-11)
Georgetown School Department, MA (K-12)
Global Youth Academy, CA (6-12)
Greenhouse Alternative High School, OR (7-12)
Harmony Lane School, OR
Harmony School, IN (pre K-12)
Highland Free School, AZ (ungraded)
Highland School, WV
Horizons School, GA (pre K-12)
Hurricane Island Outward Bound, FL (6-12)
Hurricane Island Outward Bound, ME
Lake County Learning Center, OR
Lakeside School, PA (6-12)
Little Earth School, NM (pre K-3)
Little Friends Child Care, IN
Lullwater School, GA (K-9)
Newark Center For Creative Learning, DE (K-8)
Open Meadow Learning Center, OR (7-12)
Peninsula School, CA (K-8)
Philadelphia School, PA (K-8)
Phoenix Special Programs, AZ (7-12)
Play Mountain Place, CA
Progressive School of Long Island, NY (K-6)
Project Learn School, PA
Reach School, Inc, ME (7-12)
Riley School, ME (ungraded)
River Valley Community School, OH (pre K-6)
Sandhill Crane School, CA
Sands School, Devon, England
September School, CO (9-12)
Small School, Devon, England
Southside Family School, MN (K-6)
Stonesoup School, FL (-12)

Sudbury Valley School, MA
Summerhill School, England
Synergy School, CA (K-6)
The Community School, ME (HS)
The Free School, NY (ungraded)
The Meeting School, NH (9-12)
The School Around Us, ME (pre K-6)
The School in Rose Valley, PA (pre K-6)
The Xinachtli Project, TX
Upland Hills School, MI (K-8th)
Urban Day School, WI (K-8th)
Vantage Program, PA (7-12)
Wingra School, WI (K-8)
Shalom High School, WI (9-12)
Santan High School, CA (9-12)
Community School, VA
Learning Skills Center, FL (4-12)

Montessori

ABC/International Montessori Academy, Inc, MN
Alcuin Montessori School, IL
Arborland Montessori Children's Academy, CA
Austin Montessori School, TX
Beverly Montessori School, IL
Bloomfield Hills Montessori Center, MI
Bright Star Montessori, CA
Building Blocks Montessori School, NY
Celebration Montessori Center, Inc, KS
Chesterfield Day School, MO
Children of Promise Christian Montessori, MO
Children's House, WI
Children's House of Boca Raton, FL
Claremont Montessori School, FL
Countryside Montessori, CO
Creative Montessori, Inc, AL
Croton Montessori School, NY
Daggett Middle School, TX
Discovery Montessori School, CA
Drew Model School, VA (pre K-5)
East Aurora Montessori, NY
Easton Montessori School, MD
Elementary Workshop, DE
Eton School, WA
Evergreen Academy, WA
Fox Valley Montessori School, IL
Franciscan Montessori Earth School, OR
Go Like the Wind! Montessori School, MI
Hampton Roads Montessori School, VA

Highland Community School, WI (pre K-3)
Highland Meadow Montessori Academy, TX
Infant Toddler Montessori School, AR
IUSD, Montessori Early Childhood Education, CA
Kingsley Montessori School, MA
L Robert Allen Montessori Center, HI
Lamplighter, TN
Lillie C Evans, FL
Millhopper Montessori, FL
Mitchell Montessori Elementary, CO
Montessori Centre, TN
Montessori Centres, Inc, IN
Montessori Child Development Center, CA
Montessori Day Schools, AZ
Montessori Elementary and Preschool, IL
Montessori Elementary School, IL
Montessori Family School, CA
Montessori in Redlands, CA
Montessori Learning Center, AL
Montessori Learning Center/ Alamogordo Montessori Academy, NM
Montessori of Placerville, CA
Montessori School for Shreveport, LA
Montessori School of Anderson, SC
Montessori School of Frankfort, KY
Montessori School of Fremont, CA
Montessori School of Ft Myers, FL
Montessori School of Hong Kong, Hong Kong
Montessori School of Kensington, CA
Montessori School of North Hoffman, IL
Montessori School of the Upper Valley, Inc, VT
Mountain Pathways School, NC (pre K-3)
Mt. Lebanon Montessori School, PA
Northwoods Montessori School, GA
Olivia's Montessori School, TN
Our Lady of Grace Montessori, NY
Parker Montessori Educational Institute, CO
Pierson Montessori Center, FL
Post Oak School, TX
Racine Montessori School, WI
Rainbow Montessori School, AZ
Rousseau McClellan IPS #91, IN (K-5)
Sandstone Montessori, OH
Scarborough Montessori Center, Tobago, West Indies
School of the Woods, TX
Small World Children's House, MA
South County Montessori School, RI
Southwest Suburban Montessori, IL
St Camillus Montessori, KY
St Helena Montessori School, CA
St Mary of the Springs Montessori School, OH
The Country Day School, AL
The Fleetwood Montessori School, NY
The Montessori Center, TX
The Montessori School of Champaign-Urbana, IL
The Montessory Society of Central Maryland, MD
The Vicarage School of Montessori, CT
The Village School for Children, NJ
The Walden School, PA
Trinity Montessori, NY
Villa Montessori, Inc, CA
Villa Montessori School, IL
West Side Montessori School, NY
Woodinville Montessori School, WA

Public At-Risk

Academic Community for Educational Success, NY (9-12)
A. D. Harris, FL (6-12)
AIM High School, OR (8-12)
Albert Powell Continuation High School, CA (10-12)
Alternative #1 High School, CO (9-12)
Alternative Choices in Education, MI (9-12)
Alternative Classroom, TN (7-12)
Alternative Education and Work Center (AEWC), CA (HS)
Alternative Education Center, VA (7-12)
Alternative Education Program at Braintree High School, MA (9-12)
Alternative Education Program; Halifax-S Boston, VA (7-12)
Alternative High School, AB, Canada (10-12)
Alternative Junior High School, ID (7-9)
Alternative Learning Program at Plainedge HS, NY (9-12)
Alternative Program at Willow St Vo-Tech, PA (8-12)
Axton Middle School, VA (6-8)
Bangor Alternative High School, MI (9-12)
Beachside Alternative School, VA (8-12)
Boulder Valley Schools Teen Parenting Program, CO (9-12)
Broad Horizons Educational Center, NM (8-12)
Broome-Chenango Alternative High School, NY (7-12)
Buffalo Alternative High School, NY (7-12)
CEC Alternative Schools, IA (7-12)
Centennial High School, CO (10-12)
Center for Alternative Learning, ME (9-12)
Central High School, UT (7-12)
Chesapeake Alternative, VA (7-10)
Clarksdale City School, MS (9-11)
Community Learning Opportunity Center, WA (9-12)
Community Services Consortium's Learning Opportunities Center, OR
Cottage "I" Team, CO (11-12)
DMACC Academic Achievement Center, IA (HS)
Dorchester Youth Alternative School, MA (6-10)
Dowagiac Schools Alternative Education, MI (9-12)
Dry Valley Alternative School, TN (5-12)
Earhart High School, CA (10-12)
Eastern Jackson County Alternative High School, MO (9-12)
Eclipse/Independent Redirection, CO
Even Start, CA
Excalibur Prep, MI (8-12)
EXPO High School, IA
Ferguson-Florissant Education Center, MO (K-12)
Franklin Community School, CA (6-9)
Frederick Douglass Literacy Center, NY (10)
Hampton Academy Alternative Education, ME (9-12)
Harlan Flexible Education Center, IA (9-12)
Harrell Alternative Learning Center, TX
"I" Team Estate, CO (11-12)
Ignacio Second Chance, CO (9-12)

Independent Learning Center, CA (9-12)
Indian Trails Career Center, IN (6-12)
Insights, CA (9-10)
Irwin High School, CA (9-12)
Island Academy, NY (ungraded)
Island High School, CA (9-12)
James R. Fitz Harris High School, MI (9-12)
Johnson Academy, TN
Kirkwood High Alternative, MO (HS)
Lake Pend Oreille High School, ID (9-12)
Learning Center, IA (9-12)
Lee Education Center, FL (6-12)
Lincoln Alternative High School, IA (9-12)
Lindenhurst Alternative Learning Center, NY (9-12)
Margaret Hudson Program, OK (6-12)
McDowell Education Center, IN (9-12)
McLain High School Alternative Cooperative Education, CO (9-12)
Metro High School, IA (9-12)
Metro Opportunity School, TX (HS)
Midway High School, CA (9-12)
Moneta High School, CA
Mt San Jacinto High School, CA (9-12)
Multnomah Elementary & Middle School, OR (1-8)
NE Mississippi Regional Alternative Education Coop, MS (5-12)
Neosho Evening Alternative School, MO (9-12)
New Futures School, NM (7-12)
North Babylon Alternative High School, NY (10-12)
Northern Area Alternative High School, PA (9-12)
Oasis High School, MI (9-12)
Ocean Shores High School, CA
Options Learning Center, TX (9-12)
Palisade Glacier High School, CA (9-12)
PASS Program, CA (HS)
Pegasus High School, CA (10-12)
Penobscot Job Corps, ME
Pine Belt Education Service Center, MS (5-12)
Portland Night High School, OR
Project CDA (Creating Dropout Alternatives), ID (8-12)
Project Connect, OK (9-12)
Project New Start, MS (7-12)
Prospect Alternative Center for Education, CA (9-12)
Prospect High School, CA (9-12)
REACH, MI (10-12)
Reading Recovery, Reading/Writing Lab, Math Lab, IA (1-6)
READS Academy, MA (K-12)
Revilla High School, AK (9-12)
Roberto Clemente Student Development Center, MI (8-12)
Royal Oak Teen Parent Program, MI (9-12)
Sabal Palm School, FL (4-10)
Sachem, NY (9-12+)
San Luis High School, CA
Sanford Alternative School, ME (8-10)
Satellite Academy High School, NY (9-12)
School Training At-Risk Students (STARS), TN (7-12)
Second Chance High School, ID (9-12)
Senior High Accomodations, AZ (9-12)
Sierra Vista High School, CA (9-12)
South Area High School, FL (9-12)
South Haven Alternative Education, MI (9-12)

Springdale Learning Center & "Nite" School, AR (9-12)
STAR (Student Training and Reentry) Program, OK
STC Partnership Center, IA (6-12)
STRIVE High Alternative School, SD (9-12)
Student Support Services-Iowa Lakes Community College, IA (12+)
Summit Continuation High School, CA (10-12)
Sunset High School, CA (9-12)
Take Two-AES (Alternative Education Services), OK (9-12)
Teen Parent Center, ID (7-12)
The Learning Center, MS (7-12)
The Literacy Center, VA (9)
The Log School, MA (6-8)
Triune Teaching Program, MD (8)
Twin Palms High School, CA (10-12)
Union Street Alternative Education, ME (9-12)
Vine Street Alternative High School, MI (7-12)
Wayne Enrichment Center, IN (9-12)
Wayne Township Alternative Junior High, IN
Weld Opportunity School, CO (9-12)
West School Prep Program, ME (4-12)
West Valley Academy, OR (K-12)
Window Rock Alternative Education, AZ (HS)
York County High School, PA (9-12)

Public Choice

622 Alternative High School, MN
Aldo Leopold Alternative Program at Allouez School, WI (K-8)
Albuquerque Family School, NM (1-8)
Alternative School #1, WA (K-8)
Arroyo Seco Alternative School, CA (K-8)
Ashley Falls Program, MA (3-4)
Bartlett Alternative School, OK (9-12)
Bethpage Alternative for Success Curriculum (BASC), NY (9-11)
Bishop Carroll High School, AB, Canada
Boise Evening High School, ID (9-12)
Brooklyn New School, NY (K-6)
Calgary Alternative High School, AB, Canada (10-12)
Cedar Lane Alternative Education, MI (9-12)
Center for International Studies, CO (9-12)
City-As-School High School, NY (9-12)
Coalition School For Social Change, NY (9)
Community Education Center, CA (9-12)
Continuation High School, ID (9-12)
Cooperative Alternative School, ME (7-12)
Corridor Elementary Alternative School, OR (K-5)
Crossroads School, NY (6-8)
Delta Program, PA (7-12)
Denver School of the Arts, CO (6-12)
Des Moines Alternative High School-North, IA (9-12)
Discovery at Indian Creek, IN (1-5)
Drew Model School, VA (pre K-5)
East Lansing High School, MI (9-12)
Educational Opportunity Program, CO (HS)
Enterprise High School, MI
Essential Program at R.L. Paschal High School, TX (HS)

Eugene International High School, OR (9-12)
Flower Vocational-Essential School, IL (HS)
Foreign Language Magnet, IN (HS)
Fred N. Thomas Career Education Center, CO (9-12)
Genesis School Inc, MO (6-11)
Geneva Middle School Alternative Education, NY (7-8)
Georges Valley High School, ME (9-12)
Georgetown School Department, MA (K-12)
Gordon Willard Alternative Education Center, IA (9-12)
Graham and Parks Alternative Public School, MA (K-8)
Grass Valley Charter School, CA (K-8)
HALL Program, WA (K-12)
Hall School Montessori, OR
Haslett Alternative Education, MI (9-12)
Helen Hunt Jackson Alternative School/ Alessandro High School, CA (7-12)
High School III, WY (9-12)
High School Redirection, NY
Horizons High School, CA (HS)
Independent Study, CA (K-12)
Jefferson County Adolescent Pregnancy and Parenting Program (JCAPPP), CO (8-12)
Key Elementary School-Partial Immersion, VA
Landmark High School, NY (9)
Learning Unlimited, IN (9-12)
Lester Arnold High School, CO (9-12)
Lillie C. Evans, FL
Lindblom Technical High School, IL (9-12)
Los Angeles County High School for the Arts, CA (10-12)
Maplemere Elementary, NY (K-5)
Marcy Open School, MN (K-8)
Mary Blain Elementary Key School, CO (K-5)
Mason Alternative High School, MI (9-12)
Meridian park Elementary, WA (K-6)
Middle College High School at Shelby State CC, TN (10-12)
Mitchell Montessori Elementary, CO
Mooresville Optional Year Round Program, NC (K-8)
New Orleans Free School, LA (K-8)
Nova Blanche Forman Elementary School, FL (K-5)
NYC Lab School for Gifted Education, NY (6-9)
Olympus Northwest, WA (6-8)
Open the Door to a Different Approach to Learning, TX (9-12)
Paul M. Hodgson Vocational-Technical High School, DE (9-12)
Portage Alternative High School, MI (9-12)
Porter County Career Center, IN (9-12)
Reynoldsburg High School, OH (10-12)
River Valley Alternative School, ME (9-12)
Room Nine Program
Rousseau McClellan IPS #91, IN (K-5)
Sands Montessori, OH
Scarsdale Alternative School, NY (10-12)
School for Applied Individualized Learning (SAIL), FL (9-12)
School Within a School, MA (10-12)
School Without Walls, NY (9-12)
Summit Alternative School, CO (9-12)
The Exploratory School, CO (5-6)
The Learning Community at Los Altos HS, CA (9-12)

Theatre Arts Option, NY (5-6)
University Hill Elementary, CO (K-5)
Venture School, CA (K-12)
Village School, NY (9-12)
Vista Alternative School, CA (K-12)
Walden III, WI (6-12)
Weisser Park-Whitney Young ES Fine Arts Magnet, IN (pre K-5)
Western Wyoming High School, WY (9-12)
Wilderness School, CT

Public Choice/ At-Risk

Alternative Learning Center, NE (7-12)
Caledonia Options High School, MI (9-12)
Ferguson High School, CO (9-12)
Foothills High School, CA (9-12)
International High School at LaGuardia CC, NY
Kirkwood Learning Center, IA
Lee County Schools, FL (4-12)
March Mountain High School, CA (9-12)
Meridian Academy, ID (HS)
Palmer Night School, CO (9-12)
Phoenix/Goals Alternative Schools, MI (9-12)
Saranac Alternative Education, MI (9-12)
Sem Yeto High School, CA (9-12)
Sierra Mountain High, CA (9-12)
Southwest Open High School, CO (9-12)
STRIVE Alternative High School, MI (10-12)
Training Learning Center (TLC), TN (6-12)

Quaker

Arthur Morgan School, NC (7-9)
Brooklyn Friends School, NY (pre K-12)
Delaware Valley Friends School, PA (7-12)
Friends' School, CO (pre K-5)
Friends School, NJ (pre K-8)
Friends Seminary, NY (K-12)
George School, PA (9-12)
Lincoln School, RI (pre K-12)
Pacific Oaks Children's School, CA (pre K-3)
State College Friends School, PA (K-6)

Waldorf

Antioch New England Graduate School, NH
Crossroads Waldorf School, VA (pre K-7)
Green Meadow Waldorf School, NY (nursery, K-12)
Haleakala Waldorf School, HI (pre K-8)
Hartsbrook School, MA (pre K-8)
Hawthorne Valley School, NY (pre K-12)
High Mowing School, NH (9-12)
Honolulu Waldorf School, HI (pre K-8)
Lake Champlain Waldorf School, VT (pre K-6)
Minnesota Waldorf School, MN (K-8)
Oak Meadow School, VA (K-12)
Pleasant Ridge Waldorf School, WI (K-5)
Summerfield Waldorf School, CA (K-12)

Quaker Schools

(Refer to comprehensive index for page reference of full listing)

Friends School, CA
Global Friends School Program, CA (9-12)
John Woolman School, CA (9-12)
Pacific Ackworth Friends School, CA
Pacific Oaks Children's School, CA (pre K-3)
Whittier Friends School, CA (7)
Friends' School, CO (pre K-5)
Helen Gander Friends Nursery School, CT
Hockessin Friends Preschool, DE
Willmington Friends School, DE
Friends School of Atlanta, GA (K-6)
Children's School, IN (K-5)
Friends Preschool, IN
Wichita Friends School, Inc, KS (K-5)
Cambridge Friends School, MA (K-8)
The Life Experience School, MA
Friends Community School, MD (K-6)
Friends School, MD
Thornton Friends School, MD (6-12)
Friends School in Detroit, MI (pre K-8)
Friends School of Minnesota, MN (K-6)
Arthur Morgan School, NC (7-9)

Carolina Friends School, NC
New Garden Friends School, NC (pre K-8)
Friends School, NJ (pre K-8)
Moorestown Friends School, NJ
Princeton Friends School, NJ (pre K-8)
Rancocas Friends School, NJ
Ridgewood Friends Neighborhood Nursery, NJ
Albuquerque Friends School, NM (K-3)
Brooklyn Friends School, NY (pre K-12)
Friends Seminary, NY (K-12)
Friends World Program of Long Island University, NY
Mary McDowell Center For Learning, NY (ungraded)
Oakwood School, NY (9-12+)
Scarsdale Friends Nursery School, NY
Olney Friends School, OH (9-12)
Abington Friends School, PA
Barclay Friends School, PA
Buckingham Friends School, PA (K-8)
Concord Friends Nursery School, PA (pre K)

Delaware Valley Friends School, PA (7-12)
Frankford Friends School, PA
Friends Council on Education, PA
Friends Select School, PA
George School, PA (9-12)
Germantown Friends School, PA
Goshen Friends School, PA (pre K-5)
Greene Street Friends School, PA
Greenwood Friends School, PA (pre 6)
Gwynedd Friends Preschool, PA
Lansdowne Friends School, PA
Media Providence Friends School, PA
Newton Friends School, PA
Newtown Friends School, PA
Pendle Hill, PA
Plymouth Meeting Friends School, PA
State College Friends School, PA (K-6)
Stratford Friends School, PA
The Quaker School at Horsham, PA (1-7)
United Friends School, PA (K-6)
Wrightstown Friends Nursery School, PA
Lincoln School, RI (pre K-12)
Virginia Beach Friends School, VA

Alternative Colleges

(Refer to comprehensive index for page reference of full listing)

American Open University, NY
Antioch New England Graduate School, NH
Antioch University, OH
Bank Street College, NY
Barry University, FL
Burlington College, VT
California Institute of Integral Studies, CA
Center for the Study of Educational Alternatives, NY
College of the Atlantic, ME
Columbia Pacific University, CA
Echo Springs Transition Studies Center, ID
Enriched GED Program, IL
Eugene Lang College, NY
Evergreen State College, WA
Fairhaven College, WA
Friends World Program of Long Island University, NY
Geocommons College, NH
Goddard College, VT
Hampshire College, MA
Hawthorne University, UT
Houston Montessori Center, TX
International Montessori Society, MD

Johnson Center at University of Redlands, CA
Lesley College, MA
Marlboro College, VT
Montessori Education Center of the Rockies, CO
Montessori Institute of Los Angeles, CA
Montessori Institute of Milwaukee, WI
Montessori of Las Colinas School & Training Center, TX
Naropa Institute, CO
Naropa Institute—Early Education BA, CO
National Audubon Society Expedition Institute, ME
National-Louis University's Northern Virginia/Washington, DC, Center, VA
NCACS Teacher Education Program, PA
New College of California, CA
New College, FL
New England Montessori Teacher Education Center, NH
New York Open Center, NY
Pendle Hill, PA
PLENTY, CA
Portland Community College, OR
Prescott College, AZ

Rural Education Program, HOME Coop, ME
Saybrook Institute Graduate School, CA
School for International Training, VT
School of Education, Alternative Teacher Education, IN
School of Human Service, VT
Shimer College, IL
Umpqua Community College, OR
Union Institute, OH
Waldorf Institute of Sunbridge College, NY
Warren Wilson College, NC
World University, AZ

Eureka Free University, Russia
Global Personal Teachers' Transformation, Czech Republic
Institute for Bioregional Studies, Canada
Montessori College at Mount St Mary's, Ireland
Rogers Person Centered School Foundation, Hungary
University Colleges, Canada

Waldorf Schools

(Refer to comprehensive index for page reference of full listing)

Association of Waldorf Schools, CA
Camellia Waldorf School, CA (K-3)
Cedar Springs Waldorf School, CA (K-4)
Davis Waldorf School, CA (K-7)
East Bay Waldorf School, CA
Highland Hall School, CA
Live Oak Waldorf School, CA (K-8)
Marin Waldorf School, CA
Mariposa Waldorf School, CA (K-5)
Pasadena Waldorf School, CA (K-8)
Rudolf Steiner College, CA
Sacramento Waldorf School, CA
San Francisco Waldorf School, CA
Santa Cruz Waldorf School, CA (K-8)
Santa Monica Waldorf School, CA (pre K-4)
Sierra Waldorf School, CA
Sonoma Valley Waldorf School, CA (pre K-2)
Summerfield Waldorf School, CA (K-12)
Waldorf School of Mendocino County, CA (K-8)
Waldorf School of Monterey, CA
Waldorf School of Orange County, CA
Waldorf School of San Diego, CA (pre K-5)
Waldorf School of Santa Barbara, CA
Waldorf School of the Peninsula, CA (K-7)
Aspen Waldorf School, CO (pre K-4)
Denver Waldorf School, CO
Shining Mountain Waldorf School, CO (K-12)
Waldorf School of Gainesville, FL (1-4)
The Children's Garden, GA (nursery, K, II)
Haleakala Waldorf School, HI (pre K-8)
Honolulu Waldorf School, HI (pre K-8)
Kanai Waldorf School, HI (pre K-6)
Malamalama School, HI
Pali-uli Waldorf School, HI (pre K-6)
Sandpoint Waldorf School, ID
Chicago Waldorf School, IL (pre K-8)
Cape Ann Waldorf School, MA
Hartsbrook School, MA (pre K-8)

Rudolf Steiner School of Great Barrington, MA
Waldorf School, MA (pre K-8)
Waldorf School of Cape Cod, MA (nursery-8)
Waldorf School of Baltimore, MD
Washington Waldorf School, MD
Ashwood School, ME (K-4)
The Bay School, ME
The Merriconeag School, ME (K-4)
Detroit Waldorf School, MI
Oakland Steiner School, MI (pre K-6)
Rudolf Steiner School of Ann Arbor, MI (pre K-8)
Camphill Village MN, MN
City of Lakes Waldorf School, MN (pre K-8)
Minnesota Waldorf School, MN (K-8)
Spring Hill Waldorf School, MN (pre K)
Blue Ridge Waldorf Community, NC
Antioch New England Graduate School, NH
High Mowing School, NH (9-12)
Monadnock Waldorf School, NH (pre K-8)
Pine Hill Waldorf School, NH (K-8)
Waldorf School of Princeton, NJ (pre K-8)
Santa Fe Waldorf School, NM (K-8)
Aurora Waldorf School, NY
Green Meadow Waldorf School, NY (nursery, K-12)
Hawthorne Valley School, NY (pre K-12)
Hillside Children's Garden, NY (pre K-K)
Mountain Laurel Waldorf, NY (K-7)
Rudolf Steiner School, NY (pre K-12)
Spring Hill School, NY (pre K-6)
The Waldorf School of Garden City, NY (nursery-12)
Waldorf Institute of Sunbridge College, NY
Waldorf School of the Finger Lakes, NY (pre K-8)
Cincinnati Waldorf School, OH (pre K-2)

Spring Garden Waldorf School, OH (pre K-8)
Eugene Waldorf School, OR (K-12)
Portland Waldorf School, OR (pre K-8)
The Waldorf School of the Rogue Valley, OR (pre K-8)
Kimberton Waldorf School, PA
Susquehanna Waldorf School, PA (nursery-6)
Waldorf School Association of the Delaware River Valley, PA (pre K-1)
Meadowbrook Waldorf School, RI (K-5)
Austin Waldorf School, TX (K 6)
Crossroads Waldorf School, VA (pre K-7)
Green Mountain Waldorf School, VT (pre K-6)
Lake Champlain Waldorf School, VT (pre K-6)
The Montpelier Waldorf Child's Garden, VT
Upper Valley Waldorf School, VT (K-2)
Olympia Waldorf School, WA (K-5)
Seattle Waldorf School, WA (pre K-8)
Whatcom Hills Waldorf School, WA (K-8)
Whidbey Island Waldorf School, WA
Pleasant Ridge Waldorf School, WI (K-5)
Prairie Hill Waldorf School, WI (K-8)
Waldorf School of Milwaukee, WI (K-5)
Calgary Waldorf School, AB
Kelowna Waldorf School, BC
Nelson Waldorf School, BC (K-8)
Sunrise Waldorf School, BC (pre K-8)
Vancouver Waldorf School, BC
Alan Howard Waldorf School, ON (nursery-8)
Halton Waldorf School, ON
London Waldorf School, ON
Ottawa Waldorf School, ON
Rudolf Steiner Centre, ON
Toronto Waldorf School, ON (pre K-12)
L'Ecole Rudolf Steiner de Montreal, PQ

Other Independent Schools

(Refer to comprehensive index for page reference of full listing)

Marietta Johnson School of Organic
    Education, AL
Clear Spring School, AR (pre K-6)
Headwater School, AR
Alpha Omega Institute, AZ (pre K-8)
Awakening Seed School, AZ
Carden School of Tucson, AZ (K-8)
Highland Free School, AZ (ungraded)
Kino Learning Center, AZ
Phoenix Special Programs, AZ (7-12)
Veade Valley School, AZ (9-12)
Wood Canyon School, AZ
Ala Carte, International School, CA
Ananda School, CA
Cascade Canyon School, CA (K-8)
Children's House, CA
Community Learning Center, CA
Contra Costa Alternative High School,
    CA (9-12)
Encampment for Citzenship, CA
Fresno Valley High School, CA (9-12)
Futures High School, CA (7-12)
Gateway Community School, CA (K-5th)
Global Youth Academy, CA (6-12)
Great Explorations, CA (K+)
Horizons School, CA (7-12)
Independent Study Program, CA (K-12)
Learning Forum/Supercamp, CA
Mariposa School, CA
McFarland Independent School, CA (9-12)
Nonesuch School, CA
Oratory School, CA
Park Day School, CA (K-6)
Pathfinder, CA
Pathfinder High School of Independent
    Study, CA
Peninsula School, CA (K-8)
Petrolia High School, CA (9-12)
Pioneer Christian Academy, CA (K-12)
Play Mountain Place, CA
Rivendell School, CA
Sacramento Valley School, CA (K-12)
Sandhill Crane School, CA
Santan High School, CA (9-12)
Sequoyah School, CA (K-8)
Slide Ranch, CA (K-12)
St Vincent de Paul Life Skills, CA
Synergy School, CA (K-6)
Westland School, CA (K-6)
Adult Education Center, CO
Aspen Community School, CO (pre K-8)
Eagle Rock School, CO (HS)
Eclipse Program at Denver Children's
    Home, CO (7-12)
Foothills Academy, CO
Lamborn Valley School, CO
Mountain Sage School, CO

September School, CO (9-12)
Cold Spring School, CT (K-6)
Mead School, CT
Natchaug Democratic School, CT (1-12)
Parents Place and Kids Connection, CT
Watkinson School, CT (6-12+)
Wightwood School, CT (pre K-8)
School For Friends, DC
Community Learning Institute, Inc, DE
Early Childhood Laboratory School, DE
Educational Enrichment Center, Inc, DE
EUREKA! Learning Community, Inc, DE
Independence School, DE
Joshua's Choice School, DE
King's Kids Academy, DE
Newark Center For Creative Learning,
    DE (K-8)
Oakwood Clonlara School, DE
People's Settlement Preschool, DE
Pilot School, Inc, DE (ungraded)
Rose Valley School, DE
The Child Craft Company, DE
The Idea Patch, DE
The Little School, Inc, DE
Cornerstone School, FL (pre K-5)
Edison Learning Center, FL
Full Flower Education Center, FL (K-8)
Grassroots Free School, FL
Huckleberry School, FL
Hurricane Island Outward Bound, FL
    (6-12)
Jordan Glen School, FL (K-8)
Learning Skills Center, FL (4-12)
Magnolia School, FL
Oliver's Academy, FL (pre K-12)
Stonesoup School, FL (-12)
Sunflower School, FL
Benjamin Franklin Academy, GA
Horizons School, GA (pre K-12)
Lullwater School, GA (K-9)
CORAL Ohana O Maui, HI (ungraded)
Kalani Honua, HI
Malcolm Price Laboratory School, IA (all)
Willowind School, IA
Carbondale New School, IL (pre K-8)
Dr Pedro Albizu Campos High School, IL
    (9-12)
Progressive Path School, IL (pre K-ES)
The Southern School, IL
Transitional Care program at Northwest
    Coonen High School, IL (9-12)
Harmony School, IN (pre K-12)
Little Friends Child Care, IN
Padanaram Village School, IN (K-12)
Associated Youth Services, Inc, KS (6-12)
Creative Education Center, KY (1-12)
The Children's Community School, LA

Buxton School, MA (9-12)
Center of Independent Learning, Inc,
    MA (K-8)
Experiment With Travel, MA
Full Circle High School, MA
Full Circle School, MA (ungraded)
Holyoke Street School, MA
Nantucket New School, MA (pre K-7)
Sudbury Valley School, MA
The Apple Orchard School, MA
The Common School, MA
Touchstone Community School, MA
Green Acres School, MD
Sandy Spring Friends School, MD
Hurricane Island Outward Bound, ME
National Audubon Society Expedition
    Institute, ME (HS, college, graduate
    school)
New Country School, ME (pre K-6)
Reach School, Inc, ME (7-12)
Riley School, ME (ungraded)
The Community School, ME (HS)
The School Around Us, ME (pre K-6)
Toddy Pond School, ME
Climbing Tree School, MI (pre K-5)
Clonlara School, MI (pre K-12)
New Morning School, MI (pre K-8)
Upland Hills School, MI (K-8th)
Prairie Creek Community School, MN
    (K-5th)
Second Foundation School, MN (K-12)
Southside Family School, MN (K-6)
Superlearning, MN
De La Salle Education Center, MO (HS)
East Wind Community, MO
Little Piney Schoolhouse, MO
Phoenix International School for Peace,
    MO
The Principia, MO
Avalon School, MT (pre K-6)
Clark Fork School, MT (pre K-3)
Headwaters Academy, MT (7-12)
Shining Mountain School, MT
Sussex School, MT (K-8)
Camp Elliot Therapeutic Wilderness
    Program, NC
Children's Grammar School, NC
Rainbow Mountain School, NC
Father Flanagan High School, NE
Howard Dougherty Learning Center at
    Epworth Village, NE (K-12)
Lincoln Independent Study High School
    at University of Nebraska, NE (HS)
Boynton School, NH (7-12+)
Clearway Alternative High School, NH
Community School, NH (6-12)
The Meeting School, NH (9-12)

The Well School, NH
Atlantic County New School, NJ
Montclair Cooperative School, NJ
Sprout House, NJ (ungraded)
Armand Hammer United World College, NM
Chamisa Mesa High School, NM (9-12)
Down to Earth School, NM (7-12)
Little Earth School, NM (pre K-3)
Nizhoni School for Global Consciousness, NM
School of the North Star, NM
Vista Grande Preparatory School, NM (K-6)
Akwesasne Freedom School, NY (pre K-7)
Barbara Taylor School, NY (K-8)
Blue Rock School, NY (K-6)
Children's Storefront Support Corporation, NY (pre K-8)
City and Country, NY
Cobblestone School, NY (ungraded)
Corlears School, NY
Democratic School of the Finger Lakes, NY
Duane Lake Academy, NY
EIDOS Alternative Education Program, NY
Frost Valley Environmental Education, NY
Hampton Day School, NY (pre K-8)
High Meadow School, NY (K-7)
Holy Name School, NY (pre K-8)
Integrative Studies, NY
Manhattan Country School, NY
North Country School, NY (4-8)
Omega Institute for Holistic Studies, NY
Progressive School of Long Island, NY (K-6)
Robert C Parker School, NY (4-8)
Saratoga Independent School, NY (K-3)
Shalmont High School, NY (9-12)
The Alternative Learning Center, NY
The Free School, NY (ungraded)
The House for Bright and Gifted Children, NY (nursery-K)
The New School, NY
Westchester Day School, NY (pre K-8)
Antioch School, OH (pre K-6)
River Valley Community School, OH (pre K-6)
Street School, OK
Cascade Valley School, OR (ungraded)
Drinking Gourd Elementary School, OR (ungraded)
Fire Mountain School, OR (K-6th)
Greenhouse Alternative High School, OR (7-12)
Hands On Schools, OR
Harmony Lane School, OR
Horizon School, OR (pre K-5)
Josephine County Alternative Center, OR (7-12)

Lake County Learning Center, OR
Lithia Springs School, OR (9-12)
Looking Glass Educational Services, OR (5-12)
LUNO (Learning Unlimited Network of Oregon), OR
Mt Hood Academy, OR (9-12)
North Marion Alternative High School, OR (10-12)
Open Meadow Learning Center, OR (7-12)
Pacific Child Center, Inc, OR (K-6)
Parrott Creek School/Canby Union Annex, OR (8-12)
SOCRATES, OR (HS)
The Dome School, OR (pre K-5)
The Upstairs School, Alternative Youth Activities, Inc, OR (7-12)
Waucoma School, OR
Young Parent Opportunity Program, OR (HS)
Youthworks Educational Services, OR (7-12)
AYS Day Treatment, PA (4-12)
Circle School, PA
Country Gardens, PA
Crossroads Day Treatment, PA (ES-HS)
Fairville Early Learning Center, PA
Friends Central School, PA
Lakeside School, PA (6-12)
Middle Earth, Inc, PA (9-12)
Miquon School, PA
Philadelphia School, PA (K-8)
Project Learn School, PA
The School in Rose Valley, PA (pre K-6)
Upattinas School, PA (K-12)
Vantage Program, PA (7-12)
West Branch School, PA (K-6)
West Chester Friends School, PA (K-6)
William Penn Charter School, PA
Moses Brown School, RI
School One, RI
Wellspring Community School, RI (K-3)
Laurel High School, TN
Alexander School, TX
Awty International School, TX
Bending Oaks High School, TX (9-12)
Bright Ideas School, TX (pre K-11)
Community School, TX
Dallas Learning Center, TX (9-12)
East Dallas Community School, TX
Greenbriar School, TX
Highland Academy, TX
McGuffey Academy, TX
Rapid Advancement Program, TX (infant-8)
Robert Muller School, TX (birth-12)
The Circle School, TX (pre K-5)
The Xinachtli Project, TX
Weise Memorial Academy, TX (7-12)
Blacksburg New School, VA

Blue Mountain School, VA (pre K-7)
Community School, VA
New School of Northern Virginia, VA (K-12)
North Branch School, VA (nursery-8th)
Shenendoah Country Day School, VA
Bennington School, Inc, VT
Bridge School, VT
Eckerd Wilderness, VT
Gailer School, VT
Grammar School, VT (K-8)
Green Mount Valley School, VT
Hiland Hall School, VT
Laraway School, VT
Maplehilll Community School, VT
Mountain View Community School, VT (pre K-2)
Mtn. School Program of Milton Academy, VT
New School,Inc, VT
North Hollow School, VT
Open Fields School, VT
Pine Ridge School, VT
Red Cedar School, VT
Rock Point School, VT (HS)
Saxon Hill School Inc, VT
Schoolhouse, VT (K-6)
Smokey House Project, VT
Southshire Community School, VT (K-6)
The Neighborhood Schoolhouse, VT (ungraded)
Upward Bound, VT
Bellingham Cooperative School, WA
Family Academy, WA (K-12)
Skagit Alternative High School, WA
The Little School, WA (ungraded)
Willapa Community School, WA (K-8)
Multicultural Community HS, WI
NOVA, WI (7-12)
Quest Learning Center, Inc, WI (K-12)
Shalom High School, WI (9-12)
Turning Point School, WI
Urban Day School, WI (K-8th)
Wingra School, WI (K-8)
Gesundheit Institute, WV
Highland School, WV
Cowichan Valley Trade School, BC
Wondertree Education Society, BC
Schole, NS (1-12)
Indian Way School, ON
Oneida Learning Center, ON
Pickering College, ON
Reading Circles, ON
The Schoolhouse, ON (pre K-6)
Grace Christian School, PEI
Immanuel Christian School, PEI
Au Grand Bois, PQ
Survival School, PQ
Community Folk Schools of Saskatchewan, SK

Home-Based Education Groups and Organizations

(Refer to comprehensive index for page reference of full listing)

National

Calvert School Home Instruction Department, Baltimore, MD (K-8)
Home Study Directory/National Home Study Council, Washington, DC
Home-Based Educators Accrediting Association, Cambridge, MN
Home Study International, Silver Spring, MD (pre K-college)
Islamic Home School Association of North America, Raleigh, NC
Jewish Home Educator's Network, Sharon, MA
National Association of Mormon Home Educators, Perry, UT
National Challenged Homeschoolers Associated Network, Olalla, WA
National Homeschool Association, Cincinnati, OH
National Homeschool Service, Rodeo, NM
National Institute for Christian Home Education, Rustburg, VA

State, Local

Homeschoolers of Cordova, Cordova, AK
CHEF: Christian Home Education Fellowship of Alabama, Tuscaloosa, AL
Athens Support Group, Athens, AL
Auburn/Opelika Christian Home Educators, Auburn, AL
Baldwin County Home Educators, Robertsdale, AL
Chattahoochee Valley Homeschoolers Support Group, Phenix City, AL
Christian Educators at Home in Anniston (CHEAHA), Jacksonville, AL
Covenant Academy, Montgomery, AL
East Lake UMC Academy, Birmingham, AL
Fellowship Christian Support Group, Double Springs, AL
Fellowship of Christian Home Educators, Alabaster, AL
Florence/Sheffield Area Support Group, Sheffield, AL
Homeschool Advocates, Mobile, AL
Homeschooling Network, Tallahassee, AL
Southwest Alabama Home Educators, Mobile, AL
Arkansas Christian Home Education Association, North Little Rock, AR

Headwater School, Pettigrew, AR
Crowley's Ridge Christian Parent Education Association, Jonesboro, AR
Arizona Families for Home Education, Mesa, AZ
Arches, Tucson, AZ
Bethany Home Educators, Mesa, AZ (K-12)
Circle of Angels, West Sedona, AZ
Cochise County Families for Home Education, St David, AZ
Families For Home Education, Scottsdale, AZ
Parents Association of Christian Home Schools, Mayer, AZ
Phoenix Learning Alternatives Network (PLAN), Phoenix, AZ
SPICE, Avondale, AZ
Tucson Home Education Network (THEN), Tucson, AZ
Home School Advantage, Phoenix, AZ
Christian Home Educators of California, Santa Ana, CA
Home School Association of California, Sacramento, CA
Homeschool Association of California, Petaluma, CA
Northern Alameda/Western Contra Costa Homeschool Support Group, Berkeley, CA
West Mall Alternative School, Atascadero, CA (K-12)
Park Alternative Center, Monrovia, CA (K-12)
Crossroads High Independent Study, Newark, CA
P. G. Center for Independent Study, Pacific Grove, CA (K-12)
Twin Ridges Elementary Alternative Education, N San Juan, CA
Venture School, San Ramon, CA (K-12)
Vineyard High Independent Study, Livermore, CA
Alternative Family Education Home Studies, Santa Cruz, CA (K-12)
Bay Shore School, Long Beach, CA
Central Coast Homeschoolers, Atascadero, CA
Cooperative Home Education Program Center, El Cajon, CA
Cooperative Learning Center, Vista, CA
Esparto Homeschoolers, Esparto, CA
HCL, Whittier, CA (K-12)
High Desert Alternative Education Center, Victorville, CA (7-12)

Home And Independent Study, Pico Rivera, CA
Home Education League of Parents (HELP), Los Angeles, CA
Home Study Alternative School, Newport Beach, CA (K-8)
Homeschoolers For Peace, Midpines, CA
Humboldt Homeschoolers, Trinidad, CA
Laurel Springs School, Ojai, CA (K-12)
Magic Meadow School, N San Juan, CA
Mountain Home Alternative, Oakhurst, CA
Natural Alternative, Felton, CA
Peninsula Homeschoolers, San Jose, CA
Riverside Area Home Learners, Corona, CA
Santa Clara Valley Homeschoolers, Sunnyvale, CA
South Street Centre, Boulder Creek, CA (K-12)
South Valley Homeschoolers Association, Gilroy, CA
SPICE Homeschool Support Group, Wilton, CA
Whiz Kidz, Chico, CA
Yosemite Area Homeschoolers/ Home-schoolers for Peace, Midpines, CA
Home Educator's Almanac, Morgan Hill, CA
Landmark, Fillmore, CA
Liedloff Continuum Network, Sausalito, CA
The Sycamore Tree, Costa Mesa, CA
Christian Home Educators of Colorado, Denver, CO
Colorado Home Educator's Association, Westminster, CO
Colorado Home Educators Association, Denver, CO
Colorado Home Schooling Network, Sedalia, CO
Wyoming Homeschoolers, Ft. Collins, CO
Lamborn Valley School, Paonia, CO
Agape Family Schools, Loveland, CO
Catholic Home Educators, Aurora, CO
Christian Homes Educating for Excellent Results, Castle Rock, CO
Christian Parents Who Are Teaching at Home, Durango, CO
Christian Single Home Educators' Network, Commerce City, CO
Collegiate Peaks Home Educators, Buena Vista, CO
Colorado Springs Homeschool Support Group, Colorado Springs, CO

Colorado Springs Homeschoolers, Colorado Springs, CO

Delta County Support Group, Paonia, CO

Front Range Eclectic Educators, Parker, CO

Gunnison Valley Homeschoolers, Gunnison, CO

Home Education for Excellence in Durango (HEED), Durango, CO

Home Education League of Parents, Grand Junction, CO

Homeschoolers of Central Aurora, Aurora, CO

Homeschoolers Under God, Fort Collins, CO

Idaho Springs Home Educators, Idaho Springs, CO

Ind. Network of Creative Homescoolers, Aurora, CO

Independent Network of Creative Homeschoolers, Aurora, CO

Morgan County Homeschoolers Network, Brush, CO

Mountain Area Home Educators, Evergreen, CO

North Suburban Homeschoolers, Thornton, CO

Northern Colorado Home School Association, Fort Collins, CO

Pleasant Hill Academy, Longmont, CO (K-12)

Pueblo Home School Association, Pueblo, CO

San Juan Home Educators, Montrose, CO

Sonshine Support Group, Lamar, CO

Summit County Home Schoolers, Dillon, CO

Teller County Home Education Association, Woodland Park, CO

The Children's Cooperative Homeschool, Ridgway, CO (ES)

Unschoolers Family Support Group, Colorado Springs, CO

We Are Teaching Our Children At Home, Brighton, CO

Pinewood School, Pine, CO (K-12)

Pinyon Court School, Lakewood, CO (K-12)

Connecticut Home Educators Association, Middletown, CT

The Educational Association of Christian Homeschoolers (TEACH), Bloomfield, CT

Delaware Home Education Association, Newark, DE

Tri-State Homeschoolers Association, Newark, DE

Florida Association for Schools at Home, Tallahassee, FL

Learning Skills Center, Pensacola, FL (4-12)

Alachua County Home Schoolers, Gainesville, FL

Alachua Home School Group, Alachua, FL

Chuluota First Home Schoolers, Chuluota, FL

Community Home School, Ocala, FL

Deltona Group, Deltona, FL

Family Centered Learning of Central Florida, Longwood, FL

Family Learning Exchange, Mims, FL

Family Training Fellowship, Orlando, FL

Grace Home Schoolers, Casselberry, FL

Gulf Coast Homeschool, Ft Myers, FL

HETE: Home Educators Teaching for Eternity, Orlando, FL

Hogtown Homeschoolers, Archer, FL

Open Door Private School of Pinellas Co, Inc, Dunedin, FL (K-12)

Panama Support Group at Ft Amador, APO Miami, FL

Parkland Home Educators, Winter Park, FL

Vero Beach Support Group, Vero Beach, FL

West Florida Home Education Support League, Pensacola, FL

A BEKA Correspondence School, Pensacola, FL

Florida at Home, Orlando, FL

Homeschooling Today, Melrose, FL

Christians Concerned for Education / Still Waters, LaFayette, GA

Georgia Home Education Association, Fayetteville, GA

Georgia Home Educators, Dunwoody, GA

Atlanta Alternative Education Network, Decatur, GA

Cobb County Homeschoolers, Kennesaw, GA

Free to Learn at Home, Oakwood, GA

Hall County Home Educators, Oakwood, GA

Herbst Homeschool, Woodstock, GA (K-9)

North Side Atlanta Homeschoolers, Atlanta, GA

REACH, Woodstock, GA

Christian Homeschoolers of Hawaii, Ewa Beach, HI

Hawaii Homeschool Association, Waialua, HI

Hawaii Island Home Educators, Mountain View, HI

Hawaii Military Families in Home Education, Fort Ord, HI

Friends Learning at Home, Mililani, HI

HAPPY (Homeschool Adventures: Program for Parents and Youngsters), Wailuku, HI

Ohana Community Center, Haiku, HI

Open Sky Home Education, Pahoa, HI

Kids Lib News, Naalehu, HI

Open Sky HOME Education, Pahoa, HI

Tropical Homeschooler Newsletter, Haiku, HI

Iowa Coalition for Home Educators, Des Moines, IA

Iowa Families for Christian Education, Missouri Valley, IA

Cerro Cordo County Support Group, Mason City, IA

Ida County Support Group, Ida Grove, IA

Jasper County Support Group, Newton, IA

Johnson County Support Group, Iowa City, IA

Monroe County Support Group, Albia, IA

SHEEP, Altoona, IA

Story County Support Group, Roland, IA

Home Educators of Idaho, Coeur d'Alene, ID

Idaho Home Educators, Boise, ID

Homeschooling on the Polouse, Moscow, ID

HOUSE, Evansville, IL

Illinois Christian Home Educators, Zion, IL

American School, Chicago, IL

Christian Liberty Academy Satellite Schools, Arlington Hgts, IL (K-12)

Indiana Association of Home Educators, Greenwood, IN

Fort Wayne Area Home Schools, Fort Wayne, IN

Jackson County Christian Home Educators, Seymour, IN

Lake County Christian Home School Association, Cedar Lake, IN

LEARN, Unionville, IN

River Falls Christian Association of Home Educators, Charlestown, IN

Southern Indiana Support Group, Princeton, IN

Wabash Valley Homeschool Association, Terre Haute, IN

Christian Home Educators Confederation of Kansas, Shawnee Mission, KS

Kansans for Alternative Education, Spring Hill, KS

Central Kansas Home Educators, Lyons, KS

Hesston/Canton Home Educators Association, Canton, KS

Lawrence Area Unaffiliated Group of Homeschoolers (LAUGH), Perry, KS

Manhattan Parent Educators, Manhattan, KS

Teaching Parents Association, Wichita, KS

Kentucky Christian Home School Association, Fairdale, KY

Kentucky Home Education Association, Winchester, KY

Kentucky Home Schoolers, Louisville, KY

Christian Home Educators Fellowship of Louisiana, Baton Rouge, LA

Louisiana Citizens for Home Education, Baker, LA

Beauregard/Vernon Home School Association, Leesville, LA

Homeschoolers of Massachusetts Education Club, Newton, MA

Massachusetts Home Learning Association, Lenox, MA

Massachusetts Homeschoolers Organization of Parent Educators, Wilmington, MA

Jewish Home Educator's Network, Sharon, MA

Abbington Academy, Wareham, MA (1-12)

Apple Country Homeschooling Association, Harvard, MA

Berkshire Homeschoolers Group, Berkshire, MA

Cape Ann Homeschoolers, Magnolia, MA (K-6)

Greater Boston Home Educators, Wakefield, MA

Hibbard Alternative, Pittsfield, MA

Home Education Resource Center, Pittsfield, MA

Kitchen School Group, W Boxford, MA

Metro West Homeschoolers, Framingham, MA

North Shore Homeschool Support Group, Beverly, MA

South Shore Home Schoolers, Rockland, MA

South Shore Homeschoolers, Brockton, MA

The Learning Cooperative, Amherst, MA

Worcester Area Homeschooling Organization, Worcester, MA
Holt Associates, Cambridge, MA
Maryland Home Education Association, Columbia, MD
North Country Home Educators, Pasadena, MD
Parents for Home Education, Beltsville, MD
The Glen Burnie Homeschool Support Group, Glen Burnie, MD
Home Study Institute, Takoma Park, MD
Alternative Education Association of Maine, Portland, ME
Homeschoolers of Maine, Hope, ME
Maine Homeschool Association, Portland, ME
Mount Desert Island Homeschoolers, West Tremont, ME
Peninsula Area Homeschooling Association, Deer Isle, ME
Sebago Lake Homeschoolers Support Group, Sebago Lake, ME
Southern Maine Home Education Support Network, Scarborough, ME
Brook Farm Books, Bridgewater, ME
Gentle Wind School, Surry, ME
Homeschool Associates of New England, Auburn, ME
Bay City Homeschooling Support Group, Bay City, MI
Benzie Home Educators, Benzonia, MI
Heritage Home Educators, Holly, MI
Holland Homeschool Group, Holland, MI
Learning Tree Resource Center, Atlantic Mine, MI
Mid-Michigan Homeschoolers, Grand Blanc, MI
Spencer Home Learning Center, Ypsilanti, MI
Sunnyridge Alternative Learning Center, Pelkie, MI
Ward Homeschool Fellowship, W Bloomfield, MI
Clonlara School Home Based Education Program, Ann Arbor, MI (K–12)
The Home School Manual, from Gazelle Publications, Niles, MI
Umoja*Unidad*Unity (Homeschoolers of Color), Idlewild, MI
Minnesota Association of Christian Home Educators, Anoka, MN
Minnesota Home School Network, Hastings, MN
Minnesota Homeschool Alliance, Maple Plain, MN
MN Homeschoolers Alliance, Richfield, MN
TEACH Institute, N Robbinsdale, MN
Detroit Lakes Alternative Learning Center, Detroit Lakes, MN
Families Nurturing Lifelong Learners, Maplewood, MN
Fargo-Moorehead Homeschool Association, Moorehead, MN
WOLF School, Minneapolis, MN (K–12)
Catholic Home School Newsletter, New Brighton, MN
Homeward, Lakeville, MN
New Moon Publishing, Duluth, MN
Families for Home Education, Sibley, MO
Home Schooling Network, St Louis, MO
Springfield Area Homeschoolers, Springfield, MO
Practical Homeschooling, Fenton, MO

Home Educators of Central Mississippi, Ridgeland, MS
Homeschoolers of Montana, Helena, MT
Butte Home Education Association, Butte, MT
Flathead Homeschool Association, Columbia Falls, MT
Gardiner's Homeschoolers, Gardiner, MT
Helena Area Christian Home Educators, Helena, MT
Homeschool Information, Seeley Lake, MT
Missoula Homeschoolers Association, Missoula, MT
The Grapevine (Montana Homeschool News), Seeley Lake, MT
North Carolinians for Home Education, Raleigh, NC
Carolina Superschoolers, Columbus, NC
CELO Community, Burnsville, NC
Chapel Hill Homeschoolers, Chapel Hill, NC (all)
Charlotte Home Educators Association, Charlotte, NC
CHARM: Christian Homeschool Association of Rocky Mount, Rocky Mount, NC
Christian Home Education Association of Franklin, Franklin, NC
Christian Home Education Association of Greater Durham, Durham, NC
Down East Homeschoolers, Washington, NC
ED-venturous Learning Families, Franklin, NC
Fellowship & Instruction to Home Educators, Charlotte, NC
Gaston County Homeschool Network, Gastonia, NC
Greensboro Home Educators, Greensboro, NC
Haywood County Home Educators, Waynesville, NC
Heart of Carolina, Raleigh, NC
High Point Area Home Educators, High Point, NC
Home Education Association, Durham, NC
Home Educators of Carteret, Beaufort, NC
Home Offering Meaningful Education, Fayetteville, NC
Iredell County Home Educators, Statesville, NC
Magnum Opus Developmental Education Laboratory (MODEL), Asheboro, NC
New Beginnings, Zebulon, NC
New Bern Homeschoolers, Ernul, NC
Our Greenhouse, High Point, NC (5, 8)
Pathfinders, Fuquay-Varina, NC
Profile, Elizabeth City, NC
Randolph County Christian Home Educators, Asheboro, NC
Randolph County Home Educators, Greensboro, NC
Rowan County Homeschoolers, Salisbury, NC
SHARE, Morganton, NC
Stanly/Montgomery, Albemarle, NC
TEACH of NC, Raleigh, NC
The "Y" Group, Raleigh, NC
Thomasville Home Educators, Thomasville, NC

Union Acres Alternative School, Whittier, NC
Wayne Christian Home Educators, Goldsboro, NC
Wilmington Homeschool Organization, Wilmington, NC
North Dakota Home School Association, Mandan, ND
Nebraska Home Educators Association, Lincoln, NE
Nebraska Independent Homeschoolers Network, Lincoln, NE
LEARN, Lincoln, NE
Nebraska Home School Contact, Johson, NE
Nebraska Home School Contact, Bellevue, NE
Nebraska Home School Contact, Merna, NE
Nebraska Home School Contact, Holdrege, NE
Nebraska Home School Contact, Holdrege, NE
Nebraska Home School Contact, Firth, NE
Nebraska Home School Contact, Kearney, NE
Nebraska Home School Contact, Dakota, NE
Nebraska Home School Contact, Indianola, NE
Nebraska Home School Contact, Lincoln, NE
Nebraska Home School Contact, Nebraska City, NE
Nebraska Home School Contact, Norfolk, NE
Nebraska Home School Contact, North Platte, NE
Nebraska Home School Contact, Ord, NE
Nebraska Home School Contact, Milford, NE
Nebraska Home School Contact, Oxford, NE
Nebraska Home School Contact, Miniature, NE
Nebraska Home School Contact, Herman, NE
Nebraska Home School Contact, Herman, NE
OPEN, Omaha, NE
Christian Home Educators of New Hampshire, Manchester, NH
New Hampshire Alliance for Home Education, Manchester, NH
New Hampshire Home Education Association, Nashua, NH
New Hampshire Homeschooling Coalition, Concord, NH
New Jersey Family Schools Association, Washington, NJ
New Jersey Unschoolers, Farmingdale, NJ
North Jersey Home Schoolers Association, Hillsdale, NJ (pre K–12)
Homeschoolers of South Jersey, Vincentown, NJ
Jersey Shore Christian Homeschoolers Association, Matawan, NJ
Lipman-Stern, Highland Park, NJ
Roots and Wings, Denville, NJ
Seeds of Learning, Brick, NJ (pre K)
The Tutor, Millville, NJ (pre K–12)
Unschoolers Support Group for Central NJ, Jobstown, NJ

New Mexico Christian Home Education, Albuquerque, NM

New Mexico Family Educators, Albuquerque, NM

Glorieta Family Educators, Glorieta, NM

Rocky Mountain High Academy, Flora Vista, NM

Santa Fe Learning Cooperative, Santa Fe, NM

A Voice For Children, Santa Fe, NM

Christian Home Educators of Nevada, Las Vegas, NV

Home Schools United/Vegas Valley, Las Vegas, NV

Nevada Home Schools, Inc, Reno, NV

Assistant Commissioner for Non-Public Schools, Albany, NY

Loving Education at Home (LEAH), Syracuse, NY

Parents Instructing Challenged Children, Fulton, NY

Gemini, W Nyack, NY (10-12)

Albany Area Home Schoolers, Scotia, NY

Capital District Home Educators, Schaghticoke, NY

Creamery Kids Adventure Group, New Paltz, NY

Dutchess County Homeschoolers, Poughkeepsie, NY

Families for Home Education, Cazenovia, NY (pre K-8)

Fingerlakes Unschoolers Network, Ithaca, NY

GALLAH (Green/Albany Learning At Home), Hanacroix, NY (K-6)

Grasso Homeschool, Brentwood, NY (4)

HELP Resource Center, Elizaville, NY

Home Education Exchange of the Southern Tier, Vestal, NY

Homer/Cortland Home Educators, Truxton, NY

Kid's Place of Choice, South Nassau High School Resource Room, Freeport, NY

Linda Tagliaferro, Little Neck, NY

Long Island Growing at Home (LIGHT), Freeport, NY

Long Island Home Schoolers Association, Massapequa Park, NY

Loving Education At Home, Albany, NY

Morgan Home School, Rochester, NY (12)

New Paltz Area Home Educators Collective, New Paltz, NY (K-12)

New York City Home Educators Alliance, NY, NY

Rochester Area Homeschoolers Association, Rochester, NY

Schoharie County Area Home Educators, Cobleskill, NY

Southern Tier Unschoolers, Hammondsport, NY

St Lawrence County Group, Madrid, NY

The Learning Co-op, Syracuse, NY

Tri-County Homeschoolers, Stoneypoint, NY

Tri-Lakes Community Home Educators, Raybrook, NY

Upstate Homeschoolers, Earlville, NY

Westchester Home Learners, Crestwood, NY

Western NY Homeschooling Network, Fredonia, NY

Woodstock Support Group, Lake Hill, NY

Spirit of January, Great Neck, NY

Christian Home Educators of Ohio, Columbus, OH

Ohio Coalition of Educational Alternatives Now, Thompson, OH

Cassidy and Nells, Huber Hts, OH

Growing Together, Columbus, OH

HELP- Oberlin, Oberlin, OH

Home Ed. League of Parents/HELP Unlimited, Ashland, OH

Home Education League of Parents, Perrysburg, OH

Home Education League of Parents (HELP) Columbus Chapter, Columbus, OH

Home Education League of Parents (HELP) Miami Valley Chapter, Yellow Springs, OH

Home Educator's Resource Organization, Norwalk, OH (pre K-9)

Homeschool Network of Greater Cincinnati, Maineville, OH

Ohio Home Educators Network (Cleaveland-Akron area), Chagrin Falls, OH

Special Friends, Winchester, OH

Oklahoma Christian Home Educators Association, Tulsa, OK

Cornerstone, Broken Arrow, OK

Cornerstone, Tulsa, OK

Home Educators Resource Organization, Norman, OK (pre K-12)

OK Central Home Educators Consociation, OKC, OK

Learning All Ways, McLoud, OK

Oregon Christian Home Educators Association Network (OCEAN), Portland, OR

Oregon Home Education Network, Beaverton, OR

Bend Homeschoolers, Bend, OR

Douglas County Homeschoolers Connection, Roseburg, OR

North Willamette Homeschoolers, Portland, OR

Parents Education Association, Beaverton, OR

Portland Area Tri-County Homeschoolers, Newberg, OR

The Learning Connection, Grants Pass, OR

The Learning Network, Springfield, OR

Willamette Homeschoolers, Eugene, OR

Homeschooling in Oregon, the Handbook, Portland, OR

The Teaching Home, Portland, OR

Christian Homeschool Association of Pennsylvania, Manheim, PA

Pennsylvania Home Education Network, Meadville, PA

Pennsylvania Homeschoolers, Kittanning, PA

Armstrong County Area Homeschoolers, Templeton, PA

Butler Area Homeschoolers, Marwood, PA

Center City Homeschoolers, Philadelphia, PA

Central Area Pennsylvania Home Education Network, Summerhill, PA

Chester County Homeschoolers, Exton, PA

Circle of Children Co-op

Cornucopia Enterprises, Shrewsbury, PA (pre K-12)

Creative Education Network, Carversville, PA

Endless Mountains Homeschoolers, Columbia Cross Rds, PA

Erie County Homeschoolers, Cranesville, PA

Family Resource Center, Bryn Mawr, PA

Harmony Home Educators, Dalton, PA

Homeschool Resource Center, Philadeophia, PA

Homeworks, Edinboro, PA

Lakeland Home Educators, Meadville, PA

Lancaster Home Educators Association, Red Lion, PA

Pittsburgh East Suburban Homeschoolers, Pittsburgh, PA

Southwestern Pennsylvania Home Education Network, Tarentrum, PA

Sunflower School, Grove City, PA

Puerto Rico Homeschooling Association, Santurce, PR

Parent Educators of Rhode Island, Glendale, RI

Rhode Island Guild of Home Teachers, W. Greenwich, RI

Rhode Island Guild of Home Teachers, Warwick, RI

Educational Resource Center of Rhode Island, Providence, RI

South Carolina Association of Independent Homeschools, Irmo, SC

South Carolina Home Educators Association, Lexington, SC

South Dakota Homeschool Association, Sioux Falls, SD

Home Education Association of Tennessee (HEAT), Nashville, TN

Tennessee Homeschooling Families, Oak Ridge, TN

TN Homeschool Families, Gray, TN

Educational Choices, Harriman, TN

Homeschooling Families, Oliver Springs, TN

HOT, Nashville, TN

Smoky Mountain Chapter, Tennessee Home Education Association, Knoxville, TN

The Farm School, Summertown, TN

Family Christian Academy, Madison, TN

HOPE: Home-Oriented Private Education for Texas, Austin, TX

Texas Home School Coalition, Dallas, TX

Texas Homeschool Coalition, Lubbock, TX

Basic Education, D/FW Airport, TX

El Paso Homeschoolers Association, El Paso, TX

Houston Alternative Education Alliance, Cypress, TX

North Texas Self-Educators, Colleyville, TX

Southeast Texas Homeschool Association, Houston, TX

Sing and Learn Curriculum Supplies, Garland, TX

Summit Christian Academy, Dallas, TX (K-12)

Utah Home Education Association, Provo, UT

Canyon Country Homeschoolers, Moab, UT.

FCLA Utah Spice Group, Provo, UT

Mount Vernon Academy, Murray, UT

Utah Home Education Association, Farmington, UT

Brigham Young U, Dept of Independent Study, Provo, UT

Home Educators Association of Virginia, Front Royal, VA
Community School, Roanoke, VA
Beach Educators Association for Creative Homeschooling (BEACH), Virginia Beach, VA
BRANCH: Blue Ridge Area Network for Congenial Homeschoolers, Afton, VA
Children's Circle, Mouth of Wilson, VA
Home Educators Network, Fredericksburg, VA
Home Free, Virginia Beach, VA
Home Instruction Support Group, Sterling, VA
Living Education Center for Ecology and the Arts, Charlottesville, VA
Northern Virginia Homeschoolers / LEARN, Sterling, VA
Schwartz-Gralla Homeschool, Check, VA
Seton Home Study School, Front Royal, VA (K-12)
Snakefoot School, Lexington, VA (1-7)
The Learning Community Inc, Herndon, VA
Home School Legal Defense Association, Paeonian Spgs, VA
Vermont Home Schoolers, Plainfield, VT
Vermont Home Schoolers, Montpelier, VT
Vermont Homeschool Association, Middletown Springs, VT
Vermont Homeschoolers Association, Bristol, VT
Addison County Home Schoolers, Salisbury, VT
Addison County Homeschool Group, Vergennes, VT
Caledonia County Homeschool Group, Lyndon Center, VT
Central Vermont Homeschool Group, Manchester Center, VT
Homeschool Representative, Belvidere, VT
Lamoille County Homeschool Group, Morrisville, VT
Northeast Kingdom Homeschool Group, Irasburg, VT
Rutland County Homeschoolers, Pittsford, VT
Washington County Homeschool Group, Waterbury Center, VT
Windham County Homeschool Group, Putney, VT
Washington Homeschool Organization (WHO), Seattle, WA
Port Townsend Migrant Education Program, Port Townsend, WA (K-12)
HALL Program, Gig Harbor, WA (K-12)
Ballard Homeschoolers, Seattle, WA
Blue Mountain Homeschool Association, Walla Walla, WA
Bonney Homeschool Support Group, Sumner, WA
Cathedral of Praise Home Education Support, Lacey, WA
Christian Home Educators, Sequim, WA
Clark County Christian Home Educators, Vancouver, WA
Eatonville Area Homeschool Association, Eatonville, WA
Ellensburg Homeschool Support Group, Ellensburg, WA

Everson Homeschool Support Group, Everson, WA
Family Advocates in Teaching Homes, Yacolt, WA
Family Centered Learning Alternatives, Naselle, WA
Family Learning Center, Spokane, WA
Graham Homeschool Fellowship, Graham, WA
Grant County Home Educators Association, Quincy, WA
Grays Harbor Christian Homeschool Parent Support Group, Aberdeen, WA
Greater Gig Harbor Homeschool Support Group, Gig Harbor, WA
Homeschool Support Association, Tacoma, WA
Homeschool Support for Military Families, Ft Lewis, WA
Homeschoolers in FOCUS, Lynwood, WA
Homeschoolers in Sequim, Sequim, WA
Homeschoolers On Whidbey, Oak Harbor, WA
Homeschoolers Organized for Meaningful Education, Bothell, WA
Homeschoolers Support Association, Maple Valley, WA
Homeschooling and Other Parents Encouraged, Pt Orchard, WA
Homeschooling on the Palouse, Pullman, WA
Kittitas Valley Homeschool Association, Ellensburg, WA (K-9)
Lakewood Christian Home Educators, Tacoma, WA
Lewis River Home Educators, Ridgefield, WA
Lower Valley Homeschool Support Group, Bickleton, WA
Lynden Home Learners, Lynden, WA
Mt Pilchuck Homeschoolers, Granite Falls, WA
North Olympic Homeschool Association, Sequim, WA
Olympia Home School Support Group, Olympia, WA
Orcas Homeschoolers, Eastsound, WA
Puget Sound Community School, Bellevue, WA
Puyallup Homeschool Fellowship, Puyallup, WA
Rainbow Way Homeschool Group, Seattle, WA
Seattle Homeschool Group, Seattle, WA
Shoreline Homeschoolers Co-op, Seattle, WA
Skagit Valley Homeschool Association, Mt Vernon, WA
Sky County Home Educators, Sultan, WA
Snoqualmie Valley Homeschoolers Co-op, North Bend, WA
SnoValley Homeschool Association, Duvall, WA
South Pacific County Homeschoolers, Ocean Park, WA
South Whidbey Homeschool Support Group, Langley, WA
Tacoma Homeschool Fellowship, Tacoma, WA
Trestle Homeschoolers, Everett, WA
Tri-Cities Homeschool Support Group, Pasco, WA

Valley Home Educators, E Wenatchee, WA
Whatcom Homeschool Association, Bellingham, WA
Woodland Homeschool Support Group, Woodland, WA
Zillah Homeschoolers, Zillah, WA
Hewitt Research Foundation, Washougal, WA (K-12)
Home Education Press, Tonasket, WA
Moore Academy, Camas, WA (K-12)
The Drinking Gourd, Harambee, Redmond, WA
Parent Assisted Learning Services, Tacoma, WA (1-8)
Wisconsin Parents Association, Madison, WI
Families in Schools at Home (FISH), Cottage Grove, WI
HOME, Madison, WI
The Bike Farm, Cushing, WI (7-12)
Unschooling Families, Appleton, WI
International Institute, White Lake, WI
Switch, Fontana, WI
West Virginia Home Educators Association, Inc, Charleston, WV
Alternatives in Education, Chloe, WV
Wyoming Unschoolers, Lander, WY
Alberta Home Education Association c/o Aine Stasiewich, Leduc, AB
Homeschoolers Association of Northern Alberta, Edmonton, AB
Canadian Home Educators Association of BC, Kelowna, BC
Cowichan Valley Christian Homelearners Support Group, Duncan, BC
Education Advisory, W Vancouver, BC
Gabriola Homeschoolers, Gabriola Island, BC
Greater Vancouver Home Learners Support Group, Vancouver, BC
Home Learning Resource Centre, Quathiaski, BC
Kootenay Home Educators, Nelson, BC
Manitoba Association for Schooling at Home, Winnipeg, MB
Manitoba Association for Schooling at Home, Manitoba, MB
New Brunswick Association of Christian Homeschoolers, Hillsborough, NB
Schole, Margaree Valley, NS (1-12)
Nova Scotia Support Group, c/o Laura Uhlman, Pleasantville, NS
MUDPUDL, Hamilton, ON (K-6)
Orilla Homeschoolers Support Group, Orilla, ON
Pinewood Alternative School, Millbrook, ON
Rideau Valley Home Educators Association, Ottawa, ON
Canadian Alliance of Home Schoolers, St George, ON
Catholic Homeschoolers Association, Kanata, ON
Quest, The Home Educators' Journal, Ottawa, ON
Montreal Home Schoolers, Dorval, PQ
Montreal Homeschoolers' Support Group, Montreal, PQ
Quebec Homeschool Association, Val David, PQ

Boarding Schools

Andis Alternative Education Center and Drift Creek Farm for Youth
2204 SR 217, Kitts Hill, OH 45645
Earl Hutchinson, Dir, 614-532-8882,-9068
Lawrence County
81-acres; residential services available; voc; natural resources, agri. prod, work & family; lab work in forestry, soil conservation, hydroponic horticulture, food prep, nutrition; CAI.

Arthur Morgan School (1962)
1901 Hannah Branch Rd, Burnsville, NC 28714
Johno Zakelj & Joy Montagano, Co-clerks, 704-675-4262
Type: Quaker, non-profit; tuition: $5150-10500, scholarships
12 teachers, 24 students, ages 12-15, 7-9th grade
Entrance requirements: no severe mental, emotional problems, 2 day visit.
Affiliations: NCACS, NAMTA, FEAA
Governance by staff, staff and student all-school meeting
Rare junior high boarding school, geared to meet their specific needs; challenging outdoor experiences; community service; daily work projects; caring community environment; based on Montessori's Erkinder model; no letter grades; multi-aged classes; extensive field trips; rural location; interns accepted.

AYS Day Treatment (1991)
115 S Marion St, Ebensburg, PA 15931
Thomas Prout, Exec Dir, 814-472-7874, FAX: 472-7920
Cambrie County
Type: independent, non-profit
8 teachers, 40 students, mainly at-risk, ages 11-18, 4-12th grade
Interview required
Governance by board
Very structured.

Boynton School (1964)
RR 1, Box 31B, Orford, NH 03777
Arthur Boynton Jr, Director, 603-353-4874
Type: independent; tuition: $5000
2 teachers; 7-12+
Governance by cooperative
Individualized help with languages, music, athletics; multi-aged classes; no letter grades; rural location; interns accepted.

Boys Totem Town
398 Totem Rd, St Paul, MN 55119
Dave Ardoff, 612-292-6295
Career exploration; work experience; year round.

Buxton School (1928)
PO Box 646, Williamstown, MA 01267
C. William Bennett, 413-458-3919, FAX: 413-458-9427
Berkshire County
Type: independent, non-profit; tuition: $19,500/yr, scholarships
16 teachers, 80 students, ages 14-18, 9-12th grade
Entrance requirements: Personal interview.
Governance by teachers and Principal
Teacher qualifications: Bachelor's
Sophisticated academic curriculum combined with exceptional opportunities in the arts; work program; students maintain school; entire school travels to major city for research projects and to perform touring play; no letter grades; extensive field trips; multi-aged classes; rural location.

Eagle Rock School (1993)
Box 1770, Estes Park, CO 80517
Robert Burkhardt, Head, 303-588-0600, FAX: 586-4805
Larimer County
Type: independent, non-profit; tuition: free
20 teachers, 96 students, partly at-risk, ages 15-18, HS
Affiliation: Honda
Governance by teachers, principal, democratic school meeting, board
650 acres; 1 mile from Rocky Mountain National Park; integrated; stresses service learning, outdoor ed, environmental stewardship, cross-cultural understanding; no letter grades; multi-aged classes; extensive field trips; interns accepted.

Eclipse Program at Denver Children's Home
1501 Albion St, Denver, CO 80220
David Dunn or Linda Lindsay, 303-399-4890
Type: independent, non-profit
15 teachers, 60 students, mainly at-risk, ages 11-18, 7-12th grade
Governance by teachers and principal
Integrated; thematic; internships; community service, placement; experiential; multi-aged classes; extensive field trips; urban location; interns accepted.

Eclipse/Independent Redirection
1501 Albion, Denver, CO 80220
Linda Lindsay, Dir, 303-399-4890, FAX: 303-399-9846
Type: public at-risk
24 teachers, 135 students
Governance by teachers, Principal, students. parents
Emotional support; community-based and therapeutic day programs; multi-cultural; extensive field trips; multi-aged classe; interns accepted.

Geocommons College (1991)
RR 2 Box 793 Derbyshire Farm, Temple, NH 03084
Bruce Kantner, Dir, 603-654-6705
Hillsboro County
Type: higher education, non-profit; tuition: variable, scholarships
4 teachers, 5-15 students
Entrance requirements: must be able to travel, live simply in rural India
Affiliations: UNH, Gaia Educational Outreach Institute
Governance by consensus
Teacher qualifications: background, skills, goals in harmony with program
Sustainable community; ecological literacy; bioregional, world studies; compassionate, mindful living; visits exemplary communities in USA, Europe, India; partial UNH credit; interns accepted.

George School (1893)
Box 4000, Newtown, PA 18940
Karen S. Hallowell, Adms Dir, 215-579-6500, FAX:-6549
Type: Quaker, non-profit; tuition: res:$17,900/yr
    day:$11,650/yr, scholarships
70 teachers, 525 students, ages 13-18, 9-12th grade
Entrance requirements: grades, testing, recommendations,
    interview.
Affiliation: Religious Society of Friends
Governance by consensus
Teacher qualifications: college degree
65 hours community service; work camps in developing
    countries; IB; suburban location.

Headwaters Academy (1990)
418 Garfield, Box 7258, Bozeman, MT 59715
Shawn Gant, Headmaster, 406-585-9997
Gallatin County
Type: independent, non-profit; tuition: $4850/yr, scholarships
7 teachers, 23 students, ages 12-18, 7-12th grade
Entrance requirements: interview, references, essay.
Governance by faculty and student representatives, board
Teacher qualifications: certification of advance degree
No formal grade levels; group work, art, music, adventure
    considered as important as academics; travel to Baja,
    Spain, Guatamala; grades given are A, B, C, in progress, not
    complete; multi-aged classes; extensive field trips; urban
    location.

High Mowing School (1942)
PO Box 850, Abbot Hill Rd, Wilton, NH 03086
Virginia R. Buhr, Adms Dir, 603-654-2391, FAX:-658?
Hillsborough County
Type: Waldorf, non-profit; tuition: $9,950-10,500 day,
    $16,250-18,000 boarding/yr, scholarships
20 teachers, 85 students, ages 13-19, 9-12th grade
Entrance Requirements: application, transcripts, tch recs,
    interview.
Affiliations: NEASC, NAIS, ISANNE, AWSNA, SATB
Governance by faculty
Teacher qualifications: BA, Waldorf interest/training, love
    teenagers
College prep; extensive arts; social responsibility; interna-
    tional community; multi-aged classes; rural location;
    interns accepted.

Highland School (1981)
Rt 83 Box 56, Highland, WV 26346
Dr. Charlotte Landvoigt, Director, 304-869-3250
Ritchie County
Type: independent, non-profit; tuition: day 60, bdg 560/mo
3 teachers, 14 students, ages 5-18
Entrance requirements: interview for children over 11.
Governance by democratic school meeting
Teacher qualifications: B.A. minimum; willingness to be equal
    member of democratic community
Located on 480 acres: woods, pond, streams, fields, wildlife;
    international visitors and exchanges; stresses individual
    interests, responsibility; apprenticeship program: oil and
    gas, veterinary science, office skills; PSAT administered; no
    letter grades; non-compulsory class attendance; multi-
    aged classes; extensive field trips; rural location; interns
    accepted.

Horizons School
1900 Dekalb Ave, Atlanta, GA 30307
Dr. Lorraine Wilson, Co-administrator, 404-378-2219, FAX: 404-
    373-3650
Type: independent, non-profit; tuition: $3800-8000/yr, schol-
    arships: work, need
14 teachers, 145 students, ages 4-18, pre K-12th grade
Affiliation: NCACS
Governance by democratic school meeting; some decisions
    by administration +
Students and staff designed and built new campus; alternative evaluation methods in some classes; college prep
program; wholistic approach; multi-aged classes; extensive
field trips; urban location; interns accepted.

Illinois Mathematics and Science Academy (1986)
1500 W Sullivan Rd, Aurora, IL 60506-1039
708-801-6000
Type: magnet
Student ages 13-18, 10-12th grade
State-funded; mentorships; near Fermi Accelerator Lab.

John Woolman School (1963)
13075 Woolman Ln, Nevada City, CA 95959
916-273-3183, FAX: 916-273-9028
Type: Quaker; tuition: $14,900/yr, scholarships
35 students, ages 14-17, 9-12th grade
Affiliation: NAIS
Governance by teachers, principal, board
Teacher qualifications: credentials, experience
Emphasizes truthfulness, simplicity, non-violence, respect,
    listening to the Spirit Within; nurtures inquiry, creativity,
    physical work, service; multi-aged classes; rural location.

Johnson Center at University of Redlands (1969)
PO Box 3080 1200 E Colton Ave, Redlands, CA 92373-0999
Yasuyuki Awada, Dir, 909-335-4071, FAX: 909-793-2029
San Bernardino County
Type: higher education, non-profit; tuition: $15,760/yr,
    scholarships
140 students
Entrance requirements: HS diploma, SAT/ACT scores.
Accreditation: WASC
Governance by community consensus
Teacher qualifications: PhD, ABD
Students negotiate learning contracts with faculty; no letter
    grades; student designed curriculum and majors; subur-
    ban location.

Marlboro College (1946)
PO Box A, Marlboro, VT 05344
Wayne R. Wood, Adms Dir, 802-257-4333, FAX:-4154
Type: higher education, non-profit; tuition: $17,175/yr,
    scholarships
36 teachers, 270 students, ages 17-40
Entrance requirements: HS diploma.
Governance by faculty and student reps
Self-designed curriculum; one to one tutorials; small classes;
    philosophy of self-governance, academic vigor.

National Audubon Society Expedition Institute (1981)
PO Box 365, Belfast, ME 04915
Karen Woodsum, Office Mgr, 207-338-5859
Type: independent, higher education; tuition: $9300/yr,
    scholarships
4/bus teachers, 20 students, HS, college, graduate school
Affiliation: Leslie College
Governance by consensus
Explores 1 region of US & Canada each sem; environmental
    ed degrees; values-based, holistic approach; non-
    authoritarian; self-paced, directed and evaluated; camping,
    hiking, canoeing.

Nebraska Center for Children & Youth: Whitehall School
5701 Walker, Lincoln, NE 68504
402-471-3305
Type: public at-risk
K-12th grade
Enrollment restricted to wards of the state.
Work experience; cooperative programs; behavior modifica-
    tion, contracts; vocational, group, individual counseling.

North Country School (1938)
Box 187, Lake Placid, NY 12946
Christine Lefevre, Adms Dir, 518-523-9329, FAX:-4858
Essex County

Type: independent, non-profit; tuition: $22,000/yr, scholarships
30 teachers, 55 students, ages 9-14, 4-8th grade
Affiliation: Camp Treetops
Governance by board
Teacher qualifications: BA/BS and interest/experience
School-as-village model; outdoor ed; art; work program; greenhouse; organic gardens; farm animals; maple-sugaring; no letter grades; rural location; transportation; interns accepted.

Olney Friends School (1837)
61830 Sandy Ridge Rd, Barnesville, OH 43713
Bonnie Irwin, Asst Head, 614-425-3655, FAX: 425-320?
Belmont County
Type: Quaker, non-profit; tuition: $13,230/yr, scholarships
12 teachers, 49 students, ages 13-19, 9-12th grade
Affiliations: ISACS, NAIS, FCOE
Teacher qualifications: BS with a major in subject to be taught
Whole-person approach; college prep; multi-aged classes; rural location; interns accepted.

Owosso Alternative Education (1990)
120 Michigan Ave, Owosso, MI 48429
Shirley McNier, Coord, ?-723-5598
Shiawassee County
Type: public choice
7 teachers, 65 students, mainly at-risk, ages 16-18
Enrollment restricted to resident HS dropouts age 16+; limited SE services
Affiliation: MAEO
Governance by Principal, faculty, student reps, board
Teacher qualifications: secondary certification
Electives; Glasser's control theory; reality therapy for behavior control; hands-on projects; volunteer work; suburban location; interns accepted.

Padanaram Village School (1972)
RR 1, Box 478, Williams In, IN 47470
Steven Fuson, Schoolmaster, 812-262-7252
Martin County
Type: independent, non-profit; no tuition
9 teachers, 60 students, ages 5-18, K-12th grade
Enrollment restricted to members of the community.
Governance by teachers and Principal, parent cooperative
Community shares goods communally; 3 R's and strong curricula are blended with arts, hands-on learning, community life; no letter grades; multi-aged classes; extensive field trips.

Penobscot Job Corps (1979)
1375 Union St, Bangor, ME 04401
207-990-3000, FAX: ?-942-9829
Penobscot County
Type: public at-risk; scholarships
23 teachers, 330 students, mainly at-risk, ages 16-24
Enrollment restricted by income verification; for age 16-24; no residency requirement.
Affiliation: Training & Development
Governance by training & Development Corp and Dept of Labor
Teacher qualifications: bachelor's degree
College prep; ESL; vocational training; remedial studies; community resources; culturally diverse staff with educational hands-on experience; opportunity for one-on-one attention; multi-aged classes; rural location; interns accepted.

Petrolia High School (1983)
Box 197, Petrolia, CA 95558
Seth Zuckerman, Director, 707-629-3509
Humboldt County
Type: independent, non-profit
10 teachers, 24 students, ages 14-18, 9-12th grade
Governance by teachers and Principal, democratic school meeting, board
Year starts with 2 week backpacking; 6 week intercultural trip

with home stay, often in Mexico; involvement in local environmental restoration efforts; individually designed project month; extensive field trips; rural location.

Phoenix International School for Peace
Box 336, Birch Tree, MO 65438
John Staniloiu, Dir, 314-292-3880
Type: independent
Student ages 8-16
320 acres; animals, rivers, caves; hands-on experiences.

Rock Point School
Institute Rd, Burlington, VT 05401
Russell Ellis
Type: independent
Students mainly at-risk, HS
Low ratio; counseling; tutoring; self-image/motivation; substance abuse counseling; 24 hr/day supportive environment; positive peer culture.

Sandhill Crane School (1989)
PO Box 160, Fall River, CA 96028
916-336-6582
Shasta County
Type: independent; tuition: $5,000/yr
2 teachers, 3 students, ages 9-15
Entrance requirements: independent-thinking, athletic, health-conscious.
Affiliations: Kempo International, Ch'uan Tao Assn
Governance by benevolent director
Teacher qualifications: outstanding athlete, min 7 yrs training in Chinese martial arts
Does not advocate material gain, ego enhancement; vehicle is mind-body training of Chinese martial arts; no letter grades; multi-aged classes; extensive field trips; rural location; interns accepted.

Shining Mountain Waldorf School (1982)
987 Locust Ave, Boulder, CO 80304
Nancy Jane, Enrl Coord, 303-444-7697, FAX: 444-7701
Non-profit; tuition: $3,500-5,850/yr, scholarships
25 teachers, 326 students, ages 4-18, K-12th grade
Affiliation: AWSNA
Governance by teachers, Principal, and board
Teacher qualifications: Waldorf training, certification
8 acres; extensive field trips; summer school; rural location; interns accepted.

Stonesoup School (1979)
Star Rt 1, Box 127, Crescent City, FL 32112
Deborah Rogers, 904-698-2516
Type: independent, non-profit; tuition: $700/mo, scholarships
3 teachers, 10 students, ages 8-18, -12th grade
Entrance requirements: interview, telephone or in person.
Affiliation: NCACS
Governance by democratic school meeting
Free school approach to learning and living; freedom tempered with responsibility and independence, cooperation; encourages self-reliance, character development; self paced tutorials; on 50 acres with lake; no letter grades; non-compulsory class attendance; multi-aged classes; extensive field trips; rural location; interns accepted.

The Community School (1973)
Box 555-79 Washington St, Camden, ME 04843
Emanual Pariser, Dora Lievow, Co-Directors, 207-763-3000
Knox County
Type: independent, non-profit; tuition: $17,000/yr/session, scholarships
6 teachers, 8 students, mainly at-risk, ages 16-21, HS
No untreated addicts; no suicide attempts in last 6 mo; 6 gr+ reading level.
Affiliations: NCACS, Nat Dropout Prev Net
Governance by democratic school meeting; faculty determines inalterable rules

"Real world" preparation includes work in community, maintenance of the facility, and meeting room and board costs; applied home economics; conflict resolution and anger management; competency-based academic program; new book: Changing Lives: Voices From a School that Works; no letter grades; multi-aged classes; extensive field trips; rural location; interns accepted.

The Meeting School (1957)
Thomas Rd, Rindge, NH 03461-9781
Ed Miller, Admissions Director, 603-899-3366
Cheshire County
Type: independent, non-profit; tuition: $15,000, scholarships
12 teachers, 27 students, ages 13-19, 9-12th grade
Entrance requirements: willingness on part of student; won't take extreme at-risk.
Affiliations: NCACS, ISEANNE
Governance by faculty consensus for some decisions; whole community or board for some
Students live in cooperative households with faculty, sharing cooking, cleaning; 4-hr work study: farm, childcare, office; 4 week intersession project-travel; apprenticeships, peace studies; student-run radio station, post graduates; no letter grades; multi-aged classes; extensive field trips; rural location; interns accepted.

Timber Lake Job Corps CCC (1964)
59868 E Hwy 224, Estacada, OR 97023
Juanita Morin, Mgr, 503-834-2291
Type: public at-risk
7 teachers, 234 students, ages 16-21
Intensive; voc and life skills; GED/diploma.

Upattinas School (1971)
429 Greenridge Rd, Glenmoore, PA 19343
Sandra Hurst, Dir, 215-458-5138
Chester County
Type: independent/home-based, non-profit
11 teachers, 80 students, ages 5-19, K-12th grade
Entrance restriction: no Neo-Nazi students permitted; entrance requirements: application, visit.
Governance by democratic school meeting
Teacher qualifications: individually decided by school
Enrollment, materials, support for homeschooling; international student placement; I-20 authorization; exchanges, part time programs; high school diploma for in-school and independent study students; no letter grades; non-compulsory class attendance; multi-aged classes; extensive field trips; rural location; interns accepted.

Veade Valley School (1948)
3511 Veade Valley School Rd, Sedona, AZ 86351
Roy E. Grimm, Head, 602-284-2272, FAX: 284-0432
Type: independent, non-profit; tuition: $17,325/yr, scholarships
24 teachers, 125 students, ages 13-18, 9-12th grade
Entrance restrictions: no significant psychological, drug, alcohol problems.
Affiliations: NAIS, AEE
Governance by board
Teacher qualifications: prefer BA/MA
Emphasis on anthropology, intercultural understanding, environmental stewardship; classical college prep; experiential pedagogy; multi-aged classes; extensive field trips; rural location; interns accepted.

Wil Lou Gray Opportunity School (1921)
PO Drawer 280128, Columbia, SC 29228
Dr Mary Catherine Norwood, Superintendent, 803-822-5480, FAX: 803-822-8146
Lexington County
Type: public at-risk; scholarships
23 teachers, 170 students, ages 15+, 9-12th grade

Entrance Requirements: school records, medical information, application.
Governance by board
Case management teams; outdoor education; vocational training; college residential setting; individualized instruction; suburban location; interns accepted.

Au Grand Bois (1980)
RR 1, Ladysmith, PQ, Canada J0X 2A0
A & L Prost, Co-Dirs, 819-647-3522
Type: independent, non-profit; scholarships
20 teachers, 50 students, ages 8-16
Governance by staff, co-directors, much input from campers.
Summer program; vegetarian, organic gardens; 565 acre semi-wilderness; non-competitive; campers choose avtivities; promotes understanding and respect for self, others, natural environment; rural location.

Institute for Bioregional Studies (1982)
PO Box 126, Charlottetown, PEI, Canada C1A 4P3
Phil Ferraro, Dir, 902-892-9578
Queens County
Type: higher education
1-6 teachers, 11 students, ages 17+
Application required.
Affiliation: York University
Governance by faculty, student reps, board
Teacher qualifications: MA, licensed
Integrated resource management training; summer camp; apprenticeships; community resources include organic farms, eco land trust, Fundy Folk Society; interns accepted.

Schole (1985)
Box 10 RR #1, Margaree Valley, NS, Canada
Donald Knight, 902-248-0601
Type: Independent, home-based; cost: C$12,000/yr, scholarships
2-3 teachers, 4-6 students, ages 6-16, 1-12th grade
Student letter required.
Governance by board
Wilderness setting; extensive travel, eg, to Latin America, 1994-95 to Europe; no letter grade; interns accepted.

Colegio Bilingue "Jorge Emilio Gutierez"
Apdo Aereo 101634, Bogota, DE, Columbia SA
Alejandro Acero, 011571-2150051
Type: independent
60+ students, partly international, indigenous, K-12th grade
Summerhill philosophy; outdoor classes on mountainside; exchange program.

Brockwood Park Krishnamurti Educational Centre (1969)
Bramdean, Hampshire, England SO24 0LQ
Scott Forbes, 962-771-744, FAX: 962-771-875
Type: independent, non-profit
30 teachers, 60 students, ages 14-19
Affiliation: Krishnamurti Schools
Governance by all faculty with school meeting
Holistic; in 1769 Georgian mansion and park; no letter grades; multi-aged classes; extensive field trips; rural location.

Summerhill School (1921)
Leiston, Suffolk, England IP16 4HY
Zoe Redhead, 0728-830540
Type: independent; tuition: $£5,000/yr
12 teachers, 70 students, mainly international, ages 6-17
Entrance requirements: interview.
Governance by democratic school meeting
Teacher qualifications: dictated by position
Founded by A.S. Neill as a pioneering free school and democratic community; 12 acres; no letter grades; non-compulsory class attendance; multi-aged classes; rural location; interns accepted.

Part Six

COMPREHENSIVE ALPHABETICAL INDEX

About The Editors

JERRY MINTZ has been a leading voice in the alternative school movement for over thirty years. He has a B.A. from Goddard College, and a Masters in Teaching from Antioch New England Graduate School. For seventeen years he worked as a public school teacher and as a principal in both public and alternative schools. He also founded several alternative schools and organizations. He became the first executive director of the National Coalition of Alternative Community Schools and served from 1985–1989. In 1989 he founded the Alternative Education Resource Organization, which he continues to direct, and is editor of its publication, *AERO-GRAMME*. He has lectured and consulted with schools and organizations in the United States and around the world, most recently in the Czech Republic, France, England, Israel, and Russia. He has been a guest on many radio and TV shows, and has published hundreds of articles and studies on educational alternatives.

RAYMOND SOLOMON is a partner in The Solomon Press, and works as editor, graphic designer, and science publisher. He was picture editor of the *Macmillan Illustrated Almanac for Kids*. He has published about fifty articles in various periodicals, including *The Windham Free Press, The Jewish Press, The New York Page, The Jewish Spectator,* and *United Israel Bulletin*. He often uses the pen name Reuven Solomon. He is a graduate of Forest Hills High School in New York and has a B.A. in government from Windham College. As a college student he was active on behalf of the starving people of Biafra. He is currently working on *The Science Almanac for Kids* and *The Modern Vegetarian Almanac*. He lives with his wife, Judy, in Queens, New York.

SIDNEY SOLOMON, the former Design Director of the Macmillan Publishing Company, is now a partner in The Solomon Press, book publishers. He had the benefits of several years in an experimental alternative class in a junior high school in the Bronx, with a teacher who believed that all kids could be talented—and proved it. Sidney graduated from Townsend Harris High School, City College of New York, and did graduate work at Columbia University. He was a jazz drummer and teacher in New York before going into publishing as an editor and art director. He is the co-author of the best-selling *Macmillan Illustrated Almanac for Kids*. He became a serious painter as an adult and has had eight solo shows.